SENSATION and PERCEPTION

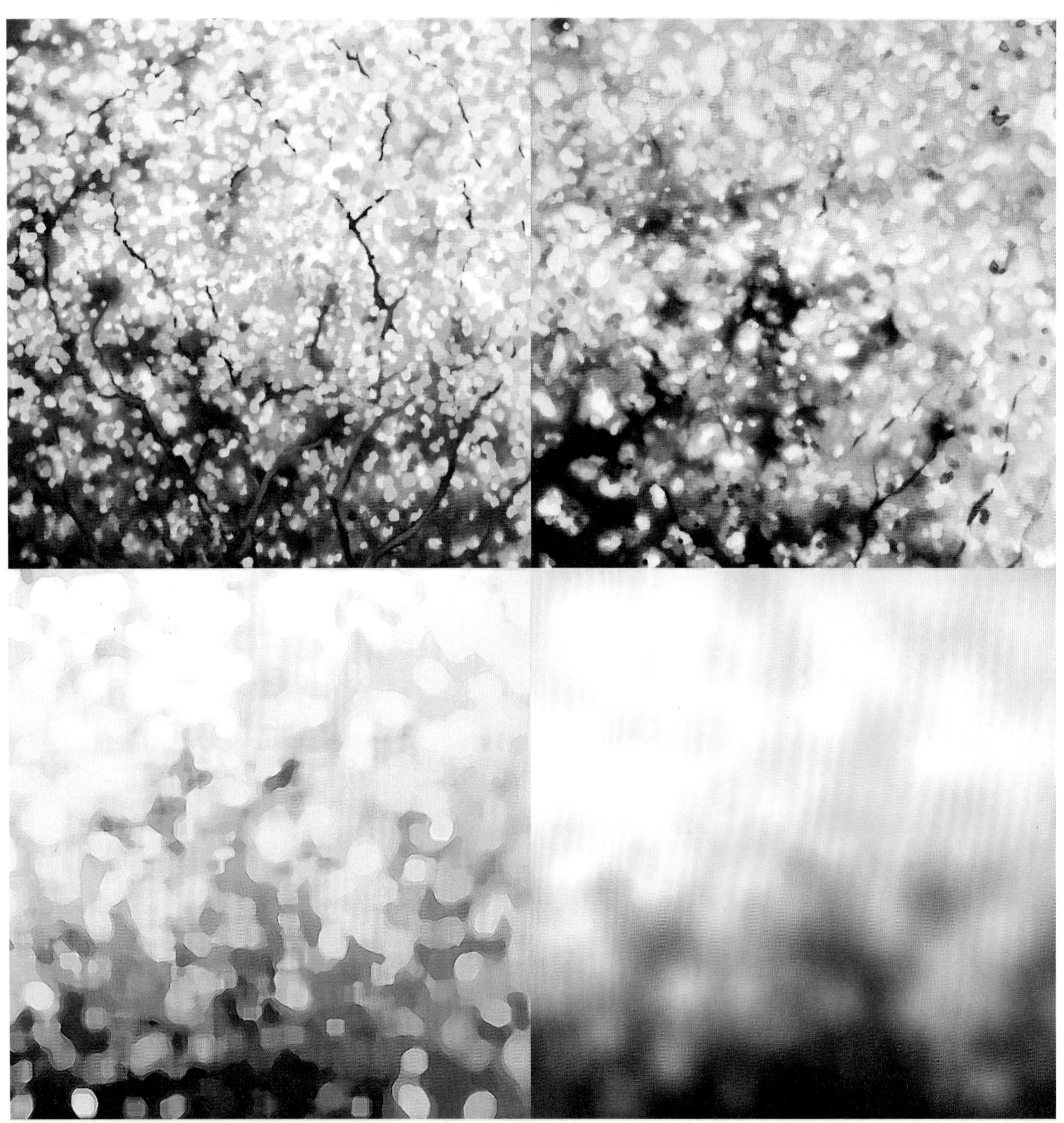

The four paintings on the front cover were created by Alison Jardine. I was drawn to these pieces because of their beauty, but I also think they reflect how our perceptual system works with light, color, and shape to create a multifaceted experience of the world. On her Web site, Jardine describes how she begins with a digital photograph that she manipulates until she has an image on which she can base an oil painting. She then takes a photo of that painting and manipulates the photo to create an image that will form the basis of the next painting, and "this feedback loop continues towards a gradual, entropic dispersal of color and light. . . ." Jardine was born and grew up in Yorkshire, England, and now lives and works in Texas.

SENSATION and PERCEPTION

Steven Yantis

Johns Hopkins University

WORTH PUBLISHERS

A Macmillan Higher Education Company

Vice President, Editorial and Production: Catherine Woods
Associate Publisher: Jessica Bayne
Developmental Editor: Len Neufeld
Editorial Assistant: Eric Dorger
Marketing Manager: Lindsay Johnson
Marketing Assistant: Julie Tompkins
Director of Print and Digital Development: Tracey Kuehn
Associate Managing Editor: Lisa Kinne
Project Editor: Kerry O'Shaughnessy
Media and Supplements Editor: Betsy Block
Photo Editor: Ted Szczepanski
Photo Researcher: Deborah Anderson
Interior and Cover Designer: Diana Blume
Illustration Coordinator: Bill Page
Illustrations: Kip Carter, MS CMI; Brad Gilleland, MS; Thel Melton; Network Graphics
Production Manager: Sarah Segal
Supplements Production Manager: Stacey Alexander
Supplements Project Editor: Julio Espin
Composition: Northeastern Graphic, Inc.
Printing and Binding: Quad/Graphics

Credit is given to the following sources for photos:

Figure 4.3 (p. 119): *first row:* iStockphoto/Thinkstock; Reflexstock; Reflexstock; Reflexstock; Imagesource; SIN/fotolia.com; *second row:* Artville; Reflexstock; Artville; Artville; Corbis; Lai Leng Yiap/fotolia.com; *third row:* Judith Collins/Alamy; Eyewire; Eyewire; Alex Mac/fotolia.com; Ensuper/fotolia.com; Artville; *fourth row:* Getty Images; Tony Cordoza/Alamy; Getty Images; mbongo/fotolia.com; Artville; PhotoSpin, Inc/Alamy; *fifth row:* Reflexstock; Artville; Getty Images; Image Source; EyeWire; Reflexstock; *sixth row:* Reflexstock; Reflexstock; Corbis; Getty Images; Eyewire; Kellis/fotolia.com.

Figure 4.4 (p. 119): *first row:* Sergio Ranalli/Getty Images; Gary Vestal/Getty Images; Frank Krahmer/Getty Images; Paul Goff/Getty Images; Brand X Pictures; *second row:* Wilfried Krecichwost/Getty Images; Wonderlust Industries/Getty Images; Reflexstock; James Young/Getty Images; Buena Vista Images/Getty Images; *third row:* Joseph Sohm/Getty Images; Joseph Sohm/Getty Images; Peter Hendrie/Getty Images; Enigma/Alamy; imagebroker/Alamy; *fourth row:* Graham Kirk/Getty Images; John P. Kelly/Getty Images; Steve St. John/National Geographic/Getty Images; David Evans/National Geographic/Getty Images; Image Source/Corbis.

Figure 4.5 (p. 120): *first row:* Philip Kramer/Getty Images; Purestock/Thinkstock; fotog/Getty Image; forcdan/fotolia.com; *second row:* fotog/Getty Images; Stephen Mallon/Getty Images; Stockbyte/Thinkstock; fotog/Getty Images; *third row:* Todd Gipstein/National Geographic/Getty Images; Robert Glusic/Getty Images; Lonny Kalfus/Getty Images; Hemera/Thinkstock; *fourth row:* Reflexstock; Grant Faint/Getty Image; iStockphoto/Thinkstock; Reflexstock.

Figure 13.1 (p. 429): *first row:* Mehmetali Uslu/Stock.xchng; Reflexstock; Reflexstock; *second row:* Photodisc/Getty Images; Reflexstock; Reflexstock; *third row:* Reflexstock; Reflexstock; Sergei Didok/iStockphoto.

Credit is given to the following sources for the vignettes that begin each chapter (see the References section for the full citations):

Chapter 1: Taylor, 2009; Chapter 2: Nordby, 1990; Chapter 3: Goodale & Milner, 2005; Chapter 4: Duchaine & Nakayama, 2006; Chapter 5: Heywood & Kentridge, 2003; Chapter 6: Barry, 2006; Sacks, 2006; Chapter 7: Zihl et al., 1983, pp. 314–315; Chapter 8: Driver & Vuilleumier, 2001; Chapter 9: Semaan & Megerian, 2010; Chapter 10: Mendez & Geehan, 1988; Chapter 11: Piccirilli et al., 2000; Chapter 12: Cole, 1995; Chapter 13: Birnbaum, 2008; Herz, 2007.

Library of Congress Control Number: 2012949534

ISBN-13: 978-0-7167-5754-2
ISBN-10: 0-7167-5754-0

Printed in the United States of America

First printing

Worth Publishers
41 Madison Avenue
New York, NY 10010
www.worthpublishers.com

Dedicated to my father, Phillip A. Yantis

ABOUT THE AUTHOR

Steven Yantis is Professor in the Department of Psychological and Brain Sciences at Johns Hopkins University, with secondary appointments in the Departments of Cognitive Science and Neuroscience. He studied experimental psychology as an undergraduate at the University of Washington in Seattle and received a PhD in experimental psychology at the University of Michigan. Following a year as a postdoctoral fellow at Stanford University, he joined the faculty at Johns Hopkins University, where he has been ever since. Yantis has research interests that include visual perception, attention, and cognition. Members of the Yantis laboratory measure behavior (response time, eye movements) and brain activity (functional MRI) as people carry out tasks that probe perception and attention. He has taught a variety of courses in human perception and attention for more than two decades. He received the Early Career Award from the American Psychological Association in 1994 and the Troland Research Award from the National Academy of Sciences in 1996.

BRIEF CONTENTS

CONTENTS

PREFACE

Understanding the human mind and brain is arguably the most exciting scientific challenge of the twenty-first century. Astonishing progress has been made in unraveling the connections between mind, brain, and behavior in all areas of cognitive neuroscience. But it is in the realm of perception that these connections are best understood. Throughout this book, we will see that our understanding of how people and other organisms perceive the world has undergone a revolution over the last two decades, driven by dazzling scientific advances, including fundamental discoveries about the genetic bases of perception and important technological breakthroughs in neuroimaging. I wrote this book to convey these achievements by integrating the classic findings of the 1950s–1990s with the more recent discoveries that have transformed our ideas about how the mind and brain function.

My aim is to tell the story of perception in a way that brings out the purposes that perception serves, showing how perceptual systems have been shaped by evolutionary pressures to help organisms survive and reproduce. Each chapter emphasizes this evolutionary basis of perception by highlighting how perception serves behavioral goals. In addition, each includes the following features

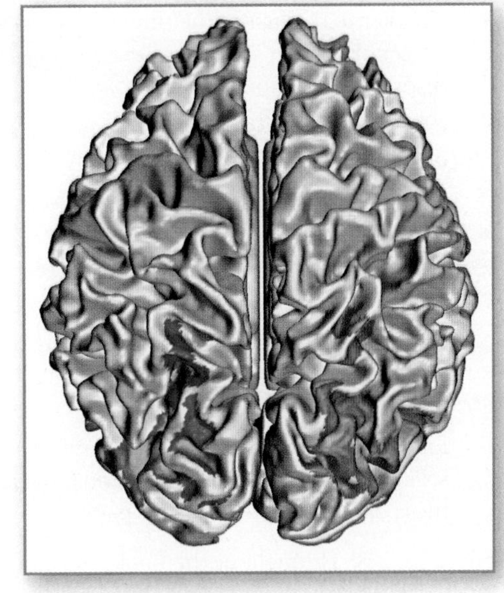

Neuroimaging reveals human brain activity during shifts of attention. (See Chapter 8; image courtesy of Y.-C. Chiu.)

- Integrated coverage of behavioral, physiological, and neuroimaging research
- An opening vignette about a clinical syndrome that results in a perceptual deficit, to demonstrate how specific aspects of perception depend on the functioning of specific parts of the central nervous system
- An Applications section showing how technology can be applied to enhance and extend perception
- Clear and detailed explanations, supported by highly effective illustrations and a strong and comprehensive array of pedagogical features and supplementary materials

Chapter 1 lays out the foundations of research in sensation and perception. It provides basic information about how neurons convey information within vast networks, and it introduces cognitive neuropsychology and functional neuroimaging (EEG, MEG, PET, and fMRI), key methods for investigating how the brain supports perception. It also introduces behavioral methods in perception research, including psychophysics and signal detection theory. The experiments discussed throughout the rest of the book all employ one or more of these methods, so a clear understanding of the methods is a critical first step.

Every subsequent chapter emphasizes how the findings from multiple research methods tend to converge, yielding a comprehensive and multifaceted view of how a given domain of perception works. A good example is the question of how the visual system supports motion perception: behavioral experiments have established the exquisite sensitivity of the visual system to moving objects of all kinds; recordings of the activity of single neurons in monkeys have revealed a brain region specialized for processing motion; people with brain damage in this region can't see motion; fMRI shows that this region is very active when humans view motion and that this activity is strongly correlated with perceptual judgments about motion; and shifts of attention toward or away from motion in a visual scene change both the neural activity in this region and the observer's ability to experience motion.

Following the foundational material in Chapter 1, the book covers the senses in a clear and logical order: first vision (Chapters 2–8), then audition (Chapters 9–11), and then the body senses (Chapter 12) and the chemical senses of smell and taste (Chapter 13).

- Chapter 2 covers light and the structure and function of the eyes, including disorders of vision.
- Chapter 3 focuses on how the brain processes the neural signals provided by the eyes.
- Chapter 4 explains object recognition, arguably the primary purpose of vision.
- Chapters 5–7 cover the perception of color, depth, and motion, respectively, as well as perception to guide action (e.g., catching a fly ball).
- Chapter 8 discusses how attention affects what we perceive, with a focus on visual attention.
- Chapter 9, the first of the three chapters on audition, explores the physical and perceptual dimensions of sound and the structure and function of the ear, including disorders of audition.
- Chapter 10 discusses how the brain processes sound, how we determine the location of sound sources, and how we analyze auditory scenes into different "auditory objects."
- Chapter 11 explains how the auditory system responds to the complexities of speech and music.
- Chapter 12 explores the body senses. The largest single topic is touch, but the body senses are amazingly diverse, including the perception of pain, temperature, and limb and hand position; the use of touch in object recognition; and the perception of balance and acceleration.
- Finally, Chapter 13 covers the chemical senses of smell and taste, where recent scientific breakthroughs have fundamentally changed our understanding of how these often-neglected senses operate.

Throughout the book, illustrations drawn in collaboration with Kip Carter (University of Georgia) provide fresh visual representations of sensory systems and phenomena. Anaglyphs that can be viewed in 3-D using the glasses provided with each copy of the book help illustrate how the visual system uses the slightly different views from the two eyes to create a vivid sense of depth.

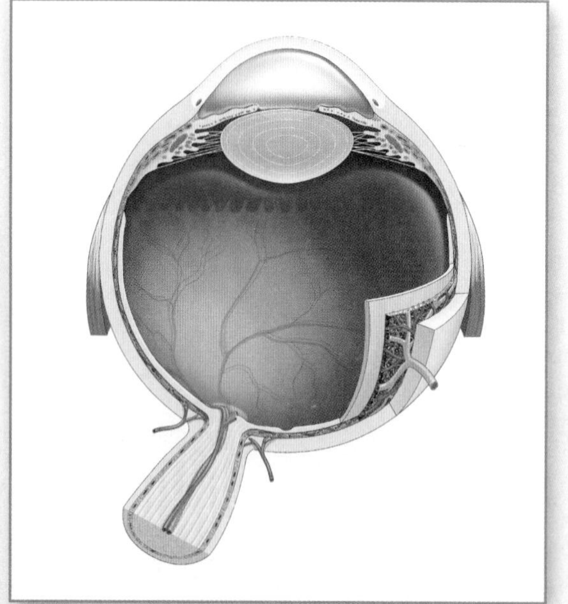

Structures of the human eye. (See Chapter 2.)

To view this anaglyph in 3-D, look at it through the glasses that came with this book. (See Chapter 6.) [Glyn Kirk/AFP/Getty Images]

Support for Learning: Interactive Demonstrations Online and Supplemental Features in This Book

More than 50 topic-relevant demonstrations, available on the book's Web site, let students view and interact with simulations of perceptual processes that are best presented dynamically rather than through static illustrations, and they give students the opportunity to participate in simulations of experiments. (Access to these online demonstrations can be obtained via the Web site at www.worthpublishers.com/yantis; the Web site also gives students free access to study quizzes and to interactive flashcards with key terms from the book.)

In addition, the following features are part of every chapter in the book:

- Key terms are highlighted in the text and defined in the margins.
- "Check Your Understanding" self-study questions appear at the end of most main sections.
- More thought-provoking "Expand Your Understanding" questions appear at the end of the chapter, offering a chance to connect ideas in new ways.
- Following the Applications section at the end of each chapter is a chapter summary, organized by the main headings in the chapter, and an alphabetical list of the key terms in the chapter, including the page on which each term is defined.
- Each chapter ends with "Read More About It," an annotated list of key additional readings on the chapter topic.

Together, these elements provide interlocking support for learning about the mind and brain and how we perceive and understand the world. Mastering this material opens a gateway for students with deeper interests in psychology, cognitive science, and neuroscience—fundamentally important fields for this century and beyond.

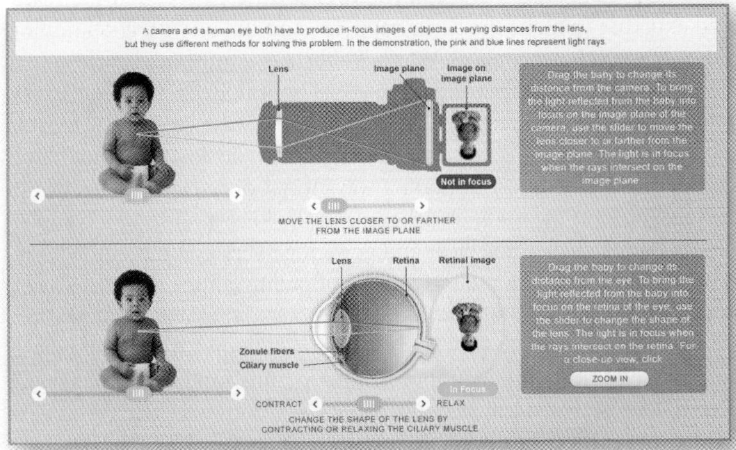

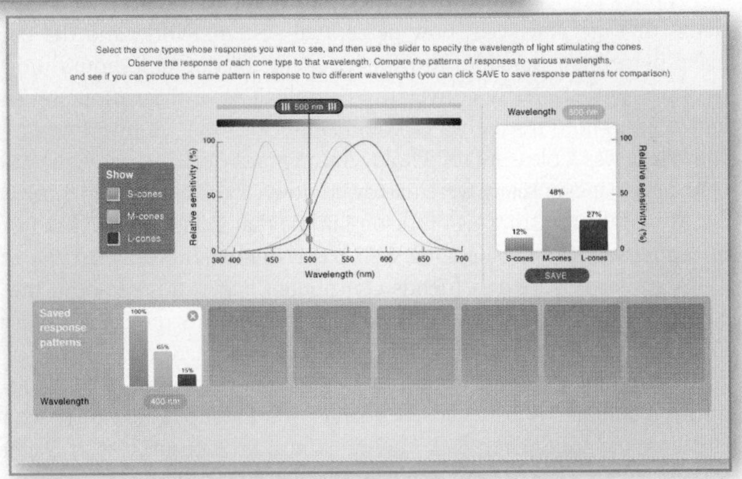

(top) From Demonstration 2.1, Focusing Light in a Camera and in the Eye. (bottom) From Demonstration 5.3, Trichromatic Color Representation. These and many other interactive demonstrations are available on the book's Web site.

Instructor's Materials

A number of ancillary materials are available free for instructors:

- Interactive Presentation Slides for instructors, including all the illustrations from the book, as well as the chapter outlines. These slides can be customized to fit your needs and can be found on the book's Web site.
- Instructor's Manual prepared by Alexis Grosofsky (Beloit College), available online and in print, includes chapter summaries, lecture discussion topics, classroom activities, handouts, and additional Web and print materials.
- Test Bank prepared by Larence Becker and Craig Clarke (Salisbury University) includes a variety of multiple-choice, true-false, short-answer, and essay questions for every chapter of the book. It is available in print or on a dual-platform CD. The computerized Test Bank in the Diploma system guides instructors through the process of creating and editing test items.
- A password-protected Web site offers teaching resources, including a digital version of the instructor's manual, answers to the midchapter and end-of-chapter study questions, and a grade book for student quizzes.

Acknowledgments

Many people have contributed to the creation of this book in ways large and small, and none more than my family. When I started this project, my daughters were in middle school; now Alyson teaches first grade and has a family of her own, and Caitlyn is in graduate school. They and especially my wife, Kathy, have been endlessly supportive and immensely patient throughout this project.

Len Neufeld, the developmental editor, has been with me every step of the way in creating this book. His clear writing, detailed and skillful editing, and genuine enthusiasm for the material have made this project a joy. Jessica Bayne oversaw the project and the many people who contributed expertise to make the book happen—and did so with good humor, equanimity, and wisdom. Many other people at Worth Publishers contributed their expert knowledge to produce a book of high quality and great visual appeal: Kerry O'Shaughnessy, the Project Editor, oversaw the production of the physical book and was occasionally flexible with deadlines. Bill Page, the Illustration Coordinator, and Ted Szczepanski, the Photo Editor, were amazingly persistent, creative, and fast in finding ways to produce clear figures. Sarah Segal, the Production Manager, kept the book on schedule in the final months of a complex production process. Diana Blume created the clear and engaging overall design of the book. Eric Dorger, Editorial Assistant, managed a million aspects of pulling all the pieces together. Patti Brecht and Linda Elliott provided careful and detailed copyediting and proofreading, respectively. Laura Pople and Barbara Brooks provided important support early in the project. Dr. Tomonori Nagano provided translation help in obtaining permission from the Japanese publisher of the Ishihara color vision test featured in Chapter 5.

A book on perception depends critically on figures and demonstrations that illustrate things that are perceived, how perceptual systems work, and the parts of the body that make perception possible. Kip Carter spent uncountable hours producing the beautiful illustrations that clearly convey the complexities of the various sensory systems covered in the text. Photo researcher Deborah Anderson's eye for fine art and for matching images with ideas was a pleasure to behold. Among many other things, she discovered a vast array of images that eventually were narrowed down to 13 chapter-opening works of art; she also discovered the arresting art of Alison Jardine that graces the book's cover. Graig Donini and his team produced the amazing Web-based demonstrations.

Many colleagues and friends contributed expert advice about the vast array of topics covered in this book. I would never have started this project without the inspiration provided by Bruce Borland and Mike McBeath over a decade ago. My friend and colleague Richard Abrams contributed enormously to the demonstrations, aided by former Johns Hopkins graduate students Robert Rauschenberger and Larence Becker. My wonderful colleagues at Hopkins, including Greg Ball, Yu-Chin Chiu, Ed Connor, Gislin Dagnelie, Howard Egeth, Stewart Hendry, Steve Hsiao, Mike McCloskey, Brenda Rapp, Melvin Rouse, Richard Schoen,

Janet Sunness, and Rudiger von der Heydt, all provided crucial insights about various domains of perception. Stewart and Steve in particular generously provided detailed and extremely valuable comments about many technical topics in perceptual neuroscience.

Several friends and colleagues (including those who hosted my very productive sabbaticals in Australia, New Zealand, New York, and Italy) provided expert knowledge about technical topics and intellectual stimulation during periods of intensive writing over the last few years. They include Francesca Bacci, Marisa Carrasco, Zhe Chen, Angelika Lingnau, David Melcher, Susanne Raisig, Suparna Rajaram, Roger Remington, Jens Schwarzbach, and Gary Van Essen.

Many people read various parts of the manuscript; some of them went above and beyond the call of duty by providing extremely useful, detailed, and good-natured comments on the text: Stewart Hendry (Johns Hopkins University); Steven Hsiao (Johns Hopkins University); Steven Roper (Miami University); Arty Samuel (Stony Brook University); Barbara Shinn-Cunningham (Boston University); and Robert Zatorre (McGill University). Taylor Chamberlain spent several hours a week for a year as a high school intern in my lab; she read every word of the manuscript and provided valuable comments that greatly improved the readability of the text.

Many experts in sensation and perception, including researchers and teachers from a variety of scientific and educational institutions, reviewed chapters and provided invaluable comments and suggestions. I am deeply grateful to each of you:

Aneeq Ahmad, *Henderson State University*
Frank Amthor, *University of Alabama at Birmingham*
Mike Babcock, *Montana State University*
Benoit-Antoine Bacon, *Bishop's University (Canada)*
Erik Blaser, *University of Massachusetts–Boston*
Barbara Blatchley, *Agnes Scott College*
Darlene Brodeur, *Acadia University (Canada)*
James Brown, *University of Georgia*
Michael Canterina, *Johns Hopkins University*
Joseph Cohen, *Mount Holyoke College*
Kathleen Cullen, *McGill University (Canada)*
David Devonis, *Graceland University*
Joshua Dobias, *University of New Hampshire*
Stephen Dopkins, *George Washington University*
Sue Dutch, *Westfield State University*
Robert Flint, *College of St. Rose*
John Flowers, *University of Nebraska–Lincoln*
Phyllis Freeman, *SUNY New Paltz*
Isabell Gauthier, *Vanderbilt University*
Kim Gerecke, *Rhodes College*
David Gooler, *University of Illinois*
Sean Green, *Medaille College*
Anthony Greene, *University of Wisconsin–Milwaukee*
Kalanit Grill-Spector, *Stanford University*
Sowon Hahn, *University of Oklahoma–Norman*
Billy Hammond, *University of Georgia*
Steven Horowitz, *Central Connecticut State University*
Steven Hsiao, *Johns Hopkins University*
Aaron Johnson, *Concordia University*
Michael Kisley, *University of Colorado–Colorado Springs*
Stephen Kitzis, *Fort Hays State University*
Fabio Leite, *Ohio State University–Lima*
Richard H. Masland, *Harvard University*
James Mazer, *Yale University*
Sandra McFadden, *Western Illinois University*
Patrick Monnier, *Colorado State University*
Cleve Mortimer, *University of South Florida*
Jonathan J. Nassi, *Harvard University*
Crystal Oberle, *Texas State University*
Andrew J. Oxenham, *University of Minnesota*
Christopher Pagano, *Clemson University*
Andrew Parker, *University of Oxford (England)*
Richard Pastore, *SUNY Binghamton*
John Philbeck, *George Washington University*
Dave Pittman, *Wofford College*
Chrislyn Randell, *Metropolitan State College of Denver*
Steven Roper, *University of Miami*
Michael Russell, *Washburn University of Topeka*
Arthur Samuel, *SUNY Stonybrook*
Lisa Sanders, *University of Massachusetts, Amherst*
Jim Schirillo, *Wake Forest University*
Barbara Shinn-Cunningham, *Boston University*
T. C. Sim, *Sam Houston State University*
Emily Skow, *Simpson College*
Gene Stoner, *Salk Institute*
Dan Swift, *University of Michigan–Dearborn*
Erik C. Tracy, *University of North Carolina at Pembroke*
Shaun Vercera, *University of Iowa*
Matt Wachowiak, *University of Utah*
Jeffrey Wagman, *Illinois State University*
Debbie Wang, *University of North Florida*
Sheree Watson, *University of Southern Mississippi*
Shannon Whitten, *University of Central Florida Palm Bay Center*
Donald Wilson, *University of Oklahoma*
Jessica Witt, *Purdue University*
Geoff Woodman, *Vanderbilt University*
Robert Zatorre, *Montreal Neurological Institute (Canada)*

Steven Yantis

Glen Arm, Maryland
September 2012

Alex Kanevsky, *Malanga II*, 2001. [Oil on board, 27.5 × 23 inches. Courtesy of Alex Kanevsky and J. Cacciola Gallery, New York and Dolby Chadwick Gallery, San Francisco.]

1

FOUNDATIONS

"I'm Having a Stroke!"

At 7:00 A.M. on December 10, 1996, Jill Taylor awoke and immediately felt a sharp and utterly unfamiliar pain behind her left eye. As she began her usual morning routine, she noticed some other things that didn't seem right: During her morning exercises, she felt like her mind was dissociated from her body, as if she were observing someone else exercising, and her movements were awkward and halting; then, when she turned on the shower, the water made a disturbingly loud roar, contributing to the headache; also, the usual "internal voice" with which we monitor, plan, and generally track our progress through the day was strangely silent. Yet, despite these odd perceptual changes, she felt a growing sense of peace and even euphoria.

Suddenly, just as she was about to sit down in the shower and enjoy the moment, her mind broke through the silence: she realized that something was wrong with her brain and that she'd better find out what it was. At that moment, she noticed that her right arm was hanging limply at her side and that she couldn't move it, and that brought the answer to her in a flash: *"I'm having a stroke!"* She suddenly felt incredibly tired, but she knew that if she lay down for even a moment she might never get up again. She had to get help.

She tried to formulate a plan but struggled to generate a coherent sequence of ideas. She got out of the shower and tried to find her doctor's number in the stack of business cards on her desk, but to her great dismay she couldn't perceive the writing on the cards as writing. She couldn't even see the shape of the cards as rectangles. She decided to call a friend at work to come and get her—but what was the number at work? After nearly an hour of effort and concentration, she managed to call, but when her friend Steve answered, she couldn't understand a word he said. She tried to say, "This is Jill. I need help!" but all that came out were grunts and groans. Despite not knowing what Steve was saying, she did grasp that his voice had a soothing and reassuring tone, so she knew that help would come.

Jill's stroke that morning resulted from a hemorrhage, bleeding from a break in a blood vessel in the left half of her brain, near regions that are involved in hearing, seeing, memory, and language. Damage due to this bleeding caused the perceptual impairments she experienced, impairments that didn't make her blind or deaf but that interrupted the normal activity of her brain in way that resulted in jumbled and incoherent perceptions of the world. In the years following her stroke, Jill recovered almost completely. *My Stroke of Insight*, her book about her experiences, provides a dramatic and educational glimpse into the unexpected ways perception can change when the brain is damaged.

In the chapters ahead, we'll discuss numerous other case studies of individuals with perceptual impairments caused by brain damage or arising in other ways, and we'll see how each case reveals the tight linkages among mind, brain, and perception.

Chapter Outline

In order to survive and reproduce, organisms must respond to the physical conditions of their environment. This is true of even the simplest organisms: some single-celled bacteria, for example, respond to the presence of toxic chemicals by paddling away with their flagella. A Venus flytrap that snaps shut on an unlucky bug is also responding to the physical conditions of its environment—in this case, a bug in its "jaws." Although we might be willing to say that these organisms are *sensing* the environmental conditions, we might be reluctant to say that they are *perceiving* those conditions. We'll apply the term "perceiving" to organisms with nervous systems—including people—in which specialized sensory cells convert physical features of the environment into electrochemical signals that motivate physiological, behavioral, emotional, and cognitive responses and can give rise to awareness.

This book is a survey of how humans and other animals sense and perceive their local environment. **Sensation** refers to the initial steps in this process—converting physical features of the environment into electrochemical signals within specialized nerve cells, and sending those signals to the brain for processing. Over the course of evolution, animals have acquired a variety of physiological functions called **senses**, each of which has its own array of specialized cells, tissues, and organs for converting particular environmental features into electrochemical signals that are then sent to the brain. For example, the sense of sight converts light into signals, and the sense of hearing converts sound into signals.

Perception refers to the later steps in the process, whereby the initial sensory signals are used to form mental **representations** of the objects and events in a scene so they can be recognized, stored in memory, and used in thought and action. In many complex organisms—including humans—perception also includes conscious awareness of the objects and events in a scene. But as we'll see over the course of our detailed explorations of the various senses, there isn't any sharp dividing line between sensation and perception, and really no need for one.

sensation The initial steps in the perceptual process, whereby physical features of the environment are converted into electrochemical signals that are sent to the brain for processing.

senses Physiological functions for converting particular environmental features into electrochemical signals.

perception The later steps in the perceptual process, whereby the initial sensory signals are used to represent objects and events so they can be identified, stored in memory, and used in thought and action.

representations Information in the mind and brain used to identify objects and events, to store them in memory, and to support thought and action.

World, Brain, and Mind

To some extent, organisms' knowledge about the world is innate—a spider emerges from its egg "knowing" how and where to spin webs and capture prey, and a human infant is born "knowing" how to nurse at her mother's breast. But other ways of knowing—awareness of current conditions or learning from experience—depend on information that is made available by the senses, whether it's knowledge acquired by touch (fingering through the change in your pocket to find a quarter), olfaction (smelling milk to find out if it's drinkable), or any other sense. Indeed, many complex tasks require knowledge obtained via multiple senses at the same time. For example, when you drive a car, you have to pick up information simultaneously from vision (where is the surrounding traffic?), audition (that ambulance siren means pull over), and touch (how firmly do I have to grip the steering wheel to turn it?).

The scientific study of perception is highly interdisciplinary. College courses on this topic are often taught in psychology departments because perception is an aspect of how the mind works. But the disciplines relevant to a complete understanding of perception include physics and chemistry, which involve the study of things that can be sensed (light, sound, chemical substances, and so forth); cognitive neuroscience, the study of the brain, cognition, and behavior; neuropsychology and neurology, the study of brain damage and its effects on perception; computer science and artificial intelligence, concerned with building computational devices that can model how organisms perceive and respond to the world; biomedical engineering and radiology, fields that are relevant to imaging the brain and building sensory prosthetics; and philosophy, which considers topics like subjective awareness, consciousness, and knowledge.

Each of these fields contributes to the story that will unfold in this book. Our goal in telling this story is to develop a scientific understanding of how perception works, a goal that we'll try to achieve by surveying the results of experiments carried out by scientists in all these disciplines. In the process, we'll discuss how scientific reasoning about perception proceeds from initial ideas and questions to the formulation of hypotheses about how particular aspects of perception work, followed by experiments in which evidence concerning the hypotheses is collected and used to draw conclusions.

Now let's briefly review some aspects of the perceptual process to get a sense of where psychologists and cognitive neuroscientists start in deciding what questions to ask.

The Perceptual Process

The starting point for perception is the world itself—the objects and events in the environment that organisms perceive. These objects and events give rise to physical phenomena that can be sensed: a tree reflects light that can be seen; a slamming door produces sound waves that can be heard; a glass of wine contains molecules that can be smelled and tasted. The objects and events that are perceived and the physical phenomena they produce are both referred to as **stimuli** (singular *stimulus*), but it's useful to make a distinction between them. The thing in the world—the tree or the slamming door—is called a **distal stimulus.** The physical phenomenon evoked by a distal stimulus—the reflected light or the sound waves—that impinges on the specialized cells of the relevant sense is called a **proximal stimulus.**

The cells of the nervous system that produce and transmit information-carrying electrochemical signals are called **neurons,** and the electrochemical signals they carry are called **neural signals.** The specialized neurons that convert proximal stimuli into neural signals are called **sensory receptors**—for example, the neurons in your eye that convert light into neural signals are called *photoreceptors,* and the neurons in your fingertips that convert pressure on your skin into neural signals are called *mechanoreceptors.*

To illustrate the process of perception, let's suppose you're playing tennis (see Figure 1.1). The various objects and events that are part of the tennis match—including the ball, the racquet you're holding, and your opponent, as well as events like a racquet striking a ball—are distal stimuli, the things that you want to perceive. The proximal stimuli produced by these distal stimuli include light reflected into your eyes from the objects in the scene; sounds entering your ears, produced by your opponent's racquet striking the ball; and the pressure of the racquet on the skin of your hand. Sensory receptors in your eyes, ears, and skin convert these proximal stimuli into neural signals that are sent to the brain.

Your brain not only processes these signals into visual, auditory, and tactile perceptions, but also combines them into an integrated conscious experience of the match as a whole. For example, neural signals containing visual information about the trajectory of the ball and signals containing information about your body position and motion are sent to the action-control centers of your brain to guide your movements. And you can store your perception of the match in memory, and tell a friend about the match the next day.

Other stimuli might also be converted by specialized receptors into neural signals—for instance, molecules from nearby pine trees might be converted into neural signals by receptors in your nose. But you might not become consciously aware of the pine smell or store it in memory, because you're not attending to the smell; after all, it's not an important part of your primary goal, which is to play the match.

Often, the speed and accuracy of perception are enhanced by the perceiver's knowledge about the current scene and by the perceiver's expectations about what kinds of things are likely to be present or to occur—for example, knowing that you arranged for your cousin to meet you for tennis will speed up the process of recognizing him when he arrives. The perceiver's knowledge and expectations about the world, as well as the perceiver's goals that determine what is important and worth attending to (the ball's trajectory) and what's not (the smell of the pine trees), are referred to as **top-down information,** which is contrasted with the **bottom-up information** contained in the neural signals from receptors. (The idea that top-down information plays a key role in perception was first proposed in 1866 by the German scientist Hermann von Helmholtz and is now well established in perceptual science.)

stimuli The objects and events that are perceived (distal stimuli) and the physical phenomena they produce (proximal stimuli).

distal stimulus A perceived object or event in the world.

proximal stimulus A physical phenomenon evoked by a distal stimulus that impinges on the specialized cells of a sense.

neurons Cells of the nervous system that produce and transmit information-carrying signals.

neural signals Information-carrying electrochemical signals produced and transmitted by neurons.

sensory receptors Specialized neurons that convert proximal stimuli into neural signals.

top-down information An observer's knowledge, expectations, and goals, which can affect perception.

bottom-up information The information contained in neural signals from receptors.

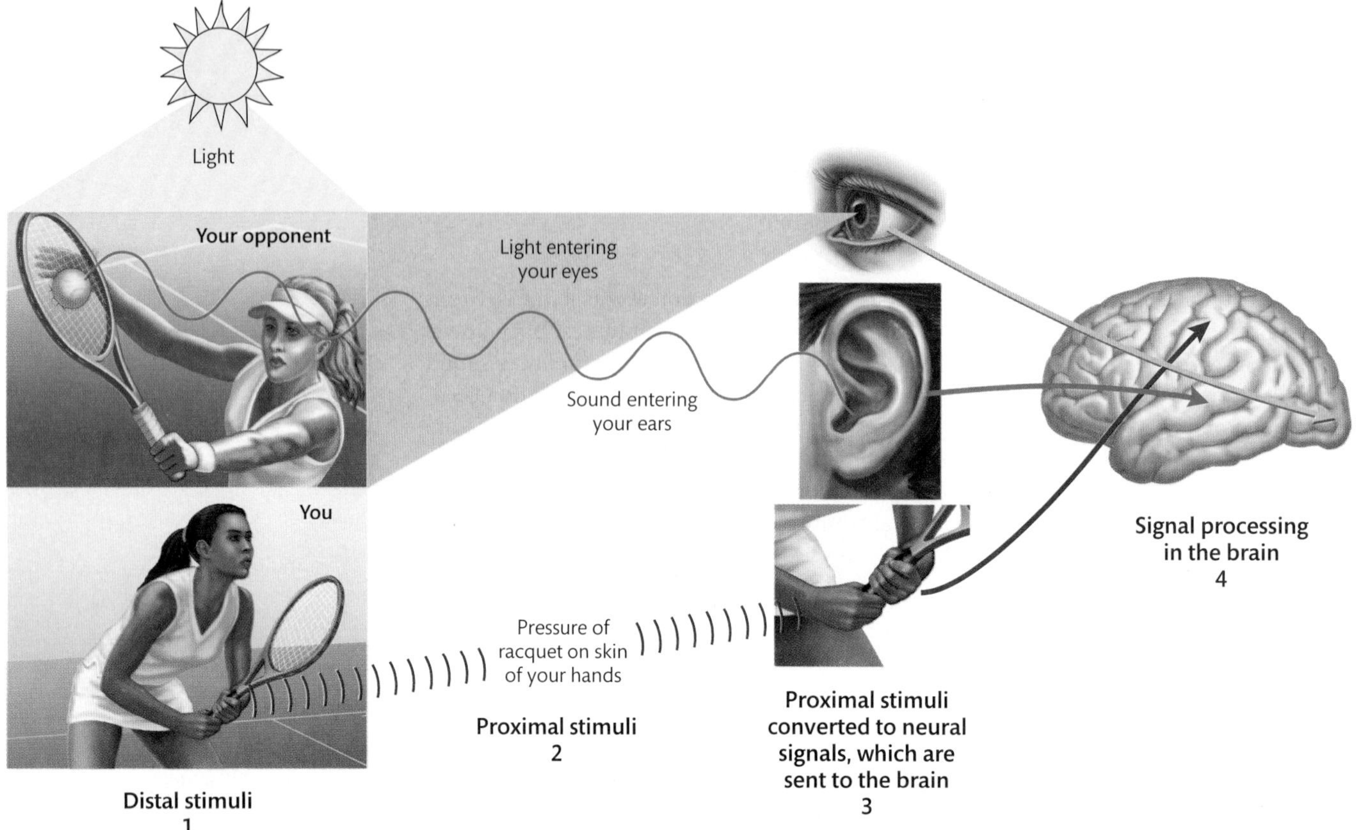

Figure 1.1 The Process of Perception (1) A tennis match contains distal stimuli—objects and events that can be perceived. (2) The distal stimuli give rise to proximal stimuli—physical phenomena such as light entering the eyes, sound entering the ears, and pressure against the skin that (3) are converted into information-carrying neural signals by specialized receptors; these signals are sent to the brain. (4) Within the brain, neural signals represent visual, auditory, and tactile perceptions that give rise to conscious awareness and provide a basis for a variety of cognitive activities, including thought and planning, memory storage, and action guidance.

Given these basic ideas about the perceptual process, we can now discuss the next important issue in our investigation of perception: What kinds of questions should we ask in order to understand perception scientifically?

Three Main Types of Questions

There are, broadly speaking, three kinds of questions that we'll need to ask as we explore perception. First, how does the proximal stimulus carry information about the thing that is perceived? For example, how does light projected into the eyes carry information about the position, shape, and color of an object in the world? How does sound carry information about an event like a clap of thunder, a spoken sentence, or a musical passage?

Second, how is the proximal stimulus (a physical stimulus like light or sound) transformed into neural signals—a process called **transduction**? How do these neural signals form a **neural code**—a pattern of signals that carries information to the brain and that can serve as a representation of the stimulus being perceived? And how is the information in the neural code processed in the brain?

Third, what is the relationship between perceptual experience—what we see or hear or feel—and the distal stimulus, the thing that is perceived? This last question falls into the realm of a field of study known as **psychophysics**, which is concerned with relating psychological experience to physical stimuli.

transduction The transformation of a physical stimulus into neural signals.

neural code A pattern of neural signals that carries information about a stimulus and can serve as a representation of that stimulus.

psychophysics A field of study concerned with relating psychological experience to physical stimuli.

To answer these kinds of questions, scientists use rigorous, quantitative, and repeatable experimental methods, including the methods of cognitive neuroscience and the methods of psychophysics. Cognitive neuroscience measures neural activity both at the level of individual neurons and at the level of groups of neurons and neural circuits in the brain. Psychophysics assesses perceptual experience on the basis of simple behavioral responses, such as reporting whether a stimulus was detected or whether two stimuli appeared to be the same or different. These methods are the tools that perceptual scientists use to investigate the relationships between distal stimuli, proximal stimuli, neural activity in the brain, and perceptual experience. By examining how these factors are related, we can develop an account of the causal chains that link them.

How Many Senses Are There?

The traditional answer to the question of how many senses there are is five: vision, audition, touch, smell, and taste. The idea of "the five senses" dates back at least to Aristotle. But senses evolve in response to the physical properties of objects and events in the world that organisms need to sense in order to survive, and a moment's thought will tell you that there are many more than just those five properties—light, sound, mechanical forces on the skin, molecules in the nose, and molecules in the mouth—that humans and other animals need to sense. In Table 1.1, for example, the "Primary Senses" column lists not only the traditional five senses but five additional senses, which, along with touch, comprise what we'll refer to as the *body senses.* These evolved to sense limb and body position, pain, skin temperature, balance, and body movement.

Moreover, Table 1.1 shows that vision, audition, and tactile perception can be further broken down into multiple physical and perceptual dimensions. Vision, for example, represents the brightness, color, shape, texture, location, and motion of objects. Audition provides information about loudness, pitch, and other dimensions of sound, as well as about the location of sound sources. Gustation provides information about taste qualities such as sweet, salty, bitter, and sour, and about the intensity and pleasantness of tastes and the texture, spiciness, and temperature of foods. And the body senses include not only the many dimensions listed in Table 1.1 but also dimensions that provide information about bodily states such as hunger (blood glucose level), thirst (body fluid levels), internal body temperature, and muscle fatigue.

Some animals have evolved the ability to sense other physical properties of the world, in response to their environments and their ways of life. Some species of fish, for example, can sense changes in electric fields emitted by their own bodies and by other fish; some species of birds can sense the earth's magnetic field; and bees can sense a property of light called *polarization.*

The point is that the question of how many senses there are is more complex than you might have thought, even considering only human senses. Differences among the senses reflect the differences in the ways that each sense evolved as our ancestors adapted to the physical stimuli in their environments.

Evolution and Perception

The biological structure and function of every organism on Earth is a result of billions of years of evolution driven by the mechanisms of **natural selection**—Darwin's influential idea, which lies at the foundation of virtually all of modern biological science (Darwin, 1859/1988). At the most general level, the modern theory of evolution based on natural selection contains these core ideas:

natural selection The basic mechanism of biological evolution, whereby adaptive traits are more likely to be passed on to offspring through genetic inheritance and to become increasingly prevalent in a population.

- Organisms have observable characteristics, or traits, called *phenotypes* (e.g., structures like eyes and ears). Phenotypes result from a genetic code called a *genotype,* carried in DNA, that uses the machinery of the cell to produce the organism's phenotypical structures and functions.

TABLE 1.1 Human Senses

Primary Senses	Physical Stimuli Transduced	Receptors	What Is Sensed: Physical Dimensions	What Is Sensed: Perceptual Dimensions
Vision (sight) (Chapters 2–7)	Light	Photoreceptors in eye	Intensity	Brightness
			Wavelength	Color
			Spatial distribution	Shape, texture, location in 3-D space
			Temporal distribution	Motion
Audition (hearing) (Chapters 9–11)	Sound	Hair cells in inner ear (in cochlea)	Amplitude	Loudness
			Frequency	Pitch
			Waveform	Timbre
			Interaural differences	Location of sound source in 3-D space
Tactile perception (touch) (Chapter 12)	Mechanical forces	Mechanoreceptors in skin	Skin indentation	Spatial pattern, texture, shape
			Skin stretch	Hand conformation
			Skin motion, low-frequency vibration of skin	Slip, grip control
			High-frequency vibration of skin	Fine texture, transmitted vibration
Proprioception (body perception) (Chapter 12)	Mechanical forces	Nerve fibers in muscles, tendons, and joints	Muscle tension	Limb position and movement
Nociception (pain perception) (Chapter 12)	Mechanical forces, molecules, extreme temperatures	Nociceptors in skin	Tissue damage	Pain quality (e.g., sharp or throbbing) and location on or in body
Thermoreception (temperature perception) (Chapter 12)	Heat	Thermoreceptors in skin	Skin temperature	Heat, cold
Balance (Chapter 12)	Gravitational force	Hair cells in inner ear (in semicircular canals)	Head orientation (tilt)	Balance
Body movement (Chapter 12)	Acceleration	Hair cells in inner ear (in semicircular canals)	Head acceleration (including rotation)	Body movement
Olfaction (smell) (Chapter 13)	Molecules	Olfactory receptor neurons in nose	Molecular structure and concentration	Odor
Gustation (taste) (Chapter 13)	Molecules	Taste receptor cells in mouth	Molecular structure and concentration	Taste

- The genetic code is transmitted in DNA from one generation to the next via reproduction. DNA can undergo random mutations, resulting in new genetic sequences that might produce new phenotypes. Occasionally a mutation yields a new trait that is advantageous (adaptive) in the organism's environment and that can be passed on to offspring.
- Organisms with adaptive new traits compete more effectively for resources in the environment and are therefore more likely to survive and reproduce than

organisms lacking these traits. Thus, through natural selection, an increasing proportion of individual organisms in a population will come to possess those traits. (Such traits are said to increase an individual's *fitness*—hence the phrase "survival of the fittest.")

Like all other traits, the senses have evolved by natural selection. Consider, for example, the human sense of vision—the perception of things that reflect light. The light that we can see—visible light—is electromagnetic radiation made up of a small range of wavelengths within the very wide spectrum of electromagnetic radiation emitted by all the different types of radiation sources in the universe. Why can we only see light within this narrow range, and not other wavelengths, like infrared or ultraviolet light or, for that matter, radio waves?

One likely answer comes from the fact that the wavelengths of visible light are the most abundant wavelengths in the light emitted by the sun. And these wavelengths are especially well transmitted in seawater, the environment in which eyes like ours are thought to have evolved in fish, some 400 million years ago (Fernald, 1997). During that period, genetic mutations led to the development of eyes that provided more and better information about objects and events in that environment (via light reflected from them), and by the process of natural selection, this adaptive new phenotype was preferentially passed on to subsequent generations.

At various points in the remaining chapters, we'll point out how evolution by natural selection may have similarly given rise to other perceptual abilities.

Check Your Understanding

1.1 Use these terms to fill in the blanks in the paragraph below: distal stimuli, neural signals, neurons, proximal stimuli, sensory receptors, top-down information.

The process of perception begins with __________ that produce physical phenomena called __________ that specialized __________ called __________ convert into __________ that are sent to the brain. The speed and accuracy of perception can be enhanced by expectations and other types of __________.

1.2 Name at least three human senses beyond the traditional five senses, and list the physical dimensions sensed by each.

1.3 Human voices tend to vary in pitch across a fairly narrow range, but people can hear sounds much higher in pitch than the highest-pitched voice and much lower in pitch than the lowest-pitched voice. Nevertheless, people are most sensitive to sounds in that same narrow range of pitches—that is, we can hear softer sounds within that range than outside that range. Briefly explain why you might expect this to be the case.

Exploring Perception by Studying Neurons and the Brain

Perception relies on the activity of neurons, beginning with the activity of receptors that transduce proximal stimuli into neural signals that are propagated through vast networks of other neurons in the brain. The idea that perception is based on neural activity can be traced in the modern era to the German scientist Johannes Müller, who in 1826 articulated what has been termed the "law of specific nerve energies," which states that the kinds of perceptions we have depend on which neurons are activated, not on what's activating those neurons. For example, receptor neurons in the eye generate visual perceptions, regardless of whether the neurons are stimulated by light entering the eye (the typical method), by the gentle pressure of your finger against the side of your eye, or even by electrical currents from retinal prosthetic devices.

Johannes Müller (1801–1858). [Mary Evans/The Image Works]

Charles Sherrington (1857–1952). [Wellcome Library, London]

In the late nineteenth century, questions about the basic structure and organization of the brain were the subject of much debate—for example, the question of whether or not neurons are physically connected, like wires (they're not). In 1906 the British scientist Charles Sherrington (who would receive the 1932 Nobel Prize in Physiology or Medicine) articulated what are now recognized as the fundamental principles of brain function, including how neurons communicate with one another in networks.

Much later, the Canadian neurosurgeon Wilder Penfield (who had been a student of Sherrington's) found that when he directly stimulated neurons in certain areas of the brain of awake patients undergoing surgery for epilepsy, the patients would report the sensation of being touched at certain places on their body. In this way, Penfield constructed a complete "touch map," showing how the perceived location of touches on the body surface corresponds to the location of neural activity in the brain (Penfield & Rasmussen, 1950).

In the 1950s and 1960s, as the relationship between neural activity and perception was further explored, neuroscientists discovered that individual neurons in the frog's brain responded to specific visual stimuli, like the movement of a fly (Barlow, 1953), and other researchers investigated how changes in physical stimuli produce corresponding, quantitatively precise changes in neural activity (Mountcastle et al., 1963). According to the **neuron doctrine,** perception depends on the combined activity of many specialized neurons, each of which responds to specific aspects of a stimulus, called *trigger features* (Barlow, 1972). For example, one visual neuron might respond to movement of an object in a particular direction and speed; another might respond to a particular contour shape. This general idea continues to be an important guiding principle of perceptual neuroscience (Parker & Newsome, 1998).

neuron doctrine The principle that perception depends on the combined activity of many specialized neurons, each of which responds to specific aspects of a stimulus.

In this section, we'll begin to consider how this principle applies in practice. First, we'll explore the structure, function, and communication methods of neurons and see how neural activity is measured, and in broad strokes we'll describe how the brain is organized. Then we'll discuss how brain functions can be assessed, both by examining patterns of impaired performance following brain damage (the field of cognitive neuropsychology) and by functional neuroimaging of brain activity in healthy volunteers carrying out carefully controlled perceptual tasks.

Neurons and Neural Signals

Neurons are cells, and like any other type of cell, each neuron has a **cell membrane** that separates what's inside the cell from what's outside the cell. Every neuron also has a nucleus (which contains DNA) and a variety of other structures that support normal cellular functioning (e.g., mitochondria). The main characteristic that distinguishes neurons from other types of cells is their ability to receive and transmit neural signals. Also, neurons are extensively interconnected: any one neuron sends signals to and receives signals from as many as several thousand other neurons.

cell membrane A cell structure that separates what's inside the cell from what's outside the cell.

Figure 1.2 shows a photomicrograph and a schematic diagram of a typical neuron. The neuron's **cell body** (or *soma,* from the Greek for "body") contains the nucleus. Two prominent types of projections emanate from the cell body: **dendrites,** which receive signals from other neurons, and an **axon,** which conducts signals to the **axon terminals,** where the signals are transmitted to other neurons. Any given axon may branch into as many as several thousand axon terminals, each of which ends immediately adjacent to a dendrite or the cell body of another neuron. A bundle of axons that travel together from one location in the nervous system to another is called a **nerve** (or, within the brain, a *tract*).

cell body The part of a cell that contains the nucleus.

dendrites Projections that emanate from the cell body of a neuron and that receive signals from other neurons.

axon A projection that emanates from the cell body of a neuron and that conducts neural signals to the axon terminals, for transmission to other neurons.

axon terminals Endings of an axon, where neural signals are transmitted to other neurons.

nerve A bundle of axons that travel together from one location in the nervous system to another.

Neurons come in many shapes and sizes and can differ in many other ways, such as the extent of their dendritic trees and the length of their axons (from less than a millimeter to more than two meters). Some types of neurons have no axon, while other types lack dendrites, but even these types still carry neural signals.

In the next two sections, we'll consider a little neurophysiology, which will help clarify, first, how signals are propagated down the axon of individual neurons and, second,

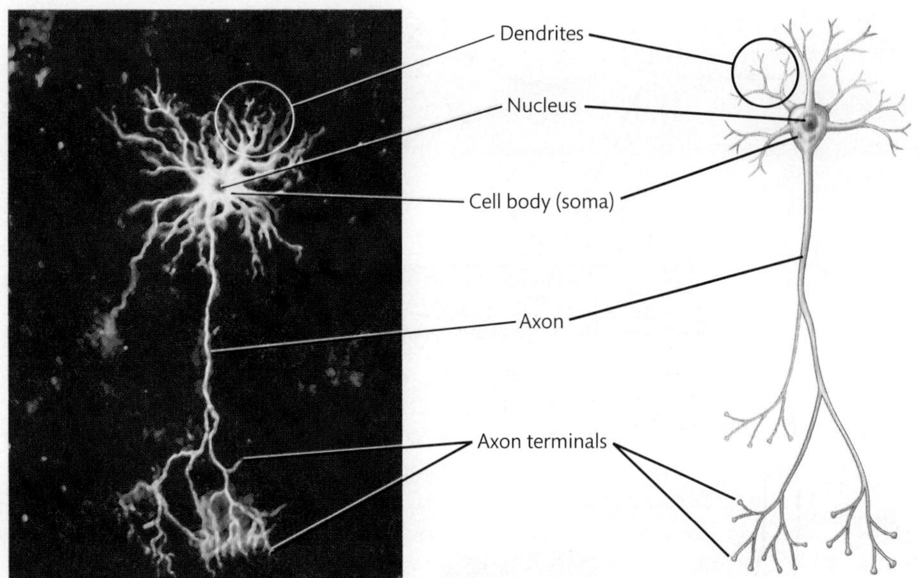

Figure 1.2 **A Typical Neuron** The labels point to the principal parts of a typical neuron in the brain. The cell body (or soma) contains the nucleus; dendrites receive signals from other neurons; and the axon conducts signals to the axon terminals, which transmit signals to other neurons. [James Cavallini/Photo Researchers]

how signals are transmitted between neurons. Because receptors in the various sensory systems (photoreceptors in the eye, hair cells in the ear, and so forth) transduce sensory input in highly specialized and varied ways, we'll postpone discussion of transduction until the relevant later chapters. Here we'll focus on the functions of neurons that are not receptors.

Action Potentials

An **action potential** is an electrochemical signal that begins in the dendrites of a neuron that has been stimulated by a signal from another neuron. The action potential then travels down the neuron's axon to the axon terminals. As we'll see next, action potentials arise though a complex and exquisitely coordinated biochemical process.

action potential An electrochemical signal that begins in the dendrites of a neuron and travels down the axon to the axon terminals.

Every atom contains one or more positively charged particles called *protons* in its nucleus, which is surrounded by a cloud of negatively charged particles called *electrons*. In its neutral state, an atom contains the same number of electrons and protons. An **ion** is an atom that has an imbalance in the number of protons and electrons, which means that an ion has an electric charge—either a positive charge (if the ion has more protons than electrons) or a negative charge (if the ion has more electrons than protons). The charge of an ion is indicated by + or − superscripts on the chemical symbol—for example, Na^+ denotes a positively charged ion of sodium, and Cl^- denotes a negatively charged ion of chlorine.

ion An atom that has an imbalance in the number of protons and electrons and that therefore has an electric charge.

The fluid within and around neurons contains various types of ions. In the production of an action potential, two types of positively charged ions are of particular importance—sodium ions (Na^+) and potassium ions (K^+)—and a variety of negatively charged ions (including Cl^-) also play a role. Differences in the concentrations of these positive and negative ions inside and outside the cell give rise to a difference in electrical potential across the cell membrane, called the **membrane potential** (measured in millivolts, or mV).

membrane potential A difference in electrical potential across the cell membrane, due to a difference in the concentrations of positive and negative ions inside and outside the cell.

Figure 1.3 illustrates the ion concentrations when a cell is at rest (i.e., when it isn't generating a neural signal). These concentrations result in a membrane potential of about −70 mV, a difference known as the **resting potential** (the number is negative because there is a higher concentration of negatively charged ions inside the cell than outside). As illustrated in Figure 1.3, the membrane potential can be measured with electrodes (thin insulated wires) placed inside and outside the cell membrane, a technique called **single-cell recording.**

resting potential The membrane potential when a neuron is at rest (about −70 mV).

single-cell recording A technique used to measure the membrane potential.

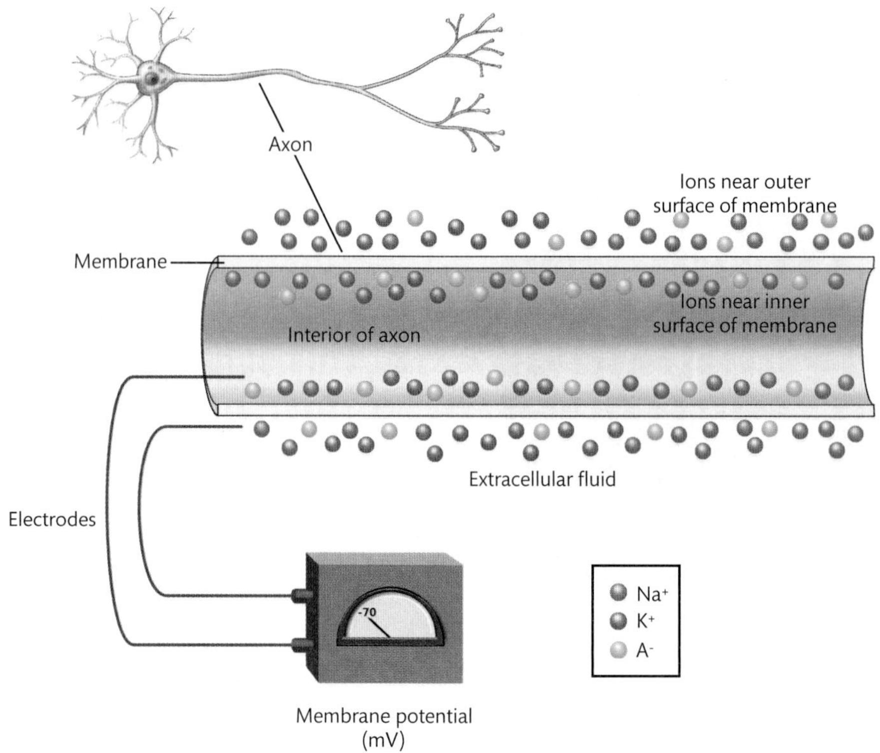

Figure 1.3 Resting Potential of a Neuron Neurons are bathed in an extracellular fluid containing positively and negatively charged ions; the interior of neurons also contains positively and negatively charged ions (this illustration shows just the axon of a typical neuron). At rest, the concentration of positively charged sodium ions (Na^+) is much higher outside the axon than inside; the concentration of positively charged potassium ions (K^+) is somewhat higher inside the axon than outside; and the concentration of various negatively charged ions (A^-) is also somewhat higher inside than outside the axon. These concentration differences lead to a membrane potential—a difference of about −70 mV across the cell membrane surrounding the axon, reflecting the higher concentrations of positively charged ions outside the membrane and the higher concentrations of negatively charged ions inside the membrane.

ion channels Small pores in the cell membrane of neurons through which certain ions can flow into or out of the cell.

The cell membrane of neurons is semipermeable: certain ions can cross the membrane through small pores called **ion channels,** each of which allows only a specific type of ion to pass through—for example, sodium channels only allow sodium ions to pass, and potassium channels only allow potassium ions to pass. These channels are *voltage-gated*—that is, they open when the membrane potential changes sufficiently, and ions can pass through only when the channels are open.

When a neuron receives a signal from another neuron, the receiving neuron undergoes an abrupt change in membrane potential, which causes voltage-gated sodium channels to open at the base of the axon, where it emerges from the cell body. This in turn allows extracellular sodium ions (Na^+) to flow into the axon. They move into the axon because the concentration of Na^+ ions is much greater outside the membrane than inside.

depolarization Part of the sequence of events of an action potential, during which an inflow of positively charged ions causes the membrane potential to become markedly more positive.

The influx of positively charged Na^+ ions causes the membrane potential to become markedly more positive (see Figure 1.4). This change in membrane potential is called **depolarization,** because the membrane potential is becoming less polarized—that is, less extreme, moving from −70 mV toward 0. However, as shown by the graph in Figure 1.4, depolarization doesn't stop at 0. The inflow of Na^+ ions continues until the difference in electric charge at the inner and outer surfaces of the membrane is reversed, with the inside of the axon becoming more positively charged than the outside, resulting in a membrane potential of about +30 mV at its peak.

Immediately after the sodium channels open, they close again, stemming the inflow of Na^+ ions, and nearby potassium channels open (in response to the depolarization of the membrane), allowing positively charged potassium ions (K^+) to flow out of the axon, again driven by the concentration difference. The outflow of K^+ ions pushes the membrane potential back toward its resting value of −70 mV, a process called *repolarization*. Like the sodium channels, the potassium channels close again immediately after opening. The membrane potential briefly exceeds the resting potential—this is termed *hyperpolarization*—before returning to the resting potential. This sequence of changes in membrane potential from −70 mV to +30 mV and finally back to −70 mV is the action potential, and the entire sequence takes place in about 5 milliseconds (msec).

The action potential causes voltage-gated sodium channels to open a little bit further down the axon, and the sequence of events repeats—in effect, the action potential travels

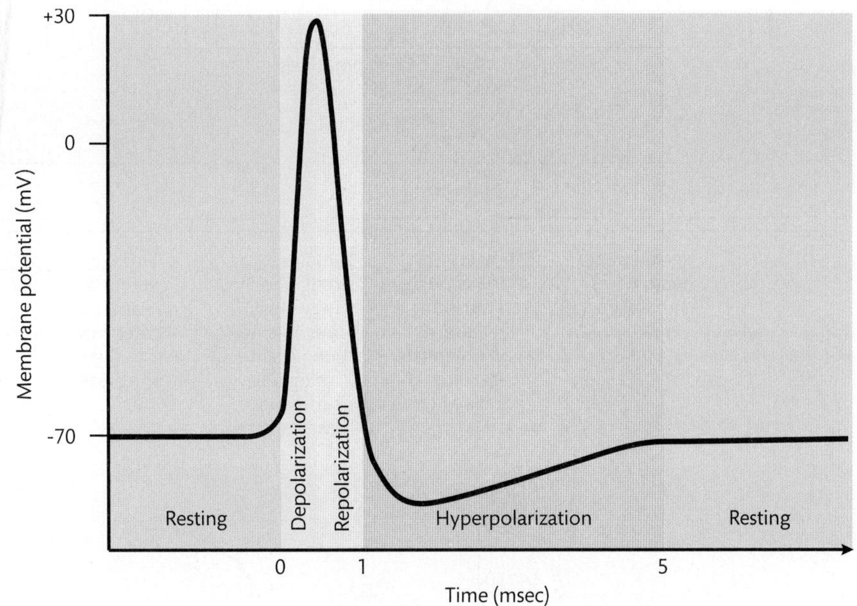

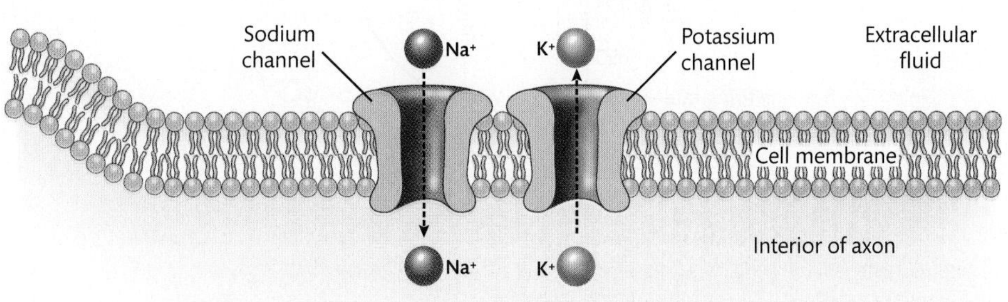

Figure 1.4 Action Potential When a neuron at rest, with a membrane potential of about −70 mV, receives a signal from another neuron, the membrane potential becomes slightly more positive, beginning the depolarization phase. This opens voltage-gated sodium channels in the membrane, allowing Na^+ to enter the cell. The inflow of these positively charged ions drives the membrane potential in a positive direction, until it reaches a peak at about +30 mV. Immediately after opening, the sodium channels close, and potassium channels open, allowing K^+ to exit the axon, which drives the membrane potential back toward −70 mV; this is the repolarization phase, which is followed by hyperpolarization, during which the membrane potential falls slightly below resting potential and then returns to it. This entire sequence of phases in the action potential takes about 5 msec.

down the axon until it arrives at the axon terminals. The action potential can travel "downstream" only, because the recently opened ion channels "upstream" are temporarily deactivated during a brief **refractory period;** this means that a new action potential cannot be initiated in the neuron until the refractory period ends.

refractory period Following an action potential, a brief period during which a new action potential cannot be initiated.

Action potentials are all-or-none—the magnitude and duration of the change in membrane potential, from −70 mV to +30 mV and back again, are always almost exactly the same. Furthermore, the speed at which the action potential travels down the axon of any given neuron is always the same, although the speed can differ in different neurons, depending on various factors. For example, large-diameter axons propagate action potentials faster than small-diameter axons, and some axons are covered with a kind of insulation called *myelin* that can dramatically increase the speed of propagation.

The fact that each action potential is all-or-none raises a question: How does the stream of action potentials produced by a neuron convey information about the physical stimulus that evoked that neural activity? The answer is that characteristics of the inducing stimulus are reflected in the neuron's **firing rate**—the rate at which the neuron produces action potentials—which is usually expressed in terms of *spikes per second* (when the time scale is highly compressed, each action potential looks like a spike; see Figure 1.5a). There are limits to a neuron's range of possible firing rates, of course: a neuron cannot fire less than zero times per second, and most neurons cannot fire more than a few hundred times per second (because of the refractory period). Most neurons exhibit a **baseline firing rate,** a low rate of spontaneous firing at fairly random intervals in the absence of any stimulus.

firing rate The rate at which a neuron produces action potentials; usually expressed in terms of spikes per second.

baseline firing rate A neuron's low rate of spontaneous firing at fairly random intervals in the absence of any stimulus.

As we'll see in later chapters, changes in the firing rates of neurons can result from a wide variety of changes in the proximal stimuli—for example, a visual neuron might

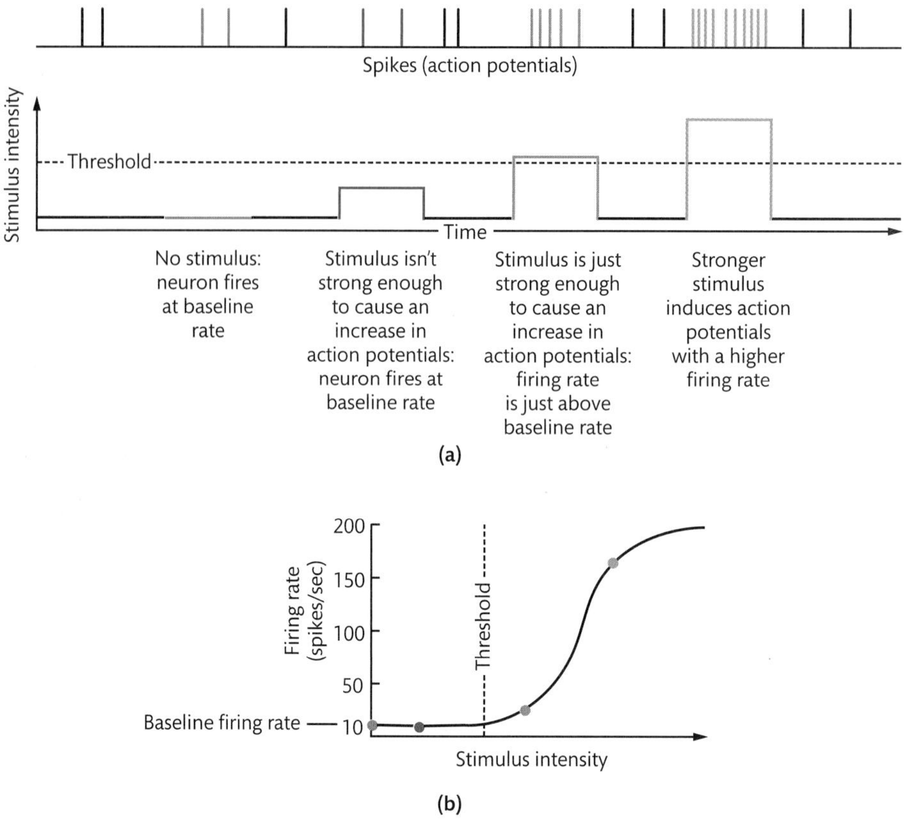

Figure 1.5 Firing Rate and Stimulus Intensity (a) Each action potential, or spike, is all-or-none; changes in stimulus intensity affect only the firing rate of a neuron (measured in spikes/second). The black spikes represent spontaneous (baseline) firing. (b) A typical neuron might have a baseline firing rate of a few spikes per second (about 10 in this illustration) when the stimulus intensity isn't great enough to induce additional action potentials. As the stimulus intensity increases, the firing rate also increases but then begins leveling off, until it reaches a maximum (in this case, about 200 spikes/second), typically producing an S-shaped curve like the one shown here.

respond most strongly to a vertical edge (and less strongly to other orientations); an auditory neuron might respond most strongly to a medium-pitch tone (and less strongly to lower- or higher-pitch tones); and so forth. In other words, the firing rate of a neuron functions as a neural code, conveying useful information about the stimulus that evoked the neural activity. But regardless of the nature of the proximal stimulus, its intensity must reach a minimal level, called the *threshold,* in order to evoke an increase in firing rate above the baseline rate. The firing rate then increases with stimulus intensity until the neuron is firing at its maximal rate (see Figure 1.5b).

Transmitting Signals Between Neurons

Neurons aren't physically connected to each other like wires in an electrical system. Rather, there is a tiny gap called a **synapse** ("SIN-apps," a term coined by Charles Sherrington) between the axon terminal of one neuron and the dendrite or cell body of another neuron. The membrane at the axon terminal of a neuron producing an action potential is called the **presynaptic membrane;** the membrane of the dendrite or cell body of the receiving neuron is called the **postsynaptic membrane.** Within axon terminals, tiny sacs called **synaptic vesicles** contain molecules of **neurotransmitters,** chemical substances that are crucially involved in the transmission of signals between neurons.

The arrival of an action potential at an axon terminal causes synaptic vesicles to merge with the presynaptic membrane, releasing neurotransmitter molecules into the synapse (see Figure 1.6). Some of these molecules float across the synapse and come into contact with the postsynaptic membrane, which contains proteins called *receptors.* The neurotransmitter molecules fit into, or *bind,* to receptors, like a key fits into a lock.

This binding causes certain *ligand-gated* ion channels in the postsynaptic membrane to open (a ligand is a molecule such as a neurotransmitter), leading to a change of membrane potential through the process of ion flow described earlier. If enough neurotransmitter binding events result in the opening of enough ion channels, the change

synapse A tiny gap between the axon terminal of one neuron and the dendrite or cell body of another neuron.

presynaptic membrane The membrane at the axon terminal of a neuron producing an action potential.

postsynaptic membrane The membrane of the dendrite or cell body receiving a neural signal.

synaptic vesicles Within axon terminals, tiny sacs that contain neurotransmitter molecules.

neurotransmitters Chemical substances involved in the transmission of signals between neurons; neurotransmitter molecules released into a synapse by the neuron sending a signal bind to receptors on the neuron receiving the signal.

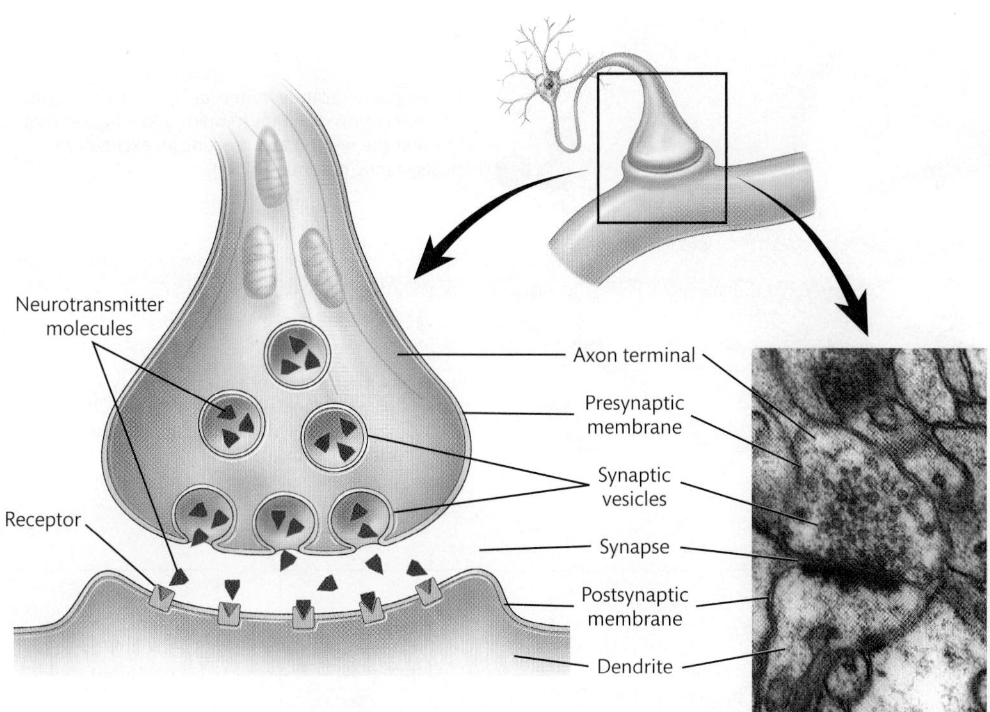

Figure 1.6 How Neural Signals Are Transmitted Across a Synapse The synapse is the gap between the axon terminal and the dendrite. Within the axon terminal, synaptic vesicles contain neurotransmitter molecules. The arrival of an action potential causes the synaptic vesicles to merge with the presynaptic membrane, which releases neurotransmitter molecules into the synapse. Some neurotransmitter molecules drift across the synapse and bind to receptors on the postsynaptic membrane (the neurotransmitter molecules fit into the receptors the way a key fits into a lock). Binding causes ion channels to open on the postsynaptic membrane (not shown). In the photomicrograph on the right, the axon terminal, vesicles, synapse, and dendrite are easily visible. [Courtesy of Jeffrey Klein]

in membrane potential in the postsynaptic neuron can reach the threshold at which an action potential is initiated by the opening of voltage-gated ion channels. This is how an action potential in a presynaptic neuron can lead to the initiation of an action potential in a postsynaptic neuron.

Dozens of different neurotransmitters participate in the transmission of signals between neurons. They can be categorized on the basis of whether they have an excitatory or an inhibitory effect on the postsynaptic neuron. The binding of **excitatory neurotransmitters** depolarizes the membrane potential and thereby increases the probability that an action potential will be generated in the postsynaptic neuron. In contrast, the binding of **inhibitory neurotransmitters** hyperpolarizes the membrane potential and thereby decreases the probability of an action potential. Thus, neurotransmitter binding sometimes promotes the initiation of an action potential and sometimes prevents it.

The illustration at the top of Figure 1.7 shows three synapses where axon terminals of presynaptic neurons meet dendrites of a postsynaptic neuron. Two of these synapses (E1 and E2) are excitatory—at these synapses, molecules of an excitatory neurotransmitter are released from the axon terminal and bind to receptors on the dendrites. This causes Na^+ ion channels to open in the postsynaptic neuron's membrane, letting Na^+ ions enter the cell, which in turn makes the membrane potential more positive (this is called an **excitatory postsynaptic potential,** or **EPSP**). The EPSP increases the probability that an action potential will be initiated in the postsynaptic neuron. The other synapse (I) is inhibitory—at this synapse, an inhibitory neurotransmitter is released and binds. This causes Cl^- ion channels to open in the postsynaptic neuron's membrane, letting Cl^- ions enter the cell, making the membrane potential more negative (this is called an **inhibitory postsynaptic potential,** or **IPSP**). The IPSP decreases the probability that an action potential will be initiated in the postsynaptic neuron.

The postsynaptic neuron's firing rate changes depending on the balance between EPSPs and IPSPs, as illustrated by the graphs at the bottom of Figure 1.7. In effect, the postsynaptic neuron is "adding up" any EPSPs and "subtracting" any IPSPs as a way of "deciding" whether or not to produce a spike. Given that a typical neuron is receiving EPSPs and IPSPs via thousands of excitatory and inhibitory synapses at which binding occurs in complex,

Demonstration 1.1 Neurons and Neural Signals Interact with depictions of neurons, synapses, and neural signals.

excitatory neurotransmitters
Neurotransmitters that have an excitatory effect on the postsynaptic neuron, increasing the probability that an action potential will be initiated.

inhibitory neurotransmitters
Neurotransmitters that have an inhibitory effect on the postsynaptic neuron, decreasing the probability that an action potential will be initiated.

excitatory postsynaptic potential (EPSP)
The effect of an excitatory neurotransmitter, making the postsynaptic neuron's membrane potential more positive.

inhibitory postsynaptic potential (IPSP)
The effect of an inhibitory neurotransmitter, making the postsynaptic neuron's membrane potential more negative.

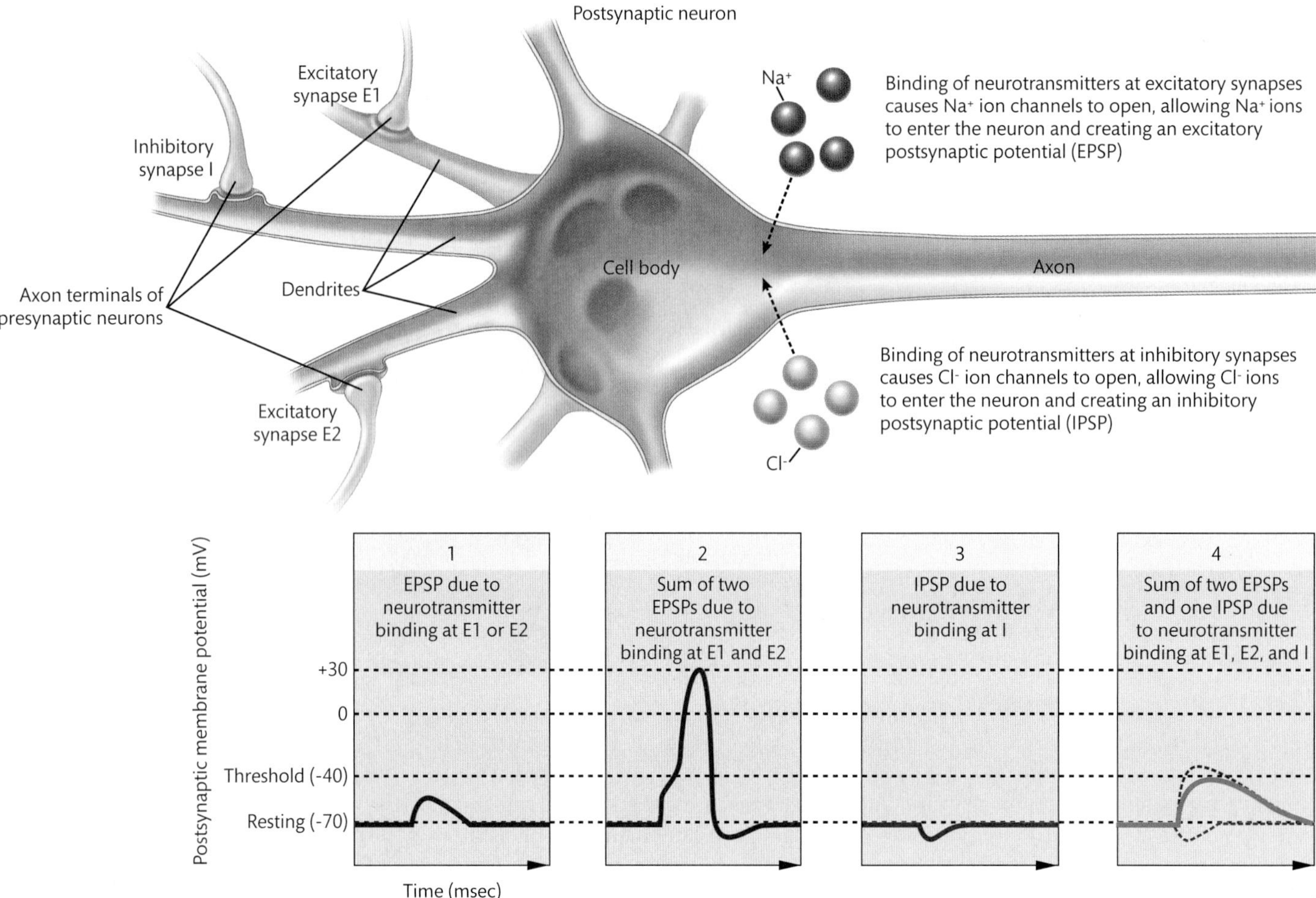

Figure 1.7 Excitatory and Inhibitory Synapses (top) Three axon terminals of presynaptic neurons make synapses with three dendrites of a postsynaptic neuron. Synapses E1 and E2 are excitatory—the binding of the neurotransmitter released at these synapses creates an EPSP in the postsynaptic neuron. Synapse I is inhibitory—the binding of the neurotransmitter released at this synapse creates an IPSP in the postsynaptic neuron. (bottom) (1) The EPSP due to binding at E1 or E2 isn't enough to move the membrane potential of the postsynaptic neuron above the threshold and initiate an action potential. (2) If binding at E1 and E2 occur at the same time, the sum of the two EPSPs drives the membrane potential above threshold, and an action potential is initiated. (3) The IPSP due to binding at I moves the postsynaptic membrane potential farther below the threshold. (4) If the IPSP from I and the EPSPs from E1 and E2 occur together, the IPSP subtracts from the sum of the two EPSPs, and the membrane potential doesn't cross the threshold; thus, the IPSP prevents an action potential from being initiated.

overlapping temporal patterns, you can see how this simple mechanism provides a powerful way to regulate neurons' firing rates as part of the process of creating perceptual representations within the brain.

The Human Brain

The human brain is complex in both structure and function. It contains some 100 billion neurons organized into dozens of anatomically and functionally distinct regions. Within and between these regions, the brain's neurons are intricately connected to one another in immense networks. Given that each neuron is connected to as many as several thousand other neurons and that each such connection typically consists of multiple synapses, the number of synapses in the brain is thought to exceed 100 trillion. Figure 1.8 lays the basic groundwork for our later discussions of the brain, its regions, and its structures and functions. This figure also establishes some of the important terminology we'll use in describing views of the brain and locations within the brain.

cerebral hemispheres The two most important divisions of the brain; separated by the longitudinal fissure.

The brain weighs about 1.3 kg and has the consistency of tofu. It consists of several major divisions; the most important are the right and left **cerebral hemispheres,** which are

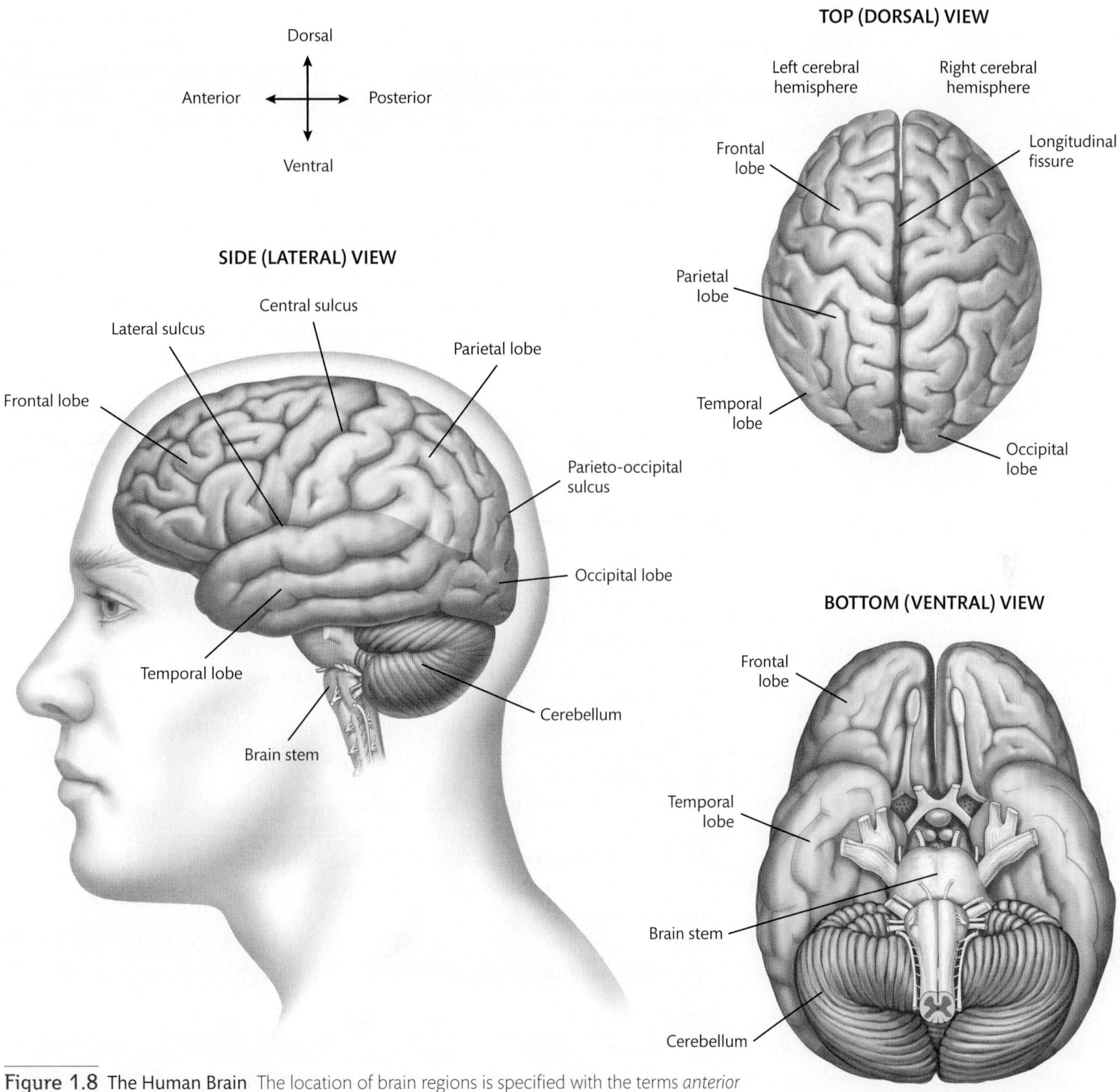

Figure 1.8 The Human Brain The location of brain regions is specified with the terms *anterior* (toward the front of the brain), *posterior* (toward the back of the brain), *dorsal* (toward the top of the brain), and *ventral* (toward the bottom of the brain). The cerebral hemispheres are separated by the longitudinal fissure, and each hemisphere consists of four lobes—frontal, temporal, parietal, and occipital. The brain stem and the cerebellum lie beneath the cerebral hemispheres.

separated by the longitudinal fissure. The two hemispheres are approximately mirror images of one another, although there are some important functional differences that we'll discuss in later chapters. The major connection between the two hemispheres is a large bundle of axons called the **corpus callosum.** The surface of the cerebral hemispheres is highly convoluted: each individual elongated bump is called a **gyrus** (plural *gyri*), and the indentation between two gyri is called a **sulcus** (plural *sulci*). The patterns of convolutions in different human brains aren't identical but are similar enough that some gyri and sulci can be used to mark the locations of brain regions with particular functions.

corpus callosum A large bundle of axons that constitutes the major connection between the two cerebral hemispheres.

gyrus An elongated bump on the surface of the cerebral hemispheres.

sulcus An indentation between two gyri on the surface of the cerebral hemispheres.

Demonstration 1.2 Anatomy of the Brain Interact with different views of the brain.

frontal lobe One of the four lobes of each cerebral hemisphere; separated from the temporal lobe by the lateral sulcus and from the parietal lobe by the central sulcus.

temporal lobe One of the four lobes of each cerebral hemisphere; separated from the frontal lobe and the parietal lobe by the lateral sulcus.

parietal lobe One of the four lobes of each cerebral hemisphere; separated from the frontal lobe by the central sulcus, from the temporal lobe by the lateral sulcus, and from the occipital lobe by the parieto-occipital sulcus.

occipital lobe One of the four lobes of each cerebral hemisphere; separated from the parietal lobe by the parieto-occipital sulcus.

cerebral cortex The outermost layer of the cerebral hemispheres; about 2–4 mm thick and consisting mostly of gray matter (neural cell bodies).

gray matter The cell bodies of neurons making up the cerebral cortex.

white matter The myelin-covered axons of cortical neurons, making up the interior parts of the cerebral hemispheres; these axons connect neurons located in different parts of the cerebral cortex.

thalamus The most important subcortical structure involved in perception; most neural signals pass through the thalamus on their paths from the sensory organs to the cortex.

Each cerebral hemisphere of the brain is divided into four lobes: the **frontal lobe, temporal lobe, parietal lobe,** and **occipital lobe.** The lateral sulcus separates the temporal lobe from the frontal lobe and the parietal lobe; the central sulcus separates the frontal and parietal lobes; and the parieto-occipital sulcus separates the parietal and occipital lobes.

The outermost layer of the cerebral hemispheres is called the **cerebral cortex** (*cortex* is Latin for "bark"). The cortex is about 2–4 mm thick and mostly consists of **gray matter,** the cell bodies of neurons. In contrast, the interior parts of the cerebral hemispheres are mostly **white matter,** consisting of the axons of cortical neurons, which carry signals from one part of the cortex to another (these axons are covered in myelin, which is white). The convolutions of the cortex give it a large surface area, about 2,500 cm^2—if you could smooth the cortex out flat on a table, it would be roughly the size of a large unfolded dinner napkin, about 18 inches square. The convolutions allow this large surface to fit inside the head in a way that permits efficient connectivity among regions.

The cerebral hemispheres also contain a number of subcortical (beneath the cortex) structures that play important roles in perception, such as the amygdala (important for emotion) and the hippocampus (important for memory). However, the most important subcortical structure involved in perception is the **thalamus;** most neural signals originating in the sensory organs pass through the thalamus (via a synapse there) on their way to the cortex.

Check Your Understanding

1.4 Give at least two reasons why the following sentence is false: Like all other types of cells, neurons have a cell body, an axon, and dendrites.

1.5 Put the following events in the sequence in which they occur from before to after an action potential is produced by a neuron:

- **A.** Potassium channels close.
- **B.** Sodium channels open in the axon.
- **C.** Potassium ions flow out of the neuron, causing repolarization.
- **D.** Refractory period.
- **E.** Hyperpolarization.
- **F.** Sodium ions flow into the axon, causing depolarization.
- **G.** Neuron receives a signal from another neuron.
- **H.** Sodium channels close, and potassium channels open.

1.6 True or false? A neuron's baseline firing rate is the firing rate evoked by a stimulus just above threshold.

1.7 The terms and descriptions in the following table relate to the process of transmitting signals between neurons. Match each term with its description:

Term	Description
A. Binding	**a.** Contained within synaptic vesicles and released by presynaptic neuron.
B. EPSP	**b.** Synaptic vesicles merge with this.
C. IPSP	**c.** Increases the probability of an action potential in the receiving neuron.
D. Neurotransmitter	**d.** Gap between the sending neuron and the receiving neuron.
E. Postsynaptic membrane	**e.** Neurotransmitters fit into receptors.
F. Presynaptic membrane	**f.** Found within axon terminal.
G. Receptor	**g.** Decreases the probability of an action potential in the receiving neuron.
H. Synapse	**h.** Protein in the postsynaptic membrane.
I. Synaptic vesicle	**i.** Contains receptors.

1.8 How many lobes make up your brain—two, four, or eight? Name them.

Cognitive Neuropsychology

In 1865 the French physician Pierre Paul Broca described the cases of two patients with damage to the left frontal lobe as the result of a stroke. In both cases, the patients exhibited an impaired ability to produce spoken language, but in virtually all other respects they remained cognitively normal. Broca argued that the site of the damage was a good candidate for a "speech center," an area in the human brain dedicated to speech production.

The logic of Broca's argument has been updated but continues to guide research today: if damage to a particular area of the brain typically causes a deficit in a specific cognitive or perceptual function, then it may be appropriate to conclude that the function in some way depends on that brain area (Coltheart, 2002). More generally, by examining what kinds of deficits always occur with damage to particular areas in the brain (and what kinds never occur), it's possible to create a detailed picture of the functional organization of the brain. This is the task of **cognitive neuropsychology,** the investigation of perceptual and cognitive deficits in individuals with brain damage in order to discover how perception and cognition are carried out in the normal, undamaged brain. (Cognitive neuropsychology is distinct from the branch of medicine called *clinical neuropsychology,* which is concerned with the diagnosis and treatment of perceptual and cognitive deficits due to brain damage.)

Pierre Paul Broca (1824–1880). [Hulton-Deutsch Collection/Corbis]

The story of Jill Taylor's left-hemisphere stroke, which appears at the beginning of this chapter, provides a real-life example of how deficits can reveal the parts of the brain that are critical for some perceptual or cognitive function. The stroke impaired her ability to understand speech, but not her ability to hear that sounds were coming from the phone or even that the sounds had a reassuring tone. This suggests that parts of the brain responsible for perceiving speech were damaged but that other parts of the brain, including those needed to understand emotional tone, were intact.

cognitive neuropsychology The investigation of perceptual and cognitive deficits in individuals with brain damage in order to discover how perception and cognition are carried out in the normal, undamaged brain.

Cognitive neuropsychology depends on the notion of **modularity,** the idea that the human mind and brain consist of a set of distinct modules, each of which carries out one or more specific functions (Fodor, 1983). Any complex task involves the coordinated activity of many modules, each contributing its part—for example, the task of typing to spoken dictation involves modules involved in audition, language, and finger movements, among others. A module processes only specific types of information, such as information about faces or about speech—that is, a module is domain specific.

modularity The idea that the human mind and brain consist of a set of distinct modules, each of which carries out one or more specific functions.

The assumption of functional modularity is often accompanied by an assumption of anatomical modularity—that is, the idea that a functional module resides in a specific region of the brain (Coltheart, 2002). For example, there is very good evidence that the function of processing information about the motion of visual objects is supported by dedicated neurons in a region of the brain known as area MT. In other cases, however, a particular function is carried out by neurons in several different brain regions working in concert—for example, the function of recognizing visual objects involves a number of different regions in the occipital and temporal lobes.

To understand the logic of cognitive neuropsychology, consider the following scenario. A man who has suffered a stroke can recognize objects but can't recognize faces—for example, when looking at his desk chair, he can identify it as his chair, but when seeing the face of someone he knows, even the face of his wife, he can't identify the person. This pattern of ability and disability could be interpreted as suggesting that there are at least two modules for visual recognition, one for faces (which would seem to have been damaged in this man) and the other for objects (not damaged). Such a pattern is called a **dissociation,** because two different functions are dissociated, or separated.

dissociation In cognitive neuropsychology, a pattern of brain damage and impaired function in which damage to some specific brain region is associated with impairment of some specific function but not with impairment of another function.

However, another interpretation of this pattern is possible. What if there were just one part of the brain (one module) that carried out the process of visual recognition for all objects, including faces? We might observe the same pattern of impairment subsequent to a stroke if face recognition were simply more difficult than recognition of other objects—that is, if the stroke had damaged the single visual recognition module to some extent but not completely, so that the module was still able to carry out the simpler process of recognizing nonface objects but could no longer accomplish the more difficult process of recognizing faces.

double dissociation In cognitive neuropsychology, a pattern of brain damage and impaired function in which damage to some specific brain region is associated with impairment of some specific function A but not with impairment of another function B, along with a pattern (in a different patient) in which damage to a different region is associated with impairment of function B but not with impairment of function A.

assumption of cognitive uniformity The assumption that the functional organization of human cognition and of the brain is essentially the same in everyone.

What evidence could help us decide between these two interpretations? Suppose we found a second stroke patient with damage to a different part of the brain who exhibits the opposite pattern of impaired perception—this patient can recognize faces but is unable to recognize nonface objects. Now we have a **double dissociation:** the two functions have been separated in both possible ways (object recognition without face recognition, and face recognition without object recognition). This eliminates the single-module interpretation in which one function is presumed to be more difficult than the other: if face recognition were more difficult, how could it be that the second patient can perform the more "difficult" process of recognizing faces but not the "easier" process of recognizing other objects? Thus, the double dissociation provides strong evidence that the two functions really are carried out by separate modules that can be separately damaged.

In this scenario, we're relying on evidence provided by only two individuals to make a strong scientific inference. Nevertheless, the inference is legitimate because it's supported by an important principle of modern neuroscience, the **assumption of cognitive uniformity**—the assumption that the functional organization of human cognition and of the brain that supports cognition is, for all practical purposes, nearly the same in everyone. Much of the knowledge that has been gained in cognitive neuroscience over the last century supports this assumption. Of course, there are individual differences in perceptual functions that can have both genetic and experiential causes, such as an inherited (genetic) ability of those with absolute pitch to identify isolated musical tones accurately and a learned (experiential) ability to perceive subtle differences in the tastes and odors of wines. And there are cases suggesting that the assumption of cognitive uniformity doesn't always hold—for example, the visual cortex of a congenitally blind person may come to serve a nonvisual function such as touch (Lewis et al., 2010).

Although cognitive neuropsychology has proven to be an extremely productive approach toward revealing the functional organization of the human brain, it has some practical limitations. Strokes are by far the most common cause of brain damage in patients who participate in cognitive neuropsychological studies, but strokes tend to occur much more often in some brain locations than in others; therefore, the effects of damage in rarely affected locations are not readily available for study. Also, if the damage due to a stroke isn't confined to a small, well-defined brain region (unfortunately, it's common for the damage to be widespread), then more than one functional module could be affected, as apparently happened in the case of Jill Taylor's stroke described at the beginning of the chapter.

Functional Neuroimaging

functional neuroimaging An array of techniques for measuring brain activity in healthy volunteers carrying out carefully designed tasks.

Another method for exploring the functions carried out by different brain regions is **functional neuroimaging,** an array of techniques that make it possible for neuroscientists to measure brain activity in healthy volunteers carrying out carefully designed perceptual and cognitive tasks. Functional neuroimaging techniques can be divided into two broad types: techniques for measuring the electrical or magnetic fields produced by populations of active neurons (electroencephalography and magnetoencephalography) and techniques for measuring the changes in blood flow and blood oxygenation that accompany brain activity (positron emission tomography and functional magnetic resonance imaging). All of these techniques rely on the same assumptions of modularity and cognitive uniformity that were discussed in the last section.

Electroencephalography and Magnetoencephalography

electroencephalography (EEG) A functional neuroimaging technique based on measurement of the electrical fields associated with brain activity.

magnetoencephalography (MEG) A functional neuroimaging technique based on measurement of the magnetic fields associated with brain activity.

Electroencephalography (EEG) and **magnetoencephalography (MEG)** exploit the fact that when many neurons are simultaneously active, the activity produces weak electrical and magnetic fields that can be measured with sensors placed on or near the surface of the scalp. These methods have very fine temporal precision—that is, measurements are taken 1,000 times per second or more, which is fast enough to provide detailed information about the time course of neural activity as it unfolds (Luck, 2005). However, the spatial resolution of EEG and MEG is relatively coarse, allowing only approximate determination of the locations in the brain of the neural activity being measured (typically, multiple locations are active simultaneously).

Positron Emission Tomography

When neurons in some part of the brain become active, more blood flows to that area to supply it with oxygen and other metabolites. **Positron emission tomography (PET)** can be used to measure changes in blood flow and thereby indirectly measure the underlying neural activity. PET involves introducing a radioactive substance into the blood (e.g., via injection). The substance is carried to the brain, and a PET scanner provides a 3-D image of the amount of radioactivity at different locations within the brain. When blood flow at a given location changes due to a change in neural activity there, the strength of the radioactive signal emitted from that location also changes, and this change can be seen on the scan. In a typical experiment, two scans are taken, one during each of two perceptual conditions, and the difference in the two images reveals the parts of the brain that are more active in one condition than the other.

positron emission tomography (PET) A functional neuroimaging technique based on measurement of the changes in blood flow associated with brain activity, using a radioactive substance introduced into the blood.

Figure 1.9 shows two PET scans from an experiment in which participants first viewed a display showing a flickering checkerboard pattern (Figure 1.9a) and then viewed a blank display (Figure 1.9b) (Posner & Raichle, 1994). The difference image (Figure 1.9c) shows that there was greater activity in certain parts of the occipital lobe when participants viewed the checkerboard pattern, which suggests that neurons in these areas play a role in visual perception.

Starting in the 1980s and into the early 1990s, PET provided extremely important information about how the brain supports perceptual and cognitive functions. However, PET has some significant drawbacks as a functional neuroimaging tool. First, it is invasive: participants must have a radioactive substance introduced into their body, which always involves some risk, even though the amount of radiation received for a PET scan is less than the amount received during a chest X-ray. Furthermore, each image provides a record of the average brain activity over 30–60 minutes, which means that changes in brain activity that happen over shorter periods of time cannot be measured.

Functional Magnetic Resonance Imaging

Magnetic resonance imaging (MRI), which was invented in the 1970s, takes advantage of the magnetic properties of molecules that occur naturally in the body (e.g., water molecules) to produce very high resolution, 3-D images of bodily structures and their internal features, including the brain. This use of MRI to obtain a single static "snapshot" of organs, bones, and joints is called *structural MRI,* and it is commonly employed to find brain tumors or to identify brain damage due to a stroke.

In the early 1990s, researchers discovered that they could use MRI to image neural activity in the brain over time, based on changes in the level of oxygen in the blood (Kwong et al., 1992; Ogawa et al., 1992). Activity in any given part of the brain produces a change in

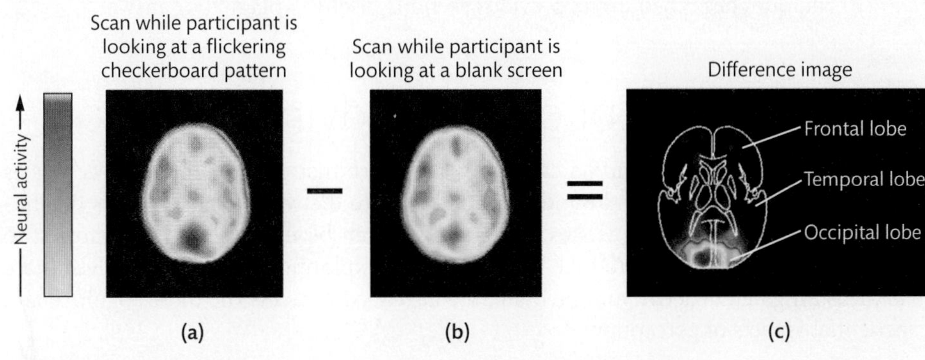

Figure 1.9 Using PET to Reveal the Functional Organization of the Brain The images in (a) and (b) are PET scans taken when the participant was (a) viewing a flickering checkerboard pattern and (b) viewing a blank screen. The difference image in (c) is the result of "subtracting" the scan in (b) from the scan in (a), to reveal visually responsive brain regions. (Adapted from Posner & Raichle, 1994.) [Marcus E. Raichle]

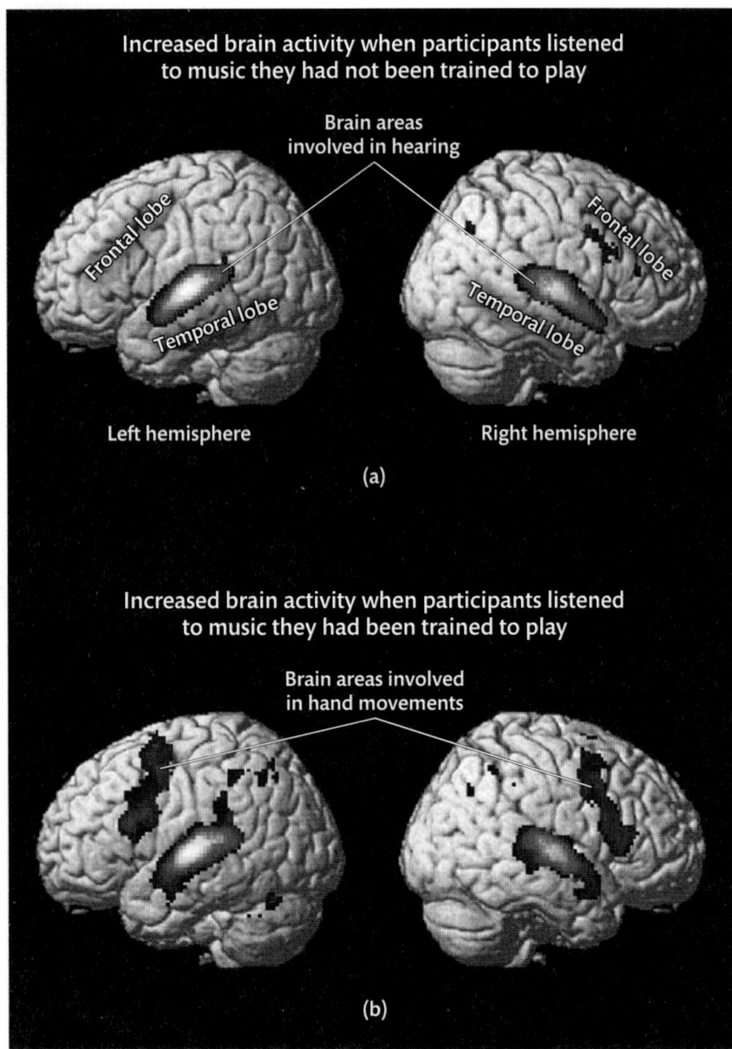

Figure 1.10 **Using fMRI to Reveal the Functional Organization of the Brain** Like the image in Figure 1.9c, the images in this figure are difference images, the result of subtracting an fMRI scan obtained while the participant wasn't listening to any music from a scan obtained while listening to music. (a) As indicated by the colored regions, when participants listened to music they hadn't been trained to play, there was increased neural activity mainly in brain areas involved in hearing. (b) When participants listened to music they had been trained to play on the piano, there was also increased activity in areas of the frontal lobe involved in controlling hand movements. (Adapted from Lahav et al., 2007, Figure 3.)

the oxygenation of the blood at that location, because higher levels of oxygen are needed to support increased neural activity. MRI can measure differences in blood oxygen levels—and thus neural activity—at each location in the brain as the activity unfolds over time. This use of MRI is called **functional magnetic resonance imaging (fMRI)** because it provides images of how the brain is functioning—that is, images of neural activity. Modern MRI scanners can obtain a high-resolution 3-D image of the entire brain every 2–3 seconds while people are engaged in a perceptual or cognitive task, thus providing a nearly real-time "movie" of the neural activity in the brain associated with that task.

As with PET, an fMRI experiment typically involves examining the differences in brain activity under two conditions that differ in only one way. Consider, for example, the study illustrated in Figure 1.10 (Lahav et al., 2007). Participants were nonmusicians who had been trained to play a simple piece of piano music and who then underwent fMRI scans under three conditions: while listening to music they hadn't been trained to play; while listening to the piece of music they had been trained to play; and at rest, with no music playing.

Figure 1.10a shows the increase in brain activity observed when participants listened to music they hadn't been trained to play (compared to rest). In this case, there was increased neural activity in the superior temporal lobe, a brain area involved in hearing. Figure 1.10b shows the increase in brain activity when participants listened to the music they had been trained to play (compared to rest). In this case also, there was increased neural activity in the superior temporal lobe; but in addition, there was increased activity in frontal lobe areas that are involved in controlling hand movements, *even though the participants' hands hadn't been moving during the scans.* The researchers concluded that listening to music that you know how to play produces activity in brain regions involved in controlling the movements associated with playing that music—as if you were mentally "rehearsing" the movements.

Check Your Understanding

1.9 Consider the question of whether the same region(s) of the brain support both speaking and understanding a language. Describe a double dissociation that would provide evidence that these two functions are supported by different regions of the brain.

1.10 "fMRI has the advantages of EEG, MEG, and PET, without any of the disadvantages." Is this a fair evaluation of the functional neuroimaging techniques described in the previous section? Briefly explain your answer.

functional magnetic resonance imaging (fMRI) A functional neuroimaging technique based on measurement of the changes in blood oxygenation associated with brain activity.

Exploring Perception by Studying Behavior

Looking back at Figure 1.1 and its caption, you can see that the perceptual process goes from the world to the brain and mind, and then back to the world, via behaviors like hitting a tennis ball. Perception evokes awareness and can be used to create memories, to participate in cognition, and to take action. Clearly, exploring perception involves more than measuring neural activity in the brain. We also need to assess the more cognitive and experiential aspects of perception.

Starting in the nineteenth century, researchers began to develop objective behavioral methods for assessing subjective perceptual experiences, methods based on simple, well-defined responses. For example, to assess whether a person can see a dim spot of light against a black background, the person is asked to say "yes" when they see the spot or "no" when they don't; similarly, the person could respond with a button press or any other observable response. Methods like these came to define the field of psychophysics.

The first requirement of these behavioral methods is that the investigator must precisely control the physical attributes of the perceptual stimuli—the intensity, wavelength, duration, and spatial pattern of a light; the source, frequency, duration, and amplitude of a sound; or the pattern, location, and magnitude of pressure against the skin. Then, by analyzing participants' responses, perceptual scientists can develop theories of how perceptual systems encode these attributes.

In the next section, we'll explore how perceptual experience varies with changes in the physical characteristics of stimuli. We'll see that some of the variation in perception involves small random fluctuations—particularly at the extremes, when people attempt to perceive a very weak stimulus. Then we'll turn to signal detection theory, which gives investigators a way to account for how people make perceptual decisions based on such imperfect information.

Psychophysics

As we noted earlier, the field of psychophysics and the principle behavioral methods used in psychophysical investigations were developed in the nineteenth century by the German experimental psychologist Gustav Fechner, who published his foundational *Elements of Psychophysics* in 1860. Psychophysics investigates the relationship between stimuli and experience in two ways:

- By investigating the thresholds of perceptual experience—that is, the points at which there are perceptual transitions, such as the transition from not perceiving a very quiet sound to perceiving the sound as it increases in amplitude. Psychophysics attempts to answer two primary questions about perceptual thresholds: How intense must a physical stimulus be for the stimulus to be detectable? And how different must two stimuli be for the difference to be detectable?
- By investigating the scaling of perceptual experience—that is, how perceptual experience changes with changes in the physical characteristics of a perceptible stimulus, such as how the perceived loudness of a sound changes as the physical intensity of the sound goes up or down.

Gustav Fechner (1801–1887). [The Granger Collection]

Absolute Threshold: Perceivable or Not?

The **absolute threshold** is the minimum intensity of a physical stimulus that can just be detected by an observer. It marks the transition from the psychological state of not detecting the stimulus to the state of detecting it. Absolute thresholds reveal which stimuli are more detectable than others, which can provide important hints about how the brain processes those stimuli. For example, medium-pitched tones are detectable at a lower intensity than high-pitched tones, and that information is useful in investigating how neurons in the auditory system respond to tones with different pitches.

absolute threshold The minimum intensity of a physical stimulus that can just be detected by an observer.

In all cases, measuring an absolute threshold involves presenting stimuli that vary in physical intensity and having participants respond to each stimulus by indicating whether they detected it. The methods for doing this differ in how the intensities are selected and the order in which they're presented. Three of these methods were developed by Fechner and are still in use today: the method of adjustment, the method of constant stimuli, and the staircase method (a variant of what Fechner called the *method of limits*).

Method of Adjustment In the **method of adjustment**—the simplest "quick and dirty" method for estimating absolute thresholds—the person observes the stimulus and adjusts a knob that directly controls the intensity of the stimulus. Let's say the stimulus is a tone of some constant pitch, heard through headphones. The experimenter starts the tone at an

method of adjustment A behavioral method used in psychophysical experiments; the participant observes a stimulus and adjusts a knob that directly controls the intensity of the stimulus.

intensity that is easy for the person to hear, and the listener lowers the intensity slowly until she can just barely no longer hear the tone—the intensity at this point is an estimate of the absolute threshold. The experimenter then sets the tone well below audibility, and the listener increases the intensity slowly until she can just barely hear the tone—the intensity at this point provides another estimate of the absolute threshold. (Typically, the various judgments will be similar but not exactly the same from one estimate to the next.) The entire procedure is repeated several times, and the average of the threshold estimates is taken as the final estimate of the absolute threshold.

Method of Constant Stimuli We called the method of adjustment "quick and dirty" because the results it gives can be obtained quickly, but they tend to vary quite a bit, even when the method is used repeatedly with the same person. For more reliable results, researchers use the **method of constant stimuli.** This method starts with the selection of a set of stimulus intensity values that cover a range likely to include the absolute threshold (based on preliminary observations). Then the stimuli are presented one after another in random order, and following each presentation, the person responds by indicating whether she detected the stimulus or not (e.g., by saying "yes" or "no"); each stimulus-and-response sequence constitutes a single trial. Stimuli with each intensity are presented many times, and the frequency of "yes" responses is plotted for each intensity. The resulting curve is then used to estimate the absolute threshold for the given stimulus.

method of constant stimuli A behavioral method used in psychophysical experiments; the participant is presented with a fixed set of stimuli covering a range of intensities that are presented repeatedly in random order, and the participant must indicate whether or not each stimulus was detected.

Figure 1.11a shows one possible outcome from this kind of experiment: the person responds "yes" to every tone with an intensity of 3 or higher but responds "no" to any tone with an intensity of less than 3. In this case, the abrupt transition at intensity 3 clearly identifies that intensity as the absolute threshold for that tone.

In actual experiments like this, however, a more typical result is an S-shaped curve like the one in Figure 1.11b. The frequency of "yes" responses is near zero for very low intensity stimuli—tones with an intensity greater than zero but too low to be heard by most participants. As the intensity of the tone increases, so does the frequency of "yes" responses, until the intensity reaches a value where almost all the responses are "yes."

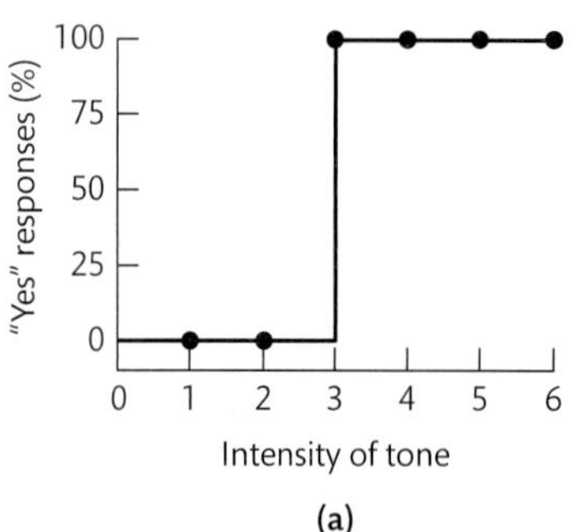

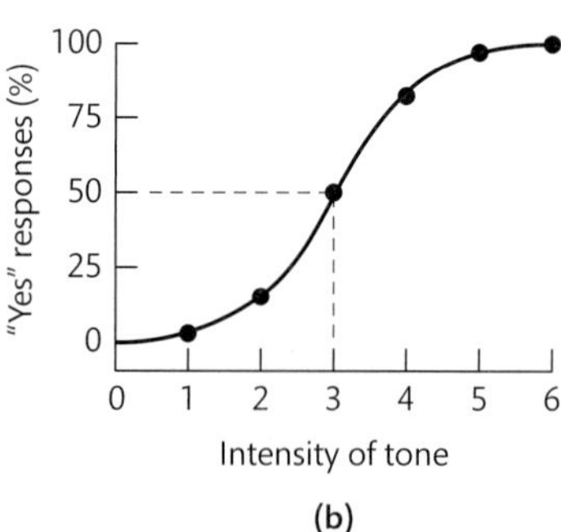

Figure 1.11 Method of Constant Stimuli and the Psychometric Function This figure shows two different hypothetical results of a psychophysical experiment using the method of constant stimuli to determine the absolute threshold for a tone. The participant listens to repeated presentations of the tone, in random order at six different intensities. After each tone is presented, the participant must respond "yes" if she heard the tone and "no" if she didn't. For tones at each intensity, the percentage of "yes" responses is plotted on a graph. The resulting curve, relating perceptual experience to physical stimulus intensity, is called a *psychometric function.* (a) In this case, tones with an intensity of less than 3 are never heard (percentage of "yes" responses = 0), and tones with an intensity of 3 or more are always heard (percentage of "yes" responses = 100). The sharp transition clearly establishes that the absolute threshold is intensity 3. (b) In this more typical case, the percentage of "yes" responses increases gradually as the intensity increases. The absolute threshold is defined as the intensity at which participants respond "yes" 50% of the time (here, at intensity 3).

This type of curve, which relates a measure of perceptual experience to the intensity of a physical stimulus, is called a **psychometric function** and is ubiquitous in psychophysics—we'll encounter it often in this book. At the end of this section, we'll examine why the psychometric function is typically S-shaped as in Figure 1.11b, rather than exhibiting an abrupt transition as in Figure 1.11a. For now, we have a practical question: How can we identify the absolute threshold, given a result that takes the form of an S-shaped psychometric function? Somewhat arbitrarily, the absolute threshold is often defined as the intensity at which people respond "yes" 50% of the time, but as long as the threshold is defined the same way with different stimuli (e.g., with higher-pitched or lower-pitched tones), the arbitrariness has little practical significance. In Figure 1.11b, as indicated by the dashed lines, this way of defining the absolute threshold yields a threshold at intensity 3.

psychometric function A curve that relates a measure of perceptual experience to the intensity of a physical stimulus.

Staircase Method The method of constant stimuli is a simple and accurate way of determining absolute thresholds, but it isn't very efficient, because it involves repeated presentations of stimuli that are already known to be well below or well above threshold (e.g., the tones at levels 1 and 6 in the previous example), so presenting these stimuli doesn't generate much useful data. Rather, the data obtained in the steepest part of the psychometric function—that is, near the absolute threshold—are most informative. Fortunately, a more efficient version of the method of constant stimuli can be used to eliminate repeated presentations of stimuli well below or above the threshold and to focus instead on presenting stimuli near the threshold. This procedure is known as the **staircase method**, because the intensity of each stimulus is either one step up or one step down from the previous stimulus. Figure 1.12 shows how the method works. Note that, with this method, only the first few tones are well below (or, on some sequences, well above) threshold.

Demonstration 1.3 Absolute Threshold Determine your absolute threshold for visual stimuli, using the method of constant stimuli and the staircase method.

staircase method A behavioral method used in psychophysical experiments; the participant is presented with a stimulus and indicates whether it was detected, and based on that response, the next stimulus is either one step up or one step down in intensity.

The staircase method is commonly used to measure possible hearing loss, particularly in older adults. For each of several tones at different frequencies (from low pitched

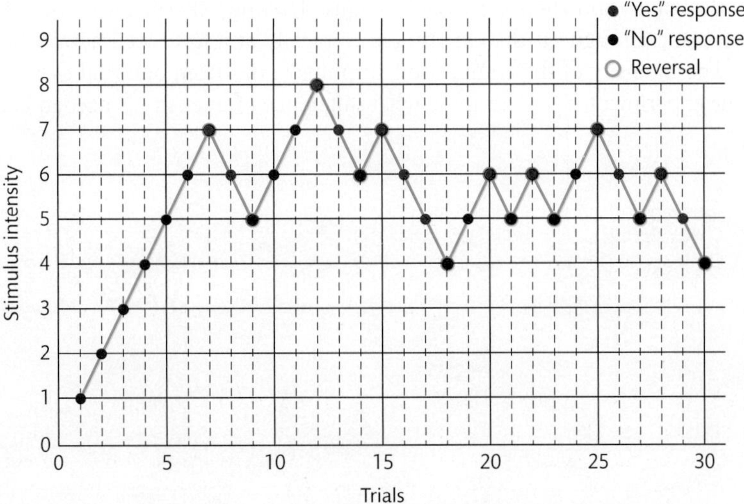

Figure 1.12 Staircase Method The stimulus in each trial is one step up or down in intensity from the stimulus on the preceding trial. The stimulus on Trial 1 is at an intensity of 1, which is known from preliminary testing to be well below the absolute threshold. Whenever there is a reversal of perceptual experience—that is, whenever the response changes from "yes" (the stimulus was perceived) to "no" (the stimulus wasn't perceived) or from "no" to "yes"—there is a corresponding reversal in the direction of the step. The intensity at each reversal is an estimate of the absolute threshold, and the final estimate is the average of all these values. In this case, the average intensity of the 14 reversals is 5.8.

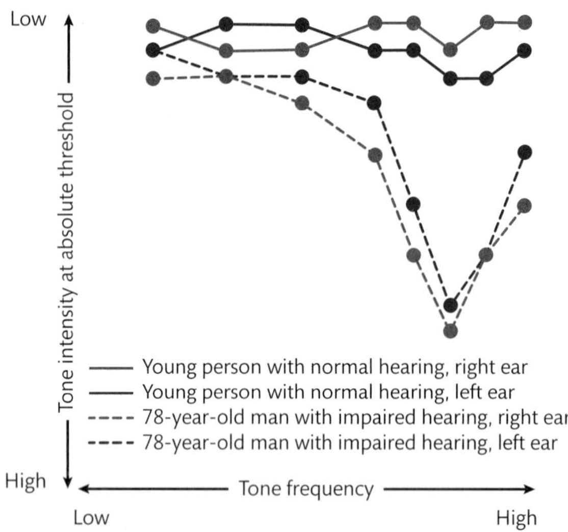

Figure 1.13 Using the Staircase Method to Measure Hearing Loss These two audiograms—one for a young person with normal hearing (solid lines) and one for an older person with impaired hearing—were constructed by using the staircase method to estimate the absolute threshold at various frequencies, corresponding to the plotted points. At every plotted frequency (especially at higher frequencies) the older person's absolute threshold is greater than that of the young person—that is, at every frequency, the intensity of a tone must be higher for the older person to detect it than for the young person (note that in this graph, as is standard in audiograms, tone intensity increases from top to bottom: louder tones indicate poorer performance).

to high pitched), an audiologist estimates the person's absolute threshold (the intensity required for the person to just detect the tone) and then plots these absolute thresholds on a graph like the one in Figure 1.13 (curves like those in Figure 1.13 are called *audiograms*).

Difference Threshold: Same or Different?

The absolute threshold provides important information about how a given perceptual system works, in terms of the absolute sensitivity of the system. However, most perception in everyday life involves stimuli that are well above absolute threshold, stimuli that we are more concerned with differentiating than just with detecting. For example, whether we're listening to music, engaging in conversation, or focusing on traffic sounds to tell if it's safe to cross the street, hearing typically involves noticing that stimuli are different (different musical notes, different speech sounds, different vehicle sounds), rather than deciding whether we're hearing something or not. It's useful to be able to measure how different two stimuli must be in order for them to be perceived as different.

Figure 1.14 illustrates this aspect of perception in the realm of vision. The square on the left appears slightly brighter (more intense) than the background, and the one on the right appears slightly darker (less intense). But there is also a square in the middle, which is impossible to see because it has the same intensity as the background. Clearly, our ability to see each square depends on our ability to tell the difference between the intensity of the square and the intensity of the background.

Now we can ask, how much less or more intense would the middle square in Figure 1.14 have to be in order to make the square visible? The answer to this question would define a **difference threshold** (or *just noticeable difference [JND]*), the minimum difference between two stimuli that allows an observer to perceive that the two stimuli are different.

difference threshold (or *just noticeable difference [JND]*) The minimum difference between two stimuli that allows an observer to perceive that the two stimuli are different.

Experiments aimed at determining a JND always involve comparing two stimuli, called the *standard stimulus* and the *comparison stimulus*. The intensity of the standard stimulus remains constant throughout the experiment, typically at a level well above the absolute threshold. The intensity of the comparison stimulus varies from one trial to the next. The object of the experiment is to determine what difference in intensity is needed between the

Figure 1.14 Just Noticeable Difference (JND) The square on the left is slightly brighter than the background, and the square on the right is slightly darker. There is a middle square that has the same intensity as the background and is therefore invisible. By how much would we have to adjust the intensity of the middle square—making it brighter or darker—to make it perceivable? The amount of the adjustment in intensity would define the *just noticeable difference*, or *difference threshold*, for the intensity of a visual stimulus against this background. The JND for a darker or lighter gray background would likely be different.

standard stimulus and the comparison stimulus for people to reliably detect that the two stimuli differ. The methods used in such experiments to determine the difference threshold are similar to the methods used to determine the absolute threshold.

Method of Adjustment To illustrate how the method of adjustment is used to measure the JND, let's consider an experiment in which two patches of light are presented side by side on a black background. One patch is the standard stimulus—it always has the same physical intensity. The other patch is the comparison stimulus—the participant adjusts its intensity by turning a knob. The experiment begins with the comparison stimulus set at the same intensity as the standard stimulus, and the participant adjusts its intensity until it appears to be just noticeably brighter than the standard. Then, starting from the same point, the participant adjusts the intensity of the comparison stimulus until it seems just noticeably dimmer than the standard. After a sufficient number of such trials, the experimenter calculates the average difference in intensity that the participant needed to just notice that the comparison stimulus differed from the standard stimulus, and this value is taken as an estimate of the JND.

Method of Constant Stimuli The same experiment can be conducted using the method of constant stimuli. Figure 1.15a shows the results of a typical experiment, in the form of a psychometric function. The intensity of the standard stimulus is 16 (in some arbitrary units of intensity). The percentage of "yes" responses starts out near zero for comparison stimuli that are much less intense than the standard. As the intensity of the comparison stimuli increases, the percentage of "yes" responses also increases until, for comparison stimuli that are much more intense than the standard, the person almost always says that the comparison appears

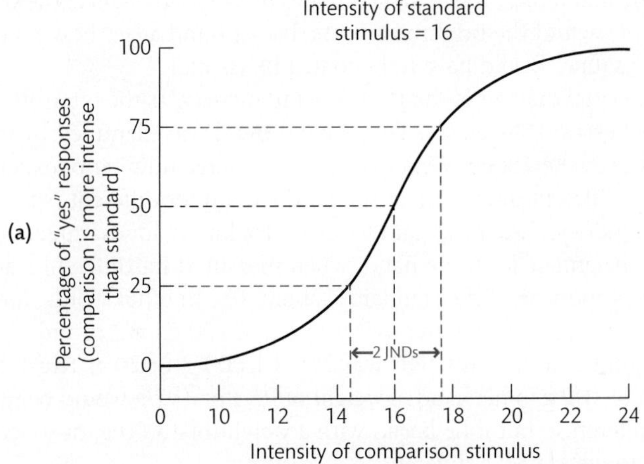

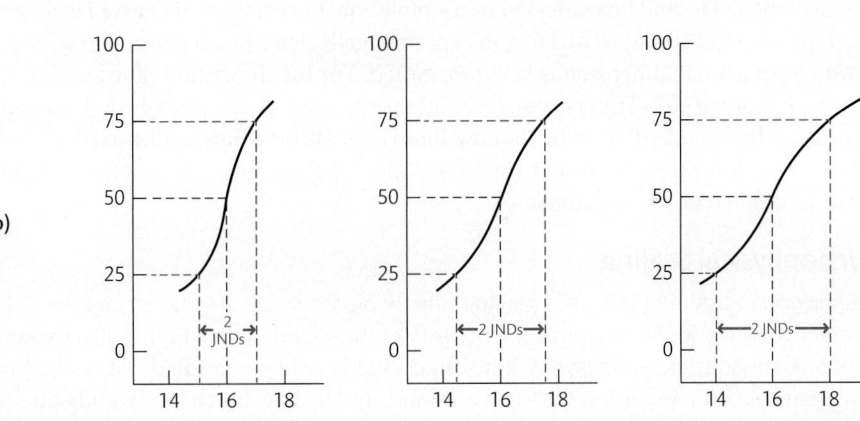

Figure 1.15 Determining the JND with the Method of Constant Stimuli (a) On each trial of an experiment, a standard stimulus with an intensity of 16 is presented next to one of eight different comparison stimuli, with intensities ranging from 10 to 24. The participant has to respond "yes" (the comparison stimulus is brighter) or "no" (the comparison stimulus isn't brighter). This graph shows the psychometric function that results from plotting the percentage of "yes" responses for each comparison stimulus. The JND is defined as the intensity at which 75% of the responses were "yes" minus the intensity at which 25% of the responses were "yes," divided by 2. Here, the JND is about 1.55. (b) The JND correlates with the steepness of the psychometric function. In the middle graph, the curve between 25% and 75% "yes" responses has the same steepness as the curve in (a); in the graph at left, the curve is steeper, and the JND is smaller; in the graph at right, the curve is less steep, and the JND is larger.

Ernst Weber (1795–1878).
[Max Planck Institute for the History of Science, Berlin/Wikipedia]

brighter. As you'd expect, when the comparison stimulus has an intensity of 16, equal to that of the standard, the participant says the comparison is brighter about half the time—the participant is just guessing.

In an experiment like this, the JND is determined by finding the point on the psychometric function where 25% of the responses were "yes" (corresponding to an intensity of about 14.4 in Figure 1.15a) and the point where 75% of the responses were "yes" (corresponding to an intensity of about 17.5), then halving the difference between these two values of intensity, which in this case yields a JND of about 1.55 units of intensity ([17.5 − 14.4] / 2 = 1.55). In other words, on average, when the standard stimulus has an intensity of 16 units, a comparison stimulus must be 1.55 units brighter or dimmer in order to be reliably perceived as different from the standard.

Figure 1.15b illustrates how the JND is reflected in the steepness of the psychometric function. A very steep psychometric function reflects a very small JND, meaning that observers can detect very small differences from the standard stimulus; in contrast, a very shallow psychometric function reflects a very large JND, meaning that observers can only detect very large differences from the standard.

Note that the staircase method—the version of the method of constant stimuli that we discussed above for determining the absolute threshold—can also be used to measure the JND. For example, in the experiment illustrated in Figure 1.15a, after each trial, the intensity of the comparison stimulus would be adjusted downward if the response on that trial were "yes" and upward if it were "no." After a sufficient number of trials, the difference between the intensity of the comparison stimulus and the intensity of the standard stimulus would be taken as a measure of the JND.

Weber's Law In the example experiment just discussed, the JND was determined in relation to a standard stimulus with a fixed intensity of 16. But what if a standard stimulus with a different intensity had been used—for example, one with an intensity just above the absolute threshold or one with an intensity much greater than 16? Would that affect the size of the JND? Or, in Figure 1.14, would the brightness of the background affect how much brighter or darker the middle square would have to be to just be visible?

The answer, it turns out, is yes: the size of the JND tends to increase as the intensity of the standard stimulus (or background) increases. This general trend was identified by the German physician Ernst Weber in the 1860s. Weber carried out a large number of experiments to estimate the JND for different intensities of standard stimuli for different perceptual dimensions (brightness, loudness, heaviness, and so forth). He found, for example, that the JND for the heaviness of weights held in the hand, when measured for different standard weights, was a constant proportion of the standard—about 2%. In other words, for a standard stimulus with a weight of, say, 100 g, the JND was 2% of 100 g, or 2 g; and for a standard stimulus with a weight of 1,000 g, the JND was 2% of 1,000 g, or 20 g. Thus, if a person were to hold a weight of 100 g in his hand, a weight of 98 g or 102 g would be just enough for him to detect a difference, but if he began with a weight of 1,000 g, he'd need a weight of 980 g or 1,020 g to just detect a difference.

Weber's law A statement of the relationship between the intensity of a standard stimulus and the size of the just noticeable difference (JND = kI, where I is the intensity of the standard stimulus and k is a constant that depends on the perceptual dimension being measured).

Weber fraction The constant k in Weber's law (JND = kI).

Weber found that the relationship between the intensity of the standard stimulus and the size of the JND could be expressed by a simple equation: JND = kI, where I is the intensity of the standard stimulus, and k is an experimentally determined constant that depends on which perceptual dimension is being measured. For the dimension of heaviness, as we just saw, k is about .02. This systematic relationship between the size of the JND and the intensity of the standard stimulus is now known as **Weber's law**, and the constant k in Weber's law is known as the **Weber fraction**. Table 1.2 shows the values of the Weber fraction in four different sensory domains.

TABLE 1.2 Weber Fraction for Four Different Perceptual Dimensions

Sensory Domain	Perceptual Dimension	Weber Fraction
Taste	Saltiness	.083
Vision	Brightness	.079
Audition	Loudness	.048
Touch	Heaviness	.020

Psychophysical Scaling

Imagine you're listening to music playing quietly on the radio. If you turn up the volume enough to exactly double the physical intensity of the sound, how will that affect your perception of the music's loudness? Will it sound exactly twice as loud? If not, will it sound more than twice as loud or less than twice as loud, and by how much? Answering questions like these is the domain of **psychophysical scaling,** the process of measuring how changes in stimulus intensity relate to changes in the perceived intensity.

psychophysical scaling The process of measuring how changes in stimulus intensity relate to changes in the perceived intensity.

Should Weber's law be part of how we answer these questions? After all, Weber's law expresses a relationship between stimulus intensity and how we perceive stimulus intensity, in the sense that it tells us by how much the intensity of two stimuli must differ for the stimuli to be perceived as different. In the next two sections we'll consider two approaches to psychophysical scaling—one that incorporates Weber's law and one that discards it.

Fechner's Law Gustav Fechner was very impressed by Weber's law and thought it could be used to quantify how people perceive stimulus intensity in general. He began by supposing that 1 JND is equivalent to 1 unit of difference in perceived intensity, which seems reasonable given that the perceptual relationship between two stimuli separated by 1 JND is always the same: the difference between the two stimuli is just barely detectable. Then, using the relationship between stimulus intensity (I) and JND in Weber's law (JND $= kI$), Fechner derived a simple equation, now known as **Fechner's law,** to express how the perceived intensity S of a stimulus changes as its physical intensity I changes: $S = k \ln I/I_0$, where k is the same as in Weber's law—that is, the Weber fraction—and where $\ln I/I_0$ is the natural logarithm of the ratio of the stimulus intensity (I) to the intensity of the same stimulus at the absolute threshold (I_0). (Note that this last term ensures that the perceived intensity S is 0 when the stimulus is at absolute threshold, because $\ln I_0/I_0 = \ln 1 = 0$—that is, the natural logarithm of 1 is 0.)

Fechner's law A statement of how the perceived intensity of a stimulus changes as its physical intensity changes ($S = k \ln I/I_0$, where S is the perceived intensity, k is the Weber fraction, and $\ln I/I_0$ is the natural logarithm of the ratio of the stimulus intensity, I, to the intensity, I_0, of the same stimulus at the absolute threshold).

Fechner's law is illustrated in Figure 1.16. As you can see, the curve is steep for low-intensity stimuli but then flattens out as the physical intensity of the stimuli increases. This means that, for low-intensity stimuli, a 1-JND increase in perceived intensity is achieved by just a small increase in physical intensity (the small distance between the red vertical dashed lines); but for higher-intensity stimuli, a much larger increase in physical intensity (the much larger distance between the blue vertical dashed lines) is needed to produce that same 1-JND increase in perceived intensity.

Given that Weber's law and Fechner's law are so closely related—in essence, Fechner's law is Weber's law plus the assumption that 1 JND equals 1 unit of difference in perceived intensity—Fechner's law is sometimes referred to as the *Weber–Fechner law,* and the graph in Figure 1.16 paints an elegant picture of how Fechner's law expresses the relationship between the physical intensity of a stimulus and its perceived intensity. But now we can ask, does Fechner's law capture a general principle of perceptual experience?

S. S. Stevens (1906–1973).
[Harvard University Archives W277900_1]

Stevens Power Law Clearly, the validity of Fechner's law depends on the validity of Weber's law, and although Weber's law is approximately correct for several perceptual dimensions, such as brightness and loudness, it doesn't do a good job of accounting for the perception of other dimensions, such as electric shock. In the mid-twentieth century, the American psychologist S. S. Stevens argued forcefully that Fechner's law must be rejected. To develop

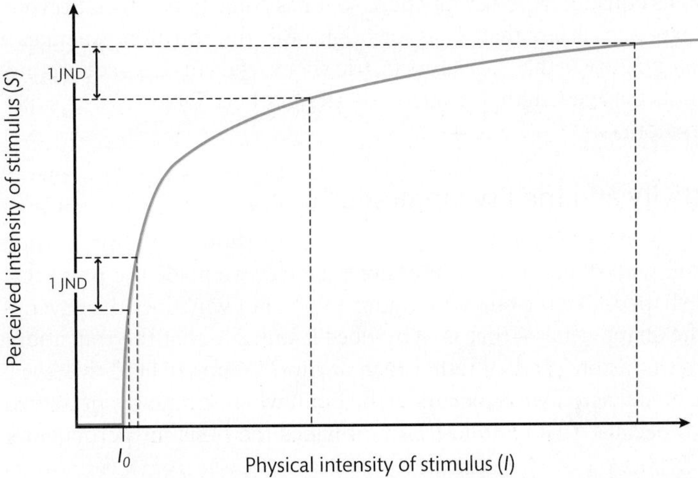

Figure 1.16 Fechner's Law Fechner's law ($S = k \ln I/I_0$) generates a curve that is initially very steep but then flattens out, showing that the increase in physical intensity needed to produce a 1-JND difference in perceived intensity is much larger for higher-intensity stimuli than for low-intensity stimuli. The exact shape of the curve will depend on the value of the Weber fraction. Note that the perceived intensity is 0 for physical stimulus intensities at and below the absolute threshold, I_0.

Figure 1.17 Stevens Power Law Stevens power law reflects the fact that the relationship between perceived intensity and physical intensity is different for different perceptual dimensions. Many dimensions, like brightness, are associated with a decelerating curve like the one for Fechner's law. But other dimensions, like electric shock, yield an accelerating curve or, like line length, a curve that is close to a straight line.

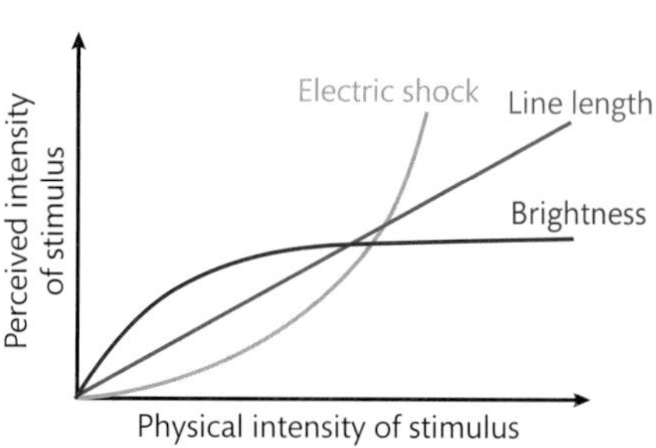

magnitude estimation A behavioral method used in psychophysical experiments to estimate perceived intensity directly; the experimenter assigns an arbitrary number (e.g., 100) to represent the intensity of a standard stimulus, and then the participant assigns numbers to other stimuli to indicate their perceived intensity relative to the standard.

an alternative, Stevens devised a method called **magnitude estimation** that uses behavioral responses to estimate perceived intensity directly (Stevens, 1961).

To use this method, the experimenter selects a set of several different stimuli varying widely in physical intensity, all above absolute threshold. A stimulus is presented with an intensity in the middle of this range that functions as a standard: the participant is told to assign the perceived intensity of this stimulus some arbitrary number, say, 100. The other stimuli are then presented to the participant one at a time in random order, and after each presentation, the participant estimates the intensity or magnitude of the stimulus by assigning it a number relative to the standard. For example, if the stimulus was perceived as twice as intense as the standard, it would be assigned 200; if half as intense, 50, and so on.

Figure 1.17 shows some typical results for three perceptual dimensions—brightness, line length, and electric shock. As you can see, the brightness curve has the same general shape as the curve in Figure 1.16—it first rises steeply and then flattens out, indicating that as the magnitude of the physical stimulus increases, its perceived magnitude increases more and more gradually. This *decelerating* curve characterizes perceptual dimensions that can be approximated by Fechner's law, such as loudness and brightness. In contrast, however, neither the curve for line length nor the curve for electric shock is decelerating, which shows that these dimensions don't conform to Fechner's law.

Stevens power law A statement of the relationship between the physical intensity of a stimulus and its perceived intensity ($S = cI^n$, where S is the perceived intensity of the stimulus, I is its physical intensity, the exponent n is different for each perceptual dimension, and c is a constant that depends on which units are being used for S and I).

Electric shock produces an *accelerating* curve, indicating that small increases in high-intensity stimuli cause a greater change in perceived intensity than do small increases in low-intensity stimuli—for example, an increase from 1 to 2 milliamperes (mA) of electric current might be barely detectable, but an increase from 5 to 6 mA is quite noticeable (for comparison, 100–300 mA is enough to cause death by electrocution). For line length, the relationship between perceived magnitude and physical magnitude is very nearly constant, resulting in a straight line on the graph in Figure 1.17. That is, just noticeable changes in perceived length are the same for short lines as they are for long lines. Stevens found that a simple equation could capture all three possibilities: $S = cI^n$, where S is the perceived intensity of the stimulus, I is its physical intensity, the exponent n is different for each perceptual dimension, and c is a constant that depends on which units are being used for S and I. The exponent makes this equation a power function, so it has come to be called **Stevens power law.** When the exponent is less than 1, as for brightness, the equation generates a decelerating curve; when it's greater than 1, as for electric shock, the curve is accelerating; and when it's equal to 1, as for line length, the curve is a straight line. Table 1.3 lists exponents for several sensory domains.

TABLE 1.3 Stevens Power Law Exponent in Different Sensory Domains

Sensory Domain	Perceptual Dimension	Exponent
Taste	Sweetness	0.8
Vision	Brightness	0.3
Audition	Loudness	0.5
Touch	Warmth	1.6
Touch	Heaviness	1.5
Touch	Electric shock	3.5

Noise in Neural Activity and the Psychometric Function

In our earlier discussion of the psychometric function, a curve showing the proportion of trials on which stimuli with different intensities are detected, we made the point that the curve is typically S-shaped, like the curve in Figure 1.11b. But why does the psychometric function have the shape it has—that is, why does it indicate that the transitions that define absolute thresholds are gradual rather than abrupt? To understand this, we'll need to think about the neural activity that occurs in the brain when stimuli are presented at levels near threshold, because this neural activity provides the basis for participants' responses.

Let's assume that, in an experiment involving tones of different intensities, each tone is presented for 1 second and that each response is based on the number of action potentials (spikes) sent along the auditory nerve from the ears to the brain during that 1-second period—after all, the listener has no other information to use in deciding whether or not a tone was presented. If the number of spikes is large, the participant responds "yes"; if the number of spikes is very low, the participant responds "no." (Recall that most neurons have a spontaneous firing rate of, say, 5–10 spikes per second even when there is no stimulus present; that means the listener can't just say "yes" whenever there's even one spike.)

Figure 1.18a shows the number of spikes sent along an auditory nerve axon on each of four presentations of a tone with a physical intensity setting of 3. Note that the number of spikes is not the same on every trial. All neurons exhibit this kind of variability, which is referred to as **noise;** noise makes neurons less-than-perfect transmitters of information. (Throughout this discussion, we'll focus on the number of spikes in just one typical auditory nerve axon, rather than the cumulative activity in the many thousands of axons that make up the auditory nerve.)

noise In the study of neural activity, slight random variation in the number of action potentials produced by neurons in response to a fixed sensory stimulus.

Figure 1.18b shows how the number of spikes per trial might vary across 1,000 tone presentations. This graph was generated simply by counting up the number of trials in which the neuron produced 0 spikes, 1 spike, 2 spikes, and so forth—for example, the neuron produced 10 spikes on 52 trials and 15 spikes on 83 trials. The total number of spikes produced in the 1,000 trials was 14,899, meaning that, on average, about 15 spikes per trial were evoked by the tone (14,889/1,000 = 14.889 ≈ 15), as indicated by the vertical dashed line. On most trials, the number of spikes was indeed around 15 (between 10 and 20 spikes were produced in 795 of the 1,000 trials, about 80% of the time), but occasionally there were a lot more or a lot fewer.

The general shape of the graph in Figure 1.18b is shown by the blue curve, the familiar bell-shaped curve of a normal distribution, with a peak at about 15 spikes per trial. In Figure 1.19, normal distributions are used to represent how the neuron's responses change

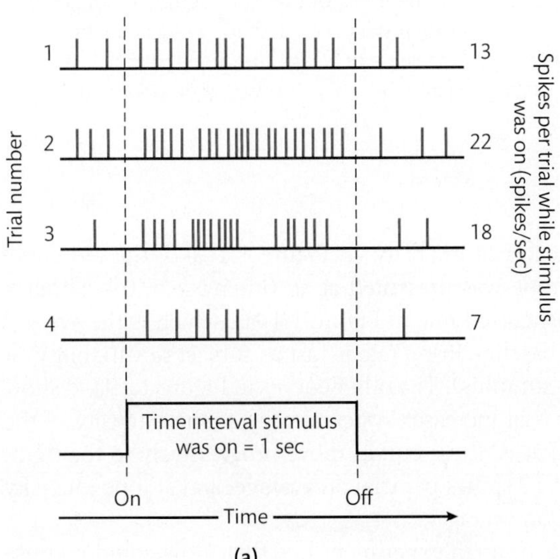

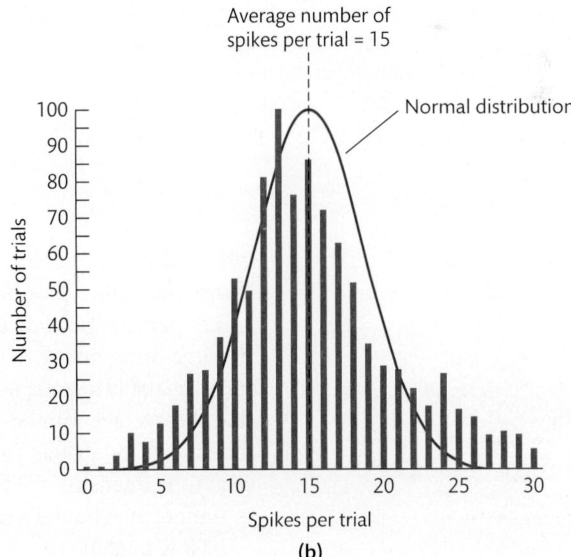

Figure 1.18 Noise in Neural Activity (a) The stimulus is a tone with an intensity of 3, presented for 1 second. The number of action potentials (spikes) evoked in a typical auditory nerve axon by four such tone presentations varies from 7 to 22 (13 on Trial 1, 22 on Trial 2, 18 on Trial 3, and 7 on Trial 4). This variability in neural activity in response to identical stimuli is called *noise.* (b) This graph shows how the number of spikes per trial varied across 1,000 trials, due to noise. The average number of spikes per trial is 15, with as few as 0 spikes produced on 1 trial and as many as 30 spikes produced on 5 trials. The general shape of this graph is like a bell-shaped curve, or normal distribution (the blue curve behind the red bars).

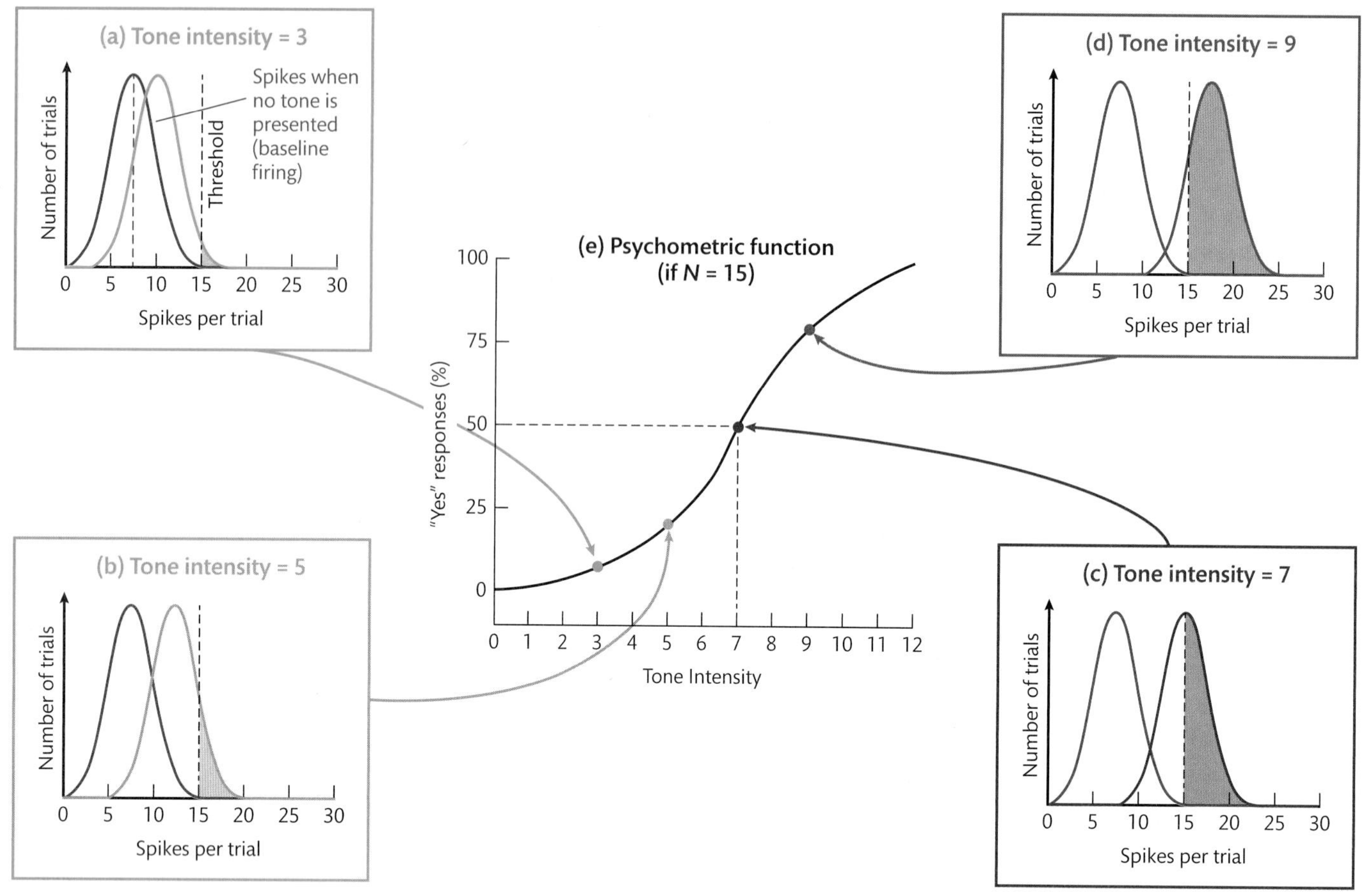

Figure 1.19 Noise and the Psychometric Function (a)–(d) The red curve shows the number of spikes produced by a neuron during trials when no tone was presented; the vertical dashed red line in (a) shows that this baseline firing rate averages about 7 spikes. In trials when a tone was presented, as the intensity of the tone increases from 3 to 9, the average number of spikes per trial increases from about 10 to about 17. Assume that the participant's threshold *N* for deciding that a tone was presented is *N* = 15 spikes per trial. The percentage of "yes" responses at each tone intensity is the proportion of the area under each curve to the right of the threshold, as indicated by shading. (e) The variability due to noise results in an S-shaped psychometric function, regardless of the value of *N*. The absolute threshold is 7, the intensity that results in 50% "yes" responses (indicated by the dashed lines).

when tones are presented at various levels of intensity. In Figure 1.19a–d, the red curve shows the spikes produced when no tone was presented at all (intensity = 0)—about 7 spikes per trial (as indicated by the dashed red line in Figure 1.19a), which is the average baseline firing rate of this neuron (the baseline firing rate is just as subject to variability, or noise, as the firing rate in response to a stimulus). The other curves in Figure 1.19a–d show that the average number of spikes per trial increases systematically as the intensity of the tone increases, just as you'd expect—that is, these curves move progressively to the right, so at tone intensity = 3 there are about 10 spikes per trial on average, and at tone intensity = 9 there are about 17 spikes per trial on average.

Now imagine that you're a participant in an experiment like this. How could you use the number of spikes during each trial to decide whether or not a tone had been presented? You need a rule like the following: if I count *N* or more spikes, I'll respond that a tone was presented; if I count fewer than *N* spikes, I'll respond that no tone was presented. If you adopt this rule with, say, *N* = 15, then whenever the neuron produces 15 or more spikes, you'll respond "yes," and otherwise you'll respond "no."

This choice of a threshold means that you'll respond "no" on about half the trials when a tone is presented at intensity 7, as shown in Figure 1.19c. Why not just lower the threshold and respond "yes" whenever the neuron produces, say, 5 spikes? The presence of noise—variability in the neuron's response—creates a problem in applying a rule with such a low threshold: it would lead to your saying "yes" even when no tone is presented—all the trials to the right of 5 spikes per trial on the red signal-absent curve in these graphs. Clearly, given the overlap of the signal-absent curve with the signal-present curves in Figure 1.19a–d, there is no "perfect" value of *N*, no value that would lead you to respond "yes" whenever a tone was presented and to respond "no" whenever no tone was presented.

The plotted points in the graph in Figure 1.19e show the percentage of "yes" responses for each of the tone intensities in Figure 1.19a–d, if $N = 15$. For example, consider the green plotted point for tone intensity = 3, with about 7% "yes" responses; this means the neuron produced 15 or more spikes on about 7% of all the trials at this intensity. Figure 1.19e shows that the best curve for connecting these plotted points (and the points that would have been plotted if other tone intensities had also been tested) is an S-shaped psychometric function like the one in Figure 1.11b.

Where does the variability in the neural response come from? There are two main sources of noise—external and internal. In a tone-detection experiment like the ones we've been discussing, external sources of noise might include slight movements by the participant, which could create small sounds that produce extra spikes; or the speaker producing the tones might be subject to minute fluctuations in the building's electrical power, which could cause the physical intensities of the tones to vary slightly from what they're supposed to be. Internal sources of noise include factors such as tiny fluctuations in body temperature affecting biochemical factors that influence ion flow, random variations in the number of neurotransmitter molecules that bind to the postsynaptic membrane, and even random fluctuations in the participant's attention, all of which can influence the number of spikes produced by neurons. And of course, the responses of neurons involved in all the senses, not just hearing, are influenced by such external and internal sources of noise.

Check Your Understanding

1.11 In each trial of a tone-detection experiment, a tone is presented that is initially too quiet to hear. The participant turns up a volume knob until he can just hear the tone, and then continues turning the knob until he can just tell that the tone has gotten louder, and the experimenter records the setting of the volume knob at both points. Is this experiment using the method of adjustment or the method of constant stimuli, and is it aimed at determining the participant's absolute threshold or difference threshold or both?

1.12 How is the staircase method more efficient than the method of constant stimuli?

1.13 Explain why both graphs in Figure 1.11 are psychometric functions.

1.14 In the section on Weber's law ($\text{JND} = kI$), we saw that k is about .02 for the perceptual dimension of heaviness. Describe two trials of an experiment using the method of adjustment, with responses indicating that k is about .05 for the dimension of loudness (use arbitrary values for loudness levels).

1.15 How does Figure 1.17 show that Fechner's law doesn't hold for the perceptual dimension of electric shock?

1.16 Which of the following sentences could be interpreted as showing the presence of noise in neural activity:

A. In a tone-detection experiment, the number of spikes per trial evoked in an auditory nerve axon increased as the loudness of the tone increased.

B. In a tone-detection experiment, the number of spikes per trial evoked in an auditory nerve axon by a tone of fixed loudness was different in different trials.

Signal Detection Theory

As we saw in our discussion of Figure 1.19, noise in neural activity makes it difficult to be certain about perceptual judgments, so perceivers have to choose some decision criterion *N*, some number of spikes above which they'll report having detected a stimulus and below which they'll report not having detected a stimulus. In this scenario, people are free to select the value of *N*. For example, in a tone-detection experiment, some participants might be liberal and select a relatively low *N*, so they respond "yes" if there's the slightest hint that a tone was presented, whereas others might be conservative and select a relatively high *N*, so they say "yes" only if they're quite sure they heard a tone. This means that the measured threshold would reflect not just the participants' perceptual sensitivity, but also their decision-making style.

The issue of how a person decides to weigh evidence—their decision-making style—matters not just in laboratory experiments but also in important real-world situations. Consider, for example, the perceptual decisions made by airport security agents screening baggage. Suppose it's unclear from the X-ray image of a carry-on bag whether the bag contains a weapon. An agent with a very liberal decision-making style would decide to hand-search the bag in such situations whenever there's the slightest hint that the bag contains a weapon-shaped object—but this slows the line and causes people to get upset. In contrast, an agent with a very conservative decision-making style would hand-search only those bags that almost certainly contain a weapon—but this would result in not finding some well-hidden weapons. The proportion of times an agent, in effect, says "yes" and performs a hand-search depends both on how liberal or conservative their decision-making style is and on how clearly the X-ray image provides evidence for the presence of a weapon.

signal detection theory A framework for measuring how people make decisions based on noisy perceptual evidence; provides a way to measure perceptual sensitivity apart from the decision-making style.

We'd like to separate the two factors of perceptual sensitivity and decision-making style, in order to measure perceptual sensitivity in a way that isn't affected by the decision-making style—both to understand perceptual sensitivity scientifically and to help people adjust their decision-making style appropriately in different practical situations. **Signal detection theory** provides a way to do just that (Tanner & Swets, 1954).

A Signal Detection Experiment

In a typical experiment based on signal detection theory, a stimulus is presented in some trials (often, a randomly selected half of the trials), and no stimulus is presented in others. Within any given experiment, the presented stimulus always has the same fixed, very low intensity. Participants respond "yes" if they perceive a stimulus and "no" if they don't.

hit In a signal detection experiment, a response indicating that a signal was detected on a trial when a signal was presented.

false alarm In a signal detection experiment, a response indicating that a signal was detected on a trial when no signal was presented.

miss In a signal detection experiment, a response indicating that no signal was detected on a trial when a signal was presented.

correct rejection In a signal detection experiment, a response indicating that no signal was detected on a trial when no signal was presented.

receiver operating characteristic (ROC) In a signal detection experiment, a curve representing the quality of a participant's performance.

As illustrated in Figure 1.20a, a participant's response in each trial of a signal detection experiment (say, a tone-detection experiment) can be classified as belonging to one of four categories:

- Saying "yes" after a signal is presented is a **hit.**
- Saying "yes" after no signal is presented is a **false alarm.**
- Saying "no" after a signal is presented is a **miss.**
- Saying "no" after no signal is presented is a **correct rejection.**

Hits and correct rejections (shown in blue) are correct responses; false alarms and misses (shown in red) are errors.

Figure 1.20b shows the hypothetical results of such an experiment. Out of 100 trials, there were 29 hits, 16 false alarms, 21 misses, and 34 correct rejections. Underneath these results, we've computed the percentage of each. For example, there were 50 trials in which a tone was presented and participants could, therefore, record a hit. The actual number of hits was 29, so the percentage of hits, or the hit rate, is 29/50 = .58, or 58%. If this result were obtained across a sufficiently large number of trials, we could say that the hit rate is an estimate of the probability of a hit under these experimental conditions.

		Stimulus	
		Signal presented	Signal not presented
Responses	"Yes"	HIT	FALSE ALARM
	"No"	MISS	CORRECT REJECTION

(a) Possible outcomes

		Stimulus		
		Tone presented	Tone not presented	Totals
Responses	"Yes"	**29 hits**	**16 false alarms**	45 "Yes"
	"No"	**21 misses**	**34 correct rejections**	55 "No"
	Totals	50 trials	50 trials	

Hit rate = 29/50 = .58

Miss rate = 21/50 = .42 (= 1.0 − hit rate)

False alarm rate = 16/50 = .32

Correct rejection rate = 34/50 = .68 (= 1.0 − false alarm rate)

(b) Sample results

Figure 1.20 A Signal Detection Experiment (a) In a signal detection experiment, a signal is presented in half the trials and no signal is presented in half the trials. This means that there are four possible types of responses: a hit (saying "yes" when a signal is presented), a false alarm (saying "yes" when no signal is presented), a miss (saying "no" when a signal is presented), and a correct rejection (saying "no" when no signal is presented). (b) These sample results are used to calculate the hit rate, miss rate, false alarm rate, and correct rejection rate.

Similarly, the miss rate is the probability of saying "no" when a tone was presented and is here equal to 21/50 = .42, or 42%. Obviously, whenever a tone is presented, the participant's response must be either a hit or a miss, so the sum of hits and misses must equal 50 (the number of trials in which a tone was presented), and the sum of the hit rate and the miss rate must equal 1.0, or 100%.

The false alarm rate (the probability of saying "yes" after no tone was presented) and the correct rejection rate (the probability of saying "no" after no tone was presented) are related in the same way. That is, the false alarm rate is 16/50 = .32, or 32%, and the correct rejection rate is 34/50 = .68, or 68%; so the sum of false alarms and correct rejections is 50, and the sum of their probabilities is 1.0, or 100%. Note that the results of the experiment are completely described by the hit rate and the false alarm rate, because once you know those rates, simple subtraction tells you the miss rate and the correct rejection rate.

To view the results of this type of experiment, we can plot the hit rate against the false alarm rate on a graph called a **receiver operating characteristic (ROC)**, as shown in Figure 1.21. (This terminology comes from the mid-twentieth century, when this method was developed by engineers and psychologists to assess the accuracy of radio operators listening to noisy signals on their receivers.) The blue point corresponds to the result of our experiment. The green point represents the best possible performance—the participant always says "yes" when the tone is presented and always says "no" when the tone is absent. The red line marks all the points at which the hit rate equals the false alarm rate, as if the participant were just guessing, responding "yes" and "no" equally often, regardless of whether a tone was presented or not. (This might well happen if the intensity of the tone were well below the absolute threshold—in other words, if the trials containing the tone sounded the same as the trials containing silence.)

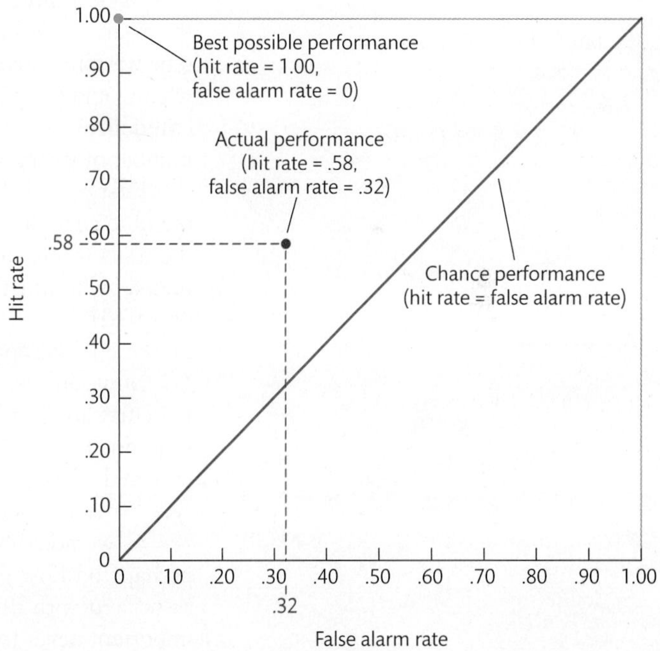

Figure 1.21 Receiver Operating Characteristic (ROC) An ROC plot is a graph of the hit rate versus the false alarm rate in a signal detection experiment. Here, reflecting the sample results in Figure 1.21, the hit rate is .58 and the false alarm rate is .32. In the best possible performance, the participant would always say "yes" when a signal was presented (hit rate = 1.00) and always say "no" when no signal was presented (false alarm rate = 0); chance performance would result from randomly saying "yes" half the time and "no" half the time (hit rate = false alarm rate), which would correspond to any point on the main diagonal. The better the actual performance, the closer the point would fall to the upper left corner of the graph.

In general, then, the quality of participants' performance in a signal detection experiment can be judged by where the point representing their performance falls on an ROC plot: the closer to the

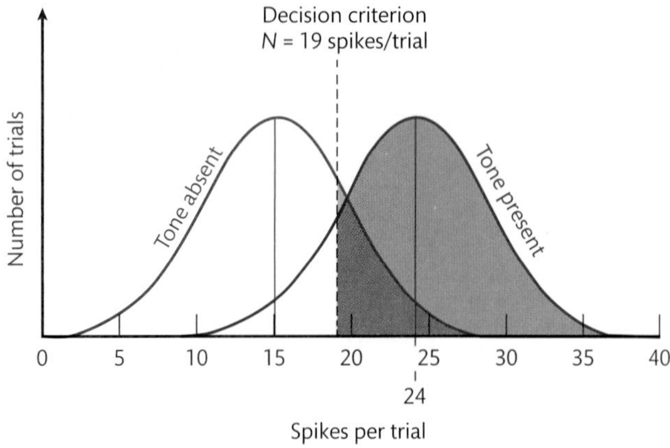

Figure 1.22 Decision Criterion, Hit Rate, and False Alarm Rate With a decision criterion of $N = 19$ spikes/trial, the participant will say "yes" on trials with 19 or more spikes and will say "no" on trials with fewer than 19 spikes. When a tone is present, 19 or more spikes occur on about 80% of the trials (the proportion of the area under the blue curve that's at or to the right of 19, shaded in blue). When a tone is absent, 19 or more spikes occur on about 25% of the trials (the proportion of the area under the red curve that's to the right of 19, shaded in red).

top and left of the graph, the better the performance (indicating a very detectable stimulus); the closer to the main diagonal, the worse the performance (indicating random guessing about a stimulus that's not at all detectable).

Sensitivity and Bias

Now let's see how we can interpret the results of this type of signal detection experiment to measure perceptual sensitivity apart from the effects of the decision-making criterion.

As discussed earlier, neural activity—that is, the number of spikes evoked by a stimulus—tends to increase as the intensity of the stimulus increases, and a perceiver can use this spike count to decide whether a stimulus has been presented or not. But as we saw in Figures 1.19 and 1.20, when a stimulus with a fixed intensity is presented over many trials, the number of spikes per trial typically varies around a central tendency. Furthermore, even in trials where no tone is presented, noise affects the baseline firing rate of neurons, resulting in a range of spike counts with a central tendency.

Figure 1.22 depicts this in a graph like those in Figure 1.19a–d. Suppose this graph represents a signal detection experiment consisting of 100 trials—50 in which a tone was presented and 50 in which no tone was presented. The blue curve represents the spikes per trial when a tone was presented; on a small number of trials, there were fewer than 15 spikes or more than 35 spikes, but on most trials the number of spikes was close to 24, the mean number of spikes per trial. The red curve represents the spikes per trial when no tone was presented; here, the range is from 0 to 30, with a mean of 15. Given this scenario, what would the participant's "yes" and "no" responses be if the participant uses a decision criterion of $N = 19$ spikes per trial? Keep in mind, that all the participant knows is the number of spikes, not whether the tone was presented.

First consider the 50 trials in which a tone was presented. In Figure 1.22, the part of the blue curve at or to the right of the decision criterion (19 spikes per trial) represents the trials where the participant responded "yes"—about 80% of the trials (this is determined by finding the proportion of the 50 tone-present trials on which 19 or more spikes occurred). In other words, the hit rate—the probability of saying "yes" when a tone is presented—is about .80 when $N = 19$ spikes per trial.

Now consider the 50 trials in which no tone was presented. In this case, the part of the red curve to the right of the decision criterion represents the trials where the participant responded "yes." The proportion of the 50 tone-absent trials on which 19 or more spikes occurred is about 25%, which means that the false alarm rate—the probability of saying "yes" when no tone is presented—is about .25.

As we noted before, people can set their decision criterion as they wish, depending perhaps on how liberal or conservative they happen to be or on any costs or benefits associated with different kinds of errors or correct responses. For example, if it's very important never to miss a tone, even if that means responding with a lot of false alarms, then a very liberal criterion of less than 10 spikes per trial might be the best choice; but if the important thing is not to make false alarms, than a very conservative criterion of more than 30 spikes per trial would be appropriate, even though that would entail a lot of misses.

Figure 1.23 shows how three different decision criteria compare. In Figure 1.23a, the decision criterion has been adjusted down to 16, which means that the participant will almost always respond "yes" when a tone is presented (hit rate = .90); however, the false alarm rate is now .42. In Figure 1.23b, the decision criterion has been held at 19 (as in Figure 1.22), yielding a hit rate of about .80 and a false alarm rate of about .25. In Figure 1.23c, the decision criterion has been adjusted up to 25; now the participant will almost never say "yes" when no tone is presented (false alarm rate = .05), but the hit rate is down to .42.

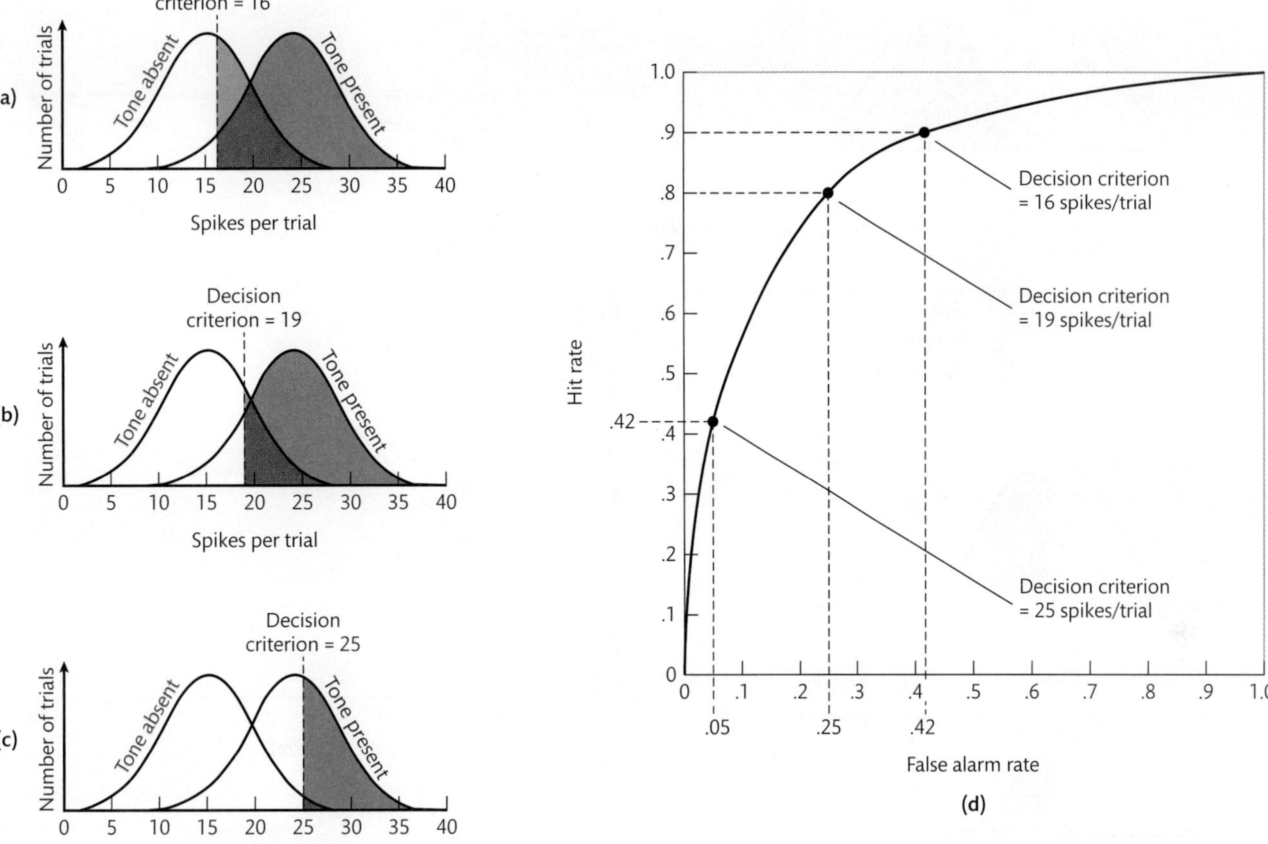

Figure 1.23 Decision Criteria and ROC Plots In (a)–(c), the blue and red curves are the same as the curves in Figure 1.22. (a) If the participant uses a liberal decision criterion of 16 spikes per trial, the hit rate is high (about.90), because in trials when a tone is presented, there are more than 16 spikes on about 90% of the trials; however, the false alarm rate is also high (about .42), because when a tone is absent, there are more than 16 spikes in about 42% of the trials. (b) As we saw in Figure 1.22, if the decision criterion is 19 spikes per trial, the hit rate is about .80 and the false alarm rate is about .25. (c) If the decision criterion is 25 spikes per trial, the false alarm rate is low (about .05), but the hit rate is also low (about .42). (d) An ROC plot of the data points corresponding to (a)–(c) produces a curve showing how the participant would respond to the tone for any given decision criterion—as the participant's decision criterion becomes more liberal, the corresponding data point would move up and to the right on the curve (higher hit rate and higher false alarm rate), and as the decision criterion becomes more conservative, the data point would move down and to the left (lower higher hit rate and lower false alarm rate).

The value of the decision criterion is said to reflect the participant's **decision-making bias** (which we've previously referred to as the participant's "style"). Using a criterion of 16 reflects a liberal bias (resulting in a higher hit rate but also a higher false alarm rate—the participant is simply more willing to say "yes" for the given amount of evidence than a more conservative participant would be), and using a criterion of 25 reflects a conservative bias (resulting in a lower false alarm rate but also a lower hit rate—the participant's tendency is to say "no" unless the evidence is very strong). Figure 1.23d is an ROC plot that compares these three cases. (The curve connecting the three points in this ROC plot shows how performance in response to this tone would vary across all possible choices of decision criterion.)

decision-making bias In a signal detection experiment, a participant's tendency to be liberal or conservative in deciding whether a signal was detected; indicated by the value of the participant's decision criterion.

Figure 1.24 reveals how signal detection theory provides a way to measure a participant's perceptual sensitivity apart from any decision-making bias. The graphs in Figure 1.24a–d show how neural activity when a signal is presented (blue curves) varies according to the intensity of the signal, in relation to neural activity when no signal is presented (red curve). In Figure 1.24a, the signal has a high intensity and neural activity is correspondingly

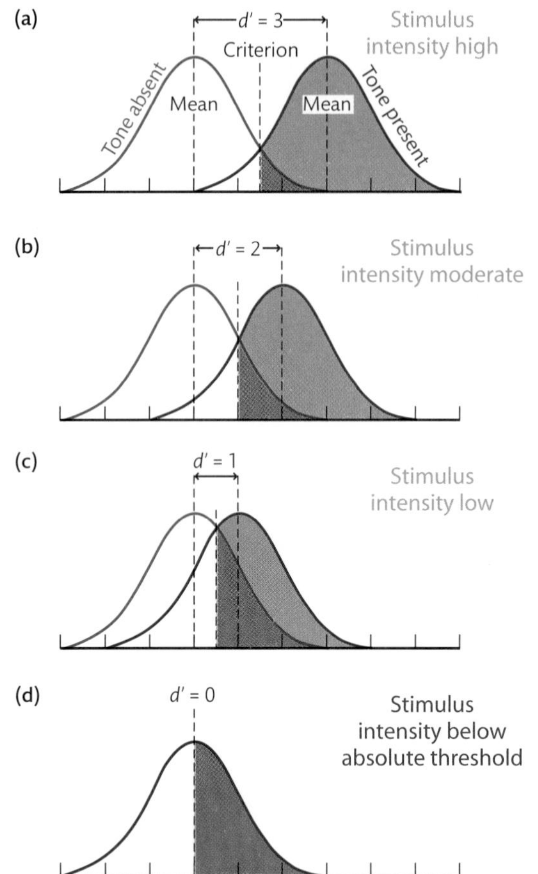

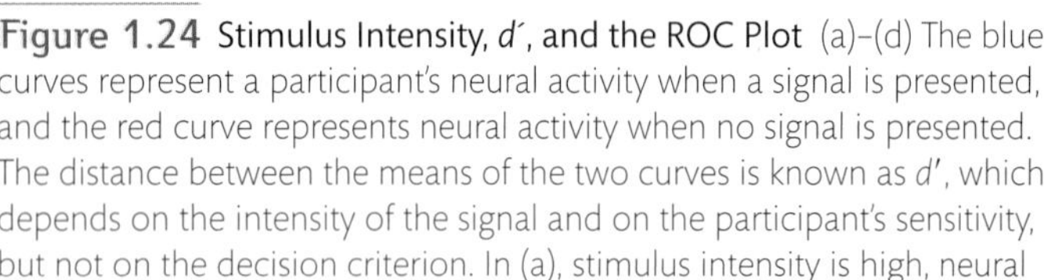

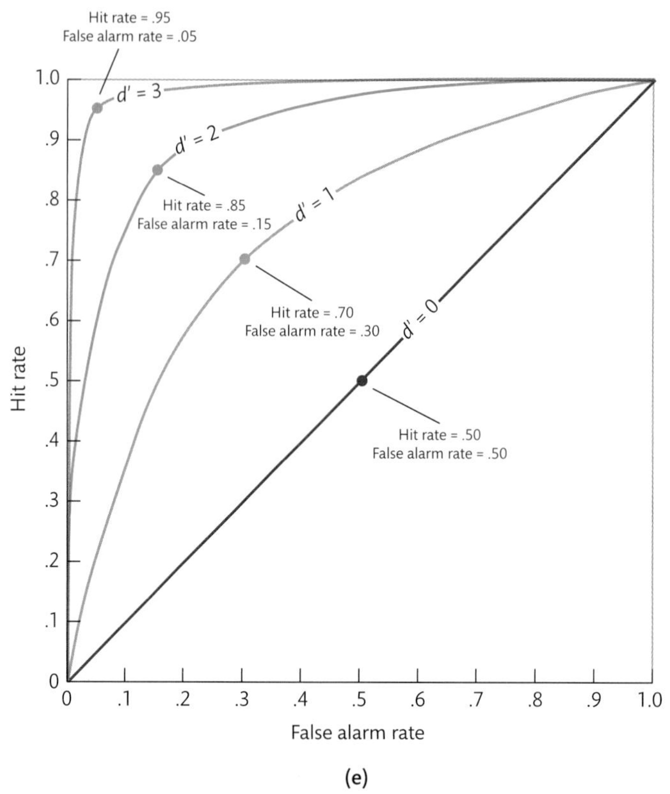

Figure 1.24 Stimulus Intensity, d', and the ROC Plot (a)–(d) The blue curves represent a participant's neural activity when a signal is presented, and the red curve represents neural activity when no signal is presented. The distance between the means of the two curves is known as d', which depends on the intensity of the signal and on the participant's sensitivity, but not on the decision criterion. In (a), stimulus intensity is high, neural activity is correspondingly high, and $d' = 3$; in (b), the intensity is moderate, and $d' = 2$; in (c), the intensity is low, and $d' = 1$; and in (d), the intensity is below the participant's absolute threshold, and $d' = 0$. (e) The ROC plots show that as the signal intensity and d' increase, the hit rate also increases and the false alarm rate decreases.

d' In signal detection theory, the difference between the mean of the curve showing the strength of perceptual evidence (e.g., the number of action potentials) when no signal is presented and the mean of the curve when a signal is presented; depends on the physical intensity of the signal and the participant's perceptual sensitivity, but not on the participant's decision criterion.

Demonstration 1.4 Signal Detection Experiment Participate in a typical signal detection experiment in which you try to detect visual targets against a "noisy" background.

high, yielding a curve in which the mean number of spikes per trial (blue dashed line) is much greater than the mean number when no signal is presented (red dashed line). The difference between these means is called $\boldsymbol{d'}$ ("*d*-prime"), and in Figure 1.24a, $d' = 3$. In Figure 1.24b, where $d' = 2$, the signal has a moderate intensity; in Figure 1.24c, where $d' = 1$, the signal has a low intensity; and in Figure 1.24d, where $d' = 0$ (i.e., where the two curves have the same mean), the intensity of the signal is below the absolute threshold, so the distribution of number of spikes per trial will be the same as when no signal is presented. In this case, no matter what decision criterion is used, the probability of a hit will be the same as the probability of a false alarm. In general, the magnitude of d' depends on the physical intensity of the signal and the participant's perceptual sensitivity, but not on the participant's decision criterion. (To see why, look back at Figure 1.23 and note that different choices of decision criterion create different hit rates and false alarm rates but have no effect on the relative positions of the blue and red curves.)

Now look at the ROC plots in Figure 1.24e, which show a curve for each of the d' values 0–3. The four plotted points each represent use of a neutral decision criterion that's halfway between the means of the tone-present and tone-absent curves in Figure 1.24a–d. Use of a lower, more liberal criterion would move each point up on its curve (higher hit rate and higher false alarm rate), whereas a larger, more conservative criterion would move each point down on its curve (lower hit rate and lower false alarm rate). However, each plotted point would stay on its curve, which means that an *ROC curve represents the participant's perceptual sensitivity apart from the choice of decision criterion.* That is, for a signal with a given intensity, regardless of the decision criterion, the performance of a participant with higher sensitivity would generate an ROC curve closer overall to the upper-left corner of the graph than would the performance of a participant with lower sensitivity.

Check Your Understanding

1.17 On a given trial of a signal detection experiment, it was possible for a participant to record a hit or a miss but not possible for the participant to record a false alarm or a correct rejection. Was a signal presented on that trial?

1.18 In a signal detection experiment, under what circumstances might a participant record a hit rate of 1.00 and a false alarm rate of 0?

1.19 True or false? In a graph like Figure 1.22, the lower the decision criterion, the more conservative the participant's decision-making bias.

1.20 True or false? The ROC plot in Figure 1.23d shows how the performance of a participant is affected by the participant's choice of decision criterion, whereas the ROC plot in Figure 1.24e shows the performance of participants with different sensitivities regardless of the decision criterion.

APPLICATIONS Optimal Decision Making: Detecting Cracks in Aircraft Wings and Diagnosing Breast Cancer

In everyday life, people are often faced with yes-or-no questions about issues ranging from matters of life or death to matters of relatively little importance: Is this criminal defendant guilty? Does this diagnostic test indicate the presence of cancer? Is there a weapon in this piece of luggage? Should this applicant be hired? Will it rain tomorrow? Is the witness lying? In all these cases, there is evidence of some kind that can be used as a basis for making a decision, but often the evidence is noisy—subject to random variation—which means that decisions will be based on probabilities, not certainties. Errors are inevitable, but some errors are more costly than others—for example, our legal system is partly based on the belief that the error of finding an innocent defendant guilty (a false alarm) is worse—more costly to society—than the error of finding a guilty defendant innocent (a miss). In deciding whether to hand-search a piece of luggage, the agent must weigh the cost of missing a weapon (potentially disastrous) versus the cost of slowing the screening process (inconveniencing passengers), given that there is a very low probability that a weapon is actually present. Signal detection theory provides a principled way to improve decision making by taking into account the costs of different kinds of errors (Swets et al., 2000).

In life situations like the ones mentioned before, just as in signal detection experiments, the best decision-making performance will result from the selection of an optimal decision criterion. But in real life—in contrast to laboratory experiments—it's not always clear how to define "best" performance. One idea is that it's the performance that maximizes **utility**—a measure of the overall satisfaction resulting from a given decision—by maximizing the payoff of correct decisions (hits and correct rejections) and by minimizing the costs associated with errors (misses and false alarms) (Swets et al., 2000). In terms of the choice of decision criterion, this means:

utility In signal detection theory, a measure of the overall satisfaction resulting from a given decision.

- Choosing a decision criterion that's based on one or more reliable sources of evidence.
- Adjusting the decision criterion depending on the a priori probability that a signal will be present—a very improbable outcome should require more evidence than a very probable one, all else being equal.
- Adjusting the decision criterion depending on the benefits of correct responses (hits and correct rejections) and the costs of errors (misses and false alarms).

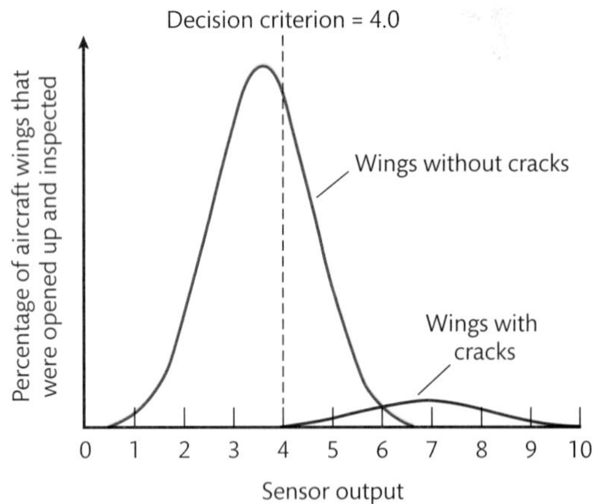

Figure 1.25 Sensor Output and Cracked Aircraft Wings Aircraft wings containing a crack tend to produce higher sensor readings than wings without cracks. But the overlap in these two curves in the range of sensor readings between about 4 and 7 shows that using sensor output to find cracks is subject to uncertainty. A decision criterion is needed to help decide whether to order a wing inspection.

Let's take as an example the detection of cracks in commercial aircraft wings. Manufacturers design aircraft to withstand virtually continuous use for decades, but the extreme mechanical stresses during countless landings and takeoffs and through rough weather can lead to cracks that, if undetected, can have terrible consequences. In this case, the "signal" is the presence of a crack in an aircraft wing. To detect cracks, engineers use a magnetic sensor that measures changes in the integrity of metal parts that are inside the wing and therefore not directly accessible. Here, the sensor output is the evidence about whether a crack is present—for simplicity, we can represent this as a single number. However, the sensor output is subject to random variation (noise), which means that the range of outputs produced by small cracks will overlap with the range of outputs produced by wings without cracks.

The cost of a miss (failing to detect a crack) could be high—in the worst case, the plane would crash and people would be killed. The cost of a false alarm (detecting a crack when there isn't one) is significant: the aircraft must be taken out of service and the wing must be opened up for inspection—an expensive procedure. (Note that in this case the benefits of hits and correct rejections can be seen as the avoidance of the costs of misses and false alarms, respectively.) The a priori probability that a crack will be present is the known prevalence of cracks over the preceding five years, which is usually quite low.

Signal detection theory can be used to help technicians make the best decisions about how to interpret the sensor output, so as to maximize utility. Figure 1.25 shows how the sensor output from wings without cracks might differ from the output from wings with cracks (assuming that every wing was then opened up and inspected to determine with certainty whether or not there were any cracks). The curves indicate that the percentage of wings without cracks was much greater than the percentage with cracks and that wings with cracks tend to produce higher sensor readings than wings without cracks. However, the overlap of the two curves in the range of 4 to 7 means that sensor readings in this range are ambiguous—they're associated with both the absence and the presence of cracks, a situation that results from noise in the sensor output. Technicians have to establish a decision criterion, a sensor reading that will tell them whether to take the aircraft out of service for inspection. (In reality, the decision would also take into account the age of the aircraft and its number of service hours, as well as other factors.)

As we saw in the previous section, when curves like those in Figure 1.25 overlap due to noise, there is no perfect decision criterion, which means that errors in diagnosis (crack detection) are unavoidable. Figure 1.26a (analogous to Figure 1.20a) uses the signal detection framework to show the possible diagnostic outcomes after testing in a hypothetical sample of 1,000 aircraft wings. A true positive (or hit) occurs if a sample with a high sensor reading (i.e., a level at or above the decision criterion) actually has a crack, a false positive (false alarm) occurs if a wing with a high sensor reading doesn't have a crack, and so forth. The goal in setting a decision criterion is to maximize the two correct outcomes (in blue) and minimize the two errors (in red), taking into account their associated costs.

To get a sense of what this involves, compare the two tables of sample results in Figure 1.26b. Both tables indicate that, in this sample of 1,000 tested wings, 30 actually had cracks and 970 didn't. In the table at the left, the decision criterion for diagnosing that a crack is present and ordering an inspection is a sensor reading of 4.0 or higher. Of the 100 wings with sensor readings of at least 4.0, 25 had cracks (true positives) and the other 75 didn't (false positives); of the 900 wings with sensor readings less than 4.0, 5 had cracks (false negatives) and 895 didn't (true negatives). Thus, there were 80 errors: 75 false positives and 5 false negatives.

In the table at the right, the decision criterion is a more liberal sensor reading of 2.5. Should engineers adjust the criterion down to this cutoff to reduce the number of false negatives? In this example, the more liberal criterion does reduce the number of false negatives by 3 (from 5 to 2), but it also leads to 25 more false positives (from 75 to 100). Here is where assessment of the associated costs of errors comes into play: is the cost of failing to

		True diagnosis: Crack	True diagnosis: No Crack
Sensor output	At or above decision criterion	**TRUE POSITIVE (TP) (HIT)**	**FALSE POSITIVE (FP) (FALSE ALARM)**
Sensor output	Below decision criterion	**FALSE NEGATIVE (FN) (MISS)**	**TRUE NEGATIVE (TN) (CORRECT REJECTION)**

(a) Possible diagnostic outcomes

Criterion = 4.0

Sensor output	True diagnosis: Crack	True diagnosis: No crack	Totals
≥ 4.0	TP = 25	FP = 75	100 wings
< 4.0	FN = 5	TN = 895	900 wings
Totals	30 wings	970 wings	

Criterion = 2.5

Sensor output	True diagnosis: Crack	True diagnosis: No crack	Totals
≥ 2.5	TP = 28	FP = 100	128 wings
< 2.5	FN = 2	TN = 870	872 wings
Totals	30 wings	970 wings	

(b) Sample diagnoses with different decision criteria

Figure 1.26 How the Decision Criterion Affects the Diagnosis of Cracks in Aircraft Wings (a) The signal detection framework can be used to classify the outcomes of diagnosing cracks in aircraft wings when using sensor output as evidence. (b) In a hypothetical population of 1,000 wings that were opened up and inspected to determine whether there were, in fact, any cracks, 30 had cracks and 970 didn't. Testing these 1,000 wings with a magnetic sensor, using a decision criterion of 4.0 in the sensor reading (left), resulted in 80 errors: 75 false positives and 5 false negatives. A more liberal decision criterion of 2.5 (right) resulted in 102 errors: 100 false positives and 2 false negatives. The question is, given the difference in associated costs between the two types of errors (false negatives can lead to catastrophic wing failure that may cost lives, while false positives can lead to unnecessary and costly inspections), is it more appropriate to use the conservative decision criterion of 4.0 or the liberal one of 2.5?

correctly detect three defective wings greater than or less than the cost of opening up and inspecting 25 wings that weren't defective? Obviously, this isn't an easy question to answer. The economic costs of unnecessary inspections may seem high but then, in hindsight, may seem inconsequential if a missed crack results in a catastrophic crash.

Signal detection theory can also be applied to more complex decision-making scenarios. In the diagnosis of breast cancer, for example, mammograms are a crucial source of evidence, but assessing a mammogram isn't like reading the output from a sensor—even experienced radiologists can find it difficult to decide whether a given mammogram indicates the presence of cancer (see Figure 1.27a).

To help make breast cancer diagnosis more accurate, researchers devised an enhanced method of mammogram assessment based on identifying 23 meaningful features of mammograms, including the presence and size of a mass, the irregularity of its shape, and so forth (Getty et al., 1988). They assigned weights to each type of feature according to how well that feature predicted the presence of cancer in cases where a subsequent biopsy had established the diagnosis with certainty. They then compared diagnoses by a group of radiologists using a standard method of assessing mammograms with diagnoses of the same mammograms made several months later by the same group of radiologists using the enhanced method. Figure 1.27b, which shows the ROC curves for the two methods, reveals that the

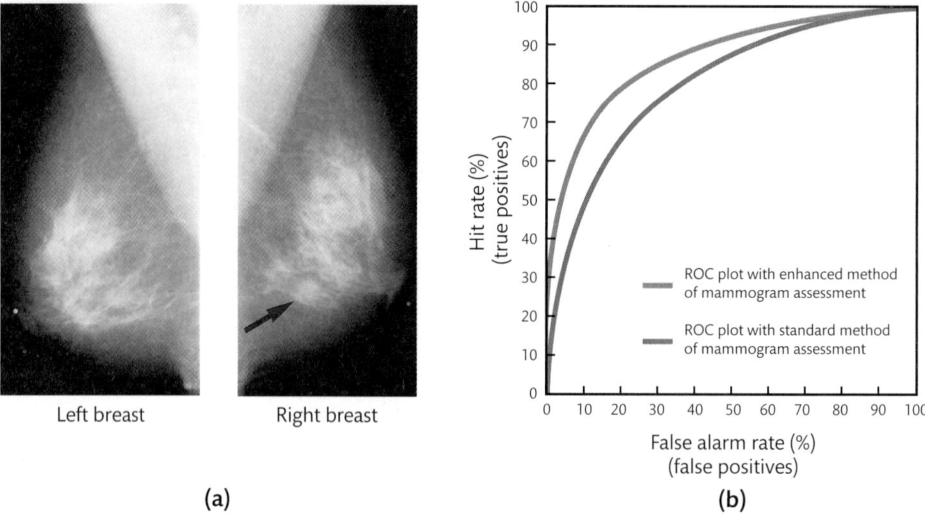

Figure 1.27 Using Signal Detection Theory in the Diagnosis of Breast Cancer
(a) Mammograms like these are extremely important in the diagnosis of breast cancer, but accurately assessing mammograms is difficult, even for radiologists with years of training and experience. Here, the arrow points to a mass in the lower part of the right breast that was diagnosed as a malignancy, a diagnosis later confirmed by a biopsy. But the clues in the mammogram that led to this diagnosis are subtle. (Adapted from Ikeda et al., 2004.) (b) Applying signal detection theory to compare a standard method of mammogram assessment to an enhanced method yielded these two ROC plots, showing that the enhanced method led to a higher hit rate for any given false alarm rate. In terms of utility, this means greater overall satisfaction—higher benefits (earlier detection of many cancers) and lower costs (less needless anxiety and fewer unnecessary biopsies). (Adapted from Swets, 1988.) [Image from Ikeda et al., 2004, courtesy RSNA]

enhanced method resulted in a significantly higher hit rate (true positives) and a significantly lower false alarm rate (false positives) (Swets, 1988; Swets et al., 1991).

Clearly, this kind of approach can have significant practical value in medical diagnosis and in many other domains where decisions are often complex and difficult. Signal detection theory provides a principled framework for assessing many of the relevant factors.

Check Your Understanding

1.21 Suppose you're at the airport getting ready to board a plane for an important business trip. You happen to know that the plane's wings were just tested with a sensor and that the sensor reading for each wing was 4.5. Based on Figure 1.25 and the discussion of it, explain why you would or wouldn't want the flight to be canceled so the plane could be taken out of service and the wings opened up for inspection.

1.22 Match the terms in the following table:

Tone-Detection Experiment	Diagnosis of Breast Cancer
Miss	True positive
Correct rejection	False positive
False alarm	False negative
Hit	True negative

SUMMARY

- World, Brain, and Mind Perception begins with objects and events in the world (distal stimuli) that produce physical phenomena (proximal stimuli) that the senses convert into neural signals that are sent to the brain. These signals evoke perceptions of individual objects and events, and in combination they evoke integrated conscious experiences of the current scene. Perceptual experiences can be stored in memory and used for planning and for purposeful action. Scientific understanding of perception involves understanding how information is contained in proximal stimuli, how proximal stimuli are converted into information-carrying neural signals, and what the relationship is between perceptual experience and the object and events being perceived. The field of psychophysics uses behavioral responses to assess this relationship.
- How Many Senses Are There? Senses evolve in response to the physical properties of objects and events that organisms must perceive in order to survive. In addition to the sensory domains covered by the traditional five senses, the body senses cover several more sensory domains. Furthermore, each sense provides information about multiple physical and perceptual dimensions. Some animals can sense physical dimensions that humans cannot sense.
- Evolution and Perception Like all other traits, senses evolve by natural selection, in response to the characteristics of the organism's environment.
- Exploring Perception by Studying Neurons and the Brain Neurons are cells like other types of cells but are distinguished by their ability to send and receive neural signals, typically via axons and dendrites. Within individual neurons, signals take the form of action potentials; information is expressed by changes in a neuron's firing rate. Signals between neurons are transmitted at synapses, via the release and binding of neurotransmitters, which can be excitatory or inhibitory. The brain contains some 100 billion neurons that are connected via some 100 trillion synapses. The most important divisions of the brain are the two cerebral hemispheres, each divided into four lobes. The cerebral cortex is the outer layer of the cerebral hemispheres. Cognitive neuropsychology—the study of perception and cognition by investigating deficits in individuals with brain damage—is based on the idea of functional and anatomical modularity, the notion that the mind and brain consist of distinct modules that carry out specific functions. Dissociations and double dissociations provide evidence linking brain regions and perceptual functions, supported by the assumption of cognitive uniformity. Additional evidence is provided by functional neuroimaging—techniques for measuring brain activity in participants carrying out carefully designed tasks.
- Exploring Perception by Studying Behavior Psychophysics uses objective behavioral methods to investigate the thresholds of perceptual experience and the scaling of perceptual experience. An absolute threshold is the minimum intensity of a stimulus that an observer can detect; a difference threshold (or just noticeable difference) is the minimum difference in intensity between two stimuli that allows an observer to perceive that the stimuli are different. Weber's law indicates that, within any given perceptual domain, the size of the just noticeable difference increases as the intensity of the standard stimulus increases. Psychophysical scaling is the process of measuring how changes in stimulus intensity relate to changes in the perception of stimulus intensity. Fechner's law indicates that a much greater increase in intensity is needed for a high-intensity stimulus than for a low-intensity stimulus in order to produce the same perceived difference in intensity. Fechner's law is valid for some but not all perceptual dimensions. Stevens power law indicates that, for some dimensions, the relationship between stimulus intensity and perceived intensity is linear, whereas for other dimensions a smaller increase in intensity is needed for high-intensity stimuli than for low-intensity stimuli. Neural firing rates show random variability, or noise, which means that observers have to choose a criterion—some minimum firing rate—as a basis for deciding whether a stimulus was detected. Signal detection theory provides a way to measure perceptual sensitivity apart from the observer's choice of criterion, by graphing the observer's responses on an ROC curve.
- APPLICATIONS: Optimal Decision Making: Detecting Cracks in Aircraft Wings and Diagnosing Breast Cancer Signal detection theory can be used to assess the quality of decision making, when decisions must be based on noisy evidence. This involves defining what's meant by the "best" decision, which can be defined as the decision that maximizes utility by maximizing the percentage of correct decisions while taking into account the benefits of correct decisions and the costs of errors.

KEY TERMS

absolute threshold (p. 21)
action potential (p. 9)
assumption of cognitive uniformity (p. 18)
axon (p. 8)
axon terminals (p. 8)
baseline firing rate (p. 11)
bottom-up information (p. 3)
cell body (p. 8)
cell membrane (p. 8)
cerebral cortex (p. 16)
cerebral hemispheres (p. 14)
cognitive neuropsychology (p. 17)
corpus callosum (p. 15)
correct rejection (p. 32)
d' (p. 36)
decision-making bias (p. 35)
dendrites (p. 8)
depolarization (p. 10)
difference threshold (or *just noticeable difference [JND]*) (p. 24)

EXPAND YOUR UNDERSTANDING

1.1 Many very simple activities involve every one of the primary senses listed in Table 1.1. For each of those senses, list a possible distal stimulus and proximal stimulus during the activity of eating dinner.

1.2 While driving home from work, Dave was talking on his cell phone to his wife. Suddenly, she screamed because she saw water coming under the bathroom door and flooding the hallway. At the same moment, the car in front of Dave slowed down unexpectedly and Dave rear-ended it. Discuss this outcome in terms of how bottom-up and top-down information figure into the perceptual process.

1.3 Explain the similarities and differences in what's shown by Figures 1.5a and 1.18a. Do the same for Figures 1.5b and 1.11b.

1.4 An investigator has proposed that when a person feels physical pain (as from a pinprick on the fingertip), the intensity of the pain is represented in one region of the brain, while the location of the pain is represented in a different region. Describe hypothetical evidence from cognitive neuropsychology and from functional neuroimaging that would provide support for this hypothesis.

1.5 Describe how a version of Figure 1.14 could be used to determine the absolute threshold for brightness perception, with each of the following methods: the method of adjustment, the method of constant stimuli, and the staircase method.

1.6 Consider the following statement: If the exponent in Stevens power law were less than 1 for every perceptual dimension, Fechner's law would be correct and we could disregard Stevens power law. Do you agree? Explain your answer.

1.7 True or false? The blue curve in Figure 1.18b is analogous to all the curves except the red curves in Figure 1.19a–d. Explain your answer.

1.8 Discuss how signal detection theory could be used to decide whether the luggage of a passenger undergoing screening at an airport should be hand-checked for a suspicious item based on an X-ray image. Here the evidence is the perceptual similarity of some feature of the image to the shape of a prohibited item (e.g., a weapon). Discuss how to define utility in this situation, including consideration of the overall prevalence of prohibited items in luggage (as well as the prevalence of features "inserted" into the images to keep inspectors on their toes) and consideration of what should be included as costs associated with errors.

READ MORE ABOUT IT

Coltheart, M. (2002). Cognitive neuropsychology. In J. Wixted (Vol. Ed.) & H. Pashler (Series Ed.), *Stevens' handbook of experimental psychology:* Vol. 4. *Methodology in experimental psychology* (pp. 139–174) New York: Wiley.

An outline of the logic of cognitive neuropsychology—that is, inferring the functional architecture of the brain from patterns of impaired perception and cognition in persons with brain damage.

Hodos, W., & Butler, A. B. (1997). Evolution of sensory pathways in vertebrates. *Brain, Behavior and Evolution, 50,* 189–197.

A brief survey of the principles underlying the evolutionary development of sensory systems.

Huettel, S. A., Song, A. W., & McCarthy, G. W. (2009). *Functional magnetic resonance imaging* (2nd ed.). Sunderland, MA: Sinauer.

A comprehensive and authoritative account of the technical foundations of fMRI, the biology and physics of imaging, the design of experiments, and the inferential logic of neuroimaging data analysis.

Macmillan, N. A., & Creelman, C. D. (2004). *Detection theory: A user's guide* (2nd ed.). Mahwah, NJ: Erlbaum.

A user-friendly treatment of signal detection theory with an emphasis on practical applications.

Parker, A. J., & Newsome, W. T. (1998). Sense and the single neuron: Probing the physiology of perception. *Annual Review of Neuroscience, 21,* 227–277.

An influential article describing experiments that focus on how neural activity can be directly linked to perceptual performance in tasks requiring the perceiver to make simple decisions about a stimulus.

Taylor, J. B. (2009). *My stroke of insight.* London: Plume.

An engaging personal account of a stroke and its aftermath, with insights derived from the author's training as a brain scientist.

Yantis, S. (Ed.). (2001). *Visual perception: Essential readings.* Philadelphia: Psychology Press.

A collection of 25 classic articles that provide a foundation for many of the core ideas in perceptual science.

Vasily Kandinsky, *Circles in a Circle*, 1923. [Oil on canvas, 38 7/8 × 37 5/8 inches. The Louise and Walter Arensberg Collection, 1950. The Philadelphia Museum of Art.

2

LIGHT AND THE EYES

A Rare Case: Vision Without Cones

Knut Nordby was born in Norway in 1942 and moved with his family to Sweden in May 1943. Even when he was an infant, his parents recognized that something was not quite right about his vision—he blinked continuously, tried to avoid bright light, and squinted when bright light got in his eyes. When he was nine months old, a doctor told the family that Knut was completely color-blind and that his ability to see things clearly was extremely poor—in other words, he was nearly blind. It turned out that Knut had been born without cones, one of the two types of receptors that transduce light in the eye.

Cones are needed for color vision and for normal vision in bright light, as in daylight. Without cones, Knut is left with only rods, which are extremely sensitive to light because they're specialized for night vision. In people with normal vision, rods effectively shut down in bright light, and cones take over. But Knut has no cones, so he has to rely on his rods even in daylight. It's as if he's always in a state you've undoubtedly experienced, having to blink and squint uncomfortably after turning on a bright light when you've been in the dark for a while. To mitigate this constant feeling of being dazzled, Knut has to wear very dark sunglasses that sharply reduce the amount of light entering his eyes.

As we'll see later in this chapter, the extreme sensitivity of rods, which is very helpful when light levels are low, also means that rods aren't very useful for seeing details clearly, so tasks like reading and recognizing faces are a challenge for Knut—just as most of us find it difficult to read or to recognize people in dim light. In order to read, Knut uses a magnifying glass and brings the reading material very close to his face. Because he's color-blind, deep reds and purples appear as very dark gray, blues and greens as medium gray, and yellow as light gray. To some extent, these differences in shades of gray let him distinguish between different colors, but he has never had the experience of actually seeing the colors of a rich sunset or of beautiful works of art.

Knut usually avoids revealing the nature of his visual impairment, and around strangers, he sometimes even simulates having normal vision so he won't be treated as "disabled." Nevertheless, he says, "In spite of my visual handicap and all the practical and social problems I encounter, I feel that I live a very rich and interesting life."

In his book *Vision*, David Marr (1982, p. 3) says that the goal of vision is "to know what is where by looking." The act of looking is effortless, but assembling a detailed account of how the visual system senses the pattern of light entering our eyes and transforms that sensation into an understanding of "what is where" is a significant scientific challenge.

Figure 2.1 shows the overall plan of the human visual system. Light enters the eye and passes through the lens, which focuses an image on the retina, the light-sensitive inner membrane of the eye. Receptors in the retina convert the light into neural signals that are processed by other retinal neurons and then sent to the brain via the optic nerve. The neural

Chapter Outline

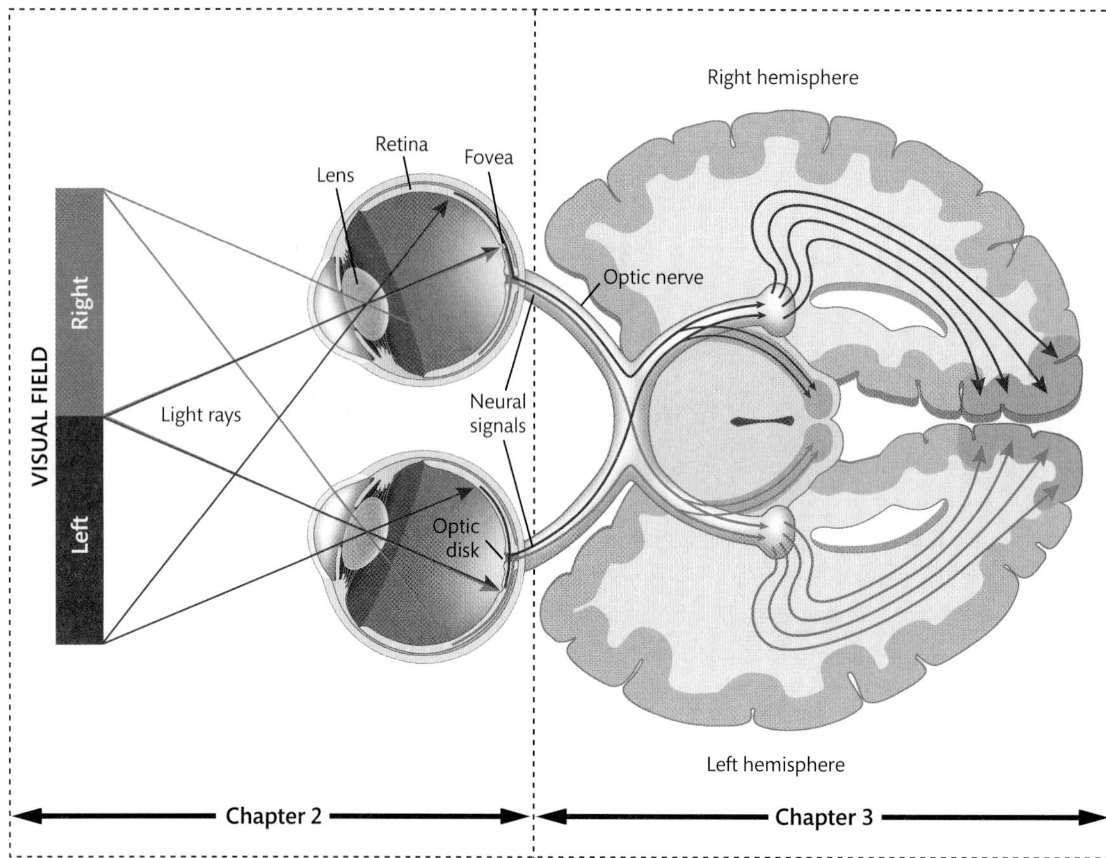

Figure 2.1 Human Visual System This chapter covers vision from its beginning, when light enters the eye, to the point where neural signals exit the eye via the optic nerve on their way to the brain. Within each eye, light from the scene is focused on the retina, where it's converted into neural signals that contain detailed information about the pattern of light on the retina. Chapter 3 explores the structures in the brain that receive the signals originating in the retina and what the brain does with the information in these signals so we can see "what is where."

signals from each eye are relayed to the visual cortex at the back of the brain, where further processing continues the transformation of neural signals into perceptions of "what is where."

In this chapter, we'll explore what scientists have learned about the first part of this process—the part that takes place in the eyes. We'll consider the nature of light and how light is focused on the retina. We'll also consider the parts of the eye and their main functions. Then we'll zoom in on the different kinds of receptors and other neurons in the retina, where they're located, how they work, and the different visual functions they support. Finally, we'll examine the last link in the chain of retinal neurons—the cells that send signals into the optic nerve. In Chapter 3, we'll follow those signals through the optic nerve and into the brain.

Light

The universe is filled with light. But what *is* light?

In everyday language, we use the word **light** to mean the visible illumination that comes from sources such as the sun, candles, or lightbulbs. The dictionary definition of this kind of light is "something that makes vision possible."

In the language of physics, light is a type of **electromagnetic radiation** (specifically, a narrow range of wavelengths, as explained below). It differs from other forms of electromagnetic radiation in that we can see it. Many other nonvisible types of electromagnetic radiation are emitted by innumerable natural and artificial sources, including the sun and other stars, radio and TV antennas, microwave ovens, and radar guns—even by warm

light Visible illumination; a type of electromagnetic radiation, corresponding to a small slice of wavelengths in the middle of the electromagnetic spectrum.

electromagnetic radiation A physical phenomenon that is simultaneously both a wave and a stream of particles.

human bodies, which emit infrared (heat) radiation. Other types of electromagnetic radiation that you probably have heard of include gamma rays, X-rays, and ultraviolet rays.

Knowing that light is a type of electromagnetic radiation still doesn't tell us what light is; it just changes the question to, what is electromagnetic radiation? Unfortunately, that's not an easy question to answer, not even for physicists. In 1905 Albert Einstein proposed that light is simultaneously both a wave and a stream of particles. Subsequent work in quantum physics has confirmed this wave–particle duality of light. Hard as it is to imagine something that's both a spread-out wave and a point-like particle, the quantum theory of light is one of the most successful theories of modern physics in terms of the wide range of phenomena it explains.

Light as a Wave

As a wave, electromagnetic radiation has a property called **wavelength,** the distance between two successive peaks of the wave. Different types of electromagnetic radiation are defined by their differences in wavelength, which depends on how the radiation was emitted by its source. Figure 2.2 shows the entire **electromagnetic spectrum**—that is, the entire range of wavelengths of electromagnetic radiation, from very short to very long. As you can see, light corresponds to a small slice of wavelengths in the middle of the spectrum, from about 370 nanometers (nm) to about 730 nm. Within this range, people with normal vision perceive differences in wavelength as differences in color. The shorter wavelengths (around 400 nm) are perceived as dark blue; as wavelength increases, the perceived color changes to lighter blue to green to yellow to orange to red; and the longer wavelengths (around 700 nm) are perceived as dark red. (See Chapter 5 for a complete discussion of color vision.)

wavelength The distance between two successive peaks of a wave; different types of electromagnetic radiation are defined by their differences in wavelength.

electromagnetic spectrum The entire range of wavelengths of electromagnetic radiation.

Light as a Stream of Particles

The particles of electromagnetic radiation are called **photons.** A photon—a single particle of light—is the smallest possible quantity of electromagnetic radiation. Thinking of light as consisting of particles is useful when we want to talk about the *amount* of light—we can specify the number of photons.

photons Single particles of light; a photon is the smallest possible quantity of electromagnetic radiation.

Consider the extremely large number of photons leaving the surface of the sun at every moment and traveling outward in all directions at the speed of light. Before photons emitted by the sun can reach the earth, they must first be transmitted through outer space and through the air in the earth's atmosphere. When they reach the earth, photons may:

- Strike a surface and be absorbed—that is, disappear into the material of the surface (e.g., the earth's surface). Since photons have energy, a surface that absorbs a photon acquires that energy, which is typically transformed into heat, causing a minute rise in the temperature of the surface.

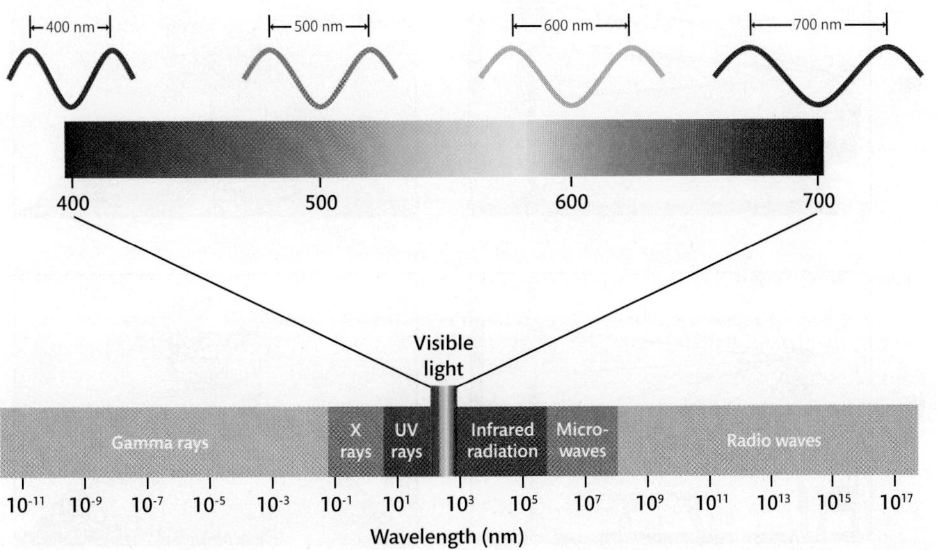

Figure 2.2 Electromagnetic Spectrum Electromagnetic radiation varies in wavelength. Wavelength is the distance between successive peaks of a wave, as illustrated at the top of the figure. Light—the type of electromagnetic radiation that humans can see—is a small slice of the spectrum, from about 370 nm to about 730 nm. A nanometer is a billionth of a meter (10^{-9} m); a nanometer is to a millimeter (10^{-3} m) as a millimeter is to 10 football fields (1,000 yards ≈ 10^3 m).

- Strike a surface and be reflected—that is, bounce off the surface (of a leaf, for example). Reflected photons are then transmitted through the air until they strike another surface and are absorbed or again reflected. Photons that aren't reflected back through the atmosphere and into outer space are ultimately absorbed. Light reflected into our eyes and absorbed by receptors in the retina is seen.
- Cross a boundary between the air and another transparent or translucent medium (such as a body of water). Photons that cross a boundary between two transparent or translucent media at an oblique angle are refracted—their direction of motion changes depending on the angle and on the physical characteristics, such as the density, of the media. (Refraction is what causes a pencil placed in a glass of water to appear bent.) Like reflected photons, refracted photons continue to be transmitted (and possibly reflected, re-reflected, and re-refracted) until they either reenter outer space or are absorbed.

The Optic Array

At every waking moment (as long as there is a source of light and your eyes are open), light enters your eyes and forms a spatial pattern on the retina. We use the term *spatial pattern* to convey the idea that the light rays entering your eyes from different locations in visual space strike the retina in a pattern that varies in brightness and color. Brightness (or intensity) depends on the amount of light (number of photons) in a light ray, while color, as we have seen, is conveyed by the wavelength of the light. This spatial pattern of brightness and color is called the **optic array,** a term coined by the influential American psychologist J. J. Gibson (1966, 1979). Note that the optic array varies not just in space but also in time—it changes from moment to moment, as you walk around and move your eyes, as the lighting conditions change, and as objects move within the scene. Figure 2.3 illustrates the optic array and how it changes as the perceiver moves.

optic array The spatial pattern of light rays, varying in brightness and color, entering your eyes from different locations in a scene.

The lines of sight depicted in Figure 2.3a define the parts of each surface that can reflect photons into the woman's eyes while she's seated in the chair. The optic array is formed by the spatial arrangement of the objects and surfaces in the room, as well as by their shape, color, texture, and other characteristics. The information in the optic array results from the fact that the different surfaces in the room reflect different amounts and wavelengths of light. When the woman stands up (Figure 2.3b), the lines of sight take somewhat different angles into her

Lines of sight

Optic array (what the person sees)

(a)

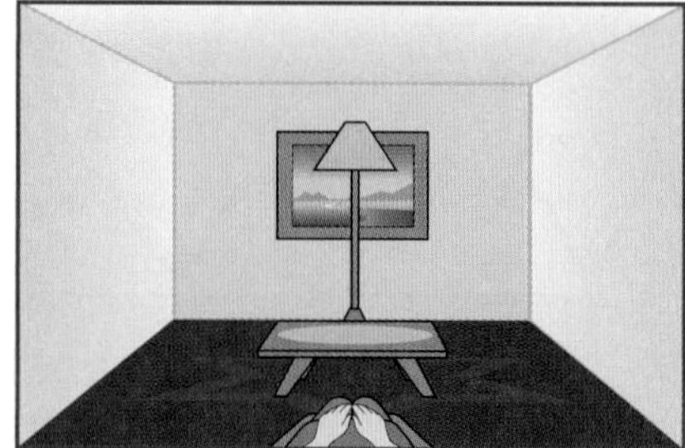

(b)

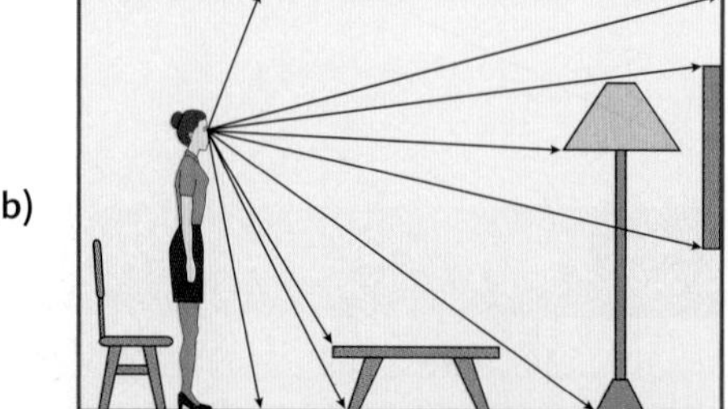

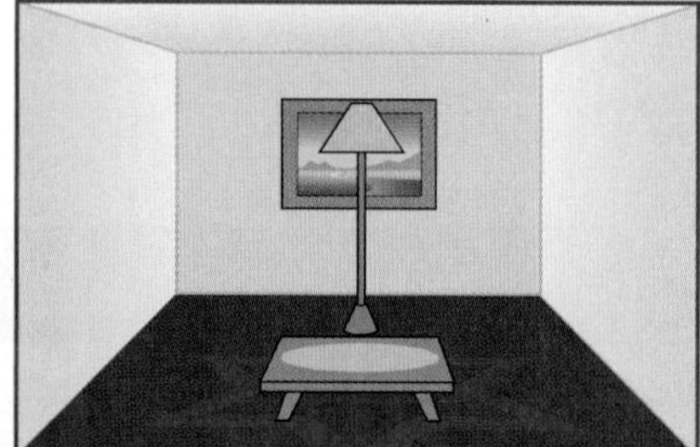

Figure 2.3 Optic Array Photons reflected from surfaces specify the optic array—the pattern of brightness and color that is visible to an observer whose eyes are at a specific location in space. The lines of sight define the parts of the various surfaces in the optic array that can be seen. (a) The woman sitting in the chair can see, among other things, part of her own lap, part of the red rug in front of the table (but not the part directly behind the table), most of the front legs of the table, and most of the lamp, except for the bottom of the base. (b) When the woman stands up, the optic array changes: now she can see part of the rug behind the table, less of the table legs, and the entire base of the lamp.

eyes, so that slightly different parts of the various surfaces reflect photons into her eyes, with corresponding changes in the optic array.

Our visual system has evolved to process the optic array in an integrated way that allows us to perceive the scene—to understand "what is where." The first step in this remarkable process is transforming the pattern of light that makes up the optic array into a pattern of neural signals that can be sent to the brain for interpretation. This step takes place in the eye.

Check Your Understanding

2.1 What range of wavelengths can we see as light?

2.2 What physical characteristics of light do brightness and color correspond to?

2.3 What are the three principal fates of a photon of light from the sun after it enters the earth's atmosphere?

2.4 What factors can cause the optic array to vary over time?

The Human Eye

To be called an eye, an organ must be capable of sensing the presence and perhaps the amount of light in the local environment—and this is all that the eyespot of an organism such as the unicellular *Euglena* can do. But eyes must do much more than that in order to support the complex, motivated, visually guided behavior of humans (Land & Fernald, 1992). Our eyes must have some way of moving, so we can point them at different parts of the environment. They must be capable of creating a focused optical image of the light in the optic array. They must have a way of measuring the brightness and color at each location in that image. And because the image is continuously changing as objects and the observer move about, our eyes must also be capable of continuously sampling the changing image. Finally, our eyes must be able to convert the light in the optic array into neural signals that can be sent to the brain.

Field of View

Humans, like most other vertebrates, have two eyes positioned horizontally in the head (in humans, about 6 cm apart). The specific position of the eyes varies across species. In humans and all other primates (and in most predatory mammals), the eyes are in the front of the head. This positioning lets you see where you're going and lets you use your eyes to guide the movements of your hands and fingers. It also allows high-resolution depth perception, which depends on looking with both eyes, in a major part of your field of view (see Chapter 6). As shown in Figure 2.4, the

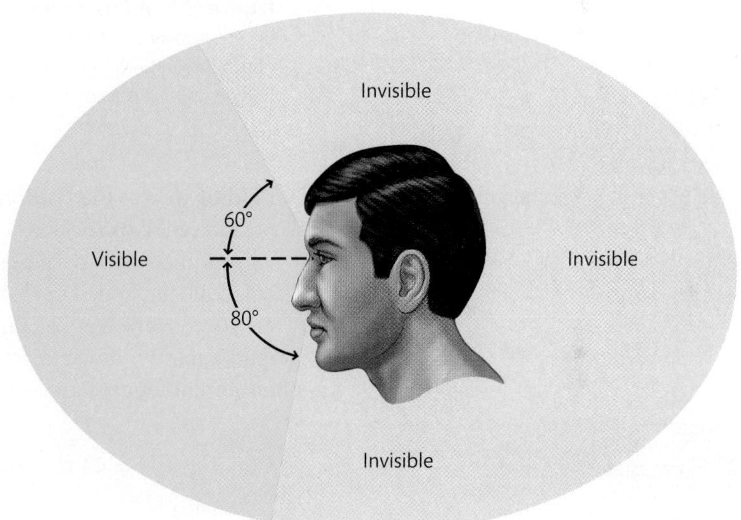

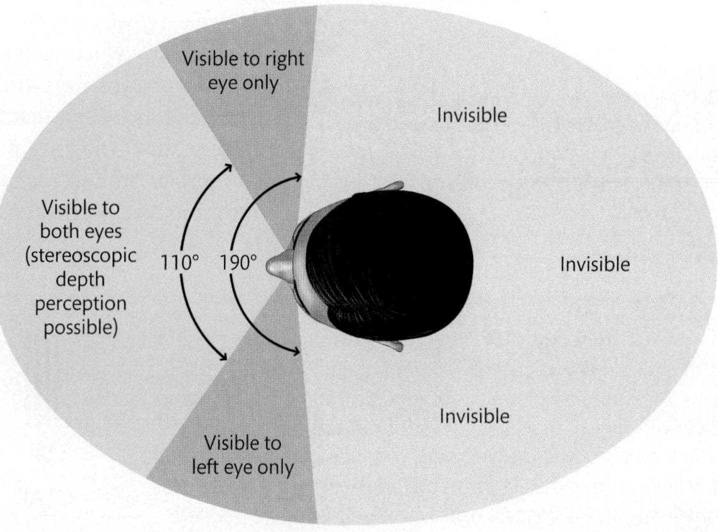

Figure 2.4 Your Field of View Your field of view is the portion of the world that you can see without moving your eyes. For humans, whose eyes are in the front of their head about 6 cm apart, the field of view extends about 140° vertically (about 60° up and about 80° down) and about 190° horizontally, from side to side. About 110° of that side-to-side field of view is visible to both eyes simultaneously, enabling high-resolution depth perception, which requires both eyes.

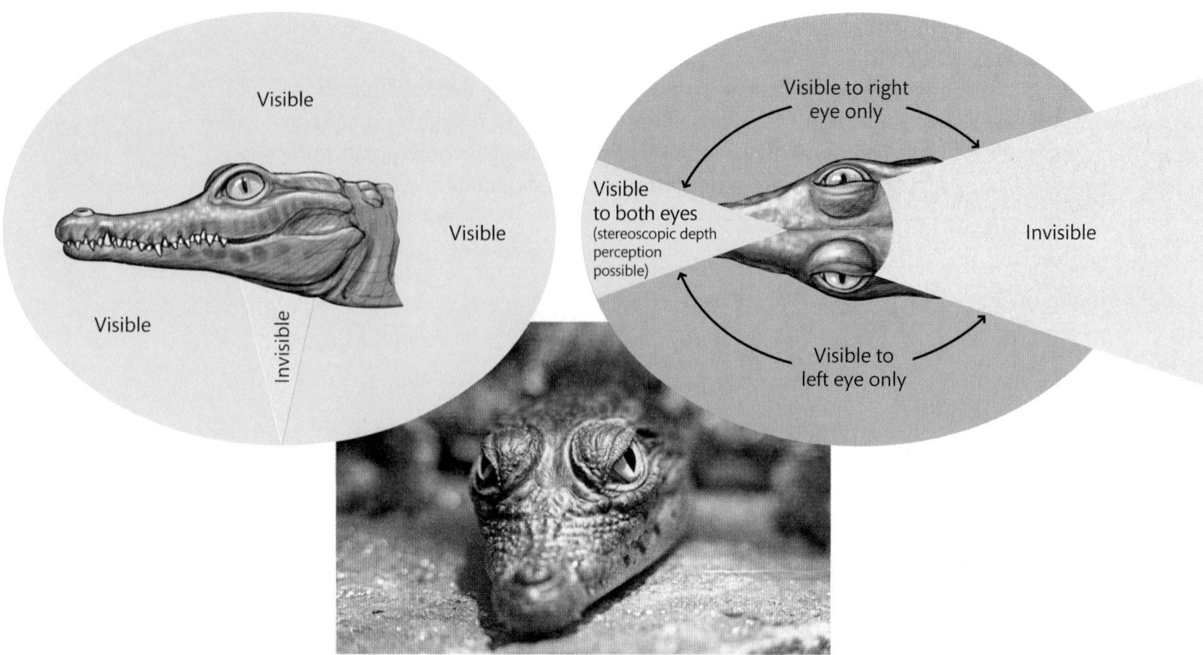

Figure 2.5 A Crocodile's Field of View Crocodiles have eyes on the sides of their heads, which provides a wide field of view so they can detect prey in almost any direction. However, the portion of the field where high-resolution depth perception is possible is much narrower than it is for humans. [Ronald Wittek/dpa/Corbis]

field of view The portion of the surrounding space you can see when your eyes are in a given position in their sockets.

field of view is the portion of the surrounding space you can see with your eyes in a given position in their sockets.

Animals with eyes positioned on the sides of the head rather than in front—like the crocodile illustrated in Figure 2.5—have a much more extensive field of view than humans do. A crocodile can see almost directly behind (very important for detecting prey) but has only a narrow range in front where high-resolution depth perception is possible—not so important for crocodiles, which use ambush, rather than pursuit, to capture prey.

Acuity and Eye Movements

acuity A measure of how clearly fine detail is seen.

extraocular muscles Three pairs of muscles around each eye that enable us to move our eyes very rapidly and accurately and keep the eyes always pointed in the same direction.

Like many other animals, we depend on vision for interacting with objects and for navigating within our environment. Often, this requires that we see things clearly and in fine detail (as when you're reading this book and have to see each letter clearly). **Acuity** is a measure of how clearly we can see fine detail, and as you know from experience, you see things much more clearly when your eyes are pointed at them (see Figure 2.6).

If our eyes were frozen in one position, we could point them at things by moving our head; however, that would be a very slow and inaccurate procedure (try reading this page without moving your eyes!). Fortunately, evolution has provided us with three pairs of muscles around each eye—the **extraocular muscles** (*extra,* meaning "outside"; *ocular,* meaning "eye")—that enable us to move our eyes very rapidly and accurately, as shown in

Figure 2.6 Acuity Hold the book at normal reading distance and look directly at the green disk on the left. You can easily count the number of lines above the disk and read the letters below it without moving your eyes from the green disk. But if you look directly at the red square on the right, you can't count the lines or read the letters on the left. Acuity—the ability to see details clearly—is greatest near where your eyes are pointed.

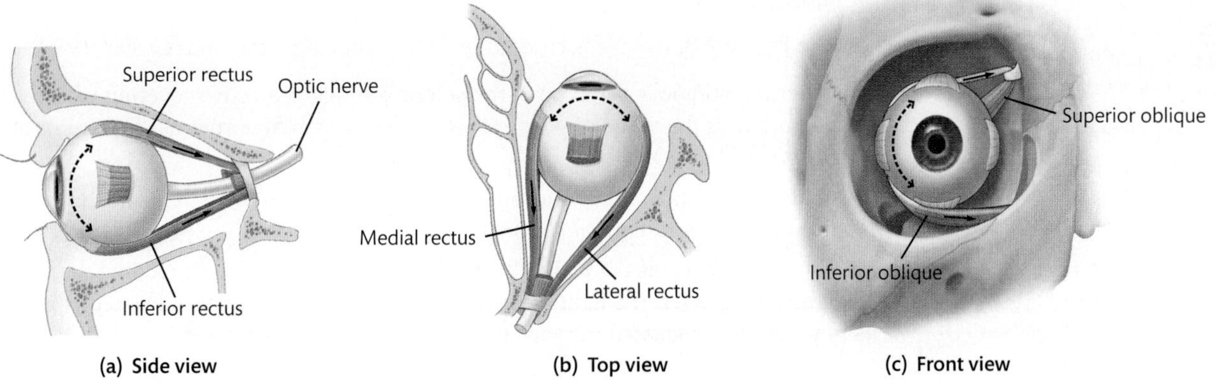

Figure 2.7 Extraocular Muscles Three pairs of extraocular muscles move the eyes. Most eye movements involve all three pairs of muscles. (a) The superior and inferior rectus muscles move the eye up (elevation) and down (depression). (b) The medial and lateral rectus muscles move the eye to the side toward the nose (adduction) and away from the nose (abduction). (c) The superior and inferior oblique muscles rotate the eye clockwise (intorsion) and counterclockwise (extorsion). Any given eye movement is the result of an exquisitely balanced interaction of these three pairs of muscles.

Figure 2.7. The extraocular muscles of the two eyes work in tandem, so the eyes always point in the same direction (except for people with *strabismus*, a disorder of the extraocular muscles; see the section on disorders of vision). In Chapter 7, we'll have more to say about how eye movements are controlled and how they permit us to pick up the information in the scene that we need for whatever we're doing.

optic axis An imaginary diameter line from the front to the back of the eye, passing through the center of the lens

Structure and Function of the Eye

Up to this point, we've discussed the nature of light, how it is reflected from objects and surfaces, and how we move our eyes to make sure the light reflected from what we want to look at enters our eyes. Now we'll begin our exploration of what happens to light after it enters the eyes. To make that process clear, we first need to describe the main parts of the eye and how they work.

Shape and Size

The human eye (see Figure 2.8) is roughly spherical, with a diameter of about 24 mm. The spherical shape makes it easy to rotate and move. The **optic axis** is an imaginary diameter line from the front to the back of the eye, passing through the center of the lens; each eye points in the direction defined by the optic axis.

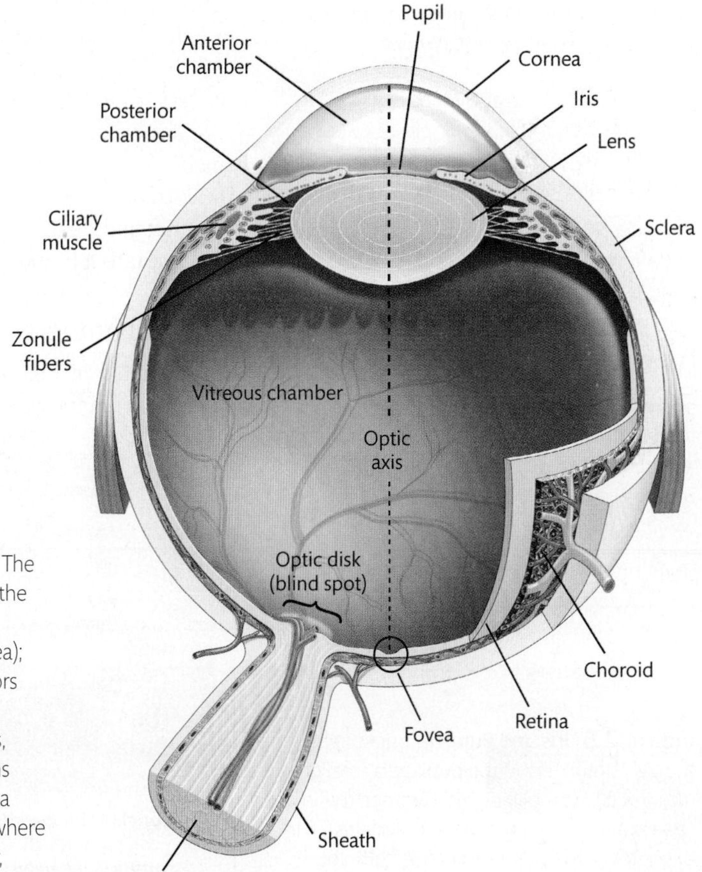

Figure 2.8 Anatomy of the Eye The right eye is shown here from above. The eye has a diameter of about 24 mm. The optic axis is an imaginary line from the front to back of the eye. Three membranes surround the eye: the sclera is a protective outer membrane with a transparent portion at the front (the cornea); the choroid contains blood vessels; the retina contains light-sensitive receptors and other neurons. Light enters the eye through the pupil, an opening in the middle of the iris. The ciliary muscles control the tension on the zonule fibers, which pull on the lens to adjust its shape, so the light passing through the lens focuses precisely on the retina. The fovea is the area at the center of the retina receiving light from objects at the center of gaze. The optic disk is the place where the optic nerve exits the eye. Fluids in the three chambers (anterior, posterior, vitreous) exert outward pressure on the eye and keep it from collapsing.

sclera The outer membrane of the eye; a tough protective covering whose visible portion is the white of the eye and the transparent cornea at the front of the eye.

choroid The middle membrane of the eye, lining the interior of the sclera and containing most of the blood vessels that supply the inside of the eye with oxygen and nutrients.

retina The inner membrane of the eye, made up of neurons, including the photoreceptors that convert the light entering the eye into neural signals.

Three Membranes

As shown in Figure 2.8, the eye is encased in three layers of membrane (Oyster, 1999):

- The outer membrane is made up of the **sclera,** a tough protective covering whose visible portion is the white of your eye, and the transparent cornea at the front of the eye (discussed below).
- The middle membrane is the **choroid;** it lines the interior of the sclera and contains most of the blood vessels that supply the inside of the eye with oxygen and nutrients.
- The inner membrane is the **retina,** which is made up of neurons, including the receptors that convert the light entering the eye into neural signals. (The retina and its functions are discussed in much more detail later in this chapter.)

cornea A transparent membrane at the front of the eye; light enters the eye by first passing through the cornea, which sharply refracts the light.

Cornea

The **cornea** is a transparent membrane at the front of the eye. Light enters the eye by first passing through the cornea, which sharply refracts (bends) the light. This refraction of light by the cornea is part of the process of focusing light on the retina—in fact, the cornea performs most of this focusing process. However, the cornea is rigid and cannot adjust how much the light passing through it is refracted. This is left to the flexible lens (discussed below), which performs the fine adjustments necessary to bring light into sharp focus.

iris The colored part of the eye—a small circular muscle with an opening in the middle (the pupil) through which light enters the eye.

pupil An opening in the middle of the iris, through which light enters the eye.

pupillary reflex The automatic process by which the iris contracts and relaxes to control the size of the pupil, in response to the relative brightness of light entering the eye.

Iris and Pupil

The **iris**—the colored part of the eye—is a small donut-shaped muscle with an opening in the middle through which light enters the eye; this opening is called the **pupil** (see Figure 2.7c for a front view of the iris and pupil). The iris controls the size of the pupil by contracting and relaxing, mainly in response to the brightness of light entering the eye. Bright light makes the iris contract, which makes the pupil smaller and thus reduces the amount of light that can enter the eye. In dim light, the iris relaxes, which makes the pupil larger and thus increases the amount of light that can enter the eye. This completely automatic process is known as the **pupillary reflex.**

The pupil can range in diameter from about 2 mm to about 8 mm; when the pupil gets smaller we say it *constricts*, and when it gets larger we say it *dilates* (see Figure 2.9). Like the extraocular muscles, the irises in the two eyes normally work in tandem, so both pupils constrict and dilate simultaneously and to the same degree. (You can see this if you shine a penlight into a friend's left or right eye: both pupils will constrict.)

anterior chamber The space between the cornea and the iris, filled with aqueous humor.

posterior chamber The space between the iris and the lens, filled with aqueous humor.

Three Chambers

As illustrated in Figure 2.8, the iris lies behind the cornea and in front of the lens. The space between the cornea and the iris is called the **anterior chamber,** and the smaller space between the iris and the lens is called the **posterior chamber.** Both chambers are filled with

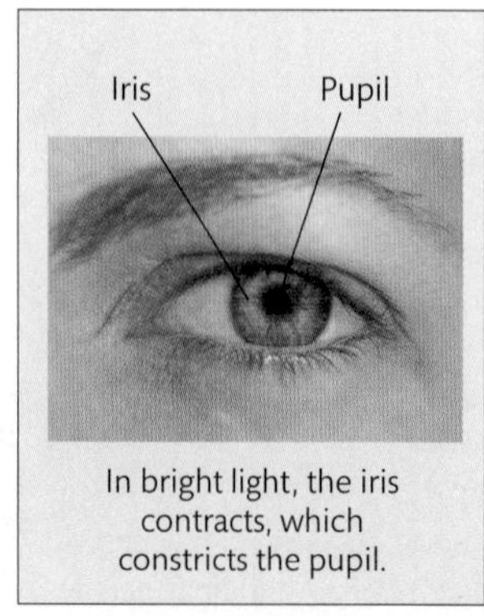

Iris
Pupil
In bright light, the iris contracts, which constricts the pupil.

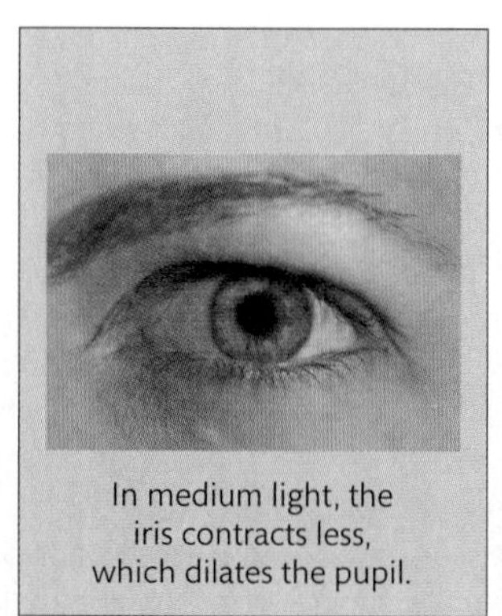

In medium light, the iris contracts less, which dilates the pupil.

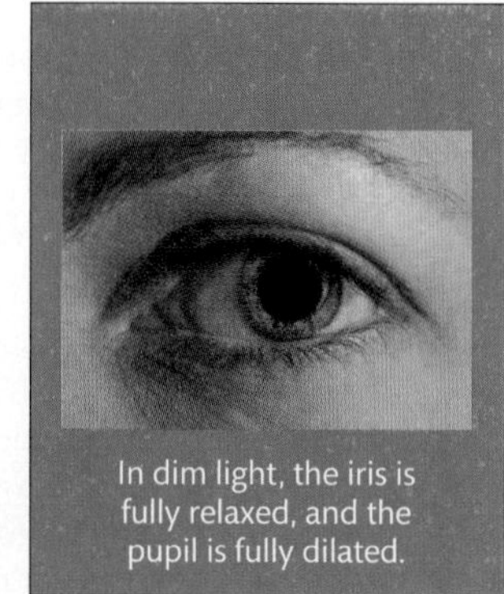

In dim light, the iris is fully relaxed, and the pupil is fully dilated.

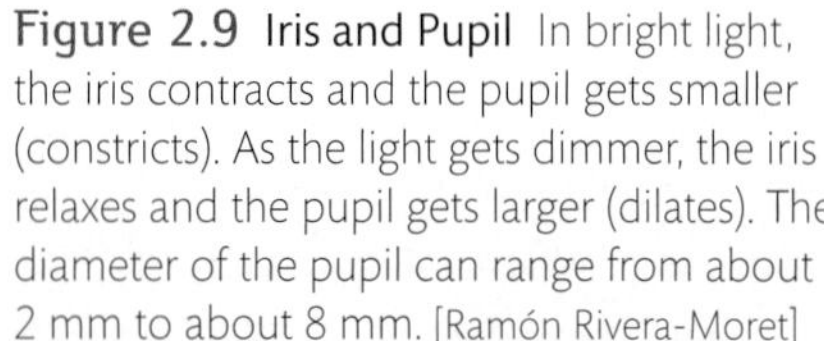

Figure 2.9 Iris and Pupil In bright light, the iris contracts and the pupil gets smaller (constricts). As the light gets dimmer, the iris relaxes and the pupil gets larger (dilates). The diameter of the pupil can range from about 2 mm to about 8 mm. [Ramón Rivera-Moret]

a clear, thin fluid called **aqueous humor** (*humor* comes from a Latin word that means "moisture"). The large **vitreous chamber**—the main interior portion of the eye—is filled with **vitreous humor,** a clear fluid that is more gel-like than the aqueous humor (despite this difference, both fluids are more than 99% water). The aqueous and vitreous humors also slightly refract light, but like the cornea, the amount of refraction they perform can't be adjusted.

The **intraocular pressure**—the pressure of the fluids in the three chambers of the eye—must be greater than air pressure to prevent the eyes from collapsing like deflated basketballs. (However, the intraocular pressure must not be too great; if it is, it can cause a condition known as *glaucoma,* which we discuss in the section on disorders of vision.)

aqueous humor A clear, thin fluid filling the anterior and posterior chambers of the eye.

vitreous chamber The main interior portion of the eye, filled with vitreous humor.

vitreous humor A clear, somewhat gel-like fluid filling the vitreous chamber of the eye.

intraocular pressure The pressure of the fluids in the three chambers of the eye.

Lens and Accommodation

As previously noted, light enters the eye by first passing through the transparent cornea, which sharply refracts the light. The light then passes through the pupil and into the **lens,** a transparent structure that further refracts the light, to ensure that light focuses properly on the retina.

The power of any lens to refract light determines its **focal length,** the distance from the lens at which the image of an object is in focus when the object is far away from the lens (i.e., at "optical infinity," where the light rays from the object are effectively parallel to one another). As illustrated in Figure 2.10, a weak lens doesn't refract light much; it is relatively thin and flat and has a large focal length. In contrast, a strong lens refracts light sharply; it is relatively thick and rounded and has a short focal length. The power of a lens is typically expressed in **diopters,** which is defined as 1/(focal length) in meters—for example, a lens with a focal length of 0.5 meters has a power of 2.0 diopters ($1/0.5 = 2.0$). The greater the power of a lens, the shorter the focal length.

For any given convex lens, as the object moves closer to the lens, the image of the object (formed on the other side of the lens) moves further away from the lens. In a camera, in order to focus light onto the image plane, you have to move the lens further from the image plane as the object gets closer (see Figure 2.11). The mammalian eye, in contrast, has evolved to solve this focusing problem in a different way: instead of moving the lens closer to or further from the retina, the eye adjusts the shape of the lens to change its focal length.

If the lens were removed from the eye and held in your hand, it would take on a roughly spherical shape, but when it's in position inside the eye, its shape is more ellipsoidal because the edges of the lens are stretched by **zonule fibers** that connect the lens to the choroid. The tiny **ciliary muscles** are also attached to the choroid. When the ciliary muscles are relaxed, the choroid can pull on the zonule fibers; this stretches the lens and causes it to

lens A transparent structure near the front of the eye that refracts the light passing through the pupil so that the light focuses properly on the retina.

focal length The distance from a lens at which the image of an object is in focus when the object is far away from the lens (at "optical infinity").

diopters Units used to express the power of a lens; diopters = 1/(focal length).

zonule fibers Fibers that connect the lens to the choroid; they pull on the lens to change its shape.

ciliary muscles Tiny muscles attached to the choroid; they relax and contract to control how the choroid pulls on the zonule fibers to change the shape of the lens.

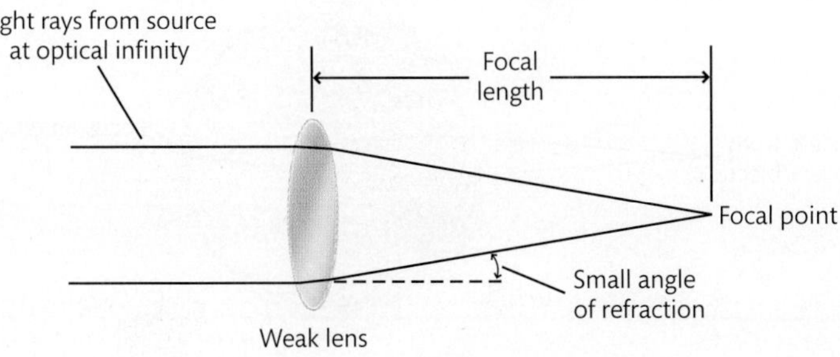

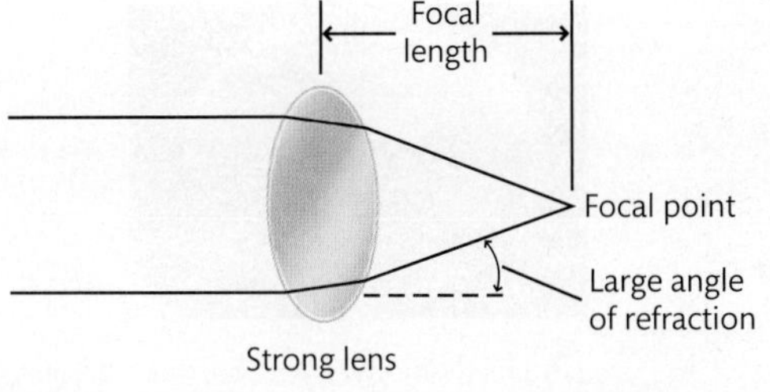

Figure 2.10 Weak and Strong Lenses The focal length of a lens—the distance from the lens to the point where light rays from a source at optical infinity come to a focus—is determined by the power of the lens. A weak lens has a relatively long focal length and doesn't bend light very much—it has a relatively small angle of refraction. A strong lens has a relatively short focal length and bends light more—it has a relatively large angle of refraction. The more parallel the front and rear surfaces of a lens, the weaker it is; a pane of glass, with perfectly parallel surfaces, is at one extreme.

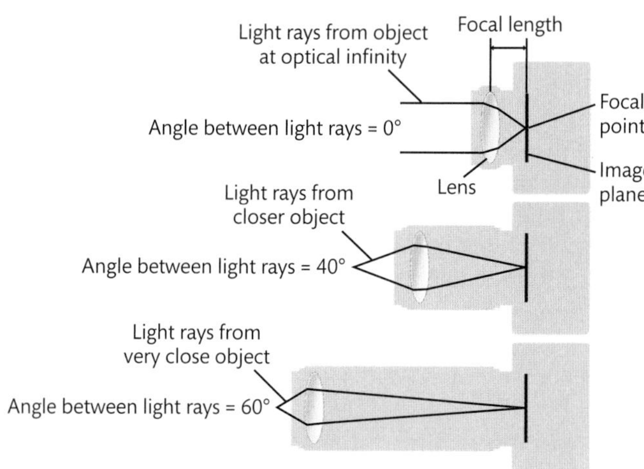

Figure 2.11 **Focusing Light in a Camera** A camera focuses light on the image plane (e.g., the sensor in a digital camera) by moving the lens closer to or further from the image plane. The shape of the lens in a camera is fixed; this determines the power of the lens, which determines the focal length. In the top illustration, light rays from an object at optical infinity are effectively parallel when they enter the lens, so the distance from the lens to the image plane has to be equal to the focal length in order to focus the light on the image plane. In the bottom two illustrations, as the object moves closer to the lens than optical infinity, the light rays enter the lens at a progressively greater angle, and the focal point moves progressively further from the lens. Thus, the lens must be moved progressively further to the left to bring the focal point onto the image plane.

Demonstration 2.1 **Focusing Light in a Camera and in the Eye** Interact with dynamic models of a camera and the human eye to see the differences and similarities in how an image is brought into focus.

accommodation Adjustment of the shape of the lens so light from objects at different distances focuses correctly on the retina.

take on a relatively thin, flat shape, making it a relatively weak lens with a relatively long focal length, appropriate for focusing light from distant objects. When the ciliary muscles contract, they oppose the pull by the choroid on the zonule fibers; the lens isn't stretched as much, so it takes on a thicker, more rounded shape, making it a stronger lens with a shorter focal length, appropriate for focusing light from nearer objects. This adjustment of the shape of the lens to focus on objects at different distances from the eye is called **accommodation** and is illustrated in Figure 2.12. (Several kinds of things can go wrong with this system of accommodation that result in the focal point being in front of or behind the retina. See the section on disorders of vision for discussion of these conditions.)

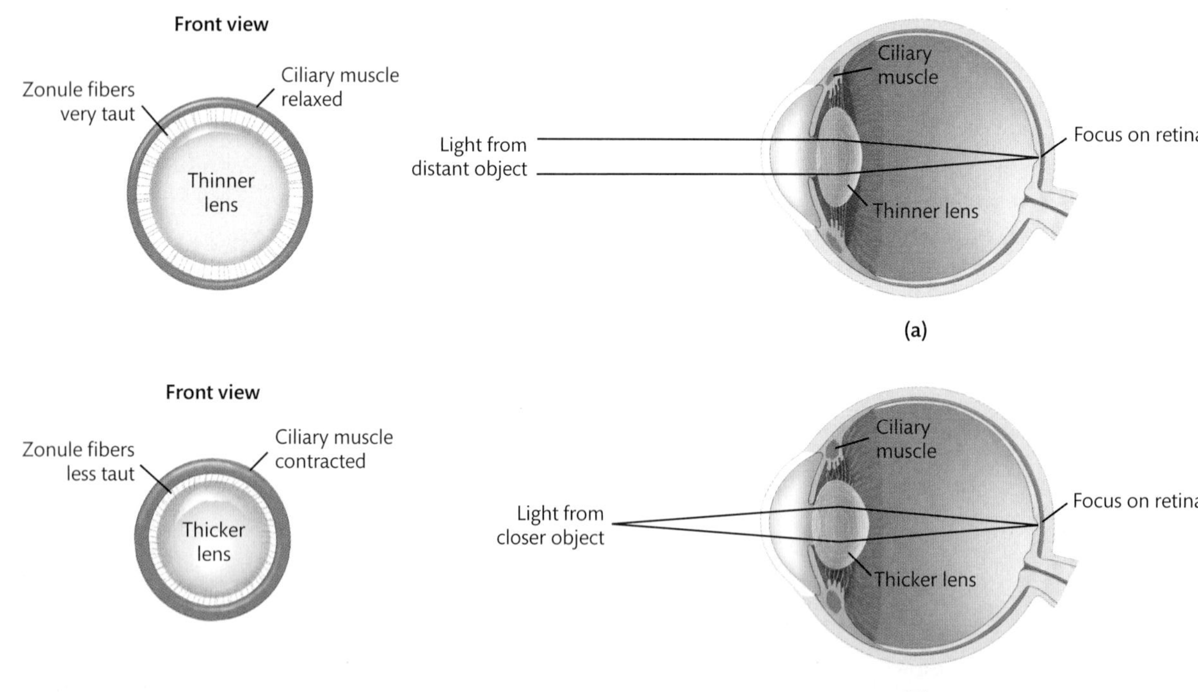

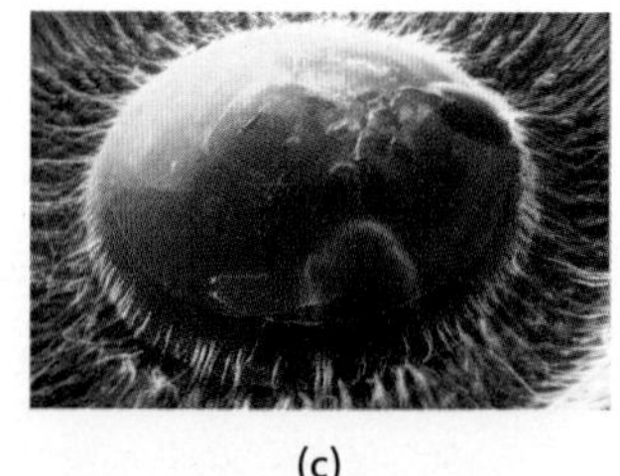

Figure 2.12 **Focusing Light in Your Eyes** Unlike a camera, which focuses light on the image plane by moving the lens, your eyes focus light on the retina by changing the shape of the lens to change its focal length (i.e., by the process of accommodation). (a) To focus light from distant objects, the lens has to be relatively weak—thinner and flatter. The eye accomplishes this by relaxing the ciliary muscles, so they don't oppose the pull of the choroid on the zonule fibers. The zonule fibers stretch the lens to thin and flatten it. (b) To focus light from closer objects, the lens has to be relatively strong—thicker and rounder. The eye accomplishes this by contracting the ciliary muscles, so they oppose the pull of the choroid on the zonule fibers, which then don't stretch the lens as much. (c) Photomicrograph of the lens and the surrounding zonule fibers. [Ralph C. Eagle, Jr./Photo Researchers]

Check Your Understanding

2.5 Define *field of view*. How does the field of view of humans differ from that of animals with eyes on the sides of their head?

2.6 How does the iris control the amount of light entering the eye?

2.7 What is accommodation? How does the lens accommodate (change) in order to focus on objects at different distances from the eye?

Retina

The goal of the eye's optical system—first, constriction or dilation of the pupil by the iris to control the amount of light entering the eye, and then accommodation by the lens to focus that light on the retina—is to form a clear image on the retina of the optic array; that is, a clear image of what you're looking at. The retina then transforms the image into neural signals to be sent to the brain (Rodieck, 1998; Wässle, 2004).

The Retinal Image In this book, we'll usually talk about and illustrate the **retinal image** as if it were like a movie projected on the retina (or like a still from a movie). We'll ignore the fact that the retina is soft, textured, living tissue, not smooth and regular like a movie screen. Likewise, we'll generally ignore the fact that the retina is a curved surface rather than flat and that the retinal image is inverted—up becomes down, left becomes right, and vice versa. The inverted retinal image is illustrated in Figure 2.13.

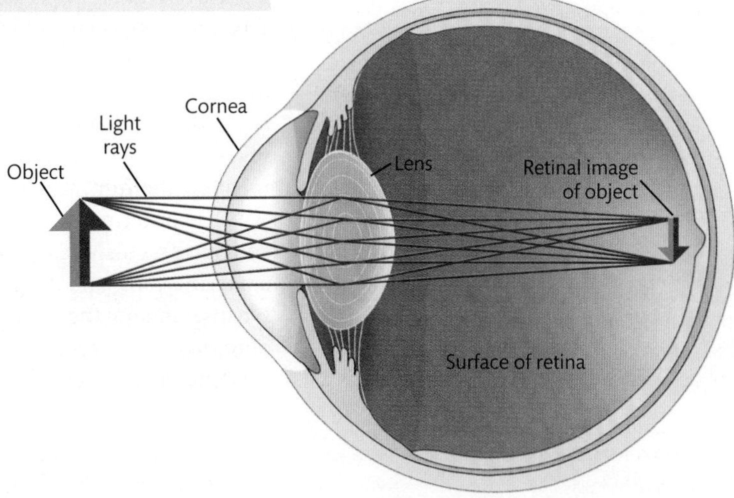

Figure 2.13 Retinal Image Light rays are reflected in all directions from each point on an object in the environment. This illustration shows how five of the rays reflected from each of two points on the object are refracted by the lens. The refraction by the lens brings all the rays from each point on the object into focus at the corresponding point of the retinal image. Note how the inversion of the retinal image results from the way the light rays are refracted. (For the purposes of this illustration, we've used simplified paths of refraction.)

Anatomy of the Retina As shown in Figure 2.8, the retina is the innermost of the three membranes enclosing the eye (see Figure 2.14, which shows the surface of the retina as seen through an ophthalmoscope). It is made up of several different classes of neurons, and each class performs a distinct function (Masland, 2001; Wässle, 2004). Within each class, multiple types and subtypes of neurons have been described by neuroscientists, each with

retinal image A clear image on the retina of the optic array.

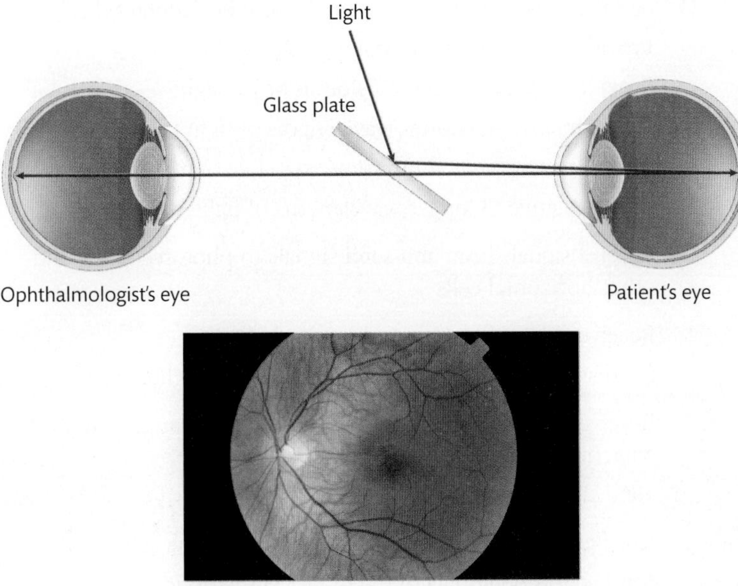

Figure 2.14 Ophthalmoscope: Looking at the Retina If you look into someone's eye, the pupil looks black because most of the light entering the eye is absorbed by the retina and not reflected back out through the pupil. You must shine a lot more light into the eye in order to see what's inside. (*top*) An ophthalmoscope—an instrument invented in 1851 by the German scientist Hermann von Helmholtz—reflects a beam of light off a glass plate that works as a "see-through mirror." The tilt of the plate is adjusted so the light goes into the patient's eye, reflects off the retina, passes back out of the patient's eye, passes through the glass plate, and enters the ophthalmologist's eye. (*bottom*) A normal human retina as seen through an ophthalmoscope. The bright circular region is the optic disk (or blind spot), which is more reflective than the rest of the retinal surface. Blood vessels and the optic nerve pass through the retina at the optic disk (only blood vessels can be seen in the photo); note that there are no blood vessels in front of the fovea, at the center of the photo. [Paul Parker/Photo Researchers]

distinct structure and function (more is known about the functions of some of these than others). Table 2.1 lists the functions of the neuron types that will play important roles in our discussions in this chapter and later (the table doesn't include the subtypes about which less is known or that aren't discussed in this chapter).

The retina is structured in layers, as shown in Figure 2.15. The three main layers—the outer nuclear layer, inner nuclear layer, and ganglion cell layer—are called **nuclear layers** because they contain the nuclei of the various types of retinal neurons described below. The nuclear layers are separated by two **synaptic layers**—the outer synaptic layer and inner synaptic layer—where the retinal neurons make synapses with each other. Closest to the back of the eye is a layer consisting of the inner and outer segments of the **photoreceptors,** the retinal neurons that transduce light into neural signals. The two classes of photoreceptors—**rods** and **cones**—are named for their distinctive shapes. The "business ends" of the photoreceptors, where transduction occurs, are embedded in a layer of cells called the **pigment epithelium,** which is itself attached to the choroid.

The **outer nuclear layer** consists of the photoreceptors (but not including their inner and outer segments); the **inner nuclear layer** contains **bipolar cells, horizontal cells,** and **amacrine cells;** and the **ganglion cell layer** consists of **retinal ganglion cells (RGCs).** The synapses among the photoreceptors, bipolar cells, and horizontal cells are contained in the **outer synaptic layer,** and the synapses among the bipolar cells, amacrine cells, and RGCs are contained in the **inner synaptic layer.**

The axons of the RGCs exit the eye at the **optic disk** (or *blind spot,* so called because there are no photoreceptors in this part of the retina). The million or so RGC axons form a bundle called the **optic nerve.**

Fovea The optic axis passes through the **fovea** (or *fovea centralis*) at the center of the retina (see Figure 2.8 for the fovea's location in the eye; in Figure 2.14, the fovea is the faint dark region in the center of the retina). This is where the light from objects at the center of our gaze strikes the retina. The anatomy of the retina in the fovea is markedly different from

TABLE 2.1 Retinal Neurons

Classes and Types of Neurons	Main Functions
Photoreceptors	Transduce light into neural signals.
	Send signals to bipolar cells.
	Send signals to and receive signals from horizontal cells.
Rods	Provide black-and-white vision in dim light.
Cones	Provide high-acuity color vision in bright light.
S-cones	Most sensitive to shorter wavelengths of light.
M-cones	Most sensitive to medium wavelengths of light.
L-cones	Most sensitive to longer wavelengths of light.
Horizontal cells	Receive signals from and send signals to photoreceptors and other horizontal cells.
Bipolar cells	Receive signals from photoreceptors.
	Send signals to amacrine cells and retinal ganglion cells.
Amacrine cells	Receive signals from and send signals to bipolar cells and other amacrine cells.
	Send signals to retinal ganglion cells.
Retinal ganglion cells	Receive signals from bipolar cells and amacrine cells.
	Send action potentials to the brain via the optic nerve.

nuclear layers The three main layers of the retina, including the outer nuclear layer, inner nuclear layer, and ganglion cell layer.

synaptic layers In the retina, two layers separating the three nuclear layers—the outer synaptic layer and inner synaptic layer.

photoreceptors Retinal neurons (rods and cones) that transduce light into neural signals.

rods One of the two classes of photoreceptors, named for their distinctive shape.

cones One of the two classes of photoreceptors, named for their distinctive shape.

pigment epithelium A layer of cells attached to the choroid; photoreceptors are embedded in it.

outer nuclear layer The layer of the retina consisting of photoreceptors (but not including their inner and outer segments).

inner nuclear layer The layer of the retina that contains bipolar cells, horizontal cells, and amacrine cells.

bipolar cells Neurons in the inner nuclear layer of the retina.

horizontal cells Neurons in the inner nuclear layer of the retina.

amacrine cells Neurons in the inner nuclear layer of the retina.

ganglion cell layer The layer of the retina that contains retinal ganglion cells.

retinal ganglion cells (RGCs) Neurons in the ganglion cell layer of the retina.

outer synaptic layer The layer of the retina that contains the synapses among photoreceptors, bipolar cells, and horizontal cells.

inner synaptic layer The layer of the retina that contains the synapses among bipolar cells, amacrine cells, and RGCs.

optic disk (or *blind spot*) Location on the retina where the axons of RGCs exit the eye; contains no photoreceptors.

optic nerve Nerve formed by the bundling together of the axons of RGCs; it exits the eye through the optic disk.

fovea A region in the center of the retina where the light from objects at the center of our gaze strikes the retina; contains no rods and a very high density of cones.

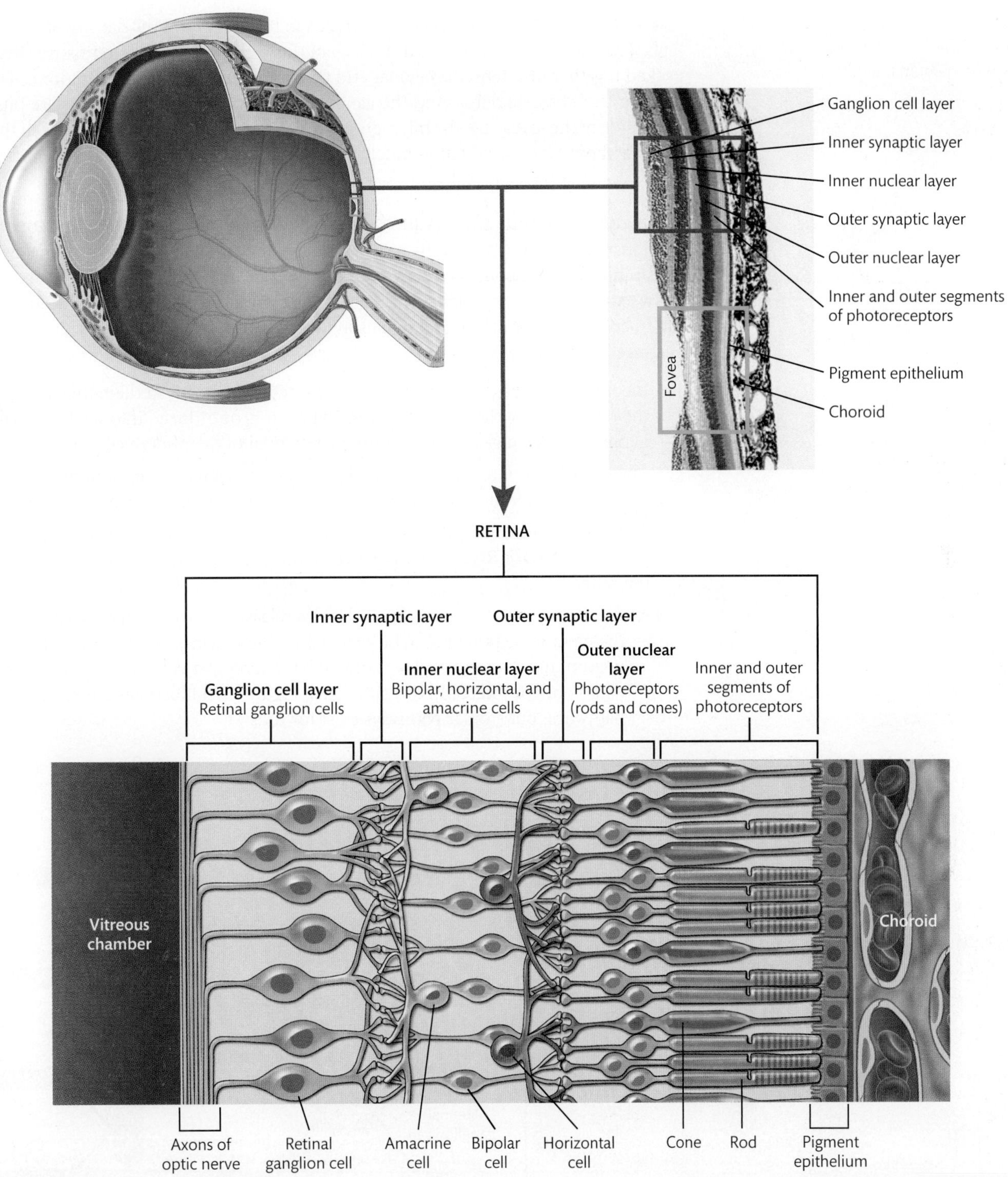

Figure 2.15 **Anatomy of the Retina** The retina is structured in three main nuclear layers—the outer nuclear layer, inner nuclear layer, and ganglion cell layer—separated by two synaptic layers containing synaptic connections among the cells in the nuclear layers. A layer at the back of the eye consists of the inner and outer segments of photoreceptors, with the outer segments embedded in the pigment epithelium, from which the photoreceptors receive nourishment. The outer nuclear layer consists of the photoreceptors (not including their inner and outer segments), and the inner nuclear layer consists of horizontal cells, bipolar cells, and amacrine cells, which form a network connecting the photoreceptors to the ganglion cell layer, which consists of retinal ganglion cells. The axons of the retinal ganglion cells come together at the optic disk and exit the eye in a bundle, the optic nerve. The micrograph shows a cross section of the retina: the part in the red box corresponds to the part of the retina illustrated below; the part in the green box is the retina at the fovea, where the ganglion cell layer and inner nuclear layer are "pushed to the side" to minimize interference with the image at the fovea by giving incoming light more direct access to the photoreceptors. [Courtesy of Dr. Deborah W. Vaughan, Histology Learning System, Boston University]

Demonstration 2.2 Functional Anatomy of the Eye Interact with a depiction of the human eye.

that in the rest of the retina. There are no rods in the fovea, and the density of cones is very high. The cones in the fovea are thinner than those elsewhere in the retina, so they can be packed together in a dense hexagonal grid (the most efficient arrangement for cells shaped more or less like cylinders). And the ganglion cell and inner nuclear layers are pushed off to the side of the fovea (see the micrograph in Figure 2.15), which lets light reach the foveal cones without being scattered as much. All of these factors contribute to maximizing high-acuity vision at the center of gaze.

Pathways of Neural Signals in the Retina: An Overview Within the retina, signals are transmitted between neurons in ways that ensure that the brain will ultimately receive useful information about the scene you're looking at (Wässle, 2004). In the sections that follow, we'll describe the nature of these transmissions in some detail. But for now, you can trace the pathways of neural signals in Figure 2.16 to get the following broad overview (also see Table 2.1):

- Incoming light passes through the other layers of neurons in the retina and strikes the outer parts of the photoreceptors, where it is transduced into neural signals, expressed as changes in the membrane potential of the photoreceptors.
- The changes in photoreceptor membrane potential alter the amount of neurotransmitter molecules that the photoreceptors release (Trifonov, 1968).
- A "through pathway" (green arrows in Figure 2.16) transmits signals from photoreceptors to RGCs via bipolar cells; this is the principle flow of signals through the retina.
    - The flow of neurotransmitter molecules released by rods and cones affects the membrane potential of bipolar cells, which changes their release of neurotransmitter molecules. (Any individual bipolar cell receives signals from cones only or rods only. For simplicity, Figure 2.16 illustrates cones-only pathways, but similar pathways exist for rods.)

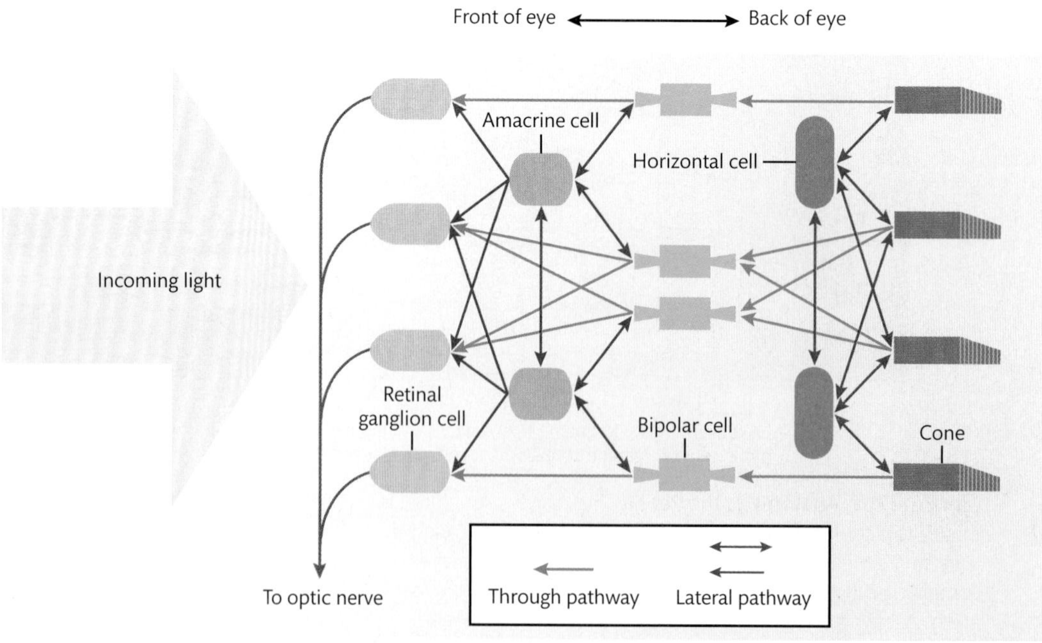

Figure 2.16 Pathways in the Retina Pathways in the retina support complex patterns of neural signal transmission. The through pathway goes from photoreceptors to bipolar cells to RGCs. The lateral pathway, involving horizontal cells and amacrine cells, allows the interaction of signals originating from photoreceptors at different locations on the retina. (For simplicity, this figure shows pathways involving cones only.)

- The change in bipolar cell neurotransmitter release affects the membrane potential of RGCs, which in turn affects their firing rates.

- A "lateral pathway" involving horizontal cells and amacrine cells (red arrows in Figure 2.16) allows the presence of light at one location on the retina to affect the responses of photoreceptors, bipolar cells, and RGCs at adjacent locations on the retina. (As we'll see later, these lateral influences provide a way for the neural signals to transmit information about **luminance contrast**—differences in the intensity of illumination at adjacent retinal locations—and this plays a critical role in detecting edges and boundaries.)
  - Horizontal cells receive signals from photoreceptors and other horizontal cells and send signals back to photoreceptors and other horizontal cells.
  - Amacrine cells receive signals from bipolar cells and other amacrine cells, send signals back to bipolar and amacrine cells, and send signals to RGCs.
- Retinal ganglion cells receive signals from bipolar cells and amacrine cells and send action potentials to the brain via the optic nerve.

These complex interconnections provide a means for signals from many different cells to interact as they flow from photoreceptors to the optic nerve. As we'll see, these interactions are an essential part of the processing of light by the retina.

luminance contrast A difference in the intensity of illumination at adjacent retinal locations.

Demonstration 2.3 Functional Anatomy of the Retina Interact with a depiction of the human retina.

Check Your Understanding

2.8 Fill in the names of the retinal layers next to their contents:

Retinal Layer	Contents
A.	bipolar cells, horizontal cells, and amacrine cells
B.	synapses among RGCs, amacrine cells, and bipolar cells
C.	synapses among photoreceptors, horizontal cells, and bipolar cells
D.	rods and cones

2.9 True or false? There are no rods in the fovea, and there are no photoreceptors in the optic disk.

2.10 Fill in the blanks:

A. Photoreceptors send signals to __________ and receive signals from __________.

B. Horizontal cells send signals to __________ and receive signals from __________.

C. Bipolar cells send signals to __________ and receive signals from __________.

D. Amacrine cells send signals to __________ and receive signals from __________.

E. Retinal ganglion cells send signals to __________ and receive signals from __________.

Photoreceptors: Rods and Cones

At this point, you know that the photoreceptors in the retina consist of two types of neurons—rods and cones—and that both the rods and the cones transduce light into neural signals. We've also mentioned that cones provide more detailed information about the light they transduce than rods do—specifically, cones carry information about differences in wavelength (color) and support greater acuity (especially the densely packed cones in the fovea). In contrast, rods are much more sensitive than cones to low levels of light but support only poor acuity and carry little information about color. These differences mean that we use our rods mainly to see in dim light (night vision) and our cones to see in bright light (daylight vision).

Another important difference between rods and cones is that there is just one type of rod but there are three types of cones; and each type of photoreceptor has a different kind of **photopigment**, a molecule with the ability to absorb light and thereby initiate transduction. The four kinds of photopigment molecules differ in their **spectral sensitivity**—that is, in their ability to absorb light of different wavelengths (perceived as different colors), as shown in Figure 2.17. Despite the differences between rods and cones, their overall anatomy is similar, as shown in Figure 2.18.

photopigment A molecule with the ability to absorb light and initiate transduction.

spectral sensitivity The degree to which a photopigment molecule absorbs light of different wavelengths.

isomers Different possible shapes of molecules, such as the all-*trans* retinal and 11-*cis*-retinal shapes of photopigment molecules.

photoisomerization A change in shape by a photopigment molecule from one isomer (11-*cis* retinal) to another (all-*trans* retinal) when the molecule absorbs a photon; initiates the transduction of light to a neural signal.

Transduction of Light

The process by which light is transduced to a neural signal is cyclical (Wald, 1935, 1968). Photopigment molecules have two possible shapes, called **isomers.** When a photopigment molecule absorbs a photon of light, it undergoes **photoisomerization**—its shape changes from one isomer (11-*cis* retinal) to the other (all-*trans* retinal), as illustrated in Figure 2.19. Photoisomerization initiates a cascade of biochemical reactions that eventually results in a reduction in the membrane potential of the photoreceptor, the first step in the transduction of light. This reduction in membrane potential produces a change in the number of neurotransmitter molecules released by the photoreceptor at the synaptic terminals (Burns & Lamb, 2004). And this change in neurotransmitter release, in turn, causes a change in the membrane potential of the bipolar and/or horizontal cells to which the photoreceptor is connected, resulting in changes in neurotransmitter release by those cells, which similarly affect the amacrine cells and RGCs to which they're connected. In this way, neural signals are propagated through the layers of the retina to the RGCs, which send action potentials into the optic nerve and then to the brain. (Photopigment regeneration, which constitutes the rest of the visual transduction cycle, transforming the all-*trans* isomer back to the 11-*cis* isomer, is discussed later in this chapter.)

Demonstration 2.4 Spectral Sensitivity of Photopigments Control the wavelength and intensity of light striking the retina, and monitor the responses of the four types of photoreceptors.

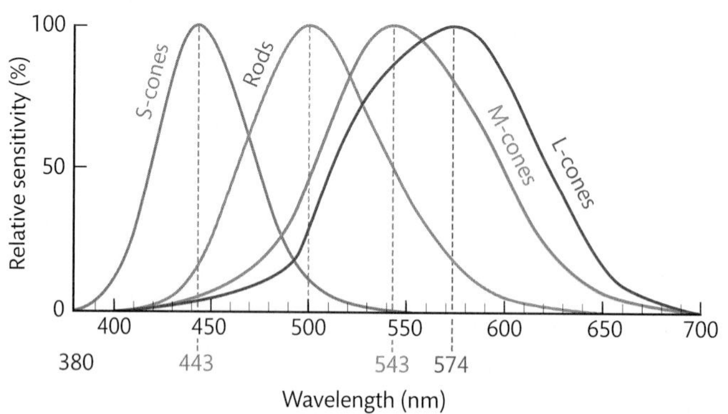

Figure 2.17 Spectral Sensitivity of Photopigments The four kinds of photopigments—one in each of the three cone types and another in rods—vary in their ability to absorb light of different wavelengths. The photopigment in S-cones is most sensitive to short-wavelength light, with a peak sensitivity at 443 nm; S-cones are quite insensitive to wavelengths greater than about 550 nm. The photopigments in M-cones and L-cones both have some sensitivity across nearly the entire spectrum of visible light, but the sensitivity of M-cones is greater toward the middle wavelengths (peaking at 543 nm), while that of L-cones is greater toward the longer wavelengths (peaking at 574 nm). The photopigment in rods is most sensitive to light with a wavelength of 500 nm. Note that these curves show the *relative* sensitivity of each photopigment (i.e., relative to its maximal response, 100%). The *absolute* sensitivities of the photopigments differ greatly—for example, maximum rod sensitivity is much greater than the maximum M-cone sensitivity, which is why rods support vision under low-light conditions. (Adapted from Stockman et al., 1993.)

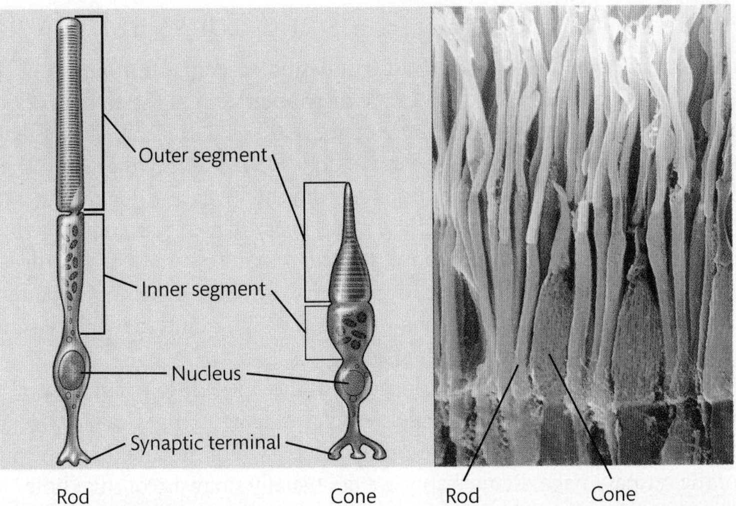

Figure 2.18 Rods and Cones Rods and cones support different types of vision (night and daylight, respectively) but, in certain other respects, are similar in structure and function. Photopigments stored in the outer segment transduce light: absorption of photons leads to changes in the rate of neurotransmitter release by the photoreceptor. These photopigments are manufactured in the inner segment, then transported to the outer segment; the inner segment also contains mitochondria and other organelles that support cellular metabolism. The nucleus contains DNA, which genetically controls the workings of the cell. Synaptic terminals at the base of the photoreceptor synapse with other cells. Changes in neurotransmitter release at the synaptic terminals signal changes in the amount of light to other neurons in the retina. The photomicrograph shows numerous thin rods and sparser, fatter cones at a location some distance away from the fovea. [Ralph C. Eagle, Jr./Photo Researchers]

The many intricate biophysical and biochemical details of the photoisomerization and photopigment regeneration processes are well understood but are beyond the scope of this book (see Rodieck, 1998, Chapter 8, for a detailed account). However, it's worth mentioning that certain steps in the biochemical cascade following the transduction of light by rods greatly amplify the signals from rods when they're exposed to even a few photons of light; this is what's responsible for the very high sensitivity of rods to low light levels.

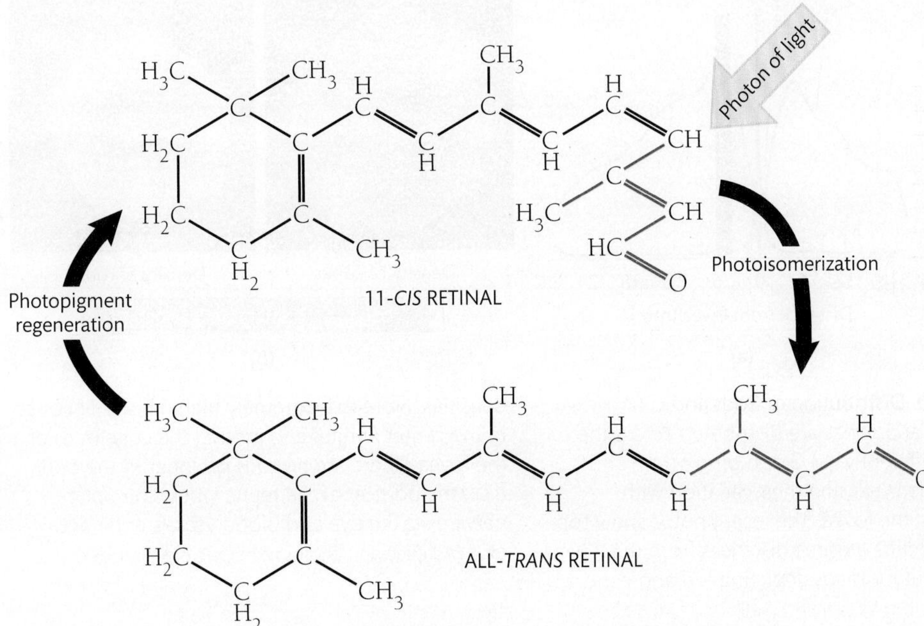

Figure 2.19 Photoisomerization This photopigment molecule has two possible shapes (isomers)—one called 11-*cis* retinal, the other called all-*trans* retinal. When the 11-*cis* retinal isomer absorbs light, it changes shape to all-*trans* retinal—a process called *photoisomerization*—and this initiates a cascade of biochemical reactions that lead to changes in the rate of neurotransmitter release by the photoreceptor. Photopigment regeneration is the process by which the all-*trans* isomer is converted back to the 11-*cis* isomer, after which the molecule is again ready to transduce light.

Number and Distribution of Rods and Cones in the Retina

Each human retina has an area of about 1,000 mm^2 and contains approximately 100 million rods and 5 million cones. Rods and cones are distributed across the retina very differently, and neither distribution is uniform (Curcio et al., 1990). Figure 2.20 shows that there are no rods at all in the fovea, while the density of cones there is very high, and that the density of cones falls off very rapidly with distance from the fovea and remains at a lower level throughout the rest of the retina. In contrast, the density of rods rises rapidly within a short distance of the fovea, reaching a high point in a ring about 6 mm from the fovea and then declining gradually as distance from the fovea increases. These distribution patterns of rods and cones reflect their different functions—cones for high-acuity daylight vision, rods for low-acuity but very light-sensitive night vision.

Demonstration 2.5 Blind Spot Explore the blind spot interactively, and map the blind spots in your own eyes.

In addition, Figure 2.20 shows the location of the optic disk, or blind spot, where the optic nerve leaves the eye and blood vessels enter and leave. This is called the "blind spot" because of the total absence of photoreceptors there, which means that we cannot sense that part of the retinal image. Remarkably, we are usually unaware of this "hole" in the retinal image, because the visual system automatically fills it in (Andrews & Campbell, 1991; Ramachandran, 1992); however, you can "see" your blind spot by looking at Figure 2.21 and following the directions in the caption. (Figure 2.22 shows what happens during this procedure.)

Adapting to Changes in Lighting

The human visual system operates within a certain (very large) range of light intensities (Packer & Williams, 2003). Below that range, not enough light strikes the retina to activate vision; above that range, the visual system is overwhelmed and we are effectively blinded by glare (in fact, if you look at the sun for more than a second, you can permanently damage your retinas). In everyday life, we might experience the lower part of the range when looking at a white piece of paper on a clear moonless night in the country, when stars provide

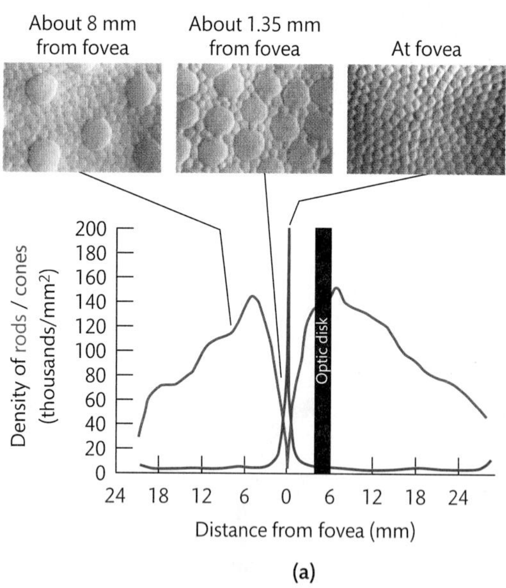

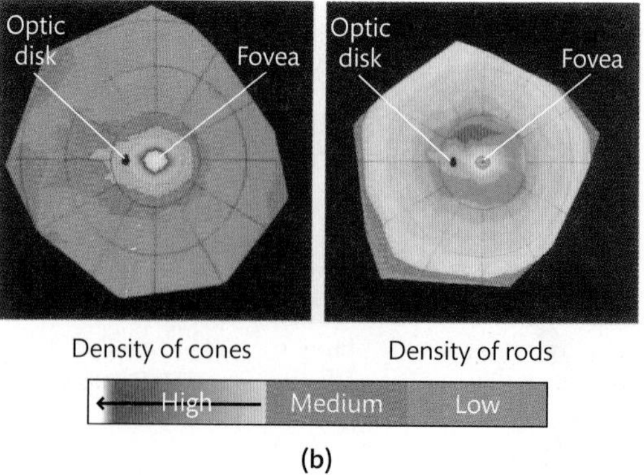

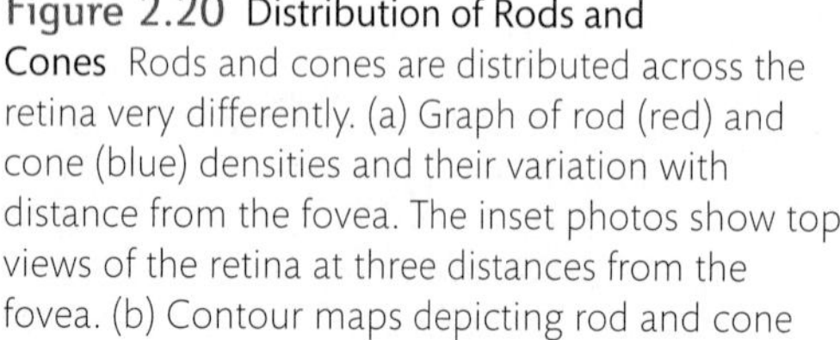

Figure 2.20 Distribution of Rods and Cones Rods and cones are distributed across the retina very differently. (a) Graph of rod (red) and cone (blue) densities and their variation with distance from the fovea. The inset photos show top views of the retina at three distances from the fovea. (b) Contour maps depicting rod and cone densities. Note the extremely high density of cones in the center (white) and around the edge (red) of the fovea. There are no rods or cones in the optic disk, the portion of the retina where the optic nerve exits the eye and blood vessels enter and exit. (Adapted and photos from Curcio et al., 1990.)

Figure 2.21 Blind Spot I: Demonstration Hold the book at arm's length, close your left eye, and look at the cross with your right eye. Slowly move the book toward your face, while continuously looking at the cross. At some point, the red disk will seem to disappear. Also, the two vertical lines may appear as a single continuous line running across the space occupied by the red disk. We don't fully understand how the visual system fills in that space, but the fact that it does so shows that the visual system doesn't just report what's in the retinal image (in this case, that would include a "hole" at the optic disk), but constructs the likeliest "explanation" of the optic array.

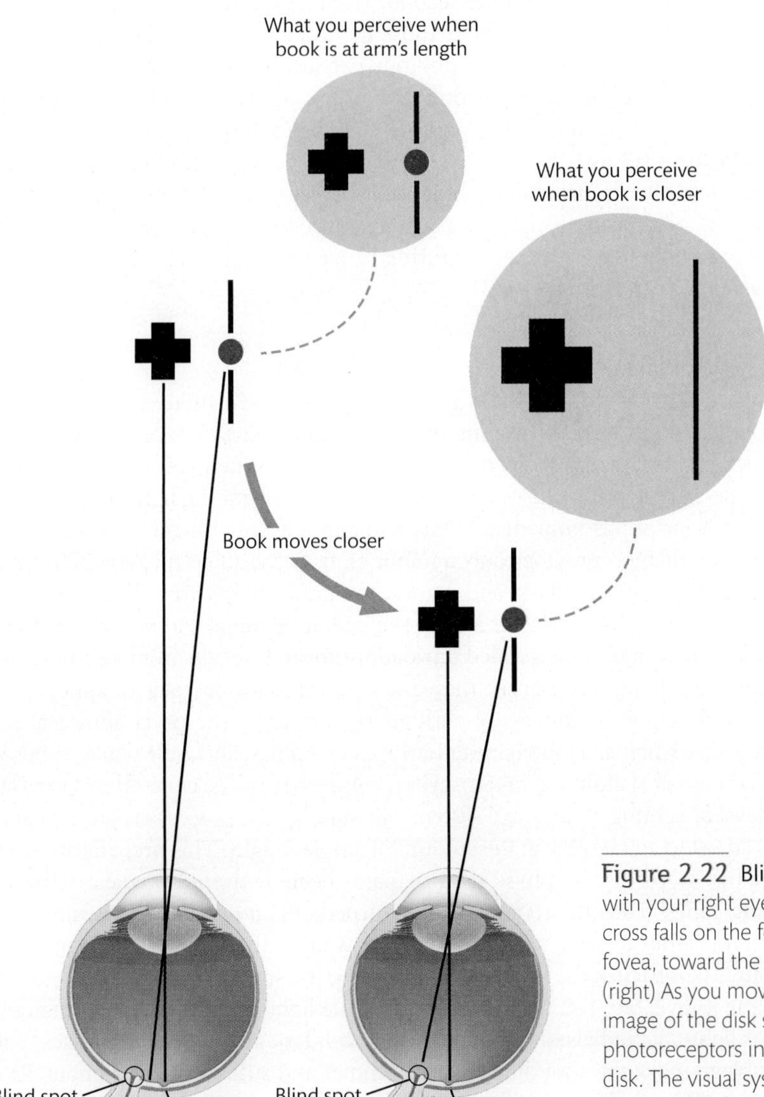

Figure 2.22 Blind Spot II: Explanation (left) When you look at the cross with your right eye and the book is at arm's length, the retinal image of the cross falls on the fovea, and the image of the red disk falls to the side of the fovea, toward the optic disk but not on it. Thus, you perceive the red disk. (right) As you move the book closer (indicated by the thick arrow), the retinal image of the disk shifts until it falls directly on the optic disk. There are no photoreceptors in that portion of the retina, so you don't perceive the red disk. The visual system fills in the hole in the retinal image with its "best guess" about what's there—in this case, the visual system guesses that the two vertical lines are really the two ends of one continuous line.

the only illumination (in these conditions, about 10^7 photons per second strike each square millimeter of our retinas—this is still a *lot* of photons!). In contrast, we might experience the upper part of the range while looking at a white piece of paper in the bright sun (when about 10^{13} photons per second would strike each square millimeter of retina). In other words, the highest level of light we commonly experience is at least a million times as great as the lowest level ($10^{13} - 10^7 = 10^6 = 1{,}000{,}000$).

Across this range, how does the visual system convey the fine distinctions in light intensity that we need in order to perceive our environment accurately? Recall that the last links in the neural pathways of the retina are the RGCs (see Figure 2.16). The rate at which these cells fire is what tells the brain how much light is present. But an RGC can fire at a rate of 1 to about 100 spikes per second—that is, the ratio of the highest to lowest firing rate is only about a 100:1. Clearly, this is inadequate to represent the 1,000,000:1 ratio of highest to lowest light intensity that we encounter in the world. As we'll see in the next section, the sensitivity of the retina automatically adjusts to deal with this mismatch in ranges in order to effectively handle the average amount of light striking the retina in any given scene.

Operating Range

On a sunny day at the beach, when you're looking at the white sand, clear water, and light blue sky, the number of photons per second striking each square millimeter of your retina might range from 10^{10} to 10^{13}; under those conditions, your RGCs might fire at or near their lowest rate in response to 10^{10} photons per second and at or near their highest rate in response to 10^{13} photons per second. If you put on dark sunglasses that transmit just 1% of the light, then the number of photons striking each square millimeter of your retina would range from 10^8 to 10^{11} per second, and your RGCs will gradually adapt to these new conditions until they're firing at or near their lowest rate in response to 10^8 photons per second and at or near their highest rate in response to 10^{11} photons per second. That is, the visual system works within an **operating range** that is most effective for current conditions (Valeton & van Norren, 1983).

operating range The visual system's sensitivity to the range of light intensities within the current scene; the visual system adjusts its operating range according to current conditions.

Dark Adaptation

In the last section, we found that the retina adjusts its sensitivity to deal optimally with the amount of light that is present in the current scene. We've all experienced how this adjustment process takes a certain amount of time. When you first enter a dark movie theater, especially if you've just come into the theater from daylight, you can't see much of anything. Your pupils immediately dilate to admit as much light as possible (see Figure 2.9), but pupil dilation provides only a minor adjustment. Over the next 30 minutes or so, your eyes "get used to" the dark, and your vision gradually returns. This process of adjusting retinal sensitivity—in effect, changing the operating range—as you move from a bright environment to a darker one is called **dark adaptation.** It results from an adjustment in the sensitivity of the photoreceptors so they can respond to lower levels of light.

dark adaptation The process of adjusting retinal sensitivity (changing the operating range) as the person moves from a bright environment to a darker one; the reverse process is called *light adaptation.*

We can measure the process of dark adaptation using the psychophysical method of adjustment (see Chapter 1). Imagine entering a perception lab where you're exposed to normal daylight levels of illumination for several minutes. If you've come from a classroom with a lower level of lighting, your visual system will undergo the process of *light adaptation*—that is, it will adjust to an increase in the amount of ambient light. This preparatory step is taken to ensure that all the psychophysical participants begin with their visual systems operating in the same range. Then the room lights are turned off, and you can see a dim spot of light on a screen in front of you. Your hand rests on a knob that controls the brightness of the light. Your task is to turn the knob in order to keep the spot of light as dim as possible without making it invisible. You begin by adjusting the light until it's just bright enough to see with your light-adapted vision. As time passes and dark adaptation progresses, you gradually are able to make the spot dimmer and dimmer and still see it. After about 30 minutes, your eyes are fully dark adapted, and the experiment ends. The adjustments you made in the brightness of the light are plotted on a graph, yielding a curve like the blue curve in Figure 2.23 (Rushton, 1965). This figure has a number of interesting features.

The blue curve represents the sensitivity of the retina as a whole (note that increased sensitivity corresponds to a *decrease* in how bright the light needs to be for the participant to just barely see it). If we trace this curve from its beginning, we see that there is an immediate rapid increase in sensitivity as soon as the lights are turned off, until about minute 3, when the curve begins to level off. Then, around minute 8, sensitivity abruptly begins to increase again, at the point labeled *rod–cone break*. After this point, sensitivity continues to increase but at a progressively slower rate, until the curve levels off again around minute 25. The most obvious question about this curve is, What causes the abrupt change in direction at the rod–cone break? The answer, of course, is contained in the name given to this point in the curve: the two different types of photoreceptors—rods and cones—have different dark adaptation curves.

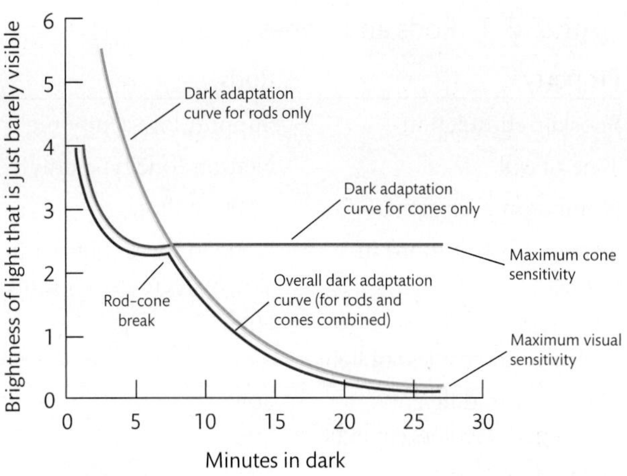

Figure 2.23 Dark Adaptation The sensitivity of the visual system increases with time in the dark during dark adaptation. The blue curve shows overall changes in sensitivity. The red cones-only curve is obtained by making sure that the spot of light falls only on the fovea, where there are no rods. The green rods-only curve is obtained by having a rod monochromat as the participant (rod monochromats have no cones in their retina).

In Figure 2.23, the dark adaptation curve for cones is shown in red and the curve for rods in green. As you can see, during the first 8 minutes or so, when the light still needs to be fairly bright to be visible, the combined dark adaptation curve matches the cone curve. The reason for this is that during this period, cones are more sensitive than rods (shown by the fact that the cone curve is below the rod curve, which means that cones can respond to dimmer lights than rods). As cone sensitivity levels off, rod sensitivity catches up to it, and after the rod–cone break, rods are more sensitive than cones, and the combined curve matches the rod curve. Clearly, this explanation depends on being able to establish the cone and rod curves separately, so we can compare them to the curve for the retina as a whole.

To establish the cone curve, we can exploit the fact that there are no rods in the fovea (see Figure 2.20). If the spot of light during the dark adaptation experiment is small enough and if the participant is instructed to look directly at it at all times, then light from the spot will fall only in the fovea, and we can obtain the dark adaptation curve for cones only. As you can see in Figure 2.23, the upper arm of this cone curve very nicely fits the upper arm of the combined curve.

However, no part of a normal retina is completely free of cones, so how can we establish the dark adaptation curve for rods? We must ask for help from **rod monochromats** like Knut Nordby, whose visual disorder was described at the beginning of this chapter. Rod monochromats have a very rare genetic disorder in which the retina develops with rods but without cones. The green rods-only curve in Figure 2.23 is the dark adaptation curve of rod monochromats, and as you can see, it closely matches the lower arm of the combined curve. Thus, we have shown that the combined dark adaptation curve is a combination of the cones-only curve and the rods-only curve.

rod monochromats Individuals with a very rare genetic disorder in which the retina develops with rods but without cones; used in dark adaptation experiments to establish the curve for rods.

Photopigment Regeneration What is going on in the retina to change sensitivity during dark adaptation? Photopigment molecules that have isomerized from the 11-*cis* to the all-*trans* shape after absorbing a photon of light require a period of time to regenerate—that is, to change back into the 11-*cis* shape so they are again capable of transducing light. This process of **photopigment regeneration** (see Figure 2.19) is relatively rapid for cones—it takes about 5 minutes for cones to go from a state in which most of the photopigment molecules are not light sensitive to a state in which most are. For rods, however, the process is considerably slower, 20–30 minutes (Rushton, 1965). These durations closely match the psychophysically established durations shown in Figure 2.23.

photopigment regeneration The process whereby photopigment molecules change back into the 11-*cis* shape after photoisomerization.

Rod Sensitivity We've noted several times that rods are very sensitive to low levels of light, particularly after full dark adaptation, but just how sensitive are they? In a classic psychophysical experiment, researchers carefully measured the absolute threshold for vision under optimal conditions (including full dark adaptation), and concluded that a rod can respond to as little as a single photon of light (Hecht et al., 1942; this finding has been confirmed more recently with physiological measurements of rod responses). In short, if you recall

TABLE 2.2 Rods and Cones

Property	Rods	Cones
Specialized function	Support low-acuity night vision	Support high-acuity daylight vision
Type of cell	Neuron (one type only)	Neuron (three subtypes)
Number in each retina	~100 million	~5 million
Density (distribution) in retina	None in fovea, highest in ring around fovea, then slowly declining with increasing distance from fovea	Very high in fovea, quickly declining within short distance of fovea, and low in rest of retina
Sensitivity to different amounts (intensities) of light	High	Low
Sensitivity to different wavelengths (colors) of light	Low	High (each subtype has a different spectral sensitivity)
Dark adaptation	Gradual over a period of 25–30 min	Rapid over a period of 3–4 min, then gradually leveling off over the next 4–5 min

that a single photon is the smallest possible amount of light, you can see that rods are as sensitive as they can possibly be!

All the differences between rods and cones that we've discussed—the differences in their sensitivity to different amounts and wavelengths of light, the differences in their distribution within the retina, and the differences in dark adaptation—contribute to the cones' support of high-acuity daylight vision in color and to the rods' support of high-sensitivity, low-acuity, noncolor night vision. Table 2.2 summarizes the main properties of rods and cones and the differences between them.

Check Your Understanding

2.11 Define *spectral sensitivity* and describe how the spectral sensitivity of rods and cones differs.

2.12 Describe how light is transduced into a neural signal.

2.13 What is the operating range of the eye? How is photopigment regeneration involved in the process of dark adaptation, by which the visual system changes its operating range to adjust to changes in overall illumination?

2.14 What is the sensitivity of human rods? How was this first determined?

2.15 In an experiment to determine the number of photons required to activate a single rod (Hecht et al., 1942), researchers shone a spot of light on part of the retina near the fovea but not on the fovea itself. Give at least two reasons why.

Retinal Ganglion Cells: Circuits in the Retina Send Information to the Brain

So far, we've constructed a picture of vision that we can outline like this:

1. Electromagnetic radiation is emitted by many different sources. Some of this radiation is visible light—our eyes can sense it.
2. Light enters our eyes after being transmitted from a source through some medium (e.g., the air) and usually after being reflected from objects and surfaces in the environment. The pattern of light entering our eyes is called the *optic array;* it contains information about the color, shape, and layout of objects and surfaces in the scene. The task of the eyes is to transform the pattern of light into neural signals carrying this information to the brain.

3. The eyes accomplish the first part of this task by regulating the amount of light reaching the retina (by adjusting the size of the pupil) and by making sure the light is properly focused on the retina (by accommodation of the lens) to form a useful retinal image.
4. The light forming the retinal image strikes photoreceptors (rods and cones) in the retina, which transduce the light into neural signals that are propagated to other retinal neurons—horizontal cells, bipolar cells, amacrine cells, and, finally, retinal ganglion cells (RGCs). The processes of dark adaptation and light adaptation ensure that this happens effectively under a wide range of environmental lighting conditions, from very dim to very bright.
5. The axons of the RGCs bundle together to form the optic nerve, which carries action potentials from the RGCs to the brain.

At first glance, the last two steps in this process might seem fairly simple and direct. For example, suppose we look at the retina as a surface divided into a grid of tiny squares, with each square corresponding to the location of a single photoreceptor. At any given moment, each photoreceptor is sensing light of a particular brightness (number of photons making up the light) and particular color (wavelengths making up the light). Each photoreceptor transduces this light into a neural signal that depends on the brightness and wavelength. We could then hypothesize that the neural signal from each photoreceptor is transmitted basically unchanged through the other retinal neurons and the optic nerve to the brain, which processes all the signals from all the photoreceptors to construct a visual perception of the retinal image.

However, a quick glance back at Figure 2.16 shows that the signals received and sent by a single RGC to the brain are the result of signals transmitted through a complex neural circuit that may involve dozens or even hundreds of other cells. A critical function of these circuits is to encode information about the location of edges—the boundaries of objects in the retinal image—as the first step in allowing us to recognize what is where in the scene we're viewing. In this section, we'll focus on two important aspects of the neural circuits of the retina: first, the role of convergence, which results from the many-to-one patterns of connection illustrated in Figure 2.16; and second, how convergent circuits that include excitatory and inhibitory synaptic connections can produce signals carrying information about useful features of the retinal image—in particular, the location of edges.

Convergence in Retinal Circuits

Figure 2.24a illustrates retinal circuits with different patterns of connectivity. The circuits at the left and in the middle have many-to-one patterns of connection—a single RGC receives signals from multiple photoreceptors (the signals are transmitted via an intervening network of horizontal, bipolar, and amacrine cells, but for simplicity, these intervening cells aren't shown in the figure). Circuits with many-to-one patterns of connection are said to exhibit **convergence,** because signals from multiple photoreceptors *converge* onto a single RGC (Stirling, 2004). As you can see, different retinal circuits can show different degrees of convergence, from high convergence involving many photoreceptors, to moderate convergence involving fewer photoreceptors, to no convergence at all, in which case the pattern of connection is one-to-one (one RGC receives signals from just one photoreceptor).

convergence A property of retinal circuits in which multiple photoreceptors send signals to one RGC.

Circuits with convergence have a property called **spatial summation.** This is illustrated in Figure 2.24b, which shows that signals from the photoreceptors in the circuit, which occupies some small space on the retina (hence, "spatial"), add up (hence, "summation") to affect the response of the RGC. That is, the firing rate of the RGC increases as the number of photoreceptors that are activated by light increases. Thus, in Figure 2.24b, the RGC has a low firing rate when a small spot of light stimulates just one of the photoreceptors in the circuit, a moderate firing rate when two photoreceptors are stimulated, and a high firing rate when all four photoreceptors are stimulated.

spatial summation A property of retinal circuits with convergence in which signals from photoreceptors in some small space on the retina summate (add up) to affect the response of the RGC in the circuit.

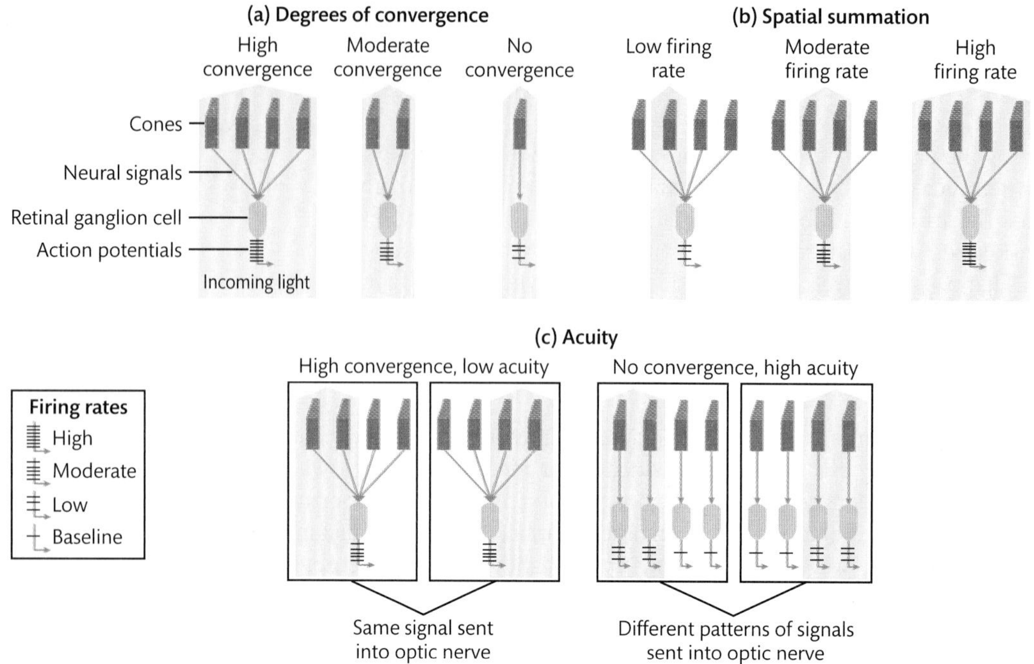

Figure 2.24 Convergence in Retinal Circuits (a) Retinal circuits differ in their degree of convergence. A highly convergent circuit might involve hundreds of photoreceptors sending signals that converge onto a single RGC, but for simplicity, the example illustrated here contains just four photoreceptors (all cones), and the circuit with moderate convergence contains just two photoreceptors. Both of these patterns of connectivity are many-to-one (multiple photoreceptors connect to one RGC). In contrast, the circuit with no convergence has a one-to-one pattern of connectivity (one photoreceptor connects to one RGC). (b) In a convergent circuit, each photoreceptor responds with neural signals when stimulated by light. *Spatial summation* means that the RGC's response is based on adding up (summating) the signals from all the photoreceptors being stimulated in the space on the retina occupied by the circuit. Thus, an RGC that receives signals from just one photoreceptor (left) responds with a low firing rate, in contrast to the moderate firing rate of an RGC receiving signals from two photoreceptor (center) and the high firing rate from four photoreceptors (right). (c) No matter which two photoreceptors are stimulated by spots of light in this convergent circuit (left), the response from the RGC is the same, thus providing no information about the difference in location of the two spots of light. In contrast, the pattern of RGC responses from the circuits with no convergence (right) is different whenever different photoreceptors are stimulated, thus providing precise information about the location of the light.

The degree of convergence affects two important characteristics of retinal circuits:

- The higher the degree of convergence, the more the circuit supports sensitivity to dim light, because the signals from all the photoreceptors in the circuit are combined by being funneled onto a single RGC.
- The lower the degree of convergence, the more the circuit supports visual acuity, because different spatial patterns of light stimulate different photoreceptors, and the responses from the different photoreceptors aren't combined but are sent to separate RGCs.

The relationship between degree of convergence and sensitivity to dim light reflects the fact that a convergent circuit acts like a funnel. In Figure 2.24a, let's suppose that the incoming light is very dim, so that the neural signals it evokes from a single photoreceptor are barely sufficient to stimulate the RGC to fire at a low rate, just above baseline. This is shown in the circuit with no convergence. In contrast, in the circuits with moderate and high convergence, light with the same low intensity evokes signals from two or four photoreceptors, which means that the signals funneled down to the RGC deliver more stimulation (in accord with spatial summation), and the RGC's firing rate is correspondingly higher. Thus, the more convergent the circuit, the stronger the response to dim light.

Now let's see why less convergent retinal circuits provide higher visual acuity than more convergent circuits. Acuity is the ability to see spatial details clearly, as when you're trying to thread a needle. In order to accomplish that task, you have to be able to tell exactly where the tip of the thread and the hole in the needle are, so you can poke the thread through the hole. Figure 2.24c illustrates a similar scenario involving spots of light instead of thread and needle. In the high-convergence circuit, a spot of light that strikes the retina at a location where it stimulates the two leftmost photoreceptors evokes the same response from the RGC as a spot of light at a location where it stimulates the two rightmost photoreceptors. In other words, the response of the RGC contains no information that the brain could use to perceive that the two spots are in different locations.

Now consider the circuits with no convergence in Figure 2.24c. The four photoreceptors in these circuits occupy the same size area on the retina as the four photoreceptors in the high-convergence circuit. In this case, however, different RGCs respond when a spot of light stimulates the two leftmost photoreceptors versus the two rightmost photoreceptors, and these different patterns of response enable the brain to perceive the spots as occupying two distinct locations.

As you can see from Figure 2.24c, the nonconvergent circuits that support high acuity require a higher density of RGCs than do convergent circuits (where density refers to the number of RGCs per unit area on the retina). In general, the density of RGCs is much greater near the fovea than in the periphery of the retina, indicating that the fovea contains mainly circuits with little or no convergence and that the periphery contains mainly circuits with greater convergence. This explains why acuity is higher in the fovea than in the periphery, whereas sensitivity to dim light is higher in the periphery than in the fovea.

Receptive Fields

The simple circuits shown in Figure 2.24 illustrate the concept of the **receptive field** of a sensory neuron: the region of a sensory surface (in this case, the retina) in which the presence of a stimulus causes a change in the neuron's firing rate (Hartline, 1938; Kuffler, 1953; Martin & Grünert, 2004; Stirling, 2004). The American physiologist H. K. Hartline, who won the 1967 Nobel Prize in Medicine or Physiology, was the first to use the term to apply to visual responses; he was also the first to record action potentials in individual axons of vertebrate RGCs (1938), and this enabled him to map the region of the retina that, when illuminated by a spot of light, produced a change in the firing rate of a single RGC (1940).

receptive field The region of a sensory surface that, when stimulated, causes a change in the firing rate of a neuron that "monitors" that region of the surface; the receptive field of an RGC is the region of the retina occupied by the photoreceptors to which the RGC is connected.

H. K. Hartline (1903–1983). [Mary Evans Picture Library/ The Image Works]

In the leftmost circuit in Figure 2.24a, the receptive field of the RGC is the region of the retina occupied by the four photoreceptors in the circuit, because the RGC's firing rate changes when that region (or any part of it) is stimulated by light. In contrast, in the rightmost circuit in Figure 2.24a, the receptive field of the RGC is the much smaller region of the retina occupied by just one photoreceptor. One can think of the receptive field of an RGC as the part of the retina monitored by that cell.

Note that the definition of a receptive field refers to a *change* in the firing rate of the neuron—not necessarily an increase. Recall from Chapter 1 that an unstimulated neuron (e.g., an RGC with a receptive field that's receiving no light) has a baseline firing rate of a few spikes per second. If an RGC is part of a circuit in which some of the neural connections are inhibitory, then stimulation of its receptive field by light could result in a decrease in the firing rate of the RGC, rather than an increase. This kind of response plays a role in representing dark objects on a light background, among other things.

Size and Distribution of Receptive Fields

Each human retina contains about 1 million RGCs, compared with about 100 million rods and about 5 million cones. That is, the ratio of photoreceptors to RGCs is roughly 100:1. However, this doesn't mean that neural circuits throughout the retina tend to have about 100 photoreceptors each and that RGCs throughout the retina tend have about the same size receptive fields. Rather, the number of photoreceptors in retinal circuits and, consequently, the size of receptive fields vary greatly with the position in the retina.

In the fovea, many RGCs have very small receptive fields, based on underlying circuits with little or no convergence, and as we have seen, such circuits support high acuity. As the distance of RGCs from the fovea increases, receptive fields get larger, because the

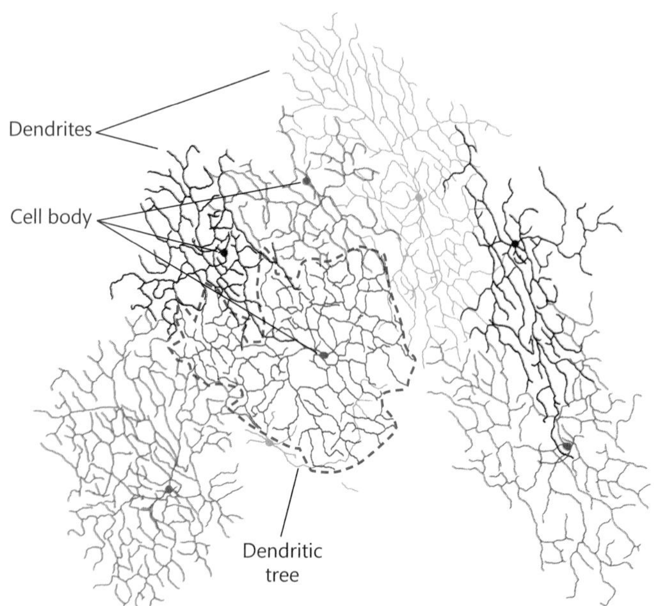

Figure 2.25 Retinal Ganglion Cell Dendritic Trees The size of an RGC's receptive field depends on the size of its dendritic tree. This micrograph shows the dendritic trees of seven RGCs in a rabbit retina. Note how the trees (and, therefore, the RGCs' receptive fields) tile this part of the retina, with few gaps. (Adapted and photo from Vaney, 1994.)

increasingly large numbers of photoreceptors in the underlying circuits take up increasingly more space (Watanabe & Rodieck, 1989). And as we have seen, this means increasing convergence and increasing sensitivity to dim light, but decreasing acuity.

The correspondence between the size of an RGC's receptive field and the number of photoreceptors in the circuit can be expressed in another way: the size of the receptive field depends on the size of the RGC's dendritic tree. To see why, look back at Figure 2.16 and imagine what this figure would look like if it included hundreds of photoreceptors and many dozens of horizontal, bipolar, and amacrine cells—each RGC would be receiving signals from a large number of bipolar cells and amacrine cells occupying some significant area of the retina. In order to receive those signals, the RGC's dendrites would have to spread across that area to make synapses with the axon terminals of all those amacrine cells and bipolar cells, resulting in a large dendritic tree. Figure 2.25 shows a top view of such dendritic trees in the retina of a rabbit.

This description of receptive field sizes is made more complex by the fact that there are over 20 different types of RGCs, each of which sends different kinds of visual information to the brain and each of which has its own characteristic receptive field sizes (Nassi & Callaway, 2009). Consider, for example, two of the more well studied types of RGCs, known as *midget RGCs* and *parasol RGCs;* both types exhibit the increase in receptive field size with increasing distance from the fovea (measured by the size of their dendritic trees), but at any given distance midget RGCs have relatively small receptive fields and parasol RGCs have relatively large receptive fields. Figure 2.26 illustrates this difference in receptive field size between midget and parasol RGCs (Watanabe & Rodieck, 1989). It also illustrates an important aspect of receptive field distributions: the receptive fields of each type of RGC (not just midget and parasol RGCs) tile the retina, with much overlap and few gaps (Gauthier et al., 2009). (In Chapter 3, we'll take a look at the functional differences between these two types of RGCs, plus a third type known as *bistratified RGCs.*)

Given the large number and variety of neurons involved in most retinal circuits, the complexity of the neural connections in those circuits, the large variety of different types of RGCs, and the near-total retinal coverage by the receptive fields of each type of RGC, it's clear that the signals sent to the brain by RGCs represent an extremely rich and sensitive response to light.

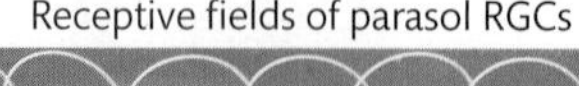

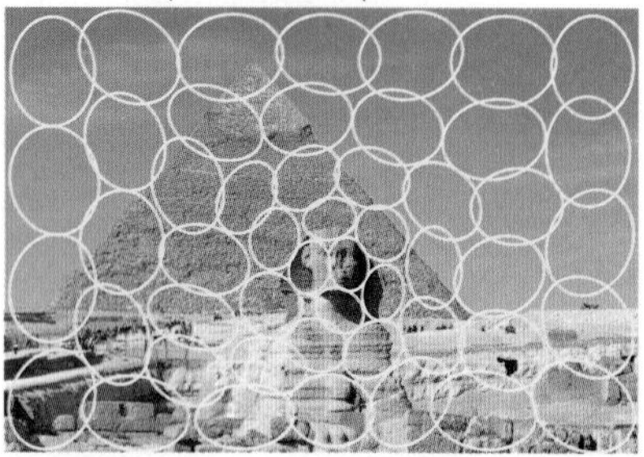

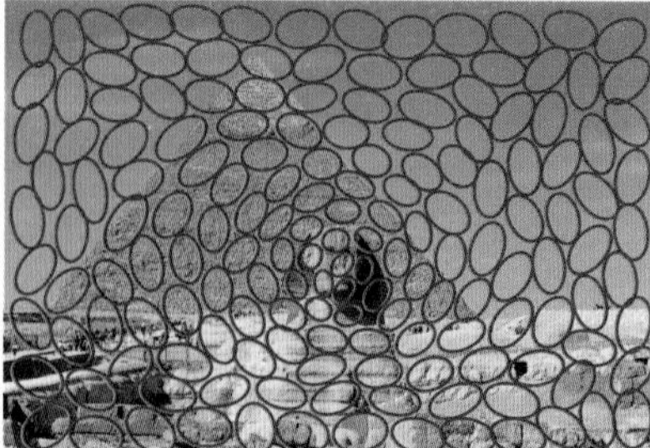

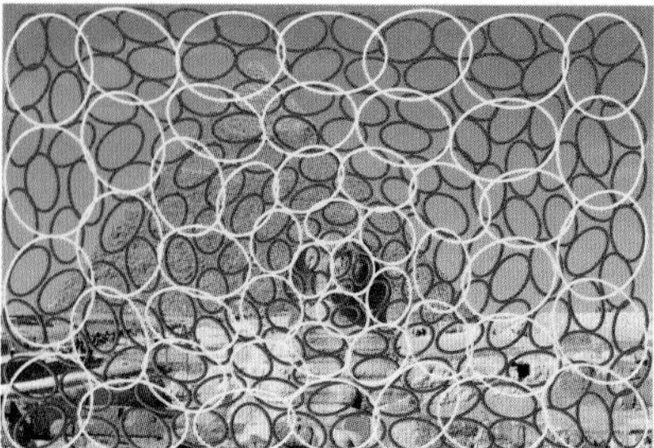

Figure 2.26 Receptive Field Sizes and Distributions This figure illustrates the average difference in size between the receptive fields of parasol RGCs (yellow) and midget RGCs (purple), two of the more than 20 different types of RGCs in the retina. Note how the receptive fields of each type increase in size from the fovea toward the periphery (here, we're assuming the eye is pointed at the center of the photo) and how the receptive fields of each type form a tight mosaic over the surface of the retina. (For clarity, the figure shows much less overlap of the receptive fields of each type of RGC than is actually the case.) (Based on Watanabe & Rodieck, 1989.) [Jon Arnold Images Ltd/Alamy]

Retinal Ganglion Cells Have Center-Surround Receptive Fields

The American physiologist Stephen W. Kuffler discovered that RGCs in the mammalian retina have a **center–surround receptive field**—stimulation of the center of the receptive field evokes a different response from the RGC than does stimulation of the surrounding portion of the receptive field. As shown in Figure 2.27, center–surround receptive fields can be either on-center or off-center, with correspondingly different patterns of response from the RGCs (Kuffler, 1953):

- Cells with **on-center receptive fields** increase their firing rate when the amount of light striking the center of the cell's receptive field increases relative to the amount of light striking the surround. This can occur either by increasing the amount striking the center (Figure 2.27a) or by decreasing the amount striking the surround (Figure 2.27d). The RGC responds in the opposite way to relative decreases of light in the center—for example, when the relative amount of light striking the surround increases, on-center cells decrease their firing rate (Figure 2.27b and c). As shown in Figure 2.27a, the **preferred stimulus** for an RGC with an on-center receptive

center-surround receptive field An RGC receptive field in which the center of the receptive field responds differently to stimulation than the surrounding portion of the field.

on-center receptive fields Receptive fields of RGCs with center-surround structure in which the RGCs increase their firing rate when the amount of light striking the center of the receptive field increases relative to the amount of light striking the surround.

preferred stimulus The type of stimulus that produces a neuron's maximum firing rate; for RGCs with on-center receptive fields, the preferred stimulus is a spot of light that exactly fills the center of the receptive field.

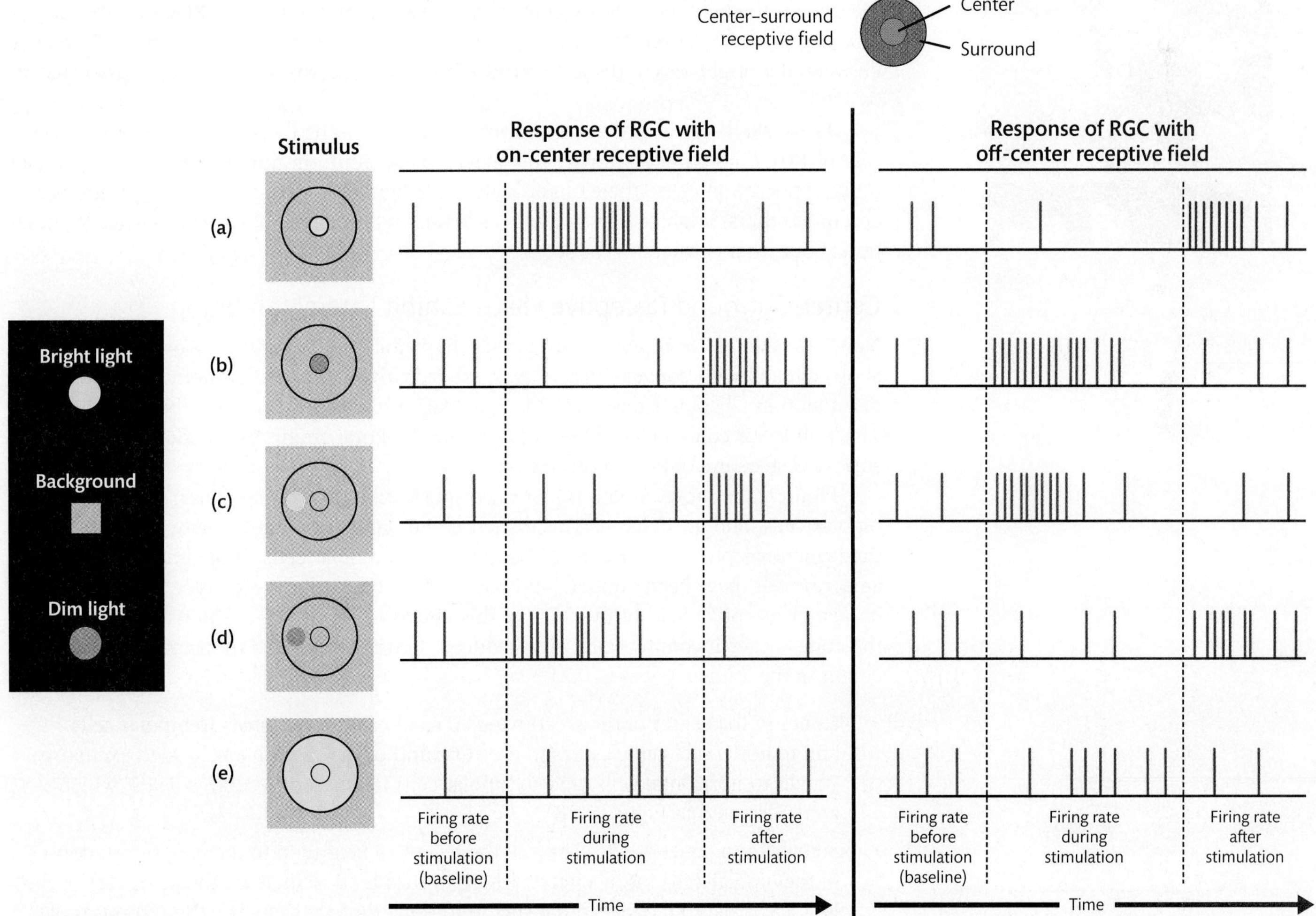

Figure 2.27 On-Center and Off-Center Receptive Fields Retinal ganglion cells have center-surround receptive fields, which can be on-center or off-center. (a)–(d) These two types of RGCs respond differently to stimuli that increase or decrease the amount of light striking the center versus the surround (the retina is illuminated by a medium gray background when the stimuli are off, as indicated by the gray square behind each stimulus). (e) When both the center and the surround are illuminated by a uniform light, neither type of RGC produces much of a change in firing rate, showing that these neurons respond most to luminance contrast—a difference in the brightness of the light striking the center versus the surround.

Demonstration 2.6 Receptive Fields of Retinal Ganglion Cells Control the intensity, size, and location of spots of light striking the receptive fields of retinal ganglion cells, to map their responses.

off-center receptive fields Receptive fields of RGCs with center–surround structure in which the RGCs decrease their firing rate when the amount of light striking the center of the receptive field decreases relative to the amount of light striking the surround.

Stephen W. Kuffler (1913–1980). [The Alan Mason Chesney Medical Archives of the Johns Hopkins Medical Institutions]

field—that is, the stimulus that causes the greatest increase in the cell's firing rate—is a spot of bright light that covers the entire center of the receptive field without touching the surround. (A smaller spot doesn't maximally stimulate the cell, and a larger spot produces a lower firing rate because the surround is partly stimulated.)

- Cells with **off-center receptive fields** increase their firing rate when the amount of light striking the center decreases relative to the amount striking the surround (Figure 2.27b and c)—a response pattern that's important when we're looking at dark objects on a bright background. These RGCs decrease their firing rate when the amount of light striking the center increases relative to the amount striking the surround (Figure 2.27a and d). For an RGC with an off-center receptive field, the preferred stimulus would be a dark spot covering the entire center without touching the surround (Figure 2.27b).

Figure 2.27e shows that for both types of RGCs, light that uniformly covers both the center and the surround causes very little change in the firing rate, because the response prompted by stimulation of the center is largely "canceled out" by the response prompted by stimulation of the surround. (In Figure 2.27e, the light covering the center and surround is bright, but the responses of the two types of RGCs would look much the same if the light were dim.) This reveals a very important point: RGCs don't respond much to uniform illumination; rather, they respond to luminance contrast, a difference between the brightness of the light striking the center versus the surround of their receptive field.

As we shall see, response to contrast is typical of sensory neurons in general. In the case of RGCs, it's easy to see why this makes sense: uniform illumination doesn't contain much information (just "there's light here"); but light that's present in some locations and absent in others, brighter now than it was before, red here and blue there, carries information about what is where in the scene.

Center–Surround Receptive Fields Exhibit Lateral Inhibition

Now let's take the concepts covered in this chapter about different types of retinal neurons, about circuits with convergence, and about receptive fields and combine them with our discussion in Chapter 1 about excitatory versus inhibitory connections between neurons. This will let us construct a picture of the type of neural circuit that underlies the center–surround structure of RGC receptive fields.

Figure 2.28 shows a convergent on-center circuit containing cones, horizontal cells, bipolar cells, and an RGC. A typical such circuit could contain as many as several hundred photoreceptors and dozens of horizontal and bipolar cells. (For simplicity, rods and amacrine cells have been omitted, and only two or three cells of each type are shown.) The on-center receptive field of the RGC in this circuit is the region of the retina occupied by the cones. After incoming light is transduced, neural signals are transmitted through the circuit in the following way:

- Cones in the center of the receptive field send excitatory signals to bipolar cells and to horizontal cells. Cones in the surround of the receptive field send excitatory signals to horizontal cells (and to bipolar cells in adjacent receptive fields, which aren't depicted in Figure 2.28).
- Signals from cones in the center of the receptive field tend to increase the responses of the bipolar cells in the circuit, which in turn tend to increase the firing rate of the RGC. Signals from cones in the surround don't directly influence the responses of bipolar cells, but they do influence the signals from horizontal cells back to cones in the center and thereby exert an indirect influence on bipolar cell responses.
- In response to signals from cones, horizontal cells send inhibitory signals back to the same cones and to adjacent cones; these inhibitory signals tend to decrease the strength of the signals sent by the cones. In addition, excitatory interconnections

between horizontal cells enable signals to spread laterally (horizontally) across the circuit. In Figure 2.28, for example, the horizontal cell on the left doesn't send inhibitory signals directly to the cone on the right, but it influences that cone indirectly via the horizontal cell on the right.

- The inhibitory influence of the horizontal cells tends to decrease the response of cones within a relatively large region, including both the center and surround of the receptive field.
- The combination of center and surround influences on the bipolar cells determines the strength of the signals that the bipolar cells send to the RGC, and this in turn determines the firing rate of the RGC as it sends action potentials into the optic nerve.

Thus, the signals sent by an RGC aren't simply the result of summing the activity of the photoreceptors in the RGC's receptive field. Rather, the RGC's response reflects a balance of the excitatory signals sent by center photoreceptors and the inhibitory signals sent by horizontal cells (Wilson, 2004). These transmissions of inhibitory signals, discovered in the 1950s, are collectively referred to as **lateral inhibition** (Hartline & Ratliff, 1958; Kuffler, 1953).

lateral inhibition Inhibitory neural signals transmitted by horizontal cells in retinal circuits.

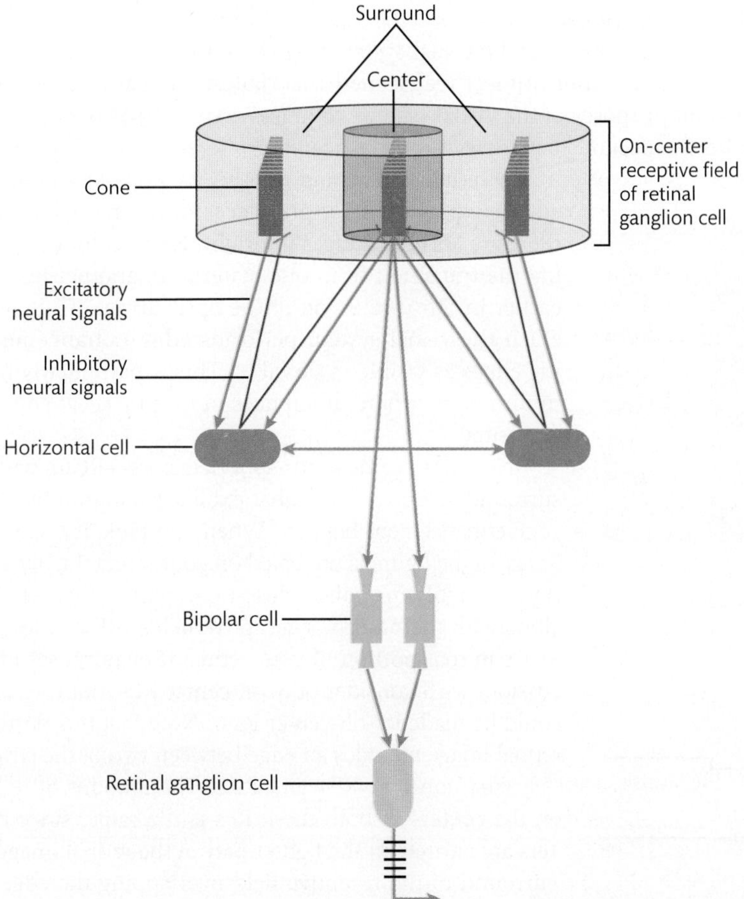

Figure 2.28 Lateral Inhibition in Circuits Underlying Center-Surround Receptive Fields *Lateral inhibition* refers to the inhibitory signals sent by horizontal cells, which modify the responses of photoreceptors and provide a way in which neural activity in one part of the circuit can influence neural activity in adjacent parts of the circuit. In this circuit underlying an on-center receptive field, signals from cones in the surround tend to reduce the responses of the bipolar cells, whereas signals from the cone in the center tend to strengthen bipolar cell responses. The RGC response is based on the signals it receives from the bipolar cells and therefore depends on the balance between the signals from cones in the center and surround.

Ernst Mach (1838–1916).
[Wellcome Library, London]

Edge Enhancement: An Example of How It All Works Together

Judging by the descriptions and discussions up to this point, an RGC with a center–surround receptive field is a "spot detector": such a cell fires most vigorously when a spot of light having a particular size, position, brightness, and color is present in the retinal image. However, most of vision does not involve correctly perceiving the location and other characteristics of little spots of light. How, then, do these spot detectors and the retinal circuits that support them actually help us see "what is where"?

Figure 2.29 illustrates a striking perceptual illusion that helps answer this question. The vertical strips in the figure range from dark gray on the left to light gray on the right. In reality, each strip is uniform in brightness across its entire width. This is indicated by the "Physical intensity" graph at the bottom of the figure, which shows that brightness takes a small step up at the edge between any two strips and then remains constant until the next edge is reached. Perceptually, however, the brightness of each strip appears to be a gradient, from slightly lighter on the left to slightly darker on the right. The "Perceived intensity" graph indicates this: brightness appears to take a big step up at each edge and then appears to gradually decline until the next edge. These illusory changes in brightness near each edge are called *Mach bands,* after their discoverer, the Austrian physicist Ernst Mach (Ratliff, 1965).

edge enhancement A process by which the visual system makes edges as visible as possible, facilitating perception of where one object or surface ends in the retinal image and another begins.

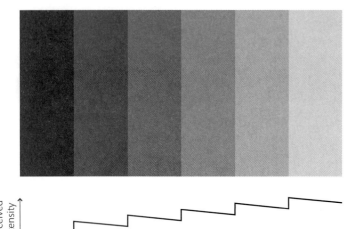

Is this illusion a failure of the visual system to give us an accurate perception of the figure? Well, yes, it is. But in most real scenes, this "failure" actually serves one of the most important purposes of the visual system: to perceive the shapes of objects and surfaces. A crucial aspect of shape perception is perceiving where one object or surface ends in the retinal image and another begins—that is, perceiving edges. Typically, edges are places in the retinal image where there are abrupt changes in brightness or color or both, marking the transition from one material to another (as described earlier in our discussion of the optic array). Thus, we'll benefit if the visual system performs **edge enhancement**, making edges as visible as possible. This is particularly important in dim light, where differences in brightness at edges may be very small.

Now let's see how our spot detectors—RGCs with center–surround receptive fields that exhibit lateral inhibition—make edge enhancement happen. When you look at Figure 2.29, an image of the figure is projected on your retina. Figure 2.30 illustrates a highly magnified close-up of part of that retinal image, along with the on-center receptive fields (RFs) of four selected RGCs in that portion of your retina. (For purposes of this discussion, we'll consider only on-center RFs, but the same point could be made for off-center RFs.) Note that this portion of the retinal image includes an edge between two of the strips.

First consider RF1 and RF2. The amount of light falling on the centers of both these RFs is the same, since both centers are entirely in the lighter part of the retinal image. But the surround of the receptive field overlapping the edge (RF1) is receiving less light than the surround of RF2, because part of RF1's surround is in the darker part of the retinal image. This means that the RGC associated with RF1 is receiving less inhibitory input from its surround (due to lateral inhibition from horizontal cells) than RF2's RGC. Therefore, the firing rate of RF1's cell will be greater than that of RF2's cell, and the part of the retinal image covered by RF1 will appear brighter than the part covered by RF2.

Figure 2.29 An Illusion with a Purpose: Edge Enhancement Each strip is uniform in brightness across its width, as indicated by the "Physical intensity" graph. But each appears to be lighter at the left and darker at the right, as indicated by the "Perceived intensity" graph. The edges where the strips meet are perceptually enhanced by an illusory increase in contrast at the edge—the apparently darkest part of the strip on the left is next to the apparently lightest part of the strip on the right. (You can verify that the individual strips are, in fact, of uniform brightness. Just look at each one separately by masking off the strips on either side of it with pieces of paper.)

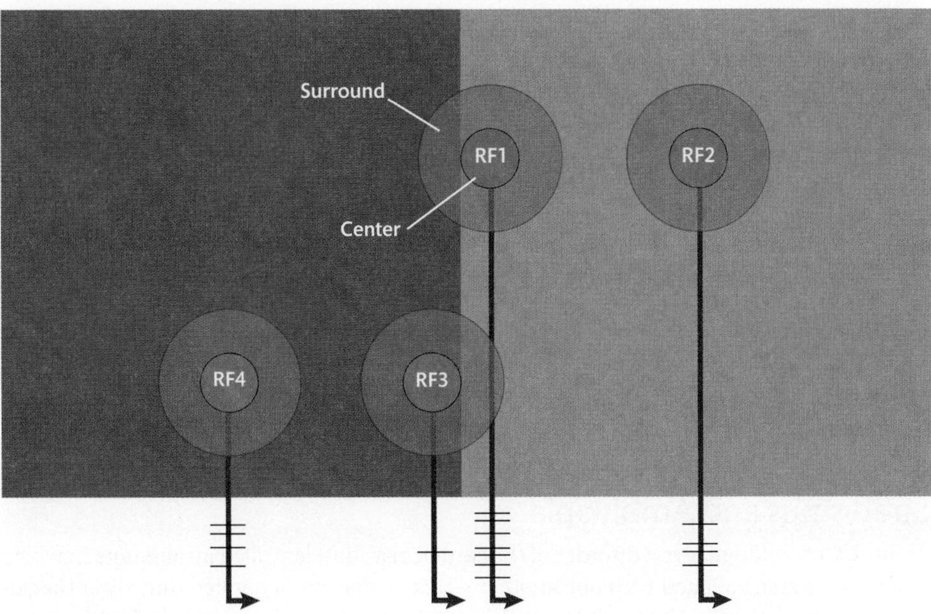

Figure 2.30 **Center-Surround Receptive Fields with Lateral Inhibition Enhance Edges** This enlargement of a small part of the retinal image of the strips in Figure 2.29 also includes the on-center receptive fields (RFs) of four RGCs near an edge between two strips. The differences in the responses of the RGCs lead to edge enhancement.

Now consider RF3 and RF4. Again, the centers are receiving equal amounts of light, since both centers are entirely in the darker part of the retinal image. But in this case, the surround of the receptive field overlapping the edge (RF3) is receiving *more* light than the surround of RF4, because part of RF3's surround is in the lighter part of the retinal image. This means that the RGC associated with RF3 is receiving more inhibitory input from its surround than RF4's RGC. Therefore, the firing rate of RF3's cell will be less than that of RF4's cell, and the part of the retinal image covered by RF3 will appear darker than the part covered by RF4.

If we extend this picture to all the RGCs with RFs near the edge, we can see that the part of the retinal image just to the right of the edge will appear lighter than parts further to the right, and the part of the retinal image just to the left of the edge will appear darker than parts further to the left. That is, the *apparent* contrast in brightness at the edge is greater than the actual contrast—our spot detectors have perceptually enhanced the edge. Thus, the visual system is accomplishing something useful through this failure of accurate vision. In this case, edges are enhanced in order to improve our ability to see shapes (the individual strips). In the chapters ahead, we'll encounter other illusions that lead to similar insights about how the visual system optimizes our ability to see "what is where."

Check Your Understanding

2.16 What is the difference between a retinal circuit with high convergence and a retinal circuit with no convergence? State one advantage and one disadvantage of high convergence. Are highly convergent circuits more common in the fovea or away from the fovea?

2.17 True or false? The receptive fields of parasol RGCs almost completely cover the retina but the receptive fields of midget RGCs are separated by large gaps.

2.18 Describe the difference between on-center and off-center receptive fields.

2.19 In retinal circuits with lateral inhibition, which types of cells are responsible for the inhibitory effects that lead to edge enhancement?

2.20 What is edge enhancement, and why is it a useful illusion?

Disorders of Vision

As we have seen throughout this chapter, the human eye is an exquisitely complex device, with mechanisms that must work together in a delicate balance to admit light, focus and transduce the retinal image, and send neural signals packed with useful information to the brain. This complexity means that there is a lot that can go wrong. In this section, we'll discuss a few relatively common disorders of vision.

Strabismus and Amblyopia

strabismus A disorder of the extraocular muscles in which the two eyes are not aligned with one another, resulting in a double image, which impairs binocular depth perception.

amblyopia A condition in which both eyes develop normally but the neural signals from one eye aren't processed properly, so that fine vision doesn't develop in that eye.

About 2% of children have a disorder of the extraocular muscles called **strabismus** in which the two eyes aren't aligned with one another—that is, one eye is pointed directly at the target, while the other is pointed off-target (Kleinstein, 1984). This results in a double image, which impairs binocular depth perception (see Chapter 6). Another possible consequence of strabismus is **amblyopia,** a condition in which both eyes develop normally but the neural signals from the misaligned eye aren't processed properly, so that fine vision doesn't develop in that eye (Kleinstein, 1984). Amblyopia can also be caused by poor uncorrected vision in one eye.

Different types of strabismus can be corrected with eyeglasses, extraocular surgery, or a combination of these methods; the goal is to balance the strength in the extraocular muscles so the eyes can work together effectively. Amblyopia is often treated by correcting the vision of the poorer eye with glasses and by patching the stronger eye so that the poorer eye is used more and becomes more functional. This treatment works best if it is started before the age of five—that is, before the early stage of neural development of the visual system is complete.

Disorders of Accommodation: Myopia, Hyperopia, Presbyopia, and Astigmatism

In the section on the lens, we saw how accommodation—the automatic process of contracting or relaxing the ciliary muscles to adjust the shape of the lens—ensures that the light entering the eye is properly focused on the retina. Some people's eyes, however, are a little too long or short (in terms of the length of the optic axis—see Figure 2.8), and accommodation can't fully compensate (Kleinstein, 1984). Figure 2.31 compares normal vision to what happens in these cases:

myopia (or *nearsightedness*) A condition in which the optic axis is too long and accommodation cannot make the lens thin enough to focus light from a distant object on the retina, so the light comes to a focus in front of the retina, and the image on the retina is blurry; the person can see nearby objects clearly but not distant objects.

hyperopia (or *farsightedness*) A condition in which the optic axis is too short and accommodation cannot make the lens thick enough to focus light from a nearby object on the retina, so the light comes to a focus behind the retina, and the image on the retina is blurry; the person can see distant objects clearly but not nearby objects.

- When the optic axis is too long and the person is looking at a distant object, accommodation makes the lens thin, but cannot make it thin enough (Figure 2.31, top): light comes to a focus in front of the retina, and the image on the retina is blurry. This condition is called **myopia** (or *nearsightedness*) because the person can see nearby objects clearly but not distant objects.
- When the optic axis is too short and the person is looking at a nearby object, accommodation makes the lens thick, but cannot make it thick enough (Figure 2.31, bottom): light comes to a focus behind the retina, and the image on the retina is again blurry. This condition is called **hyperopia** (or *farsightedness*) because the person can see distant objects clearly but not nearby objects.

Myopia and hyperopia are usually detected early in life and corrected with eyeglasses (or contact lenses). The lenses in the eyeglasses refract (bend) the light entering the eye just

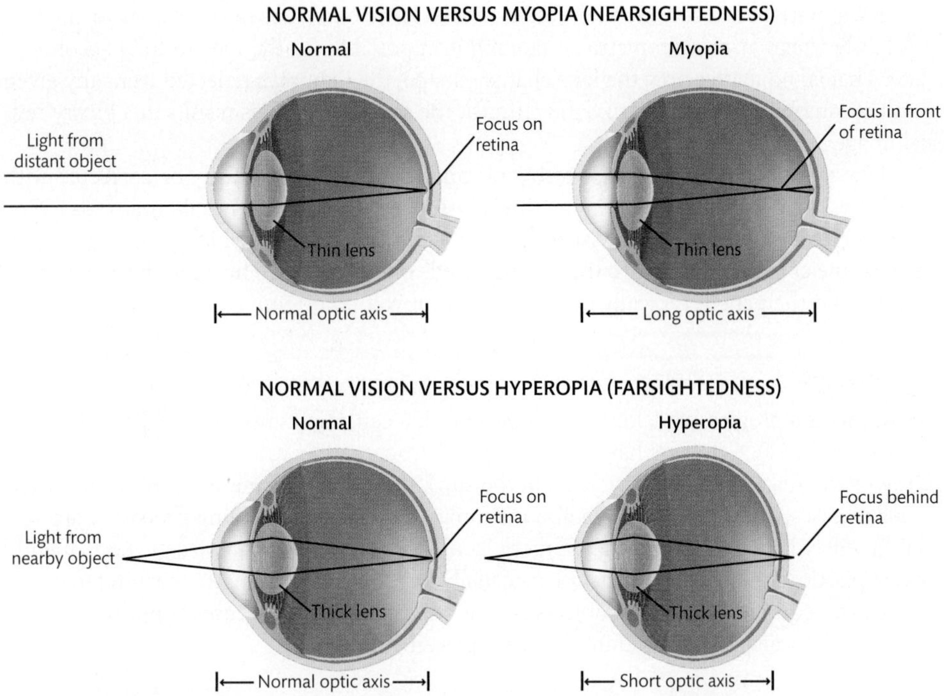

Figure 2.31 Myopia and Hyperopia (top left) Accommodation makes the lens thin so the light from a distant object focuses on the retina. (top right) But if the optic axis is too long, the lens can't become thin enough; the light focuses in front of the retina, and the image on the retina is blurry. This is myopia, or nearsightedness. (bottom left) Accommodation makes the lens thick so the light from a nearby object focuses on the retina. (bottom right) But if the optic axis is too short, the lens can't become thick enough; the light focuses behind the retina, and the image on the retina is blurry. This is hyperopia, or farsightedness.

enough to compensate for the person's eye shape, enabling the lens in the person's eye to focus the image on the retina.

Another condition involving accommodation, **presbyopia**, could be called "old-sightedness." The term is derived from Greek (*presbus,* meaning "old man"; *opia,* meaning "eye") and refers to a common occurrence—the lens becomes less elastic with age (the condition affects many people by their late 40s). As in hyperopia, the result is that accommodation can't make the lens thick enough to properly focus light from nearby objects (distance vision is usually not affected). The closest distance at which a person can bring an object into focus is called the **near point,** so presbyopia is characterized by a progressive increase in the distance from the eye to the near point as the person ages (see Figure 2.32).

presbyopia A common condition in which the lens becomes less elastic with age, characterized by a progressive increase in the distance from the eye to the near point as the person ages; as in hyperopia, accommodation can't make the lens thick enough to focus light from nearby objects.

near point The closest distance at which a person can bring an object into focus; presbyopia is characterized by a progressive increase in the distance from the eye to the near point as the person ages.

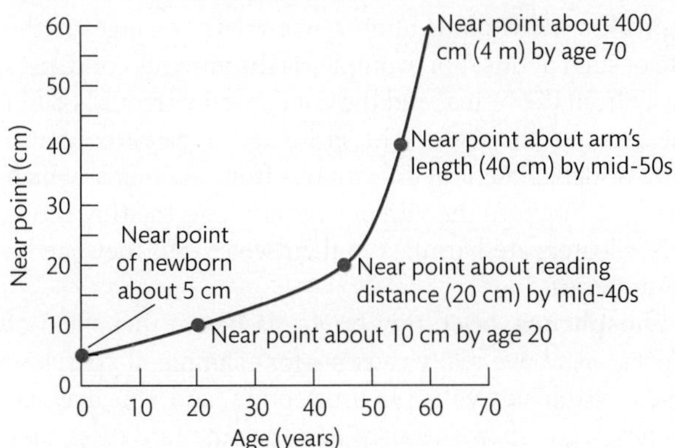

Figure 2.32 Presbyopia: The Near Point Recedes with Age The near point is the closest distance at which an object can be seen in focus. As you age, the lenses in your eyes becomes less elastic (less able to change shape during accommodation), which means that the near point gets progressively further away. This process is known as *presbyopia*. Typically, the near point approaches reading distance (20 cm) by the mid-40s, at which time many people begin to use reading glasses.

astigmatism A condition in which the curvature of the cornea or lens is slightly irregular or asymmetrical, making it impossible for the lens to fully accommodate.

LASIK Surgery to reshape the cornea in order to correct disorders of accommodation.

Astigmatism is a common condition in which the curvature of the cornea or the lens is slightly irregular or asymmetrical, making it impossible for the lens to fully accommodate. That is, no matter how the lens changes shape, the light rays reflected from any given point on an object won't all strike the retina at the same point. This results in a blurry retinal image.

Like myopia and hyperopia, presbyopia and astigmatism can easily be corrected with eyeglasses or contact lenses. An increasingly popular and cost-effective alternative is a type of surgery called **LASIK** (laser-assisted in situ keratomileusis), in which a laser is used to reshape the cornea according to the specific needs of the patient. This is an outpatient procedure, and the patient typically experiences improved vision immediately.

Cataracts

cataract A progressive "clouding" of the lens that can, if left untreated, lead to blindness.

A **cataract** is a progressive "clouding" of the lens that can, if left untreated, lead to blindness (Ginsberg, 1984). Cataracts have several possible causes: they can result from exposure to ultraviolet radiation (e.g., many years in the sun), they can be a side-effect of diabetes and other diseases, and they can come about simply as a result of the aging process. Cataracts can be effectively treated through surgery to remove the lens and replace it permanently with a plastic lens. The replacement lens usually has a fixed focal length, meaning that eyeglasses are required to focus on objects at other distances (in some cases, a multifocal lens, similar to bifocals, can be used in cataract replacement).

High Intraocular Pressure: Glaucoma

glaucoma A condition in which the intraocular pressure is too high for the person's eye, most commonly caused by blockage of the openings that let aqueous humor drain from the anterior chamber.

Intraocular pressure is the pressure of the fluids filling the chambers of the eye: the aqueous humor filling the anterior and posterior chambers and the vitreous humor filling the vitreous chamber (see Figure 2.8). **Glaucoma** is a condition in which the intraocular pressure is too high for the person's eye (Jampel, 1997). The most common cause of glaucoma is blockage of the openings that let aqueous humor drain from the anterior chamber. Fresh aqueous humor is constantly being generated by ciliary tissue, and if it can't drain, it accumulates and pushes back on the vitreous chamber, increasing the pressure there too. This can result in pressure on the head of the optic nerve, where it exits the eye through the optic disk, and it can damage retinal ganglion cells, leading to gradual visual loss that may not be noticed by the afflicted person until it is advanced. If left untreated, glaucoma can cause permanent loss of vision and even complete blindness.

Ophthalmologists measure intraocular pressure by pressing on the cornea with an instrument called a *tonometer;* if the pressure required to deform the cornea by a fixed amount is greater than normal, further testing is done to see if there is evidence of damage to the eye. Modern drug, laser, or surgical therapies are very effective in treating this disorder.

Floaters and Phosphenes

floaters Shadows on the retina thrown by debris within the vitreous humor; perceived as small, semitransparent spots or threads that appear to be floating before the person's eyes and tend to move with the eyes.

People of all ages experience **floaters**—small, semitransparent spots or threads that appear to be floating before your eyes and tend to move with your eyes. Actually, floaters are shadows on the retina thrown by debris within the vitreous humor. Age-related changes in the vitreous humor are a common cause of such debris. For example, as the vitreous condenses and shrinks with age, it can pull away from the retina, and the condensed vitreous is often perceived as a "spider web" near the center of the vision. The shrinkage of the vitreous also may cause minor tearing of the retina or detachment of the vitreous from the retina, which in turn can cause a small amount of bleeding into the vitreous humor, and the tiny drops of blood can be perceived as floaters. Floaters are harmless in themselves, but they can be annoying or distracting if they are numerous.

phosphenes Brief, tiny bright flashes in the person's field of view not caused by light but by any of a variety of other causes.

Some people also experience **phosphenes**, brief, tiny bright flashes in their field of view that are not caused by light. These can have many causes—for example, if you close your eyes and rub them, the pressure stimulates your photoreceptors, and you may see phosphenes. Occasionally, phosphenes occur spontaneously, and in some rare cases they can indicate problems such as retinal detachment.

Normal vision

Vision with macular degeneration

"Tunnel vision" with retinitis pigmentosa

Figure 2.33 Macular Degeneration and Retinitis Pigmentosa Macular degeneration results from damage to photoreceptors in the macula (a region of the retina that includes the fovea). Retinitis pigmentosa, which begins with damage in the peripheral retina, can progress to "tunnel vision" and then to complete blindness. [Marcus Brandt/epa/Corbis]

Retinal Disease: Macular Degeneration and Retinitis Pigmentosa

Macular degeneration, the leading cause of severe visual loss in the United States, is a condition characterized by damage to the photoreceptors in the *macula* (a region at the center of the retina that includes, but is somewhat larger than, the fovea). The condition takes two forms, known as *dry* and *wet.* In the dry form, cells degenerate in the pigment epithelium (see Figure 2.15), which causes loss of function of the photoreceptors overlying those cells (Stone, 2007). In advanced cases, small areas of blind spots develop, which gradually enlarge over time. In the wet form, new blood vessels grow underneath the retina, leak fluid, bleed, and ultimately scar, also leading to loss of function of the overlying photoreceptors. Macular degeneration can occur in younger adults, but it is more common in older persons. This age-related macular degeneration (AMD) occurs in about 10% of people between 66 and 74 years of age and in 30% or more of those aged 75–85. Currently, there is no treatment for the dry form of AMD. The wet form has been successfully treated with drugs that block the growth of new blood vessels.

macular degeneration A condition characterized by damage to the photoreceptors in a region at the center of the retina; the leading cause of severe visual loss in the United States.

Retinitis pigmentosa (RP) is an inherited condition in which there is gradual degeneration of the photoreceptors over many years (Pacione et al., 2003). The midperipheral retina is affected first, in a ring- or horseshoe-shaped region, with blind spots then expanding toward the center and further out into the periphery. People with RP may have night blindness from birth, even before their visual field is affected, or they may develop night blindness as they lose visual field. The rods are often affected first and then the cones. People with RP may also develop "tunnel vision," with only a small central seeing area. In some cases, RP can progress to complete blindness. There is currently no treatment for people with RP, though genetic therapy has been successful in dogs with retinal degeneration caused by the same abnormality as in one type of RP. The first trials of this gene therapy in humans are now beginning. Other treatment approaches being studied include retinal implants and replacing the lost photoreceptors with stem cells that then develop into photoreceptors. Figure 2.33 illustrates what a scene might look like to a person with macular degeneration or with the tunnel vision caused by retinitis pigmentosa, compared to normal vision.

retinitis pigmentosa (RP) An inherited condition in which there is gradual degeneration of the photoreceptors over many years, often leading to night blindness and "tunnel vision."

Check Your Understanding

2.21 How are strabismus and amblyopia related? How are they different?

2.22 What is the difference between nearsightedness and farsightedness? How are these conditions corrected?

2.23 Which of the following accommodation disorders typically relate to problems with the shape of the cornea: myopia, hyperopia, presbyopia, astigmatism?

2.24 What is the principal cause of glaucoma?

2.25 What are floaters?

2.26 What is the leading cause of severe visual loss in the United States?

APPLICATIONS Night-Vision Devices

We all know that it's harder to see at night than during the day. Dark adaptation might enable you to see shapes, but if the light is dim enough—for example, if clouds obscure the moon and stars—you'll miss a lot. The most common solution to this problem is to illuminate the scene with artificial lighting, such as streetlights, vehicle headlights, or a flashlight. However, most types of lighting can illuminate objects only within a fairly short distance of the light source, which means that more distant objects remain difficult to see. Also, in some cases, as in military operations or when observing the nighttime activities of wildlife, artificial lighting might reveal the presence of the viewer as well as the target. These types of issues have motivated the development of **night-vision devices (NVDs)**, which have been based on two different technologies: thermal imaging and image enhancement.

night-vision devices (NVDs) Devices to enable vision in total or near-total darkness.

thermal imaging A technology used in night-vision devices; infrared radiation emitted by objects and surfaces in a scene are converted into a visible electronic image.

Devices based on **thermal imaging** create an image of a scene by converting the infrared radiation (heat radiation) emitted by the objects and surfaces in the scene into a visible electronic image. If you look back at Figure 2.2, you'll see that infrared radiation is radiation with wavelengths from just above the visible range (about 700 nm) to about 30,000 nm; thus, infrared radiation is invisible to human vision. However, an array of infrared sensors can detect differences in temperature in the scene by measuring the amount of infrared radiation emitted from different locations in the scene. For example, in a street scene where a warm human body emits much more infrared radiation than the surface of a building, the sensor array can project these differences onto a display where different temperatures are depicted as different colors (see Figure 2.34a). NVDs based on thermal imaging will work

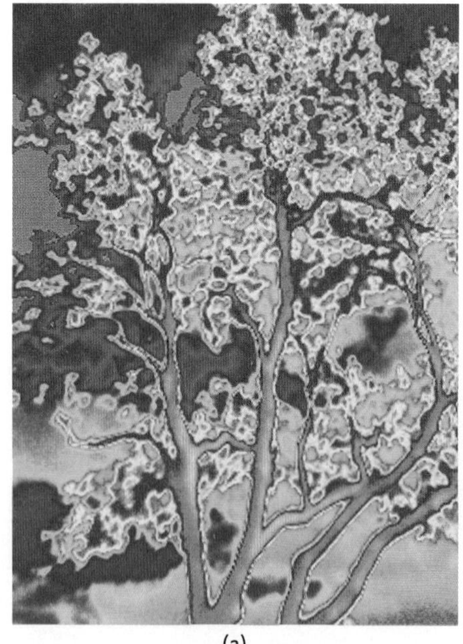

(a)

(b)

Figure 2.34 Night-Vision Devices (a) Devices based on thermal imaging detect differences in the amount of infrared radiation (heat) emitted from different locations in the scene. The devices then convert these differences into differences in color. Here, the tree's branches and leaves emit more heat than the surrounding air. (b) Devices based on image enhancement work by converting photons into electrons, amplifying the number of electrons, and then using the electrons to make a phosphor-coated screen glow. The differences in brightness in different parts of the scene are represented by differences in the intensity of the glow. [a: Tony McConnell/Photo Researchers; b: SPL/Photo Researchers]

in scenes where there is no visible light at all, because the radiation used to create the image is emitted by the objects in the scene.

Other NVDs are based on **image enhancement,** a technology that requires the presence of at least some visible light, which is then amplified to make the objects in the scene visible on a display. Photons reflected from the objects in the scene are focused into an image-intensifier tube, which converts the photons into electrons and amplifies the number of electrons by a factor of as much as 30,000 times. The electrons then strike a screen coated with phosphors, which glow with different intensities when struck by electrons with different energies. Thus, the pattern of phosphor intensities produces an image of the scene based on the differences in brightness between different parts of the scene (see Figure 2.34b). The most recent generation of image-enhancement NVDs incorporate adaptation to changes in lighting—they can automatically adjust the amount of amplification as the brightness of the scene changes, thereby protecting the user from being "blinded" by either sudden increases or sudden decreases in illumination.

image enhancement A technology used in night-vision devices; dim light is amplified by converting photons into electrons, amplifying the number of electrons, and then using the electrons to produce a pattern of varying intensities on a phosphor-coated screen

Check Your Understanding

2.27 True or false? Thermal-imaging NVDs work in total darkness, but image-enhancement NVDs don't.

2.28 Could a thermal-imaging NVD create an image of the scene inside a freezer? Explain your answer.

SUMMARY

- Light Light is a type of electromagnetic radiation. Differences in the wavelength of light are perceived as differences in color; differences in the number of particles of light are perceived as differences in brightness. Light can be transmitted, absorbed, reflected, or refracted. Light that enters your eyes forms a spatial pattern of brightness and color called the *optic array.*
- The Human Eye Your field of view is the portion of surrounding space you can see with your eyes in a fixed position. Acuity is greatest in the part of the field of view where your eyes are pointed. The extraocular muscles let you point your eyes where you want. The eye is roughly spherical and is encased in three membranes: the sclera, the choroid, and the retina. The iris constricts and dilates the pupil to control the amount of light entering the eye. The lens focuses an image on the retina, which contains photoreceptors called *rods* and *cones.* Photopigments in the rods and cones transduce light into a neural signal that is sent to retinal ganglion cells. The axons of the retinal ganglion cells form the optic nerve, which sends signals to the brain. The fovea is a region containing no rods and a very high density of cones, supporting high-acuity vision there.
- Photoreceptors: Rods and Cones There are three types of cones and one type of rod. Cones are used to see in normal daylight conditions, and rods are used in dim light. The density of cones declines rapidly with distance from the fovea; the density of rods is greatest in a ring around the fovea and declines gradually with distance from the fovea. Photoreceptors change their sensitivity under different lighting conditions.
- Retinal Ganglion Cells: Circuits in the Retina Send Information to the Brain Circuits in which a retinal ganglion cell receives neural signals from multiple photoreceptors show convergence. Convergent circuits are more sensitive to dim light than nonconvergent circuits; nonconvergent circuits support greater acuity. Most retinal ganglion cells have receptive fields with a center–surround structure, either on-center or off-center. Retinal circuits with a center–surround structure exhibit lateral inhibition, which supports edge enhancement.
- Disorders of Vision Strabismus results in the eyes not being aligned with each other. Amblyopia is a condition in which fine vision doesn't develop properly in one eye. Disorders of accommodation include myopia, hyperopia, presbyopia, and astigmatism. A cataract is a progressive clouding of the lens. Glaucoma is excessively high intraocular pressure. Floaters are visible shadows of debris in the vitreous humor; phosphenes are brief, tiny flashes not caused by light. Macular degeneration and retinitis pigmentosa are degenerative diseases that damage photoreceptors.
- Applications: Night-Vision Devices Night-vision devices based on thermal imaging don't require any visible light; they create an image of a scene by converting the infrared radiation in the scene into a visible electronic image in which different temperatures are depicted as different

colors. Devices based on image enhancement do require some visible light; they work by converting photons into electrons, then amplifying the number of electrons, and then using the electrons to produce an image on a phosphor-coated screen.

KEY TERMS

accommodation (p. 54)
acuity (p. 50)
amacrine cells (p. 56)
amblyopia (p. 76)
anterior chamber (p. 52)
aqueous humor (p. 53)
astigmatism (p. 78)
bipolar cells (p. 56)
blind spot, see **optic disk.**
cataract (p. 78)
center–surround receptive field (p. 71)
choroid (p. 52)
ciliary muscles (p. 53)
cones (p. 56)
convergence (p. 67)
cornea (p. 52)
dark adaptation (p. 64)
diopters (p. 53)
edge enhancement (p. 74)
electromagnetic radiation (p. 46)
electromagnetic spectrum (p. 47)
extraocular muscles (p. 50)
farsightedness, see **hyperopia.**
field of view (p. 50)
floaters (p. 78)
focal length (p. 53)
fovea (p. 56)
ganglion cell layer (p. 56)
glaucoma (p. 78)
horizontal cells (p. 56)
hyperopia (or *farsightedness*) (p. 76)
image enhancement (p. 81)
inner nuclear layer (p. 56)
inner synaptic layer (p. 56)
intraocular pressure (p. 53)
iris (p. 52)
isomers (p. 60)
LASIK (p. 78)
lateral inhibition (p. 73)
lens (p. 53)
light (p. 46)
luminance contrast (p. 59)
macular degeneration (p. 79)
myopia (or *nearsightedness*) (p. 76)
near point (p. 77)
nearsightedness, see **myopia.**
night-vision devices (NVDs) (p. 80)
nuclear layers (p. 56)
off-center receptive fields (p. 72)
on-center receptive fields (p. 71)
operating range (p. 64)
optic array (p. 48)
optic axis (p. 51)
optic disk (or *blind spot*) (p. 56)
optic nerve (p. 56)
outer nuclear layer (p. 56)
outer synaptic layer (p. 56)
phosphenes (p. 78)
photoisomerization (p. 60)
photons (p. 47)
photopigment (p. 60)
photopigment regeneration (p. 65)
photoreceptors (p. 56)
pigment epithelium (p. 56)
posterior chamber (p. 52)
preferred stimulus (p. 71)
presbyopia (p. 77)
pupil (p. 52)
pupillary reflex (p. 52)
receptive field (p. 69)
retina (p. 52)
retinal ganglion cells (RGCs) (p. 56)
retinal image (p. 55)
retinitis pigmentosa (RP) (p. 79)
rod monochromats (p. 65)
rods (p. 56)
sclera (p. 52)
spatial summation (p. 67)
spectral sensitivity (p. 60)
strabismus (p. 76)
synaptic layers (p. 56)
thermal imaging (p. 80)
vitreous chamber (p. 53)
vitreous humor (p. 53)
wavelength (p. 47)
zonule fibers (p. 53)

EXPAND YOUR UNDERSTANDING

2.1 At this moment, rays of light are passing left–right, up–down, and diagonally in all directions in front of your face. Why can't you see those rays? What would you need to do in order to see them?

2.2 The retinal image is upside down (see Figure 2.13). Why does the world look upright?

2.3 Write the word LEFT on an index card or a small piece of paper and the word RIGHT on another. Hold them up about a foot in front of your face and about a foot apart (LEFT on the left, RIGHT on the right). If you look straight ahead at a point between the two words, you can almost, but not quite, read them. If you shift your eyes to look at LEFT, RIGHT becomes much less distinct; similarly, if you shift your eyes to look at RIGHT, LEFT becomes much less distinct. Explain these experiences in terms of the location of the words in the retinal image and the distribution of cones in the retina.

2.4 Using the concept of operating range, explain why turning on the dome light in your car makes it more difficult to see the road and the surrounding countryside when you're driving in a rural area at night. (Ignore the effect of reflections in the car windows.)

2.5 Describe two common activities that would be difficult or impossible without dark adaptation, and explain why.

2.6 Suppose you want to sew on a button during a blackout, when the only light is provided by candles. You know that the needle is on the table, and to find it, you scan the tabletop rapidly until you notice the dim glint of the needle out of the corner of your eye. Why is this a good strategy? To pick up the needle, you focus your eyes directly on it at about arm's length. Why? To thread it, you sit next to the candle, bring the needle and the thread much closer to your eyes, and focus on the tip of the thread and the eye of the needle. Why? Your answers should be in terms of where rods and cones are in the retina, where the retinal images of the needle and thread are located, and where retinal circuits exhibit more or less convergence and spatial summation.

READ MORE ABOUT IT

Atchison, D. A., & Smith, G. (2000). *Optics of the human eye*. Boston: Butterworth-Heinemann.

A detailed account of how the eye forms an image upon the retina.

Cornsweet, T. N. (1970). *Visual perception*. New York: Academic Press.

A classic text, with a first chapter that includes a detailed, compelling description of the experiment of Hecht et al., 1942.

Oyster, C. W. (1999). *The human eye*. Sunderland, MA: Sinauer.

Thoroughly covers the structure and function of the eye, with an emphasis on anatomy.

Rodieck, R. W. (1998). *The first steps in seeing*. Sunderland, MA: Sinauer.

Detailed, beautifully illustrated coverage of the initial encoding of light by the retina. The treatment is fairly technical yet accessible.

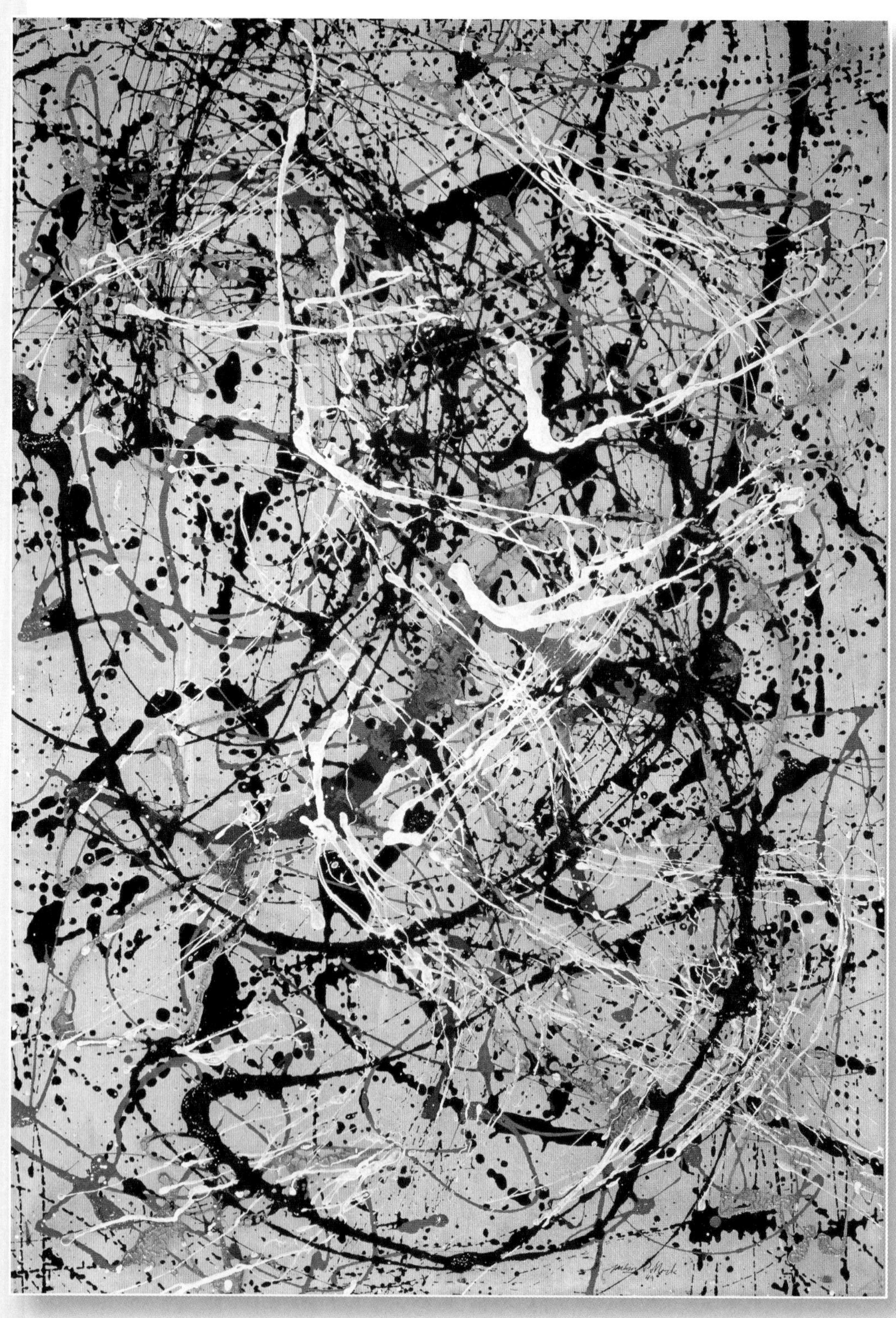

Jackson Pollock, *Number 20*, 1949. [Enamel on paper laid down on Masonite, 425 × 600 cm. Private collection/James Goodman Gallery, New York/Bridgeman Art Library. ©2012 The Pollock-Krasner Foundation/Artists Rights Society (ARS), New York.]

3

THE VISUAL BRAIN

Chapter Outline

No Thing to See

In 1988 a young woman who is known in the neurological literature as "D.F." fell into a coma as a result of carbon monoxide poisoning at her home. (The gas was released by a faulty propane heater.) She was discovered unconscious and taken to a hospital. When she awoke, she seemed alert and could speak and understand, but she couldn't see anything. Her doctors initially diagnosed cortical blindness—blindness resulting from damage to the primary visual area at the back of the brain. Within days, however, it became apparent that this diagnosis was incorrect, as certain aspects of D.F.'s vision began to return. First, she started seeing colors, like the red and green of the flowers in her hospital room. Then she began to see textures and fine details. And she had no problem seeing that something was moving. But that's where her improvement ended—she never regained the ability to see objects as recognizable wholes, to see their shape and be able to say what they were. Though she could see details like the tiny hairs on the back of her mother's hand, she couldn't see the shape of the hand as a whole. The only objects she could identify by sight were those with a distinctive color or visual texture. In contrast, her ability to identify objects by touch was normal, so it was clear that her impairment was visual, not cognitive.

Now, more than 20 years after her accident, D.F.'s world is still without visible shape or form. She can't make out printed words, recognize faces, or identify everyday objects by sight. She even has trouble separating objects from their background—objects seem to "run into each other," she says—so adjacent objects with the same color, like a knife and a fork, might look like one unrecognizable blob. Conversely, a single object with differently colored parts might look like two or more separate things.

Yet, despite these severe impairments in her ability to perceive objects, D.F. is perfectly able to use vision to guide actions like reaching for objects and grasping them. How is this possible? As we'll see later in this chapter, D.F.'s case provided crucial evidence for our current understanding of how the visual brain is organized: some brain areas involved in recognizing objects are separate from other areas involved in using vision to guide action. The carbon monoxide poisoning had damaged object-recognition areas but not vision-for-action areas in D.F.'s brain.

Vision begins in the eye. As we saw in Chapter 2, light rays forming a spatial pattern of brightness and color (the optic array) enter the eye and are focused into a sharp image on the retina. Photoreceptors in the retina transduce the light in the retinal image into neural signals that propagate through neural circuits within the retina. Lateral inhibition in the neural circuits underlying retinal ganglion cell receptive fields promotes the representation of edges at locations in the retinal image where there are abrupt changes in brightness. Signals generated by the retinal ganglion cells carry information about edges and other elementary visual features such as color. These signals flow along the retinal ganglion cells'

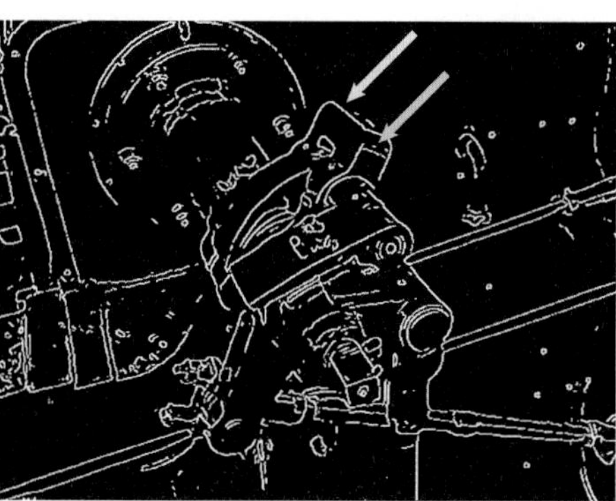

Figure 3.1 Edges and Changes in Brightness The image on the right shows where there are abrupt changes in brightness in the photo on the left. Changes in brightness often correspond to edges—that is, to the boundaries between parts of a scene. Sometimes, though, there is a change in brightness where there is no actual edge but just, for example, a highlight (pink arrows), and sometimes an edge is nearly invisible, as when an object and its background are very similar in brightness (yellow arrows). [Simpsons Contributor/ Wikipedia]

axons, which bundle together to form the optic nerve exiting each eye and carrying the signals to the brain.

Clearly, by the time neural signals leave the retina via the optic nerve, the visual system has already taken significant steps toward using the information in the retinal image to tell us "what is where." But as important as edges and other elementary features are to perception, much more neural processing is required to create representations of the shapes, locations, and identities of the objects in a scene (see Figure 3.1). How the brain does this is the subject of this chapter and the next.

As we progress through this chapter, we'll see how the neural signals originating in the retina travel along pathways deeper into the brain, through networks of increasing complexity. And we'll see that two overarching principles characterize how these pathways and networks are organized:

functional specialization The specialization of different neural pathways and different areas of the brain for representing different kinds of information.

- ***Functional specialization.*** The optic array (and the corresponding retinal image) contains many different kinds of information, including information about shape (based on the locations, orientations, and curvature of edges), color, motion, and depth. Different neural pathways and different areas of the brain are specialized for representing these different kinds of information.

retinotopic mapping An arrangement of neurons in the visual system whereby signals from retinal ganglion cells with receptive fields that are next to each other on the retina travel to neurons that are next to each other in each visual area of the brain.

- ***Retinotopic mapping.*** Vision is a *spatial* sense: the spatial arrangement of brightness and color in the retinal image is what we use to see things, and this arrangement is echoed by the arrangement of neurons throughout the visual system. That is, neural signals from retinal ganglion cells with receptive fields that are next to each other on the retina travel to neurons that are next to each other in each visual area of the brain; thus, the spatial location of visual features is explicitly reflected in the spatial arrangement of activated neurons throughout the visual system.

In the sections that follow, we'll see that signals from the eye travel first to two important subcortical structures, the lateral geniculate nucleus of the thalamus and the superior colliculus. After exploring the functions of those two structures, we'll examine the functional organization of the primary visual cortex, where visual signals are received from the lateral geniculate nucleus. Then we'll take an overall look at the visual system's areas, pathways, and modules—from the eye, to the lateral geniculate nucleus, to the primary visual cortex and beyond—to see how visual signals are processed in support of recognizing objects and acting on them.

From Eye to Brain

optic chiasm The location where the optic nerves from the two eyes split in half, with half the axons from each eye crossing over to the other hemisphere of the brain.

optic tract The continuation of the optic nerve past the optic chiasm; the right optic tract consists of axons from the retinal ganglion cells in the right half of each retina, and the left optic tract consists of axons from the left half of each retina.

Figure 3.2 shows the main pathways followed by the neural signals in the 1 million axons of the retinal ganglion cells (RGCs) that emerge from the back of each eye to form the optic nerve. The left and right optic nerves travel only a few centimeters until they meet at the **optic chiasm,** where the optic nerve from each eye splits in half. The axons from the RGCs in the right half of the right retina and the right half of the left retina—that is, from the right temporal retina (nearest to your temple) and the left nasal retina (nearest to your nose)—combine into the right **optic tract,** which continues into the right hemisphere of the brain.

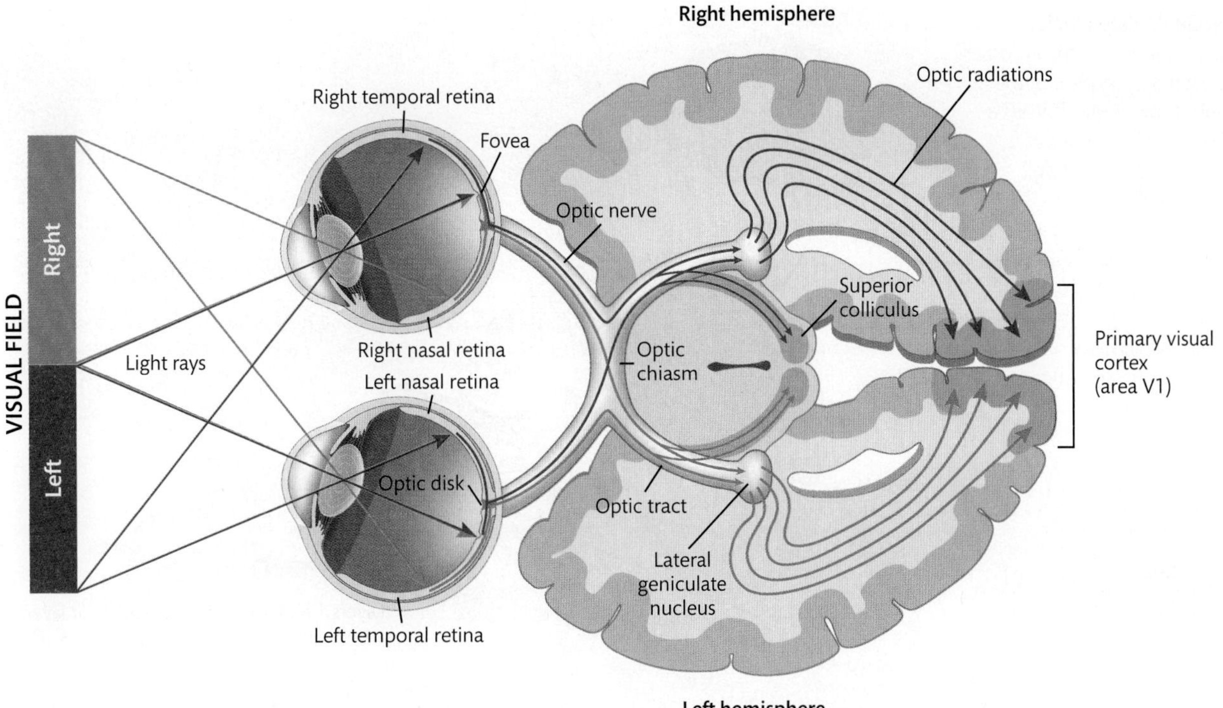

Figure 3.2 Main Pathways from Retina to Brain The optic nerves—consisting of the bundled-together axons of the retinal ganglion cells—leave the eyes at each optic disk and meet at the optic chiasm, where they split apart and rebundle as the optic tracts. Neural signals carrying information from the left half of the visual field (depicted in red)—that is, signals from the right temporal retina and the left nasal retina—are sent via the lateral geniculate nucleus and the optic radiations to the primary visual cortex (area V1) in the right hemisphere. Signals carrying information from the right half of the visual field (depicted in blue)—that is, signals from the left temporal retina and the right nasal retina—are sent to the left hemisphere. Some pathways branch off from the optic tract and travel to the superior colliculus and to other structures.

The axons from the RGCs in the left half of the right retina and the left half of the left retina (i.e., from the left temporal retina and the right nasal retina) combine into the left optic tract, which continues into the left hemisphere.

As shown in Figure 3.2, light rays from the left half of the visual field strike the right half of each retina, while light rays from the right half of the visual field strike the left half of each retina. Then, as a consequence of the splitting of the optic nerves and their recombining into the optic tracts, neural signals carrying information from the left visual field (red in the figure) go to the right hemisphere of the brain, while signals carrying information from the right visual field (blue in the figure) go to the left hemisphere. This is referred to as the *contralateral representation of visual space* and is an example of **contralateral organization** (opposite-side organization, as opposed to *ipsilateral*, or same-side, organization). About 90% of the axons in the optic tract go to the lateral geniculate nucleus, which sends signals to the primary visual cortex (area V1) via the optic radiations; most of the other axons in the optic tract branch off to the superior colliculus.

Demonstration 3.1 Visual Pathways from Eye to Brain Show how neural signals flow along the visual pathways in response to light from the left and right visual fields.

contralateral organization Opposite-side organization, in which stimulation of neurons on one side of the body or sensory organ is represented by the activity of neurons in the opposite side of the brain.

Lateral Geniculate Nucleus

The **lateral geniculate nucleus (LGN)** is a peanut-sized structure—one in each hemisphere—that is part of the thalamus (see Figure 3.3). The thalamus is a rather large structure containing several other nuclei that serve as "way stations" for different sensory systems—for example, the medial geniculate body, which is adjacent to the LGN, receives signals from the ears that are sent on to the primary auditory cortex. The LGN was once thought to be a simple relay for neural signals from the eyes, but we now know that its functions are more complex and important than the term "relay" suggests.

lateral geniculate nucleus (LGN) Part of the thalamus (one in each hemisphere); receives visual signals via the axons of retinal ganglion cells.

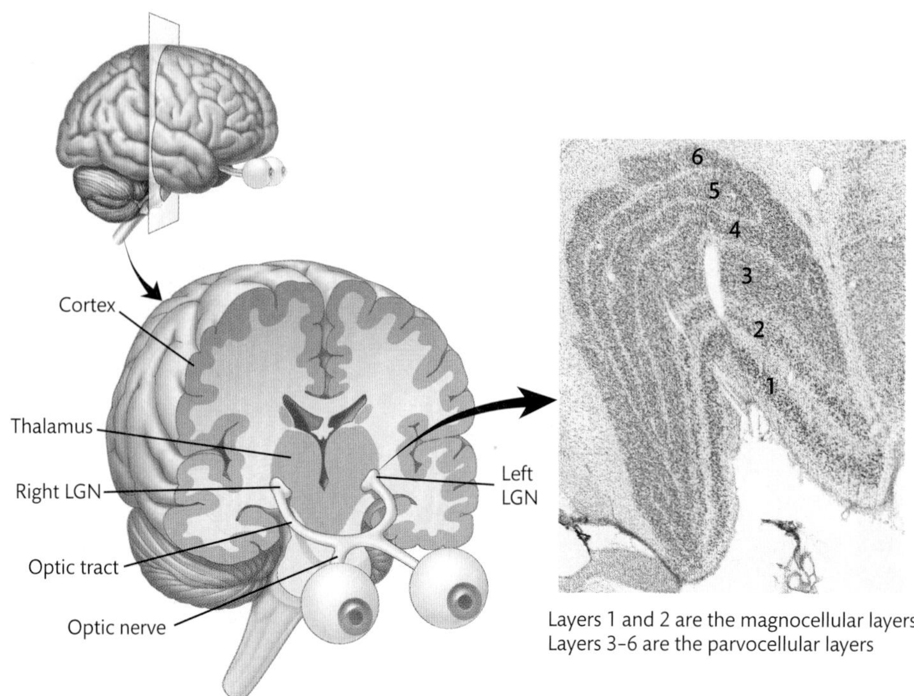

Figure 3.3 **Lateral Geniculate Nucleus (LGN)** (left) The LGN is part of the thalamus; there is one LGN in each hemisphere of the brain. (right) In this photomicrograph from a macaque monkey LGN, each purple dot is the cell body of an LGN neuron. The cell bodies in the two magnocellular layers (layers 1 and 2) are relatively large, while those in the four parvocellular layers (layers 3–6) are relatively small. The koniocellular layers are the lighter-colored layers between the other layers; the cell bodies in the koniocellular layers are too small to be seen in this image. [brainmaps.org]

The photomicrograph on the right side of Figure 3.3 shows a slice through the LGN, which is structured like a many-layered sandwich that has been folded so the layers curve. The cell bodies (purple dots in Figure 3.3) in the layers numbered 1 and 2 are larger than those in the layers numbered 3–6. For this reason, layers 1 and 2 are called **magnocellular layers** (from the Latin *magnus,* meaning "great"), and layers 3–6 are called **parvocellular layers** (from the Latin *parvus,* meaning "small"). The thinner layers between the magnocellular and parvocellular layers contain even smaller cells and are called **koniocellular layers** (from the Greek *konia,* meaning "grains of sand"). There is one koniocellular layer just under each of the six magnocellular and parvocellular layers.

magnocellular layers Layers of the lateral geniculate nucleus containing neurons with large cell bodies.

parvocellular layers Layers of the lateral geniculate nucleus containing neurons with small cell bodies.

koniocellular layers Layers of the lateral geniculate nucleus containing neurons with very small cell bodies.

Pathways from the Retina to the LGN

Figure 3.4 shows the neural pathways from the retina to the magnocellular, parvocellular, and koniocellular layers of the LGN:

- The left LGN receives signals from the right half of the visual field (i.e., signals from the left temporal retina and the right nasal retina), while the right LGN receives signals from the left half of the visual field (i.e., signals from the right temporal retina and the left nasal retina).
- Each LGN layer receives signals from one eye only: layers 1, 4, and 6 (and the koniocellular layers just under each) receive signals from the contralateral eye (the eye on the opposite side of the body), while layers 2, 3, and 5 (and the corresponding koniocellular layers) receive signals from the ipsilateral eye (the eye on the same side of the body) (Hendry & Reid, 2000).
- The magnocellular layers receive signals from **parasol retinal ganglion cells,** the parvocellular layers receive signals from **midget retinal ganglion cells,** and the koniocellular layers receive signals from **bistratified retinal ganglion cells.** (We'll have more to say about these three classes of RGCs later in this chapter.)
- Within each layer of each LGN, the neurons are arranged in a retinotopic map of the visual field. In other words, RGCs with adjacent receptive fields connect to adjacent neurons in the LGN. Furthermore, the retinotopic maps in the six layers of the LGN line up with one another, which means that an electrode penetrating through the

parasol retinal ganglion cells Retinal ganglion cells that send signals to the magnocellular layers of the lateral geniculate nucleus.

midget retinal ganglion cells Retinal ganglion cells that send signals to the parvocellular layers of the lateral geniculate nucleus.

bistratified retinal ganglion cells Retinal ganglion cells that send signals to the koniocellular layers of the lateral geniculate nucleus.

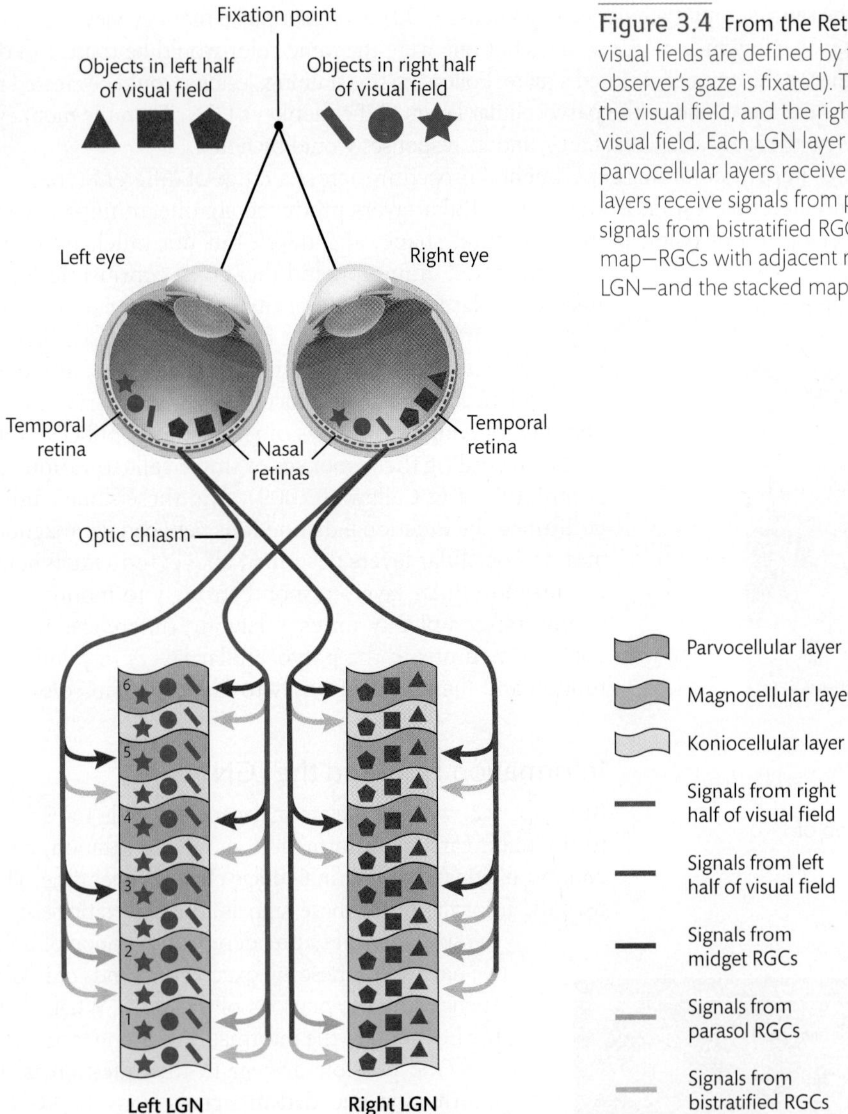

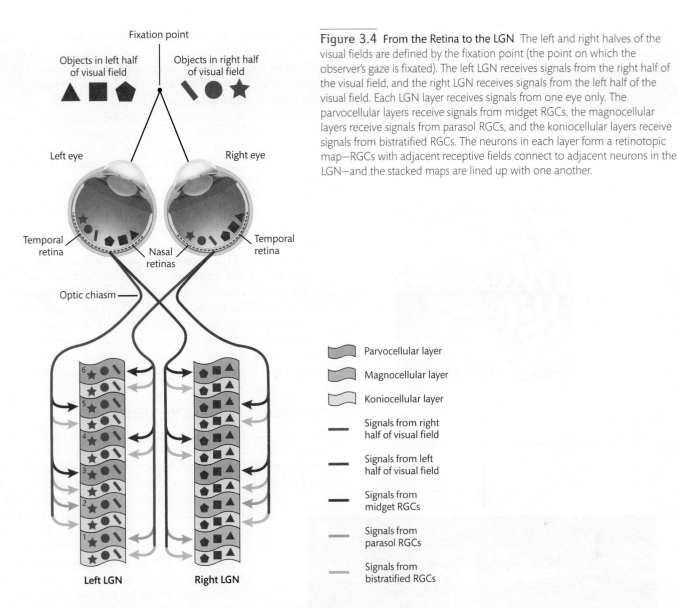

Figure 3.4 From the Retina to the LGN The left and right halves of the visual fields are defined by the fixation point (the point on which the observer's gaze is fixated). The left LGN receives signals from the right half of the visual field, and the right LGN receives signals from the left half of the visual field. Each LGN layer receives signals from one eye only. The parvocellular layers receive signals from midget RGCs, the magnocellular layers receive signals from parasol RGCs, and the koniocellular layers receive signals from bistratified RGCs. The neurons in each layer form a retinotopic map—RGCs with adjacent receptive fields connect to adjacent neurons in the LGN—and the stacked maps are lined up with one another.

layers of the LGN would encounter neurons that all respond to a stimulus at the same location in the visual field.

Functional Specialization of the Layers of the LGN

The layers of the LGN differ functionally, as well as structurally. Experiments with monkeys have provided strong evidence that the magnocellular layers are specialized for carrying information about dynamic visual properties such as motion and flicker, and the parvocellular layers are specialized for carrying information about static visual properties such as color, texture, form, and depth. Less is known about functional specialization of the koniocellular layers, but there is strong evidence that these layers are also involved in carrying information about color (Nassi & Callaway, 2009). (As we discuss functional specialization here and later in the chapter, keep in mind that it's generally an oversimplification to assume that neurons specialized for carrying information about one property, such as motion, carry no information at all about another property, such as color. Rather, neurons tend to differ in their *relative* sensitivities to different types of stimuli.)

The functional differences between the magnocellular and parvocellular layers are evident in the results of an experiment in which monkeys trained to respond to a variety of visual stimuli expressing dynamic and static properties were given lesions in specific layers of the LGN (by injection of toxins that killed neurons); they were then tested on their responses to the same stimuli (Schiller & Logothetis, 1990). For example, a monkey viewing a display of squares in which all the squares but one were the same color would be trained to direct its gaze to the uniquely colored square. Following this training, lesions would be created in either the magnocellular or the parvocellular layers of the monkey's LGN. Then the monkey would view the same array of squares, and its responses would be noted.

Repetition of this experimental procedure across a range of different types of stimuli revealed that lesions in the parvocellular layers produced significant impairment in the perception of color, pattern, texture, shape, and depth but not much impairment in the perception of motion and flicker. In contrast, lesions in the magnocellular layers dramatically impaired the monkeys' ability to perceive motion and flicker but had much less effect on their ability to perceive color, pattern, texture, shape, and depth.

Evidence that the koniocellular layers carry information about color comes from physiological studies of LGN neurons—that is, recording the responses of single cells to various types of stimuli (Nassi & Callaway, 2009). And these same studies have confirmed the functional distinctions between the magnocellular and parvocellular layers described above: individual neurons in the magnocellular layers respond strongly to motion and flicker but are completely unresponsive to differences in color; in contrast, neurons in the parvocellular layers respond poorly to motion and flicker but strongly to differences in color.

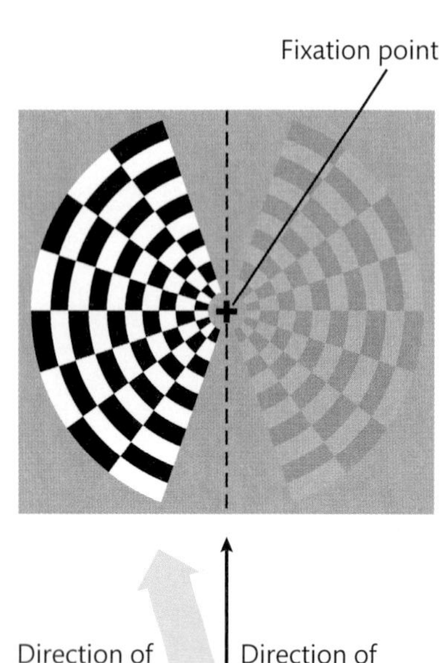

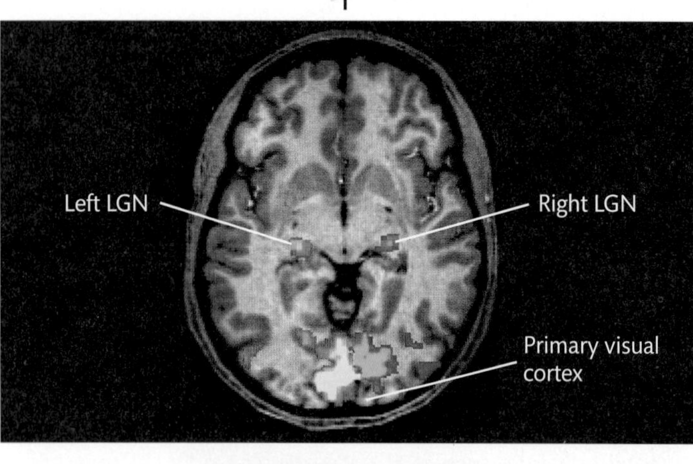

Figure 3.5 The Effect of Attention on LGN Activity In this experiment using fMRI (O'Connor et al., 2002), participants kept their eyes fixated on the cross while directing their attention to a checkerboard pattern flickering in the left or right visual field. When attention was directed to the left visual field, as illustrated here, activity increased in the right LGN and the right primary visual cortex. Conversely, when attention was directed to the right visual field, activity increased in the left LGN and left primary visual cortex. [O'Connor et al., 2002]

Information Flow and the LGN

In Chapter 2, we saw that retinal ganglion cells transmit signals to the brain carrying information about the location, color, and contrast of edges as the retinal image changes over time. The brain uses the information in these signals to create representations of the size, shape, texture, depth, and motion of objects. As we have seen, these are exactly the kinds of information encoded by the neurons of the LGN. What, then, does the LGN add to the information coming from the retina?

One possible answer to this question is that the information encoded in signals from the LGN can be modified to some degree by top-down feedback from brain structures farther along the pathways—not just the primary visual cortex, but also higher cortical areas that receive signals from the primary visual cortex and from other sensory systems. These brain structures encode information related to mental functions such as attention. Feedback from these structures can influence the LGN, so that the flow of information from the LGN to the cortex is controlled in part by what information the perceiver needs at each moment in time.

The effect of attention on LGN activity in humans was investigated in a study using fMRI (O'Connor et al., 2002). People were trained to keep their eyes fixed on the center of a computer screen while directing their attention to a flickering checkerboard pattern in the left or right half of the screen. (This is like looking at something "out of the corner of your eye.") When the person attended to the left (remember, signals carrying information from the left visual field flow to the right hemisphere), neural activity increased in both the right LGN and the right half of the primary visual cortex (as illustrated in Figure 3.5). The reverse happened when the person attended to the right. The authors of the study suggest that feedback from higher cortical areas involved in attention may serve to modulate LGN activity, as if the LGN were a "volume knob" for the brain.

To a first approximation, then, the LGN forms a sort of gateway from the eyes to the brain, providing some initial control of the flow of information from the world to the mind. In later chapters, we'll see that there are similar structures within the thalamus that perform this function for the senses of hearing and touch.

Superior Colliculus

About 90% of the axons that leave the retina connect to the LGN. The remaining 10% go to several other structures in the brain, the most important of which is the **superior colliculus (SC).** The human SC is about the size of a pencil eraser and sits near the top of the brain stem, one in each hemisphere. Its principal function is to help control rapid eye movements to visual targets—that is, to help the eyes quickly point at what you want to see.

superior colliculus (SC) A structure near the top of the brain stem (one in each hemisphere); its principal function is to help control eye movements.

Neurons in the SC can respond to just about any visual stimulus, regardless of shape or color; in other words, these cells are more concerned with *where* things are than with *what* they are. This is consistent with the principal function of SC neurons, which is to enable quick shifting of the gaze from one object to another in the field of view (Munoz & Everling, 2004). Neural signals reach the SC almost immediately after leaving the eye, giving this control system very rapid access to information about the location of visual targets—an obvious advantage for organisms that need to look at what's happening around them.

Another indication of the SC's role in controlling eye movements is that the SC also receives signals from both the auditory and somatosensory (touch) systems. In fact, certain individual neurons in the SC respond to signals from two or more sensory systems, and these signals can serve to reinforce one another. For example, such an SC neuron might respond poorly to a weak auditory stimulus alone (such as a quiet rustling sound coming from a bush) or to a weak visual stimulus alone (such as the movements of a small animal in the bush) but may respond strongly to both stimuli together. Thus, the SC is thought to be a site of **multisensory integration,** and this is supported by the fact that the SC acts in concert with a variety of cortical areas—some driven mostly by visual, auditory, and tactile properties of the stimulus, others more closely tied to the muscle commands needed to move the eyes (Stein & Meredith, 1993).

multisensory integration A function of brain areas in which signals from different sensory systems are combined.

In addition to its role in controlling eye movements, the SC sends the signals it receives from the retina to areas of the visual cortex beyond area V1, without going through area V1. The existence of this pathway helps explain a phenomenon known as *blindsight* (discussed further in Chapter 8), in which some people with damage to area V1 can perform visually guided actions in relation to objects (e.g., point at an object) without being aware of seeing the objects (Ptito & Leh, 2007).

Check Your Understanding

3.1 To show that you know what *the contralateral representation of visual space* refers to, draw a diagram depicting an object located in the right visual field, the location where light reflected from the object strikes the retina in each eye, and the pathways followed by signals carrying information about the object from the left and right retinas to the primary visual cortex.

3.2 Summarize the pattern of connections (the neural pathways) from retinal ganglion cells to the magnocellular, parvocellular, and koniocellular layers of the lateral geniculate nucleus.

3.3 Summarize the functional differences between the magnocellular, parvocellular, and koniocellular layers of the lateral geniculate nucleus.

3.4 What is the main function of the superior colliculus, and why is it thought to be a site of multisensory integration?

Primary Visual Cortex (Area V1)

That the occipital lobes of the brain are critical for vision has been known for more than a hundred years. For example, following the Russo–Japanese War of 1904–1905, the Japanese scientist Tatsuji Inouye found that soldiers who had been shot in the head and suffered nonfatal injuries in the back of the brain—that is, in the occipital lobe—had specific types of visual "blind spots" that depended on the specific location of the injury (Horton & Hoyt, 1991).

Around the same time, the German neurologist Korbinian Brodmann (1909/2005) identified 52 distinct regions of the human brain that today are called *Brodmann areas.* In the occipital lobe, Brodmann areas 17, 18, and 19 are concerned with vision. Since Brodmann's time, the boundaries of brain areas have been defined with more precision, and this has led to new labeling terminologies. For example, Brodmann areas 17, 18, and 19 are now known to include quite a few more than three functionally distinct visual areas. In the sections that follow, we'll discuss the functions of some of these principal visual areas, beginning with the **primary visual cortex,** or *V1* (see Figure 3.6), the part of the occipital lobe where signals flow from the lateral geniculate nucleus.

primary visual cortex (or *V1*) The part of the occipital lobe where signals flow from the lateral geniculate nucleus.

Response Properties of V1 Neurons

Neurons in area V1 were the subject of the first systematic studies of cortical neurons in the visual system, carried out by David Hubel and Torsten Wiesel at the Johns Hopkins University and, later, at Harvard University, starting in the late 1950s. Hubel and Wiesel had begun their scientific collaboration while working in the laboratory of Stephen Kuffler, who, in 1953, had published the initial studies of the receptive fields of RGCs. In his studies, Kuffler shone small spots of light on the retinas of cats and found that RGCs have

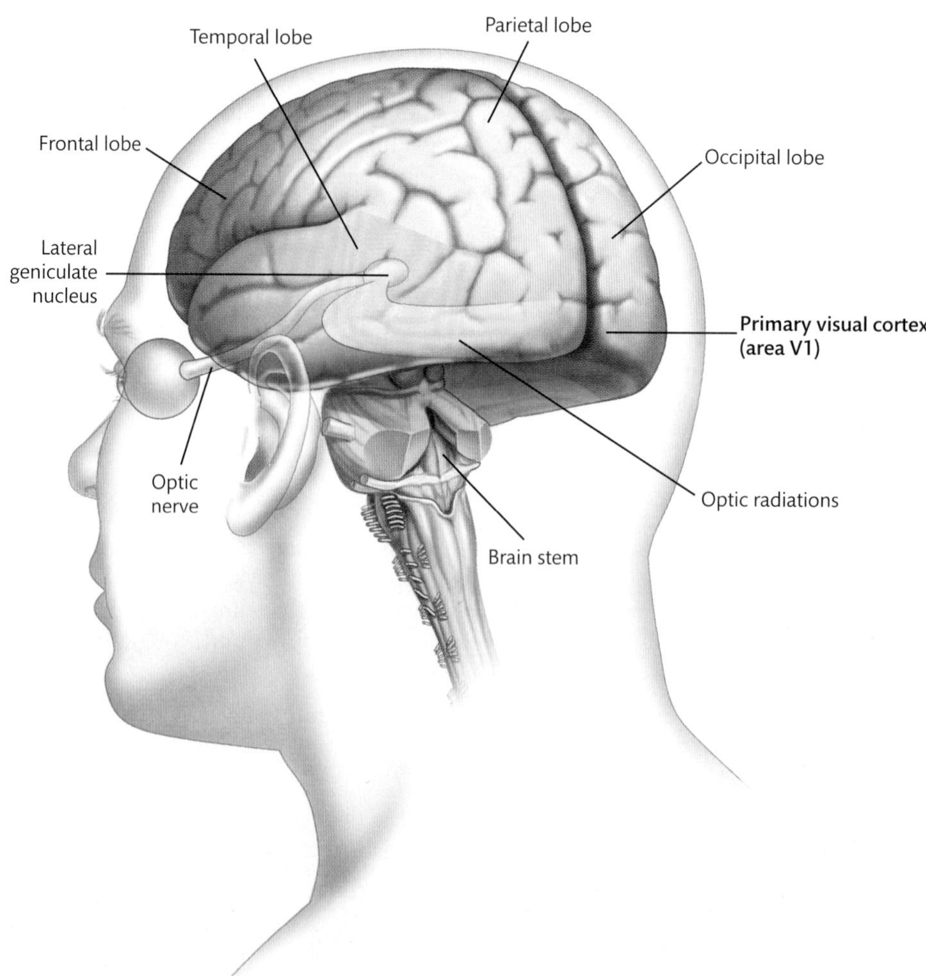

Figure 3.6 Primary Visual Cortex The primary visual cortex (area V1) is in the occipital lobe. Areas farther along the visual pathways are in adjacent regions of the occipital lobe, in the temporal lobe, and in the parietal lobe.

circular center–surround receptive fields (as described in Chapter 2). When Hubel and Wiesel decided to record from individual V1 neurons of the cat brain, they expected to find receptive fields of the same type. What they actually found, however, was very different and surprising. Quite by accident, they discovered that the neurons responded to the shadows cast by the edge of a slide as they removed and inserted the slide into a slide projector that projected spots of light into the eye (Hubel, 1995, pp. 69–70).

Hubel and Wiesel had discovered that cells in V1 are most effectively stimulated by bars or edges within a narrow range of orientations. The small spots of light that Kuffler had used to stimulate RGCs were quite poor in eliciting a response from these cortical cells. You can see why this makes sense: the center–surround receptive fields of RGCs help tell the visual system *where* light is located, while the responses of V1 neurons to oriented edges begin to tell the visual system *what* objects are at those locations. We recognize objects largely by their shape, and the shape of an object is defined by the position and orientation of its edges.

(left) David H. Hubel (b. 1926) and (right) Torsten Wiesel (b. 1924). [Ira Wyman/Sygma/Corbis]

Simple Cells

Area V1 contains two main classes of neurons, called *simple cells* and *complex cells* by Hubel and Wiesel. A **simple cell** responds most strongly to a bar of light with a particular orientation at a particular location on the retina—the location of the cell's receptive field. This location is determined by finding the area on the retina where a flashed bar causes the cell to fire. (Throughout this discussion of simple cells and complex cells, keep in mind that a bar of light is effectively an edge, a location in the retinal image where there is an abrupt change in brightness.)

The **preferred orientation** of the cell—that is, the orientation that tends to produce the strongest response—is determined by flashing bars with various orientations in the receptive field, recording the number of action potentials (spikes) evoked by each flash, and then calculating the average number of spikes evoked by each orientation. Such experiments produce results like those shown in Figure 3.7, where an **orientation tuning curve** represents the responses of each simple cell to bars with a full range of orientations.

What are the connections—from RGCs to LGN cells to simple cells in V1—that make these response patterns possible? Figure 3.8 illustrates a hypothetical and simplified neural circuit that could account for the responses of a simple cell with a preferred orientation of about 50° (based on the results of Reid & Alonso, 1995). Multiple RGCs with receptive fields aligned at an angle of 50° connect one-to-one with multiple LGN cells that all connect to the same simple cell. Each LGN neuron has a circular, center–surround receptive field corresponding to the receptive field of the RGC to which it connects. The simple cell's receptive field is an elongated shape with an excitatory central area and inhibitory surrounding area, corresponding to the way in which the excitatory centers and inhibitory surrounds of the receptive fields of the RGCs and the LGN cells overlap. As shown in the top illustration in Figure 3.8, the simple cell responds strongly when the excitatory centers of the LGN cells' receptive fields are covered by a bar of light oriented at 50°. The bottom illustration shows that if the bar is oriented at an angle of 70°, it covers less of the excitatory centers and more of the inhibitory surrounds, resulting in a weaker response from the simple cell.

simple cell A type of neuron in area V1 that responds best to a stimulus with a particular orientation in the location of its receptive field.

preferred orientation The stimulus orientation that tends to produce the strongest response from an orientation-tuned neuron such as a simple cell.

orientation tuning curve A curve on a graph that shows the average response of an orientation-tuned neuron such as a simple cell to stimuli with different orientations.

Demonstration 3.2 Responses of Simple Cells in V1 Simulate an experiment to find the location and structure of the receptive field of a simple cell in V1.

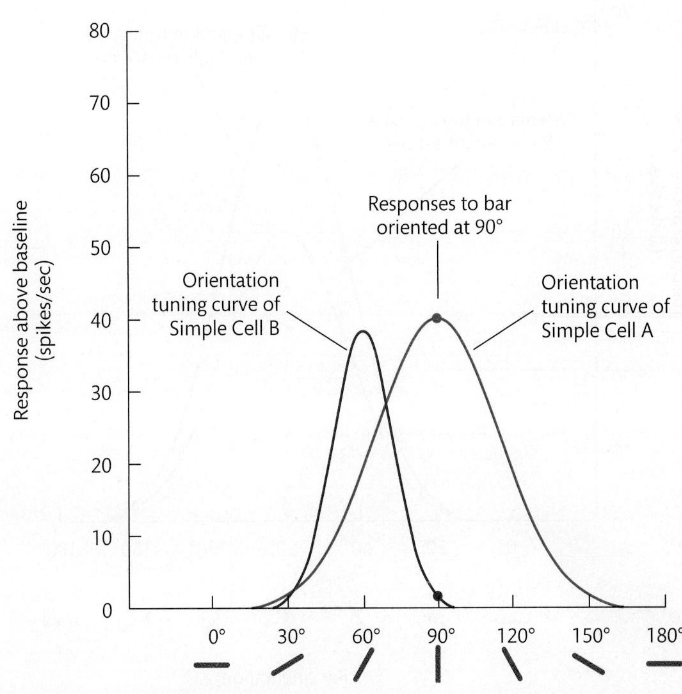

Figure 3.7 Orientation Tuning Curves of Simple Cells in V1 Responses of two simple cells to bars of various orientations flashed in their receptive fields. The vertical axis shows the number of spikes per second above the baseline firing rate following a flashed bar of light with the orientation shown on the horizontal axis. Each cell has a preferred orientation to which it tends to respond most strongly—for Simple Cell A, about 90°, and for Simple Cell B, about 60°. Thus, in response to a bar with an orientation of 90°, Simple Cell A responds strongly, and Simple Cell B responds weakly.

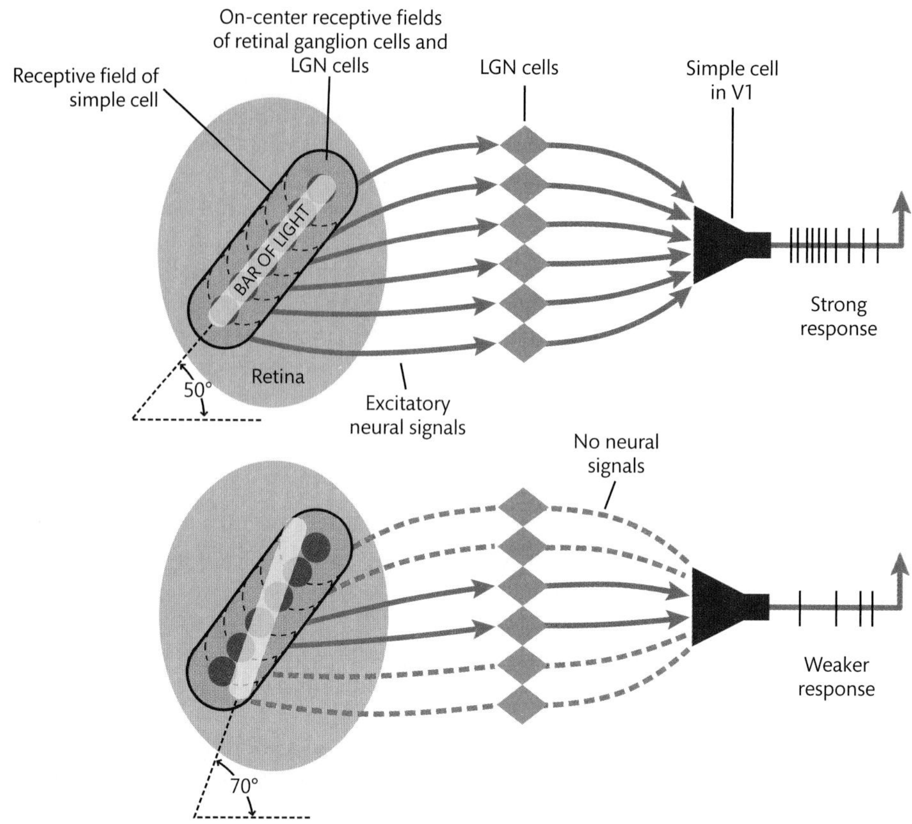

Figure 3.8 Neural Circuitry Underlying the Preferred Orientation of a Simple Cell in V1 Retinal ganglion cells with on-center receptive fields aligned at an angle of 50° each connect with LGN cells that have similar receptive field locations. These, in turn, all connect with one simple cell in V1. As shown in the top illustration, the simple cell responds most strongly to a bar of light oriented at 50° that just covers the excitatory centers of the aligned RGC receptive fields; that is, the preferred orientation of this simple cell is 50°. When the bar of light has a different orientation—say, 70°, as shown in the bottom illustration—the simple cell tends to respond less strongly, because the light is stimulating fewer of the excitatory centers and more of the inhibitory surrounds. (This model is based on results reported in Reid & Alonso, 1995.)

Despite these types of regularities in the responses of simple cells to oriented bars of light, the responses of an individual simple cell don't give the visual system enough information to unambiguously determine orientation. To understand why—and to understand how the visual system gets the information it needs—you need to keep in mind two additional factors. First, the strength of a simple cell's response is affected not only by the orientation of the bar but also by the luminance contrast of the bar with its background—that is, how much brighter or darker than the background the bar is. Generally, the greater the contrast, the stronger the response. And second, any relatively small area on the retina contains the receptive fields of many simple cells covering the full range of preferred orientations.

Consider the difficulty the visual system would face in trying to determine the orientation of a bar of light based on the response of just one simple cell—say, Simple Cell A in Figure 3.7, with a preferred orientation of 90°. As you can see in the figure, a bar oriented at 90° evokes, on average, a response of 40 spikes/sec so you might think that a 40-spikes/sec response definitely indicates a 90° bar orientation. But this reasoning doesn't take contrast into account. Figure 3.9 shows that the 40-spikes/sec maximum response is for a low-contrast bar. If a high-contrast bar were flashed in the cell's receptive field, an orientation of either 67° or 111° would generate a response of 40 spikes/sec, while an orientation of 90° would now generate a response

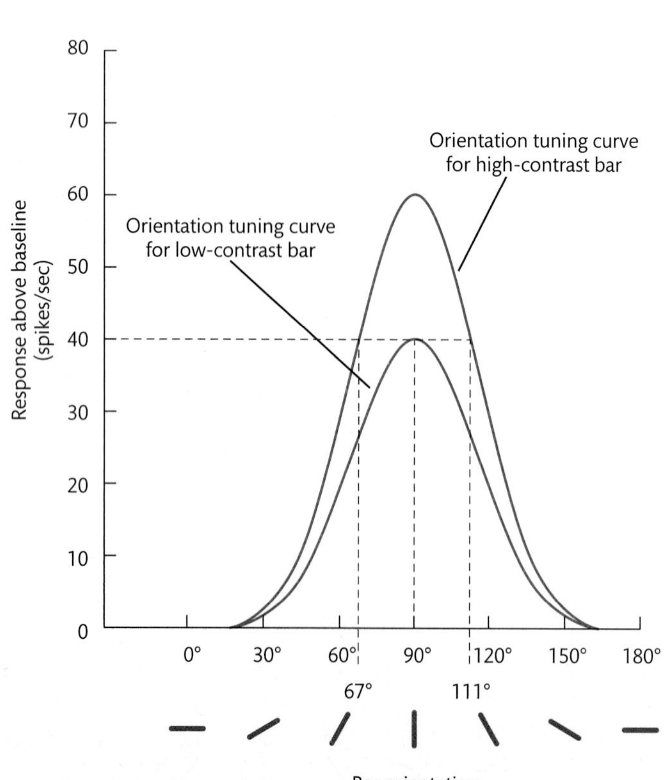

Figure 3.9 Effect of Luminance Contrast on the Orientation Tuning Curve of a Simple Cell The firing rate of a single simple cell is ambiguous because a high-contrast bar of light tends to evoke a stronger response than a low-contrast bar. In the situation illustrated here, a firing rate of 40 spikes/sec could represent the cell's response to a high-contrast bar oriented at either 67° or 111°, or to a low-contrast bar oriented at 90°.

of 60 spikes/sec. Thus, it would be impossible for the visual system to "know" the orientation of a bar of light based just on the response of a single simple cell with a known orientation tuning curve, because the simple cell has no way, by itself, of conveying information about the bar's contrast with its background separately from its orientation: a response of 40 spikes/sec could be due to a low-contrast 90° bar or a high-contrast 67° or 111° bar.

Figure 3.10 indicates how the visual system solves this problem. The figure shows the orientation tuning curves of two simple cells with receptive fields at the same location on the retina. Simple Cell A has a preferred orientation of 90°, and Simple Cell B has a preferred orientation of 75°. As shown by the graph on the left, when the stimulus is a low-contrast bar with an orientation of 90°, Simple Cell A produces a response of 40 spikes/sec above baseline, while Simple Cell B produces a much weaker response of just 17 spikes/sec above baseline. Now note the graph on the right, which shows that when the stimulus is a high-contrast bar with the same 90° orientation, Simple Cell A produces a response of 60 spikes/sec above baseline, while Simple Cell B produces a response of 25 spikes/sec above baseline. Thus, regardless of whether the 90° bar is low contrast or high contrast, the response of Simple Cell A is greater than the response of Simple Cell B.

Now compare the responses of these simple cells to low- and high-contrast bars oriented at 75°, also illustrated in Figure 3.10. In this case, when the bar is low contrast, Simple Cell B's response is greater than Simple Cell A's (30 versus 26 spikes/sec above baseline), and the same is true when the bar is high contrast (48 versus 34 spikes/sec above baseline). Again, just as with the 90° bar, the relative responses of the two simple cells are the same regardless of whether the bar is low contrast or high contrast, but now the response of Simple Cell B is consistently greater than the response of Simple Cell A.

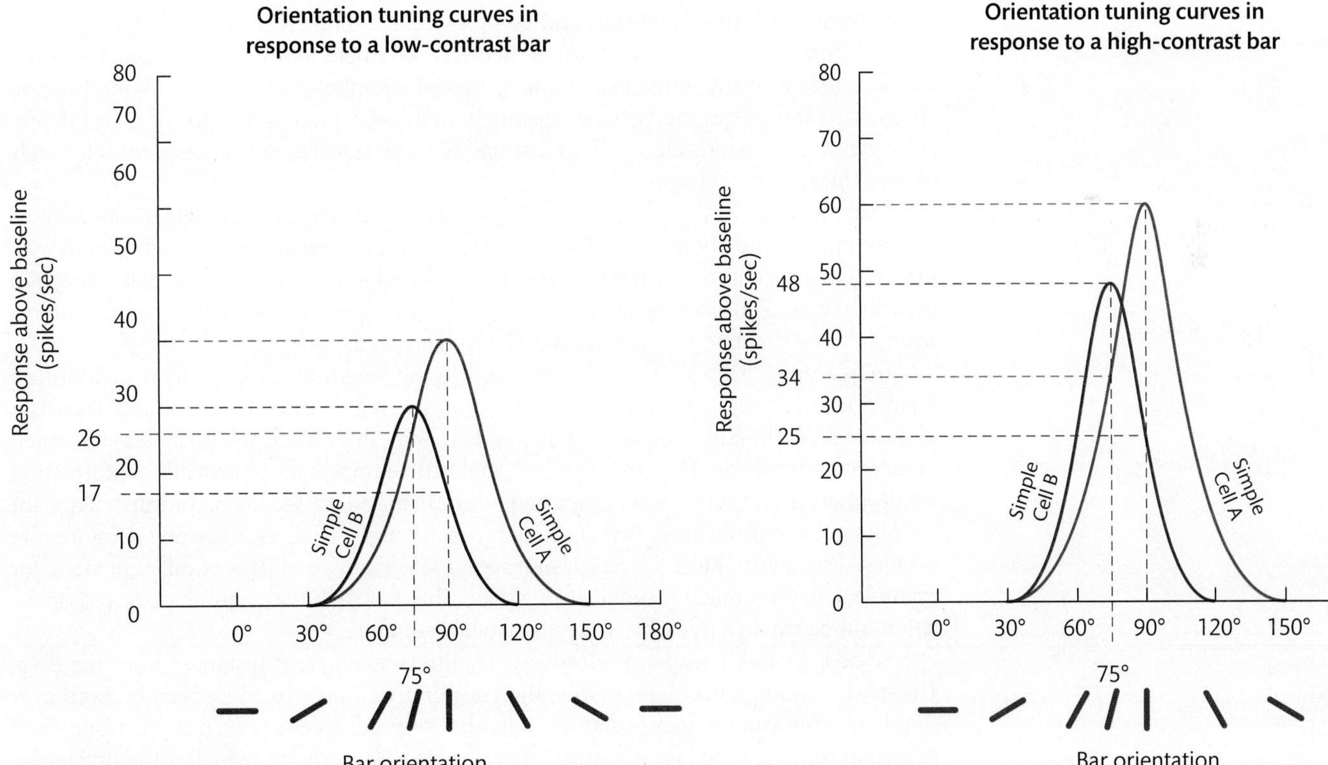

Figure 3.10 How a Population Code Specifies Orientation Despite the Effects of Luminance Contrast Simple Cells A and B have receptive fields at the same location on the retina but have different preferred orientations, as shown by these orientation tuning curves: a preferred orientation of 90° for Simple Cell A and 75° for Simple Cell B. When the receptive field location on the retina is illuminated by a bar of light oriented at 90°, the response of Simple Cell A is greater than the response of Simple Cell B, regardless of whether the bar is low contrast (left) or high contrast (right). For a bar oriented at 75°, the relative responses are reversed—the response of Simple Cell B is greater than the response of Simple Cell A, regardless of contrast. Thus, orientation but not contrast changes the response pattern of these two cells. The different patterns of responses evoked in a population of simple cells by differently oriented bars of light function as a population code, allowing the visual system to compute the orientation regardless of contrast.

Demonstration 3.3 Orientation Tuning of Simple Cells in V1, and Population Coding Control the orientation and contrast of stimuli on the receptive field of a simple cell to measure its orientation tuning curve; explore how the responses of multiple simple cells can unambiguously represent the orientation of stimuli.

population code A consistent difference in the patterning of the relative responses of a population of differently tuned neurons; used to compute perceptual features such as the orientation of a visual stimulus.

complex cells Neurons in area V1 that respond best to a stimulus with a particular orientation; differ from simple cells in the variety and location of stimuli that generate a response.

Thus, changing the contrast of the stimulus doesn't change the relative responses of these two simple cells, but changing the orientation does. This type of consistent difference in the patterning of the relative responses of neurons with different orientation tuning curves is called a **population code,** because the response patterns of a population of differently tuned neurons function as a code that lets the visual system compute a perceptual feature—in this case, the orientation of a bar of light. (Of course, the population of simple cells in V1 with receptive fields at each location in the retinal image consists not of two cells but of thousands.) In later chapters, we'll see that our perceptual system operates with population codes to compute a variety of other perceptual features, including nonvisual ones.

Complex Cells

The second main category of cells in V1—**complex cells**—are apparently the most numerous cell type in that area of the visual cortex. Like simple cells, complex cells are tuned for orientation—that is, they respond well to bars within a specific range of orientations flashed on their receptive field. However, they differ from simple cells in at least two respects. First, they respond as well to a light bar on a dark background as to a dark bar on a light background; simple cells respond well to one or the other, but not to both. Second, complex cells respond about equally well to a bar at almost any location within their receptive field; simple cells respond best to a bar at a very specific location within their receptive field. These response differences suggest that complex cells probably have functions distinct from or in addition to the function of simple cells (representing the orientation of edges), but just what those functions are remains a subject of active research.

Responses to Other Visual Features

We've seen that both simple cells and complex cells are tuned to respond to edges with particular orientations at the location of their receptive field in the retinal image. However, the responses of many individual simple cells and complex cells also convey information about other features in the visual image, including color, motion, length, size, and depth. Some neurons respond selectively to just one of these features; others respond selectively to two, three, or more features.

Many neurons in V1 are tuned to color—that is, they respond strongly to some colors but not others. And about 30% of V1 cells are tuned for direction and speed of motion—that is, a given neuron will respond strongly to an edge moving in a particular direction (usually perpendicular to the neuron's preferred orientation) at a particular speed, and less strongly to motion in other directions and at other speeds.

In addition, many V1 neurons are tuned to the length of the edge used to stimulate them. Such neurons are sometimes called *end-stopped cells* because their response increases as the length of the edge increases, up to a certain limit; then, as the length increases further, the response weakens. This property is thought to be important in providing information about where an object's corner is located—information that would be of importance for neurons in later visual areas that are tuned to particular shapes (see Chapter 4 for a more detailed discussion). Most V1 cells also respond selectively to objects of different sizes; for example, a neuron might respond strongly to a thin bar with the neuron's preferred orientation but poorly to a thick bar with the same orientation.

Some cells in V1 respond selectively to objects at different distances from the eyes. These V1 cells are binocular—that is, they respond well only to edges seen by both eyes simultaneously (unlike monocular V1 cells that respond to edges seen by just one eye). Binocular cells are tuned for a feature known as *binocular disparity,* which is the difference, if any, in the location of an object's retinal image in the two eyes. As we will see in much more detail in Chapter 6, binocular disparity is critical for perceiving depth.

Given that many cells in area V1 are tuned to multiple features, how can the visual system use the strength of a neuron's response to determine the actual features of a particular stimulus? We've already answered this question with respect to the two features of orientation and luminance contrast, where we saw how the visual system uses a population code to determine orientation despite differences in contrast; the same concept of a population code can be extended to disentangling the effects of more than two features on a neuron's response. The visual system detects patterns in the relative responses of a population of neurons that are differently tuned to, say, orientation, motion, and binocular disparity, and on the basis of those patterns determines the actual orientation, motion, or binocular disparity of the stimulus. As we'll see throughout this book, our perceptual systems have evolved to use complex codes that make the most of the information contained in the responses of neural populations.

Check Your Understanding

3.5 What determines the preferred orientation of a simple cell?

3.6 What factor in addition to the orientation of a stimulus most affects a simple cell's response?

3.7 How does the visual system determine the orientation of a bar of light despite the effects of luminance contrast on the responses of simple cells?

3.8 What is the main difference in the response patterns of simple cells and complex cells?

3.9 What information might the visual system get from the responses of end-stopped cells in V1?

Organization of V1

The cerebral cortex—the outermost layer of the cerebral hemispheres—is itself structured in layers that are characterized by different types and densities of neurons and by different patterns of connection with other neurons within the brain. Figure 3.11 shows these layers in the primary visual cortex, area V1.

The functional organization of the cortex, including area V1, is characterized by columns that run vertically through the layers. Each **cortical column** is a small volume of

cortical column A small volume of neural tissue running through the layers of the cortex perpendicular to its surface; consists of neurons that respond to similar types of stimuli and that have highly overlapping receptive fields.

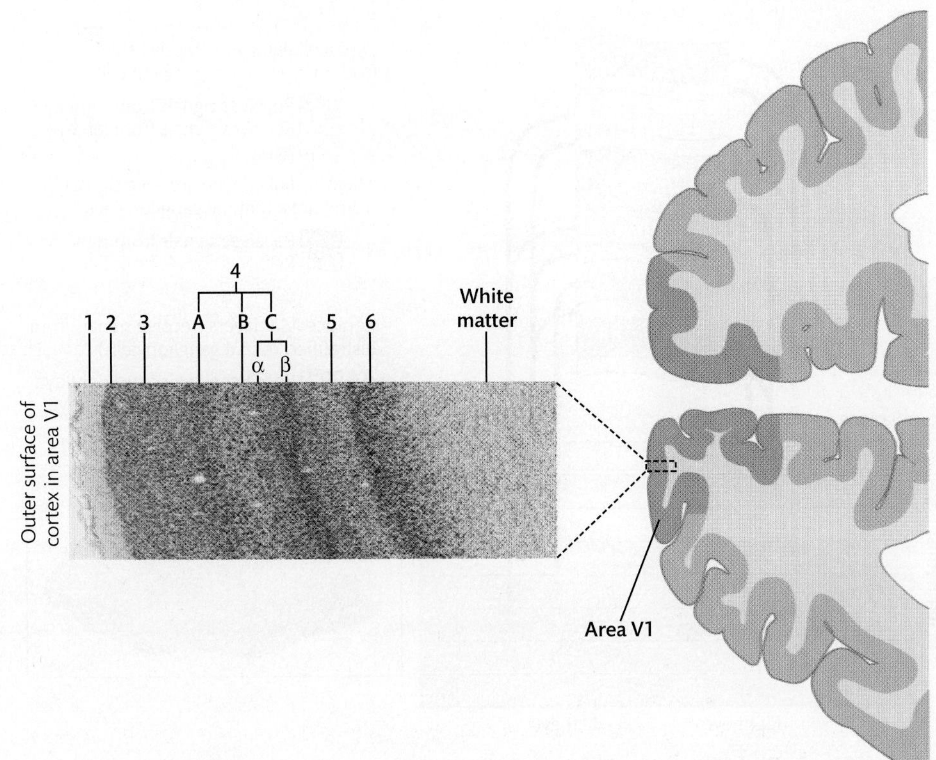

Figure 3.11 Layers of the Primary Visual Cortex (Area V1) Layers 1–6 of the primary visual cortex (area V1) were originally described by Brodmann (1909/2005). Layer 4 had to be subdivided, and then layer 4C had to be subdivided again, as more was learned about the connectivities of the neurons. [brainmaps.org]

Vernon B. Mountcastle (b. 1918).
[The Alan Mason Chesney Medical Archives of the Johns Hopkins Medical Institutions]

neural tissue like a tiny cylinder about 0.5 mm in diameter and 2–4 mm tall (corresponding to the thickness of the cortex in any given area). The existence of these functional building blocks of the cortex was first discovered by the American neuroscientist Vernon Mountcastle (1957) in his studies of the somatosensory (touch) system of the brain. He found that when he inserted a microelectrode vertically into the cortex, the neurons he encountered all responded in similar ways; in contrast, when the electrode was inserted obliquely, the neurons at successive positions had different response properties.

Hubel and Wiesel found that the primary visual cortex of the cat (1962) and the monkey (1968) are also organized into columns. Within a column, neurons have similar properties, and they monitor virtually the same area of the sensory surface (e.g., the skin in the case of touch or the retina in the case of vision)—that is, they respond to similar types of stimuli, and their receptive fields are highly overlapping.

In the next sections, we'll discuss the three types of organization involving cortical columns in V1: ocular dominance columns, consisting of neurons that receive signals from one eye only; orientation columns, consisting of neurons with similar orientation tuning; and retinotopic mapping, whereby (1) columns consist of neurons with receptive fields located in the same area of the retina, and (2) neurons in adjacent columns have receptive fields in adjacent areas. Throughout these sections, keep in mind that, in reality, the borders of cortical columns are somewhat fuzzier and the functional changes across columns are more gradual than some of the illustrations might suggest.

Ocular Dominance Columns

As discussed above and as illustrated in Figure 3.4, signals from each eye travel to separate layers in the LGN. This separation is maintained in V1, with alternating columns of neurons receiving signals originating in the left eye and the right eye. The existence of these **ocular dominance columns** can be visualized using a tracer substance that is injected into one eye. The tracer is transported up the optic nerve, across the synapses in the LGN, and on to V1, where it's deposited in the axon terminals of LGN cells. The presence of the tracer shows up in micrographs like the one at the bottom right of Figure 3.12, where the stripes are the

ocular dominance columns Cortical columns consisting of neurons that receive signals from the left eye only or the right eye only.

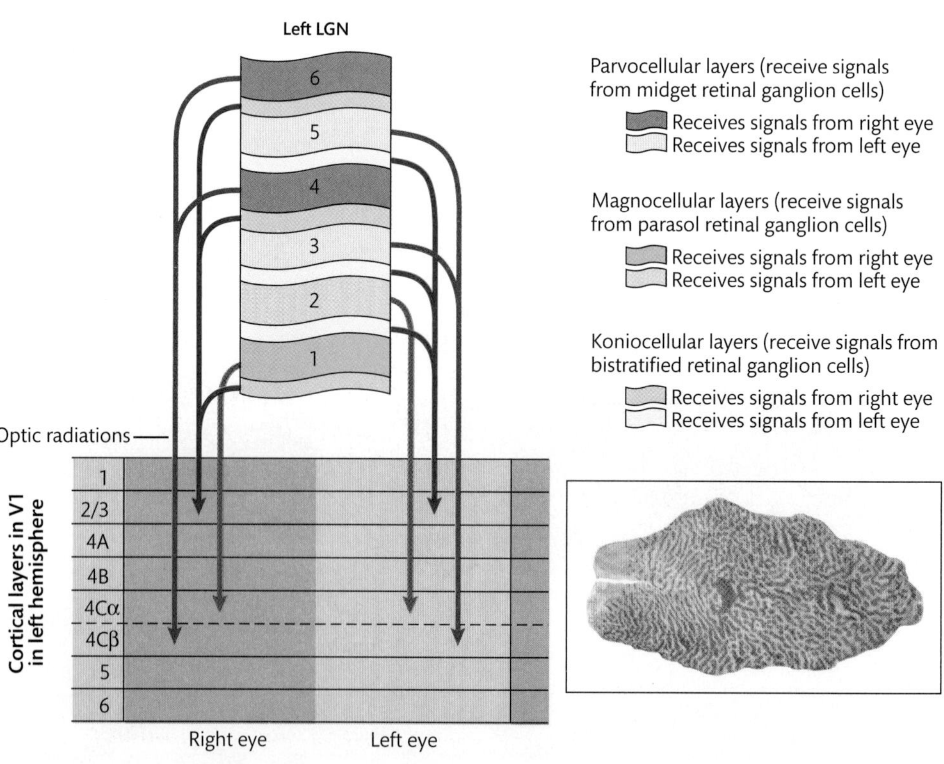

Figure 3.12 Ocular Dominance Columns in V1 Ocular dominance columns in V1 reflect the pattern of connectivity between the layers of the LGN and layers 2/3 and 4C in the cortical columns in V1. Alternating columns in V1 receive signals either from the right eye via LGN layers 1, 4, and 6 (and the koniocellular layers under them) or from the left eye via LGN layers 2, 3, and 5 (and the koniocellular layers under them). The parvocellular layers send signals to V1 layer 4Cβ, the magnocellular layers send signals to V1 layer 4Cα, and the koniocellular layers send signals to V1 layers 2/3. The micrograph shows ocular dominance columns in a human brain. (Illustration based on Nassi & Callaway, 2009.) [Micrograph: Adams & Horton, 2009, Figure 3]

alternating ocular dominance columns in V1. The rest of Figure 3.12 is a schematic illustration of how ocular dominance columns reflect the connections between the layers of the LGN and layers 2/3 and 4C of V1. Recordings from individual neurons in V1 have revealed that the cells in a border zone between ocular dominance columns respond to input from both eyes, and many of these neurons are tuned for binocular disparity (Horton & Hocking, 1998).

Orientation Columns

Hubel and Wiesel found that, just as there are ocular dominance columns in which neurons receive signals from the same eye, there are also **orientation columns**, in which neurons have the same (or very similar) orientation tuning. And just as ocular dominance columns alternate systematically between left-eye and right-eye dominance, orientation columns vary systematically across the full range of preferred orientations. This was shown by experiments in which an electrode was advanced obliquely through the visual cortex; each time a cell was encountered, its orientation tuning was determined by presenting bars of light with various orientations (Hubel & Wiesel, 1962). The diagram in Figure 3.13a depicts how the electrode was advanced through the layers of the cortex, and the graph in Figure 3.13b shows the systematic change in the orientation tuning of neurons encountered successively by such an electrode as it moves through adjacent columns.

orientation columns Cortical columns consisting of neurons with the same (or very similar) orientation tuning.

The images in Figure 3.13c show how the orientation tuning of neurons in V1 has been visualized in cats (Ohki et al., 2006; Ohki & Reid, 2007). A voltage-sensitive dye is squirted onto the surface of the cortex, and the cat is shown a display consisting of stripes, all having the same orientation. The activity of neurons in the cortex that respond when that orientation is viewed causes the dye to change color, and a photograph is then taken of the surface of the cortex. This procedure is then repeated for many different orientations, with a different color being used to show the locations of active neurons for each orientation. The color-coded bars indicate the preferred orientations of the neurons in four adjacent columns. The enlargement, which reveals individual neurons tuned to each

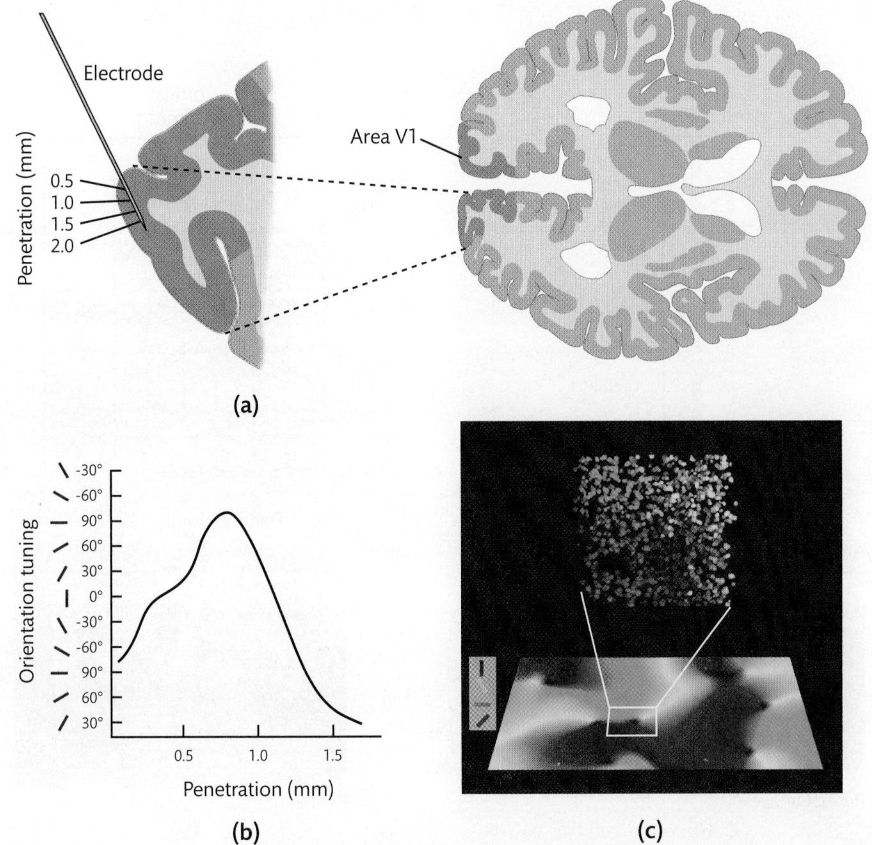

Figure 3.13 Orientation Columns in V1 (a) An electrode is advanced obliquely through the visual cortex (a human brain is depicted, but the experiments were done in cats). (b) The orientation tuning of the neurons successively encountered by the electrode changes systematically as the electrode moves from one column of cells to the next. (Adapted from Hubel, 1995.) (c) Imaging of the surface of V1 of a cat (viewed from above) reveals the organization of orientation columns: each patch of color corresponds to the location of a column of neurons, with the preferred orientation indicated by the color-coded bars at the left (and as you can see, the columns aren't arranged in a rectilinear grid, but in a kind of "pinwheel" pattern). The enlargement reveals the orientation preferences of individual neurons in the outlined area. [(c): Ohki & Reid, 2007, Figure 1a]

orientation, shows that any small region of the cortex contains neurons covering the full range of preferred orientations.

Retinotopic Maps and Cortical Magnification

A third type of organization in V1 involves the receptive field locations of neurons at adjacent locations in the cortex. Studies with nonhuman animals have shown that if a recording electrode is inserted into V1 perpendicular to the surface of the cortex, so the electrode encounters neurons within a single column, the receptive fields of those neurons will all be at about the same location on the retina—that is, the receptive fields will largely overlap (Hubel & Wiesel, 1974), as shown in Figure 3.14a. Thus, the cells within a single cortical column all monitor about the same small part of the retinal image. However, if the electrode is inserted obliquely, as shown in Figure 3.14b, so that it traverses adjacent cortical columns, the receptive fields of the neurons encountered will be at adjacent locations on the retina.

Thus, area V1 contains a retinotopic map, which can be easily seen in the human cortex through the use of fMRI (Tootell et al., 1998). This retinotopic map is constructed in polar coordinates: one dimension is the *eccentricity*—the distance from the center of the fovea—and the other dimension is the *polar angle*—the angle above or below the horizontal in a circle with the fovea at the center. To show that the visual system uses this coordinate system, two fMRI scans are required, as illustrated in Figure 3.15. The eccentricity dimension is demonstrated by having an observer in an fMRI scanner look at a visual display consisting of an expanding black-and-white checkerboard ring on a medium-gray background (Figure 3.15a). To demonstrate the polar angle dimension, the observer is shown a flickering checkerboard wedge that rotates slowly around the fovea (Figure 3.15b).

As mentioned earlier, the retinotopic map in area V1 in humans was first discovered early in the twentieth century by T. Inouye, who also discovered another phenomenon—cortical magnification—that was later confirmed by the mapping studies described above. **Cortical magnification** refers to the nonuniform representation of visual space in the

cortical magnification The nonuniform representation of visual space in the cortex; the amount of cortical territory devoted to the central part of the visual field is much greater than the amount devoted to the periphery.

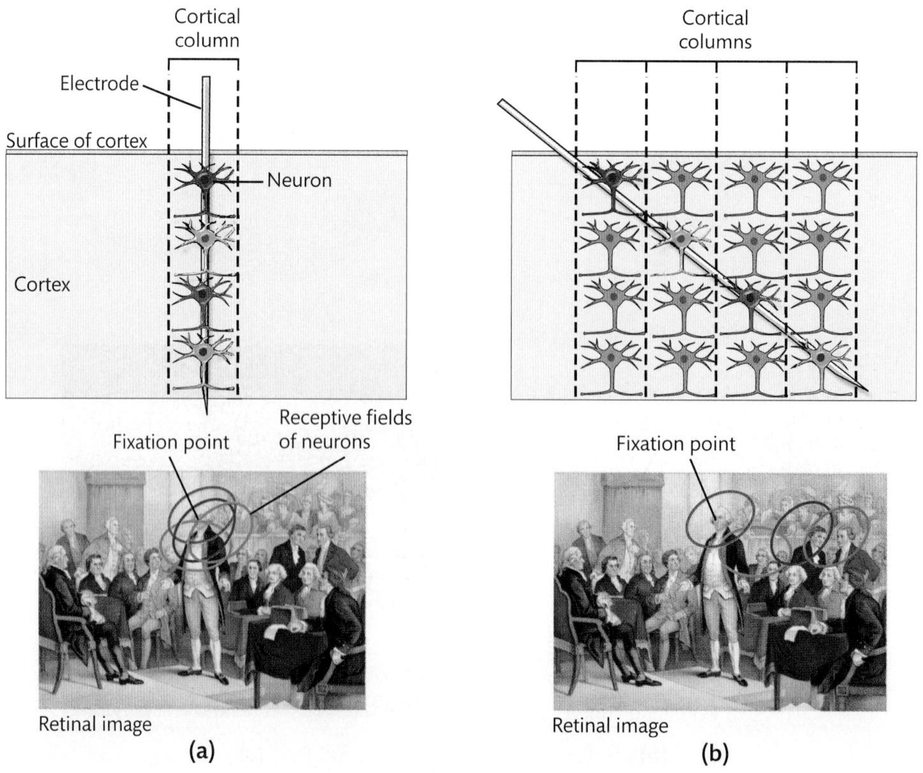

Figure 3.14 Receptive Field Locations and Cortical Columns in V1 (a) V1 neurons within a single cortical column can be found by inserting a recording electrode into the cortex perpendicular to its surface. All these neurons will have a receptive field at about the same location in the retinal image. (b) V1 neurons in adjacent columns can be found by inserting a recording electrode obliquely through the cortex; these neurons will have receptive fields at adjacent locations in the retinal image. [Painting courtesy of The Library of Congress]

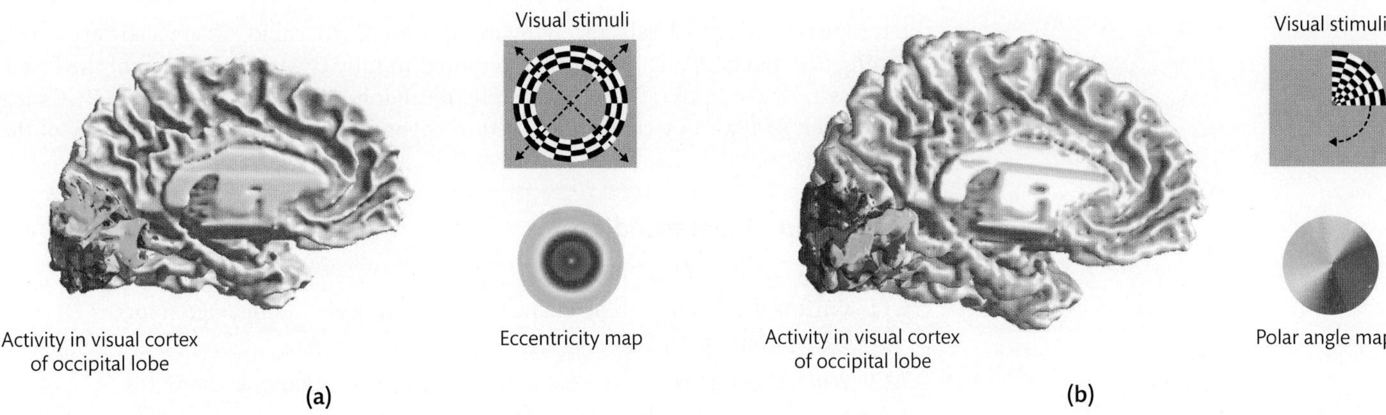

Figure 3.15 Retinotopic Map in the Visual Cortex These medial views of the left hemisphere of the human brain show the patterns of activity in the visual cortex evoked by two different types of stimuli. The patterns demonstrate that the visual cortex constructs a retinotopic map based on polar coordinates. Throughout these experiments, the participant fixates on a small square at the center of the display. (a) The stimulus consists of a checkerboard ring that slowly expands outward while the black-and-white pattern of the checkerboard reverses four times per second, a flicker rate that evokes a strong response from cortical neurons. The eccentricity map, color coded to match the activity pattern in the visual cortex, shows that the expanding ring produces a wave of activity that starts at the rearmost point of the occipital lobe, corresponding to the center of the fovea, and moves forward across the occipital lobe. (b) The stimulus consists of a checkerboard wedge that slowly rotates clockwise while the checkerboard again flickers four times per second. The color-coded polar angle map shows that, as the wedge rotates in the right visual field, it produces a wave of activity that moves from the bottom to the top of the left visual cortex (because the lower right visual field is represented at the top of the left-hemisphere visual cortex, and the upper right visual field is represented at the bottom). (Adapted and images from Dougherty et al., 2003.)

cortex. In particular, the amount of cortical territory in V1 devoted to the central part of the visual field (corresponding to the part of the retinal image over the fovea) is much greater than the amount of territory devoted to peripheral parts of the visual field (corresponding to the parts of the retinal image over the periphery of the retina). Figure 3.16 illustrates this difference—many more V1 neurons respond to a stimulus at the fovea than to a stimulus in the periphery. Or, to put it another way, many more V1 neurons have receptive fields in the fovea than in areas in the periphery of the retina.

The reason for this is that the fovea has a very high density of retinal ganglion cells, with small receptive fields, while the density of RGCs declines rapidly with distance from the fovea, with a corresponding increase in the size of their receptive fields. Thus,

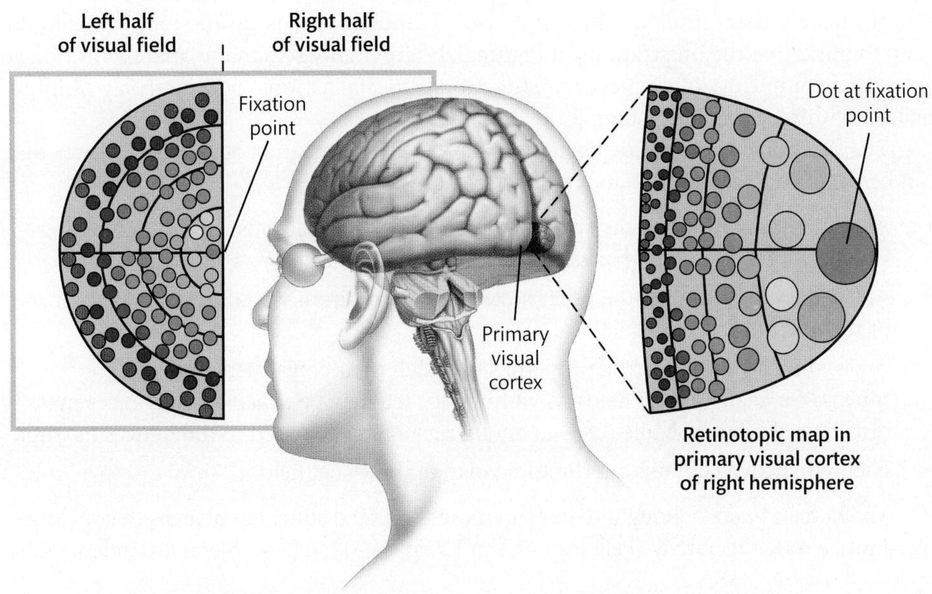

Figure 3.16 Cortical Magnification The left half of the visual field contains dots that are all the same size—that is, they occupy equal areas of the retinal image. Neurons in the observer's right-hemisphere primary visual cortex respond to the dots in the retinal image, forming a distorted retinotopic map. Each dot in the retinotopic map is sized to show how much cortical surface area (i.e., how many neurons) would respond to it, revealing the effects of cortical magnification. Much more cortical territory is devoted to visual stimuli on or near the fovea (e.g., the dark orange dot) than to stimuli in the periphery of the retinal image (e.g., the purple dots). (Adapted from an illustration by G. Boynton. Used with permission.)

the receptive fields of V1 cells receiving input from the foveal RGCs are also very small, meaning that a great many V1 cells are required to fully cover a given area of the fovea. In contrast, the receptive fields of V1 cells receiving input from peripheral RGCs are much larger, so fewer V1 cells are needed to cover a given area in the periphery of the retina.

Check Your Understanding

3.10 What is a cortical column?

3.11 What is the distinguishing characteristic of an ocular dominance column? Of an orientation column?

3.12 What does it mean to say that area V1 contains a retinotopic map?

3.13 *Cortical magnification* in V1 refers to the nonuniform representation of visual space. Explain what this means.

Functional Areas, Pathways, and Modules

Functional specialization is ubiquitous in the visual system, starting with the neurons that transduce light into neural signals, the rods and cones. Specialization continues in the different functions of midget, parasol, and bistratified RGCs, which send signals to neurons in the parvocellular, magnocellular, and koniocellular layers of the LGN, respectively. Signals from the layers of the LGN then travel to separate layers of area V1, where populations of neurons encode edge orientation and other visual features. In the rest of this section, we'll follow these pathways deep into the visual cortex.

Functional Areas and Pathways

Figure 3.17 depicts the flow of information from midget, parasol, and bistratified RGCs to the LGN, to area V1, and then on to other areas of the visual brain, including areas in the parietal and temporal lobes. The connectivity patterns shown in the illustration at the top of Figure 3.17 can be understood as consisting of a few major functional pathways for information of specific types, where a "pathway" consists of neural connections involving millions of axons and many different visual areas. Each pathway transmits neural signals containing information of particular types and connects areas of the brain that are specialized for processing those types of information. In Figure 3.17, the labels *form, color,* and *motion* indicate the broad categories of information transmitted via these pathways. (In this context, *form* refers to properties like edge orientation and curvature that ultimately determine an object's shape.) Throughout this discussion, you should keep in mind that the illustrations in Figure 3.17 are highly schematic, merely hinting at the actual complexity of connections, functional specializations, and interplay of information within the visual system.

The functional pathways depicted in Figure 3.17 connect areas of the visual cortex that can be compared according to four characteristics:

- Areas differ according to the types and distributions of neurons within them (e.g., small cell bodies densely packed versus large cell bodies more sparsely arranged).
- Areas differ according to the other areas in the brain from which they receive signals or to which they send signals.
- Areas differ according to the properties to which their constituent neurons are tuned—for example, the neurons within one area may be tuned to differences in direction of motion, while those in another area may be tuned to differences in color.
- Each visual area contains a retinotopic map of the visual field.

The human brain is thought to contain more than 30 distinct visual areas that are organized into a rough hierarchy (Felleman & Van Essen, 1991), where "hierarchy" refers to the

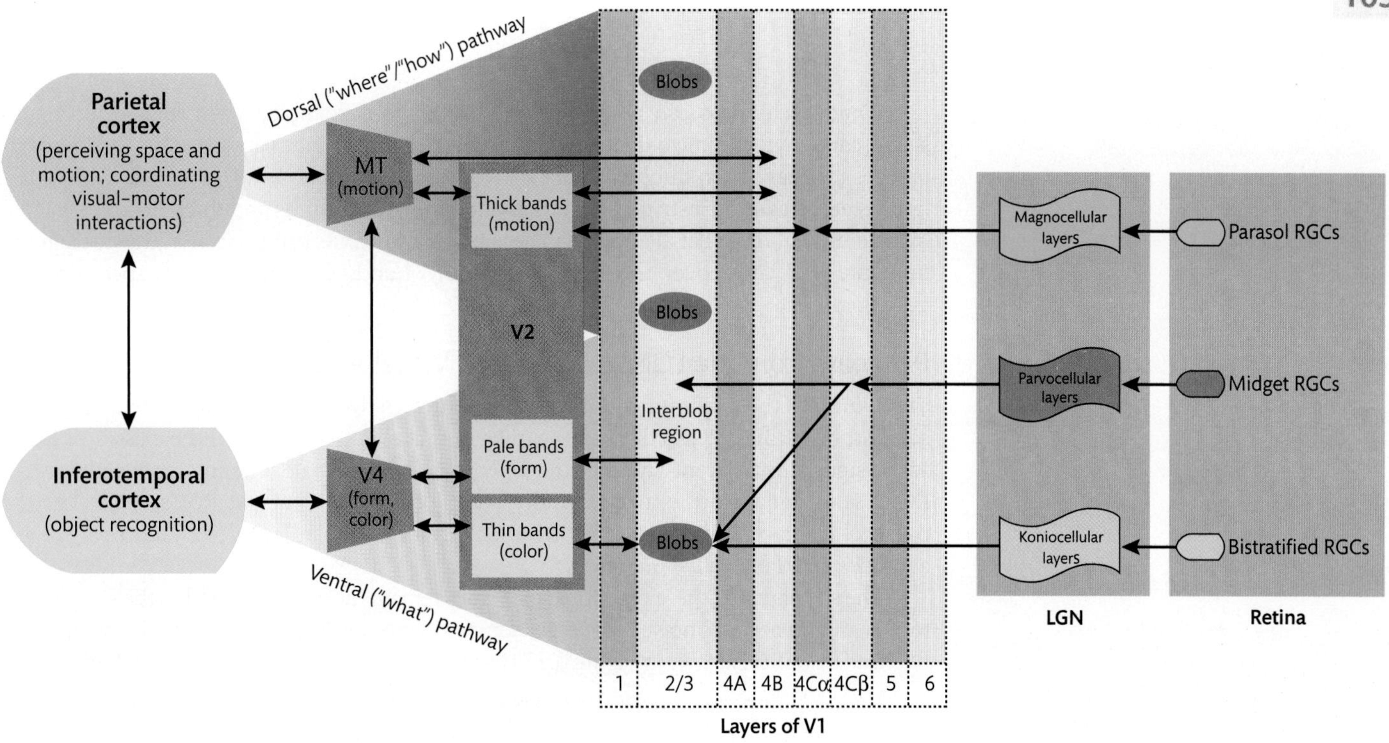

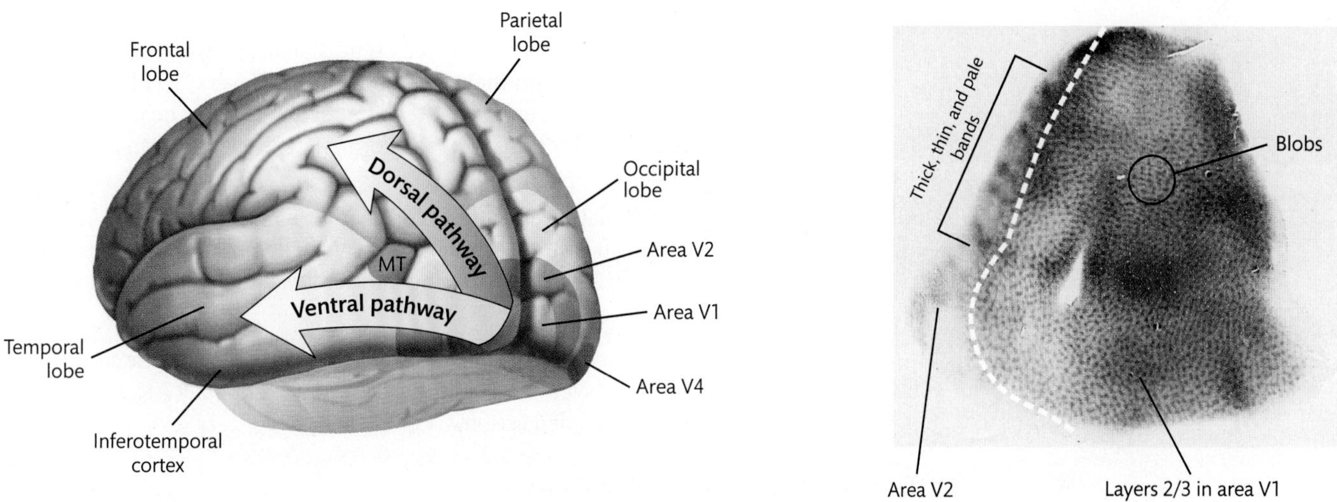

Figure 3.17 Functional Areas and Pathways in the Visual System Neural signals from parasol, midget, and bistratified RGCs remain segregated in the layers of the LGN, from which they carry information into the layers of V1, including the blobs and interblob regions of layers 2/3. From V1, these signals flow to the functionally specialized bands of V2, which transmit the separate types of information that define the two large-scale pathways: the ventral pathway and the dorsal pathway. The ventral pathway, which flows from V2 through area V4 and to the inferotemporal cortex, transmits information about form and color that is used as part of the process of object recognition—determining what the observer is looking at (hence the name "what" pathway). The dorsal pathway, which flows from V2 through area MT to the parietal cortex, transmits information about motion and location that is used as part of the process of visual-motor interactions—determining where objects are and how to interact with them (hence the name "where"/"how" pathway). (Arrows represent neural signals; double-headed arrows represent signals that flow in both directions, carrying feedback.) The micrograph is from the visual cortex of a macaque monkey; it shows part of V1 layers 2/3 and part of V2. Blobs can be seen throughout layers 2/3, and thick, thin, and pale bands can be seen in V2. The dashed white line indicates the border between V1 and V2. [Micrograph: Horton, 1984, Figure 3]

order in which areas process information coming from the retinas. Thus, as indicated in Figure 3.17, area V1 is lower in the hierarchy than area V2, which is lower than areas V4 and MT, which are lower than the visual areas in the inferotemporal cortex and parietal cortex. When two brain areas are connected (as, for example, V1 is connected to V2), the connection is always reciprocal—V1 sends signals to V2, and V2 sends signals back to V1.

Some visual areas can be further subdivided. For example, when stained for a substance called cytochrome oxidase, layers 2/3 of area V1 exhibit many small, roughly circular patches that have been dubbed "blobs" (Livingstone & Hubel, 1984). Area V2, when similarly treated, takes on a striped pattern of alternating thin bands and thick bands separated by pale bands (Tootell et al., 1983). (These blobs and bands can be seen in the micrograph in Figure 3.17.) Moreover, these subdivisions of V1 and V2 are functionally specialized, as described next.

Pathways from the LGN to the Brain's Visual Areas

The sources of the major functional pathways through the visual brain are the midget, parasol, and bistratified RGCs discussed earlier in this chapter. Each of these classes of RGCs sends signals to different layers of the LGN, where the signals remain segregated: parasol RGCs send signals to the magnocellular layers of the LGN, midget RGCs connect to the parvocellular layers, and bistratified RGCs to the koniocellular layers (see Figures 3.4, 3.12, and 3.17 and Table 3.1).

The signals along these functional pathways remain mostly segregated as the signals flow to area V1 and beyond; however, there is some evidence for "crosstalk," indicated by the double-headed vertical arrows in Figure 3.17 (Nassi & Callaway, 2009). As shown in Figure 3.17:

- Neurons in the magnocellular layers of the LGN send signals to layer 4Cα of V1; from there, signals flow to the thick bands of V2 and then to MT. The neurons in this pathway are specialized for transmitting information about movement and spatial location in the visual field.
- Neurons in the parvocellular layers of the LGN send signals to layer 4Cβ of V1; from there, signals flow to the blobs and the interblob regions of layers 2/3 of V1 and then to the thin and pale bands of V2 and to V4 (Federer et al., 2009). The neurons in this pathway are specialized for transmitting information about the form and color of objects in the visual field.
- Neurons in the koniocellular layers of the LGN send signals to the blobs in layers 2/3 of V1 from which signals flow to the thin bands of V2. The neurons in this pathway are thought to be specialized for transmitting information about the color of objects in the visual field (Nassi & Callaway, 2009).

Now let's explore the ways in which higher areas of the visual system use the information carried by the pathways labeled "dorsal" and "ventral" in Figure 3.17 to support both object perception and visually guided action.

The Dorsal and Ventral Pathways

During the 1970s and 1980s, researchers made a great deal of progress in clarifying the functions of many visual areas, but the overall organizational scheme of the visual brain

TABLE 3.1 Main Functional Pathways in the Visual System*

RGCs →	LGN Layers →	V1 Layers →	V2 Bands →	Intermediate Visual Areas* →	Higher Visual Areas	
Parasol	Magnocellular	4Cα	Thick (motion)	MT (motion)	Parietal cortex (perceiving space and motion; coordinating visual–motor interactions)	*Dorsal Pathway: "Where"/"How"*
Midget	Parvocellular	4Cβ	Thin (color) Pale (form)	V4 (form, color)	Inferotemporal cortex (object recognition)	*Ventral Pathway: "What"*
Bistratified	Koniocellular	2/3 (blobs)	Thin (color)			

*There are several different intermediate visual areas in each pathway; shown are prominent examples.

remained unclear. Then, two key studies—one from the early 1980s and the other from the early 1990s—provided an overarching framework for thinking about how visual function is organized in the primate brain. These studies suggested that there are two major pathways for the flow of information from V1 onward—the pathways labeled *dorsal* and *ventral* in Figure 3.17:

- The **dorsal pathway** passes from V1 and V2 into MT and then to the parietal cortex. This pathway is responsible for representing properties that relate to an object's motion or location, information that's also used to guide action (therefore, it has also been called the *"where" pathway* and/or the *"how" pathway*).
- The **ventral pathway** passes from V1 and V2 into V4 and then to the inferotemporal cortex. This pathway is responsible for representing properties that relate to an object's identity, such as its color and shape (therefore, it has also been called the *"what" pathway*).

dorsal pathway A visual pathway that runs from V1 and V2 into MT and then to the parietal cortex; represents properties that relate to an object's motion or location and that can be used to guide actions.

ventral pathway A visual pathway that runs from V1 and V2 into V4 and then to the inferotemporal cortex; represents properties that relate to an object's identity, such as its color and shape.

In the first experiment (Ungerleider & Mishkin, 1982), monkeys were trained to perform two different tasks—called a *landmark task* and an *object task*—that involved learning which of two covered bins contained food (see Figure 3.18). In the landmark task, the monkeys were trained to look for the food in the bin that was closer to a landmark; this task was hypothesized to engage the dorsal ("where") pathway selectively, because the monkeys had to learn where the bin with food was in relation to the landmark. In the object task, the monkeys were trained to look for the food in the bin covered by an object with a particular shape; this task was thought to engage the ventral ("what") pathway selectively, because the monkeys had to learn what object covered the bin with food.

The investigators then produced brain lesions in the parietal cortex (part of the dorsal pathway) or in the inferotemporal cortex (part of the ventral pathway) and tested the monkeys on the two tasks once again. The results showed that monkeys with damage to the dorsal pathway lost their ability to succeed in the landmark task but not the object task, whereas monkeys with damage to the ventral pathway lost their ability to succeed in the object task but not the landmark task.

This organizational scheme—the dorsal pathway as the "where" pathway, the ventral pathway as the "what" pathway—prevailed until the publication of a case study of a neuropsychological patient with the initials D.F. who had brain damage in her ventral pathway as a result of carbon monoxide poisoning (Goodale et al., 1991; see the vignette at the beginning of this chapter). The patient suffered from visual agnosia, an inability to recognize objects visually—that is, she was unable to perceive the shapes of objects she was looking at. Despite this damage, D.F. could accurately reach for and grasp objects, even though performing this action required some degree of shape perception because she had to conform her hand to the shape of the object in order to grasp it.

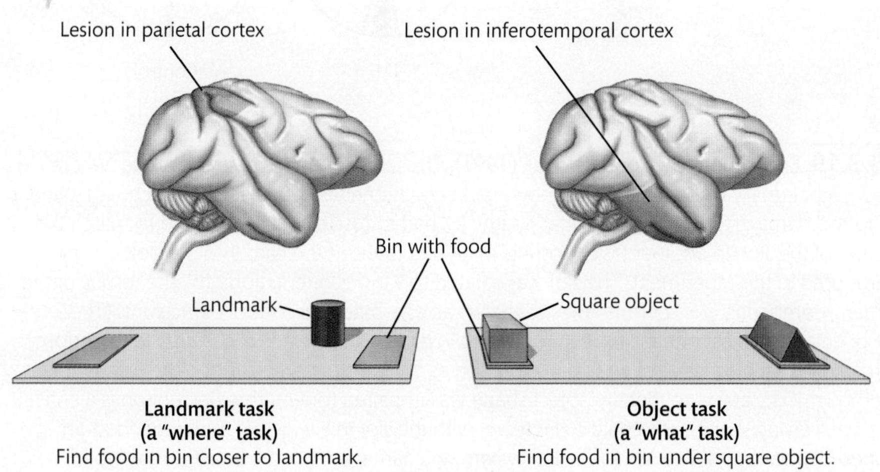

Figure 3.18 Experiment by Ungerleider and Mishkin (1982) Monkeys were trained to perform two different tasks. The monkeys were then given lesions in either their parietal cortex or their inferotemporal cortex. Those with lesions in the parietal cortex could no longer accomplish the "where" task, while those with lesions in the inferotemporal cortex could no longer accomplish the "what" task. This experiment led to the identification of two main functional pathways in the brain—the ventral pathway (or "what" pathway) and the dorsal pathway (or "where" pathway).

The researchers tested D.F. in detail to determine the precise nature of her deficit. In one test (illustrated in Figure 3.19), they found that she was unable to correctly perceive orientation—a critical aspect of shape perception—as evidenced by her inability to orient a card held in her hand to match the orientation of a rotatable slot in a board in front of her (Figure 3.19a). Her responses were almost completely random (Figure 3.19b, top left circle), whereas a control participant could match the orientation with the card almost perfectly (Figure 3.19b, top right circle). The investigators then asked D.F. to actually insert the card into the slot (similar to posting a letter through a mail slot). In this case, D.F. performed virtually as well as the control participant, regardless of the orientation of the slot (Figure 3.19b, bottom circles). Even though D.F. couldn't correctly perceive orientation (as indicated by her inability to reproduce the orientation of the slot simply by turning the card), she could accurately insert the card into the slot, an action that clearly required perception of the slot's orientation—an apparent paradox.

In another test, D.F. was asked to state which of two elongated rectangular blocks was longer, and her ability to do this was no better than chance. However, when she was asked to reach out and grasp a block, the distance between her index finger and thumb would almost perfectly match the size of the block (Goodale et al., 1991). Once again, despite her apparent lack of ability to perceive the shape (in this case, length) of an object, her ability to use information about shape was nearly intact when she had to interact with the object (in this case, by grasping it).

The researchers argued that D.F.'s impaired ability to match the orientation of a slot or compare the lengths of wooden blocks reflected the damage to her ventral object-recognition pathway: perception of an object's orientation and perception of its size are basic aspects of perceiving its overall shape. However, the fact that D.F. could still use information about orientation to interact with the slot (by posting the card in it) and use information about size to interact with the block (by grasping it) led them to the further

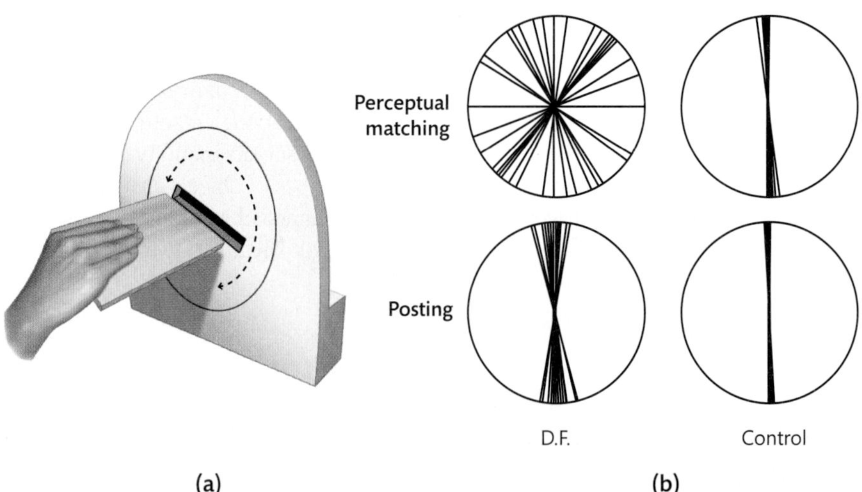

Figure 3.19 Experiment by Goodale et al. (1991) This experiment suggested that the "where" pathway might equally well be called the "how" pathway. In one task ("perceptual matching"), patient D.F., who had damage to her ventral ("what") pathway, had to rotate a handheld card to match the orientation of the slot; in another task ("posting"), she had to insert the card into the slot. (a) The apparatus used in the experiment. The slot was rotated to various orientations. (b) The results of the experiment, comparing D.F.'s performance to that of an age-matched control participant. (The correct orientation on each trial has been rotated to vertical.) Note that D.F. was unable to perform the perceptual matching task but was nearly as good as the control participant on the posting task. Thus, although D.F.'s ability to identify object shape was impaired (orientation perception is a critical aspect of perceiving shape), she could still interact with the slot in a way that also depended on perception of orientation. The ventral "what" system was damaged, but the intact dorsal "how" system was still receiving orientation information from early visual areas.

conclusion that her intact dorsal pathway had access to the information required for these tasks, information that flowed from the early visual areas of the occipital lobe, such as V1 and V2. This, they argued, would explain D.F.'s ability to use that information to interact with an object while being completely unable to use the very same information to consciously perceive the object's shape.

Other patients, with damage to the parietal lobes, sometimes exhibit a different but complementary pattern of impairment known as **optic ataxia,** a deficit in their ability to guide movements visually (Goodale, 2011). These patients can see and identify objects perfectly well, but they're unable to reach out and grasp a viewed object. Often, they'll reach out with their hands as if they were feeling for the object in the dark. They also fail at performing the task of "posting" a rectangular block into a slot—a task that D.F. could perform very accurately. Such patients do not have a motor deficit: they can accurately point to different locations on their own body with their eyes closed. Instead, they have a deficit that is in many ways the opposite of D.F.'s agnosia: an inability to guide actions with vision, with no impairment of their ability to recognize objects visually.

optic ataxia A deficit in the ability to guide movements visually.

On the basis of these striking experiments, Goodale and Milner have suggested that the dorsal pathway might more properly be called the *"how" pathway* (rather than the *"where" pathway*, as suggested by Ungerleider and Mishkin), because it's responsible not just for representing the location and motion of objects, but also for representing how to interact with objects by coordinating perception and action.

The proposals of Ungerleider and Mishkin on the one hand and Goodale and Milner on the other aren't mutually exclusive, as indicated in Figure 3.17 by the labeling of the dorsal pathway as the *"where"/"how" pathway.* The idea that the dorsal pathway may play a role in coordinating perception and action is a refinement and extension of the earlier proposal—after all, you have to know where an object is and how it's moving before you can act on it—and is perfectly consistent with the experimental observations of Ungerleider and Mishkin. (We'll explore the interplay between perception and action in more detail in Chapter 7.)

It's worth keeping in mind that this view of a hierarchical series of visual areas with two strictly segregated pathways is a simplification, for two main reasons. First, as illustrated in Figure 3.17, there is extensive feedback—information flows not just from lower to higher areas but also back from higher to lower areas, which means that the responses of any given neuron are based on a complex mixture of bottom-up and top-down information (Hegdé & Felleman, 2007). Second, the two pathways are not completely segregated; they are better described as "segregated but interacting" (Nassi & Callaway, 2009, p. 369). In order to use vision to guide an action such as grasping an object, you need information not just about the location and motion of the object, but also about its shape, size, and orientation. Similarly, information about the spatial relations among objects is a critical part of perceiving complex scenes with multiple objects.

Functional Modules

We've seen that midget, parasol, and bistratified retinal ganglion cells send signals containing different kinds of information to the magnocellular, parvocellular, and koniocellular layers of the LGN, and that LGN neurons send signals to functionally specialized layers of area V1. But taken as a whole, the retina, the LGN, and area V1 are each a general purpose part of the visual system: each must be able to process all kinds of visual information.

Beyond V1, as indicated by the functional labels in Figure 3.17, individual brain areas start to become more specialized. In this section, we'll take a look at functional specialization in four areas that have been studied in some detail. The first two are important modules on the ventral pathway: area V4, specialized for responding to color and edge curvature; and a region that includes the lateral occipital cortex and portions of the inferotemporal cortex, specialized for responding to complex shapes (within the inferotemporal cortex, smaller subareas have been identified that are even more narrowly specialized, including the fusiform face area and the parahippocampal place area). Then we'll discuss two areas that are important modules on the dorsal pathway: area MT, specialized for responding to

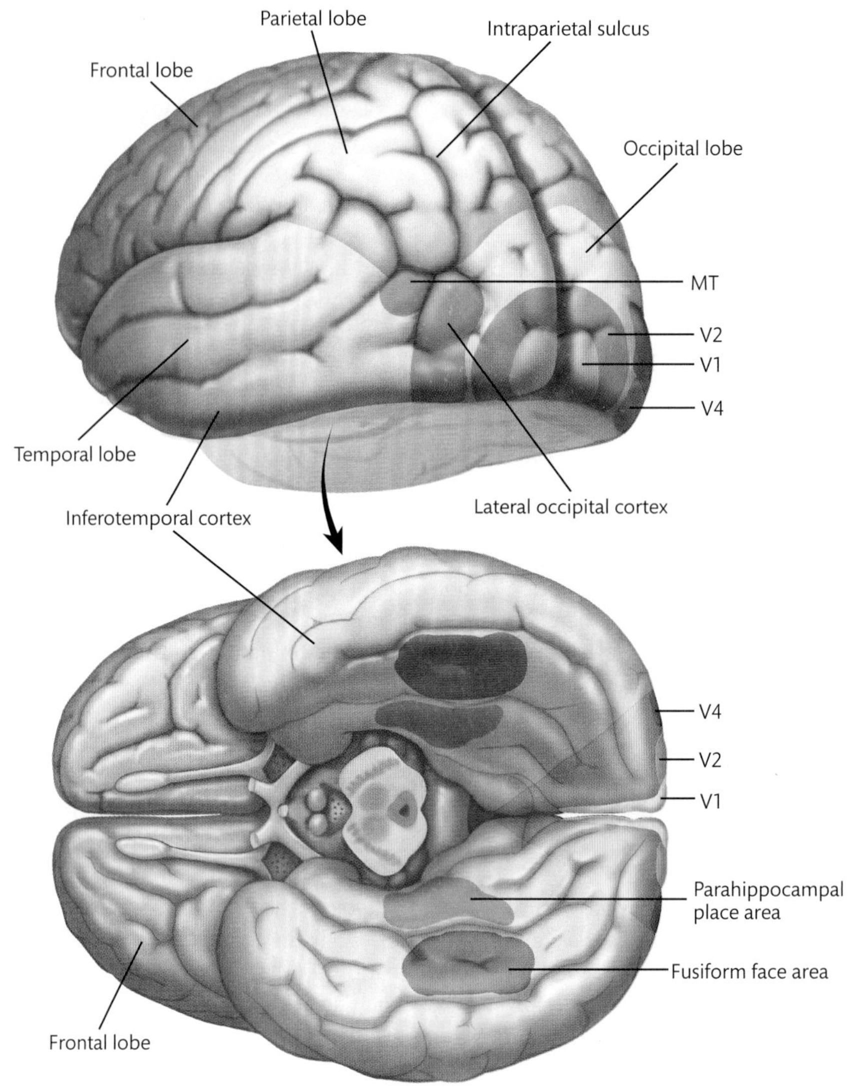

Figure 3.20 Functional Modules in the Visual System Area V4 is crucially involved in color perception and in perceiving the curvature of edges. Area MT is specialized for motion perception. The lateral occipital cortex and inferotemporal cortex (IT cortex) are responsible for representing complex shapes, including both natural objects and human artifacts. Areas located within the IT cortex include the fusiform face area, for recognizing faces, and the parahippocampal place area, for recognizing large-scale places such as landscapes, buildings, and rooms. Areas involved in visually guided action are located in the intraparietal sulcus.

motion, and the intraparietal sulcus in the parietal lobe, which contains several subregions that are specialized for supporting visually guided action. The locations of all these areas are shown in Figure 3.20.

Area V4: Color and Curvature

V4 An area in the occipital lobe consisting of neurons that respond selectively to the color of stimuli and to the curvature of edges.

Area **V4** was one of the earliest areas of the brain beyond area V1 to be investigated with single-cell recording (Van Essen & Zeki, 1978), including a study showing that V4 neurons in monkeys respond selectively to light of different colors and to edges with different curvatures (Desimone et al., 1985). A PET imaging study with human participants also showed that V4 responds selectively to color: when participants viewed a display containing a pattern of rectangles of different colors, V4 was more active than when the same pattern of rectangles was viewed in shades of gray (Zeki et al., 1991). Furthermore, damage to V4 and areas to which V4 is connected can result in a neuropsychological condition called *achromatopsia,* or *cortical color blindness,* an inability to perceive colors despite having a normal array of cones in the retina (Heywood & Kentridge, 2003; see the vignette at the beginning of Chapter 5 for a description of a case of achromatopsia).

There is also abundant evidence that neurons in V4 are tuned to the curvature of object boundaries. In a single-cell recording experiment, macaque monkeys viewed shapes that varied in the degree of curvature of an edge (Pasupathy & Connor, 2002). The study found V4 neurons that are tuned to edges with particular degrees of curvature, just as neurons in V1 are tuned to edges with particular orientations. Responding selectively to the curvature of edges is thought to be an intermediate stage in the process of recognizing the entire shape of an object.

Lateral Occipital Cortex and Inferotemporal Cortex: Objects, Faces, and Places

As we move forward from areas V1, V2, and V4 along the ventral pathway, we encounter a region of the brain with neurons that respond selectively to objects. Initial studies in monkeys using single-cell recording indicated that this region was located in the inferior (bottom) part of the temporal lobes, referred to as the **inferotemporal cortex (IT cortex).** More recent studies using fMRI in humans indicate that the object-selective regions of the human brain also include the **lateral occipital cortex** (see Figure 3.20). These areas respond strongly when the person views pictures of faces, animals, buildings, tools, appliances, or other objects but don't respond well when the person views random textures, for example (Grill-Spector, 2003). This is in contrast to earlier visual areas such as V1 and V4 that respond about equally to objects, textures, and scrambled objects, reflecting the role of these early areas in representing simple features rather than complex shapes.

Early studies of object recognition in the primate brain were modeled after those of Hubel and Wiesel, who discovered that neurons in V1 respond well to oriented bars. These studies found that many IT neurons respond best to specific shapes (Gross et al., 1972; Tanaka et al., 1991). To determine a neuron's shape preference, many different shapes—including complex objects such as toys, household implements, and random items found in the investigators' laboratory, as well as faces (of both monkeys and humans)—were presented in a monkey's visual field. In this process, it was discovered that the receptive fields of IT neurons are quite large; in some cases, an IT neuron will respond to its preferred shape almost anywhere in the visual field. Many IT neurons respond well to both frontal and profile views of monkey and human faces and less well to nonface stimuli (Desimone et al., 1984).

Subsequent studies of human participants using fMRI have revealed an area in the brain that is active in response to viewing faces but not in response to viewing a wide range of nonface stimuli (Kanwisher et al., 1997). This has been called the **fusiform face area (FFA)** because it resides in the fusiform gyrus of the IT cortex (see Figure 3.20); damage to this part of the brain results in an impairment of the ability to recognize faces (this condition, called *prosopagnosia,* is discussed further in Chapter 4). Other studies using fMRI have identified another area in the human IT cortex that appears to be selectively activated when scenes containing large-scale spatial layouts are viewed, such as landscapes, buildings, and rooms (Epstein & Kanwisher, 1998). This area, which is not too far from the FFA, has been termed the **parahippocampal place area (PPA)** because it resides in the parahippocampal gyrus, immediately adjacent to the hippocampus, the site of memory storage in the human brain. We'll return to these areas in our discussion of object recognition in Chapter 4.

Area MT: Motion

Moving forward from area V2 along the dorsal pathway brings us to area **MT** (for *middle temporal* area), sometimes referred to as *V5,* reflecting its approximate position in the visual processing stream and the order in which it was discovered. Its function is undisputed: neurons in MT respond strongly and selectively to motion in their receptive field. Single-cell recording in monkeys has shown that most MT neurons are strongly tuned for both the direction and the speed of motion (Albright, 1984). Typically, stimuli are moved across an MT neuron's receptive field in various directions and at various speeds, and the response of the neuron to each direction and speed is recorded. Figure 3.21 shows the results of plotting an MT neuron's responses to dots moving in one of 16 directions at a constant speed. The magnitude of the neuron's response to each direction of motion is indicated by the radius of the tuning function at that direction.

The motion tuning of MT neurons has been corroborated by fMRI studies of humans. For several seconds, participants view a display containing coherently

inferotemporal cortex (IT cortex) The cortex in the bottom part of the temporal lobe; one of the object-selective regions of the visual system.

lateral occipital cortex An area of the occipital lobe; one of the object-selective regions of the visual system.

fusiform face area (FFA) An area in the fusiform gyrus of the IT cortex; a functional module that responds selectively to faces.

parahippocampal place area (PPA) An area in the parahippocampal gyrus of the IT cortex; a functional module that responds selectively to large-scale spatial layouts such as landscapes and buildings.

MT An area in the middle temporal lobe consisting of neurons that respond selectively to the direction and speed of motion of stimuli.

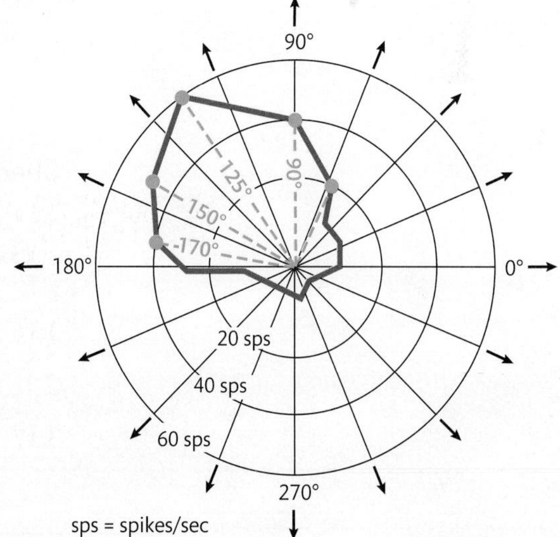

Figure 3.21 MT Neuron Motion Direction Tuning Curve Dots were moved in various directions (as represented by the arrows) across an MT neuron's receptive field. On this graph using polar coordinates, the radius of the tuning function at any direction indicates the magnitude of the neuron's response. This MT neuron responds most strongly (60 spikes/sec) to motion at an angle of 125°, with a steady falloff in response to motion in other directions. (Adapted from Albright, 1984, Figure 1.)

moving dots—for example, a "star field" of dots moving outward from the center of the screen—and then they view a display containing stationary dots. When the brain activities evoked by these two stimuli are compared, increased activity in response to the moving dots can be seen in area MT (O'Craven et al., 1997).

Additional evidence for the role of MT in motion perception comes from studies investigating perceptual deficits following damage to this area. Both monkeys and humans exhibit significantly impaired ability to detect and discriminate visual motion following MT damage (Zihl et al., 1983). All this evidence together strongly implies that MT is a "motion module" in the brain. (See Chapter 7 for further discussion about the function of area MT; the vignette at the beginning of Chapter 7 describes the experiences of a woman whose ability to perceive motion was impaired by damage to area MT.)

Intraparietal Sulcus: Visually Guided Action

As we noted before, within the parietal lobe, subregions of the intraparietal sulcus are also on the dorsal pathway and play a role in visually guided action (Culham et al., 2006; Snyder et al., 2000). These regions include the lateral intraparietal (LIP) area, the anterior intraparietal (AIP) area, and the medial intraparietal (MIP) area. (We'll discuss each of these regions in more detail in Chapter 7.)

Single-cell recording studies in monkeys and fMRI studies in humans have shown that neural activity in area LIP is associated with tasks requiring eye movements to visual targets and with tasks requiring shifts of attention (without eye movements) to locations in the visual periphery (Colby et al., 1996; Schluppeck et al., 2006).

Areas MIP and AIP are specialized for visually guided reaching and grasping, respectively (Culham et al, 2006). For example, experiments with monkeys have revealed neurons in area MIP that show increased activity associated with reaches in a particular direction (Snyder et al., 2000). Reaching can be used to point at an object or to get the hand near an object that you want to grasp. To grasp an object, you have to analyze its shape, size, and orientation so you can shape and orient your hand appropriately. Most studies of grasping actually include both reaching and grasping, because you have to reach for the object before you can grasp it. However, these two functions can be studied separately by comparing brain activity during a reach-then-grasp task with activity during a reach-then-touch task, where the participant just touches the object with a knuckle, without changing the shape or orientation of the hand. The difference in the location of brain activity between these two tasks indicates that area AIP is involved just in grasping.

Check Your Understanding

3.14 What are four characteristics on which areas of the visual cortex can be compared?

3.15 What kind of information is carried by neural signals along the dorsal pathway? Along the ventral pathway?

3.16 What conclusions did researchers draw from the fact that the patient D.F., with damage to her ventral pathway, could perform actions that depended on knowledge of objects' shape and orientation?

3.17 Pair the visual stimuli listed below with the brain areas that respond selectively to them.

Stimuli: faces; simple and complex shapes; visually guided action; color and edge curvature; houses and landscapes; motion

Brain areas: V4; MT; inferotemporal cortex; fusiform face area; parahippocampal place area; intraparietal sulcus

APPLICATIONS Brain Implants for the Blind

More than 1 million people in the United States—and more than 40 million worldwide—are legally blind (Leonard, 2002), mostly as a result of diseases that affect the eye and retina, including cataracts, glaucoma, macular degeneration, and retinitis pigmentosa (see Chapter 2 for a discussion of these conditions). Brain damage in the visual cortex—as might result from a stroke—can also lead to blindness, but such damage is actually quite rare; the parts of the brain that normally process visual information are usually intact in blind individuals. This means that if some way could be found to deliver signals to the brain that are sufficiently like the signals from healthy eyes, it might be possible for the blind to see. Over the past decade, vision scientists and engineers have made great progress toward this goal through the development of **visual neuroprosthetic devices**—that is, devices that collect visual information from a camera or other type of sensor, send the signals from the sensor to a signal processor—a computer—that converts the signals into a form appropriate for stimulating neural responses, and deliver the processed signals to the visual system via an implanted stimulator (Fernandez et al., 2005).

visual neuroprosthetic devices Devices designed to help the blind see; relay signals from a camera or photocells to implanted stimulators that activate the visual system.

In some cases, the stimulator can be placed in the retina or in the optic nerve, but retinal disease may make these approaches impossible and require that the stimulator be placed directly on the surface of the visual cortex. Electrical stimulation of the neurons in the region surrounding a stimulating electrode tip in area V1 produces the experience of a small, starlike image with a perceived size that varies according to the retinotopic organization of V1—that is, stimulation of a location corresponding to the fovea produces an image with a small perceived size (because V1 neurons receiving signals from foveal cones have small receptive fields), while stimulation of a location corresponding to the periphery of the retina produces an image with a larger perceived size (because neurons receiving signals from cones in the periphery have larger receptive fields), in accord with the cortical magnification factor (Schiller & Tehovnik, 2008; look back at Figure 3.16).

Figure 3.22 illustrates the effects of both retinotopic mapping and cortical magnification on the representation in V1 of three shapes composed of blue and green dots—an arrow and two differently positioned circles. The parts of the shape in the left visual field are represented in V1 in the right hemisphere and vice versa, and in each case, the size of the representation of

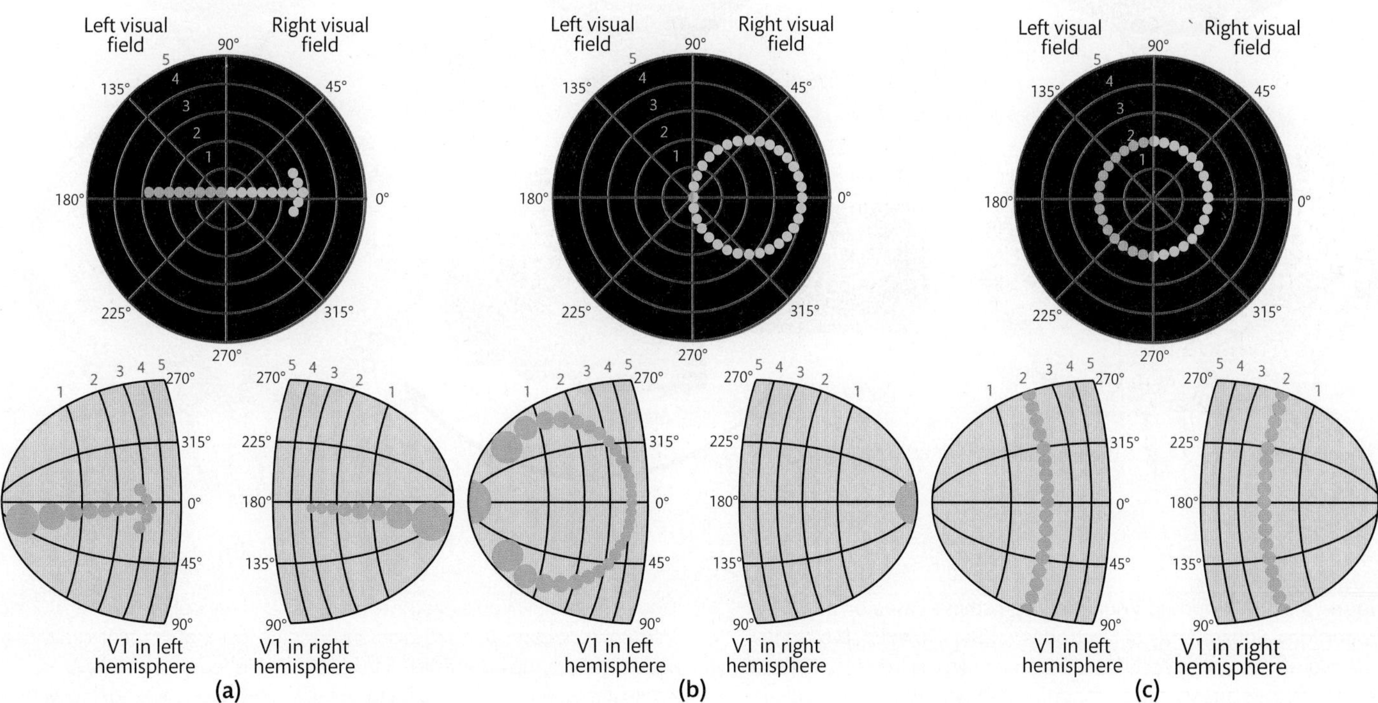

Figure 3.22 Representation of Simple Shapes in V1 In the visual field at the top of each panel is a simple shape made up of blue and green dots; the bottom of each panel shows the retinotopically corresponding location of each dot on the surface of area V1 in the left and right hemispheres of the monkey brain, using a format like that shown in Figure 3.16. (a) The contralateral representation of visual space means that the tail of the arrow in the left visual field (blue) projects to the right hemisphere, while the head (green) projects to the left hemisphere; dots near the fovea project to the occipital poles, at the far left and far right, and activate a larger part of the cortical territory because of cortical magnification. (b) A circle in the right visual field includes a dot centered on the fovea; the circle projects almost entirely to the left hemisphere, with half of the fovea-centered dot projecting to the occipital pole of the right hemisphere. (c) A circle centered on the fovea projects to a curved line of locations within each hemisphere. (Adapted from Schiller & Tehovnik, 2008, Figure 5.)

the dots making up the shape varies according to the distance from the fovea—that is, relatively large near the fovea and progressively smaller moving away from the fovea.

To account for this distortion due to cortical magnification, researchers working on visual neuroprosthetics have proposed using a *proportional square array* of electrodes in which the parts of V1 corresponding to the fovea are stimulated by relatively few electrodes and the parts corresponding to the visual periphery are stimulated by relatively many electrodes (Schiller & Tehovnik, 2008). Figure 3.23a illustrates how such an array would be set up. Figure 3.23b shows how this setup could be used to evoke a perception of the words "FIAT LUX" (Latin for "Let there be light").

A major challenge facing any visual neuroprosthetic device is to achieve a degree of spatial and brightness resolution that is comparable to what's achieved by a normal visual system. The optic nerve contains over 1 million RGC axons, whereas even the most advanced cortical neuroprosthetic device contains only a tiny fraction of this number of

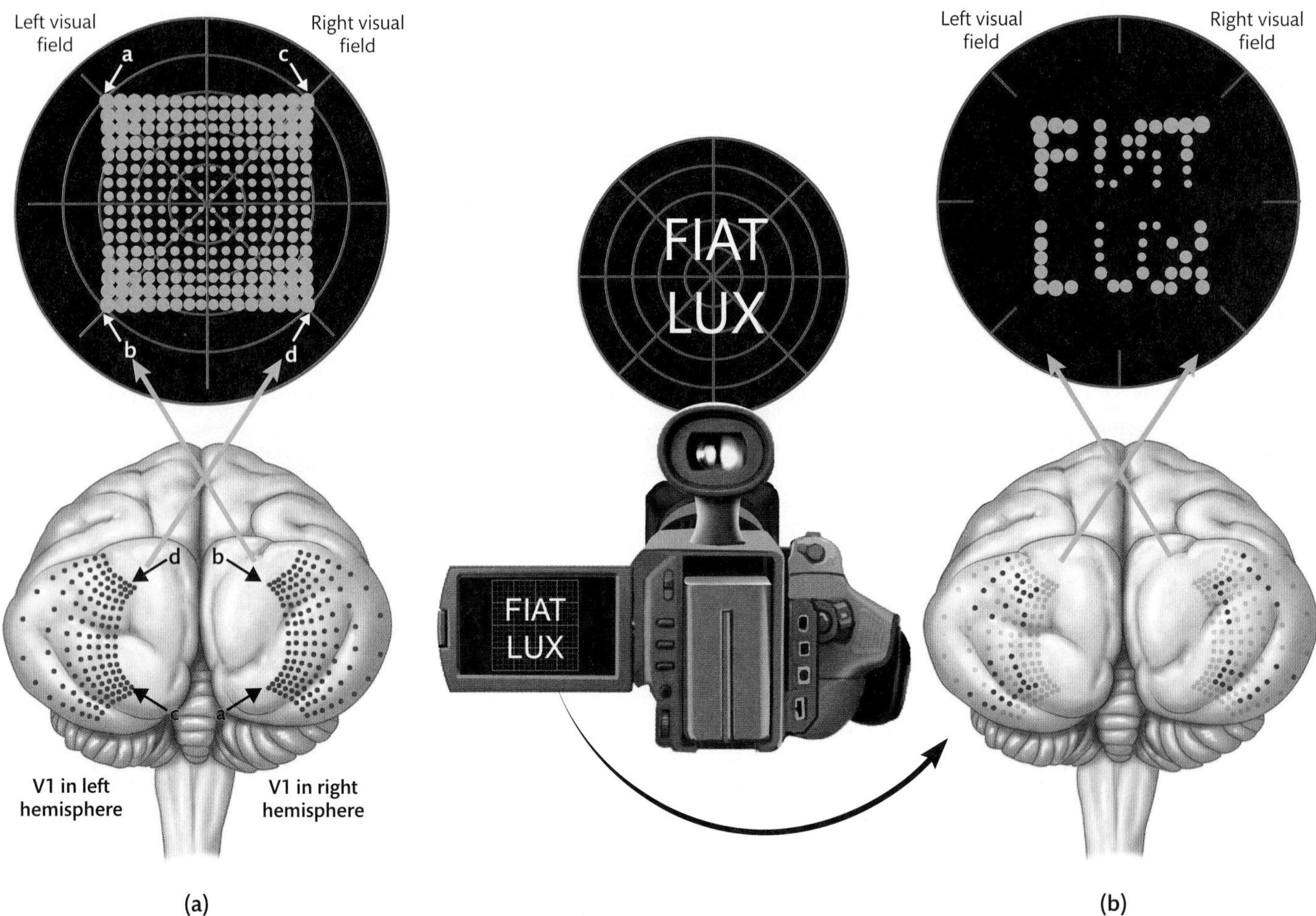

Figure 3.23 **A Proposed Visual Neuroprosthesis Based on a Proportional Square Array of Electrodes** (a) The 256 red dots on the surface of V1, each representing the location of an electrode (128 in each hemisphere), are arranged in a proportional square array—that is, stimulation of all the electrodes simultaneously would result in a perception of the square shown in the visual field above (the dots in the periphery of the square are bigger because neurons receiving signals from the periphery of the visual field have larger receptive fields than neurons receiving signals from the center of the visual field). The retinotopic organization of V1 and the contralateral representation of the visual fields in V1 account for the mapping of points **a, b, c,** and **d** in the visual fields to the similarly labeled points in V1. A macaque monkey brain is shown from the rear with the two hemispheres spread apart so V1 can be seen on the medial surface of the brain. The occipital poles, at the extreme left and right of the two hemispheres, correspond to locations near the fovea, at the center of the visual field. (b) The Latin words "FIAT LUX" are flashed on a screen. A computer-aided camera divides the image into 256 sections, each of which is connected to the retinotopically corresponding electrode in V1. The electrodes are activated in a pattern that reflects the pattern of light and dark sections in the image, as shown by the red dots (versus the unactivated gray dots), and this pattern of activation would result in the perception shown in the visual field above the brain. The examples in this figure are for the monkey brain. In humans, most of area V1 is not easily accessible for surgical implantation of electrodes (it's hidden on the medial wall of the brain), so many of the electrodes have to be implanted in area V2. (Adapted from Schiller & Tehovnik, 2008, Figure 7.)

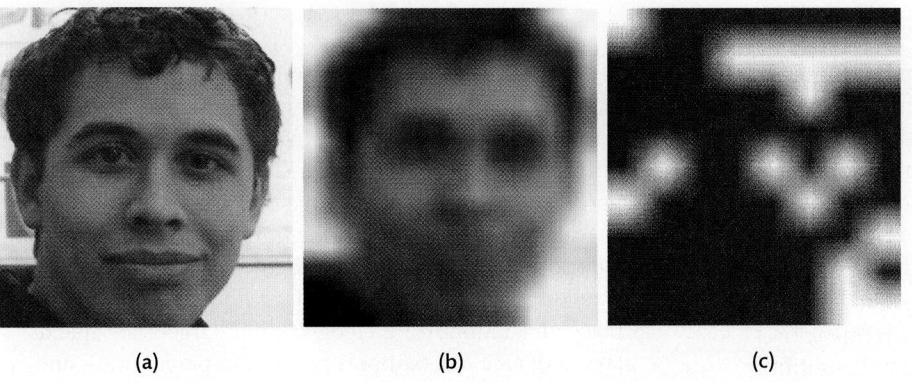

Figure 3.24 Resolution and Image Quality Three versions of the same image shown at various spatial and brightness resolutions. (a) Spatial resolution—255 × 286 pixels; brightness resolution—65,000 gray levels per pixel. (b) Spatial resolution—32 × 36 pixels; brightness resolution—256 gray levels. (c) Spatial resolution—8 × 9 pixels; brightness resolution—black and white, which would evoke a perception something like the somewhat blurry image shown (corresponding to the current capability of the most advanced devices). [Bradley et al., 2005, Figure 1]

electrodes. For example, one group is developing a system that consists of 64-electrode modules, of which as many as four might be implanted (Dagnelie, 2006). Another group implanted an array of 152 electrodes in area V1 of a monkey, and the monkey was able to make eye movements to locations corresponding to stimulated sites in V1 (Bradley et al., 2005); however, each such location represents a relatively large area of the visual field, so the spatial resolution provided by the stimulation is quite coarse. To see what this means, compare the high-resolution image in Figure 3.24a with Figure 3.24b, which depicts a resolution that would require over 1,000 electrodes, well beyond current technology, and with Figure 3.24c, which approximates what is currently achievable.

This is an exciting time for visual neuroprosthetic research, with more than a hundred laboratories worldwide working on various approaches (Dagnelie, 2006). Nevertheless, it's clear that the initial cortical prosthetic devices will support only simple visual functions, such as the ability to orient to light or, perhaps, to detect motion (Dagnelie, 2008). As the technology improves, it may become possible to support higher visual functions, such as shape and pattern discrimination. Overcoming the further challenges of enriching visual experience with color, depth, and motion will take longer, but significant successes can probably be expected over the next 10–15 years (Schiller & Tehovnik, 2008).

Check Your Understanding

3.18 Why might a blind person benefit from a neuroprosthetic device that stimulates area V1 but not from a device that stimulates the retina or the optic nerve?

3.19 Could an individual with a nonfunctional area V1 (say, due to a stroke) benefit from the visual neuroprosthetic devices described in this section? Why or why not?

3.20 Why is it difficult to achieve the same degree of spatial resolution with a visual neuroprosthetic device as with a normally functioning visual system?

SUMMARY

- **From Eye to Brain** The optic nerves meet at the optic chiasm and recombine into the optic tracts, which convey signals from the retinas to the lateral geniculate nuclei in accord with the contralateral representation of visual space. The lateral geniculate nucleus contains functionally specialized layers that relay information about different types of visual features to the brain. Some signals from the retina also flow to the superior colliculus, which controls eye movements.
- **Primary Visual Cortex (Area V1)** The primary visual cortex (area V1), in the occipital lobe, is the part of the brain to which signals flow from the lateral geniculate nuclei. It contains two main classes of neurons—simple cells and complex cells. Simple cells are tuned to respond most strongly to stimuli (such as bars of light) with a particular orientation at the location of their receptive field. The visual system uses a population code—the varying responses of a population of simple cells with different orientation tuning—to determine the specific orientation of a stimulus. Complex cells, which are also tuned for orientation, differ from simple cells in responding to a wider range of stimuli at a wider range of locations. Many V1 neurons are also tuned for visual features other than orientation, such as motion, edge length, binocular disparity, and color. Area V1 is organized into layers, with cortical columns running vertically through the layers; neurons in a cortical column receive signals from the same

eye (ocular dominance columns), have similar tuning for visual features, and have highly overlapping receptive fields. Area V1 is also organized into a retinotopic map based on polar coordinates, and V1 exhibits cortical magnification—more cortical territory is devoted to representing information coming from the fovea than from the periphery of the retina.

- Functional Areas, Pathways, and Modules Functional pathways of the visual system begin in the retina with functionally specialized parasol, midget, and bistratified retinal ganglion cells, which send signals to the magnocellular, parvocellular, and koniocellular layers, respectively, of the lateral geniculate nucleus, from which signals are sent to areas V1, V2, V4, and MT. The pathway from particular layers of V1 to the thick bands of V2 to MT and then to the parietal cortex is the dorsal pathway (or "where"/"how" pathway), which carries information related to the motion and location of objects. The pathway from other layers of V1 to the thin and pale bands of V2 to V4 and then to the inferotemporal cortex is the ventral pathway (or "what" pathway), which carries information related to the identity of objects. Functional modules of the visual system include area V4 (supporting the perception of color and of edge curvature), areas of the lateral occipital cortex and the inferotemporal cortex (supporting general object recognition), the fusiform face area (supporting face recognition), the parahippocampal place area (supporting recognition of large-scale spatial layouts), area MT (supporting motion perception), and areas in the intraparietal sulcus (supporting visually guided action).
- Applications: Brain Implants for the Blind Visual neuroprosthetic devices use neural stimulators implanted in area V1 to activate the visual system on the basis of signals received from an external camera. Major challenges facing all such devices include achieving a sufficient degree of brightness and spatial resolution to support good visual functioning.

KEY TERMS

bistratified retinal ganglion cells (p. 88)
complex cells (p. 96)
contralateral organization (p. 87)
cortical column (p. 97)
cortical magnification (p. 100)
dorsal pathway (p. 105)
functional specialization (p. 86)
fusiform face area (FFA) (p. 109)
inferotemporal cortex (IT cortex) (p. 109)
koniocellular layers (p. 88)
lateral geniculate nucleus (LGN) (p. 87)
lateral occipital cortex (p. 109)
magnocellular layers (p. 88)
midget retinal ganglion cells (p. 88)
MT (p. 109)
multisensory integration (p. 91)
ocular dominance columns (p. 98)
optic ataxia (p. 107)
optic chiasm (p. 86)
optic tract (p. 86)
orientation columns (p. 99)
orientation tuning curve (p. 93)
parahippocampal place area (PPA) (p. 109)
parasol retinal ganglion cells (p. 88)
parvocellular layers (p. 88)
population code (p. 96)
preferred orientation (p. 93)
primary visual cortex (or *V1*) (p. 92)
retinotopic mapping (p. 86)
simple cell (p. 93)
superior colliculus (SC) (p. 91)
V1, see **primary visual cortex**
V4 (p. 108)
ventral pathway (p. 105)
visual neuroprosthetic devices (p. 111)

EXPAND YOUR UNDERSTANDING

3.1 A man is sitting in a meadow looking at a grove of trees, which fills his entire field of view. A girl wearing a *blue* dress and carrying a *long-handled* net is *running quickly* through the trees at the *left*, chasing a *yellow* butterfly *flickering* among the trees at the *right*. The terms in italics represent information about the scene that the man's retinal ganglion cells (RGCs) send to his lateral geniculate nuclei (LGNs). For each term, specify which category of information is being sent by parasol or midget RGCs to the magnocellular or parvocellular layers of the right or left LGN. With regard to the *blue* dress, for example, the category of information is *color*, being sent by *midget RGCs* to the *parvocellular layers* of the *right LGN*.

3.2 A student is looking to the left at her professor, who's demonstrating how to dissect a frog, but "out of the corner of her eye," she's paying more attention to a classmate at her right, who's demonstrating some features of his new smart phone. As soon as her professor finishes and starts to clean up, the student's eyes move so she's looking directly at her classmate's phone, which has begun to emit little beeps. While she's looking at her professor, is her left LGN active? Why? Which brain structure then helps her look to the right? Why are the "little beeps" significant?

3.3 Suppose simple cell orientation tuning curves like those depicted in Figure 3.7 looked like this instead:

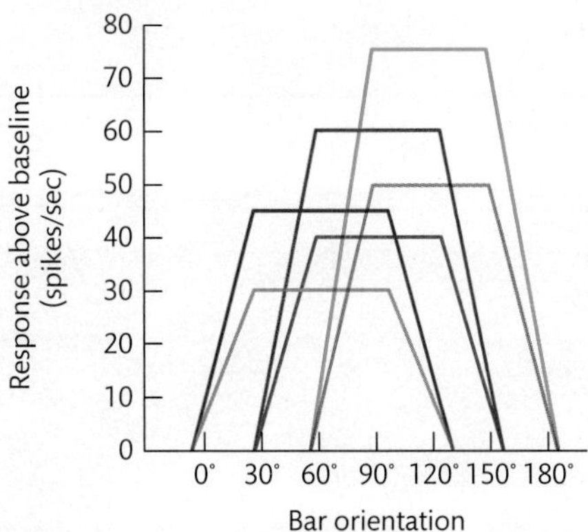

Would that make it easier or harder for the visual system to use population codes to determine the precise orientation of a stimulus? Explain your answer.

3.4 Suppose the orientation tuning curves of three simple cells in area V1 are as shown in the following graph. The average firing rates above baseline of the neurons in response to a bar of light with a particular orientation are about 13 spikes/sec for Neuron A, 36 spikes/sec for Neuron B, and 24 spikes/sec for Neuron C. The average firing rates in response to a bar with a different orientation are about 0 spikes/sec for Neuron A, 27 spikes/sec for Neuron B, and 39 spikes/sec for Neuron C. What are the approximate orientations of the two bars? Explain your answer.

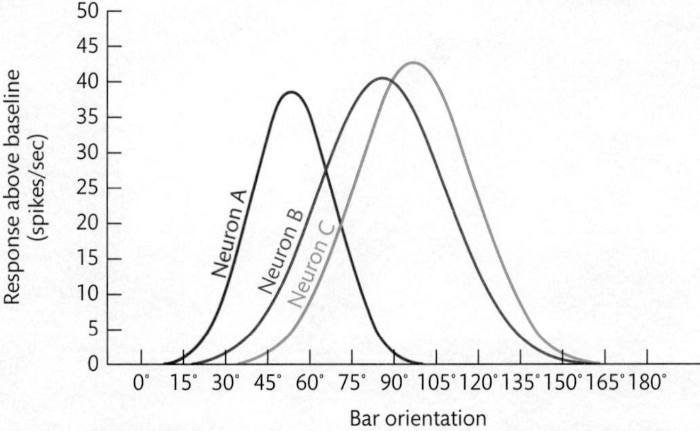

3.5 The section of this chapter on ocular dominance columns ends with this statement: "Recordings from individual neurons in V1 have revealed that the cells in a border zone between ocular dominance columns respond to input from both eyes, and many of these neurons are tuned for binocular disparity." Why does it make sense that this should be the case?

3.6 Explain the relationship between cortical magnification and visual acuity.

3.7 A blue locomotive is circling clockwise and a red locomotive is circling counterclockwise on concentric model train tracks. On top of the blue locomotive are two photographs—one of Albert Einstein and the other of Abraham Lincoln; on top of the red locomotive are two other photographs—one of an apartment building and the other of a basketball. You have to (a) pick up the blue locomotive, (b) say which picture is Einstein and which is Lincoln, (c) grab the picture of the apartment building, and (d) point to the picture of the basketball. For each of these tasks, explain how it involves the ventral and/or dorsal pathway, and explain how various functional areas and modules of the visual system are involved.

3.8 Suppose all the parasol retinal ganglion cells in your left eye suddenly stopped working. Where would an implanted visual neuroprosthetic device need to send signals in order to restore motion perception in your right visual field?

READ MORE ABOUT IT

Goodale, M. A., & Milner, A. D. (2005). *Sight unseen: An exploration of conscious and unconscious vision.* Oxford, England: Oxford University Press.

Reviews a wide range of studies that document two major functional pathways—the ventral "what" pathway and the dorsal "where"/"how" pathway—in the human visual system.

Hubel, D. H. (1995). *Eye, brain, and vision* (2nd ed.). New York: W. H. Freeman and Company.

Hubel's personal account of his groundbreaking work with Torsten Wiesel in uncovering the functions of the visual brain, with a focus on the pathway from the eye to the primary visual cortex.

Kaas, J. H., & Collins, C. E., (Eds.). (2004). *The primate visual system.* New York: CRC Press.

Detailed coverage of the structure and function of the primate visual system, from retina to object recognition.

Nassi, J. J., & Callaway, E. M. (2009). Parallel processing strategies of the primate visual system. *Nature Reviews Neuroscience, 10,* 360–372.

A recent overview of the primate dorsal and ventral visual pathways and how they support visually guided action and object recognition, respectively.

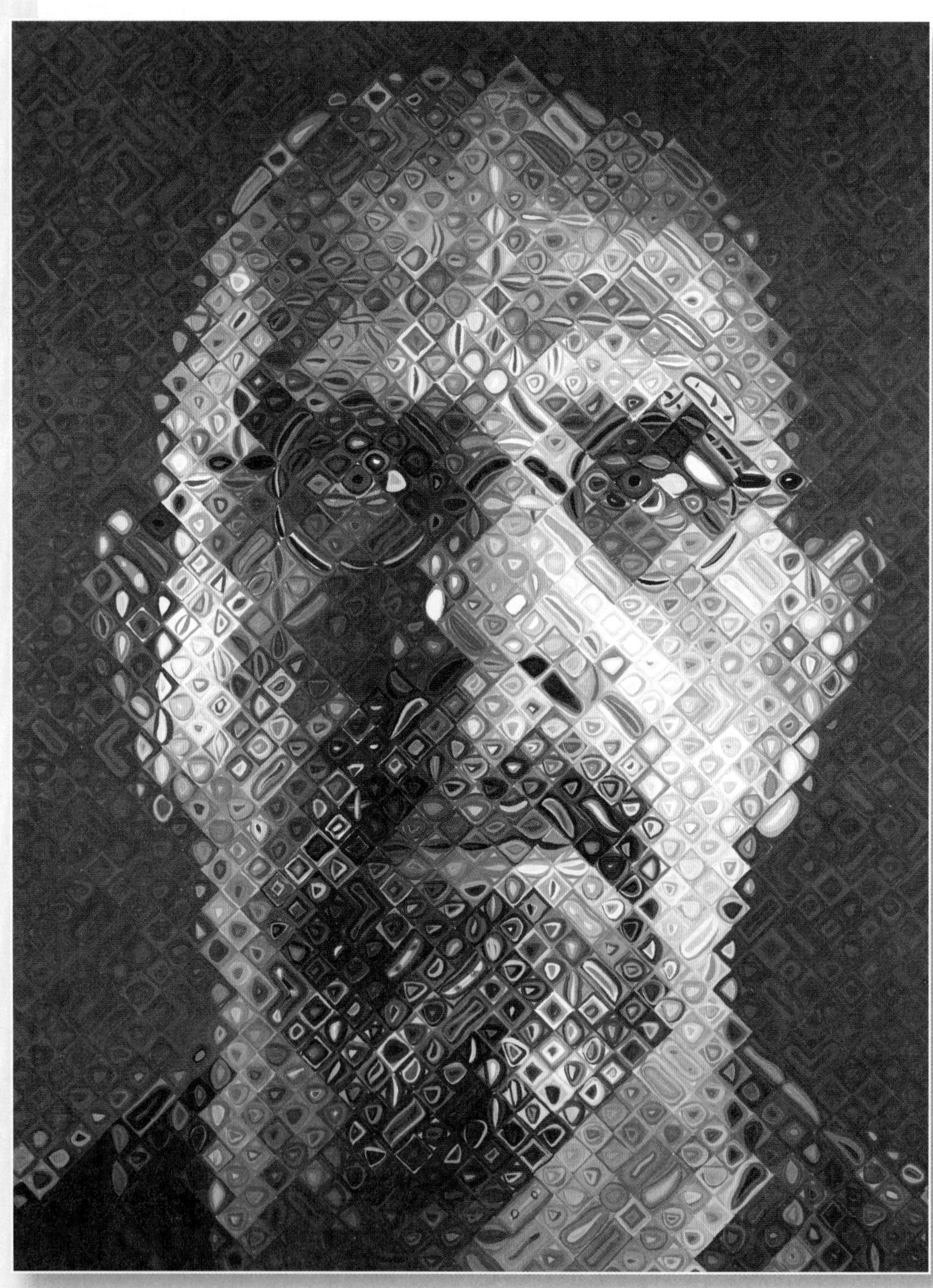

Chuck Close, *Self-Portrait*, 2000–01. [Oil on canvas, 9 × 7 feet. Courtesy of Pace Gallery.]

4

RECOGNIZING VISUAL OBJECTS

Face-Blind

Imagine you're walking along a city street, glancing at the people coming the other way on the sidewalk. Suddenly, one of them—a bearded man in his 30s—smiles at you and raises his hand in greeting, and you have no idea who he is. Just not to seem unfriendly, you too raise your hand a little and try to smile back, but your mind is racing, trying to place him. Without a doubt, he sees that you don't recognize him. Half a block later, you realize it was the guy who works at the grocery store—you've seen each other dozens of times, but outside the context of the store, recognizing him took a long time and required conscious thought. Of course, this kind of thing happens to everyone from time to time.

Now try to imagine what it would be like to have this happen *every time* you meet someone, no matter how well you know the person, including your family members, friends, teachers, office mates, all the people you see and talk to every day—to be simply unable to recognize anyone's face, to be face-blind, like the woman we'll call Beth.

Beth is not blind; indeed, she can read, drive a car, and recognize objects without difficulty. She simply cannot recognize people by their face—including herself when seen in a mirror or in a photo. She finds that this condition (called *prosopagnosia*) often produces awkward social situations because people are easily offended when not recognized. Beth goes to great lengths to conceal her disability by trying to recognize people based on other cues—their hair color and style, the sound of their voice, and the context in which she encounters them.

What does Beth's condition tell us about the visual system? Beth can easily discriminate colors, she knows whether someone is moving around or standing still, and she can recognize her pocketbook and her car, all of which suggest that important parts of her visual system—the parts that support functions such as color vision, motion detection, and general object recognition—are working normally. By the same reasoning, her deficit suggests that a part of her visual system essential for recognizing faces isn't working normally. Evidence from single-cell recording in monkeys and fMRI studies of humans indicates that this conclusion is probably correct, that there are regions of the brain specialized for the very important task of recognizing faces.

In Chapters 2 and 3, we covered two major parts of the process by which the visual system accomplishes its principle function—determining "what is where." In Chapter 2, we discussed the part of vision that takes place in the eyes, with an emphasis on the retina. In Chapter 3, we followed the neural signals sent by retinal ganglion cells into the brain. In both chapters, much emphasis was placed on anatomy and physiology. Now, in this chapter, while not abandoning the anatomical and physiological perspective, we'll focus

Chapter Outline

on perceptual functions, bringing together the information covered in Chapters 2 and 3 to present a global view of how the visual system recognizes objects.

A Few Basic Considerations

Before we begin exploring the process of object recognition, let's consider some of the factors that play into that process, as well as various issues to keep in mind as you proceed through the chapter.

Object Familiarity

Figure 4.1 An Unfamiliar Object This is a dried-out seed pod from the garden plant *Leonotis leonurus* (commonly known as lion's ear or lion's tail), but if you didn't know that, you'd probably have trouble categorizing it any more specifically than as "a roundish object with things like thorns sticking out in every direction." [Martin Harvey/Getty Images]

To understand our surroundings and behave appropriately, we need to determine, rapidly and accurately, what objects are around us, no matter whether those objects are familiar or unfamiliar. This means that the visual system has to create a mental representation of a given object and then, if the object is familiar, recognize the object by matching its representation with one stored in memory. For example, when you see a familiar suitcase, this process results in your knowing what its function is, whom it belongs to, and what it's made of.

But even an unfamiliar suitcase is familiar in the sense that we still recognize it as a suitcase, which means that all suitcases must have things in common that differentiate them visually from other types of objects. For instance, suitcases tend to be rectangular solids, which immediately differentiates them from objects like coffee mugs, which tend to be cylindrical. Then, within the realm of all rectangular solids, we can differentiate suitcases from, say, pencil cases, books, and apartment buildings on the basis of such characteristics as size and the fact that suitcases typically have a handle and a zipper or snap lock.

In the case of an object that is even more unfamiliar, the visual system must still be able to represent it in a way that lets us recognize it as an object so we can navigate around it, pick it up and move it, or interact with it in other ways. For example, if you woke up one morning and saw the object in Figure 4.1 sitting on the table next to your bed, you might have no idea what it was, but you would certainly know how to pick it up (carefully!) and how to describe it. So far, so good.

Image Clutter, Object Variety, and Variable Views

The analysis of object recognition starts to get complicated quickly, with three complications being especially important. The first is **image clutter**, which refers to the fact that most scenes contain many objects scattered in 3-D space, as illustrated in Figure 4.2. If the scene includes a book, other objects in the scene may occlude (or cover) parts of it. Somehow the visual system must organize the scene and represent both the visible elements of any given object and its occluded parts as a complete object that can then be recognized.

image clutter A characteristic of visual scenes in which many objects are scattered in 3-D space, with partial occlusion of various parts of objects by other objects.

Figure 4.2 Image Clutter Most scenes (like this one) contain many objects arrayed in 3-D space, with some objects partly covering others. This means that the shape of an object such as the book with the orange cover is incomplete in the retinal image, yet somehow we are able to recognize it as a book anyway. [Peter Dazeley/Getty Images]

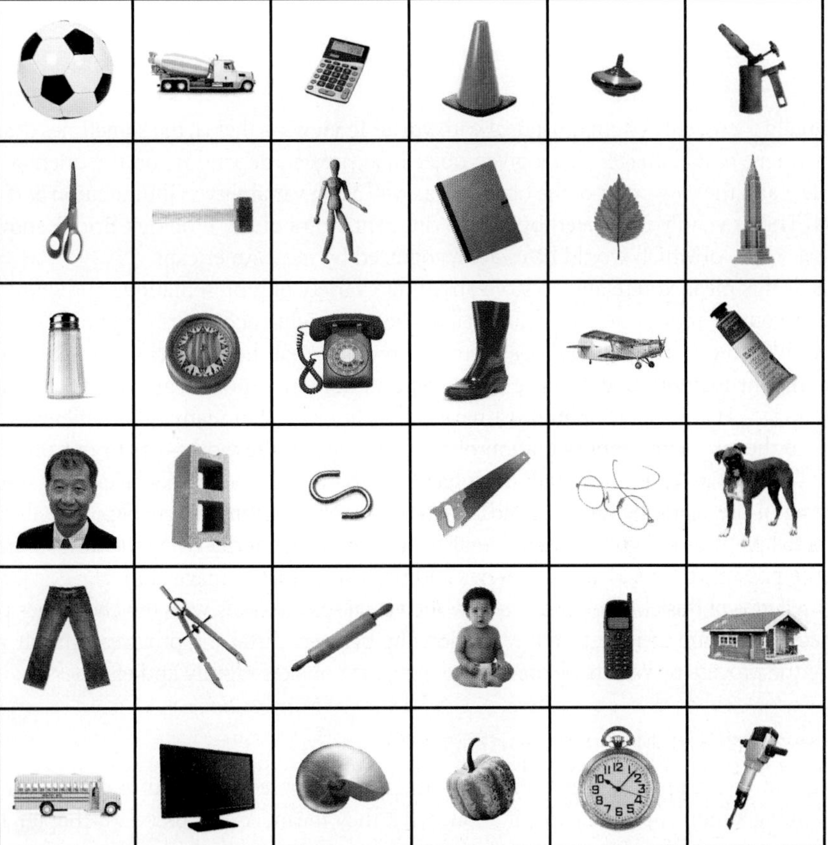

Figure 4.3 The Vast Variety of Objects Here's a miniscule subset of the types of objects we can recognize almost instantaneously. [See copyright page for photo credits]

Another complication is **object variety**, as illustrated in Figure 4.3. The world is filled with an enormous variety of objects, most of which you've never seen but can still instantly recognize—if not the specific, individual object (Joe's pet turtle), at least what type of object it is (a turtle). As we noted above with regard to Figure 4.1, the visual system has to have the flexibility to represent any object it encounters, with no restrictions. Even within a single category of objects, there is a great deal of variability in shape. Figure 4.4, for instance, merely hints at the immense variety of retinal images that almost everyone would recognize as "a tree."

object variety Refers to the fact that the world contains an enormous variety of objects.

Figure 4.4 Object Variety Within One Category: Recognizing a Tree How does our visual system recognize each of these widely differing objects as "a tree"? [See copyright page for photo credits]

variable views The different retinal images that can be projected by the same object or category of objects.

Finally, the visual system must deal with **variable views**—that is, the sometimes dramatically different retinal images that a given object can project, depending on the orientation of the object and the viewpoint of the observer, as well as on variability in illumination and other factors. This is vividly illustrated by the 16 different views of the Brooklyn Bridge shown in Figure 4.5, any of which would be easily recognized by most Americans.

Does this mean you're able to store an infinite variety of representations of the Brooklyn Bridge in your memory, one for each retinal image you might encounter? Certainly not—your brain would quickly run out of space. Rather, it must be that the representation of the bridge stored in your memory doesn't have to correspond in a one-to-one way with any particular retinal image. That is, your brain must have the ability to match many quite different retinal images to the very same representation of a single thing in the world—or to put this in the terms used in Chapter 1, your brain must have the ability to represent a single distal stimulus (the thing-in-the-world being perceived) based on any of an infinite variety of proximal stimuli (the spatial patterns of light, or retinal images, that could be produced by the distal stimulus, given the possible effects of variable views and occlusion due to image clutter).

One focus of this chapter, then, is how the visual system deals with the challenges posed by object variety and the one-to-many relationship between distal and proximal stimuli, as we explore the process by which we are able to recognize objects rapidly and effortlessly.

Representation and *Recognition*

Throughout this chapter, we frequently use the terms *representation* and *recognition,* and it's worth taking a moment to be explicit about what they mean. As discussed in Chapter 1, the term *representation* refers to a pattern of neural activity in the brain that contains information about a stimulus and gives rise to a subjective perceptual experience of that stimulus. In the visual system, the process of creating representations starts as soon as the photoreceptors in the retina begin responding to light, with representations containing information about the changing spatial pattern of brightness and color in the retinal image (the proximal stimulus). As neural signals flow to V1 and then to higher visual areas (see Chapter 3), representations are constructed that contain information about increasingly complex aspects of the retinal

Figure 4.5 Variable Views: 16 Versions of the Brooklyn Bridge The 16 very different views of the Brooklyn Bridge in these photos are all immediately recognizable. Explaining how the visual system accomplishes that is one of the major challenges to any theory of object recognition. [See copyright page for photo credits]

image—for example, the location and orientation of edges and the specification of an object's overall shape, as well as its color, texture, motion, and so on. The term *recognition* refers to the process of matching the representation of a stimulus to a representation stored in long-term memory, based on previous encounters with that stimulus or with similar stimuli. In this chapter, we'll focus on how shape (rather than color, texture, etc.) is used to recognize objects, because shape is usually the most important determinant of what an object is.

In the next section, keeping all these considerations in mind, we'll begin with an overview of the process of object recognition; this overview will serve as a kind of map to help you navigate through the more detailed discussions that will follow.

Check Your Understanding

4.1 Match each of the following concepts with the example that illustrates it.

Concepts: (1) object familiarity, (2) image clutter, (3) object variety, (4) variable views.

Examples: (A) Danny's roommate Karl was performing a headstand, but Danny still recognized him. (B) Despite the jumble of tools in the drawer, she instantly saw the monkey wrench at the bottom of the pile. (C) I still haven't learned the difference between Irish terriers and fox terriers, but of course I always know whether I'm looking at a terrier or a spaniel. (D) The first time I found one of these on an archeological expedition, I had no idea what it was:

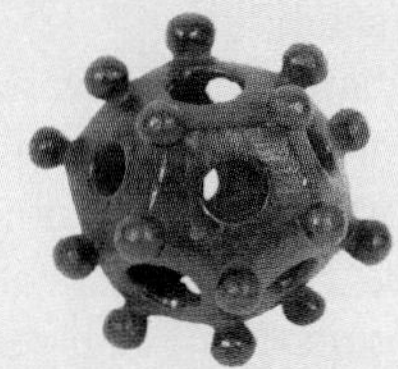

[©Birmingham Museums & Art Gallery]

Overview: The Fundamental Steps

The perceptual process that ends with matching the visual system's representation of an object to a representation stored in memory can be broadly divided into two parts—perceptual organization and object recognition. In perceptual organization, the visual system performs the operations involved in identifying those portions of the retinal image that belong to one object or another, or to the background—especially important when viewing a cluttered scene. In object recognition, the process is carried to its conclusion. These two parts and the steps that make them up are not necessarily strictly sequential—they can overlap in time and interact in certain ways—but by putting this complication aside, we can convey a general picture of the overall process, as in the following outline.

I. *Perceptual organization:*
   A. Represent edges—abrupt, elongated changes in brightness and/or color.
   B. Represent uniform regions bounded by edges.
   C. Divide these regions into figure and ground, and assign border ownership.
   D. Group together regions that have similar properties (e.g., color). Groups consisting of "figure" regions are represented as candidate objects; other groups of regions are represented as background.
   E. Fill in missing edges and surfaces—that is, edges and surfaces that are partly occluded—to obtain more complete representations of candidate objects.

II. *Object recognition:* Use higher-level processes to represent objects fully enough to recognize them, by matching their representations to representations stored in memory.

Now let's briefly describe these steps as they might be applied to the scene depicted in Figure 4.6. The photograph in Figure 4.6a shows an arrangement of seven wooden blocks. Abrupt discontinuities in color and/or brightness in the scene usually correspond to a boundary or corner of an object. These discontinuities are locations in the retinal image that exhibit color and/or luminance contrast and are represented as edges by your visual system.

Figure 4.6b labels 31 distinct regions of the image, each bounded by edges and each of approximately uniform brightness and color. None of these numbered regions by itself is something that the visual system should attempt to recognize as a complete object. For example, region 21 is part of one side of a block, and region 31 is part of the background. Background regions don't provide information about the shape of any object—for example, the trapezoidal shape of region 31 doesn't tell us anything about the shape of anything. One important step, then, is for the visual system to represent each of these 31 regions and to determine whether each is part of an object or part of the background; regions that are part of an object are identified as **figure,** and regions that are part of the background are identified as **ground.**

figure A region of an image that is perceived as being part of an object.

ground A region of an image that is perceived as part of the background.

Some of the blocks in Figure 4.6 overlap, with one block partly occluding one or more other blocks—for example, the yellow block partly occludes the orange block. When one object partly occludes another object, the border between them belongs to the occluding object (the object in front), and the surfaces and edges of the partly occluded object are perceived as continuing behind the occluding object. So the next step after identifying regions that are figure and regions that are ground is to determine **border ownership**—that is, to determine which region "owns" each border.

border ownership The perception that an edge, or border, is "owned" by a particular region of the retinal image.

In scenes like Figure 4.6, where objects overlap and partly occlude one another, a single object may be only partly visible (like the light blue block, of which only regions 13–20 are visible). In order to represent such an object as a single shape, the visual system must perform two important steps. First, it must combine, or group together, the separate regions, based on similarity of properties—regions 13–20 are all the same color (while differing in brightness); this process is called **perceptual grouping.** Second, it must "fill in" the parts of the object that can't be seen due to occlusion (like the parts of the light blue block that are occluded by the red, pink, yellow, and dark blue blocks). This process of filling in—called **perceptual interpolation**—uses the visible parts of an object, together with our knowledge about object shape and about how edges tend to relate to one another in real scenes, to represent the hidden parts of the object.

perceptual grouping The process by which the visual system combines separate regions of the retinal image that "go together" based on similar properties.

perceptual interpolation The process by which the visual system fills in hidden edges and surfaces in order to represent the entirety of a partially visible object.

(a)

(b)

Figure 4.6 Edges, Shapes, and Borders (a) Your retinal image of this arrangement of seven wooden blocks consists of 31 distinct regions bounded by edges and with uniform brightness and color. (b) Your visual system has to represent each of the regions 1–28 as part of an object's surface. But regions 29–31 aren't part of any surface; rather, they're part of the background. Your visual system must correctly organize the image into figure and ground and assign border ownership. [Ramón Rivera-Moret]

Once the steps of perceptual organization are complete, the visual system has representations of the shapes of the objects in the scene, and can, with some additional processing, match them to representations of objects stored in memory. This is the object recognition part of the process outlined above. It takes place mainly in the ventral visual pathway (the "what" pathway, as described in Chapter 3), where neurons respond selectively to objects with complex curved contours in specific configurations.

In the sections that follow, we'll describe in more detail how these steps occur.

Check Your Understanding

4.2 What features of the retinal image does the visual system use to identify edges?

4.3 Suppose your retinal image consists of 25 different regions with uniform properties bounded by edges. Why might some but not all of these regions provide information about the shapes of objects?

4.4 In real scenes, surfaces are often only partly visible, because of occlusion. In which two steps of the perceptual organization process does the visual system create representations of the entirety of such surfaces?

Perceptual Organization

Perceptual organization is the visual system's way of dealing with scenes containing multiple overlapping objects—it makes object recognition within complex scenes possible. Without perceptual organization, the visual system would be overwhelmed by the jumbled pattern of brightness and color in the retinal image of most real scenes. As outlined in the preceding section, the first step in perceptual organization is to represent edges, so that regions of uniform color and brightness bounded by edges can then be represented. These regions are the elementary units of perceptual organization and of the representations used in object recognition.

edge extraction The process by which the visual system determines the location, orientation, and curvature of edges in the retinal image.

Representing Edges and Regions

Using a simple scene in which the only contrast is in brightness, Figure 4.7 illustrates the process of **edge extraction,** in which the visual system determines the location, orientation, and curvature of edges in the retinal image, based on patterns of responses from neurons in areas V1, V2, and V4 (as discussed in Chapter 3). The figure also recalls the discussion in Chapter 3 of how shapes bounded by edges are represented in regions further along the "what" pathway.

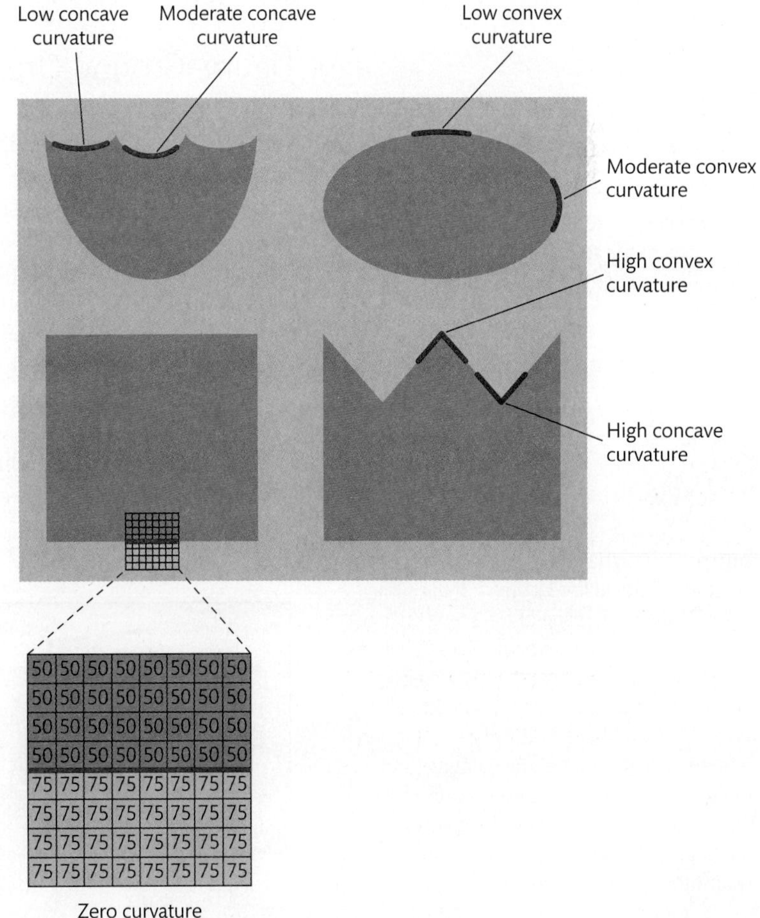

Figure 4.7 Edges and Simple Shapes in a Retinal Image This illustrates the retinal image of a scene consisting of four dark gray shapes on a lighter gray background. The brightness values in the blowup of the grid over the lower edge of the square show that each location in the retinal image has a particular brightness, forming a pattern of brightness values (in this case, 50% brightness above the edge, 75% below). As we saw in Chapter 3 (see Figure 3.8), retinal ganglion cells with receptive fields near the red edge segment in the grid send a corresponding pattern of responses to orientation-tuned neurons in area V1, and the visual system uses the pattern of V1 responses to represent a horizontal edge. Neurons in areas V2 and V4 use signals from V1 neurons to represent edges with various degrees of curvature, and neurons in regions further along the "what" pathway can represent the regions bounded by those edges—the four dark gray shapes.

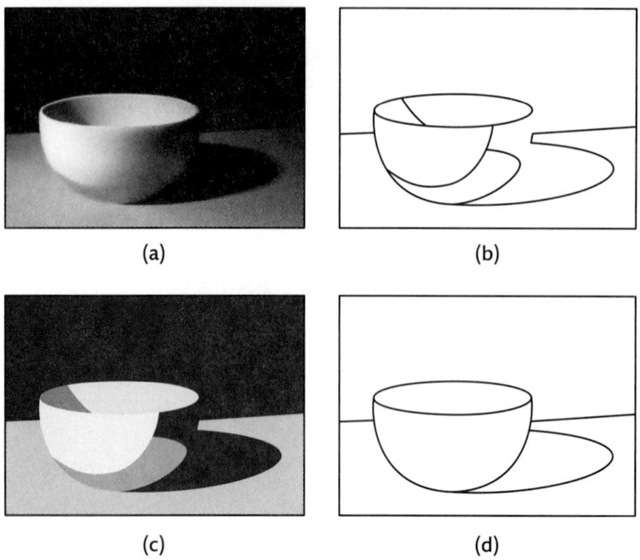

Figure 4.8 Edges and Regions, Shading and Shadows (a) A photograph of a bowl resting on a table. Shading hides the upper and lower edges of the right side of the bowl and creates apparent edges on the inside and outside of the bowl, while the bowl's shadow creates an apparent shape on the table. (b) All the edges, both real and apparent, that the visual system represents in (a). (c) The regions that the visual system represents in (a), roughly indicated by the light and dark gray areas. Each region is defined by approximately uniform brightness. (d) The true physical boundaries of the bowl, its shadow, and the table. How does the visual system derive a representation like this from a retinal image like (a)? [a: Ramón Rivera-Moret]

Edge extraction and the representation of simple shapes are relatively straightforward in scenes like the one illustrated in Figure 4.7, consisting of nonoverlapping regions with uniform brightness. But the visual system often has to deal with scenes containing shading and cast shadows, which, as illustrated by Figure 4.8a, can create brightness differences that generate the same differential patterns of response from orientation-tuned neurons as are generated by the actual edges of objects. These brightness differences can lead the visual system into representing image regions that are actually just the result of shading or shadows on a surface, like the region created by the shadow of the bowl on the table in Figure 4.8a. And they can obscure the actual edges of objects, like shading obscures the upper and lower portions of the right-hand edge of the bowl.

Occlusion, shading, and shadows all contribute to the image clutter that the visual system must deal with when organizing the scene into regions for further processing. Figure 4.8b, for example, illustrates the edges—both real and apparent, but not the "missing" edges—that the visual system initially represents within the scene shown in Figure 4.8a. These edges partition the scene into regions that exhibit **uniform connectedness** (Palmer & Rock, 1994), which simply means that the regions have approximately uniform properties (in this case, just brightness is relevant). The regions with uniform connectedness in Figure 4.8b are roughly indicated by the light gray and dark gray areas in Figure 4.8c.

Now let's explore the methods that the visual system uses to move from a representation like Figure 4.8c to one like Figure 4.8d, where the actual shapes of the objects in the scene are much more accurately represented.

Figure–Ground Organization: Assigning Border Ownership

Figure 4.9 shows a scene in which a woman is looking at a painting hanging on a wall. The scene is shown from three different viewpoints. Regardless of viewpoint, the abrupt changes in brightness, color, texture, and depth at the edge (or border) of the woman's body provide information about its shape. However, that border has nothing to do with the shape of what's on the other side—in this case, the painting, wall, and floor. This means that the borders between the woman and the painting, wall, and floor are seen as belonging to the woman and not to those other surfaces—in other words, ownership of these borders is assigned to the woman's body—and therefore your visual system identifies the woman as *figure* and the painting, wall, and floor as *ground*.

uniform connectedness A characteristic of regions of the retinal image that have approximately uniform properties.

The importance of correctly assigning border ownership is shown by Figure 4.10 (Bregman, 1990). In Figure 4.10a, where a random arrangement of Bs has been partly occluded with "spilled ink," we have little difficulty seeing the Bs. But as shown in Figure 4.10b, if the "ink" were white, so it disappears against the white page, the Bs are nearly impossible to see. The

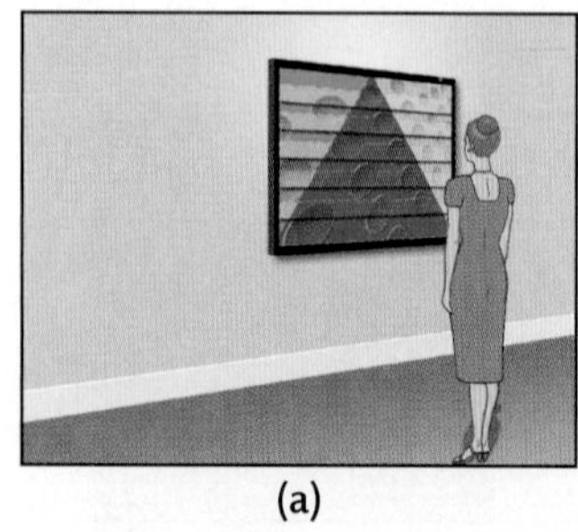

(a)

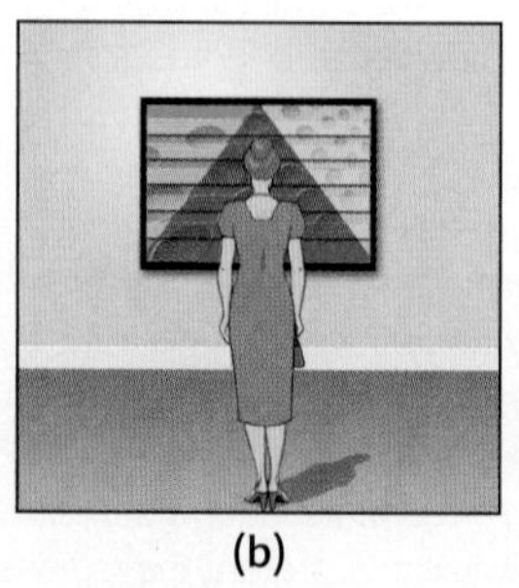

(b)

(c)

Figure 4.9 What Is Figure, and What Is Ground? Three different views of the same scene. The retinal image of the scene changes depending on your viewpoint. These changes tell you, for example, that the painting is farther away than the woman and doesn't have a woman-shaped hole in it—that is, the woman occludes part of the painting (and also occludes parts of the wall and the floor). The woman is figure against the ground of the painting, wall, and floor; the painting is figure against the ground of the wall.

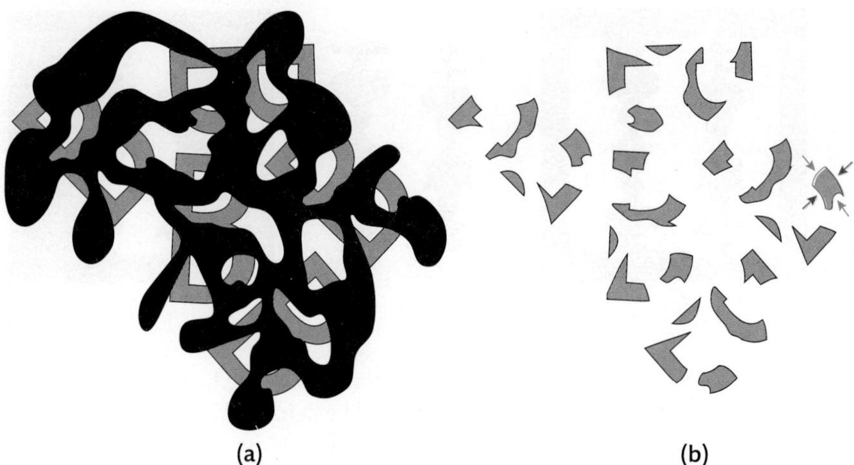

Figure 4.10 Border Ownership and Figure-Ground Organization (a) It's easy to perceive the Bs because we know which borders belong to them and which to the "spilled ink." (b) When the "ink" is white, the visual system assigns ownership of all the borders to the fragments of the Bs—including both the actual borders (e.g., the two borders indicated with red arrows) and the false borders (e.g., the two indicated by blue arrows)—and therefore perceives each fragment as a separate figure, doesn't group them into shapes, and utterly fails to perceive the Bs. (Adapted from Bregman, 1990.)

Edgar Rubin (1886–1951). [Royal Library of Denmark]

reason is that in Figure 4.10b, the borders that belong to the Bs (e.g., the two borders indicated by the red arrows) cannot be distinguished from the borders that belong to the invisible white ink (e.g., the two indicated by the blue arrows). The visual system interprets all the edges as borders belonging to the fragments of Bs, and each fragment is perceived as a separate figure.

Figure 4.11 Ambiguous Border Ownership The border between the black and white regions can be perceived as belonging to one region or the other but not to both simultaneously. When you assign border ownership to the white region, you see a vase; when you assign border ownership to the black region, you see two faces in silhouette. If you don't exert some control over which one you experience, your perception spontaneously flips back and forth between the two, but you can't see both at the same moment. When you perceive the vase, the border between the white and black parts of the image seems clearly to belong to the white region, and you perceive the black background as continuing behind the vase. But when you perceive the faces, you see the black region as owning the border, and you see the white background as continuing behind.

Principles of Figure-Ground Organization

Sometimes, a border can belong to two regions simultaneously, as when a single surface is divided by a crack or when two surfaces meet at an edge, like squares in a checkerboard. For now, however, we'll focus on the more typical situation, where an edge that separates two regions in an image is perceived as a border belonging to one of the regions and not to the other. Of course, a given region may be a figure with respect to some regions but a ground with respect to others. For example, in Figure 4.9, the painting is a figure against the wall but a ground for the woman's body.

However, it isn't *always* clear which region a border belongs to. The potential ambiguity of border ownership was first discussed by the Danish psychologist Edgar Rubin (1921/2001) with regard to images like the one shown in Figure 4.11, where a change in perceived border ownership dramatically alters the interpretation of the image. Rubin and others used images like Figure 4.11 to elucidate the following principles that the visual system uses to assign border ownership and organize visual scenes into figure and ground.

Depth As we've already noted, when one region is perceived to be in front of another, the region in front is perceived as owning the border between the regions and is perceived as figure, and the other region is perceived as ground.

Surroundedness If a region is completely surrounded by another region, then the surrounded region tends to be perceived as owning the border and, therefore, perceived as figure, while the surrounding region is perceived as ground. This is illustrated by Figure 4.12, where the gray "cloud" tends to be perceived as figure and the black rectangle as ground. Of course, it could

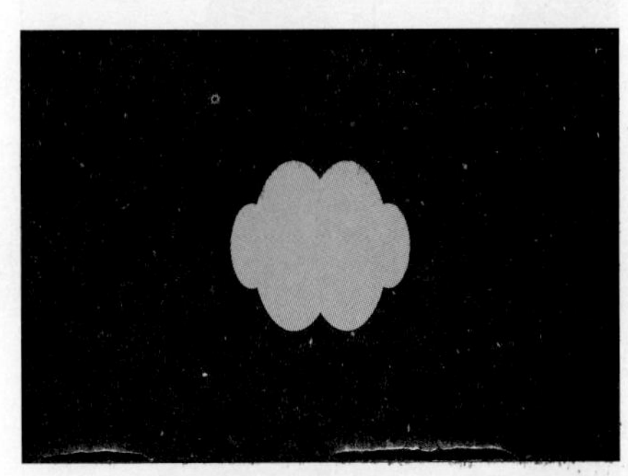

Figure 4.12 Surroundedness in Figure-Ground Organization The completely surrounded gray region tends to be perceived as figure in front of a black background—that is, the border tends to be perceived as belonging to the gray region. But if you perceive this image as a black surface with a hole in it, then the gray region is perceived as part of a more distant surface seen through the hole—that is, the border is perceived as belonging to the black region.

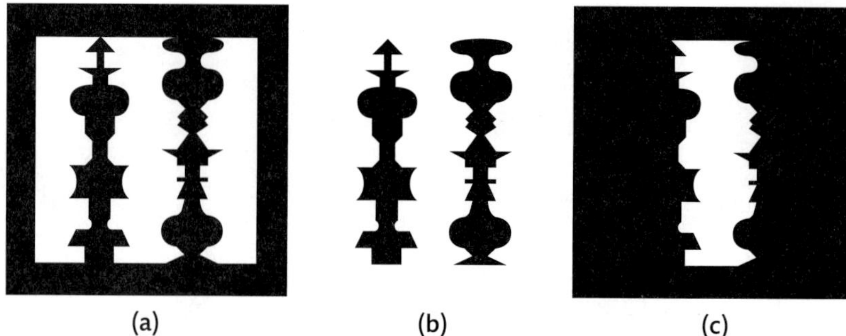

Figure 4.13 Symmetry in Figure-Ground Organization Regions that exhibit symmetry are more likely to be seen as figure than are nonsymmetrical regions. The image in (a) contains two symmetrical regions, shown in (b), and three nonsymmetrical regions, one of which is shown in (c).

easily be the case that the surrounded region is actually a hole in the surrounding region—for example, Figure 4.12 could be perceived as a black wall with a cloud-shaped window in it. Nevertheless, without additional information about the relative depths of the two regions, the figure-on-background perception is usually more compelling than the hole-in-a-surface perception.

Symmetry A region with symmetrical borders is more likely to be seen as figure than as ground (Harrower, 1936). For example, in Figure 4.13a, the black regions (isolated in Figure 4.13b) are likely to be seen as figures, whereas the white region between them (isolated in Figure 4.13c) is likely to be seen as part of the background.

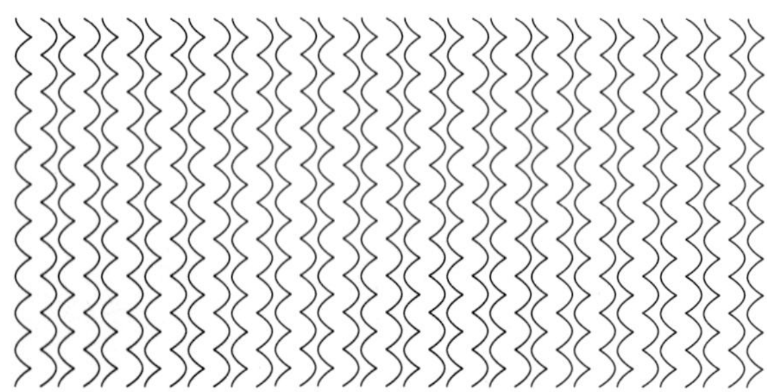

Figure 4.14 Convexity in Figure-Ground Organization Regions with convex borders are more likely to be perceived as figure than are regions with concave borders. Here, you're more likely to perceive "twisted cords" (with mainly convex borders) than "branches with thorns" (with mainly concave borders). (Adapted from Stevens & Brookes, 1988, Figure 4.)

Convexity Regions with convex (outward-bulging) borders are more likely to be perceived as figures than are regions with concave (inward-going) borders. In Figure 4.14, for example, it's possible to perceive vertical "branches with thorns," but vertical "twisted cords" are more readily perceived. This is thought to reflect the fact that most objects have smooth, convex shapes.

Demonstration 4.1 Meaningfulness in Figure-Ground Organization Participate in an experiment to assess whether the meaningfulness of shapes affects figure-ground organization.

Meaningfulness It's reasonable to suppose that, in order to represent and then recognize an object, the visual system must first represent its shape and then match that representation with a representation of an object shape stored in memory—and to do that, the visual system must first identify that shape as figure rather than ground. In other words, it's reasonable to suppose that figure–ground organization precedes object recognition. Consider, however, the three images in the top row in Figure 4.15. In each of these images, one side would be no more likely to be perceived as figure than the other side (the creators of these images attempted to equate both sides of each image for factors like convexity). Therefore, it should be the case that, in each image, the border could as easily be perceived as belonging to the white region as to the black region. Nevertheless, people are much more likely to perceive the white regions as figure in Figure 4.15a and c and the black region as figure in Figure 4.15b. This happens because the regions perceived as figure are meaningful—they correspond to object shapes stored in memory. So here it seems that the visual system recognizes object shapes *prior* to assignment of border ownership and determination of figure–ground organization. If the images are turned upside down (as in the bottom row of Figure 4.15), so that neither region has a meaningful shape, then assignment of border ownership is equally likely for the two regions (Peterson & Gibson, 1994).

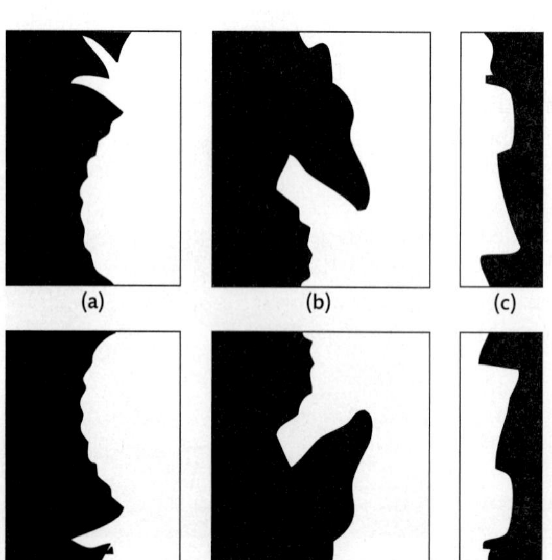

Figure 4.15 Meaningfulness in Figure-Ground Organization The visual system sometimes assesses the meaningfulness of a shape—that is, recognizes it—*before* assigning border ownership and determining figure-ground organization. In each of the images (a)-(c), the border could in principle be perceived as belonging to either the black or the white region, but in all three cases, there is a strong tendency to see the border as belonging to the region that depicts a recognizable object (a pineapple, seahorse, and woman, respectively). Turning the images upside down eliminates any meaningfulness and makes border ownership truly ambiguous. (Adapted and photos from Peterson & Gibson, 1994.)

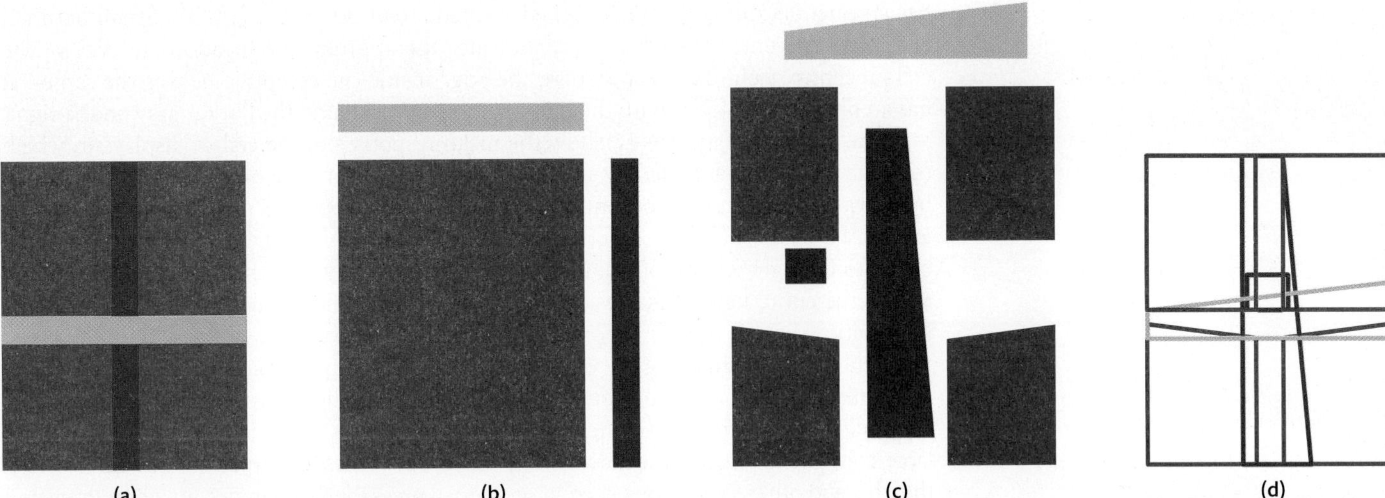

Figure 4.16 Simplicity in Figure-Ground Organization The visual system is strongly biased to interpret any given image in the simplest way it can. The simplest interpretation of the image in (a) is that it consists of the three shapes shown in (b), but of course there are an infinite number of other possibilities, such as the array of shapes in (c) arranged as shown in (d). In this case, (b) is the simplest interpretation because it shows the minimum number of shapes that could yield the image in (a). (Adapted from von der Heydt, 2004, Figure 11.)

Simplicity No matter what an image looks like, there are many different ways of segmenting it into figure and ground, although we're usually not aware of this. Take a look at Figure 4.16a, for example. Most of us would say this image consists of a horizontal light blue strip and a vertical dark blue strip on top of a red rectangle—that is, the three shapes shown in Figure 4.16b, not the seven shapes shown in Figure 4.16c, arranged as shown in Figure 4.16d, and not any other possible arrangement. The arrangement involving the shapes in Figure 4.16b has the highest possible degree of simplicity, and that's the arrangement we tend to see. In this case, *simplicity* refers to the number and placement of shapes composing the image. The interpretation depicted in Figure 4.16b involves just three shapes, and their exact positions aren't crucial—that is, moving the light blue strip up or down a bit or moving the dark blue strip left or right a bit wouldn't much change how we see Figure 4.16a. However, the interpretation depicted in Figure 4.16c involves many shapes that have to be positioned in precise ways to give rise to what we see in Figure 4.16a.

Neural Basis of Border Ownership Assignment

How does the brain represent border ownership? Single-cell recording experiments in monkeys have implicated area V2 in the process of assigning border ownership (Zhou et al., 2000). The responses of single V2 neurons with known orientation and brightness preferences were recorded while the monkeys were shown displays with various configurations of simple geometric shapes on a uniform background. Figure 4.17 shows the displays presented to a V2 neuron that

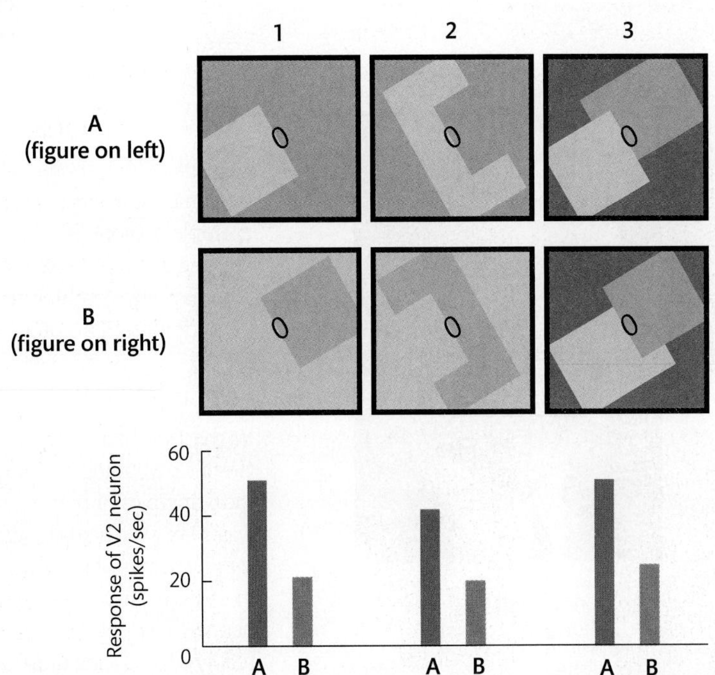

Figure 4.17 Neural Basis of Border Ownership The graphs show the responses of a single neuron in area V2 of a monkey's visual cortex to the displays above. The small outlined ellipse at the center of each display shows the size and location of the neuron's receptive field. In each display, an edge that matches the neuron's orientation preference crosses the receptive field. The graphs indicate that this neuron responds most strongly to a border belonging to a figure lying mainly to the left of the receptive field (the figures in row A, as opposed to the figures in row B, which lie to the right of the receptive field). The question is, how does the neuron "know" the location of the figure? (Adapted from Zhou et al., 2000, Figure 23, p. 6607.)

has an orientation preference for an edge tilted about 30° to the left. The small outlined ellipse at the center of each display indicates the approximate location and size of the cell's receptive field. In every display, the edge inside the receptive field is the same—it has an orientation of 30°, with the lighter gray on the left and the darker gray on the right.

The graphs in Figure 4.17 show the mean responses of the cell to displays in which the edge was a border owned by a figure to either the left or right of the cell's receptive field but always extending well beyond it. In all cases, the response is greater when the border is part of the object to the left of the receptive field (condition A) than when it's part of the object to the right (condition B). Clearly, the cell "knows" where the figure is, even though almost the entire figure lies outside the cell's receptive field. Somehow, the cell is getting information that lets it prefer a border owned by a figure to the left of its receptive field. The researchers concluded that early visual areas (V1 and V2) include specialized networks that allow important information about border ownership and figure–ground organization to be computed and transmitted very rapidly among cells whose combined receptive fields cover large contiguous areas of the visual scene. Such networks would provide the information that this and other V2 neurons need in order to express their preference for a border owned by a figure in a particular spatial relationship to the neuron's receptive field.

An fMRI experiment with human participants has also demonstrated that neurons in area V2 play a role in border assignment: activity in V2 depended on whether borders were owned by the same or different figure regions (Fang et al., 2009).

Check Your Understanding

4.5 How do shading and cast shadows complicate the process of edge extraction?

4.6 Is there a surface in your current visual scene that functions as both figure and ground? If so, describe it. If not, imagine a scene with such a surface and describe it.

4.7 Surroundedness and convexity are two principles that the visual system uses to assign border ownership and determine figure–ground organization. Describe a scene in which these principles might conflict, resulting in ambiguity of border ownership and difficulty in determining figure and ground.

4.8 Which principles of figure–ground organization lead you to interpret the image at the left as consisting of the two shapes in the middle rather than the two shapes at the right.

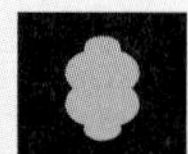  

Perceptual Grouping: Combining Regions

Look back for a moment at Figure 4.6. In this figure, as in many real scenes, single objects are broken up into separate regions, partly seen through the "holes" between occluding objects. For example, regions 21–24 in Figure 4.6b are all part of a single object. When we look at this figure, the fact that these regions are part of the same object is immediately obvious—that is, we automatically combine regions 21–24 in the process of creating a representation of the object they compose. This process of combining image regions into wholes is called *perceptual grouping*.

Max Wertheimer (1880–1943). [Bettmann/Corbis]

Principles of Perceptual Grouping

In the first half of the twentieth century, a group of German psychologists (known as the Gestalt psychologists) created demonstrations and conducted experiments aimed at clarifying the principles of perceptual grouping. Among the most important of the Gestalt psychologists was Max Wertheimer, who devised a method to examine the principles of grouping by presenting arrays of very simple elements and manipulating various relations among the elements in order to discover how those relations affect the perceived grouping of the elements (Wertheimer, 1923/2001). Figure 4.18 shows a number of such arrays and the principles of perceptual grouping they illustrate. In the next few sections, we'll discuss some of these principles in

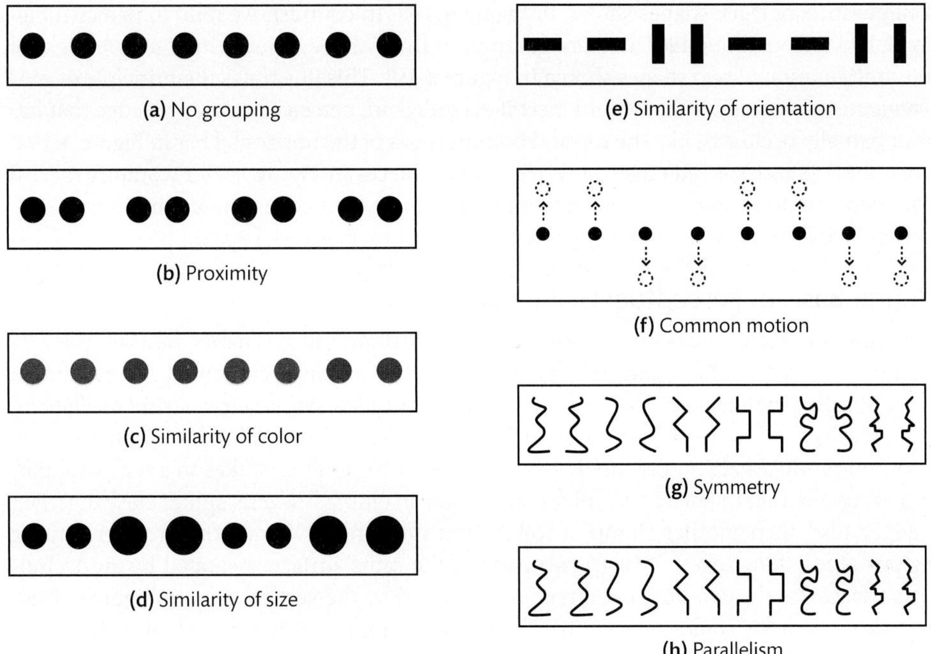

Figure 4.18 Principles of Perceptual Grouping In each panel except (a), simple elements are perceived as "going together" by virtue of one or more grouping principles. (a) No grouping. (b) Elements that are relatively close together group more readily than elements that are relatively far apart. (c) Elements that are similar in color group more readily than elements that are different in color. (d) Elements that are similar in size group more readily than elements that are different in size. (e) Elements that are similar in orientation group more readily than elements that are different in orientation. (f) Elements that move in unison group more readily than elements that move differently. (g) Symmetrical elements group more readily than nonsymmetrical elements. (h) Parallel elements group more readily than nonparallel elements.

more detail. As you read these discussions and consider the accompanying illustrations, keep in mind that our goal is to understand how people group regions in real scenes (like Figure 4.6) rather than in simplified arrays like those used by the Gestalt psychologists.

Proximity According to the principle of *proximity,* elements that are close together group more easily than elements that are far apart. In Figure 4.18b, for example, most people perceptually group the pairs of dots that are closer together.

Similarity The principle of *similarity* states that similar elements tend to group together. In Figure 4.18c, d, and e, the spacing between the elements is uniform, but the pairs of elements that have the same color, size, or orientation tend to be perceptually grouped.

Common Motion According to the principle of *common motion* (sometimes called *common fate*), elements that move in unison are likely to be perceptually grouped. This is illustrated in Figure 4.18f, where the pairs of elements that move up would form one perceptual group, while the pairs of elements that move down would form another.

Symmetry and Parallelism Elements that are symmetrical (Figure 4.18g) or parallel (Figure 4.18h) tend to group together.

Good Continuation We tend to perceive Figure 4.19a as a vertical bar partly occluding a horizontal bar—that is, we perceive the configuration of two shapes shown in Figure 4.19b, not something like the

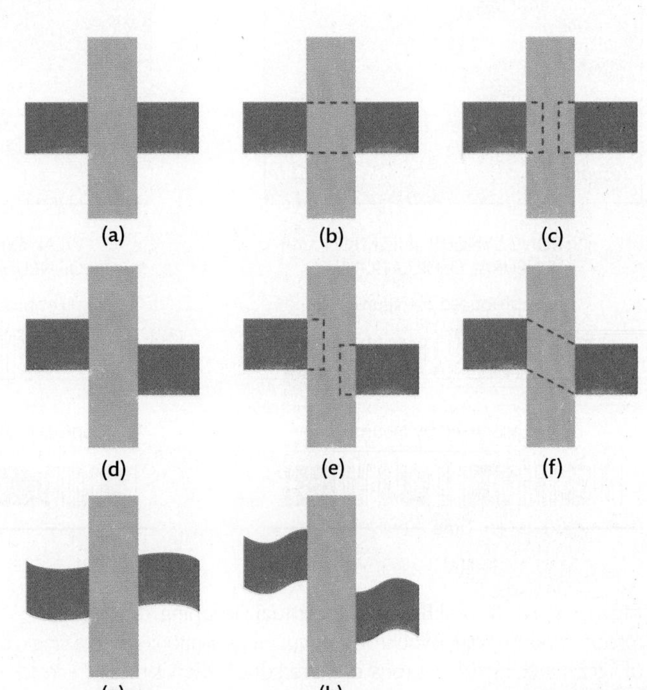

Figure 4.19 Good Continuation The top and bottom edges of the green shapes in (a) would meet if they were extended, as shown in (b). Therefore, by the principle of good continuation, we tend to perceive (a) as a blue vertical rectangle partially occluding a dark green horizontal rectangle, as opposed to perceiving two smaller dark green rectangles, as shown in (c). In (d), the top and bottom edges of the green shapes wouldn't meet if extended, so we tend to perceive two separate rectangles, as shown in (e), rather than the single "bent" shape illustrated in (f). The principle of good continuation works for curved shapes too, as shown by (g) and (h).

Demonstration 4.2 Principles of Perceptual Grouping Interact with animated displays to see how factors such as proximity, similarity, symmetry, and common motion affect how you group visual objects..

configuration of three shapes shown in Figure 4.19c. In contrast, we tend to perceive Figure 4.19d as something like the configuration of three shapes shown in Figure 4.19e, not the configuration of two shapes shown in Figure 4.19f. This illustrates the principle of *good continuation*—two edges that would meet if extended are perceived as a single edge that has been partially occluded, like the top and bottom edges of the horizontal bar in Figure 4.19a. Since the top and bottom edges of the horizontal pieces in Figure 4.19d wouldn't meet if extended, we don't tend to perceive them as the single bent edges shown in Figure 4.19f. This principle applies to curved edges too, as shown by Figure 4.19g and h.

Neural Basis of Perceptual Grouping

How does the brain represent the result of perceptual grouping? That is, how are the representations of spatially separated regions grouped in a single, combined representation of an object? One proposal involves a phenomenon called *synchronized neural oscillations*. We typically think of neural response in terms of spikes per second—that is, how rapidly a neuron produces action potentials—but neurons also produce spikes in a temporal pattern, or oscillation. In particular, spikes often come in clumps: several spikes close together, then a pause, then another clump of spikes, and so forth. If two neurons are representing regions that belong together (e.g., two parts of the same surface separated by an occluding surface, like the two horizontal regions separated by the vertical strip in Figure 4.19a), then those neurons could indicate that the regions belong together by synchronizing their oscillations—that is, by producing clumps of spikes at the same time (Gray et al., 1989).

The researchers tested this idea by recording the responses of pairs of neurons with the same orientation preference in the primary visual cortex of an anesthetized cat. The receptive fields of the two neurons in each pair were spatially separated but aligned with one another (see Figure 4.20). The stimuli were moving bars of light oriented to match the neurons'

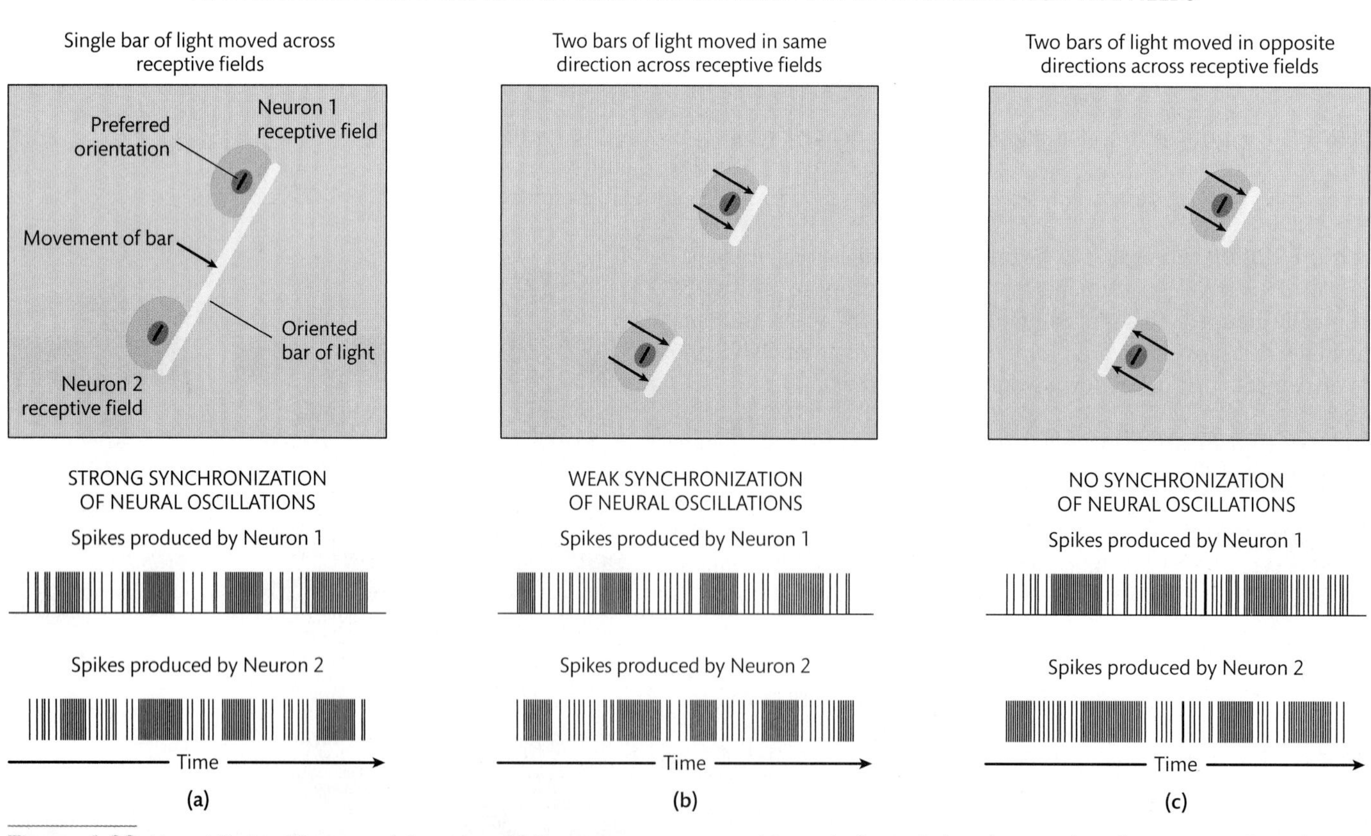

Figure 4.20 Neural Basis of Perceptual Grouping (a) Neurons respond with strongly synchronized neural oscillations when a single bar of light matching the neurons' preferred orientation is moved across their receptive fields. (b) When two separate but aligned bars of light are used instead of a single bar, the neural oscillations are still synchronized but more weakly. (c) When the two bars are moved in opposite directions, the neural oscillations show no synchronization at all. (Adapted from Gray et al., 1989.)

Figure 4.21 Perceptual Interpolation: Seeing Invisible Edges In these photographs, sections of many edges are invisible because the white on one side of the edge is nearly identical to the white on the other side. Nevertheless, we "see" these edges and correctly perceive the shapes of the objects. [Hemera/Thinkstock]

preference. When both receptive fields were stimulated by a single long bar, the neural oscillations were strongly synchronized (Figure 4.20a). Two separate bars moving together also resulted in synchronized neural oscillations, but the synchronization was weaker (Figure 4.20b)—a case of grouping by common motion. If the bars moved in opposite directions, there was no synchronization at all (Figure 4.20c). These results suggest that three important principles of perceptual grouping—similarity (of orientation), good continuation, and common motion—may be represented by synchronized neural oscillations.

The synchronized neural oscillations hypothesis remains somewhat controversial. For example, researchers have pointed out that no detailed mechanism has been proposed to explain how the synchronization would be established—in other words, how the visual system would figure out which units go together—and the same researchers also reviewed the experimental evidence for synchronized neural oscillations and argued that it isn't definitive (Shadlen & Movshon, 1999). For example, a recent experiment designed to test whether synchronized oscillations could account for perceptual grouping of different parts of the same object yielded negative results (Dong et al., 2008). The neural basis of perceptual grouping remains under active investigation.

Perceptual Interpolation: Perceiving What Can't Be Seen Directly

So far, we've described how the visual system identifies edges and regions, assigns border ownership to determine which regions are figure and which are ground, and groups "figure" regions into candidate objects. The next step is perceptual interpolation—intelligently filling in edges and surfaces that aren't visible, typically because they're occluded by other elements of the image but sometimes because they blend in with the background. To get a sense of the automatic ease with which the visual system performs this step, look at Figures 4.21 and 4.22. In Figure 4.21, many portions of the edges of the crockery and the eggs are not physically evident

(a)

(b)

Figure 4.22 Perceptual Interpolation: Seeing Occluded Surfaces (a) The grating hides a substantial percentage of the scene behind it, yet we have no trouble perceiving the scene as a continuous whole. (b) The trees give a very fragmented view of the buildings, and the fragmentation is much less regular than in (a), yet we easily perceive the buildings as single integrated objects. [a: Vibe Images/Alamy; b: Glowimages/Getty Images]

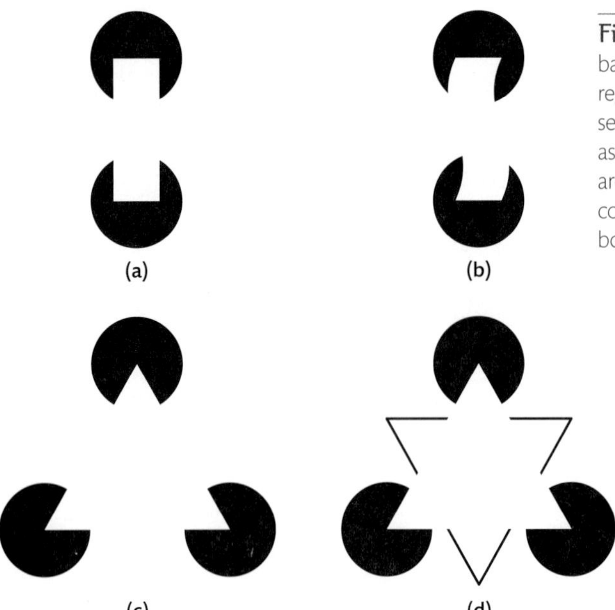

Figure 4.23 Edge Completion (a) The visual system interprets this image as a white bar partly occluding two black disks. The physically nonexistent edges of the bar in the region between the disks have a certain perceptual reality, with the interior of the bar seeming a bit whiter than the white surface of the page. (b) Nonexistent curved edges are as perceptually real as straight ones. (c) A Kanisza triangle: only the corners of the triangle are defined by actual edges, yet we perceive the triangle as complete. (d) The illusion of a complete triangle is strengthened when the nonexistent edges seem to cut off the borders of a partly occluded upside-down triangle.

because the white color matches that of the immediate background. Yet we experience these edges and can easily trace over them (Figure 4.8 also shows some "missing" edges). In Figure 4.22a, the grating gives you a highly fragmented view of the scene beyond it, yet you effortlessly perceive that scene as a continuous whole, along with the objects in it. And in case you think the straight lines and regular spacing of the grating are what make this possible, note the similar ease with which you can look through the trees in Figure 4.22b and perceive the buildings. These figures indicate that perceptual interpolation actually consists of two different operations with somewhat different perceptual consequences: the completion of edges (Figure 4.21) and the completion of surfaces (Figure 4.22).

Edge Completion

edge completion The perception of a partially hidden edge as complete; one of the operations involved in perceptual interpolation.

illusory contours Nonexistent but perceptually real edges perceived as a result of edge completion.

In Figure 4.23a, we see a vertical white bar partly occluding two black disks. The edges of the bar between the disks are not physically present on the page (a fact you can confirm by covering the two disks), but they have an explicit, if dim, perceptual reality—we seem to actually *see* the edges, and this provides a perfect example of **edge completion.** The interior of the bar appears a bit whiter than the white of the page, producing the contrast needed to "see" the edges. Nonexistent but perceptually real edges like these are often termed **illusory contours,** and you can see by Figure 4.23b that the illusion is just as strong for curved edges as for straight ones. The Kanizsa triangle in Figure 4.23c (Kanizsa, 1979) is a well-known example of this sort of perceptual interpolation. The edges of a white triangle partly occluding three black disks are perceptually real even though there are no physical edges in the white space between the disks (again, you can check this by covering the black disks). Note how the addition of an inverted triangle in Figure 4.23d makes the illusion more vivid, presumably because the cut-off edges of that triangle reinforce the reality of the illusory contours.

Surface Completion

surface completion The perception of a partially hidden surface as complete; one of the operations involved in perceptual interpolation.

The images in Figure 4.24a and b are just like those in Figure 4.23a and b except for a thin line that has been added to complete the outline of the black disks. As you can see, this line negates the perception of illusory contours and transforms the perceptual interpretation of the images into a white bar against a black background seen through a pair of "portholes." The middle of the bar is occluded by the white page in front, yet we perceive it as a complete bar; this is an example of **surface completion.** You perceive the bar as complete, but you don't perceive its edges explicitly in the same way as in Figure 4.23a and b. Rather, the edges appear to be occluded by the surface of the page, so you don't experience the white space between the disks as brighter than the white of the page.

The images in Figure 4.24c–f illustrate another aspect of surface completion. Most people would say that Figure 4.24c is a disk partly occluded by a square—that is, the two shapes in Figure 4.24d. However, it could be that the disk really has a cut-out portion that just happens to be perfectly aligned with the square, as illustrated by Figure 4.24e. Or the hidden part of the "disk" could have any of an infinite variety of shapes, like the one shown in Figure 4.24f.

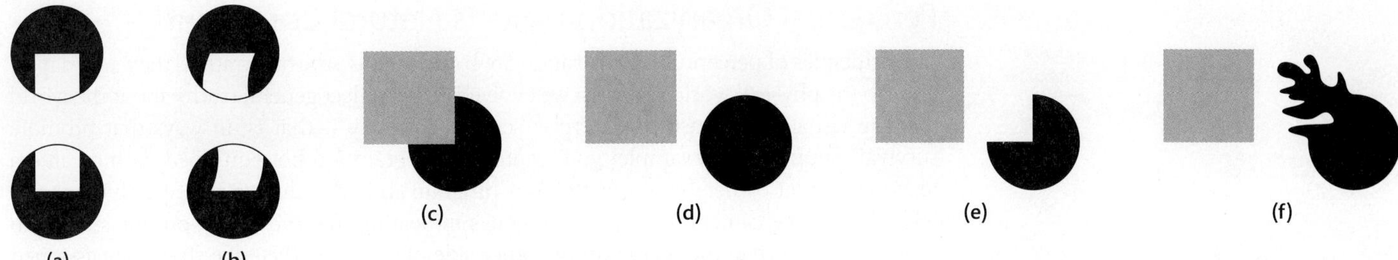

Figure 4.24 Surface Completion (a) Compare this image to Figure 4.23a. The completed outlines of the black disks change our perception to a white bar seen through two "portholes." That is, we perceive the surface of the bar as complete even though only two pieces of that surface are really there. (b) Under the same conditions, a surface with curved edges also appears complete. (c) This image is typically perceived as consisting of the two shapes in (d), but it might just as logically consist of the shapes in (e) or (f) or an infinite number of other possibilities. As with the principle of good continuation (see Figure 4.19), surface completion typically operates to lead the visual system to perceive the simplest shapes.

Neural Basis of Perceptual Interpolation

In experiments with monkeys, recordings of the responses of single neurons in area V2 have provided insights about how illusory contours are represented in the brain (von der Heydt et al., 1984). First, as shown in Figure 4.25a, the neuron's receptive field location (the ellipse) and preferred orientation (about 65°) were determined. The dense array of dots at the right of Figure 4.25a shows the neuron's strong response to a bar of light with this orientation moving across the cell's receptive field, as indicated by the red arrows. Then, as shown in Figure 4.25b, areas entirely outside the cell's receptive field were presented with two bars at the preferred orientation that were moved so as to induce an illusory edge within the receptive field. As you can see, the neuron responded robustly to this illusory edge. To show that the response was not just a result of the movement of the inducing edges, the same two bars were presented, but with their ends cut off, as highlighted by the small red circles in Figure 4.25c. In this case, the gaps at the ends of the bars destroy any perception of an illusory edge, and the neuron's response is indistinguishable from its baseline rate, shown in Figure 4.25d.

This experiment demonstrates that the experience of an illusory contour is not an abstract expectation or inference but the result of an explicit perceptual representation quite early in the visual stream. And as we saw in our discussion of the neural basis of border ownership assignment, individual neurons in early visual areas appear to base their responses on information in the scene well outside the cell's receptive field.

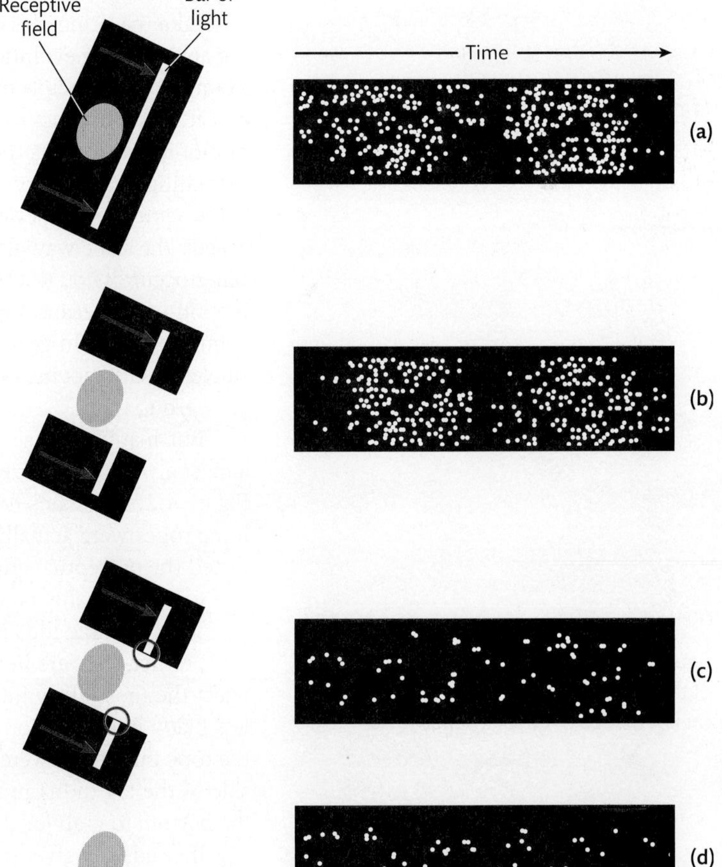

Figure 4.25 Neural Basis of Perceptual Interpolation Recordings from a single neuron in area V2 of a monkey's visual cortex suggest a neural basis for the representation of illusory contours. The neuron's preferred orientation is about 65°, as indicated by the tilt of the receptive field. (a) The two dense arrays of dots show the neuron's strong response to a bar of light at its preferred orientation making two sweeps across its receptive field, in the direction indicated by the red arrows (each dot represents a spike). (b) When two aligned bars at the preferred orientation were moved across areas outside the receptive field in a way designed to induce an illusory edge within the receptive field, the neuron responded almost as strongly. (c) When the ends of the bars of light were cut off (as highlighted by the red circles), no illusory edge was induced, and the neuron's response was essentially the same as its baseline rate, shown in (d). (Adapted from von der Heydt et al., 1984.)

Perceptual Organization Reflects Natural Constraints

The principles of perceptual organization are by no means arbitrary; rather, they are adaptations to the physical world in which we evolved. They reflect general truths about the world that the visual system uses to interpret scenes "correctly"—that is, in ways that promote survival. Suppose, for example, you wanted to program a robot equipped with a camera to assign border ownership correctly. Your program should include a rule specifying that if the image in the camera included depth cues indicating that the region on one side of an edge was closer than the region on the other side of the edge, the edge should be assigned to the closer region, because this is virtually always the correct assignment in the real world (see Chapter 6 for a detailed discussion of depth cues). In Figure 4.22b, for example, the trees are closer than the building, so ownership of any given border between a tree branch and the building should be assigned to the branch. A robot that operates according to this rule would navigate through the trees more successfully than one that doesn't use this rule, and so would an organism that, like us, has evolved with a visual system using this principle. The adaptive advantage conferred by more successful navigation (among many other advantages) has led to this principle being built into our and many other organisms' visual systems over evolutionary time.

The other principles of figure–ground organization and border assignment—for instance, the principles of surroundedness and symmetry—also undoubtedly evolved because they offer adaptive advantages. The principle of surroundedness (see Figure 4.12) reflects the fact that organisms in the natural world encounter objects situated in front of a background much more often than they encounter holes or windows in a surface. The principle of symmetry probably reflects the fact that parallel or otherwise symmetrical edges bound the opposite sides of many biological objects, because the objects themselves are symmetrical (e.g., people and tree trunks). In contrast, the edges surrounding a background region between two different objects are unlikely to exhibit symmetry (see, for example, Figure 4.13c).

Like the principles of figure–ground organization, the principles of perceptual grouping arose during evolution because of certain facts about the physical world. Consider, for example, the principle of common motion. In the real world, all the parts of a rigid moving object, like a car moving along a straight road, tend to have the same direction and speed of motion, as long as the object isn't rotating. That is, the car's left front fender and right rear taillight, and every other securely attached part of the car are all moving straight ahead at the same speed: they exhibit common motion. Unrelated objects rarely move together in exactly the same way, although, of course, common motion of separate objects does sometimes occur: if you throw a handful of rice in the air, many of the grains will have common motion—not because they are parts of the same object, but because their motion had a common cause. In general, though, elements that move together are likely to be part of a single, rigidly moving object, so it's quite sensible that the visual system should automatically group them.

But many of these "general truths" about the physical world aren't *always* true, just almost always. It is, for example, much more probable that a scene like the one depicted in Figure 4.26a contains ropes like those in Figure 4.26b than like those in Figure 4.26c. But if the ropes were actually as shown in Figure 4.26c—that is, if the actual situation contradicted the perceptual grouping principle of good continuation—the man on the side of the cliff would probably be told to grab onto the wrong rope.

This example illustrates why the principles of perceptual organization aren't absolute laws; rather, they are **heuristics**, or rules of thumb. This means that it's always possible to reject the most likely interpretation of how a scene is organized perceptually, in favor of a less likely interpretation based, perhaps, on subtle clues. For instance, if the man holding the rope on the left were to pull on it a little and notice that the piece of rope on the other side of the log didn't move, he might quickly reinterpret the scene and advise the man at the bottom to grab for the rope on the right.

heuristics In perceptual organization, rules of thumb based on evolved principles and on knowledge of physical regularities.

Indeed, any given retinal image has an infinite number of possible scenes that could have produced that image. However, it's usually the case that one of these possible scenes

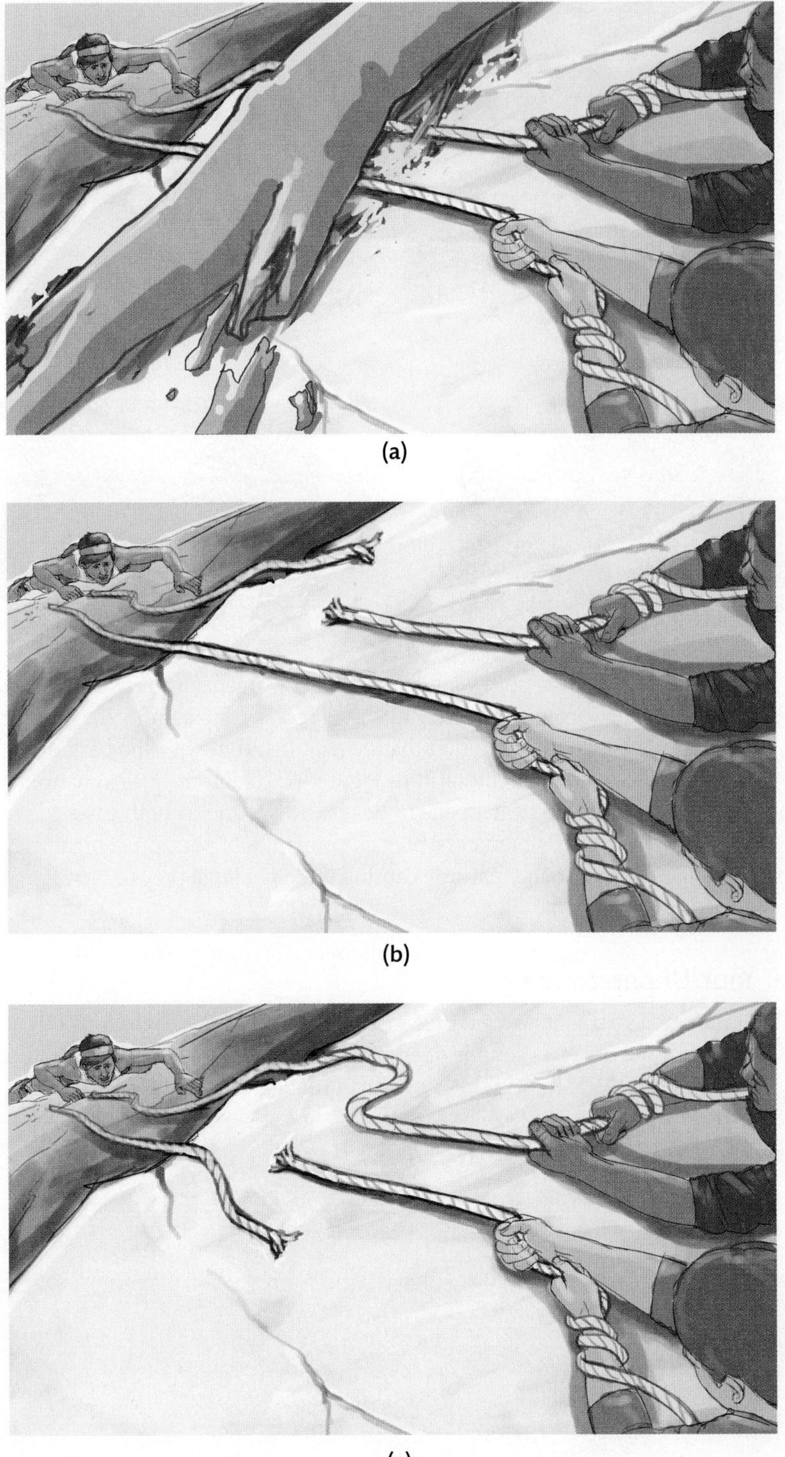

Figure 4.26 **Good Continuation?** In most cases, in the situation depicted in (a), the man on the side of the cliff would be well advised to grab for the rope on the left: the principle of good continuation says that the rope on the left continues unbroken under the log, whereas the pieces of rope on the right don't look like they're connected. This interpretation of the situation is shown in (b). But another possible interpretation is the one illustrated in (c). Like the other principles of perceptual organization, good continuation doesn't always lead to a correct interpretation of the scene.

is much more likely than all the others. In Figure 4.26, the interpretation in which the rope on the left is continuous is much more likely than the interpretation in which the rope on the right is continuous. The visual system tends to interpret any given scene as the one that is most probable given the current retinal image, even though low-probability scenes can sometimes occur. Using heuristics in this way, to guide the interpretation of a retinal image based on knowledge of physical regularities in the world, is called **perceptual inference.**

perceptual inference In vision, the interpretation of a retinal image using heuristics.

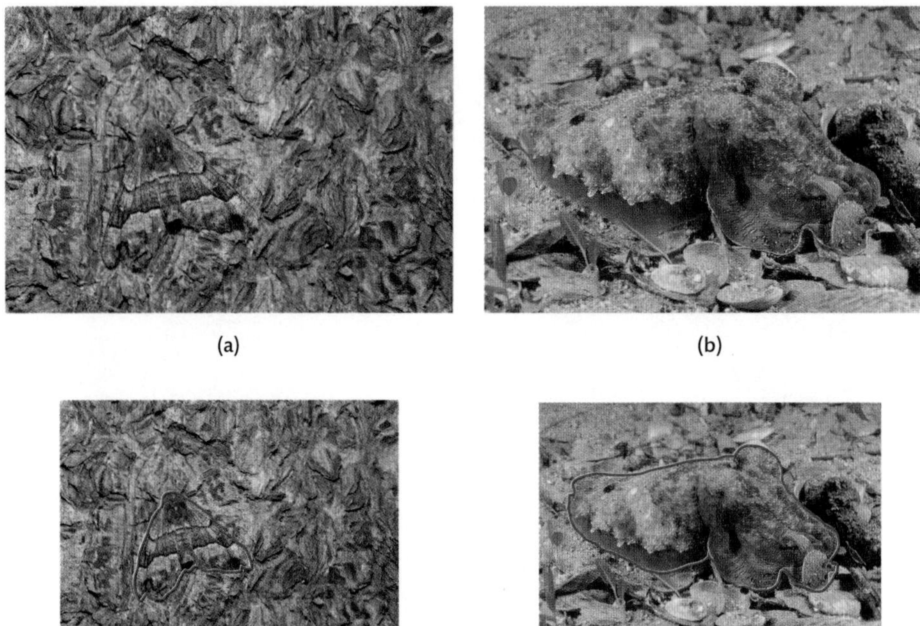

Figure 4.27 Natural Camouflage Like the moth in (a) and the cuttlefish in (b), many animals have evolved with surface coloration that leads potential predators to group them with their backgrounds and therefore fail to see (and eat) them. [a: Ralph A. Clevenger/Corbis; b: Fred Bavendam/Minden Pictures]

Of course, evolution works both ways—that is, some organisms have evolved the ability to take advantage of other organisms' perceptual inferences. For example, the moth in Figure 4.27a has a nonuniform surface coloration that helps it blend in with the bark of the tree on which it is often found, while the cuttlefish in Figure 4.27b automatically changes its coloration to match whatever surface it happens to be resting on, and in both cases the result is a kind of camouflage that exploits predators' built-in principles of perceptual organization (e.g., grouping by similarity of color and texture), causing these potential prey to blend in with their backgrounds.

Check Your Understanding

4.9 Do you perceive this image as three groups of two objects each or two groups of three objects each, or does your perception alternate between these interpretations? Which principles of perceptual grouping would lead to each interpretation?

4.10 Does this figure illustrate edge completion, surface completion, both, or neither? Explain your answer.

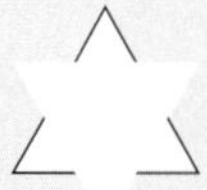

4.11 Your visual system automatically interprets the image on the left as an overlap of the two objects on the right, not the two objects in the center. Describe this interpretation in terms of a perceptual inference involving the heuristic application of a principle of figure–ground organization.

Object Recognition

In the preceding section of this chapter, we explored the steps required for perceptual organization. These steps, which aren't necessarily strictly sequential, include identifying edges and regions in the retinal image, organizing regions into figure and ground through the assignment of border ownership, grouping "figure" regions that are part of the same object, and interpolating portions of edges and surfaces that aren't physically present in the image. By the end of this process, the visual system has created representations of candidate objects—regions or groups of regions making up the objects in the scene. The visual system then has to recognize those objects, by matching them to object representations stored in memory. But how is that matching carried out, and what is the nature of the stored representations?

As we saw at the beginning of the chapter, in our discussion of Figure 4.5, the representation of an object stored in memory can't correspond to a single specific view of the object, because the retinal image of any given object changes—often dramatically—when the object is viewed from different perspectives (of course, there are exceptions, like a featureless sphere, but the exceptions tend to be rare). Clearly, the representation of an object stored in your memory must take this fact into account.

A visual system that can recognize an object as being the same despite such changes in the retinal image is said to exhibit *invariance* (the essentially equivalent term *constancy* is used in other contexts—e.g., in our discussion of color constancy in Chapter 5). In neurophysiological terms, you can think about invariance as follows: the retinal images of any two views of the Brooklyn Bridge in Figure 4.5 are very different, which means that the patterns of action potentials leaving the eyes via the two optic nerves in response to the two views are also quite different, and so are the resulting patterns of neural activity in V1 and V4. But somewhere in the brain, the patterns of neural activity evoked by these two images must be the same or at least related in some systematic way, because the images are indeed perceptually equivalent—our visual system recognizes both of these images as "the Brooklyn Bridge." So an important problem in understanding object recognition is understanding how invariance is achieved.

Two approaches to this problem have been proposed. One is based on the idea that a single representation is activated whenever an object is seen, regardless of the viewpoint, and that this single representation involves specifying the parts of the object and their spatial relationships (Biederman, 1987; Marr & Nishihara, 1978). This approach provides a way to distinguish between major categories of objects—between, say, chairs and tables, which are made up of different types of parts in different spatial relationships. However, the representations that flow from this approach tend to be too abstract—that is, they provide no straightforward way to distinguish between specific instances of a category, such as my office chair versus my kitchen chair. This is the case because different types of chairs have nearly the same parts in about the same spatial relationships, which means that their representations could easily be indistinguishable. Another way of putting this is that this approach does lead to an invariant representation of a chair across different viewpoints, but the approach often does too good a job—it leads to an invariant representation of *all* chairs, even ones that are obviously different from each other.

The other approach is based on the idea that objects are represented in a view-specific manner (Bülthoff & Edelman, 1992; Riesenhuber & Poggio, 2002; Tarr, 1995). That is, for any given object, multiple representations would be stored, each corresponding to a different possible view of the object, and the representation generated by the current view would be compared to all the stored representations simultaneously. This approach is supported by evidence that people recognize objects more easily and more quickly when they see them from a familiar viewpoint (Tarr & Pinker, 1989). Additional support comes from studies showing that single neurons in the inferotemporal cortex respond differently to different specific views (Logothetis et al., 1995), suggesting the existence of distinct, view-specific representations. One reason that this approach can work is that many views are qualitatively equivalent—for example, your view of an automobile changes continuously as you walk around it, and although the front view, rear view, and side view are all quite different, many of the intermediate views are very similar to one another. So storing representations of just a few basic views may well be sufficient to enable recognition through most of the range of views seen under normal circumstances. Nevertheless, critics have argued that in order to have enough specific views stored to recognize any object from any view, you would need a brain that is too big for your head.

In the next sections of this chapter, we'll discuss how objects are represented at different levels of the visual hierarchy—from V1 to V4 and beyond—and we'll explore the issue of whether and to what extent the patterns of neural activity that underlie object recognition tend to be distributed across many different visual areas of the brain or concentrated in modules, areas devoted to recognition of specific categories of objects. Our focus will be on the representation of object shape, rather than other attributes like color or texture, because shape is the most critical for object recognition. Throughout these discussions, note how the problem of invariance remains a central consideration.

Hierarchical Processes: Shape Representation in V4 and Beyond

Our goal in this section is to examine how shape is represented by the patterns of neural activity in the visual areas of the brain, beginning with area V1 (the primary visual cortex). As we saw in Chapter 3, each V1 neuron is tuned to respond maximally to an edge (an extended region of brightness or color contrast) within a narrow range of orientations and locations. This tuning, which results from the way V1 neurons are connected to LGN neurons (look back at Figure 3.8), is the basis for creating a representation of the location and orientation of edges in the retinal image.

Shape Representation in V4

What happens next? It's not hard to imagine that more complex contours could be represented by neurons in V4 that combine the responses of multiple V1 neurons, perhaps with input from neurons in V2. (Recall that V4 is subsequent to V1 and V2 and is the first area of the visual cortex that belongs exclusively to the ventral visual pathway, or "what" pathway, as described in Chapter 3 and illustrated in Figure 3.17.) Suppose, for example, that a group of V1 neurons each indicates the presence of a short, straight edge with a specific orientation and position. As illustrated in Figure 4.28, a V4 neuron that combines the responses of those V1 neurons could indicate the presence of a longer, curved edge built up out of the shorter, straight edges.

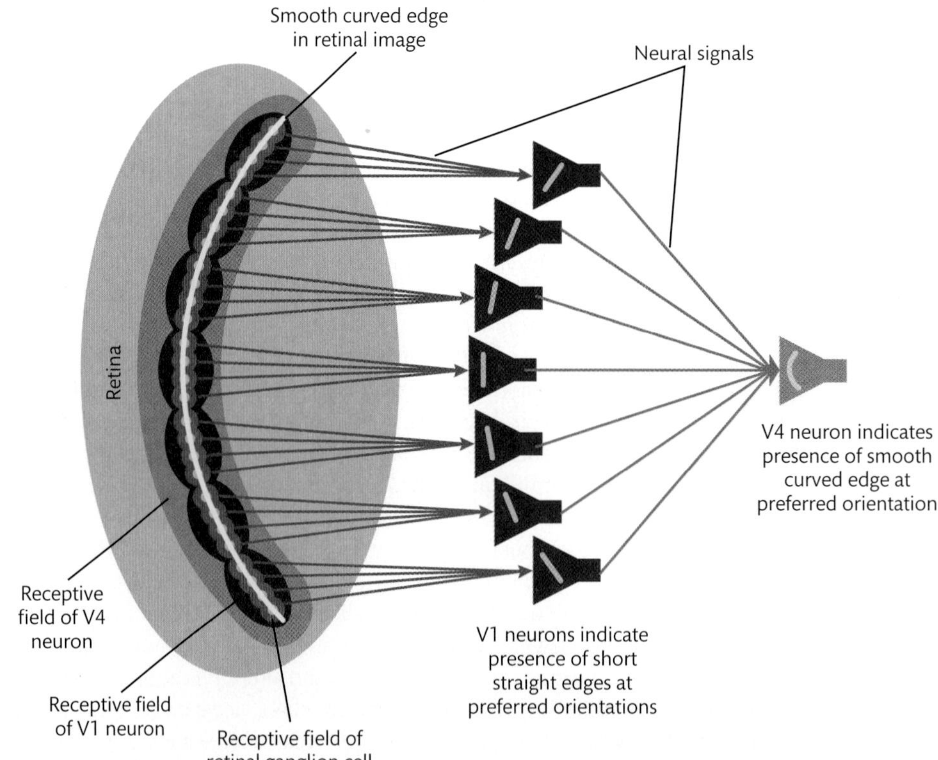

Figure 4.28 Representation of a Curved Edge by a Neuron in Area V4 In this highly schematic illustration, a smooth curved edge in the retinal image (indicated by the yellow curve) activates multiple retinal ganglion cells (RGCs), which send neural signals (via the lateral geniculate nucleus, not pictured here) to neurons in V1. Each V1 neuron receives signals from a small group of aligned RGCs and represents those signals as a short straight edge at the V1 neuron's preferred orientation (indicated by the gray line on each V1 neuron). The V1 neurons send these representations to a single V4 neuron, which combines them to create a representation of a smooth curved edge (indicated by the gray curve on the V4 neuron) corresponding to the actual edge in the retinal image. Each location in the retinal image contains the receptive fields of different neurons in V4 tuned to the full range of convex and concave curvatures and orientations.

In fact, individual neurons in area V4 respond most strongly to edges that can be more complex than those in V1 in at least three ways. First, the edges to which V4 neurons respond strongly can be straight (like the edges that elicit strong responses from V1 neurons) or they can be curved, from very broadly to very sharply. Second, like V1 neurons, they have a preferred orientation, but a contour with the preferred orientation will elicit a strong response from a V4 neuron only if the contour is at a particular angular position relative to the entire shape that the contour belongs to—for example, a V4 neuron may be tuned to respond to a contour oriented at 90° but only if the contour projects outward (a convex contour) from the top of the shape rather than inward (a concave contour) or only if it projects from the bottom of the shape. Third, again like V1 neurons, V4 neurons have a preferred location in the retinal image, but their preferred location covers a larger region of the retinal image; this means that an individual V4 neuron shows some degree of invariance with respect to location because its response to an edge with its preferred curvature and orientation will be the same across a range of locations of the edge within the retinal image.

Evidence for this type of shape tuning comes from studies of the responses of individual neurons in area V4 of the macaque monkey (Pasupathy & Connor, 2002). Figure 4.29a shows some of the systematically varying shapes presented to the receptive field of a single V4

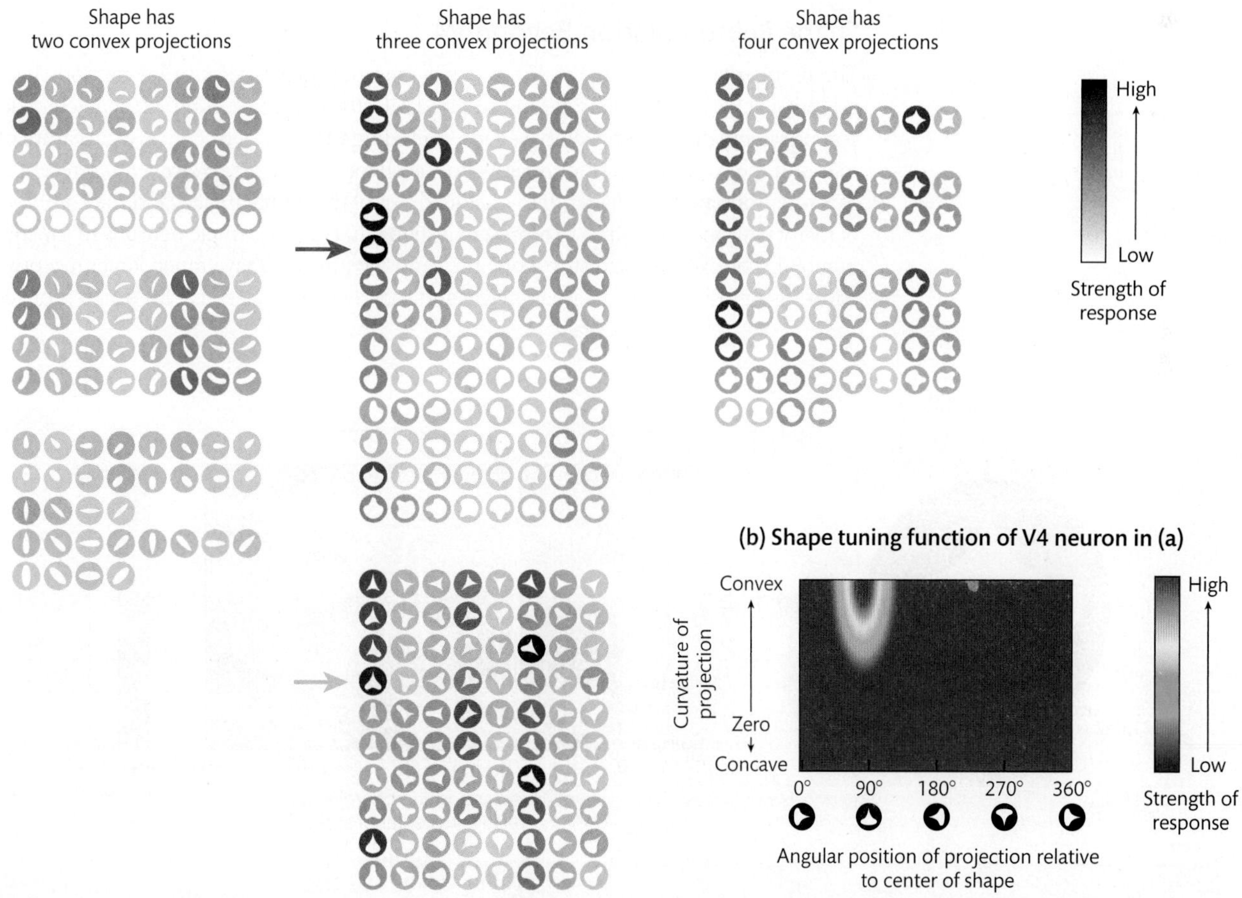

Figure 4.29 A Shape-Tuned Neuron in Area V4 of a Macaque Monkey (a) The strength of response of a single neuron in area V4 of a macaque monkey to a variety of systematically different shapes, as indicated by the shading in the circle behind each shape. This neuron responds strongly to a sharp convexity pointing directly upward from the top of the shape, regardless of the other characteristics of the shape. For example, the two shapes indicated by the red and green arrows are quite different, but both have the required upward-pointing sharp convexity, and both elicit a strong response. (b) The shape tuning function for this neuron, where color indicates the strength of the response. Note the "hot spot" for a sharp convexity at 90°. (Adapted and images from Pasupathy & Connor, 2002.)

neuron. The strength of the neuron's response to each shape is indicated by the grayscale level of the background of the shape (darker background means greater firing rate).

As you can see, this particular neuron tended to respond most vigorously to a sharp convex contour oriented at 90°, pointing directly upward from the shape. The response to this type of contour was consistent regardless of the other properties of the shape—for example, the neuron responded equally strongly to a flattened raindrop shape (indicated by the red arrow in Figure 4.29a) and to an upside-down heart shape (indicated by the green arrow). This neuron's shape tuning is summarized in Figure 4.29b. Other neurons studied were tuned to other combinations of curvature and orientation, and all exhibited some degree of invariance with respect to location.

These observations led the researchers to propose that shapes are represented in V4 by the combined activity of all the neurons responding to the contour fragments making up the shape. Consider, for example, the flattened raindrop shape in Figure 4.30a, which is made up of the contour fragments indicated by the letters A–F. The idea is that, when this shape is viewed, neurons tuned to the curvature, orientation, and location of each of these contour fragments would respond strongly, as shown by the "hot spots" that define the population response in Figure 4.30b. The white curve shows the shape of the flattened raindrop—that is, the curvature and orientation of each segment of its contour—indicating whether each contour fragment is convex or concave and relatively broad or relatively sharp for each angular position from 0° to 360°. This pattern of responses by these neurons constitutes a population code representing the entire shape.

Shape Representation Beyond V4

The representation of shape in V4 is richer than that in V1 because V4 neurons have larger receptive fields than V1 neurons and respond selectively to more complex characteristics of the contour fragments that make up a shape, including the convex or concave curvature of a contour and the contour's position relative to the shape as a whole. However, the receptive fields of V4 neurons are still smaller than one quadrant of the retinal image, and the combined firing of many neurons is required to represent a shape. In contrast, single neurons in the inferotemporal (IT) cortex—the next stop along the ventral pathway—have much larger receptive fields, covering almost the entire retinal image, and each neuron is selective for much more complex

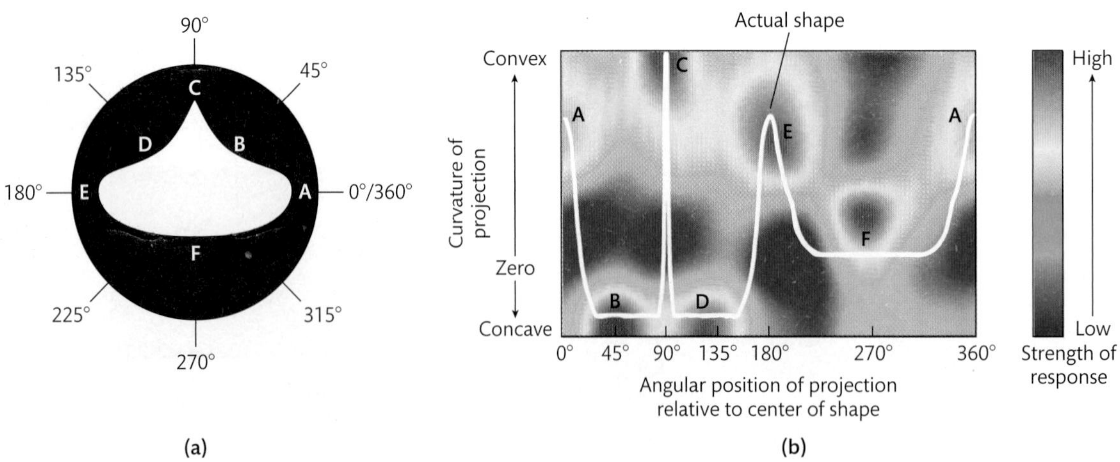

Figure 4.30 A V4 Population Code for Shape (a) This flattened raindrop shape consists of six contour fragments (A–F) that vary in curvature and position. Fragment C would be represented by shape-tuned neurons that prefer an upward-pointing sharp convexity, like the neuron illustrated in Figure 4.29; fragments B and D, by neurons that prefer broad concavities pointing diagonally to the left or right; fragments A and E, by neurons that prefer moderate convexities pointing directly right or left; and fragment F, by neurons that prefer a very broad convexity pointing directly downward. (b) Each of the "hot spots" A–F represents the response of the V4 neurons tuned to respond to the correspondingly labeled contour fragment in (a). The white line shows the actual curvatures and positions of each of the contour fragments of the shape. This pattern of responses constitutes a population code that represents the entire shape. (Adapted and images from Pasupathy & Connor, 2002.)

shapes than are V4 neurons (Brincat & Connor, 2004; Gross et al., 1972; Perrett et al., 1982; Tanaka et al., 1991). That is, individual V4 neurons are tuned to single contour fragments with specific curvatures and orientations, located in a specific part of the retinal image, whereas individual IT neurons respond most strongly to specific *combinations* of contour fragments, located almost anywhere in the visual field. For example, a single IT neuron might respond selectively to a broad concave contour below combined with a sharp convex contour above, like the upside-down heart shape indicated by the green arrow in Figure 4.29a. It is as if these individual IT neurons combine the responses of a large population of V4 neurons.

This kind of shape representation is based on a structural description—that is, a description that specifies a set of parts (contour fragments) and their spatial relations. For example, the white curve in Figure 4.30b is a structural description of the flattened raindrop and could correspond to the tuning of one neuron or a small number of neurons in the IT cortex. The story that is emerging from physiological studies suggests that the representation of shape in the brain is both parts based and view specific (Brincat & Connor, 2004; Pasupathy & Connor, 2002). This amounts to a sort of compromise between the two approaches to object recognition described at the beginning of this section.

Demonstration 4.3 Shape Representation in the Visual Cortex Stimulate different locations on the retina with different shapes to see the responses of V1, V4, and IT neurons.

The Question of "Grandmother Cells"

In the preceding sections, we've reviewed evidence that as you ascend the visual hierarchy from V1 to V4 to the IT cortex, the representations of shape become increasingly complex and receptive fields become larger. In the IT cortex, for example, neurons respond selectively to fairly complex combinations of contours, and their receptive fields can encompass almost the entire retinal image, which means that they exhibit a high degree of invariance with respect to location. Given this hierarchical progression along the ventral pathway, it seems reasonable to suppose that the final representation of a shape—the representation that you subjectively experience and that you match to an object representation stored in memory—is encoded by the response of a single neuron at the very top of the hierarchy. This is the notion of a *grandmother cell,* a term coined by Jerome Lettvin in the late 1960s: a neuron that fires whenever you look at your grandmother's face (regardless of whether it's a front or side view, with or without a hat, etc.).

This idea has been criticized because it would appear to require too many such neurons, one for each of the huge number of recognizable objects. However, evidence has recently emerged in support of a type of grandmother cell in the human brain, based on the responses of individual neurons in the medial temporal lobes of epilepsy patients who were undergoing single-neuron recording as part of their treatment (Quiroga et al., 2005). (It's worth noting that the medial temporal lobe houses the hippocampus—a structure that is important for storing and retrieving long-term memories.) Photographs were flashed on a computer screen, and single neurons were identified that responded to specific objects, regardless of viewpoint. In one case, a neuron that responded to a photograph of the Sydney Opera House also responded to the printed words "Sydney Opera House." This type of response is truly conceptual—that is, the response is invariant not just with respect to viewpoint but also with respect to whether the object is present as a picture or as words. A neuron that responds to the abstract concept of the Sydney Opera House is a good candidate for a **grandmother cell**.

grandmother cell A neuron that responds to a particular object at a conceptual level, firing in response to the object itself, a photo of it, its printed name, and so on.

However, our experience of an object can't depend just on the responses of these kinds of neurons—after all, when we look at an object (say, a toaster), we know exactly where it is (e.g., a bit to the left of where we're looking) and whether we're seeing it in side view or front view, and we know whether we're looking at an actual toaster or the word "toaster." A neuron with truly invariant responses to a toaster wouldn't provide any information about these other important details, which are essential in guiding actions—for example, the action of inserting bread into the slots of the toaster.

Thus, it must be the case that the responses of neurons *throughout the visual hierarchy* contribute to our experience. Neurons in V1 and V2 provide detailed information about the precise locations of the edges of the slots and handle of the toaster. Neurons in V4 provide information about the curvature and orientation of the toaster's various contours. IT neurons provide information about more complex aspects of the toaster's shape, and highest-level neurons—like the ones we've been discussing—provide a truly invariant representation of the concept "toaster."

Modular and Distributed Representations: Faces, Places, and Other Categories of Objects

One of the first experiments using fMRI to investigate how the human brain represents objects revealed a region of the brain that responds selectively to pictures of objects but not to simple features or textures (Malach et al., 1995). A subsequent experiment showed that this region, which researchers refer to as the *lateral occipital cortex* (see Figure 4.31), also exhibits invariance: activity in the region is not dependent on the size, position, or other features of the pictured object (Malach et al., 2002). These results strongly suggest that the lateral occipital cortex is a critical, high-level part of the brain's object recognition system. In addition, regions in the IT cortex have been identified that respond selectively to specific categories of objects, such as faces and buildings. A significant goal of subsequent research has been to understand how different categories of objects are represented within these and other higher-level visual areas.

modular coding Representation of an object by a module, a region of the brain that is specialized for representing a particular category of objects.

distributed coding Representation of objects by patterns of activity across many regions of the brain.

Two main ideas about how objects are processed have been proposed. According to the **modular coding** view, specific parts of the IT and occipital cortex along the ventral visual pathway are specialized for representing objects of specific categories (e.g., faces). These specialized portions of cortex are sometimes referred to as *modules* (following the suggestion of Fodor, 1983; see the discussion of modularity in Chapter 1 and the section "Functional Modules" in Chapter 3). In contrast, the **distributed coding** view holds that, regardless of category, objects are represented by the pattern of activity across relatively wide expanses of cortex along the ventral pathway.

Evidence for the modular view comes from fMRI experiments showing that viewing certain categories of objects (and no other categories) can strongly activate specific brain regions. For example, as we saw in Chapter 3, one region of the IT cortex responds strongly to faces but not to other categories of objects. In a typical experiment, observers viewed a sequence of 45 photographs of human faces, each presented for less than a second, then a sequence of 45 photographs of another type of object, then another sequence of faces, and so on (Kanwisher et al., 1997). Figure 4.32 shows that this region of cortex responded more vigorously to faces than to any of the other categories of objects presented. The researchers argued that this region constitutes a module specialized for representing faces; they called it the *fusiform face area* (FFA) because it's located on the fusiform gyrus along the lower surface of the temporal lobe (see Figure 4.31). Studies in monkeys using both fMRI and single-cell recording have shown that about 97% of FFA neurons are highly selective for faces (Tsao et al., 2006).

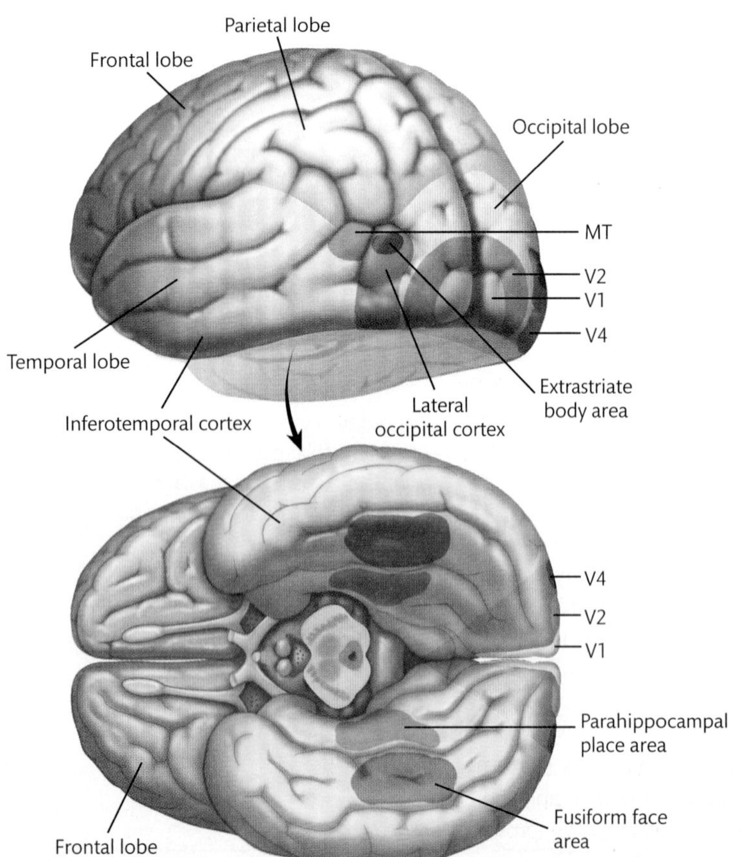

Figure 4.31 Object Recognition in the Brain Areas V1, V2, and V4 create increasingly complex representations of edges, regions, and shapes. The complexity and invariance of these representations further increase in higher visual areas along the ventral pathway, including the lateral occipital cortex and the inferotemporal cortex. The fusiform face area, parahippocampal place area, and extrastriate body area have been proposed as modules, localized areas that are specialized for representing particular categories of objects (faces, places, and body parts, respectively).

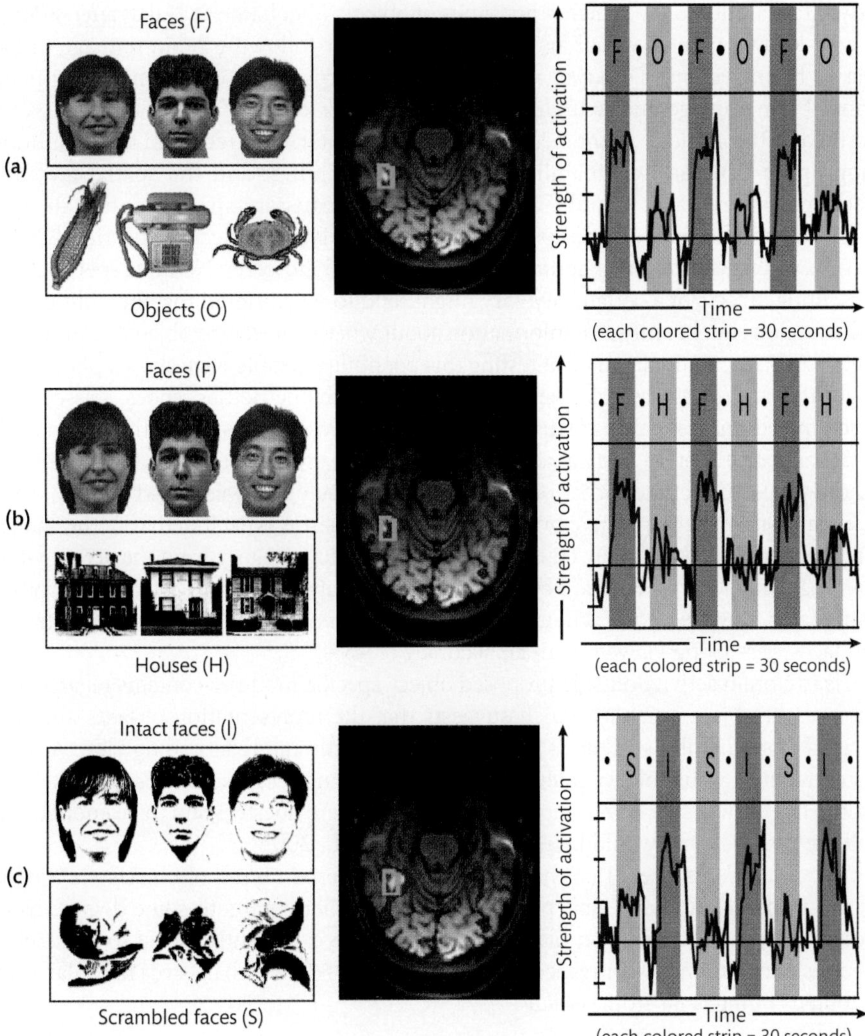

Figure 4.32 A Face-Selective Region in the Human Inferotemporal Cortex An fMRI experiment measured activity in the human brain as subjects viewed alternating 30-second sequences of faces versus other types of objects. (a) Faces versus a variety of different objects. (b) Faces versus houses. (c) Intact faces versus scrambled faces. In all cases, brain activity within a region of the fusiform gyrus in the inferotemporal cortex (outlined in green in the fMRI images in the middle column) was greater when subjects were viewing faces; this is the region that has been termed the *fusiform face area*. (Adapted from Kanwisher et al., 1997. Grateful acknowledgment to N. Kanwisher for the images in this figure.)

Other proposed modules in the ventral visual pathway have been identified that respond selectively to other categories of objects. These include the parahippocampal place area (PPA), which is activated by buildings and outdoor scenes (Epstein & Kanwisher, 1998), and the extrastriate body area, which is activated by human and animal bodies and body parts, but not by faces (Downing et al., 2001; both of these areas are shown in Figure 4.31). Some studies suggest that other parts of the ventral visual pathway respond selectively to still other categories of objects (e.g., tools and chairs).

Evidence for the existence of category-specific modules is also provided by patients with brain damage that results in **visual agnosia,** an impairment in object recognition (Lissauer, 1890/2001; Mahon & Caramazza, 2009). Visual agnosia isn't due to some form of blindness, as shown by the fact that patients can often describe the color and location of an object in front of them, but can't name it or say what its function is. Nor is it due to a loss of conceptual knowledge, as these patients can, when given the name of an object, state what it's for and what its shape is. Furthermore, they can recognize objects based on touch.

visual agnosia An impairment in object recognition.

Visual agnosias come in many varieties. The patient D. F., described in Chapter 3, exhibited a condition called *visual form agnosia,* which affected her ability to perceive shapes of any kind; this type of visual agnosia probably results from damage to relatively early parts of the ventral pathway. Other visual agnosias affect the perception of only specific categories of objects. **Prosopagnosia**—an inability to recognize faces, with a

prosopagnosia A type of visual agnosia in which the person is unable to recognize faces, with little or no loss of ability to recognize other types of objects.

nearly intact ability to recognize other types of objects (Duchaine & Nakayama, 2006)—is a well-known type of visual agnosia that can occur following brain damage in face-selective brain regions (Dricot et al., 2008) but is surprisingly common among people without brain damage and is highly heritable (Wilmer et al., 2010). (Beth, the woman described in the vignette at the beginning of this chapter, suffered from this condition.) **Topographic agnosia**—an inability to recognize buildings and the spatial layouts of streets and other spaces (Farah, 2004)—is another category-specific deficit in object recognition and could well be due to damage to the PPA (Mendez & Cherrier, 2003).

topographic agnosia A type of visual agnosia in which the person is unable to recognize spatial layouts such as buildings, streets, landscapes, and so on.

The evidence for modular coding is not unequivocal, however. Neurons specialized for representing objects of a certain category might tend to be clustered together, but neurons in other regions might still carry information about whether a viewed object belongs to that category. In an experiment aimed at testing this possibility, people were shown photographs of eight different categories of objects (faces, houses, chairs, bottles, shoes, scissors, cats, and scrambled images) during fMRI scanning, and the researchers found that by analyzing the spatial distribution of cortical activity within a large swath of the IT cortex, they could predict with 95% accuracy what object category was being viewed (Haxby et al., 2001). And even when the region where brain activity was greatest was excluded from the analysis, the researchers found that they could still reliably predict category from the activity in the remaining parts of the IT cortex. For example, when analyzing brain activity in response to viewing faces, they excluded activity in the FFA and found that they still could determine when faces were being viewed, with an accuracy of 93%.

Clearly, brain activity outside proposed object-specific modules contains reliable information about object category, which suggests that the representation of faces and other objects is more distributed than is presumed by a strictly modular coding view. Also, the sheer number of visual object categories that people can recognize makes it unlikely that each one has its own specialized module in the brain: there doesn't seem to be enough brain for all the modules that would be required (Haxby et al., 2001).

Demonstration 4.4 Modular and Distributed Representations Simulate an experiment showing that object representation in the brain is both modular and distributed.

Overall, it seems likely that the brain represents certain types of objects via modular coding—in particular, faces, and probably places and body parts to some degree. Nevertheless, distributed coding also plays a significant role even with respect to these object categories and certainly with respect to other categories. The debate over modular versus distributed coding is far from settled.

Top-Down Information

Throughout most of this chapter, we've emphasized the role of bottom-up information during the perception of scenes and objects: the flow of information from the retina to V1, V4, and beyond—that is, the flow from lower to higher regions of the visual hierarchy. This bottom-up account of object recognition, however, is incomplete, because it doesn't include the role of top-down information: the flow of information from higher regions to lower regions. Top-down information flow involves the perceiver's goals, attention, and knowledge, as well as expectations about what objects are likely to occur in the current scene.

The influence of knowledge and expectations on object recognition was brought out in an early experiment showing that whenever an object violated any of several default assumptions about the relationship between an object and its scene, the object was more likely to be misidentified or missed altogether in a brief exposure (Biederman et al., 1982). For example, if a fire hydrant was shown in a street scene floating above the sidewalk or placed on top of a car, then its identification was impaired. This suggests that there is some mechanism for rapidly assessing the "gist" of a scene, that knowing the gist sets up expectations about what objects are likely to be in the scene (and about how those objects are likely to be situated in the scene), and that such expectations can affect object recognition. This is a bit of a paradox, however, because the gist of many types of scenes is defined by the types of objects typically contained in the scene—for example, the gist of a kitchen is, essentially, the combination of a sink, a stove, a refrigerator, and so on. In such cases, it would seem that in order to perceive the gist of the scene, you would first have to identify the objects making up the scene, so how could the gist help identify those objects?

One idea is that the visual system first creates a representation of the general, overall layout of the scene and tries to match that with representations of the general layout of specific categories of scenes stored in memory (Oliva & Torralba, 2007). For example, most beach scenes contain a broad light-colored swath in the lower third (the sand), a darker-colored swath in the middle third (the water), and a light-blue colored swath in the upper third (the sky). Of course, there are many possible variants of this general layout, depending on the presence and placement of objects such as palm trees, people, and boats, but if you could create a composite of, say, 1,000 beach photographs, all the specific details that vary from one scene to the next would "average out," resulting in a picture consisting of just the general layout described above.

A general layout that can rapidly be matched to a layout stored in memory provides a gist that the visual system can use to guide the identification of specific objects in the scene, because these stored representations of general layouts are associated with specific types of objects that typically appear in such scenes, and this makes those types of objects more accessible in memory, enabling them to be more speedily recognized. For example, if the general layout was identified as a beach scene, then even a small part of a palm tree would be rapidly recognized, while an object with the shape of a fire hydrant would take longer to identify (this principle is illustrated in Figure 4.33).

Figure 4.33 What Is This Object? This is a portion of a familiar object, and it would be easily recognizable if seen in a familiar context, but can you recognize it out of context? (Turn to p. 146 to see it in context.) [Inti St Clair/Getty Images]

Thus, representations of general layouts stored in memory provide the gist of the current scene, and knowledge about scenes with different gists narrows down the range of probable objects to be recognized. This top-down information is combined with bottom-up information in the ventral pathway to speed up the process of fully recognizing the objects in the scene. The details of this process are still being worked out theoretically and experimentally, but there's no doubt that top-down information flow is an important aspect of object recognition.

What is the basis for this process of object recognition aided by top-down information? Researchers have proposed that the brain is *always* actively predicting the immediate perceptual future, using both the recent past and the current scene as evidence—that is, the brain is constantly trying to answer the question: What am I likely to see, given what I know, what I've seen during the last few minutes, and where I am at the moment? (Kveraga et al., 2007). The roots of this idea go back to the nineteenth-century German scientist Hermann von Helmholtz (1866/1925), who spoke of vision as a process of "unconscious inference." Helmholtz suggested that the mind is always trying to infer what the scene is that produced the current retinal image, based on information in the image and on information in memory about past experiences with scenes like the current one.

Recently, vision scientists have used the **Bayesian approach** (inspired by the work of Thomas Bayes, an eighteenth-century mathematician and Presbyterian minister) to develop mathematical descriptions of how this process of unconscious inference might work (Kersten et al., 2004). According to this approach, the visual system unconsciously combines two probabilities in order to infer what type of scene produced the currently experienced retinal image: (1) the prior probability of all possible scenes and (2) for each possible scene, the probability that it produced the current retinal image.

Bayesian approach In object recognition, the use of mathematical probabilities to describe the process of perceptual inference.

To see what this means, look back at Figure 4.26. The scenes depicted in Figure 4.26b and c are two of the many possible scenes that could have produced the current retinal image illustrated in Figure 4.26a (another possibility, for example, is that both ropes consist of separate pieces). The visual system assigns a lower prior probability to the scene illustrated in Figure 4.26c because it would require that the cut ends of the rope just happen to line up under the log, and the visual system "knows" that this kind of coincidence is unlikely. Given that both the scenes in Figure 4.26b and c *could* have produced the current retinal image and that the scene in Figure 4.26b has a higher prior probability, the visual system infers that the scene in Figure 4.26b has a higher probability of having *actually* produced the current retinal image. In this way, the visual system can assign the most probable interpretation (Figure 4.26b) to an ambiguous retinal image (Figure 4.26a). This general conceptual framework can be applied in much more complex situations to help explain how the visual brain combines bottom-up and top-down information to recognize scenes and objects.

Context for Figure 4.33 (p. 145) In context, a refrigerator is identifiable by just a narrow portion of its front side. [Inti St Clair/Getty Images]

Check Your Understanding

4.12 When I went to pick up my car at the repair shop, it was still up on the lift, next to another dark blue car on the adjacent lift. Because I wasn't accustomed to looking at cars from below, I wasn't sure which car was mine. How does this experience argue for view-specific object representation?

4.13 Describe two ways in which V1 neurons and V4 neurons differ in their responses to edges.

4.14 In which visual area of the brain do neurons have receptive fields large enough to represent shapes that occupy most of the visual field: V1, V4, or the inferotemporal cortex?

4.15 Where would so-called grandmother cells fit into the hierarchy of representations from lower to higher visual areas?

4.16 Briefly describe the difference between modular and distributed representations of visual objects.

4.17 Mark gets coffee and a bagel at the same diner every morning before work, and he always pays the same cashier—by now he feels as if they're old friends. But yesterday, they passed on the street and Mark wouldn't have recognized her if she hadn't said hi. How does this illustrate top-down processing in object recognition?

APPLICATIONS Automatic Face Recognition

In this era of heightened concern about security, automatic face recognition—using computers to match digital images of faces to images in a database of known faces—has taken on new importance. There is still no automated system that can recognize faces as rapidly and accurately, and under as wide a range of conditions, as the human visual system, but great progress has been made since this aspect of computer vision first emerged as a focus of research in the 1950s, and it continues to be an area of active research. Many commercial face recognition systems exist for specific applications, and their performance is surprisingly good.

Three types of approaches have been taken toward developing automatic face recognition systems: feature based, holistic, and hybrid (Zhao et al., 2003). As the accuracy and speed of these systems increase, we can expect to see them appear in a variety of applications in the years ahead.

Feature-Based Approach

The feature-based approach focuses on identifying the most prominent anatomical features of a face and the spatial relations among them (this is similar to the structural description models for object recognition illustrated in Figure 4.30). For example, prominent features might include the eyes, eyebrows, nose, mouth, lips, and chin; spatial relations might include such measurements as the width of the eyes, the distance between the top of the eyes and the bottom of the eyebrows, and the thickness of the lips. One face recognition system using this approach (Cox et al., 1996) involves first specifying the locations of 35 key points in the face and then measuring 30 spatial relations among features of the face, based on distances between selected pairs of key points (see Figure 4.34).

To implement this system, each of the face images in the database of known faces is processed in order to determine the 30 spatial relations that characterize it; thus, the representation of each face image is just a list of 30 numbers. When an image of a test face is presented to be recognized, its 30 spatial relations are measured, yielding a representation that is then compared to the representation of each face image in the database. Under ideal

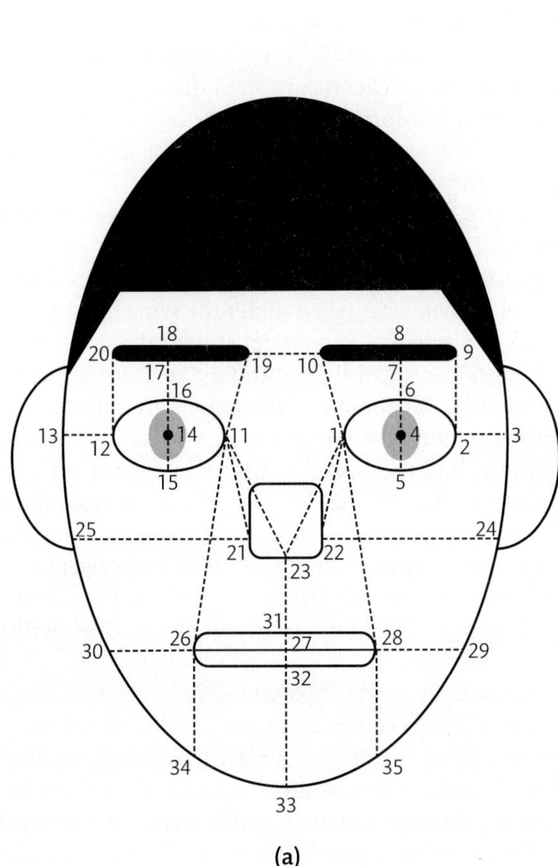

SPATIAL RELATION	DISTANCE
Average width of eyes	0.5 * [(1,2) + (11,12)]
Average height of eyes	0.5 * [(5,6) + (15,16)]
Width of face across eyes	(3,13)
Width of face across tip of nose	(24,25)
Width of face across mouth	(29,30)
Width of chin	(34,35)
Height of chin on right side	(26,34)
Height of chin on left side	(28,35)
Width of mouth	(26,28)
Height of upper lip	(27,31)
Height of lower lip	(27,32)
Height of chin at center of mouth	(32,33)
Distance from top of upper lip to bottom of nose	(23,31)
Width of nose across nostrils	(21,22)
Average distance along outer edge of upper half of cheeks	0.5 * [(3,24) + (13,25)]
Average distance along outer edge of lower half of cheeks	0.5 * [(24,29) + (25,30)]
Average distance along outer edge of jaw	0.5 * [(28,35) + (30,34)]
Average distance from inner corner of eye to edge of nostril	0.5 * [(1,22) + (11,21)]
Distance between inner ends of eyebrows	(10,19)
Average distance from outer corner of eyebrow to outer corner of eye	0.5 * [(2,9) + (12,20)]
Average width of eyebrows	0.5 * [(9,10) + (19,20)]
Average distance from inner corner of eyebrow to inner corner of eye	0.5 * [(1,10) + (11,19)]
Average distance from bottom of eyebrow to top of eye	0.5 * [(6,7) + (16,17)]
Average height of eyebrows	0.5 * [(7,8) + (17,18)]
Average width of inner portion of eyebrows	0.5 * [(8,10) + (18,19)]
Average width of outer portion of eyebrows	0.5 * [(8,9) + (18,20)]
Distance from inner corner of right eye to bottom of nose	(11,23)
Distance from inner corner of left eye to bottom of nose	(1,23)
Average distance from inner corner of eye to outer corner of mouth	0.5 * [(1,28) + (11,26)]
Average distance from outer corner of eye to edge of face	0.5 * [(2,3) + (12,13)]

(b)

Figure 4.34 Feature-Based Approach to Automatic Face Recognition (a) This schematic face shows the 35 key points used to determine the 30 spatial relations that represent a face. (b) This table shows how the 30 spatial relations are measured as distances, based on the distances between selected pairs of measurement points. The notation (1, 2), for example, means the distance between points 1 and 2; thus, the average width of the two eyes is derived by adding the width of the left eye (the distance between points 1 and 2) to the width of the right eye (the distance between points 11 and 12) and multiplying the result by 0.5; similarly, the height of the lower lip is the distance between points 27 and 32. Points 4 and 14 don't figure in any of the spatial relations because the distance between them (the distance between the centers of the irises) is used to normalize all the other distances, so the face recognition system can compare different-sized images of faces. (Adapted from Cox et al., 1996.)

conditions, if the test face is among the faces in the database, the 30 spatial relations of the test face will perfectly match those of just that face in the database (assuming that each known face has just one image in the database). Of course, conditions are rarely ideal. Many factors might make the spatial relations of the test face image differ from those of the image of the same face in the database, including differences in the pose of the face (e.g., frontal versus three-quarters), differences in the person's expression, lighting differences that change the shadows on the face and affect measured distances, and differences in the distance from the face to the camera.

Given these sources of noise (see the discussion of noise in Chapter 1), it's likely that the representation of the test face will not exactly match the representation of any face in the database. Therefore, the researchers who developed this system devised a statistical method for finding the best match and for deciding whether that best match is close enough to be considered a successful recognition. If the system decides that the best match isn't close enough, it declares that the test face isn't in the database.

Holistic Approach

The 30 spatial relations of the feature-based approach described above fail to capture many key aspects of facial appearance, including skin color and texture, hair and eye color, the presence of facial hair, and the position and prominence of the cheekbones. Given such limitations on this and other feature-based approaches, much research has focused on holistic approaches, which involve matching an image of a test face as a whole with the images of the known faces in the database. The simplest version of a holistic approach would be simply to make a pixel-by-pixel comparison of the test face image to the image of each known face and to compute a correlation. This method does not work well, however, because even if the test face is among the known faces, all the small differences between the test face image and the image in the database (due to differences in pose, expression, lighting, etc.) will add up, and the computed correlation won't indicate a match.

A more sophisticated holistic approach uses what are called *eigenfaces,* face images generated from a set of digital images of human faces taken under the same lighting conditions, normalized to line up the eyes and mouths, and rendered with the same spatial resolution. The resulting eigenface images consist of light and dark areas arranged in a pattern that may or may not resemble a face, depending on the weight given to different facial features in the process of creating the image—features such as symmetry, style of facial hair if any, location of the hairline, and the size of the nose or mouth. Any human face can be represented as the average face in the database of known faces plus a weighted combination of the other eigenfaces in the set—for example, your face might be composed of the average face plus 8% from eigenface 1 in the set, 63% from eigenface 2, −4% from eigenface 3, and so on. Figure 4.35a shows some of the images from a set of known faces in a large database, and Figure 4.35b shows some of the eigenfaces derived from those images.

Each image in the database of known faces can be represented in terms of the set of eigenfaces by starting with the average face (computed by averaging together all the images in the database) and adding a weighted sum of the other eigenfaces, as described above. The more weight a particular eigenface receives in representing an image of a known face, the more "important" that eigenface is in that representation, and it turns out that representations using only the most important eigenfaces can do a very good job of creating a recognizable image.

Systems using this type of holistic approach determine whether a test face is among the known faces in the database by first calculating how each eigenface has to be weighted to reconstruct the test face; then, if the set of weights representing the test face is similar enough to the set representing a face in the database, the system decides that the test face has been recognized. However, as with systems using feature-based approaches, noise resulting from differences in pose, lighting, and other such factors can reduce performance.

(a)

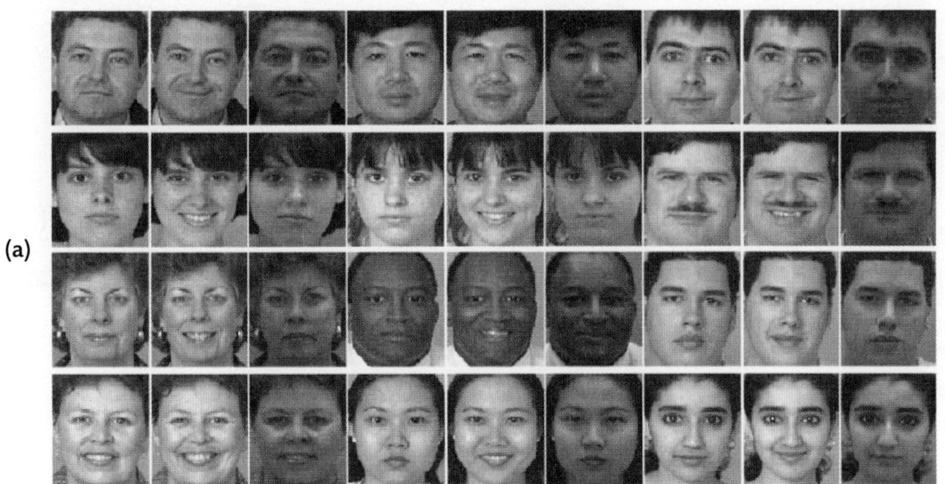

(b)

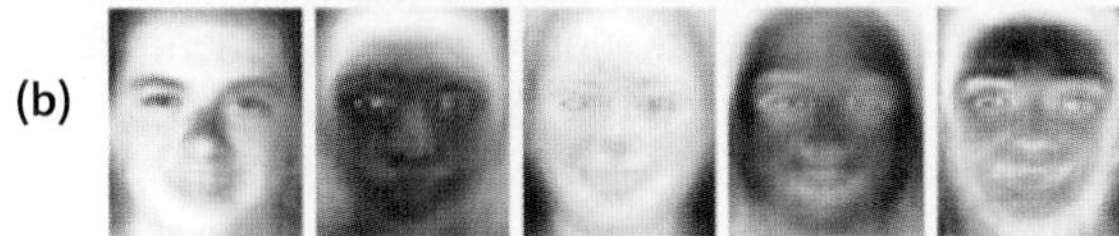

Figure 4.35 Holistic Approach: Face Recognition Using Eigenfaces (a) Some of the images that make up the set of known faces in the system's database. (b) Some of the eigenfaces obtained from the database of known faces. A face is represented by adding a weighted sum of eigenfaces to the average of all the faces in the database. The representation of any face image in the database, then, is the list of weights applied to these eigenfaces to reconstruct that image. (Adapted and photos from Kwak & Pedrycz, 2007.)

Hybrid Approach

A third, hybrid type of approach combines the best aspects of the holistic and feature-based approaches, as exemplified by a system in which eigenfaces were supplemented by eigenfeature representations—eigeneyes, eigenmouths, and eigennoses (Pentland et al., 1994). A set of eigeneyes, for example, would be generated in the same way as a set of eigenfaces, and would consist of the average eye (derived from the eyes of the known faces in the database) plus additional eigeneyes based on weights assigned to different aspects of the eyes in the database (e.g., shape and color). The system attempts to recognize a test face by first constructing an eigenface representation of the whole face and an eigenfeature representation of each feature, with both types of representations consisting of the average eigenface or eigenfeature plus a list of weights given to each remaining eigenface or eigenfeature. The eigeneye representation of the test eye is then compared to the eigeneye representation of each eye in the database, to determine which faces contain an eye like the test eye. The same procedure is used for the nose and mouth, and when this is combined with the eigenface approach, performance improves, as illustrated in Figure 4.36.

Are these automatic face recognition approaches anything like how the brain processes faces? We know that the fusiform face area (FFA) is crucially involved in recognizing faces, but we don't know in much detail how the FFA actually works. As our knowledge grows, researchers will be able to incorporate the FFA's principles of operation in automatic face recognition systems that could truly mimic the way humans recognize faces.

Test faces

Incorrect matches based on eigenfaces

Correct matches based on eigenfaces and eigenfeatures

Figure 4.36 Hybrid Approach: Adding Eigenfeatures to Eigenfaces Test faces (top) with deliberately introduced "noise" (hand to face, paint on face, and beard and mustache) were incorrectly matched by a system that used eigenfaces (middle) but were correctly matched by a system that also used eigenfeatures (bottom). (Adapted and photos from Pentland et al., 1994.)

Check Your Understanding

4.18 An image of Herb's face is in a database of known faces. After that image was made, Herb shaved his head, grew a beard, and had a big tattoo inked on his forehead. Which type of automatic face recognition system would probably be more successful at matching a new image of Herb's face to the image in the database—a system based on a holistic approach or a system based on a hybrid approach? Explain why.

SUMMARY

- A Few Basic Considerations We recognize a familiar object by matching the visual system's representation of it to a representation stored in memory, but even an unfamiliar object can be recognized as an object. Three factors complicate the process of object recognition—image clutter, object variety, and variable views.
- Overview: The Fundamental Steps The process of matching the visual system's representation of an object to a representation stored in memory can be broadly divided into two parts—perceptual organization and object recognition. The steps in perceptual organization are representing edges; representing uniform regions bounded by edges; dividing these regions into figure and ground and assigning border ownership; grouping regions with similar properties and representing "figure" regions as candidate objects; and filling in partly occluded edges and surfaces to represent candidate objects more completely. Object recognition involves the use of higher-level processes to represent objects fully enough to match them to representations stored in memory.
- Perceptual Organization Perceptual organization is the visual system's way of dealing with scene complexity. The visual system represents edges via patterns of brightness differences in the retinal image, but this process of edge extraction can be complicated by occlusion, shading, and cast shadows. Figure–ground organization, which goes hand-in-hand with assignment of border ownership, operates according to various principles, including depth, surroundedness, symmetry, convexity, meaningfulness, and simplicity. Studies indicate that border ownership is computed in V2 and other early visual areas via specialized networks of neurons whose combined receptive fields cover large contiguous areas of the visual scene. Perceptual grouping—combining the regions identified during figure–ground organization—also operates according to various principles, including proximity, similarity, common motion, symmetry and parallelism, and good continuation. One proposal regarding the neural basis of perceptual grouping involves synchronized neural oscillations. Perceptual interpolation involves edge completion (via the perception of illusory contours) and surface completion; studies with monkeys indicate that individual neurons in early visual areas respond to illusory contours based on information in the scene well outside the neuron's receptive field. The principles of perceptual organization aren't absolute laws but rules of thumb, which help us respond quickly according to the most likely interpretations of scenes and events.
- Object Recognition Because of variable views, no single retinal image of an object can be considered equivalent to the representation of that object stored in memory. Rather, the visual system must exhibit invariance, the ability to represent an object in the same way despite changes in its retinal image. One approach to explaining invariance proposes that a single representation is activated whenever an object is seen, but this approach leads to all objects in the same category being represented in the same way. Another approach proposes that specific views of each object are represented, but this raises the issue of whether there would be enough brain to hold all the representations needed. Shape representation involves hierarchical processes carried out in V1, V4, and the inferotemporal cortex (where representations based on structural descriptions are created). According to the modular coding view, specific parts of the occipital and inferotemporal cortex along the ventral visual pathway are specialized for representing objects of specific categories. The distributed coding view holds that, regardless of category, objects are represented by the pattern of activity in multiple regions of the ventral pathway.
- Top-Down Information Knowledge and expectations can influence perceptual organization and object recognition. Knowledge about the scene within which an object appears can affect the speed with which it's recognized, which suggests that there is some mechanism for rapidly assessing the gist of a scene, perhaps based on its general layout. Researchers propose that the brain is constantly making unconscious inferences about the current scene, perhaps using the Bayesian approach to assign probabilities to various types of scenes that might have produced the current retinal image.
- Applications: Automatic Face Recognition Automatic face recognition systems are based on one of three different types of approaches to matching a digital image of a face to an image in a database of known faces: feature based, holistic, and hybrid. The feature-based approach matches the spatial relationships among anatomical features to instances stored in the face database. The holistic approach, which can account for nonspatial aspects of facial appearance, is based on matching the whole image of a face to the images in the database, with more sophisticated versions of this approach making use of eigenfaces. The hybrid approach combines the other two approaches and may also make use of eigenfeatures.

KEY TERMS

Bayesian approach (p. 145)
border ownership (p. 122)
edge completion (p. 132)
edge extraction (p. 123)
distributed coding (p. 142)
figure (p. 122)
grandmother cell (p. 141)
ground (p. 122)
heuristics (p. 134)
illusory contours (p. 132)
image clutter (p. 118)
modular coding (p. 142)
object variety (p. 119)
perceptual grouping (p. 122)
perceptual inference (p. 135)
perceptual interpolation (p. 122)
prosopagnosia (p. 143)
surface completion (p. 132)
topographic agnosia (p. 144)
uniform connectedness (p. 124)
variable views (p. 120)
visual agnosia (p. 143)

EXPAND YOUR UNDERSTANDING

4.1 You and a friend plan to meet at a concert by looking for each other outside the north entrance to the concert hall. When you get there, you see hundreds of people milling around. As you s2earch for your friend, which of the following factors poses the greatest challenge to perceptual organization—object variety, image clutter, or variable views? Explain why.

4.2 Perceptual grouping of these elements into successive pairs is easiest with one of the rows of shapes below, more difficult with another row, and most difficult with the remaining row. Identify which row is which, and explain why.

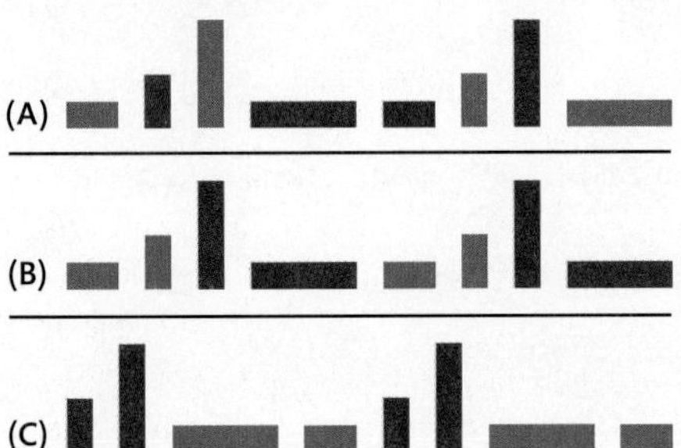

4.3 Describe a scene that might lead a person's visual system to make an incorrect perceptual inference based on incorrect perceptual interpolation (either edge completion or surface completion or both). (Draw a sketch of the scene if necessary to support your description.)

4.4 What's odd about the view of the full moon in the night sky on the left, in terms of the rules of thumb that guide perceptual organization? How is border ownership assigned differently in these two images, and how do meaningfulness and top-down processing account for the difference?

4.5 Suppose the flattened raindrop in Figure 4.30 filled a large part of your visual field. Describe in general terms how your visual system might represent its shape via a hierarchical process involving neurons in V1, V4, and the inferotemporal cortex.

4.6 People are much better at recognizing differences between upright faces than between inverted faces, which isn't the case for other types of objects. Explain how this supports the notion of a brain module that responds specifically to faces.

4.7 Typically, the database of known faces used by an automatic face recognition system includes just one image of each person's face. For each approach discussed in this chapter—feature based, holistic, and hybrid—briefly discuss whether having in the database additional images of each face would probably improve, degrade, or have no effect on the accuracy of the system.

READ MORE ABOUT IT

Connor, C. E., Pasupathy, A., Brincat, S., & Yamane, Y. (2009). Neural transformation of object information by ventral pathway visual cortex. In M. Gazzaniga (Ed.), *The cognitive neurosciences* (4th ed., pp. 455–466). Cambridge, MA: MIT Press.

A brief, accessible account of how neurons in the primate brain encode information about object shape.

Dickinson, S. J., Leonardis, A., Schiele, B., & Tarr, M. J. (2009). *Object categorization: Computer and human vision perspectives.* Cambridge, UK: Cambridge University Press.

A collection of tutorial chapters that survey the many different current approaches to understanding how the brain perceives and categorizes objects.

Palmeri, T. J., & Gauthier, I. (2004). Visual object understanding. *Nature Reviews Neuroscience, 5,* 291–303.

A review of two major research themes: object identification (how a decision is made about an object's unique identity) and object categorization (how a decision is made about an object's kind or category).

von der Heydt, R. (2004). Image parsing mechanisms of the visual cortex. In L. M. Chalupa & J. S. Werner (Eds.), *The visual neurosciences* (Vol. 2, pp. 1139–1150). Cambridge, MA: MIT Press.

A brief review of the neural basis of perceptual organization.

Mark Rothko, *Untitled*, c. 1953. [Oil on canvas, 83½ × 68 inches. Art Resource, NY. © 1998 Kate Rothko Prizel & Christopher Rothko/Artists Rights Society (ARS), New York.]

5

PERCEIVING COLOR

Colorless

P., a 68-year-old retired office worker, had been rushed to the hospital after she suffered a stroke that affected part of the occipital lobe in both hemispheres. She was discharged following a few days in the hospital but continued to experience some lingering effects from the stroke: she had difficulty recognizing faces, including the face of her husband of 35 years (although she could easily recognize his voice), and the world appeared to be without color, as if she were watching a black and white movie. She said that the clothes in her closet all looked dirty, and she had difficulty deciding what she wanted to wear. Even more disturbing, all of her food looked gray, which made it difficult for her to recognize certain foods. Some she could identify by their size and shape—peas and bananas, for example—but an omelet might look like a steak, which meant she wasn't always prepared for what something would taste like when she put it in her mouth.

When a neurologist tested her object-recognition abilities by showing her some common objects (e.g., a telephone, a coffee mug, and a pencil) and asking her to name them, P. made a few errors but for the most part seemed unimpaired. However, when the neurologist showed her a series of brightly colored objects, they all looked like pale shades of gray. And when she was given red, green, blue, and yellow cards of various brightnesses (e.g., bright, medium, and dark red) and asked to sort them into four same-color piles, she became frustrated and felt as if she was just guessing.

P.'s loss of color vision was not debilitating; she found ways to identify objects without depending on color—for example, she soon began to use her sense of smell to identify foods. But she found the world a less vivid sensory experience, and this change was depressing. She continued to go to art museums, a favorite activity before her stroke, but she focused on the sculptures because she found it too painful to view her beloved Impressionist paintings, which now looked drab and unappealing.

Color adds richness and beauty to the visual world, but that hardly explains why visual systems have evolved to perceive color. Without denying the purely aesthetic value of color, it's important to understand that color vision also serves many important practical purposes, both "natural" (e.g., letting us find red berries among green leaves or detect tawny-colored lions hiding in yellow grass) and "artificial" (e.g., enabling the use of traffic lights and the innumerable other technologies in which color perception plays a crucial role). Nevertheless, most of us take the practical aspects of color perception for granted, focusing instead on the subjective experience of color. From that point of view, vision without color is like eating without being able to taste flavors: you can certainly take in calories, but it's not much fun!

Chapter Outline

color vision The ability to see differences between lights of different wavelengths.

Color vision is the ability to see differences between lights of different wavelengths. In this chapter, we begin our exploration of color vision by considering the wavelength composition of light and by looking at how the reflection of light from different surfaces can change that composition before it enters our eyes, thus providing information about the material properties of that surface. We then consider hue, saturation, and brightness (the qualities that describe how we perceive color) and follow that with a discussion of how colors mix, in which you'll see that colored lights mix quite differently from colored substances like paints. This will lead us into the core of the chapter: an investigation of the two physiological mechanisms that create our experience of color—trichromacy and opponency.

The final sections of the chapter address color constancy and lightness constancy—our ability to see things as having the same color and brightness under different lighting conditions—and color vision deficiencies (sometimes called "color blindness"), in which people experience partial or total loss of the ability to see color.

Isaac Newton (1643–1727). [SSPL/Science Museum/Art Resource, NY]

Throughout the chapter, it will be important to keep in mind an idea first mentioned by Isaac Newton in his seminal treatise on light, *Opticks* (1704/1952), where he made the following observation about the subjective experience of color and its relation to the physical properties of light:

> The Rays to speak properly are not coloured. In them there is nothing else than a certain Power and Disposition to stir up a Sensation of this or that Colour. . . . So Colours in the Object are nothing but a Disposition to reflect this or that sort of Rays more copiously than the rest. (p. 125)

In other words, objects don't "have" color any more than substances "have" odor (for a lively debate about this, see Byrne & Hilbert, 2003). Our perception of odors comes from the interaction between receptors in the nose and volatile molecules thrown off by substances—a specific experienced odor is evoked by specific types of molecules. Similarly, our perception of color comes from the interaction between receptors in the eyes and the wavelengths of light reflected from the surfaces of objects—a specific experienced color is evoked by specific wavelengths present in the light.

Light and Color

visible spectrum The portion of the electromagnetic spectrum in the range of about 400 to about 700 nm; within this range, people with normal vision perceive differences in wavelength as differences in color.

In Chapter 2, you learned that light is electromagnetic radiation with wavelengths in the range of about 400 to about 700 nm. This portion of the electromagnetic spectrum is called the **visible spectrum.** Within this range, people with normal vision perceive differences in wavelength as differences in color.

In discussing color vision, we'll be concerned mainly with how we perceive light that is reflected from a surface into our eyes (and only occasionally with light that is transmitted directly from a source into our eyes, as when you look at a lightbulb or a campfire). It will often be convenient to refer to light of a particular color or to material things of a particular color, but you should always keep in mind—as Newton pointed out—that color isn't *in* light or material things. Rather, color is a perceptual experience evoked by the wavelengths of light reaching our eyes.

Spectral Power Distribution

spectral power distribution (SPD) The intensity (power) of a light at each wavelength in the visible spectrum.

heterochromatic light Light that consists of more than one wavelength.

monochromatic light Light that consists of only one wavelength.

For any light, we can construct a graph that depicts the light's **spectral power distribution (SPD)**—the intensity (power) of the light at each wavelength in the visible spectrum (see Figure 5.1). The SPD is a crucial determinant of the perceived color of the light.

Most light sources emit light that consists of a wide range of different wavelengths. Such light is called **heterochromatic light** (*hetero,* meaning "different"; *chromatic,* meaning "color"). Light that consists of only a single wavelength is called **monochromatic light** (*mono,* meaning "single"). The SPD of a monochromatic light is a vertical spike, as illustrated in Figure 5.1. Figure 5.1 compares the SPD of sunlight to that of light from two familiar artificial light sources, an incandescent bulb and a fluorescent bulb. All three of these light sources emit

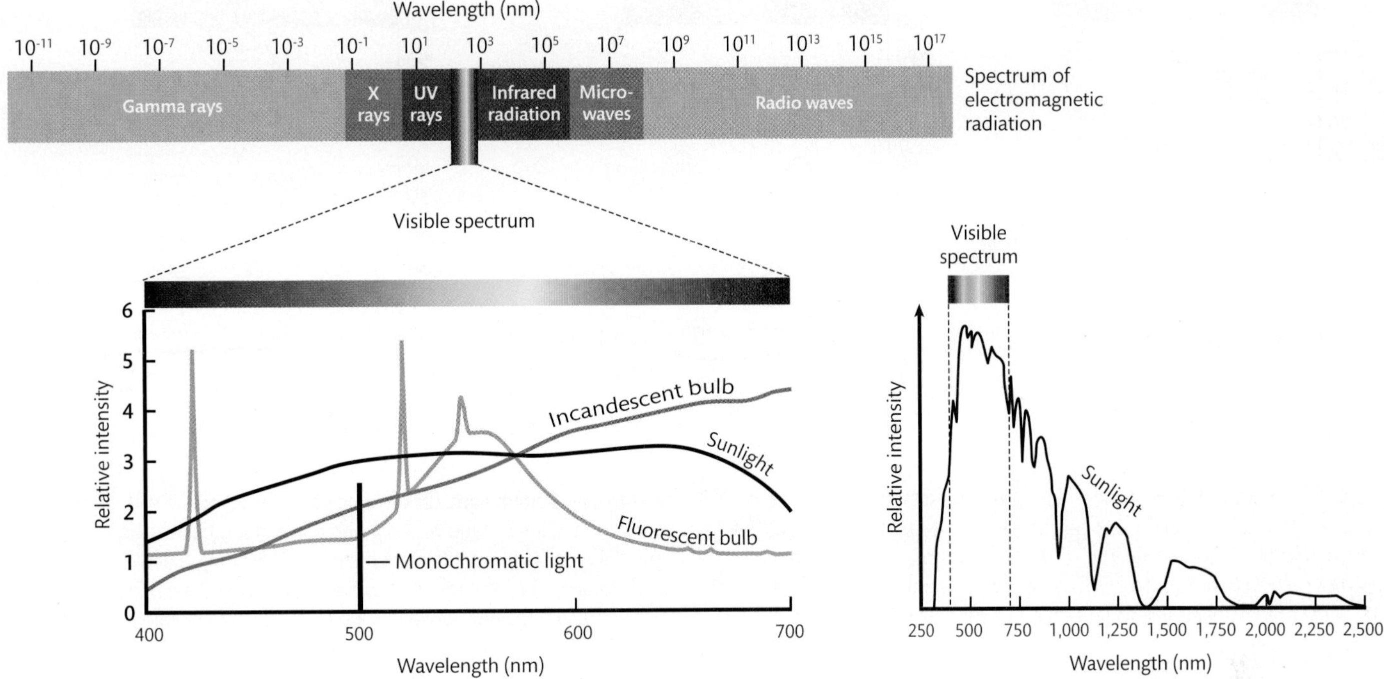

Figure 5.1 Spectral Power Distribution Electromagnetic radiation varies enormously in wavelength across the spectrum (top). The visible part of the spectrum ranges in wavelength from about 400 to about 700 nm. A graph of the spectral power distribution of a light source (like the graphs for three light sources at the bottom left of this figure) shows the relative amount (intensity, or power) of each wavelength in the light. For example, light from an incandescent bulb contains proportionately more long-wavelength (red) light than sunlight does. A fluorescent bulb contains narrow bands of high-intensity wavelengths within the blue and green regions of the spectrum. The vertical spike depicts the spectral power distribution of a monochromatic light with a wavelength of 500 nm. The graph at right shows that sunlight contains wavelengths that extend well above and below the range of the visible spectrum but that the most intense wavelengths are in this range. Most other light sources also contain wavelengths outside the visible spectrum—for example, much of the radiation from a standard lightbulb falls in the infrared range, which we can't see but instead perceive as heat.

what could be called *white light*—that is, heterochromatic light that (1) contains wavelengths from across the entire visible spectrum and (2) has no really dominant wavelengths. The SPD of an idealized white light would be a horizontal line: a light in which all wavelengths across the visible spectrum have exactly equal power. We perceive white light as more or less colorless, which is why white light is also called **achromatic light** (*a*-, meaning "without"). The SPD of sunlight is quite close to that of an idealized white light. In contrast, the SPD of light from an incandescent bulb is more intense toward the yellow and red end of the spectrum, while the SPD of light from a fluorescent bulb has "spikes" at short and medium wavelengths that make fluorescent light somewhat more bluish than sunlight. You can easily see these differences by standing outside at night and looking at the windows of rooms illuminated by incandescent bulbs, which look distinctly yellowish, and by fluorescent bulbs, which look distinctly bluish.

Demonstration 5.1 Spectral Power Distribution See the SPDs of different colored lights, and change the shape of SPDs to see how that affects the color of the light.

achromatic light (or *white light*) Light containing wavelengths from across the visible spectrum, with no really dominant wavelengths; perceived as more or less colorless (i.e., a shade of gray).

Spectral Reflectance

The SPDs shown in Figure 5.1 describe the wavelengths and intensities of the light emitted by light sources. In everyday life, however, we rarely look at light sources such as the sun and lightbulbs. Instead, we typically look at the things around us that reflect the light from whichever light sources are present. This means that the perceived color of things depends on the SPD of the light source and on how things reflect light. The way things reflect light depends on the molecular structure of the surface, which determines its **spectral reflectance,** the proportion of light at each wavelength that the surface reflects rather than absorbs (see Figure 5.2).

spectral reflectance The proportion of light that a surface reflects at each wavelength.

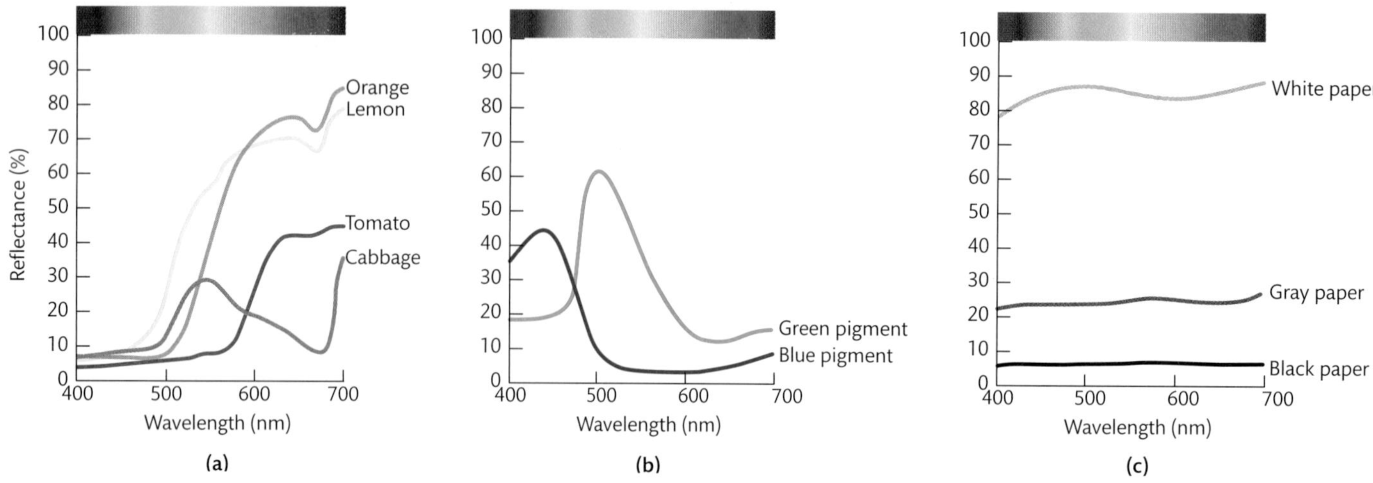

Figure 5.2 Spectral Reflectance A graph of the spectral reflectance of a surface shows the percentage of light at each wavelength that the surface reflects rather than absorbs. (a) The surfaces of lemons, oranges, and tomatoes reflect proportionately more long-wavelength light than does the surface of a cabbage, which reflects proportionately more medium-wavelength light. (b) Contrasts in reflectance are even more striking in the case of blue versus green pigments. (c) Black, gray, and white paper have similarly flat reflectance curves—indicating that they reflect about the same percentage of all wavelengths—but white paper reflects much more light overall, while black paper reflects very little light.

Figure 5.2a shows that something we perceive as green, like a cabbage, reflects a greater percentage of the light in the "green" portion of the spectrum, in the range of 500–550 nm, and a lower percentage of most other wavelengths. Similarly, something we perceive as red, like a tomato, reflects more light with longer wavelengths and less light from the rest of the spectrum. Figure 5.2b shows that some surfaces—for example, white, gray, and black paper—have reflectance curves that are approximately horizontal lines, indicating that they reflect about the same percentage of all wavelengths. However, they differ in the overall *amount* of light they reflect, as indicated by whether their reflectance curve is high or low in the graph: black paper absorbs more than 90% of the incident light and reflects less than 10%, while white paper reflects 80% or more at almost all wavelengths.

Check Your Understanding

5.1 What is the meaning of the term *visible spectrum*?

5.2 What is the difference between spectral power distribution and spectral reflectance?

5.3 True or false? In a graph like Figure 5.2c, if the gray paper were a darker gray, its reflectance curve would move up in the graph.

Dimensions of Color: Hue, Saturation, and Brightness

In the previous section, we discussed the physical properties of light and of surfaces, which determine the wavelengths of the light that enters our eyes. In this section, we consider how those physical properties of light evoke subjective experiences of color.

hue The quality usually referred to as "color"—that is, blue, green, yellow, red, and so on; the perceptual characteristic most closely associated with the wavelength of light.

The perceptual experience of color can be described in terms of three independent dimensions—hue, saturation, and brightness. **Hue** corresponds to the way we ordinarily use the word "color"—that is, to say whether something looks blue, green, yellow, red, or some other color, without specifying whether the color looks vivid or washed out or whether it looks bright or dim. In Figure 5.1, for example, it is the hue that varies from blue to red as you scan from left to right across the visible spectrum. Thus, hue is the characteristic most closely associated with the wavelength of light.

saturation The vividness (or purity or richness) of a hue.

Saturation refers to the *vividness, purity,* or *richness* of a hue. A red velvet robe, for example, is typically a much more vivid red than the pastel pink of a cherry blossom, although the robe and the blossom may have the same hue. Monochromatic hues like those

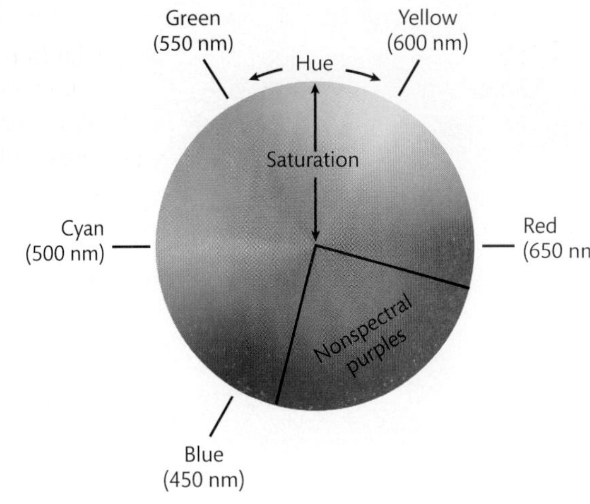

Figure 5.3 Color Circle A color circle represents two of the three dimensions of color perception: hue (around the circumference) and saturation (along any radius). The red and blue ends of the visible spectrum are joined across the range of hues labeled "Nonspectral purples"—purplish colors that are mixtures of red and violet, which are, respectively, the longest- and shortest-wavelength monochromatic lights we can see. These purplish hues are called "nonspectral" (i.e., heterochromatic) because they are created by mixtures of wavelengths, as opposed to the "spectral" (i.e., monochromatic) hues in the visible spectrum.

in the color bars used to adjust your TV picture are shown maximally saturated—that is, as vivid as possible. You can decrease the saturation of monochromatic light by adding white light to it; if enough white light is added, the light will appear to be nearly pure white with just the faintest hint of a hue, but the hue itself will not have changed.

Brightness (or intensity), as we've previously noted, refers to the amount of light; brightness is what you change when you substitute a 100-watt bulb for a 60-watt bulb.

color circle A 2-D depiction in which hue varies around the circumference and saturation varies along any radius.

color solid A 3-D depiction in which hue varies around the circumference, saturation varies along any radius, and brightness varies vertically.

Color Circle and Color Solid

We can represent the three dimensions of hue, saturation, and brightness geometrically, in a way that captures our perception of the similarities among colors. A 2-D color circle can depict the two dimensions of hue and saturation, but to include the third dimension, brightness, we need a 3-D color solid.

In a **color circle** (see Figure 5.3), hue varies around the circumference and saturation varies along any radius; the most saturated hues are at the circumference and saturation decreases as you move toward the center. The sequence of hues around the circumference matches the sequence in the visible spectrum (see Figure 5.1), but the red and blue ends of the spectrum meet at the part of the circumference labeled "Nonspectral purples" in Figure 5.3. These purple lights are mixtures of the shortest-wavelength violet and the longest-wavelength red—they're called "nonspectral" because they don't exist anywhere on the visible spectrum as single wavelengths, but can only be created as mixtures. White is also a nonspectral color: it can only be created by mixing together two or more wavelengths.

A **color solid** adds the vertical dimension to represent brightness, with brightness increasing as you move up. Figure 5.4 shows a color solid with the top tilted back. The central axis represents shades of gray light, since all the hues are equally represented at the center of the circle. Thus, the colors along this achromatic axis range from black at the bottom point to the brightest white at the top point. A color circle like the one at the cut can be produced at any given level of brightness by cutting horizontally through the color solid. Note that the radius of the color solid shrinks as you move up or down from the middle—that is, as you increase or decrease brightness. Since the radius represents saturation, a shrinking radius implies that saturation varies over a smaller and smaller range as brightness increases or decreases from its midlevel. This corresponds to our perception that as colors get very dim or very bright, they become less vivid.

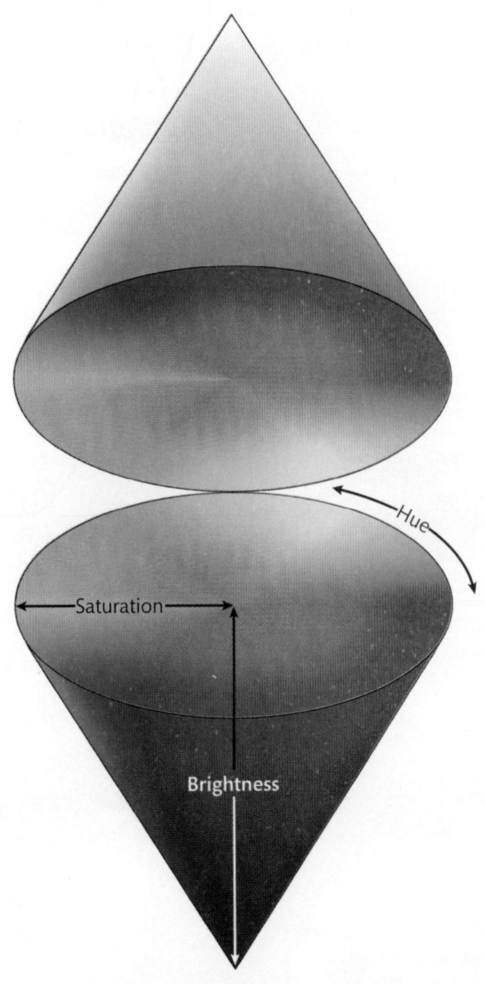

Figure 5.4 Color Solid A color solid adds the third dimension of brightness, or intensity, to the two dimensions of a color circle. Brightness varies along the central axis: the color circle at the cut through the middle of the solid is 50% gray at the center, halfway between black and the brightest white.

Color Mixtures

Children playing with crayons soon learn that colors can be combined to make other colors. For example, a child who makes a scribble with a yellow crayon and then scribbles over it with a blue crayon sees that the result looks green. Painters know how to mix combinations of two or more of the paints on their palette to make a nearly infinite variety of colors. Theatrical lighting directors combine colored spotlights to create light that will evoke particular moods during a play. Inkjet printers mix just four different inks (three colors plus black) to create all the colors needed to print color photographs. Children with crayons, painters, and inkjet printers mix substances, whereas lighting directors mix light. The results of these two types of color mixing are generally quite different.

Subtractive Color Mixtures: Mixing Substances

As we have seen, the perceived color of a substance depends on its reflectance—the percentage of light it reflects at each wavelength, with the rest being absorbed. When two or more different-colored substances are mixed, as when a painter mixes paints, the reflectance curve of the mixture can be computed by multiplying the reflectances of all the substances in the mixture at each wavelength and plotting the results on a graph. (For the purposes of this discussion, we'll assume that the illuminant is white light—i.e., light containing approximately equal amounts of all wavelengths across the visible spectrum.) To see how this works, consider a mixture of blue paint and yellow paint. In Figure 5.5a, the illustration and the reflectance curve show that blue paint looks blue because it reflects mainly the shorter wavelengths (those toward the blue end of the visible spectrum), as well as some medium (green) wavelengths, and absorbs all other wavelengths (yellow, orange, and red). Figure 5.5b shows that yellow paint looks yellow

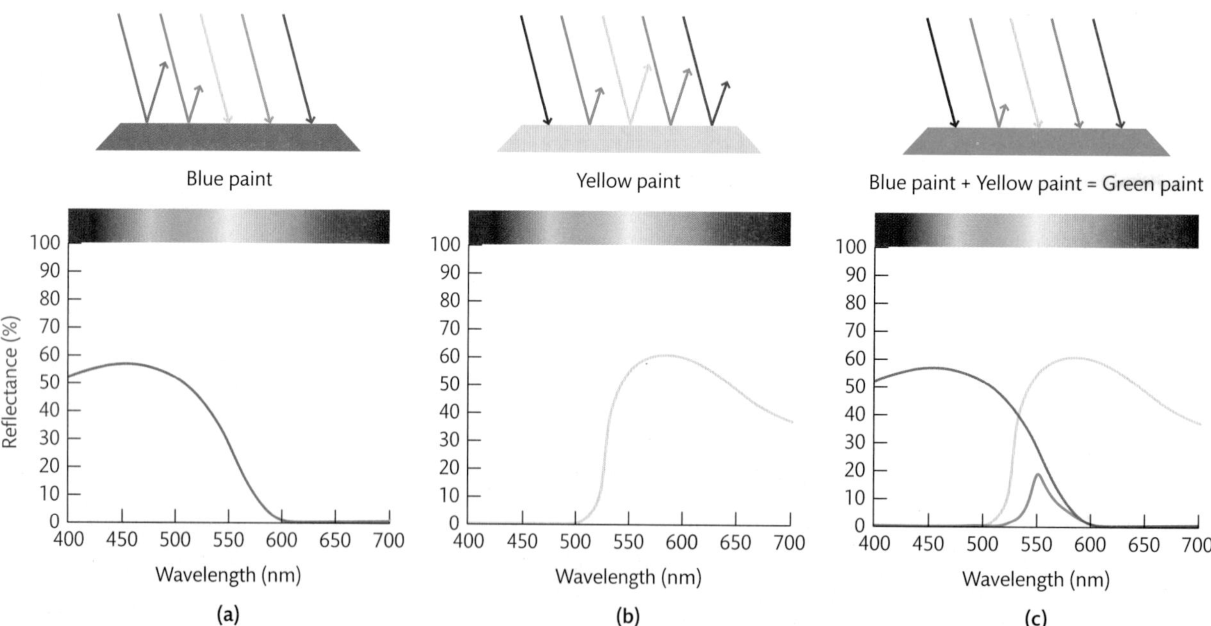

Figure 5.5 Mixing Paints: An Example of a Subtractive Color Mixture (a) Blue paint absorbs (or subtracts) all the longer wavelengths (yellow, orange, and red light). (b) Yellow paint subtracts all the shorter wavelengths (blue light). (c) A mixture of blue paint and yellow paint subtracts all but the middle wavelengths (green light). The reflectance curve of a mixture of different-colored substances—in this case, the green paint—is constructed by multiplying the reflectances of each substance in the mixture at each wavelength. For example, the peak reflectance of the green paint, at 550 nm, is about 15% because the reflectances of blue paint and yellow paint at that wavelength are about 28% and 55%, respectively ($.28 \times .55 \approx .15$). Given that most substances (such as paints) have reflectance curves that fall well below 100%, subtractive mixtures typically reflect much less light than any of the constituent substances.

because it predominantly reflects wavelengths from the yellow part of the spectrum, as well as some green, orange, and red wavelengths. In Figure 5.5c, we see that the mixture looks green because both the blue paint and the yellow paint reflect light from the green part of the spectrum, while the blue paint in the mixture subtracts (absorbs) all the yellow, orange, and red light, and the yellow paint in the mixture subtracts all the blue light. That's why a mixture of substances is called a **subtractive color mixture:** because each substance in the mixture subtracts certain wavelengths.

Figure 5.6 Mixing Lights: An Example of an Additive Color Mixture The white screen reflects all wavelengths equally, so the perceived color of any mixture of these monochromatic blue, green, and red lights depends only on the combination of wavelengths, not on the reflectance of the screen. Our perception of the reflected light results from adding (combining) the wavelengths in the projected lights, not from subtracting wavelengths as in a subtractive color mixture.

Additive Color Mixtures: Mixing Lights

Now let's consider how mixing lights differs from mixing substances like paints. Suppose a lighting director is using three equally bright theatrical spotlights, each of which emits light within a narrow range of wavelengths—say, red light, green light, and blue light. Figure 5.6 shows what happens when the three lights are projected on a white screen so they partially overlap. The screen equally reflects all the wavelengths that hit it, because the reflectance of a white surface is much the same at every wavelength. Thus, the proportions of wavelengths in the reflected light are the same as the proportions in the projected lights, and where the spotlights overlap, the reflected light contains the sum of the wavelengths in the overlapping region. This type of color mixture is called an **additive color mixture** because it results from adding wavelengths rather than subtracting them. Later in this chapter, in the section "Trichromatic Color Representation," we'll see why these additive color mixtures are perceived the way they are—for example, why a combination of red and green lights is perceived as yellow, while a combination of red, green, and blue lights is perceived as a shade of gray.

Figure 5.7 shows how you can use a color circle to predict the perceived color of an additive mixture of any two monochromatic lights. If you draw a line between the two hues in the mixture, the perceived color will fall somewhere on the line; exactly where will depend on the relative intensities of the two lights. For example, equal intensities of each hue will result in a perceived color at the line's midpoint, while a greater intensity of one hue will shift the perceived color toward that hue. Thus, the spectral power

subtractive color mixture A mixture of different-colored substances; called "subtractive" because the light reflected from the mixture has certain wavelengths subtracted (absorbed) by each substance in the mixture.

additive color mixture A mixture of different-colored lights; called "additive" because the perceived color of the mixture is the result of adding together all the wavelengths in all the lights in the mixture.

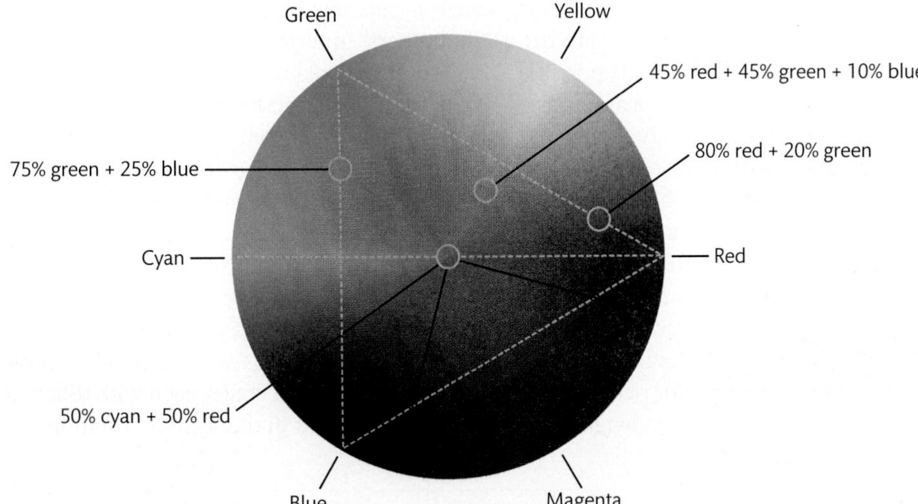

Figure 5.7 Predicting the Color of Additive Color Mixtures To predict the color of a mixture of two monochromatic lights, draw a straight line connecting any two hues on the color circle. The perceived color of the mixture will fall somewhere on that line, depending on the intensity of the two lights (e.g., the 75% green + 25% blue and 80% red + 20% green mixtures indicated in the figure). If the two lights have equal intensity, the perceived color of the mixture will be at the midpoint of the line, and if, in addition, two hues are opposite each other (i.e., if they are complementary colors, 180° apart), the perceived color will be at the center of the color circle (like the red + cyan mixture in the figure) and will therefore be a shade of gray. To predict the color of a mixture of three monochromatic lights, connect them to form a triangle, like the triangle formed by red, green, and blue. The color of the mixture will fall somewhere within the triangle, depending on the relative intensities of the three lights—for example, the 45% red + 45% green + 10% blue mixture. Any such set of three monochromatic lights makes a set of primary colors.

distributions—wavelengths and intensities—of lights determine the perceived color of additive color mixtures.

Figure 5.7 shows the results for three different additive mixtures of pairs of lights. Note that the mixtures shown in the figure all involve fully saturated hues: the lines connecting the colors all begin and end at the circumference of the color circle, representing 100% saturation. It is clear that the hue resulting from any such mixture will be less than fully saturated, because it will fall inside the color circle, nearer to the fully unsaturated center.

Demonstration 5.2 Additive Color Mixtures and Primary Colors Specify the color and intensity of pairs of lights to see the color of their mixture; select a set of three primary colors and see the colors you can produce by mixing those primaries.

What about mixtures of *three* monochromatic lights? The color resulting from such a mixture will fall somewhere within the triangle formed by connecting the three hues—exactly where depending on the relative intensities of the lights—and will again be less than fully saturated. Figure 5.7 shows such a mixture of three lights falling within a triangle connecting red, green, and blue.

Complementary Colors

complementary colors Pairs of colors that, when combined in equal proportion, are perceived as a shade of gray.

In Figure 5.7, note the line connecting red and cyan. Since these two hues are exactly opposite each other on the circumference of the color circle, the connecting line runs through the center of the circle. Thus, a 50–50 combination of this pair (and of any other pair of colors 180° apart, such as yellow and blue) would be perceived as some shade of gray, depending on the intensity of the lights—because the additive result would be at the center of the circle (recall from our discussion of the color solid that the central, achromatic axis of the solid represents all shades of gray, from white to black). Pairs of colors that combine in equal proportion to yield a shade of gray are termed **complementary colors.**

Primary Colors

primary colors Any three colors that can be combined in different proportions to produce a range of other colors.

Primary colors are any three colors that can be combined in different proportions to produce a range of other colors. As we noted above, the triangle formed by connecting red, green, and blue in Figure 5.7 defines a range of other colors that can be created by combining these colors in different proportions. Thus, red, green, and blue constitute a set of primary colors. In fact, any three hues in the color circle can be connected in this way to form a triangle enclosing other colors, which means that there is no unique set of primaries. Nevertheless, some sets are better than others, in terms of producing as many of the colors in the color circle as possible. The triangle formed by red, green, and blue, for example, has as large an area as a triangle in the color circle can have, because red, green, and blue are spaced equally around the circle; it therefore encompasses as large a range of other colors within the circle as possible. However, these three primaries are incapable of producing colors (such as a highly saturated cyan) that are outside the triangle. Red, green, and blue are the primaries conventionally used to produce additive color mixtures in color TVs and computer monitors. For technologies that use subtractive color mixtures (e.g., for color printing, as in inkjet printers), magenta, cyan, and yellow—which form as large a triangle as red, green, and blue—are conventionally used as primaries.

Why are primaries defined as sets of three colors and not, say, two or four? The simple answer is that human color perception is based on three types of cones, each with different sensitivities to different wavelengths of light, as discussed next in the section "Trichromatic Color Representation."

Check Your Understanding

5.4 What are the three perceptual dimensions of color and how are they depicted in a color solid? Which of these dimensions is lacking in a color circle?

5.5 Why are subtractive color mixtures called "subtractive" and additive color mixtures called "additive"?

5.6 Why do red, green, and blue make a better set of primary colors than cyan, green, and blue?

Color and the Visual System

To this point, we've explored some physical characteristics of light and of materials that reflect light and indicated how those characteristics relate to our perception of color. In particular, we've seen that the most important characteristics relevant to color vision are the spectral power distribution of a light and the reflectance of the material reflecting that light.

In this section, we'll discuss how the light entering the eyes evokes patterns of activity in the visual system to produce the perception of color. Color perception is a two-stage process. In the first stage, referred to as *trichromatic color representation,* light evokes different responses from the three different types of cone photoreceptors in the retina. In the second stage, known as *opponent color representation,* the responses from the cones are combined and processed by a subset of retinal ganglion cells and by color-selective neurons in the brain. The observations that led to the formulation of these two types of color representation were first made during studies of color vision in the nineteenth century. For a time, they were seen as competing accounts of color vision, but studies in the mid-twentieth century showed that both are essential parts of the color vision system.

Thomas Young (1773–1829). [J. Bedmar/Iberfoto/The Image Works]

Trichromatic Color Representation

A trichromatic account of color vision was first proposed in 1802 by the English physician and scientist Thomas Young, who wrote: "As it is almost impossible to conceive each sensitive point of the retina to contain an infinite number of particles [cones], each capable of vibrating in perfect unison with every possible undulation [wavelength], it becomes necessary to suppose the number limited." He then suggested that the number of different "particles" was three, based on the observation that any visible color can be matched by the proper mixture of three primary colors. Some 50 years later, Young's ideas were discussed and popularized by the great German scientist Hermann von Helmholtz. Thus, this is often called the *Young–Helmholtz trichromatic theory.*

Color Matching with Mixtures of Three Primary Colors

How do we know that a mixture of three primary colors can match any other color? First, we need to understand that this is a psychophysical question, not a physical one. The question is whether the right mixture of three monochromatic primary colors is perceived as identical in color to some other monochromatic light, not whether the mixture and the other light are physically identical. To show the perceptual equivalence of these lights, vision scientists conduct what are known as *metameric color-matching experiments* (Stiles & Burch, 1959). **Metamers** are any two stimuli that are physically different but are perceived as identical.

metamers Any two stimuli that are physically different but are perceived as identical.

In a metameric color-matching experiment, an observer is shown two patches of light, called the *test patch* and the *comparison patch,* side by side on a perfectly white screen that reflects all wavelengths equally (see Figure 5.8). The test patch consists of a single wavelength with a fixed intensity—say, 590 nm. The comparison patch consists of an additive mixture of three monochromatic lights, with wavelengths of, say, 645, 526, and 444 nm, which would be perceived as the colors red, green, and blue, respectively, and which function as the three primary colors in the experiment. The observer can turn three dials to adjust the intensities of the three lights in the comparison patch separately. The observer's task is to adjust the intensities so that the additive color mixture in the comparison patch appears to have the same color as the test patch. If the observer can do this, then the two patches constitute a metameric color match—that is, despite their physical difference, the two patches are perceptually identical.

Hermann von Helmholtz (1821–1894). [The Library of Congress]

In Figure 5.8, the observer has achieved a metameric color match with the test patch by setting the intensities of red, green, and blue at 228, 189, and 79, respectively. In an actual experiment, the observer wouldn't be working with numerical settings but would just turn the dials until she perceived a match. Figure 5.8 also shows two hypothetical

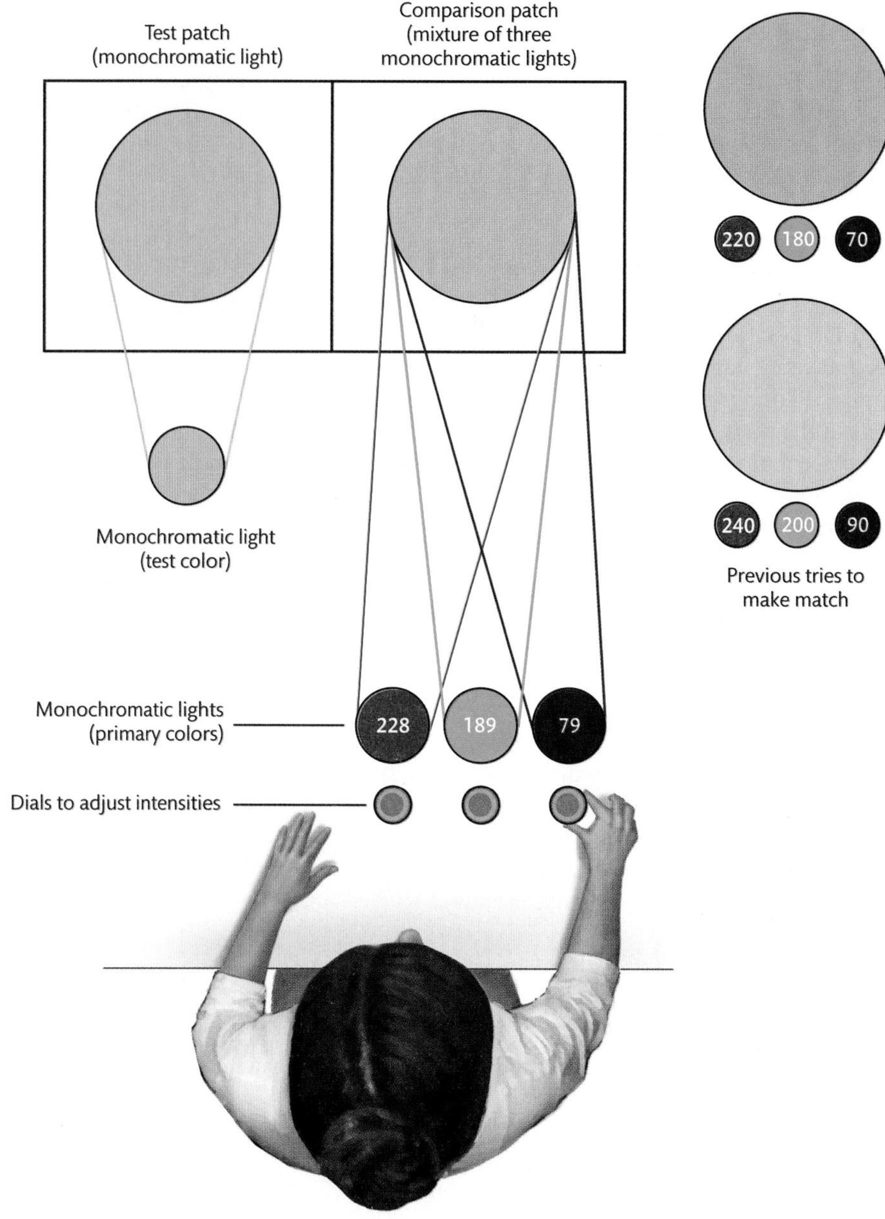

Figure 5.8 Metameric Color-Matching Experiment The participant must adjust the intensities of the three monochromatic lights so their additive mixture (the comparison patch) matches the test patch. (The number on each monochromatic light represents the intensity set by the participant.)

previous attempts to achieve a match, one appearing a little too dark (corresponding to settings of 220, 180, and 70) and the other a little too light (corresponding to settings of 240, 200, and 90). Repeated color-matching experiments like this one have shown that people with normal color vision are, in fact, able to mix three primaries in this way to achieve metameric color matches with monochromatic light from across the visible spectrum. But does this imply the need for three types of cones—as Young proposed—or could a person with only one or two types of cones also match colors successfully? To answer these questions, we need to consider how cones work.

Cones and Colors

You already know from Chapter 2 that there are three types of cones, that each type contains a different photopigment, and that each photopigment has a particular spectral sensitivity. You also know that the three types of cones are referred to as *L-cones, M-cones,* and *S-cones,* according to whether their peak sensitivity is to a long, medium, or short wavelength, respectively. Figure 5.9 shows the **spectral sensitivity function** of the photopigment in each type of cone—that is, the probability that a photon of light with any given wavelength will be absorbed by that cone's photopigment (Stockman et al., 1993). You can see from the figure that the photopigment in each type of cone is most responsive to a particular range of wavelengths, but all three respond to a wide range of wavelengths, and their spectral sensitivity functions overlap considerably.

spectral sensitivity function The probability that a cone's photopigment will absorb a photon of light of any given wavelength.

Principle of Univariance

Each type of cone varies in its sensitivity to different wavelengths of light, but it's impossible to work backward from the response of a single cone to determine the wavelength of the light that caused the response. The reason for this is expressed by the **principle of univariance** as it applies to cones: the absorption of a photon of light causes a fixed response by a cone, regardless of the photon's wavelength—in other words, the strength of the response generated by a cone when it transduces light depends only on the *amount* of light transduced, not on the *wavelength* of the light (Baylor et al., 1987; Rushton, 1972). (We previously encountered an analogous idea in Chapter 3 while discussing how neurons in area V1 represent orientation—see Figure 3.9 and the accompanying text.) The spectral sensitivity functions show that cones differ in the likelihood that they will absorb photons of light of a particular wavelength, but once a photon is absorbed, its effect is the same for all wavelengths. For example, an M-cone's response to a dim 543-nm light and to a bright 450-nm light could be identical, with the right choice of intensities. The principle of univariance means that color vision depends crucially on the relative responses of multiple cone types. Let's take a look at why that's the case.

principle of univariance With regard to cones, the principle that absorption of a photon of light results in the same response regardless of the wavelength of the light.

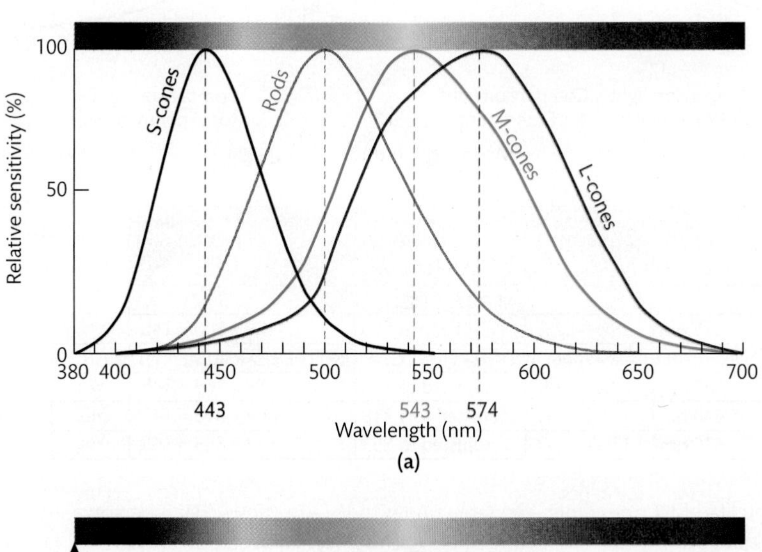

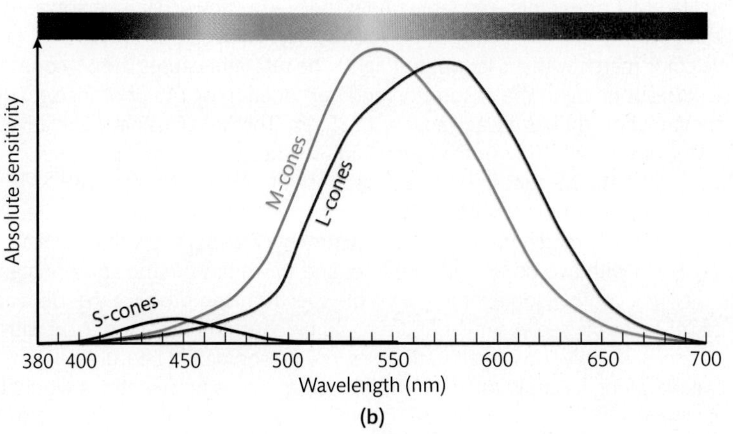

Figure 5.9 Spectral Sensitivity of Photopigments
(a) *Relative sensitivity.* In this graph, the scale of the vertical axis is normalized, so the peak of each curve is at the same height (100%). The photopigment in S-cones is most sensitive to light with a wavelength of 443 nm and almost completely insensitive to wavelengths greater than about 550 nm. The photopigments in M-cones and L-cones both have some sensitivity across nearly the entire spectrum of visible light, but the sensitivity of M-cones is higher toward the middle wavelengths (peaking at 543 nm), while that of L-cones is higher toward the longer wavelengths (peaking at 574 nm). The photopigment in rods is most sensitive to light with a wavelength of 500 nm. (b) *Absolute sensitivity.* When the scale of the vertical axis isn't normalized, it's apparent that the photopigments in M-cones and L-cones are much more sensitive to their wavelengths of peak sensitivity than is the photopigment in S-cones. The photopigment in rods is the most sensitive of all—the peak absolute sensitivity of rods is about 100 times that of the peak sensitivity of M-cones (much too high to be shown on this graph).

If You Had Only One Type of Cone (or Only Rods)

Consider how a person with only one type of cone—say, M-cones—would perceive different wavelengths of light. Figure 5.10 shows the spectral sensitivity curve of M-cones. Suppose this person participated in a metameric color-matching experiment but was instructed to try achieving a metameric color match using only one of the monochromatic lights (instead of all three, as in the experiment described earlier). Also suppose that the test patch consists of a monochromatic light with a wavelength of 615 nm and an intensity of 500 photons/sec. As you can see from the figure, the relative sensitivity of M-cones to this light is 29%; for the purposes of this example, let's assume that this means that each M-cone absorbs and transduces 29% of the photons of this wavelength that strike it. Since the intensity of the test light is 500 photons/sec, each M-cone absorbs

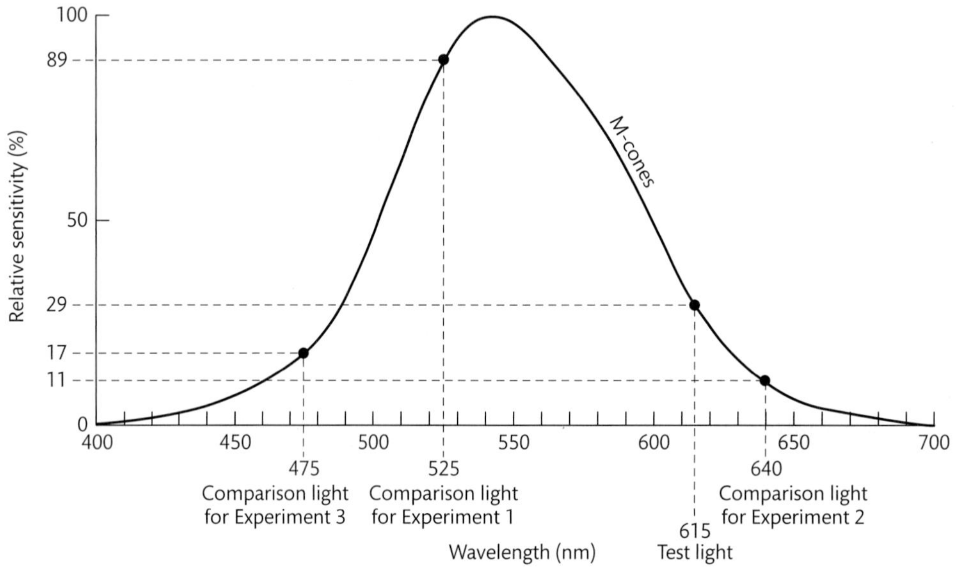

	Wavelength	Relative sensitivity of M-cones	Intensity (photons/sec)	Photons/sec absorbed and transduced by M-cones	
	FIXED TEST LIGHT				
	615 nm	29% (= .29)	fixed at 500	.29 x 500 = 145	
	ADJUSTABLE COMPARISON LIGHT (JUST ONE USED PER EXPERIMENT)				MATCH?
Experiment 1	525 nm	89% (= .89)	adjusted to 163	.89 x 163 = 145	Yes
Experiment 2	640 nm	11% (= .11)	adjusted to 1,318	.11 x 1,318 = 145	Yes
Experiment 3	475 nm	17% (= .17)	adjusted to 853	.17 x 853 = 145	Yes

Figure 5.10 If You Had M-Cones Only The table under the graph shows that a person with M-cones only could adjust the intensity of any single monochromatic comparison light to achieve a metameric color match with a 615-nm test light. The test light causes the M-cones to produce a response corresponding to the absorption and transduction of 145 photons/sec. In Experiment 1, the comparison light has a wavelength of 525 nm. The M-cones have a relative sensitivity of 89% to this wavelength. Thus, if the person adjusts the comparison light to an intensity of 163 photons/sec, the M-cones produce a response of 145 photons/sec (.89 × 163 = 145), matching their response to the test light. This means that the person can adjust the comparison light to perceptually match the test light. Experiments 2 and 3 show that such a match can also be achieved with two other lights, 640 nm and 475 nm. With the appropriate adjustments in intensity, *any* comparison light in the visible spectrum can produce the identical M-cone response of 145 photons/sec. A similar figure could be constructed for a person with only S-cones, only L-cones, or only rods. In all such cases, the person would be truly colorblind—that is, any two wavelengths could differ only in perceived intensity; everything would be perceived as shades of gray.

145 photons/sec of this light (.29 × 500 = 145) and produces a response with a strength corresponding to the transduction of those 145 photons/sec.

Now suppose the person tries using a 525-nm comparison light to create a metameric color match to the test light. As you can see in Figure 5.10, the relative sensitivity of M-cones to light with this wavelength is 89%. Experiment 1 in the table in Figure 5.10 shows that if the person adjusts the 525-nm light to an intensity of 163 photons/sec, the M-cones will absorb and transduce the same 145 photons/sec and, by the principle of univariance, will produce the same response as the response to the test light. Since the lights produce the same response, the person has no way to perceive the difference in wavelengths: the test light and comparison light will look identical. Thus, by appropriately adjusting the intensity of a light that a person with normal color vision would perceive as green (525 nm), a person with M-cones only could achieve a metameric color match with a test light that a person with normal color vision would perceive as reddish orange (615 nm).

The table in Figure 5.10 shows that the same goes for a 640-nm comparison light (Experiment 2) and a 475-nm comparison light (Experiment 3). Indeed, a person with just one type of cone can create a metameric color match between any randomly selected test light and any arbitrary comparison light (as long as both lights are in the visible spectrum) by appropriately adjusting the intensity of the comparison light.

This hypothetical experiment sheds light on one of the questions we asked before: Could a person with just one type of cone match colors successfully? The answer is yes: to a person with only one type of cone, changes in the wavelength of light are indistinguishable from changes in intensity, with the degree of apparent change in intensity depending on the relative sensitivity of the cone type at the given wavelength. Such a person would be truly color-blind—everything would appear as some shade of gray—and matching colors would simply mean adjusting the intensity of one gray light until it looked like another gray light.

The principle of univariance also applies to rods and explains why night vision is color-blind (a fact we first mentioned in Chapter 2). Recall from our discussion of dark adaptation in Chapter 2 that rods are much more sensitive to light than cones; for this reason, only rods are active in low light. In effect, therefore, in low light people have only one type of photoreceptor: rods. If you now look back at Figure 5.9 and consider the spectral sensitivity curve for rods, you can see that the situation is the same as that for M-cones illustrated in Figure 5.10. That is, lights of different wavelengths can produce identical responses from rods. For example, the relative sensitivity of rods is about 50% both to light with a wavelength of around 465 nm and to light with a wavelength of around 545 nm. Thus, a person with normal vision will perceive two lights of these wavelengths as the same if their intensities are equal, even though in daylight, when cones are active, the person would perceive the first light as blue and the second as green. And just as in the M-cones example, the intensity of light with any other wavelength could be adjusted to produce exactly the same response from rods. This is why different wavelengths of light are experienced as different shades of gray at night, when vision is based only on rods. Under equal illumination, green surfaces might look brighter than red or blue surfaces—because the relative sensitivity of rods is higher in the green portion of the spectrum than in the red or blue portion—but they will not look different in color.

If You Had Only Two Types of Cones

Now let's explore how a person with only two types of cones (say, M-cones and L-cones) would perceive different wavelengths. Figure 5.11 shows the spectral sensitivity curves for M-cones and L-cones. Suppose we conduct a metameric color-matching experiment with this person, again using a monochromatic test light with a wavelength of 615 nm, as in the experiment illustrated in Figure 5.10, and a monochromatic comparison light with a wavelength of 495 nm. The intensity of the test light is fixed at 1,000 photons/sec. Since the relative sensitivity of M-cones to the test light is 29%, they absorb 290 photons/sec and produce a corresponding response. The relative sensitivity of L-cones to the test light is 62%, so they absorb 620

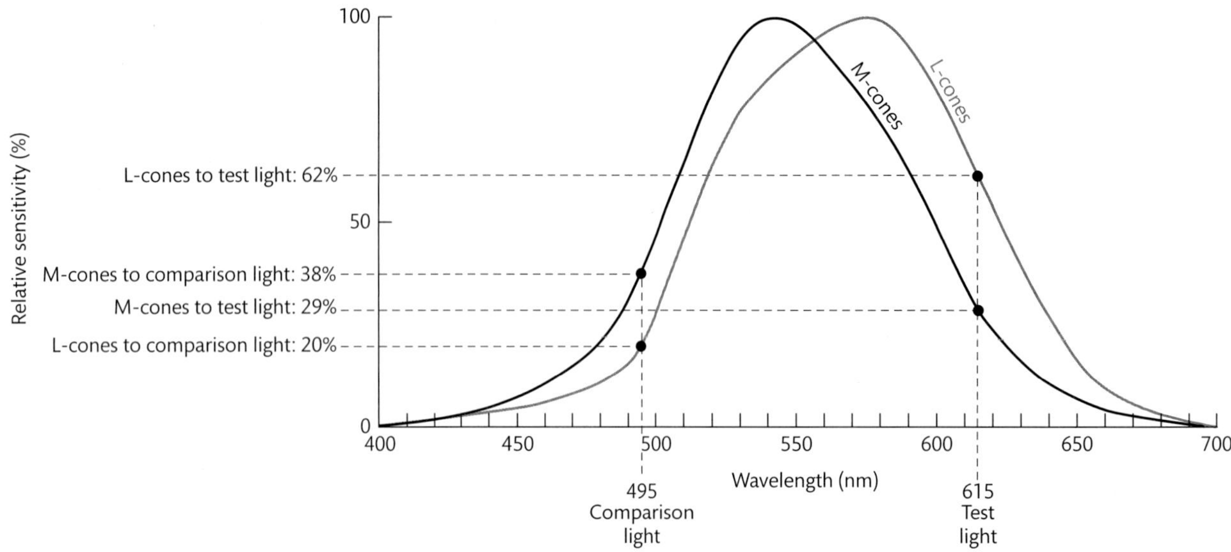

	Test light: 615 nm, with intensity fixed at 1,000 photons/sec		Comparison light: 495 nm						
	Relative sensitivity	Photons/sec absorbed	Relative sensitivity	Photons/sec absorbed with intensity adjusted to 1,000 photons/sec	Match?	Photons/sec absorbed with intensity adjusted to 763 photons/sec	Match?	Photons/sec absorbed with intensity adjusted to 3,100 photons/sec	Match?
M-cones	29% (.29)	.29 x 1,000 = **290**	38% (.38)	.38 x 1,000 = 380	No	.38 x 763 = **290**	No	.38 x 3,100 = 1,178	No
L-cones	62% (.62)	.62 x 1,000 = **620**	20% (.20)	.20 x 1,000 = 200		.20 x 763 = 153		.20 x 3,100 = **620**	

Figure 5.11 If You Had M-Cones and L-Cones Only The table under the graph shows that a person with only M-cones and L-cones would be unable to adjust the intensity of an arbitrarily chosen 495-nm comparison light to achieve a metameric color match with a 615-nm test light. A similar graph and table could be constructed for any combination of two types of cones and any test light and comparison light. Thus, a person with only two types of cones would have a form of color vision—that is, he or she would generally perceive differences in wavelength as differences in color.

photons/sec and produce a different response. These two different signals coming from the part from the retina stimulated by this test light determine the perceived color.

As shown in the table below the figure, when the 495-nm comparison light has the same intensity as the test light—1,000 photons/sec—the M-cones absorb a greater number of photons than they do with the test light (380 versus 290 photons/sec), while the L-cones absorb many fewer photons than they do with the test light (200 versus 620 photons/sec). Because the responses of the two cone types differ for the test and comparison lights, they will look different. On the one hand, if the person reduces the intensity of the comparison light to 763 photons/sec, so the M-cones absorb the same 290 photons/sec that they do with the test light, the L-cones, of course, will absorb even fewer than before. On the other hand, if the person raises the intensity of the comparison light to 3,100 photons/sec, so the L-cones absorb the same 620 photons/sec that they do with the test light, the M-cones will absorb even more than before.

Clearly, there is no way to adjust the intensity of the comparison light so the M-cones and L-cones each absorb the same number of photons as they do with the test light. Thus, unlike the situation with a person who has just one type of cone, a person with two types of cones cannot adjust the intensity of a single arbitrary comparison light to match the color of a test light with a different wavelength. Such a person has a limited form of color vision—he or she will generally perceive two different wavelengths as two different colors, not just as a difference in intensity. (The reasons why color vision with just two types of cones is described as "limited" are discussed in the section "Color Vision Deficiencies" later in this chapter.)

Metameric color-matching experiments have shown that people with two types of cones can, however, match a monochromatic test light of any wavelength if they have a mixture of *two* monochromatic comparison lights to work with, instead of just one. For a person with two types of cones, there are, in effect, only two primary colors needed to match any other color. Furthermore, metameric color-matching experiments have also shown that people with normal color vision require three monochromatic comparison lights to match any monochromatic test light, indicating that, for them, there are three primary colors (e.g., red, green, and blue, as in the metameric color-matching experiments first described above).

The pattern is clear. The number of comparison lights required to produce a match with any arbitrary test light tells us how many cone types the observer has. Since most people require three comparison lights, the normal number of cone types (and of primary colors) must also be three, and this is why normal color vision is termed *trichromatic*.

George Wald (1906–1997). [Daniel Bernstein/ Photo Researchers]

Physiological Evidence for Trichromacy

Long after scientists had used metameric color-matching experiments like those described here to provide psychophysical evidence for three types of cones, definitive physiological evidence emerged to corroborate this idea. George Wald (who was awarded the 1967 Nobel Prize in Physiology or Medicine for his discovery of the basic cycle of visual transduction, described in Chapter 2) developed a method for measuring the amount of light at each wavelength absorbed by a foveal cone, which enabled the determination of the spectral sensitivities of the three types of cones (Brown & Wald, 1964).

The mosaic of the three types of cones within the human retina can be directly visualized using a technique called *retinal densitometry* (Roorda & Williams, 1999), which produces high-resolution images of the retina (see Figure 5.12). As indicated by this figure, the retina contains a fairly small proportion of S-cones (roughly 5%); the relative number of M-cones and L-cones, however, can differ greatly from one person to the next, even for people who have normal color vision.

Additional evidence of three different types of cones comes from photocurrent measurements, in which researchers directly measure an individual cone's response to light (Baylor et al., 1987). An extremely thin electrode is used to measure electrochemical changes in a single cone that is stimulated with tiny beams of light of various wavelengths and intensities. If a large enough number of individual cones is assessed in this way, and the resulting measurements are plotted on a graph, three distinct patterns of sensitivity to light emerge—the spectral sensitivity curves of the three different types of cones (see Figure 5.9).

Demonstration 5.3 Trichromatic Color Representation Control the wavelength of a light to see how S-, M-, and/or L-cones respond to the light.

Meaning of Trichromacy

The trichromatic representation of wavelength can be thought of as a form of data compression. Rather than measure the amount of light at every wavelength at every point in the retina, the human visual system depends on the responses of just three types of cones to represent different colors. Clearly, some such compression is necessary, even though it necessarily results in a loss of information, as shown by the metameric color-matching experiments—that is, many pairs of lights that are physically different in their wavelength composition are perceived as identical. Evolution has

Retina of Person 1

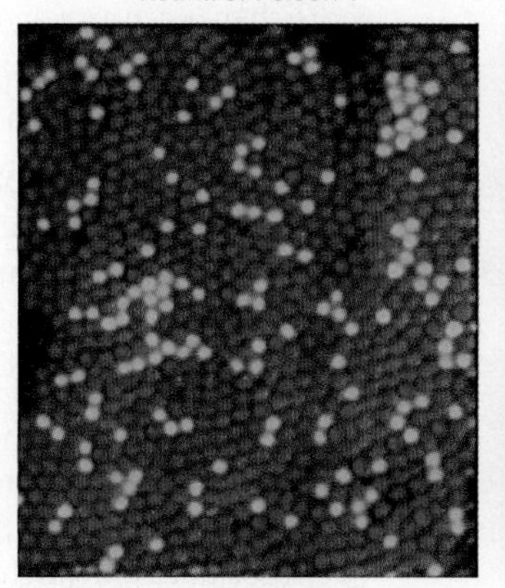

S-cones ● 4.2%
M-cones ● 20.0%
L-cones ● 75.8%

Retina of Person 2

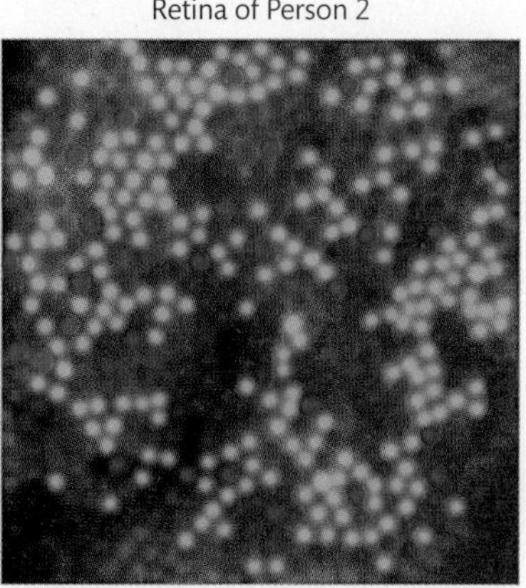

S-cones ● 5.2%
M-cones ● 44.2%
L-cones ● 50.6%

Figure 5.12 Visualizing Cones with Retinal Densitometry The imaging technique of retinal densitometry produces images like these, providing direct evidence that people have three types of cones (the colors have been added to make it easier to distinguish the different types). As shown here, the proportion of S-cones tends to be about the same across individuals, but the proportions of M-cones and L-cones can vary greatly. These images were taken of a patch of retina about 0.3 mm from the fovea. (Adapted from Roorda & Williams, 1999.)

resulted in an extremely efficient means of encoding color: just three types of cones, each with a spectral sensitivity function that spans most visible wavelengths, suffice to create fine enough distinctions in color for humans to thrive in a highly varied visual environment. Moreover, technological innovations exploit trichromatic color vision in printing and video color technology to create thousands of perceptually distinct colors with only a small number of inks or lights. This is why just three primary colors are sufficient to reproduce colors associated with wavelengths throughout the visible spectrum: if a mixture of the three primaries stimulates the three cone types in the same way as a given monochromatic light would, the visual system will be unable to discriminate that mixture from the monochromatic light.

Check Your Understanding

5.7 What is a metameric color-matching experiment designed to test?

5.8 State the principle of univariance as it applies to cones.

5.9 The answer to the question whether a person with only one type of cone could match any two colors successfully is *yes*. Explain why.

5.10 In general, how many comparison lights would a person with two types of cones need to match any given test light in a metameric color-matching experiment?

5.11 What are two sources of physiological evidence for trichromacy?

Opponent Color Representation

In the late nineteenth century, a debate arose about whether the trichromatic representation can account for all aspects of human color vision. At the center of the debate was the German scientist Ewald Hering, who pointed to several phenomena that were difficult to explain with a trichromatic approach to color vision (Hering, 1878/1964). Unfortunately, Hering's arguments were largely ignored for several decades, not only because the trichromatic mechanism proposed by Young and Helmholtz worked perfectly for color-matching experiments, but also because of its elegant simplicity. It wasn't until the late 1950s that Hering's ideas were reexamined and clearly confirmed (Hurvich & Jameson, 1957).

Ewald Hering (1834–1918). [U.S. National Library of Medicine/NIH]

Subsequent research has led to the current view of color vision as a two-stage process. In the previous section, we described the trichromatic representation, which correctly characterizes the first stage of color vision, up to the point where cones transduce light into neural signals. In this section, we'll explore the second stage, the opponent color representation, which describes what happens after that point—that is, how retinal ganglion cells and color-selective neurons in the brain process the cone signals. The opponent color representation accounts for the puzzling observations made by Hering more than a century ago.

Four Basic Colors in Two Pairs of Opposites

Hering's observations constituted psychophysical evidence for two important ideas: first, in some respects, the human visual system operates as if there were four basic colors, rather than the three implied by trichromacy; and second, these four basic colors can be divided into two pairs of complementary colors, with the members of each pair being in some sense opposites. The observations that led to these ideas included the following:

- When people are given a stack of cards, each with a different patch of color, and are asked to sort the cards into piles of similar colors, they tend to sort them into four piles—which most people would call red, green, blue, and yellow—rather than the three piles one might expect if color vision were strictly trichromatic.
- Color afterimages have a peculiar feature involving pairs of complementary colors. You can use Figure 5.13 to observe this feature of afterimages for yourself: the

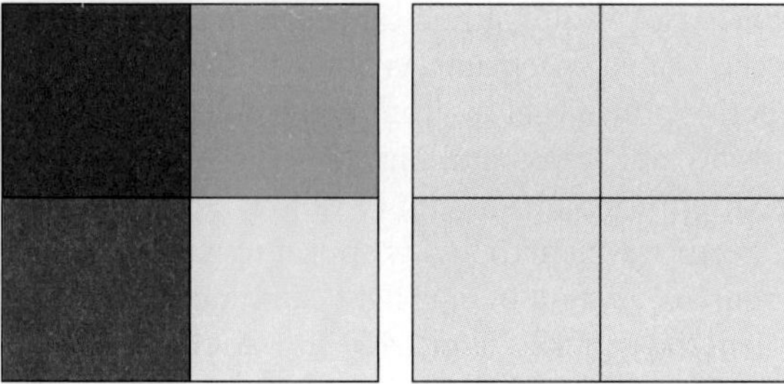

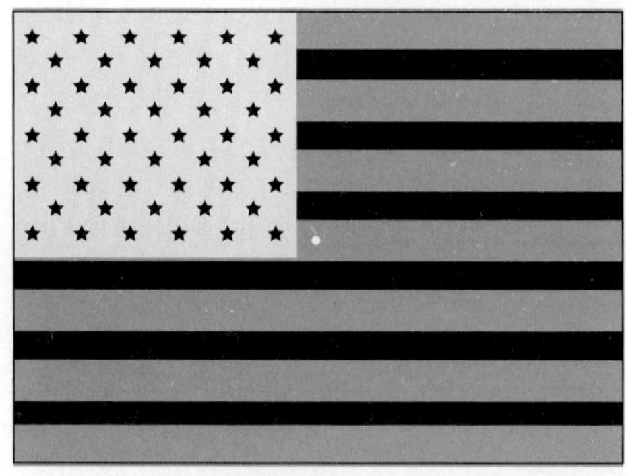

Figure 5.13 Color Afterimages (top) Under good white light, stare at the blue, green, red, and yellow squares for 20 seconds or more, minimizing blinks and keeping your eyes fixed on the central point where the four squares meet (the longer you stare, the more vivid will be the afterimage). Then shift your gaze to the four gray squares and look at the afterimage there. You'll see that, in the afterimage, the yellow and blue squares now look blue and yellow, respectively, and the same for the red and green squares. In both cases, the color of the afterimage is the complement of the original color. (bottom) Repeat this procedure with the green, black, and yellow flag, first staring at the central white dot in the flag for at least 60 seconds and then switching your gaze to the gray, flag-shaped rectangle next to it, where you'll see an afterimage with the usual flag colors (red, white, and blue, the complements of the original green, black, and yellow, respectively). Complementary-colored afterimages provide evidence for opponent color representation and against a strictly trichromatic representation.

colors in the afterimages will be the complements of the colors in the original images. These types of color afterimages suggest that the visual system intrinsically pairs complementary colors, and this is hard to explain if we assume that the visual system operates only via a trichromatic representation, because you can't make pairs with an odd number of colors.

- Colors often appear to be mixtures of two noncomplementary colors but never appear to be mixtures of two complementary colors. For example, orange looks like a mixture of red and yellow, cyan looks like a mixture of green and blue, and purple looks like a mixture of red and blue—but we can't even imagine a color that we would call reddish green or bluish yellow. Once again we see a pairing of complementary colors, and once again the trichromatic account can't explain why that is.

Hering pointed out that in all these cases, there seemed to be four basic colors, not three, and that pairs of complementary colors appeared to have an "opponent" character to them: red and green are in some sense opposites, and so are blue and yellow. These facts, Hering insisted, could not be accounted for by a trichromatic representation of color vision.

Hue Cancellation

In the 1950s, psychophysical experiments using the technique of **hue cancellation** were carried out to test the idea that some aspects of color perception are best explained by assuming that the visual system operates as if there were four basic colors consisting of two pairs of complements, red–green and blue–yellow (Hurvich & Jameson, 1957). In a hue cancellation experiment, a person is shown a monochromatic test light and instructed to neutralize, or cancel out, a perceived basic color in the light by adding its complement. For example, the person might be shown a monochromatic test light with a wavelength of about 550 nm, which would typically be perceived as a yellowish green. The person is asked to cancel perceived yellowness by adding an appropriate amount of blue light, because blue is the complement of yellow. The intensity of blue light needed to cancel the yellowness corresponds to the perceived amount of yellowness in the original 550-nm test light. Similarly, the person should be able to add a certain intensity of red light to the test light to cancel out the perceived amount of greenness.

hue cancellation An experimental technique in which the person cancels out any perception of a particular color (e.g., yellow) in a test light by adding light of the complementary color (e.g., blue).

Figure 5.14 depicts the results of hue cancellation experiments for test lights with wavelengths across the visible spectrum. As you can see, the curves in this figure very closely match our perceptions. That is, from about 400 nm to the wavelength labeled "Unique green" (typically, about 489 nm), lights are perceived as having blueness but no yellowness; adding the appropriate amount of yellow light can cancel out the blueness. Above the "Unique green" wavelength, lights appear to have yellowness but no blueness, and adding the appropriate amount of blue light can cancel out the yellowness. From the "Unique blue" wavelength (typically, about 464 nm) to the "Unique yellow" wavelength (about 572 nm), lights are perceived as having greenness but no redness, with red light needed to cancel out the greenness. And redness but no greenness is perceived at wavelengths below "Unique blue" and above "Unique yellow." We can make some sense of this split of redness perception by looking back at the color circle in Figure 5.3, where the red and blue ends of the spectrum meet in the "Nonspectral purples" range of hues, all of which are perceived as having redness.

The unique hues in Figure 5.14 are wavelengths that aren't perceived as combinations, but as purely blue, green, or yellow; that is, none of these hues are perceived as having any of their noncomplementary colors (e.g., unique green is perceived as having

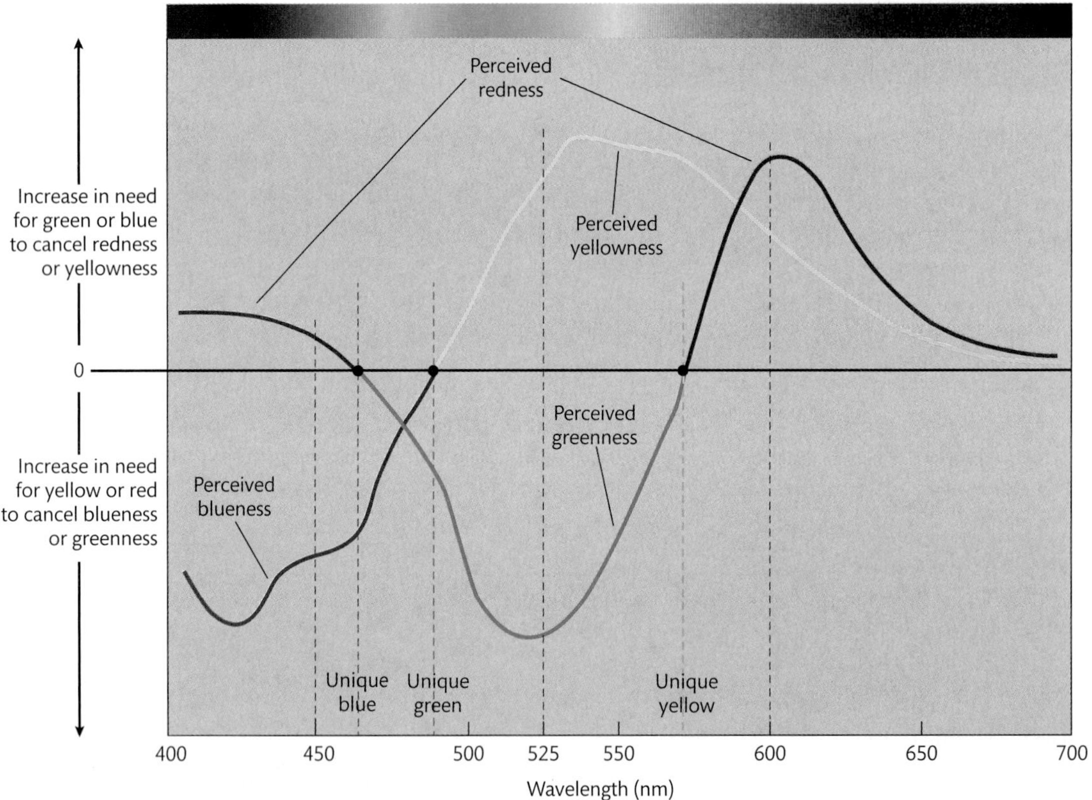

Figure 5.14 Hue Cancellation The curves in this graph show how much of each basic color people perceive in monochromatic lights of different wavelengths. As indicated by the points where the dashed vertical lines intersect the curves, at each wavelength (except the unique hues), people perceive the light as being made up of exactly two noncomplementary colors. For example, a monochromatic light with a wavelength of 525 nm is perceived as having substantial amounts of both greenness and yellowness, with green being more prominent. The unique hues are perceived as being made up of one basic color only; unique yellow, for example, is perceived as having no redness or greenness. The curves are based on hue cancellation experiments designed to determine how much of a complementary-colored light people need to add to a monochromatic light to "cancel out" the perception of a basic color. Thus, in the case of 525-nm light, people need to add a lot of red light to cancel out the greenness and somewhat less blue light to cancel out the yellowness. (Adapted from Hurvich & Jameson, 1957.)

no blue and no yellow). As you can see in the figure, the red–green curve intersects the zero line twice, with unique blue perceived at one intersection and unique yellow perceived at the other—each of these unique hues is perceived as having zero redness and zero greenness. In contrast, the blue–yellow curve intersects the zero line just once, where unique green is perceived; this corresponds to the perception that there is no truly unique red—even though the longest wavelengths all look red, they are still perceived as having a tinge of yellowness.

In Figure 5.14, all these perceptions can be illustrated with a vertical line extending up from any wavelength. Any such line intersects exactly two of the curves, indicating the basic colors perceived as making up light of that wavelength. The points of intersection indicate the relative amounts of the two basic colors perceived as making up the light. In the case of the unique hues, one of the intersection points is at zero, indicating that these hues are not perceived as combinations.

Physiological Evidence for Opponency

Until the mid-1950s, all of the evidence in support of opponent color representation was psychophysical, based either on introspection (e.g., Hering's observations) or on experiments like those just described involving hue cancellation. In the 1950s, techniques for measuring the responses of single cells in the retina and then the brain were developed and brought into wide use. First, single cones in the fish retina were found that responded in opposite ways to wavelengths from different parts of the visible spectrum, providing the first physiological evidence for opponency (Svaetichin & MacNichol, 1958). This was followed by measurements of neurons in the lateral geniculate nucleus that also responded to color in an opponent fashion (De Valois et al., 1958; recall from Chapter 3 that the lateral geniculate nucleus, in the thalamus, receives signals from retinal ganglion cells, processes those signals, and sends them on to the primary visual cortex via the optic radiations). Later research using these techniques has confirmed the existence of neural circuits underlying the opponent color representations implied by the psychophysical evidence—that is, circuits supporting color vision with four basic colors grouped in two pairs of opposites, red–green and blue–yellow.

Figure 5.15 illustrates how such circuits in the retina are thought to work (Calkins, 2004; De Valois, 2004). Nerve impulses from the three types of cones are processed by networks of other retinal neurons (bipolar, horizontal, and amacrine cells), resulting in combinations of excitatory and inhibitory inputs to retinal ganglion cells (RGCs). These patterns of neural signals create four different types of "opponent color circuits" in which the RGCs function as "opponent neurons," as described below, where + = excitatory; − = inhibitory; S = short-wavelength, or bluish-to-greenish, light; M = medium-wavelength, or greenish-to-yellowish, light; and L = long-wavelength, or yellowish-to-reddish, light:

- *+S–ML circuit.* The RGC in this type of circuit fires above its baseline rate in response to short-wavelength light (i.e., *+S*) and below its baseline rate in response to medium- and long-wavelength light (i.e., *–ML*). Figure 5.15a illustrates a +S–ML circuit.
- *+ML–S circuit.* The RGC in this type of circuit does the opposite, firing above its baseline rate in response to medium- and long-wavelength light and below its baseline rate in response to short-wavelength light. Figure 5.15b illustrates a +ML–S circuit.
- *+L–M circuit.* Here, the RGC fires above its baseline rate in response to long-wavelength light and below its baseline rate in response to medium-wavelength light. Figure 5.15c illustrates a +L–M circuit.
- *+M–L circuit.* The RGC in this type of circuit does the opposite, firing above its baseline rate in response to medium-wavelength light and below its baseline rate in response to long-wavelength light. Figure 5.15d illustrates a +M–L circuit.

Demonstration 5.4 Opponent Color Representation Explore how hue cancellation experiments reveal the perceived amounts of red, green, blue, and yellow in monochromatic light; interact with the retinal circuits that underlie these perceptions.

This opponent color model accounts physiologically for the phenomena that are problematic for trichromatic representation. +S–ML and +ML–S neurons respond

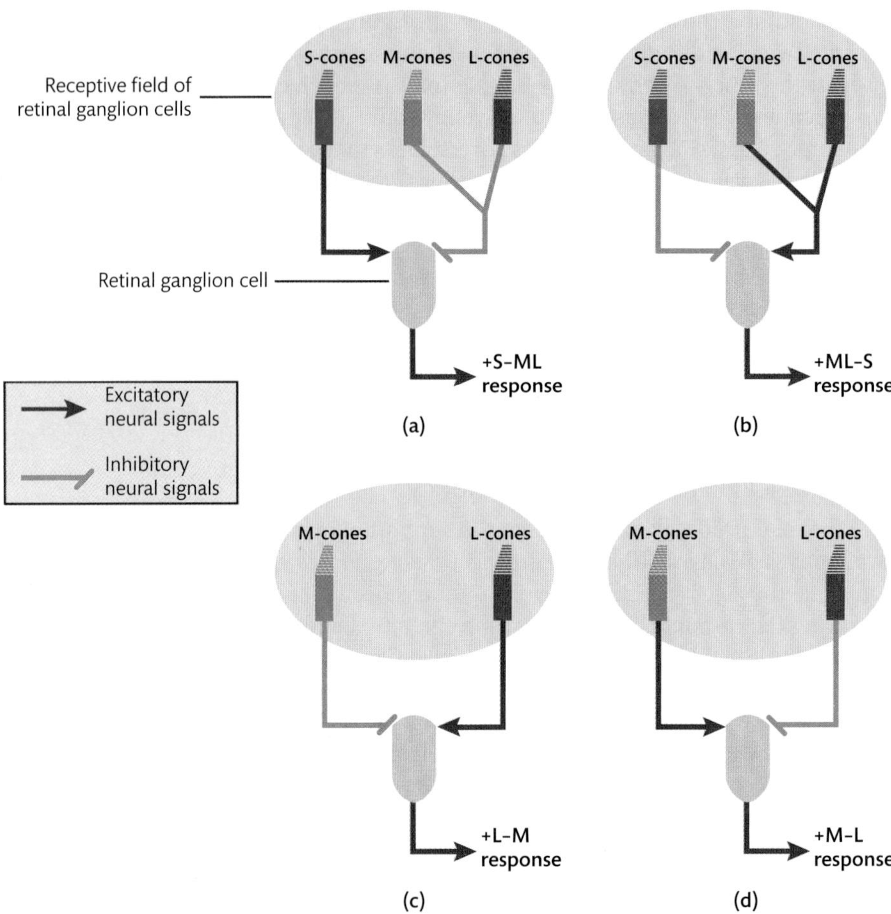

Figure 5.15 Opponent Color Circuits in the Retina Retinal ganglion cells with appropriate connections from cones in their receptive fields function as opponent neurons in four different types of opponent color circuits. (a) A +S−ML circuit consists of a retinal ganglion cell that receives an excitatory signal from S-cones in its receptive field and an inhibitory signal from M-cones and L-cones. (b) A +ML−S circuit consists of a retinal ganglion cell that receives an excitatory signal from M-cones and L-cones and an inhibitory signal from S-cones. (c) A +L−M circuit consists of a retinal ganglion cell that receives an excitatory signal from L-cones and an inhibitory signal from M-cones. (d) A +M−L circuit consists of a retinal ganglion cell that receives an excitatory signal from M-cones and an inhibitory signal from L-cones.

oppositely to blue and yellow light, so their outputs support the perception of blue and yellow as basic and opposite colors. Similarly, +L–M and +M–L neurons respond oppositely to green and red light, so their outputs support the perception of green and red as basic and opposite colors. Thus, the model includes four basic colors, rather than three; and it includes a sense in which blue–yellow and green–red are paired opposites. In addition, it makes some sense of the fact that yellowish blue and reddish green aren't possible color perceptions.

Color-Opponent Neurons in the Visual Pathway

The color-opponent RGCs described above respond with an increase in firing rate to one range of wavelengths and with a decrease in firing rate to the complementary range of wavelengths—for example, the RGC in a +L–M circuit (see Figure 5.15c) fires above its baseline rate in response to long-wavelength light and below its baseline rate in response to medium-wavelength light. The receptive fields (RFs) of these neurons are spatially uniform; that is, the neurons respond most strongly to a uniform patch of light having the preferred wavelength and are maximally suppressed by a uniform patch of light having the complementary wavelength.

In contrast, other color-selective neurons in the visual pathway—including RGCs, LGN cells, and cortical cells—have RFs that produce more elaborate patterns of response (Johnson et al., 2008). For example, the V1 cell depicted in Figure 5.16a has a *single-opponent* center–surround RF—it responds with an increase in its firing rate when the RF center is stimulated with long-wavelength (reddish) light and with a decrease in its firing rate when the RF surround is stimulated by medium-wavelength (greenish) light. Other single-opponent V1 cells have the opposite response pattern—they increase their firing rate in response to medium-wavelength light in the center and decrease it in

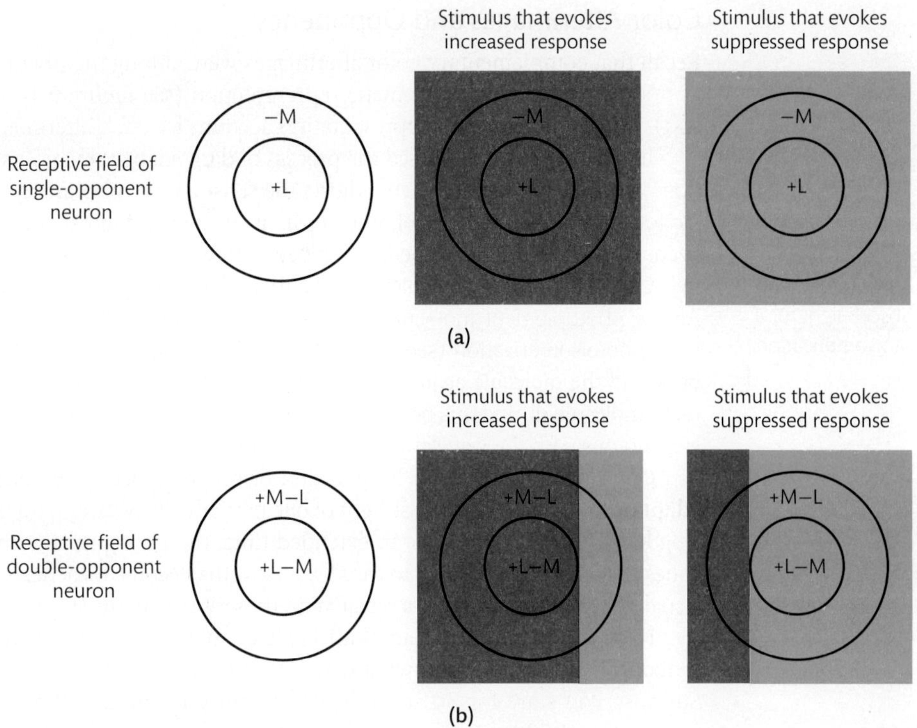

Figure 5.16 **Receptive Fields and Response Patterns of Single-Opponent and Double-Opponent Neurons in V1** Single-opponent and double-opponent neurons have been identified in area V1 in monkeys. (a) A neuron with a single-opponent center–surround receptive field (RF) responds with an increase in firing rate when the RF center is illuminated by long-wavelength (reddish) light; its response is suppressed by medium-wavelength (greenish) light in the surround. The responses of these neurons provide information about uniform illumination across the RF. (b) A neuron with a double-opponent center–surround RF responds with an increase in firing rate to reddish light in the center and/or to greenish light in the surround; its response is suppressed by greenish light in the center and/or reddish light in the surround. The responses of these neurons provide information about the location of red–green edges—an increased response is evoked when an edge is located so that the center is stimulated by reddish light and a portion of the surround is stimulated by greenish light, because the excitatory signals from these parts of the RF outweigh the inhibitory signals from the portion of the surround stimulated by reddish light; and a suppressed response is evoked when an edge is located so that the center is stimulated by greenish light and a portion of the surround is stimulated by reddish light, because the inhibitory signals from these parts of the RF outweigh the excitatory signals from the portion of the surround stimulated by greenish light. (Adapted from Johnson et al., 2008.)

response to long-wavelength light in the surround. Single-opponent neurons with L/M opponency have been the most extensively studied, but neurons with S/ML opponency are also believed to be present in the visual pathway.

The responses of single-opponent neurons carry information about the wavelength of light within uniformly colored regions of the visual scene but don't provide much information about color edges, locations where adjacent regions are illuminated by different wavelengths. In contrast, the responses of neurons with a *double-opponent* center–surround RF, like the one depicted in Figure 5.16b, do provide information about color edges. This type of RF, which is seen in many color-selective V1 neurons, produces a strong increase in firing rate when the RF center is stimulated with long-wavelength light and the RF surround is stimulated with medium-wavelength light. Conversely, its response is strongly suppressed when the RF center is stimulated with medium-wavelength light and the RF surround with long-wavelength light.

Double-opponent neurons like these, providing information about the location of edges between regions that differ in color, complement neurons that provide information about edges between regions that differ in brightness, as discussed in Chapter 3. They help us perceive objects in scenes where objects and their background have the same brightness but are of different colors.

Color Afterimages and Opponency

Recall that complementary color afterimages were among the phenomena noted by Hering as not explainable by trichromatic representation (see Figure 5.13 and the accompanying text). Can opponent color representation account for such afterimages?

In Chapter 2, we discussed the process of dark adaptation and its converse, light adaptation, in which the visual system adjusts the sensitivity of photoreceptors to a level appropriate for the current intensity of ambient light. If the lighting becomes dim, the visual system becomes more sensitive; if the lighting becomes bright, the visual system becomes less sensitive. One of the primary mechanisms of dark and light adaptation is **photopigment bleaching.** After a photopigment molecule absorbs a photon and undergoes the shape change referred to as photoisomerization (see Figure 2.19), some time must elapse before its shape changes back and the molecule again becomes light sensitive. We describe the state of the photopigment molecule during this period as *bleached,* meaning that it can't respond to light by absorbing photons with the wavelengths to which the molecule is sensitive in its unbleached state.

photopigment bleaching A photopigment molecule's loss of ability to absorb light for a period after undergoing photoisomerization.

Color afterimages result from a kind of photopigment bleaching known as **chromatic adaptation.** If relatively intense light of one particular wavelength (or a narrow range of wavelengths) strikes the retina for an extended time, the photopigment molecules in the type of cones that are most sensitive to those wavelengths become bleached en masse, rendering the visual system temporarily less sensitive to those wavelengths (Burnham et al., 1957).

chromatic adaptation A kind of photopigment bleaching that results from exposure to relatively intense light consisting of a narrow range of wavelengths.

How would chromatic adaptation affect an opponent color circuit like the one illustrated in Figure 5.15d, and what would that mean for the perceived color of afterimages? Suppose you stare for 30 seconds at a brightly lit picture of a green square with peak reflectance of 500 nm. The photopigment molecules in the M-cones in the square portion of your retina where the retinal image of the square is projected will bleach more than those in the L-cones there, so the M-cones will be relatively less sensitive than the L-cones for a period of time. If during that time you look at a white surface, which would normally elicit equal responses from M-cones and L-cones (because white light contains all wavelengths equally), the L-cones in that part of the retina will respond more strongly than the M-cones because of the bleaching. The weakened response from the M-cones there means weaker inhibitory impulses transmitted to the +L–M opponent neurons with receptive fields there. The excitatory impulses from the L-cones to those +L–M neurons now outweigh the inhibitory impulses from the M-cones, and the neurons begin to fire, signaling reddishness, which you perceive as the color of a square afterimage on the white surface. When the M-cones recover from bleaching, the balance of excitatory and inhibitory impulses is restored, and white looks white again. A corresponding account can be given for complementary-colored afterimages of green, blue, and yellow things.

Meaning of Opponency

In the section on the trichromatic representation of color, we saw that people with normal color vision have three types of cones, with three different photopigments that respond preferentially to different wavelengths of light. These physiological facts explain the results of psychophysical experiments in color matching, which show that we can mix three primary colors of monochromatic light to match light of any color.

Opponent color representation, in contrast, explains other psychophysical phenomena, such as color categorization, color afterimages, complementary colors, and the results of hue cancellation experiments—all of which imply that, at some level, people operate with four basic colors in two complementary pairs. Physiological evidence for opponency comes from the detection of opponent neurons—retinal ganglion cells and neurons in the lateral geniculate nucleus and the visual cortex whose neural circuitry supports the four-colors-in-two-pairs aspects of color vision.

Why did the visual system evolve with an opponent representation of color? A likely explanation is that it's a matter of efficient transmission of information. To see why, note that the responses of M-cones and L-cones are very similar across a broad range of the visible spectrum, as indicated by the similarity of their spectral sensitivity functions (see Figure 5.9). That is, the responses of these two cone types, considered separately, would provide the visual system with much the same information. The +L–M and +M–L opponent color circuits use subtraction to send the visual system focused information about the *difference* in the responses of these two cone types, rather than making the visual system find the buried bits of useful information among all the redundancies. Also, because the responses of M-cones and L-cones are so similar, comparing the responses of M-cones to S-cones wouldn't tell the visual system anything very different from comparing the responses of L-cones to S-cones. Here again, our actual opponent color circuits (+ML–S and +S–ML) give the visual system much more easily accessible information. Significantly, researchers have found that color opponency provides an extremely efficient code for representing the colors found in natural scenes (Lee et al., 2002), lending support to the idea that opponency is an evolutionary adaptation.

Like trichromatic representation, opponent representation is a form of data compression: the visual system combines the responses of L-cones and M-cones rather than dealing with each separately. The result is an efficient and effective mechanism for differentiating wavelengths—that is, a mechanism that allows us to see color.

Color Constancy

Suppose you're looking at a piece of paper lying on a tabletop and illuminated by the light from a lamp with an incandescent bulb. Suddenly, the bulb burns out, and you replace it with a compact fluorescent bulb. Under both types of illumination, you perceive the paper as the same shade of blue, which is not surprising because this paper predominantly reflects shorter wavelengths. But the wavelengths entering your eyes don't depend only on the spectral reflectance of the paper but also on the spectral power distribution (SPD) of the illuminating light—that is, the relative intensities of all the wavelengths present in the light. Figure 5.17 shows the SPD of incandescent light and fluorescent light and the reflectance of the blue paper.

As indicated in Figure 5.17, the amount of each wavelength reflected into your eyes by the paper—that is, the SPD of that reflected light—is determined by multiplying the

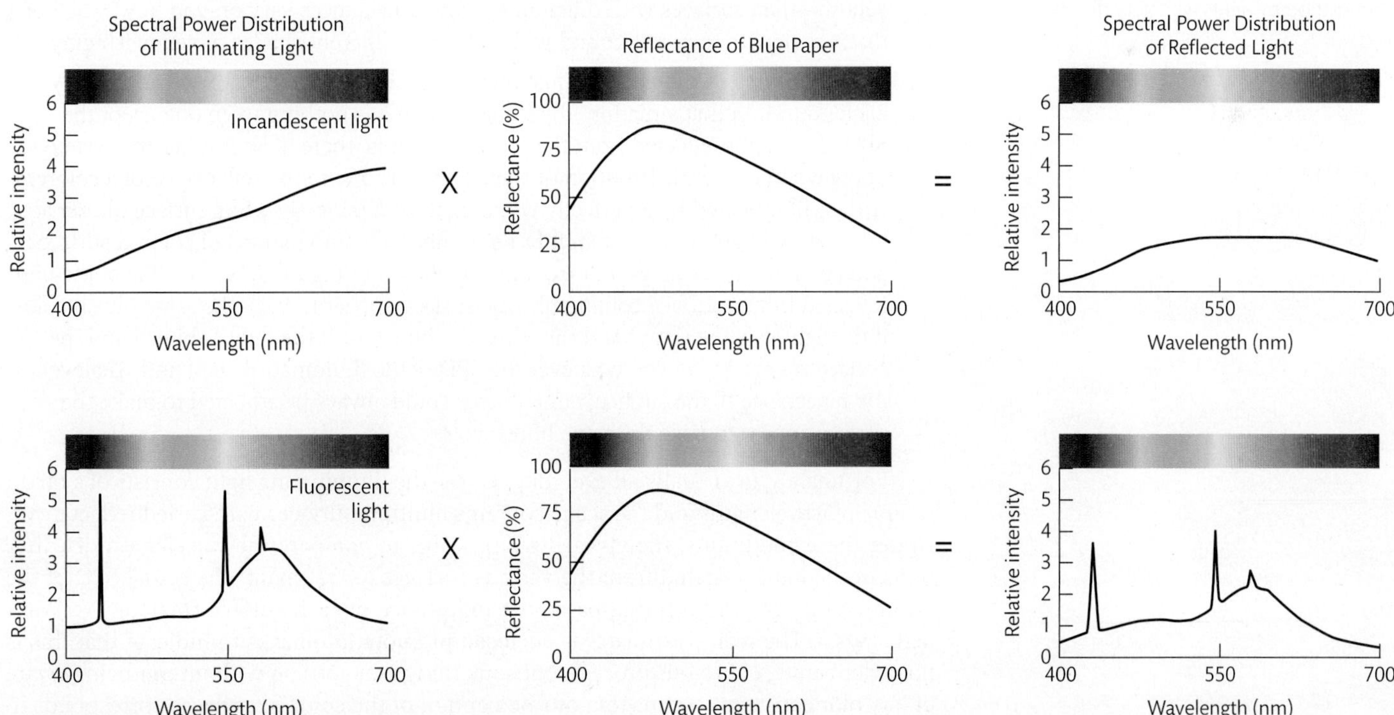

Figure 5.17 Illumination and Surface Reflectance Determine the Wavelengths in Reflected Light Incandescent light consists of a larger proportion of longer wavelengths than does fluorescent light, while fluorescent light contains narrow, high-intensity bands of medium and short wavelengths that aren't present in incandescent light. As a result, the spectral power distribution of light reflected from blue paper is quite different under the two different illuminants. Yet the paper is perceived as having the same color under both illuminants—an example of color constancy.

Figure 5.18 Color Differences Under Different Illuminants These two images illustrate the difference in the spectral power distribution of the light reflected from a panel of colored patches when the panel is illuminated by sunlight versus incandescent light. They show how you might perceive the panel under these two different illuminants if you saw it in isolation against a featureless background. But if you were in a room in which the panel was first illuminated by sunlight and then by incandescent light, you'd experience the colors as about the same in the two cases. (Adapted from Shevell & Kingdom, 2008, Figure 5.)

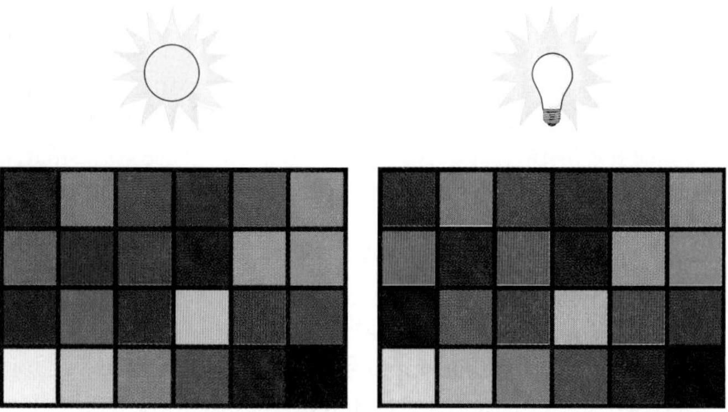

relative intensity of the illuminating light at each wavelength by the reflectance of the paper at each wavelength. And as you can see, the SPD of the light reflected by the paper in incandescent light is quite different from the SPD of the light reflected by the paper in fluorescent light. Yet you perceive little if any difference in the color of the paper after you replace the bulb. This tendency to see a surface as having the same color under illumination by lights with very different SPDs is called **color constancy.** Figure 5.18 provides a striking visual illustration of how large the differences in the SPD of reflected light can be and still result in perception of the same colors.

But how is color constancy achieved? To answer this question, it's helpful to start by noting two situations in which color constancy fails:

color constancy The tendency to see a surface as having the same color under illumination by lights with very different spectral power distributions.

- Color constancy will fail if the illuminating light consists of only a narrow range of wavelengths. In other words, the SPD of the illumination must include a reasonably broad sampling of wavelengths across the visible spectrum. If the illuminating light is nearly monochromatic—for example, the light from low-pressure sodium vapor lamps, often used as streetlights, is nearly monochromatic at 589 nm and appears yellow—then surfaces with different spectral reflectances vary only in how much of that wavelength they reflect and will look to be different shades of yellowish gray.
- Color constancy will also fail if just one surface is seen against a black and empty background. In that situation, the visual system has nothing to go on except the SPD of the light reflected from the surface—that is, there is no way for the system to know whether that distribution of wavelengths is due to the reflectance of a colored surface illuminated by a perfectly white light, or a perfectly white surface illuminated by a colored light, or any of an infinite number of combinations of colored surfaces and colored light sources. For example, as shown in Figure 5.19, the SPD of the light reflected from a surface could make the surface appear to have the same bluish color if the light is white (gray) and the surface is bluish or if the light is bluish and the surface is gray. Moreover, whatever the SPD of the illuminating light and whatever the reflectance of the surface, either factor could always be adjusted to make the surface appear to have the same bluish color.

Fortunately, in virtually all everyday scenes, the illuminating light consists of a broad sample of wavelengths and the scene contains multiple surfaces with varied reflectances. Under these conditions, the visual system is able to compare the wavelength distributions in the light reflected from the various surfaces to "estimate" the actual SPD of the illuminating light and, on that basis, the reflectance of each surface (Maloney & Wandell, 1986). The word "estimate" is enclosed in quotation marks to indicate that this is not a deliberate, conscious process, but something that goes on without our being aware of it. Color constancy means that our perception of the color of surfaces corresponds to the estimated reflectance of each surface, not to the SPD of the reflected light. Exactly how the visual system does this is not fully understood, though various theories have been proposed (Foster, 2011). One is that the visual system automatically determines the amount of each wavelength reflected from all the surfaces on average and uses this as its estimate of the SPD of the illuminant. If the SPD of the illuminant is known, then

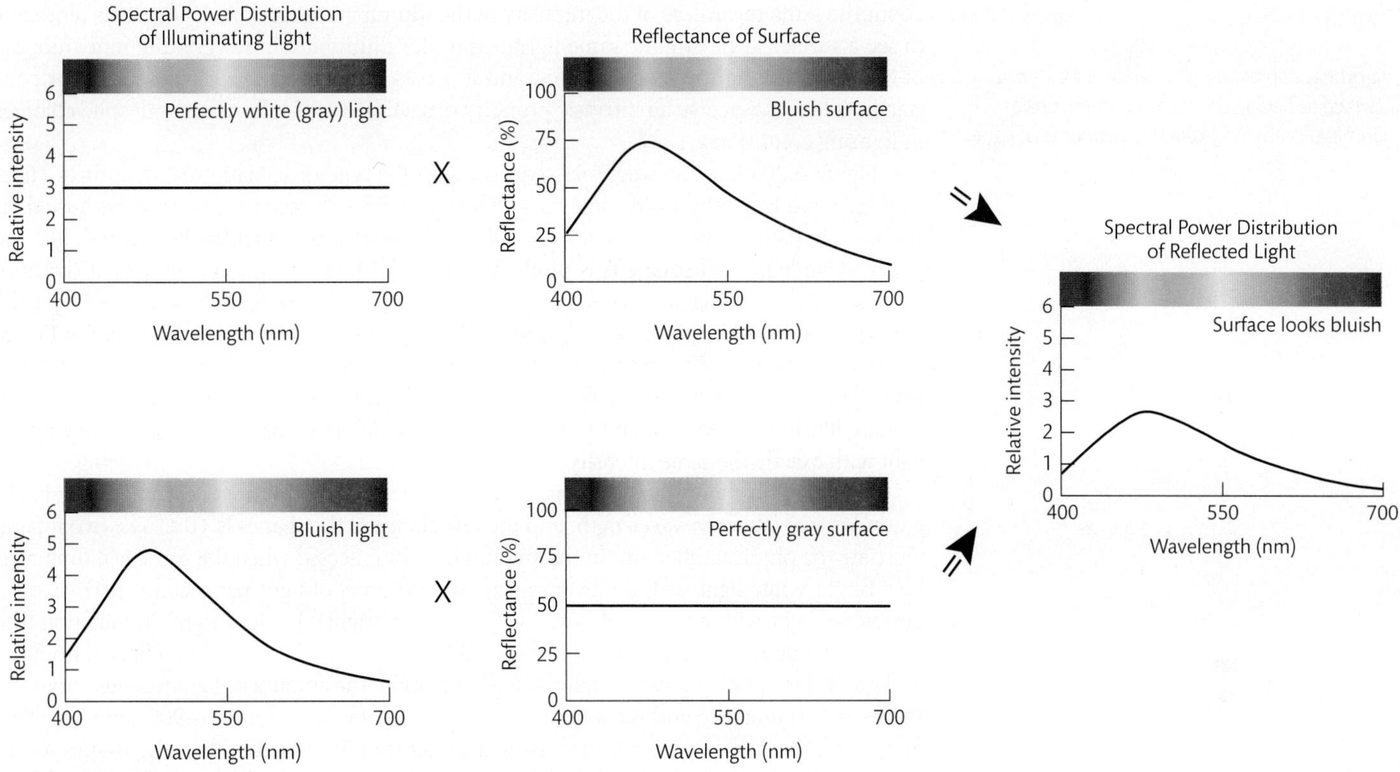

Figure 5.19 Failure of Color Constancy These graphs illustrate how color constancy can fail. In the top row, a perfectly white light (i.e., a light with a flat SPD, which would be perceived as a shade of gray) illuminates a bluish surface (i.e., a surface with higher reflectance toward the blue end of the spectrum). In the bottom row, a bluish light (i.e., a light with an SPD tilted toward the blue end of the spectrum) illuminates a perfectly gray surface (i.e., a surface with equal reflectance across the spectrum). In both cases, the SPD of the light reflected from the surface makes the surface appear bluish.

it is possible to determine the reflectance of a surface simply by dividing the amount of light reflected by that surface at each wavelength by the amount of light present in the illuminant at that wavelength. This method for achieving color constancy is often called "discounting the illuminant."

Another way the visual system tends to achieve color constancy is through chromatic adaptation, which we discussed earlier in relation to color afterimages. As we saw in that discussion, cones adapt to continuous, intense stimulation by a particular wavelength, so that their response to that wavelength becomes weaker. For example, if you were to look at a scene illuminated by bluish light with an SPD like that of the light in the bottom left graph of Figure 5.19, your cones would adapt by responding more weakly to short wavelengths. By adjusting your cones to compensate for the imbalance of wavelengths in the illuminating light (e.g., by making the cones less sensitive to the shorter wavelengths in the bluish light emitted by, say, a fluorescent lightbulb), chromatic adaptation "compensates" for nonwhite illumination, which helps you make more accurate judgments about the actual color of surfaces. That is, your eyes' response to the wavelength distribution of the reflected light will be somewhat more uniform across the spectrum because of its reduced sensitivity to short-wavelength light.

Lightness Constancy

In color constancy, when we correctly perceive the color of a surface under different illuminants, we're perceiving how the surface reflects different wavelengths differently. But what about a surface that reflects all wavelengths about equally—that is, a surface we perceive as a shade of gray? Will such a surface appear to be a lighter shade of gray when illuminated by a very intense light, like sunlight, and a darker shade of gray when illuminated by a very dim light, like candlelight? The answer is no—the lightness of a gray surface appears

lightness constancy The tendency to see a surface as having the same lightness under illumination by very different amounts of light.

about the same regardless of the intensity of the illuminant (Adelson, 1993). This tendency to see a surface as having the same lightness under illumination by very different amounts of light is called **lightness constancy**, and it serves much the same purpose as color constancy: it lets us perceive an intrinsic property of a surface—its reflectance—despite changes in lighting conditions.

Figure 5.20a illustrates lightness constancy in the type of scenario just described. Here, squares A and B are physically identical—that is, they have the same reflectance, because their surfaces are painted with the same light gray paint. Square B is brightly illuminated, like the paper in sunlight, and square A is dimly illuminated, like the paper in candlelight (because it's in shadow). This means that square A is reflecting much less light than square B, yet the two squares tend to be perceived as the same shade of gray. In the image on the right in Figure 5.20a, the vertical gray bar, which reflects the same amount of light as square A, reveals the difference in intensity of the light reflected by squares A and B. The bar also demonstrates a very striking illusion—squares A and C appear to be very different shades of gray, yet they reflect light with exactly the same intensity.

Figure 5.20b shows two versions of a simple scene; in both, the reflectance of the background is 90% at every wavelength, and the reflectance of the shapes is 10%. The two images illustrate the physical difference in the amount of light reflected when the scene is illuminated by a bright white light with a power of, say, 10,000 units of light per second (left) versus a dim white light with a power of, say, 1,000 units/sec (right). Under bright illumination, the amount of light reflected from the shapes is 1,000 units/sec and the amount reflected from the background is 9,000 units/sec. Under dim illumination, the amount of light reflected from the shapes is 100 units/sec and the amount reflected from the background is 900 units/sec. This means that the background reflects less light under dim illumination than the shapes reflect under bright illumination. Yet if you were to see this scene in reality, first illuminated by a bright light and then by a dim light, you would perceive the shapes as black and the background as white in both conditions.

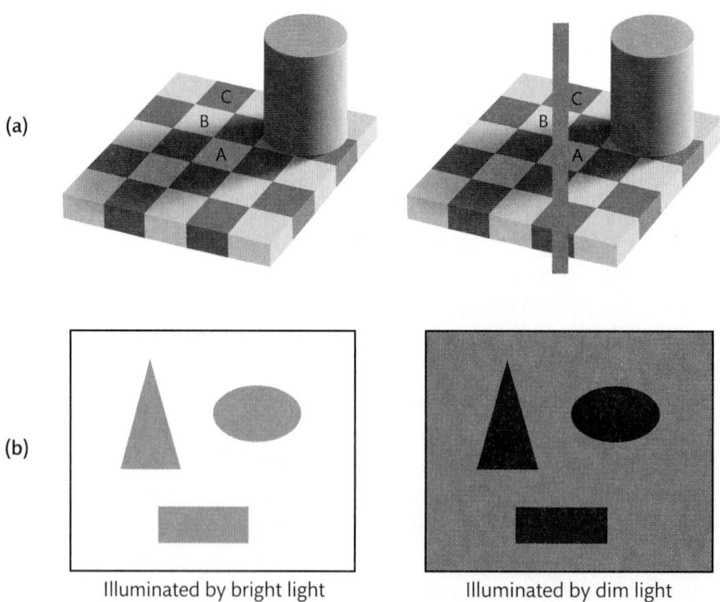

Figure 5.20 **Lightness Constancy** (a) In the image on the left, the intensity of the light reflected from squares A and B is different, yet they appear to be the same shade of gray. In the image on the right, the gray bar is a uniform shade of gray; the fact that the bar blends in with square A and contrasts sharply with square B shows how large the difference is in the intensity of the light reflected by the two squares. The bar also blends in with square C, demonstrating a powerful illusion in this well-known image: squares A and C, which look so different, reflect light with the same physical intensity. (b) When illuminated by bright light (left), the shapes reflect more light than the background reflects when illuminated by dim light (right). Yet you wouldn't perceive much change in the lightness of the shapes or the background if you first illuminated such an image with a bright light and then turned down the light to dim. (Image in panel [a] from Edward H. Adelson, http://web.mit.edu/persci/people/adelson/checkershadow_illusion.html.)

If the illumination across a scene is uniform, lightness constancy can be explained by what's known as the *ratio principle*, which says that the perceived lightness of a region is based not on the absolute amount of light reflected from the region, but on the relative amount reflected from the region and its surround (Wallach, 1948). Given that this ratio is the same (9:1) under both conditions in Figure 5.20b, the shapes are perceived as black and the background as white, regardless of the amount of light in the illuminant.

But in Figure 5.20a, the illumination isn't uniform across the scene, which means that the ratio principle can't explain why squares A and B are perceived as the same shade of gray. To address this problem, it has been suggested that the ratio principle be supplemented with a two-part anchoring rule: (1) In any given scene, the region that reflects the most light is perceived as white (or as the lightest shade of gray in the scene), and the lightness of every other region is perceived in relation to that anchor point. (2) If the scene consists of regions under different amounts of illumination (as in Figure 5.20a, where a region that includes square A is in shadow), the visual system applies the anchoring rule separately in each illumination zone (Gilchrist, 2006). Thus, in Figure 5.20a, square A reflects the most light in its region (the region in shadow) and square B reflects the most light in *its* region (not in shadow); therefore, each square is the anchor point for its region, and the two squares are perceived as being the same shade of light gray.

Figure 5.21 illustrates an experiment using an illusion of depth perception to demonstrate the anchoring rule (Gilchrist, 1977). In Figure 5.21a, the white paper target is correctly perceived as attached to the near wall and is perceived as white, like the paper attached

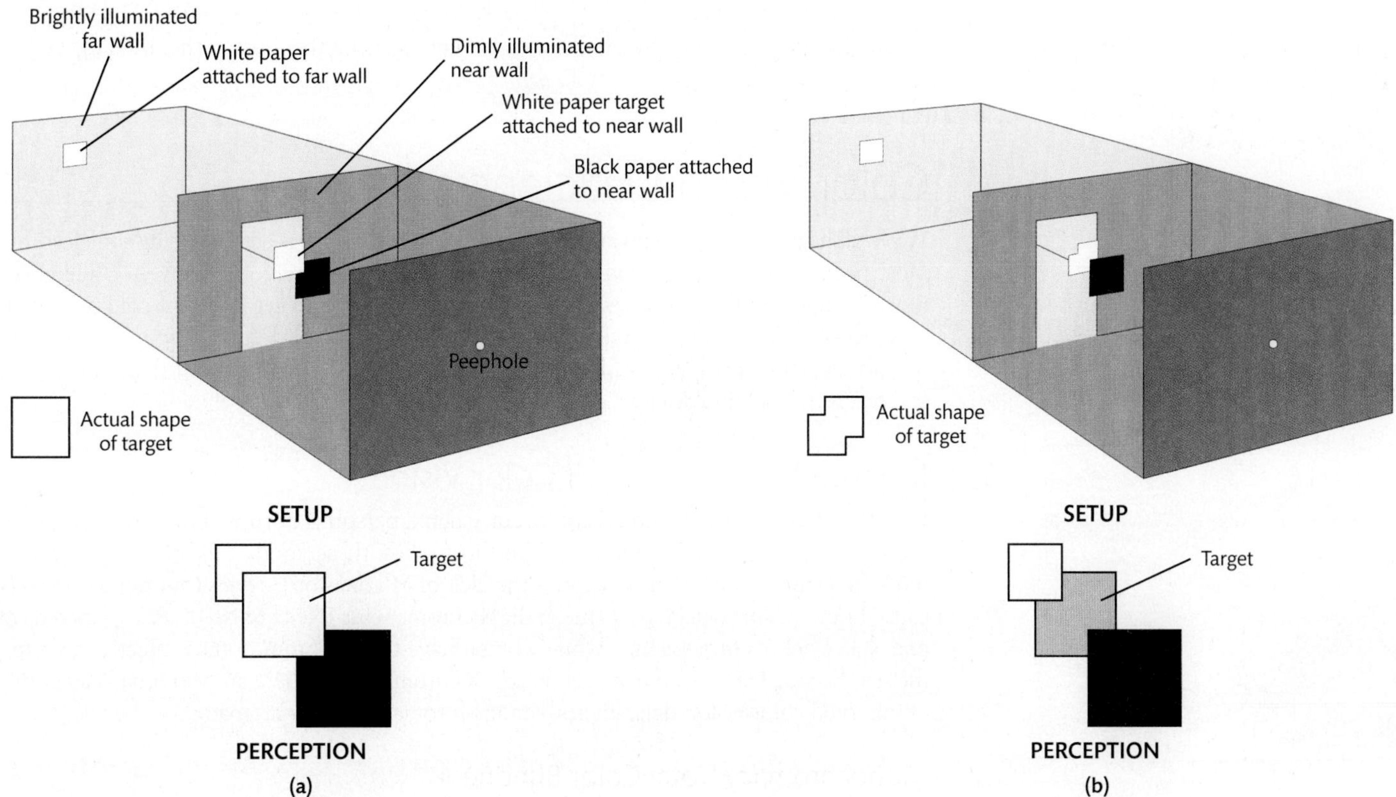

Figure 5.21 An Illusion of Depth Perception Shows How an Anchoring Rule Can Be Used to Explain Lightness Constancy In both setups, the white paper target and the black paper are attached to the dimly illuminated near wall, a white paper (with the same white as the target) is attached to the brightly illuminated far wall, and an observer looking through the peephole perceives that the scene consists of two rooms under different illumination (here, the ceiling and left side wall of the rooms have been cut away so you can see the interiors of the rooms). (a) The target is correctly perceived as attached to the near wall. It reflects more light than anything else in its region of the scene and is perceived as the region's anchor point. Similarly, the white paper attached to the far wall is perceived as its region's anchor point. And the two regions' anchor points are perceived as having the same lightness, white. (b) The notches cut out of the target create the illusion that it's attached to the far wall. The brightly illuminated white paper attached to the far wall is perceived as that region's anchor point, and the dimly illuminated target—which seems to be part of the same region—is perceived, in relation to the anchor, as dark gray. (Adapted from Gilchrist, 1977.)

to the far wall. But in Figure 5.21b, the notches cut out of the target create the illusory perception that the target is attached to the far wall, and the target is perceived as dark gray. Again, the anchoring rule can be applied to explain these perceptions. Under the reasonable assumption that the near wall and the far wall have the same reflectance, observers' visual system "understands" that the illumination across the scene isn't uniform but consists of two regions, a dimly illuminated near room and a brightly illuminated far room. In Figure 5.21a, observers see that the target reflects the most light in its region and that the white paper attached to the far wall reflects the most light in *its* region, so observers perceive each as its region's anchor point and perceive both as white. In Figure 5.21b, however, the target is perceived as being in the far room. The brightly illuminated white paper attached to the far wall reflects the most light in that region and is perceived as the anchor point, and in relation to that anchor point, the dimly illuminated target is perceived as dark gray.

Check Your Understanding

5.12 What were three observations made by Hering that could not easily be accounted for by a trichromatic representation of color vision?

5.13 In hue cancellation experiments, what does the person try to do? How do these experiments support opponent color representation?

5.14 What is the difference between a +S–ML neural circuit and a +ML–S neural circuit? Between a +L–M circuit and a +M–L circuit?

5.15 What is photopigment bleaching and how is it involved in color afterimages?

5.16 What is color constancy? Describe a situation in which color constancy fails.

5.17 In Figure 5.21b, why did the experimenters create the illusion that the target was attached to the far wall?

Color Vision Deficiencies

We've all heard of people who are "color-blind," but this term is actually a little misleading. Most people who have color vision deficiencies are not entirely insensitive to differences in wavelengths of light—that is, they aren't entirely unable to see different colors—which is what *color-blind* would literally mean. In this section, we'll describe the most common deficiencies of color vision, which are inherited, as well as noninherited deficiencies that can result from brain damage.

Inherited Deficiencies of Color Vision

Inherited deficiencies of color vision occur when a person is born without one or more of the three types of cones in the retina. In most cases, these conditions affect males much more frequently than females, because the lack of M-cones or L-cones (but not S-cones) is caused by a specific defect in a gene on the X chromosome (Neitz & Neitz, 2011); men have one X and one Y chromosome, while women have two X chromosomes, effectively giving them a "backup" for a genetic defect on one X chromosome. There are two broad categories of inherited color vision deficiencies—monochromacy and dichromacy.

Monochromacy: Total Color Blindness

monochromacy A condition in which a person has only rods or has only rods and one type of cone; in either case, the person is totally color-blind, perceiving everything in shades of gray.

rod monochromacy A condition in which a person has rods only, with no cones.

A person with **monochromacy** sees everything in shades of gray. There are two inherited conditions that result in monochromacy, and both are rare: rod monochromacy and cone monochromacy. In **rod monochromacy,** a condition that occurs in about 0.002% of the population (20 per million), the person has no cones at all and must rely on rod vision all the time. (All the percentages given in this section are from Sharpe et al., 1999.) As a result, rod monochromats are not only unable to perceive color, but are also hypersensitive to light—typically, so hypersensitive that they must wear very dark sunglasses during the day (Sharpe & Nordby, 1990; recall the vignette about Knut Nordby at the beginning of Chapter 2). If you think back to the discussion in Chapter 2 of the differences between rods and cones, you'll understand why this is so. Rods are much more light sensitive than cones, so people with normal vision use their rods to see in dim light (e.g., for night vision) and their cones to see in bright light. If rod monochromats try to see in daylight without sunglasses, their rods are overwhelmed by the amount of light—the rod photopigment is fully bleached and therefore not able to respond to light. In Chapter 2, we also noted that the densely packed cones in the fovea of people with normal vision support high visual acuity; rod monochromats, with no cones at all, have relatively low visual acuity, making reading and other tasks that demand high acuity difficult.

The other type of monochromacy—**cone monochromacy**—occurs even less frequently than rod monochromacy. Cone monochromats have both rods and cones, but only one type of cone, which can be either S-, M-, or L-cones. Like people with normal vision, they use their rods to see in dim light and their cones to see in bright light; but like rod monochromats, they entirely lack color vision. Different wavelengths appear to them as different shades of gray (see the prior section "If You Had Only One Type of Cone").

cone monochromacy A condition in which a person has rods and only one type of cone.

Dichromacy: Partial Color Blindness

More common, but still rare overall, are the three types of **dichromacy,** in which just one of the three types of cones is missing. As we saw in the section "If You Had Only Two Types of Cones," people with two types of cones can discriminate between colors that a rod monochromat would see as equivalent, but they would confuse some colors that a trichromat could tell apart. The three types of dichromacy and their frequency of occurrence are as follows:

- **Protanopia**—the person lacks L-cones; affects about 1% of males and 0.02% of females.
- **Deuteranopia**—the person lacks M-cones; affects about 1% of males and 0.01% of females.
- **Tritanopia**—the person lacks S-cones; affects about 0.002% of males and females.

Figure 5.22 shows three of the many test circles from the **Ishihara color vision test;** the full test can be used to determine whether someone has a color vision deficiency.

Most people with only two types of cones get along quite well; indeed, many dichromats are unaware of their condition. The differences between the subjective perceptual experiences of dichromats and trichromats are difficult to describe. To see why, imagine that you had four types of cones rather than three. You would look at a metameric color match produced by someone with normal trichromatic vision, and you would see the test patch and the

dichromacy A condition in which a person has only two types of cones, instead of the normal three; in all such cases, the person has a limited form of color vision but cannot discriminate as many colors as a person with all three cone types.

protanopia A condition in which a person has M-cones and S-cones but lacks L-cones.

deuteranopia A condition in which a person has L-cones and S-cones but lacks M-cones.

tritanopia A condition in which a person has L-cones and M-cones but lacks S-cones.

Ishihara color vision test A test using configurations of multicolored disks with embedded symbols; the symbols can be seen by people with normal color vision but not by people with particular color vision deficiencies.

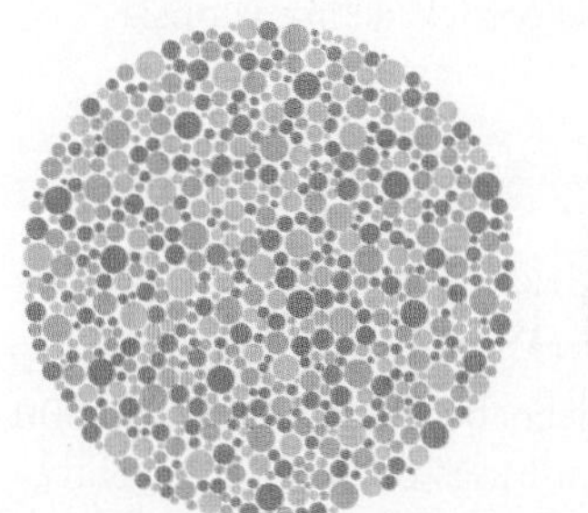
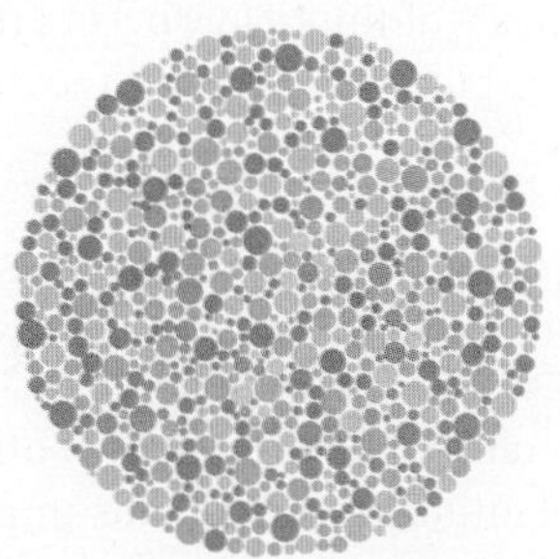
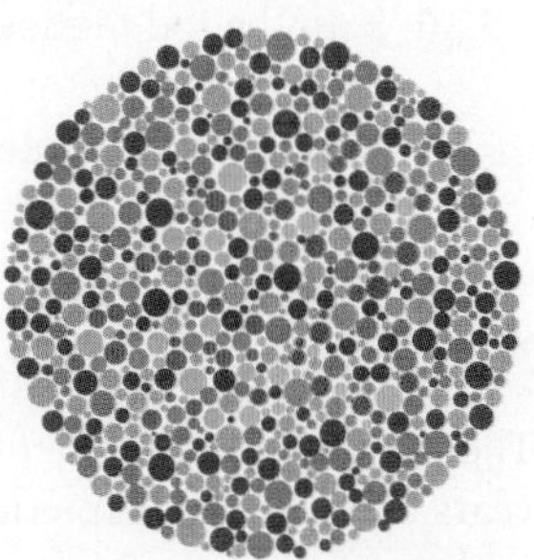

Figure 5.22 Ishihara Color Vision Test The full form of the Ishihara color vision test consists of two dozen or more color plates like these, in which the person being tested tries to detect a number. A person with a color vision deficiency may not be able to see the numbers in one or more of these plates. If you can't see an "8" in the plate on the left, you may have some form of protanopia (missing L-cones), since the "8" is formed of reddish-colored circles, and L-cones are particularly sensitive to long-wavelength (reddish) light. If you can't see a "15" in the middle plate you may have some form of deuteranopia (missing M-cones), since the "15" is formed of greenish-colored circles, and M-cones are particularly sensitive to middle-wavelength (greenish) light. In the plate on the right, containing the number "42," people with some form of protanopia may see just the "2," whereas people with some form of deuteranopia may see just the "4." [Ishihara, 2011]

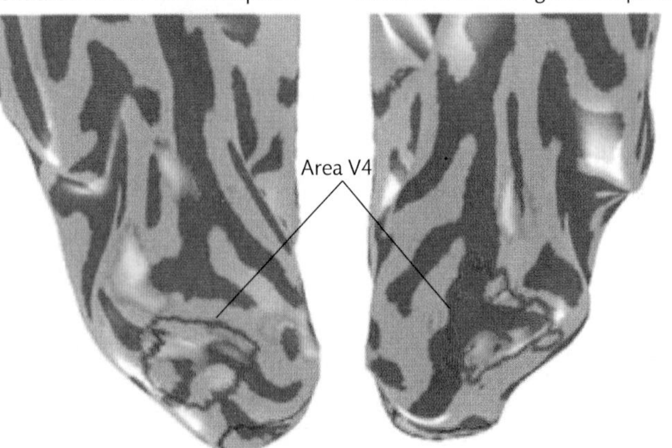

Figure 5.23 A Color Center in the Brain? Functional magnetic resonance imaging (fMRI) was used to produce scans of people's brains while they viewed either a color image like the one at top right or an otherwise identical grayscale image like the one at top left. The scans at the bottom show the ventral (bottom) surface of the left and right temporal and occipital lobes. The small yellow blobs represent the difference in activity when viewing color versus grayscale images. This suggests that area V4 and other regions play important roles in color vision. (Adapted from Wade et al., 2008.)

comparison patch as different in color. In other words, you would be able to see more colors than a trichromat. But how could you describe what those colors look like? And how would you describe the experience of red to a monochromat without using color words to do so?

Cortical Achromatopsia: Color Blindness from Brain Damage

achromatopsia Loss of color vision caused by brain damage.

Loss of color vision caused by injury to parts of the brain that are critical for representing color is called **achromatopsia,** and it occurs even less frequently than the inherited deficiencies discussed above. The vignette at the beginning of this chapter describes the case of P., whose injury included area V4, a part of the brain that is more active when people view color images than when they view black and white versions of the same images. As illustrated in Figure 5.23, researchers used fMRI to compare activity in the brains of people looking at multicolored patches to activity when they were looking at equally bright grayscale patches under otherwise identical conditions (Wade et al., 2008). Activity in several regions of the temporal and occipital lobes, including area V4, was greater when participants were looking at color patches, leading to the conclusion that these areas contribute to the perception of color. As discussed in Chapter 3, these areas are part of the ventral visual pathway—the "what" pathway—which represents information about the identity of objects, and color is certainly an important dimension of object identity.

Check Your Understanding

5.18 What are the two main kinds of monochromacy? How do they differ?

5.19 Describe the three types of dichromacy.

5.20 Both the rod monochromacy of Knut Nordby and the cortical achromatopsia of P. resulted in total color blindness. What is the difference in the way their conditions originated?

APPLICATIONS Color in Art and Technology

The use of natural pigments to reproduce the colors of objects began more than 30,000 years ago with the depiction of animals and humans in paintings on the walls of caves such as Chauvet and Lascaux in France. In more recent times, synthetic pigments have been developed to expand the range of colors in the paints and dyes used in fine art, mosaics, and tapestries, as well as in an enormous variety of manufactured goods. And the last few decades have seen the development of rapid and convenient methods for reproducing a wide range of colors in photographs taken using film, in printed materials, and in all forms of digital imaging.

Typically, artists mix paints and apply the mixtures to a canvas or other surface, and as we saw earlier in the chapter, these are subtractive color mixtures. In this section, we'll see how artists have also used paint to produce a kind of additive color mixtures, and we'll describe how color is produced by digital video displays using additive mixtures and by color printers using subtractive mixtures.

Pointillist Painting

In the late nineteenth century, pointillist artists such as Paul Signac and Georges Seurat began to experiment in their paintings with additive color mixtures. Rather than mixing pigments on a palette in correct proportion to create a desired paint color, these painters tried applying tiny flicks and dots of various colors close together on the canvas. The flicks and dots were supposed to blend together visually—if the viewer was standing far enough away—so that the light reflected from them would mix additively and the viewer would perceive the color represented by the mixture. For instance, an area on the canvas with an equal proportion of red dots and blue dots would be perceived as a rich purple. Figure 5.24 shows a painting by Seurat and a blowup of one part of the painting so you can clearly see the different colored flicks and dots.

One of the objectives in adopting this technique was to avoid the dimming effect of subtractive color mixtures, which are always less intense than the constituent pigments because of the subtraction of wavelengths (see Figure 5.5). In pointillist paintings, however, the brushstrokes don't really disappear—that is, from a comfortable viewing distance of two to three meters, the individual flicks and dots are clearly visible across most of the painting. The visual effect isn't true additive mixing but nevertheless results in a striking luminosity of a kind not previously achieved in painting.

Digital Color Video Displays

Digital color video displays such as digital television and computer screens use additive mixtures of three primary colors at each location on the screen to produce nearly the full gamut of colors you can see. They do this by taking advantage of the limited ability of the human eye to distinguish dots that are sufficiently small and close together (Wandell & Silverstein, 2003)—in a sense, these displays accomplish what the pointillist artists were trying to do.

The display screen of a digital color monitor consists of a large number of **pixels** (picture elements) arranged in a grid (see Figure 5.25a). For example, a display with a standard resolution of 1,024 × 768 is a grid 1,024 pixels wide by 768 pixels high, so that the display consists of a total of 1,024 × 768 = 786,432 pixels. As illustrated in Figure 5.25a, each pixel contains three subelements, which each emit light of a different primary color—red, green, or blue. As indicated in Figure 5.25b, the intensity of the light from each subelement can have any of 256 possible values (0–255). Each different combination of intensities from a pixel produces a different additive color mixture. Thus, the number of different colors that can be produced by each pixel is 256^3 = 256

pixels Picture elements in the display screen of a color monitor; a pixel consists of three subelements, each designed to emit the light of one of three primary colors—red, green, or blue.

Figure 5.24 Pointillist Painting George Seurat's *A Sunday Afternoon on the Island of the Grande Jatte* (1884/85) is an example of pointillism—building up objects and surfaces from thousands of tiny dots and flicks (points) of color. The magnification on the right shows a detail of the painting, which clearly reveals the dots and flicks.

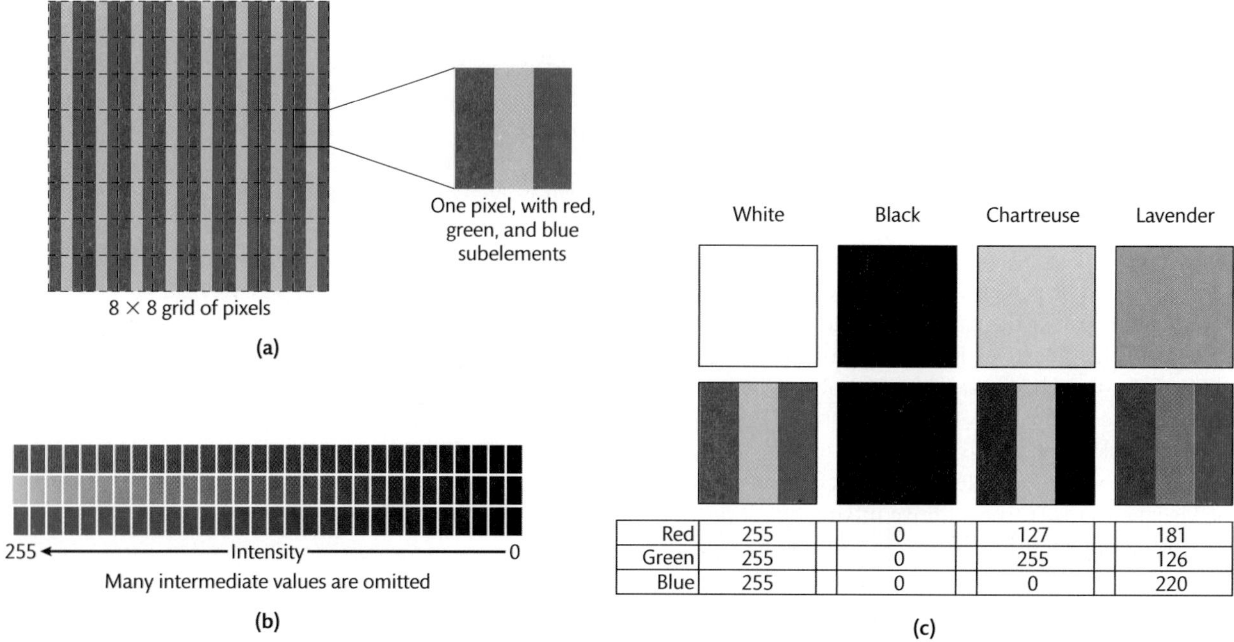

	White	Black	Chartreuse	Lavender
Red	255	0	127	181
Green	255	0	255	126
Blue	255	0	0	220

Figure 5.25 How a Computer Screen Creates Colors (a) The screen of a color monitor is a grid of pixels (picture elements). Each pixel consists of three subelements, each of which emits (nearly) monochromatic light of one primary color—red, green, or blue. The pixels are too small to be seen individually, so we perceive additive mixtures of the light emitted from them. (b) The intensity of the light emitted by each pixel can have any of 256 possible values, from 0 (no light) to 255 (maximum amount of light). (c) With every possible combination of light intensities from the three subelements, each pixel can produce $256^3 = 16{,}777{,}216$ different colors, four of which are shown here.

× 256 × 256 = 16,777,216. This is certainly greater than the number of colors we can actually distinguish as different.

At normal viewing distances, the pixels and their subelements cannot be seen individually by the human eye, and so the light from clusters of pixels blends together into additive color mixtures. If our visual systems were acute enough to see the individual subelements, current color monitors would not work—that is, we'd see a patchwork of red, green, and blue dots instead of additive color mixtures.

Digital Color Printing

Digital color printing is achieved by applying tiny droplets of different color inks to a material such as paper. In order to produce the desired patterns of color, the droplets must be applied precisely in the right locations and in layers with the right thickness (Wandell & Silverstein, 2003). Four ink colors are used: cyan, magenta, yellow, and black. As shown by the reflectance curves in Figure 5.26, the cyan ink mainly absorbs yellow and red light and mainly reflects blue and green; magenta ink mainly absorbs green and reflects blue and red; yellow ink absorbs blue and reflects green and red; and black ink absorbs all colors about equally. The thickness of the ink layer at each location determines how much of the light that ink absorbs: the thicker the layer, the more likely the ink is to absorb a photon of light in its absorption region.

When different inks are applied in layers one on top of the other, their subtractive effects combine. Suppose, for example, that a location is occupied by a thick cyan layer on top of a thin yellow layer. If a photon of red light strikes that location, it's not likely to be absorbed by the yellow layer, because yellow mainly reflects red, but it's especially likely to be absorbed by the thick cyan layer, because cyan mainly absorbs red and because the layer is thick; in contrast, a photon of green light will probably be reflected, because both cyan and yellow mainly reflect green. Given the known reflectance curves of the inks and

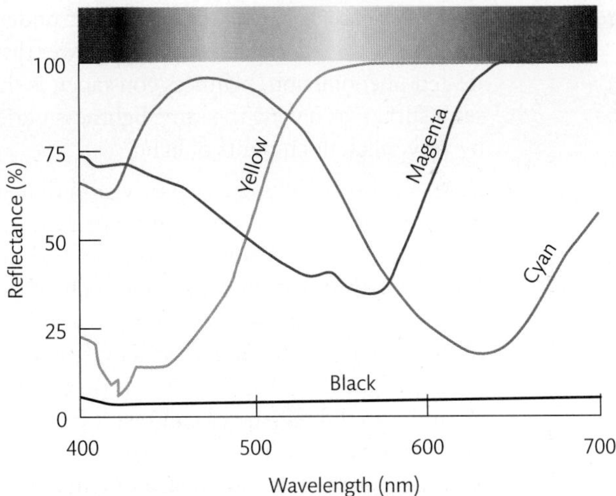

Figure 5.26 Reflectances of Inks Used in Digital Color Printing Four different inks are used in digital color printing: yellow, magenta, cyan, and black. Their reflectance curves show that each of the nonblack inks absorbs light in one of the three regions of the visible spectrum and reflects light in the other two regions: cyan absorbs long-wavelength red light, magenta absorbs medium-wavelength green light, and yellow absorbs short-wavelength blue light. Black absorbs all wavelengths about equally. (Adapted from Wandell & Silverstein, 2003, Figure 8.17.)

the known ways in which the thickness of the ink layers affects the probability that light of a given color will be absorbed or reflected, precise control of the placement and thickness of the ink droplets allows the printing of any desired color image.

If you're wondering why black ink is also used, given that shades of gray (including black) could be produced by thick overlapping layers of the other three inks to absorb light across the spectrum, the reason is economic: to avoid wasting ink. That is, it takes much less black ink to produce any desired shade of gray than it would take to combine the other three ink colors for the same effect.

Check Your Understanding

5.21 Why did pointillist painters often avoid letting the dots and flicks of different-colored paint overlap and mix together?

5.22 If you looked at a digital video display through a magnifying glass powerful enough to let you see the individual subelements in the pixels, what color light would you see being emitted by each subelement? Would these colors necessarily look equally bright?

5.23 Suppose a digital color printer is malfunctioning so that it applies yellow ink in thicker layers than it should. How would that affect the perceived color at a location where a layer of yellow ink overlies a layer of cyan ink?

SUMMARY

- Light and Color The intensity of light at each wavelength is called the light's *spectral power distribution*. Light can be heterochromatic, monochromatic, or achromatic (also called *white light*). The percentage of light reflected by a surface at each wavelength is called the *reflectance* of the surface.
- Dimensions of Color: Hue, Saturation, and Brightness The perception of color can be described by three dimensions: hue, saturation, and brightness. A color circle depicts the two dimensions of hue and saturation; a color solid also depicts brightness. The color of a mixture of substances (e.g., paints) is called a *subtractive color mixture* because the light reflected

from the mixture lacks all the wavelengths that are absorbed (subtracted) by any of the substances in the mixture. The color of a mixture of lights is called an *additive color mixture* because the mixture contains the sum of all the wavelengths that were present in the constituent lights. Pairs of colors that combine in equal proportion to yield a shade of gray are called *complementary colors*. Any three colors that can be combined in different proportions to yield a range of other colors are called *primary colors*.

- Color and the Visual System Two color representations work together in two stages to produce color perception. The first stage, trichromatic representation, involves three types of cones providing information about the wavelength composition of light. Metameric color-matching experiments provide psychophysical evidence that there are three types of cones. Physiological evidence for three types of cones comes from high-resolution images of the retina and from measuring how cones absorb different wavelengths of light. The second stage, opponent color representation, accounts for the fact that people tend to sort colors into four categories (red, green, yellow, and blue) and that these four basic colors consist of two pairs of "opposites," red–green and yellow–blue. Hue cancellation experiments provide psychophysical evidence for opponency. Physiological evidence for opponency comes from the identification of single neurons that respond to signals from the three cone types in an opponent fashion. Chromatic adaptation accounts for the opponent quality of color afterimages and is involved in color constancy, the tendency to see a surface as having the same color under illumination by lights with very different spectral power distributions. A related phenomenon, lightness constancy, is the tendency to see a surface as having the same lightness under illumination by very different amounts of light.
- Color Vision Deficiencies Color vision deficiencies can be inherited or can result from brain damage. Inherited deficiencies include monochromacies and dichromacies. Rod monochromacy and cone monochromacy result in total color blindness—everything is seen in shades of gray. In dichromacies, the person lacks just one of the three types of cones and has a limited form of color vision. Noninherited deficiencies can result from damage to parts of the brain involved in color vision, a condition known as *cortical achromatopsia*. Measurements of brain activity have identified area V4 as a region of the brain that may be important in color vision.
- Applications: Color in Art and Technology Pointillist artists applied tiny flick and dots of paint close together on the canvas to create additive color mixtures. Digital color video displays create additive color mixtures via a grid of tiny pixels, each of which consists of three subelements, each emitting red, blue, or green light at any of 256 possible intensities. Digital color printers produce subtractive color mixtures by applying tiny droplets of cyan, magenta, yellow, and black ink in precisely controlled locations and in layers with precisely controlled thickness.

KEY TERMS

achromatic light (or *white light*) (p. 155)
achromatopsia (p. 182)
additive color mixture (p. 159)
chromatic adaptation (p. 174)
color circle (p. 157)
color constancy (p. 176)
color solid (p. 157)
color vision (p. 154)
complementary colors (p. 160)
cone monochromacy (p. 181)
deuteranopia (p. 181)
dichromacy (p. 181)
heterochromatic light (p. 154)
hue (p. 156)
hue cancellation (p. 169)
Ishihara color vision test (p. 181)
lightness constancy (p. 178)
metamers (p. 161)
monochromacy (p. 180)
monochromatic light (p. 154)
photopigment bleaching (p. 174)
pixels (p. 183)
primary colors (p. 160)
principle of univariance (p. 163)
protanopia (p. 181)
rod monochromacy (p. 180)
saturation (p. 156)
spectral power distribution (SPD) (p. 154)
spectral reflectance (p. 155)
spectral sensitivity function (p. 163)
subtractive color mixture (p. 159)
tritanopia (p. 181)
visible spectrum (p. 154)
white light, *see* **achromatic light**.

EXPAND YOUR UNDERSTANDING

5.1 Suppose that a blueberry reflects 30% of the light below 450 nm and 0% above that—that is, it reflects blue light but no green, yellow, or red light. Draw the spectral power distribution of the light reflected from the surface of the blueberry when it's illuminated by a bright red light consisting entirely of wavelengths above 650 nm. What color will the blueberry appear to be under these conditions?

5.2 Suppose a person with only one type of cone is shown two monochromatic lights of different wavelengths but with the same physical intensity. Does the person, who is truly color-blind, necessarily see the two lights as identical? Why or why not?

5.3 If a perfectly achromatic (gray) light reflects off a perfectly white surface, the spectral power distribution curve of the reflected light will be a perfectly horizontal line. Describe a situation where a heterochromatic light (containing different amounts of light at different wavelengths, like the incandescent light in Figure 5.1) would reflect off a colored surface such that the spectral power distribution curve of the reflected light would still be a horizontal line. What color would the surface appear to have?

5.4 Suppose a vision scientist conducted a metameric color-matching experiment using these three monochromatic lights for producing the comparison patch: cyan, yellow, and red. Would the participant be able to match a fully saturated blue test patch? Why or why not? (Refer to Figure 5.7 in your answer.)

5.5 In a metameric color-matching experiment with a participant who has only L-cones, the test light is 500 nm with a fixed intensity of 5,000 photons/sec. The comparison light is 450 nm with an adjustable intensity. Assume that the sensitivity of L-cones to 450-nm light is 30% (i.e., L-cones absorb and transduce 30% of the photons of this light) and that their sensitivity to 500-nm light is 50%. At what intensity of the comparison light will the participant perceive a metameric color match with the test light?

5.6 Judging by Figure 5.14, there is only one wavelength at which a person would have to add equal amounts of yellow and red light to cancel out the perceived blueness and greenness, respectively, and only one wavelength at which a person would have to add equal amounts of blue and green light to cancel out the perceived yellowness and redness, respectively. Approximately what are those wavelengths?

5.7 You stare for several minutes at a large white screen illuminated with bright green light—that is, a light with maximal spectral power in the green range of the spectrum. Then you are shown a scene with many objects of various colors, illuminated with bright white light. How will chromatic adaptation affect your perception of the objects' colors?

5.8 Do you think a brain injury would be more likely to result in a color vision deficiency resembling monochromacy or dichromacy? Explain your answer.

READ MORE ABOUT IT

Gegenfurtner, K. R., & Sharpe, L. T. (Eds.). (1999). *Color vision: from genes to perception*. Cambridge, England: Cambridge University Press.

A collection of tutorial essays on a wide range of issues in color vision.

Minnaert, M. (1954). The nature of light and color in the open air. New York: Dover.

An engaging classic that explains everything from rainbows to iridescent oil slicks.

Solomon, S. G., & Lennie, P. (2007). The machinery of colour vision. *Nature Reviews Neuroscience, 8*, 276–286.

A brief, clearly written, and authoritative summary of color vision.

Francisco Diaz de Leon, *Town of Amecameca with Popocatepetl*, 1923. [© Christie's Images/Corbis.]

6

PERCEIVING DEPTH

Chapter Outline

Learning to See in 3-D

Sue Barry was born with strabismus: her eyes didn't point in the same direction, producing a double image. As a result, her visual system automatically suppressed the vision from one eye or the other at all times—not by closing one eye or the other, but by processing the neural signals from only one eye at a time. This meant that Sue was *stereoblind*, unable to experience the vivid sense of depth that occurs when the brain combines the slightly different retinal images in the two eyes into a single image. Of course, Sue was still able to judge the relative depths of objects, but only by using the types of cues available in flat photographs or paintings—for example, when a nearby object partially hides a more distant object—or the cues provided by the relative motions in her retinal image of objects at different distances when she moved past them. People with normal vision get a much richer sense of depth by combining the images in the two eyes.

For many years, Sue didn't realize that she was stereoblind, but after she grew up she decided to study neurobiology, and in her studies, she learned about stereopsis: depth perception based on combining the two retinal images. When she tried to see stereoscopic depth by looking into a View-Master, for example, she only saw flat images.

Eventually, Sue consulted an ophthalmologist, who gave her eyeglasses containing a prism in one lens to align the two retinal images. She had to practice overcoming the automatic suppression of one eye and then had to go through a series of exercises in fusing (combining) the images. After some time, she mastered the crucial technique, learning to look directly at a point in space with both eyes simultaneously.

One day she experienced something profoundly new and different: "I went back to my car and happened to glance at the steering wheel. It had 'popped out' from the dashboard." After that, she began to see stereoscopically more frequently: "I had no idea what I had been missing. . . . Ordinary things looked extraordinary. Light fixtures floated and water faucets stuck way out into space. . . . My first snowfall with my new vision was spectacular. I could see each snowflake in its own 3-D space. . . . I felt myself within the snowfall, not outside of it. This is true for the way I now perceive my surroundings in general. I feel myself within the 3-D space instead of outside, looking in."

To hit a tennis ball, drive a car, hand a friend a cup of coffee, and perform myriad other everyday tasks, we must rapidly and accurately perceive where things are in the 3-D space around us. The only visual information we have that enables us to do this is the information in the retinal images in the two eyes. The vertical and horizontal dimensions of 3-D space are explicitly represented in each retinal image: if the chair is to the left of the table and the wall clock is above the table, the retinal images show these relationships. But how can we obtain information from the retinal images about the third dimension of space, depth? For instance, how do we know that the chair is in front of the lamp? The fundamental goal of depth perception is to let us accurately perceive a 3-D world on the basis of two 2-D retinal images, one in each eye.

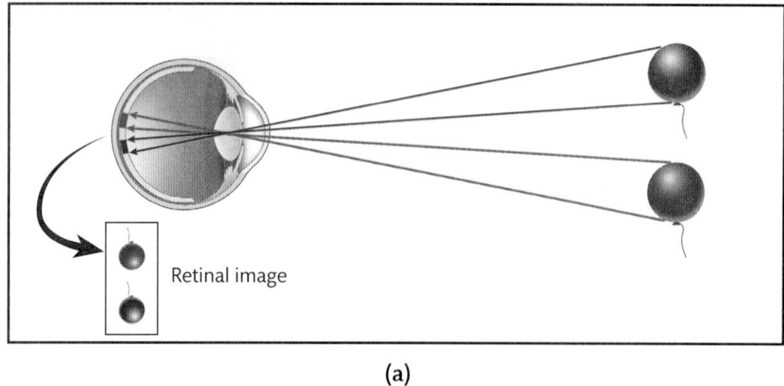

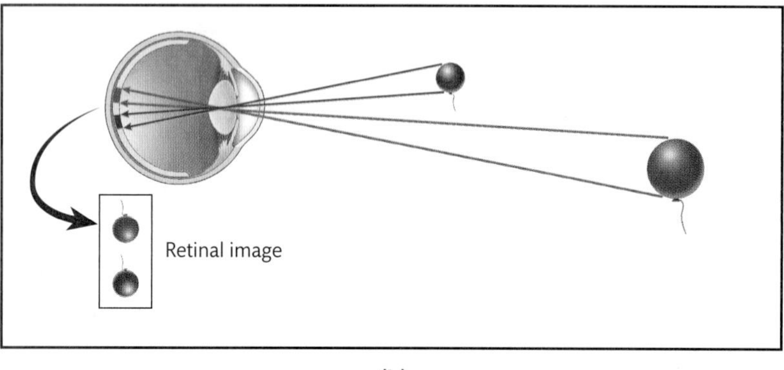

Figure 6.1 Different Scenes, Same Retinal Image (a) Two equal-size balloons at equal distance from an observer (here, viewed from the side) produce a retinal image in which the retinal images of the balloons are equal in size. (b) If one balloon is deflated to half its original size and moved twice as close to the observer along the line of sight, the two balloons produce the same retinal image.

Accomplishing this goal is a challenge because any given 2-D retinal image could be produced by an infinite variety of 3-D scenes. To understand why this is so, imagine you're looking at two balloons of the same size floating one above the other against a plain background, using just one eye, as illustrated in Figure 6.1a. If the red balloon were deflated to half its original size and moved toward you, along the line of sight, to half its original distance, your retinal image wouldn't change (see Figure 6.1b). In fact, no matter how the size of either balloon is changed, if it's moved correspondingly closer or farther away, your retinal image will remain unchanged. Clearly, there are an infinite number of ways to size and locate the balloons in 3-D space to produce the same 2-D retinal image.

In other words, the representation of 3-D space in the 2-D retinal image is *many-to-one*: many different 3-D scenes (in fact, an infinite variety of them) can produce one and the same retinal image. Figure 6.2 illustrates this in a different way, with objects of different shapes and sizes and at different distances that produce the same retinal image because of the way the objects are oriented. Taken together, these two figures illustrate not only the many-to-one relationship between 3-D scenes and the 2-D retinal image, but also the close connections between depth perception and our perception of size and shape.

Despite the inherent ambiguity in the retinal image, our visual system has evolved in a way that allows us to perceive the three dimensions of the real world with great accuracy. Depth perception is accomplished by using various properties of the retinal image as reliable (but not infallible) cues to depth. In addition, feedback from the muscles in and around our eyes also provides information about depth. Figure 6.3 shows the variety of depth cues that we use to determine the relative depths of the objects in a scene. Any given scene typically contains many of these cues, which usually provide redundant information and are combined effortlessly by the visual system to produce an accurate and unambiguous experience of depth. Just how all this works is the main topic of this chapter.

We'll begin by exploring the oculomotor cues, those based on feedback from the eye muscles. We'll then survey the rich variety of cues that the retinal image contains about depth, beginning with monocular cues—that is, cues that are available from the retinal

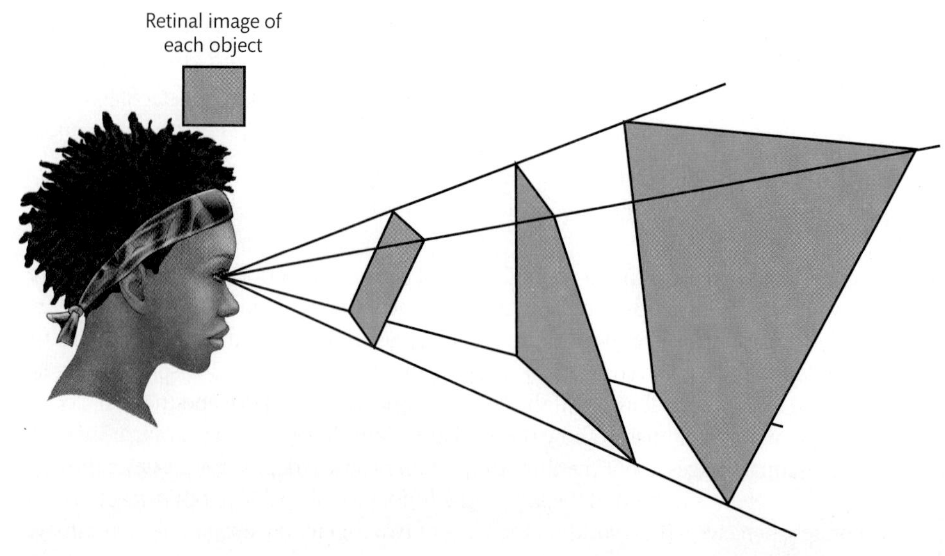

Figure 6.2 Different Objects, Same Retinal Image Three objects of very different shapes and sizes can produce identical retinal images if they are arranged appropriately in terms of distance and orientation.

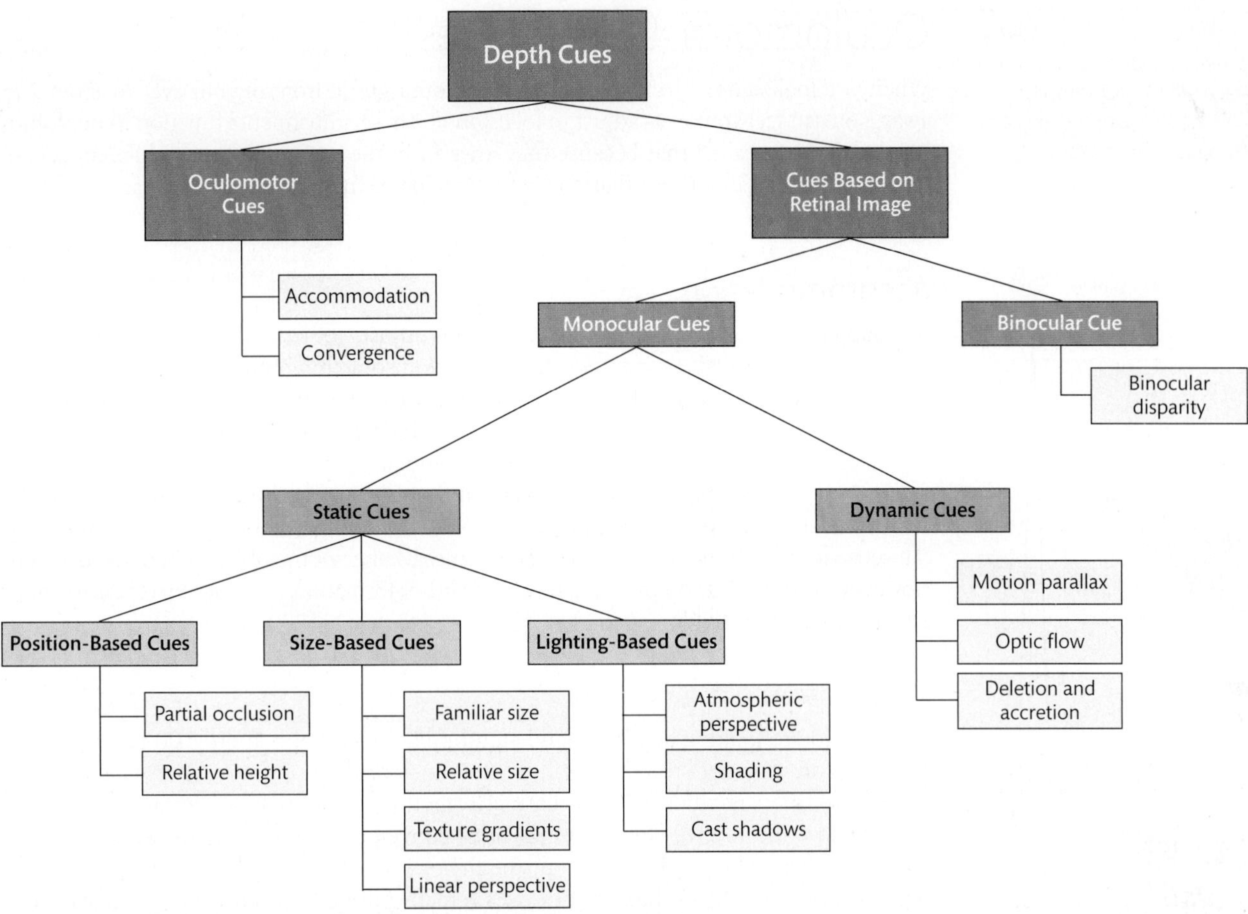

Figure 6.3 Depth Cues We perceive depth based on integrating information gained from a wide variety of cues. Oculomotor cues provide information from the muscles that move the eyes and the muscles that change the shape of the lens. All the other depth cues are contained in the retinal image. Binocular disparity provides information derived from the differences in the retinal images in the two eyes. The monocular cues, which provide information that could be derived from the retinal image in just one eye, can be broadly divided into static cues (like the cues we could get from a still photo) and dynamic cues, based on relative motion within the retinal image.

image in just one eye. The monocular cues are divided into static cues, which don't depend on movement, and dynamic cues, which do involve movement.

Then we'll consider binocular disparity, the depth cue based on the slightly different retinal images in our two eyes. Our visual system processes this difference in a way that gives us a rich and vivid sense of depth. In this context, we'll consider the correspondence problem—how do we match up the features and objects in the two slightly different retinal images?

Next we'll investigate how people integrate depth cues—how the cues work together to give us a single, accurate representation of depth in the visual scene. And we'll follow this by exploring the relationships between depth perception and the perception of size and shape. We'll see that, as in most aspects of perception, unconscious assumptions about what's most simple, natural, and probable play a large role in how we perceive depth, size, and shape in real-world scenes and situations.

We'll end with a look at some striking visual illusions, which occur when usually reliable cues produce inaccurate perceptions of depth, size, and shape. Most real-world scenes contain many depth cues that are highly redundant, all pointing to the same solution to the many-to-one problem of depth perception. But if two or more depth cues are in conflict, the visual system has to find a way to resolve the conflict—and that can lead to misperceptions. Illusions of depth, size, and shape can help us figure out which cues tend to dominate under which conditions and how the visual system combines cues when depth information is ambiguous.

Oculomotor Depth Cues

oculomotor depth cues Cues that are based on feedback from the oculomotor muscles controlling the shape of the lens and the position of the eyes.

When you look at an object that is anywhere from right in front of your eyes to about 2 m away, you can feel your eyes adjust to focus on it. These adjustments function as **oculomotor depth cues**, called that because they arise from the workings of two different sets of oculomotor muscles—those that control the shape of the lens and those that control the position of the eyes.

Accommodation

In Chapter 2, we saw how the shape of the lens adjusts to focus an image sharply on the retina, a process called *accommodation*. To focus on something more than a few feet away, you need a relatively flat lens, so the ciliary muscles relax; to focus on something closer, you need a more rounded lens, so the ciliary muscles contract (see Figure 2.12). Of course, this takes place very rapidly and completely involuntarily—your autonomic nervous system determines the lens shape needed to bring what you're looking at into focus and adjusts the ciliary muscles appropriately. Despite the involuntary nature of this muscular reaction, you can sense it and use the sensation as a cue to the distance of the object you're focusing on. However, accommodation provides reliable depth information only for objects up to about 2 m away (Wallach & Floor, 1971).

Convergence

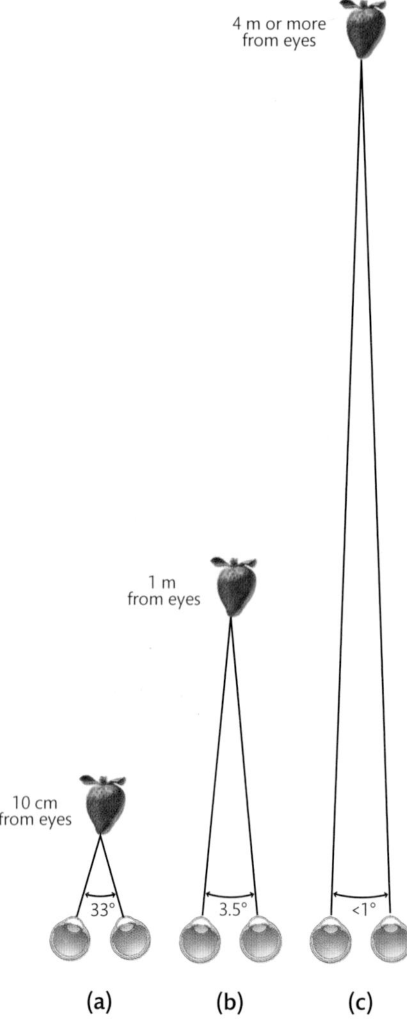

Figure 6.4 Convergence (a) Your eyes must converge (or "cross") to focus on an object 10 cm away, and you can feel your eye muscles working to form the required angle between the lines of gaze. (b) For an object 1 m away, a smaller angle is required, and the feedback from your eye muscles is much less noticeable. (c) Focusing on objects at a distance of 4 m (or more) requires virtually no convergence. (Not drawn to scale.)

Suppose you're looking at your friend standing across a field, about 100 m away. Both your eyes are pointed straight ahead, so the lines of gaze of your two eyes are almost parallel, as they are whenever you look at something more than a few meters away. As your friend walks toward you, your eyes must converge (turn inward, toward each other) in order to keep her face in focus. For the first 98 or 99 m, this convergence is so small as to be imperceptible—that is, your eyes remain pointed virtually straight ahead. But when your friend is within a meter or two, you begin to feel tension in the muscles that move your eyes, tension that serves as a cue to her decreasing distance. If she gets closer than about 10 cm, and you keep your eyes focused on the tip of her nose, your eyes become noticeably "crossed" and the feeling of tension in your eyes increases markedly.

As you can see from Figure 6.4, the angle formed between the lines of gaze of the two eyes decreases as the distance increases. For an object 10 cm away, the angle between the lines of gaze is about 33°; for an object 1 m away, it's about 3.5°. For objects more than about 2 m away, the convergence angle changes very little with increasing distance, which is why convergence is not a very significant depth cue beyond 2 m (Howard & Rogers, 2002; Wallach & Floor, 1971). Thus, convergence, like accommodation, can serve as a depth cue only over a fairly short distance in front of your eyes.

Check Your Understanding

6.1 What does "oculomotor" refer to in the term *oculomotor depth cues*?

6.2 In the process of accommodation, how does the shape of the lens change when you switch from looking at a near object to looking at a far object?

6.3 Why does convergence work as a depth cue only when you're looking at objects closer than about 2 m?

Monocular Depth Cues

monocular depth cues Cues that are based on the retinal image and that provide information about depth even with only one eye open.

Depth cues based on information in the retinal image are far more important than the oculomotor cues because they operate across a much greater range of distances. The **monocular depth cues** give you information about depth even when you're looking with only one eye (*mono*, meaning "one"; *ocular*, meaning "eye"). First we'll consider the static monocular cues—sometimes called *pictorial* cues—which are those that we see in motionless 2-D depictions of 3-D scenes, as in paintings and photographs (and, of course, in real scenes too). Then we'll consider the dynamic monocular cues, which involve motion; these provide information about depth when, for example, you're walking through a forest or watching a movie.

static monocular depth cues Cues that provide information about depth on the basis of the position of objects in the retinal image, the size of the retinal image, and the effects of lighting in the retinal image.

partial occlusion (or *interposition*) A position-based depth cue—in scenes where one object partially hides (occludes) another object, the occlusion indicates that the former is closer than the latter.

Static Cues: Position, Size, and Lighting in the Retinal Image

When you look at a photograph or a realistic painting, it's easy to judge the relative depth of the objects in the scene, despite the fact that the photographs and paintings are flat. For example, if one object is partially hidden by another, you know immediately that the partially hidden object is farther away than the one that is hiding it. This and other cues are the **static monocular depth cues**, which let you perceive depth on the basis of the position of objects in the retinal image, the size of their retinal images, and the effects of lighting in the retinal image.

Position in the Retinal Image

Two very important static depth cues are based on the position of objects in the retinal image. The first, partial occlusion, works because almost all objects are opaque. The second, relative height, lets us infer depth from the position of objects in relation to the horizon or eye level.

Partial Occlusion The scene in Figure 6.5 contains many cues to the relative depth of the objects in it. Perhaps the most powerful of these cues is **partial occlusion** (or *interposition*), where one object partially hides (occludes) another. In the figure, the fact that the umbrella partially occludes a building clearly indicates that the umbrella is in front of the building. We know that the woman must be between the briefcase and the taxi because the woman partially occludes the taxi, and the briefcase partially occludes the woman's foot. The many occlusion relations in the scene provide rich information about the relative depths of the objects.

A scene like the one in Figure 6.5 makes the cue of partial occlusion look obvious, as if it requires no explanation. In fact, however, the perception of relative depth on the basis of partial occlusion requires assumptions of which we are mostly unconscious—assumptions about the nature of the objects in a scene and assumptions about how those objects are arranged in 3-D space. Figure 6.6 illustrates some of these assumptions.

The most natural interpretation of Figure 6.6a is that a red rectangle is in front of and partly occluding a blue rectangle. Under this interpretation, if the red rectangle were moved out of the way, you would see both rectangles in full. The key features that lead to this interpretation are the intersections between the edges of the two objects, called *T-junctions* (see Figure 6.6b): the edge of the blue rectangle aligned with the stem of the T seems to continue behind the edge of the red rectangle aligned with the top of the T, as indicated by the dashed blue lines (Kellman & Shipley, 1991).

Figure 6.5 Partial Occlusion Partial occlusion is an extremely common and reliable depth cue; here, it tells us that the umbrella is in front of the building, and the woman is between the briefcase and the taxi. [Michael N. Paras/age footstock]

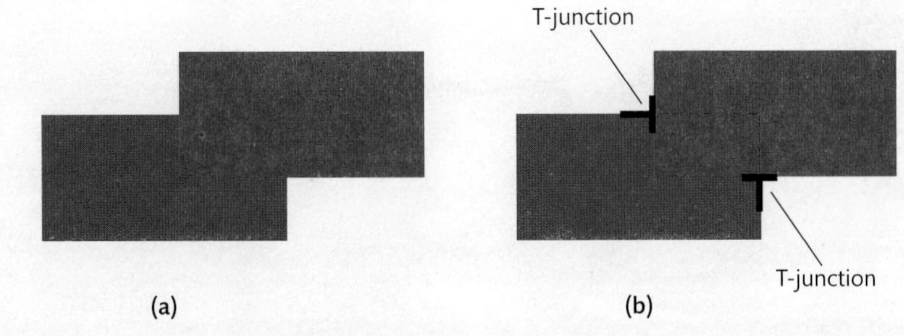

Figure 6.6 Accidental Alignment Versus Partial Occlusion (a) Our natural interpretation of this retinal image is that a red rectangle is partially occluding a more distant blue rectangle. (b) The T-junctions imply that the edges of the blue rectangle (indicated by dashed lines) continue behind the red rectangle. Under this interpretation, if the red rectangle were moved up, you would see two complete rectangles. Another possible interpretation is that a red rectangle appears to fit exactly into a notch in the blue shape; if the red rectangle were moved up, you would see that the blue shape isn't a rectangle. This isn't the usual interpretation because it requires a highly unlikely accidental alignment of the two shapes and your viewpoint.

Why is this the most likely interpretation? One explanation is that any other interpretation would require a highly unlikely accidental alignment of the shapes with your line of sight. For example, the retinal image in Figure 6.6a could be interpreted as a red rectangle next to a blue shape with one corner cut out. However, for this interpretation to be true, the shapes would have to be perfectly positioned so that the edges of the red rectangle exactly match up with the missing corner of the blue shape. Given how unlikely this is, we unconsciously assume that the hidden part of the blue shape is a simple continuation of the visible part. This is another instance of the principle of simplicity in figure–ground organization that we discussed in Chapter 4 (see, e.g., Figure 4.16).

If we now go back to Figure 6.5, we can see some of the assumptions we were making when we looked at that photo. We assumed, for example, that the part of the building occluded by the umbrella was actually there, not that there was an umbrella-shaped hole in the building—with the umbrella behind the building but viewed through the hole. We also assumed that the taxi was a whole, normally shaped automobile.

These examples show that the basic assumption we make when perceiving depth on the basis of partial occlusion is that the objects in a scene and their arrangement with respect to each other and the observer are as simple and natural as possible. You can appreciate the power of partial occlusion by noting that this cue is used by artists in virtually all cases where they want to show objects at different depths (Cutting & Vishton, 1995).

Relative Height Look straight across the room you're sitting in, at a point on the far wall that's at eye level. The bases of objects resting on the part of the floor close to you are lower in your retinal image than the bases of objects resting on the part of the floor close to the wall; the reverse is true for the ceiling (or for objects on the ceiling, such as light fixtures), with the area of the ceiling closer to you being higher in the image than the area farther from you. This type of scene is shown in Figure 6.7.

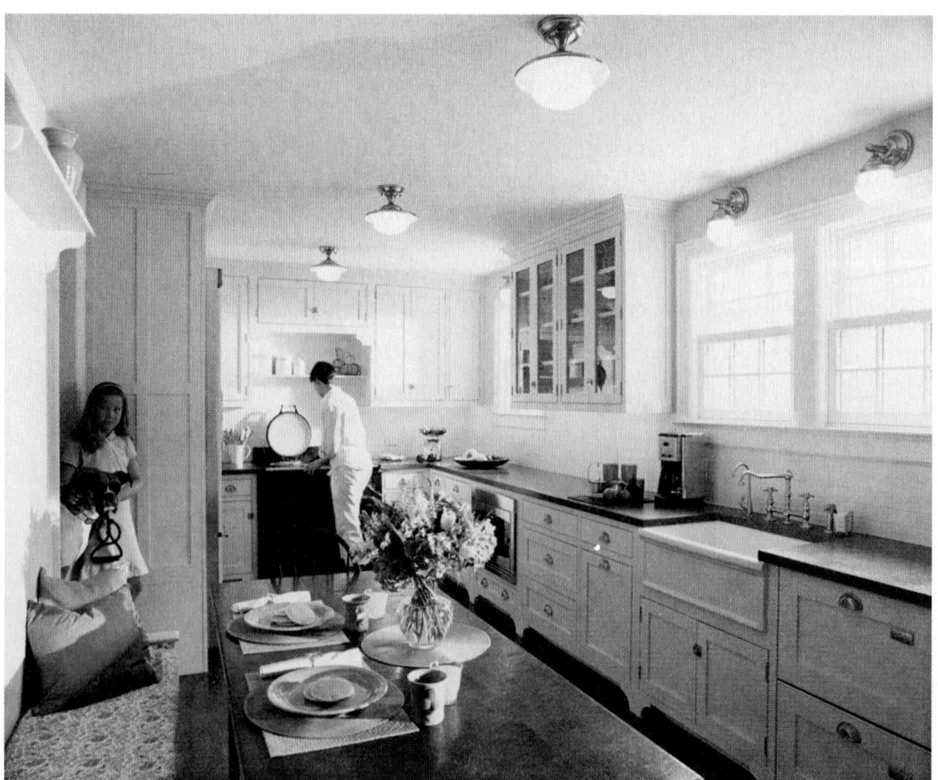

Figure 6.7 Relative Height in the Retinal Image For objects on the floor or on the table or countertop, the lower the base of the object is in the retinal image, the closer the object is to the observer. For objects on the ceiling, the reverse is true—the higher the base of the object is in the retinal image, the closer the object is to the observer. [William Geddes/Beateworks/Corbis]

This example illustrates a general principle: the **relative height** of the objects in the retinal image with respect to the horizon—or with respect to eye level if there is no visible horizon—provides information about the objects' relative distance from the observer (Ooi et al., 2001; Euclid made this observation in his *Optics* [Burton, 1945; Howard & Rogers, 2002]). Below the horizon or below eye level, objects situated lower in the image are closer to the observer; above the horizon or above eye level, objects higher in the image are closer to the observer.

relative height A position-based depth cue—the relative height of the objects in the retinal image with respect to the horizon—or with respect to eye level if there is no visible horizon—provides information about the objects' relative distance from the observer.

The power of this depth cue is indicated by the fact that relative height in the retinal image affects depth perception even in scenes where there is no visible floor or ceiling. For example, people who are shown two isolated lights above eye level in a pitch dark room perceive the one closer to eye level as farther away (Kilpatrick, 1952).

Size in the Retinal Image

If you hold this book with the center of the front cover touching your nose, its retinal image fills nearly your entire field of view. If the book is propped against the wall on the other side of the room, its retinal image is much smaller. This illustrates the **size–distance relation**: the farther away an object is from the observer, the smaller is its retinal image (Burton, 1945; Ittelson, 1951).

size-distance relation The farther away an object is from the observer, the smaller is its retinal image.

Figure 6.8 illustrates the size–distance relation in the case of a tree positioned at two distances from the eye. The retinal image size of an object can be measured in terms of its **visual angle**, the angle subtended (occupied) by the object in the visual field. As you can see from the figure, the size–distance relation is exact—the size of the retinal image decreases in the same proportion as the distance to the object increases.

visual angle The angle subtended by an object in the field of view.

Scenes in which the size–distance relation is apparent are said to contain the depth cue of **size perspective**, which simply refers to this regular decrease in the retinal image size of objects as their distance from the observer increases. Most natural scenes, as well as many artworks, exhibit this cue in its various aspects, as we'll see in this section.

size perspective A depth cue in scenes in which the size-distance relation is apparent.

Familiar Size We all have a sense of the retinal image size of a person of average height standing across the room, say, 4 m away. Now imagine you're an astronaut out for a space walk with your astronaut friend Phoebe. You see Phoebe floating in space against a black

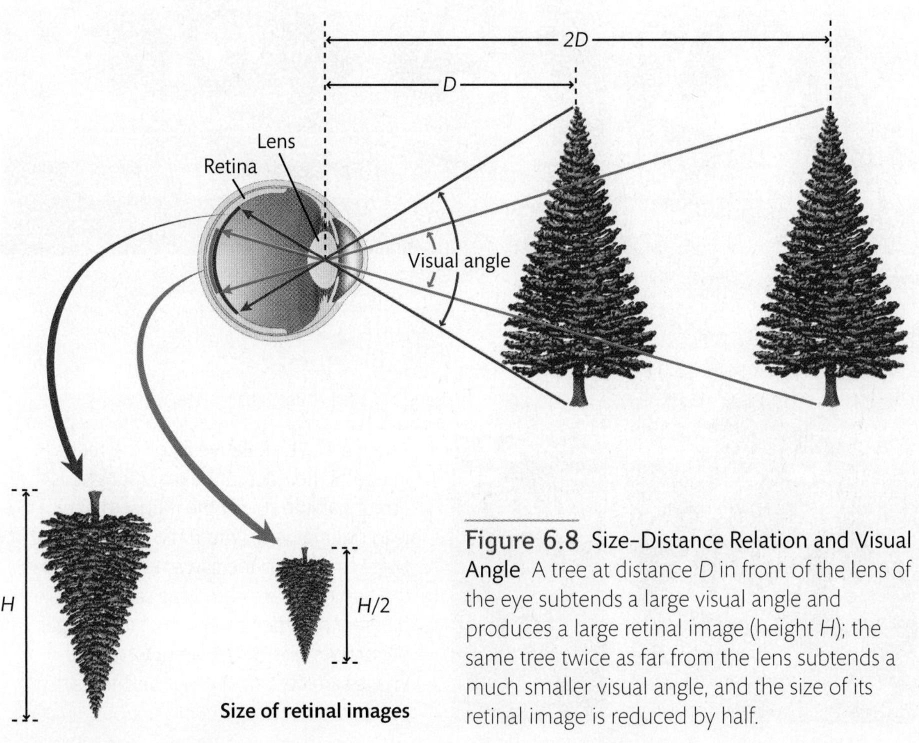

Figure 6.8 Size-Distance Relation and Visual Angle A tree at distance *D* in front of the lens of the eye subtends a large visual angle and produces a large retinal image (height *H*); the same tree twice as far from the lens subtends a much smaller visual angle, and the size of its retinal image is reduced by half.

familiar size A size-based depth cue—knowing the retinal image size of a familiar object at a familiar distance lets us use its retinal image size to gauge its distance.

relative size A size-based depth cue—under the assumption that two or more objects are about the same size, the relative size of their retinal images can be used to judge their relative distances.

background spotted with stars. Nothing else is visible, so the only cue you have as to Phoebe's distance from you is the size of her retinal image. If her retinal image is about half as big as the familiar-size retinal image of a person standing 4 m away, then the size–distance relation tells you that Phoebe is about 8 m away. This is the depth cue of **familiar size**—knowing the retinal image size of a familiar object at a familiar distance lets us use its retinal image size at an unknown distance to gauge that distance (Ittelson, 1951).

Figure 6.9 illustrates the depth cue of familiar size in a more everyday context than a space walk. Golf balls, baseballs, and basketballs are familiar objects whose sizes we know quite well—a golf ball is small, a baseball is medium-size, and a basketball is large. If their retinal images are all the same size, as they are in the figure, then we know that the golf ball must be closer than the baseball, which is closer than the basketball. However, if you'd never seen a golf ball, baseball, or basketball and didn't know their relative sizes, you'd have trouble judging their distances based on retinal size alone.

Relative Size If we assume that two or more objects are all about the same size, we can use the **relative size** of their retinal images to judge their relative distances (Ittelson, 1951). For example, adult humans tend to be approximately the same height, so if one person in a scene has a retinal image size that is half that of another person, then it is usually safe to conclude that the first person is about twice as far away as the other person. In Figure 6.10, for instance, you could use a ruler to measure the heights of the images and determine that the rider in the rear is about twice as far from the observer as the lead rider.

Note the difference between the depth cues of familiar size and relative size: the cue of familiar size is based on our familiarity with the retinal image size of objects with known sizes at known distances, whereas the cue of relative size requires only that we assume

Retinal image

Figure 6.9 Familiar Size If you're familiar with the relative sizes of a golf ball (small), a baseball (bigger), and a basketball (even bigger), then in a situation where all three produce retinal images of the same size, you know that the golf ball is closer than the baseball and that the baseball is closer than the basketball.

Figure 6.10 Relative Size The retinal image of the rider in the rear (at right) is about half the size of the retinal image of the lead rider (at left), who must, therefore, be twice as close to the camera—if we assume the two riders are about the same size. This difference in the actual size of the images becomes strikingly apparent when the images are cut out and put next to each other. [Christof Koepsel/Bongarts/Getty Images]

Figure 6.11 **Texture Gradients** A surface with repeated elements—such as a stone lakeshore, a rippled sand dune, or the heads and torsos of people in a crowd—forms a texture that projects a retinal image in which the apparent size of the texture elements (and the distance between them) decreases as distance from the observer increases, giving a strong impression of depth. [clockwise from left: Connie Ricca/Corbis; moodboard/Corbis; Spencer Platt/Getty Images]

objects are of approximately equal size but doesn't require that the objects be familiar. Thus, in Figure 6.10, if the racers were alien beings of unknown size riding alien bikes on an alien track on another planet, and if we assumed that all the aliens were approximately equal in size, we would still know which rider was twice as far away as the leader.

Texture Gradients Many surfaces have a visible texture, either because of variations in the structure of the surface (e.g., the rough texture of tree bark) or because the surface is composed of repeated elements (e.g., the texture created by stones in a dry riverbed, grains of sand, blades of grass, etc.). Typically, the surface variations or repeated elements are fairly regular in size and spacing. The retinal image size of these equal-size features decreases as their distance increases (another example of the size–distance relation), producing a **texture gradient** that serves as a cue to depth, as in Figure 6.11. This is a special case of the relative size cue described in the last section: on the assumption that the texture elements are all about the same size, we can conclude that the decrease in their retinal image size must be due to their increasing distance (Gibson, 1950b; Rosenholtz & Malik, 1997).

texture gradient A size-based depth cue—if surface variations or repeated elements of a surface are fairly regular in size and spacing, the retinal image size of these equal-size features decreases as their distance increases.

Linear Perspective Parallel lines appear to converge as they recede in depth. This well-known visual phenomenon functions as a depth cue known as **linear perspective**. Consider, for example, the images in Figure 6.12. In each, lines that are parallel in the world appear to converge in the image (e.g., the edges of the crop rows or the walkway receding into the distance). The reason for this apparent convergence is that a fixed distance (e.g., the fixed distance between the walkway edges) projects a smaller and smaller retinal image as it recedes from the observer (Burton, 1945; Clark et al., 1955).

linear perspective A size-based depth cue—parallel lines appear to converge as they recede in depth.

Figure 6.12 **Linear Perspective** In both these images, lines that are parallel and receding in the scene converge in the image, providing a compelling cue to depth. (Note that these images also illustrate texture gradients.) [left: David Frazier/Corbis; right: Francesco Borromini, Perspective Gallery. Palazzo Spada, Rome, Italy. Scala/Art Resource, NY.]

Lighting in the Retinal Image

In this section, we'll discuss three lighting effects that function as depth cues: atmospheric perspective, shading, and cast shadows.

atmospheric perspective A lighting-based depth cue—the farther away an object is, the more air the light must pass through to reach us and the more that light can be scattered, with the result that distant objects appear less distinct than nearby objects.

Atmospheric Perspective Air can hold moisture, smoke, pollen, and other particles, all of which can scatter light in a way that gives us cues about depth. This effect is called **atmospheric perspective**—the farther away an object is, the more air the light must pass through to reach us, and the more that light can be scattered. The result is that distant objects appear less distinct than nearby objects. Distant objects also can appear more bluish (see Figure 6.13, top and bottom left), because atmospheric haze tends to scatter short-wavelength blue light more than other wavelengths. When the air is very clear and dry, as it can be in the mountains in winter, atmospheric perspective can be nearly absent (see Figure 6.13, bottom right).

Shading Light falls on curved surfaces in ways that give rise to shading differences, because some parts of the surface are illuminated more directly than others. Such shading gives us information about the relative depth and orientation of the different parts of the surface (Todd & Mingolla, 1983). Figure 6.14 illustrates this with the curved surfaces of Greta Garbo's face: the shading gradient on her right cheek—the way that the shadow increases in darkness from the front of the cheek to the back—tells us that the cheek is receding in depth.

Again, unconscious assumptions play a role in how we interpret this depth cue. One such assumption is that just one primary light source is illuminating the surface and that the light source is above the scene, as the sun would be. Consider Figure 6.15, for example. If you assume that the light is coming from above, you'll see the light-colored regions in

Figure 6.13 Atmospheric Perspective Moisture and particles in the air scatter light, which makes objects appear increasingly hazy with distance, as in the photo at top. Artists routinely use atmospheric perspective to convey a sense of depth, as in the painting at bottom left (*Journey of a Lifetime*, by Richard Boyer; used with permission). The photo at bottom right shows that atmospheric perspective can be nearly absent when the air is very clear and dry. [top: Steven Yantis; bottom left: Courtesy of Richard Boyer; bottom right: iStockphoto/Thinkstock.]

Figure 6.14 Shading: Greta Garbo On a smoothly curved unblemished surface, shading conveys subtle changes in depth and surface orientation. [Clarence Sinclair Bull/Hulton Archive/Getty Images]

Figure 6.15 Ambiguous Shading Our "natural" assumption is that light comes from above, like the sun. This makes us see the light-colored regions in this woodcarving as standing out from the background, forming an array of meaningless shapes. If you turn the book upside down and view the photo with the light coming from the opposite direction, you'll interpret the image very differently. [From WALTER WICK'S OPTICAL TRICKS. Scholastic Inc./Cartwheel Books. Copyright © 1998 by Walter Wick. Used by permission.]

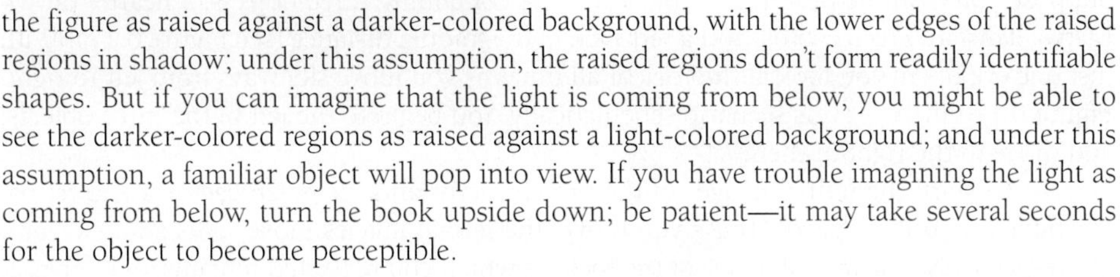

the figure as raised against a darker-colored background, with the lower edges of the raised regions in shadow; under this assumption, the raised regions don't form readily identifiable shapes. But if you can imagine that the light is coming from below, you might be able to see the darker-colored regions as raised against a light-colored background; and under this assumption, a familiar object will pop into view. If you have trouble imagining the light as coming from below, turn the book upside down; be patient—it may take several seconds for the object to become perceptible.

Cast Shadows Depth can also be signaled by the shadows cast by objects (Kersten et al., 1997). In Figure 6.16a, note how relative height indicates that the running woman is farther away than the standing man. In Figure 6.16b, the cast shadows show that the woman and the man are at the same distance and that the woman is above the ground, so relative height isn't a reliable cue.

Dynamic Cues: Movement in the Retinal Image

As you move through a scene, you see it from a constantly changing viewpoint. The changes in viewpoint result in changes in the positions of the objects in the retinal image relative to each other. These changes provide information about the layout of the objects in the scene, including their relative depths. Filmmakers, particularly animators, often introduce such motion-based depth cues to enhance the 3-D feeling of their work. For example, the classic animated Disney film *Bambi* begins with the camera panning through the forest just

(a)

(b)

Figure 6.16 Cast Shadows (a) Relative height makes it look like the running woman is at a greater distance than the standing man. (b) Cast shadows show that the running woman is at the same distance as the standing man, but she's above the ground, so relative height is misleading.

before dawn. During the pan, the nearby trees move across the screen more quickly than the trees farther away. As the nearby trees move across your field of vision, they cover and then uncover more distant parts of the forest. Later in the scene, as the camera zooms in on the small clearing where Bambi's mother has just given birth to him, the trees at the edges of the screen disappear off the screen. Overall, the depth effect from motion is extremely compelling, and the scene vividly illustrates all three types of dynamic (motion-based) cues we'll consider in this section: motion parallax, optic flow, and deletion and accretion.

The discussions in this section will be simpler if we assume that an observer is moving through a scene and that the objects in the scene are stationary or—in the case of deletion and accretion—that the observer is stationary and an object is moving. Nevertheless, you should understand that the visual effects and the depth cues would be the same—although geometrically more complex—if *both* the observer and some of the objects in the scene were moving.

Motion Parallax

Suppose you're in the desert, looking at a scene containing three objects: a nearby brown cactus, a distant green cactus, and a red rock in the middle distance (see Figure 6.17). With just one eye open, you look at the rock at all times as you move sideways from left to right. Figure 6.17 illustrates this scenario schematically. You begin to the left of the three objects, and move to the right of them.

At the start, the retinal images of the brown cactus and the green cactus are at retinal locations A and B, respectively. As you move, the retinal images move to locations C′ and D′, respectively. The retinal image of the rock on which you're fixated remains, of course, at

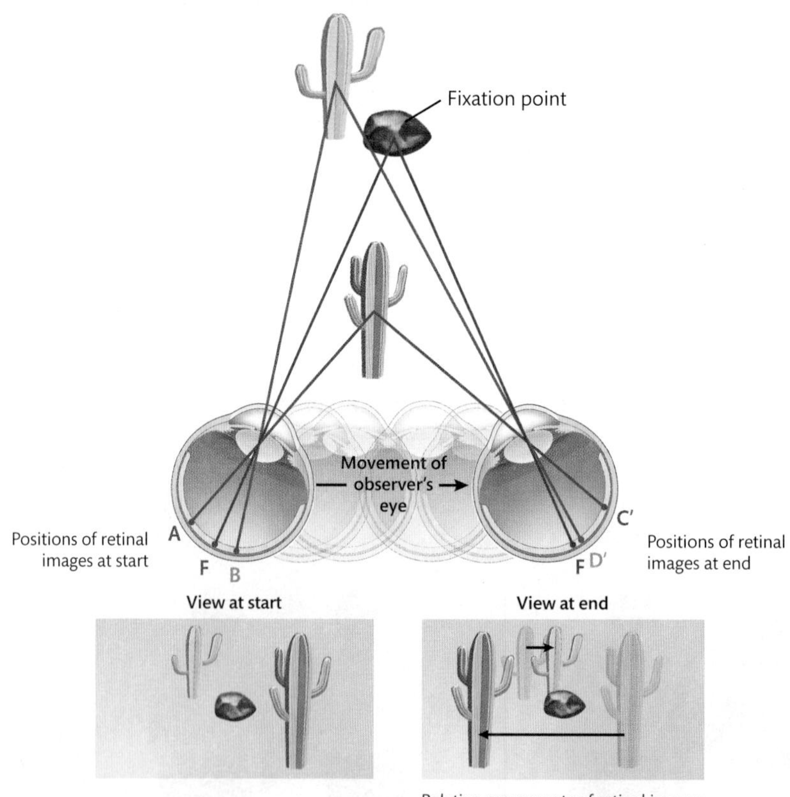

Figure 6.17 Motion Parallax With just one eye open, you move sideways across a desert landscape containing two cacti and a red rock, keeping your eye fixed on the rock. The green cactus is closer to the rock than is the brown cactus, so its retinal image moves a shorter distance (from point B to point D′), and therefore more slowly, than the retinal image of the brown cactus (from point A to point C′). The relative motion of the brown cactus (nearer to you than the rock) is to the left, opposite to your direction of motion; while the relative motion of the green cactus (farther from you than the rock) is to the right, in the same direction as you're moving. These differences in the speed and direction of motion of objects closer to or farther from the fixation point provide the depth cue of motion parallax.

retinal location F, the fovea. As you can see from the figure, the retinal image of the brown cactus moves a greater distance than that of the green cactus. Since the movements of both retinal images occur over the same period of time, the speed of the green cactus's retinal image must be less than that of the brown cactus's, because the green cactus's retinal image moves a shorter distance. Also, the brown cactus (closer than your fixation point) appears to move opposite to your direction of motion, while the green cactus (more distant than your fixation point) appears to move in the same direction as your direction of motion. In general, then, the farther an object is from the fixation point, the farther and faster will be its relative motion across the scene in the retinal image. Objects closer than the fixation point will move in a direction opposite to the observer's direction of motion; objects farther than the fixation point will move in the same direction as the observer's direction of motion. These differences in the speed and direction with which objects appear to move in the retinal image as you move within a scene provide the depth cue of **motion parallax** (Dees, 1966; Rogers & Graham, 1979).

motion parallax A dynamic depth cue—the difference in the speed and direction with which objects appear to move in the retinal image as an observer moves within a scene.

Optic Flow

The form of motion parallax we've just described comes into play when you observe a scene as you move across it. Now let's consider a form of motion parallax called **optic flow**, referring to the relative motions of objects and surfaces in the retinal image as you move forward or backward through the scene (Gibson et al., 1955; Simpson, 1993). The experience of using this type of information to perceive depth was vividly described by the German scientist Hermann von Helmholtz (1866/1925, Vol. 3):

optic flow A dynamic depth cue—the relative motions of objects and surfaces in the retinal image as the observer moves forward or backward through a scene.

> Suppose, for instance, that a person is standing still in a thick woods, where it is impossible for him to distinguish, except vaguely and roughly, in the mass of foliage and branches all around him what belongs to one tree and what to another, or how far apart the separate trees are, etc. But the moment he begins to move forward, everything disentangles itself, and immediately he gets an apperception of the material contents of the woods and their relations to each other in space, just as if he were looking at a good stereoscopic view of it. (pp. 295–296)

Figure 6.18 illustrates a different scene in which depth information is provided by optic flow. Imagine you're back in the desert, driving down a long, flat, straight road toward a distant mesa. In your peripheral vision, you can see the landscape at the side of the car

(a)

(b)

Figure 6.18 Optic Flow (a) As you drive down a long straight road with your eyes focused on the mesa straight ahead, the entire landscape flows outward in your retinal image and then disappears out the edges of your field of view. Only the point where you're looking (the focus of expansion) remains stationary in your retinal image. (b) Each arrow represents the instantaneous direction and speed of the point in the image at the location of the dot at the arrow's tail end (speed is proportional to the length of the arrow). Only a sampling of such arrows is shown here—every discernible point could have an associated arrow (only truly featureless and textureless areas such as portions of the sky and road wouldn't appear to flow). [Robert Glusic/Corbis]

whizzing by in a blur and disappearing out the edges of your field of view. A little farther ahead, the scrub vegetation and road markers rapidly flow toward the sides of your field of view until they too flash away. The more distant landscape flows outward more slowly but eventually meets the same fate, as do the clouds in the sky and the road beneath your wheels, which disappear out of the top and bottom of your field of view, respectively. Only the faraway mesa where you are looking seems fixed in position.

This optic flow is a critical cue to depth when you're driving, though it also operates, of course, when you're moving more slowly through a scene. The objects and surfaces near the point toward which you are looking (called the *focus of expansion*) move outward slowly in your retinal image. Closer objects move away from the focus of expansion much more rapidly. Indeed, every feature in the scene moves outward from the focus of expansion at a rate that depends on how far away it is from you.

As you can probably imagine, the apparent relative motion of objects that provides the depth cue of motion parallax (including optic flow) can be far more complex than in the examples we've used here. Your movement through a scene can be a combination of side to side, back and forth, and up and down, as when you're flying in a plane or simply driving around curves and up and down hills, and your eyes can move around the scene or track particular objects. Yet this complexity is what we deal with all the time in an infinite variety of situations, without even thinking about it—and we automatically translate the complex optic flow pattern into a vivid sense of the 3-D spatial layout of the scene.

Deletion and Accretion

deletion A dynamic depth cue—the gradual hiding (occlusion) of an object as it passes behind another one.

accretion A dynamic depth cue—the gradual revealing ("de-occlusion") of an object as it emerges from behind another one.

Suppose you're standing on a city street, leaning against a lamppost and watching people go by. Across the street, a man is walking along the sidewalk and approaching a newsstand. As he crosses behind the right edge of the newsstand, his body is gradually occluded by the newsstand—a process called **deletion**—and as he emerges past the left edge of the newsstand, his body is gradually uncovered—a process called **accretion** (see Figure 6.19). In either case, the dynamic occlusion or "de-occlusion" of the moving person is an unmistakable cue that the person is farther away from you than the newsstand.

Figure 6.19 Deletion and Accretion The gradual disappearance and reappearance of objects as they are occluded behind other objects and then revealed is a pervasive depth cue in real scenes.

Check Your Understanding

6.4 What is the main difference between static depth cues and dynamic depth cues?

6.5 In Figure 6.5, which depth cues other than partial occlusion indicate that the woman is in front of the taxi?

6.6 True or false? The size–distance relationship is the basis of all these depth cues: familiar size, relative size, texture gradients, and linear perspective.

6.7 Describe a scene in which motion parallax, but not deletion and accretion, would provide information about the relative depths of the objects in the scene.

6.8 Suppose this famous statue were equally illuminated from all directions. Would any lighting-based cues provide information about the relative depth of the statue's surfaces? Explain your answer.

[Andrew Horne/Wikimedia Commons]

Binocular Depth Cue: Disparity in the Retinal Images

The monocular depth cues considered in the previous sections are present not only in real scenes but also in flat depictions of real scenes, such as photographs, paintings, and conventional motion pictures. Moreover, to see these cues, a person doesn't have to view the scene with both eyes—the cues are apparent with just one eye open. However, we have two eyes, giving us two views of the world, and our visual system has evolved to process those different views in a way that provides us with an extremely rich source of information about spatial layout, including a vivid sense of depth called **stereopsis** (or *stereoscopic depth perception*). The capacity to get depth information from this cue is what Sue Barry recovered when her strabismus was corrected (see the vignette at the beginning of this chapter).

stereopsis (or *stereoscopic depth perception*) The vivid sense of depth arising from the visual system's processing of the different retinal images in the two eyes.

Binocular Disparity

You can easily see the difference in the views of the two eyes if you hold your index finger 30 cm in front of your face and look at it with your left eye only, while also noting its position relative to an object in the background (e.g., a lamp across the room). If you then close your left eye and look at the finger with your right eye, you'll see that the position of the lamp in your retinal image has changed relative to your finger (see Figure 6.20). This difference in the retinal images in your two eyes—in this case, the difference in the position of the lamp—is called **binocular disparity**.

binocular disparity A depth cue based on differences in the relative positions of the retinal images of objects in the two eyes.

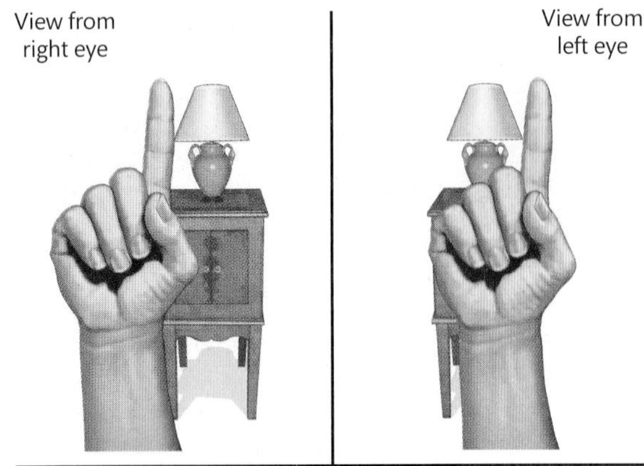

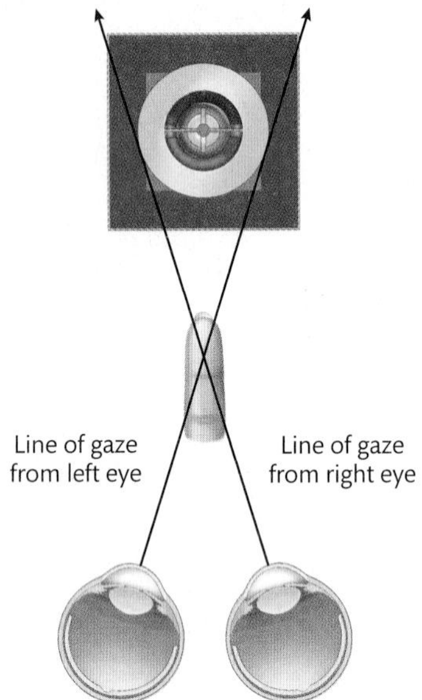

Figure 6.20 Binocular Disparity (top) Binocular disparity—the difference in the retinal images in the left and right eyes—is obvious if you hold up a single finger and look at it with first one eye closed and then the other. A lamp across the room seems to jump from one side of your finger to the other. (bottom) The reason for this binocular disparity in the relative positions of your finger and the lamp in the retinal image is also obvious—the horizontal separation between your two eyes means that the line of gaze from your left eye to your finger is quite different from the line of gaze from your right eye to your finger.

Corresponding and Noncorresponding Points, and the Horopter

Now let's look more closely at the exact positions of the images of objects on the left and right retinas. We'll begin by defining the concepts of corresponding points and noncorresponding points. A point on the left retina and a point on the right retina are **corresponding points** if they would coincide if the two retinas were superimposed—for example, the foveas of the two eyes are corresponding points, and two points that are each 4 mm to the left of the fovea in each eye are also corresponding points. Conversely, **noncorresponding points** wouldn't coincide if the retinas were superimposed. In general, two points are corresponding if they are each the same distance to the left or right of the foveas in the two eyes and the same distance above or below the foveas.

Figure 6.21 shows a schematic scene in which an observer has four objects in her field of view. The objects are of different colors but of identical size and shape, and they are all at the same height in the retinal image (so we don't have to consider the vertical dimension for the moment). The observer has *fixated* the red object—that is, she has pointed both her eyes directly at the red object, so the retinal image of that object falls on the fovea of each eye (indicated by points F and F′). The blue object is at the same distance from the observer as the fixated red object and it also produces retinal images at corresponding points in the two eyes (specifically, at points B and B′), as would any other objects located on the dashed line that passes through the red and blue objects. This dashed line is the **horopter**, an imaginary surface defined by the locations in the scene from which objects would project retinal images at corresponding points in the two retinas. Whenever an observer fixates an object (e.g., the red object in Figure 6.21), a horopter is established.

Objects that are either closer to the observer or farther from the observer than the horopter—like the brown and green objects, respectively, in Figure 6.21—will project retinal images that fall on noncorresponding points (A and D′ for the green object, C and E′ for the brown object), and will be perceived as being either nearer or farther than objects on the horopter.

corresponding points A point on the left retina and a point on the right retina that would coincide if the two retinas were superimposed—for example, the foveas of the two eyes.

noncorresponding points A point on the left retina and a point on the right retina that wouldn't coincide if the two retinas were superimposed—for example, the fovea of one eye and a point 4 mm to the right of the fovea in the other eye.

horopter An imaginary surface defined by the locations in a scene from which objects would project retinal images at corresponding points.

crossed disparity A type of binocular disparity produced by an object that is closer than the horopter—you would have to "cross" your eyes to look at it.

uncrossed disparity A type of binocular disparity produced by an object that is farther away than the horopter—you would have to "uncross" your eyes to look at it.

Crossed Disparity, Uncrossed Disparity, and Zero Disparity

Armed with the concepts of corresponding points, noncorresponding points, and the horopter, we can now explore the three types of binocular disparity—crossed disparity, uncrossed disparity, and zero disparity—as well as the magnitude of binocular disparity. Figure 6.22 shows a schematic scene in which an observer has three objects in her field of view. Again, as in Figure 6.21, the objects are of different colors but of identical size and shape, and all are at the same height in the retinal image; and again, the observer has fixated the red object. Points F and F′ (the two foveas) are corresponding points.

The brown object, which is closer to the observer than the horopter is, exhibits **crossed disparity**. It produces an image at point A in the left retina and at the noncorresponding point C′ in the right retina. Thus, the observer sees the brown object to the *right* of the fixated red object with the *left* eye and to the *left* of the fixated red object with the *right* eye. This right–left, left–right aspect accounts for the term *crossed* disparity.

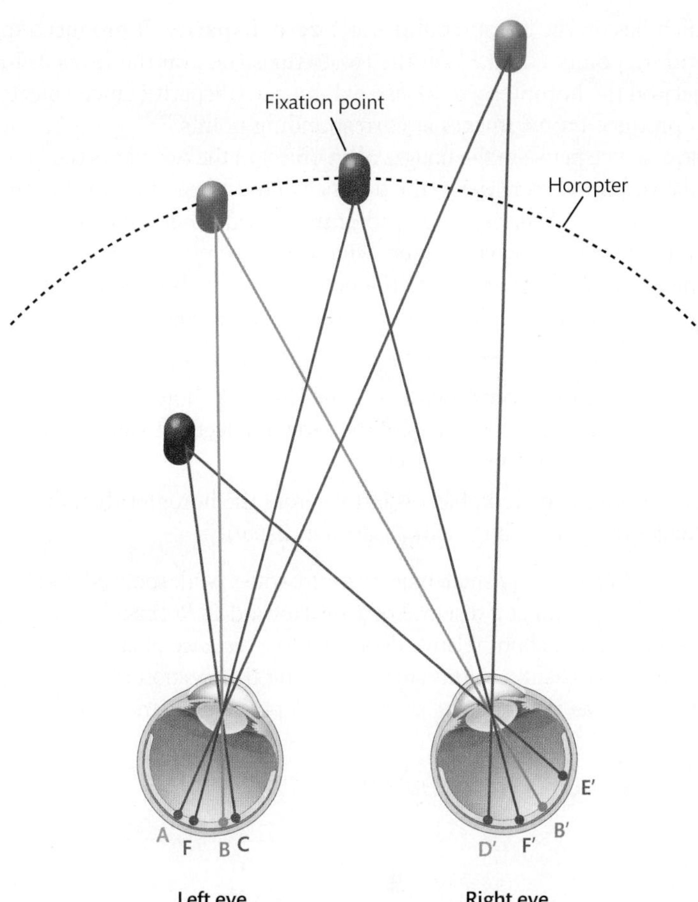

Figure 6.21 Geometry of Binocular Disparity: Corresponding and Noncorresponding Points, and the Horopter All four objects are the same size and shape, and the observer has fixated the red object.

- The retinal image of the red object is at the fovea on both retinas (points F and F′). If the two retinas were superimposed, the fovea in the left retina would coincide with the fovea in the right retina; thus, F and F′ are corresponding points.
- The retinal image of the blue object is at point B on the left retina and at point B′ on the right retina. The distance from F to B is the same as the distance from F′ to B′. Thus, B and B′ are also corresponding points, since they would coincide if the two retinas were superimposed. The blue object and the red object both lie on the horopter.
- The retinal image of the brown object is at point C on the left retina and at point E′ on the right retina. The distance from F to C is different than the distance from F′ to E′. Thus, C and E′ are noncorresponding points, since they would not coincide if the two retinas were superimposed.
- The retinal image of the green object is at point A on the left retina and at point D′ on the right retina. The distance from F to A is different than the distance from F′ to D′. Thus, A and D′ are also noncorresponding points.

The green object, which is farther from the observer than the horopter is, illustrates **uncrossed disparity**. It produces an image at point B in the left retina and at the noncorresponding point D′ in the right retina. Here, the observer sees the green object to the *left* of the fixated red object with the *left* eye and to the *right* of the fixated red object with the *right* eye. This left–left, right–right aspect accounts for the term *uncrossed* disparity. Another way to remember "crossed" versus "uncrossed" is to note that the observer would have to cross her eyes—that is, increase the angle of convergence—in order to change from fixating the red object to fixating the closer, brown object, whereas she would have to uncross her eyes—that is, decrease the angle of convergence—in order to change from fixating the red object to fixating the farther, green object.

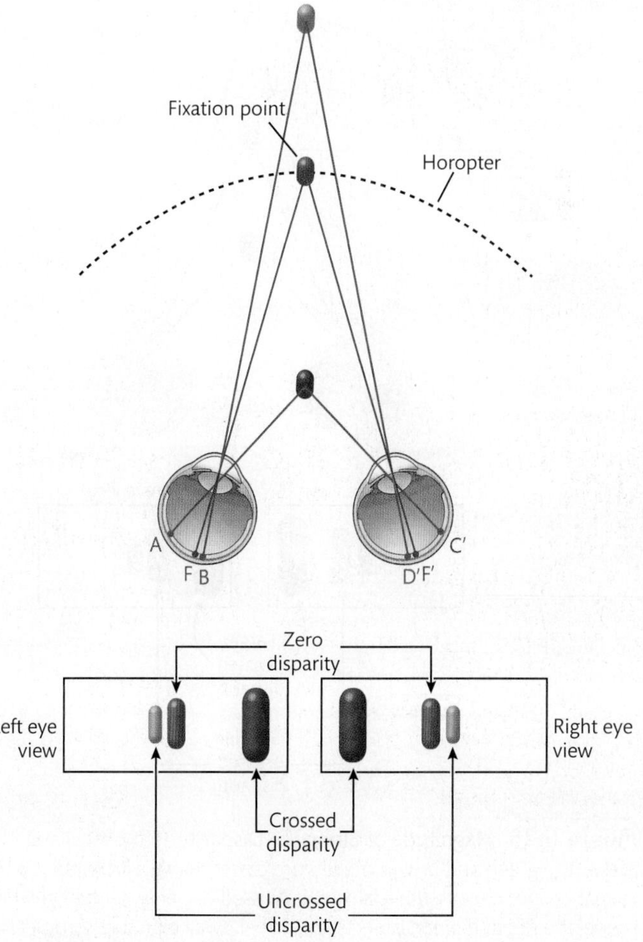

Figure 6.22 Types of Binocular Disparity: Crossed, Uncrossed, and Zero All three objects are the same physical size, and the observer has fixated the red object. This means that the retinal image of the red object is at the fovea on both retinas (i.e., at corresponding points F and F′). In the main part of the figure:

- The brown object, which lies inside the horopter, produces retinal images at noncorresponding points A and C′. It exhibits crossed disparity.
- The green object, which lies outside the horopter, produces retinal images at noncorresponding points B and D′. It exhibits uncrossed disparity.
- The red object, which lies on the horopter, produces retinal images at corresponding points (the two foveas, F and F′). It has zero disparity.

zero disparity A type of binocular disparity in which the retinal image of an object falls at corresponding points in the two eyes.

The red object, which lies on the horopter, illustrates **zero disparity**. It produces an image on the corresponding points F and F′ on the two retinas (i.e., on the foveas). In addition, any other object on the horopter would also exhibit zero disparity, since objects on the horopter always produce retinal images at corresponding points.

Finally, note that the distance between the images of an object in the two views (i.e., the *magnitude* of the binocular disparity) increases as the distance of the object from the horopter increases, regardless of whether disparity is crossed or uncrossed. This is illustrated by the two scenes in Figure 6.23. In the left-hand scene, which shows crossed disparity, both the brown object and the green object are closer to the person than the horopter is; in the right-hand scene, which shows uncrossed disparity, the green and red objects are both farther away than the horopter. As you can see:

- In the left-hand scene, where the brown object is farther from the horopter than the green object, the disparity between the images of the brown object is greater than the disparity between the images of the green object.
- In the right-hand scene, where the red object is farther from the horopter than the green object, the images of the red object exhibit greater disparity.

People are remarkably sensitive to very small binocular disparities, with some adults able to detect a difference in depth of 4 mm at a distance of 5 m (Howard & Rogers, 2002). Stereopsis typically provides information about relative depth out to a distance of about 200 m, which clearly would be extremely useful in accurately perceiving the location of predators, prey, or other food sources, such as fruit hanging at different depths amidst the branches of

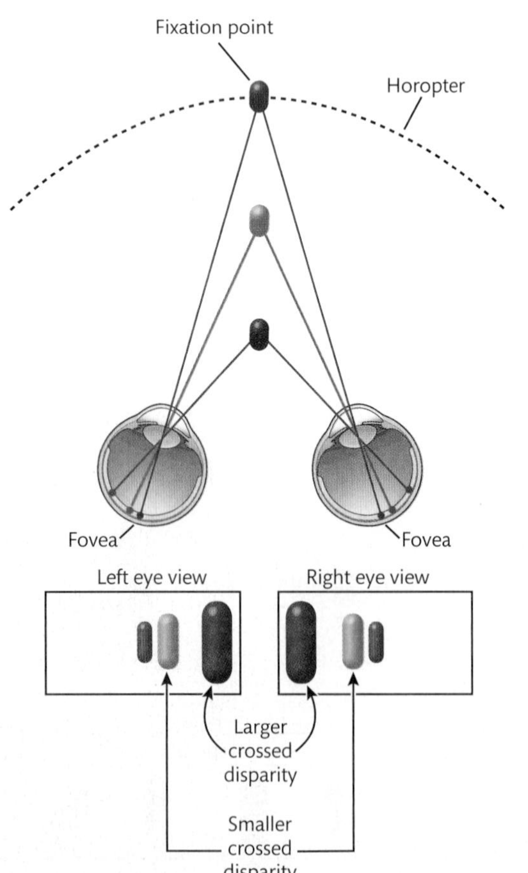

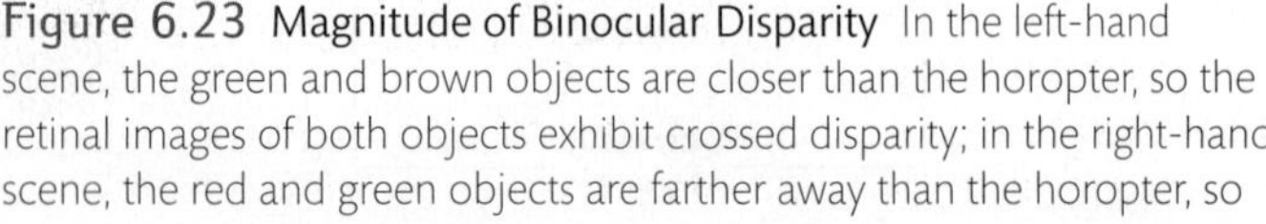

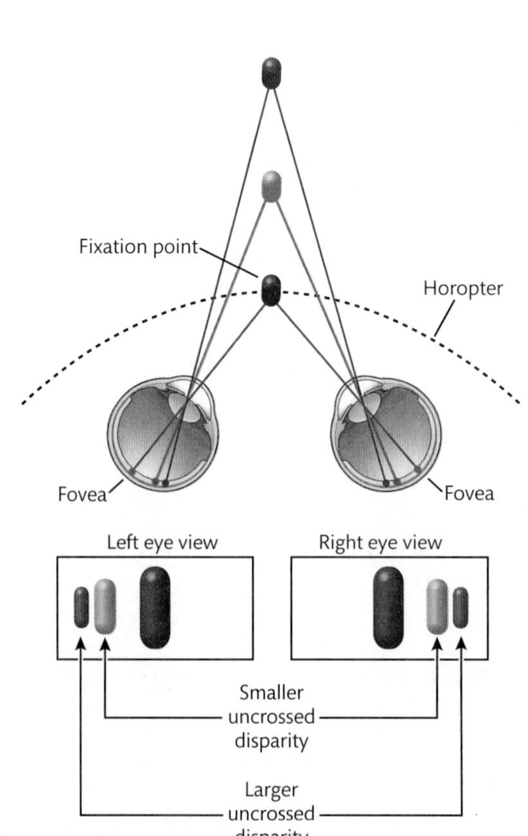

Figure 6.23 Magnitude of Binocular Disparity In the left-hand scene, the green and brown objects are closer than the horopter, so the retinal images of both objects exhibit crossed disparity; in the right-hand scene, the red and green objects are farther away than the horopter, so their retinal images exhibit uncrossed disparity. In both scenes, the farther an object is from the horopter, the greater is the disparity between its images on the two retinas.

trees. The adaptive advantage provided by this ability to detect subtle differences in depth over large distances was likely a major factor in the evolution of depth perception.

Demonstration 6.1 Binocular Disparity Explore how the binocular disparity of an object's retinal image changes as you change the depth of the object.

Correspondence Problem

Our brain automatically and unconsciously uses binocular disparity as a depth cue. If the retinal images of an object exhibit crossed disparity, our visual system perceives the object as closer than the fixated object; conversely, uncrossed disparity signals that an object is farther than a fixated object; zero disparity marks an object as being at the same depth as a fixated object; and the visual system "knows" that the greater the disparity, the greater the difference in depth from the fixated object. But when an object produces retinal images that exhibit binocular disparity of any type, how does our brain know that the image on the left retina was produced by the same object as the image on the right retina? This problem is known as the **correspondence problem**: in order to perceive depth from binocular disparity, the brain must know which part of the right retinal image corresponds with which part of the left retinal image, so it can assess the type and magnitude of the binocular disparity.

correspondence problem The problem of determining which features in the retinal image in one eye correspond to which features in the retinal image in the other eye.

The examples in Figures 6.22 and 6.23 involved an observer looking at a scene containing only a few distinctively colored objects. In these examples, it would be a trivial matter for the visual system to determine that the brown part of the left retinal image corresponded to the brown part of the right retinal image. To determine the type and magnitude of binocular disparity, the brain would simply compare the positions of the corresponding parts of the retinal images.

Real scenes, however, are not so simple. They often contain many objects of similar color; objects partially occlude other objects; some objects may be in motion; and usually there are extended, textured surfaces. All this complexity makes the correspondence problem decidedly nontrivial—it's not at all easy to explain how the brain determines which parts of the left and right retinal images correspond. Nevertheless, this is exactly what the visual system has evolved to do. There are two very different ways in which the visual system might solve the correspondence problem:

stereogram Two depictions of a scene that differ in the same way as an observer's two retinal images of that scene would differ; an observer who simultaneously views one image with one eye and the other image with the other eye (as in a stereoscope) will see a combined image in depth.

- One is that the visual system surveys the left and right retinal images and separately performs 2-D object recognition on them. The visual system in effect "labels" each feature of each retinal image as belonging to an object in the scene. For example, if the scene includes a coffee mug sitting on a table, part of the left retinal image might be labeled as the handle of the coffee mug, and part of the right retinal image might be given the same label. In this way, a labeled representation of the entire coffee mug could be built up in each retinal image, and the visual system could then assess the binocular disparity for each part of the mug.
- The other hypothesis suggests that the visual system matches parts of the retinal images based on very simple properties such as color or edge orientation before proceeding to object recognition (i.e., without assigning object labels).

The crucial difference between these two hypotheses is that, in the first, object recognition precedes correspondence matching, whereas in the second, matching precedes object recognition. A definitive experiment to resolve this question was carried out in the 1970s. Before we discuss that, however, you need to understand what a stereogram is.

Stereograms and Anaglyphs

Stereoscopic vision was first explained in scientific detail in 1838 by the English inventor and scientist Charles Wheatstone, who was already famous for having measured the speed of electricity in wire and is known for many other scientific discoveries and inventions. As part of his research into stereopsis, Wheatstone created the **stereogram**, which consists of two depictions of a scene that differ in the same way as an observer's two retinal images of that scene would differ. Wheatstone's stereograms consisted of drawings, because photography wasn't then available. A photographic stereogram can be made by mounting two cameras side by side, with the lenses separated by about 6 cm—the average distance

Charles Wheatstone (1802–1875). [Maria Platt-Evans/Photo Researchers]

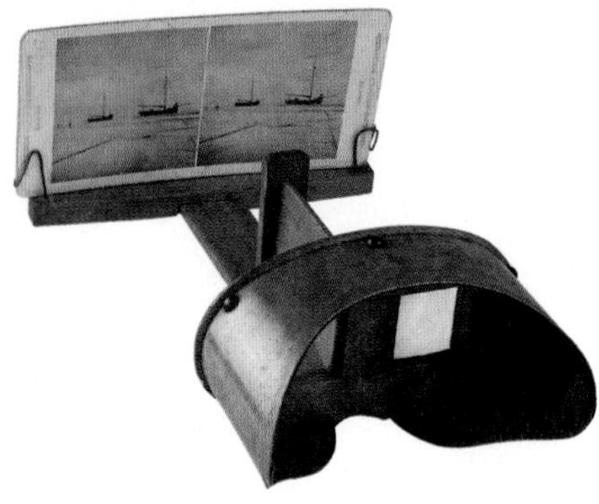

Figure 6.24 Stereoscope Two photos are simultaneously taken of the same scene with two camera lenses separated horizontally by the 6-cm interocular distance. One photo is then shown only to the left eye and the other only to the right eye, simulating the slightly different views one would experience if actually viewing the scene. The resulting binocular disparity produces a vivid perception of depth. [Brand X Pictures/Getty Images]

between the eyes of adult humans—and snapping a picture of the scene with both cameras simultaneously. The photographs are then mounted side by side in a stereoscope—also invented by Wheatstone—which is constructed to show the photo taken by the left-hand camera to the left eye only and the photo taken by the right-hand camera to the right eye only (see Figure 6.24). A person looking into the stereoscope sees a single image of the scene that gives a vivid impression of depth. This happens because the brain automatically interprets the retinal images of the photographs in terms of binocular disparity.

This book takes advantage of a different method for viewing stereograms, using the glasses that came packaged with the book. In this method, two photographs are taken just as for use in a stereoscope; then, one of the two photographs is printed in shades of one color (e.g., red) and the other is printed in shades of another color (e.g., blue). The two photographs are then superimposed, yielding an image called an **anaglyph,** like the one shown in Figure 6.25a (the three anaglyphs in Figure 6.25b aren't photos but were constructed using a computer program). First look at this figure without the glasses. You'll see double images—that is, in each anaglyph you'll see both the red image and the blue image, with some parts of the images slightly displaced from each other (in Figure 6.25a, the displacement is due to the separation of the cameras when the photos were taken; in Figure 6.25b, the program computes the displacement). Now put on the glasses and look at the figure again. The eye looking through the red lens sees only the blue image, and the eye looking through the blue lens sees only the red image. Thus, just as with the stereoscope, one eye sees one image while the other eye sees the other image; and just as with the stereoscope, your visual system interprets the difference between the images in terms of binocular disparity, and you see a single combined image giving the same vivid impression of depth.

anaglyph A stereogram in which the two photographs taken from adjacent camera positions are printed in contrasting colors and then superimposed; an observer who views an anaglyph with special glasses in which one lens filters out one of the colors and the other lens filters out the other color will see a single image in depth.

(a)

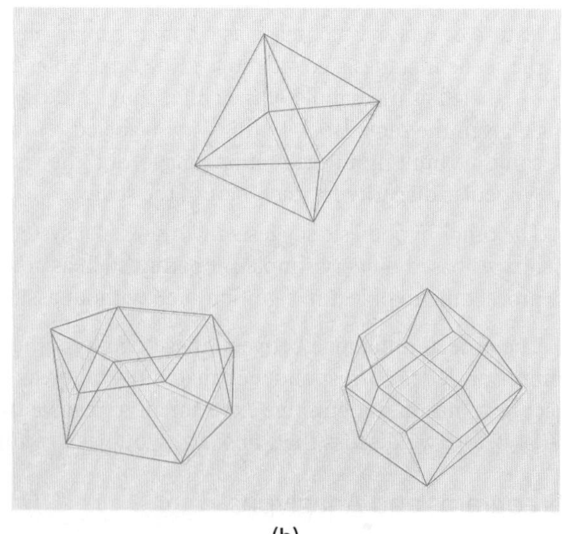

(b)

Figure 6.25 Anaglyphs (a) An anaglyph can be constructed by superimposing two photos of the same scene taken by cameras mounted 6 cm apart. (b) An anaglyph can also be constructed using a computer program to create and superimpose two drawings displaced from each other in the right way. Clockwise from the top, these three anaglyphs show solid geometrical shapes known as an octahedron, a pentagonal anti-prism, and a rhombic dodecahedron. In each anaglyph, in both (a) and (b), one photo or drawing is printed in red and the other is printed in blue. If you look at these anaglyphs through the glasses that came with this book, each eye sees only one of the two images, and you experience a single image with depth. Without the glasses, the image looks doubled. (Note: When using the red-blue glasses, place the red lens over your left eye and the blue lens over your right eye.) [a: Glyn Kirk/AFP/Getty Images]

1	2	1	2	1	2	2	1	2	1
1	2	1	1	2	1	2	2	2	2
2	1	1	2	1	2	1	1	1	2
1	2	2	2	2	1	2	1	2	1
1	2	1	1	2	1	2	2	2	1
2	1	2	2	2	2	1	2	1	2
1	2	1	1	1	2	1	2	1	1
1	2	2	1	2	2	2	1	2	2
1	2	1	2	1	2	1	1	1	1
2	1	2	1	1	1	1	2	1	2

1	2	1	2	1	2	2	1	2	1
1	2	1	1	2	1	2	2	2	2
2	1	1	2	1	2	1	1	1	2
1	2	2	2	1	2	2	1	2	1
1	2	1	2	1	2	1	2	2	1
2	1	2	2	2	1	2	2	1	2
1	2	1	1	2	1	1	2	1	1
1	2	2	1	2	2	2	1	2	2
1	2	1	2	1	2	1	1	1	1
2	1	2	1	1	1	1	2	1	2

Figure 6.26 Making a Random Dot Stereogram To create a random dot stereogram, you first make a grid of small square dots (magnified here) and color each one randomly white or black (in the figure, **1** represents a black dot, **2** represents a white dot). This array is then copied to make images of two identical arrays. Next a central portion is displaced in one image. In this schematic representation, the 4 × 4 square array of dots in the center of the left-hand image has been displaced one column to the left in the right-hand image.

Random Dot Stereograms

The crucial experiment to determine how the human visual system solves the correspondence problem, to help answer the question of whether object recognition occurs before or after matching corresponding parts of the retinal images, was carried out by Béla Julesz (1960, 1971), a Hungarian-born scientist who emigrated to the United States in 1956. The experiment involved a clever invention that Julesz called a **random dot stereogram (RDS)**, which, like any stereogram, consists of two images that exhibit binocular disparity when viewed through a stereoscope. Figure 6.26 shows simplified schematic diagrams of the two images of an RDS. The images are grids made of randomly arranged black and white square dots (in the figure, black and white are represented by 1 and 2, respectively; in an actual RDS, the grids contain many more rows and columns than these 10 × 10 grids). The two grids are identical except in their central portion: in the right-hand grid, the central portion is shifted one column to the left of where it is in the left-hand grid.

Figure 6.27 shows an actual RDS. The difference in the central portions isn't at all apparent when you look at the images with both eyes. But viewed in a stereoscope (or following the directions in the caption), the background plane of the RDS has zero disparity—that is, in the background, each dot in the left image has a paired dot in the right image of the same color and position—whereas the central portions of the two grids exhibit binocular disparity, with each dot in the left image having a pair in the right image at a slightly displaced location. Figure 6.28 shows two modern variants of RDSs

Béla Julesz (1928–2003). [Nick Romanenko]

random dot stereogram (RDS) A stereogram in which both images consist of a grid of randomly arranged black and white dots, identical except for the displacement of a portion in one image relative to the other; an observer who views a random dot stereogram in a stereoscope or as an anaglyph will see a single image with the displaced portion in depth.

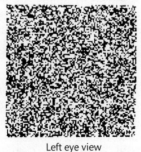

Right eye view

Left eye view

Figure 6.27 Random Dot Stereogram If you viewed this actual random dot stereogram in a stereoscope, you would see a central square in depth, floating in front of the background. In fact, with some practice, you can see the square without using a stereoscope. Relax your eyes so you're not looking at the surface of the page. Then allow your eyes to cross slightly so that you see the left image with your right eye and the right image with your left eye, as indicated by the labels under the stereogram. Once you see the square, you'll be amazed, as is everyone who sees it for the first time. [Julesz, 1971]

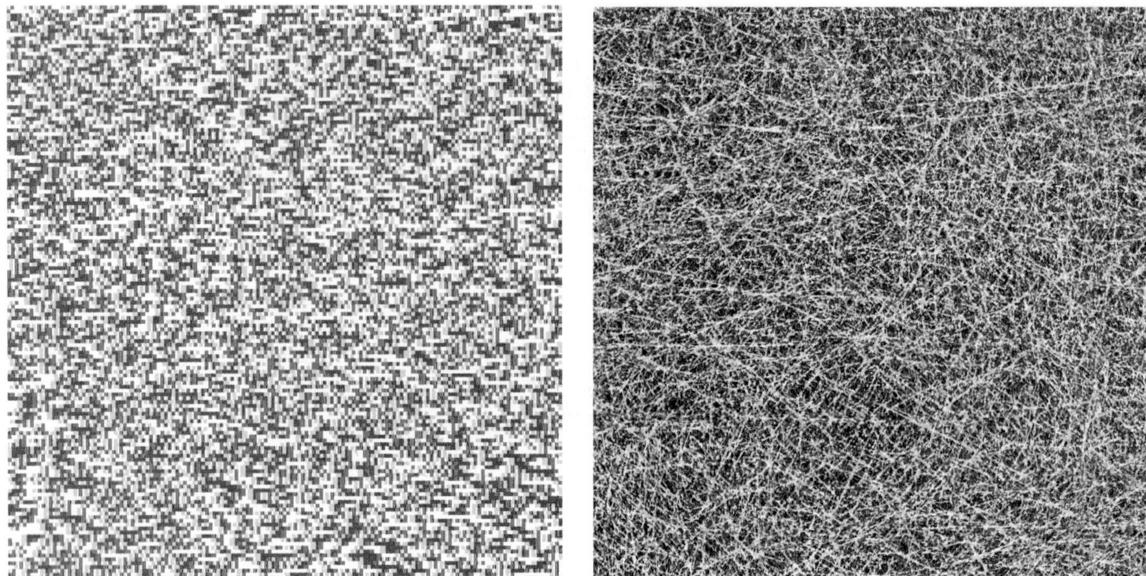

Figure 6.28 Random Dot Stereograms as Anaglyphs If you look at these anaglyphs through the red–blue glasses, you'll see an X in the left anaglyph and a heart in the right anaglyph, floating in front of the background. [David Burder, 3D Images]

rendered as anaglyphs (in the anaglyph on the right, the disparity information is carried by random scribbles rather than random dots). In each, you can see an object floating in front of the background if you look at it using the glasses provided with this book.

Now you can understand how the RDS addresses the question of whether correspondence matching precedes or follows object recognition. The argument runs like this:

1. Correspondence matching is necessary for the perception of binocular disparity.
2. If object recognition necessarily precedes correspondence matching, an RDS wouldn't produce a sense of depth, because *an RDS doesn't contain any objects*; it's just a random array of square dots or tiny scribbles, none of which can be separately labeled in either of the two images.
3. But RDSs do produce a sense of depth. Therefore, correspondence matching must precede object recognition.

Demonstration 6.2 Anaglyphs Explore a variety of anaglyphic images, including random dot stereograms.

The fact that people can see depth in an RDS doesn't explain how the brain actually solves the correspondence problem. Marr and Poggio (1979) suggested that the visual system does this by making two simple and quite reasonable assumptions about the world when matching features in the left and right retinal images (whether they're dots or scribbles in an RDS or features of objects in a real scene):

- Each feature in one retinal image will match one and only one feature in the other retinal image.
- Visual scenes tend to consist of smooth and continuous surfaces with relatively few abrupt changes in depth. For example, the entire screen of my laptop is at more or less the same distance from me; surrounding the screen in my field of view is the top of a wooden table, the front of which is much closer to me than the back, but the surface of the table recedes away from me smoothly, so any two adjacent points on the table are at almost the same depth. The only abrupt discontinuity in depth in my field of view is right at the edges of my laptop screen. That is, almost every point in my field of view is surrounded by points at about the same depth.

Marr and Poggio showed that it is possible to determine the correspondences in the two retinal images that best satisfy these two assumptions, and thus it is possible to compute the binocular disparities. The details of how this occurs are not fully understood, but it is widely believed that the brain uses constraints like these to solve the correspondence problem.

Neural Basis of Stereopsis

In the preceding sections, we showed how binocular disparity works as a depth cue; we described the correspondence problem, which the brain must solve in order to use binocular disparity; we presented evidence that the visual system solves the correspondence problem by matching corresponding features in the two retinal images before performing object recognition; and we suggested that the brain makes two simple, commonsense assumptions about the world that enable this matching of corresponding features. In this section, we'll explore how the brain measures binocular disparity in order to extract depth information from the binocular view.

In Chapter 3, we defined the receptive field (RF) of a visually responsive cortical neuron as the region of the retina that, when stimulated, causes the neuron to change its firing rate. In other words, the RF is the part of the retinal image that drives the neuron's response. That discussion considered only monocular neurons (i.e., neurons that respond to stimulation of one eye only). Here, we'll consider the many **binocular cells**, neurons that respond best to stimulation of their receptive fields in both eyes simultaneously (Barlow et al., 1967; Poggio, 1995).

binocular cells Neurons that respond best to the stimulation of their receptive fields in both eyes simultaneously.

To get a picture of how binocular cells work, look at Figure 6.29. This figure illustrates three variations of a scene in which an observer has two cacti in his field of view; he has fixated the green cactus, so an image of it is formed at the fovea of both retinas (point F).

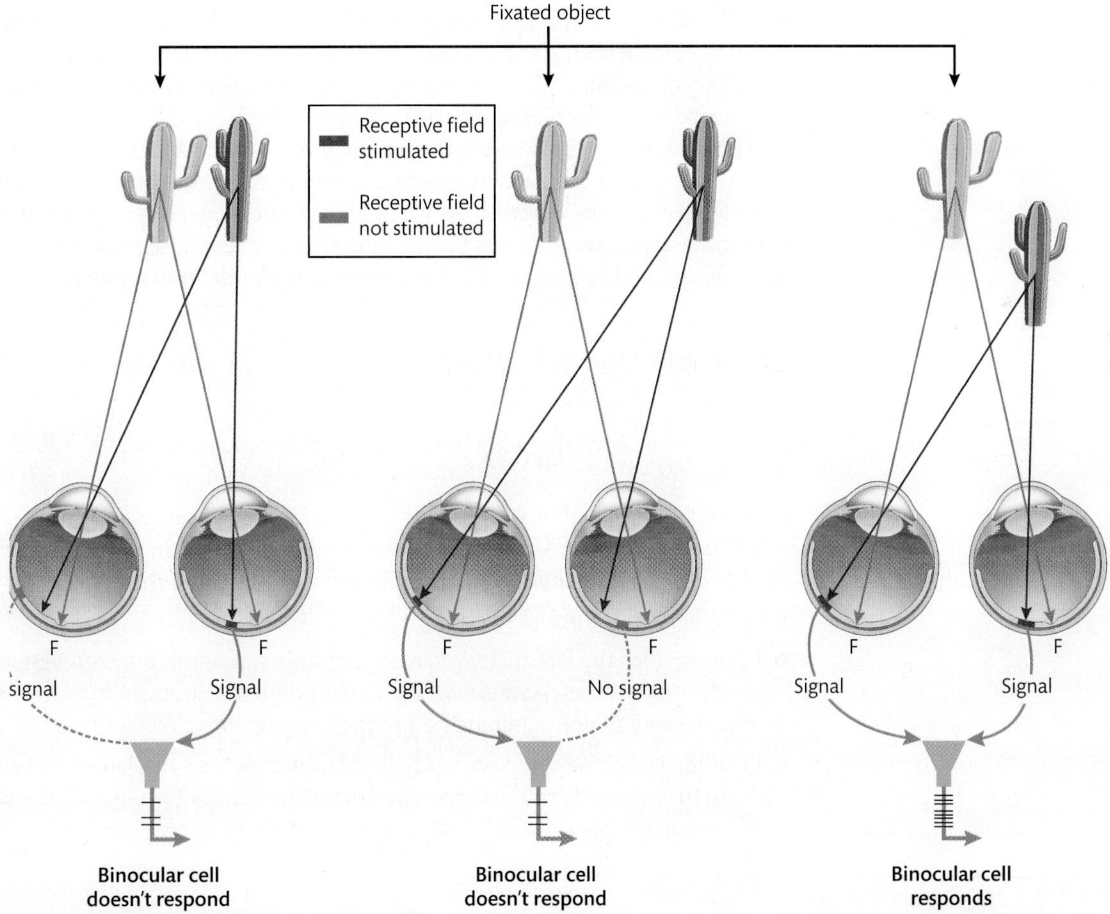

Figure 6.29 Binocular Cell's Receptive Fields The observer has fixated the green cactus. A binocular cell has a receptive field (RF) well to the left of the fovea (F) in the left eye and an RF not as far to the left of the fovea in the right eye—that is, the two RFs are at noncorresponding points. The cell will respond well only if both RFs are stimulated at the same time—that is, if an object produces retinal images with the necessary binocular disparity. (a) Light rays from a brown cactus strike the RF in the right eye but not the RF in the left eye. The binocular cell doesn't respond. (b) Light rays from a brown cactus farther to the right strike the RF in the left eye but not the RF in the right eye. Again, the binocular cell doesn't respond. (c) Light rays from a brown cactus closer to the observer strike the RFs in both eyes, and the binocular cell responds.

The figure also shows one of the observer's binocular cells and its receptive fields in the left and right retinas. Note that the receptive fields for this cell are at noncorresponding points on the retinas—the receptive field in the left retina is farther to the left of the fovea than is the receptive field in the right retina:

- In Figure 6.29a, light rays reflected from a brown cactus strike the receptive field in the right eye but not the one in the left eye; as a result, the binocular cell receives a stimulus from one eye only, and the cell doesn't respond.
- In Figure 6.29b, light rays reflected from a brown cactus farther to the right strike the receptive field in the left eye but not the one in the right eye; again, the binocular cell receives a stimulus from one eye only, and the cell doesn't respond.
- In Figure 6.29c, light rays reflected from a brown cactus closer to the observer strike the receptive fields in both eyes, and the cell responds. In other words, this particular binocular cell responds when its receptive fields are stimulated by an object that exhibits a particular degree of binocular disparity, specified by the locations of the receptive fields on the left and right retinas.

Different binocular cells are tuned to different disparities—crossed, uncrossed, or zero—and a cell tuned to crossed or uncrossed disparity will be tuned to a specific magnitude of disparity (Poggio, 1995). Since neurons tuned for binocular disparity were first discovered (Poggio & Fischer, 1977), they've been found throughout the visual pathways—in areas V1, V2, and V3; in the dorsal ("where"/"how") pathway, including the motion-selective area MT and the intraparietal sulcus, where they provide the precise depth information needed to guide reaching and grasping; and in the ventral ("what") pathway, including area V4 and the inferotemporal cortex, where they provide depth information needed to support object shape perception (Howard, 2002; Parker, 2007).

The pattern of activity across the population of binocular cells contributes to the ability to see depth and, ultimately, to the ability to judge the locations of objects that lie at different depths from the observer. As we discussed in Chapter 4, one of the most important functions of depth perception is to allow the visual system to segment a scene into distinct visual objects, and binocular cells serve an important role in that function.

Check Your Understanding

6.9 Define the terms *stereopsis* and *binocular disparity*.

6.10 What are corresponding points and noncorresponding points? What is the horopter?

6.11 If object A exhibits crossed disparity, is object A closer to the observer than the fixated object or farther away? If object B is closer to the observer than object A, which object exhibits greater binocular disparity, A or B?

6.12 What is the correspondence problem?

6.13 How does the fact that we can see depth in a random dot stereogram imply that the visual system solves the correspondence problem by performing correspondence matching before performing object recognition?

6.14 If the left-retina receptive field of a binocular cell is stimulated and sends a signal to the binocular cell, will the binocular cell necessarily respond? Explain why or why not.

Integrating Depth Cues

As we've seen, human beings estimate the depth of objects in their field of view by using a wide variety of cues (look back at Figure 6.3 for an overview of the depth cues discussed in this chapter). In most real-world situations, we use many of these cues simultaneously to obtain information about depth, and in most situations the cues are consistent with one another—they all provide the same or complementary information about the depths of the objects and surfaces in the scene.

Why does the visual system rely on so many different types of cues to provide information about depth? Taking an evolutionary perspective can help answer this question. Clearly, the accurate perception of the spatial layout of objects in the world has always been of great importance to any animal that has to survive by interacting with the physical environment—securing food and water, fleeing predators, finding shelter, and so on. Just think how dangerous driving would be, or how difficult it would be to reach out and grasp an object, if we lacked the ability to judge the relative distances of objects. So it makes sense that we should have redundant information from many different sources to ensure the accurate perception of depth (Todd, 1985).

In addition, different depth cues supply the most useful depth information under different conditions. For example, atmospheric perspective provides useful information about depth only at relatively large distances, whereas convergence and accommodation do so only within a few meters of the observer. Relative height above the horizon might provide misleading information about objects at different altitudes in the sky (e.g., a low-flying bird and a high-flying airplane), but then we can use the cue of familiar size to get a more accurate estimate of depth. And if you look back at the photos in Figures 6.5 and 6.7, you can see that monocular static cues convince us to perceive scenes in depth, despite the lack of dynamic cues and binocular disparity. Thus, the various depth cues tend to complement and compensate for one another.

How do we combine the different depth cues to yield a single coherent interpretation of a scene, even when some cues conflict with others? Researchers have examined what happens when they manipulate the number of depth cues available and the degree to which those cues conflict. Such experiments have revealed a few basic principles (Cutting & Vishton, 1995; Knill, 2007; Landy et al., 1995):

- No single depth cue dominates in all situations, and no single cue is necessary in all situations. Partial occlusion may come closest to being always dominant, as suggested in the discussion of Figures 6.5 and 6.6.
- The more depth cues that are present in a scene, the greater is the likelihood that we'll perceive the scene in depth and the greater is the accuracy and consistency of depth perception.
- Depth cues differ in the kinds of information they provide, and we use these differences to construct a more accurate view of the layout of a scene than would be possible using just one or a few of the available cues (Jameson & Hurvich, 1959). For example, partial occlusion provides good information about which object is in front of which other object, but it doesn't tell us anything about how far apart objects are. But if you're moving, you can use motion parallax to judge how far apart in depth the objects are. These cues complement one another; together, they help us build a more accurate representation of the scene.
- Depth perception based on multiple cues is a rapid, automatic process that occurs without conscious thought. The visual system employs what Hermann von Helmholtz (1866/1925) called *unconscious inference* to make a "best guess" about the layout of a scene based on the current retinal images.

In Chapter 4, we discussed how the Bayesian approach combines knowledge about the probability of possible scenes with information from the current scene to deal with ambiguous visual information—this is the modern version of Helmholtz's idea of unconscious inference. The same general approach can be applied easily to combining the information from different depth cues (Landy et al., 1995). The idea is that when multiple depth cues are available, the visual system combines the depth estimate provided by each cue in a weighted average, where the weights take into account the reliability of each cue in the given context. For example, in a region of the visual scene that contains a surface with randomly varying texture and with straight sides that converge, depth estimates based on texture gradients should carry less weight than estimates based on linear perspective. The visual system is also assumed to take into account prior knowledge of the possible depths in the scene when estimating depth—for example, if you're in your kitchen and you know your kitchen is 4 m square, you're unlikely to perceive a dollhouse chair as a real chair situated 20 m away. In other words, the visual system uses every bit of information available—including prior knowledge—to come up with the best possible understanding of 3-D layout.

Check Your Understanding

6.15 Why does the visual system use the information from many different depth cues simultaneously?

6.16 You're hiking in the mountains, looking across a valley at a range of hills in the distance. Which depth cue is likely to offer you better information about just how distant the hills are: convergence, binocular disparity, or atmospheric perspective? Why?

6.17 Describe a situation in which you could use a static depth cue and a dynamic depth cue to determine which of two objects is closer to you and how far apart the objects are.

Depth and Perceptual Constancy

Whenever you perceive some property of an object as constant despite changes in the sensory information used to perceive that property, you're experiencing what's called *perceptual constancy*. In Chapter 5, we examined color constancy and lightness constancy: the perceived color and lightness of an object tend to remain constant despite changes in the wavelengths and intensity of the light reflected into our eyes from the object due to changing lighting conditions. Here, we'll consider two other forms of perceptual constancy: size constancy and shape constancy.

Size Constancy and Size–Distance Invariance

In most real-world situations, using distance to correctly judge size is effortless and automatic, and it's difficult to suppress—for example, we automatically compensate for the different retinal image sizes of objects of the same size at different distances (see Figure 6.10). But this automatic process of size judgment based on distance doesn't always take place—it depends on the presence of depth cues that provide information about distance. This was shown by a classic experiment in which participants had to judge the sizes of different-sized disks at different distances, placed in such a way that all the disks had the same retinal image size—for example, a disk twice the size of another disk would be placed twice as far away (Holway & Boring, 1941). The results showed that people were able to judge the true sizes of the disks if they could get information about the relative distances of the disks from depth cues such as binocular disparity, motion parallax, and linear perspective. But as depth cues were eliminated—for example, by covering one eye or preventing head movement—judgments of disk sizes were increasingly based solely on the size of the retinal image.

As discussed earlier in this chapter, the size–distance relation tells us that the size of the retinal image of any rigid object depends on two factors: the object's actual size and the object's distance from the observer. This means that the retinal image of an object becomes smaller as the object recedes in depth—yet in general, objects aren't perceived as actually shrinking as they get farther away. Indeed, the immediate, unconscious perception of an object's size as unchanging as it moves away makes it difficult to perceive the changes in retinal image size. This is **size constancy**, the tendency to perceive an object's size as constant despite changes in the size of the object's retinal image due to the object's changing distance.

size constancy A type of perceptual constancy—the tendency to perceive an object's size as constant despite changes in the size of the object's retinal image due to the object's changing distance from the observer.

size–distance invariance The relation between perceived size and perceived distance: the perceived size of an object depends on its perceived distance, and vice versa.

The relation between perceived size and perceived distance is embodied in the principle of **size–distance invariance**: the perceived size of an object depends on its perceived distance, and vice versa (Kilpatrick & Ittelson, 1953). To see size–distance invariance at work, look at Figure 6.30 and follow the directions in the caption. The change in the perceived size of a retinal afterimage in proportion to the distance of the surface on which it's

Figure 6.30 Size–Distance Invariance: Emmert's Law Stare at the red disk for about a minute without moving your eyes. For some time thereafter, you'll see a greenish afterimage of the disk when you look at any light-colored surface. First look at a white piece of paper held at reading distance. Then look at a light-colored wall across the room. The afterimage on the wall appears larger than the afterimage on the paper because of size–distance invariance (this is known as *Emmert's law*); yet both retinal images are, of course, exactly the same size.

"projected" is called **Emmert's law** (Boring, 1940; the law was formulated by the Swiss ophthalmologist Emil Emmert [1844–1911], who was the first to describe the phenomenon).

Emmert's law Size–distance invariance of retinal afterimages—the perceived size of an afterimage is proportional to the distance of the surface on which it's "projected."

shape constancy A type of perceptual constancy—the tendency to perceive an object's shape as constant despite changes in the shape of the object's retinal image due to the object's changing orientation.

shape–slant invariance The relation between perceived shape and perceived slant: the perceived shape of an object depends on its perceived slant, and vice versa.

Shape Constancy and Shape–Slant Invariance

Like the retinal image size of a rigid object, the retinal image shape also depends on two factors: the object's actual shape and the object's *slant*—that is, its orientation relative to the observer's line of sight. For example, the cover of this book is a rectangle, but there is only one viewing angle at which the book's cover projects a perfectly rectangular retinal image: when the book is perpendicular to the line of sight of the observer and centered on the optic axis of the observer's eye. This is a possible viewing angle, of course, but almost always you view the cover from an oblique angle—yet you always perceive the cover as rectangular. Moreover, the perceived rectangular shape doesn't change if the book is rotated through various orientations as you watch, despite the constantly changing shape of its retinal image. This is **shape constancy**, the tendency to perceive an object's shape as constant despite changes in the shape of the object's retinal image due to the object's changing orientation. Obviously, shape constancy is very useful—we wouldn't be able to navigate among objects or manipulate them effectively if we couldn't judge their shape accurately.

Just as size constancy can be expressed in the principle of size–distance invariance, shape constancy can be expressed in the principle of **shape–slant invariance**: the perceived shape of an object depends on its perceived slant, and vice versa (Beck & Gibson, 1955). To see what this means, look at Figure 6.31, which shows how the shape of the retinal image of an object changes when the slant of the object changes. If the observer had no way of judging the slant of the object,

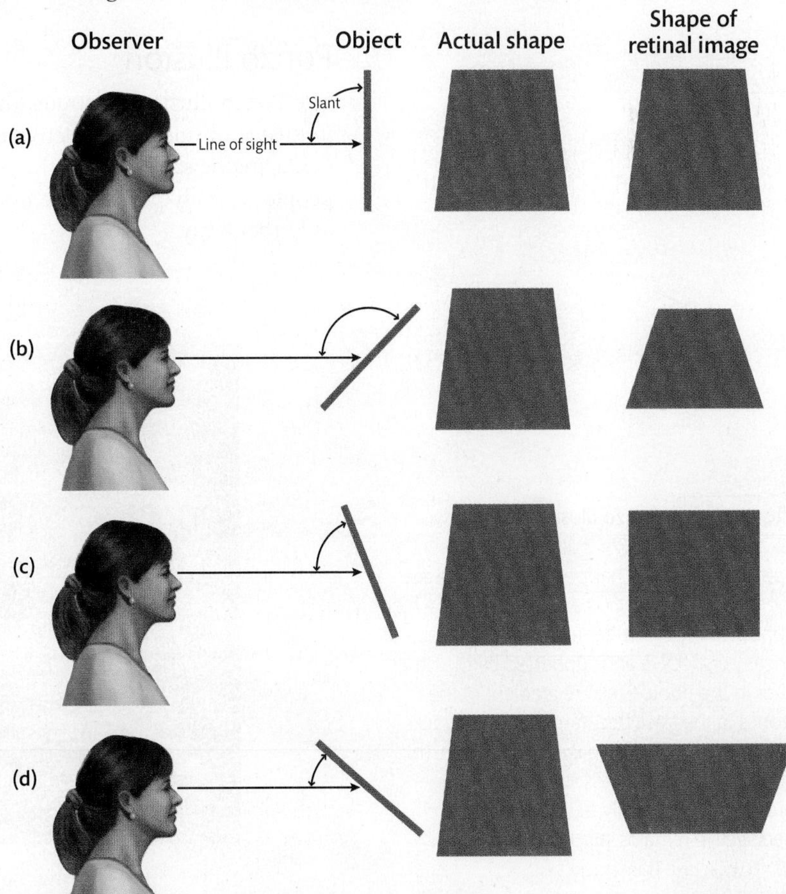

Figure 6.31 Shape–Slant Invariance: Same Object, Different Retinal Images Without slant cues, an observer looking at a single object at different slants has no way of judging its actual shape. (a) When the object is perpendicular to the line of sight, the retinal image has the same trapezoidal shape as the object. (b) If the object is slanted backward, the retinal image is still a trapezoid but not as tall and with a narrower top. (c) If the object is slanted forward the right amount, the retinal image is rectangular. (d) If the object is slanted forward even more, the retinal image is shaped like a short upside-down trapezoid.

Demonstration 6.3 Size, Distance, Shape, Slant Explore the size–distance relation and visual angle; investigate the factors involved in size constancy and size–distance invariance and in shape constancy and shape–slant invariance.

she would have no way of knowing whether the object is actually a trapezoid with the same shape as the retinal image (Figure 6.30a) or any of the other shapes in Figure 6.30—or, for that matter, any of an infinite variety of other shapes. In typical viewing conditions, however, the observer *would* be able to estimate the slant of the object using information derived from cues such as surface shading, binocular disparity, and texture gradients, and once the slant of the object is judged correctly, perception of its true shape follows automatically.

Check Your Understanding

6.18 In the Holway and Boring experiment, what was the purpose of progressively eliminating depth cues? What did the results of the experiment say about size constancy?

6.19 State the principle of size–distance invariance. Emmert's law involves size–distance invariance with what kind of "object"?

6.20 Your retinal image of the rectangular top of your desk assumes different shapes when you view the desk from different perspectives—in fact, your retinal image of it has probably never been rectangular, because you've probably never seen it from directly above. How does the principle of shape–slant invariance let you correctly perceive the desktop's true shape?

Illusions of Depth, Size, and Shape

Visual illusions often work by exploiting the perceptual strategies and operating principles that the visual system automatically relies on, which means that we can often understand how perception works by understanding how a particular illusion works. As we'll see in this section, many illusions work by exploiting the visual system's use of size–distance invariance to trick it into misperceiving distance.

Ponzo Illusion

The Ponzo illusion illustrates the principle of size–distance invariance and the powerful influence of linear perspective on size perception. The two taxis in the photo in Figure 6.32a are the same size on the page (and therefore produce equal-size retinal images), but people typically perceive the upper taxi as larger than the lower one because it's perceived as farther away.

(a)

(b)

Figure 6.32 Ponzo Illusion (a) The two taxis are the same size, but the top one appears larger. This happens because we see the taxis in relation to the railroad tracks, which appear to recede in depth based on the cue of linear perspective and supported by the other cues in the photo—texture gradient of the stones in the track bed, familiar size of tracks, relative height in the image, and so forth. (b) The illusion is much less strong (but still present) because only the cue of linear perspective remains. [tracks: Jupiter Images/Thinkstock; taxi: Thinkstock]

Of course, the tracks might also be interpreted as two lines perpendicular to the line of sight and tilted symmetrically inward (which is, in fact, what they are, as shown schematically in Figure 6.32b) rather than as two lines receding into the distance. However, the automatic perceptual strategies of the visual system evolved before the invention of photographs or realistic depictions of depth in paintings, so the visual system looks at photographs the same way it looks at the natural world, by seeking out the most likely natural interpretation. In this case, Figure 6.32a, with its array of depth cues in addition to linear perspective, enforces the interpretation of depth; in contrast, Figure 6.32b, with only the cue of linear perspective, produces a somewhat weaker size illusion.

Ames Room

Figure 6.33a diagrams the shape of a very strange room—the **Ames room**—invented in 1946 by the American ophthalmologist Adelbert Ames, Jr. (Ittelson, 1952). When viewed with one eye through a peephole in the front wall, an empty Ames room looks like an ordinary box-shaped room. In fact, however, five of its six surfaces (floor, ceiling, and the back and side walls) are trapezoids, as are any windows, floor tiles, and other apparently rectangular shapes—all very precisely constructed to appear rectangular from the perspective of the peephole.

Ames room A room specially designed to create an illusory perception of depth; when viewed with one eye through a peephole, all of the room's trapezoidal surfaces look rectangular.

As you can see from the diagram, the far right corner of the room is much closer to the observer than the far left corner, though they appear equidistant from the peephole. As a result of this illusion, a person standing in the right corner appears to be much taller than a person standing in the left corner, because the retinal image of the person in the right corner is so much larger than that of the person in the left corner (see Figure 6.33b). The illusion is so convincing that a person walking back and forth between the left and right corners actually appears to grow and shrink as she walks. Thus, in contrast to the Ponzo illusion, which works by leading the observer to perceive the lower and upper objects as being at different depths (see Figure 6.32a), the Ames room illusion works by leading the observer to perceive the people in each corner as being at the same depth. The observer is required to look through the peephole with just one eye because that eliminates the oculomotor and binocular depth cues and because the peephole is the only viewpoint from which the trapezoidal shapes all look rectangular.

The Ames room illusion can be seen as a failure of shape constancy. To see why, recall that the shape of any given retinal image could, in principle, originate from an infinite variety of shapes in the world (see Figures 6.2 and 6.31). In natural scenes, it's extremely

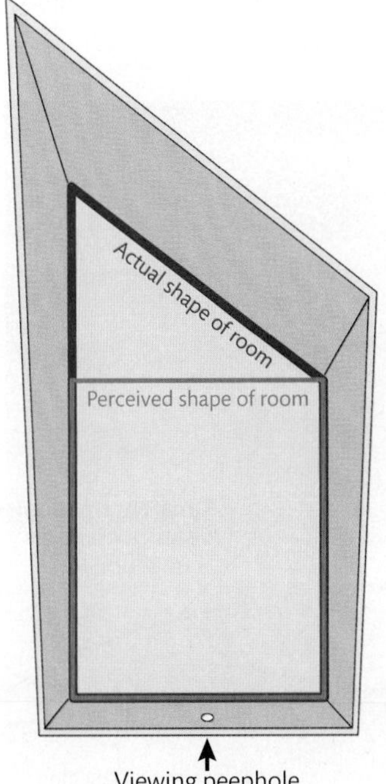

Figure 6.33 Ames Room (a) This shows the actual shape of the Ames room. Except for the rectangular wall containing the viewing peephole, all the surfaces of an Ames room are trapezoidal, but they all appear rectangular to a person looking through the peephole. Thus, the left and right corners of the wall opposite the peephole appear to be equidistant from the observer, and the wall appears to be perpendicular to the line of sight. (b) In this photo taken through the peephole in an Ames room, the girl on the right looks twice as tall as the girl on the left, but they are twins and are exactly the same height. [Mark McKenna]

unlikely that all the monocular depth cues will "conspire" to convey a false impression of the shapes of the objects in view. In the case of the Ames room, however, all the monocular depth cues lead the observer to an incorrect perception of the shape of the room, because the room is meticulously constructed to make that happen. But only a single viewpoint works—if the observer were to view the room from almost any other point, the illusion would fail.

As we have seen, the visual system has evolved to seek the most likely natural interpretation of any given scene, and the arrangement of surfaces and shapes in the Ames room is so enormously unlikely that the visual system is willing to accept that a person could grow or shrink as she walks across a room rather than accept that the complex combination of factors necessary to produce an Ames room has actually occurred.

Moon Illusion

We all know how huge the full moon looks when it's near the horizon, particularly compared to its apparent size when it's high in the sky. Many people assume that the effect is due to a kind of "magnification" caused by the atmosphere, based on the fact that the light reflected from the moon near the horizon has to travel a greater distance through the atmosphere to reach our eyes than does the light from the moon high in the sky. It turns out, however, that the physical size of the moon's retinal image doesn't change with its position in the sky (you can check this yourself by taking photos of the moon in both positions—near the horizon and at its zenith—and measuring the diameter of the moon with a ruler). Instead, the pronounced difference in perceived size is a purely perceptual phenomenon called the *moon illusion*. Why does the horizon moon seem larger than the zenith moon? This question has puzzled scientists for centuries, and we still don't have a definitive answer (Ross & Plug, 2002).

Perhaps the most widely accepted explanation of the moon illusion is that, like most other size illusions, it results from a misperception of distance. In this sense, it's closely related to Emmert's law (see Figure 6.30). The actual distance from an observer on the earth's surface to the moon is virtually the same when the moon is at the horizon and when it's directly overhead. However, researchers have argued that the *perceived* distance to the moon is greater when it's on the horizon (Kaufman & Rock, 1962; a similar proposal was made by the Arab scientist Alhazen in the eleventh century), perhaps because we perceive the moon to be at the height of the clouds (see Figure 6.34). The depth cue of relative height in

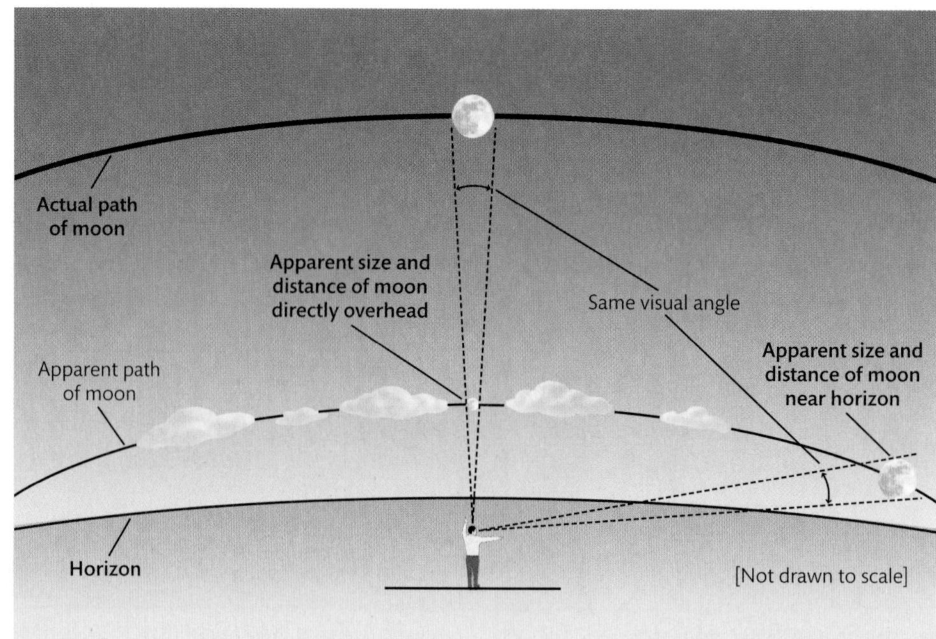

Figure 6.34 Moon Illusion The actual distance from an observer to the moon and, therefore, the size of the retinal image projected by the moon are constant, whether the moon is near the horizon or directly overhead. But if you perceive the moon as being at the height of the clouds (as indicated by the apparent path of the moon), then it's apparently more distant when it's near the horizon. As a result, the size-distance relation leads us to perceive the moon near the horizon as larger.

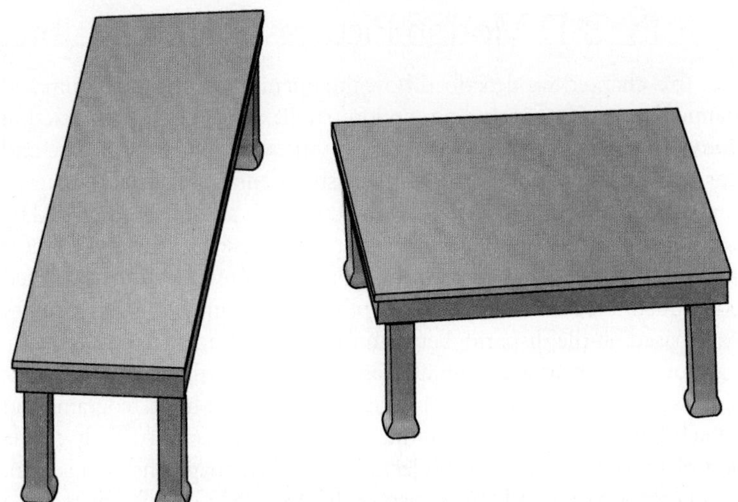

Figure 6.35 **Tabletop Illusion** The two tabletops in this figure are exactly the same shape and size. Thus, their retinal images are the same shape and size too, but because of the perceived slants, we perceive them as very different. (Adapted from Shepard, 1990, p. 48.)

the retinal image tells us that the clouds near the horizon are farther away than the clouds directly overhead. If the moon is perceived to be at the height of the clouds, then the fixed size of the moon's retinal image will lead us to perceive the moon as bigger near the horizon, based on the principle of size–distance invariance.

This seemingly straightforward explanation is not entirely satisfactory, however, because experiments aimed at measuring the perceived distance of the moon at its horizon and zenith positions have often found that the moon is perceived as *closer* when it's at the horizon. Part of the challenge in this kind of experiment is that the larger perceived size of the moon at the horizon may affect its perceived distance, making it seem closer. Similarly, experiments aimed at answering the question "how high is the sky?"—that is, determining the perceived distance of the sky directly overhead and at the horizon—have also proven difficult to conduct rigorously (Ross & Plug, 2002).

Tabletop Illusion

Figure 6.35 shows an illusion of shape sometimes called the *tabletop illusion* (Shepard, 1990, p. 48). The two tabletops are identical in shape and size—you can verify this by tracing one of the tabletops and then fitting the tracing over the other tabletop, which it will cover exactly. The shapes look so different because of their perceived slants.

The tabletop on the left is perceived as slanting back in depth lengthwise, which means we perceive the length as being foreshortened—that is, our visual system assumes that the actual length of the table is greater than its length on the page. The lengthwise (front) edge of the tabletop on the right, in contrast, is perceived as being at a constant depth, so our visual system assumes the table is exactly as long as it appears to be. The reverse is true with respect to width. These opposite perceptual exaggerations of length and width change the perceived shapes in a way that cannot be overcome even if you know the retinal images have the same shape.

Demonstration 6.4 **Illusions of Depth, Size, and Shape** Interact with a variety of illusions based on the principles of size–distance invariance and shape–slant invariance.

Check Your Understanding

6.21 Based on the Ponzo illusion, would you say that the principle of size–distance invariance is an important strategy used by the visual system to assess the size of objects? Explain your answer.

6.22 Why would the Ames room illusion diminish if the peephole was moved to a different position on the front wall?

6.23 If people perceive the moon as being farther away when it's near the horizon than when it's overhead, how does this explain the moon illusion?

APPLICATIONS 3-D Motion Pictures and Television

In an earlier section of this chapter, we described how the opening scene of the animated film *Bambi* uses dynamic depth cues—including motion parallax, optic flow, and deletion and accretion—to convey a sense of depth. Of course, in virtually all motion picture and television productions, these cues have always been the basis for enriching viewers' perception of the relative depth of the objects in a scene, beyond the depth perception provided by static cues based on position, size, and lighting, such as partial occlusion, relative size, linear perspective, and shading. But since its earliest days the motion picture industry has worked to develop stereoscopic technology for conveying depth with the lifelike 3-D vividness provided by stereopsis, based on the disparity between the retinal images in the two eyes.

The images on a movie screen or a TV monitor are flat—that is, they're 2-D—but as we have seen, 3-D stereoscopic perception of flat images can be evoked by stereograms and anaglyphs, both of which have been known since the mid-nineteenth century. Early efforts to achieve 3-D motion pictures were based on projecting red–green anaglyphs on a screen, to be viewed by an audience wearing red–green glasses. In the 1950s, a different method of creating 3-D movies was developed that relied on polarized light—that is, light in which the wave oscillations are confined to a particular direction such as up and down or side to side (most light sources emit waves that oscillate in all possible directions mixed together). Two motion picture cameras with lenses that polarize light in different directions are used to film each scene; a viewer wears glasses in which one lens admits light with one direction of polarization and the other lens admits light with the other direction of polarization. Thus, as with an anaglyph, the two eyes see the slightly different views from the two cameras, and this produces the binocular disparity that evokes stereoscopic depth perception. But unlike anaglyphs, this method allows the photographs to be rendered in full color. This is the method used today to produce 3-D high-definition digital motion pictures that combine live action and computer animation.

(a)

(b) (c)

Figure 6.36 3-D Glasses (a) A 1950s audience watching a 3-D film through glasses made with polarized lenses mounted in a frame. (b) Contemporary 3-D glasses with polarized lenses. The left lens only admits light that's polarized at a specific angle, and the right lens only admits light that's polarized at an angle that differs by 90°; when a left lens is placed at a right angle to a right lens, the view through the two lenses looks black because all light is filtered out. (c) Liquid-crystal shutter glasses rapidly and alternately open and close shutters over the two eyes. They require battery power and a wireless connection to the projector to maintain synchronization. [a: The National Archives/SSPL/Getty Images; b: Ted Szczepanski/Worth Publishers; c: Eduard Härkönen/Fotolia.com]

The 1980s saw the development of a different technology that has since been used to produce 3-D motion pictures, television programs, and video games. As with the technology just described, the film or video is shot by two cameras. When projected, the frames originally shot from one camera alternate at a precisely controlled rate with the frames from the other camera. Viewers wear what are known as *liquid-crystal shutter glasses*, which allow light to pass through only one lens at a time, alternating in sync with the projector so that the left eye sees only the frames taken with the left camera, and the right eye sees only the frames taken with the right camera. This method doesn't require the special screen that's required by the polarized-light method. However, the shutter glasses are much more expensive than the polarized filter glasses; also, they require batteries and a wireless connection with the projector to ensure perfect synchronization between the glasses and the projector. Figure 6.36a and b show some of the differences between 1950s-style and contemporary 3-D glasses using polarized lenses; Figure 6.36c shows a pair of liquid-crystal shutter glasses.

A technology called *autostereoscopy* has been developed to permit 3-D viewing of television or computer monitors without special glasses. On the monitor, alternating columns of pixels display the images originally taken by each camera, and the images are then channeled separately to the two eyes. A version of this technology called the *parallax barrier method* involves placing a barrier with vertical slits in front of the monitor. If the viewer is situated at just the right place, the vertical slits in the barrier admit the images from the left camera to the viewer's left eye and the images from the right camera to the right eye. A different version uses what are called *lenticular lenses*—instead of a barrier with slits, a series of semicircular lens "strips" are placed in front of the monitor. Each lens strip is precisely aligned to cover two adjacent columns of pixels, and the lens sends the images from one column to one eye and the images from the other column to the other eye. This method works for multiple viewers but only at certain specific viewpoints; viewers at other viewpoints will

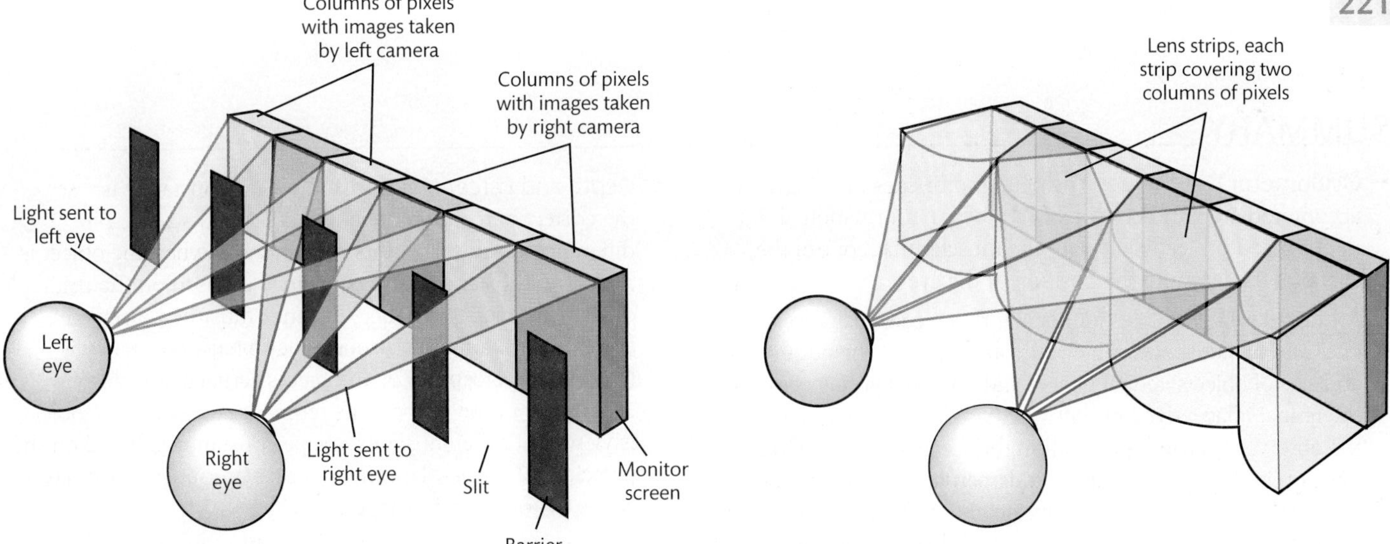

Figure 6.37 Two Methods for Autostereoscopy In the parallax barrier method, the barriers and slits ensure that the images taken by the left and right cameras are sent to the left and right eyes, respectively. This method works only for a single viewer situated at a particular viewpoint, as with handheld video games. In the method using strips of lenticular lenses, each covering two adjacent columns of pixels, the lenses are precisely designed to send the images taken by the left and right cameras to the corresponding eyes, by refracting the light from each column in the right direction. This method works for multiple viewers but only at certain specific viewpoints.

see either double images or no image at all. Figure 6.37 illustrates some of the similarities and differences in the two methods.

All these methods for producing 3-D motion pictures or video provide the same stereoscopic view of the scene to every viewer, because the scene is originally captured by a single pair of cameras positioned at one location. In a theater showing a 3-D movie, it makes no difference where a person is sitting—everyone in the audience sees the movie from the same perspective. Similarly, viewers in different locations looking at a display using lenticular lenses all see the same view of the scene on the monitor. In contrast, the next generation of 3-D video will be based on a technology called *holography* and will present a different view of the scene to viewers in different locations. That is, a viewer will be able to get different views of the scene by moving her head or walking around the display, bringing into play dynamic depth cues such as motion parallax and deletion and accretion that result from the viewer's own motion, not just from the motion of objects in the scene.

Holographic images are created by capturing a scene with many cameras positioned around the scene. Although current displays can be refreshed only once every 2 seconds, which is too slow to depict normal motion, researchers predict that advances in laser technology and materials will permit much more rapid refreshing within the next 5–10 years (Blanche et al., 2010). The first applications are likely to be in science and medicine; home consumer devices will no doubt follow as production becomes less expensive.

Check Your Understanding

6.24 In 3-D motion pictures, which type of depth cue provides the "extra" sense of depth as compared to the sense of depth provided by conventional motion pictures?

- **A.** Binocular
- **B.** Static
- **C.** Dynamic

6.25 Why wouldn't either method of autostereoscopy (the parallax barrier method or the method with lenticular lenses) work for showing a 3-D motion picture to a large audience in a theater?

6.26 Motion parallax is a depth cue in conventional motion pictures, in 3-D motion pictures viewed through polarizing glasses, and in holographic displays. How does holography differ from the other two technologies in the use of this depth cue?

SUMMARY

- Oculomotor Depth Cues The oculomotor cues of accommodation and convergence provide information about depth based on feedback from the muscles that control the shape of the lens and the position of the eyes.
- Monocular Depth Cues Monocular depth cues include static cues and dynamic cues. Static cues are based on the position and size of objects' retinal images and on how lighting affects the retinal image; dynamic cues are based on the motion of the observer and/or objects within the scene. Cues based on position in the retinal image include partial occlusion of one object by another and the relative height of objects in the retinal image. Cues based on the size of objects' retinal image include familiar size, relative size, texture gradients, and linear perspective. Lighting cues include atmospheric perspective, shading, and cast shadows. Dynamic cues include motion parallax, optic flow, and deletion and accretion.
- Binocular Depth Cue: Disparity in the Retinal Images The two eyes have slightly different retinal images of the same scene; this difference is called *binocular disparity*. The visual system processes the different retinal images in a way that provides a vivid sense of depth, called *stereopsis*. Corresponding points on the two retinas are points that would coincide if the retinas were superimposed; noncorresponding points wouldn't coincide if the retinas were superimposed. The horopter is the surface in the field of view that consists of all the locations from which objects would project retinal images at corresponding points. In the combined retinal image, objects that exhibit crossed or uncrossed disparity project images at noncorresponding points. The distance between the images in the two eyes defines the magnitude of the binocular disparity. The visual system can use binocular disparity as a depth cue only if the parts of the two retinal images that correspond can be determined—this is known as the *correspondence problem*. Cortical neurons called *binocular cells* provide a means by which the visual system can measure binocular disparity.
- Integrating Depth Cues Different cues provide different types of information about depth and work under different conditions, but the information they provide tends to be complementary, adding up to a single, consistent, strongly supported representation of the spatial layout.
- Depth and Perceptual Constancy Size constancy is the correct perception of an object's actual size despite differences in the size of its retinal image when the object is at different distances; size constancy is based on the principle of size–distance invariance; distance must be perceived correctly to maintain size constancy. Shape constancy is the correct perception of an object's actual shape despite differences in the shape of its retinal image when the object is viewed at different slants; shape constancy is based on the principle of shape–slant invariance; slant must be perceived correctly to maintain shape constancy.
- Illusions of Depth, Size, and Shape Illusions work by exploiting the operating principles of the visual system; by understanding how an illusion works, we can also understand these operating principles. The Ponzo illusion illustrates how the visual system depends on size–distance invariance to judge the size of an object by the size of its retinal image together with its apparent distance. The Ames room illusion shows what happens when shape constancy fails and when the assumption of naturalness leads us to accept the unnatural. The moon illusion is thought to result from perceiving the moon as being farther away when it's near the horizon than when it's overhead; thus, this illusion also is based on the principle of size–distance invariance. The tabletop illusion shows that perceived slant affects perceived shape.
- Applications: 3-D Motion Pictures and Television The first 3-D motion pictures were based on projecting red–green anaglyphs to be viewed by an audience wearing red–green glasses. In the 1950s, full-color 3-D films made using polarized light reflected from a special screen and viewed through polarized glasses became popular. A technology using liquid-crystal shutter glasses eliminates the need for a special screen but requires that the glasses contain a battery and have a wireless connection with the projector. Autostereoscopic techniques, including the parallax barrier method and a method using lenticular lenses, allow 3-D viewing of television or computer monitors without special glasses but are limited to one viewer or just a few viewers at a time. Holography creates 3-D images that can be seen in different perspectives from different locations.

KEY TERMS

accretion (p. 202)
Ames room (p. 217)
anaglyph (p. 208)
atmospheric perspective (p. 198)
binocular cells (p. 211)
binocular disparity (p. 203)
correspondence problem (p. 207)
corresponding points (p. 204)
crossed disparity (p. 204)
deletion (p. 202)
Emmert's law (p. 215)
familiar size (p. 196)
horopter (p. 204)
interposition, see partial occlusion.
linear perspective (p. 197)
monocular depth cues (p. 192)
motion parallax (p. 201)
noncorresponding points (p. 204)
oculomotor depth cues (p. 192)
optic flow (p. 201)
partial occlusion (or *interposition*) (p. 193)
random dot stereogram (RDS) (p. 209)
relative height (p. 195)
relative size (p. 196)
shape constancy (p. 215)
shape–slant invariance (p. 215)

size constancy (p. 214)
size–distance invariance (p. 214)
size–distance relation (p. 195)
size perspective (p. 195)
static monocular depth cues (p. 193)
stereogram (p. 207)
stereopsis (or *stereoscopic depth perception*) (p. 203)
stereoscopic depth perception, see **stereopsis**.
texture gradient (p. 197)
uncrossed disparity (p. 205)
visual angle (p. 195)
zero disparity (p. 206)

EXPAND YOUR UNDERSTANDING

6.1 Of the three depth cues that depend on lighting—atmospheric perspective, shading, and cast shadows—which one would be least affected in a scene where the illumination came from more than one direction? Explain why.

6.2 Suppose you're sitting at a four-foot-square table having dinner with two friends. If you're looking at the friend seated on the side next to you and then switch your gaze to focus on the friend seated across from you, does accommodation or convergence (or both) tell you that the friend across from you is farther away than the friend next to you? Explain your answer.

6.3 Describe the movements of an observer and one object in a scene where the dynamic depth cues of motion parallax and deletion and accretion come into play simultaneously.

6.4 When you look at the right-hand image in Figure 6.28 with the red lens on the left and the blue lens on the right, you see a heart floating in front of the background. What do you see when you reverse the lenses? Why?

6.5 You're standing motionless, looking at a scene containing five stationary objects (object A through object E) and fixating on object A. Objects A and C exhibit zero disparity, object D exhibits crossed disparity, and objects B and E exhibit uncrossed disparity (with object B's disparity being larger than object E's). List the objects in order of their increasing distance from you. If you shifted your gaze to object E, which object(s) would now exhibit uncrossed disparity?

6.6 This chapter discusses a problem that two-eyed people have to solve but one-eyed people do not. What is that problem and why don't one-eyed people have to solve it? Why didn't Sue Barry (from the vignette at the beginning of the chapter) have to solve it before she acquired stereopsis, despite having two eyes?

6.7 When you look at a person walking back and forth in an Ames room, you see them apparently growing and shrinking (and you see the room as rectangular). How would your perception change if you could look at the room with both eyes instead of just one?

6.8 Even if holography were developed to the point where a high-quality motion picture could be shown to a large audience in a theater, the experience of each individual member of the audience wouldn't be much different from the experience of watching a 3-D movie through polarized glasses, but comparing the experiences of all audience members would reveal that many of those experiences were quite different from each other. Explain why.

6.9 The figure below illustrates the Pulfrich effect, a visual illusion in which a viewer keeps one eye covered with a filter (like the lens of a pair of sunglasses) while looking at a pendulum swinging back and forth. The dark lens has the effect of delaying the neural signal from that eye on its way to binocular cells in the brain. The illusion is that the pendulum appears to move not in a flat plane, but in an elliptical fashion, swinging toward and then away from the viewer. Explain why the illusion happens.

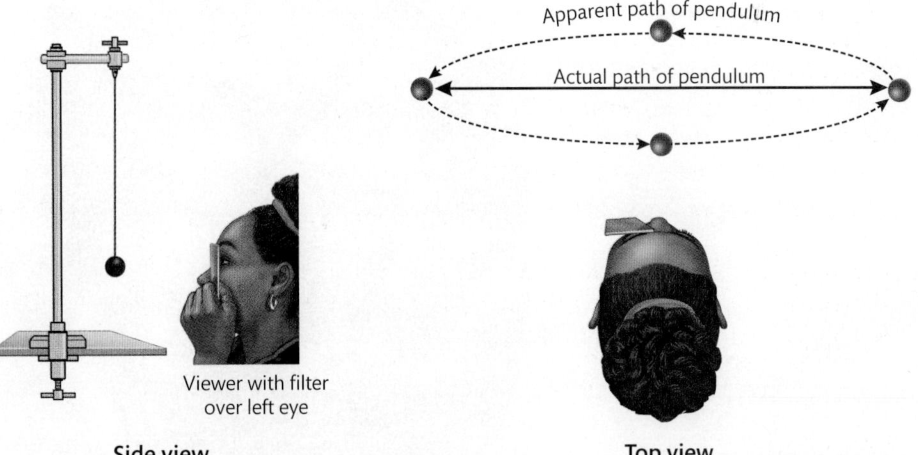

READ MORE ABOUT IT

Cumming, B. G., & DeAngelis, G. C. (2001). The physiology of stereopsis. *Annual Review of Neuroscience, 24,* 203–238. Parker, A. J. (2007). Binocular depth perception and the cerebral cortex. *Nature Reviews Neuroscience, 8,* 379–391.

Two articles that, together, provide a comprehensive review of the neural basis of stereopsis.

Howard, I. P. (2002). *Seeing in depth:* Vol. 1. *Basic mechanisms.* Toronto: I. Porteus. Howard, I. P., & Rogers, B. J. (2002). *Seeing in depth:* Vol. 2. *Depth perception.* Toronto: I. Porteus.

Two volumes that stand as the definitive, comprehensive reference on human depth perception.

Ikahl Beckford, *Windy Day*. [Mixed media, 431 × 600 cm. Private collection. The Bridgeman Art Library.]

7

PERCEIVING MOTION AND PERCEPTION FOR ACTION

Still Life

In 1978, L.M., a 43-year-old woman, suffered a stroke that affected both hemispheres of her brain, in the regions where the occipital and temporal lobes join. She recovered sufficiently to leave the hospital, but the stroke had left her with a range of problems. More than 18 months later, these problems brought her back to the hospital for further examination. She complained of becoming easily fatigued and of memory and concentration problems, but her most serious complaint was the loss of her ability to see motion. Extensive testing showed that virtually all of her other cognitive and perceptual abilities were completely normal, with that one exception: she couldn't see motion. For example, she had great difficulty pouring tea into a cup because she couldn't perceive the level of the tea rising and filling the cup (the tea would look frozen, like a glacier), so she would often make the cup overflow. She was very uncomfortable in places where people were walking about, because "people were suddenly here or there but I have not seen them moving"; she would usually leave the room in these circumstances, and of course she avoided crowded streets and other public places. Moving vehicles presented an even more serious problem because she couldn't estimate the speed of oncoming traffic when trying to cross the street: "When I'm looking at the car first, it seems far away. But then, when I want to cross the road, suddenly the car is very near." Over time, she learned how to compensate for this by relying on the increasing loudness of the sounds made by approaching cars, but in most other aspects of her life there was little she could do to ameliorate the effects of her condition. The region of L.M.'s brain damaged by the stroke includes area MT, a "motion center" discussed in detail in this chapter.

Much of our discussion of visual perception in the last few chapters has been limited to static scenes. But the world is filled with objects in motion. People, animals, and vehicles all move across our visual field, and even shrubs and trees sway in the wind. We must be able to not only recognize moving objects but also judge their trajectories, so we can determine, for example, whether there's enough time to make a left turn in front of oncoming traffic. Frogs must be able to capture moving insects with a flick of their tongue, and baseball players have only a tenth of a second in which to coordinate the swing of their bat with an oncoming fastball. Moreover, we ourselves are continuously moving—walking or driving, moving our heads and, several times a second, our eyes. Thus, the retinal image—even for objects that are stationary—is changing all the time.

Chapter Outline

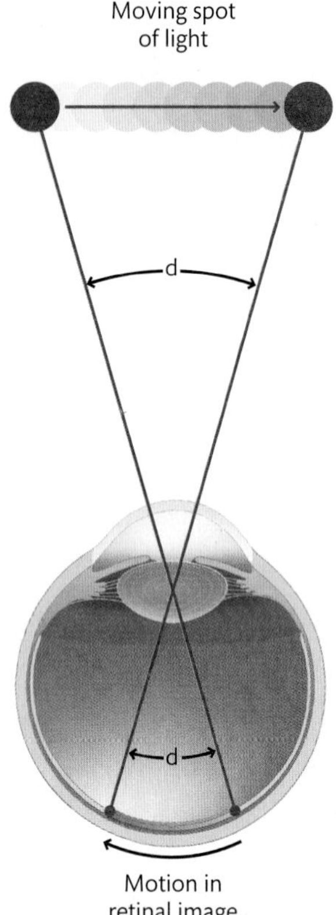

Figure 7.1 Motion in the Retinal Image A spot of light moving from left to right traverses a distance **d** (measured in degrees of visual angle) across the visual field, and the retinal image of the light traverses the same distance **d** from right to left across the retina.

To approach the complexity of motion perception, we'll start with the simplest case: a stationary observer looking at an otherwise static scene containing a single visual feature (e.g., a point, an edge, or an object) moving in a straight line at a constant speed. Our examination of this simplest case will allow us to begin to understand the neural mechanisms in the brain that respond to motion. We'll follow this with a discussion of how motion perception contributes to perceptual organization, including figure–ground organization and the perception of moving biological objects (e.g., people). Then we'll go beyond the simple case of a stationary observer and look at what happens when the observer's eyes move to explore a scene or to track a moving object. Finally, we'll look at what happens when the entire observer or part of the observer's body moves through the environment—that is, we'll explore how perceptual information is used to guide actions such as reaching, grasping, and navigating.

Motion Perception in Area V1 and Area MT

If the retina of an observer is absolutely stationary, then the motion of a visual feature such as a spot of light—that is, its change in position over time—produces an exactly corresponding change over time in the corresponding part of the retinal image. Figure 7.1 illustrates this in the case of a spot of red light that moves from left to right across the visual field. If you wanted to adjust your behavior according to the motion of this spot of light—say, to trace its motion with your finger—you would need to know three things: its position, its direction of motion, and its speed. We saw in Chapters 3 and 4 that the visual system uses *retinotopic mapping* to represent the positions of features in the retinal image; in this section, we'll explore how the visual system represents direction and speed of motion.

A Simple Neural Circuit That Responds to Motion

In order to detect and represent the motion of some feature in the retinal image, a neural circuit must monitor at least two different retinal locations and must register the order in which those locations were stimulated and how far apart in time they were stimulated. For a feature moving in a straight line at a constant speed (as we're assuming throughout this section), these pieces of information specify its direction and speed: the direction is specified by the line connecting the two retinal locations and the order in which the locations are stimulated, and the speed is specified by the distance between those locations and the time between the stimulation of one location and the next.

At first glance, you might think that the neural circuit illustrated in Figure 7.2a is a plausible model for a circuit that could respond to motion. Assume that neuron M responds strongly only when it receives simultaneous signals from Neuron 1 and Neuron 2. Neurons 1 and 2 have receptive fields RF_1 and RF_2, respectively, separated by some distance on the retina. Thus, Neuron M monitors the two different retinal locations RF_1 and RF_2. However, Neuron M in Figure 7.2a won't exhibit a motion-selective response—that is, in this circuit Neuron M can't be tuned to represent a particular direction and speed of motion. Let's see why.

A spot of red light moving left to right across the retina at a certain speed strikes RF_1 at Time 1, causing Neuron 1 to send a signal to Neuron M. This signal stimulates Neuron M at Time 2. At Time 3, the spot of light strikes RF_2, causing Neuron 2 to send a signal that stimulates Neuron M at Time 4. Since the signal from Neuron 1 arrives at Neuron M before the signal from Neuron 2, Neuron M doesn't respond strongly. In this circuit, Neuron M will respond strongly only if RF_1 and RF_2 are stimulated simultaneously, which clearly isn't what we want from a motion-selective neuron.

Werner Reichardt (1924–1992).
[Max Planck Institute for Biological Cybernetics, Tübingen, Germany]

However, as was pointed out by the German neuroscientist Werner Reichardt (1961), Neuron M will respond selectively to the direction and speed of motion if the circuit includes a *delay* in the signals from either Neuron 1 or Neuron 2. Figure 7.2b illustrates such a circuit in which Neuron M is tuned to motion in a left-to-right direction at a specific speed. A spot of light moving in this way stimulates RF_1 at Time 1, causing Neuron 1 to send a signal to Neuron M. This signal is delayed by just the right amount to ensure that

(a) Circuit in which signals from Neurons 1 and 2 have equal transmission times to Neuron M

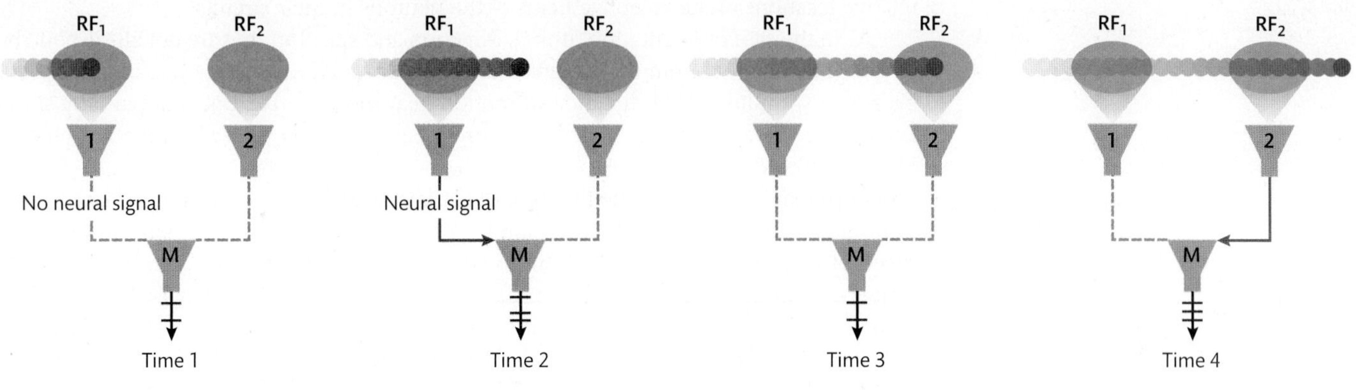

(b) Circuit with a delay in the transmission of signals from Neuron 1

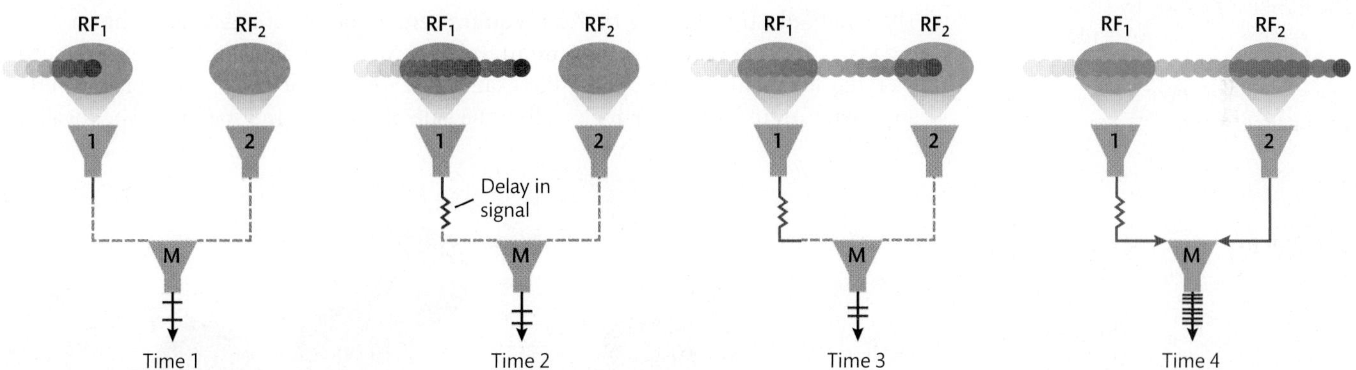

Figure 7.2 A Simple Neural Circuit That Responds to Motion A spot of red light is moving from left to right across the retina, first stimulating the receptive field RF_1 of Neuron 1 and then stimulating the receptive field RF_2 of Neuron 2. Both neurons send signals to Neuron M, which responds strongly only if signals from Neuron 1 and Neuron 2 arrive simultaneously. (a) In a circuit in which the signals from Neurons 1 and 2 take equal amounts of time to travel to Neuron M, the signal from Neuron 1 reaches Neuron M at Time 2, but the signal from Neuron 2 doesn't reach Neuron M until Time 4, and Neuron M doesn't respond strongly. In this circuit, the response of neuron M won't provide information about motion. (b) In a circuit in which the signal from Neuron 1 is delayed, the signals from Neurons 1 and 2 arrive at Neuron M simultaneously. In this case, Neuron M's strong response indicates that there is motion from left to right at a certain speed (the speed at which the red spot is traveling across the retina) in the portion of the visual field between RF_1 and RF_2.

it arrives at Neuron M at Time 4, simultaneously with the signal from Neuron 2, causing Neuron M to respond strongly.

Thus, in this circuit, Neuron M is tuned for both the direction and speed of motion: if the spot of light were moving from right to left, it would stimulate RF_2 before it stimulated RF_1, and the resulting signals would arrive at Neuron M far apart in time; and if the spot of light were moving left to right but at a different speed, the given delay wouldn't be correct—the signals from Neurons 1 and 2 would arrive at Neuron M at somewhat different times. A delay in the transmission of neural signals could be based on various mechanisms—for example, Neuron 1 might have a longer axon than Neuron 2, or Neuron 1's axon might be unmyelinated, in either case causing action potentials to take a longer time to travel from Neuron 1 to Neuron M than from Neuron 2 to Neuron M.

This example shows that direction tuning is determined by whether the delay is built into the transmission of signals from Neuron 1 or Neuron 2, and that speed tuning is determined by the length of the delay. Note that in the example we've discussed, the motion-selective neuron is tuned to only one speed. Other neurons with different delays built into

Demonstration 7.1 A Neural Circuit That Responds to Motion Explore how motion-selective neurons can represent the speed and direction of moving spots of light.

their circuits would be tuned to other speeds, both slower and faster. And of course, other motion-selective neurons would be tuned to other directions of motion, depending on the relative locations of the receptive fields of the neurons in their circuits.

As in the case of orientation tuning, direction and speed tuning are not all-or-none but have a gradual falloff from the preferred direction or speed to nearby directions or speeds, because a stimulus with a direction of motion near the preferred one will partially stimulate the receptive fields in the circuit and produce a moderate increase in the firing rate of M (see Figure 7.3).

In primates, area V1 is the first part of the visual pathway where neurons like Neuron M in Figure 7.2b have been found. Many neurons in V1 are tuned for both direction and speed of motion (Orban et al., 1986), in addition to being tuned for orientation, like the simple cells discussed in Chapter 3, or disparity, like the binocular cells discussed in Chapter 6. In several nonprimate species—including the rabbit, cat, and mouse—retinal ganglion cells have been found that respond selectively to direction of motion (first reported in the rabbit by Barlow et al., 1964). Such neurons have not yet been found in the primate retina, but they are thought likely to exist.

motion aftereffect (MAE) A visual illusion in which a stationary element of the visual scene appears to be moving in a direction opposite to the direction of motion experienced during the immediately preceding time interval.

The Motion Aftereffect

The circuit illustrated in Figure 7.2b requires certain modifications to account for a striking visual illusion called the **motion aftereffect (MAE)**, an illusion often experienced in everyday life (Mather et al., 1998). For example, if you stare at a waterfall for a few minutes and then turn to look at the rock wall to the side of the falls, the stationary rock wall may

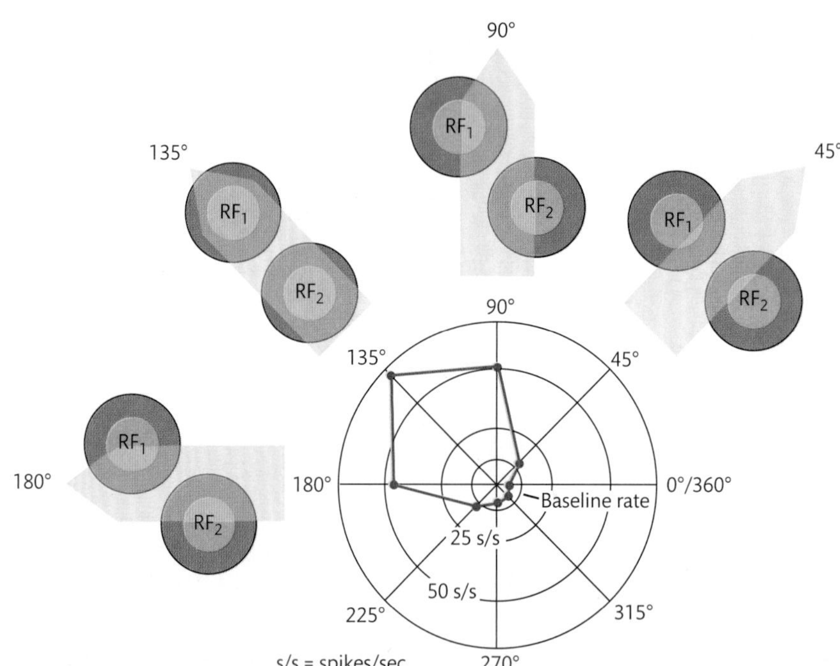

Figure 7.3 Direction Tuning of a Motion-Selective Neuron The polar plot shows the response of a direction-tuned neuron in spikes per second (s/s) as a function of the direction of a moving bar of light. The red line indicates that this neuron responds most strongly to motion at an angle of 135° (its preferred direction) but still responds significantly to motion in other directions between 90° and 180°, showing that direction tuning isn't all-or-none but falls off gradually from the preferred direction. The response is slightly *below* baseline for motion more or less opposite to the preferred direction, between 270° and 360°. Surrounding the polar plot are illustrations of a bar of light passing over the receptive fields (RFs) of the two neurons from which the direction-tuned neuron receives signals. A bar of light moving at an angle of 135° sweeps across the entire excitatory center of each receptive field. A bar of light moving at 90° or 180° covers less of the excitatory centers and more of the surrounds. A bar moving at 45° barely touches the excitatory centers and stimulates both receptive fields at about the same time; hence, the neuron's response to this stimulus is barely above baseline.

appear to be moving slowly upward—that is, opposite to the direction of the falling water, and this is why the MAE is sometimes referred to as the "waterfall illusion." Or if, while traveling by train, you gaze straight out the window as the landscape flows by, when you stop at a station you may have the impression that the platform is drifting slowly forward or, equivalently, that the train is now moving slowly backward.

Figure 7.4 illustrates a neural circuit that can account for the MAE (Mather & Harris, 1998), based on an idea first tested in the rabbit retina (Barlow & Hill, 1963). The circuit

Demonstration 7.2 Motion Aftereffect Experience the motion aftereffect, and explore the neural circuitry that underlies it.

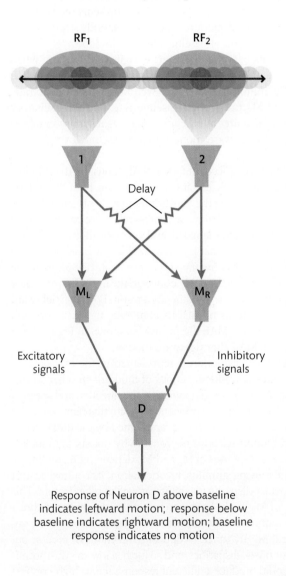

Light moves either leftward or rightward across RF_1 and RF_2

RF_1 RF_2

1 2

Delay

M_L M_R

Excitatory signals

Inhibitory signals

D

Response of Neuron D above baseline indicates leftward motion; response below baseline indicates rightward motion; baseline response indicates no motion

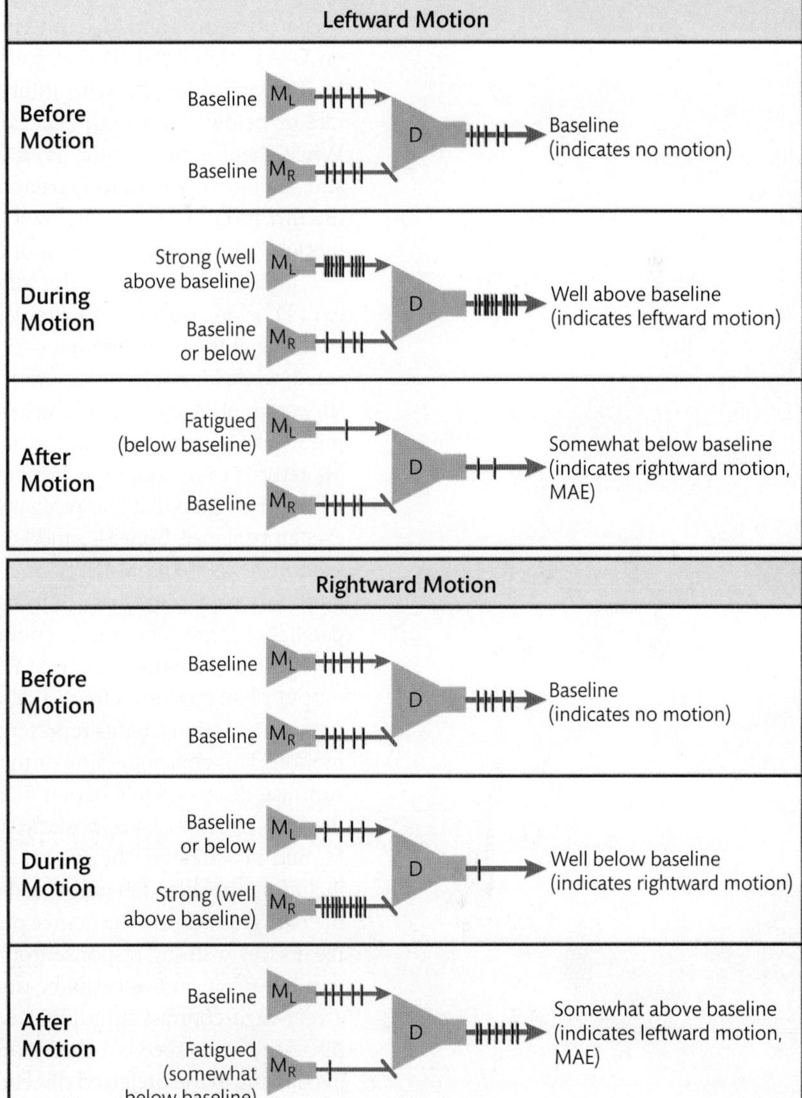

Figure 7.4 A Neural Circuit That Accounts for the Motion Aftereffect (left) The circuit contains two subunits—one consists of Neurons 1, 2, and M_L, and the other consists of Neurons 1, 2, and M_R. The subunit with M_L responds to leftward motion (from right to left); the subunit with M_R responds to rightward motion (from left to right). M_L's signals to D are excitatory; M_R's signals to D are inhibitory. This means that the response of neuron D represents the *difference* in the responses of M_L and M_R. (right) During leftward motion, excitatory signals outweigh inhibitory signals, and D responds strongly, well above baseline. During rightward motion, inhibitory signals outweigh excitatory signals, and D responds well below baseline. A motion aftereffect occurs if either leftward or rightward motion continues long enough for the strongly responding M neuron (M_L or M_R) to become fatigued. After the motion stops, the fatigued neuron's response rate falls below baseline; now the baseline response of the other M neuron predominates, and D's response indicates the opposite direction of motion for a time, until the fatigued neuron recovers.

contains two subunits, each like the circuit in Figure 7.2b but tuned to represent motion in opposite directions:

- The subunit with the motion-selective neuron M_L responds strongly to leftward motion, in which RF_2 is stimulated first; during rightward motion, M_L just continues to fire at its baseline rate or may even be slightly inhibited.
- The subunit with the motion-selective neuron M_R responds strongly to rightward motion, in which RF_1 is stimulated first; during leftward motion, M_R just continues to fire at its baseline rate or may even be slightly inhibited. (This subunit is the same as the circuit illustrated in Figure 7.2b.)

Neurons M_L and M_R both send signals to neuron D: M_L's signals have an excitatory effect on D, while M_R's signals have an inhibitory effect, and D's response represents the *difference* in the responses of M_L and M_R. During leftward motion, when M_L responds strongly with excitatory signals and M_R's inhibitory signals come at baseline rate or below, the overall effect on D is excitatory, so D fires well above its baseline rate. During rightward motion, when M_R responds strongly with inhibitory signals and M_L's excitatory signals come at baseline rate or below, the overall effect on D is inhibitory, so D fires well below its baseline rate. When there is no motion, both M_L and M_R fire at their baseline rate, and the excitatory and inhibitory signals to D balance, so D also fires at baseline. Thus, D's response indicates the direction of motion: below baseline for leftward motion, above baseline for rightward motion, and baseline for no motion.

Figure 7.4 shows how this kind of circuit can account for the MAE. Consider the responses of D before, during, and after leftward motion. Before any motion occurs, both M_L and M_R are firing at their baseline rate—so D is, too. During the leftward motion, M_L is strongly activated, while M_R continues to fire at baseline or even below, so D fires well above baseline. If the leftward motion continues long enough, M_L becomes fatigued, and when the motion stops, M_L produces very few spontaneous action potentials—that is, it fires well below baseline—while M_R returns to or continues firing at its normal baseline rate (Petersen et al., 1985). Now the inhibitory signals that D is receiving at baseline rate from M_R outweigh the lower-than-baseline excitatory signals from M_L, and D's response is below baseline. As a result, D signals rightward motion—this is the MAE. Soon, M_L returns to its normal baseline rate, the excitatory and inhibitory signals to D return to balance, and the MAE disappears. As shown in Figure 7.4, a parallel sequence of events accounts for the MAE after rightward motion.

This explanation of the MAE suggests that motion is represented in the brain by the output of an *opponent* circuit that compares opposite directions of motion—in other words, opponent motion circuits represent *motion contrast,* or differences in the direction and speed of motion. This concept is similar to the concept of how opponent color circuits represent color contrast, discussed in Chapter 5. But why should motion be represented by the difference in the responses of two oppositely tuned motion-selective neurons? Why not simply monitor M_L and M_R directly? The answer is that the responses of M_L and M_R depend on many things, including the direction and speed of the moving stimulus, its orientation, its contrast against the background, and the degree of binocular disparity it exhibits, as well as other factors. This means that a strong response from M_L or M_R might be due to motion in the preferred direction but might just as easily be due to motion in a somewhat nonpreferred direction by, say, a very-high-contrast stimulus. If M_L and M_R are tuned to opposite directions of motion but tuned to similar speeds, orientations, contrasts, disparities, and so forth, a low-contrast stimulus moving in the preferred direction would produce a different response than a high-contrast stimulus moving in a nonpreferred direction. Thus, the circuit shown in Figure 7.4 is an elegant solution to the problem of representing motion, given the many different factors that can affect the responses of motion-selective neurons. From this point of view, the MAE is simply an odd but not especially maladaptive consequence of how motion perception has evolved.

Area MT

As we noted above, many neurons in area V1 are tuned to direction and speed of motion—but many other V1 neurons aren't. Also, V1 neurons have very small receptive fields, so even motion-selective cells in V1 can respond to motion only in a highly restricted region of the retinal image. As soon as a moving stimulus passes out of that small region, the V1 cell stops responding. This means that individual V1 neurons can't represent motions of large objects moving over extended distances. In this section, we'll explore a region of the brain known as *area MT* (for *middle temporal* area, also called *V5,* first discussed in Chapter 3), which receives signals from V1 and V2, as well as from the superior colliculus (which controls eye movements).

MT Neurons Respond Selectively to Motion

Single-cell recording in monkeys has shown that almost all the neurons in area MT are tuned for direction of motion (Zeki, 1974), and the receptive fields of MT neurons are 5–10 times as large in diameter as those of V1 neurons (Born & Bradley, 2005), so MT neurons are well suited for representing larger-scale motions. Also significant is the fact that neurons in other areas at the higher levels of the primate visual pathways are tuned to features such as color and curvature (in area V4) or shape (in the inferotemporal cortex) but not to direction of motion, whereas MT neurons are tuned to direction of motion but not to color, curvature, or shape—that is, MT neurons respond about the same to objects that differ in those features (however, it's worth noting that there is some evidence that MT neurons may play a role in the representation of stereoscopic depth, as well as other features [Chowdhury & DeAngelis, 2008]). Taken together, these observations lead to the idea that area MT is a critical "motion center" in the primate brain (Britten, 2004).

Studies of the human brain using fMRI have revealed that area MT—unlike area V1—is much more active when a person looks at a moving stimulus than at a stationary one (Tootell et al., 1995), as shown in Figure 7.5a. Figure 7.5b is an fMRI image indicating the location of area MT and showing this difference in activity in response to motion (Becker et al., 2008). If a stimulus containing both moving and stationary dots is presented to a human participant who is instructed to attend to either the moving dots or the stationary dots, the response in area MT is greater when the participant is attending to the moving

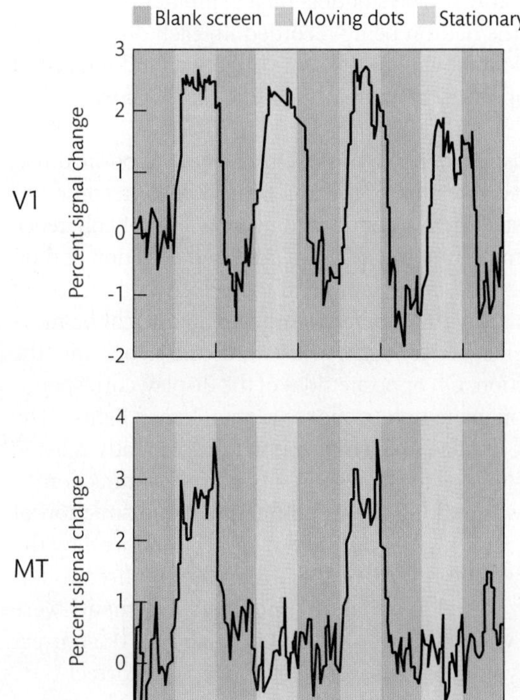

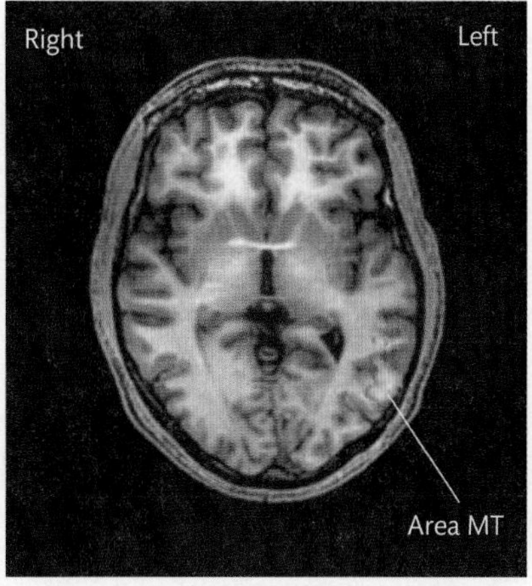

Figure 7.5 Activity in Area V1 Versus Area MT in Response to Stationary Versus Moving Stimuli (a) These graphs compare human brain activity in area V1 to activity in area MT while observers were viewing displays showing moving dots, stationary dots, or a blank screen. In area V1, stationary dots generate about as much activity as moving dots, compared to a blank screen. In area MT, only moving dots produce a significant burst of activity. (Adapted from Tootell et al., 1995.) (b) In this fMRI image, the orange area shows that left-hemisphere area MT responds more strongly to a moving stimulus in the right visual field than to a stationary stimulus. (Adapted and image from Becker et al., 2008.)

dots (O'Craven et al., 1997). In other experiments, participants were presented with stimuli moving in different directions and had to attend to motion in one of the directions. The results showed that the pattern of activity within area MT differed according to the attended direction of motion (Kamitani & Tong, 2006; Liu et al., 2011). All these observations confirm that area MT is specialized for representing motion and that MT neurons are tuned to different directions of motion.

Activity of MT Neurons Causes Directionally Selective Motion Perception

The single-cell recording and fMRI measurements described in the previous section show that when a monkey or a person views motion, MT neurons respond selectively. But in principle this could be merely a "side effect" of motion perception—that is, it could be that the activity of neurons elsewhere in the brain produces motion perception while also causing MT neurons to increase their activity. To establish that the activity of MT neurons does, in fact, cause the perceptual experience of motion, different methods are needed. In one study, monkeys were trained to press a bar to indicate the direction of motion of dots presented on a computer screen (Salzman et al., 1992). After training, their performance was highly accurate. An electrode was then placed in the monkeys' area MT, and the responses of individual MT neurons were recorded to determine each neuron's motion-direction selectivity. Finally, a very tiny current was applied to each neuron—a technique called *microstimulation*—and it was found that the monkeys tended to respond as if they had seen the direction of motion that corresponded to the stimulated neuron's directional selectivity. Given that only MT neurons were activated by this procedure, these results are strong evidence that motion perception is caused by neural activity in area MT.

William T. Newsome (b. 1952). [Courtesy of William Newsome]

Further evidence for the role of MT neurons in motion perception comes from experiments carried out by William Newsome and colleagues (1989). The activity of single MT neurons in a monkey's brain was recorded while the monkey was making judgments about direction of motion. The results showed a clear, quantitative relationship between the neural activity and the monkey's judgments, which supports the idea that the activity of MT neurons plays a causal role in directionally selective motion perception.

In these experiments, a monkey was shown arrays of dots on a computer screen, with each array covering the receptive field of the neuron being recorded. In each display, some of the dots (ranging from 0% to 100%) were moving in the same direction, and the rest of the dots were moving randomly. The proportion moving in the same direction was called the *coherence* of the motion.

The coherently moving dots in each display were moving in either of two opposite directions, corresponding either to the preferred direction of the MT neuron being recorded or to the opposite direction. Each display lasted for 2 seconds, and at each level of coherence the monkey would see 60 trials with the motion in the neuron's preferred direction and 60 trials with the motion in the opposite direction. For example, if the preferred direction of the neuron was left to right, then in one display the coherently moving dots might be moving rightward and in the next display either rightward again or leftward, and so on, until the monkey had seen 60 displays in each direction. On opposite sides of the display, corresponding to the two possible directions of motion, were two "response points" (small lights). The monkey was trained to look at the display, decide in which direction the coherently moving dots were moving, and then move its eyes to look at the response point in that direction.

At the same time that the monkey was making these judgments about direction of motion in each display, a computer was counting the number of spikes produced by the neuron being recorded. Figure 7.6 shows the results of this counting for three different levels of motion coherence—12.8%, a level at which the monkey's judgments were more than 95% correct; 3.2%, a level at which the monkey had only about 70% correct judgments; and 0.8%, where the monkey's judgments were just above 50% correct (i.e., mostly guesses).

At a coherence level of 12.8%, the cell's response to motion in its preferred direction was clearly greater than its response to motion in the opposite direction—the gray bars in Figure 7.6a are almost all to the right of the black bars. To put the same results in

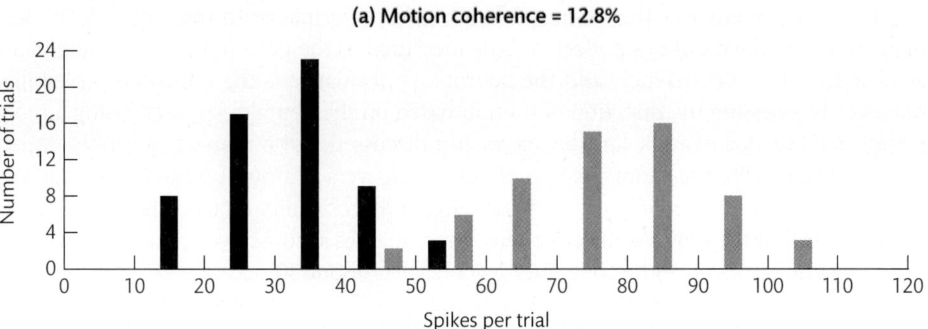

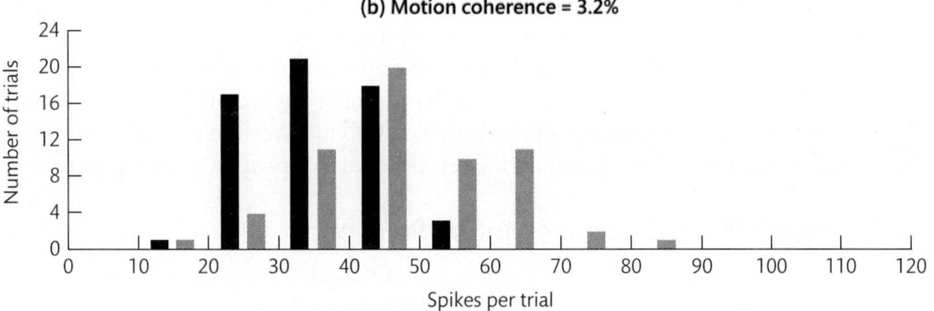

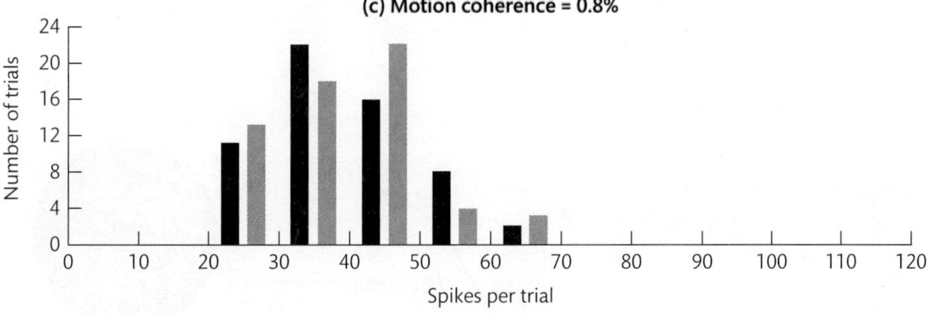

Figure 7.6 Responses of a Neuron in a Monkey's Area MT to Motion at Different Levels of Coherence Each panel shows a histogram indicating the number of trials in which the neuron produced a given number of action potentials from a minimum of 10–20 to a maximum of 100–110 when the motion was in the neuron's preferred direction (gray) or opposite to its preferred direction (black). (a) At a coherence level of 12.8%, the neuron's response to motion in its preferred direction was distinctly greater than its response to motion in the opposite direction. (b) When coherence was reduced to 3.2%, the stronger response to motion in the preferred direction was much less distinct. (c) At 0.8% coherence, there was no significant difference in the neuron's responses. (Adapted from Newsome et al., 1989.)

numerical terms, the neuron produced an average of about 80 spikes per trial when the motion was in the preferred direction, compared to about 30 spikes per trial when the motion was in the opposite direction. Let's think about this in terms of a decision criterion, noise, and signal detection theory, as discussed in Chapter 1. Suppose the monkey set a criterion of 50 spikes per trial: if the neuron produced 50 or more spikes, the monkey would respond that the motion was in the neuron's preferred direction, and if it produced fewer than 50 spikes, the monkey would respond that the motion was in the opposite direction. At the coherence level of 12.8%, this rule almost always gives the correct answer (a *hit* or a *correct rejection,* in the terminology of signal detection theory). The few trials in which this rule yields an incorrect response—a *miss* or a *false alarm*—are due to noise.

Now look at Figure 7.6b, showing the results for a coherence level of 3.2%. The response of the neuron to motion in the nonpreferred direction is close to what it was for the 12.8% coherence level (an average of about 35 spikes per trial), but the response to motion in the preferred direction is quite a bit less on average (about 50 spikes per trial), which you can see graphically as the gray bars being more intermixed with and less to the right of the black bars.

Figure 7.6c shows that when the coherence level was 0.8%, the neuron's response was about the same for motion in either direction, an average of about 40 spikes per trial. In this case, obviously, any rule based on the number of spikes will lead to an incorrect answer in about 50% of the trials, just as the monkey's perceptual judgments were about 50% correct at this coherence level.

Figure 7.7 compares the monkey's behavioral performance to the neuron's "performance," where the monkey's performance is measured as the percent of correct judgments at various levels of coherence, and the neuron's performance is the estimated probability of correctly assessing the direction of motion based on the neural responses, using a more complicated version of a rule like the one we just discussed. As you can see, when the coherence is close to 0%, the monkey's rate of correct answers is around 50%—that is, at low levels of coherence the monkey is just guessing, and probability dictates that it will guess correctly 50% of the time. As the coherence rises, so does accuracy, with the monkey making almost no errors once the coherence level reaches about 30%.

The *motion coherence threshold* referred to in Figure 7.7 was defined as the level of coherence at which performance was 82% correct. In this case, the neuron's threshold was somewhat lower than (better than) the monkey's—that is, this neuron required a slightly lower level of coherence than did the monkey to correctly judge the direction of motion 82% of the time. Overall, however, the researchers found that the performance of the individual neurons wasn't significantly different from that of the monkey across all levels of coherence. This suggests that the monkey's perceptual judgments about direction of motion are about what you'd expect if they were based on the responses of this population of MT neurons.

Disruption of Area MT Impairs Motion Perception

What happens when area MT is damaged or when neural activity there is disrupted in some way, as in the case of L.M., the woman in the vignette at the beginning of this chapter? The researchers who studied L.M. found that she had lost virtually all her ability to

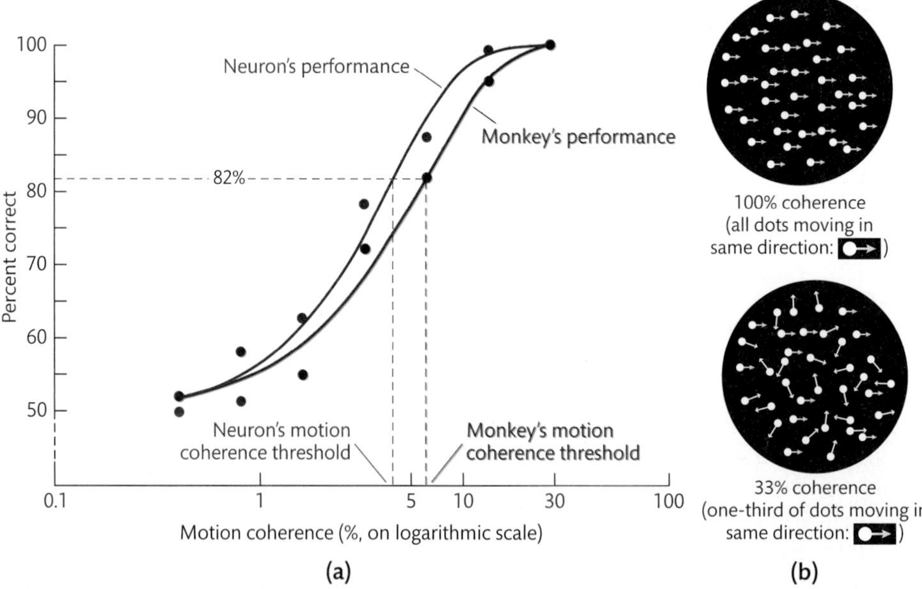

Figure 7.7 Monkey's Performance Versus Neuron's Performance (a) The blue curve, representing the monkey's performance, shows that at low levels of motion coherence, the monkey's judgments of direction of motion were near chance, with about 50% correct—that is, the monkey was just guessing. Accuracy increased as coherence increased, with the monkey approaching 100% correct as coherence approached 30%. The red curve shows the "performance" of one example neuron, measured as the probability of correctly identifying the direction of coherent motion based on the neuron's responses. In both cases, the curve that best fits the observed data points is a psychometric function. (b) These are static illustrations of the displays of moving dots used in this experiment, with arrows indicating the direction of motion; in the actual displays, of course, there were no arrows, just dots. Motion coherence is the percentage of dots moving in the same direction, while all the other dots in the display move randomly (here, green arrows identify the coherently moving dots). (Adapted from Newsome et al., 1989.)

perceive motion visually, though her other visual functions were unimpaired and she had no difficulty perceiving motion through hearing or touch (Zihl et al., 1983).

Not surprisingly, a deliberate temporary deactivation of MT—if done at just the right moment relative to the presentation of a moving-dot stimulus—also dramatically impairs the perception of motion (Beckers & Zeki, 1995). Such a deactivation can be induced by a technique called *transcranial magnetic stimulation,* in which a brief magnetic pulse, precisely targeted at MT, is transmitted through the skull of a human participant.

Consistent with these findings in humans, another study found that monkeys with lesions in MT are dramatically impaired in their ability to perceive motion, while their other perceptual abilities are unaffected (Newsome & Paré, 1988). The restriction of the deficit to motion perception is consistent with all the other evidence we've encountered indicating that motion perception is the central function of area MT.

The Aperture Problem: Perceiving the Motion of Objects

In many of the experiments discussed in preceding sections, the stimuli consisted of small moving dots. However, more typically, we must perceive the direction of motion of more extended objects. This may seem simple enough—after all, when a rigid, nonrotating object is moving in a straight line (which is the type of motion we're considering here), every part of that object is moving in the same direction. But if we look at this situation a little more carefully, a perceptual challenge emerges, particularly for direction-tuned neurons in area V1.

Consider Figure 7.8a, which illustrates the retinal image of a square object moving across the receptive field of a V1 neuron tuned to respond to motion to the right. Like all V1 neurons, this neuron has a small receptive field, which means that it monitors just a small part of the retinal image. In the sequence at the top, the object is moving directly to the right; in the sequence at the bottom, the object is moving diagonally down and to the

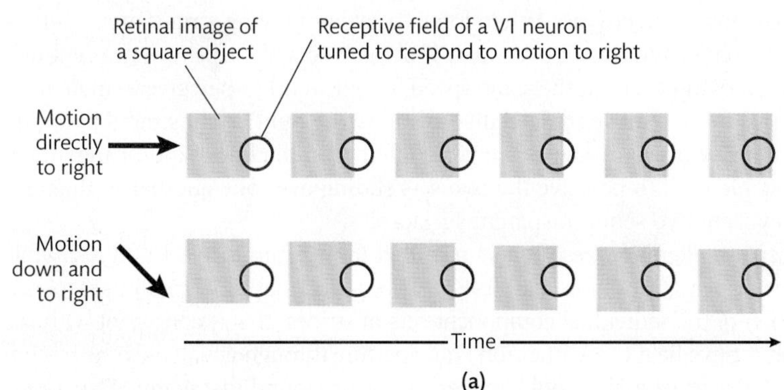

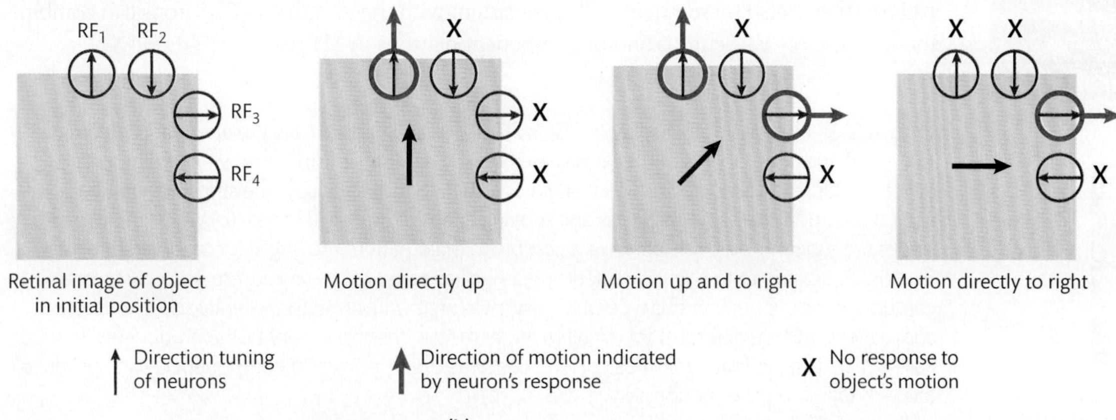

Figure 7.8 Aperture Problem (a) Regardless of whether the object moves directly to the right or down and to the right, the V1 neuron "sees" the same thing—a vertical edge moving to the right across its receptive field. This illustrates the aperture problem: V1 neurons see the world through a small aperture, which means that their responses often fail to indicate the true motion of larger objects. (b) This illustrates the solution to the aperture problem: an MT neuron that receives signals from the four V1 neurons with receptive fields RF_1–RF_4 and responds according to the *pattern* of their responses. Such a neuron could unambiguously indicate which way the object is moving, because the pattern would be different for each possible direction.

right. But all that the V1 neuron "sees" is what's happening within its receptive field, and as the figure shows, the V1 neuron sees the same thing in both cases—a vertical edge moving to the right across its receptive field.

aperture problem The impossibility of determining the actual direction of motion of a stimulus by the response of a single neuron that "sees" the stimulus only through a small "aperture" (the neuron's receptive field) and "sees" only the component of motion in the neuron's preferred direction.

This is called the **aperture problem,** because a V1 neuron, in effect, views the world through a small aperture and has no way of "knowing" what's going on elsewhere in the retinal image. Because of the aperture problem, any given direction-tuned V1 neuron will often fail to produce an accurate representation of the direction of motion of an object with a retinal image larger than the neuron's receptive field.

Now consider Figure 7.8b, which shows the same square object in relation to the receptive fields RF_1–RF_4 of four direction-tuned V1 neurons, each of which is tuned to a different direction of motion (up, down, to the right, or to the left). In its initial position, the object's upper and right-hand edges bisect all four receptive fields. As shown in the figure, each neuron responds only to the component of the motion in its preferred direction. For example, the neuron with RF_1 indicates motion up regardless of whether the actual motion is directly up or up and to the right, and the neuron with RF_3 indicates motion to the right regardless of whether the actual motion is directly to the right or up and to the right. These responses reflect the aperture problem: it's impossible to know the actual direction of motion of the object based on the response of any one of these four direction-tuned V1 neurons.

To solve the aperture problem, the visual system needs to combine the information contained in the signals from multiple V1 neurons in order to assess motion over a larger area of the retina than that seen by individual V1 neurons. This is a process that neurons in area MT are well suited to carry out. Neurons in MT have much larger receptive fields than those in V1, which means they receive signals from multiple V1 neurons. For the situation illustrated in Figure 7.8b, an MT neuron that could combine the information in the signals from the four V1 neurons could unambiguously indicate the object's direction of motion based on the different patterns of responses by the V1 neurons.

Demonstration 7.3 Aperture Problem Interact with animated displays to explore the aperture problem.

You can see a simple version of this kind of combination-of-motions effect when viewing two superimposed sets of moving stripes (Adelson & Movshon, 1982). Figure 7.9a illustrates one possible setup: a set of vertical stripes moves directly to the right, and a set of horizontal stripes moves directly up. When the two sets of moving stripes are superimposed, the result is perceived in one of two ways: if the two sets of stripes are near enough in thickness and are moving at about the same speed, people tend to perceive a single integrated pattern—a plaid—that moves diagonally up and to the right, as illustrated in Figure 7.9b. In contrast, if the two sets of stripes are very different in thickness and/or moving at different speeds, people tend to perceive the two sets sliding over one another in different directions, as if they were two semitransparent surfaces.

Using plaid displays like these, researchers recorded from neurons in V1 and MT while monkeys viewed the displays (Movshon et al., 1985). They found that all V1 neurons responded only to the motion of the individual component sets of stripes; this is consistent with the idea that the small receptive field of a V1 neuron is an aperture through which only the motion of a small portion of one set of stripes could be seen. They also found that many MT neurons responded only to one or the other of the components (they called these *component cells*); however, about one-third of the MT neurons responded best to the combined motion of the plaid pattern (they called these *pattern cells*), consistent with the idea that MT neurons can combine the responses of V1 neurons and/or component neurons in MT itself.

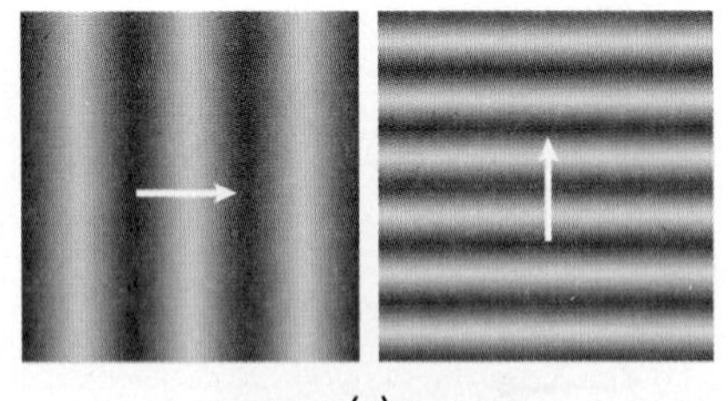

(a)

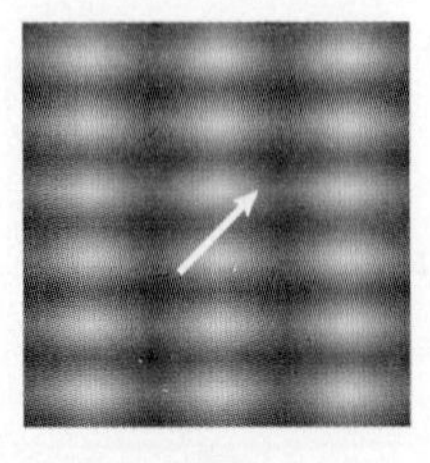

(b)

Figure 7.9 Plaid Motion Display A display like this can illustrate how the aperture problem is solved. (a) The components of the display are two separate sets of stripes moving in different directions (here, one set moves directly right and the other directly up). The stripes in the two sets need to be about the same thickness and moving at about the same speed. (b) When the two sets of stripes are superimposed, we perceive a combined plaid pattern moving in a combined direction (diagonally, up and to the right). V1 neurons, as well as some MT neurons, respond only to one component or the other in this type of display, presumably because the receptive fields of these component cells are apertures too small to let them "see" the motions of both components at once. Researchers suggest that pattern cells in MT combine the responses of component cells to produce the perception of plaid motion.

Check Your Understanding

7.1 A simple neural circuit for detecting motion would consist of two neurons with receptive fields in different locations on the retina, and a third neuron that receives signals from the other two. Why would a delay in the transmission of signals from one of those neurons be necessary?

7.2 Describe the difference between a simple neural circuit like the one referred to in Question 7.1 and a more complex circuit that can account for the motion aftereffect.

7.3 Describe two types of experimental evidence supporting the idea that the responses of MT neurons are the basis for perceiving the direction of motion.

7.4 Why is it necessary to combine information from multiple neurons in order to solve the aperture problem?

Perceptual Organization from Motion

In Chapter 4, we discussed perceptual organization, the process by which the visual system identifies those portions of the retinal image that belong to one object or another. In this section, we'll see how motion perception is involved in various aspects of perceptual organization, including perceptual grouping, figure–ground organization, and the perception of moving biological objects (people and animals).

Perceptual Grouping Based on Apparent Motion

A motion-sensing circuit like the one in Figure 7.2b responds to a stimulus moving at the preferred speed in the preferred direction—that is, from RF_1 to RF_2. However, there is no obvious reason why such a circuit shouldn't respond just as well to a brief flash at RF_1, followed by a delay, followed by a brief flash at RF_2, as shown in Figure 7.10. And in fact, within limits, we *do* experience motion as a result of such discontinuous stimuli—a phenomenon termed **apparent motion.** Actually, many of us experience apparent motion continuously for a good part of our day, since this is the basis for our sense of motion when watching movies or TV, each of which consists of sequences of still frames, presented at a rate of 24 frames per second for movies and 30 frames per second or higher for TV.

apparent motion A visual illusion in which two stimuli separated in time and location are perceived as a single stimulus moving between the two locations.

Apparent motion plays a key role in perceptual grouping by providing a link between the retinal images of an object that appear in two different locations at two different times. When the retinal images of an object activate a motion circuit like the one in Figure 7.10 and produce the perceptual experience of motion, the link provided by the motion circuit

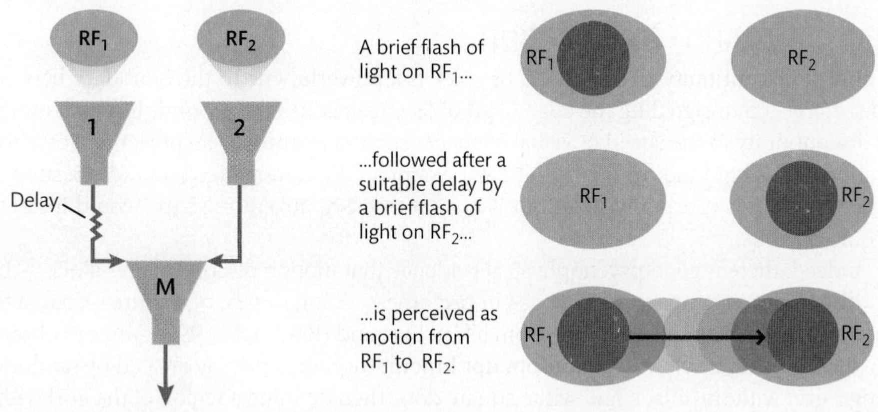

RF_1
RF_2
1
2
Delay
M
A brief flash of light on RF_1...
...followed after a suitable delay by a brief flash of light on RF_2...
...is perceived as motion from RF_1 to RF_2.
RF_1
RF_2

Figure 7.10 Apparent Motion To a motion-selective neuron like M in a circuit such as the one illustrated in Figure 7.2b (shown here at left), a flash of light on RF_1 followed after a suitable delay by a flash of light on RF_2 is indistinguishable from a single light moving from RF_1 to RF_2.

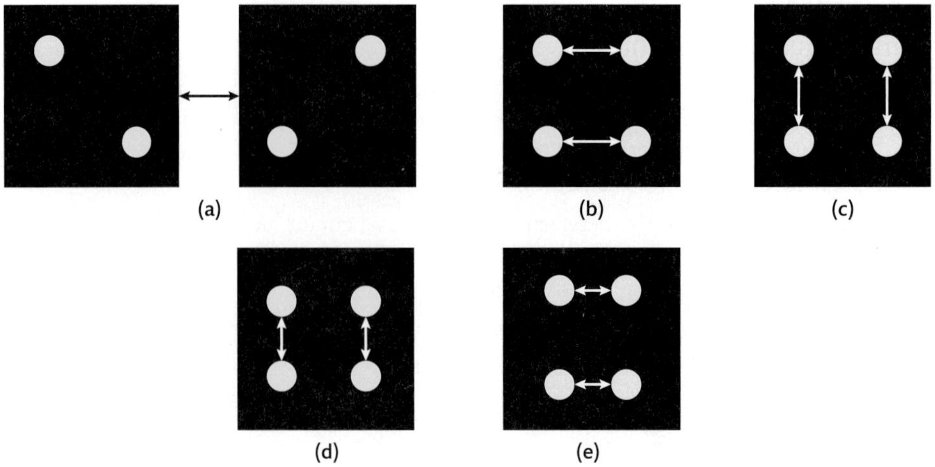

Figure 7.11 Apparent Motion Quartet (a) The display known as the apparent motion quartet consists of two frames like these presented in rapid alternation. (b) The display can be perceived as dots moving rapidly back and forth horizontally. (c) The display can also be perceived as involving vertical motion. The viewer's perception can spontaneously flip from horizontal to vertical motion and back again. (d) When the vertical distance between the dots in the two frames is less than the horizontal distance, perception is strongly biased toward vertical motion. (e) Conversely, when the horizontal distance is less, the perceptual bias is toward horizontal motion.

(a) (b) (c)

(d) (e)

gives the visual system a basis for grouping those retinal images and perceiving them as belonging to a single object.

To get a more concrete sense of how apparent motion contributes to perceptual grouping, consider a display known as the **apparent motion quartet,** in which two frames, each containing two symmetrically placed dots, are presented in rapid alternation. As illustrated in Figure 7.11a, in one frame the dots are in the upper left and lower right corners, and in the other frame the dots are in the lower left and upper right. As the frames alternate, an observer may see either of two possible directions of apparent motion. Either the dots appear to move back and forth horizontally, as illustrated in Figure 7.11b, or they appear to move up and down vertically, as illustrated in Figure 7.11c. If you look at the apparent motion quartet in action for a few minutes, you may find that your perception flips spontaneously from horizontal motion to vertical motion and back again, with the flips separated by 10 or 20 seconds. You can "force" the perception of horizontal motion by covering the top or bottom half of the display with a piece of paper or your hand, so only two dots are visible, and you can similarly force the perception of vertical motion by covering the left or right half of the display. When you remove the covering, the same direction of motion continues to be seen, at least for several seconds.

apparent motion quartet A display in which four symmetrically placed stimuli presented at alternating moments in time are perceived as two stimuli in apparent motion.

A powerful factor in determining the perceived direction of motion in the apparent motion quartet is the relative distances between the dots. If the dots are closer together vertically than horizontally, perception is very strongly biased toward vertical motion, as illustrated in Figure 7.11d; conversely, if the dots are closer together horizontally than vertically, perception is biased toward horizontal motion, as illustrated in Figure 7.13e. This is analogous to the perceptual grouping principle of proximity, which we discussed in Chapter 4 in relation to static displays (see Figure 4.18): when it can, the visual system interprets apparent motion in a way that minimizes the distance over which the stimuli appear to move.

Demonstration 7.4 Apparent Motion Interact with animated displays including the apparent motion quartet.

Figure-Ground Organization

An abrupt discontinuity in brightness or color is a powerful cue to the boundary between two surfaces, often signaling the edge of an object against its background. Just as powerful is a discontinuity in the speed of visual elements such as textures as an object moves across a stationary background. In Figure 7.12, for example, the camouflaged flounder resting on a sandy bottom is nearly invisible, but if it were to move, its entire shape would instantly become obvious.

Indeed, there is good psychophysical evidence that motion discontinuities alone—that is, without any accompanying changes in brightness, color, depth, or texture—enable the visual system to distinguish a shape from its background (Braddick, 1993). You can observe this phenomenon by viewing a **random dot kinematogram,** a display created by randomly filling a grid with tiny black and white square dots, then defining a region of the grid with a

random dot kinematogram A display in which a grid is filled with tiny, randomly placed black and white square dots and in which the dots in a region of the grid are then moved rigidly together as a group; the shape of the region is visible when the dots move but not when they're still.

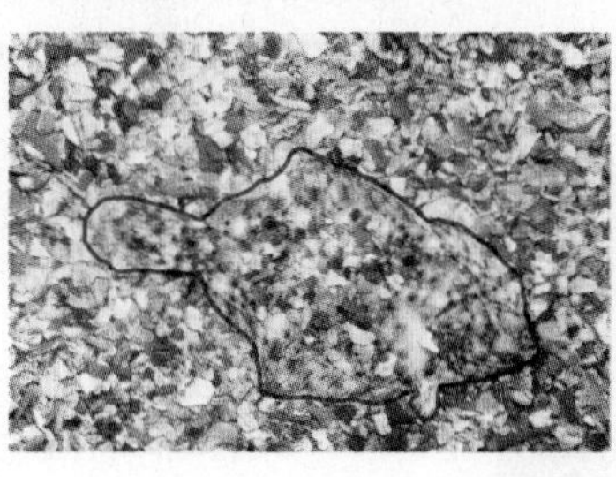

Figure 7.12 Figure-Ground Organization from Motion I: Camouflage This flounder's body is virtually the same color and texture as the sandy sea bottom, making the fish nearly invisible when it's at rest. If it were to move, the motion discontinuities at the boundaries of its body would instantly let your visual system organize its shape perceptually as a figure against the ground of the sand.

particular shape (say, a rectangle), and then moving the dots in that region rigidly together as a group (see Figure 7.13). When the defined region isn't moving, its shape is undetectable, but motion makes its shape perfectly clear. In fact, the shape is defined only by the relative motions at its edges—that is, when it's not moving, the shape doesn't exist.

Demonstration 7.5 Random Dot Kinematogram Interact with an animated display to see if you can identify the "object" in a random dot kinematogram.

Form Perception from Biological Motion

Motion can be an extremely powerful cue to the 3-D form of an organism, but to understand why this is so, we need to be able to look at just the organism's motion, without seeing its body. How is this possible? Gunnar Johansson (1973) found an ingenious method: the **point-light walker** display. He placed small lights (point-lights) at critical locations on a person's body—shoulders, elbows, wrists, hips, knees, and ankles—and shot videos of the person walking, running, or dancing in complete darkness. In the videos, only the point-lights could be seen—the person's body was completely invisible—so

point-light walker A display in which biological motion is made visible by attaching small lights at critical locations on an organism's body (e.g., at a person's arm, leg, and hip joints) and then shooting a video of the organism in motion in darkness.

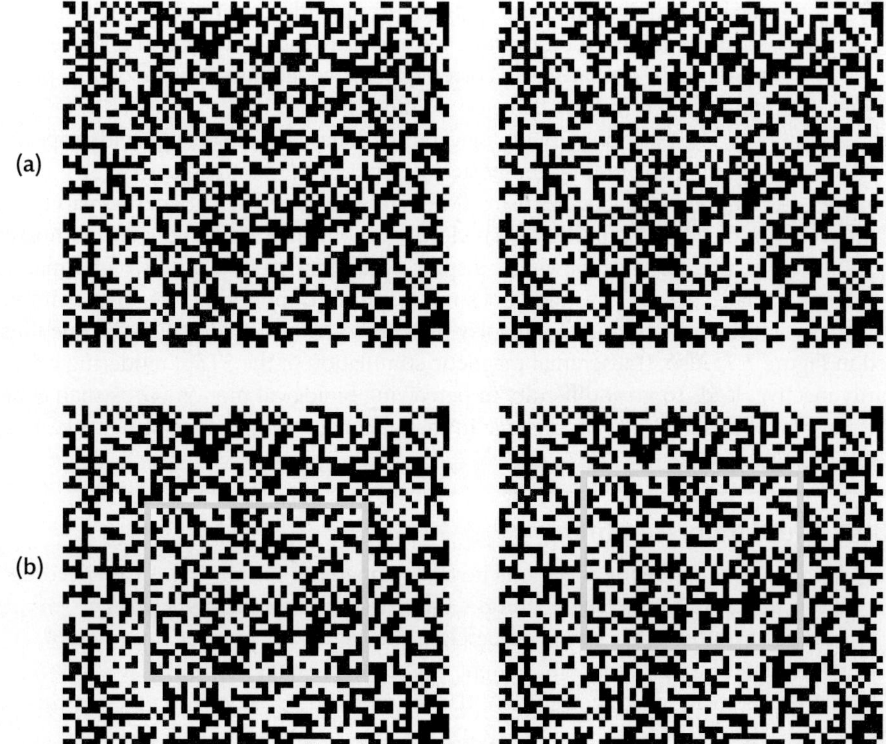

Figure 7.13 Figure-Ground Organization from Motion II: Random Dot Kinematogram (a) A random dot kinematogram (RDK) consists of a grid of tiny, randomly arranged black and white squares in which a central region with a particular shape moves as a unit. Here, you're looking at two still images of an RDK with a rectangular central region that is five rows of squares higher in the image on the right than in the image on the left. Can you discern the central rectangle? If you saw the RDK in motion, with the central rectangle shifting up and down, it would be perceptually obvious. (b) The central rectangle is outlined in yellow.

Figure 7.14 **Point-Light Walker Display** A point-light walker display is created by placing small lights on the joints of a person and then filming the person in an otherwise dark room, so only the point-lights are visible, as the person performs an activity such as walking, running, or dancing. Still images from a point-light display, like the two shown here, appear to be more or less randomly arranged dots of light, but when the film is played the nature of the motion is instantly clear.

there was no explicit information about the shape of the object (see Figure 7.14). Any one frame of such a video looks like randomly scattered dots. But as soon as the video starts to play and the dots begin to move, the structure becomes apparent—the visual system is so attuned to the perception of biological motion that it almost immediately understands the complex pattern of moving dots as the motion of a person engaging in some specific activity.

Indeed, not only is it possible to look at a point-light walker display and recognize whether you're seeing a runner, a dancer, or a walking dog, but you can also tell if a person is a man or a woman; in addition, you can recognize different specific individuals and even discern facial expressions, if point-lights are attached to key points on the face. If you view someone lifting something, you can judge the weight of the lifted object and the effort required to lift it (Shim et al., 2004), and you can assess the elasticity of a surface (e.g., a sidewalk versus a mattress versus a trampoline) by watching the motions of a person walking on it (Blake & Shiffrar, 2007).

As you might expect, the ability to make sense out of a point-light display gets better as the number of points increases, and points on the joints are more helpful than points elsewhere. However, the recognizability of point-light displays depends most crucially on the coordinated timing of the point motions. This is shown by displays created using computer animation where the time at which each point starts to move is varied randomly. Even if the trajectory of each individual point remains unchanged, the motion looks random. This is hardly surprising: it is the coordination of the moving points that conveys the swinging movements of arms and legs.

Although the body of a moving person is not rigid overall, it is "piecewise rigid"—that is, as a person walks, the distance between the elbow and the wrist, for example, remains constant, as does the distance between the knee and the ankle, while the distance between the wrist and the ankle changes dramatically. But even this piecewise rigidity isn't absolute, because the distance between, say, the elbow and the wrist appears foreshortened if the forearm tilts backward in depth. Apparently, in conjunction with knowledge about the structure of the human body, the visual system is able to pick up on these regularities to correctly perceive the invisible person in a point-light walker display (Blake & Shiffrar, 2007).

The perception of biological motion has been associated with a specific region of the brain—the posterior superior temporal sulcus (STSp), in the temporal lobe. Studies using fMRI show increased activity in that part of the brain while the participant is viewing a point-light walker display, compared to activity while viewing a display of randomly moving dots (Grossman & Blake, 2002). This area does not respond to motion per se—for example, it doesn't respond to a display of coherently moving dots like the one illustrated in Figure 7.7. Also, transcranial magnetic stimulation of the STSp, rendering it temporarily inactive, leads to great difficulty in perceiving biological motion (Grossman et al., 2005), and individuals with brain damage in that area show similar impairments (Cowey & Vaina, 2000).

Demonstration 7.6 Biological Motion Interact with animated point-light walker displays where you can control different aspects of the motion in the display.

Check Your Understanding

7.5 Which of the following situations involves apparent motion: **(A)** A car speeding along a highway disappears behind a billboard and then, a moment later, reappears on the other side; you perceive the car as moving from one side of the billboard to the other. **(B)** A light flashes on one side of a billboard and then, a moment later, another light flashes on the other side; you perceive this as a single light moving from one side of the billboard to the other. Explain your answer.

7.6 If the central portion of the object on the left rotated clockwise through the position shown in the middle until it reached the position shown on the right, you would probably perceive the object as consisting of a surrounding square surface of horizontal slats with a smaller square piece lying at its center. This illustrates what type of perceptual organization through motion?

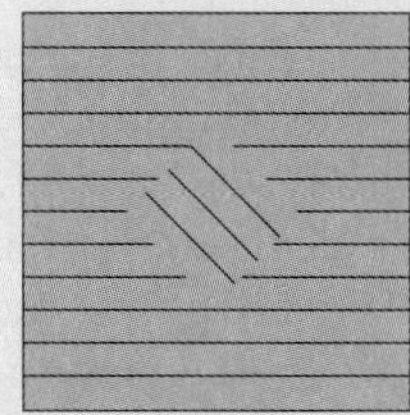
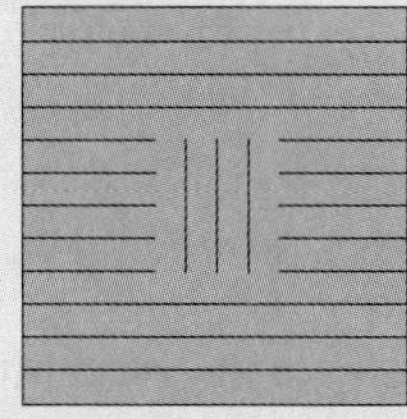

7.7 How do experiments with point-light walker displays reveal that we are able to interpret biological motion based on motion cues only, without the aid of cues based on seeing the body of the moving organism?

Eye Movements and the Perception of Motion and Stability

In the preceding sections, our discussion has been restricted to motion perception in the simplest case, by a stationary observer with unmoving eyes. However, humans and other animals must sample the optic array actively in order to gather the information they need to achieve their behavioral goals. We do so by moving our eyes so as to bring the retinal image of objects of interest to the center of our gaze, at the fovea, where vision is most acute. We can move our eyes by moving our body (e.g., turning our head or rotating at the waist) and by moving the eyes themselves, using the small extraocular muscles. Often, of course, we execute these two kinds of movements together in complex, coordinated ways.

In this section, for simplicity, we'll ignore head movements and consider only the role of eye movements themselves in the perception of motion and stability. To begin, we'll briefly consider the three different types of eye movements:

- **Saccadic eye movements** (or *saccades*) are brief, rapid movements that change the focus of gaze from one location to another in the visual scene. Saccades occur about three times per second throughout the waking hours, and each saccade lasts less than one-twentieth of a second. These are the movements you use while reading or when visually searching for a pencil on a cluttered desktop.
- **Smooth pursuit eye movements** occur when you track a moving object continuously with your eyes or when you track a stationary object while your head is moving.
- **Vergence eye movements** occur when you shift your gaze from a nearby object to a more distant object or vice versa. As discussed in Chapter 6, the directions of gaze of the two eyes are very nearly parallel when you look at an object more than about two meters away, but as you shift your focus to a closer object, your eyes both turn inward (i.e., their directions of gaze *con*verge), and as you shift your focus to the more distant object again, your eyes both turn outward (i.e., their directions of gaze *di*verge).

saccadic eye movements (or *saccades*) Brief, rapid eye movements that change the focus of gaze from one location to another.

smooth pursuit eye movements Eye movements made to track a moving object or to track a stationary object while the head is moving.

vergence eye movements Eye movements that occur when the gaze shifts between focusing on objects at different distances.

Here, we'll focus our attention on saccadic eye movements and smooth pursuit eye movements because they challenge us to explain how our perception of the world remains stable even when eye movements cause changes in the retinal image. But before proceeding to this issue, let's briefly consider an obvious question posed by eye movements: Why

saccadic suppression The visual system's suppression of neural signals from the retina during saccadic eye movements.

don't eye movements cause motion blur on the retina—particularly saccadic movements, which are so fast that the retinal image motion they produce could only be perceived as a blurry "streak" of movement? The answer is that the visual system in effect shuts down retinal input during saccadic eye movements, a phenomenon called **saccadic suppression** (Matin, 1974).

Now let's return to the main question raised by eye movements: Why doesn't a stationary scene appear to move when we move our eyes? Figure 7.15 shows two different situations involving a moving object. In Figure 7.15a, the eye remains stationary—that is, the direction of gaze remains fixed directly ahead while the retinal image of a red object moves across the retina—this is the situation covered in earlier sections of this chapter. In Figure 7.15b, the eye executes a smooth pursuit movement to track the red object as it moves across a scene that contains a stationary blue object. In this situation, the retinal image of the moving red object remains fixed at the fovea (this is what it means to track a moving object) while the retinal image of the stationary blue object sweeps across the retina—and yet the observer perceives the moving object as moving and the stationary object as stationary.

These perceptions lead immediately to the conclusion that the perception of motion and stability can't just depend on motion or lack of motion in the retinal image but must also take into account *extraretinal information*—that is, information that does not originate in the retinal image itself (in this context, the prefix *extra-* means "outside of"). Specifically, perception must also be based on information about the position and movement of the eyes. Two types of such information have been proposed: information from the extraocular

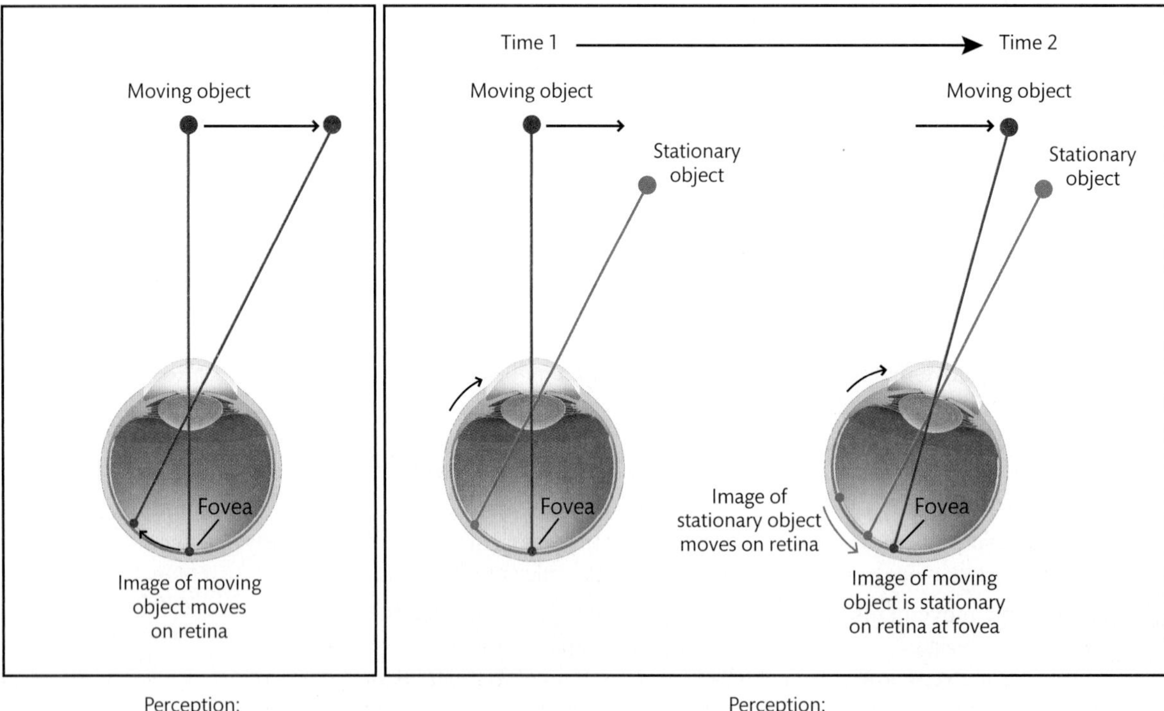

Figure 7.15 Moving and Stationary Eye, and Moving and Stationary Objects (a) When the eye is stationary, the retinal image of a moving object moves across the retina, and we perceive the object as moving. (b) When the eye rotates to track a moving object, the retinal image of the object is stationary on the retina—at the fovea—while the retinal image of a stationary object in the scene moves across the retina. Yet the moving object is still perceived as moving, and the stationary object is perceived as stationary.

muscles and information from the superior colliculus, the part of the brain that controls eye movements by sending motor commands to the extraocular muscles. Let's discuss these two proposals in that order.

Sensors in the extraocular muscles provide information about how stretched or relaxed the muscles are, and this in turn provides information about the position and movement of the eyes. In principle, the brain could combine this information with information from the retinal image to construct an accurate perception of movement and stability in the visual scene. For example, if the signals from the extraocular muscles say that the eyes are moving from left to right at 2° per second, and the signal from the retina says that the image of an object is stationary on the retina, then the information in these two signals could, in principle, be combined in some region of the brain to indicate that the object is moving at a rate of 2° per second from left to right. Figure 7.16a illustrates this type of information flow and processing.

Figure 7.16b illustrates the other proposed scenario, in which the superior colliculus sends eye-movement commands to the extraocular muscles (say, a signal that instructs the eyes to move to the right at 2° per second, a smooth pursuit movement), and a copy of those commands—termed the **corollary discharge signal (CDS)**—is sent to some region of the brain that combines the information in the CDS with the information in the signals from the retina to indicate that the object is moving left to right at 2° per second. In principle, the information in the CDS could be more useful than information from the extraocular muscles, because the CDS would be sent *before* the eyes actually move, whereas the signal from the extraocular muscles is sent during the movement of the eyes and would arrive in the brain *after* that movement. Surely, this "advance warning" about where the eyes are about to go could be useful in maintaining an accurate perception of motion and stability in the visual scene.

corollary discharge signal (CDS) A copy of an eye-movement command from the superior colliculus to the extraocular muscles, sent to the brain to inform the visual system about upcoming eye movements; used to ensure a stable visual experience even during eye movements.

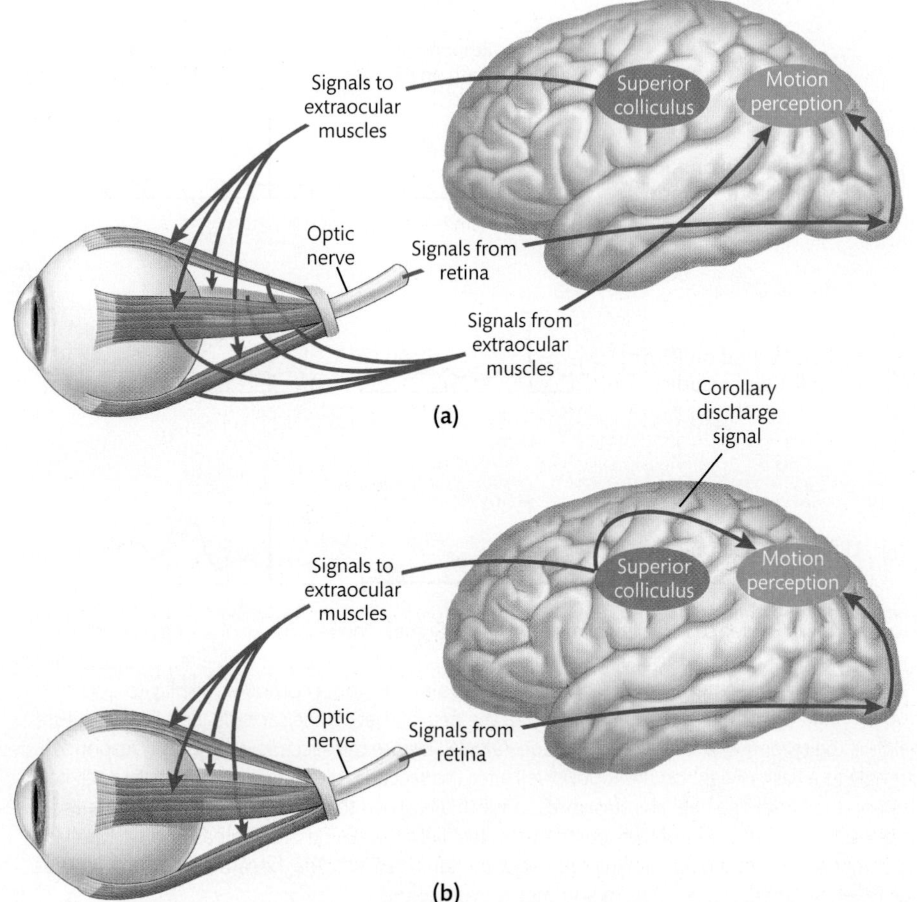

Figure 7.16 Extraretinal Information in the Perception of Motion and Stability: Two Proposals The perception that moving objects are moving and that stationary objects are stationary, regardless of whether or not the eye itself is moving, means that the perceptual system must have access to extraretinal information about the position and movement of the eyes. (a) In one proposal, this extraretinal information consists of signals from the extraocular muscles. (b) In another proposal, the extraretinal information is contained in a corollary discharge signal (CDS), a copy of the eye-movement commands from the superior colliculus to the extraocular muscles. Evidence supports the proposal involving a CDS.

Either of these mechanisms could work, but the evidence strongly points to the mechanism using the CDS. One important piece of this evidence is the surprising fact that some visual neurons change their receptive field locations just before a saccadic eye movement, as shown in a study in which experimenters recorded from single neurons in the frontal eye field (FEF) of monkeys' prefrontal cortex (Sommer & Wurtz, 2006). As illustrated in Figure 7.17, the monkeys were trained to make a saccade from an initial fixation point (FP_1) on a computer display to a final fixation point (FP_2) as soon as FP_2 appeared. At various points in time before or after the saccade, a spot of light was flashed either in the location of the neuron's receptive field (RF in Figure 7.17) before the saccade or in the location the receptive field would occupy after the saccade (FF, for "future field").

Figure 7.17a shows that a spot flashed on the RF well before the saccade evoked a strong response from the neuron being recorded, as you would expect from a flash of light in the neuron's receptive field, whereas a flash on the FF evoked no response at all. Similarly, as shown in Figure 7.17b, when the spot was flashed on the FF well after the saccade, it also evoked a strong response in the neuron, whereas a flash on the original RF evoked no response—again as you would expect, since the FF was the neuron's receptive field after the saccade. But now consider Figure 7.17c, which shows the neuron's responses to a flash *just before* the saccade. The strong response to a flash on the FF and the lack of response to a flash on the RF indicate that the neuron was, in effect, anticipating—before the eye actually began moving—where its receptive field would be once the saccade was complete. Clearly, this anticipatory remapping of the neuron's receptive field could minimize any disruption in visual perception resulting from the eye movement.

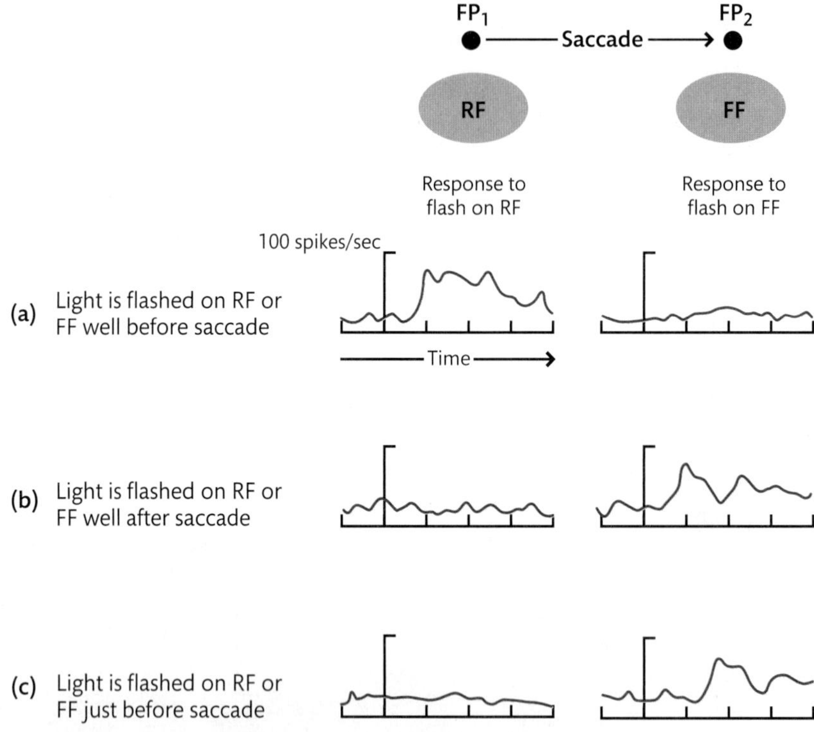

Figure 7.17 **Evidence for a Corollary Discharge Signal** The responses of a single neuron in monkeys' prefrontal cortex to flashes of light were recorded well before, well after, and just before an eye movement (a saccade) from an initial fixation point (FP_1) on a computer display to a second fixation point (FP_2). RF is the receptive field of the neuron before the saccade, and FF (for "future field") is the receptive field after the saccade. (a) Well before the saccade, the neuron responds strongly to a flash of light on the RF. (b) Well after the saccade, the neuron responds strongly to a flash on the FF. (c) The neuron's strong response to a flash on the FF just *before* the saccade indicates an anticipatory relocation of the neuron's receptive field that could only be based on a corollary discharge signal containing information about the intended saccade, because the actual saccade hasn't yet occurred. (Adapted from Sommer & Wurtz, 2006.)

The fact that remapping begins even before the eye starts to move strongly implies that the part of the brain that controls the remapping of the neuron's receptive field has received information about the *intended* eye movement—that is, a CDS—because signals from the extraocular muscles would necessarily *follow* the initiation of the saccade and would therefore be too late to support an anticipatory remapping. This study strongly suggests that we maintain accurate perception of the position and motion of objects in the visual scene, despite frequent eye movements, via a mechanism by which the information in a CDS—a copy of the eye-movement signals from the superior colliculus—is combined with the information in signals from the retina. It is believed a similar mechanism operates to compensate for head movements (Corneil et al., 2004).

Check Your Understanding

7.8 Briefly describe the differences between the three types of eye movements.

7.9 At the airport, your eyes are tracking a plane coming in for a landing. As it approaches, it whizzes past the hills beyond the runway. In your retinal image, the image of the plane remains fixed at the fovea, while the images of the hills move rapidly across the retina. Yet you perceive the plane as moving and the hills as stationary. This indicates that your visual system must make use of what kind of extraretinal information in the perception of motion and stability?

7.10 Why do vision scientists believe that extraretinal information in motion perception is more likely carried by a corollary discharge signal than by signals from the extraocular muscles?

Perception for Action

At various points in preceding chapters, we've brought up the idea that the principal purpose of vision is to let us know what is where in the scene before us—that is, to recognize objects and to determine their locations in 3-D space. At this point, however, we need to consider that this idea lacks an important element—namely, the element of action, of *doing* something with our knowledge of what is where. After all, perception evolved to effectively guide actions such as finding food and shelter, avoiding predators, finding a mate, and so on. Simply knowing what is where—"Oh, look, there's a lion jumping out at me from behind that rock!"—is hardly enough to ensure survival. Indeed, some have argued that our conscious awareness of objects and scenes is nothing but a side effect of this primary need to have perceptual systems that can guide behavior. Many perceptual scientists have emphasized the role of perception in guiding action in the world.

Usually, we think of perception as something that happens *before* action: we look at a scene and create an internal representation of it, and then we use that representation, along with a set of goals, to plan and execute movements. Until recently, most scientific research concerning perception has been based on this idea, at least implicitly—that is, researchers have focused on the creation of representations without worrying too much about what those representations are used for.

Over the last few decades, however, it has become increasingly clear that perception and action cannot be so neatly separated. On this view, perception isn't something that we passively experience; rather, it's something we actively *do*. In other words, perception is a kind of action. Moreover, perception and other forms of action happen together, in tight coordination, as is obvious in the case of eye movements. What we see depends on where we point our eyes, and that in turn provides visual input that can motivate other actions, including the next eye movement. For example, while driving down the street, you see something moving out of the corner of your eye, so you direct the next eye movement over there to bring the retinal image of that object onto the fovea for a detailed look. If you perceive a child walking into the path of your car, you move your eyes to check your rearview mirror, and if you perceive no other cars near you, you swerve into the next lane to avoid hitting the child, and so on—it's an endless loop.

James J. Gibson (1904–1979). [Courtesy of the Division of Rare and Manuscript Collections, Cornell University Library]

The influential American psychologist J. J. Gibson (1966, 1979) drew attention to the crucial link between perception and action by pointing out, for example, that animals don't judge distances by sitting still but by moving their eyes, heads, and bodies. Such actions generate changing perceptions—like the changing perceptions due to motion parallax (see Chapter 6)—that provide critical information about the layout of the scene. Gibson realized that much of the information about the locations of surfaces in the environment was specified by the ever-changing geometry of the retinal image, as when a pilot uses the ever-changing image of the landscape below to judge the distance to a runway.

In this section, we'll examine the various ways in which perception and action operate together, focusing on three types of action: eye movements, reaching and grasping, and navigation.

The Role of the Parietal Lobe in Eye Movements, Reaching, and Grasping

As discussed in Chapter 3 and illustrated in Figure 3.17, the visual system beyond area V1 splits into two functionally distinct pathways. The ventral pathway—which we referred to in Chapter 3 as the "what" pathway—travels through area V4 and into regions of the lateral occipital cortex and inferotemporal cortex that are specialized for various aspects of object recognition. The dorsal pathway—which we referred to as the "where"/"how" pathway—travels through area MT and into the parietal lobe. The description of this pathway as the "where"/"how" pathway is based on experiments with monkeys (Ungerleider & Mishkin, 1982; see Figure 3.18) and on evidence from patient D.F. (Goodale et al., 1991; see Figure 3.19). Monkeys with lesions in the parietal cortex were unable to carry out tasks related to knowing the location—the "where"—of objects. Patient D.F., with damage in the temporal lobe, was unable to carry out tasks such as identifying the orientation of a slot but was able to perform tasks like putting a letter through the slot or hitting a nail with a hammer, which involve the coordination of visual information—the "how"—needed to guide action. The position of the parietal lobes makes them well suited for the purpose of guiding action, because they are very near the motor regions of the prefrontal cortex, just as the lateral occipital cortex and inferotemporal cortex are well positioned to deliver visual information to structures of the medial temporal lobe, such as the hippocampus, that are involved in memory and categorization.

The parietal lobe can be divided into two major parts, the anterior parietal lobe and the posterior parietal lobe, separated by the postcentral sulcus, as shown in Figure 7.18.

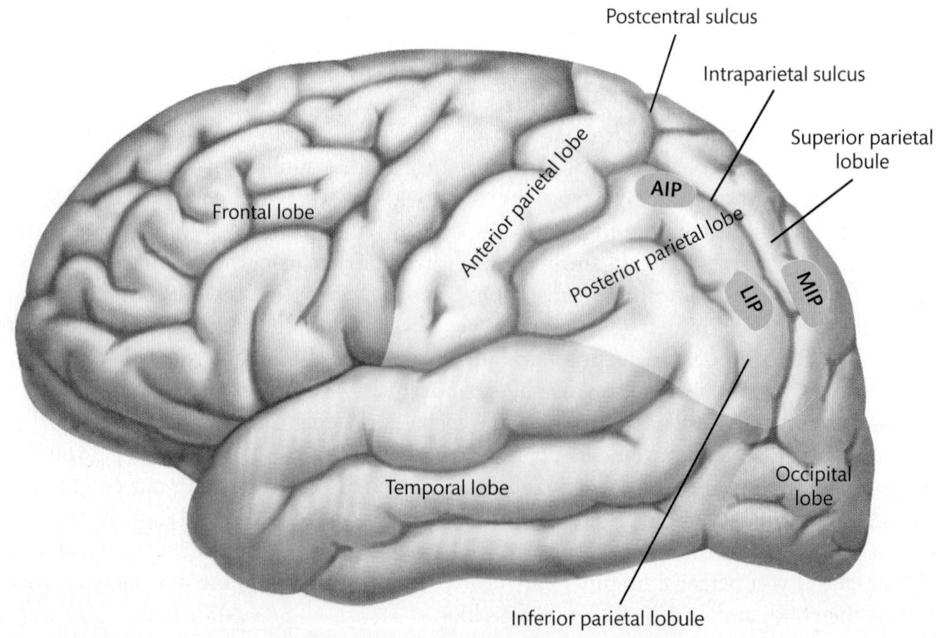

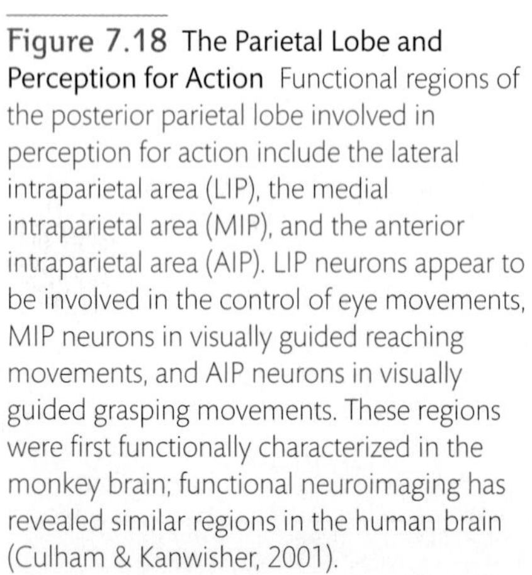

Figure 7.18 The Parietal Lobe and Perception for Action Functional regions of the posterior parietal lobe involved in perception for action include the lateral intraparietal area (LIP), the medial intraparietal area (MIP), and the anterior intraparietal area (AIP). LIP neurons appear to be involved in the control of eye movements, MIP neurons in visually guided reaching movements, and AIP neurons in visually guided grasping movements. These regions were first functionally characterized in the monkey brain; functional neuroimaging has revealed similar regions in the human brain (Culham & Kanwisher, 2001).

The anterior parietal lobe contains a somatosensory representation of the body's surface—the brain's map for touch (see Chapter 12); the posterior parietal lobe contains a variety of functionally specialized regions that support perceptually guided action and other functions (Snyder et al., 2000). Its major anatomical landmark is the intraparietal sulcus (IPS), which runs more or less horizontally through the middle of the posterior parietal lobe and divides it into the superior parietal lobule and the inferior parietal lobule. Many of the functional specializations of the parietal lobe were first characterized in studies of the monkey brain, but human fMRI experiments have revealed similar functional organization in the human brain (Culham & Kanwisher, 2001; Grefkes & Fink, 2005).

A region of the posterior parietal lobe known to be involved in the control of eye movements has been studied in detail in monkeys. Called the **lateral intraparietal area** (**LIP**, shown in Figure 7.18), it lies at about the midpoint of the IPS and contains neurons that respond to visual stimuli in their receptive fields. The activity of these neurons is sustained during delayed-saccade tasks (see Figure 7.19a), when a monkey is holding in mind the location to which it will be required to make an eye movement (Colby et al., 1996). As shown in Figure 7.19b, when the target spot first appears (time t_1), it evokes a strong response in the LIP neuron, because LIP neurons are driven by visual stimuli in their receptive fields. During the interval after the spot disappears (time t_2 to t_3), the LIP neuron sustains its increased activity at a lower level than the stimulus-driven response but still well above baseline, reflecting its role in maintaining a representation of the goal of the intended eye movement. After the monkey makes the saccade, the firing rate of the LIP neuron returns to its baseline level, because the monkey is no longer maintaining the location of the neuron's receptive field as the goal of an intended eye movement.

lateral intraparietal area (LIP) A region of the posterior parietal lobe in monkeys that is involved in the control of eye movements, including intended eye movements; an analogous region exists in the human brain.

The human brain also contains a region—analogous to the LIP in monkeys—that appears to be specific for representing the direction of an upcoming eye movement (Schluppeck et al., 2006). In other words, in both monkeys and humans, this region contains

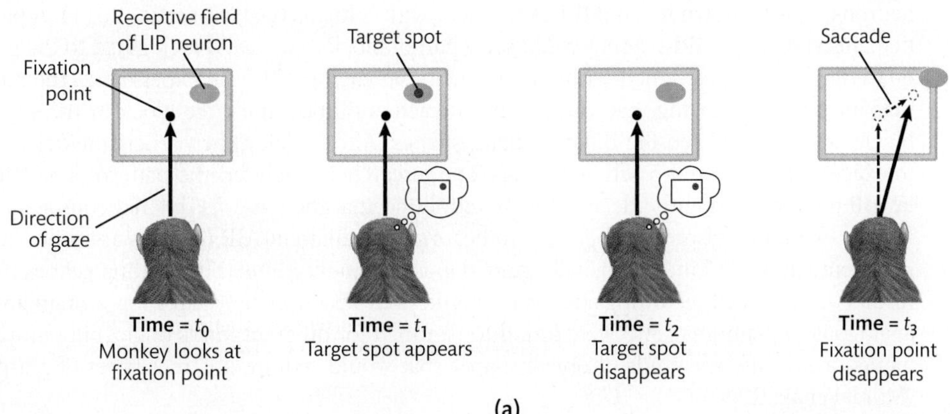

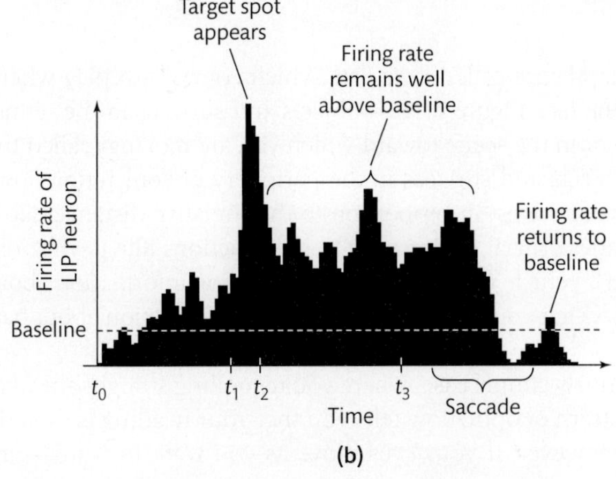

Figure 7.19 Activity of LIP Neuron Reflects Intended Eye Movements (a) This illustrates a delayed-saccade task. At time t_1, the monkey memorizes the location of the target spot, which is kept in mind through time t_2 to t_3. The disappearance of the fixation point at time t_3 cues the monkey to make a saccade to the remembered location of the target spot, and this saccade causes the location of the LIP neuron's receptive field to shift correspondingly. (b) An LIP neuron being recorded increases its activity in response to the appearance of the target spot in its receptive field. Significantly, the neuron maintains its increased activity after the target spot disappears, during the time when the monkey is remembering its location and *intending* to make a saccade after the fixation point disappears. (Data from Snyder et al., 2000.)

neurons whose activity reflects an *intended* eye movement. As you would expect for an area that uses visual information to plan an action like an eye movement, these neurons respond both to spatially specific visual input and to spatially specific planned eye movements.

medial intraparietal area (MIP) A region of the posterior parietal lobe involved in planning reach movements.

An adjacent region of the posterior parietal lobe, called the **medial intraparietal area** (**MIP**, shown in Figure 7.18), contains neurons that are active when a monkey or human is planning a reach to a specific location—hence, this area is sometimes called the *parietal reach region* (Buneo et al., 2002). A study with monkeys, in which the responses of individual MIP neurons were recorded, provided evidence that MIP neurons are crucially involved in determining the direction of visually guided reaching movements (Eskander & Assad, 2002). The monkeys were required to move a cursor on a computer screen by moving a joystick while recordings were made from MIP neurons and from neurons in a motion-selective brain area called the *medial superior temporal region* (MST). In one condition, the joystick controlled the cursor in a compatible fashion (e.g., moving the joystick up caused the cursor to move up), and in another condition, the mapping was reversed (e.g., the monkey had to move the joystick down to move the cursor up). MST neurons responded selectively according to the direction of motion of the cursor on the screen, no matter what direction of joystick movement was needed to make the cursor move. In contrast, MIP neurons responded according to the direction of the hand movement controlling the joystick. This pattern of results provides evidence that MIP neurons are selectively tuned for the production of reaching movements in specific directions. Studies using fMRI have indicated that a corresponding region of the posterior parietal cortex in the human brain is responsible for the visual guidance of reaching (Prado et al., 2005).

anterior intraparietal area (AIP) A region of the posterior parietal lobe thought to be involved in grasping movements.

Yet another region of the posterior parietal lobe, called the **anterior intraparietal area** (**AIP**, shown in Figure 7.18), is thought to be specialized for grasping movements. Once your arm moves your hand close enough to an object to pick it up or manipulate it in some other way, you must form your hand into the appropriate configuration—for example, to pick up a softball your fingers must be far apart, but to pick up a pen they must be close together. These kinds of differences in hand configuration appear to be controlled by AIP neurons, as was shown by an fMRI experiment with humans (Gallivan et al., 2011). A participant lying in an MRI scanner could see a pair of blocks—a small block glued to the top of a large block—positioned within easy reach. On each trial of the experiment, the participant, without moving, had to prepare to reach and grasp the large block or the small block, which would require different hand shapes. After a delay, the participant was told to execute the prepared reach-and-grasp. The researchers analyzed the pattern of activity in AIP neurons during the delay interval and found that the patterns differed consistently for the two kinds of prepared grasps, indicating that different AIP neurons are tuned for producing different kinds of visually guided grasping movements. This finding echoes the results of single-cell recording studies in monkeys in which many neurons in a brain area analogous to the human AIP were found to be tuned for different kinds of grasping movements or for different kinds of object shapes that would require different types of grasps (Murata et al., 2000).

Optic Flow

In Chapter 6, we discussed the depth cue called *optic flow,* which comes into play whenever you're moving through a scene (see Figure 6.18)—objects and surfaces in the retinal image move outward from the point in the scene toward which you are moving (called the *focus of expansion*), with nearby objects and surfaces in the periphery of your retina flowing outward more rapidly than distant ones, in proportion to their relative distance. Now we'll see that optic flow also provides crucial information to guide actions like navigation, as when you're walking or driving a vehicle (Gibson, 1950a), including information about heading—that is, the direction in which you're moving—as well as information about balance and body orientation.

Figure 7.20a illustrates a relatively simple case, where you're looking straight ahead at your navigation goal; here, the pattern of optic flow tells you that your heading is directly toward the focus of expansion. However, if your eyes move as you walk forward—say,

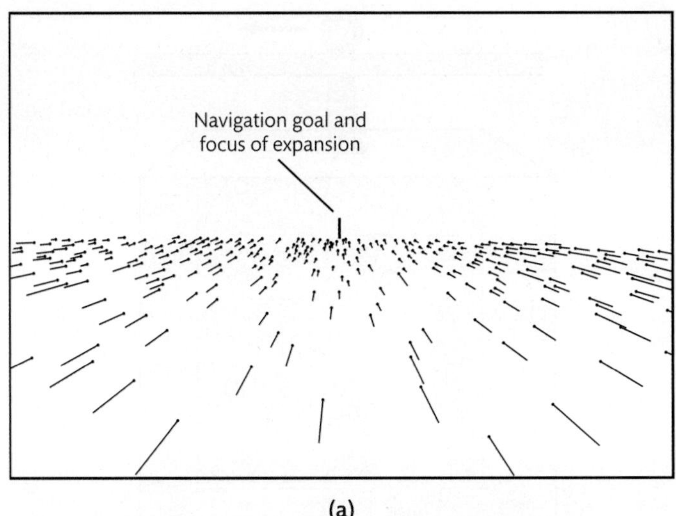

(a)

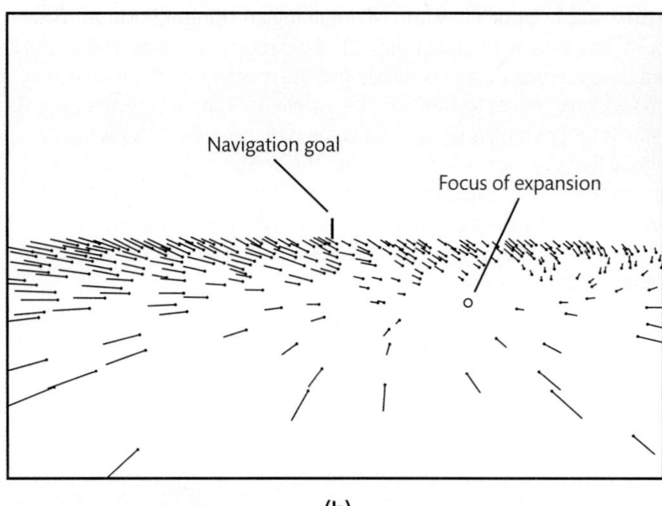

(b)

Figure 7.20 Optic Flow (a) As you walk (and look) straight ahead toward your navigation goal, everything in the retinal image flows outward from the center, which is called the *focus of expansion.* In this relatively simple and symmetrical pattern of optic flow, objects at the visual periphery, far from the point of expansion, appear to move most rapidly (as indicated by the length of the lines, representing the speed and direction of features in the retinal image at the positions of the dots at the ends of the lines), and objects close to the center, near the focus of expansion, appear to move most slowly. (b) This illustrates the more complex and unsymmetrical optic flow pattern if you're walking directly toward the navigation goal while your eyes are moving to track a stationary object (the small circle). Now the focus of expansion corresponds to the position of the stationary object. (Adapted from Warren & Hannon, 1988.)

to track a stationary object off to one side—the optic flow pattern becomes much more complex, as illustrated in Figure 7.20b; yet experiments have shown that people moving in this way can still judge their heading accurately (Warren & Hannon, 1988).

Knowing your heading lets you determine whether your heading matches your goal—that is, whether you're navigating correctly by moving in the direction you intend; if your heading doesn't match your goal, you can adjust your direction of movement as necessary. An experiment using a virtual-reality setup demonstrated that people do, in fact, use optic flow to navigate while walking (Warren et al., 2001). Participants wore a stereoscopic head-mounted display that projected a simple computer-generated scene into their eyes as they walked about within a room 12 meters square. Each participant was asked to walk toward a goal—a vertical red line projected in the scene. When the experimenters changed the optic flow pattern in the display so that the focus of expansion was displaced from where it would naturally fall, participants changed their path in a way that depended both on the location of the goal in the display and on the location of the focus of expansion within the pattern of optic flow.

Optic flow also helps you maintain a stable upright body orientation, which clearly matters whenever you're trying to execute an action. Consider, for example, the mere task of standing still. Executing this action requires information in signals from neurons at the bottoms of your feet that detect changes in pressure there as your body tilts one way or another, neurons in your muscles and joints that provide information about the positions of your limbs, and neurons in the semicircular canals and otolith organs in your inner ear that provide information about the motion and orientation of your body (discussed in Chapter 12). To see that visual information is also important in standing upright, try the following task. Stand on one foot with your eyes open for about 30 seconds, paying attention to the small adjustments you make to maintain your position. Now close your eyes. You'll notice that the adjustments are larger and it's a bit harder to maintain your position.

The role of optic flow in standing upright has been demonstrated experimentally using a room with four walls and a ceiling but no floor, suspended from above so that the room

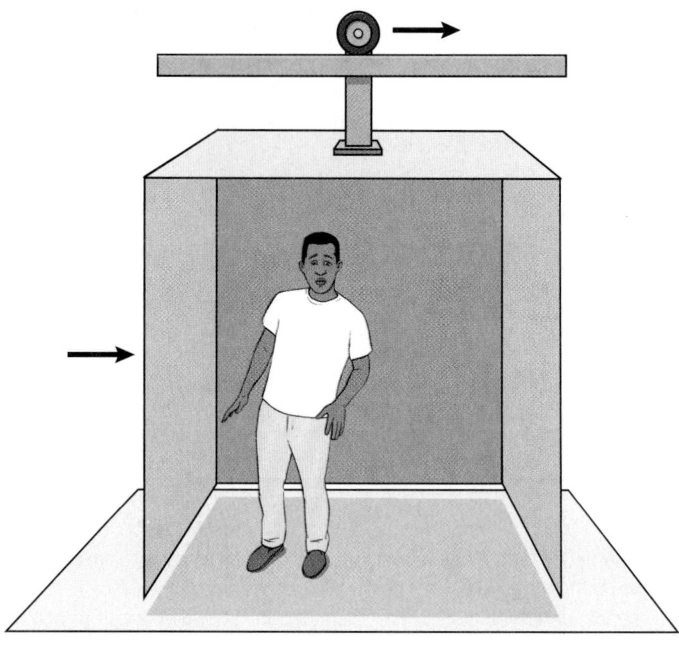

Figure 7.21 Optic Flow and Maintaining an Upright Position This "room" has a stable floor, but the rest of the room can be moved across it. If an unsuspecting person is standing in the room when the wall in front of him suddenly moves toward him, he experiences an unexpected optic flow that tells his brain he is tilting toward the wall, because it seems highly unlikely that the room itself is moving. The person responds reflexively by leaning sharply backward to compensate for the perceived sway, often to the point of staggering or even falling down. A similar result would be obtained by suddenly moving the wall away from the person—he would reflexively lean forward.

can be moved around a person standing within it on a floor that seems to belong to the room but isn't actually attached to the walls, as illustrated in Figure 7.21 (one wall is missing from the illustration so you can see the person inside). If the room is moved abruptly so that the front wall approaches the person, he experiences optic flow that carries the (incorrect) information that he is swaying forward toward the wall, and he compensates by staggering backward. When this experiment is carried out with small children, it's easy to make them fall down (Lee & Aronson, 1974).

Check Your Understanding

7.11 Would damage in the dorsal pathway be more likely to cause difficulty in reaching for and grasping an object or in identifying an object by touching it?

7.12 How does a delayed-saccade experiment show that the activity of LIP neurons reflects intended eye movements?

7.13 How does optic flow help you determine your heading?

APPLICATIONS Motion Perception in Baseball: Catching a Fly Ball and Hitting a Fastball

The principles of perception for action discussed in this chapter come into play at almost every waking moment when performing such everyday actions as picking up a cup of tea or reaching for a doorknob. More complex actions involve multiple sources of visual information—for example, when you're driving a car, the vehicle and your head and eyes move continuously within an environment containing both stationary and moving objects. Here, a combination of learned skills and moment-by-moment perception and response produces fluent and usually successful performance. In this section, we'll examine two actions of intermediate complexity that many of us can perform with some success and that professional athletes can perform amazingly well: catching and hitting a baseball.

How to Catch a Fly Ball

A baseball hit into the air follows a path shaped approximately like a parabola (air resistance, wind, and the spin on the ball make the path not quite a true parabola). One strategy for catching a fly ball would be to watch the initial trajectory and predict where the ball will land, run to that point, and catch it. However, balls with very different landing points can have very similar initial trajectories, so it's difficult to judge a fly ball's landing point based just on perceiving the initial trajectory. How, then, do fielders catch fly balls?

Researchers have proposed that fielders use a strategy called **linear optical trajectory (LOT)** to ensure that they arrive at the ball's landing point at the same time as the ball (McBeath et al., 1995). Figure 7.22 shows what a fielder must do to use this strategy: while keeping his or her eye on the ball, the fielder must run in a path and at a speed such that the ball appears to travel upward in a straight line at a constant speed—that is, such that the ball's optical trajectory is linear. In order to test whether this is a strategy that fielders actually use, the researchers recorded on video the running movements of fielders attempting to catch fly balls, while simultaneously recording the trajectory of the ball from the fielders' perspective via a video camera mounted on the fielders' shoulder. The videos showed that if the fielders followed a curved path, as predicted by the LOT strategy, while adjusting their speed so the ball follows a linear optical trajectory, they would arrive at the ball's landing point in time to catch the ball. Also as predicted by the LOT proposal, if the ball seemed to slow down—that is, if the optical trajectory began to curve down—the ball would land in front of the fielder; and if the ball seemed to speed up—if the optical trajectory began to curve up—the ball would land behind the fielder. A subsequent study found that a dog running to catch a Frisbee apparently uses the same LOT strategy (Shaffer et al., 2004).

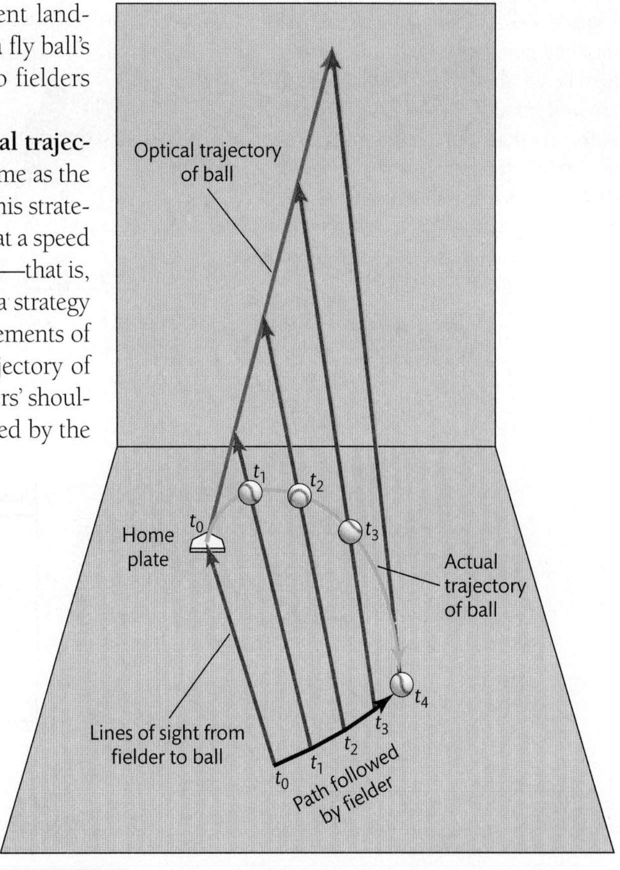

Figure 7.22 **Using the LOT Strategy to Catch a Fly Ball** Using the linear optical trajectory (LOT) strategy, fielders can ensure that they arrive at a fly ball's landing point in time to catch the ball. While visually tracking the ball, the fielder must run so that the ball appears to travel upward in a straight line at a constant speed. (Adapted from McBeath et al., 1995.)

The LOT strategy is probably not the only method fielders use to catch a fly ball, as shown by the fact that fielders often are able to station themselves at the ball's landing point before the ball arrives (Dannemiller et al., 1996), but the experiment just described shows how tightly coordinated perception and action are: fielders adjust their running path and speed while tracking the ball, to ensure that the ball maintains a linear optical trajectory; deviations from that trajectory lead to further adjustments in the running path. The detailed analysis of this situation is complicated by additional factors that were ignored in the initial studies—for example, how do the fielders' eye and head movements and their up-and-down running movements affect the perceived trajectory, and how might their choice of running paths be affected by their knowledge that the outfield fence is just behind them or that another player might be approaching? Addressing all these questions will require further investigation. Nevertheless, it's clear that perception-and-action calculations like those embodied in the LOT strategy are an everyday part of our lives and that our brains have evolved to perform such calculations automatically and effortlessly.

linear optical trajectory (LOT) A strategy for catching a fly ball by which the fielder runs in a path and at a speed such that the ball appears to travel upward in a straight line at a constant speed.

How to Hit a Fastball

Professional baseball pitchers routinely throw a fastball at 90 miles per hour (mph) or faster. The pitcher keeps one foot on the pitching rubber, 60 feet 6 inches from home plate, and strides toward the batter before releasing the pitch, so the distance from the release point to the plate is less than 60 feet. This means that a 90-mph fastball arrives at the plate less than half a second after it leaves the pitcher's hand. The batter trying to hit the ball faces a serious perceptual estimation problem, because it takes at least two-tenths of a second to swing the bat—the batter must initiate the swing after having seen only the start of the ball's trajectory, as illustrated in Figure 7.23.

Furthermore, the batter's eyes cannot track quickly enough to track a fastball all the way from its release point to the plate. In one study, measurements of eye and head position showed that a professional baseball player could track the ball only until it was about 6 feet in front of the plate (Bahill & LaRitz, 1984). This means that the ball must be hit when it's well outside the center of gaze. So how is it possible to swing and make contact with a fastball even 25–30% of the time, especially given that pitchers vary the speed and trajectory of the ball in order to maximize the batter's perceptual estimation problem?

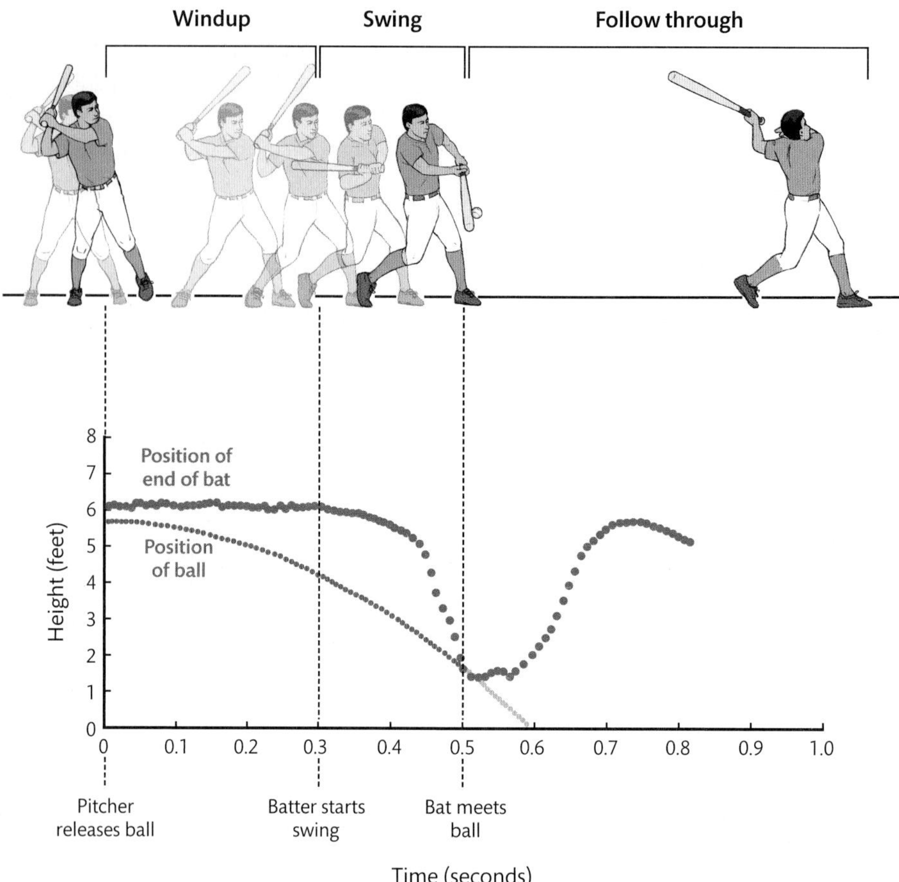

Figure 7.23 Swinging at a Fastball A baseball swing involves the coordination of legs, torso, and arms. The bat starts to move forward about 0.2 second before the baseball arrives, which is about 0.5 second after being released by the pitcher. The shaded circles at the end of the ball's flight path show the trajectory the ball would have followed to the ground if not hit. (Adapted from Gray, 2004, Figure 2.)

Part of the answer is that the batter doesn't wait until the pitch is released to plan his swing. Experienced batters know what pitches are likely to be thrown by the particular pitcher in the given situation, and batters report that they routinely prepare for a specific kind of pitch—for example, a batter expecting a fastball will be ready to begin swinging sooner than a batter expecting an off-speed pitch. Experiments have shown that the timing of a batter's swing is much better when the type of pitch matches the batter's expectation (Gray, 2002).

Once a pitch is on the way, the batter can still make small adjustments in his swing based on the perceived trajectory of the ball, but what visual information can the batter use to make those adjustments? Both the change in the size of the ball's retinal image and the change in binocular disparity during the ball's flight can give the batter information that's useful in determining the time at which the ball will arrive at the batter's position (Gray, 2002). Batters also estimate the speed of the ball in order to predict its height when it crosses the plate (slower pitches drop further), and they try to see the direction of the ball's rotation—its spin—in order to estimate the ball's trajectory. A ball with little or no spin, like a knuckleball, has a highly unpredictable trajectory because of the uneven forces exerted by the air on the ball's surface; a rapidly spinning ball produces different aerodynamic forces that affect the ball's trajectory in more predictable ways, with the direction of spin determining whether the ball will curve to one side or the other, or drop more rapidly, or both. In one study using a computerized pitching simulator, batters performed significantly better when they could accurately see the spin of the ball than when the ball had no spin (Gray, 2002).

The pitcher, of course, attempts to thwart the batter's preparations by throwing a pitch that the batter isn't expecting. If the pitcher is successful, and the batter doesn't recognize in time that the pitch is an unexpected one, the batter can experience the illusion that the ball makes an abrupt, late change in its trajectory. Consider, for example, the so-called rising fastball, which appears to rise abruptly just before it reaches the plate. A thrown ball can abruptly sink or curve in accord with the aerodynamic forces on the ball, but it cannot rise. So what's going on? One proposal is that the batter underestimates the pitch speed,

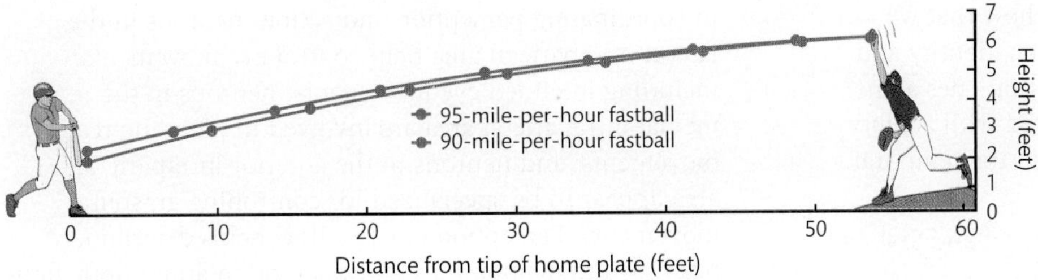

Figure 7.24 Illusion of the Rising Fastball A fastball traveling at 90 mph arrives at the plate about 3 inches lower than a fastball traveling at 95 mph. If the batter estimates that a 95-mph fastball is traveling at 90 mph, he'll misestimate the height at which the ball will arrive at the plate. As his bat passes 3 inches under the ball, he is likely to experience an illusion: the ball will seem to move upward abruptly. If a 95-mph pitch is estimated to be traveling at 75 mph, the batter would misestimate the height of the ball by nearly a foot. (Adapted from Bahill & Karnavas, 1993, Figure 1.)

and because depth cues such as retinal image size and binocular disparity are inexact, the true position of the ball can easily be misperceived until it is very close to the plate (Bahill & Karnavas, 1993). Figure 7.24 compares the trajectory of a pitched ball traveling at 95 mph with that of a ball traveling at 90 mph. The slower pitch will arrive at the plate about 3 inches lower than the faster pitch. This means that if a pitch is actually traveling at 95 mph and the batter estimates the speed as 90 mph, a swing designed to hit a ball at that slower speed will pass 3 inches below the actual pitch. When this happens, the visual system resolves the conflict between the estimated and actual height of the ball by "perceiving" an abrupt upward movement of the ball at the very last moment.

The factors that contribute to success in catching or hitting a baseball are complex and multidimensional, involving both deliberate preparation and anticipation based on experience and knowledge, as well as rapid perception of the ball's trajectory. Of course, once a person has become skilled at these complex perceptual–motor activities, very little of the "thinking" involved takes place consciously and deliberately. Indeed, one study found that skilled batters hit better when they don't think about what they're doing (Castaneda & Gray, 2007).

Check Your Understanding

7.14 Baseball outfielders often arrive at the landing point of a fly ball before the ball actually gets there. Explain why this shows that the linear optical trajectory strategy is probably not the only method fielders use to gauge a ball's landing point.

7.15 Why can perceiving the spin of a pitched ball make it easier to hit the ball?

SUMMARY

- **Motion Perception in Area V1 and Area MT** Neural circuits that respond to stimuli moving in a preferred direction at a preferred speed must include a delay in the transmission of signals from one neuron in the circuit, so signals arrive simultaneously at the motion-selective neuron. To account for the motion aftereffect, such circuits must consist of two subunits that are selective for opposite directions of motion. In area V1, many neurons are tuned to direction and speed of motion, and neurons have small receptive fields; in area MT, almost all neurons are motion selective, and their receptive fields are much larger. Single-cell recording experiments in monkeys strongly support the idea that MT neurons play a causal role in perception of the direction of motion. Damage to or disruption of MT selectively impairs motion perception. The aperture problem arises because V1 neurons can't unambiguously indicate the direction of motion of a stimulus; the problem is solved via MT neurons that combine the information from multiple V1 neurons.

- **Perceptual Organization from Motion** Apparent motion plays a key role in perceptual grouping by linking the retinal images of objects that appear in different locations at different times, as demonstrated by the apparent motion quartet. That motion can contribute to figure–ground organization is shown by animals that hide themselves using camouflage but become visible when they move. Random dot kinematograms demonstrate this point even more clearly—movement creates a figure that otherwise doesn't exist. Point-light walker displays show that we have a highly developed ability to assess the identity and actions of a biological object based on motion cues alone. Perception of biological motion is associated with activity in the posterior superior temporal sulcus in the temporal lobe.

- Eye Movements and the Perception of Motion and Stability The world doesn't appear to move when we move our eyes, even though the retinal image moves. Therefore, perception of motion and of stability can't just depend on motion or the lack of motion in the retinal image but must also depend on extraretinal information. Experiments indicate that some such information comes from corollary discharge signals—copies of eye-movement commands that tell the brain about intended eye movements, before the movements actually occur.
- Perception for Action Perception and action cannot be neatly separated—perception is a kind of action. Areas in the posterior parietal lobe play a crucial role in coordinating perception and action: neurons in the lateral intraparietal area help control eye movements, including intended eye movements; neurons in the medial intraparietal area are involved in planning reach movements; and neurons in the anterior intraparietal area appear to be specialized for controlling grasping movements. Perception of optic flow helps determine heading and maintain upright body orientation; optic flow can also produce an illusory perception of self-motion.
- Applications: Motion Perception in Baseball: Catching a Fly Ball and Hitting a Fastball Catching a fly ball is a complex, real-world example of the close relationship between perception and action; linear optical trajectory is one strategy fielders use to arrive in time at the spot where the ball will come down. Hitting a fastball requires learned skill, knowledge, experience, and quick perception of the ball's trajectory. The ball's spin can help the batter determine the trajectory. The illusion of the rising fastball is based on an underestimation of the ball's speed.

KEY TERMS

anterior intraparietal area (AIP) (p. 248)
aperture problem (p. 236)
apparent motion (p. 237)
apparent motion quartet (p. 238)
corollary discharge signal (CDS) (p. 243)
lateral intraparietal area (LIP) (p. 247)
linear optical trajectory (LOT) (p. 251)
medial intraparietal area (MIP) (p. 248)
motion aftereffect (MAE) (p. 228)
point-light walker (p. 239)
random dot kinematogram (p. 238)
saccadic eye movements (or *saccades*) (p. 241)
saccadic suppression (p. 242)
smooth pursuit eye movements (p. 241)
vergence eye movements (p. 241)

EXPAND YOUR UNDERSTANDING

7.1 In Figure 7.3, showing the responses of a motion-selective neuron in a circuit like the one in Figure 7.2b, the preferred direction of motion is 135° (from RF_2 to RF_1). Assume the following: the distance between RF_1 and RF_2 is 2° of visual angle; the preferred speed of motion is 5° per second; the transmission time for a nondelayed neural signal from one of the receptive fields to the motion-selective neuron is 0.01 sec. For this circuit to exhibit the stipulated preferred direction and speed, a delay must be built into the transmission of signals from one of the receptive fields. How long must the delay be, and from which receptive field?

7.2 Simon and Simone are sitting together on a train and looking out the window. Simon is keeping his eyes pointed straight ahead as the landscape streams by. Simone, using binoculars, is examining a distant mountaintop, hoping to see the old mansion she knows is there. The binoculars have a narrow field of view, which is almost entirely filled by the mountaintop. Suddenly, the train pulls to a halt; Simone puts down her binoculars, and the two friends continue looking out the window, trying to see what's going on. Is Simon or Simone more likely to experience the motion aftereffect? Explain why.

7.3 Figure 7.8 indicates how a neuron in area MT could combine the responses of four direction-tuned V1 neurons to unambiguously determine the direction of motion of the square object. If the MT neuron combined the responses of just two V1 neurons, those with RF_1 and RF_4, would it still be able to unambiguously determine the direction of motion of the square? Why or why not?

7.4 Each of the displays below shows the two frames of an apparent motion quartet, which would be shown in alternation to produce apparent motion. Which quartet would produce vertical motion and which would produce horizontal motion? Explain your answer.

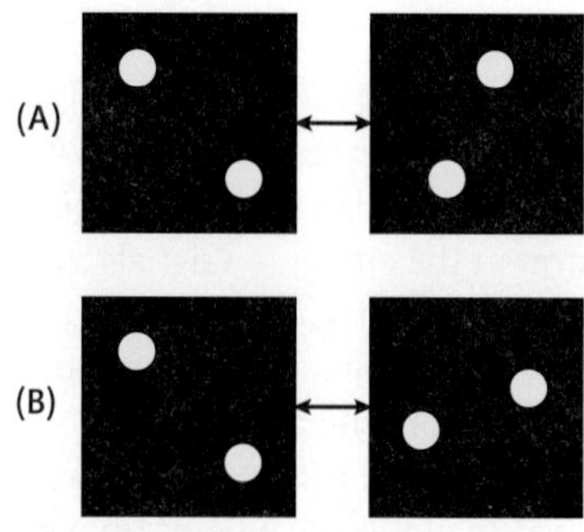

7.5 At night, an airplane flying overhead with lights on its wings and fuselage is easily seen even if you can't hear it, but in a photo it's invisible—the lights just look like more stars shining in the sky. How does this illustrate perceptual organization from motion?

7.6 In the section of this chapter on eye movements, two proposals are discussed about how the visual system gets extraretinal information on eye movements—via signals from the extraocular muscles or via a corollary discharge signal. Suppose you were looking for your cell phone, which you had put down somewhere in your kitchen. First you look at the counter by the sink, but it's not there; then you decide to look on the windowsill—but before you can move your eyes to do so, your extraocular muscles suddenly become paralyzed! What do you think the visual effect of now attempting to look at the windowsill would be under each of the two proposals?

7.7 Suppose you were bending down to pick up a suitcase when it suddenly lifted itself smoothly off the floor and came up to meet your hand. How might this affect your balance? Explain in terms of optic flow and your assumptions about the physical world.

7.8 In baseball, the batter has to hit the pitch, the catcher has to catch the pitch, and the outfielders have to catch fly balls. Which tasks do you think are more similar in terms of the perceptual strategies involved: (A) hitting the pitch and catching the pitch, or (B) catching the pitch and catching a fly ball? Explain your answer.

READ MORE ABOUT IT

Born, R. T., & Bradley, D. C. (2005). Structure and function of visual area MT. *Annual Review of Neuroscience, 28,* 157–189.

A comprehensive review of recent findings concerning the functional properties of the motion-selective brain region area MT.

Milner, A. D., & Goodale, M. A. (2006). *The visual brain in action* (2nd ed.). New York: Oxford University Press.

A very readable description of the perceptual deficits of patient D.F. and others who have provided key insights into the role of the parietal cortex in supporting visually guided action.

Newsome, W. T., Britten, K. H., & Movshon, J. A. (1989). Neuronal correlates of a perceptual decision. *Nature, 341,* 52–54.

A landmark study showing how the responses of neurons in area MT of a monkey brain can predict the monkey's decision about the direction of motion of moving dots.

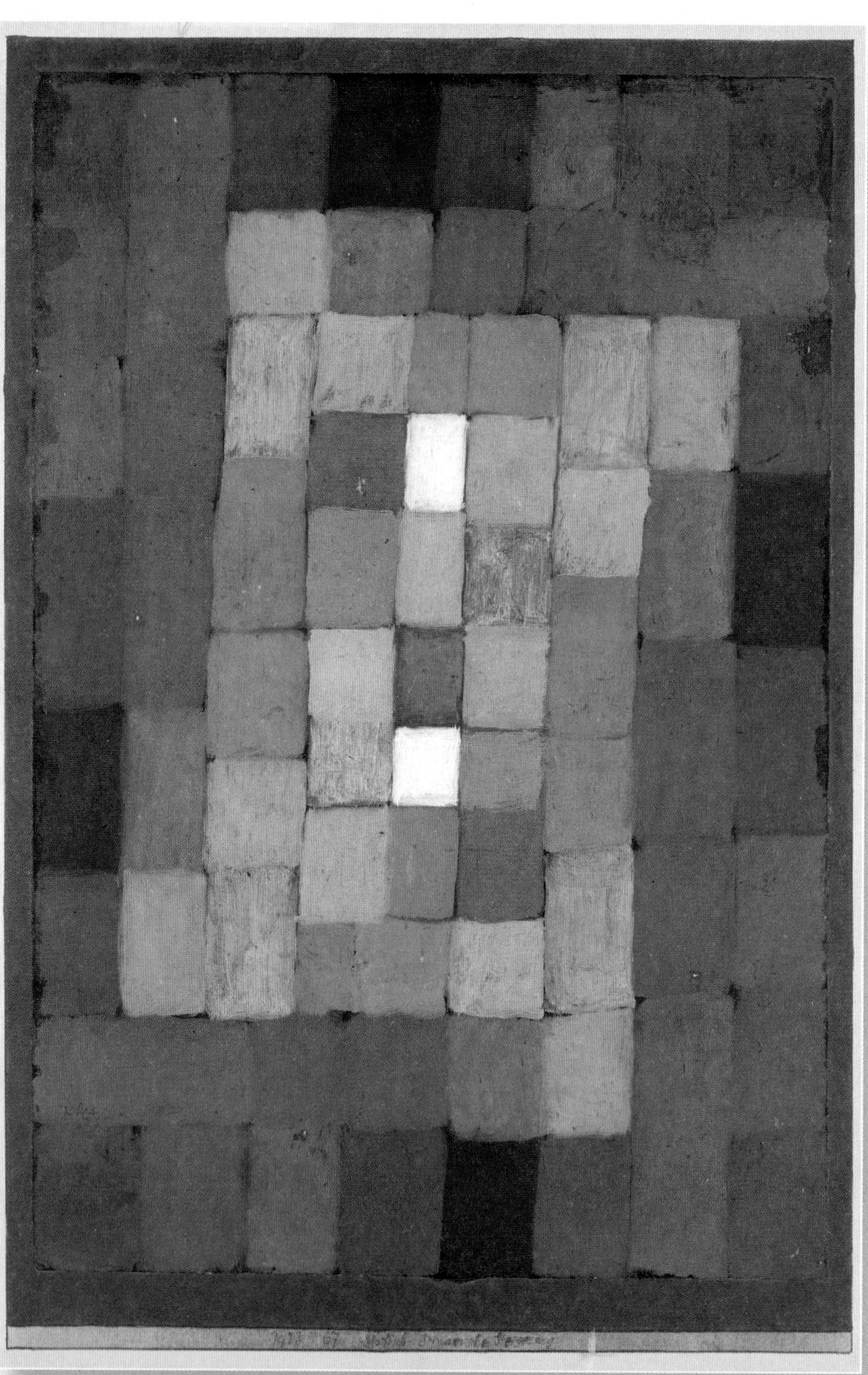

Paul Klee, *Static-Dynamic Gradation,* 1923.[Oil and gouache on paper, bordered with gouache, watercolor, and ink, 15 × 10¼ inches. The Berggruen Klee Collection, 1987 (1987.455.12). © The Metropolitan Museum of Art/Art Resource, NY.]

8

ATTENTION AND AWARENESS

Out of Mind, Out of Sight

Lloyd, a 68-year-old retired commercial airline pilot, had always prided himself on his sharp vision and his awareness of the events around him—abilities crucial to his professional success as a pilot. One night, shortly after falling asleep, he awoke suddenly with a severe headache that seemed to be centered in the upper right side of his head toward the back—a headache so severe that Lloyd and his wife decided he should go to the nearby hospital emergency room. Lloyd was quickly seen by the attending neurologist, who suspected Lloyd might be having a stroke; the neurologist administered medications to minimize its effects and admitted Lloyd to the hospital.

The next day, soon after Lloyd had finished his breakfast, his wife arrived. She quietly entered his hospital room from the door to Lloyd's left, and she was surprised that he didn't seem to notice her arrival. Then she walked around to the other side of his bed, and he finally noticed her and said he was glad to see her. His breakfast tray was still in front of him, and, with an uneasy feeling, she saw that he had eaten everything on the right half of his plate but hadn't touched anything on the left.

Then the neurologist arrived to examine Lloyd, entering through the same door, and when Lloyd failed to notice him, the neurologist's first thought was that the stroke had damaged the visual areas of Lloyd's brain, leaving him blind in his left visual field. But he also considered the possibility that the stroke had instead rendered Lloyd unable to notice—to pay attention to—things in his left visual field. As a test, the neurologist said, "Good morning, Lloyd," in a loud voice. Lloyd immediately moved his eyes to focus on him and replied, "Good morning, doctor." The neurologist then held out his hand to his right and, while wiggling his fingers, asked Lloyd if he could see this hand; Lloyd said that he could. Clearly, Lloyd wasn't blind in his left visual field. Rather, Lloyd's stroke had left him with a condition called *unilateral visual neglect*. As we'll see in this chapter, studies of patients with this condition—not uncommon among those who suffer certain kinds of strokes—have provided evidence about which parts of the brain control our ability to pay attention.

Chapter Outline

As you read the words on this page and absorb their meaning, you're continuously sensing many aspects of your external and internal environment: the warmth of the sun coming in through a window; the faint sounds of the room's ventilation system and a distant airplane; the pressure of the chair against your back and legs; the lingering pain where you bit your tongue yesterday; the slight aftertaste of the tea you sipped a few moments ago; and perhaps the smell of dinner wafting in from the kitchen. Despite the fact that all these sources

awareness Active thinking about or concentration on some source of stimulation.

attention The selection of some source of sensory stimulation for increased cognitive processing.

selective attention Attention to some things and not to others.

of stimulation are evoking activity in your sensory system, you have **awareness** of—that is, you're actively thinking about—just a small subset of them. Without moving a muscle, you can concentrate on any one of these things, for understanding, evaluation, planning, enjoyment, or some other purpose. This selection of one source of sensory input for increased cognitive processing—including for use in guiding actions such as performing a reach or an eye movement, storing the sensory input in memory, and increasing your awareness of it—is what we call **attention.**

Of course, it's possible to pay attention to more than one thing at a time. If you decide to walk from the room where you're studying to the kitchen to see what's cooking, and you go through the living room where a TV is on, you can pay attention to the room's layout, so you don't bump into the furniture, and at the same time pay attention to what the newscaster is saying on the TV. This is called *divided attention,* and it's clearly common in everyday life. Equally common is *focused attention,* being acutely aware of only one thing at a time, such as this sentence as you read it, or maybe a few closely related things, such as the taste, smell, and warmth of your cup of tea. But regardless of whether attention is divided or focused, it is always **selective attention**—that is, attention to some things and not to others. When your attention is divided between noticing the layout of the room and listening to the TV, you're probably not paying attention to the color of the rug, even if your eyes happen to be pointing at the rug. And when your attention is focused on what you're reading, you completely tune out the smell of dinner cooking. Such acts of selective attention determine the contents of your thoughts at every waking moment.

This chapter is about attention as a mechanism for perceptual selection. Attention provides a way to select what to be aware of, what to store in memory, and what information to use in guiding action. Throughout the chapter, we'll focus almost entirely on attention to visual and auditory stimuli, as those are the domains in which most of the relevant studies have been done. First, we'll take a look at some studies showing that we're aware of—and can respond effectively to—only what we attend to. Despite the impression that we're constantly aware of everything in the current scene—all the sights, sounds, smells, and other immediately available sensory stimuli—we are, at any given moment, really aware of very limited parts of the scene, while also having a more or less vague awareness of the *gist* of the environment as a whole. Then we'll consider some of the mechanisms behind this perceptual limitation, as we explore how attention is directed to specific spatial locations and perceptual features. Next we'll discuss the key function of attention—to resolve the competition among perceptual objects for neural representation in the brain. We'll then consider attentional control, exploring both voluntary shifts of attention—as when you decide to listen to the violins and ignore the piano during a classical music concert—and involuntary shifts of attention—as when a door slamming causes you to look up. Finally, we'll look at recent research aimed at shedding light on an ancient mystery: How does the mental experience of awareness arise from the activity of a material object, the brain?

Selective Attention and the Limits of Awareness

Imagine you're at a crowded, noisy party where you're trying to talk with a friend—straining to hear her voice, watching her lips to get clues to her words, and doing your best to ignore the clamor around you. Suddenly, in a conversation off to your left, you hear someone say your name. This immediately captures your attention, and as you focus on this other conversation, you lose all awareness of what your friend is saying, while you continue to smile and nod at her. If she asks you a question, you're in trouble.

The challenge of comprehending speech in a noisy environment was dubbed the *cocktail party problem* by Colin Cherry (1953), who took this situation into the laboratory for rigorous examination. As illustrated in Figure 8.1, participants in this study wore headphones that transmitted one spoken message into one ear and a different spoken

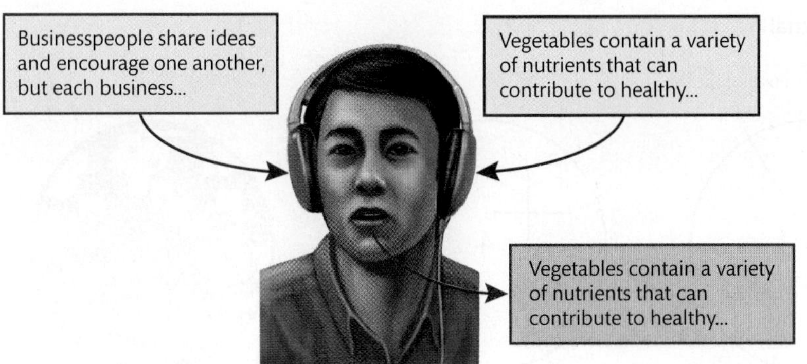
Businesspeople share ideas and encourage one another, but each business...
Vegetables contain a variety of nutrients that can contribute to healthy...
Vegetables contain a variety of nutrients that can contribute to healthy...

Figure 8.1 Dichotic Listening: Attention Affects Recall A person listens through headphones to two different messages, attending to one while ignoring the other; attention is ensured by having the person repeat (shadow) the attended message. Generally, people are able to recall little or nothing about what they heard in the unattended message.

message into the other ear (e.g., two different mundane newspaper articles that didn't include any proper names or unusual words), a procedure called **dichotic listening.** They were asked to repeat back (or *shadow*) the message heard in one ear as the message unfolded, in order to ensure that they were perceiving and understanding that message. After shadowing one message for a minute or two, participants would be asked to state what they had heard in the other, ignored ear. Consistently, participants were able to report almost nothing about the content of the ignored message. In fact, even changing the language being spoken in the ignored ear, or playing the message in reverse, was often not noticed. However, some changes were noticed immediately—for example, when the unattended message was replaced by a tone or when a man's voice was replaced by a woman's. Thus, the experiments suggested that low-level sensory changes in the ignored ear (e.g., a change from a low-pitched voice to a high-pitched voice) are noticed, but changes related to meaning aren't.

dichotic listening Listening to one message in the left ear and a different message in the right ear.

Demonstration 8.1 Selective Attention Participate in a visual version of a dichotic listening experiment to explore the factors involved in selective attention.

This conclusion, of course, raises a question: If meaning isn't registered when you're attending to one among many conversations, why do you notice your own name spoken in an unattended conversation at a party? Later studies suggested that certain words (e.g., your own name) have a default high priority: when they occur, they often capture your attention (Moray, 1959; Treisman, 1969). This suggests that the semantic content of the ignored message is processed to some degree, but unless that message has particular importance for you, it's discarded and unavailable for later recall. Later in this chapter, we'll see other examples of how certain kinds of high-priority sensory events can capture attention even when it's focused elsewhere.

Inattentional Blindness

The cocktail party problem demonstrates the dependence of awareness and comprehension on attention. To appreciate the *degree* of that dependence, consider laboratory experiments that have revealed a phenomenon termed **inattentional blindness** (Mack & Rock, 1998)—the failure to perceive a fully visible but unattended visual object. A typical experiment consisted of three or four noncritical trials followed by one critical trial, as illustrated in Figure 8.2. Participants were asked to fix their gaze on the fixation point at the center of the display and were told that after a short time a large cross would appear briefly somewhere in the display; the participants' task was to judge whether the vertical arm or the horizontal arm of the cross was longer. The difference in length was small, so the task was challenging, and the cross was presented for just one-fifth of a second before being masked by a random pattern, so there was no time for participants to move their eyes to it. In the critical trial, a small shape (e.g., a diamond) unexpectedly appeared at the fixation point at the same time as the large cross appeared; this small shape was termed the *critical stimulus,* because assessing participants' awareness of it was the whole point of the experiment.

inattentional blindness Failure to perceive a fully visible but unattended visual object.

In the critical trial, after the participants stated which arm of the cross was longer, they were asked if they had seen anything in the display other than the large cross.

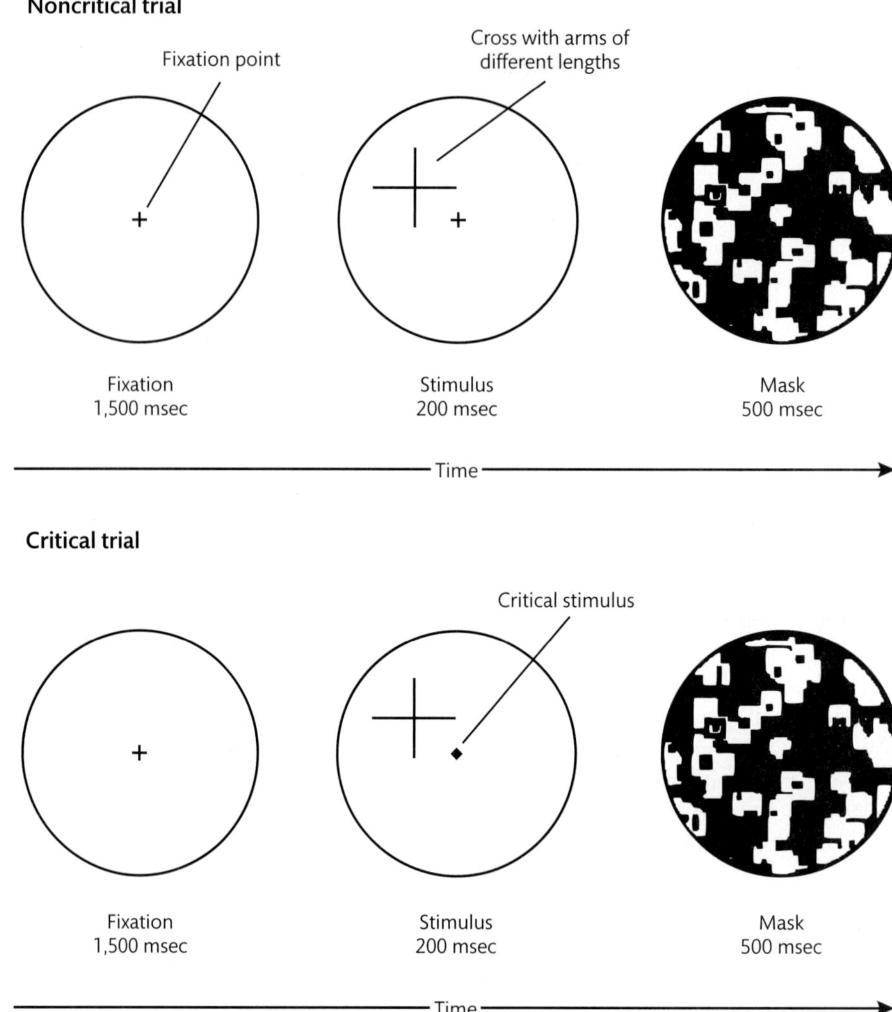

Figure 8.2 Inattentional Blindness In experiments demonstrating inattentional blindness, participants were required to judge whether the vertical or horizontal arm of a large, briefly flashed cross was longer. After each critical trial, participants were asked whether they'd noticed the critical stimulus. Typically, 60%–80% of participants showed no awareness of the critical stimulus, because their attention was directed to the large cross. (Adapted from Mack & Rock, 1998.)

Between 60% and 80% of the participants indicated that they had not seen anything except the large cross. In contrast, when participants were told to ignore the large cross and just report the shape and location of anything else that appeared in the display, performance was nearly perfect, showing that the small shape was easy to see and identify when it was attended. These experiments show that even when you're looking directly at something, you're quite likely not going to see it if you're paying attention elsewhere.

Change Blindness

Another type of example suggests that selective attention isn't simply a matter of choice—as when you choose to attend to one conversation and ignore another—but is in some sense unavoidable. This is illustrated by a kind of puzzle you may recall working on as a child, in which two complex drawings that look identical at first glance are shown side by side, and your job is to find all the small differences between them. The fact that you can't immediately see all the differences suggests that you don't have detailed simultaneous awareness of everything in the two pictures.

A version of this puzzle has been created in the perception lab that focuses on our ability to detect just a single change between two scenes. A photograph of a complex scene is taken, and a duplicate version is created that has a single change in it—for instance, an object is in different positions in the two photos, or an object is present in one photo and absent in the other. The photos are then shown in alternation, for about a quarter of a second per exposure, over and over again, with a brief blank interval after each exposure (without the blank interval the change looks like apparent motion and is immediately obvious). The observer's job is to find the difference between the two photos as quickly as possible. Figure 8.3 shows two such photos, and even here, where you can see both pictures at once instead of in alternation, you might not see the difference right away.

In such experiments, observers often require 10 or 20 seconds or even more—that is, a dozen or more alternation cycles—to detect the difference (Rensink et al., 1997). Typically, people keep their attention focused on one object in the scene for one alternation cycle to determine whether the change involves that object; if they conclude that it doesn't, they move their eyes to another object, and so on until they notice the change (Henderson & Hollingworth, 1999).

Demonstration 8.2 Change Blindness See how long it takes you to notice a difference between two alternating photos of a complex scene.

As in the case where the person has to detect multiple small differences between two scenes that are viewed simultaneously, people's inability to immediately detect a single big difference between scenes viewed in alternation indicates that they aren't simultaneously aware of everything in a scene. In addition, the alternating-photos task shows that this inability isn't merely an effect of limited visual acuity, where it's difficult to see things in the periphery of the visual field, because observers often fail to notice the difference between the two scenes even when their eyes are pointed right at the critical object, which puts the retinal image of the object on the fovea, where vision is most acute. The obvious explanation for this is that even when you're looking directly at something, you might be paying attention to something else, or you might be paying attention to one feature of an object when the change involves some other feature. This inability to quickly detect changes in complex scenes is called **change blindness**, and the research we've

change blindness Inability to quickly detect changes in complex scenes.

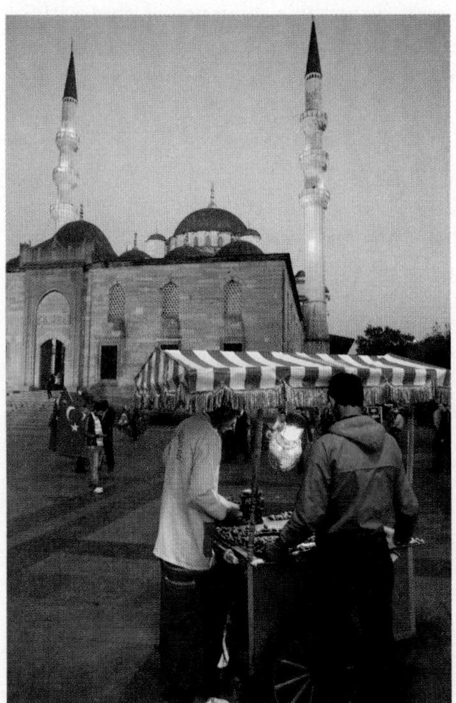

Figure 8.3 Change Blindness To demonstrate change blindness, two scenes like these are shown in rapid alternation, separated by a brief blank interval. Observers have to say what is different between the two scenes. Even when you can see both scenes at once, it may take you a while to see the single big difference. [Jordi Cami/Alamy]

just described shows that change blindness reflects our limited ability to pay attention to multiple things at the same time.

Another experiment provides an even more dramatic demonstration of the role of attention in change blindness (Simons & Levin, 1998). A member of the research team (termed a *confederate*) would approach an unknowing person on a busy street and ask for directions. After 10–20 seconds, two other confederates posing as workmen and carrying a large piece of plywood would somewhat rudely walk right between the two conversants. As they passed, one of the "workmen" would change places with the confederate asking directions, by quickly handing him the plywood while momentarily hidden by it from the person's view. The two confederates who switched places would both be adult white males but would differ in height, hairstyle, clothing, and so on. Often, the person giving directions wouldn't notice the change, even though the person had spoken to the first confederate for 10–20 seconds and looked at his face several times. Clearly, looking at something isn't the same as *seeing* it, just as letting the sound of a conversation into your ears isn't the same as *hearing* it. You have to pay attention to be aware of and fully understand what your eyes are pointed at or what your ears take in.

Gist Awareness

The examples described so far suggest that awareness is limited to just those things we're actively attending to. Yet this goes against our intuition that when we open our eyes, we become aware of a rich, full, complete scene, not just of some small part of the scene where our attention happens to be directed. How can we reconcile this apparent contradiction? The answer is that we can be aware of a scene in two different ways. On the one hand, we typically have a background awareness of the gist of the scene; this general sense of what the scene is "about" is the awareness that comes at a glance, as when we first enter a room. On the other hand, for real awareness—in order to pick up and remember detailed information—we have to attend to particular parts of the scene, noting the specific identities of objects, their spatial relations, and so forth (Oliva, 2005).

rapid serial visual presentation (RSVP) An experimental procedure in which participants must note whether a particular type of scene occurs in a series of photographs presented at a very high rate (3 to 10 photos per second).

Our ability to assess the gist of a scene on the basis of a very brief exposure has been demonstrated in **rapid serial visual presentation (RSVP)** experiments, in which people are asked to note whether a particular type of scene occurs in a sequence of photographs presented at a very high rate (3 to 10 photos per second); for example, people might be asked, Is there a picnic scene somewhere in the sequence you're about to see?—note that a wide range of specific scenes could fit this description. People can detect scenes in response to such questions with an accuracy well above chance, suggesting that the gist of a scene can be extracted within a fraction of a second (Potter, 1976).

Furthermore, in these experiments, little about the other scenes in the sequence is retained in memory. This is demonstrated by having participants complete a recognition memory test after just viewing an RSVP sequence of, say, 16 photographs. Participants are shown a group of 32 photos consisting of the 16 photos just seen, along with 16 new photos, randomly intermixed. They are permitted to look at each photo as long as they like and then must say whether it's old (i.e., among the 16 photos in the RSVP sequence just viewed) or new. In this task, participants perform near chance (Potter & Levy, 1969).

Together, these experiments show that brief exposure to a scene allows us to get its gist but doesn't give us any significant enduring perception of specific elements in the scene. For that, we have to direct our attention to the specific elements themselves.

Check Your Understanding

8.1 What does it mean to say that attention is selective?

8.2 In a dichotic listening experiment, which of the following changes would probably be noticed in the unattended ear and which would probably not be noticed: **(A)** a change from meaningful sentences to nonsense; **(B)** a change from normal conversation to a loud argument; **(C)** a change from a dog barking to a cat meowing; **(D)** a change from a list of common household appliances to a list of the names of countries?

8.3 Describe a scenario in everyday life that demonstrates inattentional blindness and another scenario that demonstrates change blindness.

8.4 Describe a scenario in everyday life that demonstrates gist awareness versus awareness of details.

Attention to Locations and Features

In the preceding section, we saw that attention is necessarily selective and that this places strict limits on our awareness and memory of what's in a scene. In this section, we'll dig a little deeper and review experimental evidence, both behavioral and neurophysiological, about how attention works in two important domains: attention to spatial locations, like an attentional "spotlight," and attention to features, such as an object's shape, color, or motion or the pitch or loudness of a sound.

Donald Broadbent (1926–1993).

Attention to Locations

The objects and surfaces around us are arrayed in 3-D space. You constantly move your gaze from one spatial location to another in patterns that depend a great deal on what kind of information you're looking for. And even without changing the direction of your gaze, you can change the location of your visual attention—for example, while speaking with a friend, you can look at a clock on the wall "out of the corner of your eye"—or you can direct your auditory attention to a location other than where you're looking, as when you start listening to a nearby conversation at a party while continuing to look at the person you're talking with.

Let's consider some studies showing not only that people can direct their attention to spatial locations, but also that doing so both enhances their ability to detect or recognize things in the attended location and impairs their perception of things in other locations. The dichotic listening experiments described earlier show that we can direct our auditory attention to one of two locations—in this case, in order to register information coming from the left or right side of space. These experiments led Donald Broadbent (1958) to propose the **filter theory of attention,** which asserts that all information from the senses is registered as physical signals but that only the signals selected for access to a "limited-capacity system" are interpreted for meaning, while the unselected signals are filtered out and the information in them is lost. In this proposal, the mechanism that performs the selection is attention, which serves as a filter, and the limited-capacity system supports awareness and the storage of information in memory. This extremely influential idea continues to play a role in most theories of attention.

filter theory of attention The theory that all sensory information is registered as physical signals but that attention selects only some of those signals to be interpreted for meaning, with the rest being filtered out.

In the 1950s and 1960s, many experiments were aimed at determining just what is involved in this process of selecting some signals while ignoring others. In one dichotic listening experiment, people were instructed to shadow a message in one ear, while ignoring the other ear. Each ear heard a different 50-word message (e.g., a passage from a novel in one ear and a passage from a technical discussion in the other). Occasionally, the two passages would switch ears in midstream, and often the person listening would "follow the message" and start shadowing the to-be-ignored ear (Treisman, 1960). In another experiment, people were asked to shadow a list of words in one ear and then to report what they had heard, if anything, in the other ear. They failed to notice when the ignored message consisted of the same set of words repeated many times, but about a third of the time they noticed when their own name appeared in the ignored message (Moray, 1959). These findings suggest that the meaning of the ignored message must be processed to some extent and that when the meaning either is of great personal interest (e.g., the listener's own name) or is highly related to the message being shadowed (e.g., when the shadowed message switches ears), then the message in the unattended ear can "break through" and enter awareness.

Later, researchers began to study visual attention using **attentional cuing**—providing a cue about the location and timing of an upcoming stimulus—to examine how the spatial

attentional cuing Providing a cue (e.g., an arrow or tone) about the location and timing of an upcoming stimulus.

location of a person's attention affects the speed with which the person can become aware of something and respond to it. In a typical experiment (Posner et al., 1978), the participant was instructed to fixate on a point at the center of a visual display (Time 1 in Figure 8.4a). One of three cues then appeared in the display for one second (Time 2 in Figure 8.4a): a left- or right-pointing arrow indicated that the participant should direct her attention to the corresponding side of the fixation point, because she'd been told that a target was likely to appear in that location; a plus sign was a neutral cue, indicating that the target was equally likely to appear in either location. Regardless of where she directed her attention, the participant was required to keep her gaze on the fixation point; a device known as an *eye tracker* was used to confirm that the participant maintained this fixation. The target then appeared (Time 3 in Figure 8.4a), and the participant had to press a button as soon as she saw it.

Demonstration 8.3 Shifting Spatial Attention Participate in an experiment aimed at assessing how long it takes to shift your attention.

Each such sequence—cue followed by target followed by button press—constituted a trial; each trial was followed by a brief pause and then a new trial. When the cue indicated that the participant should direct her attention to the left or the right, the target appeared on that side in 80% of the trials (the cues in these trials were called *valid cues*) and on the other side in 20% of the trials (*invalid cues*); when the cue was neutral, the target appeared equally often on either side. The results of this study, as shown in Figure 8.4b, were that the time

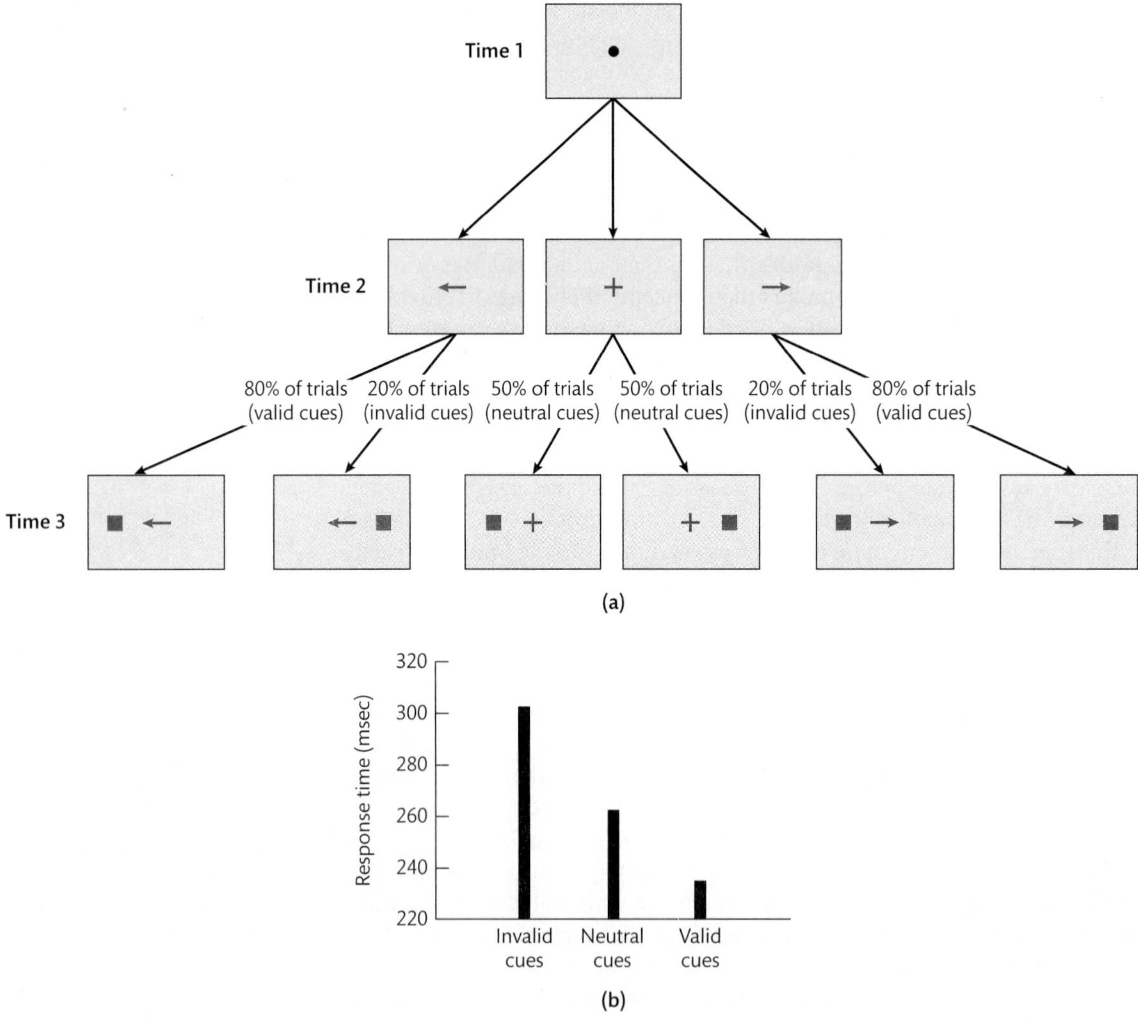

Figure 8.4 Cuing Visual Attention (a) The experimental procedure: At Time 1, a fixation point appears on a display, and the participant looks at it without moving her eyes. At Time 2, a cue appears—either a left arrow, a right arrow, or a plus sign (equally often, in random order). After 1 second, at Time 3, a target appears to the left or right of the fixation point, and the participant has to press a response button as soon as she sees the target. If the cue was an arrow, the target appears in the cued position 80% of the time (valid cues) and in the uncued position 20% of the time (invalid cues). If the cue was a plus sign (a neutral cue), the target appears half the time to the left of the fixation point and half the time to the right. (b) Typical response times: Responses to valid cues are faster than responses to invalid cues, and responses to neutral cues are about midway between. (Adapted from Posner et al., 1978.)

required to press the button—the response time—was significantly faster when the target followed a valid cue than when it followed an invalid cue, with the response time to targets following neutral cues somewhere in between. This indicates that detecting the target is significantly faster when it appears in an attended location than when it appears in an unattended location, even when the stimuli are equally distant from the fixation point and therefore equally visible. It's as if an "attentional spotlight" is directed to the cued location, and this speeds perception.

Many other studies have since confirmed and extended the results of this early behavioral research into the relationship between awareness and attention to spatial locations, leading neuroscientists to ask what changes occur in the brain when attention is directed to a location. In one influential study (Moran & Desimone, 1985), researchers recorded the activity of single neurons in area V4 of a monkey's brain in response to the presentation of two stimuli in the neuron's receptive field (RF), as illustrated in Figure 8.5. One of the stimuli was termed *effective,* because when it was presented alone, it evoked a strong response from the neuron; the other was termed *ineffective,* because it evoked only a weak response when presented alone (as discussed in Chapter 4, V4 neurons are tuned to stimuli with particular colors and orientations, so the experimenters first determined the neuron's tuning in order to establish the two stimuli to be used). The monkey was trained to direct his attention to one or the other of the two stimuli when both were present, while always keeping his gaze focused on a fixation point in a location different from that of either stimulus. The researchers found that the neuron's response depended on where the monkey was attending: the response was much stronger when the monkey attended to the effective stimulus than when it attended to the ineffective stimulus. In fact, when the monkey attended to one of the two stimuli, the neuron's response was similar to what it would have been if only that stimulus had been present in the RF. It was as if attention could select which of the two stimuli would drive the neural response in the visual system.

Another experiment compared the response rate of a V4 neuron under two conditions: when attention shifts from a location outside the neuron's RF to a location inside the RF versus when attention shifts from inside the RF to outside the RF (Motter, 1994). While the responses of a single V4 neuron were being recorded, a monkey was initially presented with a display containing a fixation point that was red on some trials and blue on others, as illustrated by

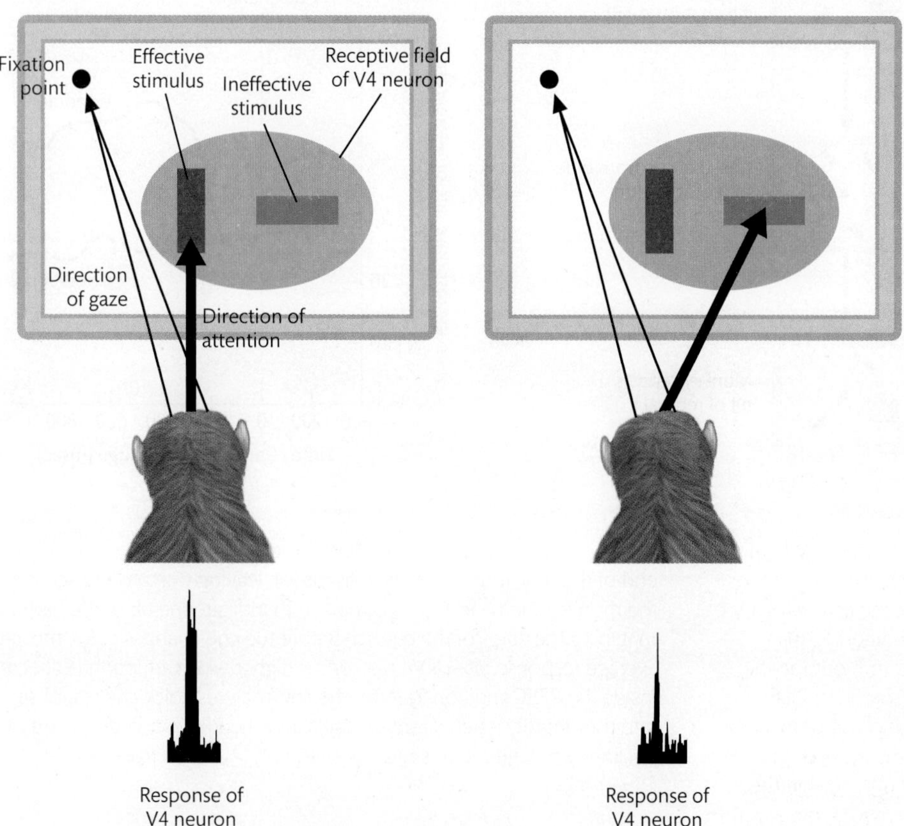

Figure 8.5 Attention Affects Neural Responses in V4 A monkey looks continuously at a fixation point while attending to one of two stimuli in the receptive field of a V4 neuron whose activity is being recorded. The neuron responds strongly when attention is directed to the effective stimulus (a red vertical bar, which evokes a strong response when presented alone) and weakly when attention is directed to the ineffective stimulus (a blue horizontal bar, which evokes a weak response when presented alone), even though both stimuli are present in the receptive field. (Adapted from Moran & Desimone, 1985.)

Conditions 1 and 2 in Figure 8.6a. Then six tilted bars appeared in the display, three red and three blue, with one of the blue bars located so that its retinal image fell within the RF of the V4 neuron. At all times, the monkey had to keep his gaze focused on the fixation point, which also functioned as an attentional cue: the monkey had been trained to attend to the blue bars when the cue was blue and to the red bars when it was red.

About a second after the bars appeared in the display, the cue would sometimes change color, from red to blue or from blue to red, which meant that the monkey would have to shift his attention from the bars of one color to the bars of the other color. When a trial began with a red cue (Condition 1 in Figure 8.6), the monkey's attention was initially directed toward the red bars; then, when the cue changed to blue, the monkey's attention would shift to the blue bars, including the one inside the neuron's RF. In contrast, when a trial began with a blue cue (Condition 2 in Figure 8.6), the monkey's attention was initially directed toward the blue bars, and when the cue changed to red, attention would shift to the red bars, outside the neuron's RF. At the end of each trial, four of the bars disappeared, leaving one red bar and one blue bar, tilted in different directions, and the monkey then had to press a button to indicate the tilt of the bar whose color matched that of the cue.

The average firing rate of individual V4 neurons across many trials is depicted in Figure 8.6b, which clearly shows that attention affects the firing rate of neurons in V4 in response to

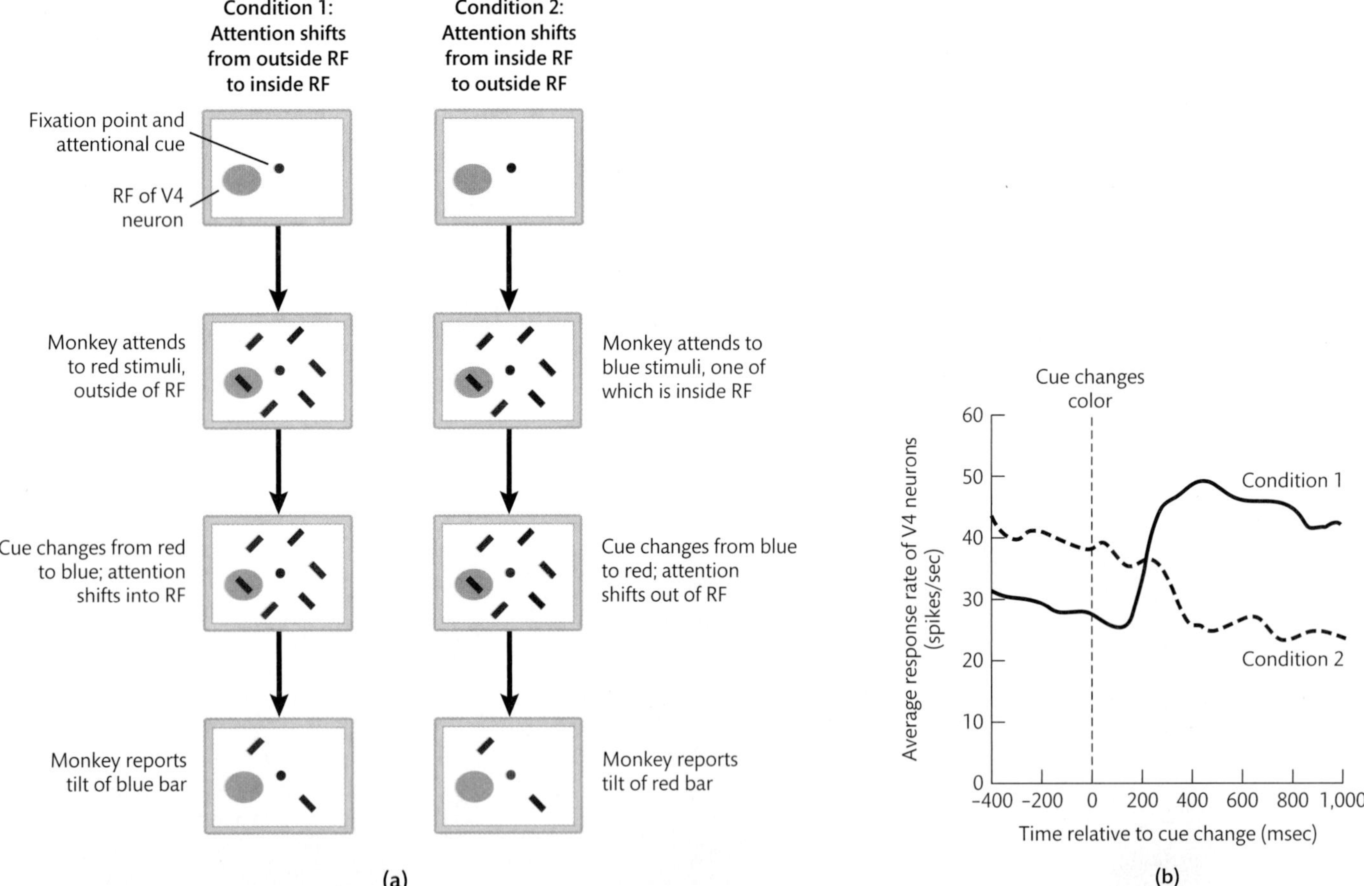

Figure 8.6 Shifts of Attention Affect Neural Responses in V4 (a) A monkey looks continuously at a fixation point (which also functions as an attentional cue) at the center of the display while the activity of a V4 neuron is being recorded. When the cue is red (Condition 1), the monkey directs attention to the red bars, all of which are outside the neuron's receptive field (RF); when the cue is blue (Condition 2), the monkey directs attention to the blue bars, one of which is inside the RF. In both conditions, the cue changes color, causing the monkey to shift his attention to the bars matching the new color—that is, to shift the location of attention from outside to inside the RF or vice versa. At the end of the trial, four of the bars disappear, leaving one bar of each color; the monkey then has to press a button to indicate the tilt of the bar matching the color of the cue. (b) Before the cue changes color, the average response rate of V4 neurons is higher when attention is directed inside the RF (Condition 2). After the cue changes color, the response rate rises rapidly when attention shifts into the RF (Condition 1) and declines when attention shifts out of the RF. (Adapted from Motter, 1994.)

stimuli in their RF, probably via feedback from higher areas of the brain that are involved in directing attention.

Later studies with humans have used fMRI to measure changes in brain activity as people directed attention to different spatial locations. In one study, participants kept their eyes fixed on the center of a display as they directed their attention to rapidly changing letters and digits on either the left side or the right side of the display (Chiu & Yantis, 2009). If the participant was attending to the stimuli on the left side, the appearance of the letter "R" on that side would cue the participant to switch attention to the right side; conversely, for a participant attending to the right side, the appearance of the letter "L" was a cue to switch attention to the left side. Figure 8.7a shows that activity was greater in the left hemisphere when attention was directed to the right (blue-green) and greater in the right hemisphere when attention was directed to the left (yellow-orange). Figure 8.7b shows that the changes in brain activity in this experiment mirrored those shown in Figure 8.6b. Thus, directing attention to a particular spatial location, *without moving your eyes,* causes corresponding changes in brain activity.

These and many other studies show not only that attention can be directed to different spatial locations, enhancing awareness of and other cognitive responses to stimuli that appear in those locations, but also that attention affects the responses of sensory neurons with receptive fields in attended locations. In effect, attention selects which of many competing stimuli will be represented for further cognitive operations.

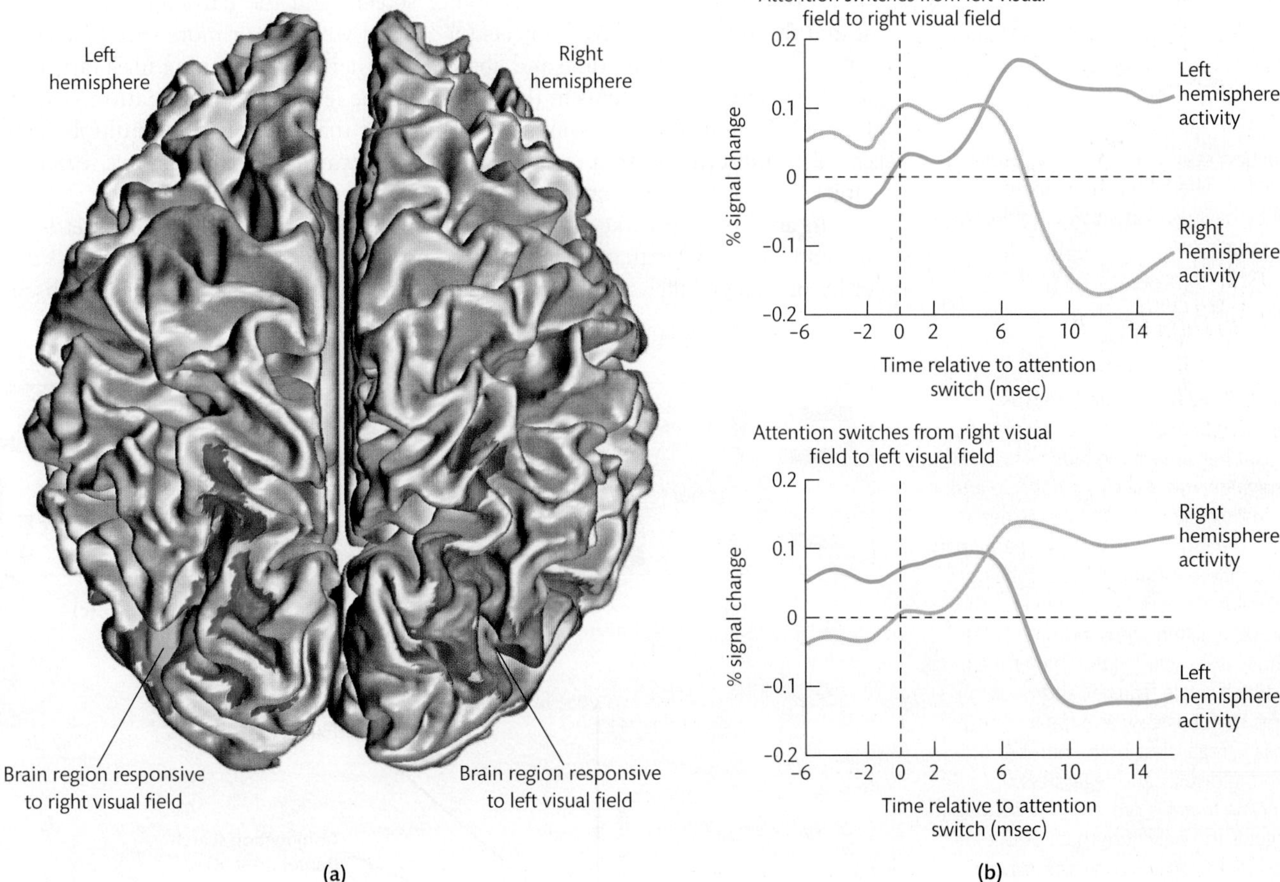

Figure 8.7 **Attention and Human Brain Activity** Participants kept their gaze fixed on the center of a computer display and, every few seconds, shifted their attention from left to right or from right to left. (a) This fMRI image of the surface of the cortex (slightly inflated to provide a view down into the sulci) shows how the location of brain activity correlated with the direction of attention. (b) The graphs show the time course of brain activity in the left and right visual cortex as participants shifted attention from left to right (green) or right to left (orange). In the left hemisphere, shifting from left to right caused an increase in brain activity, and shifting from right to left caused a decrease; this is what you'd expect because the left visual cortex represents the right side of space. The pattern was reversed in the right visual cortex. (Adapted from Chiu & Yantis, 2009.) (a: Image courtesy of Y.-C. Chiu)

Attention to Features

In Chapters 5–7, we explored the perception of color, depth, and motion, and not surprisingly, just as we can direct attention to locations, we can direct attention to these and other features of both visual and nonvisual stimuli. Consider the case of attention to voices. People's speaking voices differ in many ways, but perhaps the most important feature that distinguishes one person's voice from another's is the range of pitches over which the voice tends to vary. Back at the noisy party at the beginning of this chapter, one way you could keep track of your friend's voice would be to attend to the range of pitches, which would generally be different from the range of other nearby voices. This is an example of attending to a feature of a stimulus other than its location.

Psychophysical experiments have shown that our ability to detect a very faint sound is enhanced if we know beforehand what pitch the sound will have and direct our attention toward listening for a sound with that pitch. In one experiment, observers listened for a near-threshold tone over headphones, in some cases having previously been given a cue indicating what the pitch of the tone would be. Getting a cue enabled observers to detect much fainter tones (Hübner & Hafter, 1995).

In the arena of vision, searching for, say, a yellow pencil on a cluttered desktop would likely be quite efficient if it was guided by attention to yellow, especially if there were no other yellow objects on the desk. Laboratory tasks requiring this type of **visual search** have been used to investigate feature-based attention. A display containing multiple objects is presented on a computer screen, and the participant is instructed to search through the displayed objects for a target with one or more specific features; the target is present half the time and absent the other half. Searching for a target that differs from all the other items in the display in one feature is called **feature search** (as in Figure 8.8a and b), while searching for a target that is defined by multiple features is called **conjunction search** (as in Figure 8.8c), because the participant is searching for a target that consists of a conjunction of features in a single object.

visual search Searching for a specific target in a scene containing one, a few, or many objects.

feature search Searching a display for an item that differs in just one feature from all other items in the display.

conjunction search Searching a display for an item that differs from all other items in the display by having a particular combination of two or more features.

In an experiment like the one illustrated in Figure 8.8, where the target is the blue horizontal bar, the participant responds by pressing a button as soon as she finds the target or by pressing a different button as soon as she determines that the target is absent. This

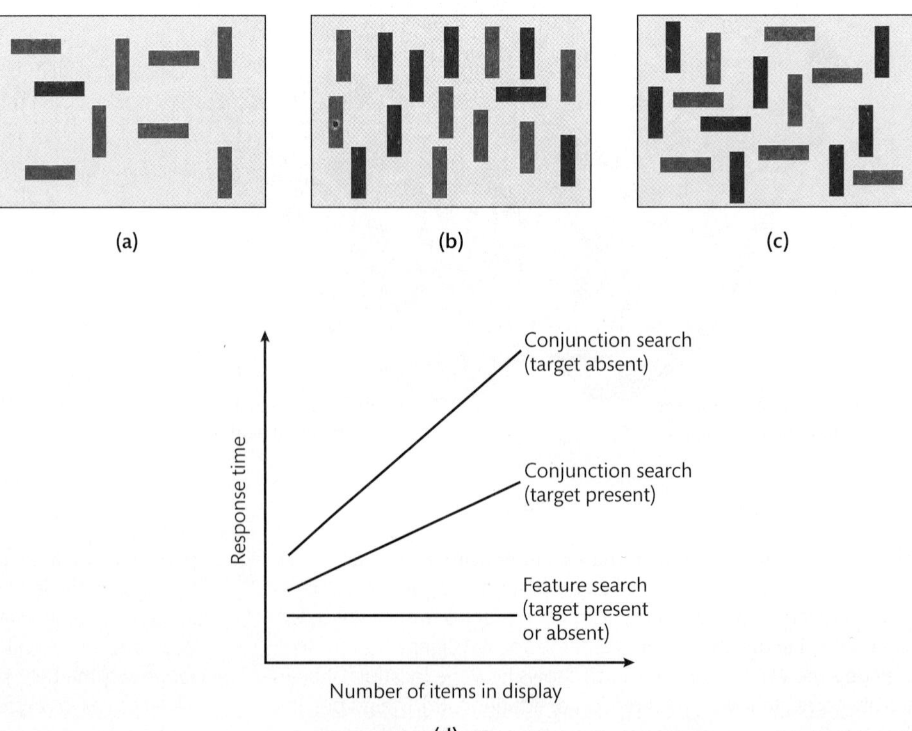

Figure 8.8 Feature Search Versus Conjunction Search For each display, the participant has to find the blue horizontal bar—the *target*—as quickly as possible and then immediately respond by pressing a button; if the target is absent, the participant presses a different button. In (a), the target is the only blue item; in (b), the target is the only horizontal item; thus, both (a) and (b) illustrate feature search (searching for a target defined by a single feature), and in both cases the search is easy and the response time is fast, regardless of the number of items in the display and regardless of whether the target is present or absent. In (c), the target is the only item that's both blue *and* horizontal, in a display that has red horizontal and blue vertical distractors, so this illustrates conjunction search. In this case, the search is more difficult and the response time increases with the number of items, as shown in (d). The response time to confirm that the target is absent in conjunction search is even longer. (Adapted from Treisman & Gelade, 1980.)

procedure is repeated many times, with a different number of items in the display each time (e.g., 4, 8, 16, or 32 items), and the time required to make each response is recorded. Feature search (as in Figure 8.8a and b) is easy—the target feature "pops out" of the display—and Figure 8.8d shows that the response time is fast regardless of the number of items in the display.

Conjunction search (as in Figure 8.8c) is much more difficult than feature search. Now the response time increases as the number of items increases, as shown in Figure 8.8d. Together, these results suggest that, in a feature search, the observer can detect the unique feature by attending to the entire visual scene—the target "pops out." In contrast, conjunction search requires the observer to direct attention to one item at a time, sequentially, to determine whether each item contains the required conjunction of features. This distinction between rapid, efficient feature search and slow, inefficient conjunction search provides good evidence that binding features together requires attention to the spatial location of those features, to make sure that the features are in the same location and belong to the same object (Treisman & Gelade, 1980). An experiment that detected neural activity related to attention shifts confirmed that conjunction search requires a sequence of attention shifts from one item to the next (Woodman & Luck, 2003).

Demonstration 8.4 Searching for Features and Conjunctions Participate in an experiment on visual search for features or conjunctions of features.

Just as attention to spatial locations affects brain activity, so does attention to features. This was shown in a human fMRI experiment that measured brain activity in area MT, the part of the brain that responds to visual motion (O'Craven et al., 1997). Observers were required to keep their gaze constantly focused at the center of a display consisting of randomly arranged stationary black dots and moving white dots (see Figure 8.9a). Every 20 seconds, the observer heard the word "white" or "black," in alternation, through headphones, which meant that he should shift his attention to the corresponding set of dots. Figure 8.9b shows that the average brain activity in area MT increased

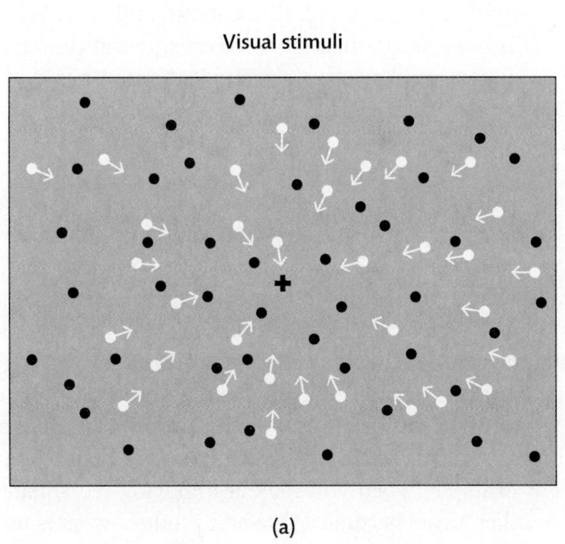

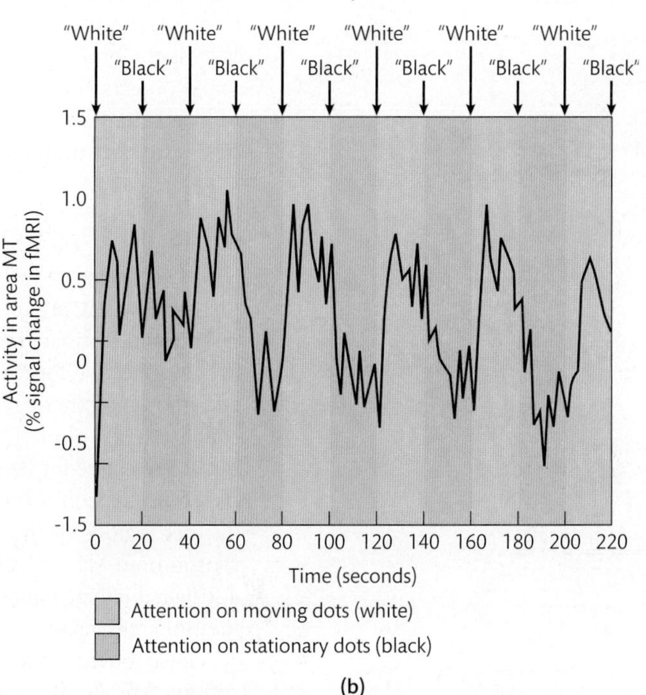

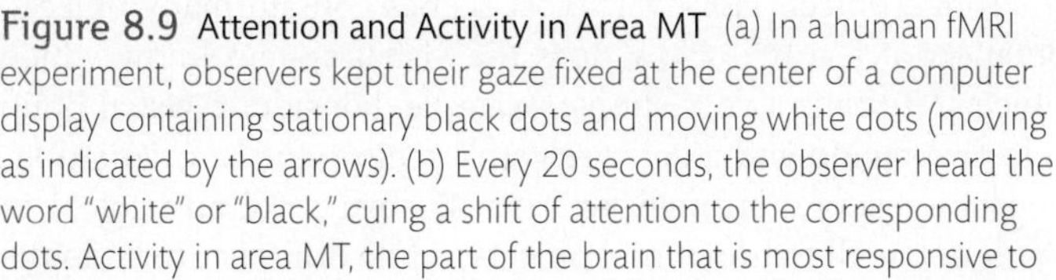
Figure 8.9 Attention and Activity in Area MT (a) In a human fMRI experiment, observers kept their gaze fixed at the center of a computer display containing stationary black dots and moving white dots (moving as indicated by the arrows). (b) Every 20 seconds, the observer heard the word "white" or "black," cuing a shift of attention to the corresponding dots. Activity in area MT, the part of the brain that is most responsive to visual motion, rose when attention was directed to the moving dots and fell when attention was directed to the stationary dots, even though both moving and stationary dots were always present. This shows how attention to a visual feature (motion) can affect brain activity. (Adapted from O'Craven et al., 1997.)

after attention shifted to the moving dots and decreased after attention shifted to the stationary dots. Given that both the moving white dots and the stationary black dots were always present and scattered throughout the display, the changes in brain activity were likely due to the shifts in attention to particular features (motion or rest) and not to shifts in the spatial location of attention.

Check Your Understanding

8.5 The filter theory of attention asserts that all sensory information is registered as physical signals but that only attended information is processed for meaning. How do dichotic listening experiments indicate that ignored sensory information is processed for meaning at least to some extent?

8.6 What do attentional cuing experiments show about the effect of attention on the awareness of stimuli in spatial locations and on the activity of neurons with receptive fields in those locations?

8.7 You're watching a TV broadcast of the 400-meter hurdles event at the Olympics—runners dashing across the screen, leaping over the stationary hurdles. How do you think the activity of an MT neuron with the entire TV screen in its receptive field would vary as you shifted your attention back and forth between the runners and the hurdles?

Why Attention Is Selective

So far in this chapter, we've seen evidence that we aren't simultaneously aware of everything in the current scene. We get the gist of a scene pretty quickly, but detailed awareness of specific objects often requires selective attention to one thing at a time. Attending to one thing means not attending to other things, which raises the following question: Why is the brain so limited in its ability to be aware of, think about, and act in relation to many objects simultaneously? This is a crucial question because it gets at the very heart of how attention works. In this section, we'll see that selective attention has evolved to deal with constraints on perception that result from how the brain represents objects.

The Binding Problem

Most objects in the real world are composed of many features, including color, size, shape, texture, motion, and others. We saw in Chapter 3 that some features are most clearly represented in distinct regions of the visual parts of the brain. For example, neurons in area MT are selective for the direction and speed of motion, responding well to some motions and poorly to others, but MT neurons are generally unselective for color, responding about equally to all colors. In contrast, neurons in area V4 are generally unselective for motion but are selective for color and curvature. This means that the full representation of a complex object requires information that is represented in the firing rates of neurons in many distinct regions of the brain. For example, when you look at a moving red square, neurons in both MT and V4 (and in other areas) become active and produce what is termed a *distributed representation* of that object—that is, a representation that is distributed across multiple regions of the brain.

Distributed representations are fine for scenes containing a single object—the visual system "knows" that the signals coming from the many different active regions must all relate to the features of that lone object. However, most scenes contain many objects, each with its own combination of features. How does the visual system know which features go with which objects? To take a very simple example, consider a visual brain that has an orientation-selective region and a color-selective region. In the orientation-selective region, some neurons respond strongly to vertical objects (of any color) in their receptive field (RF) and not at all to horizontal objects, while other neurons do the opposite. Similarly, in the color-selective region, some neurons respond strongly to green and not to red (of any orientation), while others do the opposite.

Suppose four neurons have their RFs in the same location—a vertical-preferring neuron, a horizontal-preferring neuron, a red-preferring neuron, and a green-preferring neuron. When a vertical red bar appears at that location, the vertical-preferring neuron in the orientation region and the red-preferring neuron in the color region respond strongly, whereas the other two neurons don't respond at all. This pattern of neural responses represents a vertical red object, and it's clear how other patterns of neural responses would represent the other three possibilities (horizontal red object, vertical blue object, or horizontal blue object). But what happens when a vertical bar of one color and a horizontal bar of the other color both appear together at the RF location? All four neurons respond. How, then, does the visual system know whether the stimulus is a red vertical object and a blue horizontal object, or a red horizontal object and a blue vertical object? Put another way, how does the visual system bind the features that belong to the same object? This is called the **binding problem** (Roskies, 1999).

binding problem The problem faced by the visual system of perceiving which visual features belong to the same object.

feature integration theory (FIT) The theory that the brain solves the binding problem by selectively attending to one object and ignoring any others.

The British-born psychologist Anne Treisman developed **feature integration theory (FIT)** to solve the binding problem, proposing that people must selectively attend to one object at a time during visual search for objects defined by a conjunction of two or more features (Treisman & Gelade, 1980). According to FIT, when attention is directed to an object, neurons with an RF at the attended object's location respond to that object's features only and not to the features of ignored objects. Thus, there is no ambiguity—the neural responses are all related to the features of a single object at that location, the object being attended to. Because FIT is based on the idea that conjunction search requires directing attention to one item at a time, it predicts the linear increase in response times shown in Figure 8.8d. FIT has been refined and extended over the years (Quinlan, 2003, Wolfe, 1994), but it stands as a core idea in our understanding of visual attention.

Anne Treisman (b. 1935). [Courtesy of Anne Treisman]

Competition for Neural Representation

The second issue requiring selective attention has to do with the fact that many neurons in the visual regions of the brain have RFs large enough to contain multiple objects and parts of objects, especially when the scene is cluttered. In this situation, it's frequently the case that the features of one object in a neuron's receptive field match the neuron's preferences, while the features of other objects don't. When this occurs, what would we expect the neuron's response to be?

The object with features that match the neuron's preferences drives the neuron to produce a strong response, while objects with features that don't match the neuron's preferences evoke only a weak response. This is termed *competition for neural representation,* and the competition must be resolved; otherwise, the neuron's response will be some sort of average or compromise that doesn't correspond to the features of any of the competing objects. The higher we go in the visual hierarchy, the more intense this competition becomes, because neurons in higher visual areas have larger receptive fields with more objects or object features within them. The question, then, is how can the competition for neural representation be resolved?

Just as feature integration theory proposes that the brain solves the binding problem by selectively attending to one object at a time, **biased competition theory** proposes that the brain uses selective attention to resolve the competition for neural representation by attending to one object at a time (Desimone & Duncan, 1995). According to this theory, attention biases the competition so that only the features of the attended object are represented, as if only the attended object were present. Figure 8.10 shows the results of an experiment that provides an especially clear example of how biased competition works (Reynolds et al., 1999). The experimenters measured the responses of a single neuron in area V4 of a macaque monkey while the monkey viewed displays like those shown in Figure 8.10a. The monkey was trained to keep his eyes on the fixation point at all times and to direct his attention in various ways while the experimenters presented either an effective stimulus, an ineffective stimulus, or both in the RF of the V4 neuron.

biased competition theory The theory that the brain resolves the competition for neural representation by selectively attending to one object and representing the features of just that object.

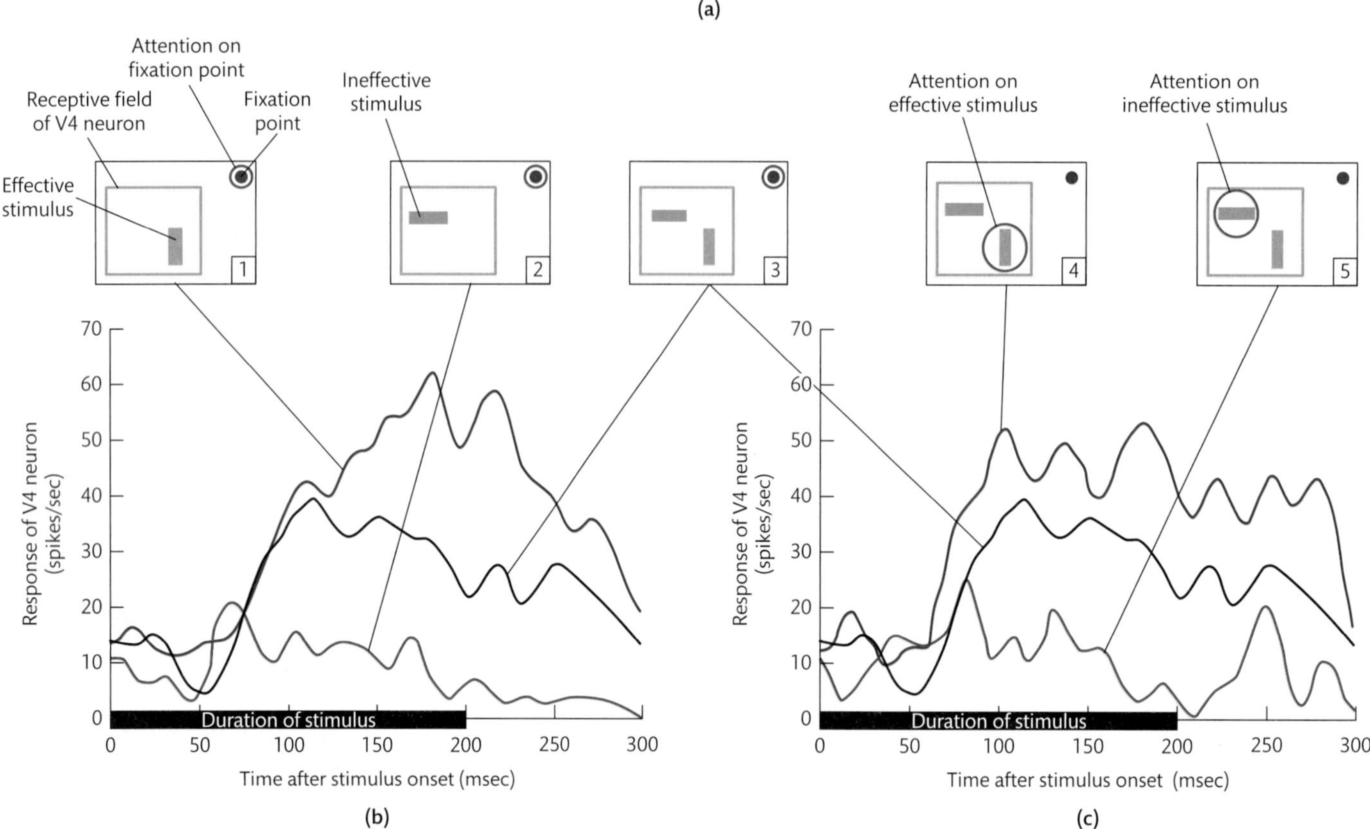

Figure 8.10 Attention and the Competition for Neural Representation (a) While the activity of a V4 neuron was being recorded, monkeys trained to keep their gaze focused on the fixation point at all times were presented with these displays containing the effective stimulus, the ineffective stimulus, or both, in the neuron's receptive field. In displays 1–3, the monkey attended to the fixation point and ignored the stimuli. The monkey attended to the effective stimulus in display 4 and the ineffective stimulus in display 5. (b) The neuron responds strongly to an effective stimulus (blue curve), weakly to an ineffective stimulus (red curve), and somewhere in between to both stimuli (black curve). (c) These three curves show the neural response in the presence of both stimuli under three different attention conditions. The black curve is the same as the black curve in (b), when the monkey was ignoring both stimuli. The blue curve shows that when attention is directed to the effective stimulus, the neuron's response is enhanced, as if only the effective stimulus were there; and the red curve shows that when attention is directed to the ineffective stimulus, the neuron's response is suppressed, as if only the ineffective stimulus were there. (Adapted from Reynolds et al., 1999.)

With just a single stimulus in the RF and the monkey's attention on the fixation point (displays 1 and 2 in Figure 8.10a), the researchers were able to establish the neuron's response to each stimulus alone, without any effect due to attention on the stimulus. As shown in Figure 8.10b, the neuron responded strongly to the effective stimulus alone (blue curve) and weakly to the ineffective stimulus alone (red curve)—this is as expected, because these stimuli had been specifically chosen to either match or not match the neuron's tuning function.

When both stimuli were in the RF while the monkey continued to attend to the fixation point (display 3 in Figure 8.10a), the neuron's response was a compromise: neither as strong as the response to the effective stimulus alone, nor as weak as the response to the ineffective stimulus alone (black curve in Figure 8.10b). The stimuli were competing for neural representation, and the neuron's response didn't correspond to either stimulus.

But when the monkey—still always keeping his eyes on the fixation point—directed his attention to one or the other of the stimuli, the competition for neural representation was resolved. With attention directed to the effective stimulus (display 4 in Figure 8.10a), the neuron's response was nearly as strong as when the effective stimulus was presented alone (blue curve in Figure 8.10c), whereas attention to the ineffective stimulus (display 5 in Figure 8.10a) resulted in a response nearly as weak as when the ineffective stimulus was presented alone (red curve in Figure 8.10c). In effect, directing attention to either stimulus when both were present caused the neuron to respond as if only the attended stimulus was present, and this is exactly what biased competition theory predicts. Note the similarities between this experiment and the experiments discussed in the section on attention to locations and illustrated in Figures 8.6 and 8.7.

How does this experiment relate to real-world situations in which a person is looking at a cluttered visual scene? Every neuron in the visual system that has an RF large enough to include two or more objects or object features—that is, most neurons beyond V1—has to resolve the competition for representation by attending to one object and ignoring the rest. Whenever the person chooses to attend to a particular object in the scene, even if only fleetingly, then all the neurons with that object in their RF will respond as if *only* that object were there. Neurons that would respond strongly to the attended object if it were presented by itself will produce a robust response; neurons that would respond weakly to the attended object if it were presented by itself will remain quiet. Keep in mind that when a neuron is quiet, it's conveying information: "My preferred feature is *not* present."

Neurons throughout the visual hierarchy respond to the attended object, forming a distributed representation of that object. For that moment, however fleeting, it's as if that object is the only thing in the visual field. Of course, this is an exaggeration: the field does not go dark with a single spotlight on the attended object. The observer still has a background awareness of the gist of the entire scene. But as we found earlier, detailed awareness of other objects in the scene would require a redeployment of attention.

Check Your Understanding

8.8 Suppose your brain were suddenly unable to solve the binding problem. How might that affect your conscious experience of seeing a red ball rolling across a green tabletop?

8.9 Suppose your brain were suddenly unable to resolve the competition for neural representation. How might that affect your conscious experience of looking at a cluttered desktop?

Attentional Control

Up to this point, we've considered a variety of studies and experiments showing that:

- Attention is inherently selective—we can really pay attention to only one thing at a time, or perhaps a few closely related things; and selective attention puts limits on awareness and cognition—we can be fully aware of and effectively respond to only those things we really pay attention to.
- Attention can be directed to different spatial locations and different features of perceptual objects. This can be demonstrated both behaviorally, in terms of how people perform on tasks requiring these types of attention, and neurophysiologically, in terms of how paying attention in these ways affects the activity of single neurons or of different brain areas.
- Selective attention is the brain's mechanism for dealing with two challenges to awareness of and effective cognition about the environment: solving the binding problem—determining which features belong to which perceptual object—and resolving the competition for neural representation.

Now let's explore how the brain controls attention—that is, how the brain directs attention to locations and features that are of interest to the person. We'll consider two different forms of attentional control—top down and bottom up—and where attentional control signals originate in the brain.

Top-Down and Bottom-Up Attentional Control

When you think about paying attention to something, you probably think of making a deliberate choice: you strain to hear what your friend is saying at a noisy party and to ignore all other sounds, or you search for a pencil on a cluttered desk. Indeed, in all the examples and experiments we've discussed so far, attention has been directed voluntarily and purposefully. This **top-down attentional control** (or *voluntary attentional control*) involves deliberately paying attention to something in order to get information needed to achieve a goal. But a second form of attentional control is just as important—and in some situations more so.

top-down attentional control (or *voluntary attentional control)* Deliberately paying attention to something in order to get information needed to achieve goals.

Consider a classroom during a final exam. Fifty students are hunched over their test booklets; all have their attention focused on what they're thinking and writing. Suddenly, a late-arriving student rushes in, letting the door slam loudly behind him, and all the other students look up, their attention having been captured by the sudden loud sound. There is nothing voluntary about this redirection of attention; rather, it is almost completely automatic, and none of the students can stop it from happening. This **bottom-up attentional control** (also called *stimulus-driven attentional control*) involves the involuntary, unavoidable capture of attention by a salient perceptual stimulus. Of course, this form of attentional control evolved for a good reason: sudden changes in the environment are often accompanied by salient perceptual stimuli (e.g., an abrupt sound or a sudden movement) and might well require a rapid response—for example, to avoid an approaching predator or to seize some passing prey. This kind of rapid, automatic response, which you can think of as a "perceptual reflex," bypasses the relatively slow mechanisms for deliberately directing attention via top-down control.

bottom-up attentional control (or *stimulus-driven attentional control*) The involuntary, unavoidable capture of attention by a salient perceptual stimulus.

The difference in speed and efficiency between top-down and bottom-up attentional control was assessed in an experiment that examined how the abrupt onset of a visual stimulus captures attention (Jonides & Yantis, 1988). As illustrated in Figure 8.11a, participants searched through an array of letters for a particular target letter. In each display, one letter had an abrupt onset and was therefore perceptually salient—a visual version of the door slamming in our earlier example. The other items were less salient because they did not have abrupt onsets but were instead revealed by removing camouflaging line segments of block eights. The participant had to press a button as quickly as possible after either finding the target letter or determining that the target letter wasn't in the display. In each trial,

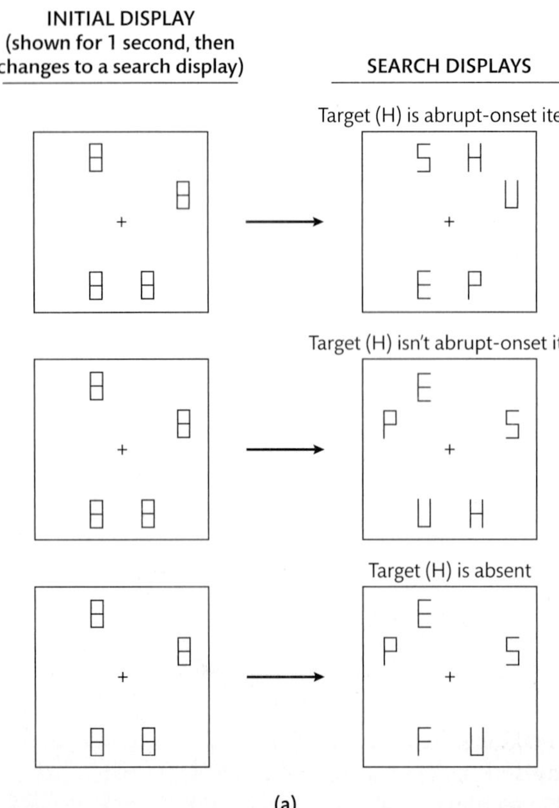

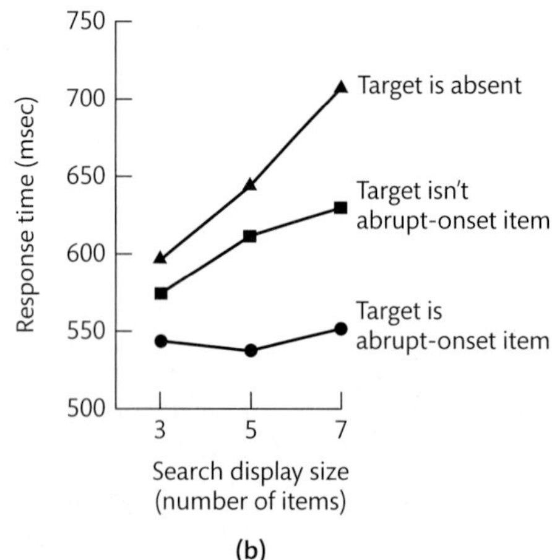

Figure 8.11 Attentional Capture by Abrupt Onsets (a) The initial display of block eights changes to a search display of letters in the same positions, but with an additional letter called the *abrupt-onset item*. The participant searches this display for a target letter. (b) Response time is fast when the target is the abrupt-onset item, regardless of the display size. Response time is slower when the target isn't the abrupt-onset item and slowest when the target is absent, and in both these cases the response time increases with the display size. (Adapted from Jonides & Yantis, 1988.)

the participant's response time was measured from the presentation of the display to the button push.

The main findings of this experiment are shown in Figure 8.11b. When the target was present but wasn't the abrupt-onset item, the response time increased as the number of letters to search increased. This is what you'd expect if the participant has to evaluate each item separately, shifting attention from one to the next in a serial fashion, until the target is found. In this case, obviously, the more items there are to evaluate, the longer the search takes—just as it would take longer to find your friend in a large crowd than a small one. In contrast, when the target happened to be the abrupt-onset item, is frequently the response time was fast and didn't increase as the number of letters to search increased. This suggests that the abrupt-onset item is frequently the first item to be searched, because its abrupt onset automatically captures the participant's attention, and if it's the target, the participant presses the button right away; it doesn't matter how many other items are present in the display. Responses are slowest when the target is absent, because the participant has to check every item in the display to confirm that fact. The results of this experiment show how bottom-up attentional control can produce a quick response to sudden events.

Bottom-up attentional control can be evoked by certain types of stimuli that might, at first glance, seem more likely to lead to top-down control. Consider an experiment in which people had to find a target that appeared randomly and equally often on the left or right side of a display. Immediately before the target appeared, a photograph of a face appeared in the center of the display, with eyes looking either right or left, again equally often and randomly. Even though the direction of the eyes didn't provide any information about where the target would appear, people found the target faster when it appeared on the side where the eyes were pointed (Friesen & Kingstone, 1998). This experiment suggests that seeing another person looking in a particular direction functions like a loud noise, automatically directing our attention in that same direction. Evolution has evidently built in an automatic tendency to rely on the attention of others to direct our own attention: if someone is looking intently somewhere, it's likely that what they're looking at is interesting or important.

Demonstration 8.5 Attentional Capture Participate in a simulated experiment showing that stimuli with abrupt onsets tend to capture your attention.

Sources of Attentional Control in the Brain

Where do the signals that control attention come from? Current research points to two areas of the brain: the posterior parietal cortex (PPC) (Behrmann et al., 2004) and an area in the frontal cortex called the *frontal eye field* (Awh et al., 2006), both of which are shown in Figure 8.12. Major evidence for the involvement of the PPC comes from patients who suffer stroke damage to the right PPC that results in **unilateral visual neglect** on the left side of visual space, a condition in which the patient has difficulty attending to objects in the left visual field—like Lloyd, the patient in the vignette at the beginning of this chapter. (Right-side neglect is much more rare, perhaps because there is some redundant processing of the right visual space by both the left and right cerebral hemispheres, whereas in most brains the left space is processed by the right hemisphere only.) Such patients don't respond to people sitting in their left visual field, they leave the food on the left side of their plate, and if they're asked to draw something from memory, they'll often omit elements from the left side (see Figure 8.13). Yet they are not *blind* on the left: it is possible to get them to see sufficiently salient visual stimuli there (Driver & Vuilleumier, 2001), suggesting that attention, not vision, is the issue and, therefore, that this region of the brain may be important for the control of attention.

unilateral visual neglect A condition in which a person has difficulty attending to stimuli in one half of the visual field (almost always the left half), as a result of damage to the contralateral posterior parietal cortex.

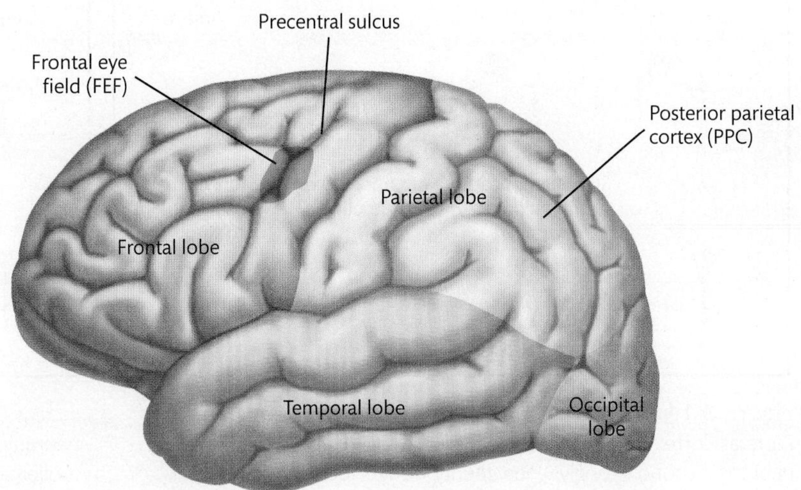

Figure 8.12 **Brain Areas Involved in Attentional Control** The posterior parietal cortex and frontal eye field are two important sources of attentional control signals in the human brain.

Research with monkeys has shown that the activity of many PPC neurons is correlated with where the monkey is attending. In one experiment, the activity of single PPC neurons was recorded as the monkey

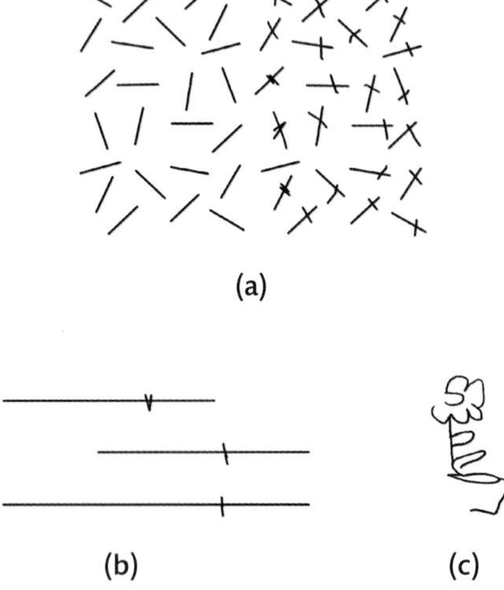

Figure 8.13 Behavioral Responses by People with Left-Side Visual Neglect People with damage to the right posterior parietal cortex may suffer from unilateral visual neglect on the left side—that is, difficulty in attending to the left visual field. (a) A patient was given a paper with many randomly placed lines and was asked to place a mark across every line, with no time limit. The patient didn't mark the lines on the left side of the paper. (b) Three patients were asked to place a mark at the center of the line; in each case, the patient placed the mark too far to the right, indicating that the left end of the line was neglected. (c) A patient asked to draw, from memory, a flower in a pot omitted elements on the left side. (Adapted from Driver & Vuilleumier, 2001, Figure 1.)

performed various tasks—termed the *fixation task, saccade task,* and *peripheral attention task*—which involved hand movements, eye movements, and the direction of the monkey's attention (Bushnell et al., 1981). As illustrated in Figure 8.14, all three tasks began, at Time 1, with the monkey looking at and attending to a fixation point at the center of a display; then, at Time 2, a salient visual stimulus appeared in the periphery of the display, within the RF of the PPC neuron being recorded. In the fixation task (Figure 8.14a), the monkey had to ignore the visual stimulus; the fixation point dimmed at Time 3, and this was a cue for the monkey to make a hand movement. As you can see, the PPC neuron continued to fire at its baseline rate throughout this task, which didn't involve any shift of attention.

In the saccade task (Figure 8.14b), when the stimulus appeared at Time 2, the fixation point disappeared, and this was a cue for the monkey to shift his attention to the stimulus and to make an eye movement (a saccade) to the stimulus; in this case, the PPC neuron's firing rate increased with the shift of attention at Time 3, before the

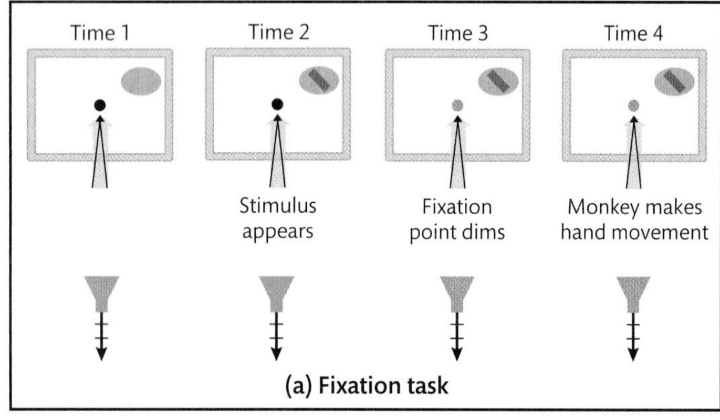

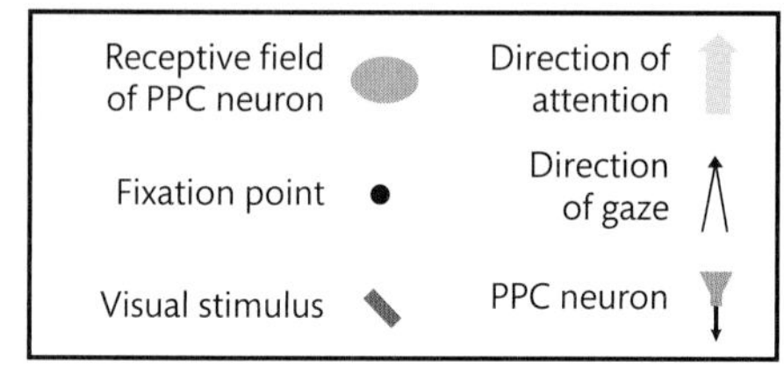

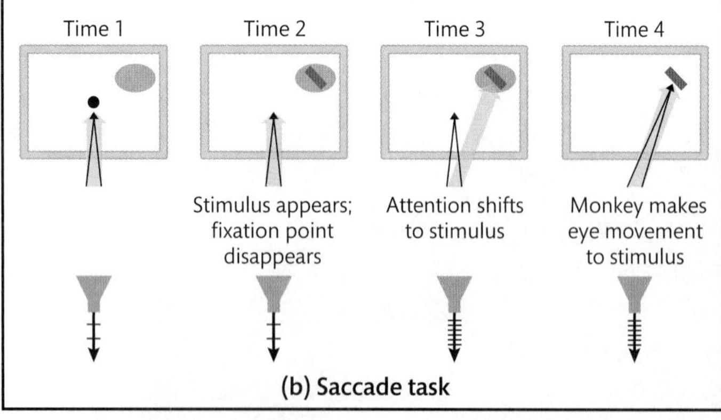

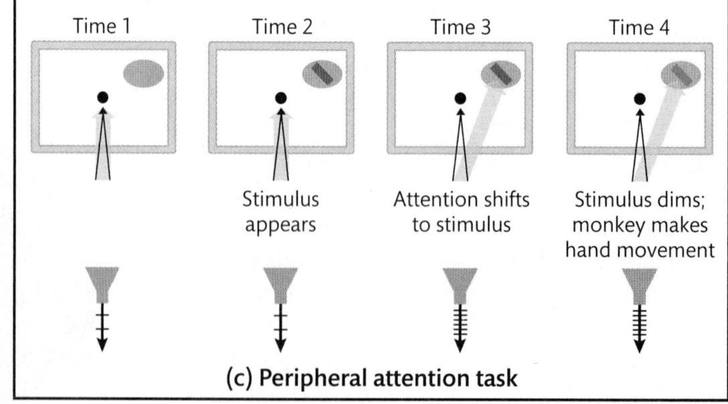

Figure 8.14 Attentional Control and Activity in the Posterior Parietal Cortex (PPC) This experiment showed that monkey PPC neurons respond strongly when attention shifts to a visual stimulus located in the neuron's receptive field, before the monkey can execute an eye or hand movement to the stimulus. (a) In the fixation task, the monkey never shifts its direction of attention, and the PPC neuron never increases its firing rate above baseline. (b) In the saccade task, the PPC neuron's firing rate increases with the shift of attention, before the eye movement. (c) In the peripheral attention task, the PPC neuron's firing rate again increases with the shift of attention, before the hand movement. (Based on Bushnell et al., 1981.)

eye movement occurred at Time 4. In the peripheral attention task (Figure 8.14c), the appearance of the stimulus at Time 2 was a cue for the monkey to shift his attention to the stimulus without changing the direction of gaze; the stimulus then dimmed at Time 4, cuing the monkey to make a hand movement; and again, the PPC neuron's firing rate increased with the shift of attention, well before the hand movement. These results show that the neuron's activity is not tied to a motor act (an eye or hand movement) but to the shift of attention to the stimulus in the neuron's RF location.

Studies of brain activity in humans using functional neuroimaging have confirmed that the PPC is an important component of the brain's ability to control spatial attention. One study, using fMRI, examined brain activity while people directed attention to visual stimuli at different spatial locations without moving their eyes (Silver et al., 2005). Activity in the occipital lobes depended mainly on the brightness and contrast of the stimuli; activity in the PPC depended mainly on whether the stimuli were being attended or not.

Other studies have shown that the frontal eye field (FEF) (see Figure 8.12), which is involved in the control of eye movements, also plays a role in controlling shifts of attention without eye movements. In one study, stimulation of a given location in a monkey's FEF with an electrode evoked an eye movement to a visual field location that was termed the *response field* for that FEF location (Moore & Fallah, 2004). The absolute threshold for detecting a spot of light in the response field was then determined under two conditions: (1) without any FEF stimulation and (2) with FEF stimulation reduced to a level where it no longer evoked an eye movement. The results showed that, with this reduced FEF stimulation, the monkey could detect a dimmer spot of light in the response field than it could without FEF stimulation, presumably because the stimulation had directed attention there. The investigators concluded that the FEF is involved in controlling the direction of visual attention.

Studies using fMRI have also shown that the human PPC and FEF are important sources of attentional control. In one study, people were instructed to attend to the left or the right side of a display in preparation for detecting a briefly flashed target (Sylvester et al., 2009). Activity increased on the contralateral side of the brain in both the PPC and the FEF, well before the target appeared. This is the brain activity that you'd expect if these regions were sources of attentional control signals.

The experiments reviewed in this section provide strong evidence that the PPC and FEF are important sources of signals that control visual attention. Of course, there are still many unanswered questions about how attentional control works. For example, how are goals stored in active memory transformed into commands about what should be attended? How does voluntary attention interact with involuntary attention? How do deficits arise in the ability to pay attention, as in children with attention-deficit/hyperactivity disorder or in older adults with mild cognitive impairment? And how can we design instruments (e.g., air traffic control displays) that take into account the limitations on our ability to control attention? Clearly, this will continue to be an exciting area of scientific investigation.

Check Your Understanding

8.10 Briefly describe the difference between top-down and bottom-up attentional control.

8.11 You've just set the table for dinner and are looking it over to make sure all the utensils are in the right place. Which might you be likely to notice more quickly: **(A)** a knife suddenly turns into a fork, or **(B)** a fork suddenly appears in the middle of the table? Explain why in terms of attention to stimuli with abrupt onsets.

8.12 Describe two types of evidence in support of the idea that the posterior parietal cortex is involved in the control of attention.

8.13 In the Moore and Fallah (2004) experiment involving reduced stimulation of monkeys' frontal eye field, what was the stimulation reduced from, and why was it significant that the stimulation was reduced?

Awareness and the Neural Correlates of Consciousness

In the chapters on vision, as well as in this chapter on attention, we've drawn an increasingly detailed picture of how the brain represents the features of visual objects—their orientation, color, size, motion, and so on—and how it combines those representations in complex patterns of neural activity all the way from V1 to the object-selective regions of the temporal lobes, in order to build up what we've called distributed representations of visual objects. But in all these discussions we haven't touched on a critical question: How can the activities of physical things—the neurons in our brain—produce conscious, subjective experiences like the awareness of objects?

Needless to say, this is a hard question. Indeed, it has been called "the hard problem" of consciousness by the philosopher David Chalmers (1995), to distinguish it from "the easy problems" of the mind, like explaining how color vision works, how we know one object is farther away than another, or how we are able to shift our focus of attention. For each of these and many similar problems, we can either refer to more or less well understood structures and functions of the brain or at least see how to approach the problem scientifically.

In contrast, the hard problem—the problem of how experiences like the redness of red or the sharp sensation of pain arise from neural activity—seems to defy scientific analysis. Chalmers (2004) argues that the easy problems of consciousness involve objectively observable data, which he calls "third-person data," that can be investigated using standard scientific methods. The hard problem involves subjective experiences, which he calls "first-person data," that cannot be observed by others and that have been difficult, if not impossible, to address scientifically. Nevertheless, Chalmers claims that scientific progress on the hard problem is possible, and among the projects he advocates is a search for the **neural correlates of consciousness (NCCs)**—correspondences between neural activity and conscious awareness. The idea is that if we can find brain activity that is systematically correlated with conscious experience, and if we can also discover what it is about that activity that makes it different from brain activity that is *not* correlated with consciousness (e.g., a type of neuron, a kind of neurotransmitter, or some other functional or anatomical property), then we will have made progress in addressing the hard problem.

neural correlates of consciousness (NCCs) Correspondences between neural activity and conscious awareness.

How can we do this? In this section, we'll review two different approaches. The first focuses on situations in which visual awareness fluctuates while the visual stimulus and the retinal image do not change; in this case, brain activities that fluctuate systematically with the fluctuations in awareness are candidates for NCCs (Crick & Koch, 1990; Kim & Blake, 2005). The other approach involves research on people with brain damage who lack aspects of conscious awareness, in order to determine how their brains differ from those of people with normal awareness. Each of these approaches deliberately addresses just one aspect of the "hard problem," avoiding such issues as the sense of self, the problem of free will, and other aspects of consciousness that are notoriously difficult to decipher. In Chalmers's terms, the idea is to tackle consciousness with minimal reliance on first-person data and maximal reliance on third-person data, but even so, we must rely to some extent on what people tell us about the contents of their awareness, because we have no way of observing those contents for ourselves.

Seeking the NCCs in Perceptual Bistability

In earlier parts of this chapter, we reviewed a variety of studies of what happens in the brain when attention shifts from one location to another in an unchanging visual scene: awareness of the contents of the scene changes according to the location of attention, and activity in many visual areas also changes. Clearly, such changes in activity could be considered NCCs—for instance, we could argue that increased activity in area MT when we attend to a moving stimulus (see Figure 8.9 and the accompanying discussion) is evidence that MT activity is a neural correlate of our conscious awareness of motion. In this section, we'll consider evidence from a phenomenon known as **perceptual bistability**, in which an unchanging visual stimulus leads to repeated alternation between two different perceptual experiences.

perceptual bistability A phenomenon in which an unchanging visual stimulus leads to repeated alternation between two different perceptual experiences.

Many perceptual illusions are examples of perceptual bistability (Attneave, 1971); perhaps the best known is the Necker cube (below left), which alternates between being perceived with one face forward or another (below middle and right). You may find in looking at the ambiguous cube on the left that you can maintain one perception or the other, or even control when the perception switches.

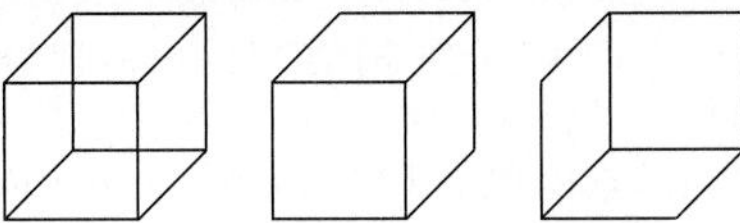

In perceptual bistability, the retinal image remains constant but conscious experience changes over time. Presumably, when we look at the Necker cube, activity in some parts of the visual system corresponds to the unchanging retinal image, while activity in other parts of the visual system corresponds to perceptual experience, so that in these areas, the activity changes when perceptual experience flips from one form of the cube to the other. So it makes sense to ask which parts of the visual system reflect the unchanging retinal image, which follow perceptual experience, and what is the difference between them?

The phenomenon of **binocular rivalry**, in which two different images presented to the two eyes result in perceptual bistability, has been used to investigate these questions. With binocular rivalry, you don't see a simple blending of the two images; instead, the images alternate every few seconds on an irregular basis—that is, they produce perceptual bistability; to experience this yourself, follow the instructions in the caption for Figure 8.15a. In an fMRI study (Tong et al., 1998), the experimenters located the regions in an observer's brain that responded well to faces (the fusiform face area, or FFA) and to houses (the parahippocampal place area, or PPA). The observers then viewed the face–house composite image in Figure 8.15a through red–blue glasses, in order to evoke perceptual bistability. Each time the observer perceived the face, he would press a button; each time he perceived the house, he would press a different button. The graph in Figure 8.15b shows that activity in the FFA and PPA correlated closely with these alternating perceptual experiences.

binocular rivalry A phenomenon in which two different images presented to the two eyes result in perceptual bistability.

This study shows that activity in both the FFA and the PPA looks more like the observer's conscious experience than like the stimulus, but what about activity in earlier visual areas? Activity as early as area V1 appears to reflect conscious visual experiences, as shown by a study that successfully predicted observers' reports of their conscious experience

(a)

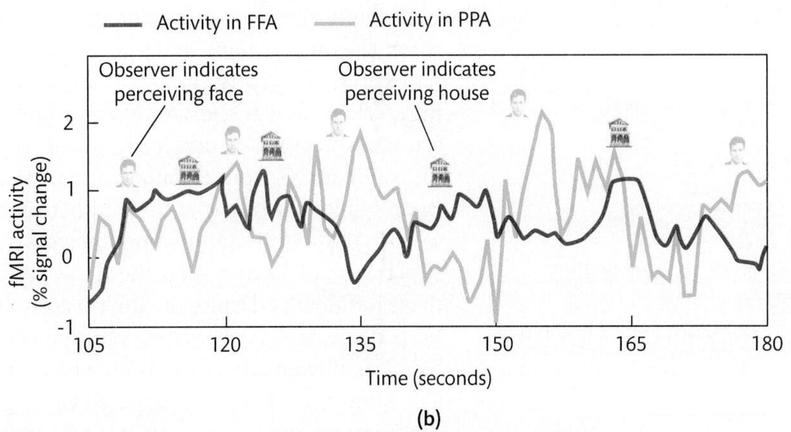

(b)

Figure 8.15 Binocular Rivalry, Perceptual Bistability, and the Neural Correlates of Consciousness (a) Use the red-blue glasses that came with this book to view this composite image (an anaglyph) of a blue face and a red house. The eye looking through the red lens will see only the face, and the eye looking through the blue lens will see only the house. This will create binocular rivalry (your visual system will be receiving conflicting information from the two eyes about the contents of the retinal image), and this will lead to perceptual bistability—your perception will fluctuate from seeing a face to seeing a house and back again. (b) Participants in an experiment viewed the image in (a) through red-blue glasses, and fMRI was used to measure activity in the face-selective FFA and the house-selective PPA. The curves show that when the observer was perceiving a face, FFA activity increased while PPA activity fell, and vice versa when the observer was perceiving a house. (Adapted from Tong et al., 1998.) [face: Ingram Publishing/Reflexstock; house: DigitalVues/Alamy]

during binocular rivalry on the basis of mathematical analysis of the pattern of activity in area V1 over time (Haynes & Rees, 2005).

What is required in addition to activation of visual areas to create conscious visual awareness? One possibility is the involvement of areas in the posterior parietal cortex that can direct attention to visual objects (Kanwisher, 2001); the fact that damage to the posterior parietal cortex can result in visual neglect—a failure of awareness—is consistent with this idea. Another proposal is that conscious perceptual experience requires a closed loop of neural activity that begins with stimulus-driven activity in lower-level visual areas, which leads to a feed-forward sweep of activity into higher-level visual areas, followed by a feedback sweep to lower-level areas (Lamme & Roelfsema, 2000). Yet another idea is that synchronized neural firing rates within and across many distinct brain regions may be a key property of conscious awareness (see the discussion in Chapter 4 of synchronized neural oscillations as a possible basis for perceptual grouping). These and other hypotheses about NCCs are under active investigation (Tononi & Koch, 2008).

What Blindsight Reveals About Awareness

People sometimes suffer brain damage that completely destroys area V1 but leaves the rest of the brain intact, and such people typically report that they can see nothing—that they are blind. This finding alone suggests that V1 is necessary for conscious vision. However, it has been known since at least the first half of the twentieth century that patients with such V1 damage do respond in certain ways to the presence of light. For example, the pupillary reflex (constriction or dilation of the pupil) in response to changes in illumination persists following loss of area V1 (Stoerig & Cowey, 1997). This is not magic: visual information leaving the eyes travels to many parts of the brain in addition to V1, including to the superior colliculus, which is important for the control of eye movements, and to other subcortical structures that mediate such functions as the pupillary reflex. But is higher visual function possible in the absence of area V1?

Consider the case of D.B., a 34-year-old man whose area V1 in his right hemisphere was surgically removed to treat severe headaches that were thought to be caused by a circulatory malformation in that part of the brain (Weiskrantz et al., 1974). After the surgery, the patient reported that he couldn't see anything in his left visual field. Standard tests for visual ability, in which D.B. was shown small spots of light at various locations in the left visual field, indicated no ability to detect stimuli there. However, tests in which D.B. was *required* to point to the places in his left visual field where spots of light were being presented—despite his conviction that he was unable to see the spots and was simply guessing—revealed that he could locate the spots quite accurately, especially when they were relatively large. As the authors put it: "When he was shown his results he expressed surprise and insisted several times that he thought he was just 'guessing.' When he was shown a video film of his reaching and judging . . . he was openly astonished" (Weiskrantz et al., 1974, p. 722). In addition, D.B. showed an ability to discriminate *X*'s from *O*'s and horizontal lines from vertical lines in the left visual field, again while insisting that he couldn't see the stimuli and was just guessing. This ability to correctly localize and sometimes discriminate visual stimuli, without any subjective experience of having seen them, is called **blindsight.** The fact that D.B. could make these judgments despite having no conscious awareness of the stimuli suggests that area V1 is necessary for awareness but that other aspects of vision, including the guidance of reaching movements, do not require a functional area V1.

blindsight The ability to point to and sometimes discriminate visual stimuli without any conscious awareness of them.

Another patient, T.N., suffered two strokes in succession, about one month apart, that caused permanent damage to area V1 in both hemispheres, resulting in blindness throughout his visual field. Functional MRI of T.N.'s occipital cortex revealed no residual brain response to visual stimulation. Nevertheless, fMRI measurements revealed activity in T.N.'s amygdala when he was shown emotionally expressive faces compared to when he was shown neutral faces, suggesting that visual information could bypass area V1 to evoke an emotional response in the brain (Pegna et al., 2005). In another study of T.N.'s blindsight, he was asked to navigate down a long hallway containing many obstacles (boxes, chairs, etc.) and could do so almost perfectly (de Gelder et al., 2008).

There is now good evidence that the residual vision in blindsight demonstrated by D.B. and T.N. is based on signals that pass from the retina to the superior colliculus, through the thalamus, and on to the visual cortex (Ptito & Leh, 2007). This pathway apparently cannot support conscious vision, but it provides sufficient visual information to support visually guided action and, in some cases, categorization of emotionally charged objects. It's worth noting that the experimental evidence concerning blindsight has at times been controversial (Cowey, 2010).

The investigation of the neural correlates of consciousness has stimulated a fascinating convergence of behavioral and neurophysiological studies together with philosophical analysis of what it means to be aware of something. This topic has achieved a degree of scientific respectability that would have been almost unthinkable 20 years ago, when virtually any investigation of unobservable phenomena, such as the contents of another person's awareness, would have been considered unscientific by many. Of course, much remains to be discovered.

Check Your Understanding

8.14 According to philosopher David Chalmers, what is "the hard problem" of consciousness and what would be one approach to shedding light on it?

8.15 Which of these two figures illustrates perceptual bistability? Explain why.

8.16 How do the binocular rivalry experiments described in this section of the chapter reveal possible neural correlates of consciousness?

8.17 Does blindsight show that all neural signals from the eyes flow to area V1? Explain your answer.

APPLICATIONS Multitasking

Multitasking is usually thought of as performing two or more tasks at the same time. However, almost all cases of multitasking actually involve **task switching**—rapid shifting of attention from one task to another and back again. Psychologists have devised methods to measure the time cost of these mental switches, providing a way to assess the efficiency of this type of "multitasking." Our understanding of the limits of multitasking is crucial to a real-world situation like flying an aircraft (with the need to monitor a complex array of instruments and the conditions outside the windshield, while also communicating with the air-traffic controller), as well as to common situations such as trying to study and stay in touch with your friends at the same time or, more dangerously, driving while talking on a cell phone.

task switching A rapid shifting of attention from one task to another and back again.

Task Switching

Consider the following scenario: Olivia, a college student, is reading a chapter in a textbook, studying for an exam. She's sitting with the book on her desk, her laptop next to it, and her cell phone next to the laptop. Every few minutes, the phone buzzes with an incoming text message from one friend or another, and she immediately responds to each message. At the same time, she's engaging in a computer chat conversation with her sister—and the laptop produces a tone to announce the arrival of each incoming chat message. This is the essence of multitasking, and Olivia is quite sure that she can effectively study and communicate with her friends and her sister at the same time.

Now let's analyze what's happening in this scenario as Olivia switches between tasks. Figure 8.16 illustrates an experiment involving a simplified multitasking situation aimed at measuring the cost of switching between two simple tasks (Rogers & Monsell, 1995). On the first trial of the experiment, a pair of characters, one letter and one number ("G7" in the figure), would appear in one quadrant of a display; on the next trial, a pair ("K2" in the figure) would

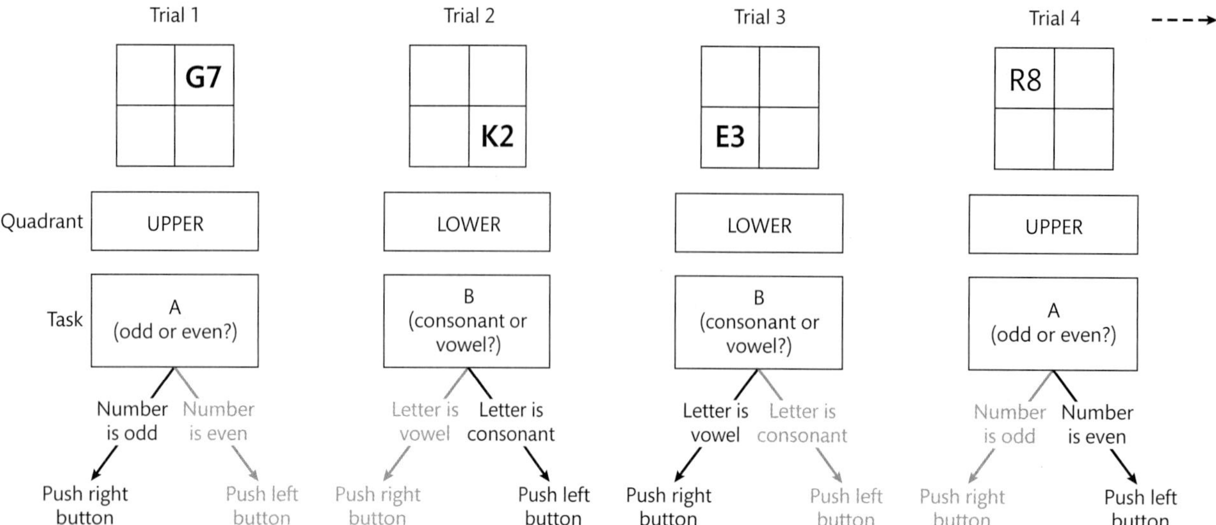

Figure 8.16 Task Switching Participants in an experiment were given the following instructions about how to respond to the character pair in the displays at top:

If the character pair is in an upper quadrant, perform Task A:

- If the number is even, press the left button.
- If the number is odd, press the right button.

If the character pair is in a lower quadrant, perform Task B:

- If the letter is a consonant, press the left button.
- If the letter is a vowel, press the right button.

The character pair marched clockwise around the display from one trial to the next. The pattern of responses illustrated at the bottom shows that task switching was necessary between Trials 1 and 2 but not between Trials 2 and 3, and then was necessary again between Trials 3 and 4, and so on. In trials that involved task switching (here, Trials 2 and 4), response time was more than 33% longer than in trials that didn't involve task switching. (Based on Rogers & Monsell, 1995.)

appear in the next quadrant going clockwise; and so on. Participants had to carry out one of two tasks, depending on the location of the quadrant where the character pair appeared (the two tasks, A and B, are described in the caption).

These instructions led to the following sequence of Task A and Task B: ABBAABBA . . . . In other words, the participant had to switch from Task A to Task B or from Task B to Task A on some trials but didn't have to switch on other trials. In trials where task switching was necessary, participants' mean response time was more than 33% longer than in trials where no switching was needed.

The difference in response time can be attributed largely to the need to switch attention between two different tasks, "a sort of mental 'gear-changing'" (Monsell, 2003, p. 135). Switching takes time, even for very simple tasks, and is only magnified for more complex tasks like reading or arithmetic (Rubinstein et al., 2001). If Olivia is in the middle of a paragraph about, say, task switching, and then has to turn her attention to a text message for 30 seconds, and then has to switch back to reading, she'll most likely have to reread a few sentences in order to recall what point was being made. Similarly, when she goes to answer the next text message, she'll probably have to spend some extra time remembering her answer to the previous one, so she doesn't repeat herself or wander off track. Figure 8.17 shows how such task switching would increase the total time Olivia spends reading the chapter in her textbook even with only one interrupting text message. If we were to factor in multiple text messages and Olivia's ongoing computer chat, you would see how multitasking can dramatically prolong the time spent on each task. And this doesn't even factor in the possible cost to Olivia of not being able to spend a prolonged time thinking deeply about the content of what she's reading.

Driving While Talking on a Cell Phone

Multitasking doesn't just add to the time required to complete a task but can have more serious consequences in many areas of everyday life—for example, when driving a car while talking on a cell phone. Driving is a complex task involving many senses and requiring attention to multiple sources of information. One study found that the risk of having an accident while

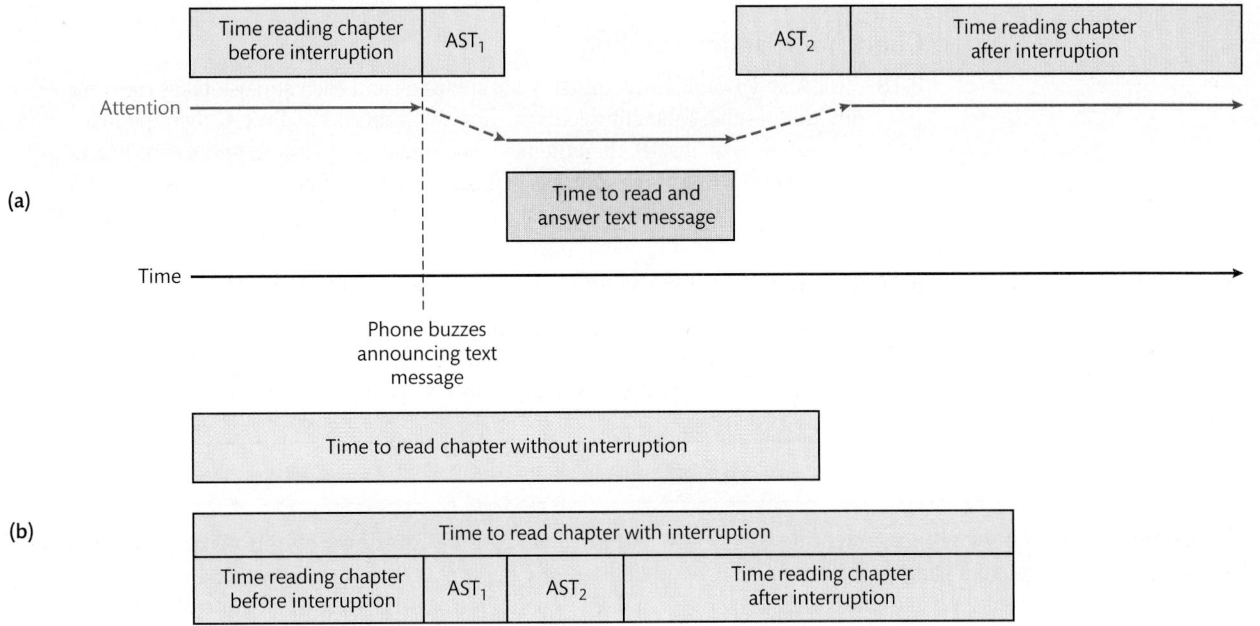

Figure 8.17 Anatomy of a Task Switch (a) Olivia begins reading a chapter in her textbook, and her attention is fully on what she's reading. Then her phone buzzes to announce an incoming text message. If she decides to interrupt her reading and answer the message, it takes her a certain amount of attention switch time (AST_1) to switch her attention to that task. When she finishes answering the message, it takes her an additional amount of time (AST_2) to switch her attention back to the task of reading the chapter, including the time to move her eyes to the correct position on the page and the time to remember what she was reading about before she switched away. (b) Adding in AST_1 and AST_2 makes reading the chapter take considerably longer than it would have without any interruption.

talking on a cell phone was increased by a factor of 4 compared to not talking on a phone, regardless of whether the phone was handheld or hands-free (Redelmeier & Tibshirani, 1997).

Another study clarified the role of attention in this situation (Strayer & Johnston, 2001). People in a driving simulator had to drive through the streets of a virtual city, stopping when appropriate, avoiding pedestrians, and generally following traffic regulations. Driving performance—for instance, the time required to respond to a brake light coming on in the vehicle ahead—was measured on an easy driving course and on a complex and unpredictable course, both while the person was just driving and while the person was engaged in one of two secondary tasks, each involving the use of a cell phone but requiring different levels of attention.

In the first task, the driver had to listen to a list of words over the phone and repeat them back (i.e., shadowing, as in the dichotic listening experiments), which requires some minimal level of attention just to hear and repeat the words. The second task also involved listening to a list of words over the phone, but after hearing each word in the list, the driver had to think of and say a word beginning with the last letter of the word just heard (e.g., in response to hearing "stapler," the driver could say "radio"). Both tasks required the driver to understand and speak words, but in the second task the driver also had to come up with a suitable response, not just repeat something. Thus, the second task resembled a simple version of what happens when a driver is engaged in a cell phone conversation and has to come up with appropriate responses to the utterances of the person on the other end of the call. The results of this study showed that both of the secondary tasks impaired driving performance compared to performance while just driving, but the task that required the driver to come up with appropriate responses impaired performance significantly more than the simple shadowing task, especially while driving on the complex and unpredictable course.

A later study showed that the impairment in driving performance while talking on a cell phone was similar to the impairment in driving performance while legally intoxicated (Strayer et al., 2006). Conversation with a passenger in the vehicle doesn't impair performance as much as a cell phone conversation (Drews et al., 2008), perhaps because the passenger is aware of traffic conditions and can stop talking when the driver has to pay full attention to the road or can even alert the driver to risks, something a cell phone conversant cannot do. The overall conclusion of these studies is that although people can share attention between two different activities—in this case, driving and engaging in a phone conversation—a loss in awareness is incurred that can have important, even deadly, consequences.

Demonstration 8.6 Divided Attention and Response Time Play a game that divides your attention between a task similar to driving and a task similar to talking on a cell phone.

Check Your Understanding

8.18 Task A and Task B each consist of six subtasks, and each subtask takes the same amount of time. John completes the first two subtasks of Task A, then the first two subtasks of Task B, then the next two subtasks of Task A, and so on. Joanne completes the first three subtasks of Task A, then the first three subtasks of Task B, then the last three subtasks of Task A, and finally the last three subtasks of Task B. Who would probably take longer to complete both tasks? Explain why.

8.19 Which do you think would impair a driver's performance more? Explain why.

A. Singing along with a familiar song on the radio.

B. Giving perfunctory responses ("uh-huh," "cool," "too bad," etc.) during a hands-free cell phone conversation with a talkative friend.

SUMMARY

- Selective Attention and the Limits of Awareness Attention is highly selective, as shown by the cocktail party problem and dichotic listening experiments. Inattentional blindness and change blindness show the degree and inevitability of this selectivity—not only do we often fail to notice fully visible stimuli, but we often fail to notice them even when we're alerted to their presence. Rapid serial visual presentation experiments show that we can assess the gist of a scene on the basis of a very brief exposure, but noticing details about a scene requires longer, more focused attention.
- Attention to Locations and Features The filter theory of attention proposes that only some sensory stimuli are selected by attention and processed for meaning; however, dichotic listening experiments suggest that even ignored messages are sometimes processed for meaning to some extent—so you notice your own name even when it's part of the ignored message. Attentional cuing experiments show that we can direct our attention to a spatial location to enhance our perception of a stimulus there. Neurophysiological recordings in the primate brain have shown that attention modulates the activity of single neurons that have receptive fields in an attended location. Human neuroimaging has shown a similar change in brain activity during shifts of spatial attention. We can also attend to nonspatial features of an object, but experiments comparing feature search and conjunction search show that binding together features requires attention to their spatial location.
- Why Attention Is Selective Different features of an object are represented in different parts of the brain (distributed representation), so how does the brain know that all the features belong to the same object? This is the binding problem. Feature integration theory proposes that the brain solves the binding problem by selectively attending to one object and ignoring others. Another issue is the competition for neural representation—objects "compete" to have their features represented. Biased competition theory proposes that attention biases the competition so that only the features of the attended object are represented, a proposal that has received strong support from single-neuron recording experiments with monkeys.
- Attentional Control Top-down attentional control involves deliberately paying attention to something in order to achieve goals. Bottom-up attentional control involves the involuntary capture of attention by a salient perceptual stimulus. Experiments comparing attention to stimuli with abrupt onsets (involving bottom-up attentional control) versus stimuli without abrupt onsets (involving top-down attentional control) have shown that bottom-up attentional control is significantly more rapid. Other experiments have shown that bottom-up attentional control can be evoked by apparently nonsalient stimuli such as seeing another person looking in a particular direction. Studies of patients with unilateral visual neglect show that the posterior parietal cortex is involved in attentional control. Single-neuron recording experiments with monkeys and functional neuroimaging studies in humans have confirmed the importance of the posterior parietal cortex in attentional control and have shown that the frontal eye field is also an important source of attentional control signals.
- Awareness and the Neural Correlates of Consciousness Philosopher David Chalmers argues that "the hard problem" of consciousness—explaining how brain activity produces conscious experiences—can be approached by searching for the neural correlates of consciousness, correspondences between neural activity and conscious experience. Experiments involving binocular rivalry and perceptual bistability have shown that at least some neural activity in the fusiform face area and parahippocampal place area correlates with the observer's conscious experience. Other experiments with both humans and monkeys indicate that the same is true for at least some activity in earlier visual areas. Patients with damage to area V1 have no conscious awareness of visual stimuli, yet they can point to and discriminate objects visually at a level above chance, suggesting that a functional area V1 is necessary for awareness of visual objects.
- Applications: Multitasking Multitasking in real life actually involves task switching, and experiments suggest that the very act of switching attention from one task to another significantly increases the time spent on each task.

Multitasking that consists of performing a complex task like driving a car while conversing on a cell phone can have serious consequences, as shown by experiments in driving simulators—just listening to words over the phone and repeating them back impairs driving performance, but not as much as having to come up with appropriate responses.

KEY TERMS

attention (p. 258)
attentional cuing (p. 263)
awareness (p. 258)
biased competition theory (p. 271)
binding problem (p. 271)
binocular rivalry (p. 279)
blindsight (p. 280)
bottom-up attentional control (or *stimulus-driven attentional control)* (p. 274)
change blindness (p. 261)
conjunction search (p. 268)
dichotic listening (p. 259)
feature integration theory (FIT) (p. 271)
feature search (p. 268)
filter theory of attention (p. 263)
inattentional blindness (p. 259)
neural correlates of consciousness (NCCs) (p. 278)
perceptual bistability (p. 278)
rapid serial visual presentation (RSVP) (p. 262)
selective attention (p. 258)
stimulus-driven attentional control, see **bottom-up attentional control**
task switching (p. 281)
top-down attentional control (or *voluntary attentional control)* (p. 274)
unilateral visual neglect (p. 275)
visual search (p. 268)
voluntary attentional control, see **top-down attentional control**

EXPAND YOUR UNDERSTANDING

8.1 If the pair of photos below were used in a change blindness experiment, they would be presented in alternation with a brief blank interval between them. What do you think would happen if the blank interval were omitted? Explain why, in terms of an attentional phenomenon discussed in this chapter.

[clock tower: Doug Houghton/Alamy; airplane: iStockphoto/Thinkstock]

8.2 If your brain were completely unable to solve the binding problem, could you perform the search illustrated in Figure 8.8c? If not, why not? If so, how—and how would the average search time compare to the average search time if your brain could solve the binding problem?

8.3 What does the experiment illustrated in Figure 8.10 show about the role of attention in determining the response of V4 neurons that isn't shown by the experiment illustrated in Figure 8.5?

8.4 In an experiment involving detection of a target stimulus in a display with an abrupt-onset item, participants were told in advance that the target was likely to appear in a specific location in the display (Yantis & Jonides, 1990). The result was that the response time for finding the target in the expected location was not slowed by an abrupt onset elsewhere in the display—in other words, the abrupt-onset item didn't capture attention. Describe this result in terms of bottom-up and top-down attentional control, and describe a real-world scenario showing why the result makes adaptive sense.

8.5 You're participating in an experiment involving functional neuroimaging of the brain during sleep. When neural activity in your parahippocampal place area increases, the experimenter awakens you, and you tell her you were dreaming about a nice little house in the woods. When neural activity in your fusiform face area increases, the experimenter again awakens you, and you tell her you were dreaming about the face of a childhood friend. Write a paragraph discussing the question of whether these types of neural activity are candidates for neural correlates of consciousness.

8.6 Which would be more likely to impair driving performance: (A) trying to figure out a complicated math problem in your head or (B) remembering with pleasure the good answer you wrote to the essay question on yesterday's psychology exam? Explain why.

READ MORE ABOUT IT

Duncan, J., Humphreys, G., & Ward, R. (1997). Competitive brain activity in visual attention. *Current Opinion in Neurobiology, 7,* 255–261.

A description of the biased competition theory of attention and a review of supporting evidence.

Metzinger, T. (Ed.). (2000). *Neural correlates of consciousness: Empirical and conceptual questions.* Cambridge, MA: MIT Press.

A collection of articles surveying this burgeoning area of neuroscience research.

Pashler, H. (1998). *Attention.* East Sussex, England: Psychology Press.

A collection of tutorial chapters surveying the key topics in attention and a wide range of experimental evidence on how attention affects perception.

Roskies, A. L. (Ed.). (1999). The binding problem [Special issue]. *Neuron, 24,* 7–125.

A collection of articles covering a wide range of empirical and theoretical approaches to feature binding.

Strayer, D. L., & Drews, F. A. (2007). Cell-phone-induced driver distraction. *Current Directions in Psychological Science, 16,* 128–131.

A review of the scientific evidence concerning the effects of mobile phone use on driving performance.

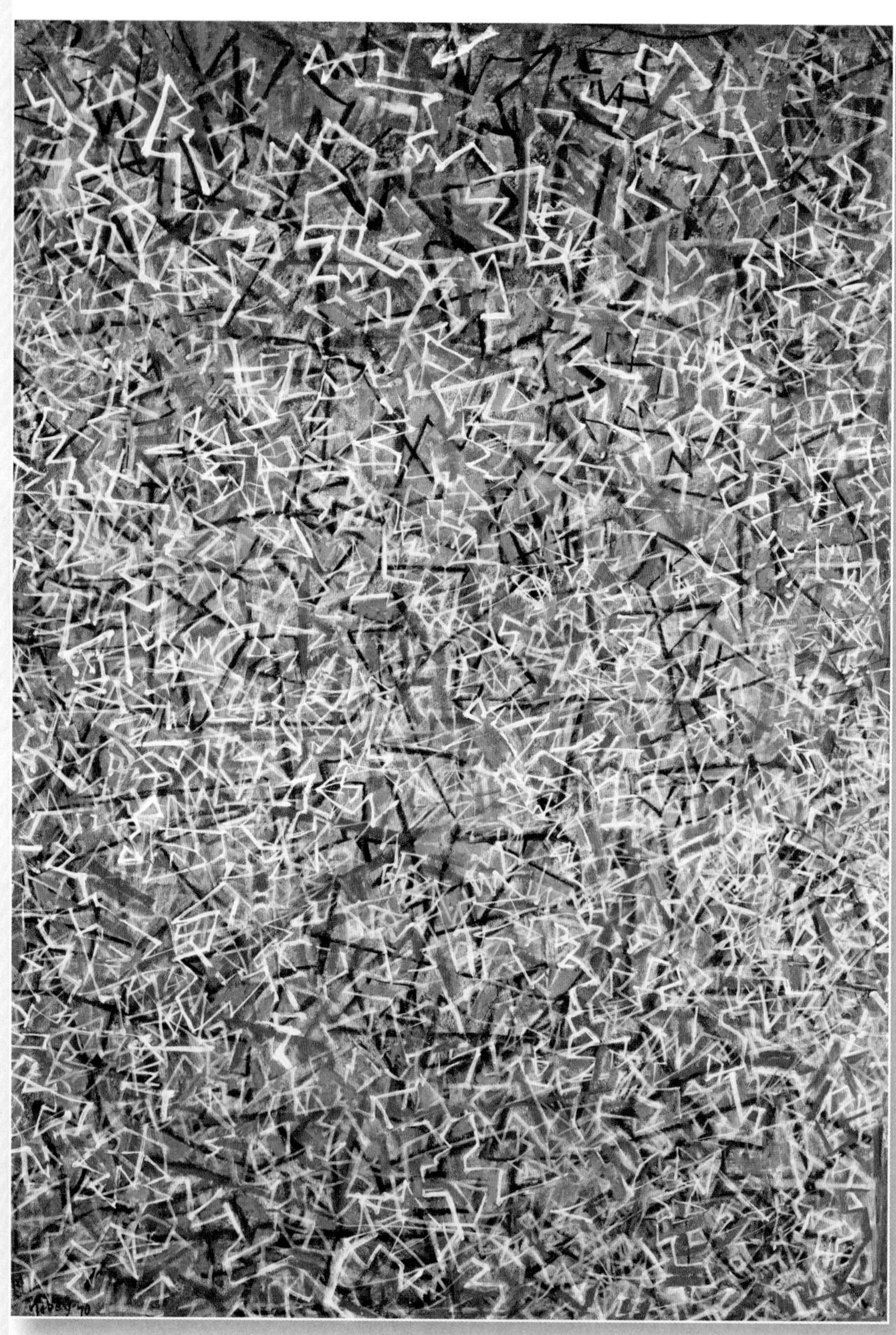

Mark Tobey, *Coming and Going,* 1970. [Tempera and pastel on cardboard support, 39½ × 27¼ inches. Charles Clifton Fund, 1970. Albright-Knox Art Gallery/Corbis. © 2012 Estate of Mark Tobey/Artists Rights Society (ARS), New York.]

9

SOUND AND THE EARS

Dizzy

L., a cellist for the symphony orchestra in a medium-sized New England city, was 45 years old when she began hearing a low-pitched roaring sound in her left ear—she couldn't seem to escape it, and it was becoming quite annoying and distracting, even interfering with her ability to rehearse. Then, as she was getting out of bed one morning about a week after the sound started, she felt the room begin to spin—an overwhelming dizziness took hold of her and she fell to the floor, where she remained for a very unpleasant 20 minutes, until the dizziness abated. She only suffered a bruise, but of course she was worried. Not only had she never before experienced an episode of dizziness like this, but she also noticed that she had begun having difficulty hearing music—or anything else—coming from her left, almost as if her left ear was somehow plugged up. The next day, she experienced another episode of severe dizziness that lasted for nearly an hour. She was able to avoid falling by sitting in a chair, but she knew something was very wrong and went to see her doctor.

The doctor said that her symptoms sounded like Ménière's disease, and he referred L. to a specialist, who found that L. had significant hearing loss in her left ear. An MRI of L.'s head revealed no tumors or other abnormalities, so the specialist concluded that L.'s symptoms indeed pointed to Ménière's disease, which is caused by a buildup of fluid in the parts of the ear that support both hearing and balance.

The specialist said that the symptoms of Ménière's disease go away on their own in roughly half of all cases, so the best treatment would be to control the dizziness with medication and just wait to see whether the hearing-related symptoms disappeared. After three months, however, L.'s symptoms were continuing to interfere with everyday life, including her ability to play the cello, so she underwent surgery to relieve the fluid buildup. Within a few weeks, her hearing was much improved, the roaring in her ear was almost inaudible, and the dizziness was gone.

Chapter Outline

As I type these words, the most salient sound is the clicking of the keys on the keyboard, but if I listen carefully, I can hear a wide range of other sounds—the hum of the building's ventilation system, the soft ticking of the wall clock, a quiet conversation down the hall, an occasional door opening and closing, and in a sign of early spring, birds in the tree outside my window. Hearing complements vision—it processes sound to provide information about events that need not be within our current field of view.

In this chapter, we'll begin by examining the physical nature of sound—pressure changes in air that propagate in waves from sound sources and are detected and processed by our auditory system. We'll explore the dimensions of sound—both the physical dimensions and the related perceptual dimensions—and we'll take a detailed look at how sound waves travel into the ear and are transduced there into neural signals, with a particular focus on how those neural signals represent the physical dimensions of frequency and amplitude. At the end of the chapter, we'll see how hearing sensitivity is measured, and we'll examine different types of hearing impairments and how they arise.

Sound

The experience of sound can be as rich and full as the cheering crowd at a baseball game or the music produced by a symphony orchestra. It can be as small and subtle as leaves rustling gently in the wind. Physically, however, sound is nothing more than changes in pressure over time, transmitted in a medium such as air or water. Here, we'll examine the causes, or sources, of sound and the physical dimensions of sound related to different dimensions of auditory perception.

Sources of Sound

Sound is usually initiated by movement that disturbs air molecules, causing them to collide with other air molecules, resulting in changes in air pressure that propagate outward from the source. For example, consider what happens when a tuning fork is struck and begins to vibrate (see Figure 9.1). As the tine of the tuning fork moves to the right, it pushes on the air molecules to its right, which then push on the molecules to *their*

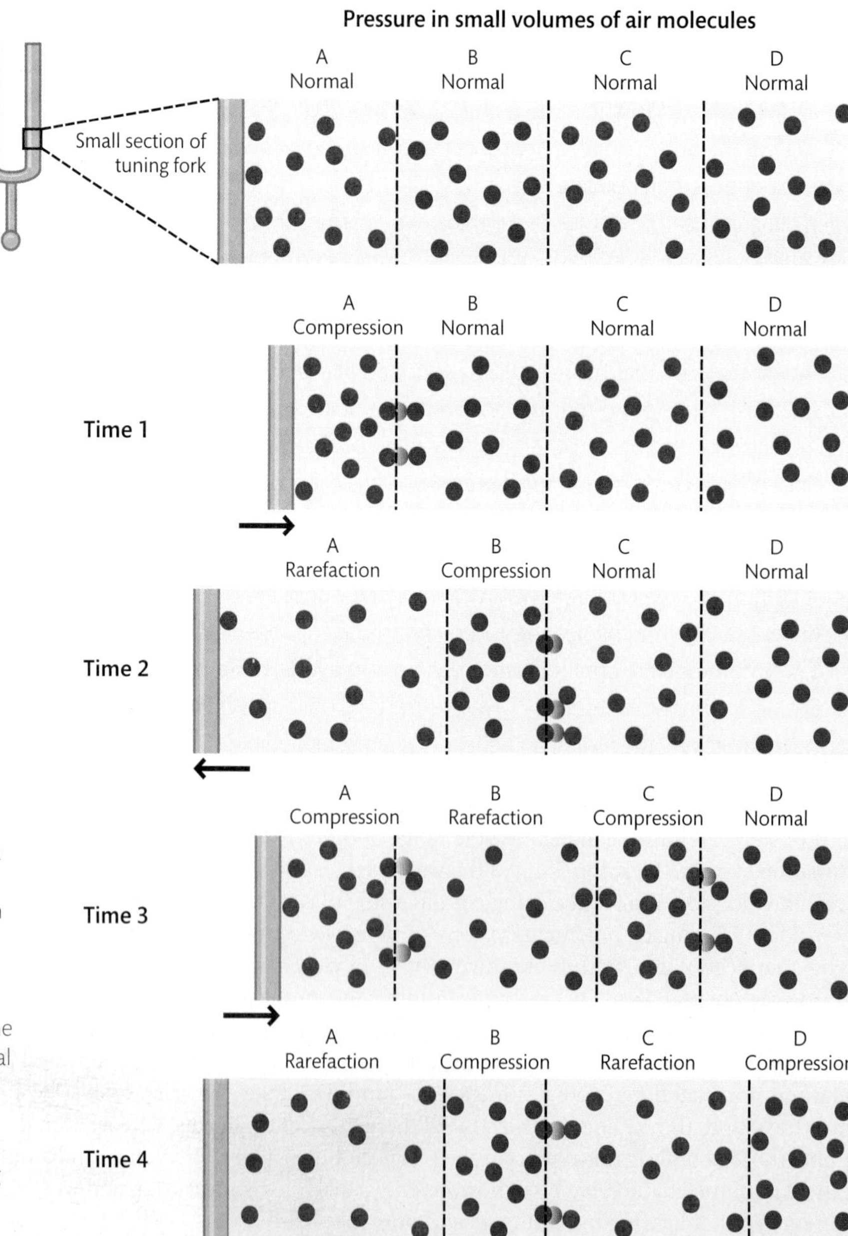

Figure 9.1 How Sound Propagates Through the Air Consider four small volumes of air (A–D) to the right of a tuning fork. When the fork is struck at Time 1, the tine pushes against the air molecules to its right, forcing them over and initiating a chain of collisions to the right in volume A, with the result that for a brief time all the air molecules there are compressed closer together, increasing the air pressure within volume A. At Time 2, the vibrating tine has moved back to the left, beyond its initial position, making volume A bigger and resulting in rarefaction, a less-than-normal air pressure in volume A. At the same time, the effects of the initial collisions in volume A have been transmitted into volume B, resulting in compression there. Mirroring the vibrations of the tuning fork, this succession of compressions and rarefactions propagates outward in all directions.

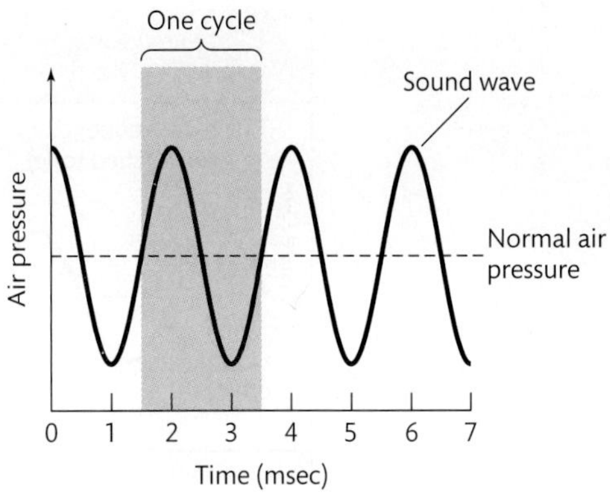

Figure 9.2 Air Pressure in a Sound Wave The regular vibrations of an object like a tuning fork set up regularly varying cycles of increasing and decreasing air pressure at a point just to the right of the fork, as illustrated by the cycles of compression and rarefaction (high and low air pressure) in volume A in Figure 9.1. One cycle is a repeating portion of the wave, shown here as a portion during which the wave varies from normal air pressure to a maximum, then to a minimum, and then back to normal.

right, and so on, resulting in an increase in air pressure in the space to the right of the tine (i.e., the air molecules are compressed into a smaller space). When the tine moves back to the left, it makes more space for the air molecules rebounding from the collisions, resulting in a decrease in air pressure in that space (rarefaction); meanwhile, the effects of the initial collisions continue propagating to the right. The tuning fork can vibrate back and forth hundreds or thousands of times per second, with waves of compression and rarefaction propagating outward in all directions. The air molecules themselves don't travel far as they oscillate back and forth, but the waves of pressure changes, which are called **sound waves,** can be detected at great distances from their source.

sound waves Waves of pressure changes in air caused by the vibrations of a source.

Figure 9.2 illustrates how the air pressure varies at a fixed location next to the tine of a vibrating tuning fork. The horizontal line labeled "Normal air pressure" marks the air pressure in the absence of sound. One **cycle** of the sound wave is a repeating segment of air pressure changes. As the sound wave travels outward from the source in all directions, the wave front resembles a sphere that grows continuously larger, like the surface of a balloon that's being inflated; thus, the total energy of the colliding air molecules at the wave front is constantly spread over a larger and larger area, which means that the sound energy at any given point on the wave front decreases with distance from the source. The falloff in sound energy with distance is known as the *inverse square law,* because the energy of the sound decreases in proportion to the square of the distance from the source—this is why distant sounds are so much quieter than nearby sounds.

cycle In a sound wave, a repeating segment of air pressure changes.

Physical and Perceptual Dimensions of Sound

Just as light can be considered in terms of physical properties such as intensity and wavelength and in terms of the related perceptual experiences (brightness and color, respectively), so can sound. The three most important physical dimensions of sound are frequency, amplitude, and waveform. They are most important because each of these dimensions is closely related to one of the major perceptual dimensions: pitch, loudness, and timbre (or sound quality), respectively. In our discussions of these dimensions of sound, we'll focus on **periodic sound waves**—that is, waves in which the cycles of compression and rarefaction repeat in a regular, or periodic, fashion—as opposed to aperiodic sound waves, the sound waves associated with an abrupt or turbulent event such as a slamming door or a roll of thunder. The simplest periodic sound wave is a **pure tone,** a sound wave in which air pressure changes over time according to a mathematical formula called a *sine wave,* or *sinusoid* (the sound wave in Figure 9.2 is a sinusoid). Pure tones can be produced, for example, by an electronic signal generator and can be approximated by the sound of a flute. Figure 9.3 uses sine waves to illustrate frequency, amplitude, and waveform.

periodic sound waves Waves in which the cycles of compression and rarefaction repeat in a regular, or periodic, fashion.

pure tone A sound wave in which air pressure changes over time according to a mathematical formula called a *sine wave,* or *sinusoid.*

Frequency and Pitch

The **frequency** of a pure tone is the physical dimension related to the perceptual dimension of **pitch.** Tones with high frequency sound high pitched, like a piccolo, and tones with low frequency sound low pitched, like a tuba. Frequency is expressed in units called **hertz (Hz),** the number of cycles per second—for example, a tone that goes through 1,000 cycles per second has a frequency of 1,000 Hz.

Young adults with unimpaired hearing can detect sounds that range from about 20 to 20,000 Hz; outside that range, sounds aren't audible to human listeners, no matter how loud. Other species can hear very different ranges of frequencies—for example, elephants can hear

frequency The physical dimension of sound that is related to the perceptual dimension of pitch; expressed in hertz, the number of cycles per second of a periodic sound wave.

pitch The perceptual dimension of sound that corresponds to the physical dimension of frequency; the perceived highness or lowness of a sound.

hertz (Hz) The number of cycles per second of a sound wave; the physical unit used to measure frequency.

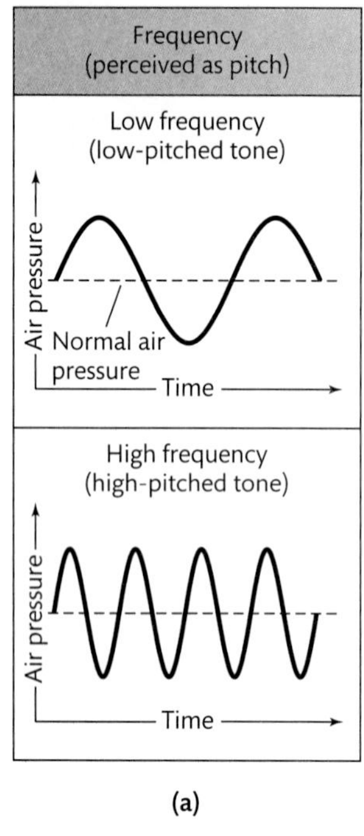

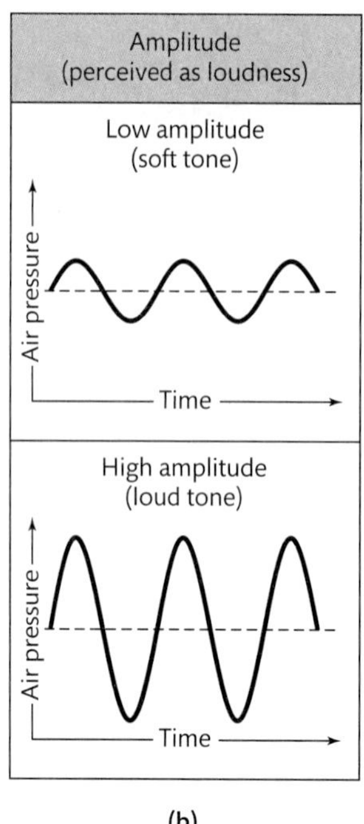

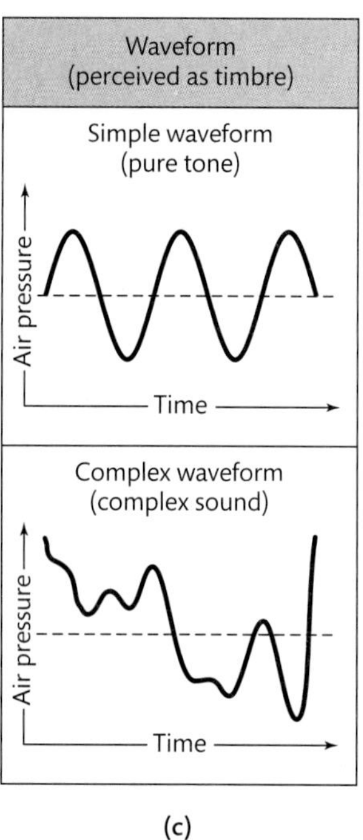

Figure 9.3 **Three Dimensions of Sound** (a) Frequency specifies the number of cycles of a periodic wave per unit of time, typically expressed as cycles per second, or hertz; differences in the frequency of a pure tone are perceived as differences in pitch. (b) Amplitude specifies the amount of air pressure change from maximum to minimum; differences in amplitude of a pure tone are perceived as differences in loudness. (c) Waveform specifies the manner in which air pressure changes over time; differences in waveform are perceived as differences in timbre, or sound quality.

very low frequency sounds (as low as 1 Hz), dogs can hear frequencies well above 50,000 Hz, and bats can hear the very high frequency clicks and squeaks they emit in echolocation, ranging up to 100,000 Hz and beyond.

Amplitude and Loudness

amplitude The difference between the maximum and minimum sound pressure in a sound wave; the physical dimension of sound that is related to the perceptual dimension of loudness.

loudness The perceptual dimension of sound that is related to the physical dimension of amplitude; how intense or quiet a sound seems.

decibels (dB) A physical unit used to measure sound amplitude; logarithmically related to sound pressure measured in micropascals.

The **amplitude** of a pure tone is the difference between the maximum and minimum sound pressure in the wave—for example, the vertical distance from a peak to a trough in the waves in Figure 9.3b. (In the following discussions of sound waves, we'll use the term "sound pressure" instead of "air pressure," because sound waves can propagate in any medium, not just in air, as when you hear sounds underwater or by pressing your ear to a wall.) The physical dimension of amplitude is related to the perceptual dimension of **loudness**—how intense or quiet a sound seems—although perceived loudness also depends on the frequency of the sound and other factors.

Periodic sounds that aren't pure tones—and this includes many natural sounds, like those produced by musical instruments or the human voice—have peaks and troughs that vary in height (as in the complex waveform shown in Figure 9.3c), in which case the *peak amplitude* within some time interval is defined as the largest peak-to-trough difference during that interval. Amplitude is expressed in units called **decibels (dB).** Because amplitude is measured in terms of sound pressure, the decibel must also be based on sound pressure, but the relationship between decibels and sound pressure is logarithmic, not linear (linear measures of sound pressure are typically expressed in a unit called *micropascals*).

As you may recall, the logarithm of any number N (the notation is $\log N$) is the power to which 10 must be raised to yield N. Thus, $\log 1 = 0$ because $10^0 = 1$; $\log 1{,}000 = 3$ because $10^3 = 1{,}000$; and so forth. Using logarithms, we express the amplitude (or peak amplitude) of a sound in decibels as

$$\text{dB SPL} = 20 \log(p/p_0)$$

where p is the measured sound pressure in micropascals (μPa) and p_0 is an internationally agreed-upon reference sound pressure of 20 μPa, which is approximately the sound pressure of a 1,000-Hz tone at the threshold of audibility for a typical healthy young adult. The notation dB SPL (decibel sound pressure level) means that p_0 is set at the agreed-upon 20 μPa. Thus, the amplitude of a sound with a pressure $p = 20{,}000$ μPa is

$$20 \log(20{,}000/20) = 20 \log 1{,}000 = 20 \times 3 = 60 \text{ dB SPL}$$

One reason logarithms are used to express amplitude is simply to reduce the size of the numbers that would have to be used if micropascals were the units—the amplitude of the loudest sounds we can safely hear is about 1 million times as great as the amplitude of the softest audible sounds. But a more important reason is that as the physical amplitude (the sound pressure measured in micropascals) of a sound doubles, the perceived loudness increases (approximately) by a constant amount, no matter whether the sound is doubling from a low level or a high level. Similarly, the just noticeable difference in the intensity of a sound is about 1 dB, whether the change is made from a quiet sound or a loud sound (this is an instance of Weber's law, which we discussed in Chapter 1). Thus, measuring amplitude in decibels rather than in micropascals more closely expresses how changes in perceived loudness relate to changes in amplitude.

The approximate amplitudes of several different types of sounds are shown in Figure 9.4. Note that 0 dB SPL (or 20μPa) corresponds to the threshold of hearing for healthy young adults. Sounds with a physical sound pressure of less than 20 μPa are inaudible and have negative sound pressure levels expressed in decibels, because the log of a value between 0 and 1 is negative—for example, a sound of 10 μPa would have a sound pressure level of $20 \log(10/20) \approx -6$ dB SPL.

Audibility Curve: The Absolute Threshold for Hearing As discussed in Chapter 1, the absolute threshold of any sensory modality is the intensity of the least intense stimulus that can be detected by that modality. For hearing, then, the absolute threshold is the intensity of the least intense sound that can be heard. But this is not a single value; it depends on the sound's frequency (just as the absolute threshold for vision—the intensity of the least intense light that can be seen—depends on wavelength).

The absolute threshold for hearing pure tones of different frequencies is measured in psychophysical experiments carried out under conditions in which, as much as possible, all other sounds have been eliminated. For example, the observer sits in a sound-attenuating chamber containing a high-fidelity speaker 2 m in front of the head at ear level. The chamber both reduces sounds from outside and absorbs sound waves from the speaker that strike the walls, reducing echoes. This doesn't completely eliminate all extraneous sound, however—the observer's heartbeat is ever present—but it does create an environment close to that ideal. The amplitudes of the tones produced by the speaker are measured by removing the observer from the chamber and placing a microphone attached to a sound-level meter at the location formerly occupied by the center of the observer's head.

With this setup, the method of constant stimuli (see Chapter 1) can be used to determine the minimum amplitude of a pure tone of, say, 1,000 Hz that can be detected, say, 75% of the time by young adults with normal hearing. This minimum amplitude is the audibility threshold for

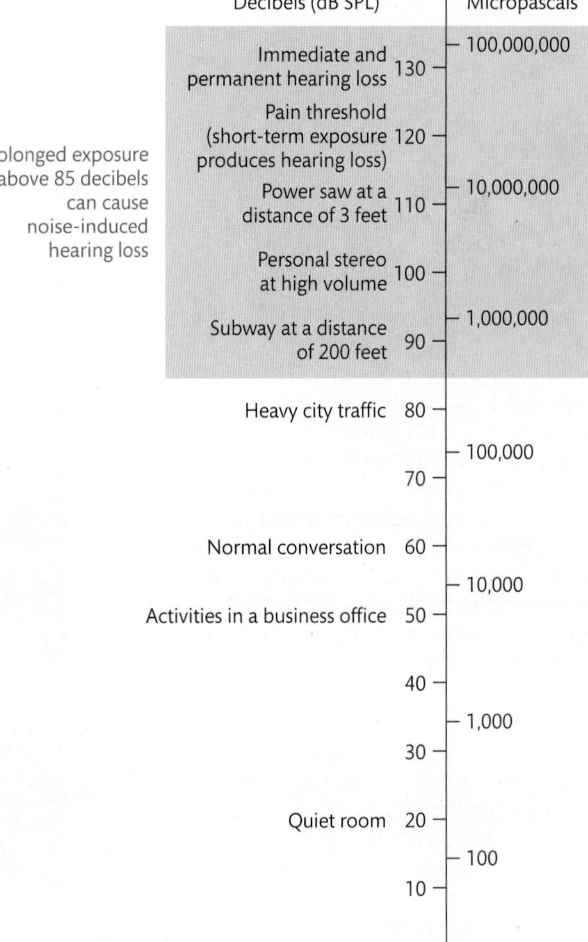

Figure 9.4 Amplitudes of Sounds in Decibels and Micropascals Because of the way decibels are calculated, exponential changes in amplitude expressed in micropascals correspond to linear changes expressed in decibels. The loudest human-made sounds are well above the pain threshold, and certain natural events, such as volcanic eruptions, can produce still louder sounds. The Occupational Safety and Health Administration has specified that continuous exposure to sounds at 85 dB SPL must be limited to eight hours per day, and above that level the duration must be reduced accordingly.

hearing a 1,000-Hz tone, which turns out to be about 0–5 dB SPL. In contrast, a 100-Hz tone would require an amplitude of about 40 dB SPL to be detectable 75% of the time by the same young adults—this means that they are much more sensitive to 1,000-Hz tones than to 100-Hz tones.

audibility curve A curve showing the minimum amplitude at which sounds can be detected at each frequency.

Conducting this type of experiment for many frequencies between 20 Hz and 20,000 Hz yields the **audibility curve** shown in Figure 9.5—the minimum amplitude that can be detected at each frequency. Note that the audibility threshold at the lower and higher frequencies that people can hear (frequencies approaching 20 Hz at the low end and 20,000 Hz at the high end) is much greater than it is at frequencies near the middle, around 500–5,000 Hz. That is, auditory sensitivity is maximal in this middle range, which happens to be the range of frequencies present in most human speech sounds.

Equal Loudness Contours The audibility curve tells us about the sensitivity of human hearing to pure tones of different frequencies. However, it doesn't tell us how to quantify the loudness of such sounds or how the loudness varies with frequency. Because loudness is a perceptual dimension of sound (i.e., a subjective phenomenon), the only way we can measure it is to ask people for their judgments about the relative loudness of different tones. To do this, we might simply ask people to assign numbers to tones of different loudnesses—for example, 1 to the softest possible sound and 100 to the loudest possible sound. This method, however, wouldn't be ideal because people might assign numbers differently from one another—for example, person A might assign 50 to tone 1, and person B might assign 50 to tone 2, but there would be no good way to know whether tone 1 seems as loud to person A as tone 2 seems to person B.

A better method is to ask people to make loudness-matching judgments—that is, to say when two different tones seem equally loud—because such judgments tend to be quite consistent across similar listeners (e.g., healthy young adults), and people can make these judgments despite differences in frequency, or pitch. An agreed-upon way of doing this is to

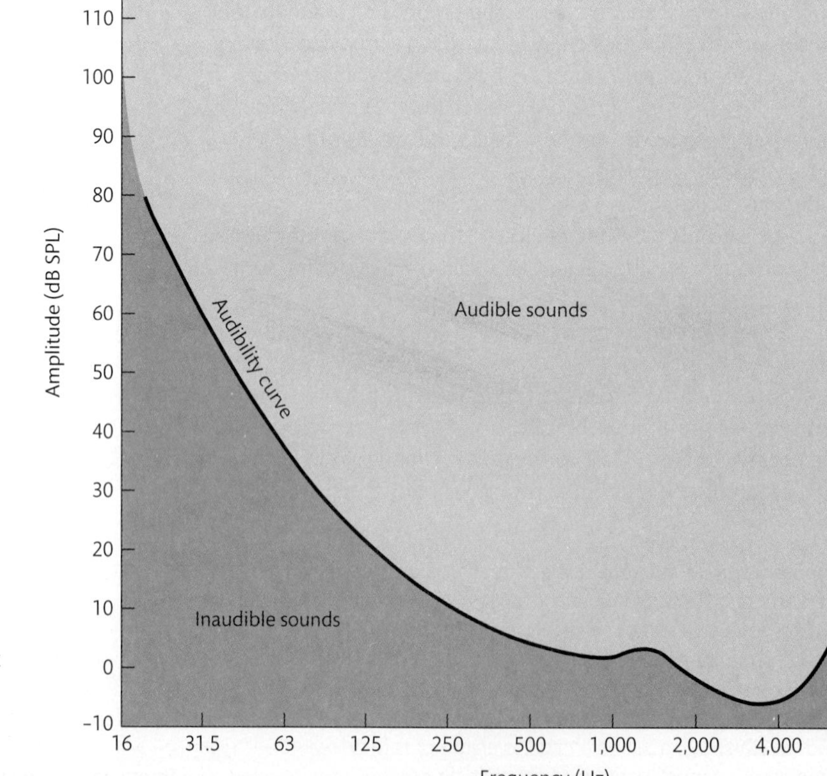

Figure 9.5 Audibility Curve The horizontal axis of this graph uses a logarithmic scale to allow the clear presentation of a wide range of frequencies. Every point in this graph represents a tone having a particular frequency and amplitude. The audibility curve plots the amplitude of the tones at each frequency that are just barely detectable—that is, the absolute threshold for hearing at each of the frequencies from around 20 to 16,000 Hz. The curve shows that frequencies toward the high and low ends of the range have to be louder than frequencies near the middle of the range in order to be heard. Any sound with a frequency and amplitude that places it below the curve will be inaudible to a typical young adult with normal hearing. Any sound above the curve will be audible. (Adapted from Suzuki & Takeshima, 2004, Figure 6.)

match the loudness of all frequencies to the loudness of a 1,000-Hz tone at a given amplitude (say, 40 dB SPL), which serves as a standard. We can ask, for example, at what amplitude a 100-Hz tone sounds just as loud as this standard tone. In such an experiment, if we begin with the 100-Hz tone set at the same 40 dB SPL, it will sound much softer than the standard—indeed, at that level, the 100-Hz tone is at threshold, just barely audible. If we then ask listeners to adjust the amplitude of the 100-Hz tone (using a knob—this is an instance of the method of adjustment, as discussed in Chapter 1) until its loudness is the same as that of the standard tone, they'll have to increase it to about 60 dB SPL.

This experiment is performed for all frequencies, to determine what amplitude each must have in order to sound just as loud as a 1,000-Hz tone set at 40 dB SPL. Plotting the results on a graph yields a curve called an **equal loudness contour.** All the tones specified by this curve sound about equally loud. The experiment is then performed using a 1,000-Hz tone set at other amplitudes as a standard, with each amplitude producing its own equal loudness contour, as shown in Figure 9.6. The unit of loudness is the *phon,* defined as numerically equal to the amplitude of a 1,000-Hz tone—that is, a 1,000-Hz tone at 10 dB SPL has a loudness of 10 phons, a 1,000-Hz tone at 20 dB SPL has a loudness of 20 phons, and so on. The similarity in shape of all the curves in Figure 9.6 reflects the sensitivity of our auditory systems to different frequencies, as we noted above with regard to the audibility curve—that is, our hearing is best for frequencies between 500 and 5,000 Hz, with sensitivity decreasing markedly at the low and high ends of the range of audible frequencies.

equal loudness contour A curve showing the amplitude of tones at different frequencies that sound about equally loud.

Demonstration 9.1 Equal Loudness Contours Generate equal loudness contours to explore the sensitivity of your auditory system to different frequencies of pure tones.

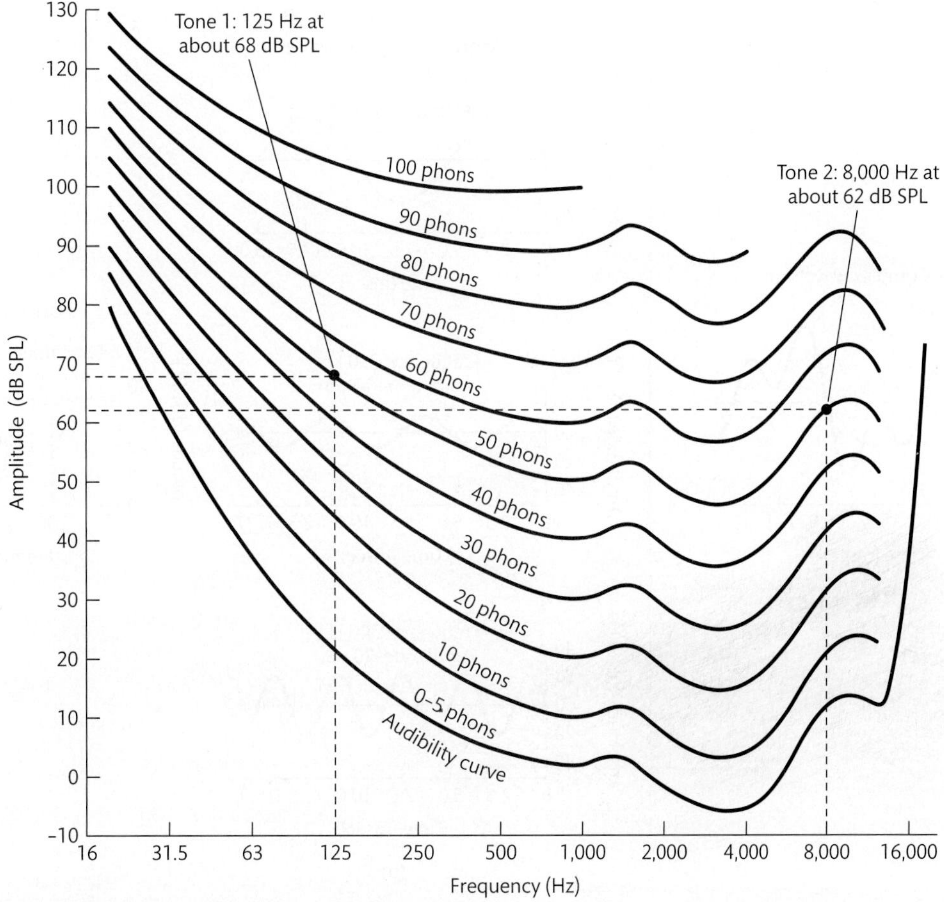

Figure 9.6 Equal Loudness Contours These equal loudness contours were determined by adjusting the amplitude of a tone with a given frequency until it sounds as loud as a 1,000-Hz tone with a given amplitude (a standard tone), and repeating this procedure with tones of all frequencies matched to 1,000-Hz standard tones across the range of amplitudes from 0 to 100 db SPL. Loudness is measured in phons—by convention, a 1,000-Hz tone with an amplitude of *x* db SPL has a loudness of *x* phons. Thus, a 1,000-Hz tone with an amplitude of 50 dB SPL has a loudness of 50 phons, and all the tones on the 50-phon contour sound equally loud—for example, a 125-Hz tone with an amplitude of about 68 dB SPL (Tone 1) sounds just as loud as an 8,000-Hz tone with an amplitude of about 62 dB SPL (Tone 2), with both having a loudness of 50 phons. The audibility curve (shown by itself in Figure 9.5) represents the absolute threshold for hearing as a function of frequency—every tone on this curve is just barely audible. (Adapted from Suzuki & Takeshima, 2004, Figure 11.)

Joseph Fourier (1768–1830). [Giraudon/The Bridgeman Art Library]

Fourier analysis A mathematical procedure for decomposing a complex waveform into a collection of sine waves with various frequencies and amplitudes.

Fourier spectrum A depiction of the amplitudes at all frequencies that make up a complex waveform.

fundamental frequency The frequency of the lowest-frequency component of a complex waveform; determines the perceived pitch of the sound.

Waveform and Timbre

In the previous two sections, we used pure tones to illustrate the physical/perceptual dimensions of frequency/pitch and amplitude/loudness. Very few commonly heard periodic sounds approximate pure tones, however—although certain birdsongs come close. Rather, most periodic sounds—that is, sounds produced by the vibrations of objects such as vocal cords, foghorns, and clarinets—consist of multiple pure tones added together. The waveforms of such sounds have a more complex shape than a sine wave (like the complex waveform in Figure 9.3c); nevertheless, as proved by the French mathematician and physicist Joseph Fourier, all such waveforms can be decomposed into a collection of sine waves with various frequencies and amplitudes (called the frequency components of the complex wave) by applying a mathematical procedure now known as **Fourier analysis.** For example, Fourier analysis of the complex waveform in Figure 9.7a shows that it consists of three pure tones, shown together in Figure 9.7a and individually in Figure 9.7b. Figure 9.7c shows a graphical way of representing the **Fourier spectrum** of this complex waveform—the full array of its component frequencies with their specific amplitudes (each sine wave is represented as a vertical line, a single frequency with a given amplitude).

The frequency of the lowest-frequency component of the complex waveform is called the **fundamental frequency** (in this case, 100 Hz), and this frequency is what determines the perceived pitch of the sound. Each of the components is called a **harmonic.** The first harmonic is the fundamental frequency, the second harmonic is the next-lowest-frequency

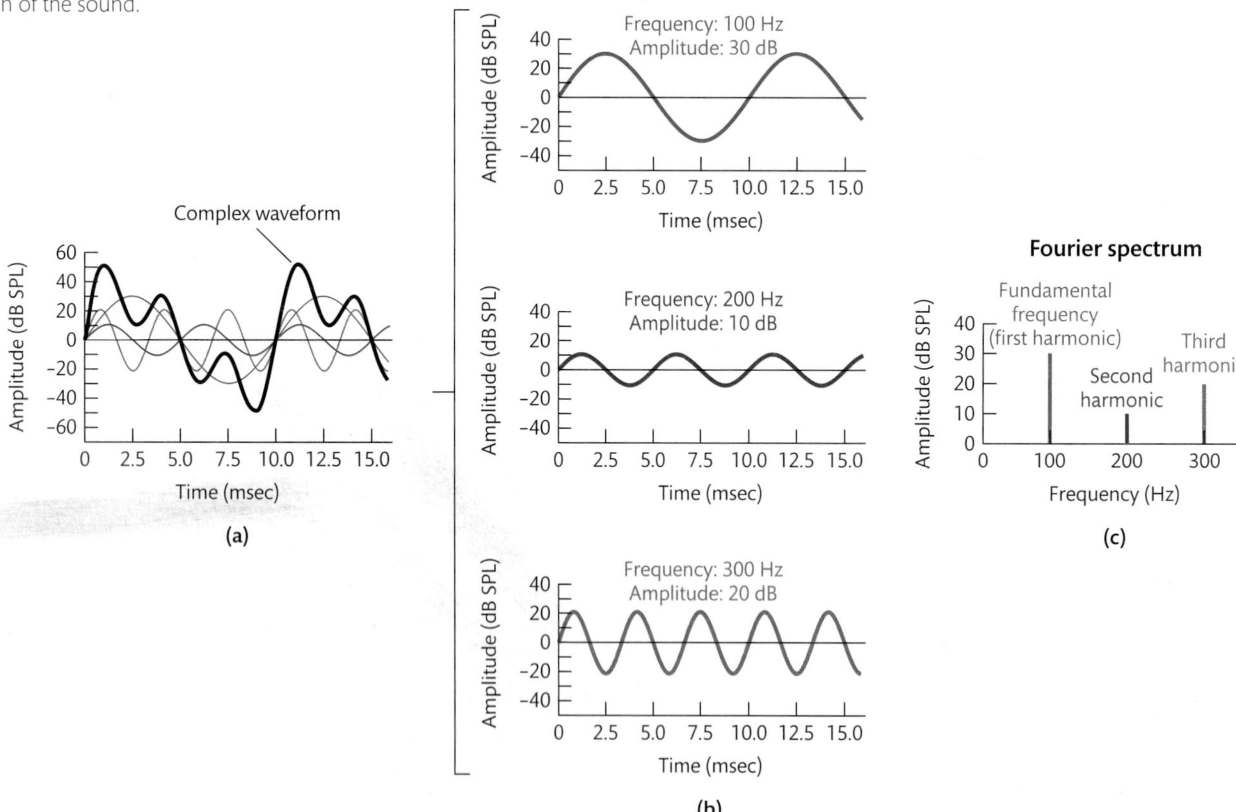

Figure 9.7 Fourier Analysis of a Complex Waveform Fourier analysis shows that the complex waveform in (a) is the sum of three sine waves, shown individually in (b). The amplitude of the complex waveform at any given time is simply the sum of the amplitudes—positive or negative—of the component waves at that time. The Fourier spectrum of the complex waveform can be graphically represented as shown in (c), where each of the three component sine waves is a single spike at the given frequency with the given amplitude. The fundamental frequency determines the perceived pitch of the complex sound; here, the complex waveform will be perceived as having the same pitch as a 100-Hz pure tone.

component, and so on. For many periodic sounds (e.g., notes produced by string or wind instruments, vowel sounds produced by the human voice, birdsong), the second and higher harmonics are integer multiples of the fundamental frequency—for example, if the fundamental frequency of the note A880 produced by a clarinet is 880 Hz, then the second harmonic has a frequency of 880 × 2 = 1,760 Hz, the third has a frequency of 880 × 3 = 2,640 Hz, and so forth, as illustrated in Figure 9.8 (which also shows that the second and higher harmonics can be referred to as *overtones*). Figure 9.8a shows one cycle of the complex waveform produced by the clarinet, one cycle of the fundamental frequency, and the first 19 of the many overtones that, when added to the fundamental frequency, make up the complex waveform (Figure 9.8b illustrates part of the Fourier spectrum—the fundamental frequency and the next 11 harmonics—of the complex waveform).

harmonic A component frequency of a complex waveform that is an integer multiple of the fundamental frequency; the first harmonic is the fundamental frequency; the second harmonic is twice the fundamental frequency, and so on.

Complex periodic sounds—that is, sounds with complex waveforms like those shown in Figures 9.7 and 9.8—don't sound like pure tones. Rather, the quality of their sound depends on the frequency and amplitude of their fundamental frequency and of each overtone. Two complex sounds that have the same pitch (i.e., the same fundamental frequency) and the same loudness but that don't sound the same are said to differ in **timbre** (pronounced "tamber"), mainly due to differences in the relative amplitudes of the various overtones. Although a potentially infinite number of overtones may be required to perfectly reproduce a complex waveform, only the overtones with frequencies within the range of human hearing will contribute to the timbre; also, very low amplitude

timbre The difference in sound quality between two sounds with the same pitch and loudness; for complex periodic sounds, timbre is mainly due to differences in the relative amplitudes of the sounds' overtones; the perceptual dimension of sound that is related to the physical dimension of waveform.

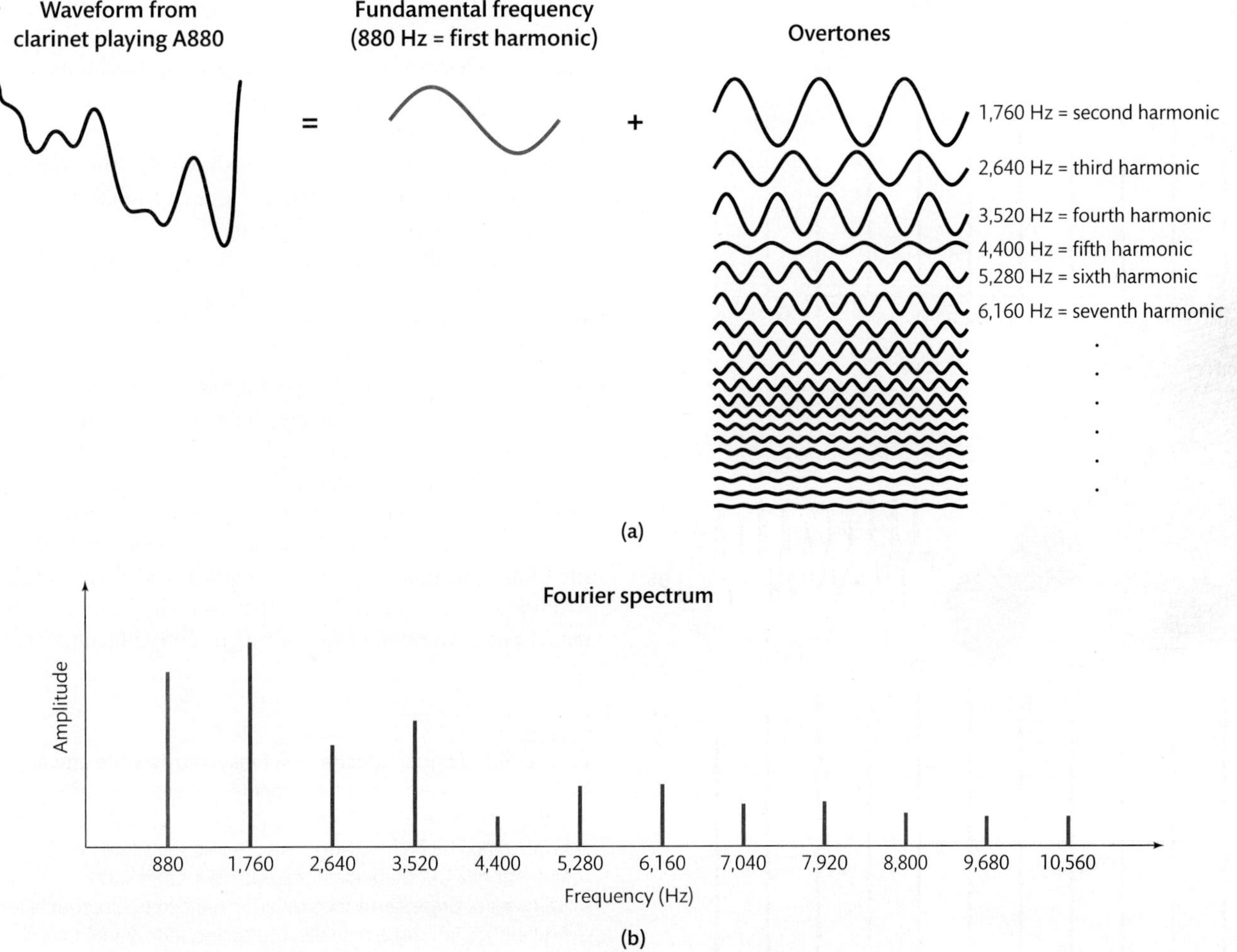

Figure 9.8 Fourier Analysis of a Clarinet's Sound (a) Fourier analysis of the sound of a clarinet playing a single sustained note (A880, a high A with a fundamental frequency of 880 Hz) shows that this complex waveform is made up of the fundamental frequency plus many higher harmonics (overtones). (b) This partial Fourier spectrum of the complex waveform in (a) shows the fundamental frequency and the next 11 harmonics.

overtones contribute less to timbre than higher-amplitude overtones. For example, the quality of the sound represented by the complex waveform in Figure 9.8a will be little affected by the tenth and higher harmonics, because they are very low amplitude, and will not be at all affected by the twenty-third and higher harmonics, because their frequencies will be greater than 20,000 Hz (the upper limit of human hearing).

Figure 9.9 shows the Fourier spectra of a flute and a violin playing the same musical note, G4. The two notes are perceived as having the same pitch (because they have the same fundamental frequency, 392 Hz) and about the same loudness, but they sound quite different. The second and higher harmonics in these two spectra are the same integer multiples of the fundamental frequency, but the relative amplitudes of these harmonics differ considerably. The flute spectrum is dominated by the first two or three harmonics, and this is what gives the flute a sound quality closer to that of a pure tone. The violin spectrum, in contrast, has significant energy at many of the higher harmonics, giving the violin a "richer" sound quality than the flute. Such differences in the relative amplitudes of harmonics are what give each sound its distinctive timbre.

With computer-generated sounds, you can selectively remove each of the harmonics to hear how this affects the sound quality. For example, removing all the harmonics except the fundamental frequency of a complex periodic sound (like either of the sounds in Figure 9.9) will produce a pure tone—in this case, a pure tone with a frequency of 392 Hz. But what happens if *only* the fundamental frequency is removed, without removing any of the other harmonics? The surprising result is that, although there is a difference in the sound quality, the pitch of the sound seems to be the same as before, even though the fundamental frequency, which determines the pitch of a complex periodic sound, is not actually present! This is called the *illusion of the missing fundamental.* It shows that the auditory system uses the pattern of frequencies in a sound's harmonics as part of the perception of pitch.

However, the perception of timbre doesn't depend just on the harmonic structure of a periodic sound; another contributing factor is the manner of its onset and offset (called the *attack* and *decay,* respectively). For example, when you strike a note on a piano, the sound has a rapid attack and a rapid decay—that is, it quickly attains its maximum amplitude and then quickly fades—whereas the same note played by a violin has a more gradual attack and decay. If you were to hear the two notes played one right after the other, you would probably find it easy to tell which was which. But if the initial and final segments (the attack and decay) of the two notes were trimmed off, so that you only heard the sustained parts, you would find it much more difficult to per-

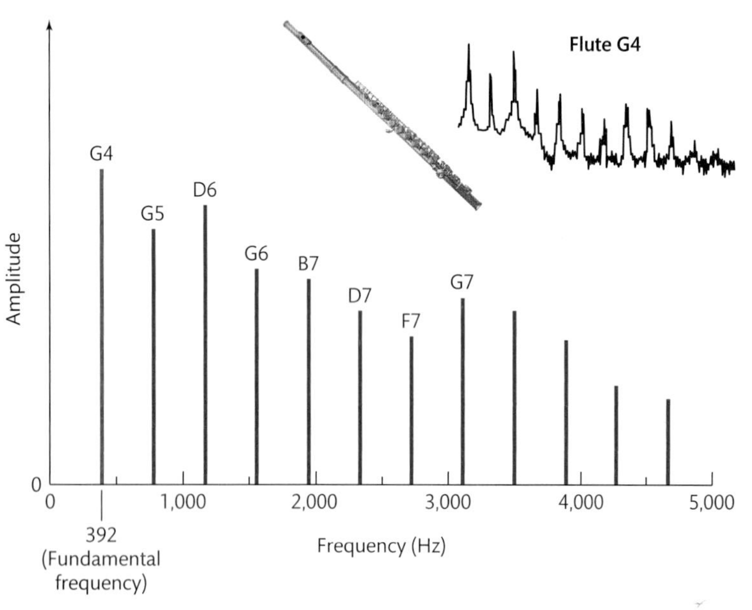

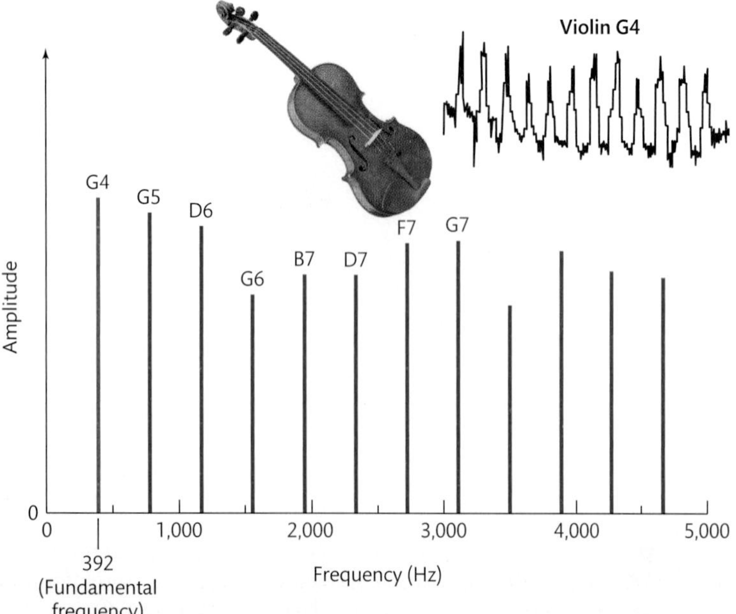

Figure 9.9 Fourier Spectra of G4 Played by a Flute and a Violin. In both spectra, the fundamental frequency is 392 Hz, and the amplitude of this fundamental frequency is the same in both spectra. The higher harmonics are also the same integer multiples of the fundamental frequency, but the relative amplitudes of these harmonics differ. This difference accounts for the difference in timbre between the two sounds. (Note that these Fourier spectra are simplified for the purpose of this illustration. The actual spectra are continuous curves with peaks around the harmonic components, as shown by the insets.) [Dmitry Vereshchagin/Fotolia.com]

ceive the difference in timbre between the two instruments and to say which note was produced by the piano and which by the violin.

The complexities involved in the perception of timbre aren't confined to periodic sounds such as musical notes; many nonperiodic sounds, such as the sounds of explosions, slamming doors, and barking dogs, differ in ways that we typically attribute to timbre, yet they can't be easily characterized in terms of fundamental frequencies and harmonics (or in terms of attack and decay). Complications like this have led one researcher to comment: "We do not know how to define timbre, but it is not loudness and it is not pitch" (Bregman, 1990, p. 93).

Demonstration 9.2 Frequency, Amplitude, and Waveform Explore how changes in the physical dimensions of sounds affect your perception of them.

Check Your Understanding

9.1 Why is a given sound much quieter at a distance than near the sound source?

9.2 What are the three main physical dimensions of sound and the related perceptual dimensions?

9.3 Why is it usually more useful to measure the intensity of a sound in decibels than in micropascals?

9.4 Suppose one person has an absolute threshold of −3 dB SPL for a 1,000-Hz tone and another person has an absolute threshold of 0 dB SPL for the same tone. Which person is more sensitive to 1,000-Hz tones? Explain why.

9.5 Both the audibility curve and equal loudness contours are at low amplitudes in the range of frequencies between 500 and 5,000 Hz. What commonly heard sounds tend to consist of this range of frequencies?

9.6 Explain the relationships among the terms Fourier analysis, Fourier spectrum, fundamental frequency, and harmonic.

The Ear

We usually think of our ears as the roughly elliptical things that stick out on the sides of our head, but of course there's much more to our ears than that. The ear is the peripheral part of the auditory system; it is the structure that transduces sound into neural signals that are sent to the brain. In this sense, the ear is analogous to the eye: it carries out the first steps in the process of hearing, just as the eye does in the process of seeing, and like the eye, the ear is a rather complex structure. As illustrated in Figure 9.10, the ear is conventionally divided into three parts—the outer ear, middle ear, and inner ear.

The outer ear refers to the parts—the pinna, the auditory canal, and the outer surface of the tympanic membrane—that can be seen from outside the body, either with the naked eye or with an otoscope, the instrument your physician uses to look into your ear (*oto-* is from the Latin root for "ear"). The principal function of the outer ear is to funnel sound from the environment onto the tympanic membrane, which vibrates in response to the sound waves. Those vibrations are transmitted into the middle ear, a tiny air-filled chamber containing three small bones, the ossicles.

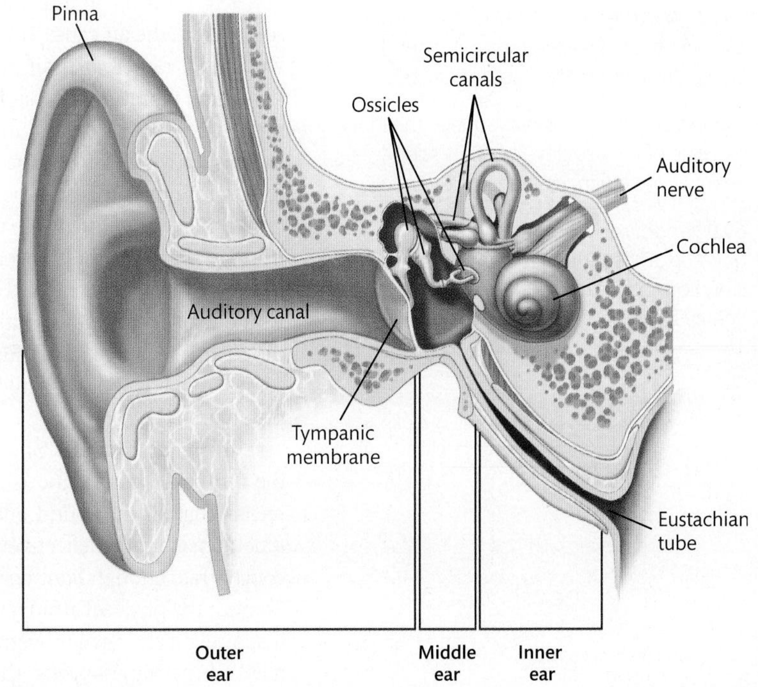

Figure 9.10 Anatomy of the Ear The outer ear is the visible part of the ear. The pinna (the part of the ear attached to the side of your head) and the auditory canal funnel sound onto the tympanic membrane, or eardrum. The tympanic membrane vibrates in response, and those vibrations are transmitted via the ossicles in the middle ear into the cochlea in the inner ear, where they are transduced into neural signals sent along the auditory nerve to the brain. The semicircular canals aren't involved in audition but in our sense of balance and acceleration.

The ossicles pick up and amplify the vibrations of the tympanic membrane and transmit them into the inner ear—specifically, into the cochlea, a specialized structure containing neurons that transduce the vibrations into neural signals that are then sent to the brain via the auditory nerve. (The inner ear also contains the semicircular canals, which aren't involved in our sense of hearing but in our sense of balance and acceleration, as we'll discuss in Chapter 12.)

Pinna, Auditory Canal, and Tympanic Membrane

pinna The outermost portion of the ear.

The **pinna** (plural *pinnae*)—the outermost portion of the ear (see Figure 9.10)—is shaped somewhat like a funnel and consists of fat and cartilage with various random-looking folds and ridges in it. Although it is sometimes said that the main function of the pinnae is to hold up your eyeglasses, they do contribute functionally to hearing, beyond just catching sound waves from the environment. Careful measurements taken with tiny microphones placed in the ear have shown that the shape of the pinnae can modify the incoming sound in a way that contributes to sound localization (discussed in Chapter 10).

auditory canal A narrow channel that funnels sound waves gathered by the pinna onto the tympanic membrane and that amplifies certain frequencies in those waves.

As shown in Figure 9.10, the pinna leads to a narrow channel called the **auditory canal,** which, in humans, is about 25 mm long and 6 mm in diameter (Møller, 2006). The auditory canal not only funnels the sound waves gathered by the pinna onto the tympanic membrane, but also amplifies frequencies in the range of 2,000–5,000 Hz, which contributes to the high sensitivity to those frequencies shown in Figure 9.5.

tympanic membrane (or *eardrum*) A thin, elastic diaphragm at the inner end of the auditory canal that vibrates in response to the sound waves that strike it; it forms an airtight seal between the outer ear and the middle ear.

The auditory canal dead-ends at the **tympanic membrane** (also called the *eardrum*), a thin, elastic diaphragm that forms an airtight seal between the outer ear and the middle ear and that vibrates in response to the sound waves that strike it.

Ossicles and Sound Amplification

ossicles Three small bones (the malleus, incus, and stapes) in the middle ear that transmit sound energy from the tympanic membrane to the inner ear.

malleus (or *hammer*) A small bone in the inner ear; one of the ossicles; transmits sound energy from the tympanic membrane to the incus.

incus (or *anvil*) A small bone in the inner ear; one of the ossicles; transmits sound energy from the malleus to the stapes.

stapes (or *stirrup*) A small bone in the inner ear; one of the ossicles; transmits sound energy from the incus to the oval window.

oval window A membrane-covered opening at the base of the cochlea; vibrations of the membrane transmit sound energy from the ossicles into the cochlea.

The **ossicles**—the three smallest bones in the human body—transmit sound energy from the tympanic membrane to the inner ear. The three bones—the **malleus** (or *hammer*), the **incus** (or *anvil*), and the **stapes** (or *stirrup*)—are connected to one another, and the malleus is connected to the tympanic membrane, so when the tympanic membrane pushes on the malleus, the malleus pushes on the incus, which in turn displaces the stapes, which then pushes in on the **oval window,** a membrane-covered opening at the base of the cochlea, as illustrated in Figure 9.11a.

Why did evolution produce this complicated and delicate mechanical arrangement of bones to transmit sound from the tympanic membrane into the cochlea? Why not simply let sound from the air cause vibrations in the oval window? The answer is that the cochlea is filled with fluid, rather than air, and sound vibrations in the air have insufficient energy to cause significant vibrations in that fluid. Think about the last time you were swimming at a crowded pool or beach. The shouts and laughter of the people around you are easily audible when your head is above water but are almost completely muffled when your head is submerged. The reason for this is that the sound waves that strike the surface of the water are largely reflected, rather than transmitted, because of the different physical properties of water and air. Similarly, if sound waves in the air were transmitted directly to the fluid-filled cochlea, there would be about a 30-dB loss in sound energy. Without any mechanism to compensate for this loss, we would fail to hear many relatively quiet sounds that make up the acoustic environment, as you can see by looking back at Figure 9.4—with a 30-dB loss in sound energy, heavy traffic would sound about as loud as activities in a business office, and many quiet sounds would be completely inaudible.

Two characteristics of ear anatomy help compensate for this loss of sound energy. First, the tympanic membrane is about 15–20 times larger in area than the oval window, which means that all the sound energy collected by the tympanic membrane is concentrated on a much smaller area, effectively amplifying its effect there (just as a large magnifying glass can concentrate enough light energy on a small spot on a piece of paper to set the paper on fire). Second, the physical arrangement of the ossicles produces a sort of lever action, with the result that a relatively small movement of the malleus ends up by causing a relatively large displacement of the stapes—thus, the action of the ossicles magnifies the vibrations of the tympanic

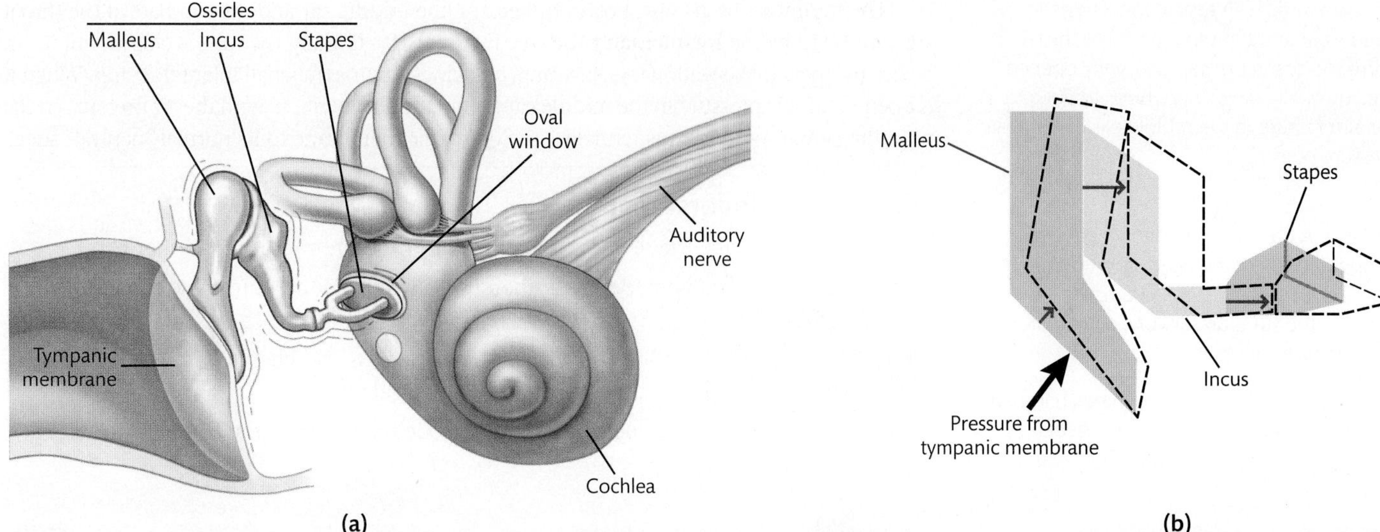

Figure 9.11 Sound Amplification (a) When the tympanic membrane vibrates, the vibrations are transmitted and amplified by the ossicles, causing vibrations of the membrane covering the oval window, which conveys the vibrations into the fluid-filled cochlea. Amplification also results from the size difference between the tympanic membrane and the oval window—the energy spread out over the tympanic membrane is concentrated on the much smaller oval window. (b) The lever action of the ossicles: a small displacement of the malleus translates into a large displacement of the stapes, as indicated by the lengths of the red arrows.

membrane (see Figure 9.11b), just as a small movement of one end of a lever can cause a much larger movement of the other end. Together, these two anatomical characteristics of the ear amplify the sounds in the air by 20–30 dB, just about completely offsetting the loss in the transmission from air to fluid.

Acoustic Reflex

When high-intensity sounds strike the tympanic membrane, two tiny muscles in the middle ear contract, pulling on the malleus and the stapes and thereby restricting their movements. This contraction is called the **acoustic reflex,** and it serves to dampen the movements of the ossicles, which helps protect the auditory system from damage due to loud noises. However, this reflex has only a limited capacity to prevent damage and occurs mainly in response to lower frequencies, leaving us vulnerable to damage from exposure to loud high-frequency noises. Also, the reflex takes more than one-tenth of a second to occur, making it too slow to protect the auditory system from sudden, brief high-intensity sounds (like a nearby clap of thunder). Beyond its protective function, another possible role for the acoustic reflex is to reduce the interference produced by our own speech sounds and by other self-produced noises such as coughing and chewing.

acoustic reflex A reflexive contraction of two tiny muscles in the middle ear in response to high-intensity sounds; it dampens the movements of the ossicles, which helps protect the auditory system from damage due to loud noises.

Eustachian Tube

In order for the tympanic membrane to vibrate effectively in response to incoming sound, the air pressure on the outer side of the membrane (i.e., the prevailing exterior air pressure) must be approximately equal to the air pressure on the inner side (i.e., the pressure in the middle ear). You experience the effect of unequal air pressures when you ascend a tall building in an elevator. As the elevator enters lower-pressure air, the air pressure on the outer side of the tympanic membrane goes down, while the air pressure in the middle ear doesn't change (because the tympanic membrane makes an airtight seal). The greater pressure on the inner side of the membrane makes the membrane stretch, which dampens its vibrations and causes a muffling of sound.

Eustachian tube A tube connecting the middle ear and the top part of the throat; normally closed but can be briefly opened (e.g., by swallowing or yawning) to equalize the air pressure in the middle ear with the air pressure outside.

cochlea A coiled, tapered tube within the temporal bone of the head, partitioned along its length into three chambers; contains the structures involved in auditory transduction.

vestibular canal One of the three chambers in the cochlea; separated from the cochlear duct by Reissner's membrane; filled with perilymph.

cochlear duct One of the three chambers in the cochlea; separated from the tympanic canal by the basilar membrane; contains the organ of Corti; filled with endolymph.

tympanic canal One of the three chambers in the cochlea; separated from the cochlear duct by the basilar membrane; filled with perilymph.

The muffling doesn't last, however, because the middle ear and the top part of the throat are connected by the **Eustachian tube** (see Figure 9.10). Usually, the tube is closed, but it can be briefly opened by swallowing, yawning, chewing gum, or (in small infants) crying. When it is opened, the air pressure in the middle ear automatically equalizes with the air pressure in the prevailing environment, thus returning the tympanic membrane to its normal "neutral" state.

Check Your Understanding

9.7 Briefly describe the different functions of the outer, middle, and inner ear.

9.8 What does the pinna do in addition to funneling sound onto the tympanic membrane?

9.9 How is sound amplified by the combined actions and characteristics of the tympanic membrane, the ossicles, and the oval window?

9.10 What are the main functions of the acoustic reflex and of the Eustachian tube?

Cochlea

The **cochlea** is a snail-shaped compartment—a coiled tube—within the temporal bone of the head. As illustrated in Figure 9.12, the structure of the cochlea can be visualized in different ways. If it could be uncoiled (Figure 9.12b), it would be a tapered tube about 33 mm long, with a diameter of about 5 mm at the wide end (the base) and 2 mm at the narrow end (the apex, the inner tip of the coil). Figure 9.12b and c show that the cochlea is partitioned along its length into three chambers—the **vestibular canal,** the **cochlear duct,** and the **tympanic canal**—with Reissner's membrane separating the vestibular canal from the

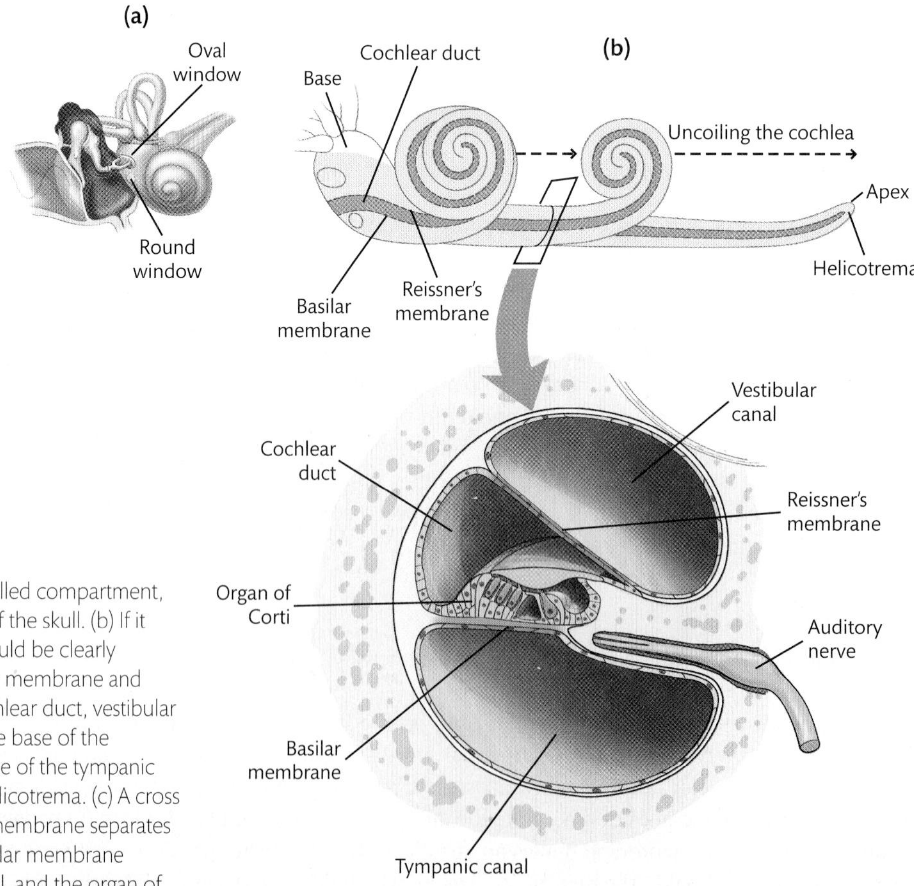

Figure 9.12 Cochlea (a) The cochlea is a fluid-filled compartment, coiled like a snail's shell, within the temporal bone of the skull. (b) If it were possible to uncoil the cochlea, its structure would be clearly revealed as a tapered tube partitioned by the basilar membrane and Reissner's membrane into three chambers—the cochlear duct, vestibular canal, and tympanic canal. The oval window is at the base of the vestibular canal, and the round window is at the base of the tympanic canal, and these two canals are connected at the helicotrema. (c) A cross section through the cochlea reveals that Reissner's membrane separates the vestibular canal from the cochlear duct, the basilar membrane separates the cochlear duct from the tympanic canal, and the organ of Corti rests on the basilar membrane.

cochlear duct, and the basilar membrane separating the cochlear duct from the tympanic canal. Resting on the basilar membrane within the cochlear duct is the structure responsible for auditory transduction, the organ of Corti, as shown in Figure 9.12c. The cochlear duct is filled with endolymph, a fluid with electrochemical properties that facilitate auditory transduction.

The vestibular and tympanic canals are filled with perilymph, a fluid similar to cerebrospinal fluid. These two canals are connected at the **helicotrema**, an opening in the partitioning membranes at the apex of the cochlea. This provides an open pathway for the perilymph to carry vibrations through the cochlea: when the stapes presses in on the membrane-covered oval window at the base of the vestibular canal, it initiates a wave of pressure in the perilymph that ultimately presses out on the membrane-covered **round window**, which serves as a kind of "relief valve" at the base of the tympanic canal. The vestibular and tympanic canals are sealed off from the cochlear duct by the partitioning membranes.

helicotrema An opening in the partitioning membranes at the apex of the cochlea; provides an open pathway for the perilymph to carry vibrations through the cochlea.

round window A membrane-covered opening at the base of the tympanic canal in the cochlea; serves as a kind of "relief valve" for the pressure waves traveling through the perilymph.

Basilar Membrane

The **basilar membrane** is a very thin strip suspended between the walls of the cochlea and running the length of the cochlear spiral (as shown in Figure 9.12b and c). Figure 9.13 shows that the membrane is somewhat thicker, narrower (about 0.1 mm), and stiffer at the base of the cochlea, and thinner, wider (about 0.5 mm), and less stiff—you might call it floppy—at the apex. The thickness, width, and stiffness change gradually and continuously from one end to the other.

basilar membrane A tapered membrane suspended between the walls of the cochlea; thicker, narrower, and stiffer at the base than at the apex.

As illustrated by steps 1–4 in Figure 9.13, pressure waves in the perilymph set up traveling waves in the basilar membrane, displacing the membrane to various degrees along its length, depending on the frequencies in the traveling waves—which ultimately reflect the frequencies in the incoming sound waves. (The term "traveling wave" simply refers to the fact that the wave "travels" from the base of the membrane toward the apex.) As with a guitar string that produces higher-frequency sounds if you tighten it (making it stiffer) and lower-frequency sounds if you loosen it (making it floppier), it is the stiffness of the membrane at each location

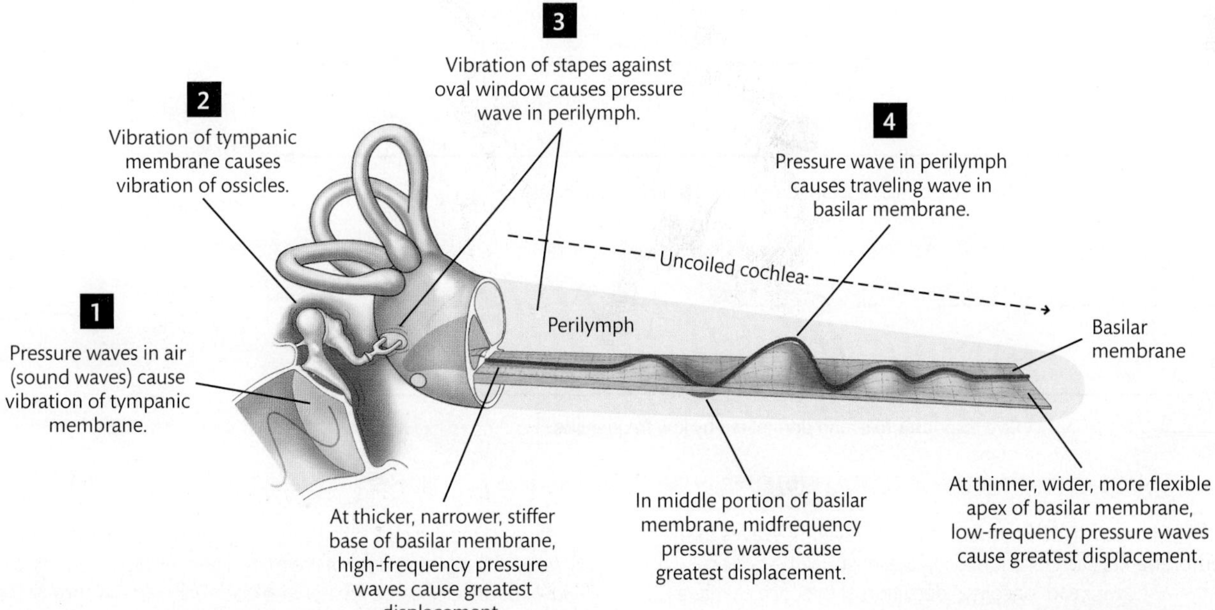

Figure 9.13 How Sound Waves Affect the Basilar Membrane The basilar membrane is thicker, narrower, and stiffer near the base of the cochlea, and thinner, wider, and less stiff near the apex. The frequency composition of the pressure waves in the perilymph is determined by the frequency composition of the incoming sound waves. The stiffness of the basilar membrane at each point along its length determines how much it's displaced in response to these different frequencies, as the wave of movement travels from the base toward the apex.

along its length that is the main determinant of how much the membrane moves at that location in response to different frequencies: the stiff base of the membrane responds most readily to high frequencies, and the floppy apex responds most readily to low frequencies, with a gradual, continuous change in response from base to apex.

characteristic frequency The frequency to which each location on the basilar membrane responds most readily.

Thus, each location along the length of the basilar membrane has a **characteristic frequency,** the frequency to which that location on the membrane responds most readily, as shown in Figure 9.14a. The traveling wave displaces the basilar membrane by some amount at each location, depending on the amplitudes of the various frequencies composing the incoming sound wave and on the characteristic frequency at each location (see Figure 9.14b). In other words, the basilar membrane separates out the frequencies of the sinusoidal components of the complex wave, performing what amounts to a Fourier analysis of the original sound wave (von Békésy, 1960). The dashed lines in Figure 9.14b and c show the maximal displacement at each point along the basilar membrane in response to various incoming sounds as the traveling wave moves from the base of the membrane toward the apex.

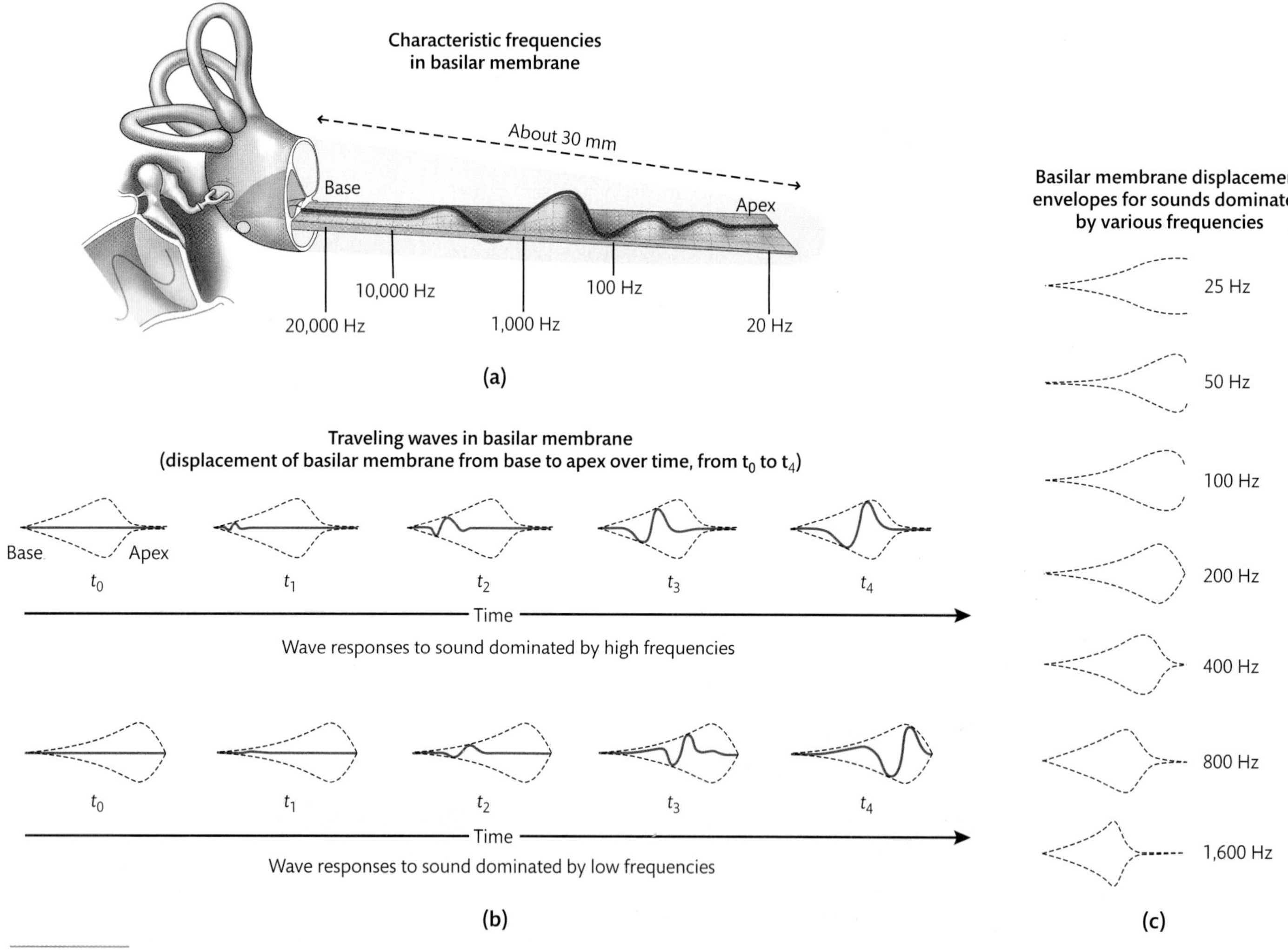

Figure 9.14 Characteristic Frequencies and Traveling Waves in the Basilar Membrane (a) Each location along the length of the basilar membrane (here shown in an "uncoiled" depiction of the cochlea) has a characteristic frequency, the frequency to which it responds most readily. Locations near the base of the membrane respond best to high-frequency waves, and locations near the apex respond best to low-frequency waves. (b) The characteristic frequency at each location determines the displacement of the membrane at that location in response to any given incoming sound. Sounds dominated by high frequencies cause greater displacement near the base of the membrane, whereas sounds dominated by low frequencies cause greater displacement near the apex of the membrane. The dashed lines show the shape of the envelope of maximal displacement, tracing the locations of the highest and lowest peaks in the traveling wave at each moment in time. (c) The envelopes of displacement for pure tones of various frequencies (adapted from von Békésy, 1960, Figure 11-43).

Organ of Corti

Within the cochlear duct, resting on and extending along the length of the basilar membrane, is the structure responsible for auditory transduction, the **organ of Corti,** first described in detail by the Italian anatomist Alfonso Corti in 1851. The organ of Corti consists of three critical components: two sets of neurons—**inner hair cells** and **outer hair cells**—and the **tectorial membrane,** which lies above them (see Figure 9.15a). There is one row of about 3,500 inner hair cells, and there are three rows of about 12,000 outer hair cells total. Each hair cell has 50–150 hairlike **stereocilia** protruding from the top (see Figure 9.15b).

Inner and outer hair cells differ in a number of ways, both anatomically and functionally. For example, as shown in Figure 9.15a, outer hair cells are cylindrical while inner hair cells are more pear shaped, and the tips of the outer hair cell stereocilia are attached to the tectorial membrane while the tips of the inner hair cell stereocilia aren't, but instead float free in the endolymph. Most importantly, only the inner hair cells are responsible for transducing sound into neural signals; the outer hair cells serve to amplify and sharpen the responses of the inner hair cells.

The **auditory nerve** conveys signals from the hair cells to the brain. As shown in Figure 9.15a, inner hair cells are connected to Type I auditory nerve fibers (each Type I fiber connects to just one or two inner hair cells; each inner hair cell connects to multiple fibers), while outer hair cells are connected to Type II auditory nerve fibers (each Type II fiber connects to as many as 30–60 outer hair cells). Of the approximately 30,000 nerve fibers that bundle together to form the auditory nerve of each ear, about 95% are of Type I and only about 5% of Type II. Type I fibers are thick and myelinated, which promotes rapid conduction of action potentials; Type II fibers are thinner and unmyelinated, which results in relatively slower conduction of action potentials.

organ of Corti A structure in the cochlea situated on the basilar membrane; consists of three critical components—inner hair cells, outer hair cells, and the tectorial membrane.

inner hair cells Neurons in the organ of Corti; responsible for auditory transduction.

outer hair cells Neurons in the organ of Corti; serve to amplify and sharpen the responses of inner hair cells.

tectorial membrane A membrane that lies above the hair cells in the organ of Corti.

stereocilia Small hairlike projections on the tops of inner and outer hair cells.

auditory nerve The nerve that conveys signals from the hair cells in the organ of Corti to the brain; made up of Type I and Type II auditory nerve fibers bundled together.

Demonstration 9.3 Functional Anatomy of the Ear Interact with depictions of the human ear.

Organ of Corti

Stereocilia
Outer hair cell
Tectorial membrane
Endolymph
Inner hair cell
Type I nerve fiber
Auditory nerve
Type II nerve fiber
Basilar membrane
Movements of basilar and tectorial membranes, resulting in shearing force on stereocilia

Hair cells and stereocilia

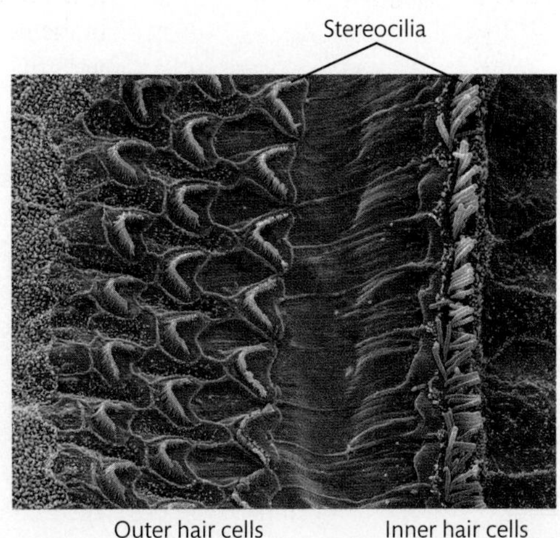

Figure 9.15 Organ of Corti (a) The organ of Corti consists of one row of inner hair cells (connected to Type I auditory nerve fibers), three rows of outer hair cells (connected to Type II auditory nerve fibers), the tectorial membrane, and various supporting structures. Open spaces within the organ of Corti are filled with endolymph, the fluid inside the cochlear duct. The stereocilia atop the hair cells are bent back and forth as a result of the movements of the basilar and tectorial membranes. (b) A photomicrograph of the organ of Corti with the tectorial membrane removed, revealing the rows of inner and outer hair cells. The stereocilia of outer hair cells are in V-shaped clusters; those of inner hair cells are in broader U-shaped clusters. [SPL/Photo Researchers]

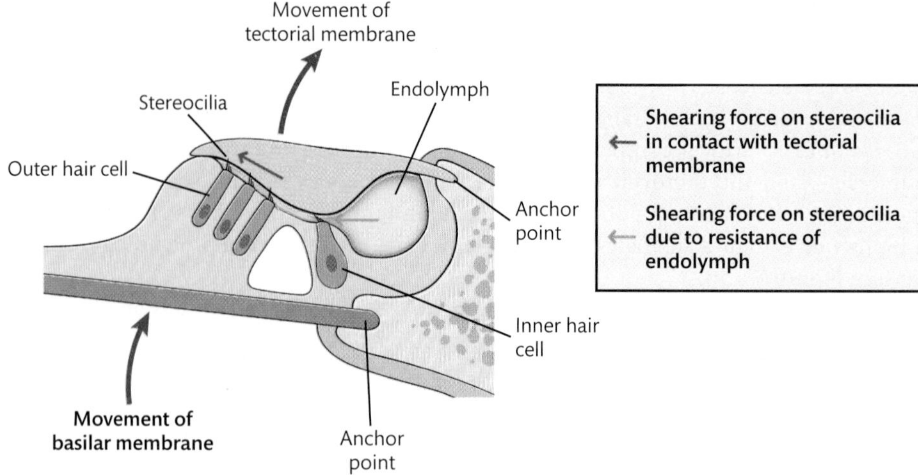

Figure 9.16 When the Basilar Membrane Moves, the Stereocilia Bend The basilar membrane and the tectorial membrane have different anchor points, so when the basilar membrane moves, the tectorial membrane moves in a somewhat different way, creating a shearing force that causes the stereocilia of the outer hair cells to bend. The stereocilia of the inner hair cells bend as they sweep through the endolymph as a result of the movement of the basilar membrane. The extent of all these movements is greatly exaggerated in this illustration.

This difference in neural connections reflects the important functional difference between the inner and outer hair cells, a difference that was elucidated only fairly recently. It had been known for decades that hair cells were responsible for auditory transduction, but it wasn't until the 1980s that it became clear that only inner hair cells participate directly in the transduction of sound (Brownell et al., 1985), a process initiated by the bending of their stereocilia due to the movements of the basilar membrane. Outer hair cells have an entirely different function, though one also dependent on the bending of the stereocilia.

Stereocilia Bending and Tip Links As illustrated in Figure 9.16, when the basilar membrane moves upward, the stereocilia at the tips of the outer hair cells, which are in contact with the overarching tectorial membrane, are bent by a shearing force due to the different motions of the two membranes, which have separate anchor points. The stereocilia of the inner hair cells are bent in the same direction by the resistance of the surrounding endolymph as the stereocilia move through the fluid (just as your hair would be swept backward if you walked along the bottom of a swimming pool with your head underwater). Figure 9.16 makes it easy to see the bending of the stereocilia, but you should keep in mind that these movements are greatly exaggerated in the illustration. For sounds near the auditory threshold, the stereocilia actually move less than 1 nanometer (nm, 1-billionth of a meter).

tip links Tiny fibers connecting the tips of adjacent stereocilia on hair cells; increased tension on tip links pulls open ion channels in the membranes of the stereocilia.

The tips of adjacent stereocilia are connected to one another with tiny fibers called **tip links**, as shown in Figure 9.17. When the stereocilia bend, the distance between the attachment points of the tip links increases; this increases the tension on the tip links, which pull open channels in the membranes of the stereocilia to which they're attached (Vollrath et al., 2007). Positively charged potassium and calcium ions then enter the hair cell through the open channels, causing the cell membrane potential to depolarize, which leads to critical reactions in both types of hair cells, as we'll see in the next section.

Inner Hair Cells and Outer Hair Cells Auditory transduction—the conversion of sound waves into neural signals—occurs when inner hair cells release neurotransmitters as a result of the depolarization of the cell membrane by the process described above. The neurotransmitter release initiates action potentials in Type I auditory nerve fibers, which carry information to the brain about the frequencies and amplitudes in the incoming sound waves (see the sections below on frequency representation and amplitude representation). And as we'll see next, this auditory information is enhanced by the action of the outer hair cells.

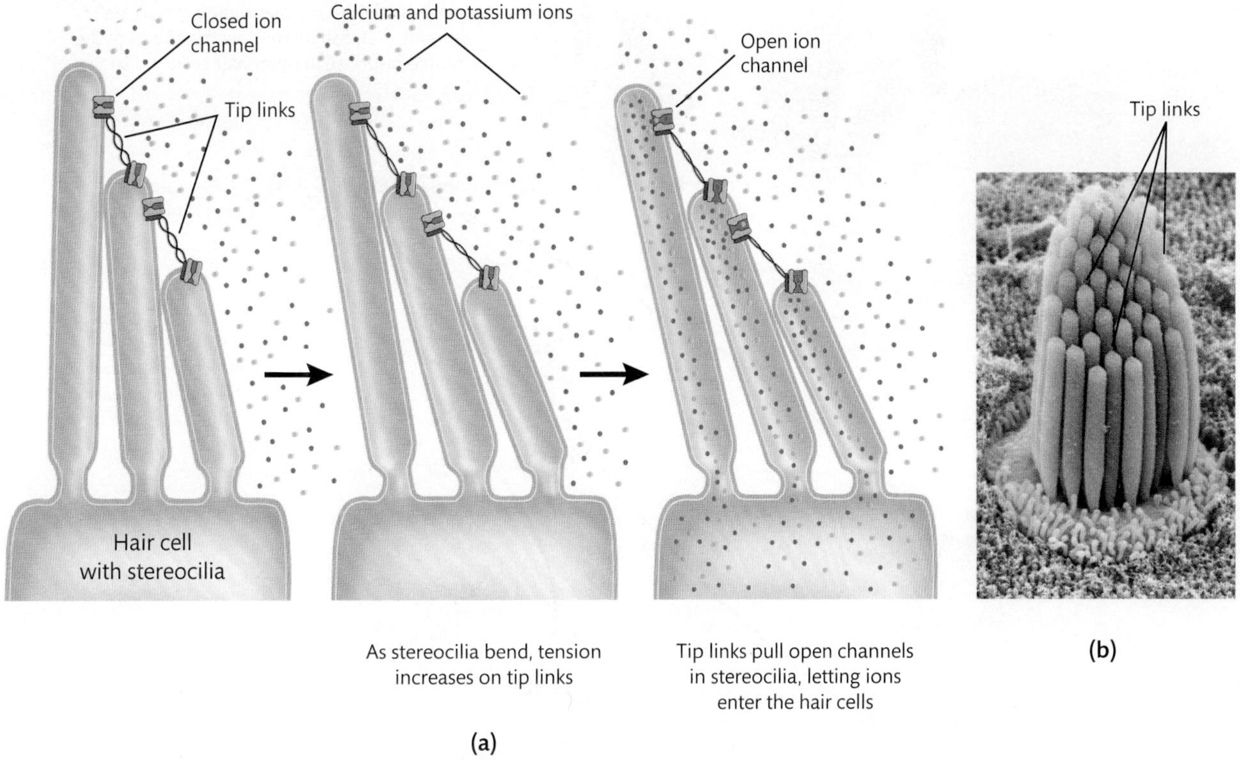

Figure 9.17 Tip Links Open Ion Channels (a) The bending of hair cell stereocilia increases the tension on the tip links connecting them. The tip links pull open channels through which positively charged calcium and potassium ions enter the hair cell. (b) Micrograph showing the tip links between hair cell stereocilia. [Leonardo Andrade and Bechara Kachar, NIDCD/NIH]

The movements of the basilar membrane caused by sound are extremely small. A sound near absolute threshold displaces the basilar membrane by less than 0.1 nm (about the width of a single hydrogen atom); even an extremely loud sound—for example, the sound of a jet engine at about 120 dB SPL—displaces the membrane by only 10 nm (Hudspeth, 2008). However, the auditory system has evolved an amazing way of mechanically amplifying and sharpening the movements of the basilar membrane and thereby producing much more information-rich signals from the inner hair cells.

In outer hair cells, depolarization of the cell membrane by the process illustrated in Figure 9.17 results in a change in the shape of a protein called *prestin* in the membrane. This shape change causes the cell body and its stereocilia to execute physical movements similar to stretching and contracting, called a **motile response** (Dallos et al., 2008; Hudspeth, 2008; Zheng et al., 2000)—the cell's length changes by as much as 2–3%. The motile response of outer hair cells has two important effects on the signals sent by inner hair cells in response to a given sound:

motile response A response by outer hair cells that magnifies the movements of the basilar membrane, amplifying sounds and sharpening the response to particular frequencies.

- The changes in the length of outer hair cells magnify the movements of the basilar membrane in the regions with characteristic frequencies corresponding to the frequencies in the sound, which means that the inner hair cells in those regions send stronger signals in response to the sound—thus, the motile response amplifies sounds.
- The magnified movements occur only in very narrow regions of the basilar membrane, covering very narrow ranges of characteristic frequencies, which means that the inner hair cells in those regions send signals that are more frequency specific—thus, the motile response sharpens the response to the frequencies in sounds.

Figure 9.18 illustrates how the motile response fits into the entire process by which the ear converts incoming sound waves into information that can be sent to the brain.

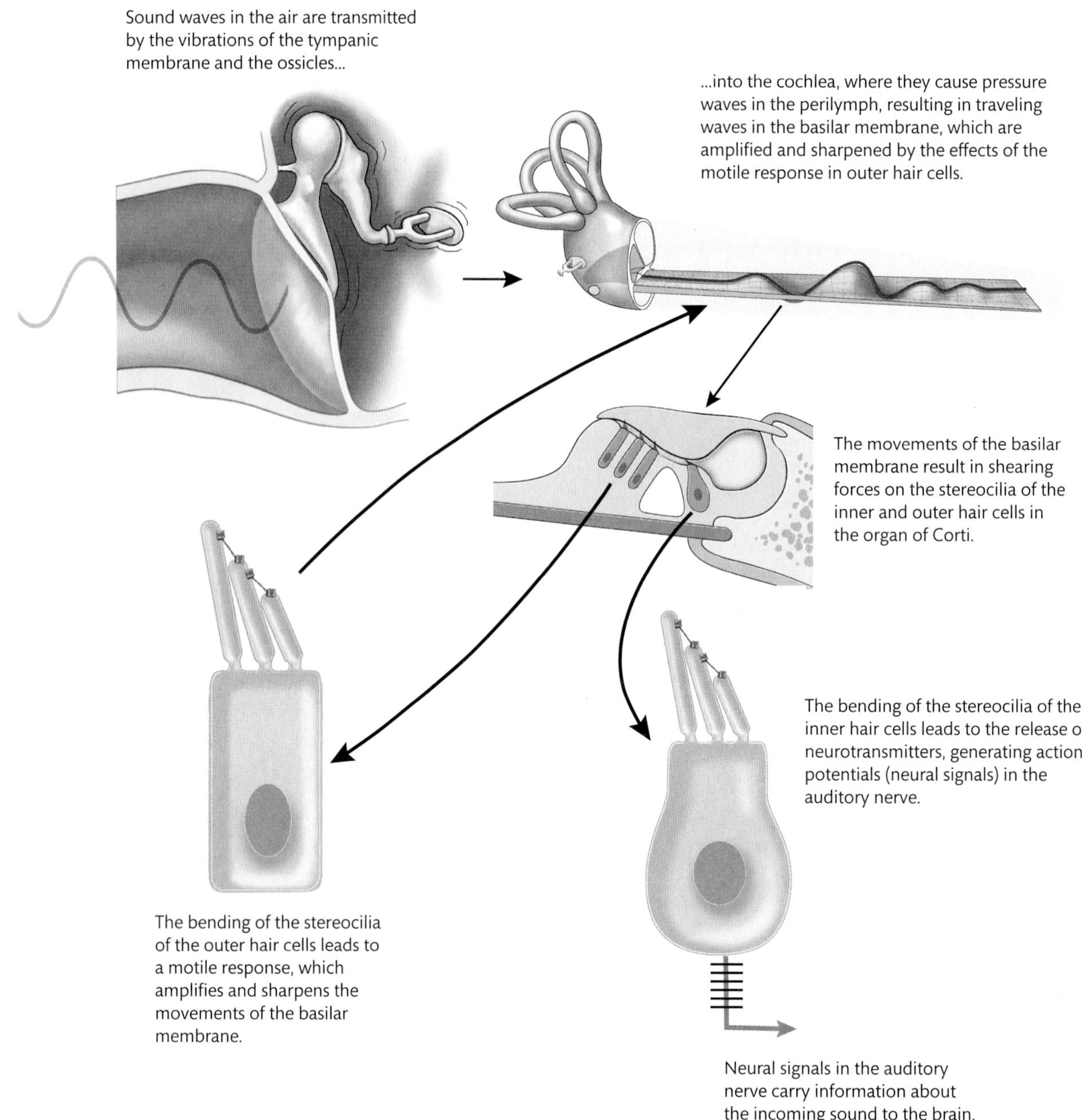

Sound waves in the air are transmitted by the vibrations of the tympanic membrane and the ossicles...
...into the cochlea, where they cause pressure waves in the perilymph, resulting in traveling waves in the basilar membrane, which are amplified and sharpened by the effects of the motile response in outer hair cells.
The movements of the basilar membrane result in shearing forces on the stereocilia of the inner and outer hair cells in the organ of Corti.
The bending of the stereocilia of the inner hair cells leads to the release of neurotransmitters, generating action potentials (neural signals) in the auditory nerve.
The bending of the stereocilia of the outer hair cells leads to a motile response, which amplifies and sharpens the movements of the basilar membrane.
Neural signals in the auditory nerve carry information about the incoming sound to the brain.

Figure 9.18 **The Role of the Motile Response of Outer Hair Cells in the Process of Auditory Transduction** The motile response of the outer hair cells contributes crucial information to the neural signals sent to the brain by the inner hair cells: it magnifies the movements of the basilar membrane, thereby amplifying sounds, and it narrows the region of the basilar membrane activated by a given frequency of sound, thereby sharpening the response to the frequencies in sounds.

The role of the outer hair cells in amplifying and sharpening the movements of the basilar membrane has been confirmed by experiments showing that displacement of the basilar membrane is reduced when the motile response is eliminated (Ruggero & Rich, 1991). Furthermore, other experiments show that basilar membrane movement is suppressed and the signals sent by inner hair cells into Type I auditory nerve fibers are thereby reduced when the superior olivary complex of the brain stem is stimulated, because the outer hair cells receive inhibitory neural signals from the superior olivary complex, and these inhibitory signals cause a reduction in the motile response (Guinan & Cooper, 2008).

Except for the motile response, little is known about the function of outer hair cells in hearing, in part because the Type II fibers to which they're connected constitute only about 5% of auditory nerve fibers and are technically difficult to isolate. One recent study found that Type II auditory nerve fibers respond only to very intense sounds, and the authors speculated that Type II fibers may play a role in the perception of sounds that are loud enough to be painful (see Figure 9.4), perhaps playing a role similar to that of neurons involved in pain perception in other parts of the body (Weisz et al., 2009). As with other painful stimuli, detection of potentially damaging sounds is important in prompting listeners to take action to prevent further damage.

Check Your Understanding

9.11 What is the helicotrema and why doesn't it result in a mixing of perilymph and endolymph in the cochlea?

9.12 What are the correspondences between the stiffness and characteristic frequency of locations from the base to the apex of the basilar membrane?

9.13 Describe the two causes of stereocilia bending in the organ of Corti.

9.14 What are tip links, and how are they involved in auditory transduction by hair cells?

Neural Representation of Frequency and Amplitude

So far in this chapter, we've examined in some detail how sound entering the ear is transformed into neural signals to be sent to the brain. Now it's time to examine just how the critical properties of sound—frequency and amplitude—are represented in the neural signals by the anatomical and physiological machinery of the cochlea.

Frequency Representation

The auditory system uses two different mechanisms to encode frequency in the neural signals sent to the brain. First, frequency is represented by the displacement of the basilar membrane at different locations, with different degrees of displacement resulting in correspondingly different rates of action potentials being sent along the Type I auditory nerve fibers at those locations—this is called the **place code.** Second, frequency is represented by a match between the frequencies in the incoming sound waves and the timing of action potentials sent by Type I auditory nerve fibers to the brain—this is called the **temporal code.** As we shall see, both codes play a role in representing the frequencies of most sounds.

place code Frequency representation based on the displacement of the basilar membrane at different locations.

temporal code Frequency representation based on a match between the frequencies in incoming sound waves and the firing rates of auditory nerve fibers.

Place Code for Frequency

The place code for frequency—the idea that different locations along the basilar membrane respond selectively to different frequencies of sound—was first suggested by the nineteenth-century German scientist Hermann von Helmholtz (1866/1925), whom we've encountered several times before in this book. The physical basis for the place code—that is, how the stiffness of the basilar membrane at each location determines its response to different sound frequencies—was established in the 1940s and 1950s by the Hungarian biophysicist Georg von Békésy. Among other things, von Békésy (1960) was the first to directly determine the envelopes of basilar membrane displacement in the inner ear, as illustrated in Figure 9.14c (von Békésy was awarded the 1961 Nobel Prize for Physiology or Medicine for his seminal discoveries).

Physiological Frequency Tuning Curves The measurements of basilar membrane movements taken by von Békésy were made in the mid-twentieth century using a microscope and a strobe light. Since that time, much more precise measurements of the movement of the basilar membrane at different locations in response to different frequencies have been taken using laser interferometry, and these have been compared with the responses of Type I auditory nerve fibers to those same frequencies (Narayan et al., 1998). The characteristic frequency of an auditory nerve fiber is like the characteristic frequency of a location on the basilar membrane: it's the frequency to which the auditory nerve fiber is most sensitive. Figure 9.19 shows

Georg von Békésy (1899–1972). [Emilio Segre Visual Archives, American Institute of Physics, W. F. Meggers Gallery of Nobel Laureates Collection]

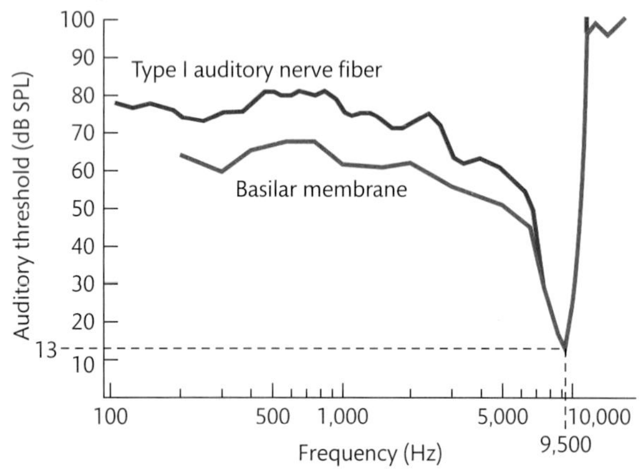

Figure 9.19 Type I Auditory Nerve Fiber and Basilar Membrane Frequency Tuning Curves The blue curve shows that an auditory nerve fiber with a characteristic frequency of 9,500 Hz requires a 13 dB SPL tone at that frequency to produce a firing rate just above baseline; higher-level tones are required at all other frequencies to produce the same response. The red curve was derived by measuring the displacement of a location on the basilar membrane produced by a 9,500-Hz, 13 dB SPL tone (2.74 nm), and then determining the sound level required to produce the same displacement at all other frequencies. (Based on data from research with chinchillas in Narayan et al., 1998.)

the frequency tuning curve of a Type I auditory nerve fiber with a characteristic frequency of 9,500 Hz (blue curve) compared to the frequency tuning curve of a location on the basilar membrane with the same characteristic frequency (red curve). These curves show the intensity of pure tones at various frequencies required to produce some predetermined minimal response. That the two frequency tuning curves are nearly identical shows that the frequency tuning of Type I auditory nerve fibers can be almost entirely accounted for by the frequency tuning of the basilar membrane, a purely mechanical factor.

Figure 9.20 shows the frequency tuning curves of several different Type I auditory nerve fibers (the dashed lines indicate the characteristic frequency of each fiber). A striking feature of these curves is that they become progressively narrower as the characteristic frequency increases, which means that nerve fibers with higher characteristic frequencies are more sensitive to frequency differences between incoming sounds near their characteristic frequency than are nerve fibers with lower characteristic frequencies. Thus, the place code provides relatively better frequency representation of high-frequency sounds than of low-frequency sounds.

Figure 9.21 shows that Type I auditory nerve fibers with different characteristic frequencies project to correspondingly different positions along the basilar membrane. This figure comes from an experiment in which single-cell recordings were used to measure the characteristic frequency of individual auditory nerve fibers (Liberman, 1982). Each fiber was then injected with a dye to make it visible under a microscope (see Figure 9.21a), so the position of the hair cell connected to that fiber could be determined. Figure 9.21b plots these positions as a function of each fiber's characteristic frequency, providing clear evidence for a place code for frequency.

Psychophysical Frequency Tuning Curves The frequency tuning curves shown in Figure 9.20 were derived by directly measuring the firing rates of auditory nerve fibers using physiological techniques such as single-cell recording. Psychophysical methods can also be used to generate frequency tuning curves, based on the perceptual judgments of human listeners. In such a procedure, the experimenter presents a target tone—a pure tone with a given frequency (say, 1,000 Hz) and a fairly low amplitude (say, 10 dB above absolute threshold)—against a silent background, so it's easily detectable. Then narrowband white noise is presented simultaneously with the target tone. (White noise, consisting of sound waves with equal amplitude at all frequencies, sounds like static on a radio that's tuned between stations; *narrowband white noise* refers to sound waves with equal amplitude at all frequencies within a narrow band of frequencies.)

The narrowband white noise presented along with the target tone is called a *noise masker* and is characterized by its center frequency and its level. With a target tone of 1,000 Hz, the experimenter first presents a noise masker with a 1,000-Hz center frequency, such as a masker covering a range of 900–1,100 Hz. The level of the masker is then

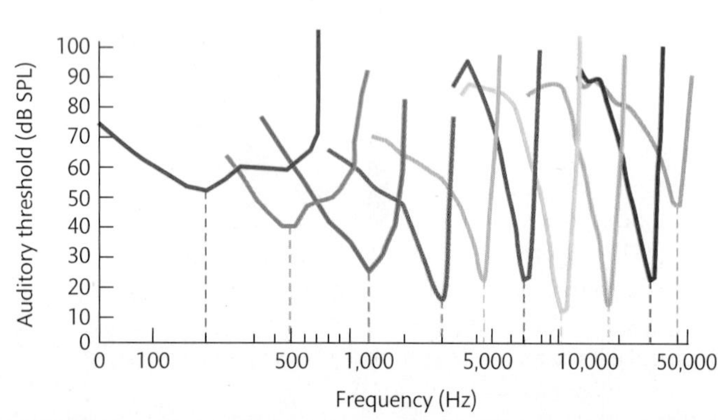

Figure 9.20 Frequency Tuning Curves for 10 Type I Auditory Nerve Fibers Each of the 10 cat auditory nerve fibers represented here has a different characteristic frequency, ranging from around 200 to 40,000 Hz, as indicated by the dotted lines. Each curve shows the sound level required for a tone of a given frequency to evoke an increase in the fiber's firing rate just above baseline. (Adapted from Palmer, 1987, Figure 1.)

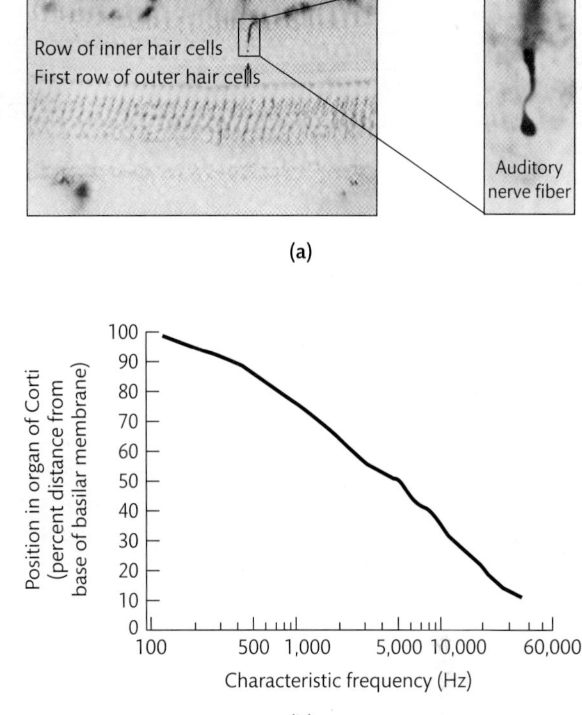

Figure 9.21 Mapping of Type I Auditory Nerve Fibers to Position in the Organ of Corti (a) A cat Type I auditory nerve fiber was labeled with a dye after its characteristic frequency was measured, so the position of the inner hair cell to which the fiber is connected could be determined. (b) A graph developed by applying the process described in (a) to numerous Type I auditory nerve fibers with a wide range of characteristic frequencies. The very regular correspondence between the characteristic frequency of auditory nerve fibers and the position of the connecting inner hair cell in the organ of Corti (measured as a percentage of the distance from the base of the basilar membrane to the apex) provides strong evidence for place coding in frequency representation in the cochlea. (Adapted and photo from Liberman, 1982, Figures 1 and 6.)

adjusted so it just barely prevents the listener from detecting the target tone, a level called the *masked threshold.* The center frequency of the noise masker is then changed in increments across a range of frequencies surrounding the frequency of the target tone, and the masked threshold is determined for each center frequency. Then the whole procedure is repeated for different target tones.

Figure 9.22 shows the results of such an experiment, using six target tones with frequencies of 250–7,000 Hz. As you can see, the lowest-level masked threshold is typically associated with a masker that has a center frequency equal or very nearly equal to the frequency of the target tone, and the masked threshold generally increases as the center frequency of the masker increasingly departs from the frequency of the target tone. For example, with a target tone of 2,000 Hz at a level of about 5 dB SPL (the purple dot in Figure 9.22), the masked threshold of a noise mask with a center frequency of 2,000 Hz is about 20 dB SPL; as the center frequency of the noise masker is changed away from 2,000 Hz, the masked threshold increases (e.g., in order to mask the tone, the level of the masker must be adjusted upward to just under 70 dB SPL for a masker center frequency of 1,000 Hz and to more than 75 dB SPL for a masker center frequency of 3,000 Hz, as shown by the purple curve in Figure 9.22).

Across all target tones, these patterns generate center frequency tuning curves that closely resemble the frequency tuning curves of auditory nerve fibers (e.g., those shown in Figure 9.20), presumably because listeners' perceptual judgments are based on the responses of Type I auditory nerve fibers. That is, when a noise masker has a center frequency at or near the frequency of the target tone, the masker activates the Type I auditory nerve fibers in the region of the basilar membrane with a characteristic frequency corresponding to the frequency of the target tone. Since those nerve fibers are already responding to the noise masker, they can't also indicate the presence of the target tone. But as the center frequency of the masker moves away from the target tone frequency, the auditory nerve fibers in that region are freed up to respond to the target tone. When

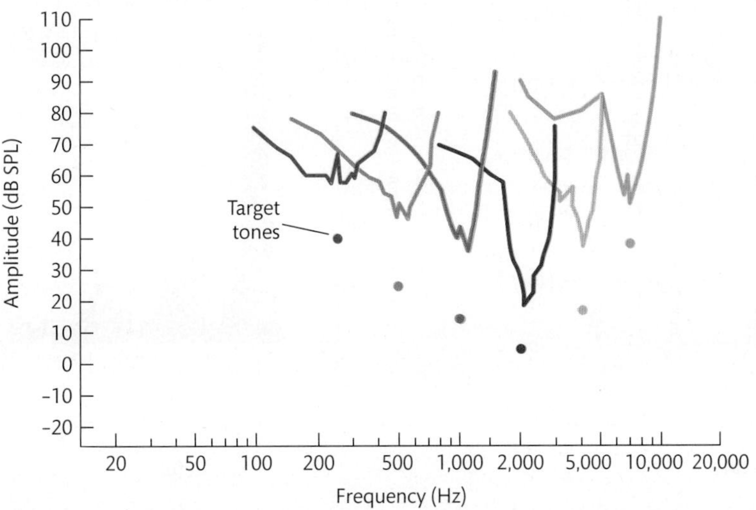

Figure 9.22 Psychophysical Frequency Tuning Curves Listeners were presented with one of six target tones (indicated by the colored dots) with frequencies ranging from 250 to 7,000 Hz, at an amplitude just high enough to make the tone easily detectable against a silent background. Each of the solid lines plots the center frequencies and amplitudes of narrowband white noise maskers that just prevent detection of the corresponding target tone. When the center frequency of a masker is very near the frequency of the target tone, the masker threshold is low—that is, the amplitude of the masker has to be just a few decibels greater than the amplitude of the target tone to prevent detection of the target tone. As the center frequency of the masker gets farther away from the target tone, the masker must be louder to prevent detection of the target tone. The shapes of these psychophysical tuning curves are strikingly similar to the shapes of the physiological frequency tuning curves of individual Type I auditory nerve fibers shown in Figure 9.20. (Based on data from Vogten, 1974.)

the masker is made louder, it begins to activate nearby auditory nerve fibers, including those most sensitive to the target tone. Thus, these psychophysical frequency tuning curves provide supporting evidence for the place code for frequency.

Temporal Code for Frequency

As we mentioned at the beginning of this section, the temporal code for frequency is based on a match between the frequencies in incoming sound waves and the firing rates of Type I auditory nerve fibers. The possibility of representing frequency in this way arises from the fact that the movements of inner hair cell stereocilia are caused by and time locked to the displacements of the basilar membrane, which are themselves time locked to the changes in air pressure of an incoming sound wave.

Consider, for example, an incoming sound wave that consists of a pure tone with a frequency of 500 Hz. This sound wave would make the tympanic membrane vibrate at a rate of 500 vibrations per second, and these vibrations would be transmitted via the ossicles into the cochlear duct, setting up a 500-Hz pressure wave in the perilymph there. This pressure wave would cause the location on the basilar membrane with a characteristic frequency of 500 Hz to be maximally displaced 500 times per second. If the Type I auditory nerve fibers connected to the inner hair cells at that location along the basilar membrane produced one action potential every time the basilar membrane there underwent its peak displacement, then the train of action potentials would have a frequency that matches the sound itself.

Things aren't quite this simple, however. We are able to hear sounds at frequencies approaching 20,000 Hz, but neurons cannot produce action potentials at a rate above a few hundred spikes per second (see the discussion of action potentials in Chapter 1). This means that the simple time-locking mechanism described above cannot be used for frequencies much greater than about 1,000 Hz. However, a time-locking mechanism can work as long as each nerve fiber produces action potentials in phase with the incoming sound stimulus—that is, as long as action potentials are produced at the same time as the peaks in the incoming sound wave, even if not at every peak. This is illustrated in Figure 9.23a, which shows the hypothetical collective activity of a population of such auditory nerve fibers. Not every fiber produces an action potential at *every* peak of the wave, but when a fiber does fire, it's at a peak. Physiological evidence for this idea can be seen in Figure 9.23b, which shows that a population of cat Type I auditory nerve fibers tended to fire in phase with a 416-Hz tone, with spikes occurring mostly at the peaks of the sound wave.

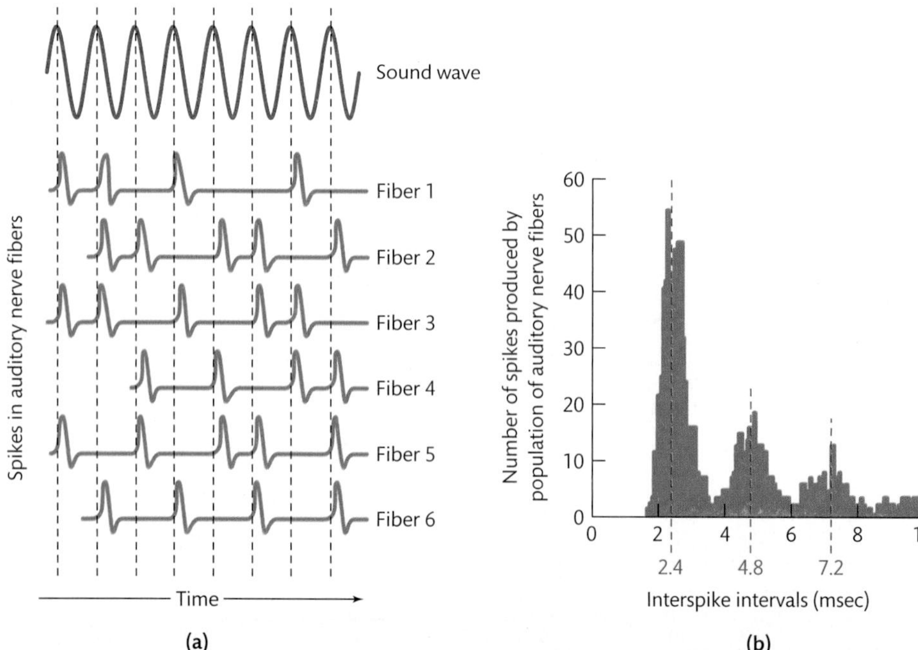

Figure 9.23 Phase Synchronization of Type I Auditory Nerve Fibers (a) Action potentials (spikes) in auditory nerve fibers are time locked to displacements of the basilar membrane, which are time locked to peaks in the incoming sound wave. When a fiber responds, the spike is (very nearly) in phase with the sound wave—that is, it occurs at the same time as a sound wave peak. Across this hypothetical population of fibers, spikes are produced in bursts that are synchronized with the sound wave—for example, fibers 1, 3, and 5 fire in phase with the leftmost peak of the sound wave, and fibers 2, 4, 5, and 6 fire in phase with the rightmost peak. (b) A population of cat Type I auditory nerve fibers was exposed to a pure tone of 416 Hz, in which the peaks of the sound wave are separated by 2.4 msec. This histogram shows the number of spikes that were separated in time by various interspike intervals. The spikes tend to be separated by integer multiples of 2.4 msec ($2.4 \times 2 = 4.8$; $2.4 \times 3 = 7.2$), in phase with the peaks of the sound wave. (Adapted from Clark, 2006, Figure 4.)

In experiments with squirrel monkeys, it was found that this type of phase synchronization breaks down for frequencies above about 4,000–5,000 Hz because the precision of the phase locking is not great enough (Rose et al., 1967). To see why, look again at Figure 9.23a and imagine that the peaks of the sound wave are much closer together, as they would be for a higher-frequency sound. In that case, if the nerve fibers weren't firing precisely in phase with the peaks, it's likely that multiple fibers—just by chance—would often be firing at about the same time between the peaks, giving the auditory system imprecise information about the timing of the peaks.

Thus, a temporal code, with phase locking, can precisely represent frequencies up to about 5,000 Hz, while the place code described in the previous section provides the sharpest representations for frequencies above about 5,000 Hz (see the discussion of Figure 9.20). Together, these two codes provide a robust representation of frequency across the entire range that humans can hear.

Demonstration 9.4 Phase Synchronization of Auditory Nerve Fibers Explore animations showing how the responses of a population of auditory nerve fibers can provide a temporal code for the frequency of a sound.

Amplitude Representation

Generally speaking, the rate of action potentials produced by auditory nerve fibers increases with the amplitude of the incoming sound wave. However, the relationship between loudness and neural firing rate is not a simple, linear mapping, mainly because the range of amplitudes that we can hear and discriminate—called the **dynamic range** of hearing—is much greater than the range of firing rates of any one auditory nerve fiber. That is, we can discriminate sounds that differ over a range of more than 1 million micropascals (see Figure 9.4), but auditory nerve fibers can differ in firing rate over a range of only a few hundred spikes per second. That means the firing rate of any one nerve fiber (or some small number of nerve fibers) is not sufficient to represent all the different amplitudes we can discriminate.

dynamic range The range of amplitudes that can be heard and discriminated; when applied to an individual auditory nerve fiber, the range of amplitudes over which the firing rate of the fiber changes.

This issue should sound familiar, because we encountered a similar problem in our discussion of the perception of brightness by the visual system. We can discriminate small variations in light intensity over an enormous range, but any given retinal ganglion cell operates over a much more limited range, with a maximum firing rate of about 100 spikes/sec.

How does the auditory system cope with the limited range of firing rates of auditory nerve fibers, given the need to represent sounds with a much greater number of discriminable amplitudes? One way is based on the increase in the number of nerve fibers that respond to a tone of a given frequency as its amplitude increases (Phillips, 1987). This is illustrated in Figure 9.24, which shows how some of the Type I auditory nerve fibers from Figure 9.20 respond to tones of different frequencies as the amplitude of the tones increases:

- For a 500-Hz tone, fiber B begins firing when the tone reaches an amplitude of about 37 dB SPL, fiber A at about 55 dB SPL, and fiber C at about 58 dB SPL.
- For a 5,000-Hz tone, fiber E begins firing at about 48 dB SPL, fiber F at about 69 dB SPL, and fiber G at about 81 dB SPL.

The increase in the number of nerve fibers responding to a given tone as the tone's amplitude increases is based on the fact that an individual nerve fiber doesn't respond just to tones with the fiber's characteristic frequency; rather, each fiber responds to a range of frequencies. But as shown in Figure 9.24, as the tone increasingly departs from the fiber's

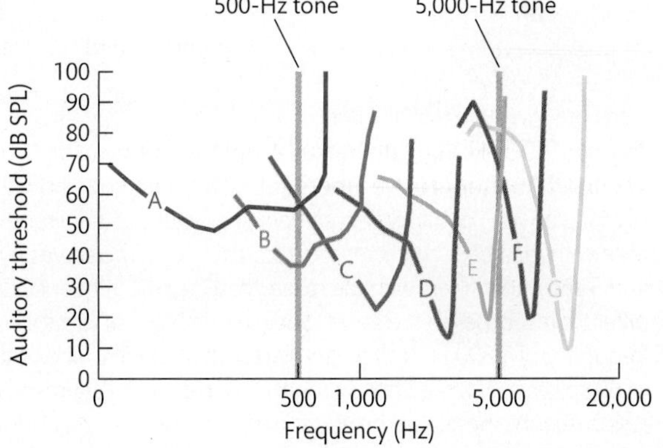

Figure 9.24 Patterns of Auditory Nerve Fiber Responses to Tones with Different Amplitudes The frequency tuning curves of seven of the Type I auditory nerve fibers shown in Figure 9.20 illustrate how the auditory system represents amplitude via the patterns of responses to tones with a given frequency. Here, for example, if fiber B is the only fiber responding when a 500-Hz tone is presented, the auditory system "knows" the tone has an amplitude of more than about 37 dB SPL and less than about 55 dB SPL, because if the tone was below 37 dB SPL, fiber B would not respond, and if it was above 55 dB SPL, then fibers A and C would also respond. The amplitude of a 5,000-Hz tone would be represented in much the same way. In reality, of course, many more fibers fire in response to a given tone than are shown here, giving the auditory system enough information to discriminate very small differences in amplitude.

characteristic frequency, it typically must have a higher amplitude to produce a response. For a very low level tone, only a small subpopulation of auditory nerve fibers will fire at all—and these will be the fibers with characteristic frequencies near the tone's frequency.

The auditory system can use patterns like those shown in Figure 9.24 to determine the amplitude of sounds of different frequencies because such patterns include the responses of hundreds or thousands of auditory nerve fibers that fire in response to a given tone. The number of possible patterns of different fibers firing at different rates is enormous, and this enables the auditory system to discriminate very small differences in amplitude.

Another property of Type I auditory nerve fibers that contributes to the auditory system's ability to discriminate sounds with different amplitudes is that fibers can differ in how they respond to tones that match their characteristic frequency. This is illustrated in Figure 9.25a, which shows the responses of five auditory nerve fibers to tones that match their characteristic frequency (note that fibers 4 and 5 have the same characteristic frequency of 1,800 Hz).

For any given nerve fiber, there is a range of low-amplitude (quiet) sounds that evoke no increase in firing rate—the fiber simply continues to fire at its baseline rate in response to those sounds. In Figure 9.25a, the baseline firing rate of each fiber corresponds to the lower endpoint of the curve—for example, fiber 3, with a characteristic frequency of 822 Hz, has a baseline firing rate of less than 10 spikes/sec. Fiber 3 doesn't begin increasing its firing rate in response to an 822-Hz tone until the tone reaches the fiber's threshold for that tone—an amplitude of about 33 dB SPL. After the tone's amplitude passes the fiber's threshold, the firing rate increases steadily as the amplitude increases, until the firing rate reaches the fiber's *saturation level*—that is, its maximum firing rate—after which the firing rate doesn't increase no matter how loud the tone becomes. The saturation level of fiber 3 is about 95 spikes/sec, which it reaches when

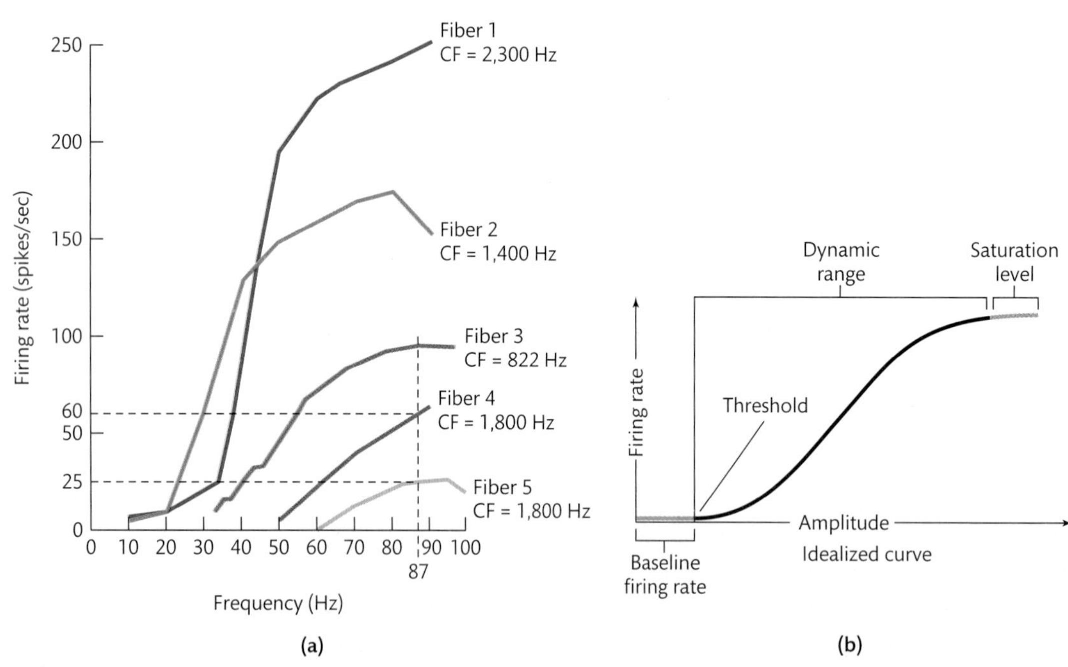

Figure 9.25 Firing Rate Versus Amplitude Curves for Actual and Idealized Auditory Nerve Fibers (a) Each curve shows how the firing rate of a single Type I auditory nerve fiber varies with the amplitude of a pure tone with the fiber's characteristic frequency (CF). The curves for fibers 4 and 5 show that fibers with the same characteristic frequency can have different responses to the same tone (i.e., in response to a tone with a frequency of 1,800 Hz and an amplitude of 87 dB SPL, fiber 4 fires at a rate of 60 spikes/sec, while fiber 5 fires at 25 spikes/sec). Patterns of differential responses like these give the auditory system information about the amplitude of an incoming sound. (b) This idealized curve represents how a typical auditory nerve fiber responds to a tone with its characteristic frequency as the amplitude of the tone increases. An auditory nerve fiber has a baseline firing rate (the fiber's response in complete silence), a threshold level (the minimum amplitude of a given tone required to produce a response above baseline), a dynamic range over which the fiber's firing rate increases as the tone's amplitude increases, and a saturation level (the amplitude at which the fiber begins firing at its maximum rate). (Adapted from Rose et al., 1971, Figure 9.)

the amplitude of an 822-Hz tone increases to about 87 dB SPL. The range of amplitudes over which the nerve fiber's firing rate increases from baseline to saturation is called that fiber's *dynamic range* (thus, the dynamic range of fiber 3 is about 33–87 dB SPL). The curve in Figure 9.25b shows that, when firing rate is plotted against amplitude across a large number of fibers, the resulting curves tend to be S-shaped, although individual fibers like those in Figure 9.25a can generate curves that depart somewhat from that idealized shape.

As you can see in Figure 9.25a, different auditory nerve fibers have different thresholds and different dynamic ranges. Just as the auditory system can use the patterns of response of nerve fibers with different characteristic frequencies to gauge the amplitude of an incoming sound (as illustrated in Figure 9.24), so it can also use the patterns illustrated in Figure 9.25a to gauge amplitude—for example, if fibers 4 and 5 are firing at rates of about 60 and 25 spikes/sec, respectively, the auditory system has good evidence that the incoming sound has an amplitude of about 87 dB SPL.

Check Your Understanding

9.15 How do physiological frequency tuning curves of auditory nerve fibers and of the basilar membrane provide support for the place code for frequency?

9.16 In a noise-masking experiment that generates psychophysical frequency tuning curves, what is the relationship between the frequency of the target tone, detection of the target tone, and the center frequency of the noise masker?

9.17 How does phase synchronization within a population of auditory nerve fibers play a role in the temporal code for frequency?

9.18 True or false? Two factors that the auditory system uses to represent the amplitude of a sound are (a) the number of auditory nerve fibers that respond to the sound and (b) the extent to which individual fibers respond to the sound.

Disorders of Audition

The delicate structures and neural pathways of the auditory system sometimes stop working properly, leading to **hearing impairment**—a decrease in a person's ability to detect or discriminate sounds, compared to the ability of a healthy young adult—including **tinnitus**, a persistent perception of sound in one's ears, such as a ringing or buzzing, not caused by any actual sound. Very few of us have "perfect" hearing, for a variety of reasons, and as we will see, some kinds of hearing disorders are preventable—and many are treatable.

hearing impairment A decrease in a person's ability to detect or discriminate sounds, compared to the ability of a healthy young adult.

tinnitus A persistent perception of sound, such as a ringing or buzzing, not caused by any actual sound.

Hearing Tests and Audiograms

Audiologists test people's hearing with an instrument called an **audiometer**, which presents pure tones with known frequency and amplitude to the right or left ear using high-quality headphones, when the person is in a quiet environment (for very precise measurements, the audiologist may have the person sit in a sound-attenuating booth). In effect, the audiologist uses the staircase method (see Chapter 1) to estimate the person's absolute threshold for each of six to eight frequencies, ranging from 250 to 8,000 Hz.

The result of such a test is an **audiogram**, a graphical depiction of auditory sensitivity (expressed as *hearing level*) compared to that of a standard listener at each of the tested frequencies for each ear (see Figure 9.26). By convention, the hearing level is measured relative to the audibility curve of the standard listener; so the standard listener would have a hearing level of 0 dB SPL at every frequency. If the listener can just detect a tone of, say, 4,000 Hz at about the same amplitude required for detection by the standard listener, then the person is said to have hearing in the normal range in the tested ear at that frequency. If the listener can detect the tone only if it's 50 dB louder than the level required by the standard listener, then the person is said to have a 50-dB hearing loss

audiometer An instrument that presents pure tones with known frequency and amplitude to the right or left ear; used in estimating the listener's absolute threshold for specific frequencies and to construct an audiogram.

audiogram A graphical depiction of auditory sensitivity to specific frequencies, compared to the sensitivity of a standard listener; used to characterize possible hearing loss.

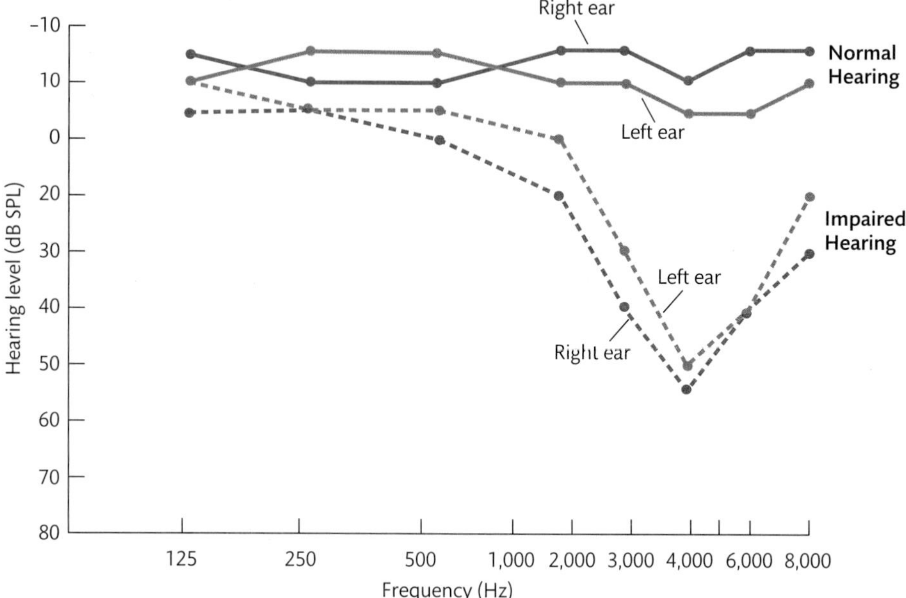

Figure 9.26 Audiogram Hearing level in each ear of a listener with hearing in the normal range compared with that of a listener whose hearing has been impaired by prolonged exposure to high-intensity, high-frequency noise. Normal hearing—the auditory sensitivity of a "standard listener," a typical young adult—is 0 dB SPL at each frequency The points plotted show how much louder (or softer) than normal a tone must be for the listener to just detect it. For example, for a 3,000-Hz tone, the listener with impaired hearing has a hearing loss of just under 40 dB in the right ear and just under 30 dB in the left ear. It is typical that the two ears have similar but not identical audiograms, due to normal random variations in function.

in the tested ear at 4,000 Hz (as in the impaired left ear in Figure 9.26). Whatever the degree of hearing loss, hearing impairments can be broadly organized into two general categories, depending on how they arise: conductive hearing impairments and sensorineural hearing impairments.

Conductive Hearing Impairments

conductive hearing impairments Hearing impairments characterized by a loss of sound conduction to the cochlea, as a result of problems in the outer or middle ear.

Conductive hearing impairments—impairments characterized by a loss of sound conduction to the cochlea—arise as a result of problems in the outer or middle ear, including a blockage of the auditory canal, a perforated or torn tympanic membrane ("punctured eardrum"), and damage to the ossicles. Conductive hearing loss can also be caused by otosclerosis, a growth of bone in the middle ear that interferes with the movement of the ossicles; in advanced stages, the most effective treatment is to remove the stapes and replace it with an artificial prosthetic stapes. Temporary conductive hearing loss can accompany inflammation of the middle ear, a condition called *otitis media* or, more commonly, an *earache*. Another fairly common cause of conductive hearing loss is a buildup of cerumen (commonly called *earwax*) that partially or almost completely blocks the auditory canal. In some cases, a physician may need to remove an excessive buildup of cerumen. (The use of cotton swabs is generally not recommended, as this usually just pushes the cerumen more deeply into the canal.)

Conductive hearing loss is usually not what is called *profound* (i.e., a loss of 90 dB or more), because even if the ear canal is blocked or the ossicles are not working properly, sound is still conducted to the cochlea via vibrations in the bones in which the cochlea is embedded. The ability to hear and understand most sounds can often be maintained in people with conductive hearing impairments by suitably amplifying sounds, as with a hearing aid.

Sensorineural Hearing Impairments

sensorineural hearing impairments Hearing impairments caused by damage to the cochlea, the auditory nerve, or the auditory areas or pathways of the brain

Sensorineural hearing impairments arise through damage to the cochlea, the auditory nerve, or the auditory areas or pathways of the brain (these areas and pathways are discussed in Chapter 10). Such impairments can be congenital (i.e., present at birth) or acquired and can range from minor deficits in hearing some sound frequencies to profound, nearly total deafness. Perhaps the most significant consequence of profound hearing loss is its effect on a person's ability to communicate with others through spoken language. Congenital deafness occurs in about 1 of 1,000 births and is usually due to a recessive gene inherited from both parents (Petit et al., 2001). Young infants are now routinely tested for hearing impairments so that early intervention can be used to prevent delayed language acquisition. Acquired sensorineural hearing impairments are much more common and have many causes, the most common of which are the effects of normal aging and the effects of exposure to loud noise.

Age-Related Hearing Impairment

Many environmental and biological factors contribute to age-related hearing impairment, or presbycusis. Among the most significant of these is lifelong exposure to noise; other factors include exposure to certain industrial chemicals, smoking and alcohol abuse, diabetes and cardiovascular disease, head trauma, and poor nutrition. Recent evidence also suggests that there may be a genetic component (Van Eyken et al., 2007). Figure 9.27 shows the median hearing loss for men and women at ages ranging from 20 to 80 years; the loss is most pronounced at higher frequencies and is greater for men than for women.

Noise-Induced Hearing Impairments

As discussed earlier in this chapter (and illustrated in Figure 9.4), prolonged exposure to sounds with an amplitude greater than about 85 dB SPL is likely to cause noise-induced hearing loss; when sounds reach a level of 120 dB SPL or higher, even short-term exposure, besides being painful, is likely to cause hearing loss. The U.S. Occupational Safety and Health Administration (OSHA) has established 85 dB SPL as the maximum safe level for daily, eight-hour exposure. Beyond that level and duration, OSHA requires industries to either reduce the duration of exposure or provide hearing protection to ensure that workers are not at risk for permanent hearing impairment. Of course, OSHA can't regulate the behavior of private citizens as they mow their lawns, attend stock car races, or listen to loud music, but anyone who values their hearing would do well to heed these guidelines in the course of their everyday lives.

Noise-induced hearing loss can be temporary and reversible or permanent, depending on the noise level and its duration. Even a single brief but very high intensity impulse, like a gunshot or a firecracker explosion—either of which can reach a level of 150 dB SPL or more—can cause permanent hearing loss across certain ranges of frequencies. Prolonged exposure over years and decades to noise levels in the range of 90–120 dB SPL can also cause permanent hearing loss. Noise-induced hearing loss is often maximal at 4,000 Hz and less severe at 8,000 Hz, leading to a V-shaped audiogram, like the dashed lines in Figure 9.26 (Møller, 2006). This is different from the pattern seen in age-related hearing loss, which tends to become progressively more severe as the frequency increases (see Figure 9.27).

There are several ways in which the delicate cells and membranes of the cochlea can be damaged by loud noise (Henderson et al., 2006). One broad category of such causes is mechanical damage due to very high amplitude pressure waves pulsing through the cochlea. Such waves can tear the basilar membrane, separating it from the walls of the cochlea, or can damage outer hair cells by pulling their stereocilia out of their insertion points in the tectorial membrane or by breaking the tip links between stereocilia.

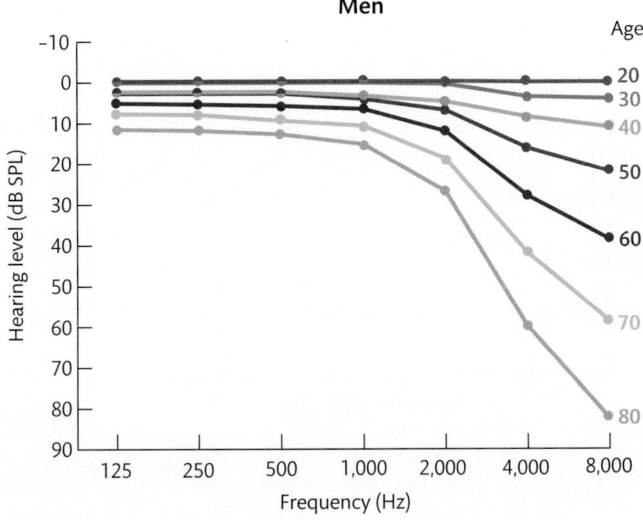

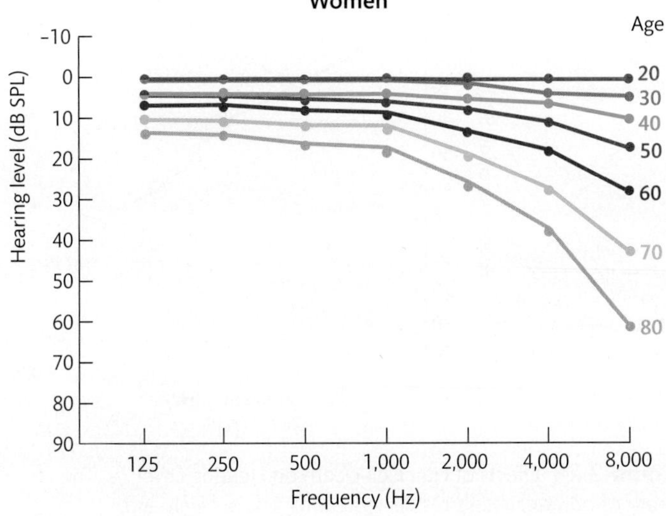

Figure 9.27 Age-Related Hearing Impairment These audiograms show median hearing level as a function of frequency for men and women aged 20 to 80 years. As expected, 20-year-old adults have unimpaired hearing levels—that is, a hearing level of 0 dB SPL at every frequency. As people age, the sound level required to just barely detect tones increases for all frequencies, but particularly for higher frequencies. For example, for 80-year-old men, the median hearing loss for 8,000-Hz tones is more than 80 dB.

Another category of cochlear damage is hair cell death, which can take hours or days to occur following noise exposure. Specific causes of such cell death include:

- Excitotoxicity, in which excessive amounts of the neurotransmitter glutamate are released, causing swelling in and damage to auditory nerve fibers, with death of the hair cells to which the fibers connect.
- Reduced cochlear blood flow due to mechanical damage to the wall of the cochlea, which can kill hair cells.
- Production of oxygen-based free radicals, molecules that can destabilize other molecules, damaging tissues and causing hair cells to die.

When outer hair cells die, their critical amplification function is lost, significantly reducing auditory sensitivity at the frequencies corresponding to the positions of the dead hair cells along the basilar membrane; when inner hair cells also die, hearing loss is even more dramatic. Figure 9.28 shows the hearing loss associated with death of just outer hair cells (Figure 9.28a) versus loss associated with death of both outer and inner hair cells (Figure 9.28b).

The fact that cochlear damage can evolve over days or weeks means that even after the temporary effects of noise exposure wear off, a gradual, almost unnoticeable loss in sensitivity can occur over time.

How can noise-induced hearing loss be prevented? Some contributing factors aren't avoidable, such as exposure to unexpected noises like the sudden onset of a jackhammer on the street or a nearby clap of thunder. However, many loud noises are quite predictable, and their effects on hearing loss are entirely avoidable—for example, by using hearing protection such as earplugs or earmuffs when operating a lawnmower or a chain saw or when banging away with a hammer and by keeping the volume at a safe level when you listen to recorded music. Earplugs, typically made of elastic foam, are inserted into the ear canal and are usually

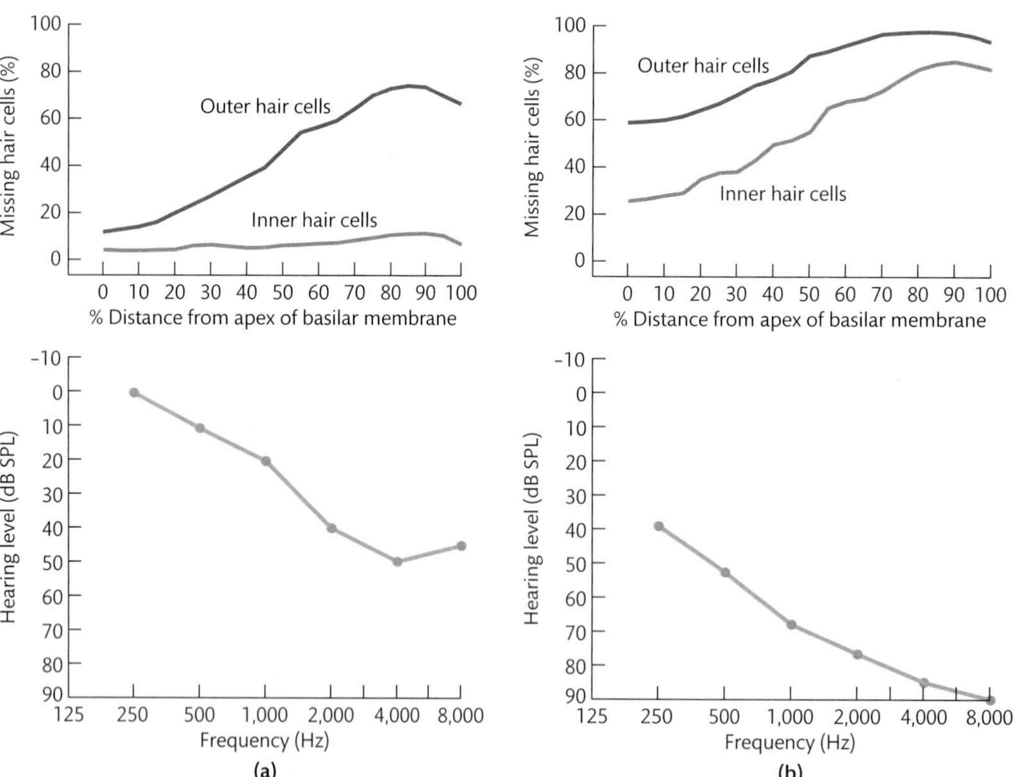

Figure 9.28 Effects of Hair Cell Death on Hearing Level (a) The death of outer hair cells results in hearing loss at levels and frequencies corresponding to the degree of loss at different positions along the basilar membrane. In this case, there has been extensive damage to the outer hair cells at the base of the membrane, the end that normally responds to high-frequency sounds. (b) Extensive death of both outer and inner hair cells along the entire length of the basilar membrane (with the percentage of missing hair cells increasing with distance from the apex) results in correspondingly extensive hearing loss, with greater loss at higher frequencies. (Based on data from research with chinchillas in Henderson et al., 2006.)

most effective in protecting against low-frequency noises. Earmuffs, which cover the entire outer ear and are held in place with an adjustable band, are usually most effective in protecting against high-frequency noises. Earplugs or earmuffs can reduce noise levels by 15–30 dB; when used together, protection is increased by another 10–15 dB.

Tinnitus

More than 50 million Americans experience some degree of tinnitus—the perception of a sound in the absence of sound waves in the environment—and more than 5% of adults over age 50 have the condition severely enough that it can cause difficulty falling asleep (Nondahl et al., 2002). The sound experienced can range from a barely perceptible hiss or ringing to an intense roar, can be perceived in one or both ears, and can be intermittent or continuous. Mild cases may only be slightly annoying, but severe cases can be debilitating, interfering with the normal activities of daily life. In some cases, tinnitus leads to depression.

The causes of tinnitus are variable and still poorly understood (Langguth et al., 2007). They include damage to the cochlea, irritation of or pressure on the auditory nerve by a blood vessel or a tumor, and changes in neural circuits within the auditory cortex. Tinnitus is also often associated with noise-induced hearing loss, although there is no clear correlation between the severity of tinnitus and the magnitude of the hearing loss (Møller, 2006).

The treatments for tinnitus are equally variable, and not surprisingly, no single treatment works in all cases. Various drugs are aimed at reducing neural activity in the auditory nerve or in the auditory cortex; hearing aids allow desirable sounds like speech to compete more effectively with the interference of tinnitus; and electrical stimulation of the auditory nerve or magnetic stimulation of the auditory cortex is aimed at reducing the excitability of these parts of the auditory system.

Check Your Understanding

9.19 What does an audiogram show?

9.20 What is the difference between conductive hearing impairments and sensorineural hearing impairments, and what are the most common causes of sensorineural hearing impairments?

9.21 Briefly describe the two main types of cochlear damage due to loud noises.

APPLICATIONS Cochlear Implants

Cochlear implants are devices designed mainly to enable deaf individuals to hear spoken language, as the inability to communicate verbally is clearly the most distressing and debilitating aspect of deafness. As illustrated in Figure 9.29, a cochlear implant has both external and internal components. The external components consist of a directional microphone, a sound processor (a tiny computer), and a transmitter placed on the surface of the scalp. The internal components are a combination receiver–stimulator surgically implanted in the mastoid bone of the skull (behind the ear) and an electrode system that starts from the receiver–stimulator, enters the cochlea via the round window, and then spirals around the cochlea inside the cochlear duct.

The microphone is typically placed above the ear and pointed forward, to pick up sounds from in front of the head, as listeners typically face the talker they are trying to understand during normal conversation. The sounds picked up by the microphone are sent to the sound processor, which performs a Fourier analysis, continuously calculating how the amplitudes of various frequencies in the sound are varying over time. The sound processor translates this information into streams of voltages that are sent to the transmitter, which in turn sends them via radio waves to the receiver–stimulator. The receiver–stimulator then sends the streams of voltages into the electrode system that has been inserted into the cochlea.

The electrode system consists of equally spaced bands of metal separated by an insulator, as shown in the blowup and the X-ray at the right of Figure 9.29. Each band is a channel that can be separately activated by one of the streams of voltages to stimulate auditory nerve fibers at a particular location along the cochlea.

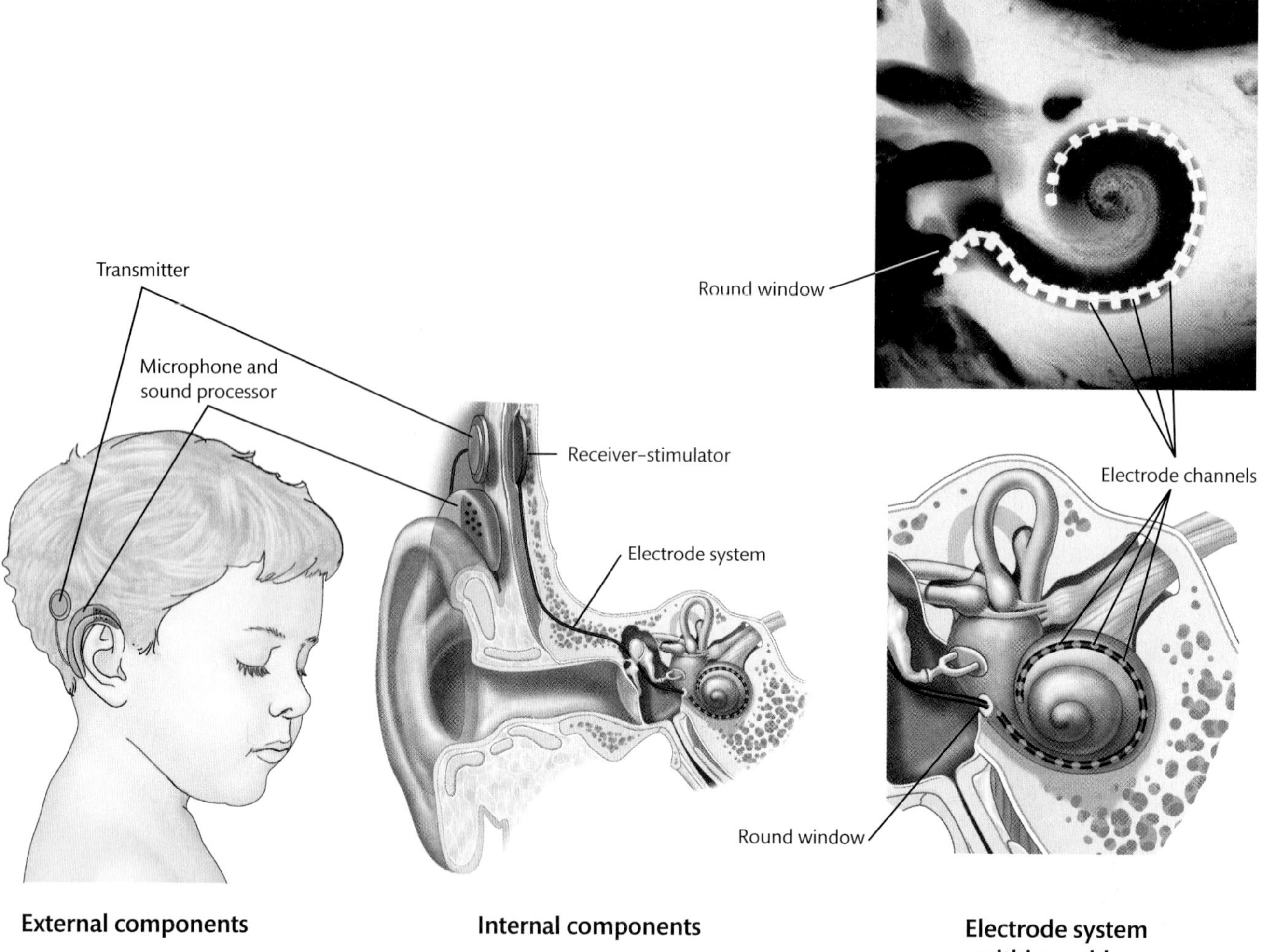

Figure 9.29 Cochlear Implant A cochlear implant has external and internal components. A directional microphone worn on the ear picks up environmental sounds and sends them to a sound processor (a small computer) that performs a Fourier analysis of the sounds and translates this into streams of voltages corresponding to the frequencies and amplitudes making up the incoming sounds. The voltage streams are sent to a small transmitter that sends them via radio waves to the implanted receiver-stimulator. The receiver-stimulator sends the voltages to the electrode system that has been inserted into the cochlea. Different voltage streams stimulate different electrode channels that then stimulate different auditory nerve fibers at spaced locations along the cochlea. The locations stimulated are essentially those at which the basilar membrane has characteristic frequencies corresponding to the frequencies present in the sounds. The X-ray at the upper right shows the electrode array after it has been inserted into the cochlea. (Adapted and photo from Clark, 2003, Figure 8.43.)

The electrode system must be inserted far enough into the cochlea to stimulate auditory nerve fibers with characteristic frequencies that span the range of frequencies in most speech sounds—typically, an insertion depth of 20–25 mm. In order to optimize the person's ability to hear and understand speech, both place coding and temporal coding are used to represent frequency (Clark, 2006). For medium to high frequencies, which are most important for understanding consonant sounds, a place code is used—auditory nerve fibers at different locations are stimulated with the appropriate stream of voltages. For lower frequencies, which are important for representing vowels and other speech sounds that involve vocal cord vibrations, a temporal code is used: auditory nerve fibers are stimulated with bursts of current presented at a rate that matches the frequency of the sound itself. Thus, a sound with a frequency of 200 Hz would be represented by current bursts directed at the appropriate location and presented at a rate of 200 bursts/sec.

Methods for stimulating the auditory nerve fibers so as to maximize the ability to perceive speech sounds began to be developed in the 1980s. Two of these methods—Multipeak and SPEAK—are illustrated in Figure 9.30. The sound spectrogram in the figure shows the frequencies over time for the spoken word "choice," with the relative amplitude of each frequency at each moment indicated by relative brightness. The initial burst of relatively high frequencies (2,000–5,000 Hz) at relatively low amplitudes corresponds to the "ch" sound;

next come three simultaneous frequency bands corresponding to the vowel sound "oi," one band at 0–1,500 Hz (high amplitude) and the other two bands at about 2,200 and 3,200 Hz (both very low amplitude); and this is followed by a final high-frequency, low-amplitude burst between about 3,500 and 5,000 Hz, corresponding to the final "s" sound.

The two electrodograms in Figure 9.30—graphs of the voltages sent through each of the 20 electrode channels in a cochlear implant over time, with the intensity of the current indicated by relative brightness—show how the sounds in "choice" are represented by the Multipeak and SPEAK methods. Each electrode stimulates auditory nerve fibers at a different location along the cochlea. Tests with adults who lost their hearing relatively later in life (after they had learned to perceive spoken language) showed that the Multipeak approach produced good results, with comprehension rates as high as 60% in one study (Hollow et al., 1995); and results with the SPEAK strategy were even better (Clark, 2006), as indicated in Figure 9.30 by the more nuanced representation of the sound spectrogram by the SPEAK electrodogram than by the Multipeak electrodogram.

A critical question is whether children born severely or profoundly deaf—that is, with little or virtually no hearing—can learn to understand spoken language with a cochlear

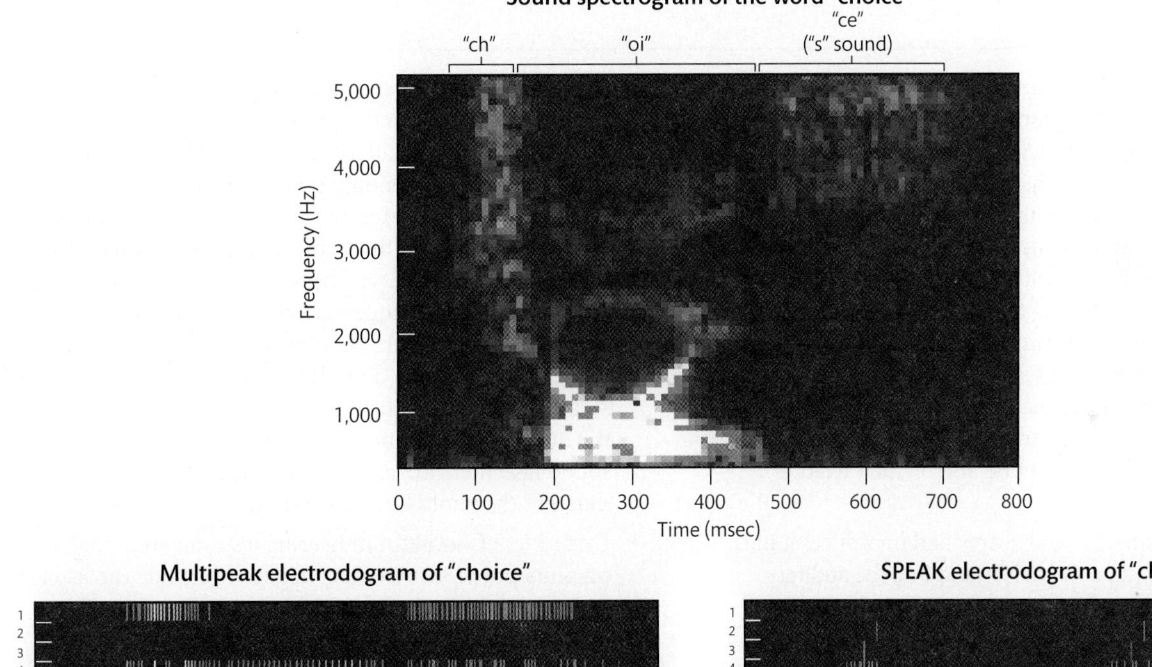

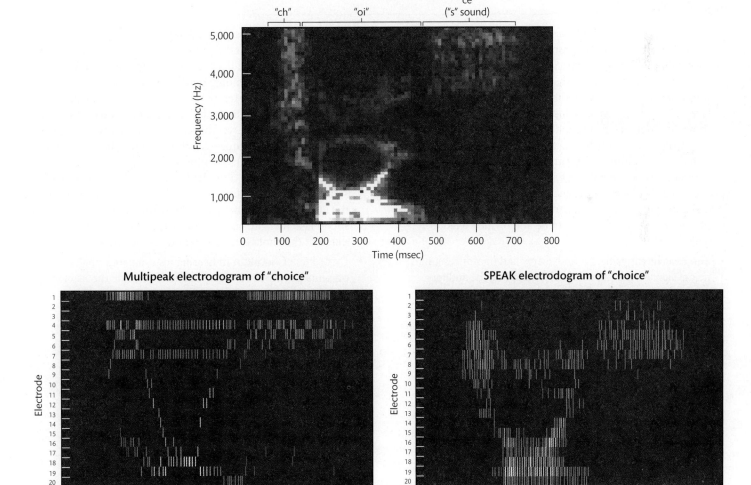

Figure 9.30 Multipeak and SPEAK Methods of Stimulating Auditory Nerve Fibers in a Cochlear Implant The sound spectrogram shows the frequencies present in the sound of the spoken word "choice" over time; brightness indicates relative amplitude. The electrodograms show the voltages sent through each of 20 electrode channels in a cochlear implant over time; brightness indicates the relative strength of the current. Electrode 1 stimulates auditory nerve fibers at a cochlear location associated with higher-frequency speech sounds and electrode 20 at a location associated with the lowest frequencies. (Adapted and photo from Clark, 2003, Figure 8.43.)

implant. For many patients, the answer is yes (Clark et al., 1987), with the age at which the patient receives the implant being among the most important factors (Clark, 2006). The brain is highly plastic very early in life, ready to learn language in a way that the adult brain cannot duplicate. If this critical period can be enriched with the sounds of spoken language via a cochlear implant, the child has a good chance of adapting to the stimulation and learning to understand speech. Current medical practice is to put a cochlear implant in place within the first year of life if possible.

Check Your Understanding

9.22 Explain why a person with a typical cochlear implant might have trouble hearing/discriminating sounds with frequencies much higher than 5,000 Hz.

9.23 Look back at Figure 9.30 and describe how the electrodograms are related to the spectrogram.

9.24 For children born severely or profoundly deaf, why do cochlear implants work better when implanted at an earlier age?

SUMMARY

- **Sound** Sound is a wave of pressure changes in a medium such as air, propagating outward from a source such as a vibrating tuning fork. The related physical and perceptual dimensions of sound are frequency and pitch, amplitude and loudness, and waveform and timbre. An audibility curve shows the audibility threshold of any given frequency. Equal loudness contours show the amplitude that sounds of different frequencies must have to be perceived as having the same loudness. A periodic sound with a complex waveform can be decomposed by Fourier analysis into a Fourier spectrum, the combination of pure tones of different frequencies with different amplitudes making up the sound. Timbre depends mainly on which harmonics are present in the sound and on their relative amplitudes.
- **The Ear** The ear gathers sound energy and transduces it into neural signals. The pinna funnels sound into the auditory canal and onto the tympanic membrane. The vibration of the tympanic membrane transfers the sound energy to the ossicles, which then transmit the energy onto the oval window, which sends the energy into the cochlea. The acoustic reflex helps protect the auditory system from very loud sounds by dampening the movements of the ossicles. The Eustachian tube can be opened to maintain normal air pressure in the middle ear. The cochlea is partitioned into three chambers—the vestibular canal, cochlear duct, and tympanic canal. The basilar membrane separates the cochlear duct and the tympanic canal and is thicker, narrower, and stiffer at the base than at the apex. Pressure waves in the perilymph displace the basilar membrane to different degrees at different locations, depending on the characteristic frequency at each location. The organ of Corti, resting on the basilar membrane within the cochlear duct, contains the structures involved in auditory transduction, including the inner and outer hair cells.
- **Neural Representation of Frequency and Amplitude** Frequency is represented by both a place code and a temporal code. The place code is based on the displacement of the basilar membrane to different degrees at different locations, resulting in the production of action potentials by Type I auditory nerve fibers connected to inner hair cells at those locations, depending on the characteristic frequency at each location. The temporal code is based on a match between frequencies in the incoming sound wave and spike timing in auditory nerve fibers. Place coding provides good representations of frequencies above about 5,000 Hz, while temporal coding works best for lower frequencies. Amplitude representation is based on the fact that as the amplitude of a sound increases, the firing rate of auditory nerve fibers and the number of auditory nerve fibers firing in response to the sound also increase, and on the fact that different fibers have different thresholds and different dynamic ranges.
- **Disorders of Audition** In hearing tests, an audiometer presents pure tones to a listener, to determine the listener's auditory sensitivity across a range of frequencies. The result is depicted by an audiogram, which shows the degree of hearing loss at each frequency, compared to a standard listener. Conductive hearing impairments arise because of problems in the outer or middle ear, with a loss of sound conduction to the cochlea. Sensorineural hearing impairments arise through damage to the cochlea, the auditory nerve, or the auditory areas or pathways of the brain and are typically age related or noise induced. Exposure to loud noise can damage the cochlea mechanically and by causing the death of hair cells. Tinnitus—the perception of sound in the absence of actual sound—is common and can be severe enough to disrupt everyday life. Various causes and treatments of tinnitus have been identified.
- **Applications: Cochlear Implants** Cochlear implants are designed primarily to help deaf or severely hearing impaired individuals hear speech. The external components of a cochlear implant consist of a microphone, sound processor, and transmitter; the internal components consist of a

receiver–stimulator and an electrode system that spirals around the cochlea and stimulates selected locations along the basilar membrane, using both place coding and temporal coding. For children born deaf, cochlear implants tend to work better when implanted at an earlier age, during the critical period for acquiring language.

KEY TERMS

acoustic reflex (p. 299)
amplitude (p. 290)
anvil, see **incus**
audibility curve (p. 292)
audiogram (p. 313)
audiometer (p. 313)
auditory canal (p. 298)
auditory nerve (p. 303)
basilar membrane (p. 301)
characteristic frequency (p. 302)
cochlea (p. 300)
cochlear duct (p. 300)
conductive hearing impairments (p. 314)
cycle (p. 289)
decibels (dB) (p. 290)
dynamic range (p. 311)
eardrum, see **tympanic membrane**
equal loudness contour (p. 293)
Eustachian tube (p. 300)
Fourier analysis (p. 294)
Fourier spectrum (p. 294)
frequency (p. 289)
fundamental frequency (p. 294)
hammer, see **malleus**
harmonic (p. 295)
hearing impairment (p. 313)
helicotrema (p. 301)
hertz (Hz) (p. 289)
incus (or *anvil*) (p. 298)
inner hair cells (p. 303)
loudness (p. 290)
malleus (or *hammer*) (p. 298)
motile response (p. 305)
organ of Corti (p. 303)
ossicles (p. 298)
outer hair cells (p. 303)
oval window (p. 298)
periodic sound waves (p. 289)
pinna (p. 298)
pitch (p. 289)
place code (p. 307)
pure tone (p. 289)
round window (p. 301)
sensorineural hearing impairments (p. 314)
sound waves (p. 289)
stapes (or *stirrup*) (p. 298)
stereocilia (p. 303)
stirrup, see **stapes**
tectorial membrane (p. 303)
temporal code (p. 307)
timbre (p. 295)
tinnitus (p. 313)
tip links (p. 304)
tympanic canal (p. 300)
tympanic membrane (or *eardrum*) (p. 298)
vestibular canal (p. 300)

EXPAND YOUR UNDERSTANDING

9.1 If the moon exploded one night in a brilliant flash of light, observers on earth would see the explosion but would hear nothing, no matter how violent the event or how long they waited. Explain the difference.

9.2 An old riddle asks, If a tree falls in the forest when no one is around to hear it, does it make a sound? Explain why the answer is yes, and then explain why the answer is no.

9.3 Suppose multiple computers simultaneously started producing a pure tone of the same frequency, but each tone had a different amplitude. Would the sound entering your ear be a pure tone? Would the amplitude of that sound be greater than the amplitude of any of the individual tones? Explain your answers.

9.4 Is the audibility curve an equal loudness contour? Explain your answer.

9.5 The pinna, the ossicles, the difference in area between the tympanic membrane and the round window, and the outer hair cells all contribute to sound amplification. Discuss some of the reasons why sound amplification is so important.

9.6 True or false? The inner and outer hair cells in the organ of Corti are analogous to the cones and rods in the retina. Explain your answer.

9.7 The temporal code for frequency and the place code for frequency depend on activity in the very same set of Type I auditory nerve fibers connected to inner hair cells. How do these two methods of representing frequency differ?

9.8 As discussed in this chapter, an increase or decrease in the amplitude of an incoming sound wave is represented by a corresponding change in the firing rate of auditory nerve fibers. But the temporal code for frequency representation is also based on a change in the pattern of auditory nerve fiber spiking. How can phase synchronization help explain why the auditory system doesn't become "confused" about whether a change in firing pattern represents a change in amplitude or a change in frequency?

9.9 Do you think cochlear implants are more typically used in people with conductive hearing impairments or sensorineural hearing impairments? Explain why.

READ MORE ABOUT IT

Møller, A. R. (2006). *Hearing: Anatomy, physiology, and disorders of the auditory System* (2nd ed.). Amsterdam: Elsevier.
A detailed description of the ear and the process of transduction, as well as a thorough discussion of the causes and treatment of hearing impairments.

Moore, B. C. J. (2012). *An introduction to the psychology of hearing* (6th ed.). Bingley, UK: Emerald Group.
A comprehensive and accessible text on auditory perception.

Plack, C. J., Oxenham, A. J., Fay, R. R., & Popper, A. N. (Eds.). (2005). *Pitch: Neural coding and perception.* New York: Springer.
Includes reviews of how the auditory system encodes and processes pitch, with topics ranging from neurophysiology to psychophysics.

von Békésy, G. (1960). *Experiments in hearing.* New York: McGraw-Hill.
A collection of seminal research papers by a Nobel Prize–winning scientist that makes fascinating reading.

Giacomo Balla, *Mercurio passa davanti al sole (Mercury passes before the sun)*, 1914. [Canvas, 120 × 100 cm. The Solomon R. Guggenheim Foundation, Peggy Guggenheim Collection, Venice, Italy. Erich Lessing/Art Resource, NY. © 2012 Artists Rights Society.]

10

THE AUDITORY BRAIN AND PERCEIVING AUDITORY SCENES

Chapter Outline

Hearing Without Recognition

One day, Mr. L.—a healthy 60-year-old—told his wife that he suddenly felt an intense headache; within minutes, he was unconscious. His wife called for an ambulance, which rushed him to a local hospital, where he was treated for a likely stroke. When he awoke the next day, he was alert but said that he couldn't hear anything. A brain scan revealed that the stroke had damaged important centers of auditory processing in the temporal lobe on both sides of his brain.

Mr. L.'s neurologist found that Mr. L. could still speak fluently—although he tended to talk in a monotone—and could still read and write without difficulty, but he didn't respond to spoken questions or commands. Nor did he seem to hear environmental sounds, not even loud noises. Also, his ability to detect pure tones was severely impaired: his hearing loss immediately after the stroke was 70 dB.

After several weeks, Mr. L.'s hearing loss had improved to about 30 dB, but he reported that even though he could hear sounds, he couldn't recognize them—that is, he perceived sounds as "an annoying buzz," "the banging of tin cans," or "rattles and squeaks," without being able to say what was producing the sounds. Mr. L.'s ability to recognize sounds was then tested by having him listen to recorded environmental sounds (a car horn, a dog barking, an ocean wave breaking on a beach, etc.) and try to match each one with a picture that corresponded to the sound. Mr. L.'s matching performance was nearly at chance. In further testing, Mr. L. was asked whether two environmental sounds were the same or different, or whether two spoken words were the same or different, and again he responded correctly only at chance. Mr. L. could hear, but the damage resulting from the stroke had left him unable to recognize what he was hearing, no matter whether the sounds were speech, music, or any of the vast array of environmental sounds.

As we saw in Chapter 9, much has been learned about how pure tones of different frequencies and amplitudes are transduced by the structures of the ear into neural signals that carry information to the brain. But the sounds we encounter in everyday life are rarely pure tones. Instead, we hear speech, music, the roar of traffic, ventilation systems, footsteps, wind blowing, dogs barking, birds singing, and myriad other natural and artificial sounds, all starting, continuing, stopping, and restarting at different times, and all mixed together at the ear into an ever-changing complex sound wave. Yet, for the most part, we don't experience the sounds of our environment as a complex mixture. Rather, with little difficulty, we attend to each sound source separately, identifying it, determining its location, and gleaning information from it. We can note the location of the barking dog, appreciate the beauty of the birdsong, and understand what someone is saying. Moreover, we can perform a much finer analysis of the auditory scene, grouping related sounds that emanate from the same source and segregating unrelated sounds. Thus, we know that the low-frequency rumble of a truck's engine and the high-frequency squealing of its brakes "go together," that the same person is producing both low- and high-frequency speech sounds, and that the blowing noises of the wind and the ventilation system are similar sounds that come from very different sources.

In this chapter, we'll begin by examining the structures and pathways of the auditory brain that underlie these effortless feats of acoustic understanding. Then we'll take a detailed look at how we locate sound sources in 3-D space and at the principles we use to analyze auditory scenes. Throughout the chapter, we'll point out the many similarities and differences between the functioning of the auditory and visual systems, and we'll end the chapter by reviewing some recent and exciting research on the use of sound to convey visual information about shape as a sensory aid for blind individuals.

The Auditory Brain

The neural signals arising in the cochlea carry information about sound to the brain via the auditory nerve. Within the brain, the signals are processed and combined with signals from the other senses as they travel via ascending pathways from structures in the brain stem to auditory areas in the cerebral cortex. In addition, feedback signals from the brain travel all the way back to the cochlea via descending pathways. In this section, we'll survey these pathways and discuss how the brain structures they traverse play a role in sound perception.

The discussions and illustrations in this section, as well as in subsequent sections of this chapter, will often involve studies of monkeys, cats, bats, and other mammals. Keep in mind that research strongly supports the idea that, beyond differences in the range of audible frequencies (bats, for example, can hear much higher frequencies than humans can), the structure and functioning of the auditory system are similar across the groups of mammals in these studies and that extrapolating the results of these studies to humans probably makes sense.

Ascending Pathways: From the Ear to the Brain

Figure 10.1 shows the principal brain structures in the auditory pathways from the right ear to the cortex. As in the visual pathways, the structures in the auditory pathways come in pairs, one for the right hemisphere of the brain and one for the left hemisphere. Type I auditory nerve fibers carry signals from inner hair cells in the cochlea to the ipsilateral **cochlear nucleus** in the brain stem—for example, signals from the left cochlea travel to the left cochlear nucleus. From there, the main pathways (heavier arrows in Figure 10.1) carry signals to the contralateral side of the brain, but signals in the secondary pathways (lighter arrows) remain mostly on the ipsilateral side.

cochlear nucleus A structure in the brain stem (one on each side of the brain); it receives signals via Type I auditory nerve fibers from inner hair cells in the ipsilateral ear.

As shown in Figure 10.1, the signals on the main pathways from the ipsilateral cochlear nucleus:

- Travel directly to the contralateral **inferior colliculus** (via a nerve tract called the *lateral lemniscus*), then to the contralateral **medial geniculate body (MGB),** and then to the contralateral auditory cortex.
- Travel directly and indirectly (via a synapse in the contralateral trapezoid body) to the contralateral **superior olivary complex,** then to the contralateral inferior colliculus, and then (like the direct signals from the cochlear nucleus to the inferior colliculus) to the contralateral MGB and auditory cortex.

inferior colliculus A structure in the midbrain (one on each side of the brain); a stop on the ascending auditory pathway.

medial geniculate body (MGB) A structure in the thalamus (one on each side of the brain); the next stop on the ascending auditory pathway after the inferior colliculus.

superior olivary complex A structure in the brain stem (one on each side of the brain); a stop on the ascending auditory pathway receiving signals from both cochlear nuclei.

Figure 10.1 also shows that the signals on the secondary pathways from the ipsilateral cochlear nucleus travel to the ipsilateral superior olivary complex and then to the ipsilateral inferior colliculus, from which some signals cross over to the contralateral MGB while other signals travel to the ipsilateral MGB and then to the ipsilateral auditory cortex. In addition, some secondary-pathway signals travel from the contralateral inferior colliculus to the ipsilateral MGB.

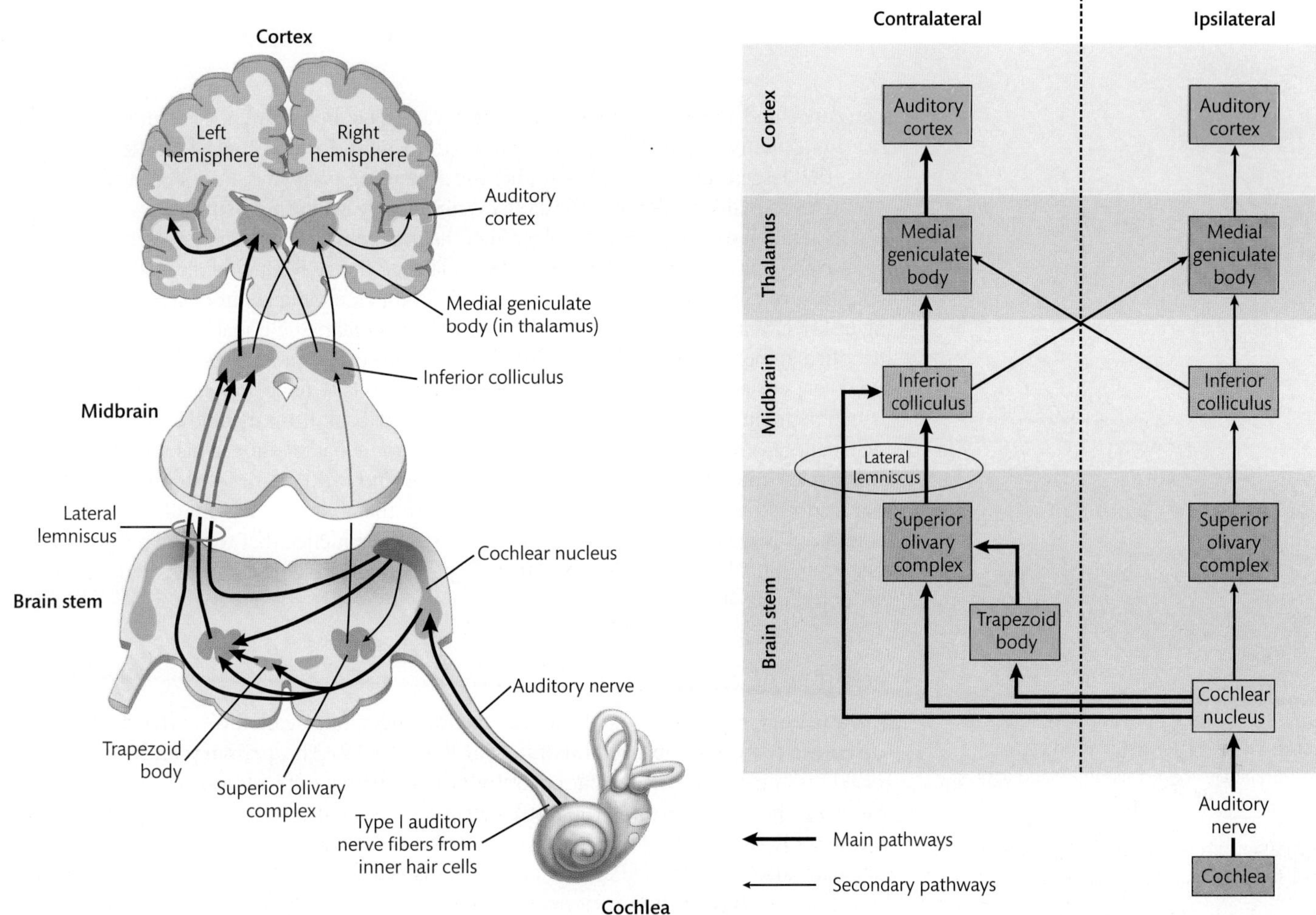

Figure 10.1 **Ascending Auditory Pathways from Cochlea to Cortex** The anatomical illustration at left shows the main and secondary pathways of auditory signals from the cochlea of the right ear to the auditory cortex; the same pathways are depicted in the simplified schematic diagram at right. The pathways from the left ear are exactly symmetrical. (Brain structures aren't drawn to scale; the midbrain is the part of the brain lying immediately above the brain stem.)

Neurons within the subcortical structures on the auditory pathways differ in their responses to signals evoked by sounds of different frequencies and durations. In response to incoming sounds with their preferred frequency, inner hair cells typically produce a large burst of action potentials in the Type I auditory nerve fibers to which they're connected, followed by a sustained slower firing rate (but still above the baseline rate). Within the cochlear nucleus, which receives these signals via the Type I fibers, many neurons show a similar response; others, however, show the same initial strong response but then quickly return to their baseline rate; and still others respond just by gradually increasing their firing rate to a moderate level, without any initial burst of activity (Carney, 2002). And neurons in the later subcortical structures—the trapezoid body, superior olivary complex, inferior colliculus, and MGB—show similarly varied patterns of response. The exact functions served by the different subcortical structures and the different response patterns of their neurons are the subject of considerable ongoing research and debate, but it's clear that these structures and the neural signal processing that takes place within them along the auditory pathways play a critical role in encoding, with exquisitely high fidelity, the rapidly changing stimuli that typically make up the auditory environment (Carney, 2002).

Descending Pathways: From the Brain to the Ear

In Chapter 9, we briefly discussed inhibitory neural signals from the superior olivary complex back to outer hair cells, signals that appear to play a role in modulating the outer hair cells' motile response. These are but one example of the signals that flow along the abundant descending pathways between the auditory cortex, subcortical auditory structures, and the ears. Overall, these pathways have been much less studied than the ascending pathways, in part because in anatomical and physiological studies with animals, the descending pathways—unlike the ascending pathways—are relatively inactive when the animal is under anesthesia (as is often the case in these studies).

In addition to their apparent role in modulating the motile response, descending signals are also thought to help protect the ear from damage (by activating the acoustic reflex) and to be involved in attention by blocking task-irrelevant ascending auditory signals while passing task-relevant ones (He, 2003; Yu et al., 2004). A similar attentional mechanism has been identified in the visual system, where feedback from the cortex modulates activity in the lateral geniculate nucleus to block task-irrelevant visual signals (O'Connor et al., 2002).

Experiments carried out in bats suggest that feedback from the auditory cortex to the MGB reflects a top-down mechanism for increasing the bat's ability to discriminate similar frequencies from one another (Suga & Ma, 2003). And fMRI studies with humans indicate that feedback-related MGB activity correlates with the ability to discriminate different syllables (von Kriegstein et al., 2008), providing strong evidence that top-down signals from the cortex can affect subcortical structures (e.g., the MGB) according to the demands of the perceptual task at hand.

Auditory Cortex

The **auditory cortex** is tucked into the lateral sulcus (also called the *Sylvian fissure*) on top of the temporal lobe, as illustrated in Figure 10.2. The **primary auditory cortex** (or *A1*) is one of three areas that constitute the **auditory core region** (the other two are known as the *rostral core* and the *rostrotemporal core*), as shown in the enlargement at the bottom of Figure 10.2. The auditory core region is situated within the transverse temporal gyrus (also called *Heschl's gyrus*, after the Austrian anatomist Richard Heschl). Signals from the core flow to two regions wrapped around it, the **belt** and the **parabelt**, each of which also contains distinct subareas (Kaas & Hackett, 2000; Woods et al., 2009). (Many of these anatomical regions were first identified in monkey brains; corresponding structures have been found in the human brain.)

auditory cortex Part of the cerebral cortex, tucked into the lateral sulcus on top of the temporal lobe; it consists of the auditory core region, belt, and parabelt.

primary auditory cortex (or *A1*) Part of the auditory core region.

auditory core region Part of the auditory cortex, located within the transverse temporal gyrus in each hemisphere; it consists of the primary auditory cortex, the rostral core, and the rostrotemporal core.

belt Along with the parabelt, a region of cortex wrapped around and receiving signals from the auditory core region.

parabelt Along with the belt, a region of cortex wrapped around and receiving signals from the auditory core region.

tonotopic map An arrangement of neurons within auditory brain regions such that the characteristic frequencies of the neurons gradually shift from lower at one end of the region to higher at the other end.

Figure 10.2 also shows that neurons within each of the auditory core regions are arranged into a **tonotopic map**, with characteristic frequencies that gradually shift from low at one end of the region to high at the other end (Bendor & Wang, 2008; Formisano et al., 2003; Recanzone & Sutter, 2008). This arrangement echoes the arrangement of characteristic frequencies along the basilar membrane (see Figure 9.14). In area A1 and in the rostrotemporal core, neurons with high characteristic frequencies are located at the posterior (back) end, while neurons with low characteristic frequencies are located at the anterior (front) end. In the rostral core, the arrangement is opposite: posterior neurons have low characteristic frequencies, while anterior neurons have high characteristic frequencies. As you might expect, each of the subcortical structures in the ascending auditory pathways shown in Figure 10.1 also has a tonotopic organization (Kandler et al., 2009). Thus, just as the visual cortex and subcortical structures on the visual pathways (e.g., the lateral geniculate nucleus) are organized retinotopically, according to spatial location in the visual field, so the auditory cortex and subcortical structures on the auditory pathways are organized tonotopically, according to frequency.

Moreover, just as the orientation tuning of neurons in the visual cortex can be broad or narrow, so can the frequency tuning of neurons in the auditory cortex, as well as in subcortical auditory regions (Møller, 2006). Figure 10.3, for example, shows frequency tuning curves for two neurons in area A1 of a cat in response to pure tones of varying frequencies and amplitudes (Schreiner et al., 2000). For the narrowly tuned neuron, only a narrow band of frequencies on either side of the neuron's characteristic frequency produced a response, no matter how high the amplitude of the tone. For the broadly tuned neuron, when the amplitude of the stimulating tone was fairly low (less than about 30 dB SPL), the band of frequencies surrounding the characteristic frequency that produced a response was also fairly narrow, but as the amplitude of the stimulating tones increased, the band became much broader. The researchers speculated that neurons with broad tuning widths might be

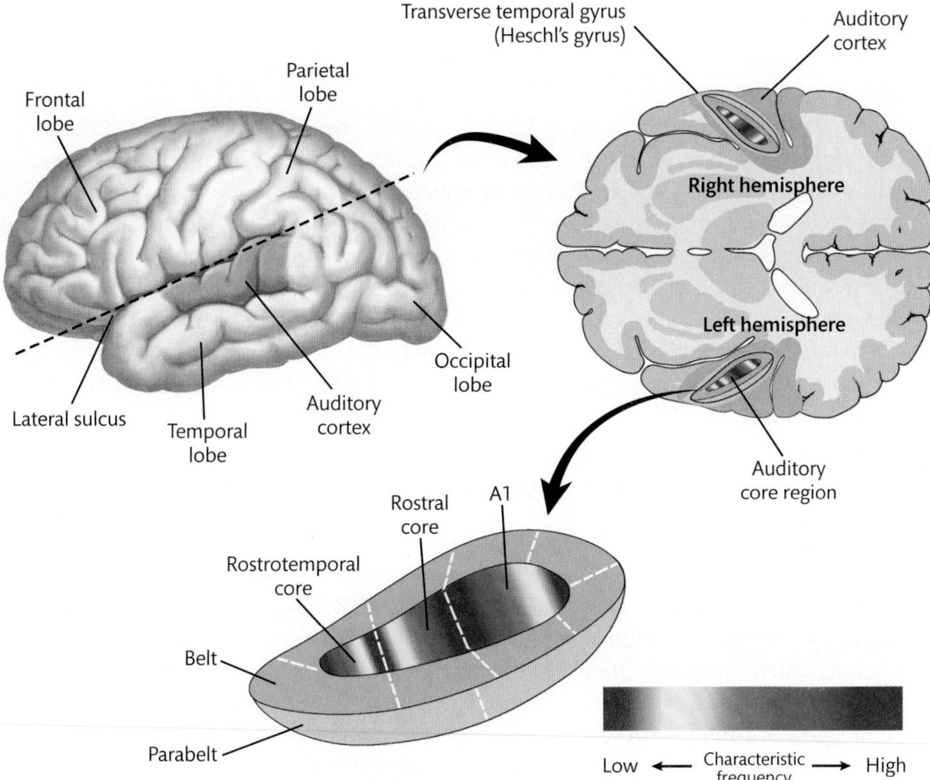

Figure 10.2 Auditory Cortex As shown in the side view at top left and the section through the lateral sulcus at top right, the auditory cortex is located on the upper surface of the temporal lobe, tucked into the lateral sulcus, which separates the temporal lobe from the frontal and parietal lobes. The enlargement at bottom shows the auditory core region, belt, and parabelt (adapted from Recanzone & Sutter, 2008, and Kaas & Hackett, 2000). The auditory core is made up of the primary auditory cortex (A1), the rostral core, and the rostrotemporal core (*rostral/rostro-* means "toward the front"; *temporal* means "toward the temple," i.e., toward the side of the head). The belt and parabelt, which wrap around the core, are each divided into distinct subregions, as indicated by the dashed lines. All three regions have a tonotopic organization, with alternating progression from low to high characteristic frequencies.

involved in integrating component frequencies of complex sounds, as part of the process of discriminating and recognizing sound sources.

This discrimination and recognition process appears to be carried forward in the belt and parabelt, which are thought to be analogous to areas beyond V1 in the visual pathways (e.g., V4, MT, and the inferotemporal cortex). As we saw in Chapter 3, neurons in V1 are mainly tuned to the orientation of edges, with some neurons also tuned

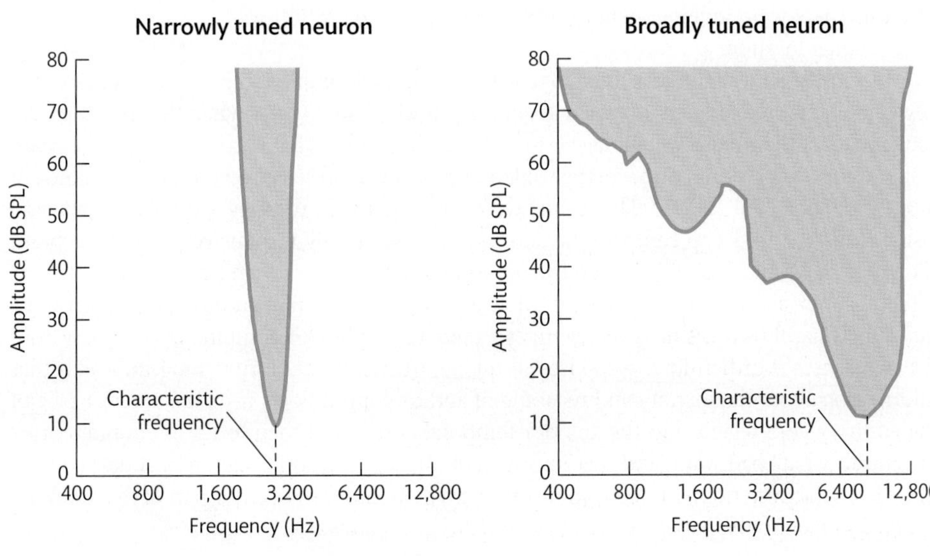

Figure 10.3 Narrow and Broad Frequency Tuning in Cat Area A1 These graphs show the responses of two neurons in cat area A1 to pure tones of varying frequency and amplitude. The green areas represent the frequency–amplitude combinations evoking a response above the baseline firing rate; combinations falling outside the green areas don't evoke a response above baseline. The frequency that produces a response at the lowest amplitude is the neuron's characteristic frequency. (Adapted from Schreiner et al., 2000, Figure 1.)

Demonstration 10.1 Functional Anatomy of the Auditory System: From Cochlea to Cortex Interact with depictions of the structures and pathways from the cochlea to the auditory cortex.

to features such as motion, length, depth, and color; neurons beyond V1 (in the ventral pathway) are tuned to one or more of these features and to more complex shapes. Similarly, unlike neurons in the auditory core region (including A1), neurons in the belt and parabelt don't respond strongly to pure tones (analogous to simple visual stimuli like oriented edges) but instead appear to be tuned to more complex stimuli containing multiple frequencies, which are, of course, the type of stimuli we're most likely to encounter in everyday life (Rauschecker, 1998). The details of how complex natural sounds are processed by successive levels of the auditory cortex are only now being worked out, and the final story is likely to be as complex as the story of visual object recognition told in Chapters 3 and 4.

"What" and "Where" Pathways and Other Specialized Regions of the Auditory Brain

The distinction between a ventral "what" pathway and a dorsal "where"/"how" pathway is well established in the visual system (see Chapter 3). The auditory system appears to exhibit a similar organization: a "what" pathway, specialized for representing the identity of sound sources, extends from the core regions into the belt and parabelt and then into anterior parts of the temporal cortex; and a "where" pathway, specialized for representing the location of sound sources, extends from the core regions into posterior parts of the auditory cortex and eventually into the posterior parietal cortex (Rauschecker & Scott, 2009). It's likely that the stroke suffered by Mr. L., described in the chapter-opening vignette, damaged important parts of his auditory "what" pathway.

Evidence for distinct "what" and "where" auditory pathways in the human brain comes from patterns of impaired performance in patients with brain damage. In one study, four patients with normal ability to identify sound sources were severely impaired in their ability to localize them, whereas a separate group of three patients could localize sound sources accurately but had difficulty identifying them (Clarke et al., 2002). This pattern of impaired performance—a double dissociation—supports the conclusion that distinct brain regions are responsible for the ability to identify and localize sound sources.

A meta-analysis of many human neuroimaging studies has corroborated this distinction (Arnott et al., 2004). In one such study, listeners were presented with pairs of spoken syllables that came from either of two locations—straight ahead or 45° to the right (Ahveninen et al., 2006). The syllables could be the same or different and could come from the same or different locations. On each presentation, the listener had to perform either an identity task or a location task—that is, the listener had to judge whether the syllables were the same (and ignore the locations) or whether the locations were the same (and ignore the identity of the syllables). They found that two distinct regions in the auditory cortex were selectively active as listeners performed these two distinct tasks (see Figure 10.4, left): a more anterior region was active when listeners were judging identity, and a more posterior region was active when listeners were judging location.

In another study, monkeys listened to a wide variety of complex sounds—including monkey calls, human voices, environmental sounds, music, and so on—while the metabolically active parts of their brain were imaged, in order to determine what parts of the primate brain respond to auditory input and whether different parts respond selectively to different kinds of input (Poremba et al., 2003). The results were compared with those of a similar study using visual stimuli, in order to compare the auditorially and visually responsive parts of the brain (Poremba & Mishkin, 2007). As you can see in Figure 10.4 (right), large areas of the primate cerebral cortex are multimodal—that is, these areas respond to both auditory and visual stimuli. This is hardly surprising given monkeys' (and our) ability to combine information from the two senses. Furthermore, responses to different types of auditory stimuli indicated that information about the identity and meaning of auditory input flows from the anterior part of the auditory core region into the anterior temporal cortex and then to the prefrontal cortex (a ventral "what" pathway), and that information about the spatial location of sound sources flows from the posterior part of the auditory core region into the posterior part of the temporal cortex and then to the parietal cortex (a dorsal "where" pathway).

HUMAN BRAIN

Anterior ROI (responds to "what" tasks)

Posterior ROI (responds to "where" tasks)

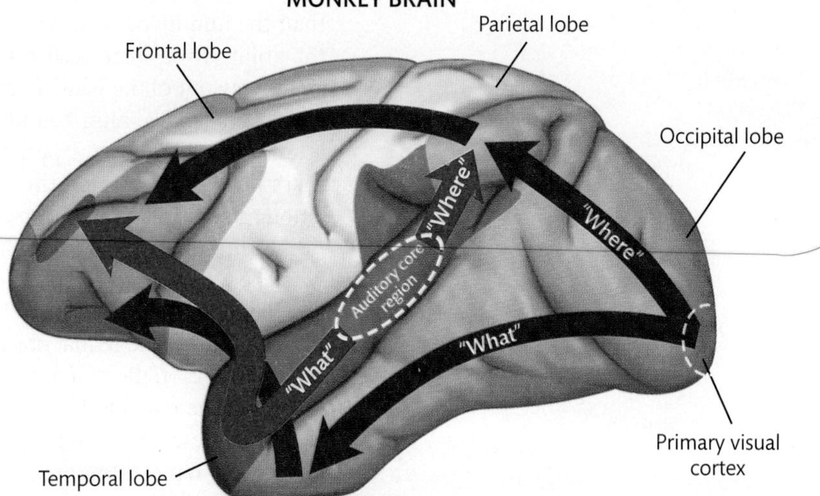

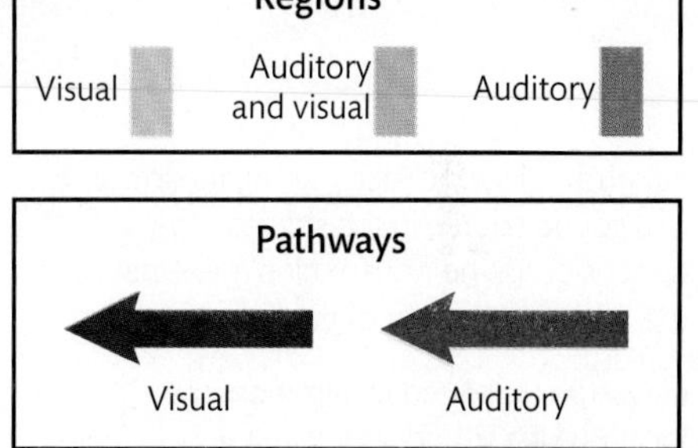

Figure 10.4 "What" and "Where" Regions and Pathways in the Human and Monkey Brain (left) Two regions of interest (ROIs) within the human auditory cortex are depicted on this inflated cortical surface. The posterior ROI contains neurons that responded more strongly when the listener was performing a "where" task, judging the location of a sound source (straight ahead versus 45° to the right). The anterior ROI contains neurons that responded more strongly when the listener was performing a "what" task, judging the identity of a sound (the vowel sound in *put* versus the vowel sound in *cat*). (right) The results of neuroimaging studies of monkey brains as the monkeys listened to a wide variety of auditory stimuli have been combined with the results of similar studies with visual stimuli. Large portions of the primate cerebral cortex are multimodal (blue)—neurons in those regions respond to both auditory and visual stimuli. The results for different types of auditory stimuli indicate that assessing the locations of sound sources involves neurons in a "where" pathway running from the posterior part of the auditory core region up into the parietal cortex, whereas assessing the identity of sound sources involves neurons in a "what" pathway running from the anterior part of the core to the anterior temporal lobe and then to the prefrontal cortex. (Adapted and photo from Ahveninen et al., 2006, Figure 3.)

Check Your Understanding

10.1 In what order do these structures appear in the ascending pathway from the ear to the brain: **(A)** inferior colliculus, **(B)** cochlear nucleus, **(C)** auditory cortex, **(D)** medial geniculate body, **(E)** cochlea, **(F)** superior olivary complex?

10.2 Of the brain structures listed in Question 10.1, which one seems to be involved in discriminating small differences in frequency based on feedback from the auditory cortex?

10.3 True or false? The auditory core region is part of the primary auditory cortex.

10.4 Which two lobes of the primate brain appear to contain large areas that are multimodal, involved in processing both auditory and visual stimuli?

Localizing Sounds

In everyday life, Where is that sound coming from? is often the first question we ask when we hear a novel or unexpected sound. After all, once we determine the location of a sound source, we can use our other senses—primarily vision—to help identify the source, which in turn will help us decide how to respond to it.

Suppose, for example, that you're sitting in your room and you suddenly hear a rapid low clicking and grinding sound. Is it coming from outside the window? If so, it's not very worrisome—you might not even feel any curiosity about exactly what it is. But if it's coming from the top of your desk, that's another matter—it might be the fan or the hard drive inside your computer, an alarming possibility.

Of course, the auditory brain evolved in the context of much more important factors than the imminent failure of a computer—as a matter of survival, our ancestors needed the ability to localize sound sources rapidly and automatically in order to avoid collisions, stay out of the way of predators, and capture prey. Less critical but often extremely important is localizing sound sources in a noisy environment, so you can direct your attention optimally and perhaps use vision to get information from the sound source that's being obscured by the noise. For example, if you're trying to listen to one voice among many in a crowded room, it helps to localize the speaker so you can pay attention to lip movements that might help you follow what's being said.

The way in which the auditory system localizes sound sources is less direct than the way in which the visual system localizes visual objects. In vision, location is explicitly represented in the image on the retina: objects in adjacent locations within a scene project light to adjacent locations on the retina, and this retinotopic organization is maintained as neural signals flow from the retina to higher visual areas. In audition, however, there is no corresponding explicit representation of location—the cochlea is organized tonotopically, with position in the cochlea representing frequency, not spatial location. To represent the location of sound sources, the auditory system has instead evolved an exquisitely sensitive method based on comparing aspects of the sound arriving at the two ears (in vision, stereoscopic depth perception uses an analogous comparison of information in the two retinal images).

As shown in Figure 10.5, a polar coordinate system based on two mutually perpendicular planes centered on the head is used to specify the locations of sound sources in 3-D space. In the horizontal plane, **azimuth** refers to the side-to-side dimension, the angle left or right of the median plane; in the median plane, **elevation** refers to the up–down dimension, the angle above or below the horizontal plane; **distance** simply refers to the distance from the center of the head in any direction. In this section, we'll explore the ways in which the auditory system localizes sounds in each of these three dimensions.

azimuth In sound localization, the location of a sound source in the side-to-side dimension in the horizontal plane—that is, the angle left or right of the median plane.

elevation In sound localization, the location of a sound source in the up–down dimension in the median plane—that is, the angle above or below the horizontal plane.

distance In sound localization, how far a sound source is from the center of the head in any direction.

minimum audible angle The minimum angular separation between a reference sound source and a different sound source emitting a tone of the same frequency that yields 75% correct judgments about the relative horizontal positions of the two sources.

Perceiving Azimuth

People's ability to perceive azimuth accurately—that is, to localize sounds in the horizontal plane—can be quantified psychophysically (using the method of constant stimuli), by situating a listener at the center of a circle of closely spaced speakers (Mills, 1958). A pure tone, called the *reference tone,* is emitted by one of the speakers, followed by a tone of the same frequency emitted by a different speaker to the left or right of the reference tone speaker, whereupon the listener must decide whether the second tone came from the left or right of the reference tone. When the two speakers are separated by a large angle, the listener almost always decides correctly, but as the two tones are emitted by speakers that are closer and closer together, the listener begins to make errors. The minimum angular separation between two different speakers that yields 75% correct judgments is called the **minimum audible angle** for that frequency at the azimuth of the speaker emitting the reference tone. Thus, the smaller

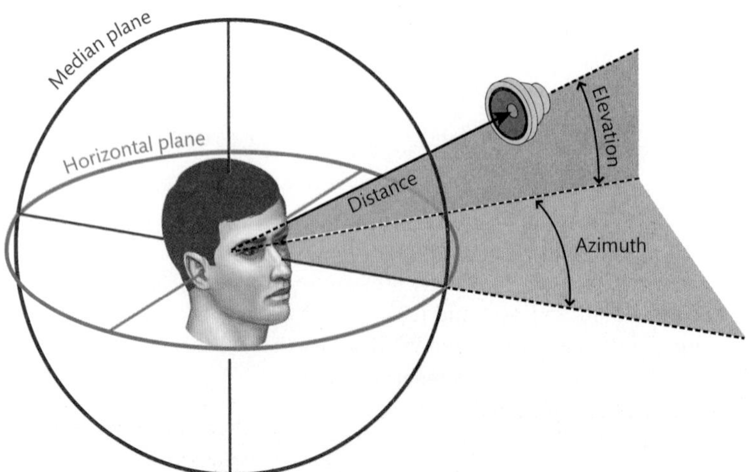

Figure 10.5 Coordinate System for Sound Localization The parameters of azimuth, elevation, and distance correspond to measurements in a polar coordinate system based on two mutually perpendicular planes (horizontal and median) centered on the head. The horizontal plane bisects the head parallel to the ground at the level of the centers of the auditory canals. The median plane is perpendicular to the ground and bisects the head midway between the two ears. Distance is the distance in any direction from the center of the head to the sound source.

the minimum audible angle, the more accurately the listener can perceive the azimuth of the sound source. For a wide variety of sounds, the minimum audible angle is under 10° and in some cases as little as 1°. What information does the auditory system use to determine the azimuth of a sound source?

Interaural Level Differences

A sound emitted by a source located on the median plane (e.g., directly in front of or behind the listener) is equally intense in the two ears because it is equally distant from them. Sources to the left or right of the median plane emit sounds that are more intense in the closer ear, for two reasons. First, the intensity of sounds decreases with distance from the source, according to the inverse square law (see Chapter 9); however, given that the extra distance to the far ear can never be more than the width of the head (about 14 cm), the difference in intensity in the two ears due to this effect is insignificant except when the sound source is relatively close to the head (like a mosquito homing in on your left ear). Second, and more important, is the fact that the head produces an **acoustic shadow**—that is, the head partially blocks the sound waves traveling to the far ear. However, as illustrated in Figure 10.6, the acoustic shadow has a much greater effect on high-frequency sounds than on low-frequency sounds.

acoustic shadow An area on the other side of the head from a sound source in which the loudness of the sound is reduced because the sound waves are partially blocked by the head; it has a much greater effect on high-frequency sounds than on low-frequency sounds.

The difference in sound level at the two ears—called the **interaural level difference (ILD,** also sometimes called the *interaural intensity difference,* or IID)—is shown in Figure 10.7 for pure tones of various frequencies originating from various directions. Regardless of frequency, sounds at 0° azimuth—directly in front of the listener—exhibit zero ILD; ILD increases steadily for sound sources from 0° to 90° azimuth; and then ILD decreases steadily back to zero at 180° azimuth—directly behind the listener. Because of the effects of the acoustic shadow, ILD typically increases with frequency at any given azimuth—for example, at 90° azimuth (directly to the right), ILD ranges from about 3 dB for a 500-Hz tone to about 20 dB for a 6,000-Hz tone. Because it's much easier for the auditory system to detect large ILDs than

interaural level difference (ILD) The difference in the sound level of the same sound at the two ears.

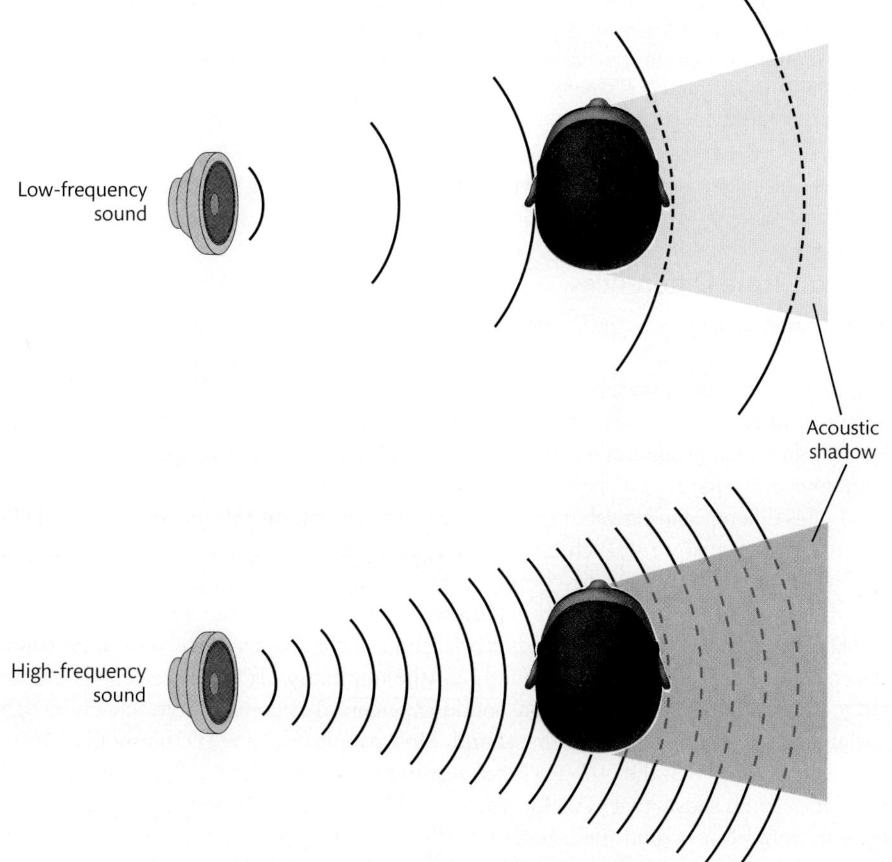

Figure 10.6 Acoustic Shadow A low-frequency sound has a longer wavelength than a high-frequency sound, as indicated by the distance between successive peaks (the curved lines) in this illustration. When a sound wave encounters an object that's smaller than the wavelength (like this listener's head in relation to the low-frequency sound wave), the sound wave diffracts (bends) around the object with little loss of energy: the sound is almost as intense in the ear on the side away from the sound source as in the ear on the side toward the source. But when the object is large compared to the wavelength, as with the high-frequency sound, the sound wave doesn't diffract much, and the sound is significantly more intense in the ear toward the source than in the far ear. We can say that the listener's head throws an acoustic shadow that attenuates high-frequency sounds much more than low-frequency sounds in the far ear.

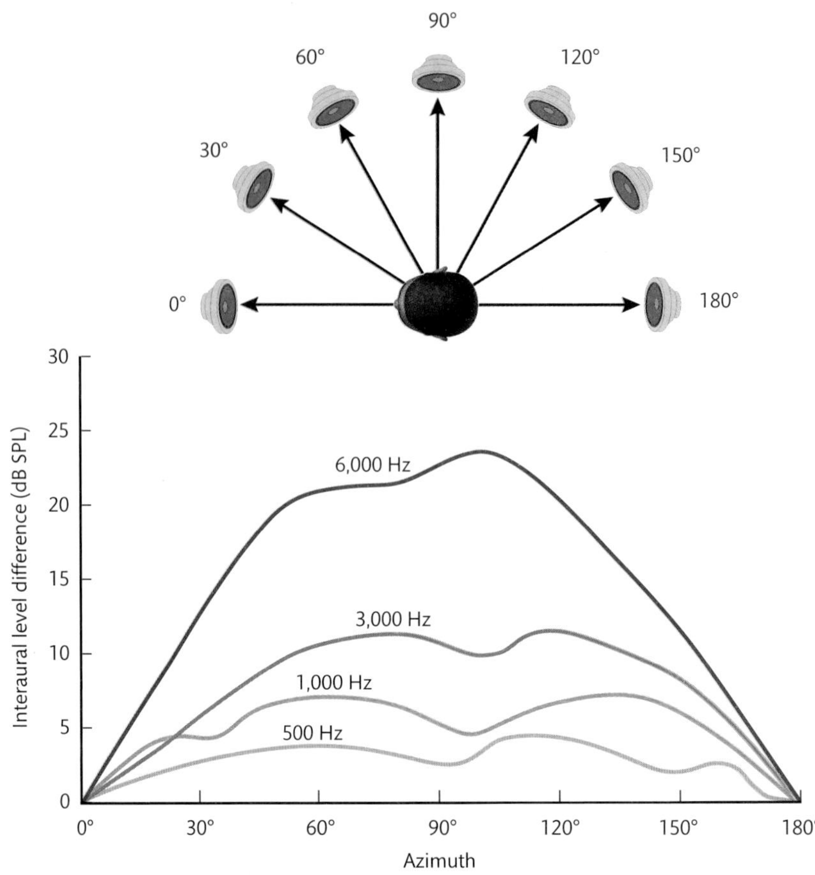

Figure 10.7 Interaural Level Difference for Different Azimuths The interaural level difference (ILD) is 0 for sounds from sources at 0° and 180° azimuth, because the distances from the sound source to the left and right ears are equal. The ILD is at a maximum at 90° azimuth, where the difference in the distances to the two ears is also at a maximum. Overall, for any given azimuth (except 0° and 180°), the ILD is greater at higher frequencies than at lower frequencies, because of the effects of the acoustic shadow (see Figure 10.6). (Adapted from Feddersen et al., 1957.)

Demonstration 10.2 Interaural Level Differences Explore sound localization.

small ones, this pattern tells us that ILD is a good cue for perceiving the azimuth of pure tones at high frequencies but not as good at low frequencies.

Interaural Time Differences

Sounds emitted by sources to the left or right of the median plan must travel different distances to the two ears, which means that such sounds arrive at the two ears at different times (see Figure 10.8a). Consider, for example, the sound from a source at 45° right azimuth. The speed of sound in air is 343 m/sec, and the left ear is about 10 cm (0.10 m) further away than the right ear from a sound source at 45° right azimuth, so the sound will arrive at the left ear about 292 microseconds (μs) after it arrives at the right ear (0.10 m ÷ 343 m/sec = 0.000292 sec = 292 μs). This difference in arrival times is referred to as the **interaural time difference (ITD).**

interaural time difference (ITD) The difference in arrival time of the same sound at the two ears.

Can people actually use such small time differences to judge the azimuth of a sound source? Consider the results of psychophysical experiments in which people wearing headphones hear two closely spaced bursts of narrowband white noise, one in each ear (Gabriel et al., 1992). If the time between the sounds is brief enough, the listener perceives a single sound. And depending on the listener's ITD threshold (the minimum ITD that the listener can use to judge azimuth), this single perceptual sound is perceived as coming from the left or right, according to which ear received the first sound. Most people have an ITD threshold of 100 μs or less, which means that the 292-μs ITD of a sound at an azimuth of 45° is more than sufficient. Figure 10.8b shows that ITDs for sounds at different azimuths vary from 0, for sounds directly in front of or behind the listener (at 0° or 180° azimuth), which arrive at both ears simultaneously, to about 600 μs for sounds directly to the side (at 90° azimuth). Together, ITD

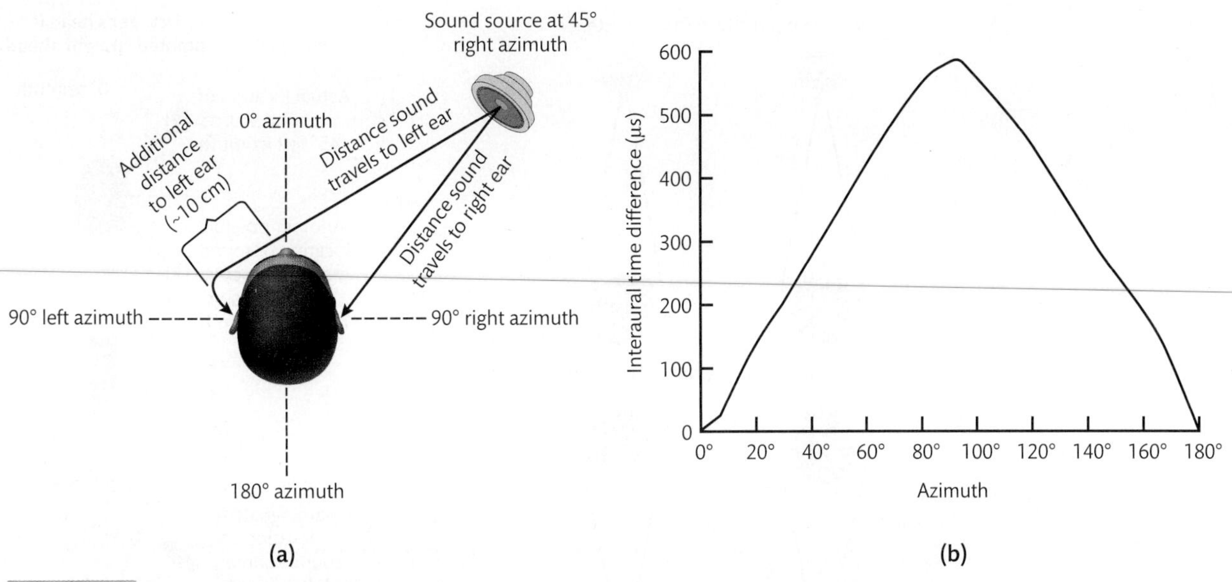

Figure 10.8 Interaural Time Difference for Different Azimuths (a) A sound from a source located at 45° right azimuth will arrive at the right ear before it arrives at the left ear, because it has to travel about 10 cm farther to the left ear. This difference in arrival times is called the *interaural time difference* (ITD). (b) The auditory system can use the ITD as a cue to localize sound sources in the horizontal plane because ITD varies systematically with azimuth: 0 at 0° and 180° azimuth and increasing to a maximum of about 600 μs at 90° azimuth. (Adapted from Feddersen et al., 1957.)

and ILD provide complementary sources of information about the location of a sound source in the horizontal plane.

Head Motion and the "Cone of Confusion"

Suppose there's a sound source behind you and to your left, at 135° left azimuth. How would you know that the sound isn't coming from a source in front of you and to your left, at 45° left azimuth? Identical sounds from sources at these two locations would have nearly identical ILD and ITD (see Figures 10.7 and 10.8b, respectively), so you wouldn't be able to use those factors to disambiguate the azimuth. In fact, the azimuth of any sound source located on the surface of a **cone of confusion** (see Figure 10.9) is confusable with

cone of confusion A hypothetical cone-shaped surface in auditory space; when two equally distant sound sources are located on a cone of confusion, their locations are confusable because they have highly similar ILD and ITD.

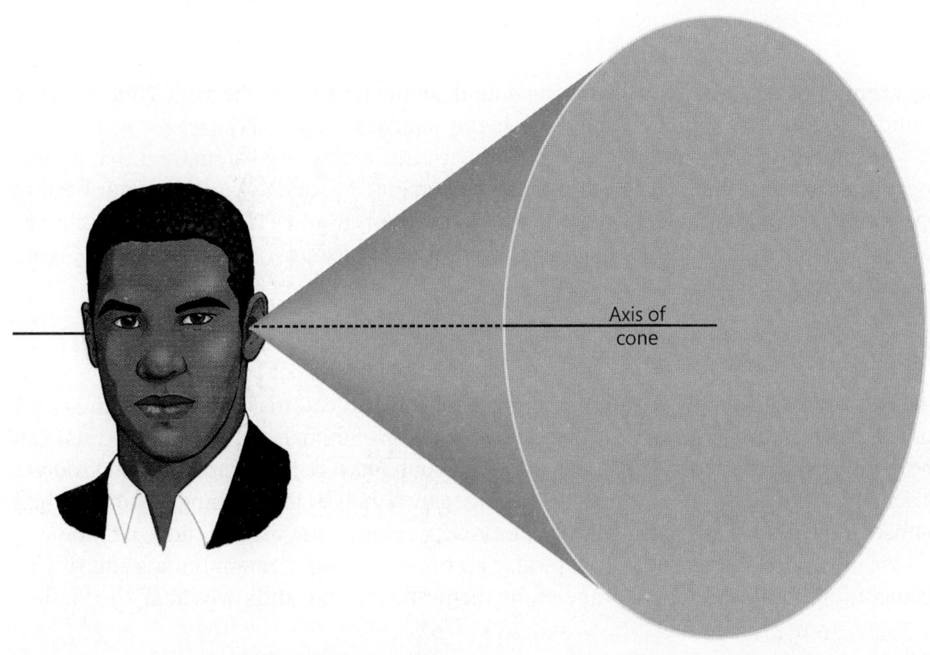

Figure 10.9 Cone of Confusion Sound sources at the same distance from the head and located anywhere on the surface of an imaginary cone of confusion produce nearly the same ITD and ILD. There are an infinite number of cones of confusion—any cone with an axis that passes through the two auditory canals.

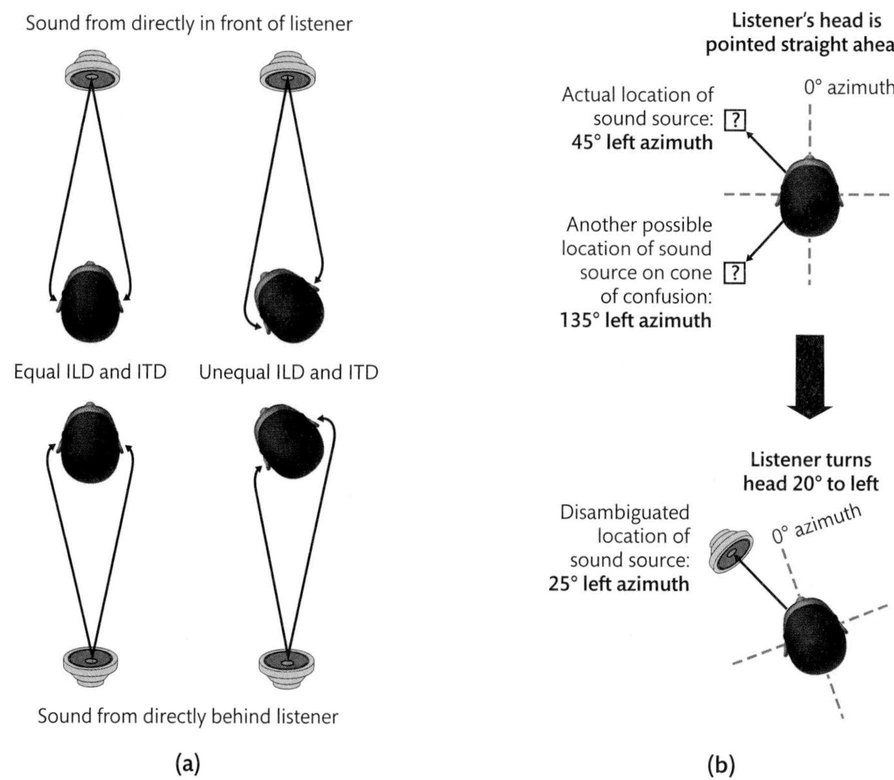

Figure 10.10 Head Motion Helps Determine the True Azimuth (a) A sound source located directly in front of the listener produces the same ILD and ITD as a source directly behind the listener (left illustration). If the listener rotates his head to the left, the ILDs and ITDs will change in a way that depends on the true location of the sound source (right illustration): if the sound source is in front of the listener, the level will be greater in the listener's right ear than in the left ear (ILD), because of the acoustic shadow, and the sound will arrive at the right ear before it arrives at the left ear (ITD); and vice versa if the sound source is behind the listener. Thus, turning the head immediately reveals the true location of the sound source. (Adapted from Blauert, 1997, Figure 2.95.) (b) Similarly, a sound source at 45° left azimuth can be localized mistakenly as an equally distant source at 135° left azimuth, as both locations are on a cone of confusion. Turning the head eliminates the possible location at 135° left azimuth: the ILD changes such that the level is higher in the right ear and lower in the left ear than before the head turn, and the ITD changes such that the sound arrives sooner in the right ear and later in the left ear than before the head turn (if the source had been at 135° left azimuth, the ILD and ITD would have changed in the opposite ways).

the azimuth of any other equally distant sound source located on the same cone, because sounds from all such sources would have highly similar ILD and ITD.

Fortunately, there's an easy way to deal with this ambiguity—a method that people use almost without thinking about it: head movement. As soon as you turn your head to one side or the other or tilt it to the left or right, the ILD and ITD of the sound change in a way that instantly disambiguates the azimuth of the source, as illustrated in Figure 10.10 (Blauert, 1997).

Perceiving Elevation

The ears of many animals, including human ears, have an external part—the pinna—that funnels sound waves into the auditory canal; and some animals (e.g., domestic cats) can move their pinnae independently, like little radar antennas, to focus on interesting sources of sound in their environments without having to turn their head. Humans can't move their pinnae in the same way, but the pinnae do provide information used to judge elevation.

As illustrated in Figure 10.11a, pinnae aren't smooth but contain bumps and ridges. As incoming sound waves are funneled by the pinna into the auditory canal, they reflect

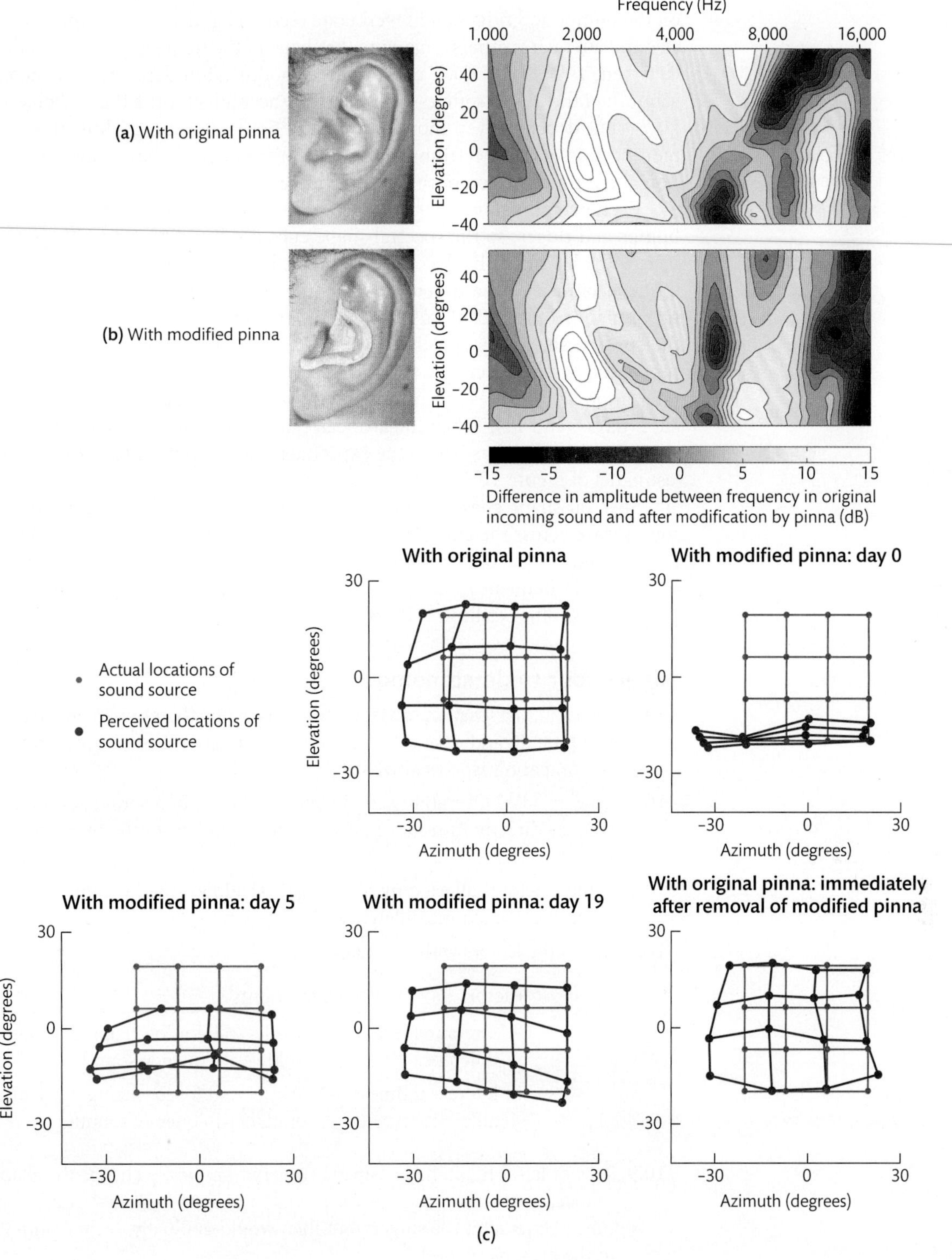

Figure 10.11 Spectral Shape Cue for Perceiving Elevation (a) The amplitudes of the various frequencies making up a broadband sound are modified by the bumps and ridges of the pinna before the sound enters the auditory canal. The graph shows how sound intensity increases (yellow to white) or decreases (orange to black) with the elevation of the sound source from 40° below horizontal to 40° above horizontal for frequencies ranging from 1,000 to 16,000 Hz, altering the shape of the frequency spectrum. The auditory system can use this spectral shape cue to determine the elevation of sound sources. (b) When a molded plastic insert is placed in the ear, modifying the shape of the pinna, the spectral shape of the sound changes—compare the graph with the one in (a). (c) The change in the spectral shape affects the accuracy with which the listener is able to judge the elevation of sound sources. In all five graphs, the red circles pinpoint the actual locations (azimuth and elevation) of sound sources, while the blue circles show the listener's corresponding localization judgments. The first panel shows localization accuracy with the listener's own pinna; the following panels show performance with a modified pinna on the day it was inserted (day 0) and on days 5 and 19, and the last panel shows performance with the original pinna immediately after removal of the mold. (Adapted and photos from Hofman et al., 1998, Figures 1 and 2.)

off the bumps and ridges and reverberate (echo) slightly, which amplifies some frequencies and attenuates others, changing the shape of the frequency spectrum (Middlebrooks & Green, 1991). The exact nature of the modification depends to some extent on the azimuth of the sound source—which largely accounts for the ILD asymmetries in Figure 10.7—but depends even more particularly on its elevation. Thus, this pinna-induced modification of the spectrum—often called the **spectral shape cue**—provides information about the elevation of the sound source.

spectral shape cue A pinna-induced modification in a sound's frequency spectrum; it provides information about the elevation of the sound source.

Each person's pinnae are unique, both in overall shape and in the configuration of bumps and ridges, so the spectral shape cues produced by your own particular pinnae have to be learned. This has been confirmed by experiments in which a person wears artificial pinnae with a different pattern of bumps and ridges from the person's natural pinnae (Hofman et al., 1998). Figure 10.11b shows one such artificial pinna and the spectral shape cue associated with it. Figure 10.11c shows that, with the artificial pinna, the person's accuracy at judging elevation is at first greatly impaired (day 0) but then improves again as the person's auditory system adapts to the new spectral shape cues (days 5 and 19). When the artificial pinna was removed, elevation judgments were immediately as good as before the experiment, with no need to relearn, as shown in the last panel of Figure 10.11c.

Spectral shape cues depend on hearing how the pinna modifies the shape of the sound wave across the entire spectrum, so this cue works best for broadband sounds—that is, sounds that contain a wide range of frequencies—as opposed to pure tones, with only a single frequency; and people are indeed quite poor at judging the elevation of pure tones (Roffler & Butler, 1968).

Check Your Understanding

10.5 In vision, the location of visual stimuli is explicitly represented via retinotopic mapping. In audition, the location of sound sources is less directly represented, by comparing aspects of what?

10.6 True or false? Our ability to judge the azimuth of a sound source is best for sources directly in front of us and is independent of the frequency of the sound.

10.7 Which factor is affected by the acoustic shadow—the interaural level difference or the interaural time difference? Explain why.

10.8 Match the factors with the statements:

Factors	Statements
A. Interaural level difference	**C.** Works well for localizing the source of lower-frequency sounds.
B. Interaural time difference	**D.** Works well for localizing the source of higher-frequency sounds.

10.9 True or false? If you had cosmetic surgery to radically change the shape of your pinnae, your ability to judge the elevation of sound sources would probably be much better after the surgery but then would gradually decline until it returned to the presurgery level.

Perceiving Distance

Often we'd like to know not just the azimuth and elevation of a sound source, but also its distance—how far away from us it is. Unfortunately, the sound localization cues we've discussed so far—ILD, ITD, and the spectral shape cue—provide little information about distance.

If the listener knows the sound level of the source, then the perceived loudness can be used to judge at least whether the source is relatively near or far. For example, normal conversation has a fairly predictable range of sound levels, so if you hear two people talking (not yelling or whispering), you can roughly judge whether they're near or far away. This is just the effect of the inverse square law—the amplitude of a sound decreases in proportion to the square of the distance to the source—and we use this effect to judge the distance of many familiar sounds. Moreover, the reduction in level is greater for high frequencies than for low frequencies, which results in a progressive "blurring" of a sound as the source grows more distant. So even if the level of the sound at the source is unknown, listeners can use this "blurring" cue to judge the distance of the sound source (Coleman, 1968). This is analogous to using atmospheric perspective as a depth cue in vision (Lewis & Maler, 2002).

An important cue for distance is provided by echoes in situations where there are many hard surfaces to reflect sound waves—for instance, inside rooms or on the streets of a city. In these environments, where you can distinguish the sound arriving directly from the source and the sound echoing off surfaces (because the spectral shape of the sound is modified by reflection, as we saw in our discussion of the spectral shape cue), you can perceive the relative proportion of each type of sound energy, direct versus reflected. If the proportion is more direct than reflected, the sound source is near; if the proportion is more reflected than direct, the sound source is farther away (Moore & King, 1999).

Other cues to distance—involving loudness and frequency—are provided by the movement of sound sources toward or away from the listener. The loudness cue is also a result of the inverse square law—as a sound source approaches a listener the loudness increases, and as the source recedes from the listener the loudness decreases. The frequency cue is a result of the **Doppler effect**—the frequency of a sound emitted by a moving sound source is higher in front of the sound source than behind it (think about a train whistle or the sound of race cars zooming past); the frequency rapidly decreases as the sound source passes the listener.

Doppler effect The frequency of a sound emitted by a moving sound source is higher in front of the sound source than behind it; the frequency rapidly decreases as the sound source passes the listener.

These effects of a moving sound source on loudness and frequency don't tell you exactly how far away the source is at any given moment, but the change in loudness does tell you whether the source is approaching or receding, and both cues tell you when an approaching source reaches its closest point, because that's when loudness stops increasing and starts decreasing and when the rate of change in frequency is maximal.

Echolocation by Bats and Humans

Bats that forage for flying insects at night have to locate small, nearly invisible moving targets in 3-D space with pinpoint accuracy. They do this by **echolocation,** emitting a sequence of high-frequency sounds (in the range of 20,000–100,000 Hz) and then processing the echoes to determine whether the sound was reflected off potential prey and, if so, to continuously track the prey's location as they close in on it (Ulanovsky & Moss, 2008). Echolocation provides information about azimuth, elevation, and distance, as well as information about the size and shape of the target and about the physical characteristics of the target's surface, such as its hardness and texture (Schnitzler & Kalko, 2001). For these bats, accurate sound localization is fundamental to survival. Figure 10.12 illustrates a prey-capture maneuver by a bat of the species *Pipistrellus pipistrellus.*

echolocation Sound localization based on emitting sounds and then processing the echoes to determine the nature and location of the object that produced the echoes.

Humans can use echolocation quite accurately to judge their distance from walls or other objects. In one classic study, two blind and two sighted but blindfolded individuals were placed in a large room at various distances from the far wall (Supa et al., 1944). They were pointed in the direction of the wall and asked to walk forward and report when they could first detect that there was a wall in front of them and then stop as close as possible to the wall without touching it. The participants were not allowed to speak or make other vocal sounds, but they could use the sounds of their own footsteps on the wooden floor as auditory cues.

The blind participants reported that they could sense the wall when they were 2–5 m away from it, and they stopped within 15 cm of the wall, never colliding with it. With no practice, the sighted but blindfolded individuals did not report sensing the wall until they were less than a meter away, and they walked into the wall more than half the time (however,

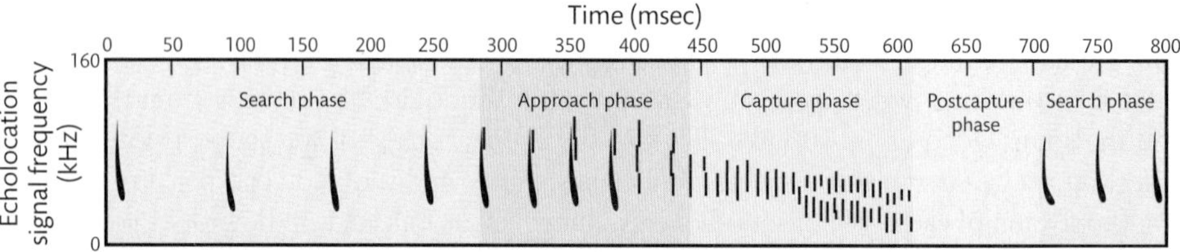

Figure 10.12 Prey Capture by Echolocating Bats Echolocating bats capture prey in flight (and in total darkness) by emitting sounds and using echoes to determine the prey's location. The photo at top shows a common pipistrelle (*Pipistrellus pipistrellus*); the sequence of exposures at bottom shows a greater horseshoe bat (*Rhinolophus ferrumequinum*) capturing a moth. The spectrogram shows how the echolocation signals emitted by a common pipistrelle vary over time, both in frequency (kHz) and in how close together the individual chirps come. Prey capture by echolocation involves four distinct phases. During the search phase, the chirps are far apart in time, as the bat flies about waiting for an echo indicating potential prey. In the approach phase, the bat has detected potential prey and emits signals more rapidly, to track the movements of the prey and close in on it. In the capture phase, as the bat gets close to the insect, very rapid signals help it determine the prey's precise location until capture occurs. During the postcapture phase, no signals are emitted; then the search phase begins again. This entire sequence of events occupies less than a second! (Spectrogram adapted from Schnitzler & Kalko, 2001, Figure 6.) [top: Stephen Dalton/Minden Pictures; bottom: blickwinkel/Alamy]

they rapidly improved with practice). When required to wear earplugs, preventing them from hearing echoes, both the blind and the blindfolded participants were unable to detect the wall and collided with it every time (they walked slowly!).

Blind individuals sometimes emit clicks with their mouth and tongue (as a bat emits high-frequency chirps) to aid in echolocation. One study found that both blind and sighted individuals could use such echoes to detect the presence of a small disk placed at different distances in front of them, although the blind participants' performance was better, presumably because they had much more experience with this form of perception (Schenkman & Nilsson, 2010).

Looking While Listening: Vision and Sound Localization

Our efforts to localize sound sources are often accompanied by looking, and looking is often rewarded by finding—that is, we see the apparent source of the sound, which would seemingly make further localization efforts by the auditory system unnecessary.

However, consider what's going on, for example, when you hear a conversation between a man and a woman on a monaural TV with a single speaker to the side of the screen. The sound originates from the same location for both voices—it comes from the TV speaker—and if you were sitting in front of the TV with your eyes closed, your auditory system would localize the sound source at the position of the speaker. But as soon as you opened your eyes, you would experience each person's voice as coming from his or her mouth. In other words, when the visual system and the auditory system give you conflicting information about the location of a sound source, your perception tends to be dominated by the visual information, and you hear the sound as coming from the visually determined location. This **ventriloquism effect** is especially powerful when the visual information matches your previous experience, as in this case, where you "know" that voices come from moving mouths and that men's voices characteristically sound one way and women's voices another.

ventriloquism effect The tendency to localize sound on the basis of visual cues when visual and auditory cues provide conflicting information.

The degree to which vision can bias the perceived location of a sound depends on three factors (Recanzone & Sutter, 2008):

- The visual and auditory events must be reasonably close together in time (and, if anything, the visual event should precede the auditory event). Thus, in the situation just described, the voices must come from the speaker reasonably in sync with the man's and woman's mouth movements; the more out of sync, the more you'd tend to localize the voices as coming from the TV speaker.
- The two events must be plausibly linked—that is, the sound must be something that the visual event could be the source of. Thus, if the auditory events corresponding to the man's and woman's mouth movements were the barking of a dog and the meowing of a cat, you'd be likely to localize the sound at the TV speaker.
- The two events must be plausibly close together in space. That is, if the TV were hooked up to a speaker behind you or in another room, rather than just to the side of the screen, you'd be highly likely to localize the sound at that speaker and not at the moving mouths.

Lloyd A. Jeffress (1900–1986). [American Institute of Physics/The Dolph Briscoe Center for American History UT Austin]

Neural Basis of Sound Localization

In humans, a brain structure called the *medial superior olive* (MSO), part of the superior olivary complex in the brain stem (see Figure 10.1), is thought to contain neurons that function as a mechanism for detecting specific ITDs and thus representing the azimuth of sound sources. According to an account first proposed more than 60 years ago by the American psychologist Lloyd A. Jeffress (1948), neurons in both the left and right MSO receive signals from both the left and right cochlear nuclei. These MSO neurons can be termed *coincidence detectors:* they fire only if the signals from the two cochlear nuclei arrive at the same time. Figure 10.13 illustrates how three of these proposed coincidence detectors in the left MSO would respond to a sound with an ITD of 350 microseconds—neuron B is tuned to that ITD and responds strongly, whereas neurons A and C are tuned to different ITDs and respond weakly. Of course, the auditory system would contain many more such circuits than the three illustrated in Figure 10.13, enabling highly accurate auditory localization based on population coding.

The mechanism illustrated in Figure 10.13 is known to exist in barn owls, which hunt at night and use hearing to locate prey. In these birds, a structure in the brain stem called the *nucleus laminaris* contains neurons that function as coincidence detectors for encoding specific ITDs (Carr & Konishi, 1990). In cats, neurons in the superior olivary complex are known to be tuned for ITDs (Yin & Chan, 1990), but the mechanism by which this tuning is accomplished is still under investigation (McAlpine, 2005).

Like ITDs, ILDs are also represented in the brain. Neurons in the auditory cortex are tuned for different ILDs, and the responses of a population of differently tuned neurons provide a neural code for sound localization using ILDs (Mendelson & Grasse, 2000).

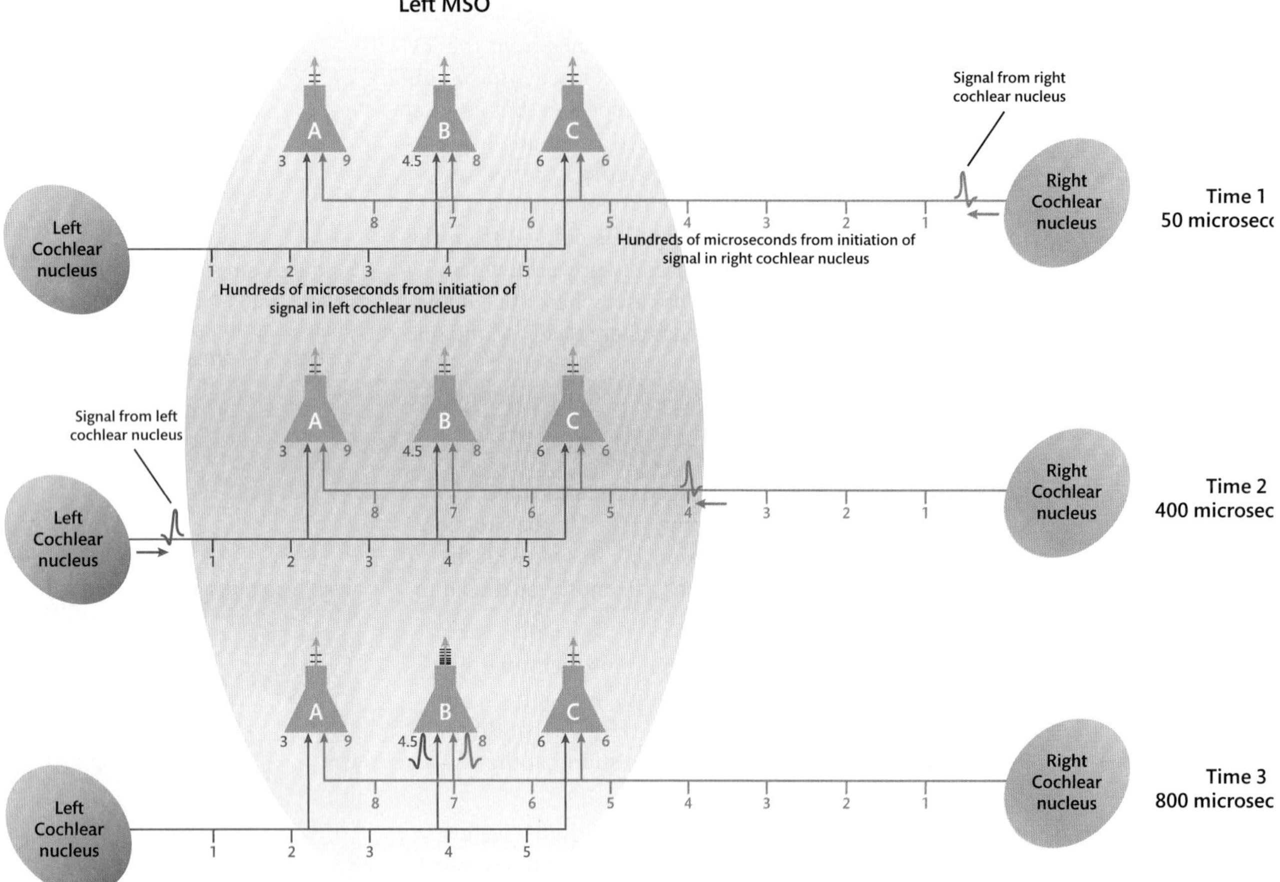

Figure 10.13 How the Brain Computes Interaural Time Differences Neurons in the medial superior olive (MSO) of mammals are tuned for different ITDs. Each neuron in the MSO receives signals from both the left and the right cochlear nucleus and fires most strongly when the signals arrive simultaneously. This illustration shows how three neurons in the left MSO respond to a sound with an ITD of 350 μs, at about 45° right azimuth (as illustrated in Figure 10.8). At Time 1, 50 μs after the initiation of the signal in the right cochlear nucleus, the signal has emerged from the right cochlear nucleus, but no signal has yet been initiated in the left cochlear nucleus. At Time 2, a signal has emerged from the left cochlear nucleus, 350 μs behind the signal from the right cochlear nucleus; meanwhile, the signal from the right cochlear nucleus has traveled some distance toward the MSO. At Time 3, the two signals reach neuron B simultaneously, and it fires strongly. Thus, neuron B is tuned to an ITD of 350 μs. Neuron A, in contrast, is tuned to an ITD of about 600 μs, because a signal from the right cochlear nucleus takes about 600 μs longer to get to neuron A than does a signal from the left cochlear nucleus. And neuron C is tuned to an ITD of 0 μs, because signals take the same amount of time to arrive from both cochlear nuclei. (Adapted from Jeffress, 1948, Figure 1.)

Check Your Understanding

10.10 Explain why, when standing in an open space on a dark night, most people would be better at judging the distance of a crying baby than the distance of a trumpeting elephant.

10.11 True or false? The relative proportion of direct versus reflected sound can help you judge whether a sound source is near or far, and the Doppler effect can help you judge when a sound source is at its closest point.

10.12 In the ventriloquism effect, does auditory perception dominate visual perception or vice versa?

10.13 In Figure 10.13, the initiation of a signal in the left cochlear nucleus occurs

A. at Time 1
B. at Time 2
C. between Time 1 and Time 2

Explain your answer.

Auditory Scene Analysis

Suppose you're sitting in your room listening to a friend telling you an amusing story about a professor; it's hot in the room, so you've got a small fan going; your printer is printing out a term paper you just finished working on; and your alarm clock has just started ringing, to remind you that it's time to get ready for class. Each of these four sound sources—friend, fan, printer, and alarm clock—is producing a sound wave over time, and each of these sound waves contains multiple frequencies. The combination of these four sound waves makes up the current **auditory scene**—all the sound entering your ears during the current interval of time, as illustrated in Figure 10.14. Somehow, with little conscious effort, you extract from this mixture the frequencies associated with each of the sound sources in the scene—so you can pay attention to your friend's voice telling the story, to the printer if you want to check that it's working properly, or to the alarm clock because you want to turn it off. This remarkable ability—called **auditory scene analysis** by the Canadian psychologist Albert S. Bregman (1990)—is the basis for our use of hearing to make sense of the auditory world.

auditory scene All the sound entering the ears during the current interval of time.

Albert S. Bregman (b. 1936). [Courtesy of Albert S. Bregman]

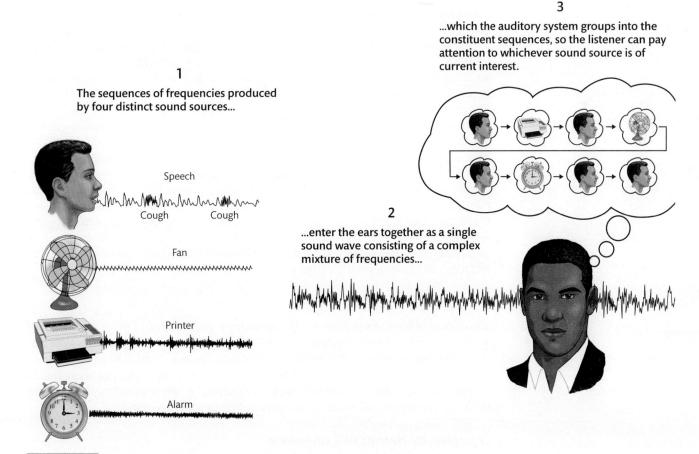

The first and most important step in auditory scene analysis is to organize the auditory scene perceptually into a set of distinct auditory streams. An **auditory stream** is an assortment of frequencies occurring over time that all "go together" because they were emitted by the same sound source or by related sources. For example, in the scene illustrated in Figure 10.14, the frequencies in your friend's voice all go together and are perceived as an auditory stream, distinct from the auditory stream of frequencies produced by the fan. This process of perceptual organization of the auditory scene into a set of distinct auditory streams is analogous to perceptual organization in vision, where the visual system organizes the visual scene into a set of

1
The sequences of frequencies produced by four distinct sound sources...
Speech
Cough
Cough
Fan
Printer
Alarm
2
...enter the ears together as a single sound wave consisting of a complex mixture of frequencies...
3
...which the auditory system groups into the constituent sequences, so the listener can pay attention to whichever sound source is of current interest.

Figure 10.14 Auditory Scene Analysis Sound waves from four sound sources enter the listener's ear as a complex mixture of frequencies. The listener can separate the mixture into its original constituents and attend to the sounds produced by each of the sound sources separately, a process called *auditory scene analysis*.

auditory scene analysis The process of extracting and grouping together the frequencies emitted by specific sound sources from among the complex mixture of frequencies emitted by multiple sound sources within the auditory scene.

auditory stream An assortment of frequencies occurring over time that were all emitted by the same sound source or related sound sources.

distinct objects. (It's worth mentioning that the wonderful demonstration of perceptual organization in vision shown in Figure 4.10 was created by Bregman.)

Just as two visual objects may overlap in space, two auditory streams may overlap in frequency. In vision, the visual system must group the regions that belong together into a single visual object, while separating out the regions that belong to other, overlapping visual objects (see Figure 4.6). The auditory system faces a similar task—it must group the frequencies that go together as frequencies belonging to a single auditory stream, while separating out the frequencies that belong to other, simultaneous auditory streams, despite the occurrence of all these frequencies in the same stretch of time.

On what basis can the auditory system decide whether a complex sound wave, made up of multiple frequencies, is being produced by a single source or by multiple sources? And if the answer is that the scene contains multiple sources, how does the auditory system decide which frequencies were produced by which source?

You might think that auditory localization would provide an important basis for grouping sounds into streams emitted by different sources—for example, if the fan is to your left and your talking friend is to your right, then the frequencies in the mixture that can be localized as coming from the right could reasonably be grouped into a stream belonging to your friend's voice. However, perceptual grouping of frequencies is almost as good even when all the sounds in a scene are coming from a single location. For example, if the sound of your friend's voice and the sound of the fan were recorded together and played back over a single speaker, you'd have no problem grouping the frequencies correctly. Therefore, localization is clearly not the only basis for grouping—nor, as it turns out, is localization even the most important basis.

Consider an auditory scene in which all the sounds come from one location. The scene begins in silence, and then several frequency components appear all at the same time. How should this be interpreted by the auditory system? There are at least two possibilities. One is that all the frequency components were produced by a single sound source (e.g., a door slamming), that they mark the beginning of a single auditory stream; this would explain why they all began simultaneously. The other possibility is that multiple independent sound sources all happened, by chance, to begin producing sounds at the same moment in time. Both of these situations are possible, but the former is much more likely than the latter, and the auditory system would do well to use the simultaneous onset of all the frequency components as a basis for concluding that they are part of a single auditory stream.

Principles like simultaneous onset for grouping frequencies—used by the auditory system to make a "best guess" about the auditory streams making up the current auditory scene—are analogous to the principles used by the visual system to group visual features in order to make a best guess about the objects making up the visual scene. Like the visual principles, auditory grouping principles aren't infallible, but they're often correct, especially when several principles lead to the same answer. And like the visual principles, they reflect certain physical regularities in the world that we have become expert at detecting, as a result of natural selection and evolution. Table 10.1 summarizes some of these regularities and indicates how they correspond across the two senses. Auditory regularities like the ones in this table lead directly to the various grouping principles that we'll explore next.

Simultaneous Grouping

The mixture of frequencies arriving at the ear within a given interval of time can be grouped according to two different principles. One is harmonic coherence—frequencies that are harmonics (i.e., integer multiples) of the same fundamental frequency tend to be grouped together as part of the same auditory stream. The other is synchrony—frequencies that begin, end, or change at the same time also tend to be grouped together (e.g., when an auditory scene begins in silence and then several frequency components appear simultaneously).

Grouping by Harmonic Coherence

The human voice, most musical instruments, and a variety of other types of sound sources produce complex sound waves consisting of a fundamental frequency and a series of harmonics that are all integer multiples of the fundamental (see Figure 9.8). When the auditory system is presented with such a sound wave, it can entertain two possibilities—that all the harmonics

TABLE 10.1 How Auditory and Visual Regularities Correspond

Audition	Vision
Unrelated auditory streams rarely start or stop at exactly the same time.	Unrelated visual objects rarely have exactly coinciding boundaries.
The features of a single auditory stream (frequency, amplitude, and timbre) tend to change slowly and gradually over time. An abrupt change often signals a new auditory stream.	The surface features of a single object (e.g., color and texture) tend to change slowly and gradually across adjacent locations. An abrupt change often coincides with the boundary between two objects.
All the frequency components of a single auditory stream tend to change in the same way at the same time (e.g., by growing louder as the sound source approaches the listener).	All the parts of a single object tend to change in the same way at the same time (e.g., by moving together, if the object is rigid).

Adapted from Bregman (1993).

are coming from a single source or that many independent sources are emitting frequencies that, completely by chance, are related to each other in precisely this way. Clearly, this is another situation is which both scenarios are possible, but the former is much more likely and is the interpretation that the auditory system strongly tends to prefer.

Figure 10.15 illustrates an experimental setup that reveals this principle at work. A listener is presented with a sound consisting of several frequencies that are all multiples of the same harmonic—for example, five pure tones comprising the first five harmonics of the fundamental frequency of 220 Hz, as shown in Figure 10.15a. The listener's auditory system will group together these frequencies, and the listener will perceive the mixture as one sound—that is,

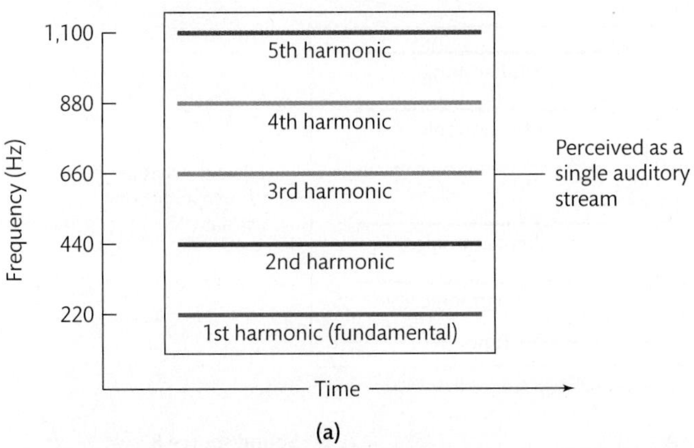

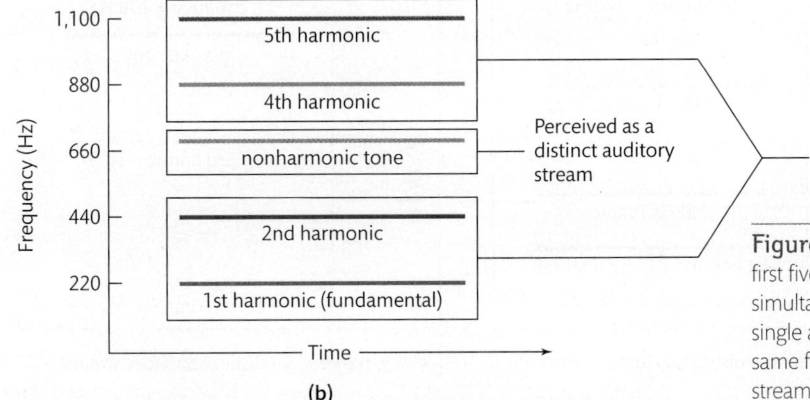

Figure 10.15 Grouping by Harmonic Coherence I (a) When the first five harmonics of the fundamental frequency 220 Hz are presented simultaneously, the listener's auditory system groups the five tones into a single auditory stream. (b) If one of the five tones isn't a harmonic of the same fundamental frequency, that tone stands out as a separate auditory stream against the harmonic background.

as a single auditory stream; indeed, without some training, listeners find it difficult to hear the individual tones. But if one of the tones isn't part of the harmonic sequence, as shown in Figure 10.15b, that tone will stand out as a separate auditory stream against the background of the mixture of the other tones (which will still group into a single stream).

Figure 10.16 illustrates a different setup that demonstrates this same principle in operation. If two sound sources produce tones that are all harmonics of the same fundamental frequency—as shown in Figure 10.16a, where the fundamental frequency is again 220 Hz, one sound source produces the first, second, and fourth harmonics, and the other sound source produces the third and fifth harmonics—the listener will perceive the mixture as a single auditory stream coming from a single sound source (presuming that the two sound sources are reasonably close to each other in space). But if, as shown in Figure 10.16b, one of the sound sources produces harmonics of a different fundamental frequency (200 Hz)—where neither fundamental frequency is an integer multiple of the other—the listener will perceive the mixtures of tones from the two sound sources as two distinct auditory streams.

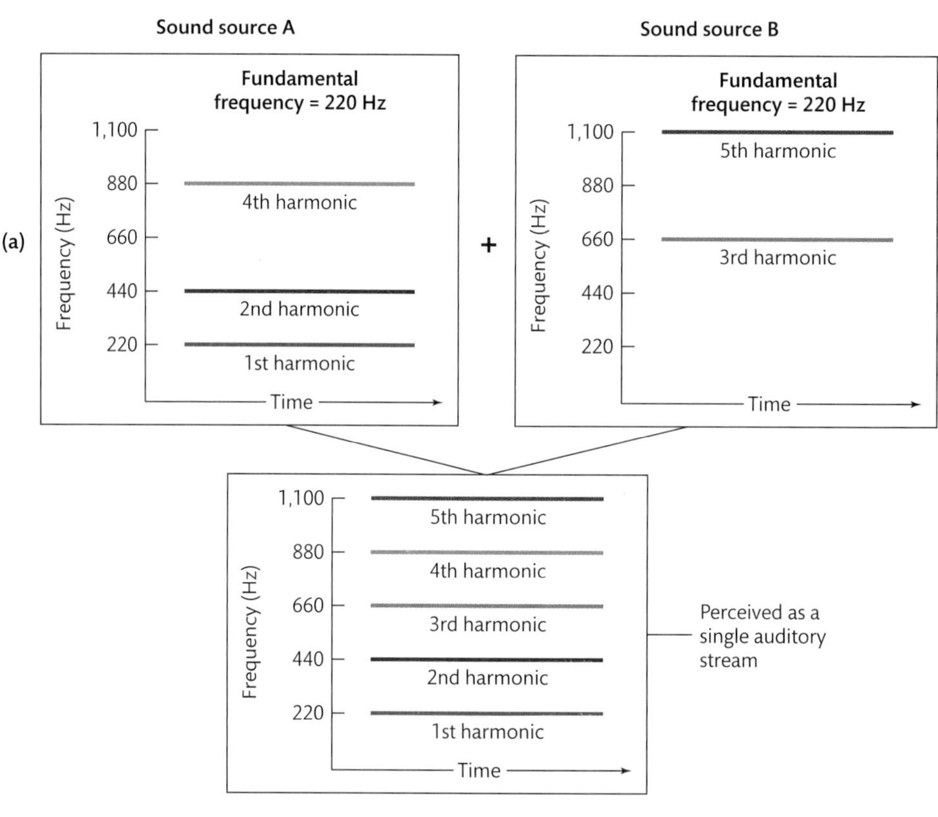

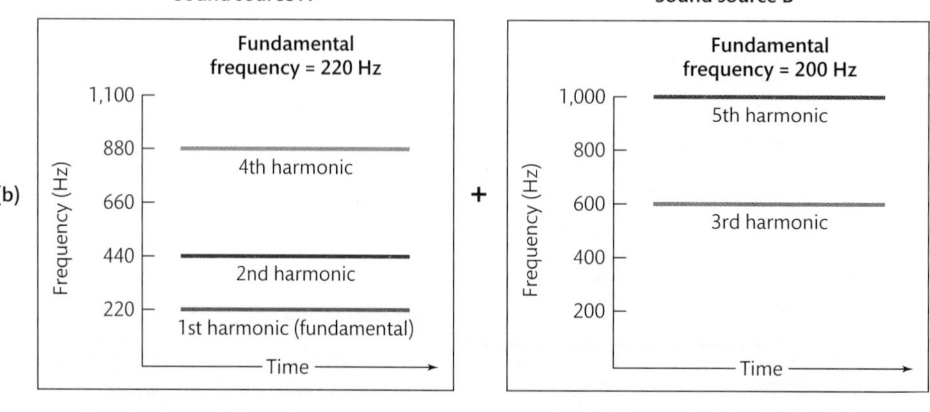

Figure 10.16 Grouping by Harmonic Coherence II (a) The first five harmonics of the fundamental frequency 220 Hz are presented simultaneously from two different sound sources; the listener groups the five tones, which are perceived as a single auditory stream. (b) If the two sound sources produce harmonics of different fundamental frequencies, the tones from each source are grouped separately and perceived as separate auditory streams.

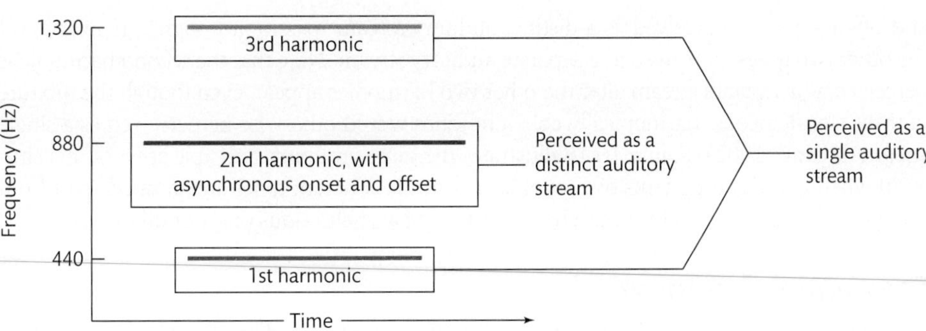

Figure 10.17 Grouping by Synchronous Onset and Offset If a listener is presented with three harmonics of the same fundamental frequency (in this case, 440 Hz), but one frequency begins before and ends after the other two—that is, it has an asynchronous onset and offset—it's perceived as a distinct auditory stream that "passes through" the background of the other two harmonics, which are grouped together. (Adapted from Vicario, 1982.)

Grouping by Synchrony or Asynchrony

Two unrelated auditory events rarely begin, end, or change at exactly the same time in the same way. For example, in heavy traffic two drivers might occasionally start blowing their horns simultaneously, but one will typically stop before the other or switch from a long continuous honk to rapid short honks. In a situation like this, a listener might have the initial impression that one loud horn is blowing but will quickly perceive that two sound sources are at work. In contrast, all the frequency components of a single auditory stream (e.g., the many frequency components produced by the clarinet in Figure 9.8) do start, stop, and change in synchrony. Grouping based on such synchrony or asynchrony is not unlike visual grouping based on the principle of common motion. The auditory system uses these regularities as very powerful grouping principles, as illustrated in Figures 10.17 and 10.18.

Figure 10.17 shows a setup in which a listener is presented with three harmonically coherent pure tones—the first three harmonics of the fundamental frequency 440 Hz. If the tones began and ended simultaneously, the mixture would be perceived as a single auditory stream (analogous to the situation illustrated by Figure 10.15a), but in this case the second harmonic begins before and ends after the other two—that is, it has an asynchronous onset

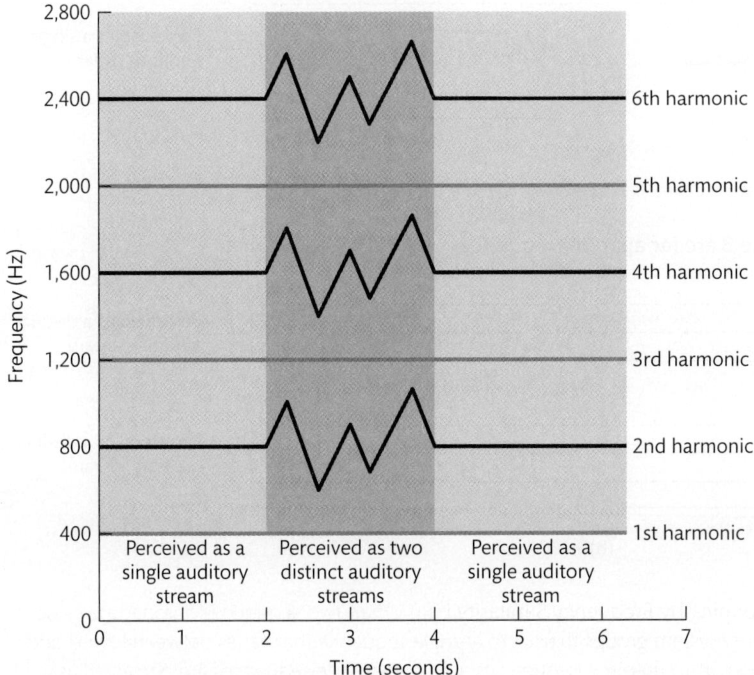

Figure 10.18 Grouping by Synchronous Change The first six harmonics of the fundamental frequency 400 Hz begin together; the listener's auditory system groups all six frequencies and perceives the mixture as a single auditory stream. Then three of the harmonics begin changing up and down in frequency together while the remaining three remain steady; during this period of synchronous change, the three changing harmonics are grouped apart from the rest. After the changing stops, and the six harmonics return to their previous steady state, they are again grouped as a single stream.

and offset—and it's perceived as a distinct auditory stream "passing through" the mixture of the other two tones, perceived as a separate auditory stream. Note that the second harmonic is perceived as a separate stream after the other two harmonics appear, even though the mixture of three simultaneous, harmonically coherent tones would otherwise be perceived as a single stream (Vicario, 1982). Figure 10.18 illustrates the same grouping principle at work in a situation where some components of a set of harmonically coherent tones are grouped apart from the others because of synchronous change instead of asynchronous onset or offset.

Sequential Grouping

By its very nature, sound unfolds in time, so it's important to understand the principles that the auditory system uses to group frequencies that occur at different times—that is, sequentially rather than simultaneously. In this section, we'll see how the auditory system uses both similarity in the frequencies of sequential tones and their temporal proximity (how close together in time they occur) to determine which tones should be grouped together and perceived as part of a single auditory stream.

Grouping by Frequency Similarity

As I write this, a bird is singing enthusiastically from its perch in a tree outside my window. If I could listen to a single note of this song and then stop time and ask myself to guess the frequency of the next note, I would do well to pick a frequency close to the frequency of the note I just heard. In fact, if the next note was *very* different in frequency, my auditory system would be likely to conclude that a different bird had started singing (or that a dog had started barking)—in other words, that a different auditory stream had begun.

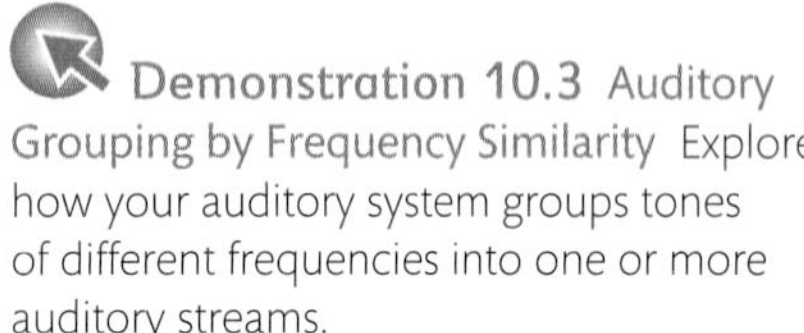
Demonstration 10.3 Auditory Grouping by Frequency Similarity Explore how your auditory system groups tones of different frequencies into one or more auditory streams.

Figure 10.19 illustrates how the auditory system uses the frequency similarity of sequential tones to group those tones into a single auditory stream or into multiple separate auditory streams. When a listener hears a sequence of pure tones that vary between two frequencies, and the alternating frequencies are close to one another, then the listener often perceives the sequence as a single auditory stream, warbling up and down. This is shown in Figure 10.19a, where the frequencies of tone A and tone B are close and the sequence A B A A B A . . . is perceived as a single stream. In contrast, if the two alternating tones are far apart in frequency, as

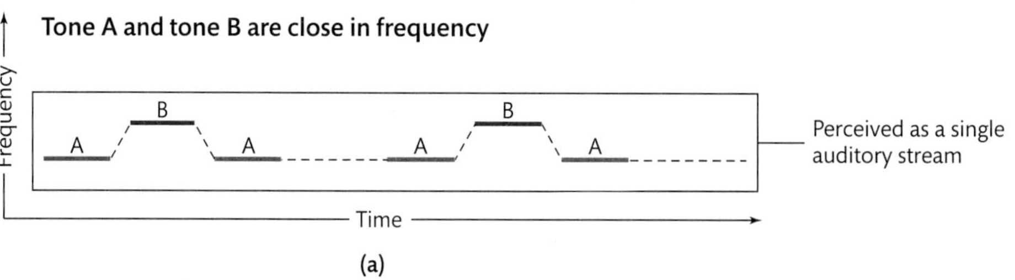

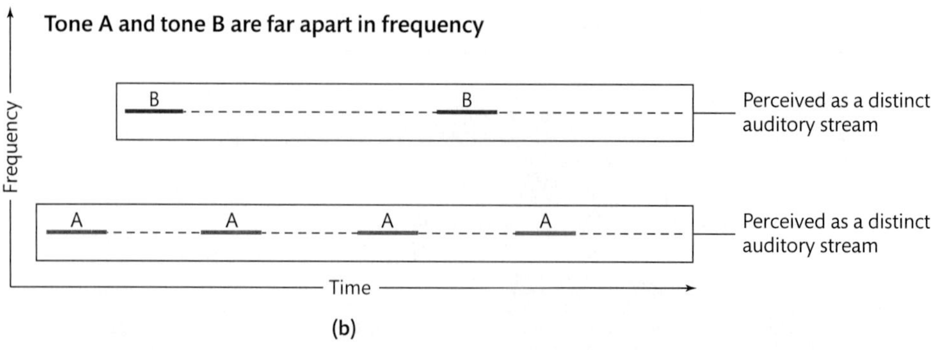

Figure 10.19 Grouping by Frequency Similarity I (a) When two sequences of tones are close in frequency, the auditory system groups them into a single sequence that varies between lower- and higher-frequency tones. (b) When the frequencies are far apart, the sequences are perceived as separate auditory streams.

shown in Figure 10.19b, then the listener perceives two separate auditory streams, a lower-frequency sequence A A A . . . and a higher-frequency sequence B B B . . . .

Figure 10.20 illustrates a different experimental situation in which frequency similarity is used as a grouping principle. The listener is presented with two target tones—a lower-frequency tone A and a higher-frequency tone B—and is required to judge whether the pair of tones rises or falls in frequency. As shown in Figure 10.20a, when the target tones are presented in isolation—that is, without any other tones also being presented—listeners find it easy to judge the order of the tones.

However, when two same-frequency flanker tones are also presented, as illustrated in Figure 10.20b, judging the order of tones A and B becomes much more difficult. Finally, when the two flanker tones are preceded and followed by a sequence of captor tones of the same frequency as the flanker tones, as shown in Figure 10.20c, judging the order of tones A and B is once again easy.

Obviously, the sequence in Figure 10.20a is easy because all the listener has to do is listen to two tones and judge whether the frequency rises or falls. In Figure 10.20b, the difficulty arises from the fact that there are three upward or downward transitions in frequency—from the first flanker tone to the first target tone, from the first target tone to the second target tone, and from the second target tone to the second flanker tone—so the listener can't just listen for an isolated upward or downward transition but must listen for and remember the middle of three transitions.

But what accounts for the ease of judgment in Figure 10.20c? Here is where grouping by frequency similarity comes into play. The captor tones "capture" the flanker tones—that is, the flanker tones and captor tones now are perceived as a sequence of tones of similar (in

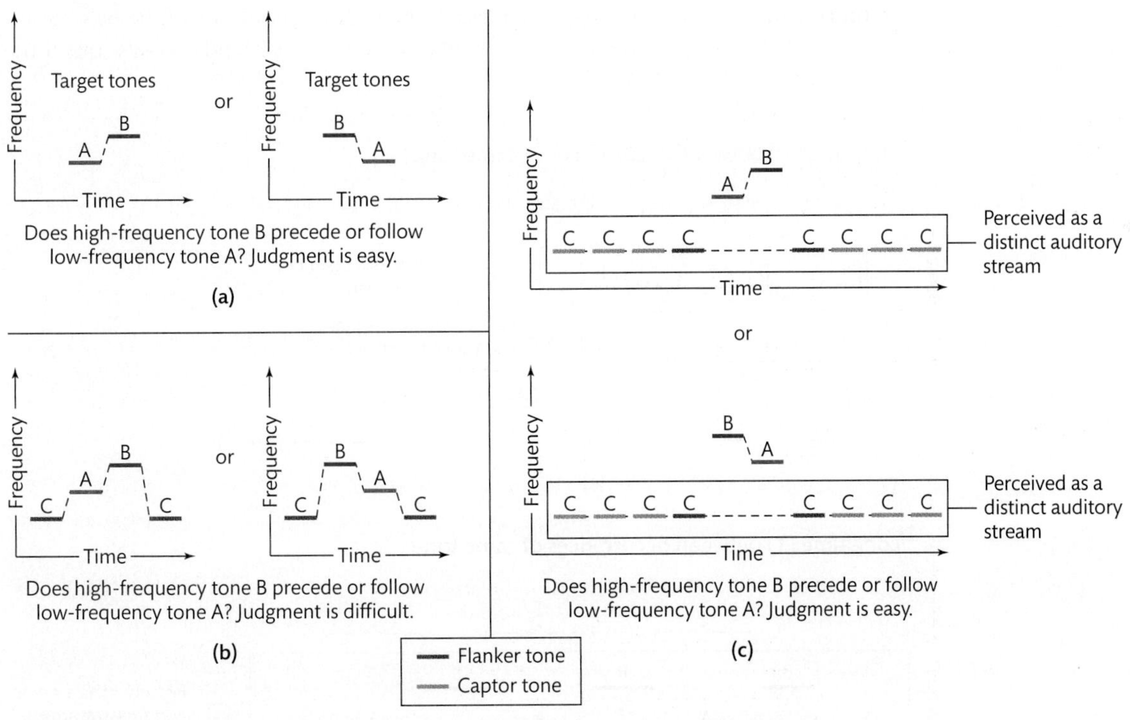

Figure 10.20 **Grouping by Frequency Similarity II** (a) The listener hears two target tones—a lower tone A and a higher tone B. Regardless of the order in which the target tones are presented, the listener finds it easy to judge whether the pair is rising (A–B) or falling (B–A) in frequency. (b) When two flanker tones C are presented before and after the target tones, the listener finds it difficult to judge the order of the target tones, because the flanker tones group with the target tones, producing a rising sequence at the beginning and a falling sequence at the end, which makes the rising or falling sequence in the middle hard to pick out. (c) When captor tones of the same frequency as the flanker tones precede and follow the flanker tones, the captor tones and flanker tones are grouped into a single sequence that's perceived as a separate auditory stream, apart from the target tones. Now the target tones are perceived in isolation, and judging their order is once again easy. (Adapted from Bregman & Rudnicky, 1975.)

fact, identical) frequency, and the auditory system automatically groups this sequence into a distinct auditory stream, leaving the target tones to be once again perceived in isolation, as in Figure 10.20a, and the transition from the first to the second target tone is once again easy to hear. It's as if the flanker tones—and the transitions between the flanker tones and the target tones—were simply part of the background, not interacting with the target tones to produce rising or falling transitions that would compete with the transition between the target tones (Bregman & Rudnicky, 1975).

Grouping by Temporal Proximity

Demonstration 10.4 Auditory Grouping by Temporal Proximity Explore how your auditory system groups alternating tones based on the temporal proximity of the tones.

Just as sequences of tones that are close together in frequency tend to be grouped together, while sequences that are far apart in frequency tend to be grouped separately (see Figure 10.19), so do tones that are close together or far apart in time. Consider, for example, two sequences of tones—a lower-frequency sequence and a higher-frequency sequence—where a relatively short time separates successive tones in each sequence, as illustrated by the sequences of tones A and B in Figure 10.21a. Here, the listener would tend to perceive the two sequences as two distinct auditory streams. But if successive tones in the two sequences are farther apart in time, as shown in Figure 10.21b, the listener tends to group together the two sequences into a single auditory stream, a single sequence bouncing slowly up and down in frequency.

Perceptual Completion of Occluded Sounds

We are often confronted with auditory scenes in which some sounds, like the speech sounds of a friend with whom you're talking, are occluded (hidden) by other sounds, like the sounds made by a passing bus. Of course, if the occluding sounds of the bus last for a long time, it's likely that you'll fail to perceive some of your friend's words, but if the

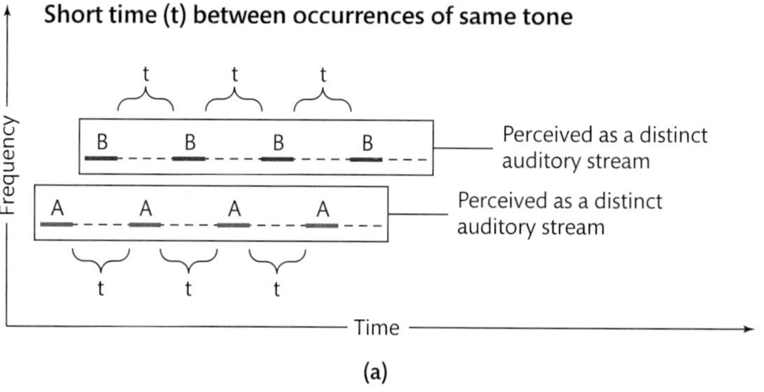

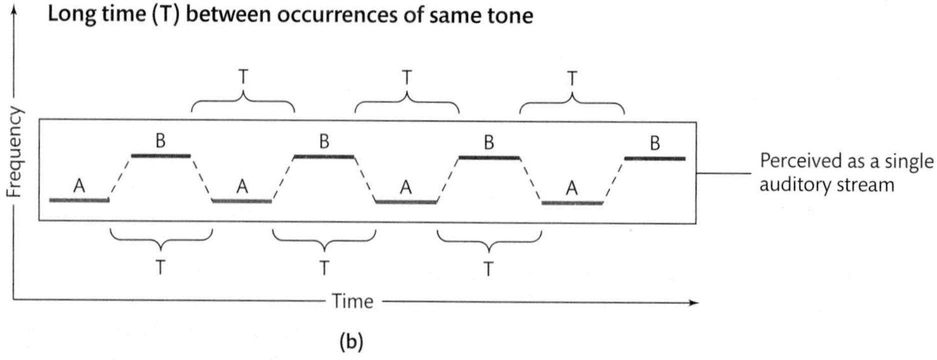

Figure 10.21 Grouping by Temporal Proximity Two sequences of tones are presented—a lower-frequency sequence of tones A and a higher-frequency sequence of tones B. (a) When a relatively short time separates successive tones of the same frequency, each frequency sequence is grouped as a distinct auditory stream. (b) When the time between successive tones gets longer, the two frequency sequences are grouped together into a single auditory stream.

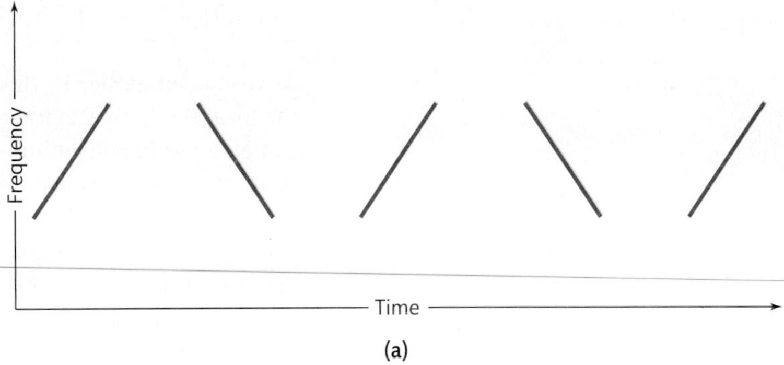

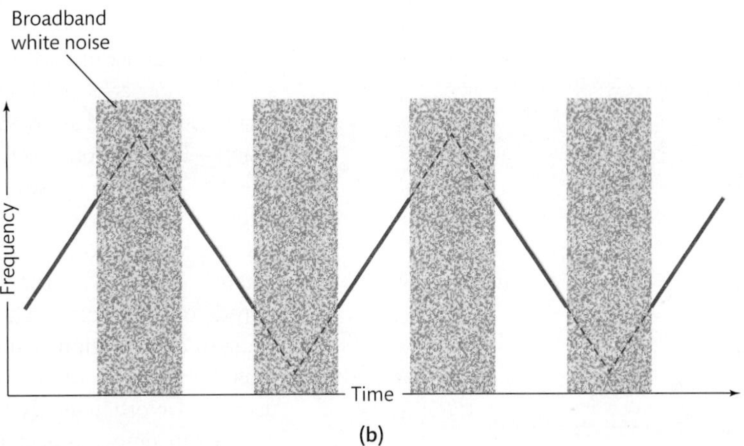

Figure 10.22 Perceptual Completion of Occluded Sounds (a) Pure-tone glides (red lines) are separated by silent gaps. Both the glides and the gaps are perceived. (b) When the gaps are filled with broadband white noise, illusory glides (dashed red lines) are perceived "behind" the noise.

interruption is brief enough, you may not even notice it—that is, you'll seem actually to perceive the occluded words.

This phenomenon is illustrated in Figure 10.22. A listener is presented with a sequence of pure-tone glides—that is, pure tones that glide smoothly up or down in frequency—separated by brief gaps of silence, as shown in Figure 10.22a. In this condition, the listener perceives both the glides and the gaps. Then, in the condition illustrated in Figure 10.22b, the gaps are filled with broadband white noise, which sounds like static, and the listener perceives the glides as continuing "behind" the noise. In other words, the listener's auditory system automatically assumes that the glides are making an uninterrupted sound that rises smoothly to a high frequency, declines smoothly to a low frequency, rises smoothly again, and so on—just as when you seem actually to perceive your friend's words when the bus goes by.

This auditory phenomenon is analogous to the visual phenomenon of perceptual interpolation, where the observer perceives partly occluded edges or surfaces as continuing behind an occluder (see Figures 4.23 and 4.24). Also, note what this type of perceptual interpolation implies: our auditory and visual systems have evolved to automatically make "best guesses" about what's really going on behind occluding sounds and shapes, because making those guesses usually enables us to respond to environmental conditions more quickly and accurately than we otherwise would. The experimental situation described here, with listeners perceiving nonexistent tones behind white noise, simply exploits this automatic process in order to reveal it.

Demonstration 10.5 Perceptual Completion of Occluded Sounds Explore the conditions under which you seem to perceive tones or words that are occluded by white noise.

Check Your Understanding

10.14 Write a sentence that relates the terms *auditory scene, auditory scene analysis,* and *auditory stream.*

10.15 Describe a scenario that shows that sound localization isn't always the basis for grouping frequencies into distinct auditory streams.

10.16 Suppose that a computer is producing three pure tones simultaneously, with frequencies of 1,000, 1,500, and 4,000 Hz, and that the 1,500-Hz tone starts one-half second before and ends one-half second after the other two tones. Into how many distinct auditory streams would listeners tend to group these tones, and which tones would be in each stream?

10.17 After which sequence of events would listeners tend to be more accurate at recalling whether the sound of the train whistle preceded or followed the sound of the foghorn?

A. car horn – train whistle – foghorn – car horn

B. car horn – car horn – car horn – train whistle – foghorn – car horn – car horn – car horn

10.18 You're watching *Jaws* on TV for the hundredth time, but it's still a very tense and exciting experience. It's the scene where the police chief (played by Roy Scheider) says, "You're gonna need a bigger boat." Just as he says the word "boat," your dog barks, completely masking the sound of the TV. Explain why you're likely to think you heard the word "boat."

APPLICATIONS Seeing by Hearing

As discussed earlier in this chapter, echolocating bats can use sound to sense not only the location of objects in their environment, but their shape and texture as well. Humans can also use echolocation to determine whether they're in an open space, as in a field, or in an enclosed space, as in a tunnel, and to determine how far away a wall or large object is. Blind people, in particular, can develop this ability quite highly. This has motivated scientists and engineers to explore ways of enhancing blind individuals' ability to use sound to perceive the spatial layout of scenes, including the ability to perceive the shapes of individual objects.

sensory substitution device (SSD) Any artificial aid in the process of acquiring information via one sense that is usually acquired via another sense.

The use of one sense, such as audition, to acquire information that's usually obtained via another sense, such as vision, is known as *sensory substitution,* and any artificial aid in this process is termed a **sensory substitution device** (**SSD**). Perhaps the most familiar example of sensory substitution is reading, where writing is the SSD, the artificial aid that lets you use vision to acquire information that's usually obtained via audition (i.e., by listening to speech). For people without vision, Braille is an SSD used to get the same information, and a cane can be used as an SSD to get information via touch that is usually obtained through vision—information about the location of objects (Bach-y-Rita & Kercel, 2003).

The different sensory modalities make use of different types of stimuli to acquire information from the environment—for example, vision acquires information about a scene via the location and brightness of light reflected from surfaces in the scene, whereas audition acquires information about sound sources via the frequency and amplitude of sound caused by events in the auditory scene, and touch acquires information via skin deformations caused by touched surfaces. Thus, in designing an SSD, choices must be made about how to map the stimuli used by one sense onto stimuli that can be used by the other sense.

For instance, in designing an SSD to substitute touch for vision, a natural approach would be to map the spatial array of brightnesses in a visual scene onto a spatial array of skin indentations on the fingertips, because the spatial resolution of touch receptors there is very high. But for an SSD aimed at substituting sound for vision, the most appropriate mapping is not spatial-to-spatial, because the spatial resolution of hearing is much lower than that of vision. Instead, researchers have made use of the exquisite sensitivity of the auditory system to differences in frequency (pitch) and amplitude (loudness) to design SSDs that map a spatial array of pixels with different locations and brightnesses onto temporal sequences of sound waves with different frequencies and amplitudes. Location maps onto time and frequency, and brightness maps onto amplitude, as illustrated in Figure 10.23 (Meijer, 1992).

A listener using an SSD based on a mapping like this (as illustrated in Figure 10.23, bottom) would first hear the complex sound wave corresponding to the pixels in column 1, followed by the wave corresponding to column 2, and so on through column 8. In order to "see" the array, the listener must learn to translate the changes in the complex sound waves into a mental representation of the spatial array. With sufficient practice (up to 60 hours), listeners using a similar SSD were able to achieve an accuracy of 53–86% in identifying novel images, where chance performance would have been 25% correct (Amedi et al., 2007).

To what extent are the quotation marks around the word "see" in the preceding paragraph actually needed—in other words, do blind users of such an SSD actually construct *visual* representations in their brains and thereby actually *see* the images? To answer this question, researchers used fMRI to measure brain activity in five sighted individuals and two blind individuals who had been trained to recognize shapes using this type of SSD (Amedi et al., 2007). As a control, they also used fMRI to measure brain activity in a different group of five sighted individuals who had learned to relate the same sounds to the names of the objects those sounds depicted. That is, these individuals did not form visual representations of the objects in response to the sounds; instead, they recalled from memory the names of the objects.

None of the sighted individuals in the control group exhibited activation in the lateral occipital area, which is associated with the recognition of visual shapes. In contrast, strong

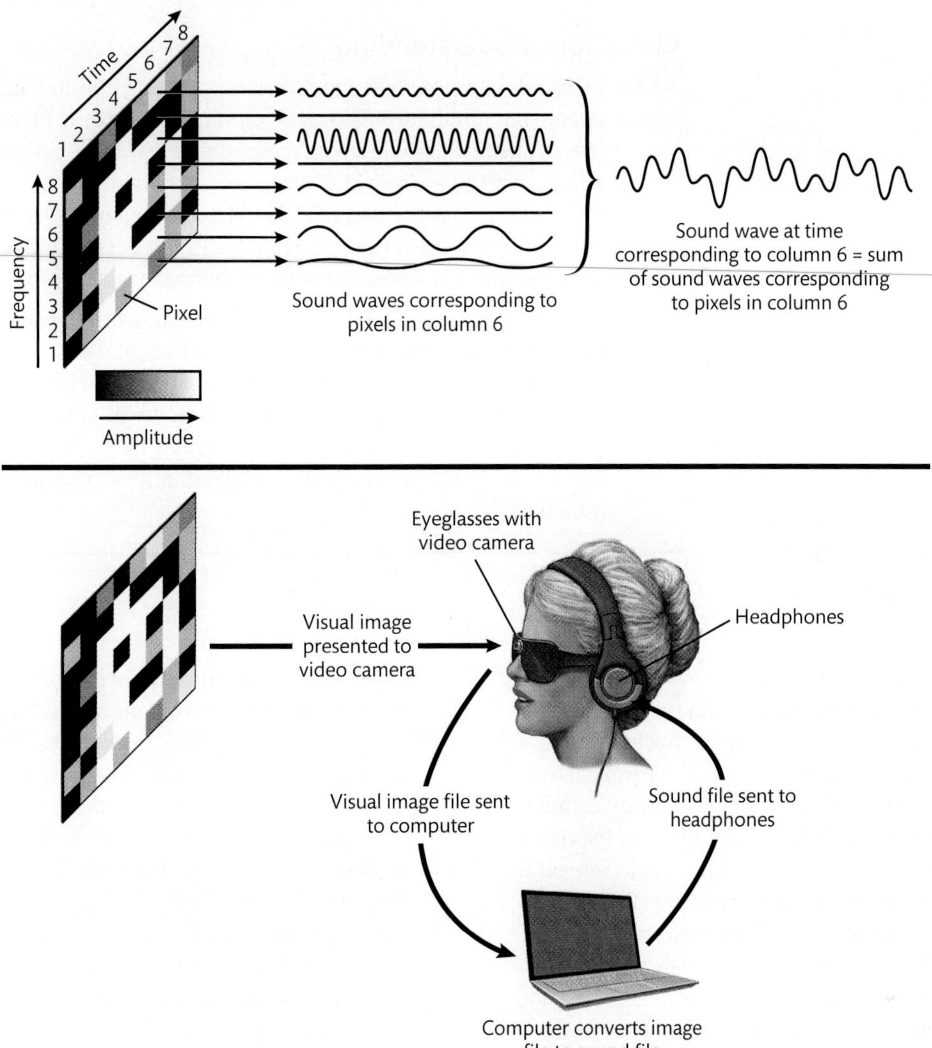

Figure 10.23 A Visual-to-Auditory Sensory Substitution Device (top) A visual image consists of an 8 × 8 array of pixels, each with a fixed brightness level, ranging from black through various shades of gray to white. Each pixel corresponds to a sinusoidal sound wave. The frequency of the wave is determined by the row the pixel is in (row 1, at the bottom, is the lowest frequency, row 8 is the highest frequency); the amplitude is determined by the brightness of the pixel (black is 0 amplitude, different shades of gray are intermediate amplitudes, and white is high amplitude). The entire array corresponds to sounds produced over time, where time is determined by the column number (time flows from column 1, at the left, to column 8). Here, we see the sound waves produced by the pixels at the time corresponding to column 6: the dark gray pixel in row 1 produces a very low frequency wave with a low amplitude; the white pixel in row 2 produces a slightly higher frequency wave with a much higher amplitude; the black pixel in row 3 produces a wave with 0 amplitude; and so on. The combined sound wave produced at this time is the sum of the waves produced by the eight pixels in that column. (bottom) The array is presented to a person wearing a visual-to-auditory sensory substitution device consisting of a video camera mounted on eyeglasses, a computer, and headphones. The camera translates the visual image into a video image file; the image file is sent to the computer, which is programmed to convert it into sound, using the pixel-to-sound correspondences described above; the sound is sent to the person's ears via the headphones. (Adapted from Meijer, 1992, and Amedi et al., 2007.)

activation in this brain region was observed in both the sighted and the blind individuals who had learned to use the SSD, including one individual who had been blind from birth. The researchers concluded that the users' brains had learned to automatically translate the sounds produced by the SSD into visual representations, using some of the same neural machinery normally used to construct visual representations. These results provide promising evidence that SSDs may eventually enable blind individuals to regain some visual function in everyday life, not just in the laboratory.

Check Your Understanding

10.19 In an exhibition. a chess grandmaster is playing blindfolded against 20 expert opponents simultaneously—and winning every game! (This is actually often the case in such exhibitions.) The grandmaster learns his opponents' moves from a referee, who tells him which piece each opponent has moved to which square, and the grandmaster then tells the referee which move to make in response. In this scenario, what is the sensory substitution device, and which sense is being used to acquire information usually obtained via which other sense?

10.20 Look back at Figure 10.23. Over the period from time 1 to time 8, how many different complex sound waves would a user of this sensory substitution device have to analyze into their component pure tones? How many different pure tones would each of these complex sound waves contain? Is it likely that all the occurrences of a pure tone with a particular frequency would have the same amplitude? What characteristic of light is represented by the amplitude of the pure tones?

SUMMARY

- The Auditory Brain Auditory information travels via ascending pathways that begin at the inner hair cells in the cochlea, which send signals to the ipsilateral cochlear nucleus in the brain stem. Then, signals travel from each cochlear nucleus to both the ipsilateral and contralateral superior olivary complex, also in the brain stem. From there, signals go to the inferior colliculus in the midbrain, then to the medial geniculate body in the thalamus, and then to the auditory cortex. Beginning with the superior olivary complex, all the brain structures on the ascending auditory pathways receive signals from both ears. Descending signals appear to play a role in attention and in fine discrimination of frequencies. The auditory cortex, located on the upper part of the temporal lobe, contains the auditory core region, which consists of area A1, the rostral core, and the rostrotemporal core. The belt and the parabelt are wrapped around the auditory core region and receive signals from it. Neurons in area A1 and in the rostral core are arranged into tonotopic maps, and, probably, so are neurons in the rostrotemporal core. Frequency-tuned neurons in these areas can have narrow or broad tuning widths. The auditory system appears to exhibit a "what" and "where" organization like that of the visual system—information flows along a ventral "what" pathway toward the anterior part of the temporal lobe and then into the frontal lobe, and along a dorsal "where" pathway into the parietal lobe. Large areas along both these pathways are multimodal, responding to both auditory and visual information.
- Localizing Sounds Sound localization is based on comparing aspects of the sound arriving at the two ears. Accuracy in determining the azimuth (left–right position) of a sound source varies with both azimuth and frequency and is measured in terms of the minimum audible angle. The interaural level difference (the difference in the level of a sound at the two ears)—mainly an effect of the acoustic shadow—is a good cue for perceiving the azimuth of pure tones at high frequencies but not low frequencies. The interaural time difference (the difference in the arrival times of a sound at the two ears) is a good cue for perceiving the azimuth of pure tones at low frequencies but not high frequencies. Head motion is used to disambiguate azimuth, to determine whether a sound is coming from one location or another on a cone of confusion. The spectral shape cue—an effect of pinna shape—is used to determine elevation. For familiar sounds, loudness can help determine the distance of the sound source. In enclosed spaces, echoes can help determine distance. When the sound source is moving, the Doppler effect provides cues to distance. Echolocating bats track and capture prey by emitting sounds and processing the echoes, and people—especially the blind—can use echolocation to detect and judge the distance of walls and other objects. When audition and vision provide conflicting information for sound localization, the visual cues tend to predominate—this is the ventriloquism effect. In humans, neurons in the medial superior olive are thought to function as coincidence detectors, providing a neural basis for sound localization.
- Auditory Scene Analysis Auditory scene analysis involves perceptual organization of the auditory scene into distinct auditory streams. As in vision, the principles of perceptual organization are based on best guesses and reflect the physical regularities that we have evolved to detect. Principles of simultaneous grouping include grouping by harmonic coherence (frequencies that are all integer multiples of a fundamental frequency are grouped together) and grouping by synchrony or asynchrony (frequencies that start and/or stop at the same time are grouped together; frequencies that start and/or stop at different times are grouped separately). Principles of sequential grouping include grouping by frequency similarity (sounds with similar frequencies are grouped together) and grouping by temporal proximity (grouping depends on how close together or far apart in time sounds are). In many situations, listeners perceptually complete occluded sounds—they tend to perceive sounds that are masked by other sounds

or to perceive sounds "behind" a masking sound even when those sounds are not actually present.

- Applications: Seeing by Hearing Blind people can learn to use audition to acquire visual information, with the help of a sensory substitution device consisting of a digital camera, a computer, and headphones. The camera sends an image file to the computer, which converts it into a sound file, which is sent to the headphones. The person learns to analyze the sound coming through the headphones so as to perceive the image. Experiments using fMRI indicate that the brains of individuals using such a device actually construct representations of visual images.

KEY TERMS

A1, see **primary auditory cortex.**
acoustic shadow (p. 331)
auditory core region (p. 326)
auditory cortex (p. 326)
auditory scene (p. 341)
auditory scene analysis (p. 341)
auditory stream (p. 341)
azimuth (p. 330)
belt (p. 326)
cochlear nucleus (p. 324)
cone of confusion (p. 333)
distance (p. 330)
Doppler effect (p. 337)
echolocation (p. 337)
elevation (p. 330)
inferior colliculus (p. 324)
interaural level difference (ILD) (p. 331)
interaural time difference (ITD) (p. 332)
medial geniculate body (MGB) (p. 324)
minimum audible angle (p. 330)
parabelt (p. 326)
primary auditory cortex (or *A1*) (p. 326)
sensory substitution device (SSD) (p. 350)
spectral shape cue (p. 336)
superior olivary complex (p. 324)
tonotopic map (p. 326)
ventriloquism effect (p. 339)

EXPAND YOUR UNDERSTANDING

10.1 Is there contralateral representation of auditory space, as there is of visual space? Explain your answer.

10.2 Describe how the response to pure tones of a neuron with a narrow tuning width differs from that of a neuron with a broad tuning width.

10.3 The speed of sound is about 343 m/sec in air and about 1,500 m/sec in water. Would using interaural time differences to determine the azimuth of sound sources work across a wider range of frequencies in air or in water? Explain why.

10.4 A car is speeding past you while the driver is honking the horn (and your eyes are closed). About 100 feet beyond you, the driver comes to a stop but continues to honk. Describe the auditory cues that tell you when the car is at its closest point to you and the auditory cues that tell you the car has stopped.

10.5 Do you think a bat with complete loss of hearing in one ear could still use echolocation to track and capture prey? Explain your answer.

10.6 A TV commercial for ChowHound dog food features a "talking" French poodle with a pink bow on its head—the dog's mouth opens and closes in synchrony with a woman's voice saying, "My name is Charmaine, and I cherish my ChowHound chow!" As a joke, your older brother, who has an exceptionally deep voice, puts his face next to the TV screen and, in perfect synchrony with the voice-over, silently mouths the same words. Discuss the question of whether you'd be more likely to perceive the words as coming from your brother's mouth or from the dog's mouth. Give some reasons for and against each answer.

10.7 Suppose the sequence of tones in Figure 10.20c looked like this:

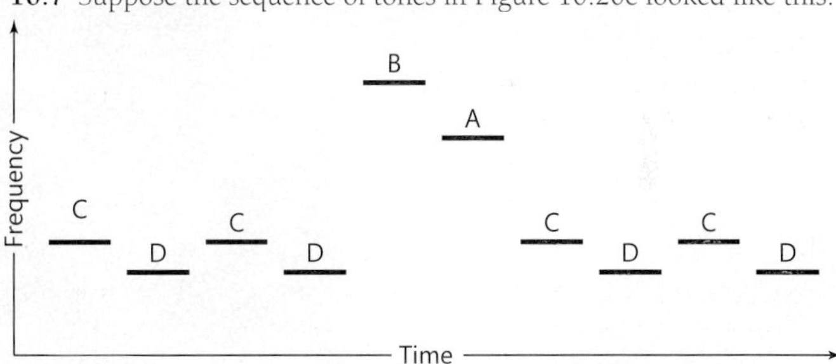

After listening to this sequence, would it be easy or difficult to judge whether tone B preceded or followed tone A? Explain your answer.

10.8 A person successfully using the sensory substitution device illustrated in Figure 10.23 is demonstrating the ability to perform auditory scene analysis. Explain why.

READ MORE ABOUT IT

Blauert, J. (1997). *Spatial hearing: The psychophysics of human sound localization.* Cambridge, MA: MIT Press.
A comprehensive resource on how the human auditory system localizes sound sources.

Bregman, A. S. (1990). *Auditory scene analysis.* Cambridge, MA: MIT Press.
A landmark book describing a program of creative research designed to uncover the principles of auditory perceptual organization.

Kaas, J. H., & Hackett, T. A. (2008). The functional neuroanatomy of the auditory cortex. In P. Dallos & D. Oertel (Eds.), *The senses: Vol. 3. Audition* (pp. 765–780). Amsterdam: Elsevier.
An up-to-date review of the primate auditory cortex.

Møller, A. R. (2006). *Hearing: Anatomy, physiology, and disorders of the auditory system* (2nd ed.). Amsterdam: Elsevier.
A comprehensive treatment of the auditory pathway from cochlea to brain.

Moore, B. C. J. (Ed.). (1995). *Hearing.* San Diego, CA: Academic Press.
A collection of tutorials by experts in the topics covered in this chapter.

Raoul Dufy, *La fée électricité*, 1937, left detail: singers, conductor. [Musée d'Art Moderne de la Ville de Paris, Paris. Bridgeman-Giraudon/Art Resource, NY. © 2012 Artists Rights Society (ARS), New York/ADAGP, Paris.]

11

PERCEIVING SPEECH AND MUSIC

"Singing Sounds Like Shouting to Me"

One afternoon, a healthy, left-handed young man of 20 (we'll call him T.) experienced a sudden, intense, sharply localized headache that seemed to be originating behind his left ear. A friend took him to the emergency room, where he was treated for an acute stroke, which a CT scan later revealed to have been caused by a malformation of veins and arteries in his left superior temporal lobe. In the days following the stroke, T. seemed to have some difficulty understanding what was said to him and some tendency to use the wrong words when talking, but these symptoms completely disappeared over the course of the next month.

However, within a few days after the stroke, T. started complaining that he could no longer hear music—all the notes sounded the same. He had been a music lover all his life, he owned thousands of CDs, and although he knew he was not a particularly talented musician, he played guitar and sang in a band he had formed with some friends. But now the sound of music, which he had always loved, had become unpleasant: "Sounds are empty and cold. Singing sounds like shouting to me. When I hear a song, it sounds familiar at first but I can't recognize it. I think I've heard it correctly, but then I lose its musicality. I can recognize the guitar but not the melody."

Three months after the stroke, detailed testing confirmed that T.'s ability to understand and produce speech had returned to normal and that his ability to recognize nonmusical, nonspeech sounds (e.g., a barking dog, a bubbling brook, or a speeding motorcycle) was also normal. But his ability to perceive music was profoundly impaired: although he could recognize different musical instruments and could recognize and reproduce rhythms (e.g., a waltz versus a tango), he was completely unable to recognize or reproduce even simple, familiar melodies, either by singing or by playing the guitar. This very specific disability suggests that the stroke had damaged a part of the brain that is specialized for processing melodies while leaving all other aspects of auditory perception unaffected.

Chapter Outline

In the last two chapters, we saw how our auditory system senses sound and transduces it into neural signals and how we use various types of cues to locate sound sources and to analyze the auditory scene. Of course, many species besides humans possess these abilities, which confer an obvious evolutionary advantage in detecting predators and prey and in perceiving the environment at a distance.

Here, we'll consider the advantages conferred by the ability to use sound for communication, another area where humans aren't alone. Broadly defined, communication is the transmission of information between individuals, and in this sense communication using sound is critical for a very wide variety of species, from insects to primates. For us, the idea of communicating with sound is almost automatically associated with language, the human system for transmitting information by connecting speech sounds to meanings. Spoken language, which has been a part of human culture for at least 50,000 years (Lieberman, 2007), undoubtedly provides much more powerful fitness advantages than nonhuman communication systems, by enabling the expression of extremely refined aspects of meaning that can promote cooperative activities and the efficient teaching of new ideas and skills.

In this chapter, we'll focus on those aspects of language that relate specifically to sound and audition—the production, characteristics, and perception of speech sounds. The psychological and linguistic aspects of how people make sense of language—that is, how they represent sequences of sounds as meanings—are topics for a different course. We'll also explore another sound-based phenomenon with profound meaning—music. We'll examine the physical and perceptual dimensions of sound that we experience as music and consider how music is processed in the brain.

One aspect of speech and music perception that sets it apart from almost all other aspects of perception is that the sensory stimuli being perceived are often ones produced by the actions of other people. That's why, in the two major sections of this chapter, we'll start with a brief discussion of the sounds of speech or music and how those sounds are produced.

Speech

Why do we talk? In most cases, we use spoken language to express thoughts and emotions—to make statements ("I'm on my way to the library"), ask questions ("Which way is the library?"), convey surprise ("The library burned down?!"), and so on. For example, if you want to let your roommate know you're going to the library, you transform the idea into a specific sequence of words, expressed as sequences of sounds associated with the words. In order for your roommate to understand the idea you want to express, she must perform similar steps in reverse order—that is, she must perceive the sequences of sounds and perceive them as the sequence of words "I'm on my way to the library," which convey your intended meaning. In the following sections, we'll examine the acoustic properties of individual speech sounds, how they're produced and perceived, and how the brain represents them.

The Sounds of Speech: Phonemes

phonemes The smallest units of sound that, if changed, would change the meaning of a word.

The basic sounds of a language—called that language's **phonemes**—are the smallest units of sound that, if changed, would change the meaning of a word. For example, we can change the word "cat" to "bat" by changing the initial sound, to "cut" by changing the middle sound, or to "cap" by changing the final sound. This shows that "cat" consists of three phonemes—represented by the three letters in the written word—and that the "b" sound in "bat," the "u" sound in "cut," and the "p" sound in "cap" also represent phonemes.

In each of these words—"cat," "bat," "cut," and "cap"—there is a simple one-to-one correspondence between phonemes and letters, but this kind of correspondence isn't always the case. For example, "that" and "chat" also consist of three phonemes but have four letters. Moreover, the same letter in written words often corresponds to two or more different sounds (e.g., in the word "icicle" the two letters "i" sound quite different and represent different phonemes, as do the two letters "c"), or letters might correspond to no sound at all (e.g., the "h" and the "e" in "rhyme").

International Phonetic Alphabet (IPA) An alphabet in which each symbol stands for a different speech sound; provides a distinctive way to write each phoneme in all the human languages currently in use.

To get around these confusing differences between sound and spelling, we use a special set of symbols known as the **International Phonetic Alphabet (IPA)** in which each symbol stands for a different speech sound. Using IPA symbols—including combinations of symbols and various types of accent marks—there is a distinctive way to write each of the more than 850 distinct sounds used as phonemes in the roughly 7,000 human languages currently in use around the world (Ladefoged & Maddieson, 1996). Table 11.1 shows how phonemes of standard American English are written in the IPA. Based on this table, the words "cat," "that," and "chat" would be written /**kæt**/, /**ðæt**/, and /**tʃæt**/, and the words "icicle" and "rhyme" would be written /**aɪsɪkəl**/ and /**raɪm**/ (slashes indicate IPA spellings).

With this as background, we can now begin a more detailed exploration of the sounds of speech—considered both as sounds and as products of the human vocal apparatus.

TABLE 11.1 Phonemes of Standard American English

Vowels		Consonants	
IPA Symbol	Example Words	IPA Symbol	Example Words
ʌ	cup, luck	b	bad, lab
a	arm, father	d	did, lady
æ	cat, black	f	find, if
ə	away, cinema	g	give, flag
ɛ	met, bed	h	how, hello
ɪ	hit, sitting	j	yes, you
i	see, heat	k	cat, back
ɔ	call, bought	l	leg, little
ʊ	put, could	m	man, lemon
u	blue, food	n	no, ten
aɪ	five, eye	ŋ	sing, finger
aʊ	now, out	p	pet, map
oʊ	go, home	r	red, try
ɛɪ	say, eight	s	sun, miss
oɪ	boy, join	ʃ	she, crash
		t	tea, getting
		tʃ	check, match
		θ	think, both
		ð	this, mother
		v	voice, five
		w	wet, window
		z	zoo, lazy
		ʒ	pleasure, vision
		dʒ	just, large

Note: The bold red letters correspond to the speech sound specified by the IPA symbol.

Producing the Sounds of Speech

Figure 11.1 illustrates the human vocal apparatus—the parts of the body used in producing the sounds of speech. Most speech sounds begin with an exhalation of air from the lungs. The air then flows through the trachea (or *windpipe*) and into the **larynx** (or *voice box*). Within the larynx, the air passes through a pair of membranes called the **vocal folds** (also known as the *vocal cords*). The air then flows from the larynx into the **pharynx** (the uppermost part of the throat) and from the pharynx up into the oral and nasal cavities, from which it exits the body via the mouth and nose. The **uvula,** a flap of tissue that hangs off the posterior edge of the soft palate, can bend upward to close off the nasal cavity, directing all exhaled air into the oral cavity and out the mouth (as we'll see below, this closure of the nasal cavity is important in the production of many speech sounds).

larynx (or *voice box*) The part of the vocal tract that contains the vocal folds.

vocal folds (or *vocal cords*) A pair of membranes within the larynx.

pharynx The uppermost part of the throat.

uvula A flap of tissue that hangs off the posterior edge of the soft palate; it can close off the nasal cavity.

The vocal folds can be relaxed and open, allowing air to pass silently, or can be tensed, which causes them to vibrate when air passes. The fundamental frequency of vocal fold vibration depends on the size and thickness of the vocal folds and the size and shape of the larynx, as well as on the current degree of contraction or relaxation of muscles in the throat. Typically, adult males produce vibrations with fundamental frequencies in the range of 85–180 Hz, adult females in the range 165–255 Hz, and children over 300 Hz. Most vocalization involves changing the fundamental frequency of vocal fold vibrations—for example, raising the pitch of your voice at the end of a question or singing high or low notes—and this can

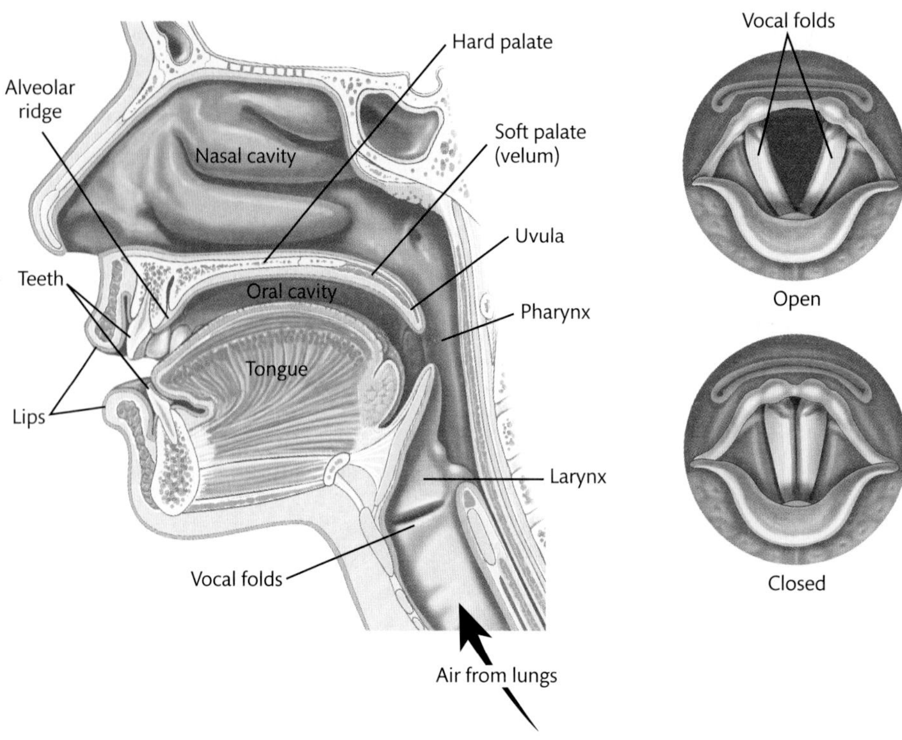

Figure 11.1 Speech Production System
Most speech sounds are initiated by air expired from the lungs into the larynx, which contains the vocal folds, which can vibrate at different frequencies to produce different voice pitches. Speech sounds are further modified by changing the shape of the pharynx and the oral cavity and by raising or lowering the uvula to block off or open the nasal cavity. The shape of the oral cavity is determined by opening or closing the jaw; by raising, lowering, or changing the shape and position of the tongue; and by opening or closing the lips.

be done by contracting or relaxing the muscles in the throat, which changes the tension of the vocal folds and thus their rate of vibration (the greater the tension, the faster the vibration and the higher the pitch).

Speech sounds can be divided into vowels and consonants. **Vowels** are produced with a relatively unrestricted flow of air through the pharynx and the oral cavity, with different vowels produced by varying the size and shape of the oral cavity. **Consonants,** in contrast, are produced by restricting the flow of air at one place or another along the path of the airflow from the vocal folds. In the next sections, we'll explore in more detail how the human vocal apparatus produces these different types of speech sounds.

vowels Speech sounds produced with a relatively unrestricted flow of air through the pharynx and oral cavity.

consonants Speech sounds produced by restricting the flow of air at one place or another along the path of the airflow from the vocal folds.

Producing Vowels

Like vibrating guitar strings, vibrating vocal folds produce sounds containing harmonic frequencies in addition to the fundamental frequency (harmonic frequencies are integer multiples of the fundamental frequency). For example, the sound wave of an adult male whose voice has a fundamental frequency of 125 Hz contains higher harmonics of 250 Hz, 375 Hz, 500 Hz, and so on, with amplitudes that tend to decrease as their frequency increases. Figure 11.2a shows an idealized version of the relative amplitudes of harmonics contained in the basic sound produced by typical male vocal folds.

In order to produce different vowel sounds, a speaker has to modify the basic sound produced by his or her vocal folds, by modifying the shape of the oral cavity in order to attenuate certain harmonics more than others, with a different pattern of modification for each different vowel (Lieberman & Blumstein, 1988). The oral cavity is the chamber through which the sound wave travels from the vocal folds to the mouth. Chambers with different shapes have different resonances, and the particular resonance determines which frequencies are attenuated by how much. The speaker modifies the shape of the oral cavity by opening the jaw to different degrees, adjusting the shape and position of the tongue, and shaping the lips. (You can demonstrate this yourself by saying aahhhhh . . . while opening and closing your mouth and changing the position of your tongue to produce a variety of vowel-like sounds.)

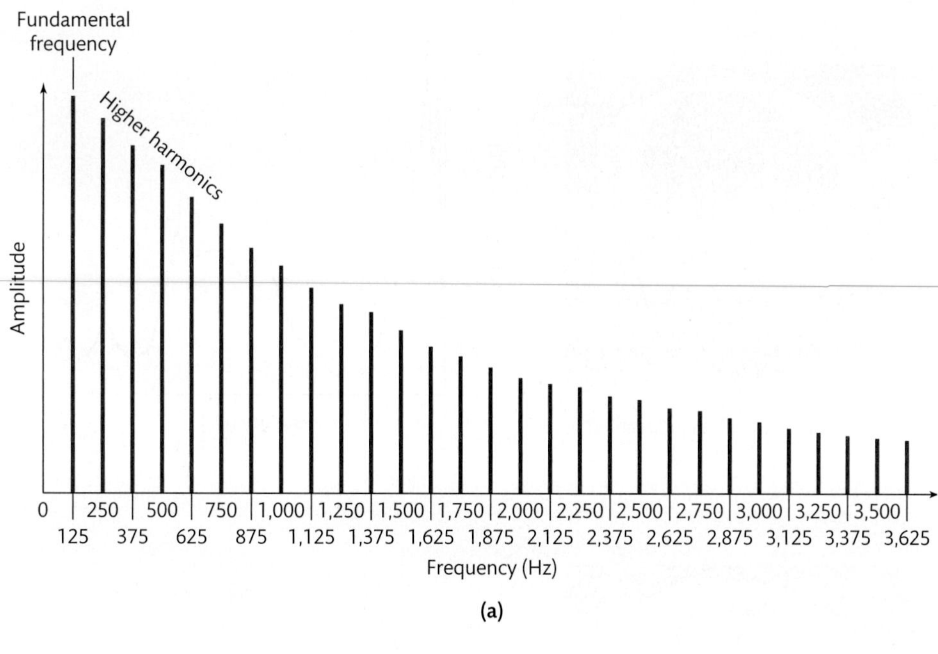

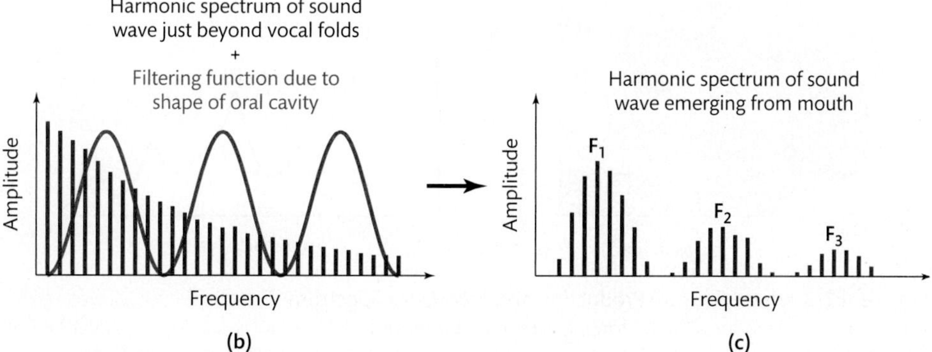

Figure 11.2 Harmonic Spectrum of a Vowel (a) When the vocal folds are tensed, they vibrate as air passes through them (as when saying "aah" for a doctor), and the sound produced has a fundamental frequency (here, 125 Hz, typical for an adult male) and has higher harmonics with amplitudes that tend to decrease as their frequency increases. This is the harmonic spectrum of the sound just beyond the vocal folds. (b) The shape of the oral cavity modifies this sound by attenuating some frequencies more than others. This pattern of modification produced by shaping the oral cavity for a vowel is depicted as a filtering function overlying the harmonic spectrum of the sound at the vocal folds. A differently shaped oral cavity, and hence a different filtering function, is associated with each different vowel. (c) The filtering function changes the harmonic spectrum of the sound to a pattern of peaks (formants) and valleys. This illustration depicts the first, second, and third formants (**F_1**, **F_2**, and **F_3**, respectively) of the vowel sound. (Adapted from Lieberman & Blumstein, 1988, Figure 4.7.)

Figure 11.2b and c illustrates how each particular shape of the oral cavity serves as a filtering function, so that the sound wave emerging from the mouth has the distinctive harmonic spectrum associated with the vowel that the speaker is trying to produce. The individual peaks in the harmonic spectrum—labeled F_1, F_2, and F_3 in Figure 11.2c—are called **formants**, the frequency bands with relatively high amplitude in the spectrum of a vowel sound. Most vowel sounds contain two or three prominent formants.

formants Frequency bands with relatively high amplitude in the harmonic spectrum of a vowel sound.

Figure 11.3 (top) shows how the different positioning of the tongue and opening of the mouth create differences in the shape of the oral cavity in the production of the vowel sounds in the words "bead" and "bad"; Figure 11.3 (bottom) shows how this results in the different complex sound waves with different formants that characterize these two sounds.

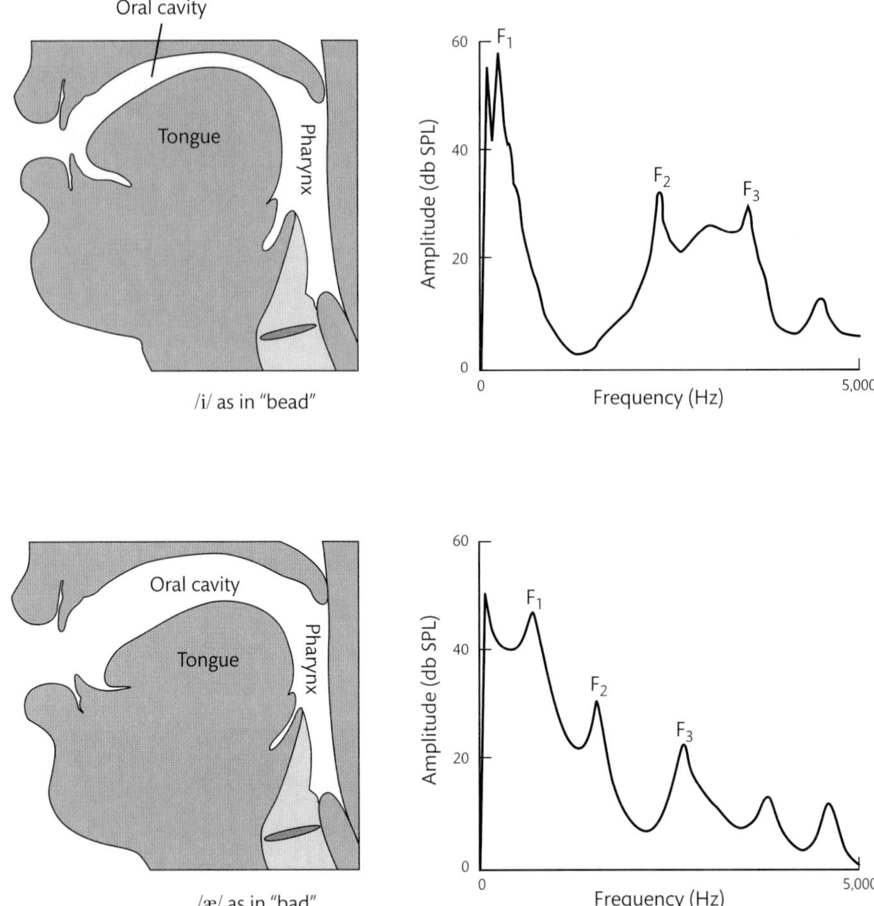

Figure 11.3 Vowel Sounds: Production and Frequency Spectrum The production of two vowel sounds. For /i/ (as in "bead"), the tongue is high in the mouth and the jaw is relatively closed. For /æ/ (as in "bad"), the tongue is lower in the mouth and the jaw more open. The differences in the shape of the oral cavity result in different relationships between the frequencies of the formants. (Adapted from Patel, 2008, Figure 2.17.)

In this section, we've implicitly assumed that the frequency spectrum of a vowel sound is constant over time, which it might well be when you produce a vowel sound all by itself and hold it for a couple of seconds—for example, when you say "aah" so a doctor can look at your throat. But in natural speech, the frequencies corresponding to each vowel sound in the utterance change rapidly over time. These types of changes in the frequency spectrum can be depicted with a **sound spectrogram,** a graph that includes the time dimension in addition to frequency and amplitude. Figure 11.4 shows sound spectrograms for several words with different vowels.

sound spectrogram A graph that includes the dimensions of frequency, amplitude, and time, showing how the frequencies corresponding to each vowel sound in an utterance change over time.

place of articulation In the production of consonants, the point in the vocal tract at which airflow is restricted, described in terms of the anatomical structures involved in creating the restriction.

manner of articulation In the production of consonants, the nature of the restriction of airflow in the vocal tract.

voicing In the production of consonants, specifies whether the vocal folds are vibrating or not (i.e., whether the consonant is voiced or voiceless).

Producing Consonants

Consonants, as defined above, are produced by restricting the flow of air coming from the vocal folds—that is, by narrowing or completely closing the vocal tract at one or more points along the path of the airflow. The production of every consonant sound can be defined in terms of three characteristics: place of articulation, manner of articulation, and voicing. **Place of articulation** describes the point at which this restriction occurs and the anatomical structures involved in creating the restriction; **manner of articulation** describes the nature of the restriction; and **voicing** specifies whether the vocal folds are vibrating or not (i.e., whether the sound is voiced or voiceless). Table 11.2 shows how English consonants are classified along these three dimensions, and Figure

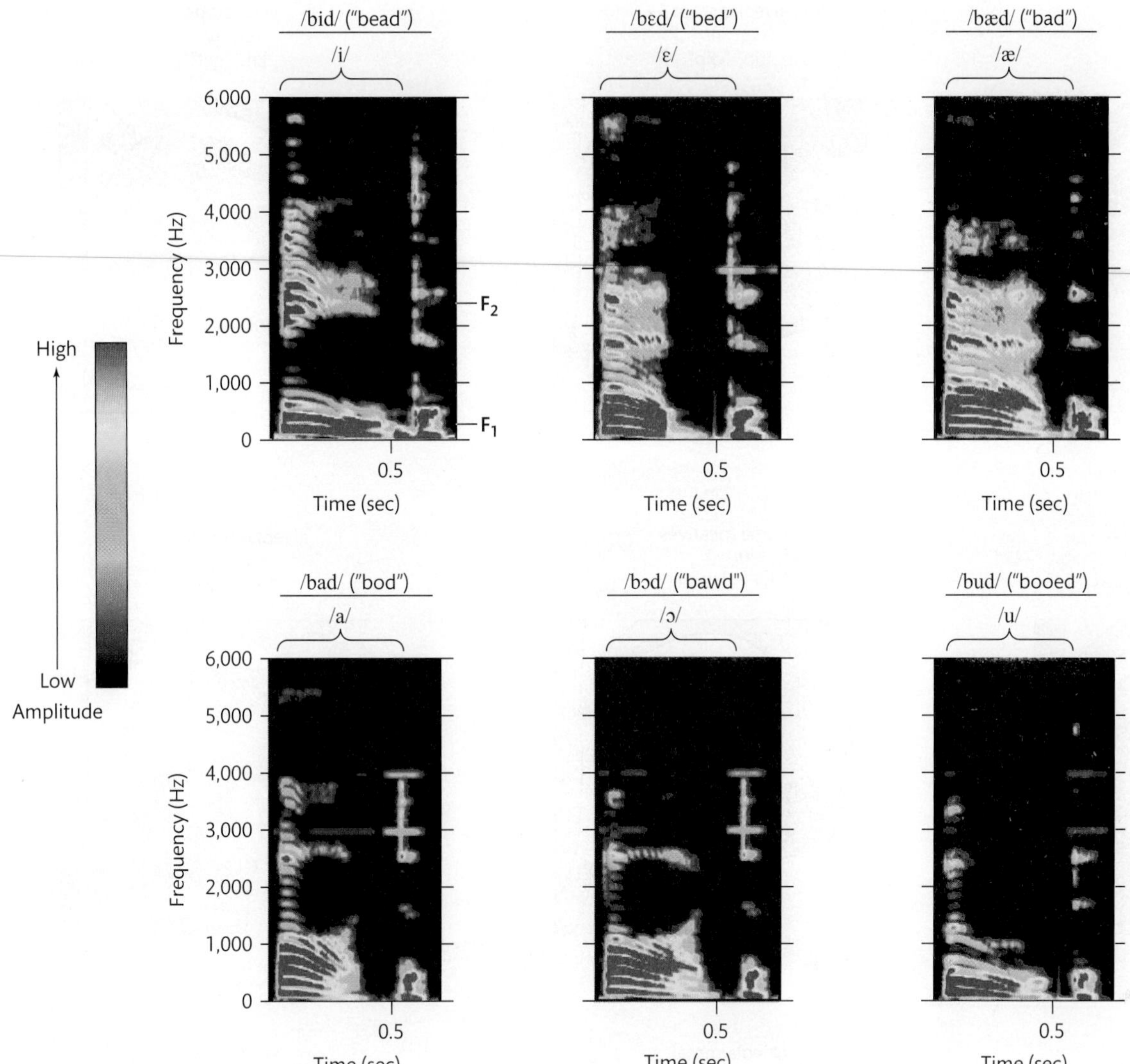

Figure 11.4 Sound Spectrograms of Some English Vowels These sound spectrograms for several spoken vowels embedded in syllables show how the formant pattern changes over time for each vowel. A sound spectrogram contains three dimensions: time is on the horizontal axis, frequency is on the vertical axis, and amplitude—the amount of energy present at each frequency at each moment of time—is indicated by the color, with dark regions indicating little energy and reds and yellows indicating a lot of energy. The formants appear as horizontal bands of higher energy at different frequency levels, as indicated by the arrows pointing to $\mathbf{F_1}$ and $\mathbf{F_2}$ in the upper-left spectrogram. [Melvin Rouse, Jr.]

11.5 shows how lips, teeth, tongue, palate, and velum are used to create the restrictions involved in producing English consonants.

Table 11.2 has many empty slots, and as you might expect, some of these would be filled if the table were showing all the consonants in all the world's languages. In fact, a table of all the world's consonants would contain many additional rows and columns specifying additional places and manners of articulation. For example, some languages, such as Hindi, include retroflex consonants, where the place of articulation is the tip of the tongue curled back and placed against the middle of the hard palate; some languages include trilled consonants, where the manner of articulation is the tongue rapidly vibrating as air flows past it, like the trilled alveolar "rr" sound in the Spanish word "perro" (meaning "dog"); and some African languages include clicks, distinguished by a manner of articulation in which outside air is abruptly drawn into the oral cavity, with an accompanying popping or clicking sound.

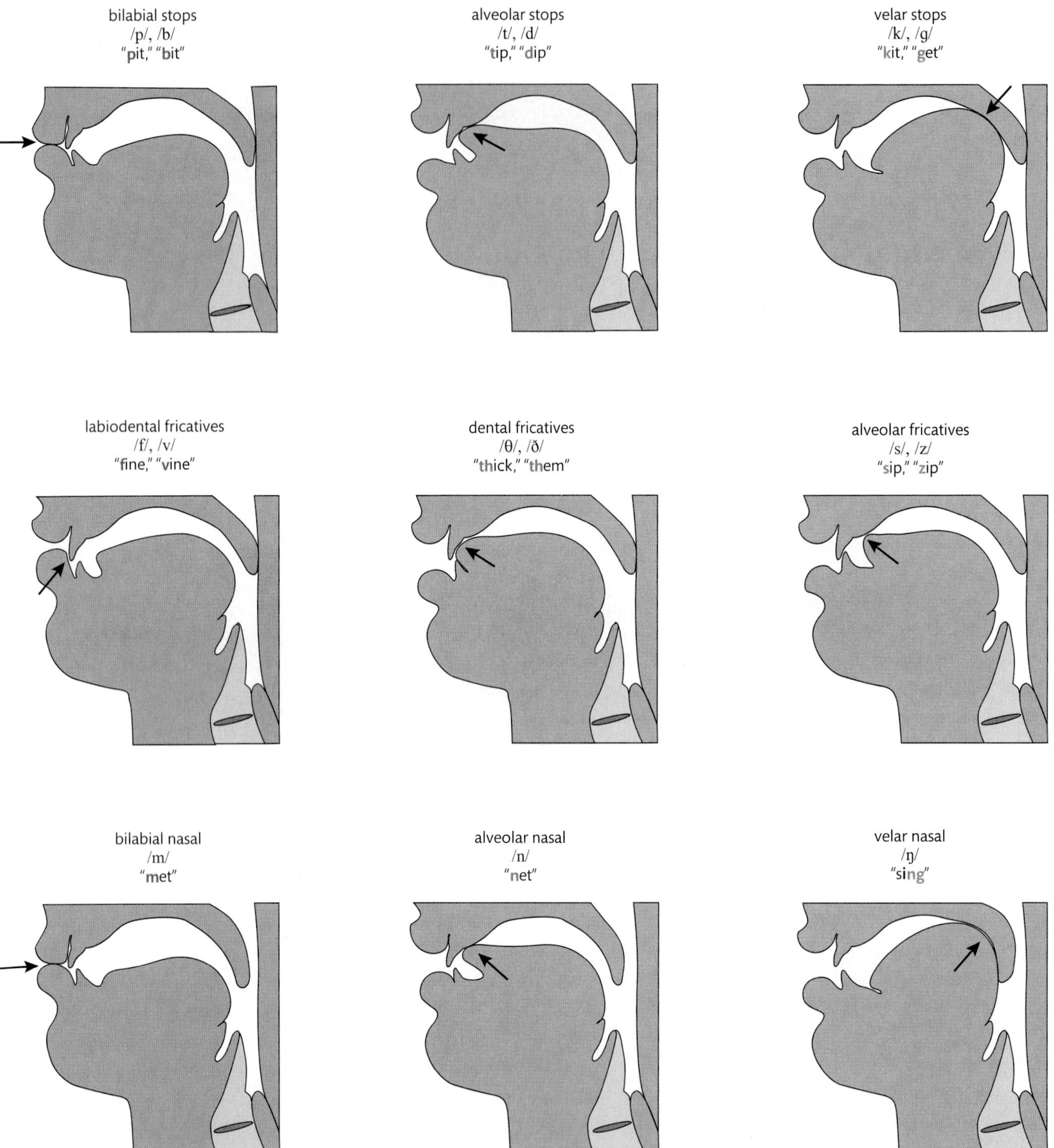

Figure 11.5 Articulation of Some English Consonants The articulation of consonants is defined by three parameters: place of articulation, manner of articulation, and voicing—for example, for the bilabial stops /**p**/ and /**b**/, the place of articulation is between the two lips, the manner of articulation is complete closure of the lips, as indicated by the arrow, and /**p**/ is voiceless whereas /**b**/ is voiced.

TABLE 11.2 Patterns of Articulation for English Consonants

Place of Articulation	*Manner of Articulation; Voicing* Stops[a]		Fricatives[b]		Affricates[c]		Nasals[d]		Approximants[e]	
	Voiceless	Voiced	Voiceless	Voiced	Voiceless	Voiced	Voiceless	Voiced	Voiceless	Voiced
Bilabial[f]	/p/ pit	/b/ bit						/m/ sum		/w/ wit
Labiodental[g]			/f/ fine	/v/ vine						
Dental[h]			/θ/ thick	/ð/ them						
Alveolar[i]	/t/ tip	/d/ dip	/s/ sip	/z/ zip				/n/ sun		/l/ let
Postalveolar[j]			/ʃ/ ship	/ʒ/ vision	/tʃ/ chip	/dʒ/ jet				/r/ rip
Palatal[k]										/j/ yet
Velar[l]	/k/ kit	/g/ get						/ŋ/ sing		
Glottal[m]			/h/ hit							

[a]Produced by completely closing the vocal tract at a place of articulation.

[b]Produced by narrowing the vocal tract at a place of articulation to create a buzzing (voiced) or hissing (voiceless) sound.

[c]Produced by first completely closing the vocal tract at a place of articulation (as for a stop) and then slightly releasing the closure.

[d]Produced by stopping the flow of air at some point in the oral cavity and allowing air to flow through the nasal cavity.

[e]Produced by narrowing the vocal tract at a place of articulation—somewhat less than the narrowing used to produce a fricative.

[f]Between the two lips.

[g]Between the lower lip and the upper teeth.

[h]Between the tongue and the teeth.

[i]Between the tongue and the alveolar ridge.

[j]Between the tongue and the part of the hard palate just behind the alveolar ridge.

[k]Between the tongue and the central portion of the hard palate.

[l]Between the tongue and the velum, or soft palate.

[m]Between the two vocal folds.

Check Your Understanding

11.1 Consider the letters *a, f, h, i, n, s,* and *v,* which make up the words "van," "fan," "fin," and "fish." In these words, which letters correspond to phonemes and which don't? Which combination of letters corresponds to a phoneme?

11.2 Which of these anatomical structures is *not* involved in the production of speech sounds: teeth, uvula, larynx, esophagus?

11.3 True or false? All speech sounds involve vibration of the vocal folds.

11.4 The formants in the speech spectrogram of a vowel sound result from

- **A.** The special characteristics of each speaker's vocal cords.
- **B.** The way the speaker modifies the shape of the oral cavity in producing the vowel.
- **C.** Random variations in the relative amplitudes of the harmonics in the sound wave.

11.5 Describe the three consonant sounds in "father" (/f/, /ð/, and /r/) in terms of place of articulation, manner of articulation, and voicing.

Perceiving the Sounds of Speech

As the stream of sounds produced by a talker arrives at a listener's ears, the listener must analyze the stream into a sequence of phonemes (which must then be grouped into subsequences that match up with words). This task of analyzing the stream of speech into phonemes may sound simple, but it's actually quite challenging, because there is no one-to-one correspondence between the sounds produced by talkers and the phonemes that those sounds represent—that is, many different acoustic events may all represent the same phoneme.

One obvious reason for this lack of one-to-one correspondence is that, as we noted before, different talkers produce sounds with different fundamental frequencies—for instance, the frequencies of an adult male and a child producing the same sentence differ substantially throughout the utterance. Another perceptual challenge arises because the sounds of specific phonemes differ in different dialects—for example, many vowel sounds are pronounced quite differently by speakers of the American English dialects prevalent in New York, Houston, and Los Angeles, and yet speakers from those places would have little trouble understanding one another. And even the same phonemes produced at different times by the same speaker can differ significantly—the person might be whispering, shouting, singing, or sounding hoarse because of a cold.

A different type of perceptual challenge relates to the indistinct boundaries between words in the sound stream of normal speech, as illustrated by the two spectrograms in Figure 11.6. In the top spectrogram—of a speaker slowly and deliberately saying "What will you

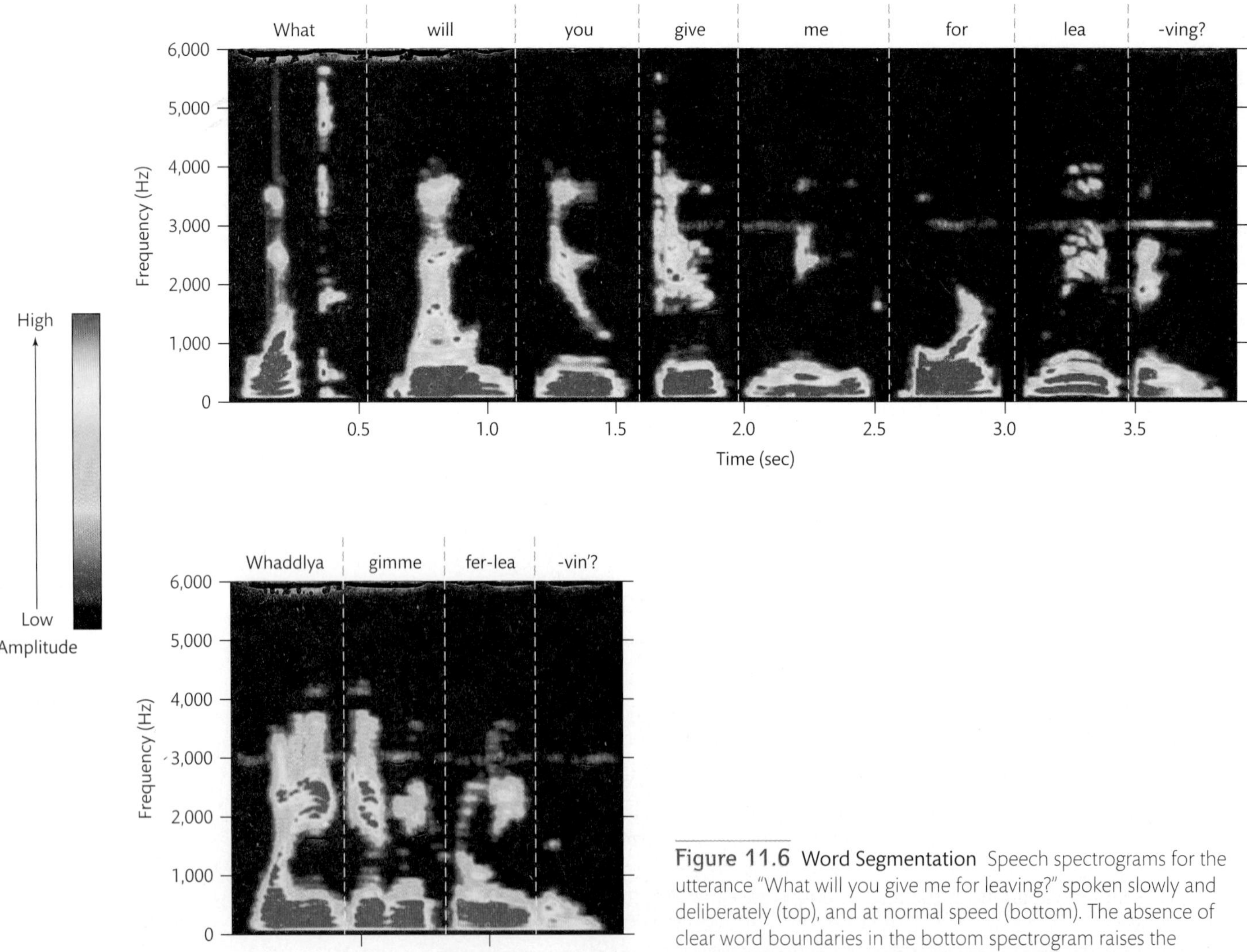

Figure 11.6 Word Segmentation Speech spectrograms for the utterance "What will you give me for leaving?" spoken slowly and deliberately (top), and at normal speed (bottom). The absence of clear word boundaries in the bottom spectrogram raises the question of how listeners segment one word from the next in normal streams of speech. [Melvin Rouse, Jr.]

give me for leaving?"—each word is followed by a brief silence, helping the listener perceive where one word ends and the next begins. In the bottom spectrogram—of a speaker saying the same sentence at normal speed (so it sounds like "Whaddlya gimme fer leavin'?")—there are no silences between words (except for the brief break after *gimme*), and some of the phonemes represented in the utterance on top are missing or modified (e.g., the /w/ in "will" and the /v/ in "give" are missing, and the /ŋ/ at the end of "leaving" has been modified to /n/).

Clearly, our auditory system cannot identify phonemes by simply mapping specific frequencies to specific phonemes. Instead, the auditory system must be using the *relative* positions of frequencies (such as the formants in vowel sounds) in the context of the entire speech stream, as well as other patterns of acoustic features, to identify the phonemes in speech. Furthermore, the listener's knowledge of the language and understanding of the context of what is being said also provide important information. In the next sections, we'll explore the various mechanisms and strategies that help listeners recognize patterns of acoustic features and accurately perceive the sounds of speech.

Demonstration 11.1 Speech Spectrograms Create spectrograms of your own voice.

Coarticulation and Perceptual Constancy

Compare the movements of your articulatory organs when you say /di/ ("dee") and /du/ ("doo"). The first part of each syllable—the consonant /d/—starts with the tip of your tongue against the alveolar ridge behind your teeth (see the diagram for /d/ in Figure 11.5). To then produce the /i/ sound in "dee," you widen your lips and move them closer together while also moving your tongue forward; this tongue placement for /i/ results in a vowel sound in which the first formant is relatively low frequency and the second formant is relatively high frequency. In contrast, to produce the /u/ sound in "doo," you must move your articulatory organs from the /d/ configuration to a configuration in which your lips are rounded and your tongue is further back in your mouth than for /i/, which results in a vowel sound with a much lower frequency second formant. The influence of one phoneme on the acoustic properties of another, due to the articulatory movements required to produce them in sequence, is called **coarticulation.**

coarticulation The influence of one phoneme on the acoustic properties of another, due to the articulatory movements required to produce them in sequence.

In fact, even as you start to say either syllable, the configuration required for the final vowel is already influencing the configuration used to form the initial /d/; in other words, the consonant and vowel productions overlap in time. This means that coarticulation affects not only flow across the transition from one phoneme to the next, but also flow "backward," from an upcoming phoneme to the phoneme currently being produced. Thus, because of coarticulation, a given sound (in this case, /d/) is regularly associated with different acoustic features—in this case, the frequencies transitioning to the second formant of the following vowel, as shown in Figure 11.7. Nevertheless,

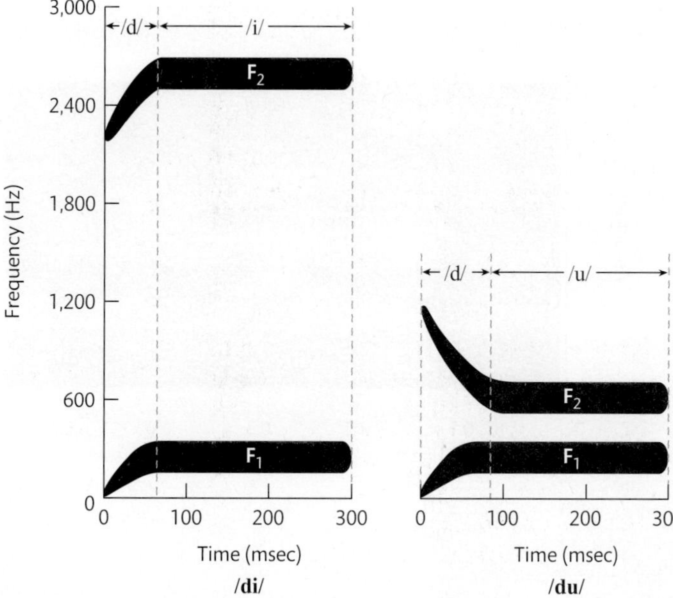

Figure 11.7 Coarticulation in Consonant Production Schematic spectrograms for /di/ ("dee") and /du/ ("doo"). The second formant for the vowel /i/ is much higher frequency than that for the vowel /u/, because of the different tongue positions for the two vowels. The different tongue positions have coarticulation effects on the preceding consonant, /d/. Specifically, there are effects on the transition from /d/ to the second formant of the vowel: the transition has a high and rising profile for /di/ and a low and declining profile for /du/. The fact that we perceive the /d/ as sounding the same in the two syllables is an example of perceptual constancy.

in both syllables listeners perceive exactly the same sound, the phoneme /d/. This is a type of perceptual constancy—different sensory stimuli regularly resulting in identical perceptions—a phenomenon that we've encountered in previous contexts (e.g., in the discussions of color constancy and lightness constancy in Chapter 5 and of size constancy and shape constancy in Chapter 6). Here, the auditory constancy that leads us to hear two different sounds as the same consonant is an important mechanism underlying the correct perception of speech.

Categorical Perception of Phonemes

categorical perception Perception of different sensory stimuli as identical, up to a point at which further variation in the stimulus leads to a sharp change in the perception.

voice onset time (VOT) In the production of stop consonants, the interval between the initial burst of frequencies and the onset of voicing.

Categorical perception refers to the perception of different sensory stimuli as identical, up to a point at which further variation in the stimulus leads to a sharp change in the perception. For example, in a video image presented to a viewer at a rate of 24 frames per second (fps), the motion of objects and people looks perfectly smooth, as does motion in video images presented at higher frame rates—that is, different stimuli (video images with different frame rates above 24 fps) are perceived as identical (motion looks smooth in all cases). But below the rate of 24 fps, motion begins to look jumpy and uneven—perception changes sharply as the frame rate crosses the limiting condition of 24 fps. Thus, choppy versus smooth categorical perception is defined by a boundary at about 24 fps.

Categorical perception is opposed to continuous perception, in which there are no sharp changes in perception as the stimulus varies. For example, our perception of the frequency of pure tones is continuous—as the frequency of a tone increases so does our perception of the pitch of the tone; two tones of different frequency are perceived as having different pitches, with no sharp discontinuities in perceived pitch as the frequency changes.

Research suggests that our perception of certain speech sounds is categorical rather than continuous, where the categories are different phonemes. To see why, let's begin by looking at the waveforms in Figure 11.8, which illustrate what happens acoustically when you produce isolated syllables that begin with stop consonants, in this case the voiceless and voiced alveolar stops /t/ and /d/ (as part of the syllables /ta/ and /da/). The figure shows an obvious difference between the voiceless /t/ and the voiced /d/ in their **voice onset time (VOT),** the interval between the initial burst of frequencies corresponding to the consonant and the onset of the following vowel /a/. As you can see, the VOT in this particular utterance of /ta/ was about 74 msec, whereas the VOT for /da/ was about 5 msec. Pairs of voiceless and voiced stop consonants are always differentiated by this pattern of a relatively long VOT for the voiceless stop and a relatively short VOT for the voiced stop.

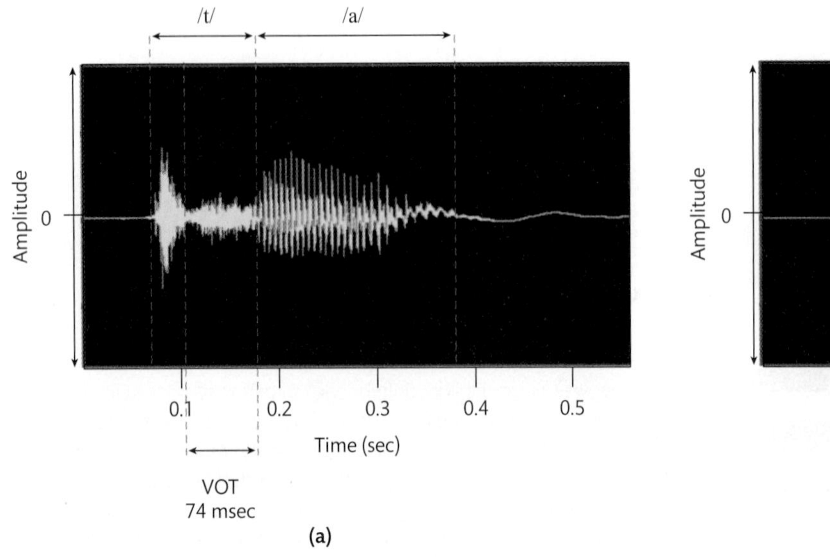

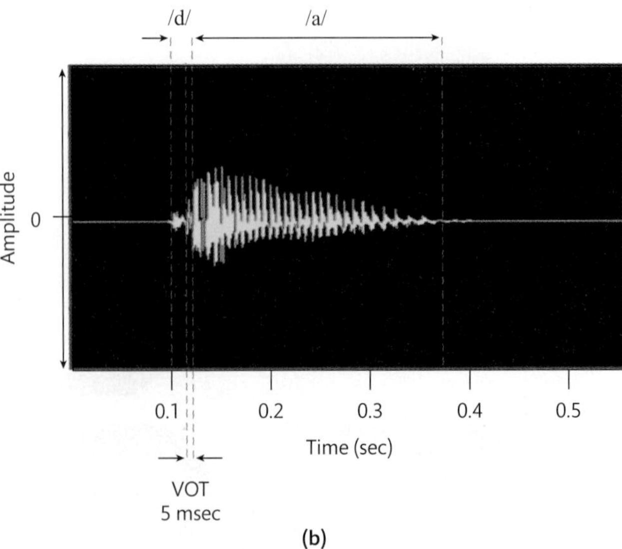

Figure 11.8 Voice Onset Time in Voiced and Voiceless Stop Consonants (a) Waveform of the syllable /ta/, which begins with the voiceless alveolar stop /t/. The initial brief burst of broadband sound is followed by a 74-msec period of near silence—the voice onset time (VOT)—before the portion of the waveform corresponding to the vowel sound /a/ begins. (b) Waveform of the syllable /da/, which begins with the voiced alveolar stop /d/. Here, the VOT lasts just 5 msec. Pairs of voiceless and voiced stop consonants in consonant-vowel syllables consistently differ like this in VOT. [Melvin Rouse, Jr.]

To investigate the precise relationship between VOT and the perception of stop consonants, experimenters created synthetic stop consonants that are identical except for differences in VOT. They combined these sounds into syllables with synthetic vowel sounds, and they then asked listeners to decide whether each syllable sounded like it began with a voiceless or voiced stop (Eimas & Corbit, 1973). Figure 11.9 shows the result of this procedure when it was done with syllables in which the synthetic stop (followed by the vowel /a/) could be perceived as either /p/ or /b/, depending on the VOT. As you can see, when the VOT was less than 25 msec, virtually every listener labeled the syllable as /ba/), and when the VOT was more than 35 msec, almost every listener labeled the syllable as /pa/. As the VOT increased from 25 to 30 to 35 msec, listeners gave a decreasing percentage of /ba/ responses and an increasing percentage of /pa/ responses, with the responses split about fifty-fifty at 30 msec. This transition at 30 msec VOT from mostly perceiving /ba/ to mostly perceiving /pa/ is called the **phonemic boundary.**

Demonstration 11.2 Categorical Perception Based on Voice Onset Time Participate in a simulated experiment demonstrating categorical perception.

What might be the mechanism behind this categorical perception? One idea is that there are "detectors" in the auditory system tuned to respond to certain ranges of VOTs. For example, a /b/ detector would respond about equally to all VOTs of 35 msec or less (with a somewhat weakening response toward the upper end of that range), and a /p/ detector would respond to VOTs of about 25 msec or more (with a somewhat weakening response toward the lower end of that range). This would explain why VOTs in the range of 25–35 msec lead to uncertainty about the perception of /b/ or /p/ (/ba/ or /pa/)—both types of detectors are responding (with a similar level of response to VOTs of about 30 msec). Overall, the results of this study suggest that the perception of voiceless versus voiced stop consonants is categorical and is based on VOT. Moreover, researchers believe that other dimensions of speech are also categorical—that is, they don't change with small variations in the timing or frequency content of the sounds except at or around boundaries such as phonemic boundaries (Raizada & Poldrack, 2007).

phonemic boundary The voice onset time at which a stop consonant transitions from being mainly perceived as voiced to being mainly perceived as voiceless.

Vision and Speech Perception: The McGurk Effect

Speech perception is, of course, primarily an auditory activity, with no visual involvement required. Nevertheless, there is good evidence that we use information from vision, when it's available, to help reinforce auditory perception, including speech perception. In some cases, seeing a person talking can strongly affect what phonemes we perceive. A vivid demonstration

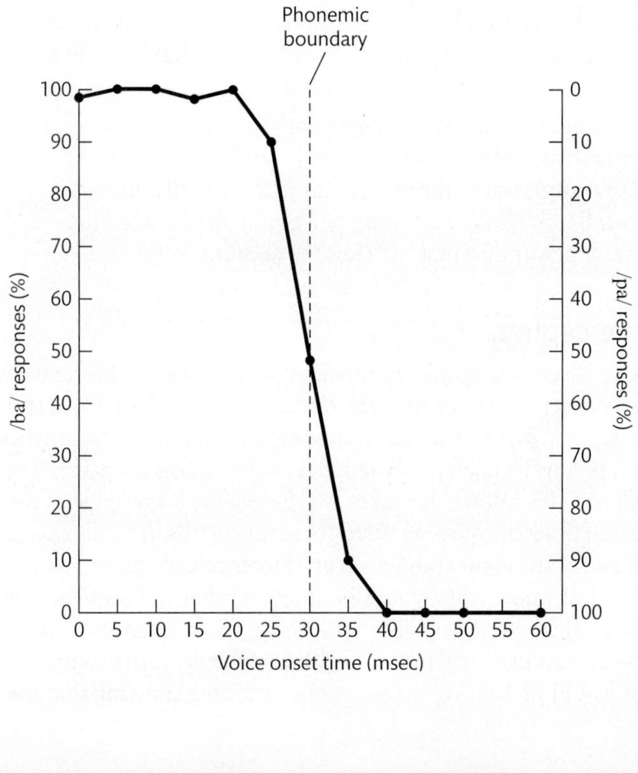

Figure 11.9 Categorical Perception Based on Voice Onset Time Listeners were presented with synthesized syllables consisting of a bilabial stop (/p/ or /b/) followed by the vowel /a/, in which the voice onset time (VOT) of the stop varied from 0 to 60 msec. After hearing each syllable, the listener had to indicate whether it sounded more like /pa/ or /ba/. The curve shows that there was a rather sharp transition around 30 msec VOT (termed the phonemic boundary)—syllables with consonants with shorter VOTs were perceived as more /pa/-like, whereas those with consonants with longer VOTs were perceived as more /ba/-like. (Adapted from Eimas & Corbit, 1973.)

of the influence of vision on the perception of speech sounds is provided by a study involving dubbed video clips (McGurk & MacDonald, 1976). The researchers prepared video clips of a woman saying the repeated syllable /**ba-ba**/, /**ga-ga**/, /**pa-pa**/, or /**ka-ka**/ and then dubbed the sound track for one syllable onto the video clip for another. Participants either watched and listened to the clips or just listened to the sound tracks while facing away from the screen; in both conditions, the participants had to respond by repeating what they perceived the woman to be saying. A response was scored as correct if it corresponded with the sound track.

People performed almost perfectly when just listening to the sound tracks without watching the clips. However, when they also watched the clips, the error rate was over 90%. The errors made by the participants were quite systematic and were related to the mismatches between the articulatory movements of the woman's mouth in the clip and the place of articulation of the consonant in the syllables on the sound track. For example, when hearing the woman produce /**ba-ba**/ and seeing the woman produce /**ga-ga**/, many people reported that she was producing /**da-da**/. To see what accounts for this kind of error, first note the nature of the conflict: the acoustic signal /**ba**/ would require a bilabial place of articulation, but the video depicts a velar place of articulation, at the back of the mouth. The speech perception system appears to come to a compromise by perceiving the consonant as being articulated in the middle of the mouth and hence experiences the phoneme as /**da**/.

Demonstration 11.3 The McGurk Effect Participate in a simulated experiment on the interaction between vision and speech perception.

These results illustrate what has come to be called the **McGurk effect:** in the perception of speech sounds, when auditory and visual stimuli conflict, the auditory system tends to compromise on a perception that shares features with both the seen and the heard stimuli; if no good compromise perception is available, either the conflict is resolved in favor of the visual stimulus or there is a conflicting perceptual experience—for example, when seeing /**ba-ba**/ and hearing /**ga-ga**/, listeners either perceive /**ba-ba**/ (the visual stimulus) or perceive /**ba-gba**/ or /**ga-ba**/ (conflicting perceptual experiences).

McGurk effect In the perception of speech sounds, when auditory and visual stimuli conflict, the auditory system tends to compromise on a perception that shares features with both the seen and the heard stimuli; if no good compromise perception is available, either the conflict is resolved in favor of the visual stimulus or there is a conflicting perceptual experience.

Check Your Understanding

11.6 Give three reasons for the lack of a one-to-one correspondence between sounds (frequencies) and phonemes.

11.7 The phoneme /**b**/ occurs in the words "saber" and "sober." Describe the coarticulation effects that would cause differences in the frequencies corresponding to the /**b**/ in the two words, even if the words were spoken one right after the other by the same person.

11.8 Fill in the blanks: In spoken syllables consisting of a stop consonant followed by a vowel, the __________ is the interval between the initial burst of frequencies and the onset of __________. The transition at the __________ from perceiving a voiced stop to perceiving a voiceless stop is an example of __________.

11.9 Explain what is incorrect about the following statement of the McGurk effect: In speech perception, when auditory and visual stimuli conflict, the listener's auditory system tends to compromise on a perception that shares features of both types of stimuli, but if no good compromise perception is possible, then the listener tends to have a perception that matches the auditory stimulus.

Knowledge and Speech Perception

In the preceding sections, we've discussed purely auditory aspects of speech perception (perceptual constancy despite coarticulation effects, categorical perception of phonemes) and how speech perception also involves interactions between audition and vision (the McGurk effect). Now we'll explore how listeners' knowledge provides a basis for perceiving phonemes and words. As you'll see, this knowledge takes two forms: (1) knowledge of the probability of various sequences of phonemes within words or across words in the language they're hearing and (2) knowledge of the context in which an utterance is being produced.

An example of the first kind of knowledge would be knowing that the sequence of phonemes /**brf**/ isn't a possible English word, so a listener hearing this sequence might—consciously or unconsciously—instead perceive /**bʌf**/ (i.e., the word "buff"). An example of the second kind of knowledge would be hearing the sequence /**brf**/ and knowing that the speaker is talking about her dog and that the dog's name is Duff, in which case the listener would—again, consciously or unconsciously—instead perceive /**dʌf**/ (i.e., the dog's name). In the following sections, we'll expand on these simple examples.

Word Segmentation As noted earlier, the stream of speech sounds uttered at normal conversational speed often contains no brief silent intervals to mark where one word ends and the next begins (see Figure 11.6); so how is it that we can segment the speech stream into perceptually distinct words? And even more puzzling is the question of how infants learn to segment speech correctly, given that they start out with no experience with the language.

One possibility is that listeners guess that a new word has started when they hear a sound that is unlikely to be part of the same word as the preceding sound. Within any given language, only certain phoneme sequences can occur in word-initial, midword, or word-final position, and some of those possible sequences are much more unlikely than others. For example, in English, the sequence /**kt**/ cannot occur at the start of a word, and although this sequence can occur in midword or word-final position (in words like "doctor" or "fact"), it's much more commonly heard when a word ending in /**k**/ is followed by a word starting with /**t**/ (in sentences like "Give it back to me" and "I'm feeling sick today"). In contrast, the sequence /**kɛɪ**/ (sounds like "kay") very commonly occurs in word-initial position (in words like "cape," "cane," "kale," "cable," "came," and "case") but occurs much less frequently in midword or word-final position (in words like "became" and "bouquet") or across two words (in a phrase like "pick acorns").

Patterns like these can be translated into **phoneme transition probabilities** for any particular sequence of phonemes—the chances (expressed as percentages) that the sequence occurs at the start of a word, in the middle of a word, at the end of a word, or across the boundary between two words. Thus, the phoneme transition probabilities for the sequence /**kt**/ would be 0% at the start of a word, fairly low in the middle of a word or at the end of a word, and quite high across two words; in contrast, the probabilities for the sequence /**kɛɪ**/ would be quite high at the start of a word and fairly low in each of the other three possible positions.

phoneme transition probabilities For any particular sequence of phonemes, the chances that the sequence occurs at the start of a word, in the middle of a word, at the end of a word, or across the boundary between two words.

If infants were able to learn probabilities like these early in the process of acquiring their native language, they could use them to construct rules for recognizing sequences that mark word boundaries—for example, based on the probabilities given above, an infant hearing the sequence /**kt**/ would, over a large number of different utterances, be correct a high percentage of the time in going by the rule that the sound /**k**/ marked the end of one word and the sound /**t**/ marked the beginning of the next word. Studies with young infants have shown that they can rapidly learn transition probabilities when they are first exposed to new combinations of speech sounds, which could give them a basis for segmenting speech (Saffran et al., 1996).

However, listeners cannot rely on this type of cue alone (Jusczyk, 1999). Consider, for example, the phoneme sequence /**zn**/, which is common across word boundaries—as in sequences such as "is new" and "was never")—but is quite rare within English words, although it does occur in the word "business" (/**bɪznɪs**/). A listener relying on transition probabilities alone would therefore perceive a word boundary between the /**z**/ and the /**n**/, an error that actual listeners don't make. People probably use a combination of cues, including their knowledge of individual words, to find word boundaries when listening to rapid, fluent speech.

Perceptual Completion: Phonemic Restoration In Chapter 10, we discussed auditory perceptual completion in relation to the perception of tone glides that seem to continue "behind" white noise (see Figure 10.22 and the accompanying text). A similar kind of perceptual completion can occur in speech perception, when parts of the speech stream are obscured or replaced by other sounds—for instance, when you're having a conversation on a street corner and a car horn obscures part or all of a word (as in "Look at that *HONK*-tiful sports car"). Similarly, when you're listening to a lecture in a quiet lecture hall, a cough by one of your fellow students can mask part of the lecturer's stream of speech (as in "Lincoln's Gettys-COUGH address was brief but powerful"). Yet in most such situations, we seem to perceive the obscured or missing speech sounds—a phenomenon known as **phonemic restoration**—and

phonemic restoration A kind of perceptual completion in which listeners seem to perceive obscured or missing speech sounds.

in many cases, we don't even become aware of the masking noise. (If you can make yourself notice your own automatic restoration of masked speech sounds, you'll probably be surprised at how frequently this occurs.)

Phonemic restoration was first demonstrated by presenting listeners with a recording of the spoken sentence "The state governors met with their respective legislatures convening in the capital city," in which the first "s" sound in the word "legislatures," with a duration of 120 msec, had been replaced by a recording of a cough with the same duration (Warren, 1970). The listeners were asked where in the sentence the cough occurred and whether it masked the sound it coincided with. None of the listeners correctly reported the location of the cough (in fact, half the listeners said it occurred outside the word "legislatures"), and all the listeners reported that no sounds had been masked (i.e., that the sentence had been completely intact). The same results were obtained using a pure tone as the masking sound; however, when the "s" sound was simply deleted and replaced with 120 msec of silence, all the listeners correctly reported the location of the silence and correctly reported that the first "s" sound in "legislatures" was missing.

Demonstration 11.4 Phonemic Restoration Participate in a simulated experiment on the perception of occluded phonemes in speech.

Given that the listeners were all adult American native speakers of English, it's not surprising that they all "heard" the masked sound as the phoneme /s/—their knowledge of English would have told them that only /s/ could fill the blank in "legi_latures" to make an English word, and as adult Americans they would be expecting a word with a meaning like "legislatures" in the context of the meaning of other terms in the sentence ("state," "governors," "convening," and "capital city"). But it is striking that none of the listeners even realized the sound was missing. Their auditory system filled in the missing phoneme automatically, without any accompanying conscious awareness, based both on the auditory system's inherent tendency toward perceptual completion of auditory stimuli (bottom-up processing, as in the perceptual completion of tone glides described in Chapter 10) and on the listeners' knowledge about language and context (top-down feedback). A recent study using fMRI to investigate the brain's activity during phonemic restoration provided evidence for two distinct brain circuits that appear to correspond to these bottom-up and top-down functions—one for establishing perceptual continuity and the other for filling in the missing sound given context and knowledge (Shahin et al., 2009).

Although top-down feedback clearly plays a role in phonemic restoration, it's also clear that the process is to some degree dependent on the particular sounds involved. This was shown by an experiment in which either a fricative (e.g., the "sh" sound in "ship"—see Table 11.2) or a vowel was masked by either white noise (like the sound of radio static) or a pure tone (Samuel, 1981). The restoration of fricatives was better when the masking sound was white noise, while the restoration of vowels was better when the masking sound was a pure tone. Why should this be? The frequency spectrum of fricatives resembles that of white noise, with energy distributed fairly randomly across the spectrum; in contrast, the formant structure of vowels gives them a frequency spectrum with horizontal bands of energy at just a few frequencies (see Figure 11.4), which more closely resembles the spectrum of a pure tone. Phonemic restoration works better when the masking sound and the masked sound have similar frequency spectra than when they don't.

Carl Wernicke (1848–1905). [Rue des Archives/ The Granger Collection, NY]

Neural Basis of Speech Perception and Production

In Chapter 1, we briefly discussed the work of the French physician Pierre Paul Broca (1865/1986), describing two patients with damage to a region in the left inferior frontal cortex who could produce only a few words of speech but whose ability to comprehend speech was largely unimpaired. About a decade later, the German neurologist Carl Wernicke (1875/1995) described patients with damage to a region in the left superior temporal cortex who were affected in the opposite way—they had deficits in speech comprehension but not in speech production (although at times their spoken utterances made little sense). Not only were these observations among the first to show how brain damage can selectively affect cognition, but they also provided evidence for the existence of distinct brain regions that are critical for the production and comprehension of speech. Damage to these regions of the left hemisphere causes **aphasia,** an impairment in language ability, including speech production or comprehension (or both).

aphasia An impairment in speech production or comprehension (or both) caused by damage to speech centers in the brain.

Building on Broca's and Wernicke's observations, and on many subsequent studies, modern neuroimaging research has provided a more detailed picture of how speech processing is organized in the human brain. Speech sounds and nonspeech sounds are transduced by the cochlea in the same way, and the resulting neural signals are sent along the same pathways to the auditory cortex, as described in Chapter 10. In the primary auditory cortex, activity is no different for speech sounds than for nonspeech sounds. However, beyond the primary auditory cortex, various brain regions, primarily in the left hemisphere (including the regions identified by Broca and Wernicke), are thought to form a specialized network for processing speech (Zatorre et al., 1992). Speech-related neural signals are channeled through these regions via two distinct pathways—a ventral pathway and a dorsal pathway (Hickok & Poeppel, 2007; Rauschecker & Scott, 2009), as illustrated in Figure 11.10, which also shows the locations of Broca's area and Wernicke's area.

According to this model, the ventral pathway includes regions involved in representing the meanings of words and of combinations of words. Thus, it's analogous to the visual system's ventral "what" pathway, which includes regions involved in representing the "meaning" of visual objects—that is, in representing the identity of objects and in recognizing them. The dorsal pathway includes regions dedicated to the production of speech by the motor system. Thus, it's analogous to the visual system's dorsal "where"/"how" pathway, which is concerned with locating and acting upon visual objects.

Evidence for these distinct functions of the regions and pathways discussed here has been obtained in fMRI studies of individuals engaged in speech comprehension or production tasks. In one such study, participants listened to three brief sounds in succession and had to judge which of the first two sounds matched the third (test) sound (Liebenthal et al., 2005). The sounds were either synthesized speech sounds or synthesized nonspeech sounds

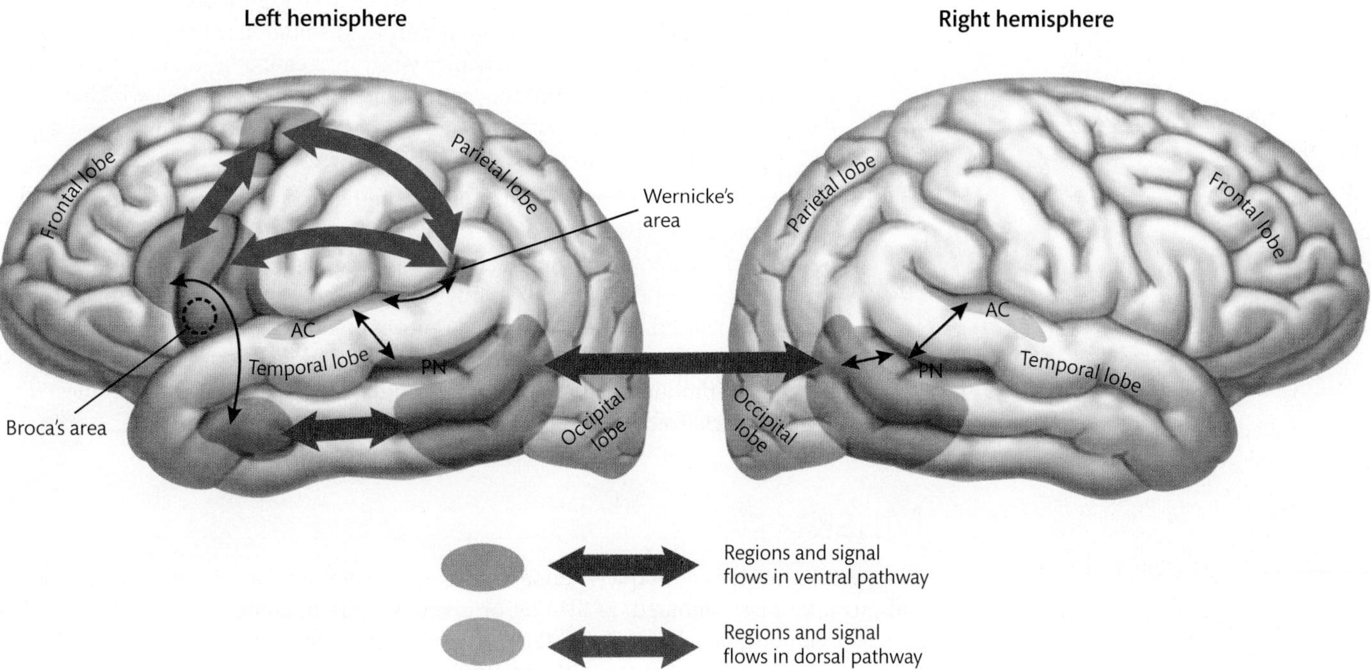

Figure 11.10 Brain Regions and Pathways for Speech Perception and Production The regions of the left and right hemispheres of the human brain—and the connections between them—that are important for speech perception and production (including Broca's area and Wernicke's area). The cochlea transduces incoming sounds (including speech) into neural signals that are sent to the auditory cortex. The auditory cortex (AC) processes these signals and creates representations of the frequencies in the incoming sound waves as they vary over time. The phonological network (PN) translates those into representations of sequences of phonemes, which are sent along two different pathways, ventral and dorsal. Regions in the ventral pathway represent phoneme sequences as meaningful words, and combine word meanings into the meanings of phrases and sentences. Regions in the dorsal pathway use the representations from the phonological network to initiate the process of speech production in response to the heard speech. Speech production is then carried forward by motor areas. (Adapted from Hickok & Poeppel, 2007.)

with frequencies and amplitudes that were similar to the speech sounds. The researchers found that a region of the left superior temporal sulcus—the left phonological network (labeled PN in Figure 11.10)—responded more when the test sound was a speech sound than when it was a nonspeech sound, confirming that this region is important for processing phonemes. In contrast, a region in the location of the auditory cortex in both hemispheres responded about equally to both kinds of sounds, confirming that this region processes sounds of all kinds and isn't specialized for speech. This study (and other similar studies) suggests that the parts of the brain specialized for processing speech are more strongly represented in the left hemisphere than in the right hemisphere (this is the case for about 95% of right-handed people and about 75% of left-handed people [Knecht et al., 2000]).

The dorsal pathway is also thought to coordinate perceived speech with the production of speech, as indicated by an fMRI study in which participants listened to spoken syllables and then produced the same syllables (Wilson et al., 2004). The motor regions of the prefrontal cortex that were strongly activated during the production of the syllables were also activated while the participants just listened to the syllables (and weren't activated when the same participants listened to nonspeech sounds). In other words, simply hearing speech activates the motor centers of the brain responsible for producing speech. Of course, speech is very often produced "from scratch," that is, not directly in response to an utterance by someone else. It seems reasonable to suppose that a conceptual network creates representations of thoughts and ideas that flow into both pathways and provide a basis for spontaneous speech production.

Check Your Understanding

11.10 The four possible positions at which a sequence of phonemes can occur are word initial, midword, word final, and across words. For each of the following sequences, at which positions does the phoneme transition probability in English equal zero: /bn/, /nb/, /pr/, /rp/?

11.11 You're listening to a recording of a fellow student saying, "I like this sensation and perception class very much"—but during this utterance the phoneme /v/ in "very" is either replaced by silence, masked by a cracking sound (like a stick breaking), or masked by a buzzing sound (like a bee flying by). In which of these cases would you be most likely and least likely to perceive the masked or missing sound as the phoneme /v/? Explain why.

11.12 Choose the correct term from each of the alternatives in parentheses: Along the speech-processing pathways of the brain, speech sounds are processed just like other sounds up to the (primary auditory cortex / right hemisphere), but then various regions of the brain, primarily in the (temporal lobes / left hemisphere), form a specialized network for speech processing, with information flowing along two pathways—a ventral pathway that includes regions specialized for speech (production/comprehension) and a dorsal pathway that includes regions specialized for speech (production/comprehension).

Music

Like speech, music is a uniquely human method for communicating with sound. Speech and music can be combined, as in song or opera, to enrich, emphasize, or contrast what each is communicating. At one level, there is a clear difference between the communications transmitted via speech and those transmitted via music. Music by itself, without words, cannot be used to communicate specific ideas, to make specific statements, or to ask specific questions. In some ways, however, the uses of speech and music can be very similar, to express moods and emotions.

In this section, we'll first examine the various dimensions of sound that characterize music, then we'll consider how humans experience music perceptually, and finally we'll examine how the brain's auditory system processes music. Throughout, our discussion will be based on Western music—on the notes, scales, melodies, and other musical elements that have characterized the music of the Western world for the past millennium or more—because that is the music most familiar to most readers of this book. However, in all cultures, music consists of notes arranged in rhythmic sequences that listeners respond to intellectually, emotionally, and physically, and that is the very general level at which we'll consider the perception of music.

Dimensions of Music: Pitch, Loudness, Timing, and Timbre

A musical composition consists of sequences and combinations of notes played with different durations and with different relative emphasis, unfolding over time in patterned ways, and produced by a particular musical instrument, combination of instruments, and/or voices. Although we'll discuss each of these dimensions of music separately, they all contribute to the overall aesthetic and emotional experience of the listener, and the sum total of their effect is complex and interactive. A composer may move from a somber section of a composition, with slow, quiet, and low pitches, to a more joyful section, with an increase in tempo, pitch, and loudness, changing gradually or abruptly over time. A complete understanding of music requires an appreciation of the almost infinite variety of pitch, loudness, timing, and timbre combinations that composers can use to create a musical experience.

Pitch

The most fundamental dimension of music—the single characteristic that most clearly distinguishes one musical composition from another—is pitch. To get a sense of how music is structured on the basis of pitch, look at Figure 11.11, which shows a representation of the

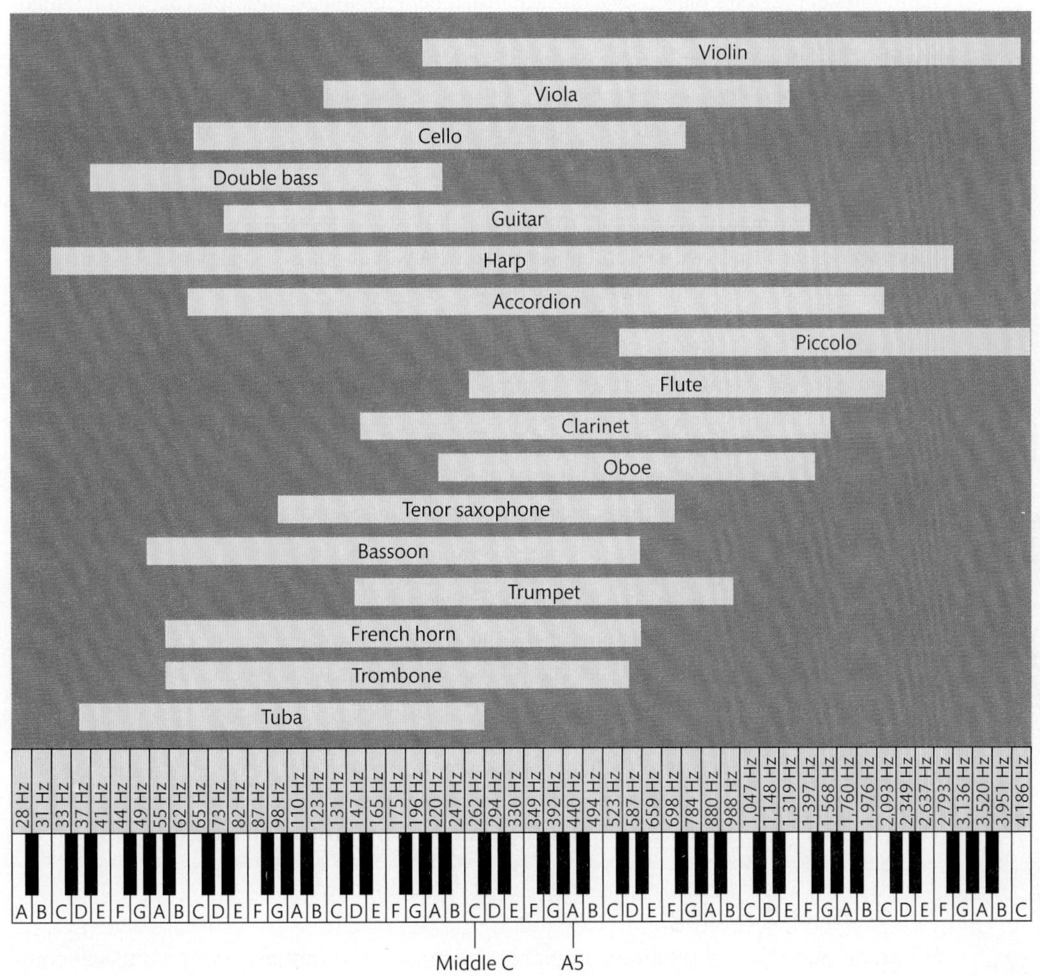

Figure 11.11 **Musical Notes and the Range of Pitches of Musical Instruments** The bottom of the figure shows the notes and fundamental frequencies produced by the white keys of a piano (frequencies are rounded to the nearest whole number of hertz). The note produced by each key (white or black) has a fundamental frequency about 6% higher than that of the preceding key, which means that frequency doubles over the span of an octave—for example, A5 has a fundamental frequency of 440 Hz, and A6 (the A one octave higher) has a fundamental frequency of 880 Hz. The range of pitches produced by the piano spans the range typically heard in Western music. The top of the figure compares the range of pitches produced by a variety of other musical instruments.

keyboard of a piano, along with the note associated with each white key (the *natural* notes A–G) and the fundamental frequency associated with each natural note (in hertz, rounded to the nearest whole number). The black keys are the sharps and flats—each black key is the sharp of the white key to its left and the flat of the white key to its right (e.g., the leftmost black key is both A sharp and B flat). The range of pitches produced by the piano spans the range of pitches typically heard in Western music. (Recall that the difference in sound quality, or timbre, between two different instruments playing the same sequence of notes is due to differences in the pattern of higher harmonics produced with each note. Two instruments playing the same note produce the same fundamental frequency but an array of higher harmonics with different amplitudes, as illustrated for a flute and a violin in Figure 9.9.)

octave A sequence of notes in which the fundamental frequency of the last note is double the fundamental frequency of the first note.

semitones The 12 proportionally equivalent intervals between the notes in an octave.

Western music is typically based on notes that are organized into octaves. An **octave** contains a sequence of notes in which the fundamental frequency of the last note is double the fundamental frequency of the first note (e.g., the octave beginning with A4, at 220 Hz, and ending with A5, at 440 Hz). In Western music, each octave consists of 13 notes separated by 12 proportionally equivalent intervals called **semitones.** (The 13 notes consist of 8 natural notes, corresponding to the white keys on a piano keyboard, and 5 sharps and flats, corresponding to the black keys. An interval is the frequency difference between two notes.)

This organization into octaves with notes separated by proportionally equivalent intervals has a twofold perceptual basis. First, notes separated by an octave are perceptually more similar than notes separated by some other interval—for example, C4 (middle C, labeled on the keyboard in Figure 11.11) is perceptually more similar to C3 (12 keys to the left) than it is to B4 (the next key to the left), even though the frequency difference between C4 and B4 is much less than the frequency difference between C4 and C3. The reason for this is that the harmonics of the notes played by a musical instrument are integer multiples of the fundamental frequency. The first harmonic (which is also the fundamental frequency) of an A4 is 220 Hz; its second harmonic is 440 Hz, which is also the fundamental frequency of A5, the note one octave higher. The harmonics of A5 are also harmonics of A4.

Second, the semitone intervals are perceptually equivalent to one another—that is, the difference in pitch between any two successive notes is perceived as constant even though the actual difference in fundamental frequency between successive notes increases as notes increase in frequency. For example, the difference between A1 (the leftmost key on the keyboard in Figure 11.11, with a fundamental frequency of about 27.50 Hz) and A1 sharp (the adjacent black key, with a fundamental frequency of about 29.14 Hz) is less than 2 Hz; in contrast, the difference between A8 (the rightmost A key, with a fundamental frequency of about 3,520 Hz) and A8 sharp (the adjacent black key to the right, with a fundamental frequency of about 3,729 Hz) is almost 210 Hz; yet these two semitone intervals are perceived as equal differences in pitch. (This perceptual equivalence depending on constant ratios rather than constant differences illustrates Weber's law, as discussed in Chapter 1: a just noticeable difference between two levels of some perceptual dimension is approximately a constant fraction of the lower of the two levels.) In each case, the higher frequency is about 6% greater than the lower frequency.

These two ideas—that notes separated by an octave have similar sound qualities and that the perceived difference in pitch between successive notes is constant—are illustrated by the pitch helix in Figure 11.12. The pitch helix illustrates the similarity among pitches geometrically. *Tone chroma* (illustrated by the color of the helix) refers to differences in pitch within an octave; *tone height* refers to the octave in which a tone appears, which increases from the bottom to the top of the helix. Each full turn of the helix covers one octave and one complete change of tone chroma, so notes that are one octave apart are vertically aligned and have the same chroma, representing their perceptual similarity. The distance between successive notes along the helix is constant, representing the perception of constant difference in pitch.

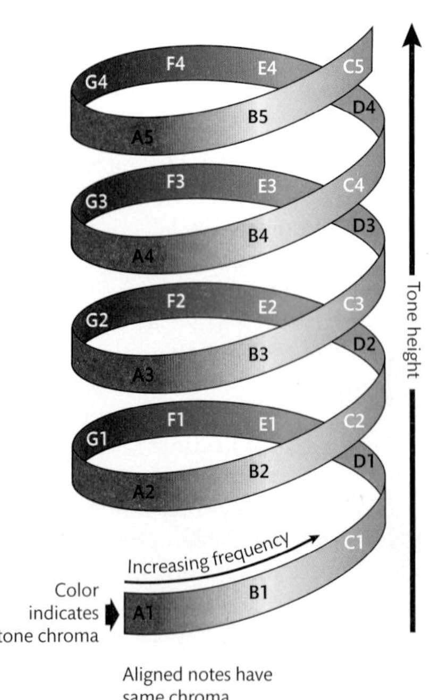

Figure 11.12 Pitch Helix The pitch helix provides a geometrical depiction of the relationships among musical notes. (Adapted from Shepard, 1982.)

Loudness and Timing

While the sequence of pitches is arguably the most important aspect of a musical composition, a composition would hardly be recognized as music if pitch were the only difference between the notes; musical compositions also vary in the loudness and timing of the constituent notes. **Dynamics** refers to the manner in which loudness varies as a piece of music progresses. It is a major factor in the artistic interpretation of a musical composition. Control over dynamics, both by composers and by performers, is achieved by specifying the loudness of different sections of music and by indicating sequences of notes over which the loudness increases or decreases abruptly or gradually. And, of course, changes in loudness are often combined with changes in timing, in order to achieve particular artistic or emotional effects.

dynamics The manner in which loudness varies as a piece of music progresses.

Rhythm refers to the temporal patterning of events in a musical composition. The *tempo* of a piece of music refers to its overall pace—that is, how fast or slow it is. The *beat* refers to equally spaced pulses that can express a fast or slow tempo (Large & Palmer, 2002). The *meter* refers to the temporal patterning of strong and weak pulses in the beat over time. Composers and performers often use a rapid tempo to establish an upbeat, joyful mood, whereas slower tempos are associated with wistful or somber moods. Indeed, some of the words used in music to indicate tempo also refer to mood—for example, the term *allegro* to indicate a rapid tempo is the Italian word for "joyful."

rhythm The temporal patterning of events in a musical composition, encompassing tempo, beat, and meter.

Timbre

In Chapter 9, we defined *timbre* as the difference between complex sounds that have the same pitch—that is, the same fundamental frequency—and the same loudness but that don't sound the same, like a violin and clarinet playing the same note. We saw that this difference can be attributed largely to differences in the relative amplitudes of the various overtones (or harmonic frequencies), along with differences in attack and decay (the ways in which the harmonic components begin and then fade away). Composers and performers use the timbres of different musical instruments and different voices to help shape the overall expressiveness of a piece of music.

Melody

In the simplest, most general terms, a **melody** (or *tune*) is a sequence of musical notes arranged in a particular rhythmic pattern, which listeners perceive as a single, recognizable unit. Complex melodies consist of a series of such recognizable sequences, forming a combination that is perceived as a larger recognizable unit and may be repeated throughout a composition in various forms—for example, with variations in timing or in the instruments or voices producing the melody.

melody (or *tune*) A sequence of musical notes arranged in a particular rhythmic pattern, which listeners perceive as a single, recognizable unit.

The most salient aspect of a melody is the relative positions of the pitches in the sequence, not the absolute pitches. For example, the melody of "Over the Rainbow" could start with middle C (C4) as the first note or it could start with C3 (or indeed any other note at all), and as long as the intervals—the number of semitones higher or lower—between consecutive notes remained the same, the sequence would be perceived as the same melody.

Two such versions of the same melody—versions containing the same intervals but starting at different notes—are called **transpositions** of one another, and even young infants appear to respond to transpositions as being perceptually equivalent. In one study, six-month-old infants were exposed to a melody repeatedly over seven days; then, on the eighth day, the infants either heard the familiar melody transposed to a different starting note or heard an unfamiliar melody (Plantinga & Trainor, 2005). Young infants, when given a choice, tend to look toward novel stimuli for a longer time than they look toward familiar stimuli, and in this case they looked longer toward the speaker playing the unfamiliar melody than they did toward the speaker playing the transposed version of the familiar melody. Even though both melodies were, strictly speaking, new, the transposed version of the familiar melody was apparently less interesting to the infants because it sounded similar to the familiar melody. Moreover, when the researchers played either the familiar, untransposed melody or the transposed version, the infants looked equally toward both. These results strongly suggest that the infants perceived the untransposed and transposed versions as very similar and thus suggest that the infants perceived and remembered the melody in terms of relative, not absolute, pitches.

transpositions Two versions of the same melody, containing the same intervals but starting at different notes.

Scales and Keys; Consonance and Dissonance

scale A particular subset of the notes in an octave.

key The scale that functions as the basis of a musical composition.

As discussed earlier, an octave spans 13 notes separated by 12 pitch intervals (semitones). A musical **scale** consists of a subset of those notes. For example, the C major scale consists of all the natural notes in an octave, beginning and ending with C: C–D–E–F–G–A–B–C. The **key** of a musical composition refers to the scale that functions as the basis of the composition—for example, a composition in the key of C major contains notes *mostly* from the C major scale (of course, the composer may also use other notes to evoke an emotional response by violating expectations and creating musical tension).

A few of the major and minor scales commonly used in Western music are shown in Table 11.3, and as you can see, each scale is named after the note with which it begins and ends (e.g., the C-flat major scale begins and ends with C flat). The major and minor scales are differentiated by the pattern of intervals (number of semitones) between successive notes—for the major scales, the pattern is 2–2–1–2–2–2–1, and for the minor scales, it's 2–1–2–2–1–2–2. Many musicians say that the major and minor scales are also differentiated by the emotional tone, or mood, evoked by compositions using one type of scale or the other; specifically, compositions based on minor scales are said to sound more serious or even sad than compositions based on major scales.

There is a rich literature discussing how Western music came to use the major and minor scales and how composers employ them to achieve particular musical effects. One important perceptual principle embodied in the use of a particular scale in a piece of music is that of consonance and dissonance. When two or more notes from a scale are played simultaneously (i.e., in a chord) or sequentially, the combination may exhibit **consonance**—the combination sounds pleasant, as if the notes "go together"—or may exhibit **dissonance**—the combination sounds unpleasant or "off."

consonance The quality exhibited by a combination of two or more notes from a scale that sounds pleasant, as if the notes "go together."

dissonance The quality exhibited by a combination of two or more notes from a scale that sounds unpleasant or "off."

As discussed earlier, musical notes have a peak in their acoustic spectrum at the fundamental (lowest) frequency and peaks at integer multiples of the fundamental—the harmonics. An important factor in the perception of consonance and dissonance is the degree to which the harmonics of the notes in the combination coincide, a factor termed *harmonicity* (McDermott et al., 2010). Figure 11.13 (left) shows two notes—C and G—with exactly coinciding harmonics. As you can see, this doesn't mean that every harmonic of C coincides with a harmonic of G but that all the harmonics of both C and G coincide with harmonics of a note with a lower fundamental frequency than C and G (this note is labeled Q in the figure). Combinations of notes with harmonicity are judged as more consonant than combinations without it and are preferred by most listeners, particularly musically experienced listeners. In contrast, the two notes shown in Figure 11.13 (right)—C and D flat—don't exhibit harmonicity, which means there isn't any note like Q with harmonics that coincide with the harmonics of C and D flat. Combinations like this are judged as dissonant and tend not to be preferred by listeners. Different

TABLE 11.3 Some of the Major and Minor Musical Scales in Western Music

Scale	Notes in Scale							
C major	C	D	E	F	G	A	B	C
C♯ major	C♯	D♯	E♯	F♯	G♯	A♯	B♯	C♯
C♭major	C♭	D♭	E♭	F♭	G♭	A♭	B♭	C♭
D major	D	E	F♯	G	A	B	C♯	D
D♭major	D♭	E♭	F	G♭	A♭	B♭	C	D♭
E major	E	F♯	G♯	A	B	C♯	D♯	E
E♭major	E♭	F	G	A♭	B♭	C	D	E♭
F major	F	G	A	B♭	C	D	E	F
F♯ major	F♯	G♯	A♯	B	C♯	D♯	E♯	F♯

Note: ♯ = sharp; ♭ = flat.

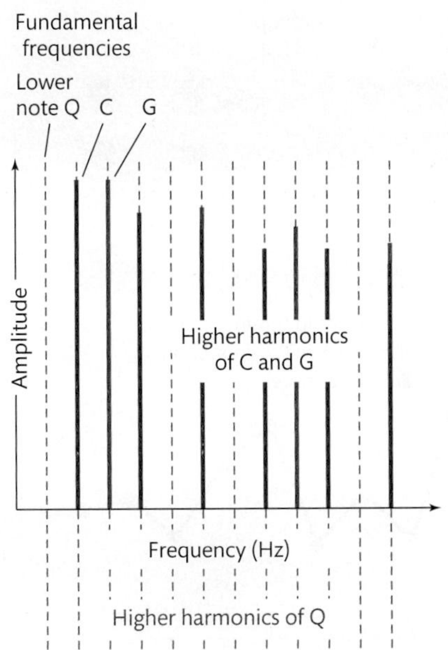

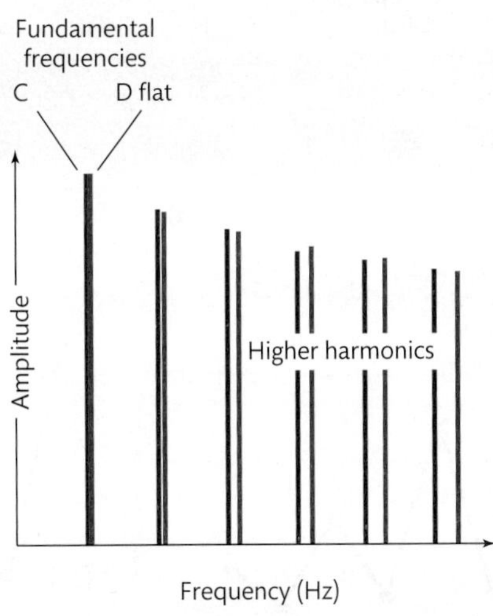

Figure 11.13 Consonance, Dissonance, and Harmonicity (left) The blue bars and red bars show the frequency spectra for the notes C and G, respectively. In this case, there exists a note Q with a lower fundamental frequency than both C and G and with higher harmonics that coincide with the higher harmonics of C and G. This pattern characterizes consonant pairs of notes like C and G. (right) The blue bars and red bars show the frequency spectra for the notes C and D flat, respectively. In this case, no note exists with a lower fundamental frequency than both C and D flat and with higher harmonics that coincide with the higher harmonics of C and D flat. This characterizes dissonant pairs of notes like C and D flat. (Adapted from McDermott et al., 2010, Figure 1.)

combinations of notes can exhibit greater or lesser degrees of consonance or dissonance, depending on the degree of harmonicity—that is, on how closely the harmonics of the notes in the combination coincide.

Knowledge and Music Perception

Our ability to understand speech depends to a large degree on the knowledge that we've accumulated in a lifetime of experience with speech—our (mostly implicit) knowledge of how language works, together with our knowledge about what to expect in a given conversation. Our perception of music also depends on our accumulated knowledge—our knowledge about how music works, together with our knowledge about what to expect in a given musical composition.

The knowledge that leads to musical expectations can be very specific. Suppose, for example, that you've heard Judy Garland sing the first line of "Over the Rainbow" 10 times or more over the course of your life. The knowledge you've gained through this experience will, the next time you hear the song, lead you to have the very specific expectation that the note corresponding to "rain-" will be followed by a note one semitone higher in pitch, corresponding to "-bow."

Other, less specific expectations are based on the general knowledge that even nonmusicians gain through repeatedly listening to compositions in the familiar scales and keys of Western music. Often, the first few notes of a piece of music enable the listener to recognize—even if only implicitly, without conscious awareness—the scale in which the piece is written and played, because the notes within that scale tend to occur more frequently than other notes. In particular, the *tonic,* or base note, of the scale (the note that the scale begins with—see Table 11.3) tends not only to occur more often but also to be played with longer duration.

To assess how this type of knowledge is reflected in listeners' perception of music, researchers conducted an experiment in which participants had to rate how well various single notes "fit" with chords from various scales (Krumhansl & Kessler, 1982). Figure 11.14a shows the notes in the C major and C minor scales. Figure 11.14b shows some of the experimental results. Each participant first listened to a chord made up of notes from the C major scale (consisting of the notes C, E, and G) or C minor scale (C, E flat, and G) and then listened to a single note, which might or might not belong to the scale from which that chord comes. The participant then rated how well the note fit with the chord (i.e., the extent to which the note sounded consonant or dissonant with the chord), on a scale of 1 (*fits poorly*) to 7 (*fits well*). As you can see, the notes of the chord itself (outlined circles) were

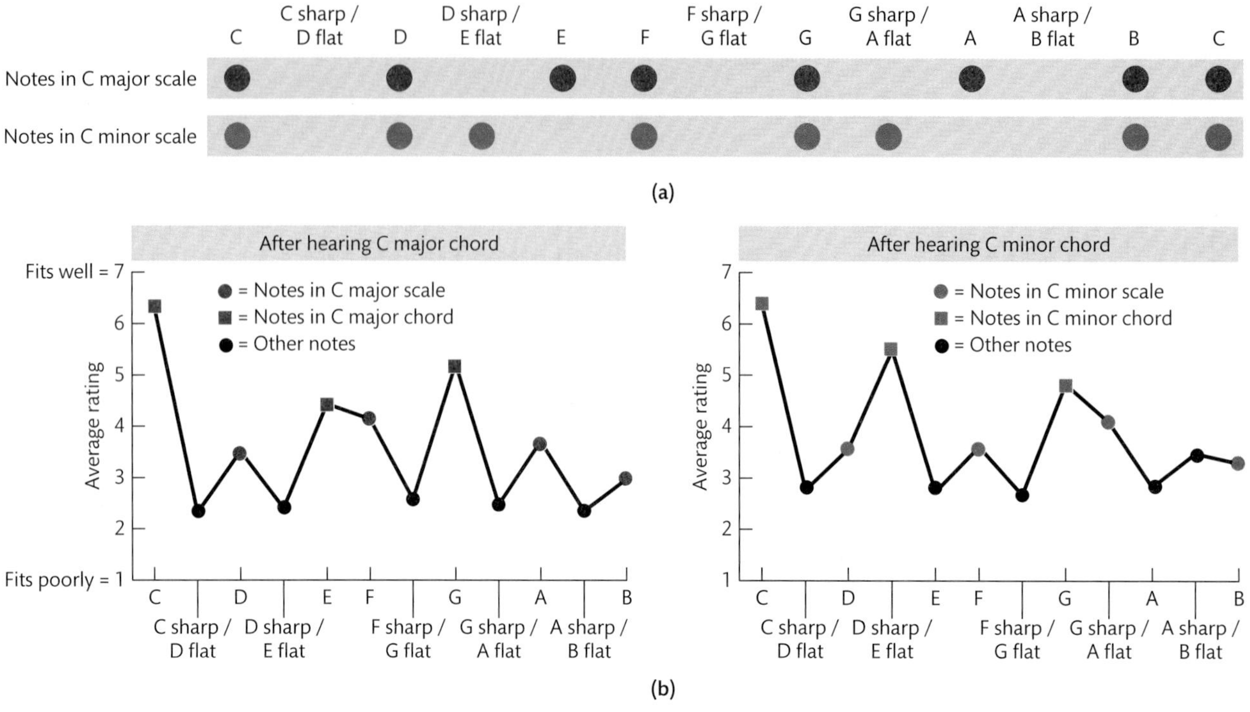

Figure 11.14 Perception of Musical "Fit" (a) The notes within an octave starting at C, along with the subsets of those notes that form the C major and C minor scales. (b) Listeners were asked to rate how well each note in the octave "fit" with a chord from either a C major scale or a C minor scale. In both cases, the tonic of the scale, C, was perceived as the best fit; notes that were part of the chord (squares) were rated higher than other notes; notes that were part of the same scale as the chord (red or blue circles) were consistently rated higher than other notes (black circles). (Data in graphs from Krumhansl & Kessler, 1982, Figure 2.)

rated as fitting best with the chord, but among the other notes, those that belonged to the same scale as the chord were, on average, almost always rated higher than those that didn't (black circles). This suggests that knowledge of Western music provides a context in which hearing a chord from a particular scale makes all the notes in that scale become salient.

Composers often take advantage of listeners' musical knowledge by creating effects based on violating expectations. For example, just as listeners quickly recognize the scale and key of a particular composition, so too do they often pick up the rhythm of a composition early on—which they may show by tapping their toes in time with the emphasized beats—and composers can use this to create musical effects by including off-rhythm notes that come at unexpected times. Similarly, composers may take advantage of listeners' scale or key recognition by introducing, near the end of a piece, a sequence of notes that aren't part of the current key. This tends to build up psychological tension as the listener waits for a resolution—a return to the notes in the current key.

Neural Basis of Music Perception

As noted earlier, the auditory system processes all sounds—including music, speech, and all other types of sound—in the same way from the cochlea to the primary auditory cortex, where the frequencies in incoming sounds are represented in a series of tonotopic maps (Peretz & Zatorre, 2005). Beyond the primary auditory cortex, however, specialized areas in the two hemispheres play important roles in processing different types of sounds. We've seen that the left hemisphere is more active than the right hemisphere in processing speech (look back at Figure 11.10), and it's been suggested that the left auditory cortex is specialized for representing the fine differences in timing that are crucial in speech perception (Zatorre et al., 2002), as illustrated in Figures 11.8 and 11.9. It's natural, therefore, to ask which areas of the cortex are responsible for representing the fine differences in pitch that are crucial in music perception.

In one fMRI study (Hyde et al., 2008), the brain activity of a group of nonmusicians was recorded while they listened passively to sequences of pure tones that either all had the same pitch (fixed-pitch sequence) or that increased and decreased in pitch (changing-pitch sequence), as illustrated in Figure 11.15a. Figure 11.15b shows that both the left and right auditory cortex were more active (and about equally active) when participants were listening to a fixed-pitch sequence versus silence, as you'd expect—these are, after all, auditory areas. In contrast, only the right auditory cortex responded more strongly when participants were listening to a changing-pitch sequence versus a fixed-pitch sequence, as shown in Figure 11.15c. In other words, the left auditory cortex responds about the same to both fixed-pitch and changing-pitch sequences, whereas the right auditory cortex is especially active when the listener is processing changes in pitch, a core function of music perception.

Thus, as evidenced by the results of this and other studies, auditory areas in the left hemisphere appear to be specialized for representing fine differences in the timing of sounds, whereas areas in the right hemisphere are specialized for representing fine differences in pitch (Zatorre et al., 2002). Of course, pitch differences are important in speech, just as timing differences are important in music, but this general statement does reflect how the auditory system divides the responsibility for representing the most fundamental aspects of speech and music, respectively.

Now recall a study we discussed in Chapter 1 (Lahav et al., 2007), which showed that when nonmusicians listened to music that they had learned to play on a piano, brain activity was observed both in the regions of the brain responsible for music perception and in the regions that control hand and finger movements, as if listening automatically primed them to play that same music. Like the intimate connection between the perception and production of speech (illustrated in Figure 11.10), there is a close tie between the perception and production of music (Zatorre et al., 2007). Thus, music perception is no exception when we consider the importance of perception in general for guiding action, a recurring theme throughout this book.

A final question related to the neural basis of music perception concerns individual differences in music-related ability. Some people (less than 1% of the population) have an ability known as *absolute pitch*—they can listen to isolated notes and name them accurately and effortlessly (Levitin & Rogers, 2005)—not unlike the way most people can look at and name isolated colors. People with absolute pitch can, for example, listen to the note produced by the third black key to the right of middle C on a piano keyboard (see Figure 11.11) and respond by saying "F sharp above middle C."

Other people (an estimated 4% of the population) have profound impairments in perceiving and remembering melodies and in distinguishing one melody from another; yet such individuals are typically normal in their ability to perceive speech and other nonmusical

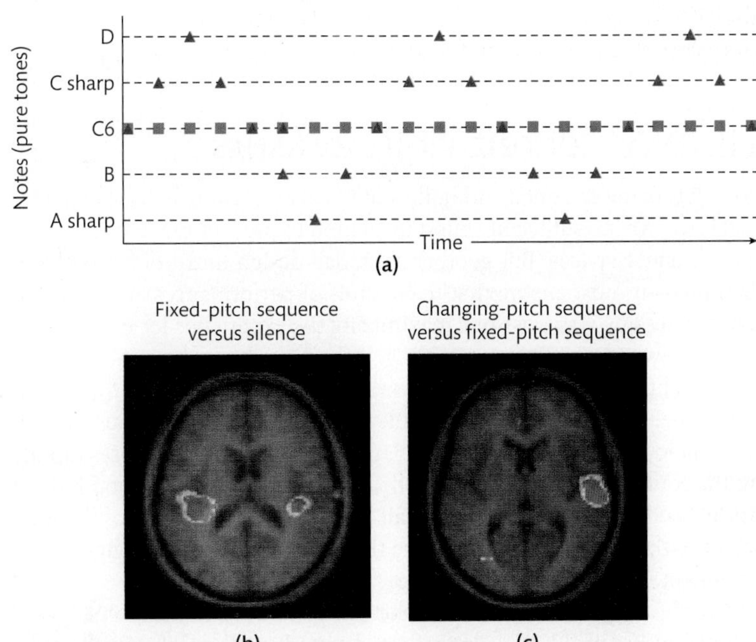

Figure 11.15 Cortical Activity in Response to Changes in Pitch (a) Participants listened to sequences of 21 evenly spaced pure tones, all of equal duration. In some cases, all the tones were of the same frequency (fixed-pitch sequence, as shown by the blue squares); in other cases, the tones increased and decreased in a patterned way (changing-pitch sequence, as illustrated by the red triangles). (b) This fMRI image was produced by subtracting the image during silence from the image during the fixed-pitch sequence, to show that the left and right auditory cortex both responded to the fixed-pitch sequence. (c) This image was produced by subtracting the image during the fixed-pitch sequence from the image during the changing-pitch sequence, to show that the right auditory cortex responded more strongly to the changing-pitch sequence (above and beyond simply hearing sounds). (Adapted and photos from Hyde et al., 2008, Figures 2 and 5.)

amusia A profound impairment in perceiving and remembering melodies and in distinguishing one melody from another.

sounds (Stewart, 2008). This condition, called **amusia,** can come about as the result of a stroke, as in the case of T., the young man in the vignette at the beginning of this chapter, but is more often congenital (i.e., present at birth) and typically persists through adulthood. People with amusia have difficulty in telling apart different notes and particularly in judging whether a sequence of notes increases or decreases in pitch. This, in turn, impairs their ability to perceive the pitch contour of a melody or to notice when specific notes are out of tune. Neuroanatomical studies have found that individuals with congenital amusia tend to exhibit thickening of the right inferior frontal cortex and right auditory cortex (Hyde et al., 2007). The thickened cortex is thought to be associated with reduced neural connections between the auditory cortex and frontal cortex, which in turn impairs music perception.

Researchers have also found that differences in musical ability and in the brain structures that support it arise though musical training and experience (Dawson, 2011). One study used magnetoencephalography to measure brain activity in a group of experienced musicians and a control group of nonmusicians listening to pure tones (Pantev et al., 1998). The two groups showed equivalent *patterns* of activity, but the *magnitude* of the activity was significantly greater in the experienced musicians—an indication that a significantly larger population of neurons was activated by musical sounds in this group. Moreover, the magnitude of the activity depended on when the person began musical training: the effect was largest in people who had started at the youngest ages.

Check Your Understanding

11.13 Consider the octave spanning E2 to E3. Which two notes in this octave have a fundamental frequency ratio of 1:2? Which note in this octave has a fundamental frequency approximately 6% higher than the fundamental frequency of G2?

11.14 Would the difference in pitch between E2 and F2 be perceived as less than, greater than, or equal to the difference in pitch between F2 and G2? Explain your answer.

11.15 Would a singer be more likely to vary the meter or the tempo to change the mood of a song?

11.16 Consider three notes X, Y, and Z, where X has the lowest fundamental frequency. The 2nd, 4th, and 6th harmonics of X coincide with the 1st, 2nd, and 3rd harmonics of Y, and the 3rd, 6th, and 9th harmonics of X coincide with the 1st, 2nd, and 3rd harmonics of Z. Do Y and Z exhibit harmonicity? Explain your answer.

11.17 True or false? The left auditory cortex seems to be more important than the right auditory cortex in representing fine differences in pitch.

APPLICATIONS Concert Hall Acoustics

When a new concert hall is being designed and built—or when an existing hall is being renovated—a major goal is to provide sufficient sound insulation to prevent unwanted sounds from entering the performance spaces. But good concert hall design must, of course, provide much more than this—it must ensure that the sounds of performances are conveyed to audiences in the most pleasing way possible, maximizing the experience for each person in the audience, no matter where the person is sitting. Achieving this goal turns out to be a highly complex task (Mehta et al., 1999).

Loudness is a fundamental concern—the sound level of the performance must be sufficiently high at every seat in the hall. As we saw in Chapter 9, sound level decreases rapidly as the distance from the sound source increases; without augmentation, the sound level at a distance equivalent to the back row of a concert hall could be as little as 1% of the level at a distance equivalent to the front row. To overcome this problem, acoustic engineers use reflected sound to augment the sound from the stage.

Sound produced inside an enclosed space like a concert hall travels to the listener along many paths, as illustrated in Figure 11.16a. The reflected sound is a form of amplification, just like the amplification provided by a simple cone-shaped megaphone, where sound waves that would otherwise dissipate out to the sides are reflected back toward the listener by the inner surface of the cone. In order to serve as effective sound reflectors, the walls, ceiling, and other surfaces in a concert hall need to be constructed to reflect sound as efficiently as possible from the stage to each seat.

Much of the focus in concert hall design is on a single factor, **reverberation time (RT)**—conventionally defined as the time for a sound to decay effectively to zero (you can think of this as "how long the echoes last"). To understand why this is such an important factor, let's begin by looking at Figure 11.16b, which illustrates how an abrupt sound on the stage of a concert hall decays over time, as measured by a microphone in the seating area of the hall. The sound that travels directly from the stage to the microphone is the first brief, loud impulse (shown in red)—all the remaining sound is reverberation, sound reflected into the microphone from the various surfaces in the hall. The main reason why the sound level decreases over time is that sound waves lose energy each time they reflect

reverberation time (RT) The time for a sound to decay effectively to zero.

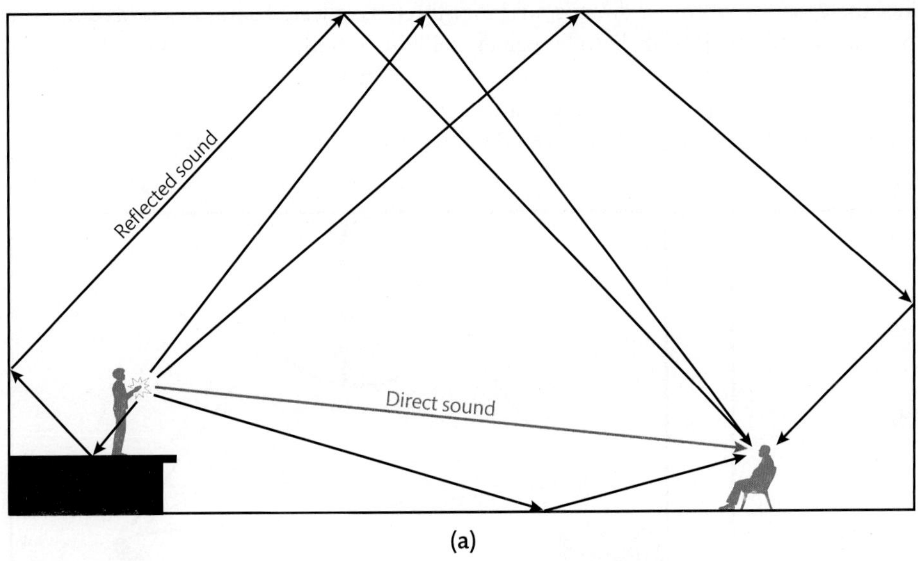

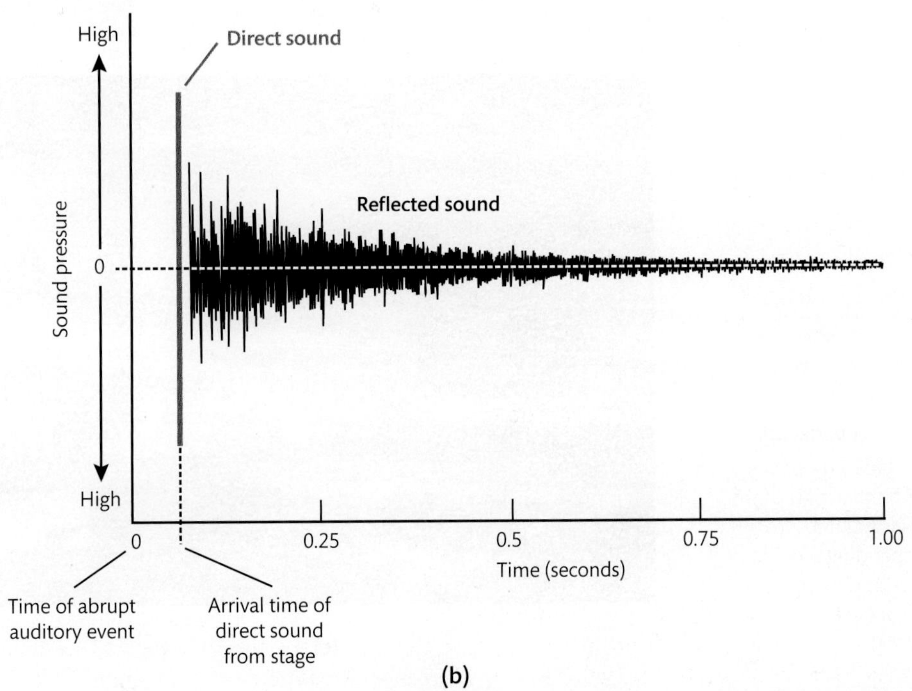

Figure 11.16 Direct and Reflected Sound, and Sound Decay (a) In an enclosed space like a concert hall, sound is reflected from hard surfaces such as the floor, walls, ceiling, and stage, reaching listeners' ears via many different paths (black arrows) in addition to the direct path (red arrow). (b) The graph shows the sound level at a microphone in the seating area of a concert hall, about 25 meters away, following an abrupt auditory event on the stage, such as a person clapping their hands once. The first sound arriving at the microphone is the sound that travels via the shortest path, directly from the stage—this is the impulse shown in red. Subsequent impulses arrive at the microphone after being reflected from one or more surfaces, such as the walls, floor, and ceiling of the hall. This reverberant sound decays over time because each reflection absorbs a little bit of energy.

off a surface. After a sufficient number of reflections, the sound energy decays effectively to zero. In Figure 11.16b, for example, very little energy is left after 1 second.

Reverberation time depends on the volume of the space (large space = long RT) and the degree to which the surfaces in the space absorb sound (hard surfaces with low absorption = long RT). In a small space with many soft, absorbent surfaces, like a bedroom, RT is typically less than half a second. In a large space with mostly hard, nonabsorbent surfaces, like a cathedral with stone walls, RT can be more than 10 seconds (which might be ideal for Gregorian chants but not for most other types of music). A short RT increases the intelligibility of speech, because echoes of previous phonemes don't overlap with the sounds of subsequent ones. However, a short RT reduces the fullness, or richness, of sounds, which is especially noticeable with orchestral music—a performance space with a short RT is said to be acoustically "dead." Many concert halls are designed to have an RT of about 2 seconds.

Acoustic engineers sometimes place sound reflectors within a hall to give a desired feeling of intimacy, or musical presence. In very large spaces, people seated in parts of the hall distant from the stage tend to feel "isolated" from the music if there is a delay of more than about 50 msec between the arrival of the direct sound from the stage and the arrival of the first echoes off the ceiling and walls, called the *first reflected sound*. This is partly because when the delay between the direct sound and the first reflected sound exceeds about 50 msec, the sounds are less likely to be perceptually fused and, therefore, more likely to be perceived as coming from different locations—like echoes. As illustrated in Figure 11.17, this problem can be addressed with reflectors (sometimes called "clouds") suspended below the ceiling, to shorten the delay between the direct sound and the first reflected sound.

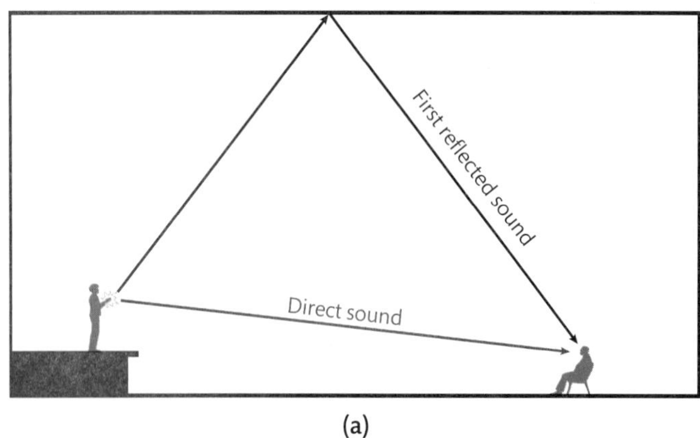

(a)

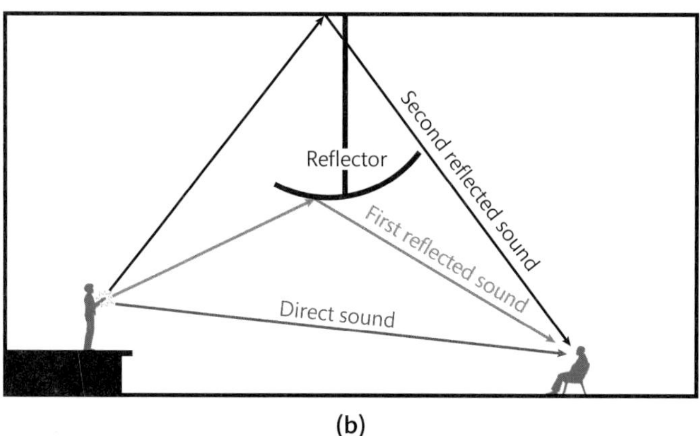

(b)

(c)

Figure 11.17 Reflectors to Reduce Delay in the First Reflected Sound (a) In a large space, listeners far from the stage experience a long delay between the arrival of direct sound and the arrival of the first reflected sound, which can make listeners feel "isolated" from the music. (b) The delay can be shortened by suspending a reflector from the ceiling. (c) The concert hall at the Culture and Congress Center in Lucerne, Switzerland, has an adjustable acoustic canopy that serves as a reflector. [Prisma Bildagentur AG/Alamy]

Check Your Understanding

11.18 True or false? Concert hall designers attempt to maximize the direct sound heard by audience members and minimize reflected sound.

11.19 For orchestral music, what is an undesirable effect of reverberation time that's (A) too long or (B) too short?

11.20 How is a listener's musical experience likely to be affected if the delay between the arrival of direct sound from the concert hall stage and the arrival of the first reflected sound is more than about 50 msec?

SUMMARY

- **Speech** Phonemes are the basic sounds of speech. To represent each phoneme in a distinctive way, we use the International Phonetic Alphabet. Phonemes are produced by the vocal apparatus, the anatomical structures that direct and modify the flow of air from the lungs through the oral and nasal cavities. Speech sounds can be divided into vowels (produced with a relatively unrestricted flow of air) and consonants (produced with some restriction in the flow of air) and can be voiced or voiceless (produced with vibrating vocal folds or not). Different vowels are produced by modifying the shape of the oral cavity, which changes the peaks (formants) in a vowel's harmonic spectrum. Sound spectrograms show how the frequency spectra of vowels vary over time. Consonants can be defined in terms of three parameters: place of articulation, manner of articulation, and voicing. Perceiving the sequences of phonemes in speech is challenging because of differences between speakers, because of differences between the same speaker at different times, and because speakers tend to blur the boundaries between phonemes and between words in rapid everyday speech. Coarticulation refers to the way in which the articulation of phonemes affects the acoustic properties of surrounding phonemes. The perception of phonemes as the same despite coarticulation effects is a type of perceptual constancy. Studies involving the manipulation of voice onset time indicate that phoneme perception is categorical rather than continuous and that the auditory system has "detectors" tuned to different voice onset times. The McGurk effect indicates that, when visual cues and auditory cues conflict, the auditory system tends toward a "compromise" perception. Listeners learn to segment the speech stream into words on the basis of having learned phoneme transition probabilities—the probabilities that given phoneme sequences will occur at various positions within words or across word boundaries. Infants have a remarkable ability to quickly learn phoneme transition probabilities. Phonemic restoration is a form of perceptual completion in which listeners perceive phonemes that have been masked or replaced by other sounds, based on their knowledge of which phonemes are likely to occur in the given position. Speech processing in the brain occurs primarily in the left hemisphere (but also to some extent in the right hemisphere) and is organized into a ventral pathway through regions specialized for speech comprehension and a dorsal pathway through regions specialized for speech production.

- **Music** The primary dimensions of music are pitch, loudness, timing, and timbre. The most fundamental dimension is pitch—the sequence of pitches is what most clearly distinguishes one piece of music from another. The notes used in producing music can be organized into octaves (sequences of notes in which the last note has twice the frequency of the first note). Notes separated by an octave are perceived as having similar sound qualities, and the perceived difference in pitch between successive notes in an octave is constant. Music exhibits rhythm, based on regular patterns of variation in the loudness, spacing, and duration of notes. Dynamics—how loudness varies over the course of a piece of music—is a major aspect of the artistic interpretation of music. Rhythm—the temporal patterning of a musical composition—encompasses tempo, beat, and meter. Variations in tempo are used to express mood. Differences in timbre arise from the use of different instruments or voices. A melody is a sequence of notes arranged in a particular rhythmic pattern and perceived as a recognizable unit. Listeners tend to recognize melodies on the basis of the sequence of relative pitches rather than on the basis of absolute pitches. Transpositions—different versions of the same melody—are recognized as similar by infants. A scale is a particular subset of the notes in a particular octave. Combinations of notes from a scale exhibit varying degrees of consonance and dissonance, mainly based on the degree of harmonicity of the combination. Music perception is also based on the knowledge and expectations accumulated through experience with music, which composers can take advantage of to create various musical effects. In the brain, the right auditory cortex is important in representing fine differences in pitch contour (more important in music perception than in speech perception), whereas the left auditory cortex is important in representing fine differences in timing (more important in speech perception). Studies of brain activity reveal a close tie between the perception and production of music. Less than 1% of people have absolute pitch. About 4% of people have amusia, an impairment of the ability to distinguish melodies and identify differences in pitch.

- Applications: Concert Hall Acoustics The goal of concert hall design is to maximize the musical experience for all the people in the audience, regardless of where they are sitting in relation to the stage. One fundamental issue is loudness, which declines rapidly with distance. Amplification is achieved by ensuring that sufficient reflected sound is directed to all locations in the hall. Another fundamental issue is reverberation time, which must be neither too long nor too short. The interval between the arrival of direct sound at the listener's ears and the arrival of the first reflected sound should be no greater than about 50 msec in order to give the listener a pleasing sense of intimacy with the music.

KEY TERMS

amusia (p. 380)
aphasia (p. 370)
categorical perception (p. 366)
coarticulation (p. 365)
consonance (p. 376)
consonants (p. 358)
dissonance (p. 376)
dynamics (p. 375)
formants (p. 359)
International Phonetic Alphabet (IPA) (p. 356)
key (p. 376)
larynx (or *voice box*) (p. 357)
manner of articulation (p. 360)
McGurk effect (p. 368)
melody (or *tune*) (p. 375)
octave (p. 374)
pharynx (p. 357)
phonemes (p. 356)
phoneme transition probabilities (p. 369)
phonemic boundary (p. 367)
phonemic restoration (p. 369)
place of articulation (p. 360)
reverberation time (RT) (p. 381)
rhythm (p. 375)
scale (p. 376)
semitones (p. 374)
sound spectrogram (p. 360)
transpositions (p. 375)
tune, see **melody.**
uvula (p. 357)
vocal cords, see **vocal folds.**
vocal folds (or *vocal cords*) (p. 357)
voice box, see **larynx.**
voice onset time (VOT) (p. 366)
voicing (p. 360)
vowels (p. 358)

EXPAND YOUR UNDERSTANDING

11.1 Write the words "through" and "breathe" using the IPA symbols shown in Tables 11.1 and 11.2. How many phonemes make up each word? Which two-letter sequences represent a single phoneme? Which letters don't represent any phoneme?

11.2 Could a human language include labiovelar stop consonants? Labiodental stop consonants? Explain your answers.

11.3 You're watching a video clip of someone facing the camera and repeatedly pronouncing one syllable while a dubbed sound track plays a different syllable. Which scenario (A or B) is more likely, due to the McGurk effect? Explain why.

	Video Clip	Sound Track	Syllable You Perceive
A	/na-na/	/ma-ma/	/ma-ma/
B	/ma-ma/	/na-na/	/ma-ma/

11.4 In the language spoken by the people of the lost continent of Atlantis, the following sequences of phonemes never occur within words but always across words: /if/, /is/, /of/, /os/. All other two-phoneme sequences always occur within words and never across words. Given this information about phoneme transition probabilities, how would you segment the following sequence of phonemes into words: /fumumosabifumosabibifufumosabisabifumofumosasabi/?

11.5 In an experiment on phonemic restoration, in a recording of the sentence "Every creature needs a teacher," the sound represented by the "t" in the word "creature" is replaced either by the sound of the "t" in "matter" or by the sound of the "sh" in "masher." Which replacement is more likely to result in a perception of the word "creature"? Explain why.

11.6 Judging by Table 11.3, would listeners familiar with Western music tend to find the note F♯ more consonant with chord 1 or chord 2?

Chord 1: D—E—B

Chord 2: F—C—D

Explain why.

11.7 Suppose a sound synthesizer could produce only pure tones with frequencies of 20 Hz to 20,000 Hz with increments of 10 Hz (i.e., 20, 30, 40, 50, . . . , 19,990, 20,000 Hz), over a wide range of amplitudes. Could the melody (or a transposition of the melody) of "Happy Birthday" (or any other familiar song) be produced with this machine? What dimension of "real" music would be lacking? Would the relationships between the notes be fundamentally different from or basically the same as the relationship between the notes in a performance of the melody on a piano? Explain your answers.

11.8 Suppose you were the only person sitting in a concert hall listening to a symphony orchestra. How would your auditory experience change if the hall were suddenly filled with other audience members? How would it change if the hall suddenly disappeared, so that the orchestra and you were in the middle of an empty field? Explain your answers.

READ MORE ABOUT IT

Greenberg, S., & Ainsworth, W. A. (Eds.). (2006). *Listening to speech: An auditory perspective*. Mahwah, NJ: Erlbaum.

A collection of chapters by leading researchers covering a broad range of topics in speech perception, from acoustics and physiology to auditory scene analysis and speech perception by the hearing impaired.

Hickok, G., & Poeppel, D. (2007). The cortical organization of speech processing. *Nature Reviews Neuroscience, 8,* 393–402.

A clear account of the current state of the art on how the brain processes speech.

Levitin, D. J. (2006). *This is your brain on music*. London: Plume.

A lively survey of the psychology and neuroscience of perceiving, performing, and enjoying music.

Patel, A. D. (2008). *Music, language, and the brain*. New York: Oxford University Press.

A comprehensive and scholarly review of the relationship between human comprehension of speech and music.

Laura Knight, *A Dark Pool,* c. 1908–1919. [Oil on canvas, 46 × 45.8 cm. Laing Art Gallery, Newcastle-upon-Tyne, UK. The Bridgeman Art Library.]

12

THE BODY SENSES

Watch Yourself!

One day when Ian Waterman was 19 years old, he suddenly started feeling extremely fatigued and weak—more than he could ever remember. He was initially diagnosed as having the flu and was advised to rest in bed to recuperate. But shortly thereafter, when he tried to get out of bed, he fell onto the floor in a heap. He was taken to an emergency room, where his condition baffled the attending doctors. Except for sensations of temperature and pain, he was completely numb from the neck down—he couldn't feel anything when he was touched, and the only way he could know the positions of his limbs was by looking at them.

Although Ian could move his arms and legs, he had little control over them. If he tried to pick up an egg, either he would crush it or it would slip from his fingers. He soon discovered that even the simplest movements required intense visual concentration—for example, in order to grasp a teacup, he had to keep close watch on his arm as he moved it toward the cup and then had to watch his fingers as he positioned them. The act of standing still with his eyes closed was impossible, because he couldn't feel the changes in pressure on the soles of his feet when his body began to tilt—these pressure changes provide the information we need to make the constant little muscular adjustments that let us maintain an upright posture. Lacking this information, Ian had to use vision to check whether he was beginning to tilt to one side, and he had to learn to use that visual information to adjust his posture.

Doctors eventually diagnosed Ian's condition as an extremely rare form of peripheral neuropathy, or pathology of the peripheral nerves (the nerves outside the brain and spinal cord), affecting only the nerves that convey neural signals from the skin and joints with information about touch and about the positions and movements of the limbs. The nerves conveying signals to the muscles were not affected, and neither were the nerves carrying information about pain, temperature, and muscle fatigue.

Over a period of many months, Ian learned to use vision to control his movements and to maintain an upright position in order to walk. Eventually, following years of physical therapy, he was able to develop a variety of strategies for controlling his muscles effectively enough to lead a full and rewarding life.

Traditionally, the body senses are grouped under the term "touch," which is described as one of "the five senses"—the others, of course, being vision, audition, smell, and taste. But this description is misleading, because the body senses are much more diverse than any of the other four, each of which monitors just one aspect of the environment and responds to just one type of stimuli—light, sound, molecules floating in the air, or molecules dissolved in saliva, respectively. In contrast, the body senses monitor the effects on the body of many aspects of the external and internal environments, and they involve responses to many different types of stimuli. Indeed, the body senses extend the traditional five senses by at least another five,

Chapter Outline

depending on how you count (see the discussion of this question in Chapter 1). One defensible way to count is by the different kinds of things that are sensed:

- skin deformation (tactile perception, or what is commonly meant by "touch")
- muscle stretch and joint angle, for monitoring limb position and movement (proprioception)
- pain, for detecting actual or potential tissue damage (nociception)
- temperature, of something contacting the skin (thermoreception)
- object shape, perceived through touch and proprioception together (haptics)
- balance and acceleration of the body

In this chapter, we'll discuss touch and each of these additional senses in turn, including the specialized sensory receptors associated with them, and we'll explore the pathways that each uses to send information to the regions within the brain where that information is processed.

Tactile Perception: Perceiving Mechanical Stimulation of the Skin

Tactile perception (or *touch,* in the narrower sense discussed above) is perception that results from the mechanical deformation—indentation, vibration, or stretching—of the skin. Figure 12.1 shows that human skin can be divided into two main types, skin with hairs (*hairy skin,* as on the head and forearms) and skin without hairs (*glabrous skin,* as on the lips and palms), and that skin consists of two main layers, the epidermis and the dermis. Within these layers (mainly in the dermis), in both glabrous and hairy skin, are a variety of sensory receptors, including the four main types of **mechanoreceptors,** which transduce mechanical deformations of the skin into neural signals that are sent to the brain.

tactile perception (or *touch*) Perception that results from the mechanical deformation–indentation, vibration, or stretching–of the skin.

mechanoreceptors Sensory receptors that transduce mechanical deformations of the skin into neural signals that are sent to the brain.

SAI mechanoreceptors Slow-adapting mechanoreceptors with Merkel cell endings; they have relatively small receptive fields and are relatively densely arranged near the surface of the skin.

SAII mechanoreceptors Slow-adapting mechanoreceptors; they have relatively large receptive fields and are relatively sparsely distributed relatively deeply in the skin.

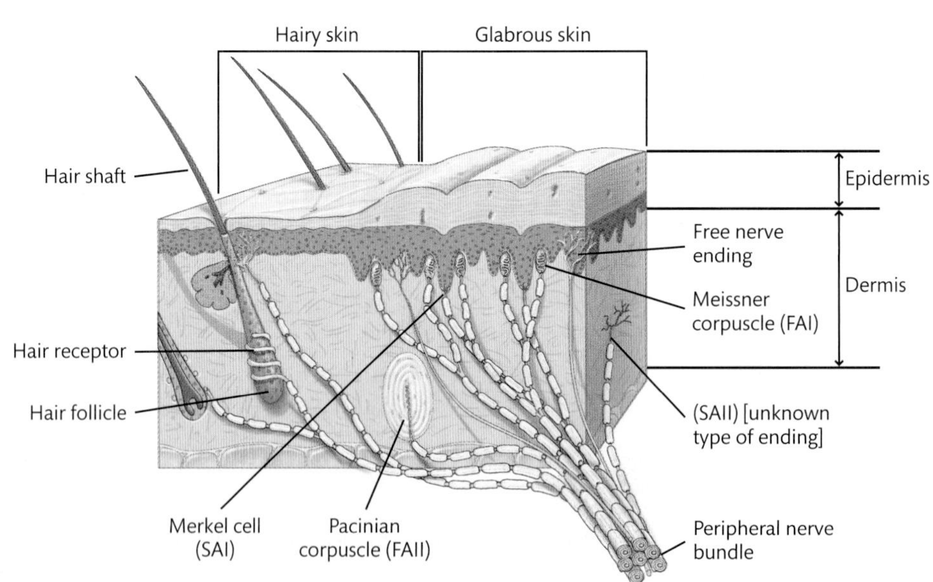

Figure 12.1 Sensory Receptors in a Cross Section of Human Skin The two main types of skin are hairy skin and glabrous (hairless) skin. The two main layers of the skin are the epidermis (the outermost surface of the skin) and the dermis. The specialized endings of two of the four main types of mechanoreceptors–Merkel cells (SAI) and Meissner corpuscles (FAI)–are densely distributed in the upper part of the dermis and lower part of the epidermis. The endings of SAII mechanoreceptors and the FAII endings (Pacinian corpuscles) are more sparsely distributed in the dermis; Pacinian corpuscles tend to be located lower in the dermis than SAII endings. (In this illustration, SAII endings are depicted as resembling free nerve endings, but their actual form is currently unknown.) Hairy skin contains mechanoreceptors called *hair receptors,* which are wrapped around the hair follicles and which respond to movements of the hair shafts (caused, for example, by objects touching the tips of the hairs). Free nerve endings (nerve fibers without specialized endings), which mediate perception of pain and temperature, tend to be located very near the surface of the skin, in the epidermis and upper dermis.

The four types of mechanoreceptors differ in the timing of their responses: the two slow-adapting (SA) mechanoreceptors—**SAI mechanoreceptors** and **SAII mechanoreceptors**—produce a burst of action potentials at the onset of skin deformation but then a lower and sustained response until the stimulus is removed from the skin; in contrast, the two fast-adapting (FA) mechanoreceptors—**FAI mechanoreceptors** and **FAII mechanoreceptors**—produce a burst of action potentials only at the onset and offset of skin deformation. The term "adapting" refers to the fact that sensory fibers tend to reduce their firing rate during prolonged, unchanging stimulation from an initial high level to either a lower, sustained level (SA) or virtually to zero (FA).

The four types of mechanoreceptors also differ in the size of their receptive fields and their typical position (depth) within the layers of the skin. SAI and FAI mechanoreceptors have relatively small receptive fields and are densely arranged near the surface of the skin. These characteristics give them relatively high spatial resolution (i.e., they can respond to fine spatial detail). In contrast, the SAII and FAII mechanoreceptors have larger receptive fields and are more sparsely distributed more deeply in the skin, which accounts for their lower spatial resolution. The sensitivity of FA mechanoreceptors to abrupt changes in stimulation makes them well suited for detecting vibration and motion. Each type of mechanoreceptor has an axon, or nerve fiber, that terminates in a specialized ending where transduction takes place. As shown in Figure 12.1, the endings of three of the mechanoreceptor types are called **Merkel cells** (on SAI mechanoreceptors), **Meissner corpuscles** (on FAI mechanoreceptors), and **Pacinian corpuscles** (on FAII mechanoreceptors); the ending associated with SAII mechanoreceptors is currently unknown. Table 12.1 summarizes all this information.

FAI mechanoreceptors Fast-adapting mechanoreceptors with Meissner corpuscle endings; they have relatively small receptive fields and are relatively densely arranged near the surface of the skin.

FAII mechanoreceptors Fast-adapting mechanoreceptors with Pacinian corpuscle endings; they have relatively large receptive fields and are relatively sparsely distributed relatively deeply in the skin.

Merkel cells Specialized endings of SAI mechanoreceptors, where transduction takes place.

Meissner corpuscles Specialized endings of FAI mechanoreceptors, where transduction takes place.

Pacinian corpuscles Specialized endings of FAII mechanoreceptors, where transduction takes place.

TABLE 12.1 The Four Main Types of Mechanoreceptors

	Slow Adapting		*Fast Adapting*	
	SAI (Small receptive field)	SAII (Large receptive field)	FAI* (Small receptive field)	FAII* (Large receptive field)
Specialized ending	Merkel cell	[unknown]†	Meissner corpuscle	Pacinian corpuscle
Position in skin layers	Upper dermis	Dermis	Upper dermis	Lower dermis
Density of distribution	Relatively dense, especially in fingertips	Relatively sparse	Relatively dense, especially in fingertips	Relatively sparse
Spatial resolution	High	Low	High	Low
Sensitivity to temporal variation	Low	Low	Medium	High
Skin deformation that elicits strongest response	Indentation by edges, curves, and textures	Stretch	Motion and low-frequency vibration	High-frequency vibration
Functions supported	Perceiving pattern, texture, and shape	Perceiving skin stretch and hand conformation	Perceiving slip; maintaining grip control	Perceiving fine textures through transmitted vibration
Timing of response‡	Firing rate / Time; Begin deformation; End deformation		Firing rate / Time; Begin deformation; End deformation	

*In many scientific publications, the FAI and FAII mechanoreceptors are called RA (for "rapidly adapting") and PC (for "Pacinian corpuscle"), respectively.

†SAII receptors were once thought to terminate in a structure called a *Ruffini corpuscle*, but careful anatomical analysis hasn't found any evidence for Ruffini corpuscles in the palm or fingertip (Paré et al., 2003).

‡ Graphs adapted from Hsiao, 1998, Figure 1.

Demonstration 12.1 Touch and Human Skin Interact with a depiction of human skin and the mechanoreceptors and other elements located in the layers of skin.

Demonstration 12.2 Receptive Fields of Mechanoreceptors Map the receptive fields of different types of mechanoreceptors with large versus small receptive fields.

In the next four sections, as we discuss in more detail the kinds of stimuli that each type of mechanoreceptor responds to most strongly and the main functions that each supports, it will become apparent that there is considerable overlap. That is, tactile perception in the real world—outside the laboratory—almost always involves input from all four types of mechanoreceptors, which work together to give us information about the things we touch.

Slow-Adapting Type I (SAI) Mechanoreceptors: Perceiving Pattern, Texture, and Shape

SAI mechanoreceptors, with Merkel cell endings that respond most strongly to indentation of the skin, are specialized for the detailed perception of spatial patterns on surfaces, such as bumps, scratches, and other types of irregularities (including dot patterns like Braille); textures, which are, in effect, fine-grained patterns; and surface curvature, including corners and edges, which defines shape. To assess the spatial resolution of tactile perception, a measure known as the *two-point threshold* can be determined by touching two nearby skin locations with a pair of pointed probes and asking the person to judge whether one or two locations were touched. The minimum distance at which the person's judgments are 75% correct is defined as the two-point threshold for that area on the skin. Figure 12.2 shows the average two-point threshold on different parts of the body (Weinstein, 1968). Not surprisingly, the threshold is smallest (i.e., spatial resolution is greatest) on the fingertips and lips and is much larger (lower resolution) on the arms, legs, and torso.

In order to examine the role of SAI and other mechanoreceptors in pattern perception (including the perception of two-point stimuli), investigators have recorded from

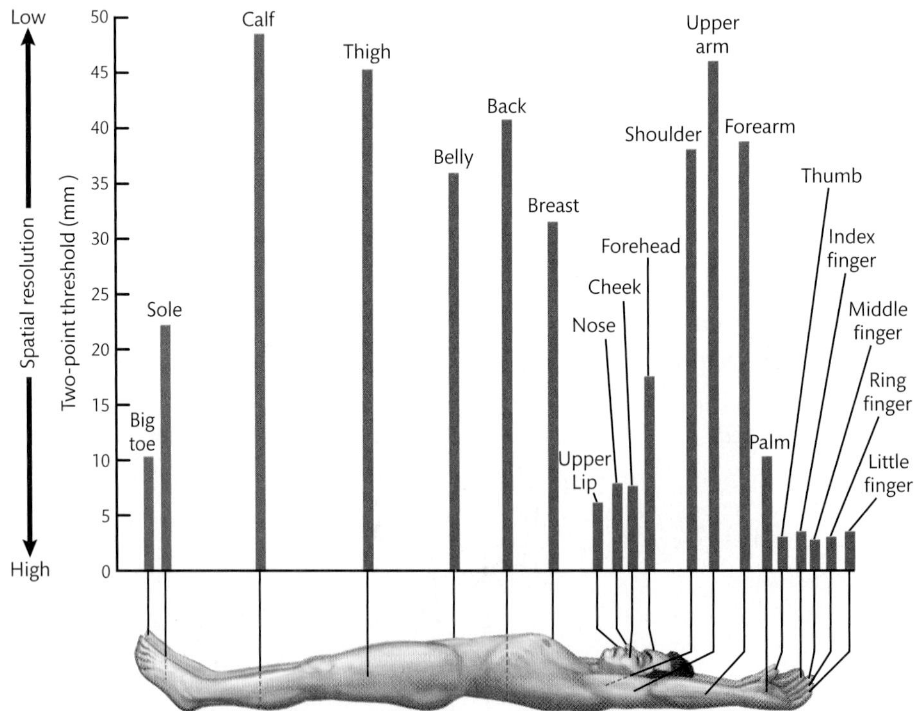

Figure 12.2 Spatial Resolution of Touch: The Two-Point Threshold The person is touched on various parts of the body with two pointed probes a small distance apart. The two-point threshold is the minimum distance at which the person can judge correctly 75% of the time that two distinct locations are being touched. Two-point thresholds are similar for males and females and for the left and right sides of the body. (Adapted from Weinstein, 1968, Figure 10-4.)

individual fibers while stimulating the skin with different patterns. The Canadian-born neuroscientist Kenneth O. Johnson, who spent most of his career working in the United States, pioneered the study of how neurons represent tactile patterns. In one such study with monkeys (Johnson & Lamb, 1981), Braille-like patterns were repeatedly passed across the fingertip using a rotating cylinder, as illustrated in Figure 12.3 (one pass of the cylinder caused the pattern to move across the receptive field on the fingertip once). After each pass, the cylinder was moved down by 0.2 mm, in preparation for the next pass. This type of tactile stimulation is similar to the stimulation a person would get from reading a Braille pattern with his or her fingertips. As the pattern moved across the receptive fields of SAI fibers, the responses of individual fibers were recorded. In this way, it was possible to generate a depiction known as a *spatial event plot* showing how the pattern of action potentials produced by an individual SAI fiber matched up with the entire pattern of the stimulus. The spikes in the spatial event plot in Figure 12.3 reveal a very close match:

Kenneth O. Johnson (1938–2005). [Justin Killebrew]

- In the first pass, when the bottom edge of the bottom dot in the Braille pattern just crosses the top of the receptive field, the fiber responds with a single action potential.
- By the third pass, the whole top dot is sweeping across the middle of the receptive field, and the fiber responds with a burst of four action potentials.
- In the seventh pass, the three center dots are crossing the middle of the receptive field, and the three bursts are correspondingly more robust.

Figure 12.4 shows spatial event plots (in a different format from the plot in Figure 12.3) for a variety of Braille stimuli that were passed over human fingertips while

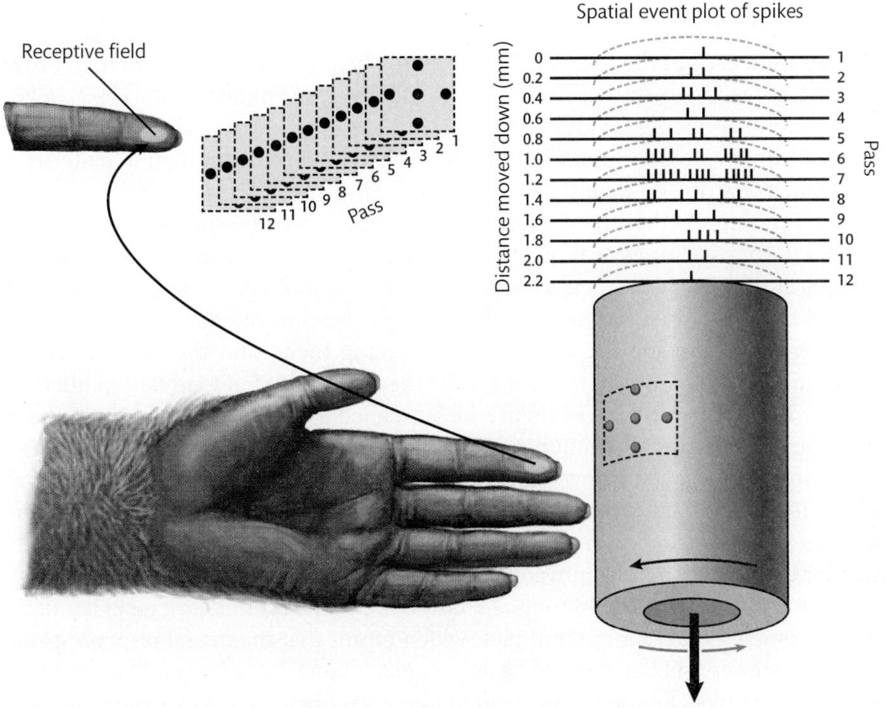

Figure 12.3 Response of an SAI Fiber to a Braille-like Pattern: A Spatial Event Plot A Braille-like pattern of bumps embossed on a plastic cylinder was passed repeatedly across a monkey's fingertip while the response of a single SAI fiber was recorded. Before each new pass, the pattern was moved down 0.2 mm. The spatial event plot shows that the pattern of spikes produced by the fiber closely matches the pattern of bumps.

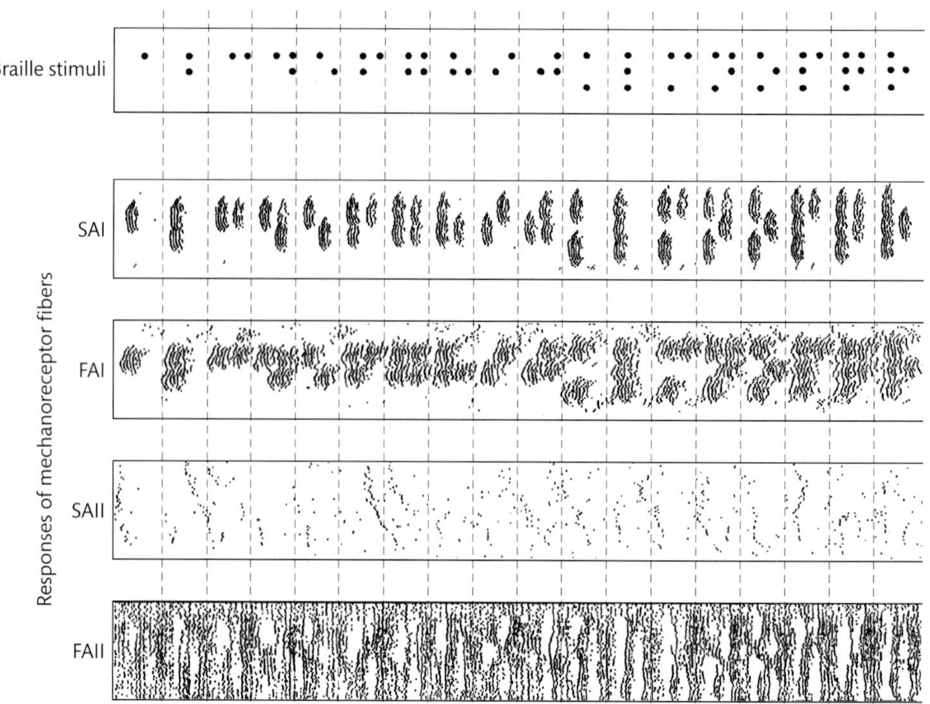

Figure 12.4 Responses of Four Mechanoreceptor Types to the Same Braille Patterns These spatial event plots from human mechanoreceptor fibers show that only the responses of the SAI fiber provide a precise representation of the stimulus patterns (the Braille letters A–R). (Adapted and art from Phillips et al., 1990.)

responses from each of the four mechanoreceptor fiber types were recorded, in order to compare SAI responses to those of the other three types (Phillips et al., 1990). Clearly, the SAII and FAII fibers provide no useful information about the patterns of the stimuli. The FAI fibers provide somewhat blurry representations of the Braille patterns, but they're much less precise than those produced by the SAI fibers.

To determine whether the neural responses represented by such spatial event plots correspond to psychophysical judgments, experimenters compared the behavioral responses of people and the neural responses of monkeys (Vega-Bermudez et al., 1991). Letters of the alphabet embossed on plastic strips were moved across the fingertips of people who had to name the letters without seeing them, and the same letters were moved across the fingertips of monkeys while the responses of individual SAI fibers were recorded. The table at the top of Figure 12.5 is called a *confusion matrix*—it shows how often people confused each stimulus letter with every other letter.

The spatial event plot below the confusion matrix shows the responses of a monkey SAI fiber to the same letter stimuli. If you compare the plots for R, H, and N, you can see why these particular confusions might have been made. The plots for B and D reveal the reason for the asymmetry of confusions between these two letters (B was called D 27% of the time, whereas D was called B only 2% of the time): the central horizontal bar of the B is almost completely absent in the B plot, which means that the neural response patterns for B and D are very similar and that both look much more like a D than like a B. Overall, the spatial event plots for the responses of monkey SAI fibers in this experiment match up very well with the patterns of errors shown in the confusion matrix.

Other experiments indicate that SAI mechanoreceptors also provide information about texture and shape, in addition to information about patterns like embossed letters and Braille dots. For example, the difference in response rates of monkey SAI fibers to textures with different roughness almost perfectly matched the difference in human judgments about the roughness of the same textures (Blake et al., 1997; Connor et al.,

Behavioral responses (%)

Stimuli	A	B	C	D	E	F	G	H	I	J	K	L	M	N	O	P	Q	R	S	T	U	V	W	X	Y	Z
A	**71**	1	·	·	·	1	·	·	·	1	3	1	2	8	·	·	·	5	·	·	·	3	1	2	·	1
B	2	**18**	2	27	1	·	5	2	·	·	1	·	2	6	6	4	3	6	3	·	6	·	1	·	·	·
C	·	1	**46**	3	·	·	15	·	·	·	·	·	·	·	15	·	15	2	1	·	2	·	·	·	·	·
D	1	2	2	**49**	1	·	2	1	·	·	·	·	1	·	22	5	4	1	1	·	7	·	1	·	·	·
E	2	6	1	1	**60**	2	1	2	·	·	8	·	1	2	·	·	1	8	1	·	1	1	1	1	·	1
F	1	1	·	·	7	**57**	1	1	1	·	4	·	·	2	·	11	·	3	3	2	·	2	·	1	2	·
G	1	11	2	3	1	·	**41**	·	·	·	·	·	4	1	6	1	18	6	5	·	·	·	·	·	·	·
H	1	1	·	1	1	1	1	**49**	·	·	4	·	9	15	·	1	1	5	·	·	6	1	4	1	·	·
I	·	·	·	·	·	·	·	·	**98**	1	·	·	·	·	·	·	·	·	·	·	·	·	·	·	·	·
J	·	1	·	1	1	1	1	·	1	**84**	1	·	·	·	·	·	·	·	3	·	1	1	·	1	1	2
K	1	1	2	·	10	1	·	·	·	·	**57**	·	3	1	·	1	·	9	·	·	1	·	2	7	·	4
L	1	·	1	·	·	·	·	·	·	1	1	**93**	·	·	·	·	·	1	·	·	·	·	·	·	·	1
M	1	4	·	·	2	1	2	2	·	·	8	·	**34**	4	·	·	1	5	1	·	6	1	30	·	·	
N	·	5	·	1	1	1	·	12	·	·	7	·	20	**15**	·	1	·	9	2	·	4	·	19	2	·	·
O	·	1	2	6	·	·	4	·	·	·	·	·	·	·	**83**	1	3	·	·	·	·	·	·	·	·	·
P	·	2	1	1	1	23	2	1	·	·	3	·	·	2	·	**44**	1	2	4	5	·	3	1	·	4	1
Q	·	2	2	8	·	·	7	·	·	·	·	·	·	1	49	1	**28**	1	1	·	·	·	·	·	·	·
R	6	4	1	4	1	·	2	17	·	·	3	·	8	14	1	2	·	**31**	·	·	4	·	1	·	·	·
S	·	21	2	6	2	·	14	1	·	·	1	1	2	1	5	3	6	8	**25**	·	1	·	2	·	·	1
T	1	1	1	·	·	2	·	·	1	1	1	1	1	·	·	1	·	·	3	**61**	·	2	·	4	15	3
U	·	1	·	2	·	·	1	1	·	·	·	·	1	1	2	1	1	1	1	·	**80**	4	2	·	·	1
V	·	·	·	1	·	·	·	·	·	·	3	·	·	2	·	2	·	·	1	·	3	**62**	3	1	21	1
W	1	1	·	·	1	1	1	1	·	·	3	·	11	2	·	1	·	1	2	·	1	1	**71**	·	·	1
X	1	1	1	·	5	1	·	·	·	1	11	·	2	1	·	·	1	3	1	1	·	·	2	**57**	1	12
Y	·	·	·	·	·	2	1	·	·	2	5	·	1	2	·	1	·	1	1	6	·	15	·	3	**58**	3
Z	1	·	·	·	3	3	1	1	1	2	7	·	·	1	·	·	·	2	1	2	·	·	1	31	2	**41**

Neural responses

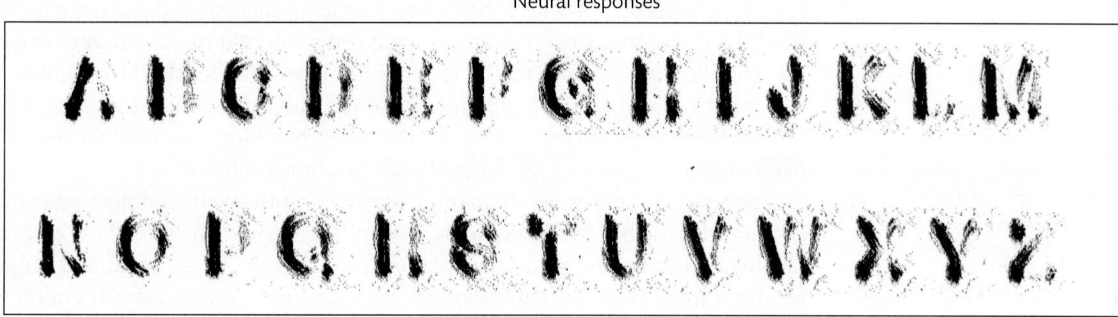

Figure 12.5 **Behavioral and Neural Responses to Embossed Letters of the Alphabet** Letters of the alphabet 6 mm high embossed onto a plastic surface were moved across the fingertips of human participants and of monkeys. (top) The table (a confusion matrix) shows the responses of the human participants, who had to name each letter they felt (without looking). The stimulus letters are in the left-hand column, and the possible responses are along the top. The numbers in the cells show the percentage of times each stimulus letter was perceived as itself (the boldface numbers running diagonally from upper left to lower right) or as any of the other letters in the top row—for example, A was perceived as A 71% of the time, as B 1% of the time, as K 3% of the time, and so on (dots represent 0%). The highlighted boxes show letter pairs with a mean confusability of more than 8% (e.g., N was perceived as R 9% of the time, and R as N 14% of the time, for a mean confusability of 11.5%). (bottom) These spatial event plots show the responses of a monkey SAI fiber to the same letters (each dot represents an action potential). Letter pairs that are highly confusable (as indicated by the highlighted boxes in the table at top) tend to produce highly similar spatial event plots—for example, compare the patterns for P and F, which have a mean confusability of 17%. (Adapted and bottom image from Vega-Bermudez et al., 1991.)

1990). A study of the neural responses produced by different-sized spheres pressed against the skin with different degrees of force showed that SAI mechanoreceptors provide reliable information about aspects of surface shape such as curvature (a small sphere has greater curvature than a large sphere) (Goodwin et al., 1995). And another study showed that although individual SAI fibers don't respond selectively to the orientation of edges pressed into the skin, the responses of a population of many SAI fibers do provide reliable information about orientation (Khalsa et al., 1998). Together, these and other studies showing that SAI fibers provide rich representations of patterns, textures, and shapes indicate that SAI responses are critically involved in identifying touched surfaces and objects.

Check Your Understanding

12.1 Which of the four main types of mechanoreceptors are slow adapting, and which are fast adapting? Which have relatively large receptive fields, and which have relatively small receptive fields? Which are relatively sparsely distributed, and which are relatively densely distributed? Which has an undetermined type of specialized ending, and what are the specialized endings associated with the other three types?

12.2 Circle the correct choice in parentheses: A mechanoreceptor that keeps responding to a stimulus after the stimulus has been present for a period of time is (slow adapting / fast adapting).

12.3 Judging by Figure 12.2, would a person probably be better at identifying a pattern (say, a raised letter) by pressing it against his cheek or his forehead?

12.4 In Figure 12.5, the spatial event plots for the letters G and Q look quite similar, and both look more like Q than like G. Do the results for G and Q in the confusion matrix correspond with this description of the spatial event plots? Explain your answer.

Fast-Adapting Type I (FAI) Mechanoreceptors: Perceiving Slip and Maintaining Grip Control

FAI mechanoreceptors, with Meissner corpuscles as their specialized endings, respond most strongly to low-frequency vibrations, conveying information about very small motions of the skin. Because they are fast adapting, FAI fibers don't respond to sustained stimulation but only to changes in stimulation (e.g., to the onset or offset of stimulation or to low-frequency vibration). This makes FAI mechanoreceptors ideally suited for perceiving slip and maintaining control over the force of one's grip on an object.

Suppose, for example, that you're playing tennis. At the moment your racquet makes contact with the ball, the sudden increase in force against the face of the racquet makes the racquet handle begin to turn and slip against the skin of your hand and fingers; based on feedback from FA1 mechanoreceptors, you automatically increase the force of your grip enough to stop the racquet from turning. Similarly, when you pick up an egg, you apply just enough force to prevent the egg from slipping out of your hand but not so much force that you crush the egg, and the force required for this is finely calibrated by feedback from FAI mechanoreceptors (Witney et al., 2004).

Figure 12.6 illustrates this function of FAI mechanoreceptors during the process of gripping a small object, lifting it off a surface, and then putting it back down (Johansson & Flanagan, 2008). You can see that the FAI fibers are active at just two points in the process: first, during the load phase, when the fingers touch the object and then grip it with enough force to lift it off the surface without having it slip through the fingers; and second, during the unload phase, when the fingers release the object after setting it back down. The spikes during the load phase reflect microscopic slippages that indicate more grip force is needed to keep the object from slipping further. In the unload phase, the FA1 fiber responds at the moment the object comes back into contact with the table, which exerts an upward "slip" force on the skin, indicating that the grip can now be released.

The other fast-adapting mechanoreceptors, FAII, are also active only at certain points in the process of grasping, raising, and lowering the object. In contrast, the slow-adapting SAI and SAII mechanoreceptors are active at about the same level throughout the process, indicating their role in signaling the surface texture of the object and perhaps its edges and corners (SAI) and in signaling the conformation of the hand (SAII). Thus, Figure 12.6 not only reveals the role of FAI mechanoreceptors in grip control, but also illustrates a point made earlier—that all four types of mechanoreceptors work together in the execution of even the simplest actions involving tactile perception.

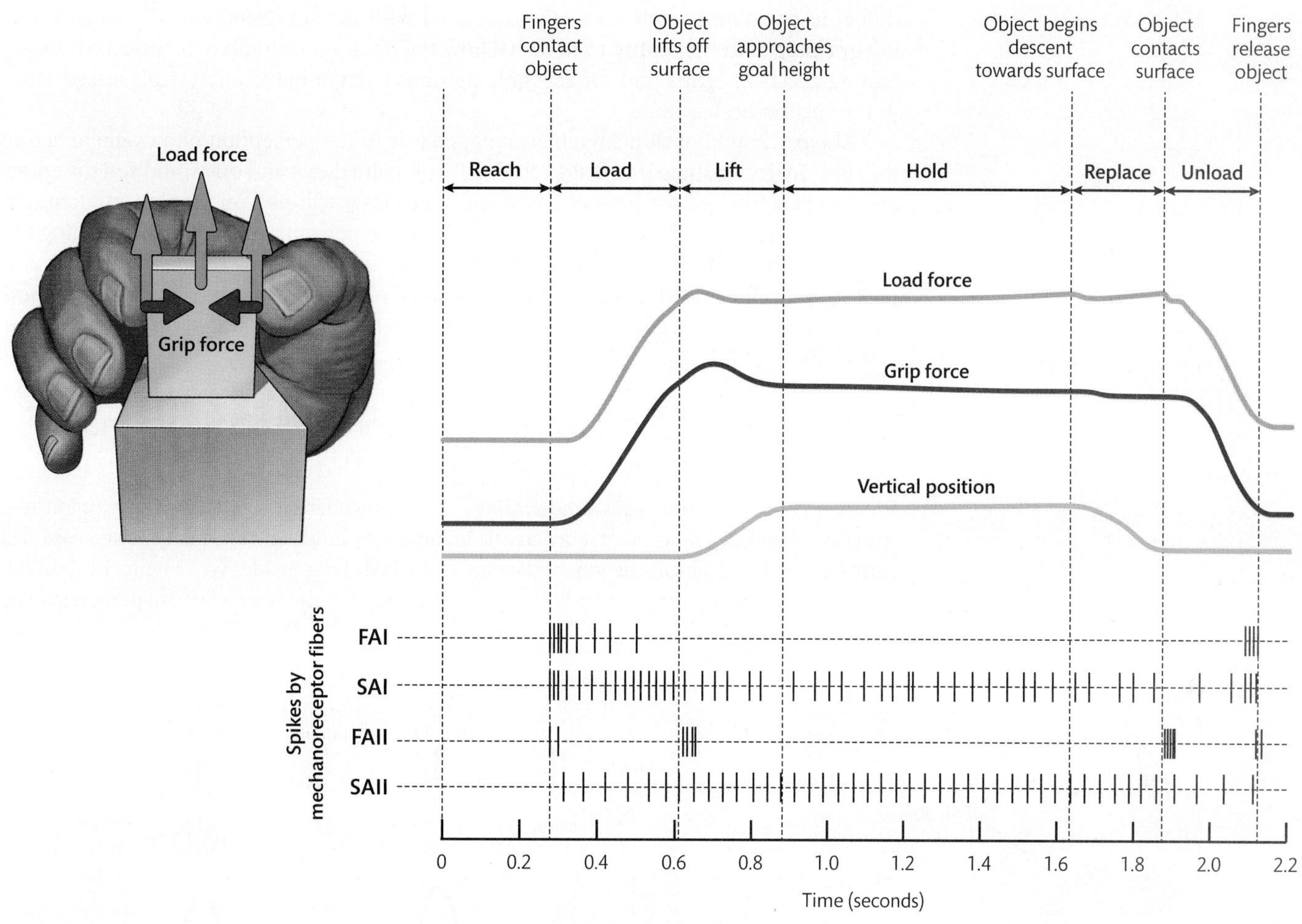

Figure 12.6 FAI Fibers and Grip Control The responses of the four main types of mechanoreceptor fibers are shown while a person grips a small object between the fingers as illustrated, raises it to a goal height, and then puts it back down. FAI fibers are active at the two points in the process when slip is an issue. (Adapted from Johansson & Flanagan, 2008, Figure 1.)

Slow-Adapting Type II (SAII) Mechanoreceptors: Perceiving Skin Stretch and Hand Conformation

The large receptive field size of SAII mechanoreceptors (five times the size of SAI receptive fields) is reflected in their unselective response to different Braille patterns (see Figure 12.4). Although their responses provide little information about patterns and textures, they provide important information about skin stretch (Edin, 1992).

Skin stretch is involved in the perception of hand conformation (how the hand is configured—e.g., flattened out against a tabletop or rounded to pick up a glass). Whenever you open or close your hand or move your fingers, the skin covering different parts of your hand stretches differently, and perception of this stretch gives you information about hand conformation. To experience this, close your eyes and hold your right hand in front of you with the fingers spread and the palm fully open and facing downward. You can feel how the skin of your palm is tightly stretched across the width of your hand just below the fingers and how the skin between your fingers is stretched tight too. In contrast, the skin on the top of your hand is unstretched and wrinkled. Now close your hand tightly into a fist. The feeling of skin stretch on the palm and between the fingers is gone, but now you can feel that the skin over your knuckles is tightly stretched, the same skin that was wrinkled and loose when the palm was open. Perception of such differences in skin stretch is closely associated with the conformation of the hand during grasping, and the ability to perceive how the hand is configured is critical for maintaining precision grips and for recognizing object shape haptically (as discussed later, in the section on haptics).

The perception of skin stretch also plays a role in the perception of movement across the skin. To demonstrate this, hold your hand out, palm down and open, and run the eraser end of a pencil across the back of your hand. The eraser will pull on the skin, stretching it a bit, and perception of this stretch contributes to the perception of motion, including the direction of motion, across the skin (Olausson et al., 2000). When you grasp an object and pick it up (as illustrated in Figure 12.6), the force of the object pulls the skin downward steadily and provides feedback that lets you know whether the object is slipping from your grip (Johnson, 2002).

Fast-Adapting Type II (FAII) Mechanoreceptors: Perceiving Fine Textures Through Transmitted Vibration

Pacinian corpuscles, the specialized endings of FAII mechanoreceptors, have an onion-like structure containing multiple layers of tissue separated by fluid—that is, many nested capsules surrounding a central capsule where the end of the FAII fiber resides (see Figure 12.7a). The layered tissue surrounding the end of the fiber is what gives the fiber a fast-adapting response

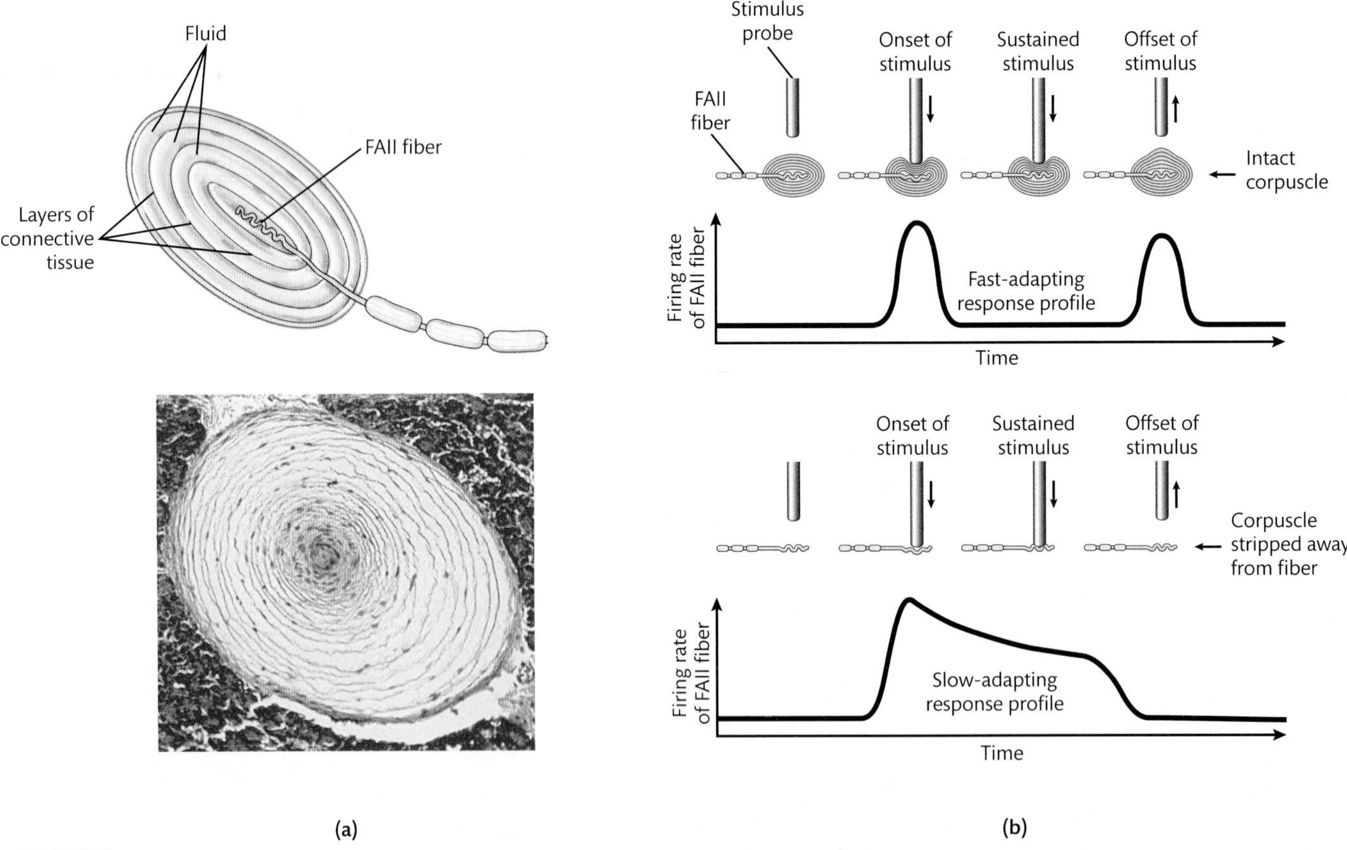

Figure 12.7 Pacinian Corpuscles (a) Pacinian corpuscles—the specialized endings of FAII mechanoreceptors—have an onion-like structure of nested capsules. Each capsule consists of a layer of connective tissue; the spaces between the layers are filled with a gelatinous fluid. The drawing and the micrograph reveal this structure in a slice through the corpuscle. (b) When the corpuscle is intact (top), the fiber shows a fast-adapting response profile: it responds strongly at the onset of the stimulus, then the response declines rapidly while the stimulus is sustained, and then it strengthens again at the offset of the stimulus. But if the corpuscle is stripped away from the end of the fiber (bottom), the fiber's response profile is slow adapting: a strong response at stimulus onset; a continuous, slowly declining response during the sustained stimulus; and a final rapid decline at stimulus offset. This is powerful evidence that the layered corpuscle is what makes the fiber fast adapting. [Ray Simons/Photo Researchers]

profile, as you can see by comparing the two graphs in Figure 12.7b. FAII mechanoreceptors are exquisitely sensitive—a vibration with an amplitude of as little as 10 nanometers is sufficient to increase the firing rate of an FAII fiber (Brisben et al., 1999). This sensitivity, combined with the fact that vibrations are transmitted across large distances within the dermis, results in the large receptive field that characterizes FAII fibers.

The ability of FAII mechanoreceptors to sense minute vibrations makes them ideal for mediating the perception of objects and surfaces via the vibrations transmitted by tools or probes held in the hand. For example, when you write with a pen, you can sense the extremely small vibrations conveyed through the pen, as if your awareness has migrated out to the tip of the pen itself, and this lets you judge the texture of the paper on which you're writing. When you use tongs to grasp and manipulate food or pliers to bend metal or hold a small screw, FAII mechanoreceptors respond to tiny vibrations in the tool and send signals that you use to perceive and maintain the stability of the grasp (Brisben et al., 1999).

Similarly, you can judge the roughness of fine textures based on the vibrations transmitted to FAII mechanoreceptors through a rigid probe, such as a thimble placed on the finger, which obviously would prevent SAI fibers from perceiving the texture based on the spatial distribution of surface elements (Klatzky & Lederman, 1999). The role of vibration sensitivity in detecting fine textures is confirmed by experiments in which a finely textured surface is surreptitiously vibrated while someone is touching it, and the surface is perceived as being rougher than it would be otherwise (Hollins et al., 2001).

Perceiving Pleasant Touch

The nerve fibers of the four main types of mechanoreceptors (SAI, FAI, SAII, and FAII) are myelinated, which means that the signals they send to the brain travel relatively rapidly, carrying information about the kinds of tactile perceptions discussed in the previous sections. Recently, a category of unmyelinated mechanoreceptors has been described, one that provides information about skin stimulations experienced as pleasant, or pleasurable (Olausson et al., 2010). These **C-tactile mechanoreceptors (CT mechanoreceptors)** are a type of free nerve endings only present in hairy skin, and therefore absent on the palms and fingertips, lips, soles of the feet, and other hairless parts of the body (other types of free nerve endings, such as those that encode painful stimuli, are found in both hairy and glabrous skin). Being unmyelinated, they carry signals relatively slowly to the brain. CT mechanoreceptors respond to slow, gentle touch, sending signals to the insular cortex, an area of the brain that is also involved in perception of the pleasant–unpleasant dimension of taste and smell, as we'll see in Chapter 13.

C-tactile mechanoreceptors (CT mechanoreceptors) Mechanoreceptors that are a type of free nerve endings only present on hairy skin; they respond to slow, gentle touch and send signals to the insular cortex.

Mechanoreceptor Transduction

In our discussion of the kinds of skin deformations that elicit responses from the four types of mechanoreceptors, and of the kinds of information provided by their neural signals, we haven't addressed a basic question: How are mechanical forces on the skin transduced into neural signals? This has turned out to be a difficult question to answer. It is thought that mechanical forces cause ion channels to open in the mechanoreceptor cell membrane (Kung, 2005); then, ion flow across the cell membrane initiates the cascade of biochemical reactions that results in action potentials being sent through the nerve fiber. Molecular biologists have begun to identify the specific molecular components involved in this process, using genetically modified animals that lack certain molecules and that exhibit reduced somatosensory sensitivity (Lumpkin & Caterina, 2009; Tsunozaki & Bautista, 2009). Some researchers have measured mechanoreceptor cell membrane potential while directly applying mechanical force to the cell (Hu & Lewin, 2006) or while deforming the cell by stretching the elastic substrate on which it has been cultured (Bhattacharya et al., 2008). There is evidence—still inconclusive, but suggestive—that the mechanism by which mechanoreceptors transduce mechanical force is analogous to the mechanism by which hair cells in the cochlea transduce movement of their stereocilia into neural signals sent through auditory nerve fibers (Kung, 2005; Lumpkin & Caterina, 2009) (see Chapter 9).

Check Your Understanding

12.5 Which is the most important property of FAI mechanoreceptors in the perception of slip: that they have small receptive fields, that they're relatively densely distributed in the upper dermis, or that they're fast adapting?

12.6 Cross out the incorrect choice(s) in parentheses: SAII mechanoreceptors have large receptive fields, which would enable them to provide information about (whether the hand is open or closed / a pattern of bumps distributed across a large surface / how much the skin is stretched).

12.7 You've just painted the wooden fence around your front yard. After it's dry, you put your hand against it to feel its nice smooth surface. Just then, the wind starts to blow, causing the board you're touching to vibrate slightly, and the surface suddenly feels a bit rougher than when you first touched it. This perception of increased roughness is probably based on signals from which type of mechanoreceptor?

12.8 In contrast to the four main types of mechanoreceptors, CT mechanoreceptors are:

A. Myelinated and found only in hairless skin
B. Unmyelinated and found only in hairy skin
C. Unmyelinated and found only in hairless skin
D. Myelinated and found only in hairy skin

Proprioception: Perceiving Position and Movement of the Limbs

In previous chapters, our discussions of vision and audition have focused on how these senses provide us with information about the world around us—through light reflected from objects and through sound waves caused by events. Similarly, so far in this chapter, we've focused on how we get information about the world through our sense of touch. But our need for information extends not only to the world around us, but also to the world within us—that is, we have a critical need to sense bodily states in order to know where we are in space, how we're oriented, whether or not we're moving, and what our limbs are doing. Clearly, vision and audition—especially vision—play some role in this: we can see where our hands and feet are, look in a mirror to see if we're standing straight, and localize the various sounds around us to sense where we are in relation to the sources producing those sounds. But a more direct sense of our bodies comes from **proprioception,** the perception of the position and movement of body parts (limbs, fingers and toes, head, eyes, etc.) based on the information in neural signals from specialized sensors within those body parts. (The term *kinesthesis* is sometimes used to refer specifically to the perception of movement of the limbs.)

proprioception Perception of the position and movement of body parts, based on the information in neural signals from specialized sensors within those body parts.

The story of Ian Waterman at the beginning of this chapter highlights the importance of proprioception for even the simplest aspects of everyday life. Consider, for example, this simple question: How do you know (without looking) where your right hand is relative to the center of your body? Your right arm is attached to your body at your right shoulder joint. The arm has a joint in the middle (the elbow) and at the end (the wrist), where your hand is attached. Assuming that your brain "knows" the length of your upper arm and forearm and the position of your shoulder joint relative to the center of your body and that it can sense the angles formed by the joints at your shoulder, elbow, and wrist, it can compute the position of your hand relative to the center of your body.

Three different types of sensory organs provide information about joint angles, which depend on the position and movement of the limbs and joints: **muscle spindles, Golgi tendon organs,** and **joint receptors** (Proske & Gandevia, 2009). All three types are illustrated in Figure 12.8, which shows that muscle spindles produce signals in afferent nerve fibers in response to changes in muscle length; in addition, muscle spindles produce signals in response to isometric forces on a muscle, as when you simply hold a weight in your hand.

muscle spindles Sensory organs that provide information about muscle length, as well as information about isometric forces on muscles, for proprioception.

Golgi tendon organs Sensory organs that provide information about muscle force for proprioception.

joint receptors Sensory organs that provide information about joint angle, probably to signal when a joint has reached the limit of its normal motion.

The figure also shows that Golgi tendon organs produce signals in response to changes in muscle force, which often also involve changes in length, and these signals

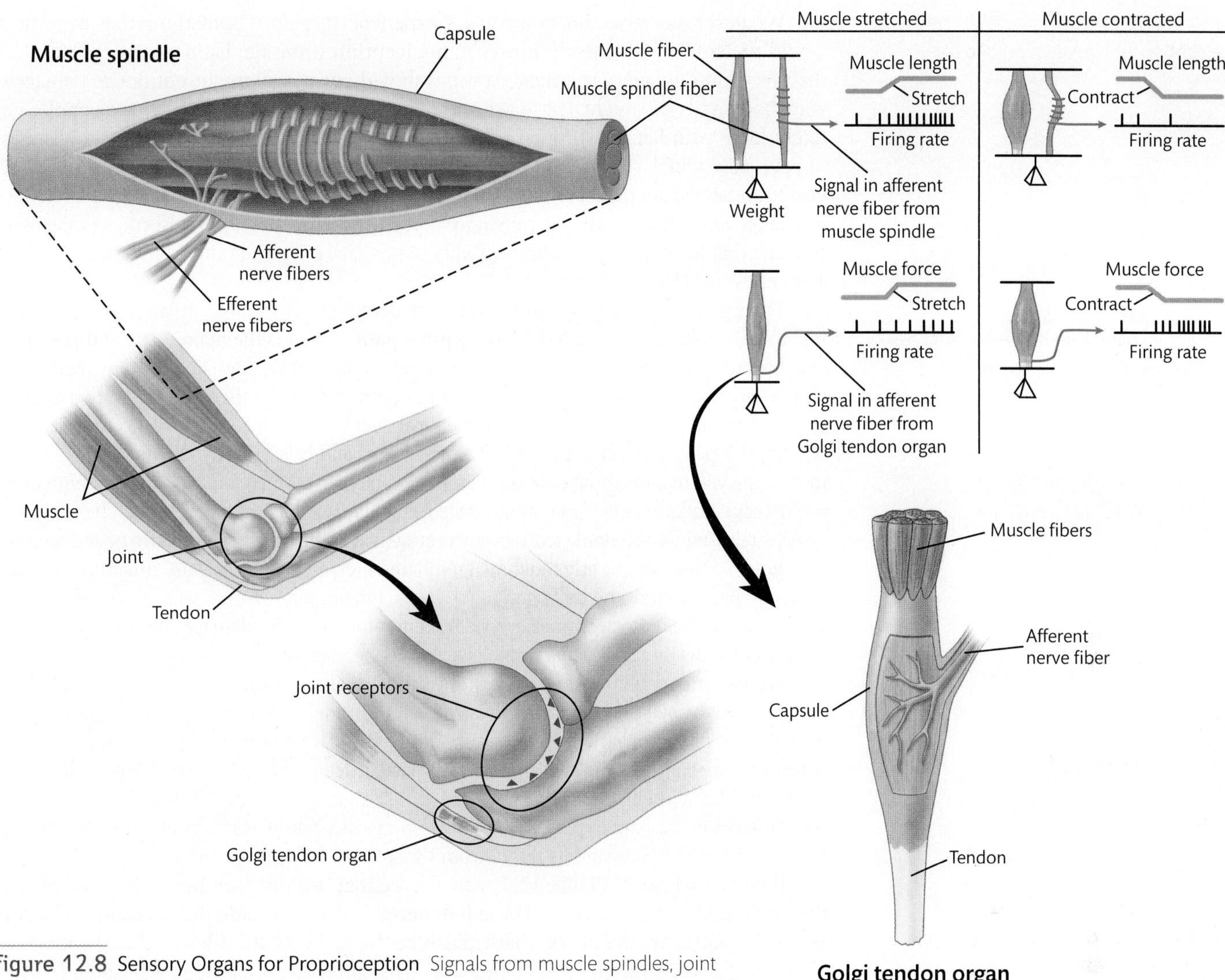

Figure 12.8 Sensory Organs for Proprioception Signals from muscle spindles, joint receptors, and Golgi tendon organs carry information used in perceiving the position and movement of the limbs. (Adapted from Gordon & Ghez, 1991.)

convey information about joint angle. When the angle of a joint changes, the muscles attached at the joint are stretched or contracted, which changes both muscle force and muscle length; thus, signals with information about muscle length also supply information about joint angle. Joint receptors also provide information about joint angle, but probably only to signal when a joint has reached the limit of its normal motion (Proske & Gandevia, 2009). It is generally believed that muscle spindles provide the most important information for proprioception (Lackner & DiZio, 2000), including the critical information for sensing both limb position and limb motion (Proske et al., 2000). (As discussed in the last section, the responses of SAII receptors provide information about skin stretch, and this information also contributes to the perception of limb position and movement.)

Nociception: Perceiving Pain

Pain is an unpleasant sensory and emotional experience that is most often caused by potential or actual tissue damage. This definition of pain emphasizes both the sensory and emotional aspects of pain and reflects the fact that pain can arise from a wide range of different causes and can evoke an equally wide range of perceptual experiences.

pain An unpleasant sensory and emotional experience caused by potential or actual tissue damage; pain can arise from a wide range of different causes and can evoke an equally wide range of perceptual experiences.

nociception The perception of pain.

Whatever its cause and however it's experienced, pain is something that most of us would prefer to avoid. Clearly, however, **nociception** (from the Latin *nocere*, "to harm")—the perception of pain—is critical to survival: without it, you might not notice damage to your body and you might fail to withdraw from damaging situations—for example, you might leave your hand resting on a hot stove, without noticing the burning and blistering of your skin. Quick recognition of damage to the body is so fundamentally important that evolution made pain perception extremely salient; organisms generally are highly motivated to change any situation that is causing pain as quickly as possible. Indeed, a rare genetic disorder that leaves a person with no ability to perceive pain leads almost invariably to death at an early age (Manfredi et al., 1981).

nociceptive pain Pain that arises from tissue damage due to physical trauma.

Three general categories of pain have been identified: nociceptive, inflammatory, and neuropathic (Scholz & Woolf, 2002). **Nociceptive pain,** which is the main focus of this section, arises from tissue damage due to physical trauma—for example, trauma caused by mechanical events such as cutting, tearing, pinching, or puncturing the skin; thermal events such as burning or exposure to extreme cold; and chemical events such as contact with corrosive acids. Nociceptive pain is detected by specialized receptors and is your body's early warning system, motivating you to take immediate action to make the pain stop, along with any consequent tissue damage. Inflammatory pain arises once tissue damage has occurred, when chemical substances released by the damaged tissue either activate pain receptors directly or reduce their threshold, so that even lightly touching an inflamed region can cause pain. Inflammatory pain generally persists until the damaged tissue heals. Finally, neuropathic pain is caused by damage to the peripheral or central nervous system—for example, damage due to a spinal cord injury, a disorder such as carpal tunnel syndrome, or a stroke.

We experience pain along two quite different dimensions: one consists of affective perceptions—that is, unpleasant physical or emotional experiences—which motivate us to make the pain stop; the other consists of discriminative perceptions, which allow us to determine where the pain is coming from, what it feels like (burning, sharp, dull, throbbing), and how intense it is. Later, we'll see that signals carrying information about these two dimensions of pain experience follow two distinct pathways within the brain. But first let's consider how pain signals travel from the skin to the spinal cord.

nociceptors Sensory receptors that transduce the physical stimuli associated with damaging mechanical, thermal, or chemical events; included among the free nerve endings in the epidermis and dermis.

If you look back at Figure 12.1, you can see that free nerve endings are found in both the epidermis and the dermis. These free nerve endings include the specialized sensory receptors, called **nociceptors**, that transduce the physical stimuli associated with damaging mechanical, thermal, or chemical events. (Free nerve endings also include other types of receptors not involved in pain perception, such as the receptors involved in the perception of pleasant touch, discussed earlier in this chapter.)

sensitization A mechanism that decreases the response threshold of nociceptors, so that even very low level stimulation of an injury site can cause pain.

Nociceptors, which are found in nearly every tissue in the body (but not, for example, in the brain), normally have a relatively high threshold—that is, they respond only to stimuli intense enough to make tissue damage likely. However, a mechanism called **sensitization**—often associated with inflammation—decreases the threshold for hours and sometimes weeks following injury, so that even very low level stimulation of the injury site, such as a light touch against a bruise or a warm shower on sunburned skin, can cause pain. Sensitization can lead an organism to favor a damaged part of the body, which can make healing occur more quickly and more completely.

A-delta fibers Myelinated axons of nociceptors that transmit pain signals relatively rapidly, to produce a rapid response to potentially damaging mechanical stimuli and to excessive heat.

C fibers Unmyelinated axons of nociceptors that transmit pain signals relatively slowly.

Nociceptors transmit pain signals to the spinal cord via two different types of fibers (axons)—small myelinated **A-delta fibers,** which transmit action potentials relatively rapidly (about 2–4 m/sec), and unmyelinated **C fibers,** which transmit action potentials relatively slowly (about 1 m/sec). A-delta fibers produce a rapid response to potentially damaging mechanical stimuli and to excessive heat, whereas C fibers produce a slower response to a wide range of pain stimuli. For example, when you stub your toe, you first experience an immediate, sharp pain carried by A-delta fibers, followed after several seconds by a prolonged burning or dull, throbbing pain carried by C fibers. The two different types of fibers activate distinct types of cells in the spinal cord, maintaining the distinction between "first pain" and "second pain" signals (Craig, 2003).

Signals produced by nociceptors travel into the brain along a different pathway from that followed by signals carrying information about tactile perception and proprioception, but along the same pathway used for thermoreception, which we turn to next.

Thermoreception: Perceiving Temperature

Thermoreception, the ability to sense the temperature of objects and surfaces in contact with the skin, plays an important role in perceiving their material properties: a steel beam and another person's skin, for example, differ not only in hardness but also in temperature—steel is cool, skin is warm. Sensing the temperature of the external environment is essential for survival, because the external temperature affects the internal temperature of your body, which can function normally only if that internal temperature is maintained within a very narrow range.

thermoreception The ability to sense the temperature of objects and surfaces in contact with the skin.

The skin contains sensory receptors called **thermoreceptors**, for the detection of temperatures within the range of about 17–43°C (63–110°F). (Temperatures below and above this range are often experienced as painful, in response to signals produced by A-delta fibers, nociceptors discussed in the preceding section.) There are two types of thermoreceptors—warm fibers and cold fibers—both of which, like nociceptors, are included among the free nerve endings illustrated in Figure 12.1. **Warm fibers** fire at an ongoing moderate rate in response to sustained skin temperatures in the range of 29–43°C (Darian-Smith et al., 1979), and **cold fibers** fire at an ongoing moderate rate in response to sustained skin temperatures in the range of 17–40°C (Darian-Smith et al., 1973). If skin temperature is abruptly warmed from a sustained neutral temperature, the firing rate of warm fibers increases, and if skin temperature is abruptly cooled from a sustained neutral temperature, the firing rate of cold fibers increases (see Figure 12.9).

thermoreceptors Sensory receptors for the detection of temperatures within the range of about 17–43°C; included among the free nerve endings in the epidermis and dermis.

warm fibers Thermoreceptors that fire at an ongoing moderate rate in response to sustained skin temperatures in the range of 29–43°C.

cold fibers Thermoreceptors that fire at an ongoing moderate rate in response to sustained skin temperatures in the range of 17–40°C.

Both types of fibers maintain their increased firing rate for several seconds but then adapt to the new temperature, and their firing rate falls back to the baseline level (Schepers & Ringkamp, 2009). Thus, temperature is typically perceived in terms of a change from a neutral condition, where the neutral condition can be any of a wide range

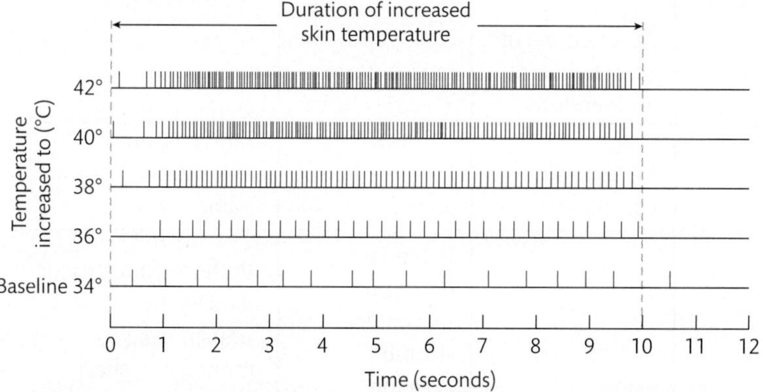

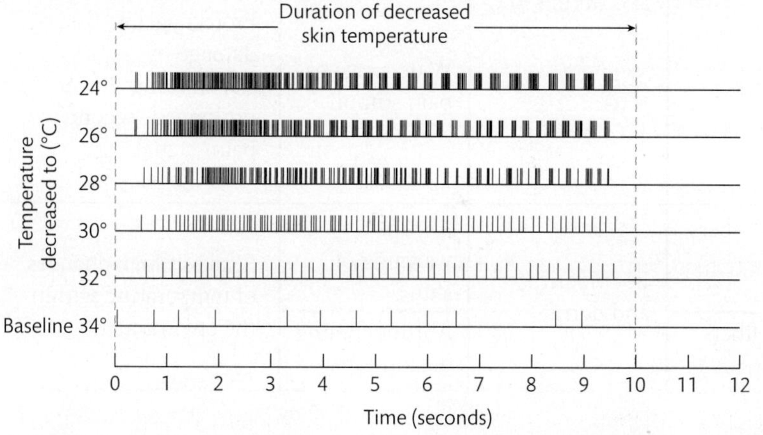

Figure 12.9 Thermoreceptor Responses to Changes in Skin Temperature (top) The response of a single warm fiber in the arm of a monkey was recorded while the skin temperature was abruptly increased from a sustained temperature of 34°C to various higher temperatures. The greater the increase in temperature, the greater the increase in firing rate, with the maximum firing rate occurring for a temperature of about 42°C. (Adapted from Darian-Smith et al., 1979.) (bottom) The response of a single cold fiber was recorded while the skin temperature was abruptly decreased from a sustained temperature of 34°C to various lower temperatures. The greater the decrease in temperature, the greater the increase in firing rate, with the maximum firing rate occurring for a temperature of about 24°C. (Adapted from Darian-Smith et al., 1973.)

of values. For example, when you arrive at the beach on a warm summer day and your bare feet hit the sand, it feels quite hot, but as soon as your thermoreceptors adapt, you "get used to" the temperature. Then, when you take that first dive into the waves, the water initially feels very cold, but after your skin temperature stops decreasing and your thermoreceptors adapt, you "get used to" the cold.

This type of sensitivity to contrasting stimuli (i.e., different skin temperatures) is similar to perception in other sensory domains. For example, in Chapter 2 we saw that retinal ganglion cells respond relatively weakly when the visual field is illuminated uniformly; instead, they are tuned to respond to contrast between dark and bright regions. Such changes in brightness occur at the boundaries of objects, and so these are the regions of the image that convey important information about object shape. Similarly, in the perception of temperature (at least within the range of temperatures that humans can tolerate), abrupt changes in temperature signal that some feature of the environment has changed (and perhaps needs to be responded to).

Table 12.2 summarizes important characteristics of the sensory receptors involved in proprioception, nociception, and thermoreception.

TABLE 12.2 Sensory Receptors for Proprioception, Nociception, and Thermoreception

Perceptual Dimension	Sensory Receptors		Locations	Respond To	Function
Proprioception	Muscle spindles		Within muscles	Change in muscle length	Provide information used in determining limb position and movement and in regulating muscle contractions.
	Golgi tendon organs		At junctions of muscle fibers and tendons	Change in muscle force	
	Joint receptors		Within joint capsules	Extreme joint angles	Protect against overextending joints
Nociception	Nociceptors	A-delta fibers	In epidermis and dermis	Potentially damaging mechanical stimuli; extreme temperatures	Protect against tissue damage by transmitting immediate, sharp "first pain" signals
		C fibers		Wide range of pain stimuli	Protect against tissue damage by transmitting slower, prolonged "second pain" signals
Thermoreception	Thermoreceptors	Warm fibers	In epidermis and dermis	Abrupt warming of skin	Sense sudden changes of temperature within the environment
		Cold fibers		Abrupt cooling of skin	

Check Your Understanding

12.9 Suppose your brain is receiving signals *from* your arm normally but is suddenly unable to send signals *to* your arm, so you can't move it. If someone lifts up your arm and bends it slightly at the elbow, you would perceive the movement and new position of your arm based on signals from which type(s) of proprioceptive sensory organ(s)—muscle spindles, Golgi tendon organs, and/or joint receptors? Explain your answer.

12.10 Circle the correct choices in parentheses: If a bee stings you on your ear, (affective / discriminative) perceptions let you know that the pain is in your ear and that it's a sharp pain, and (affective / discriminative) perceptions motivate you to put ice on your ear.

12.11 Nociceptors and thermoreceptors are both included among which types of nerve endings in the skin?

Between Body and Brain

If you look back at Figure 12.1, you can see that the axons of mechanoreceptors and other types of sensory receptors (including nociceptors and thermoreceptors) within a small area of the skin converge into a peripheral nerve bundle. Similarly, the axons of sensory neurons involved in proprioception within a muscle or joint converge into a nerve bundle. Then all the nerve bundles from each region of skin and each region of muscle tissue enter the spinal cord via one of the spinal nerves. As illustrated in Figure 12.10, the cell bodies of all these bipolar neurons are clustered together into a single dorsal root ganglion (which is why they're collectively referred to as *dorsal root ganglion cells*). Each dorsal root ganglion is adjacent to a single vertebra; each vertebra has one ganglion on the left side and one on the right (the micrograph in Figure 12.10 shows just a left-side ganglion). The dorsal root—the bundled-together axons of dorsal root

Demonstration 12.3 Between Body and Brain Interact with depictions of the structures and pathways involved in tactile perception, proprioception, nociception, and thermoreception.

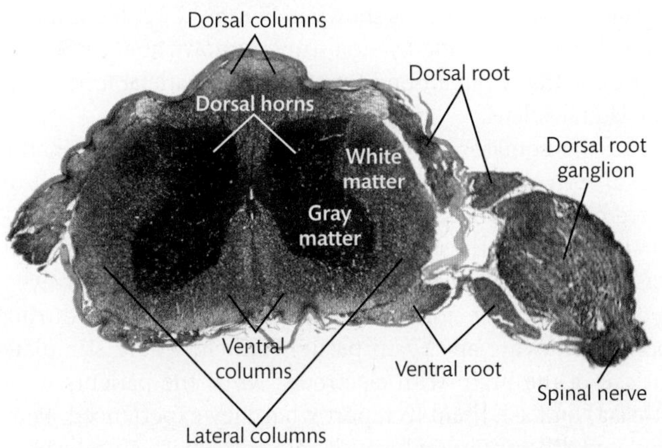

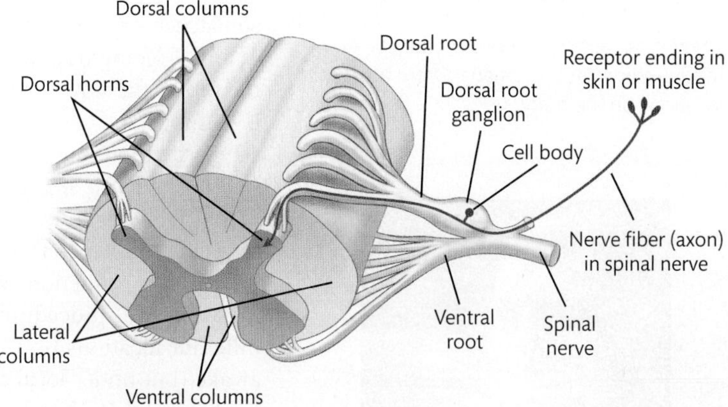

Figure 12.10 Dorsal Root Ganglion (top) A micrograph of a cross section through the spinal cord, with the back of the cord at the top, along with the left dorsal root ganglion (the ganglion at the right isn't shown). The dorsal horns of the spinal cord consist of gray matter (mostly the cell bodies of neurons, supporting cells, and capillaries), whereas the two dorsal (rear), ventral (front), and lateral (side) columns consist of white matter (mostly the myelinated axons of somatosensory and other neurons). (bottom) A 3-D depiction of the structures in the micrograph. The greatly enlarged schematic neuron (consisting of a receptor ending, nerve fiber, and cell body) shows that somatosensory neurons are bipolar neurons, with receptor endings in the skin and muscles and with cell bodies in the dorsal root ganglion; the axon (nerve fiber) of each of these neurons runs from the receptor ending, past the cell body, through the dorsal root, and into the ipsilateral (same-side) dorsal column of the spinal cord. Nerve fibers enter the dorsal root ganglion bundled together into a spinal nerve; the dorsal root is the continuation of the spinal nerve as it exits the dorsal root ganglion and enters the spinal cord. [Photo courtesy of David B. Fankhauser, Ph.D.]

ganglion cells—enters the dorsal part of the spinal cord (the ventral root consists of the axons of motor neurons sending signals from the brain to the muscles).

Within the spinal cord and then from the spinal cord into the brain, sensory signals follow two different pathways: the **dorsal column–medial lemniscal pathway (DCML pathway)** for signals involved in tactile perception and proprioception and the **spinothalamic pathway** for signals involved in nociception and thermoreception (see Figure 12.11). Nerve fibers in the DCML pathway (for touch and proprioception—blue arrows) travel up the dorsal column of the spinal cord on the ipsilateral side (the same side as the originating sensory neurons); make a synapse in the medulla, in the brain stem; then cross to the contralateral side in the medulla; and then ascend via the medial lemniscus. Nerve fibers in the spinothalamic pathway (for pain and temperature—red arrows) make a synapse when they enter the spinal cord, cross over to the contralateral side of the spinal cord, and then ascend via the spinothalamic tract. Thus, neurons in both pathways cross to the contralateral side after the first synapse, but the spinothalamic pathway has its first synapse in the spinal cord, whereas the DCML pathway has its first synapse in the medulla. Both pathways then travel through the **ventral posterior nucleus (VP nucleus)** of the thalamus and on to the **somatosensory cortex**, in the anterior parietal lobe.

Thus, just as the visual system has a contralateral organization in the visual cortex, with signals carrying information from the right half of the visual field flowing to the left-hemisphere visual cortex and vice versa, the somatosensory system also has a contralateral organization in the somatosensory cortex, with signals from the right half of the body flowing to the left-hemisphere somatosensory cortex and vice versa. And just as in both the visual system and the auditory system, where signals from the eyes and ears flow through a structure in the thalamus (the lateral geniculate nucleus and the medial geniculate body, respectively), somatosensory signals from the skin and muscles flow through a structure in the thalamus (the VP nucleus) before traveling to the cortex.

Somatotopic Cortical Maps

The somatosensory cortex is located in the postcentral gyrus, a strip at the anterior (front) of the parietal lobe, just behind the central sulcus, and consists of two main subregions—the **primary somatosensory cortex (or *S1*)**, which is the first somatosensory cortical area to receive somatosensory signals from the VP nucleus, and the **secondary somatosensory cortex (or *S2*)**, which receives signals from area S1. As shown in Figure 12.12, the primary somatosensory cortex is itself divided into four side-by-side strips—known as areas 3a, 3b, 1, and 2 (going from front to back)—that wrap around the side of the parietal lobe, from the top all the way down to the lateral sulcus.

Important characteristics of the somatosensory cortex were first revealed in the 1940s by the Canadian neurosurgeon Wilder Penfield, who pioneered an approach to treating epileptic seizures caused by uncontrolled firing of brain neurons. Penfield's treatment involved removing brain tissue where those malfunctioning neurons were thought to reside, but of course it was critical to avoid removing healthy brain tissue involved in important functions such as producing or understanding speech. Therefore, during these surgical procedures, before removing any brain tissue, Penfield would stimulate different locations on the surface of the brain with electrodes while the patients were awake (but under local anesthesia) and ask them to report what they experienced. Penfield found that when he stimulated different brain locations along the postcentral gyrus, patients would report being touched at different locations on their body (Penfield & Rasmussen, 1950).

Subsequent to Penfield's work, studies with monkeys have clearly shown that within any small region of any of the areas and subareas of the somatosensory cortex, adjacent locations receive tactile signals from adjacent locations on the body surface, forming a **somatotopic map** on the cortex (Fitzgerald et al., 2004; Krubitzer & Kaas, 1990). Other studies have reported evidence for the somatotopic representation of proprioceptive signals from joints in response to limb movements (Kapreli et al., 2007). The somatotopic

dorsal column–medial lemniscal pathway (DCML pathway) Pathway for signals involved in tactile perception and proprioception; travels up the spinal cord on the ipsilateral side, crosses to the contralateral side in the medulla, and then goes through the ventral posterior nucleus of the thalamus and on to the somatosensory cortex.

spinothalamic pathway Pathway for signals involved in nociception and thermoreception; crosses over to the contralateral side within the spinal cord and then goes through the ventral posterior nucleus of the thalamus and on to the cortex.

ventral posterior nucleus (VP nucleus) A nucleus of the thalamus; part of both the DCML pathway and the spinothalamic pathway.

somatosensory cortex A region of the cerebral cortex in the anterior parietal lobe; receives signals carrying sensory information via the ventral posterior nucleus of the thalamus.

primary somatosensory cortex (or *S1*) A subregion of the somatosensory cortex; the first area to receive somatosensory signals from the ventral posterior nucleus of the thalamus; divided into four side-by-side strips known as areas 3a, 3b, 1, and 2.

secondary somatosensory cortex (or *S2*) A subregion of the somatosensory cortex; receives signals from area S1.

somatotopic map A mapping of the body surface onto the somatosensory cortex, whereby adjacent locations on the cortex receive somatosensory signals from adjacent locations on the body.

Wilder Penfield (1891–1976). [National Institutes of Health]

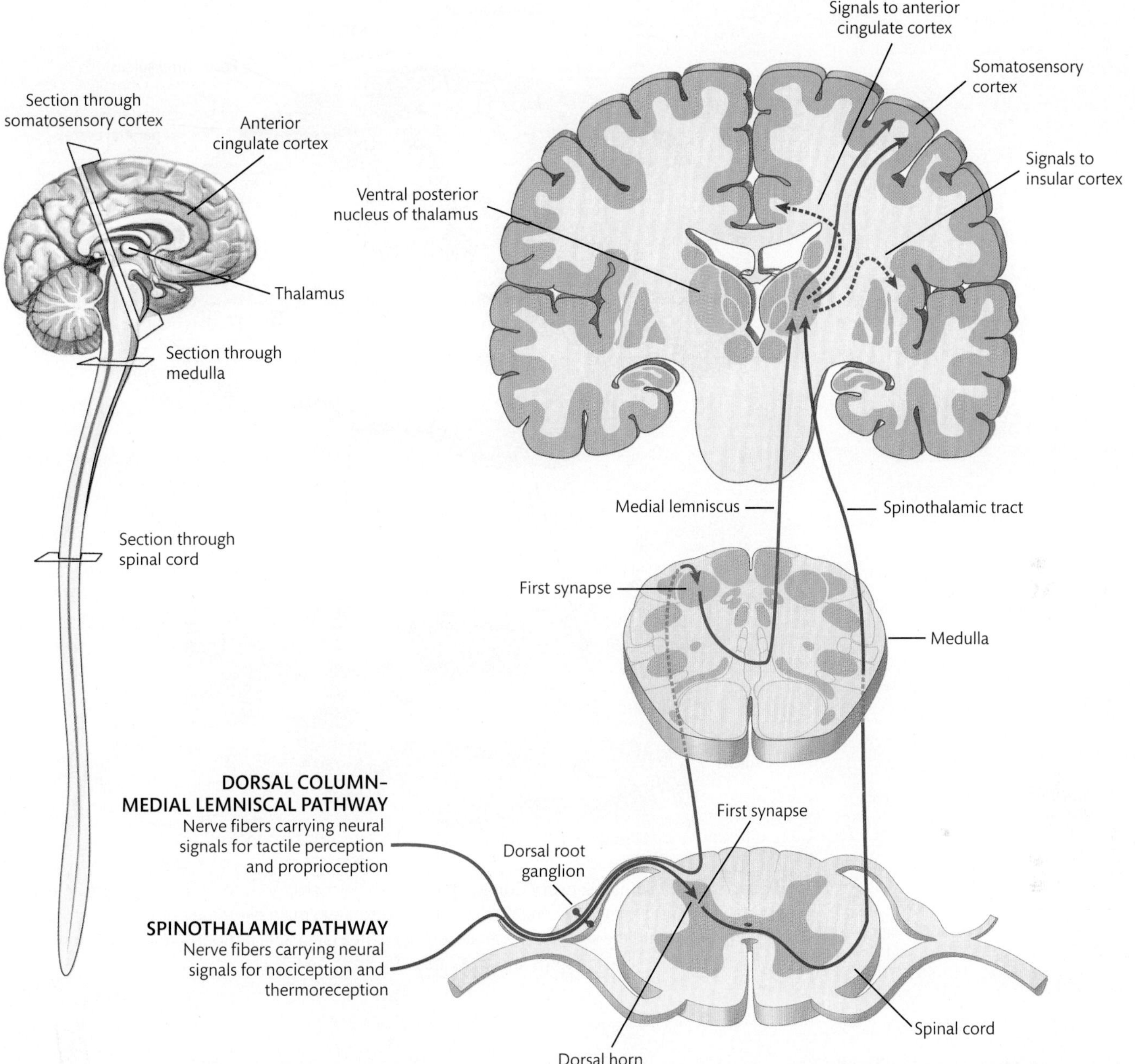

Figure 12.11 Two Somatosensory Pathways to the Brain The dorsal column–medial lemniscal (DCML) pathway carries neural signals for tactile perception and proprioception (blue arrows). A somatosensory nerve fiber in this pathway begins at its receptor ending in the skin or muscle, enters the ipsilateral dorsal column of the spinal cord, and runs up the dorsal column into the medulla, in the brain stem, where it makes a synapse with a relay neuron. The axon of the relay neuron crosses to the contralateral side in the medulla and then, as part of a bundle of axons called the *medial lemniscus*, runs up to the ventral posterior (VP) nucleus of the thalamus, where it makes a synapse. From this synapse, a connecting neuron carries signals into the contralateral somatosensory cortex. The spinothalamic pathway carries neural signals for nociception and thermoreception (red arrows). A somatosensory nerve fiber in this pathway begins at its receptor ending in the skin or muscle and enters the ipsilateral dorsal horn of the spinal cord, where it makes a synapse with a relay neuron. The axon of the relay neuron crosses to the contralateral side of the spinal cord and then, as part of a bundle of axons called the *spinothalamic tract*, runs up the spinal cord and into the brain, to the VP nucleus of the thalamus, where it makes a synapse. From this synapse, connecting neurons carry signals into the contralateral somatosensory cortex (providing information about the discriminative aspects of pain perception and thermoreception) and to the insular cortex and the anterior cingulate cortex (providing information about the affective aspects of pain perception). The pathways into the insular cortex and anterior cingulate cortex are represented by dashed arrows because the brain section shown here wouldn't reveal these regions of the cortex, which are considerably more anterior. The inset side view of the brain and spinal cord shows the locations of the sections in the main illustration.

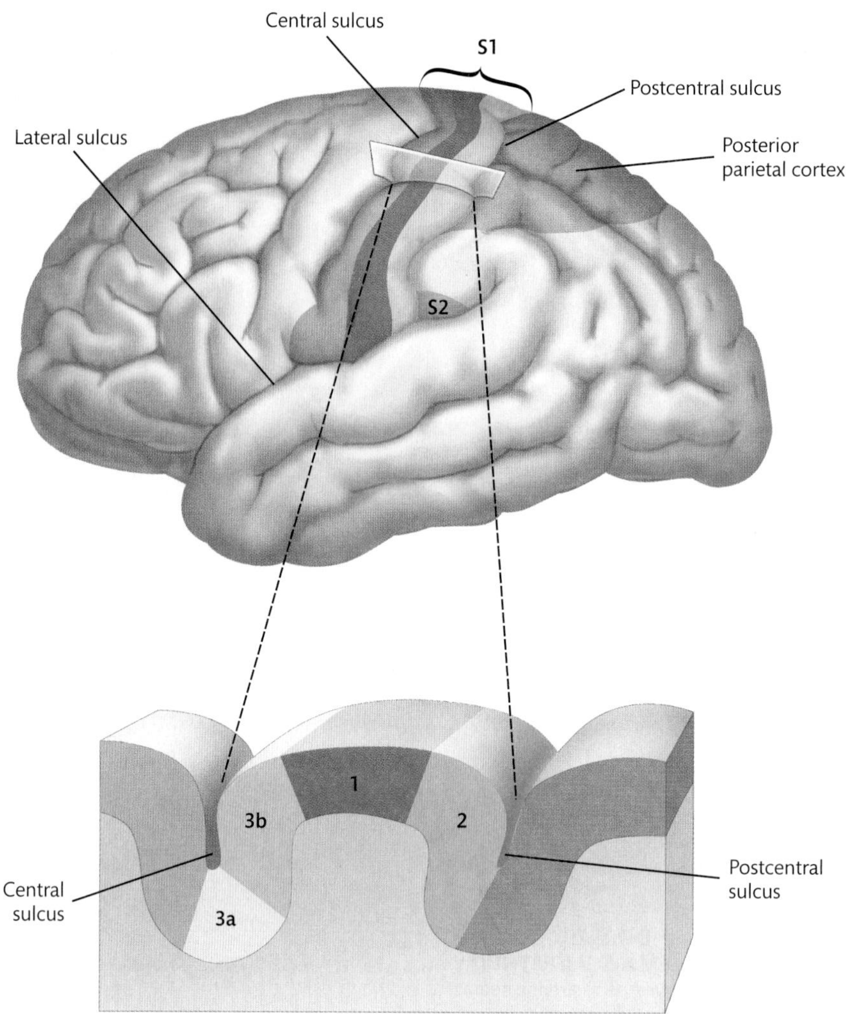

Figure 12.12 Somatosensory Cortex (top) The somatosensory cortex is located in the anterior parietal lobe, just behind the central sulcus. It consists of two main parts: the primary somatosensory cortex (area S1) and the secondary somatosensory cortex (area S2). (bottom) Area S1 is divided into four subareas, side-by-side strips known as areas 3a, 3b, 1, and 2.

organization of touch is illustrated in Figure 12.13, which shows that the somatotopic map in the somatosensory cortex is somewhat disarranged and distorted. It's disarranged in that adjacent regions of the cortex don't necessarily receive signals from adjacent parts of the body—for example, the cortical region that receives signals from the face is adjacent to the region that receives signals from the hand and fingers. And it's distorted in that relatively more cortical space is devoted to receiving signals from body parts where sensory receptors are densely distributed and have small receptive fields, such as the fingertips and lips, while relatively less space is devoted to body parts with fewer receptors that have larger receptive fields, such as the torso, arms, and legs. The size of the cortical representation of a body part corresponds with the spatial resolution of touch on that part (look back at Figure 12.2 and compare it to Figure 12.13).

This mapping of the parts of the body onto the somatosensory cortex is analogous to retinotopic mapping by the visual system (see Chapter 3) and tonotopic mapping by the auditory system (see Chapter 10). And the disproportionate amount of cortical space devoted to certain body parts is analogous to cortical magnification in the visual system,

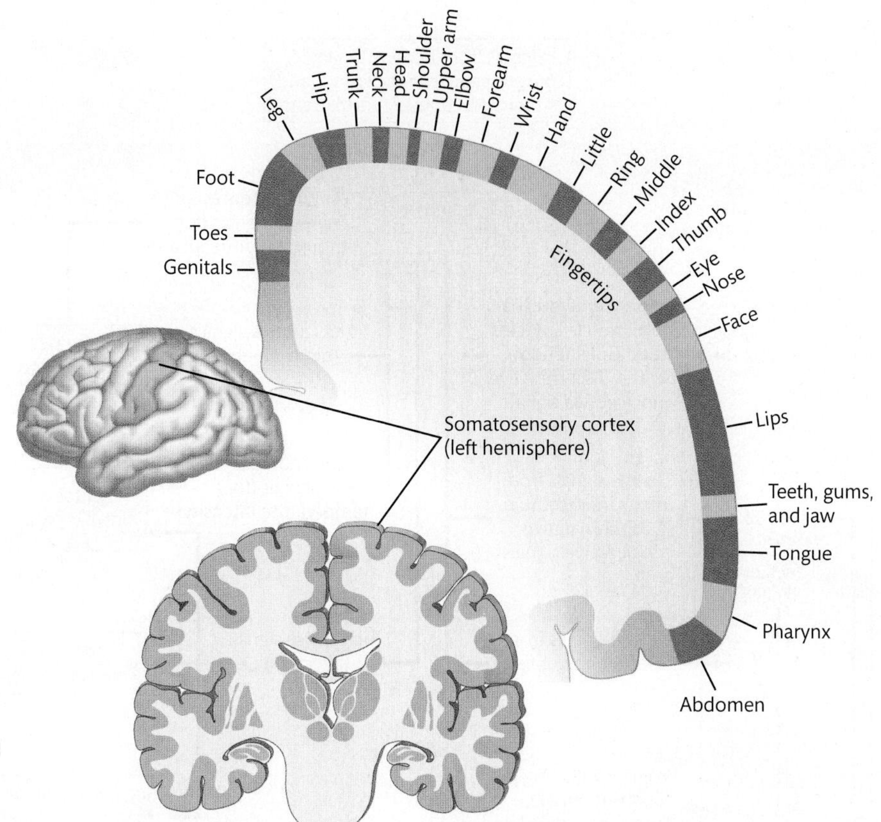

Figure 12.13 Somatotopic Maps in the Somatosensory Cortex Each of the four subareas of area S1 (i.e., areas 3a, 3b, 1, and 2) contains a full somatotopic map of the body (only one map is depicted here because all four are aligned and essentially identical). Parts of the body with high spatial resolution (e.g., the fingertips and lips) have a larger representation in the somatosensory cortex than parts of the body with low spatial resolution (e.g., the upper arm). (Adapted from Penfield & Rasmussen, 1950.)

where the amount of cortical space devoted to processing signals from the fovea, with a high density of receptors with small receptive fields, is disproportionately greater than the space devoted to the periphery of the retina, with a lower density of receptors with larger receptive fields. For both the somatosensory system and the visual system, the general point is that the parts of the body with high spatial resolution (many receptors with small receptive fields) require many cortical neurons to process their signals, and those cortical neurons take up a lot of space in the brain; in contrast, body parts with low spatial resolution (relatively few receptors with relatively large receptive fields) don't need as many cortical neurons and so take up less space in the brain.

Demonstration 12.4
Somatotopic Cortical Maps Apply tactile stimuli to a human figure and see where signals are received in the somatosensory cortex.

Responses and Representations in the Somatosensory Cortex and Beyond

Not only are the subareas of area S1 (and area S2) organized into separate somatotopic maps, but they receive signals from various types of specialized neurons, which send signals to several different areas of the brain. Figure 12.14 summarizes these information flows and pathways for tactile, proprioceptive, thermoreceptive, and nociceptive signals, as we'll discuss in the following sections.

Signals carrying tactile information from mechanoreceptors flow mainly to areas 3b and 1, whereas proprioceptive signals flow to areas 3a and 2. From S1, tactile and proprioceptive signals travel along two pathways: a dorsal pathway carries tactile information used to

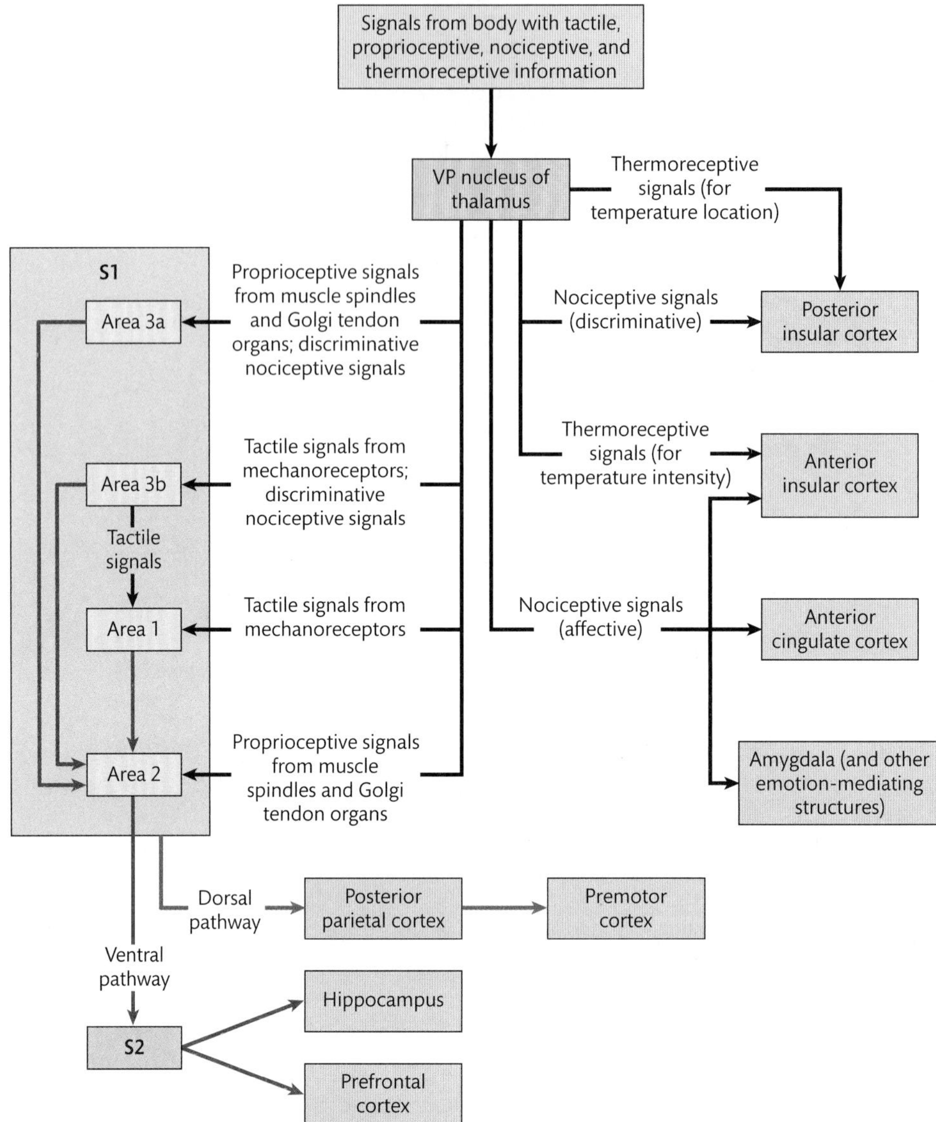

Figure 12.14 Somatosensory Information Flows: From the Body to the Brain Somatosensory signals from the body all go through the VP nucleus of the thalamus. Tactile and proprioceptive signals, as well as discriminative nociceptive signals, flow from the VP nucleus into area S1. Certain types of signals are known to flow to specific subareas of S1—tactile signals to areas 3b and 1, proprioceptive signals to areas 3a and 2, and discriminative nociceptive signals to areas 3a and 3b. The dorsal pathway (a "where"/"how" pathway, carrying information used in planning action) goes from S1 to the posterior parietal cortex and then to the premotor cortex. The ventral pathway (a "what" pathway, carrying information used in perceiving object shape and identity) consists of signals from areas 3a, 3b, and 1 to area 2, then to area S2, and then to the hippocampus (for storage in memory) and the prefrontal cortex (for use in decision making). Nociceptive and thermoreceptive signals also flow from the VP nucleus to other brain areas: the posterior insular cortex receives signals carrying discriminative nociceptive information and thermoreceptive information for locating nonpainful temperature sensations (used, for example, in maintaining homeostasis); the anterior insular cortex, anterior cingulate cortex, and amygdala all receive signals carrying affective nociceptive information; and the anterior insular cortex also receives signals carrying thermoreceptive information for evaluating the relative intensities of temperature sensations.

support touch-based action, and a ventral pathway carries both tactile and proprioceptive information used to support somatosensory object recognition and the formation of new somatosensory memories.

Nociceptive signals carrying discriminative information about the location and intensity of painful stimuli also flow to areas 3a and 3b and then to area S2, whereas signals carrying information about the unpleasantness of pain don't flow to either S1 or S2 but to several other regions of the brain (see the section below on the pathways for pain perception).

Neural Responses in Areas S1 and S2

The subareas of S1—3a, 3b, 1, and 2, each containing a full somatotopic map of the body (Kaas et al., 1979)—all receive somatosensory signals directly from the VP nucleus of the thalamus. However, as briefly described before, each of these areas receives only certain types of signals, and each contains neurons that are specialized for representing the different types of information in those signals (see Figure 12.14):

- Neurons in area 3a respond to proprioceptive information carried by signals from muscle spindles and Golgi tendon organs located in tissues below the skin, but not to tactile stimulation of the skin (Krubitzer et al., 2004 ; Moore et al.,

2000). (As mentioned earlier, areas 3a and 3b also receive some signals containing discriminative nociceptive information.)

- Neurons in areas 3b and 1 respond to tactile information carried by signals from mechanoreceptors in the skin; area 1 neurons also receive somatosensory signals from area 3b (Hsiao, 2008).
- Neurons in area 2 respond to proprioceptive information carried by signals from muscle spindles and Golgi tendon organs and to tactile information carried by signals from mechanoreceptors in the skin; area 2 neurons also receive signals from areas 3a, 3b, and 1 (Hsiao, 2008).

Many studies with monkeys have examined how S1 neurons respond to tactile stimulation. For example, in one such experiment, researchers recorded from single neurons in areas 3b and 1 of monkey area S1 (Phillips et al., 1988), using as stimuli embossed letters of the alphabet moved across the fingertips; the same stimuli were also used to examine the responses of mechanoreceptor fibers from the skin, as in the experiment illustrated in Figure 12.5. The spatial event plots in Figure 12.15 illustrate some of the results of this experiment: SAI and FAI mechanoreceptors (Figure 12.15, bottom row) produced trains of action potentials that were sufficient to discriminate between these different spatial patterns and that corresponded well to the behavioral responses documented in the confusion matrix shown in Figure 12.5. In area 3b, some neurons showed sustained responses and produced very accurate spatial event plots (Figure 12.15, top left)—some of these were virtually indistinguishable from the plots from SAI mechanoreceptors. Other neurons in area 3b showed transient responses and produced plots that didn't correspond as well to the shapes of the letters (Figure 12.15, top right). In area 1, neither sustained-response nor transient-response neurons produced plots that corresponded well to the letter shapes.

Many neurons in S1 respond selectively to specific orientations of tactile stimuli—that is, they exhibit orientation tuning not unlike the orientation tuning of simple cells in area V1 of the visual system (DiCarlo et al., 1998). In addition, many S1 neurons respond according to the direction of motion of stimuli. In one study examining the responses of single neurons in monkey area 3b, a small bar was moved in one of eight directions over the receptive field of the neuron on the surface of the fingertip, and the responses depended strongly on the direction of motion (DiCarlo & Johnson, 2000).

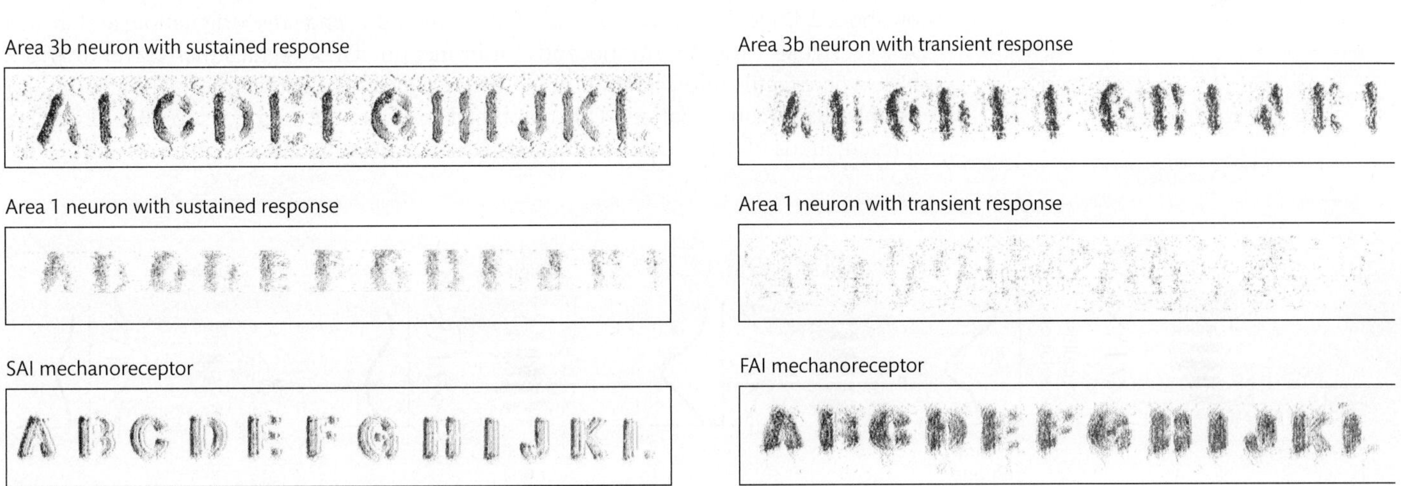

Figure 12.15 Spatial Event Plots from Single Neurons in S1 Areas 3b and 1 Embossed letters of the alphabet were moved across the fingertips of monkeys while the responses of SAI and FAI mechanoreceptors, as well as neurons in S1 areas 3b and 1, were recorded as spatial event plots. The responses of S1 neurons in both areas were either sustained or transient (similar to slow-adapting versus fast-adapting mechanoreceptor responses, respectively). Area 3b neurons with sustained responses produced the highest-fidelity representations of the letters, suggesting that area 3b may be important in using touch to perceive shape. (Adapted and images from Phillips et al., 1988.)

The specialized involvement of area 3a in proprioception was highlighted by an fMRI study of human brain activity comparing responses to tactile versus proprioceptive stimuli (Moore et al., 2000). Tactile stimulation consisted of touching participants' palm or finger with a stiff bristle; proprioceptive stimulation consisted of having participants flex their hand as if they were squeezing an imaginary tennis ball, without allowing their fingers to touch their palms. Areas 3b, 1, and 2 all showed increased activity during both types of stimulation, but area 3a showed increased activity during proprioceptive stimulation only. This corroborates findings in single-cell recording studies with monkeys indicating that area 3a is specialized for processing proprioceptive and not tactile information (Krubitzer et al., 2004).

In area S2, which receives signals from all four areas of S1, many neurons respond selectively based on the orientation of an edge pressed against the skin on multiple fingers, as illustrated in Figure 12.16 (Fitzgerald et al., 2006a). Such orientation tuning in S2 could provide part of the basis for judging the shape of a complex object held in the hand and touching several fingers (like a pencil). This possibility is supported by studies showing that many of these S2 neurons do respond to stimulation of multiple fingers (Fitzgerald et al., 2006b), suggesting that they integrate information from large regions of the fingers and hand.

Dorsal and Ventral Pathways

From area S1, signals travel along two pathways—a dorsal pathway and a ventral pathway, like the dorsal and ventral pathways of the visual system—as illustrated in Figure 12.17 (also see Figure 12.14). The dorsal pathway carries information used to guide actions that require tactile and proprioceptive input, such as the perception of slip needed to adjust grip force or the perception of shape needed to position your hand to grasp an object. Thus, it is directly analogous to the dorsal "where"/"how" pathway of the visual system, which carries visual information needed to guide actions (see Chapter 3). The dorsal pathway goes from S1 to the posterior parietal cortex—including specifically to the anterior and lateral intraparietal areas, which, as we saw in Chapter 7, are involved in perception for action—and from there into the premotor cortex (Cavada & Goldman-Rakic, 1989; Hsiao, 2008).

The ventral pathway carries tactile and proprioceptive information used in perceiving and remembering object shape and identity, and thus is analogous to the ventral "what" pathway of the visual system, which carries visual information about object shape and identity. The ventral pathway begins in S1 areas 3b and 1, with signals carrying information about 2-D tactile features such as texture, curvature, and edge orientation, and in area 3a, with signals carrying proprioceptive information. These signals then travel to area 2 of S1, where tactile information is combined with proprioceptive information about, for example, hand conformation. This combined information then goes to area S2, where representations of 3-D shape are created (Hsiao, 2008). From S2, signals are sent to the

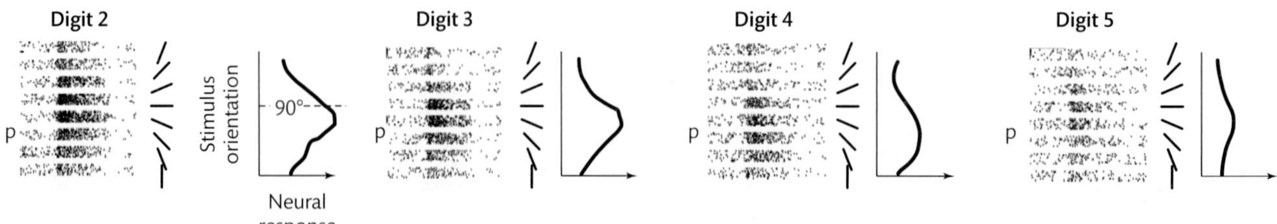

Figure 12.16 Orientation Tuning in Area S2 This figure shows the responses of a single neuron in monkey area S2 when bars with eight different orientations were pressed against the fingertips of the four digits of the hand (excluding digit 1, the thumb). In the four plots, the strength of the neuron's response to each of the eight orientations is indicated by the density of spikes; p indicates that the preferred orientation on each of the fingertips was around 90°. The curves next to the plots show that the neuron's tuning is increasingly broad going from digit 2 to digit 5. (Adapted and images from Fitzgerald et al., 2006a, Figure 1.)

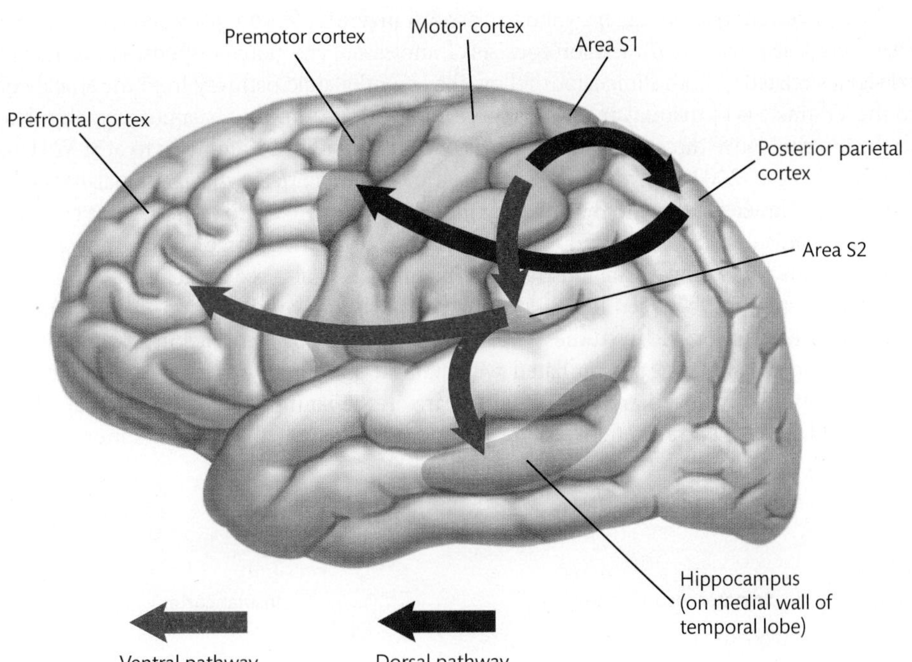

Figure 12.17 **Dorsal and Ventral Pathways** The dorsal pathway (analogous to the dorsal "where"/"how" pathway in vision) carries somatosensory information used in guiding actions; it goes from area S1 into the posterior parietal cortex and then into the premotor cortex, where motor plans are formed. The ventral pathway (analogous to the ventral "what" pathway in vision) carries somatosensory information used in perceiving object shape and identity; it goes from area S1 to area S2, and then to the prefrontal cortex (for perceptual decision making) and the hippocampus (for storage in long-term memory).

prefrontal cortex (for perceptual decision making) and to the hippocampus (for storage in long-term memory).

The evidence for this organization into a dorsal "where"/"how" pathway and ventral "what" pathway in tactile and proprioceptive perception has largely come from studies with monkeys, but these findings have been corroborated by fMRI studies with humans (Reed et al., 2005).

Cortical Representation of Temperature

As shown in Figure 12.11, thermoreceptive signals carry information about temperature from the skin into the spinal cord and then along the spinothalamic pathway to the VP nucleus of the thalamus. From the thalamus, these signals travel to S1 and to other regions of the cortex (see Figure 12.14). In one study that identified a cortical target of thermoreceptive signals, researchers applied a nonpainful cooling stimulus to the right palms of several volunteers while they underwent PET imaging of the brain (Craig et al., 2000). Over several runs, each participant's right palm was cooled from a baseline temperature of 33°C to 30°C, 28°C, 26°C, 24°C, and 20°C. In each run, the participant was asked to rate how cold the stimulus was on a 10-point scale (as you might expect, the colder the stimulus, the greater the coldness rating). The brain images showed activation in the left posterior insular cortex (contralateral to the hand that was cooled) that varied with the temperature applied to the hand; the insular cortex is a region located deep within the lateral sulcus of the brain. In the right (ipsilateral) anterior insular cortex, the intensity of activation was also correlated with the stimulus temperature and even more strongly correlated with the participants' coldness ratings. These results led the researchers to suggest that the contralateral insular cortex is a site where nonpainful temperature sensations are represented in a somatotopic map (Hua et al., 2005) and used for, among other things, maintaining homeostasis (e.g., constant body temperature), whereas the ipsilateral insular cortex is a site where the relative intensities of temperature sensations are evaluated.

Pathways for the Discriminative and Affective Dimensions of Pain Perception

As we mentioned in the section on nociception, pain is experienced along two different dimensions—discriminative and affective. The discriminative dimension consists of perceptions that enable the person to locate the pain and to classify it in terms of its intensity and type (burning, sharp, etc.). The affective dimension consists of unpleasant emotional responses to pain. Neural signals related to both dimensions follow the spinothalamic pathway from the spinal cord to the VP nucleus of the thalamus (see Figure 12.11), but from the thalamus, signals related to the discriminative dimension flow to areas 3a and 3b within S1 and then to area S2 (Duncan & Albanese, 2003), as well as to the posterior insular cortex, whereas signals related to the affective dimension flow to the anterior cingulate cortex (ACC), to the amygdala and other emotion-mediating structures, and to the anterior insular cortex (Price, 2000; Tracey, 2005). These regions and pathways are illustrated in Figure 12.18 (also see Figure 12.14).

This distinction between the discriminative and affective dimensions of pain perception has been supported by studies with human participants. Studies in which different locations on the body were stimulated with painful stimuli have provided evidence that somatotopically organized areas in S1 and S2 are on the pain pathway (Bingel et al., 2004; Chen et al., 2009; Ferretti et al., 2004), and it's thought that the representations created

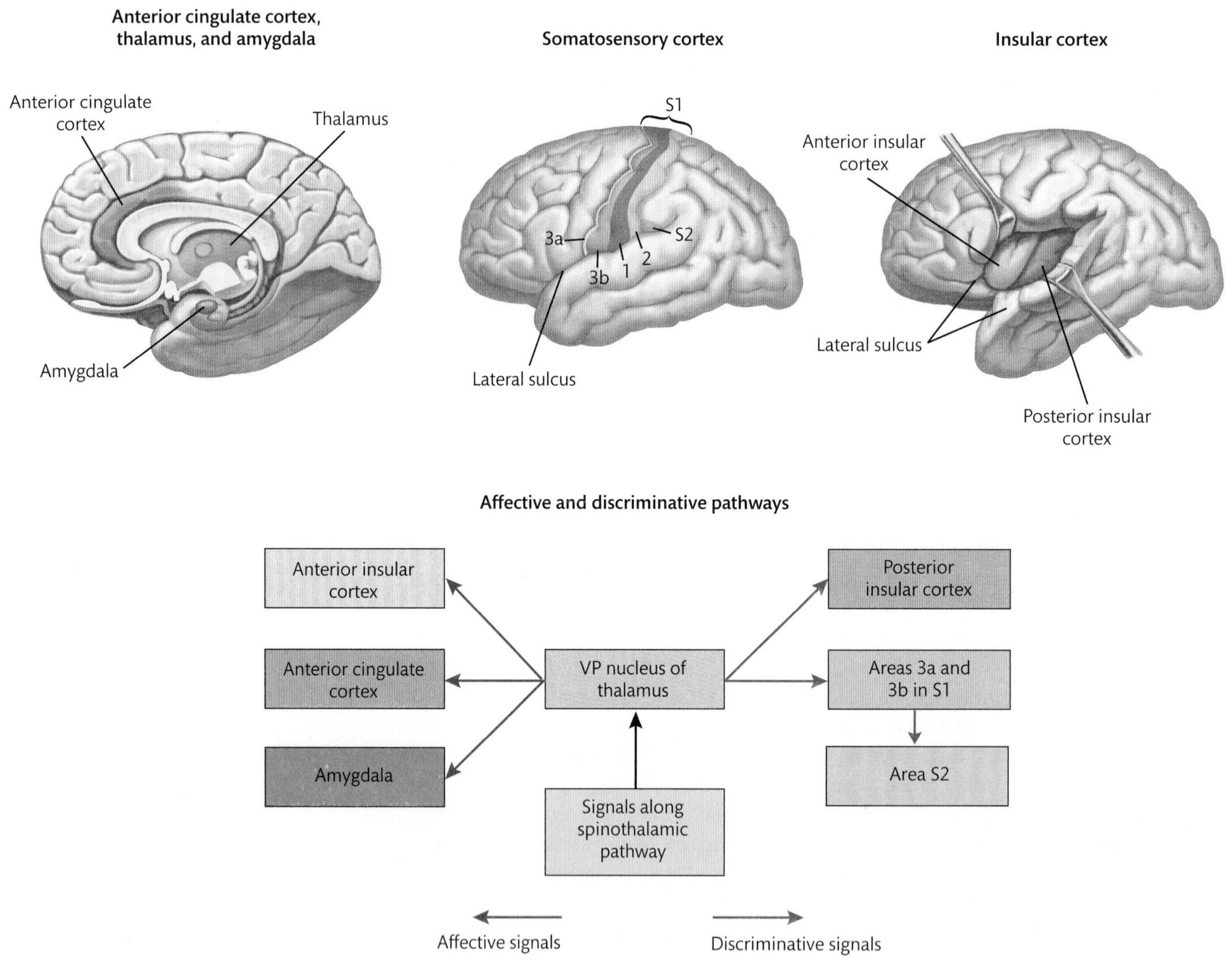

Figure 12.18 **Brain Regions and Pathways Involved in the Affective and Discriminative Dimensions of Pain Perception** (top) Three views showing the locations of the principal brain regions involved in the affective and discriminative dimensions of pain perception. Regions involved in affective perceptions include the anterior insular cortex, the anterior cingulate cortex, and the amygdala. Regions involved in discriminative perceptions include area S1 (specifically, areas 3a and 3b), area S2, and the posterior insular cortex. (bottom) This schematic representation shows how signals flow along both the affective and discriminative pathways.

in these areas provide information about the discriminative dimension but not the affective dimension. The role of the ACC in representing the affective dimension was shown in a single-cell recording study of brain-surgery patients that revealed neurons in the ACC that strongly responded to painful stimuli, including excessive heat or cold, pinpricks, and pinches (Hutchison et al., 1999). In another study with brain-surgery patients, microstimulation of the insular cortex evoked unpleasantly painful sensations (Ostrowsky et al., 2002).

In a pair of studies using PET, participants under hypnosis were induced to experience moderately painful heat stimuli as being more or less unpleasant, without experiencing any change in intensity (Rainville et al., 1997), or were induced to experience the stimuli as more or less intense, without experiencing any change in unpleasantness (Hofbauer et al., 2001). Participants who perceived differences in unpleasantness showed changes in activity in the ACC, whereas those who perceived differences in intensity showed changes in activity in S1. This double dissociation, together with the studies described here, provides strong evidence that the discriminative dimension of pain is distinct from the affective dimension and that the two dimensions are represented in different areas of the brain.

The distinction between these two dimensions of pain and their different pathways also appears to relate to feelings of empathy. This was shown by an fMRI study in which one group of participants experienced a painful stimulus themselves (an electric shock applied to the back of the hand), whereas another group observed their significant other experiencing the stimulus (Singer et al., 2004). Both groups exhibited brain activity in the ACC and the anterior insular cortex, but only the group directly experiencing the pain exhibited activity in the posterior insular cortex, as well as in the somatosensory cortex. These results support the idea that the pathway for the discriminative dimension of pain perception—what kind of pain is it? how intense is it? where is it located on the body?—runs through the somatosensory cortex and the posterior insular cortex, whereas the pathway for the affective dimension runs through the ACC and the anterior insular cortex. The study also shows that the affective dimension—involving unpleasantness and motivation to "make it stop"—is present whether the person is experiencing pain directly or empathically.

Top-Down Mechanisms of Pain Reduction

Top-down feedback from the brain plays an important role in reducing sensitivity to pain by modulating the intensity of pain signals, an effect known as *analgesia.* This modulatory feedback occurs naturally when the body releases compounds known as **endogenous opioids,** such as **endorphins,** which have an inhibitory effect on pain-related neural signals in many areas of the central nervous system (CNS). Endogenous opioids belong to a class of substances called *opiates,* which includes analgesic drugs like morphine and heroin (endogenous opioids are opiates produced within the body). Endogenous opioids are released by the pituitary gland, by the hypothalamus, and by descending nerve fibers within the spinal cord, in response to painful or stressful experiences, including painful injuries and stresses such as high-intensity exercise and sexual activity. Many regions of the CNS contain opiate receptors, which take up endorphins and other endogenous opioids and inhibit the release of neurotransmitters by pain-carrying neurons, thus reducing the perceived intensity of pain.

endogenous opioids Compounds that belong to a class of substances called *opiates;* released by the body in response to painful or stressful experiences.

endorphins Endogenous opioids that have an inhibitory effect on pain-related neural signals in many areas of the central nervous system, reducing the perceived intensity of pain.

Endorphins are readily measurable in the circulating blood following strenuous exercise, which has led to the hypothesis that endorphins produce the sense of internal harmony and euphoria—the "runner's high"—often associated with high-intensity exercise such as running a marathon. Runners also have reduced sensitivity to pain following a strenuous run, and this is associated with increased concentrations of endorphins in the blood (Janal et al., 1984).

Endogenous opioids have been proposed as a source of pain reduction following a significant injury in a high-stress situation. From an evolutionary perspective, an animal that has been injured and is in extreme danger could benefit from being able to ignore pain and escape, but the pain should return once the stressful situation is resolved, so the animal will favor the injured body part to permit healing and prevent further injury. This phenomenon, known as *stress-induced analgesia,* has been documented in both humans and other animals (Butler & Finn, 2009).

The periaqueductal gray (PAG) region of the midbrain seems to be involved in this feedback system, as indicated by experiments in which the PAG was electrically stimulated (Reynolds, 1969). Animals that have undergone PAG stimulation are still sensitive to touch, but their sensitivity to pain is greatly reduced (Stamford, 1995). The same analgesic effects are observed when opiates such as morphine and codeine are injected into the PAG or the raphe nucleus, in the brain stem, or directly into the dorsal horn of the spinal cord, activating the same circuit as in the electrical stimulation studies (Millan, 2002). A drawback of using opiate drugs for analgesia is that long-term use can lead to tolerance, in which increasing doses are required to produce the same degree of pain reduction.

Finally, recent investigations of the cognitive and emotional dimensions of pain experience have revealed a number of other top-down factors that affect the intensity and duration of pain (Tracey & Mantyh, 2007). For example, the deployment of attention away from a painful stimulus reduces both the perceived intensity of pain (Miron et al., 1989) and the level of activity in parts of the brain associated with the discriminative dimension of pain (Bantick et al., 2002). Likewise, the placebo effect—based on the expectation that a treatment, even one with no objective therapeutic value, will be effective—can lessen both the experience of pain (Colloca & Benedetti, 2005) and the associated pain-related brain activity (Wager et al., 2004), whereas negative mood and anxiety can increase the intensity of perceived pain (Tracey & Mantyh, 2007).

Cortical Plasticity and Phantom Limbs

The brains of fetuses and young children go through a period of rapid development during which the brain grows dramatically, while the intricate networks of neural connections, to a large extent specified in the genetic code but also influenced by experience, become fully expressed. Until about 20 years ago, it was widely believed that once the brain reached a certain level of maturity—and certainly once a person or animal had reached adulthood—very little additional change in brain connectivity occurred.

cortical plasticity The ability of the adult cortex to change the way it's organized.

This view has now been thoroughly revised in light of the evidence for adult **cortical plasticity**—the ability of the adult cortex to change the way it's organized (*plasticity* refers to the capacity for change). This type of brain "rewiring" was first documented in the somatosensory cortex of primates, where the somatotopic organization of the hand region in area S1 was found to change if the sensory nerve from a finger was cut (Merzenich et al., 1983). The parts of S1 that were no longer receiving signals from that finger began to respond to signals arriving in adjacent parts of S1.

phantom limb Perception of a missing limb, as if it were still there, even though the part of the somatosensory cortex that previously received signals from the limb no longer does so.

Another, even more striking example of cortical plasticity arises in people who have had a limb amputated. It is quite common for such people to experience a **phantom limb**—that is, they can feel the missing limb, as if it were still there, even though the part of the somatosensory cortex that previously received signals from the limb no longer does so.

People who have had an arm amputated sometimes report that stimulation of their face (e.g., with a cotton swab) results in a feeling that both their face and a specific location on the phantom arm are being stimulated (Ramachandran et al., 1992). Why should this be? Look again at the somatotopic map in Figure 12.12, which shows that the region of area S1 devoted to the face is very near the extensive region devoted to the arm (from the thumb to the shoulder). After the arm is amputated, of course, the missing part no longer sends signals to the corresponding region of S1. Over time, however, the brain's circuitry is rearranged in such a way that signals from the face activate not only the region of S1 devoted to the face but also the region formerly devoted to the now-missing arm. However, the person doesn't "know" about this reorganization of his brain, and continues to experience signals coming from the arm region of S1 as feelings in the arm, just as Penfield's patients experienced feelings in their arm when that region was stimulated directly (i.e., without any actual stimulation of the arm).

Loss of sensory input from the body due to a severed nerve or to amputation is not the only cause of the brain's rewiring itself; cortical plasticity also arises as a result of experience. For example, researchers measured the somatotopic map of monkeys in area

S1 before and after the monkeys learned to make very fine tactile discriminations using the tip of their index finger (Jenkins et al., 1990). Not surprisingly, the monkey's performance on this task improved as a result of practice, but the more interesting result was that the part of the somatotopic map devoted to the fingertip that had been used during learning expanded dramatically, whereas the parts devoted to the adjacent fingers did not change significantly (see Figure 12.19). Thus, as the monkeys became expert at the task, the brain, in effect, rewired itself to allocate more cortical neurons to the part of the skin surface that was needed to perform the task.

The same sorts of changes in brain organization have also been seen in humans. In one study, investigators used magnetoencephalography (measuring the strength of magnetic fields generated by electrical activity in the brain) to see how large a region of area S1 was devoted to the left and right hands of people who were either expert stringed-instrument players or novices (Elbert et al., 1995). In playing the violin, for example, manual dexterity—the ability to make precisely controlled movements with the hand and fingers—and the ability to discriminate minute changes in the position of the fingers are much more important for the left hand (which performs the fingering) than for the right hand (which holds the bow). In line with this required difference in ability between the two hands, the cortical region devoted to the left hand of expert string players was larger than that of novices, whereas the region devoted to the right hand was about equally large in the two groups. Furthermore, among the experts, the area devoted to the left hand depended on how long they had been playing their instrument: those who had started before age 13 exhibited a significantly larger magnetic signal. This suggests that the parts of the brain that are involved in making fine perceptual discriminations rewire themselves as needed.

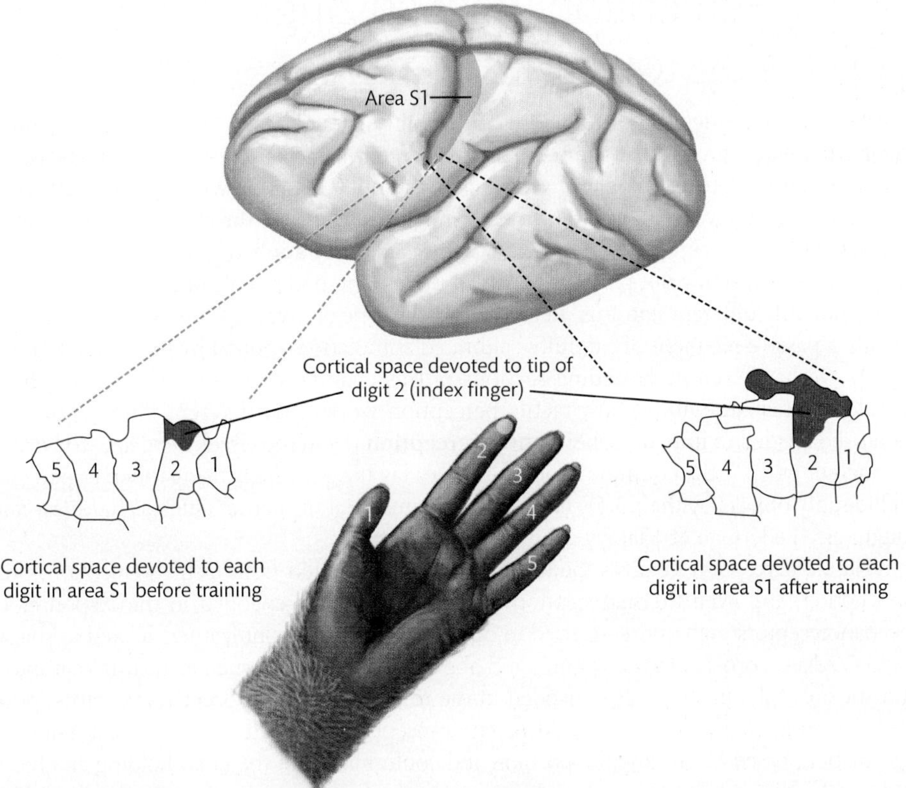

Figure 12.19 Cortical Plasticity: How Learning Affects Cortical Organization A monkey's somatotopic map in the hand region of area S1 was measured before and after the monkey trained for several months to make a very fine tactile discrimination using the tip of finger 2 (the index finger). As indicated by the difference in size of the red areas, the amount of cortical space devoted to that fingertip increased markedly after training. (Adapted from Jenkins et al., 1990.)

Check Your Understanding

12.12 Why are sensory receptors also called *dorsal root ganglion cells*?

12.13 Describe how the DCML pathway and the spinothalamic pathway differ in terms of **(A)** the types of signals that flow along each pathway, **(B)** the point at which signals cross from the ipsilateral to the contralateral side, and **(C)** the point at which the sensory receptor neurons make their first synapse.

12.14 Given that the somatotopic cortical map illustrated in Figure 12.13 shows that the cortical area devoted to the face lies next to the cortical area devoted to the thumb, in what sense can this be considered a map of the body?

12.15 Many neurons in area S1 and area S2 are tuned to the orientation of tactile stimuli (e.g., an edge pressed against the skin). How do these S1 and S2 neurons differ in the information represented in their responses?

12.16 What is the analogy between the dorsal and ventral somatosensory pathways and the dorsal and ventral pathways of the visual system?

12.17 Cross out the incorrect choices in parentheses: When you see someone you care about in pain, there's likely to be activity along the (affective/ discriminative) pathway of pain perception, in (area S2 / the anterior cingulate cortex / the anterior insular cortex / the posterior insular cortex).

12.18 Briefly explain how the experience of a phantom limb relates to the concept of cortical plasticity.

Haptic Perception: Recognizing Objects by Touch

The scientific investigation of touch began, sensibly enough, with studies of how simple touch stimuli are perceived and represented by the central nervous system. Scientists would touch a location on the skin or apply vibration or stimulate the skin with a small paintbrush or cotton swab or tweezers, in order to determine how sensitive the skin is to such stimuli and how mechanoreceptors responded to them. Later, they applied spatial patterns against the skin, such as Braille dot patterns or sets of ridges, and had people or monkeys discriminate or identify different patterns. Regardless of the type of investigation, the perceiver was usually a passive recipient of carefully calibrated stimulation applied by the experimenter.

As we have seen in preceding sections of this chapter, experiments like these have revealed a great deal about how tactile perception works; but different kinds of experiments are needed to fully decipher **haptic perception** (from the Greek *haptikos,* "to be able to touch or grasp"), the common process in everyday life of actively using touch to perceive and identify objects by their 3-D shape and other material properties, such as hardness and roughness (Lederman & Klatzky, 2009).

haptic perception Actively using touch to perceive and identify objects by their 3-D shape and other material properties; involves the integration of information from tactile perception, proprioception, and thermoreception.

Haptic perception involves the integration of information from tactile perception, proprioception, and even thermoreception. Tactile perception—encoded in the responses of mechanoreceptors in the skin—is used to obtain information about features related to shape, such as edges, corners, and curvature, and about surface features such as texture, hardness, and stickiness. Proprioception—encoded in the responses of proprioceptive receptors, principally muscle spindle fibers, and skin stretch receptors—is used to acquire shape-related information, based on sensing the position and conformation of the hand holding an object, and weight-related information, based on sensing the forces the object applies to the limbs. Thermoreception provides information about the material properties of objects (e.g., wood versus metal).

You can experience the involvement of these aspects of perception if you sit at a table with your eyes closed while a friend puts some small object down in front of you, which you then try to pick up, still with your eyes shut. You will probably start by opening your hand wide, with the palm down, and then lowering your hand slowly until it touches the top of the object, at which point you'll slowly close your hand around the object, allowing your detection of skin deformation (tactile perception) to guide the enclosing movements of your hand and fingers, while your detection of muscle stretch (proprioception) and skin stretch on the back of your hand (via SAII mechanoreceptors) tells you the final shape of your grasp. If you really pay attention to how often you handle objects without looking at them, you'll appreciate the importance of haptic perception in helping you not just to identify objects by their shapes but also to grasp objects with appropriate force, without inadvertently dropping heavy objects or inadvertently crushing fragile objects. The ability to take your house key (and not your car key) from your pocket or purse without looking is an impressive achievement of haptic perception (Johnson, 2002).

People are remarkably proficient at recognizing objects rapidly by touch. In one study, for example, people were asked to name 100 random objects while blindfolded, and accuracy was near 100% with just 2 or 3 seconds of exploration per object (Klatzky et al., 1985). How are people able to do this? To take an analogy from vision, it might be that people perceive the position and orientation of edges, corners, and curved parts, based on the responses of mechanoreceptors in the skin, and integrate these perceptions—along with the proprioceptive perception of the object's weight and overall shape, based on picking up the object—into a representation involving contours and their relative positions and orientations.

To examine this possibility, researchers asked people to identify the shapes of rigid objects that had been fastened to a surface, thus depriving the participants of information about weight and center of mass (Klatzky et al., 1993). Also, the participants were required to wear a glove that allowed them to feel the edges of the object but didn't allow detection of its surface texture or temperature, both of which could help in identifying the material of which the object was made. Under these conditions, if people were allowed to touch the object using only one finger, accuracy of identification was reduced to less than 50%; if they were allowed to use the whole hand, accuracy increased to 93%, but the average time required to identify the object was more than 15 seconds. These results imply that haptic perception of an object depends on information about its weight and center of mass, along with *simultaneous* information about shape (both of which can be acquired most readily if the object can be picked up and enclosed in the hand) and probably on information about surface features such as texture and temperature.

Depending on the size and shape of an object, its location, its movability, and other such factors, it may not be possible to touch its entire surface all at once; in these cases, as well as in cases where objects are entirely touchable, people typically move their hands and fingers over the object using what have been called **exploratory procedures (EPs)** (Lederman & Klatzky, 1987). As shown in Figure 12.20, eight different types of EPs were proposed, with

exploratory procedures (EPs) Hand and finger movements typically used by people to identify objects haptically.

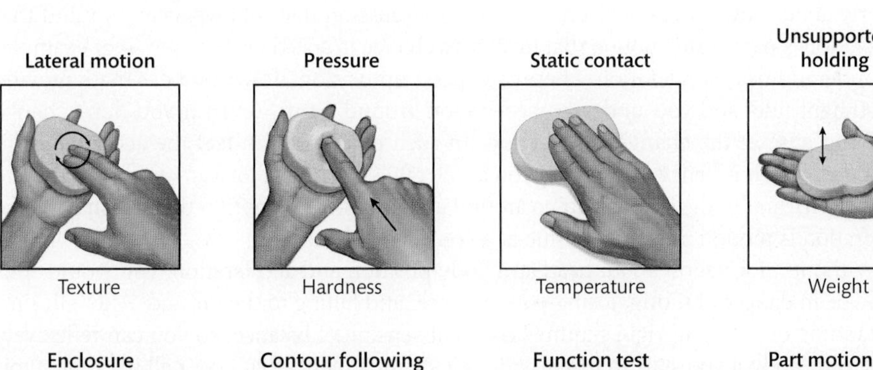

Figure 12.20 Haptic Exploratory Procedures People use different exploratory procedures when trying to determine the shape and identity of an object by touching it, depending on what information they're looking for at any given moment. (Adapted from Lederman & Klatzky, 1987.)

people using the different types to acquire different kinds of information about the object being examined.

For example, information about texture is typically obtained by the EP called *lateral motion,* which involves rubbing the skin along the object's surface; the EP *pressure* (pressing on the object) is used to get information about hardness; while information about shape is typically obtained via two different EPs, running the fingers over an edge (*contour following,* for information about the exact shape of some part of the object) and grasping the whole object in the hand (*enclosure,* for information about the shape of the object as a whole).

In the experiment described before, in which objects were fastened to a surface and participants had to wear a glove while touching them (Klatzky et al., 1993), many of the EPs could not be used effectively, requiring the participants to build up internal representations of the objects' shape and other properties using less natural ways of getting the necessary information, and as you'd expect, that took longer and was less accurate.

tactile agnosia An inability to recognize objects by touch, which can result from damage to the parietal cortex, specifically to area S2.

What parts of the brain are involved in integrating tactile and proprioceptive information? An important clue is provided by people with a condition called **tactile agnosia,** an inability to recognize objects by touch, which can result from damage to the parietal cortex (Reed et al., 1996). Consider, for example, the case of E.C., a woman who suffered a stroke in her left inferior parietal cortex. When asked to identify objects using her right hand (contralateral to the damage caused by the stroke), she was correct only half the time, but when she used her left hand, her performance was normal (90% correct). Her visual abilities remained normal following the stroke, and she could detect and identify simple tactile stimuli such as light touches, pinpricks, and different textures. She could also tell the difference in the sizes of different objects using her right hand. Her impairment was limited to recognizing objects by touch—that is, to haptic perception. The region of E.C.'s brain that was damaged by the stroke is near the usual location of area S2, and this, together with the findings of studies with monkeys (described previously), showing that S2 neurons respond to signals carrying both tactile and proprioceptive information, strongly implicates S2 in the process by which simple, local somatosensory information is integrated into an understanding of an object's entire shape and material properties.

The Vestibular System: Perceiving Balance and Acceleration

As you perform any of a nearly infinite variety of physical activities—playing tennis, dancing, bending over to tie your shoelace, or just sitting and reading at your desk—information about the position of your head and body relative to the direction of the pull of gravity is essential, as is information about how your head and body are (or are not) moving, particularly about how they're accelerating. In the discussion that follows, keep in mind that acceleration is part of any motion that involves a change in speed or direction—for example, you undergo linear acceleration when you speed up or slow down in a car that's moving in a straight line, and you undergo acceleration around a turn (even if you don't change speed) because of the change in direction. In each case, you can feel the acceleration in your body, which is bent backward as you accelerate (speed up), forward as you decelerate (slow down), and to the side as you go around a turn. The only motion that doesn't involve acceleration is motion in a straight line at a constant speed.

vestibular system The sense organs used to produce neural signals carrying information about balance and acceleration; includes the semicircular canals and the otolith organs.

semicircular canals Part of the vestibular system; three mutually perpendicular hollow curved tubes in the skull filled with endolymph; responsible for signaling head rotation.

Without information about head and body position and acceleration, you would constantly be in danger of tilting, losing your balance, and falling to the ground. After all, simply standing or sitting upright requires constant sensing of balance, so you can reflexively adjust your body if you start to lean to one side—adjustments that occur all the time, typically without any need to think about them. The neural signals carrying information about balance and acceleration are produced by hair cells within a specialized collection of sensory organs in the inner ear, adjacent to the cochlea on both sides of the head and collectively referred to as the **vestibular system.**

As shown in Figure 12.21, the sense organs that make up the vestibular system are the semicircular canals and the otolith organs. The **semicircular canals,** which are responsible

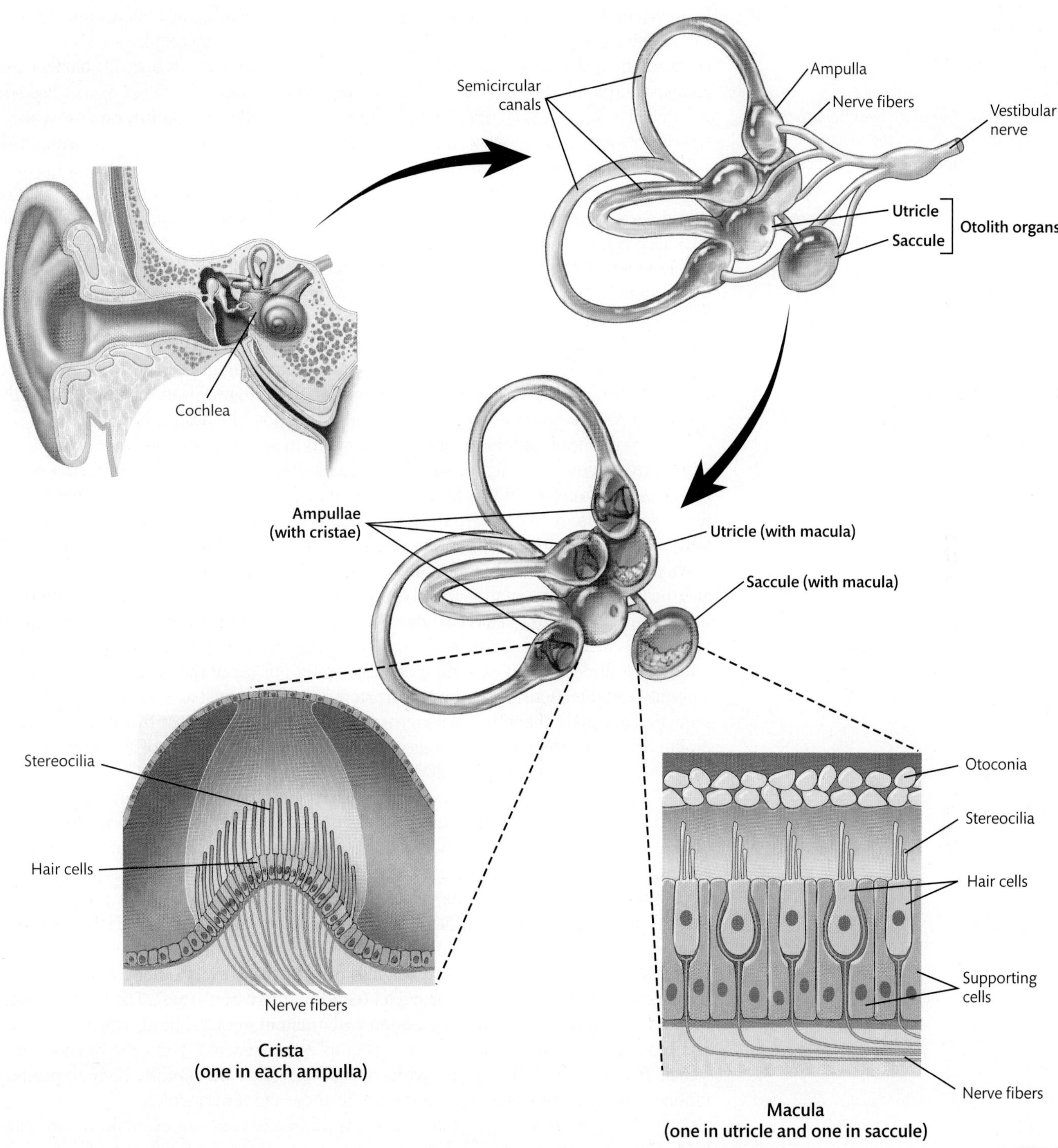

Figure 12.21 The Vestibular System Structures next to the cochlea, in the inner ear, contain hair cells that produce the neural signals used by the vestibular system in the perception of balance and acceleration. Hair cells in the cristae within the ampullae of the fluid-filled semicircular canals produce signals indicating how the head is rotating, either when turning to one side or the other or when tilting forward, backward, or to the side. Hair cells within the maculae of the fluid-filled utricle and saccule produce signals according to the direction in which the head is accelerating or the angle at which the head is tilted. The nerve fibers carrying all these signals bundle together to form the vestibular nerve, which carries the signals into the brain.

for signaling head rotation, consist of three mutually perpendicular hollow curved tubes in the skull filled with a fluid called endolymph (parts of the nearby cochlea are also filled with endolymph, as discussed in Chapter 9). At the base of each canal is a small chamber called an *ampulla* (plural *ampullae*), also filled with endolymph and containing a specialized structure called a *crista* (plural *cristae*), where the hair cells reside. The **otolith organs**, which are responsible for signaling when the head is undergoing linear acceleration or being held in a tilted position, consist of the utricle and the saccule, each of which contains a specialized structure with hair cells called a *macula* (plural *maculae*). Within each macula, the hair cells are oriented in different directions and are embedded in a viscous fluid containing tiny crystals called *otoconia*.

otolith organs Part of the vestibular system; consist of the utricle and the saccule; responsible for signaling when the head is undergoing linear acceleration or being held in a tilted position.

Rotation of the head causes the endolymph within one or more of the semicircular canals to move; the movement of the endolymph causes the stereocilia of the hair cells to bend, which in turn causes the hair cells' rate of neurotransmitter release to increase above baseline or decrease below baseline, depending on the direction of head rotation. Because the three canals are perpendicular to each other, each different head rotation evokes a different pattern of relative neurotransmitter release by the hair cells in the three canals; thus, each such pattern serves as a neural code indicating how the head is rotating.

When the head undergoes linear acceleration in any direction, as when you speed up while driving down a straight road, the otoconia drag on the fluid in the macula, and the consequent movement of this fluid causes the stereocilia of the hair cells to bend, with a resulting increase or decrease in the rate of neurotransmitter release by the hair cells. Similarly, when the head is held in a tilted position, as when you're admiring your new shoes, gravity pulls on the otoconia in a different direction than when the head is held upright, and the force of this gravitational pull causes the otoconia to drag on the macular fluid, with resultant bending of the hair cells' stereocilia and changes in neurotransmitter release corresponding with the particular tilt of the head. The stereocilia in the maculae are oriented in different directions, so each different acceleration or tilt of the head results in different amounts and directions of bending of the stereocilia. Thus, just as with the hair cells of the semicircular canals, the different patterns of neurotransmitter release by the hair cells of the otolith organs function as a code indicating the degree and direction of acceleration and tilt of the head (Angelaki & Cullen, 2008).

As shown in Figure 12.21, nerve fibers carrying neural signals from the hair cells in the semicircular canals and the otolith organs bundle together to form the vestibular nerve, which carries these signals to the vestibular complex in the brain stem. The vestibular complex contains multiple vestibular nuclei, which receive signals not only from the vestibular system, but also from the visual system, the system that controls eye movements, and the motor systems responsible for neck movements. Signals from the vestibular nuclei go to several brain regions, including the parietal insular vestibular cortex (PIVC), deep in the lateral sulcus, which also receives signals from virtually every other cortical region that receives signals from the vestibular nuclei (Guldin & Grüsser, 1998). The PIVC is thought to provide a representation of the position and orientation of the head, which can be used as a basis for maintaining balance during complex movements. Thus, the brain combines signals from the vestibular system with signals from other parts of the body to produce a unified perception of whole-body position, balance, and movement.

Other regions receiving signals from the vestibular nuclei—for example, the frontal eye field—are involved in controlling eye movements in order to maintain a stable gaze, which is among the most important functions of the vestibular system. Typically, when redirecting the gaze, the first movement is a saccade, a rapid movement of the eyes only (not the head), to point the eyes at a new target. The saccade is often followed by a turn and/or a tilt of the head, so the eyes and head end up aligned with one another, both pointing at the new target. The hair cells in the semicircular canals produce signals in response to this head movement, which in turn cause signals to flow from the vestibular complex to the oculomotor system, which moves the eyes in a direction opposite to the direction of the head movement in order to keep the eyes pointed at the target while the head is moving. This unconscious compensating movement of the eyes during head movements is known as the **vestibulo–ocular reflex.** As the basis for the remarkable stability of visual experience

vestibulo-ocular reflex An unconscious compensating movement of the eyes during head movements in order to maintain a stable gaze.

despite the nearly constant movement of the head, this reflex must occur almost instantaneously—the elapsed time from the beginning of a head movement to the beginning of the compensating eye movement is just 5 msec (Huterer & Cullen, 2002).

Check Your Understanding

12.19 You're sitting blindfolded with your arm and open hand extended in front of you, palm up. Someone drops a small, cool, light object onto your palm, and you close your hand around it. You can feel that the object has numerous edges and smooth, flat surfaces. You move the object from your palm to between the tips of your fingers, so you can feel the edges and surfaces in detail. After a few seconds, you perceive, correctly, that the object is a plastic cube, like a die. Describe the different types of tactile and proprioceptive perceptions that you've combined to produce this haptic perception.

12.20 Cross out the incorrect choices in parentheses: An ampulla containing a (crista / macula) is at the base of each (semicircular canal / otolith organ). The otolith organs consist of the (utricle / macula / saccule), each of which contains a (utricle / macula / saccule). Hair cells reside in the (crista / utricle / macula / saccule).

12.21 Hold your thumb up in front of you and move your head so that your nose traces a small circle in front of your face, while keeping your gaze fixed on your thumb. Describe how the vestibulo–ocular reflex accounts for your ability to do this.

APPLICATIONS Haptic Feedback in Robot-Assisted Surgery

Computers, video games, smartphones, and personal music players all have interface devices that allow the user to issue commands (by typing, by moving a mouse, or by using some other controller) and to receive feedback, which can be visual, auditory, or, increasingly, tactile. For example, some computer video games offer tactile and proprioceptive feedback, with vibration on joysticks or force feedback on steering wheels, simulating the "feel of the road" in racing games or providing a "jolt" when your virtual vehicle hits a virtual wall. All these forms of feedback can enrich the user's experience and provide a more complete sense of immersion in the activity, especially haptic feedback that results from the stimulation of both tactile and proprioceptive receptors. In surgery, however—unlike racing games—the presence or absence of haptic feedback can be a matter of actual, not virtual, life and death.

In traditional surgery, the surgeon makes a large incision in the skin to gain access to the interior of the body—whether to repair damage, remove diseased tissue, or replace an organ. The surgeon manipulates the surgical instruments, such as a scalpel and forceps, directly with her hands, which means that haptic feedback is a natural part of the experience of performing surgery. When she cuts a piece of tissue with a scalpel, the changes in the forces on the scalpel during the cut are transmitted through the scalpel's handle to her skin and ultimately to her brain, which combines the information in these tactile and proprioceptive signals into haptic perceptions that help the surgeon know, for example, when to stop applying force to the scalpel handle, so that she doesn't cut more tissue than she intends.

Since the mid-1980s, surgical practice has been transformed by the techniques of minimally invasive surgery (MIS)—also called *laparoscopic surgery*—in which a tiny incision is made in the skin, and small instruments mounted on long, thin shafts are inserted into the incision and guided to the appropriate location. Perhaps the most well-known form of MIS is arthroscopic surgery, which is frequently in the news when it's used to repair problems in knee, shoulder, and other joints of injured athletes. One advantage of MIS over traditional surgery is that the external incision is much smaller than in traditional surgery, resulting in much less trauma to the patient and, often, more rapid recovery.

Over the last decade, some hospitals have begun to employ robot-assisted minimally invasive surgery (RMIS), in which remotely controlled robotic sensors and manipulators are used to visualize and perform surgical procedures. The advantages of RMIS can include improved dexterity (the surgeon is no longer trying to physically manipulate an instrument at the end of a long handle), the ability to reach areas inside the body that are inaccessible to traditional laparoscopic instruments, and reduction in hand tremor (Hager et al., 2008). But an obvious potential disadvantage is the complete absence of haptic feedback, because the surgeon never touches the surgical instruments; instead, the surgeon uses handles (manipulators) that are connected to computer-run sensors that translate the surgeon's movements into motion commands that are sent to one or more robot arms controlling the surgical instruments within the patient.

To overcome this disadvantage, RMIS systems are being developed that provide haptic feedback via specialized sensors mounted on the surgical instruments (Hannaford & Okamura, 2008), as illustrated in Figure 12.22. In such systems, the forces encountered

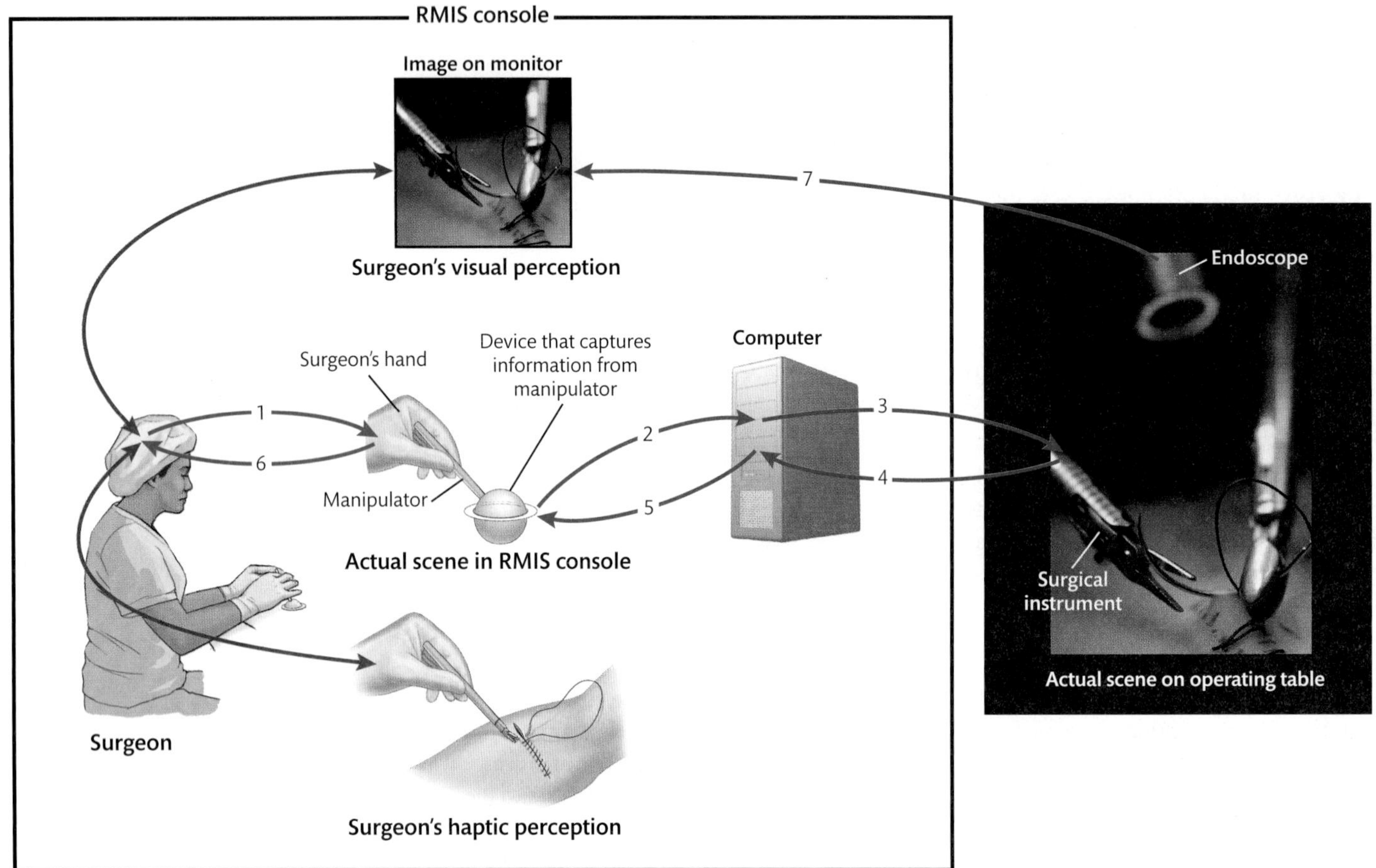

Figure 12.22 An RMIS System with Haptic Feedback (1) Movement commands are sent from the surgeon's brain to the surgeon's hand, which grasps and moves a manipulator, which is attached to a device that measures its position and orientation and the forces applied to it by the surgeon. (2) Signals with this information are sent to a computer, which translates them into (3) movement commands sent to a robotic arm controlling the actual surgical instrument. The robotic arm moves the surgical instrument in the same way that the surgeon's hand moves the manipulator. Sensors mounted on the robotic arm and on the surgical instrument register the forces exerted on the instrument by the surfaces it contacts, as well as the physical properties of those surfaces, such as hardness and texture. (4) Signals with information from these sensors are sent back to the computer, which translates them into (5) commands to the device connected to the manipulator and commands to sensors within the manipulator. These commands cause the device to exert forces on the manipulator corresponding to the forces exerted on the surgical instrument and cause the sensors within the manipulator to respond in ways that correspond to the physical properties of the surfaces encountered by the surgical instrument (e.g., by vibrating at a rate that corresponds to the texture of a surface). The forces exerted on the manipulator and the responses of the sensors are registered by receptors (mechanoreceptors, muscle spindles, etc.) in the surgeon's hand and arm. (6) Signals from these receptors travel to the surgeon's brain, which combines them into a haptic perception, giving the surgeon the experience of directly manipulating the actual surgical instrument. At the same time, (7) images taken by an endoscope are displayed on a monitor, giving the surgeon a 3-D view of the surgical field. The surgeon's brain integrates the visual and haptic perceptions into a precise understanding of the actual surgical situation, which the surgeon uses to modify (1) the movement commands sent to her hand, recommencing the cycle. In an actual surgical situation, the surgeon would use her two hands to control the two instruments and her feet to control the endoscope. (Adapted from Hannaford & Okamura, 2008, Figure 30.1, and Hager et al., 2008, Figure 3.) [Mark Harmel FAP/Alamy]

by the instruments—as well as the physical properties of the surfaces in contact with the instruments—are sensed and transmitted back to the manipulator, where they can be experienced by the surgeon. In principle, any property of the surfaces encountered by the surgical instrument could be conveyed to the surgeon—not only the positions of surfaces, but also their texture, their hardness, and even their temperature—as long as the right types of sensors are mounted on the surgical instrument.

The presence of haptic feedback is critical for certain surgical procedures, where the surgeon must apply precisely calibrated forces, as in the following examples:

- If the surgeon has to cut through cartilage, some extra force may be required to accomplish the cut, but the force must be removed immediately upon completing the cut, to avoid cutting into adjoining tissue. In this case, visual feedback is useful—the surgeon can see where her scalpel blade is—but the surgeon also needs rich haptic feedback to feel precisely how the forces she's exerting on the scalpel have to be increased, lessened, or redirected.
- If the surgeon has to grasp a piece of tissue with forceps, she must apply enough force to maintain a firm grasp but not enough to cause damage, and here again haptic feedback is vital and visual feedback much less useful.
- If the surgeon has to tie a secure knot in a suture, the knot must be tight but not too tight. A force sensor can measure the force with which the threads of the suture are being pulled by robotically controlled forceps, and that force can be indicated with colors on a visual display (e.g., blue means too loose, red too tight, and green just right).

In a study of the effectiveness of haptic feedback in RMIS, two groups of surgeons were asked to perform a cannulation—that is, to insert one tube into another—either with or without haptic feedback from grippers with force sensors attached to the grippers' jaws (Wagner & Howe, 2007). One of the groups was experienced in RMIS (but without haptic feedback), while the other wasn't. Both groups performed the task more accurately with haptic feedback, but the inexperienced group took significantly longer to perform the task with haptic feedback than without—possibly indicating that although haptic feedback from an RMIS system does indeed lead to better surgical performance, it takes some getting used to.

Engineers who are working to develop haptic sensors for RMIS face many challenges (Okamura, 2009): the sensors must be small enough and the right shape to be usable in surgery; they must be sterilizable; they must provide realistic and rapid feedback (long delays for computer processing can make feedback useless or even detrimental); and of course, cost is always a factor. Most applications of haptic feedback in RMIS are still in the development phase. Engineers and physicians are working together to find the best methods for providing haptic feedback and for training surgeons to use the feedback effectively.

Check Your Understanding

12.22 In traditional surgery, as well as in laparoscopic surgery, the surgeon naturally receives haptic feedback, but there is no haptic feedback in robot-assisted minimally invasive surgery (RMIS) unless special sensors provide it. What accounts for this difference?

12.23 Briefly explain why surgeons need haptic feedback.

SUMMARY

- Tactile Perception: Perceiving Mechanical Stimulation of the Skin Tactile perception results from the mechanical deformation of the skin. The skin contains mechanoreceptors, which transduce skin deformations into neural signals sent to the brain. The four main types of mechanoreceptors are divided into two kinds, slow adapting (SA) and fast adapting (FA), and each kind is divided into two types—SAI and SAII, and FAI and FAII—and each type supports different functions. SAI mechanoreceptors support detailed perception of spatial patterns, textures, and surface curvatures. FAI mechanoreceptors support the perception of slip across the skin and the maintenance of grip control. SAII mechanoreceptors support the perception of hand conformation. FAII mechanoreceptors support the perception of fine textures through transmitted vibration. In addition, there are C-tactile mechanoreceptors, which support perception of pleasant or pleasurable skin stimulation.

- Proprioception: Perceiving Position and Movement of the Limbs Proprioception is the perception of the position and movement of body parts—most importantly, the limbs—based on the information in neural signals from specialized sensors within those body parts. These sensors include muscle spindles, Golgi tendon organs, and joint receptors, with the most important information coming from muscle spindles.
- Nociception: Perceiving Pain Nociceptive pain—pain that arises from tissue damage due to physical trauma—is detected by nociceptors, which transduce the traumatic physical stimuli into neural signals. After injury, sensitization decreases the threshold at which nociceptors respond, so that even very low level stimulation of the injury site can cause pain. There are two types of nociceptors—A-delta fibers, which produce a rapid response to potentially damaging stimuli, and C fibers, which produce a slower response to a wide range of painful stimuli.
- Thermoreception: Perceiving Temperature Thermoreceptors detect temperatures within the range of about 17–43°C. Warm fibers fire at an ongoing moderate rate in response to sustained skin temperatures of 29–43°C; if the skin is abruptly warmed, the firing rate of warm fibers increases. Cold fibers fire at an ongoing moderate rate in response to sustained skin temperatures of 17–40°C; if the skin is abruptly cooled, the firing rate of cold fibers increases. Both types of fibers adapt after several seconds.
- Between Body and Brain Within the spinal cord and into the brain, sensory signals follow two different pathways—the dorsal column–medial lemniscal pathway for signals involved in tactile perception and proprioception, and the spinothalamic pathway for signals involved in nociception and thermoreception. Both pathways go through the ventral posterior nucleus of the thalamus on their way to the somatosensory cortex, which is organized into a somatotopic map of the body surface. The somatosensory cortex consists of two main subregions, area S1 and area S2. Many S1 neurons are tuned to a specific orientation and a specific direction of motion of tactile stimuli. Many S2 neurons are tuned to the orientation of an edge pressed against the skin on multiple fingers. From area S1, signals travel along a dorsal pathway (which carries information used to guide actions that require tactile and proprioceptive input) and a ventral pathway (which carries information used in perceiving and remembering object shape and identity). Nociceptive signals carry information about two different dimensions of pain perception—discriminative perceptions (for locating and classifying the pain) and affective perceptions (unpleasant emotional and physical perceptions that motivate the person to make the pain stop). Top-down feedback causes the release of endogenous opioids, such as endorphins, which reduce sensitivity to pain. Other top-down effects, based on attention and expectations, can also lessen the experience of pain. Adult cortical plasticity can account for the experience of a phantom limb. Plasticity also arises as a result of experience.
- Haptic Perception: Perceiving Objects by Touch Haptic perception involves the integration of information from tactile perception, proprioception, and thermoreception. People typically move their hands and fingers in different types of exploratory procedures to acquire different kinds of information about an object. Studies of people with tactile agnosia have strongly suggested that area S2 is crucially involved in haptic perception.
- The Vestibular System: Perceiving Balance and Acceleration The vestibular system, which consists of the semicircular canals and the otolith organs, is responsible for our sense of balance and acceleration. Hair cells within these organs produce the neural signals carrying information about how the head and body are oriented and moving, and these signals are used to keep the body in balance. Neural signals from hair cells flow to vestibular nuclei in the vestibular complex in the brain stem, which also receive signals from the visual system, the system for eye movements, and the motor systems for neck movements. Signals from the vestibular nuclei are involved in controlling eye movements in order to maintain a stable gaze. The vestibulo–ocular reflex is the unconscious compensating movement of the eyes during head movements.
- Applications: Haptic Feedback in Robot-Assisted Surgery In traditional surgery, the surgeon manipulates the surgical instruments directly, and naturally receives haptic feedback from the instruments. In robot-assisted minimally invasive surgery (RMIS), however, the surgeon never touches the surgical instruments, so there is a complete absence of haptic feedback. RMIS systems are being developed that provide haptic feedback via specialized sensors mounted on the surgical instruments. Haptic feedback is critical for surgical procedures where the surgeon must apply precisely calibrated forces.

KEY TERMS

A-delta fibers (p. 400)
C fibers (p. 400)
cold fibers (p. 401)
cortical plasticity (p. 414)
C-tactile mechanoreceptors (CT mechanoreceptors) (p. 397)
dorsal column–medial lemniscal pathway (DCML pathway) (p. 404)
endogenous opioids (p. 413)
endorphins (p. 413)
exploratory procedures (EPs) (p. 417)
FAI mechanoreceptors (p. 389)
FAII mechanoreceptors (p. 389)
Golgi tendon organs (p. 398)
haptic perception (p. 416)
joint receptors (p. 398)
mechanoreceptors (p. 388)
Meissner corpuscles (p. 389)
Merkel cells (p. 389)
muscle spindles (p. 398)
nociception (p. 400)
nociceptive pain (p. 400)
nociceptors (p. 400)
otolith organs (p. 420)

EXPAND YOUR UNDERSTANDING

12.1 In Table 12.1, you can see that the slow-adapting mechanoreceptors have low sensitivity to temporal variation and that the fast-adapting mechanoreceptors have medium or high sensitivity to temporal variation. Explain why.

12.2 The two-point threshold of the tip of the tongue isn't indicated in Figure 12.2. Do you think the tip of the tongue would have a high or low two-point threshold? Explain why.

12.3 Cross out the incorrect choices in parentheses: When you accidentally touch a red-hot coal, (warm fibers / A-delta fibers) respond with signals that lead to an immediate, sharp sensation of pain that makes you pull your hand away; then, the responses of (C fibers / cold fibers) lead to a prolonged sensation of pain. For days afterward, the burned area of skin hurts a lot if it's just very lightly touched or even if sunlight hits it directly—this phenomenon, which is called (analgesia / sensitization), results from a lowered response threshold of the (nociceptors / thermoreceptors) in the burned area.

12.4 Suppose that you break a small rough branch off a dead tree and are holding it in your right hand and that someone then pulls it out of your hand, leaving you with a painful splinter in your index finger. Which types of sensory receptors provide which kinds of information about this experience, from the moment you grab the branch to break it off to the moment you realize you have a painful splinter in your index finger? Which areas of your brain are involved in processing this information?

12.5 Suppose you're walking with a close friend who trips and skins her knee. When you see the bloody scrape, you cringe empathetically and can almost feel her pain. Are you having an affective or discriminative perception of pain? Then you realize that her injury looks fairly serious and that she should be taken to an emergency room, and you experience an immediate lessening of your empathic pain as you focus on dealing with the situation. Describe at least two top-down mechanisms that might be responsible for this reduction in your empathic pain.

12.6 Do you think that someone born without a right arm could experience the missing arm as a phantom limb? Explain why or why not.

12.7 Suppose you were blindfolded and wearing earplugs, and someone put the object pictured below on a table in front of you so you could touch it, pick it up, and try to determine what it is. Which of the exploratory procedures illustrated in Figure 12.20 would be useful in this task, and what kinds of information would you get from each procedure?

[Laurie Stephens/Dreamstime.com]

12.8 Standing up in front of your desk, touch the tip of your nose with your left thumb. Then put your left hand on the desktop with your thumb sticking up, bend over, and put the tip of your nose against your thumb. Which types of sensory receptors give you the same information during the two actions, and what is that information? Which types of sensory receptors give you information that lets you perceive which of the two actions you're executing, and what is that information?

READ MORE ABOUT IT

Goldberg, J. M., Wilson, V. J., Cullen, K. E., Angelaki, D. E., Broussard, D. M., Büttner-Ennever, J. A., Fukushima, K., & Minor, L. B. (2012). *The vestibular system: A sixth sense.* New York: Oxford University Press.

A detailed and comprehensive review of the functional anatomy, physiology, and clinical disorders of the vestibular system and how it supports the perception of head position, motion, and acceleration.

Johnson, K. O. (2002). Neural basis of haptic perception. In H. Pashler (Series Ed.) & S. Yantis (Vol. Ed.), *Stevens' handbook of experimental psychology: Vol. 1. Sensation and perception* (3rd ed., pp. 537–583). New York: Wiley.

A systematic review of the physiological foundations of tactile perception by one of the seminal figures in this field.

McMahon, S., & Koltzenburg, M. (2005). *Wall and Melzack's textbook of pain* (5th ed.). Edinburgh: Elsevier/Churchill Livingstone.

A comprehensive overview of the neurobiology of pain, the diverse types of pain, and the clinical assessment and treatment of pain.

Pam Ingalls, *Clink*, 2008. [Oil on board, 10 x 8 inches. © Pam Ingalls.]

13

THE CHEMICAL SENSES: PERCEIVING ODORS AND TASTES

Chapter Outline

When the Nose Knows Nothing

One afternoon in 2003, a 34-year-old New York City attorney whom we'll call B. was in the passenger seat of her best friend's car. Just as she was leaning forward to change the radio station, a delivery truck ran a red light and collided with the car. B's forehead hit the dashboard violently and she lost consciousness. When she awoke in the hospital, she learned that she had suffered a concussion. Her neurologist told her that an MRI of her brain hadn't revealed any significant damage, and after conducting several neurological tests, he declared that B. had been very lucky to escape the collision with no major ill effects. B. was relieved but troubled—something seemed not quite right, but she couldn't put her finger on it.

After B. was released from the hospital, a couple of her friends came to her apartment to prepare a comforting dinner of lasagna, accompanied by a bottle of B.'s favorite wine; they even brought a loaf of freshly baked bread, still warm from the oven. It was only when B. sniffed the wine that she realized what was wrong: she couldn't smell the wine's fragrance. The aroma of dinner cooking in the kitchen was absent, as was the odor of the fresh bread. B. had lost her sense of smell.

When B.'s head hit the dashboard, thousands of tiny nerve fibers connecting neurons in her nose to structures in her brain were severed, leading to total loss of her sense of smell, a condition known as *anosmia*. Not only that, but her ability to taste her favorite foods was nearly gone, too, because—as we'll see in this chapter—the perception of flavor is strongly influenced by our sense of smell. She found this condition deeply depressing. Things that had been important parts of her personal life—good food and fine wine—no longer brought her pleasure. Even her morning espresso was mostly just bitter. Her friends tried to console her, pointing out that she might have lost her hearing or eyesight, or even her life—but B. was not so sure it was a good deal.

One afternoon about three years later, as B. was walking from the subway to her apartment, she passed a small Italian restaurant where she had eaten frequently before her accident. Suddenly, she experienced the aroma of sautéed garlic. She was thrilled, and the memory of that moment stayed with her the rest of the day. Over the coming weeks, she found that her ability to smell certain odors was coming back to her, one odor at a time. An orange. Baby powder. Baking bread. With each new aroma, B. found her world expanding, enriching, as if she were slowly regaining the ability to see colors after seeing everything in black and white. The neurons in her nose were reconnecting with her brain, and she was beginning to feel whole again.

The senses we've discussed previously are based on the transduction of light (photons absorbed by rods and cones in the visual system) or on the transduction of mechanical forces (forces that bend the stereocilia of hair cells in the auditory system and vestibular system, forces that displace skin and other tissues in the somatosensory system). Now we turn our attention to the senses of smell (olfaction) and taste (gustation), both of which are based on the transduction of molecules in the air we breathe or in the food and liquids we ingest. Whether you're smelling a rose, tasting ice cream, or using both senses to fully appreciate a glass of wine, transduction occurs when molecules activate receptors in the nose or mouth, resulting in neural activity that evokes the subjective experience of an odor or a taste.

The chemical senses are among the most phylogenetically ancient of the senses (Hodos & Butler, 1997). Many of the earliest animals relied on smell for survival—before vision or hearing had evolved—and many animals still do today, even many that also possess the more "recent" senses. Humans use smell—and to a lesser extent, taste—to detect hazardous environmental conditions, such as bad air or spoiled food, as well as to identify nutritious food (Stevenson, 2010). In addition, many organisms, possibly including humans, use smell to recognize others and, in some cases, to select mates.

The chemical senses are often relegated to "second class" status compared to vision, audition, and the body senses. Indeed, the American Medical Association (2008) guidelines for assessing permanent impairments state that complete loss of the sense of smell is equivalent to a 3% impairment of a whole person, compared to a 35% impairment for a complete loss of hearing and an 85% impairment for a complete loss of vision. And almost everyone would say that, if they had to choose, they would prefer to lose their sense of smell or taste than to become deaf or blind. Yet, the chemical senses can hardly be considered "minor." Not only are they crucial to individual and group survival, but they also lend a significant richness to life. The importance of that richness can be seen in the energy we devote to seeking out certain smells and tastes, from expensive perfumes to great wines to decadent chocolates—and as suggested by the vignette at the beginning of this chapter, the loss of that richness can lead to serious depression (Stevenson, 2010).

Over the last century, the amount of research devoted to vision, hearing, and touch has dwarfed the amount devoted to the chemical senses. However, recent advances have greatly increased our understanding of how the chemical senses work. In particular, the discovery of the gene family that governs the development and functioning of olfactory receptors (Buck & Axel, 1991) provided a basis for the use of new techniques in molecular biology and cellular imaging to make unprecedented advances in uncovering the neural code for smell.

In this chapter, we'll examine the ability to detect, discriminate, and identify different odors and tastes. We'll consider how prolonged exposure to an odor leads to adaptation—that is, a reduction in the perceived intensity of the odor. We'll take a detailed look at how smells and tastes are encoded by specialized receptors and how odor and taste perceptions are represented in the brain. We'll also explore some of the fascinating relationships between odor, memory, and emotion; individual differences in odor and taste perception; and the interaction of smell and taste to produce flavors.

Perceiving Odors

Our sense of smell lets us perceive odors, but what is an odor? In this section, we'll begin by answering that question and then consider how much of an odor must be present to be detected and identified, and then how we "get used to" odors and become virtually unaware that they're still present. We'll also review the basic anatomy of our olfactory system, in the nose and in the brain, and we'll see that, unlike the other senses, olfaction is based on the responses from a very large variety of receptors—about 350 different receptor types, in contrast to the four receptor types that enable vision (rods and three types of cones), the two types that enable audition (inner and outer hair cells), and the dozen or so types that underlie the body senses. We'll see how olfactory receptors encode odors, how signals from receptors are organized, and where in the brain those signals are sent.

Then we'll end by considering some of the more cognitive, emotional, and behavioral aspects of odor perception—how odors are learned rapidly, producing long-lasting and vivid memories and powerfully motivating emotional responses, and how individual animals, perhaps including humans, produce odors that can motivate specific behaviors by other individuals of the same species.

What Is an Odor?

Many substances, particularly organic substances, and probably all terrestrial plants and animals emit molecules that mix with air at normal environmental temperatures. If we draw these molecules into our nose when we inhale, bringing them into contact with our olfactory receptors, we may perceive an odor, depending on whether two conditions are met: first, the molecules must be **odorants**—that is, the kinds of molecules that our olfactory receptors can "recognize" and respond to; and second, the molecules must be present at a great enough concentration to evoke a response. Figure 13.1 illustrates the enormous variety of things that emit odorants we can smell.

odorants Molecules that olfactory receptors "recognize" and respond to by producing neural signals that the brain represents as perceptions of different odors.

molecule Two or more atoms bound together by electromagnetic forces.

A **molecule** consists of two or more atoms that are bound together by the electromagnetic forces between them—for example, two atoms of hydrogen bound to one atom of oxygen make a molecule of water (H_2O). Of course, the number of atoms in a molecule can vary widely—from two, as in carbon monoxide (CO), which consists of one atom of carbon bound to one atom of oxygen, to hundreds of millions or even billions, as in DNA—and the 3-D shapes of molecules are equally varied, depending on how the electromagnetic forces interact.

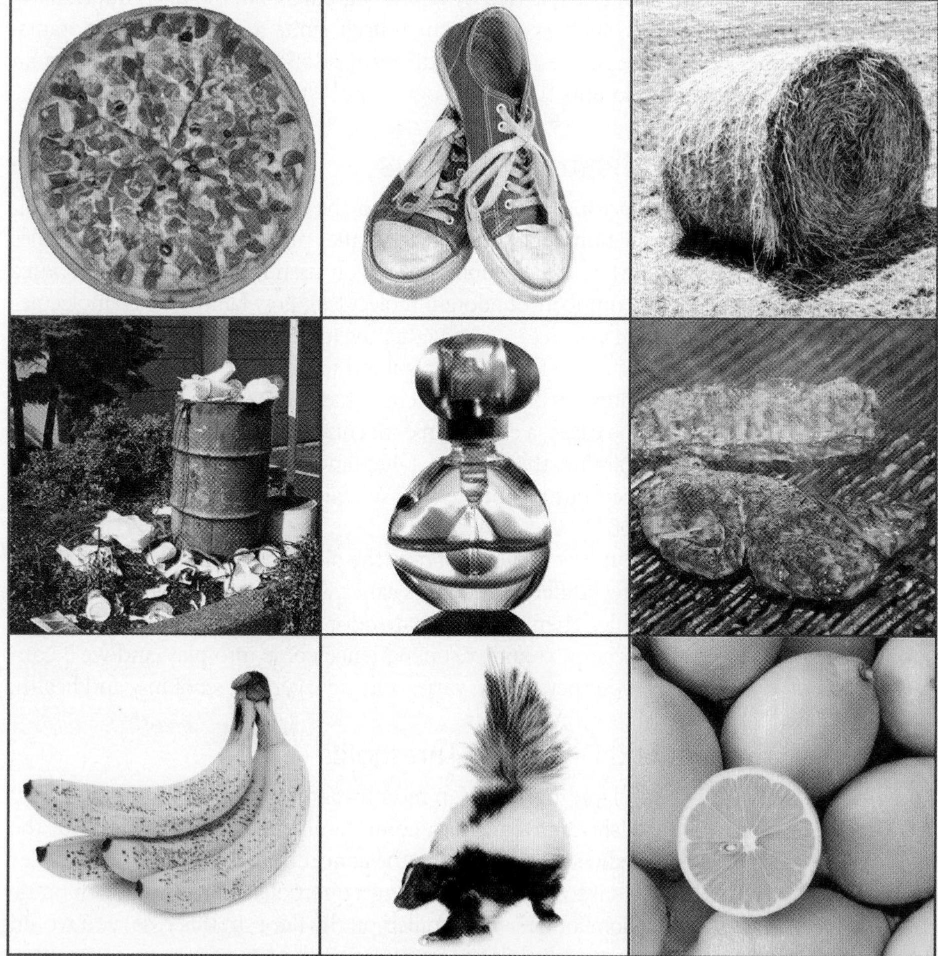

Figure 13.1 Some Common Sources of Odorants Food, animals, plants, natural landscapes, and many other kinds of things emit odorants that we can detect and recognize. [See copyright page for photo credits]

Animals can smell the odorant molecules that their evolutionary ancestors needed to smell in order to survive and reproduce, such as the molecules given off by food and, in many species, the molecules given off by potential mates. Odorants also include the molecules given off by potentially toxic substances. For example, when meat decomposes, the amino acids in the meat break down, and molecules are emitted that have (for us) a putrid smell that we find disgusting; this smell provides a strong warning signal, leading us to avoid eating decomposing meat and the toxic bacteria it may contain.

Thus, just as in vision and audition, where only some wavelengths and frequencies are detectable, in olfaction only some molecules are detectable—and these capabilities are largely determined by the conditions under which different organisms evolved. For humans, most odorant molecules are made up of combinations of just five kinds of atoms—carbon, hydrogen, oxygen, nitrogen, and sulfur—but there are, of course, vast numbers of ways these atoms can be combined to produce different molecules. Contrary to what you might expect, however, odorant molecules with similar molecular structures can smell very different, and odorants with very different structures can smell almost the same (Laing et al., 2003).

Any given environment typically contains a mixture of many different odorant molecules. Indeed, even a single source, such as a rose, typically emits hundreds of different odorants, some of which are more important than others to the overall odor perceived. To get a sense of what's meant by "overall odor," consider this common experience: You're preparing dinner in your kitchen, with multiple dishes cooking simultaneously, and each dish (and perhaps each individual ingredient in each dish) is giving off multiple different odorant molecules. Yet, you can somehow pick out not only the distinctive smell of each dish (the overall smell of all the odorants released by all the ingredients in the dish) but also the smell of individual ingredients, such as garlic, which itself emits many different odorants. Clearly, we are able to organize the vast array of different odorants typically present in an environment into groups of odorants that we recognize as belonging to different sources.

Detection and Identification of Odors

As mentioned before, a crucial factor in detecting an odor is the concentration of odorant molecules, typically measured as the number of odorant molecules present in 1 million molecules of air, or parts per million (ppm). Concentration depends on such factors as what the source is (some sources give off greater numbers of odorant molecules); how far away it is (molecules disperse as they travel away from a source); and whether the molecules are confined to a small space, as in a kitchen, or are floating in the open air, subject to dispersal by the wind.

In general, the perceived intensity of an odor increases as the concentration of the odorant molecules increases. In some cases, a change in concentration can also affect the quality of an odor. In one study, for example, the odorant 1-heptanol was described as *sweet, light,* and *medicinal* at very low concentrations, but as *oily, sickening,* and *dirty linen* at very high concentrations (Laing et al., 2003).

In this section, we'll start our investigation of how the olfactory system works by examining how people's ability to detect different odorants varies with concentration and with the structure of the odorant molecule. Then we'll compare odor detection with odor identification, to see how factors such as context and past experience come into play, and we'll conclude with a brief look at how odor perception varies with age, gender, smoking, and health.

Detection Thresholds and Difference Thresholds

Which smells stronger, menthol (an ingredient in mouthwashes and many other medicinal products) or acetone (nail polish remover)? Both compounds have a sharp odor, but the question can't really be answered without specifying the concentration. To see why, consider the following scenario: You walk into a room containing a quart of acetone in an open bottle and an ounce of menthol that someone has just spilled on the floor. In this case, you would detect a strong odor of menthol and little of acetone. But if the situation were reversed—a quart of menthol in an open bottle and an ounce of acetone spilled on the floor—your perception would also be reversed: a strong odor of acetone and little of menthol. Clearly, more of the spilled substance than of the bottled substance escapes into the air where you can detect it. So, to really see which substance smells stronger, you'd have to make sure you were smelling the same amount of each—that is, you'd have to make sure the two substances were at the same concentration.

The "strength" of an odorant is described in terms of its **detection threshold**, the concentration necessary for a person to detect the odorant, say, 75% of the time. An odorant's detection threshold is determined by having a participant sniff two equal volumes of air, one containing an odorless substance (e.g., the vapor given off by distilled water) and the other containing the target odorant at a given concentration (repeated across a range of different concentrations). The participant must choose which of the two samples contains the odorant and might be asked to make 10 or 20 judgments at each concentration. Chance performance in this case would be 50% correct: if the concentration is below threshold, performance will be near chance. Generally, as the concentration increases, the proportion of correct responses also increases, and the concentration that leads to a predetermined performance level (e.g., 75% correct) is defined as the participant's detection threshold for that substance. In this type of experiment, the air samples are delivered to the participant by an olfactometer, as illustrated in Figure 13.2.

Figure 13.2 Measuring Olfactory Detection Thresholds An olfactometer delivers samples of clear, humidified air containing either a calibrated amount of an odorant or no odorant at all. The participant must decide which sample contains the odorant. [Dr. Suresh Relwani/R&K Associates]

detection threshold The concentration of an odorant (or tastant) necessary for a person to detect it.

As shown in Table 13.1, different odorants can have very different detection thresholds (averaged across participants). For example, the threshold for acetone (15 ppm) is 375 times the threshold for menthol (0.04 ppm), which is itself 121 times the threshold for *t*-butyl mercaptan (0.00033 ppm)—this very low threshold makes *t*-butyl mercaptan well suited for adding to natural gas so people can easily detect even small gas leaks.

The detection threshold tells us the just-detectable concentration of a substance, but it doesn't tell us by how much the concentration must change to make a just noticeable difference (JND). Early studies suggested that the olfactory difference threshold was quite high—that is, that the concentration of an odorant had to change substantially before people noticed a difference in the intensity of its odor—but these studies suffered from poor control over odorant concentration (Dalton, 2002). More carefully controlled studies have revealed difference thresholds as low as 5% for some odorants—that is, if such an odorant is presented at a concentration of 10 ppm and then at various slightly higher or slightly lower concentrations, people will, on average, reliably notice a difference when the concentration is at least 5% higher (i.e., at 10.5 ppm or greater in this example) or at least 5% lower (i.e., at 9.5 ppm or less). Thus, at a concentration of 10 ppm, the JND is about 0.5 ppm (5% of

TABLE 13.1 Absolute Detection Threshold for Various Odorants

Substance	Description	Threshold in Air (ppm)
Vanillin	Flavoring extracted from vanilla bean	0.000035
t-butyl mercaptan	Added to natural gas to aid in detection of leaks	0.00033
Hydrogen sulfide	Colorless, poisonous, flammable gas	0.017
Menthol	Active ingredient in various medicinal compounds	0.04
Camphor	Active ingredient in various medicinal compounds	0.05
Chlorine	Disinfectant	0.50
Formaldehyde	Disinfectant and embalming agent	0.87
Isopropyl alcohol	Solvent and cleaning fluid	10
Acetone	Nail polish remover	15
Methanol	Antifreeze and solvent	141

Data from Devos et al. (1990).

10), while at a concentration of 1 ppm, the JND is about 0.05 ppm (5% of 1). The fact that the difference threshold is typically a fixed proportion—in this case, 5%—of the odorant concentration is another example of Weber's law (see Chapter 1): at low concentrations, a very small difference in concentration is detectable, but at high concentrations, a larger change is required to make a detectable difference.

Identifying and Discriminating Odors

Try this: Pick a food with a very familiar, very noticeable odor, such as peanut butter, and put some on a spoon. Then ask a friend to close his eyes and keep them closed while you put something under his nose for him to sniff. (Don't tell him that the "something" is food.) After he sniffs the food, ask him if he can tell you what it is. If you do this a few times with a few different foods and a few different friends, you and your friends will be surprised by how often they fail to identify the food correctly, or even to identify it as some kind of food. This will confirm what various properly controlled studies have shown: When people are presented with an odor out of context—that is, without any information that would help them determine even what *kind* of odor it is—their ability to identify even familiar odors is quite poor (Cain, 1979; Herz & Engen, 1996).

However, if you try the same "experiment" again, but this time give people choices and ask them to select the right one—for example, "Is this leather, banana, gasoline, or peanut butter?"—you'll find that their performance will often be perfect, as long as their sense of smell isn't impaired in some way, as by a stuffed nose from a head cold. And once again, this confirms what's been shown by properly controlled studies (Stevenson, 2010).

Giving people choices to select from provides very specific contextual information: the person knows that the odor is one of the choices. But even when it's not so specific, context tends to generate expectations that usually help us identify odors. For example, when you're in a kitchen, your expectations about what you might smell are different from your expectations when you're walking in a park in early spring, and these expectations affect your ability to identify odors—that is, when you're in a kitchen, you'll likely be much better at identifying food-related smells than park-related smells, and vice versa when you're in a park.

Furthermore, the ability to identify odors, as well as the ability to discriminate between similar odors, depends not just on context but also on training and experience. This can be seen in the case of professional wine tasters, who may spend many years developing their ability to identify very subtle components in the complex mixture of odors in wine, as well as their ability to discriminate between very similar smelling wines. Typically, an experienced wine taster trying to identify a wine on the basis of its odor will begin by sniffing the wine in order to categorize it at a fairly coarse level—red versus white, pinot noir versus cabernet sauvignon—and then perhaps by country and region of origin, by vineyard, and by vintage. At that point, the taster can focus her olfactory attention on even more subtle variations in odor that may allow her to identify the specific wine or at least narrow the possibilities to a few very similar wines.

These abilities may partly derive from wine tasters' practice of giving names to the component odors in a wine, to mark their similarity to other, already familiar odors, such as *lead pencil, straw, grass,* and *leather*—undoubtedly, this practice gives structure to what otherwise could be a rather vague and jumbled olfactory perception. Professional wine tasters are also better than nonprofessionals at identifying and discriminating the odors of substances other than wine, such as lemon, pine needle, and anise (Bende & Nordin, 1997), suggesting that their olfactory expertise is not domain specific. This raises the question of whether professional wine tasters are better than nonexperts at the task of merely detecting the presence of odorants.

This question was addressed in a study that examined the ability of wine experts and wine novices to detect a non–wine-related odorant and their ability to discriminate, remember, and identify wine-related odorants (Parr et al., 2002). Experts were defined as people who were established winemakers, wine researchers, and/or wine professionals (wine writers, judges, or retailers). Novices were defined as people who regularly drank wine but had no specialized training. The results showed that there was no difference in absolute detection threshold for the expert and novice groups. The story was different, however, when the experts and novices were asked to discriminate, remember, and identify different wine-related odors—in this case, the experts performed significantly better than the novices.

Olfactory Impairments: Age and Other Factors

Olfactory performance declines with age, just as performance declines with age in all the other senses. In one study of age and olfaction, almost 2,000 people were tested for their ability to identify a wide range of 40 odors using the University of Pennsylvania Smell Identification Test, or UPSIT (Doty et al., 1984). Each odorant was embedded in a "scratch and sniff" pad; after sniffing an odorant, the participant had to select from four written choices to identify the odor. A perfect score would be 40; random guessing would, on average, yield a score of 10. "Normal" was defined as a score of 35 or greater. As shown in Figure 13.3a, average performance was consistently normal for healthy adults aged 20–60, with small decrements in performance (on average) beginning to appear around age 60, followed by dramatic decreases after age 70; overall, women perform better than men. A score of 18 or lower is the criterion for clinical **anosmia**—the loss of smell—and Figure 13.3a shows that it isn't until the ninth decade of life that men (but not women) tend to show that degree of impairment.

anosmia Loss of the ability to perceive odors.

Figure 13.3b shows the results of a study of olfaction and cigarette smoking, in relation to the amount and duration of smoking and the number of years, if any, since the person quit smoking (Frye et al., 1990). As you can see, smokers on average suffer from a decline in olfactory performance that increases with the number of pack-years; however, once people quit smoking, olfactory performance tends to recover, with the degree of recovery increasing over time.

Of course, olfactory impairments can have many different causes in addition to cigarette smoking. Congenital anosmia is often associated with deformed or absent olfactory bulbs (Yousem et al., 1996), the first brain areas to receive olfactory signals from the nose. Many diseases and clinical syndromes—including schizophrenia, Alzheimer's disease, Parkinson's disease, Down syndrome, and others—are associated with impairments in the ability to identify smells (Doty, 2001), whereas many other diseases have no effect on olfaction. In some cases, diseases that otherwise have some similar symptoms (e.g., Alzheimer's disease and major depression) may differ in their effects on olfaction, providing an additional basis for diagnosis (McCaffrey et al., 2000). Among older adults, loss

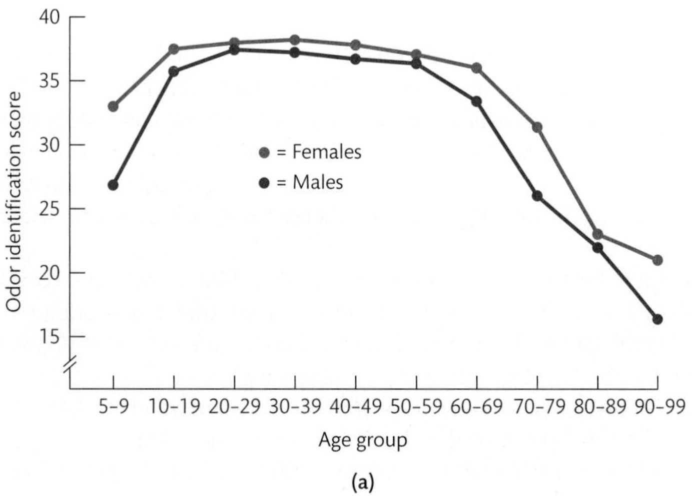

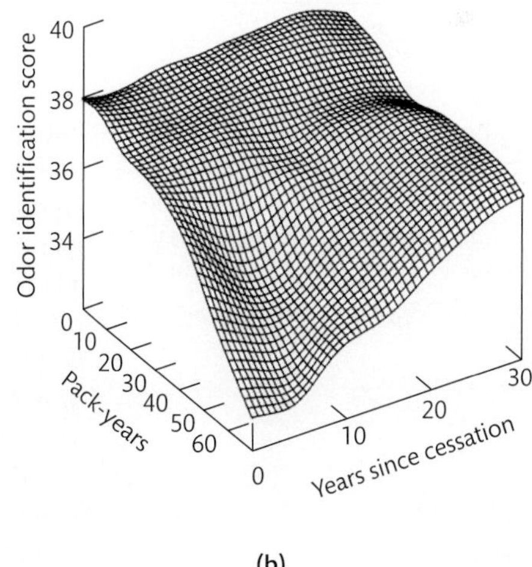

Figure 13.3 Changes in Odor Identification Ability with Age and Smoking In both parts of this figure, odor identification ability was scored using the University of Pennsylvania Smell Identification Test (UPSIT). The maximum possible score is 40, and pure guessing would produce a score of about 10. A score between 35 and 40 is considered normal, and a score of 18 or less is considered the clinical criterion for total anosmia, or a complete lack of smell. (a) Throughout the life span, females tend to have higher odor identification scores than males. For both groups, scores rise to normal during the second decade (ages 10–19), remain there through the seventh decade (ages 60–69), and, by the eighth decade (ages 70–79), decline steeply. (Adapted from Doty et al., 1984, Figure 1.) (b) This graph shows that odor identification scores tend to decline steadily the more people smoke and the longer they smoke ("pack-years" is the number of packs of cigarettes smoked per day multiplied by the number of years of smoking at that rate), but that scores tend to rise again over time after people quit smoking ("years since cessation" is the number of years since the last cigarette was smoked). (Adapted and graph from Frye et al., 1990, Figure 2.)

of the ability to identify smells can sometimes predict cognitive decline more accurately than can scores on cognitive tests (Graves et al., 1999).

In the vignette that opened this chapter, we learned about another possible cause of olfactory impairment: injury to the anatomical structures that support olfaction. Happily for B., who eventually recovered her sense of smell, the olfactory system is remarkably self-healing. Studies carried out in mice and rats have shown that when receptor neurons in the nose are damaged, they degenerate over a period of several days. However, stem cells in the nose soon become new receptor neurons that reconnect the nose to the brain (Cummings et al., 2000).

A rare genetic mutation that leads to an inability to experience pain also leads to anosmia in humans and mice (Weiss et al., 2011). People with this mutation report that they cannot smell either pleasant or unpleasant odors, and they perform at chance levels on the UPSIT. Mice that have been bred without the associated gene fail to engage in any odor-guided behaviors—they don't approach food odors or avoid predator odors, and newborn pups don't exhibit suckling behavior.

Adaptation to Odors

We have all had the experience of walking by a bakery and smelling the wonderful aroma of freshly baked bread—indeed, many bakeries make a point of venting some of that aroma onto the sidewalk outside their shops to attract customers. The next time this happens to you, enter the bakery. At first, you'll continue to enjoy the smell of the bread, and your digestive system might even gear up for a quick purchase that can be rapidly ingested. But even as your eyes scan the shelves, you'll notice that the intensity of the smell is fading. You are adapting, and quickly, to the odor of the bread.

Like all senses, olfaction is especially sensitive to change, for the same reason as the other senses: organisms must rapidly detect the presence of something new, orient to that new thing, and decide what to do about it. Smell is an early warning system for things both seen and unseen—this is why gazelles orient to the odor of an African lion and why lions approach gazelle herds from the downwind direction. But once a smell has been continuously present for a while, or repeatedly present over a short period of time, it has most likely already been identified, evaluated, and, if necessary, responded to. The organism no longer needs to perceive the smell in order to assess the current situation. Indeed, by adapting to the smell, so that it's no longer perceived, the organism is better prepared to detect new smells, because the background of odors is relatively clear.

Not only does continuing or repeated exposure to an odor result in reduced sensitivity (adaptation) to that same odor, but it can also result in reduced sensitivity to other, similar odors—a phenomenon called **cross-adaptation.** Figure 13.4 is based on a study that reveals both adaptation and cross-adaptation: a rat is put into a chamber in which a vial containing an odorant has been placed; the rat naturally investigates (sniffs) the vial, and the experimenter measures how long the investigation lasts (Cleland et al., 2002). Figure 13.4a reveals adaptation: when the experimental procedure is repeated five times with the same odorant (the adapted odorant), the rat's investigation time declines from about 10 seconds on the first trial to less than 4 seconds on the fifth trial. On the sixth trial, a new odorant (the test odorant) is placed in the chamber, and the rat's investigation time goes back up to about 10 seconds, showing that the adaptation is specific to the adapted odorant.

cross-adaptation In olfaction, reduced sensitivity to odorants that are chemically or perceptually similar to odorants to which the person has been continuously or repeatedly exposed.

Figure 13.4b reveals cross-adaptation. After the rat is adapted to acetic acid (the adapted odorant), the rat is put into the chamber with a vial containing one of five test odorants or a control odorant. The test odorant is either acetic acid itself or one of four other acids with molecular structures that are nearly identical to the structure of acetic acid, differing only in the length of the carbon chain. The control odorant is *n*-amyl acetate, a nonacid with a very different type of molecular structure. (A carbon chain is a sequence of chemically bonded carbon atoms to which other atoms can attach in various ways to form different types of molecules.)

The investigation times shown for the test odorants in Figure 13.4b are thought to reflect the degree of perceptual similarity between the adapted odorant and each test odorant: investigation time is greatest for test odorants that are most dissimilar to the adapted odorant. The fact that investigation time increases with the difference in carbon chain length

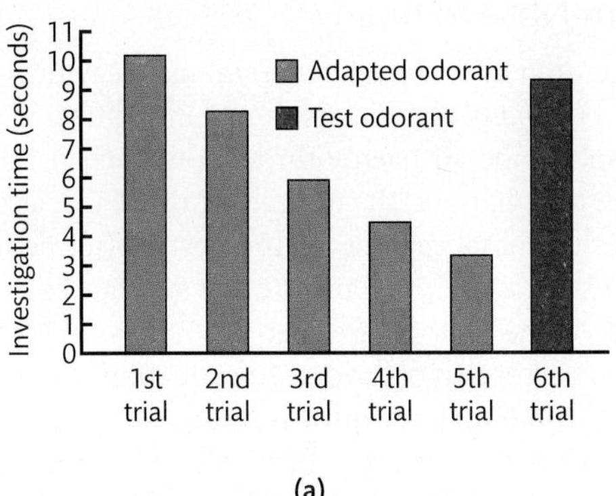

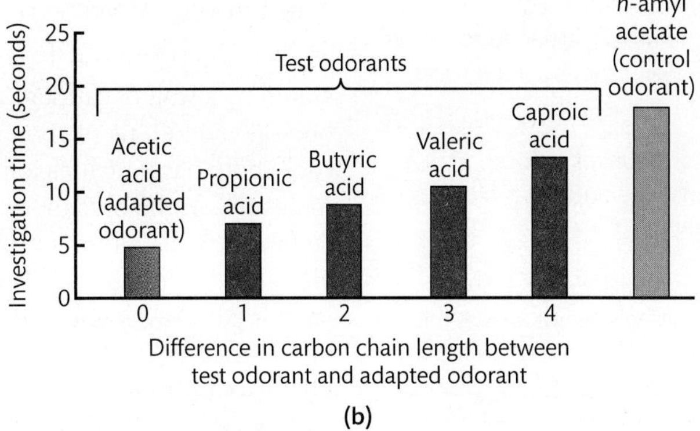

Figure 13.4 Olfactory Adaptation and Cross-Adaptation A rat is placed in a chamber with a vial containing an odorant, and the experimenter records the rat's investigation time (amount of time spent sniffing the vial). (a) To demonstrate adaptation, the rat is put into the chamber with a vial of the same odorant (the adapted odorant) on five consecutive trials, and the rat's investigation time decreases from about 10 seconds on the first trial to less than 4 seconds on the fifth trial. On the sixth trial, a vial with a different odorant (the test odorant) is in the chamber, and the investigation time is again about 10 seconds, showing that the decline in investigation time is specific to the adapted odorant. (b) To demonstrate cross-adaptation, the rat is first adapted to acetic acid (the adapted odorant). Then the rat's investigation time is measured for five different test odorants (including acetic acid itself) that differ only in the length of the carbon chain. Investigation time increases as the difference in carbon chain length increases, and investigation time is even greater for a control odorant with a very dissimilar molecular structure (*n*-amyl acetate). (Adapted from Cleland et al., 2002.)

suggests that this physical property of the molecules is at least partly responsible for perceptual similarity.

Although this seems like a nice, simple story, it turns out to be a little too simple. A study with human participants has demonstrated cross-adaptation between some perceptually similar odorants but not between others, despite similarity in molecular structure; furthermore, there are many situations in which two odorants that are perceptually very dissimilar can nevertheless produce cross-adaptation (Stevenson & Boakes, 2003). These findings confirm a point made earlier: there is no simple relationship between the molecular structure of an odorant and the perceived odor—a fact that has been a source of consternation to olfactory scientists, and perfume makers, for decades—and perceptually dissimilar odors can evoke responses suggesting that the odors are somehow similar.

Check Your Understanding

13.1 What are the two factors that determine whether a particular type of molecule will evoke a response in a normally functioning olfactory system?

13.2 If two odorants were present in an environment at equal concentrations, which would a person be more likely to perceive: **(A)** the odorant with the higher detection threshold or **(B)** the odorant with the lower detection threshold?

13.3 Which choice(s) would make the following statement false? Training and experience help people (detect / identify / remember / discriminate) odors.

13.4 True or false? People who smoke heavily for 10 years or more, even if they then quit, typically suffer severe, permanent olfactory impairments.

13.5 Odor A and odor B are similar. After repeated exposure to odor A, a person has trouble perceiving either odor. Does this illustrate adaptation, cross-adaptation, both, or neither?

Anatomical and Neural Basis of Odor Perception

Odor perception begins in the nose, which funnels stimuli to the neurons responsible for transduction. In olfaction, the stimuli are odorant molecules, and the neurons that transduce them are located near the most environmentally exposed part of your brain.

turbinates Bony convolutions of tissue protruding into the nasal cavities, functioning to disperse air evenly throughout the nasal cavities.

olfactory receptor neurons (ORNs) Neurons that transduce odorant molecules into neural signals.

olfactory epithelium A patch of tissue in the upper reaches of each nasal cavity; the epithelium contains ORNs and is covered by a layer of olfactory mucus.

Demonstration 13.1 Functional Anatomy of the Olfactory System Interact with depictions of the structures and pathways involved in olfactory perception.

The Olfactory System: From Nose to Brain

The left and right nostrils are the entrances to the left and right nasal cavities, which are separated by a wall of cartilage called the *nasal septum* . As shown in Figure 13.5a, **turbinates,** bony convolutions of tissue, disperse the air evenly throughout each nasal cavity. At the back, both nasal cavities join with the pharynx (the upper part of the throat); thus, odorant molecules in the outside air enter the nasal cavities via the nostrils (termed the *orthonasal pathway*), while odorant molecules released from food or other substances in the oral cavity are carried into the nasal cavities via the pharynx (termed the *retronasal pathway;* olfaction via this pathway is essential for the perception of flavor). Transduction of odorant molecules into neural signals is carried out by **olfactory receptor neurons (ORNs)** embedded in the **olfactory epithelium,** a patch of tissue with an area of about 2 cm^2 in the upper reaches of each nasal cavity, a few centimeters behind each eye (see Figure 13.5a).

As illustrated in Figure 13.5b, the olfactory epithelium contains supporting cells, basal cells, and Bowman's glands, in addition to ORNs. The supporting cells provide a structural matrix for the ORNs. Each ORN dies after a few weeks and is replaced by a new ORN; basal cells are the precursors of new ORNs. Bowman's glands continually secrete mucus, which covers the olfactory epithelium. The mucus flows toward the back of the nasal cavity and into the pharynx, and then is swallowed (the mucus is completely regenerated about every 10 minutes). This process effectively washes out odorant molecules from the epithelium, which otherwise could create a problem by continuing to stimulate odor perceptions after the sources of the molecules are no longer present in the environment (Dalton, 2002). In addition, the mucus layer provides a barrier against irritants and against harmful microorganisms that might otherwise penetrate into the central nervous system.

olfactory receptors G-protein coupled receptors in the cilia of ORNs.

G-protein coupled receptors (GPCRs) A large family of proteins that function as receptors; they provide a mechanism for molecules outside a cell to influence the inner workings of the cell.

olfactory nerve The axons of ORNs, carrying neural signals from ORNs to the olfactory bulb via tiny holes in the cribriform plate.

cribriform plate The part of the skull immediately above the nasal cavity; the axons of ORNs pass through a grid of tiny holes in the plate.

glomeruli Small, more or less spherical structures in the olfactory bulb; within the glomeruli, the axons of ORNs make synapses with the dendrites of mitral cells and tufted cells.

mitral cells Relay neurons within the glomeruli in the olfactory bulb; the axons of mitral cells and tufted cells form the olfactory tract.

tufted cells Relay neurons within the glomeruli in the olfactory bulb; the axons of tufted cells and mitral cells form the olfactory tract.

olfactory tract The axons of mitral cells and tufted cells, carrying neural signals from the olfactory bulb to higher areas of the brain.

Olfactory Transduction and the Large Variety of Olfactory Receptors Each ORN has numerous hairlike cilia, which project into the mucus layer. The enlargement in Figure 13.5b shows that the surface of each cilium is studded with **olfactory receptors** and that odorant molecules contact these receptors when they dissolve into and flow through the mucus. Olfactory receptors are members of the large family of **G-protein coupled receptors (GPCRs)**, which provide a mechanism for molecules outside a cell to influence the inner workings of the cell. When an odorant molecule binds to an olfactory GPCR, ion channels in the ORN's cell membrane open, positively charged calcium and sodium ions enter the cell, and the cell membrane slightly depolarizes (Kleene, 2008; Schild & Restrepo, 1998). If odorant molecules bind to many receptors on an ORN's cilia at the same time, the cell membrane depolarizes enough to generate an action potential in the ORN's axon. This is the process by which odorant molecules at sufficient concentration are transduced into neural signals.

The axons of the ORNs form the **olfactory nerve.** As shown in Figure 13.5b, these axons travel to the olfactory bulb through a grid of tiny holes in the **cribriform plate,** the part of the skull immediately above the nasal cavity. Within the olfactory bulb, the ORN axons enter small, more or less spherical structures called **glomeruli** (singular *glomerulus*), where they make synapses with the dendrites of two types of relay neurons—**mitral cells** and **tufted cells**—the axons of which form the **olfactory tract**, carrying signals with olfactory information to higher areas of the brain.

Humans have approximately 350 different types of olfactory receptors (Buck, 2004); each type can be activated by only a restricted set of odorant molecules. Each ORN has only one type of receptor on its cilia (thus, there are also about 350 different types of ORNs). Humans have an estimated 10,000–20,000 of each type of ORN, for a total of about 3–7 million ORNs, which send their axons to about 5,000 glomeruli in the olfactory bulb. The 350 different receptor types involved in olfaction make a distinct contrast to the much more limited number of receptor types involved in the other senses—for example, just four types in vision (rods and three types of cones) and two types in audition (inner and outer hair cells).

Given that much of the important research on the neural basis of odor perception has been done with mice, it's interesting to compare the anatomy of the olfactory system in mice and humans. As in humans, each mouse ORN contains just one type of olfactory receptor on its cilia, but mice have about 1,100 different types of olfactory receptors (and ORNs).

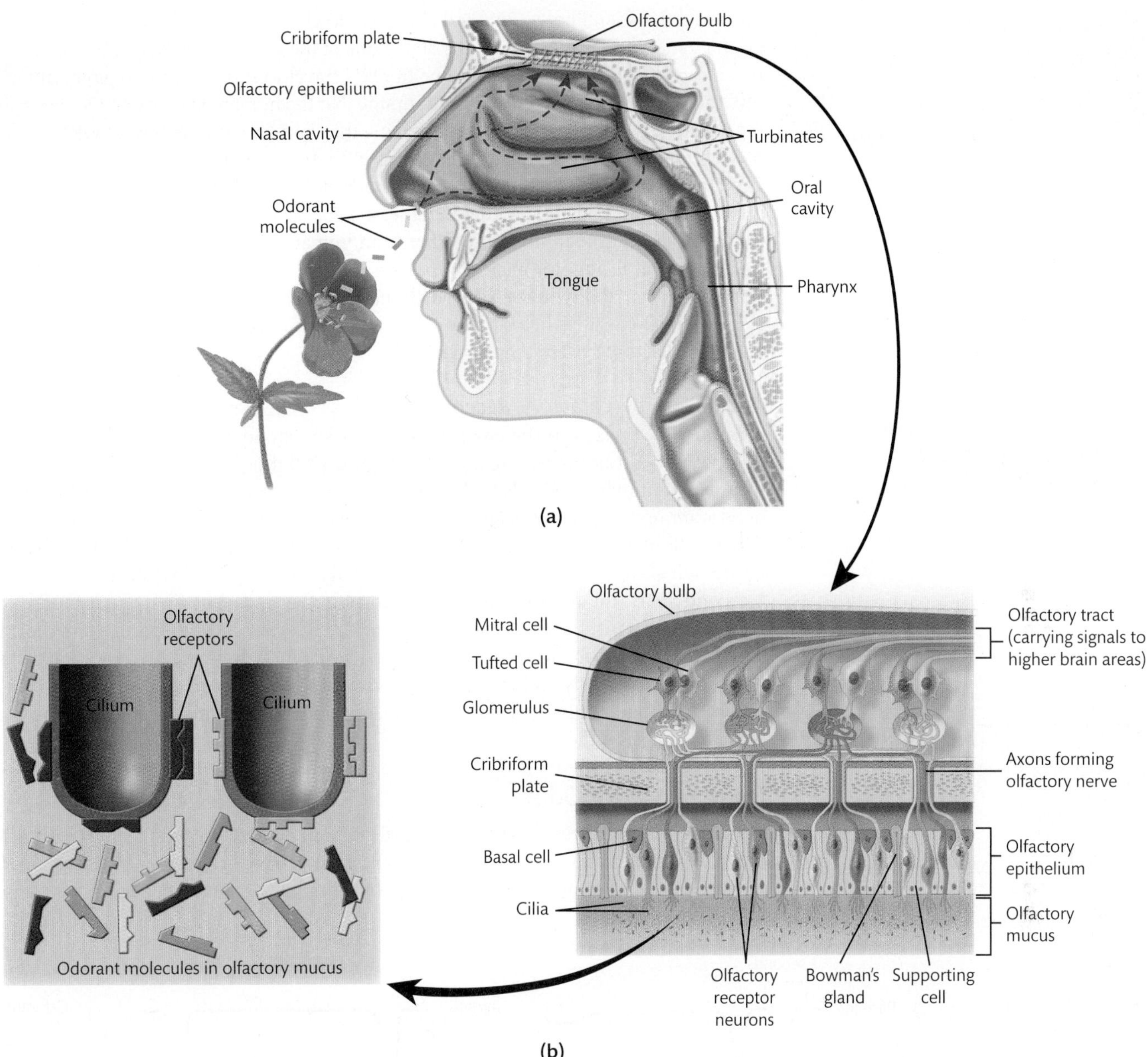

Figure 13.5 **Anatomy of the Olfactory System** (a) A front view showing how the nasal septum divides the nasal cavity into left and right halves, into which air enters through the left and right nostrils. The turbinates—bone covered with epithelial tissue—protrude into the nasal cavity. (b) Odorant molecules in the air enter the nasal cavity when the person inhales or sniffs (odorant molecules released from food or other substances in the mouth enter the nasal cavity via the pharynx). Olfaction begins when odorant molecules reach the olfactory epithelium, at the top of the nasal cavity. (c) The cell bodies of olfactory receptor neurons (ORNs) are embedded in the olfactory epithelium, which also contains supporting cells, basal cells, and Bowman's glands. ORNs have hairlike cilia that project into the olfactory mucus, a protective lining on the olfactory epithelium. The cilia have olfactory receptors on their cell membrane (as shown in the enlargement at left); transduction takes place when odorant molecules bind to olfactory receptors. The ORNs' axons, which together constitute the olfactory nerve, pass through holes in the cribriform plate and enter small structures called *glomeruli* within the olfactory bulb. Each glomerulus receives the axons of a single ORN type. Within the glomeruli, the ORN axons make synapses with mitral cells and tufted cells, and the axons of these cells form the olfactory tract, carrying signals with olfactory information to higher areas of the brain.

Mice have 10–20 million ORNs and about 1,800 glomeruli in each olfactory bulb and any given glomerulus receives the axons of just one of the approximately 1,100 types of ORNs; this means that the axons of each type of ORN travel to just one or two glomeruli in each olfactory bulb (Maresh et al., 2008). Assuming that the human olfactory system has a similar organization, with each glomerulus receiving the axons of just one type of ORN, the axons of each type of ORN in humans would travel to 10–20 glomeruli in each olfactory bulb. Despite these anatomical differences, it's widely accepted that the rodent olfactory system provides a good functional model for at least some aspects of the human system.

Animals other than mice also differ from humans with respect to the total number of ORNs. A typical dog, for example, possesses some 1 billion ORNs—and bloodhounds, known for their ability to track by smell, have as many as 4 billion. This difference in the sheer number of ORNs helps explain why some animals possess a much more exquisitely sensitive olfactory system than others.

Adaptation by Olfactory Receptor Neurons As discussed earlier, when an odor is continuously present in the environment over an extended period of time, we adapt to it—that is, we stop perceiving the odor. Figure 13.6 illustrates how adaptation works at the level of individual ORNs (Takeuchi et al., 2003). An ORN's response to brief pulses of odorant molecules is measured by the decrease in membrane potential from baseline, which reflects the rate at which the ORN transduces the odorant molecules. The graph on the left shows that, when an ORN is stimulated by two pulses of the same odorant 1 second apart, the response to the second pulse is much less than the response to the first pulse—that is, the ORN has adapted to the odorant and barely registers the stimulation, meaning that the rate of transduction declines dramatically. The graph on the right shows that ORNs recover relatively quickly from this adaptation—when the two pulses are separated by 5 seconds, the response to the second pulse is almost as great as the response to the first.

Neural Code for Odor

The 2004 Nobel Prize in Physiology or Medicine went to the American neuroscientists Richard Axel and Linda Buck for their work on the genetic basis of olfactory transduction (Buck & Axel, 1991). They discovered the family of genes that express the GPCRs that transduce

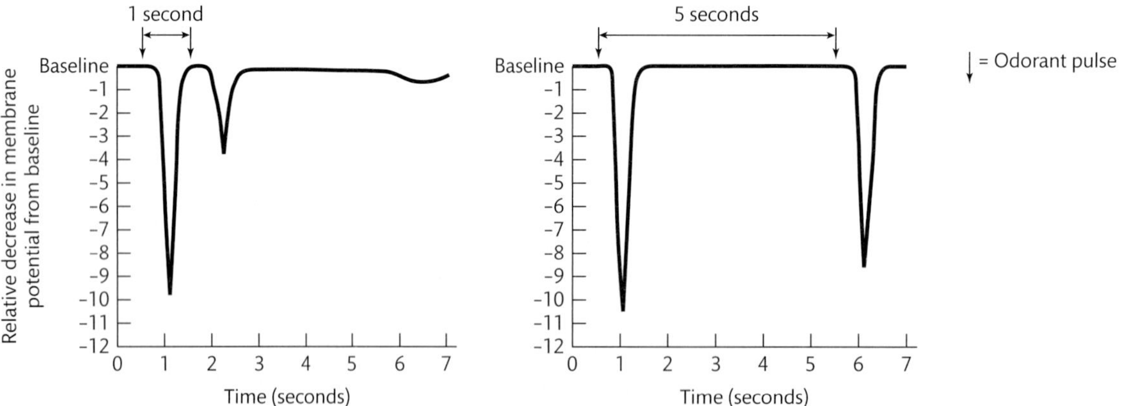

Figure 13.6 **Adaptation by Olfactory Receptor Neurons** These two graphs illustrate olfactory adaptation in single ORNs of the newt, in response to two brief pulses (each lasting 0.01 second) of the same odorant. Adaptation to the first pulse is indicated by the ORN's response to the second pulse, measured by the size of the decrease in membrane potential. (left) When the pulses come 1 second apart, the decrease in membrane potential in response to the second pulse is only a third the size of the decrease in response to the first pulse, showing significant adaptation. (right) When the pulses come 5 seconds apart, the response to the second pulse is almost as great as the response to the first pulse, showing that individual ORNs recover relatively quickly from adaptation. (Adapted from Takeuchi et al., 2003, Figure 6.)

odorants in the cell membranes of ORNs. About 1,000 genes are devoted to the genetic code for our approximately 350 different receptor types (Malnic et al., 1999), a surprisingly large proportion—an estimated 4%—of the entire human genome (which consists of some 24,000 genes). It was this seminal discovery by Buck and Axel that led to subsequent breakthroughs in our understanding of the neural code for odors.

Richard Axel (b. 1946) and Linda B. Buck (b. 1947). [Don Hamerman/CUMC/Sipa Press/Newscom]

How many different odorants can humans discriminate? Despite frequently cited estimates of 10,000–100,000 or more, nobody really knows the answer to this question (Gilbert, 2008), but the number is clearly in the thousands. This raises another question: How is this large array of odorants encoded by the 350 or so different types of ORNs? Obviously, it can't be that each type of odorant molecule binds to a single type of ORN and that a response by that ORN type indicates the presence of that odorant—this sort of one-to-one scheme won't work because it predicts that only 350 different odorants could be discriminated. Something more complex is needed.

A hint as to what this might be comes from the way color is coded by the visual system. Recall from Chapter 5 that the visual system uses a population code to discriminate a very large number of different wavelengths of light based on the responses of only three types of cones. The key to this trichromatic system is that each type of cone is quite broadly tuned, but the spectral sensitivity functions of the three cone types are different from each other—that is, each type responds to a wide range of wavelengths, but the three types tend to respond at different levels to any given wavelength. This allows for a unique pattern of response to each of a great many different wavelengths.

Olfaction also uses a population code, but one based on the responses of about 350 different types of ORNs, in contrast to the three types of cones involved in color vision. The increased number of receptor types means that each type can be relatively narrowly tuned to respond to only a few different odorant molecules.

Much of what is known in detail about olfactory encoding comes from studies of mice and rats, but there is good reason to believe that the findings from these studies also apply to other mammals, including humans (Mombaerts, 2004). Figure 13.7 shows some of the results of one such experiment (Malnic et al., 1999). Olfactory receptor neurons were exposed to two different odorant molecules in each of four different chemical families (indicated by the different background colors), and the responses of individual ORNs were measured to determine which ORNs responded to which odorants.

Two complementary findings emerged from this procedure: any given odorant molecule evoked a response from some ORNs but not from others, and any given ORN might respond strongly to some odorant molecules, weakly to others, and not at all to still others. For example, none of the odorant molecules shown in Figure 13.7 evoked a response from more than 8 of the 11 ORNs, and none of the ORNs responded to more than 7 of the 8 odorant molecules.

These results indicate that odorant molecules of a specific type activate a specific subset of the 350 different types of ORNs. Odorant molecules of a different type activate

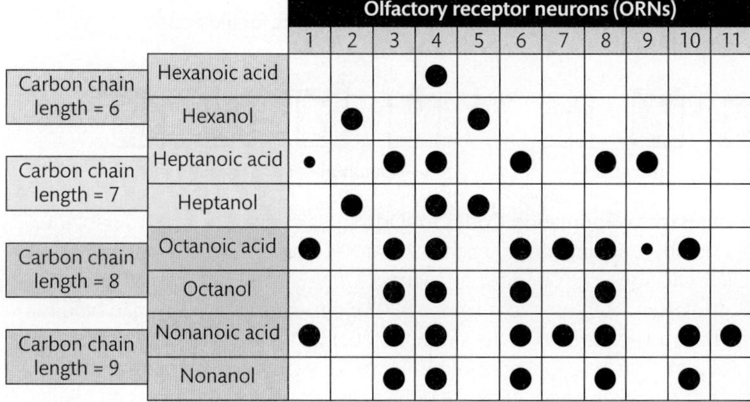

		Olfactory receptor neurons (ORNs)										
		1	2	3	4	5	6	7	8	9	10	11
Carbon chain length = 6	Hexanoic acid				●							
	Hexanol		●			●						
Carbon chain length = 7	Heptanoic acid	•		●	●		●		●	●		
	Heptanol		●		●	●						
Carbon chain length = 8	Octanoic acid	●		●	●		●	●	●	•	●	
	Octanol			●	●		●		●			
Carbon chain length = 9	Nonanoic acid	●		●	●		●	●	●		●	●
	Nonanol			●	●		●		●		●	

Figure 13.7 Population Code for Odor This shows the responses of 11 different mouse ORNs that were exposed to pairs of odorants from four different chemical families (corresponding to carbon chain length). The pattern of ORN responses evoked by an odorant constitutes a population code for that odorant. The members of each pair have similar molecular structures, but their population codes are different, so it's likely that mice would perceive them as smelling quite different. (Adapted from Malnic et al., 1999, Figures 1, 6, and 7.)

a different subset. The *pattern* of ORN responses—that is, the particular subset of ORN types activated and the relative strength of their responses—determines how that odorant smells.

Figure 13.7 also shows that these patterns of ORN responses can be quite different for odorant molecules that are structurally similar. The two odorants in each pair have similar molecular structures, with the same carbon chain length, yet they evoke responses in distinct subsets of ORNs—compare, for example, nonanoic acid, which evokes responses from ORNs 1, 3, 4, 6, 7, 8, 10, and 11, and nonanol, which evokes responses from ORNs 3, 4, 6, 8, and 10. This helps explain why odorants with similar molecular structures can smell very different from one another.

Figure 13.8 provides a schematic model of how this type of population coding for odor is thought to work at the molecular level. Each of the eight types of odorant molecules has certain specific features, represented by the colored shapes. Each of the four types of ORNs responds when molecules with particular features bind to their receptors, represented by the shapes of their indentations. As you can see, even this tiny array of ORNs can respond in enough different patterns to uniquely encode the presence of each of the eight different odorants (in fact, four ORN types could encode 15 different odorants in this way). With 350 different ORN types, a population code based, say, on responses by just four ORN types per odorant (as in Figure 13.8), would be sufficiently powerful to encode almost 15 billion different odorants (Malnic et al., 1999)—and

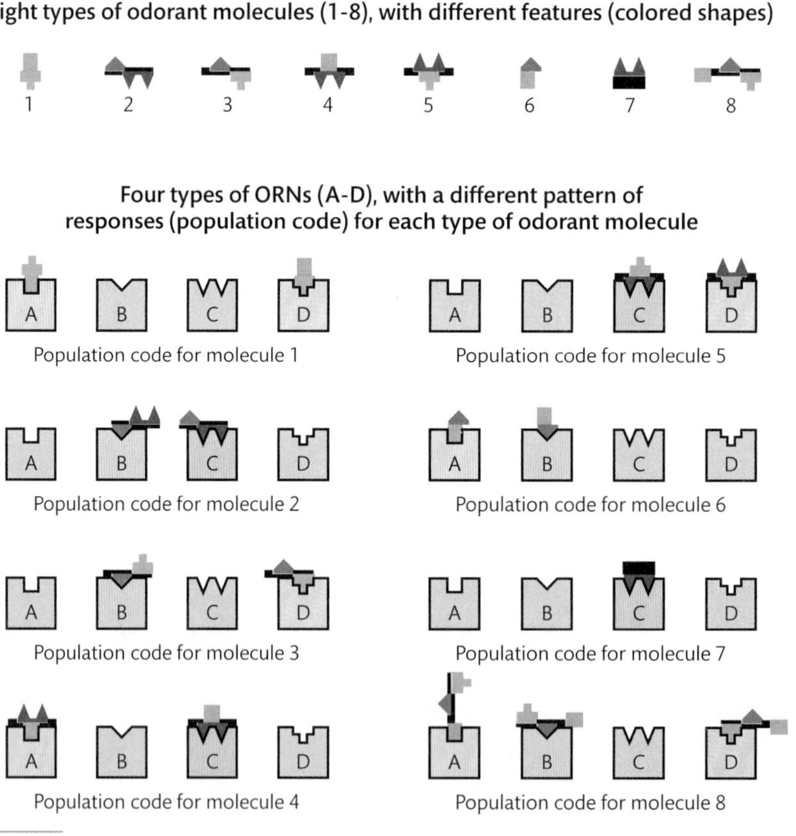

Figure 13.8 Molecular Basis of Population Codes for Odors Eight different types of odorant molecules are distinguished by combinations of chemical features (colored shapes) that can bind to (fit into) the receptors (indentations) on four different types of ORNs. Molecule 8 can bind to three of the four ORN types, Molecule 7 can bind to only one ORN type, and all the others can bind to two ORN types, but no two molecules bind to the same subset of ORNs. In this simple model, there are only eight molecules, with from one to three chemical features each, and just four types of ORNs. In reality, we have about 350 types of ORNs, and there are thousands of odorant molecules with a very large number of feature combinations. (Adapted from Malnic et al., 1999, Figure 8.)

this number would be even greater if the code also took into account differences in the strength of the ORN responses.

As previously noted, each glomerulus within the mouse olfactory bulb receives the axons of just one type of ORN; thus, the population code for each particular odorant, based on a unique pattern of responses across all the different ORN types, is maintained within the bulb. This is illustrated in Figure 13.9a, which shows the activity of mitral and tufted cells in the mouse olfactory bulb when mice were exposed to four different odorants with similar molecular structures (Fletcher et al., 2009). Each odorant produces a characteristic pattern of responses within a subset of glomeruli in the olfactory bulb, and this pattern is sent to higher areas of the brain via the tufted and mitral cell axons, which together form the olfactory tract.

Some odorants smell very different at low concentrations than at high concentrations—for example, thioterpineol, which is typically described as *tropical fruit* at low to moderate concentrations, is often described as *stench* at very high concentrations. This change in odor quality can be seen in the pattern of ORN responses in the olfactory bulb. For example, Figure 13.9b shows that an odorant at a very low concentration of 0.13% evoked relatively weak responses from relatively few mitral and tufted cells, but at higher concentrations of 1% and of 10%, the same odorant evoked progressively stronger responses from much greater numbers of cells.

The distribution of glomeruli in the olfactory bulb isn't random; rather, this distribution exhibits a coarse chemotopy (Johnson & Leon, 2007): the axons of ORNs activated by odorants with similar molecular structures tend to travel to glomeruli in the same part of the olfactory bulb, and conversely, glomeruli in different parts of the bulb tend to receive the axons of ORNs activated by odorants with different molecular structures.

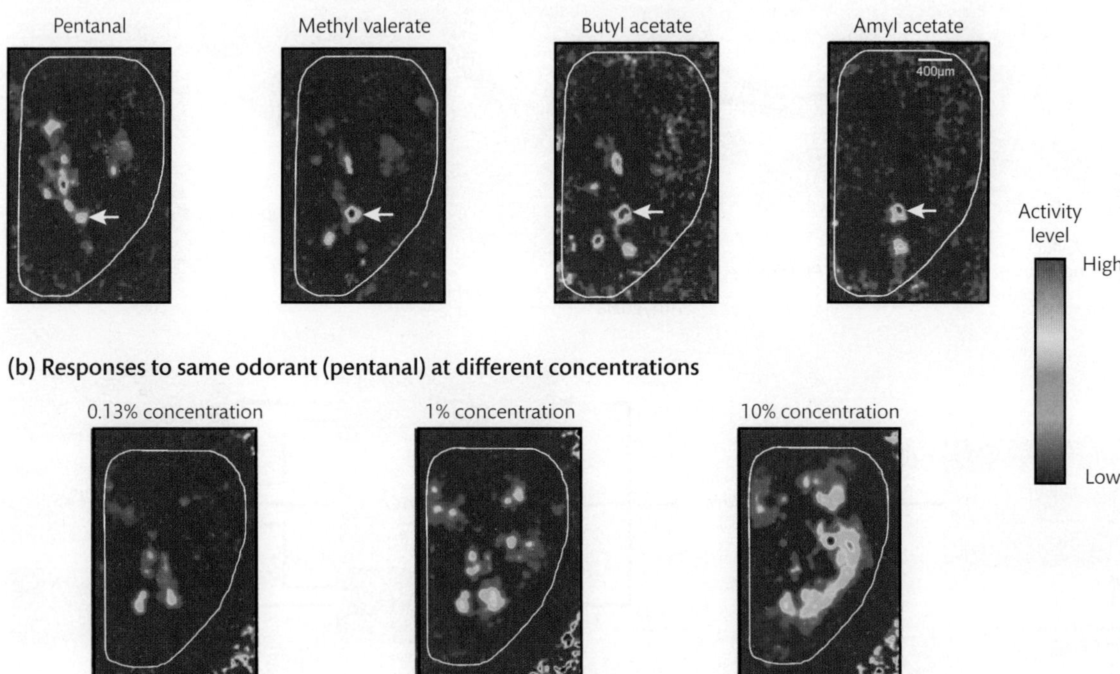

Figure 13.9 **Patterns of Activation in the Olfactory Bulb** (a) Optical imaging of mouse olfactory bulb shows regions of increased mitral cell and tufted cell activation in response to four different odorants with similar molecular structures (the molecules differed only in their carbon chain length). The white arrows point to the same location in each image, a location where the mitral and tufted cells responded to all four of the odorants. (b) Three different concentrations of the same odorant evoke different patterns of mitral cell and tufted cell activation—there is much more activation of mitral and tufted cells at the higher concentrations than at the lowest concentration. This helps explain why some odorants smell very different at low and high concentrations. (Adapted and photos from Fletcher et al., 2009, Figures 6B and 7A.)

Representing Odors in the Brain

piriform cortex The brain region considered to be the primary olfactory cortex, because it's the only region that both receives signals directly from the olfactory bulb and is known to be dedicated solely to olfaction.

The axons of mitral cells and tufted cells carry signals via the olfactory tract from the olfactory bulb to a number of brain regions, including the piriform cortex, the amygdala, and the entorhinal cortex (see Figure 13.10). The **piriform cortex**—the only region that both receives signals directly from the olfactory bulb and is known to be dedicated solely to olfaction—is considered the primary olfactory cortex (Yeshurun & Sobel, 2010). In contrast, the amygdala and entorhinal cortex are both involved in other functions in addition to olfaction (both receive signals from and send signals to many nonolfactory brain regions, as discussed below).

The amygdala is crucially involved in emotional responses (Zald, 2003) and can be activated by emotional stimuli across various sensory modalities, including by visual, auditory, and olfactory/gustatory stimuli (Costafreda et al., 2008). However, unpleasant

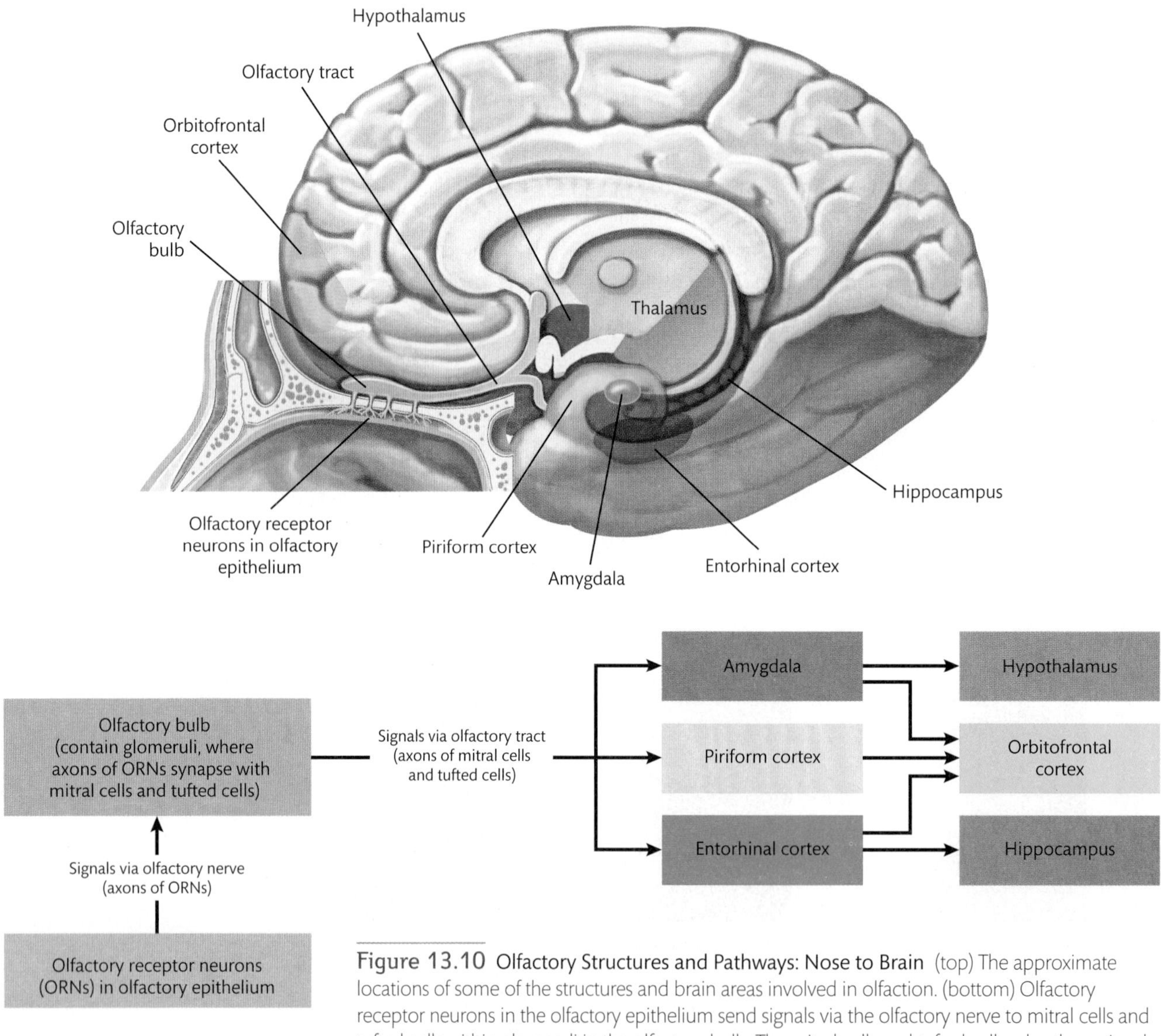

Figure 13.10 Olfactory Structures and Pathways: Nose to Brain (top) The approximate locations of some of the structures and brain areas involved in olfaction. (bottom) Olfactory receptor neurons in the olfactory epithelium send signals via the olfactory nerve to mitral cells and tufted cells within glomeruli in the olfactory bulb. The mitral cells and tufted cells relay these signals via the olfactory tract to the piriform cortex (the primary olfactory cortex), the amygdala (important for signaling emotional responses), and the entorhinal cortex. These regions all send signals to the orbitofrontal cortex. In addition, the amygdala sends signals to the hypothalamus, and the entorhinal cortex sends signals to the hippocampus (for memory storage).

and pleasant smells are more effective at activating this emotional center of the brain than are sights and sounds (Royet et al., 2000). The amygdala sends signals to the hypothalamus, an almond-sized region just below and in front of the thalamus. The hypothalamus is involved in a wide range of functions through the release of hormones and through neural activity, including the regulation of thirst, hunger, and sexual behavior. The entorhinal cortex is the gateway to the hippocampus, where long-term memories are stored and retrieved (Eichenbaum, 1998).

As shown in Figure 13.10, the piriform cortex, amygdala, and entorhinal cortex send signals to the orbitofrontal cortex, which, among other things, plays a role in evaluating incoming stimuli as positive or negative (i.e., rewarding or unpleasant). Interestingly, the olfactory system is the only sensory system in which the pathways from the sensory receptors to the cortex don't go through a nucleus within the thalamus—the visual pathway goes through the lateral geniculate nucleus, the auditory pathway goes through the medial geniculate body, and the somatosensory pathway goes through the ventral posterior nucleus. This is thought to reflect the fact that the olfactory system evolved first among the senses (Eisthen, 1997), and the thalamus didn't emerge as part of the sensory pathways until after the olfactory pathway was established.

Separate Cortical Representations of Odor Identity and Pleasantness The piriform cortex consists of two subdivisions that have different functions in olfaction (Kadohisa & Wilson, 2006a). The **anterior piriform cortex (APC)** represents features of the chemical structure of odorant molecules—for example, the length of the carbon chain, which, as we saw earlier, affects detection thresholds, cross-adaptation, and the perceptual similarity of odorants. Information about such features of odorants is analogous to information about the features of visual stimuli represented by neurons in area V1 of the visual system, such as the orientation of edges (see Chapter 3). APC neurons tend to be narrowly tuned, which means that odorant features are represented in fine enough detail to support odorant identification.

anterior piriform cortex (APC) The anterior (front) portion of the piriform cortex; it produces representations of features of the chemical structure of odorant molecules.

The **posterior piriform cortex (PPC),** in contrast, represents the quality of an odor as a whole, regardless of whether the odor is simple (resulting from the presence of just one type of odorant molecule) or complex (reflecting the presence of many different types of odorant molecules). For example, the PPC tells you that the odorant 1-heptanal smells oily while the odorant 1-heptanol has a citrus smell, or that the complex mix of odorants coming from the flower you're smelling has the odor of a rose. In effect, the PPC represents odors as "olfactory objects" that can be named and that have associated representations in long-term memory—analogous to the representation of visual objects in the lateral occipital cortex and inferotemporal cortex and their associated representations in memory (see Chapter 4).

posterior piriform cortex (PPC) The posterior (rear) portion of the piriform cortex; it produces representations of the quality of an odor as a whole, regardless of whether the odor is simple or complex.

Evidence for this distinction between the functions of the APC and the PPC in humans was provided by an fMRI study in which patterns of activity in four different olfactory brain regions were recorded while participants sniffed three odorants from each of three different odor categories—minty, woody, and citrus (Howard et al., 2009). The odorants within each category had very different molecular structures despite their perceptual similarity, and the recorded areas were the APC, PPC, amygdala, and orbitofrontal cortex (OFC). The results showed that the patterns of PPC activity were very similar for odorants within a category and different for odorants in different categories, but that activity in the other areas exhibited no such differences corresponding to differences in odor category. This experiment provides evidence that the PPC represents odor quality (minty, woody, etc.) and not merely the chemical structures of odorants.

In a different study (Zald & Pardo, 1997), responses in two of the same areas—the amygdala and the OFC—were recorded using PET while participants sniffed odors that varied along the emotional dimension of aversiveness (or unpleasantness). It's well known that odors can elicit powerful emotional responses, both pleasant and unpleasant, and in this study the odorants varied from mildly to intensely unpleasant. In both the amygdala and the OFC, the magnitude of the activation correlated with participants' subjective ratings of

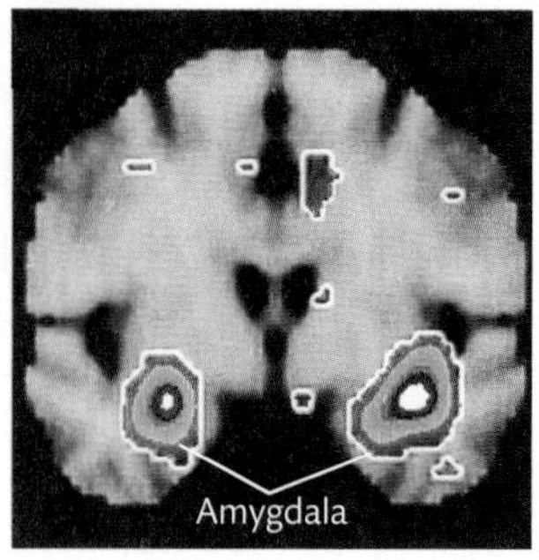

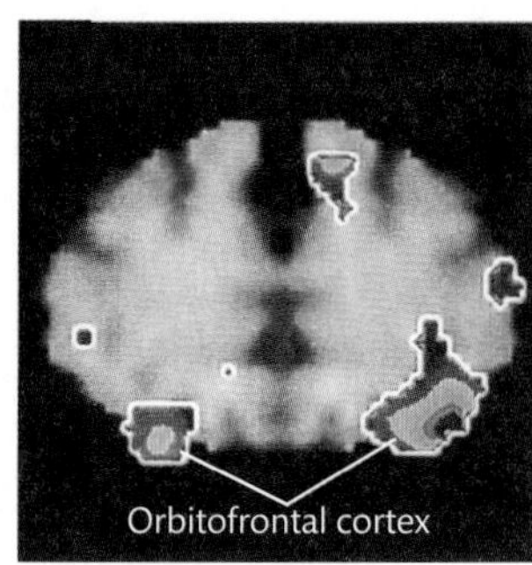

Figure 13.11 Brain Activity in Response to Aversive Odors These PET images show strongly increased responses in the amygdala and the orbitofrontal cortex when participants smelled an intensely aversive odorant—a "sulfide cocktail" that participants described as smelling like rotting vegetables—compared to smelling a neutral odor. In this experiment, participants smelled a range of aversive odors, from mild to intense, and the magnitude of the response in both areas correlated with the participants' rating of the aversiveness of the odor. (Adapted and photos from Zald & Pardo, 1997, Figure 1.)

the aversiveness of the odor—for example, the PET images in Figure 13.11 show strongly increased activation in both areas when participants sniffed an odor rated as highly aversive, compared to activation when smelling a neutral odor.

In the study described earlier (Howard et al., 2009), activity in the amygdala and the OFC didn't reflect differences in the quality of minty, woody, and citrus odorants, all of which are rated as mildly pleasant. Thus, taken together, the results of these two studies strongly support the idea that the amygdala and the OFC are involved in representing the emotional dimension of odor perception and not the identity of odors, whereas the PPC plays a role in representing the perceptual identity of odors.

As we noted earlier, there is a coarse chemotopic organization in the olfactory bulb—odorants with similar molecular structures activate adjacent glomeruli. Is there a corresponding chemotopic map in the piriform cortex? This question was addressed by a study in which the olfactory epithelium of mice was exposed to different odorants while the responses of populations of neurons in the piriform cortex were recorded (Stettler & Axel, 2009). As illustrated in Figure 13.12, the experiment revealed that each odorant

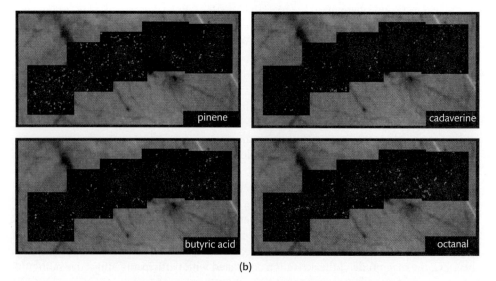

Figure 13.12 Activation in the Piriform Cortex (a) A mouse brain showing the location of the piriform cortex. (b) Four structurally distinct odorants (pinene, butyric acid, cadaverine, and octanal) evoked different patterns of responses by neurons in the piriform cortex, as shown by optical imaging. However, in all four cases, the responses seem randomly distributed, not clustered, suggesting no significant chemotopic organization in the piriform cortex (compare the clustering observed in the olfactory bulb in Figure 13.9). (Adapted and photos from Stettler & Axel, 2009, Figure 5.)

evoked a highly consistent pattern of activity in piriform cortex neurons but that there was no consistent clustering in the location of this activity—that is, no apparent chemotopic organization.

Cortical Adaptation to Odors As we discussed earlier, olfactory receptor neurons adapt to odors (see Figure 13.6), but this kind of adaptation occurs rapidly and lasts for only a few seconds. In contrast, adaptation that can last for several minutes—for example, adaptation to the smell of baking bread after you enter a bakery—appears to be mediated by the responses of neurons in the piriform cortex. This kind of adaptation is essential for detecting the presence of a new odor in an otherwise unchanging olfactory background—for instance, after adaptation to the smell of bread in a bakery, you're better able to detect the odor of a distinctive perfume on a person entering the bakery (Kadohisa & Wilson, 2006b). In an fMRI study of human olfaction, the investigators found that there is strong activation in the piriform cortex in response to the introduction of a new odor, but the activation declines over 40–50 seconds, presumably as a result of adaptation by neurons in that cortical region (Sobel et al., 2000).

Check Your Understanding

13.6 Comparing humans and other animals such as mice and dogs, what are two anatomical differences involving olfactory receptor neurons that help explain why those other animals can discriminate more odors and detect odors at lower concentrations than humans can?

13.7 Which choices match up to make two different correct statements: The axons of (**[A]** olfactory receptor neurons / **[B]** mitral cells and tufted cells) form the (**[C]** olfactory tract / **[D]** olfactory nerve). A–C and B–D? or A–D and B–C?

13.8 Explain how population coding enables humans to discriminate thousands of different odors with just 350 different types of olfactory receptor neurons.

13.9 Why is the piriform cortex considered the primary olfactory cortex, and how do the anterior and posterior piriform cortex differ in the kind of olfactory information they represent?

13.10 In which of the following scenarios is olfactory adaptation likely mediated by olfactory receptor neurons and in which is it likely mediated by neurons in the piriform cortex? **(A)** A man smoking a strong-smelling cigar walks past you, and the odor makes you feel slightly sick, but a moment later another man smoking an identical cigar walks past and you hardly notice the odor. **(B)** A man smoking a strong-smelling cigar gets in line for a movie ticket just behind you. At first, the odor makes you feel slightly sick, but after a minute or so you stop smelling it.

Odors, Emotion, and Memory

As we saw earlier, people aren't very good at identifying odors without some context or some expectation about what the odor might be. Furthermore, people's judgments about odor quality—whether about the actual identity of odors or even just the familiarity of odors—can be easily influenced by such factors as visual or verbal cues. One study, for example, showed that a bit of odorless red food coloring added to white wine dramatically affects how even experienced wine tasters describe the wine's aroma (Morrot et al., 2001). And in another study, a mixture was rated as more familiar when it was labeled "Parmesan cheese" than when the same mixture was labeled "vomit" (Herz & von Clef, 2001).

In contrast to their relatively poor ability to identify odors, people are very good at consistently assessing an odor as pleasant or unpleasant. From an evolutionary perspective, of course, this makes a great deal of sense, given the importance to organisms of being able to use olfaction to distinguish between substances that are positive (desirable, edible, beneficial) and substances that are negative (undesirable, inedible, harmful). Looked at in this way, then, the most important perceptual dimension of olfaction is the emotional one of pleasantness versus unpleasantness (Yeshurun & Sobel, 2010), and this conclusion is reinforced by the fact that two important centers of emotional processing in the brain—the amygdala and the OFC—are on the olfactory pathways.

Some odors are experienced as pleasant or unpleasant depending on the state of the smeller—for example, the odor of food can be intensely pleasant when you're very hungry but uninteresting or even unpleasant if you've just finished a big meal. Other odors, however, seem always to be experienced in the same way—for example, the smell of a predator invariably evokes fear in a prey animal, causing the animal to orient and prepare to flee. The odors given off by substances such as bodily waste, decomposing animals, and spoiled food are an interesting case in this regard: you would probably expect people to consistently experience such odors as disgusting, but research indicates that disgust reactions to at least some such substances are actually learned, not innate.

In one study, the facial expressions of adults and of children between the ages of 2 and 15 years were recorded while they sniffed fecal and urinous odorants, with the adult participants also providing a disgust rating for each odorant (Stevenson et al., 2010). More than 65% of the adult participants spontaneously produced facial expressions of disgust, but only a small percentage of children under the age of 5 did so (older children responded similarly to the adults). A comparison of the responses of children and their parents revealed that the children with the most obvious disgust reactions were those of parents with the most obvious disgust reactions, both in their facial expression and in their ratings of disgust. Other studies have shown that disgust reactions aren't inherited (Rozin & Millman, 1987), so this study suggests that the similar disgust reactions of children and their parents were learned.

One of the most striking aspects of human olfaction is our ability to rapidly acquire long-lasting memories of odors. This ability was demonstrated by a study in which people were first asked to smell and name 20 quite different substances (e.g., baby powder, banana, coffee, and leather) and then, after an interval of 10 minutes, 1 day, or 7 days, were asked to smell, in random order, the original 20 substances and 20 new substances (e.g., coconut, ginger, and mothballs) and to decide, for each odor, whether it was old (one of the original 20) or new (Rabin & Cain, 1984). Performance after 7 days was only slightly worse than performance after 10 minutes, indicating that memories for specific odors are formed quickly and decline slowly. However, the results also showed that substances more accurately named when first smelled were more accurately identified as old when smelled again. This suggests that the odors might have been, to some degree, remembered as names rather than as smells—for example, when smelling banana after a week, a participant might think, "OK, this smells like bananas. I don't remember this particular odor, but I do remember saying that one of the initial odors was banana, so this must be an *old* smell."

To check this possibility, another study compared memory for odors that varied in familiarity—that is, in how "nameable" they were (Murphy et al., 1991). After 6 months, familiar, easily named odors were remembered a little better than unfamiliar odors, but even the unfamiliar odors were remembered well above chance. This suggests that naming probably does play some role in memory for odors but that "pure" odor memory is nevertheless quite good.

Our memory for odors, as well as our assessment of the quality of odors, is also affected by the olfactory context—that is, by whether odors are smelled alone or in combination with other odors. Consider, for example, a study in which people first smelled and described various odors individually, then smelled pairs of these same odors mixed together in various combinations, and then again smelled and described the same individual odors (Stevenson, 2001). Results showed that the original odors, when smelled again, tended to acquire the characteristics of the odors they had been combined with, and that the pairs of combined odors could even be mistaken for one another. For example, participants who first smelled a cherry odor and a smoky odor individually and then smelled the two odors in combination, later tended to describe the cherry odor as a little smoky and the smoky odor as a little cherry-like, and sometimes even completely reversed the descriptions, calling the cherry odor "smoky" and/or the smoky odor "cherry."

Apparently, not only does smelling odors in combination influence our later perception of the individual odors, but also the combination of odors undergoes a kind of perceptual grouping, where the distinct odors are bound together into a single olfactory object, analogous to grouping in the perceptual organization of vision and audition (Wilson & Stevenson, 2003). For example, when you smell the combination of many different types of odorant molecules in a particular kind of wine, you experience the combination as a unified whole, which you can then remember as the aroma of that wine and can perceive as distinct from the aromas of other wines. Only careful attention to the constituent odors, which takes effort and practice, can break down the aroma into its components.

A phenomenon analogous to another aspect of perceptual organization in vision (figure–ground organization) is seen in piriform cortex activity. When a new odor arrives at the nose against an unchanging odor background, it evokes a distinct pattern of responses in the piriform cortex that is thought to reflect the representation of an odor "object" for potential identification and evaluation (Kadohisa & Wilson, 2006b).

In the laboratory studies of odor memory described earlier, as well as in many other such studies, people smelled and tried to identify specific odors and then, after various time intervals, tried to recognize and again identify the odors, with results showing recognition performance above chance after long intervals, even when the odors couldn't be reliably identified. However, these studies don't touch on a very familiar, emotional aspect of odor memory—the experience of smelling a specific, distinctive odor, such as a particular type of perfume or medication, and being immediately transported back in time to a youthful, emotionally charged experience involving that odor, like a moment of young love or an episode of illness or injury.

This property of odor memory was examined by a study in which people aged 65–80 smelled 20 different substances, including whiskey, tobacco, chlorine, snuff, tar, anise, and clove (Willander & Larsson, 2006). For each odor that evoked an autobiographical memory, the participant provided a brief written description of the memory and, whenever possible, indicated the age decade that the memory dated from. Two control groups underwent the same procedure, but instead of smelling odors, they saw words or pictures describing the odors. Figure 13.13 shows the percentage of memories from each decade of life for the three groups, computed by dividing the total number of evoked memories into the number of

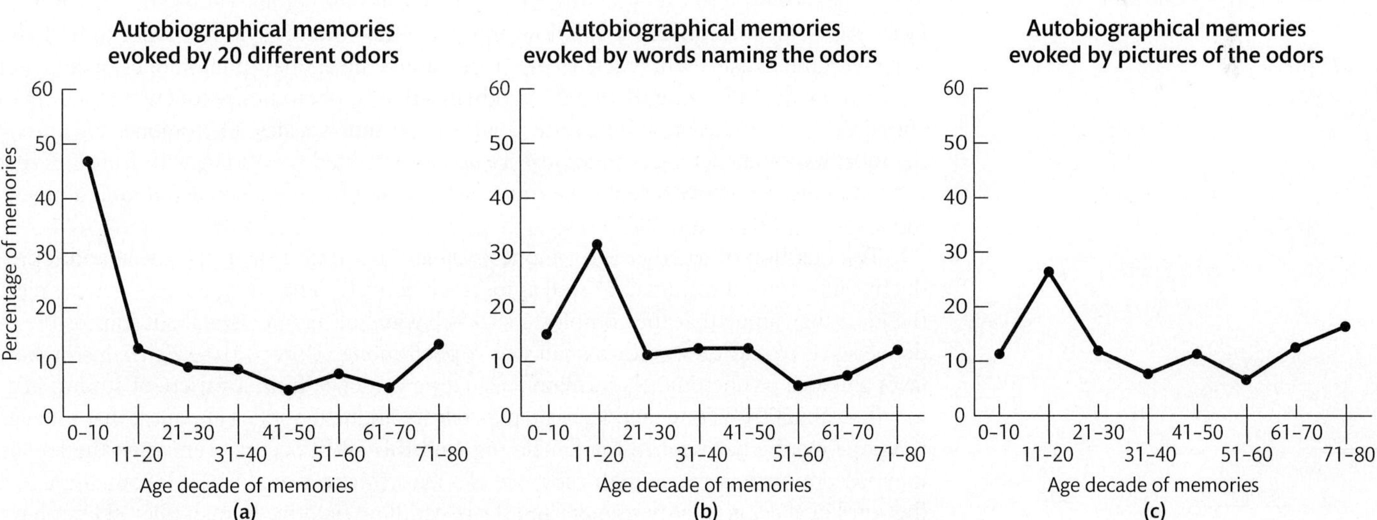

Figure 13.13 Memories Evoked by Odors Versus Memories Evoked by Words or Pictures In this experiment, participants were 65–80 years old. One group smelled 20 different odors; two other groups saw words or pictures corresponding to the odors. Each participant provided descriptions of any autobiographical memories evoked by the odors, words, or pictures and, if possible, indicated when each memory dated from. (a) For the group that smelled the odors, the largest percentage of evoked memories (nearly 50%) dated from the first decade of life. (b, c) For the groups that saw words or pictures, the largest percentage of evoked memories came from the second decade of life. Not only did odors tend to evoke earlier memories than words or pictures did, but odor-evoked memories were also rated by participants as more strongly inducing the feeling of being "brought back in time." In all three graphs, the high percentage of evoked memories from the most recent decade of life is a recency effect. (Adapted from Willander & Larsson, 2006.)

memories assigned to each decade—for example, as shown in Figure 13.13a, for the group that actually smelled the odors, almost 50% of the evoked memories were related to experiences from the first decade of life.

Two features of this figure are worth noting. The first is that, for all three groups, the percentage of memories is higher for the most recent decade than for earlier decades: this is known as a *recency effect* and is often seen in studies of memory. The second is that, as noted before, for the odors group, nearly half of all memories came from the first decade of life (ages 0–10), whereas for the words and pictures groups, the highest percentage of memories came from the second decade (ages 11–20). The participants in the odors group also more strongly indicated feeling as if they had been "brought back in time" than did the participants in the pictures and words groups. And a similar study showed that the memories evoked by odors are also more emotionally charged than those evoked by words or pictures (Herz & Schooler, 2002).

Why are odor-evoked memories acquired so quickly, so long lasting, and so emotionally vivid? One possible answer lies in brain anatomy: not only are centers of emotion (the amygdala and the orbitofrontal cortex) on the olfactory pathways, but so is an important center for memory, the hippocampus (Eichenbaum, 1998). Olfactory information travels to these brain structures more directly than does information from any other sensory modality, and this anatomical organization is thought to be a consequence of the fact that olfactory systems evolved earlier than did most other sensory systems, which tend to be centered in the more elaborately developed areas of the cerebral cortex (Niimura, 2009). The survival value of this brain organization is clear: emotionally charged experiences need to be quickly engraved in memory so that when the situations that gave rise to the memories recur, the organism can take appropriate action without delay, such as fleeing a predator or courting a potential mate.

Pheromones

pheromone A chemical substance emitted by individual organisms that evokes behavioral or hormonal responses in other individuals of the same species.

In the late 1950s, the term **pheromone** (from the Greek *pherein*, "to transfer," and *hormon*, "to excite") was coined to refer to chemical substances emitted by individual organisms that evoke behavioral or hormonal responses in other individuals of the same species (Karlson & Lüscher, 1959). For example, the female silkworm moth emits a substance called *bombykol;* male silkworm moths will follow an odor plume of bombykol in order to find and mate with the female (Schneider, 1974). Thus, unlike hormones, pheromones operate not on the individual secreting them, but on others—that is, pheromones function as a form of chemical communication among individuals of the same species. Pheromones are among the most important odorants in an insect's life, as indicated by studies with fruit flies that have identified olfactory receptor neurons that respond to only a single odorant, a pheromone (Schlief & Wilson, 2007).

The question of whether pheromones play an important role in the social and reproductive functions of mammals as well as insects is actively debated. Some researchers reject the idea: they argue that the complex social behaviors of mammals make it impossible to define what would or wouldn't qualify as a pheromone (Doty, 2010). Other researchers favor the idea of pheromones in mammals, citing evidence from a variety of studies (Tirindelli et al., 2009). For example, male pigs release androstenone, a chemical that initiates receptive mating behavior in the female pig, and this effect occurs even when the female is exposed to androstenone in the absence of a male (Melrose et al., 1971). Something like this kind of effect is what perfumers and those peddling putative human pheromones have in mind when they market their products, but the question of whether humans actually release and respond to pheromones is still very much open, as we'll see below.

vomeronasal olfactory system In many species, an olfactory system that senses pheromones; it is distinct from the main olfactory system used to smell most substances.

In many species, chemicals that would seem to qualify as pheromones are sensed via a **vomeronasal olfactory system,** which is distinct from the main olfactory system used to smell most substances. Mice, for example, have a vomeronasal organ located in a bony capsule near the nostrils (Ma, 2007). Like the main olfactory epithelium, the vomeronasal organ contains receptor neurons, support cells, and basal cells; the axons of the vomeronasal receptor neurons synapse with relay cells in a structure called the *accessory olfactory bulb,* which is distinct from the main olfactory bulb. From there, signals travel to the amygdala and the hypothalamus—structures involved in emotional processing and in the release of hormones—but not to the brain areas thought to be involved in identifying odors, such as the piriform cortex. Many animal species in addition to mice possess a vomeronasal system, including some nonhuman primates, but the balance of evidence suggests that humans do not have a functional vomeronasal system (Bhutta, 2007).

The question of whether human pheromones exist and, if so, what effects they have and how they work has been highly controversial (Jacob et al., 2002). In the early 1970s, a study found that the menstrual cycles of women living in the same college dormitory tended to become more synchronized over the course of an academic year (McClintock, 1971), an effect that could have been a result of pheromones released and sensed by the women; however, no candidate pheromones were identified, and the effect could have been the result of other factors (e.g., a common diet).

In a later study, underarm secretions of donor women were applied to the upper lips of recipient women who had never met the donors (Stern & McClintock, 1998). Secretions from donors in the late follicular phase of their menstrual cycle had the effect of shortening the menstrual cycle of the recipients (the follicular phase is the phase following menstruation and preceding ovulation), whereas secretions from donors in the ovulation phase had the effect of prolonging recipients' cycle. The researchers concluded that these effects provide definitive evidence for the existence of substances that fit the definition of human pheromones—chemicals released by individuals that evoke hormonal responses in other individuals. However, the secretions undoubtedly included sweat, exfoliated skin, bacteria, and other complex substances, each of which consists of a large number of different types of molecules, so the experiment provided no definitive indication of which chemical or chemicals actually produced these effects.

Another study compared the responses of men who had sniffed tears produced by women watching sad films to the responses of men who had sniffed a neutral salt solution (Gelstein et al., 2011). The men who had sniffed tears rated photos of women as less sexually appealing, reported reduced levels of sexual arousal, and exhibited reduced levels of testosterone. Furthermore, fMRI revealed reduced brain activity related to sexual arousal among the men who had sniffed tears. These effects occurred even though the men hadn't seen the women who had produced the tears and didn't know they were being exposed to tears. This study suggests that women's tears contain a chemical substance that reduces sexual arousal in men.

A more specific question than whether human pheromones exist—and to many people, a more interesting question—is whether individual humans emit substances, analogous to pheromones emitted by pigs and other mammals, that can have positive effects on the sexual thoughts, moods, or behaviors of other individuals. Presumably, if such substances exist, actual "love potions" could be compounded from them. Claims have been made that estratetraneol and androstadienone, steroids derived from hormones produced by women and men, respectively, have strong sexual effects on the opposite sex, by increasing the recipient's sexual receptivity and perception of the emitter's sexual attractiveness. However, although carefully conducted studies have revealed significant improvements in mood in women in response to smelling androstadienone, they have not consistently found a significant increase in either men or women in their desire to interact socially or sexually (Jacob et al., 2002).

A recent study found that women who sniffed samples of androstadienone, which is found in male sweat, reported both an elevated mood and an increase in sexual arousal (Wyart et al., 2007). And an fMRI-based study in which women smelled male sweat found that certain parts of the brain were more activated in response to smelling sweat samples taken while the donors were watching erotic videos than in response to smelling sweat taken while the donors were watching neutral videos (Zhou & Chen, 2008). However, the women in these studies (who were unaware of the nature of the compounds they were smelling) didn't perceive the sexual sweat as being especially pleasant or intense.

In another study, aimed at examining the effects of female pheromones on males, a group of 37 male college students (ages 18–23) smelled T-shirts that had been worn under different conditions by four women (ages 18–19) as they slept (Miller & Maner, 2010).

None of the men and women had ever met. Some of the T-shirts had been worn during the nights closest to ovulation in the woman's menstrual cycle (when the woman is most fertile), and some had been worn during the nights farthest from ovulation; as a control, the men also smelled T-shirts that had never been worn at all. The men's testosterone levels before and after smelling each T-shirt were measured in saliva samples, and the men were also asked to rate the pleasantness of the odor of each T-shirt. On average, the men who smelled the T-shirts worn by ovulating women had higher levels of testosterone after smelling and rated the odor as more pleasant than did the men in the other two groups. The researchers concluded that the results "provide evidence for a chemosensory signaling mechanism potentially mediating romantic courtship behavior" (Miller & Maner, 2010, p. 281).

Taken together, these three studies provide evidence that substances emitted by individuals of one sex and sensed via the olfactory system by individuals of the other sex can indeed evoke changes in sex-related mood, levels of arousal, and hormone levels. Of course, human sexual behavior is complex and multifaceted and is dependent on a variety of cognitive and social factors, as well as on physiological factors such as hormones and pheromones. Thus, human pheromones are more likely to have subtle shaping effects on sexual behavior than to directly cause specific behaviors (Jacob et al., 2002).

Check Your Understanding

13.11 Suppose participants in an olfaction experiment smell the same odor on many different occasions, across a number of months. If participants aren't given any hints about what the odor is, which of the following outcomes is more likely? **(A)** The participants almost always identify the odor in the same way (e.g., as banana or gasoline). **(B)** The participants almost always rate the odor in the same way, as pleasant or unpleasant.

13.12 True or false? Our perception of a particular odor isn't much affected by whether we've previously smelled the odor alone or smelled it in combination with other odors.

13.13 Which choice makes the statement correct? The memories evoked by odors tend to be memories of emotionally charged experiences from the (earliest / most recent) decade of life.

13.14 Suppose that humans, when engaging in strenuous physical activity on hot days, secreted a substance in their sweat that escaped into the air and was absorbed through the skin of other humans, and suppose that this substance caused the humans absorbing it to feel hot and thirsty. Would this substance fit the definition of a pheromone? Explain your answer.

Perceiving Tastes and Flavors

To survive, animals must eat substances that will provide them with the nutrients required to grow, recover from injury, and maintain appropriate chemical balances (and that won't make them sick). The main way many animals select healthy foods is by perceiving their flavors—things that taste good are usually edible and healthful, whereas things that taste bad are often inedible and potentially toxic. But this description is somewhat misleading, because it implies that taste and flavor are the same thing.

In this section, we'll begin by distinguishing between taste and flavor, and we'll see that flavor perception is more complex and multidimensional than taste perception—in brief, flavor = taste + olfaction. We'll discuss the stimuli for taste and the qualities of taste perceptions they produce, such as sweet and sour. Then we'll explore the anatomical and neural basis of taste—the distribution and structure of taste buds, the various types of taste receptor cells found in the taste buds, and how taste receptor cells transduce taste stimuli into neural signals that are sent to the brain. This will provide a basis for examining how taste and flavor are represented in the brain. We'll end by describing differences in taste perception among individual people, including people who can be classified as "supertasters."

What Is Taste? What Is Flavor?

As we have seen, the stimuli for olfactory perception are odorants—molecules with specific chemical features—which bind with receptors on olfactory receptor neurons and are transduced into neural signals that the brain represents as perceptions of different odors. Taste perception works in a very similar way: molecules called **tastants** dissolve in saliva and activate taste receptor cells within taste buds, which then produce neural signals that the brain represents as perceptions of different tastes. Moreover, just as different odorants have different detection thresholds, so do different tastants. Table 13.2 shows the detection thresholds of 15 different tastants, three from each of the five well-established taste categories, often referred to as the five **basic tastes:** sweet, salty, umami, sour, and bitter. (It's worth noting that additional categories of taste have been proposed, such as "fatty" and "carbonated," but these aren't yet well established.) The qualities sweet, salty, umami, and mild sour are typically associated with tastants that fill particular nutritive needs, whereas strong sour and bitter serve to warn us of toxic or inedible substances.

tastants Molecules that taste receptors "recognize" and respond to by producing neural signals that the brain represents as perceptions of different tastes.

basic tastes The five well-established taste categories—sweet, salty, umami, sour, and bitter.

Sweet taste is evoked by tastant molecules from the sugar family (sucrose, glucose, fructose, and many others), as well as by some amino acids and proteins (e.g., aspartame, an artificial sweetener, is partially built from amino acids). Glucose is an essential nutrient, needed for many bodily functions, including normal brain function, and sugars generally carry needed calories (needed, that is, in moderation!).

TABLE 13.2 Absolute Detection Threshold for Various Tastants

Taste Category	Substance	Description	Threshold in Water (ppm)
Sweet	Sucrose	Table sugar	11.70
	Fructose	Sweetener	16.02
	Glucose	Biological energy source	131.94
Salty	Sodium chloride	Table salt	18.36
	Potassium chloride	Fertilizer	113.58
	Lithium chloride	Various industrial uses	162.0
Umami	Monosodium glutamate	Food additive; flavor enhancer	9.0
	L-arginine	Natural amino acid	22.14
	L-glutamine	Natural amino acid	175.86
Bitter	Quinine	Various medicinal uses	0.025
	Caffeine	Stimulant	9.0
	Propylthiouracil (PROP)	Used to study perception of bitter	10.8 (nontaster); 0.36 (taster)*
Sour	Citric acid	Flavoring; preservative	1.26
	Acetic acid	Fermentation product in vinegar	1.48
	Hydrochloric acid	Main component of gastric acid	2.88

*The distinction between tasters and nontasters is discussed in the section on individual differences.

Adapted from Breslin (2000), Table 16.1.

Salts are molecules containing a positively charged ion and a negatively charged ion that together have no net charge. Salty taste is typically evoked by salts containing the sodium ion (salts containing certain other ions, such as potassium and lithium ions, also taste salty). A molecule of common table salt (sodium chloride, or NaCl) contains two ions, a positively charged sodium ion (Na^+) and negatively charged chloride ion (Cl^-), that are essential biological nutrients; among other functions, they regulate blood pressure and blood volume and play a role in the normal functioning of neurons (see Chapter 1). Because sodium is excreted—principally in sweat and urine—it must be included in one's diet to maintain healthy levels.

umami A basic taste evoked by tastants such as MSG and certain amino acids found in meats; it generally signals the presence of protein in food.

Umami (pronounced "oo-MAH-mee"; derived from a Japanese word best translated as "savory") is a relatively recent addition to the other four basic taste qualities (Shigemura et al., 2009). It's typically evoked by tastants such as MSG (monosodium glutamate) and certain amino acids found in meats (see Table 13.2) and generally signals the presence of protein in food. The prototypic example of an umami taste is that of beef broth.

Sour taste, which is evoked by acids, can be pleasant and desirable when relatively mild, as in the case of pickles, or in combination with sweet taste, as in ripe fruits, or in certain other combinations, such as the combination of vinegar (sour) with oil in salad dressing. However, very acidic substances, such as spoiled food, have a strong, aversively sour taste and are typically avoided.

Bitter taste is evoked by many different types of molecules. Although a wide variety of edible plants contain molecules that taste bitter (e.g., Brussels sprouts), this taste quality is most often associated with toxic substances, and the natural aversion to bitter taste is thought to have evolved because of the survival advantage gained by avoiding the ingestion of such substances. (Genetic differences among individuals in sensitivity to bitter taste are discussed later in this chapter.)

flavor The total sensory experience evoked by ingesting something; it includes the perception of the basic tastes, the perception of other attributes of tastants such as pleasantness and intensity, and other sensory properties, the most important of which is smell.

These five taste qualities aren't the only attributes of tastants that determine our overall perception of taste. The quality of a tastant helps us identify the substance we're tasting, but tastants also differ in hedonics (the degree to which the taste is pleasant or unpleasant), in intensity, in onset and aftertaste (how the taste unfolds over time), and in localization (where in the mouth the taste is sensed). Figure 13.14 depicts all these dimensions of taste, plus a wide variety of other sensory perceptions—the most important of which is olfaction—that combine in the perception of **flavor,** the total sensory experience evoked by ingesting something. The flavor of a food strongly depends on its

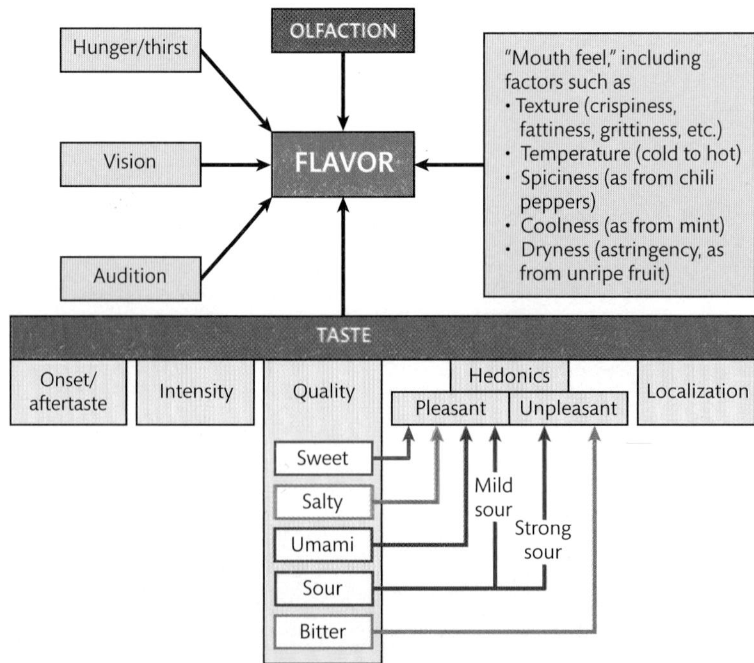

Figure 13.14 Taste and Flavor The five taste qualities (sweet, salty, umami, sour, and bitter) are important in helping us identify what we're eating or drinking, but taste also has other important attributes, including onset and aftertaste (some tastes evolve slowly over time and have a lingering aftertaste), intensity, localization (where in the mouth we experience a taste), and hedonics (whether the taste is experienced as pleasant or unpleasant). Sweet, salty, umami, and mildly sour tastes tend to be experienced as pleasant, while bitter and strongly sour tastes tend to be unpleasant. Taste strongly contributes to flavor—the total sensory experience evoked by ingesting something—but so does olfaction. The aromas of food and drink, which we perceive both before we put something in our mouth and afterward (via the retronasal pathway), have a powerful influence on our experience of flavor. Other important factors in flavor perception include our state of hunger and thirst, vision (food that looks good has a better flavor), audition (like the appealing sound of biting into a crisp pickle), and the "mouth feel" of food and drink. (Adapted in part from Breslin & Spector, 2008, Figure 2.)

taste, to be sure, but it also strongly depends on the food's aroma, which comes both from the odorants released by the food before it is placed in the mouth, which enter the nasal cavity via the nostrils, and from the odorants released while the food is in the mouth and being chewed and swallowed, which enter the nasal cavity via the retronasal pathway, as described earlier in this chapter.

The "mouth feel" of food, perceived via somatosensory receptors inside the mouth (Simon et al., 2006), is important, too—its texture, its temperature, and even its ability to slightly irritate the interior of the mouth (think chili peppers or curry). Food has a better flavor when we're hungry—we might be repelled by a plateful of macaroni and cheese if we've just eaten a big meal but might devour the same dish with intense pleasure after a long day of hiking. And vision and audition also play a role: food that *looks* appetizing (like a colorful salad) often seems especially flavorful, and the crunch of a crisp pickle or a potato chip can sound very appetizing.

The importance of smell for our experience of flavor is easily demonstrated—simply hold your nose while eating, which prevents odorant molecules from entering the nasal cavity via the nostrils. Studies have shown that the accuracy with which people can identify tastes is significantly reduced in people who have impaired olfactory sensitivity (Landis et al., 2010). Indeed, as we saw in the case of B. in the vignette at the beginning of this chapter, people with acquired anosmia often experience their loss of smell primarily as a loss of the ability to experience the flavor of food.

Anatomical and Neural Basis of Taste and Flavor Perception

Taste perception starts with the transduction of tastants into neural signals by specialized cells within taste buds on the tongue and other surfaces of the mouth. Depending on the location of the taste bud, the neural signals are transmitted by one of three cranial nerves to a nucleus in the brain stem and eventually to various parts of the cortex, where the information in these signals is combined with information in signals from the olfactory and somatosensory systems. (In addition to the specialized cells that transduce sweet, salty, umami, sour, and bitter tastants, the mouth also contains free nerve endings that transmit signals with information about nontaste factors such as the heat of chili peppers and the coolness of menthol, as well as somatosensory receptors that let us detect the texture and temperature of food in the mouth.)

Taste Buds and Taste Receptor Cells

On average, individual humans have 3,000–12,000 **taste buds,** about a third of which are on the soft palate, epiglottis, and upper esophagus, with the remaining two-thirds on the tongue, within small structures called **papillae** (pronounced "puh-PIL-ee"; singular, *papilla*) (Halpern, 2002). As shown in Figure 13.15 (left and center), there are three different types of papillae on the tongue that contain taste buds:

- **Fungiform papillae** are tiny mushroom-shaped structures located along the edges and top of the front two-thirds of the tongue. Each fungiform papilla contains 3–5 taste buds on its upper surface.
- **Foliate papillae** are small ridgelike folds of tissue located on the sides of the tongue near the back; a few hundred taste buds are tucked into each fold.
- **Circumvallate papillae** are mushroom shaped like fungiform papillae but are much larger. The mouth contains only 8–12 of these papillae, all situated in a row at the back of the tongue. Each circumvallate papilla contains 200–700 taste buds around its sides.

A fourth type, called *filiform papillae,* which don't contain taste buds, cover much of the tongue's surface; they contain somatosensory receptors thought to provide information about the texture of food (Oakely & Witt, 2004).

Each taste bud contains 40–100 **taste receptor cells (TRCs),** elongated neurons with cilia at their outer ends and without axons (Halpern, 2002). As illustrated in Figure 13.15

taste buds Structures that contain taste receptor cells, within papillae in the mouth.

papillae Tiny structures on surfaces in the mouth, mainly on the tongue; three different types of papillae contain taste buds.

fungiform papillae Tiny mushroom-shaped structures located along the edges and top of the front two-thirds of the tongue; each fungiform papilla contains 3–5 taste buds on its upper surface.

foliate papillae Ridgelike folds of tissue located on the sides of the tongue near the back; a few hundred taste buds are tucked into each fold.

circumvallate papillae Mushroom-shaped structures (much larger than fungiform papillae) situated in a row at the back of the tongue; each circumvallate papilla contains 200–700 taste buds around its sides.

taste receptor cells (TRCs) Elongated neurons, packed within taste buds, that transduce tastants into neural signals.

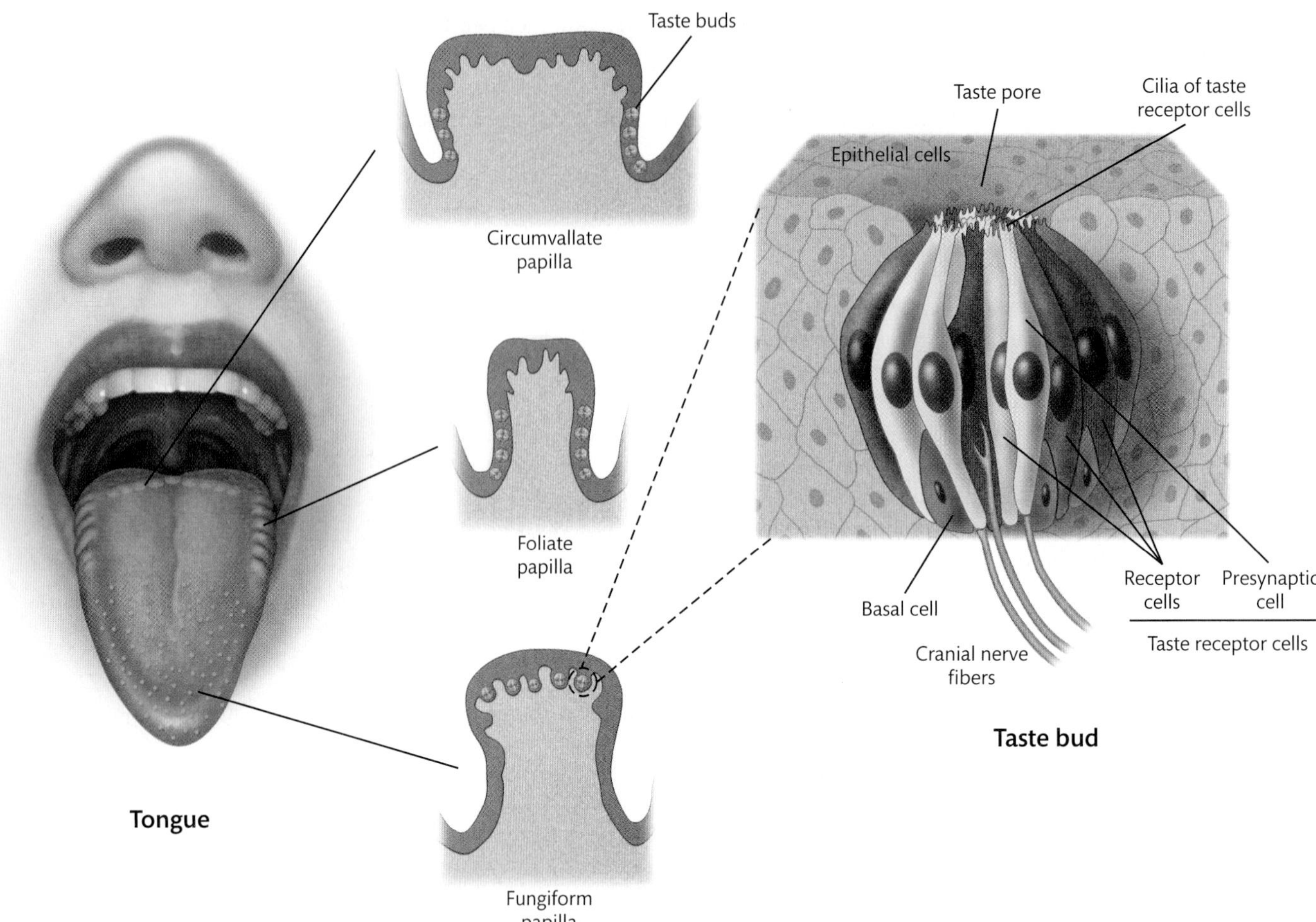

Figure 13.15 Tongue, Papillae, and Taste Buds The human tongue contains three types of papillae that house taste buds. In circumvallate papillae, at the back center of the tongue, and in foliate papillae, at the rear sides of the tongue, hundreds of taste buds are found along the inner sides of the folds. Fungiform papillae, small bumps on the edges and top of the front two-thirds of the tongue, have 3–5 taste buds on their upper surface. Each taste bud contains 40–100 taste receptor cells (TRCs)—many more than the few depicted in the enlargement here. TRCs have cilia at the outer end, protruding into a taste pore, an opening onto the surface of the tongue that allows tastant molecules dissolved in saliva to come into contact with receptors on the cilia. There are two main types of TRCs: receptor cells, which come in three subtypes (indicated by different colors here) and which don't have synapses with cranial nerve fibers, and presynaptic cells, which do have synapses with cranial nerve fibers. TRCs live for just a week or so and then are replaced by new TRCs that develop from basal cells in the taste bud.

(right), each taste bud is structured like a head of garlic, with the TRCs analogous to the garlic cloves. Each TRC lives for only a week or so and is then replaced (new TRCs develop from basal cells in the taste bud). The cilia of the TRCs project into a taste pore (an opening onto the surface of the tongue) at the top of the taste bud, where the cilia come into contact with tastant molecules dissolved in saliva.

receptor cells A type of taste receptor cells containing receptors that initiate transduction of sweet, umami, and bitter tastants.

presynaptic cells A type of taste receptor cells in which the receptors take the form of ion channels where transduction of salty and sour tastants is initiated.

There are two types of TRCs: **receptor cells** and **presynaptic cells** (DeFazio et al., 2006). The membranes of receptor cell cilia contain receptors that initiate transduction of sweet, umami, and bitter tastants; typically, each receptor cell contains only a single category of receptors on its cilia (Chandrashekar et al., 2006). Receptor cells do not have synapses with cranial nerve fibers. In presynaptic cells, receptors take the form of ion channels in the cilia membrane, where transduction of salty and sour tastants is initiated; each presynaptic cell contains channels for both these types of tastants. The inner ends of presynaptic cells release neurotransmitters into synapses with cranial nerve fibers that send taste signals to the brain (Tomchik et al., 2007).

The receptors in the membranes of receptor cell cilia are GPCRs, related to the GPCRs that function as olfactory receptors, as discussed earlier in this chapter. The GPCRs involved in taste perception have been characterized biochemically and genetically and have been linked via behavioral and genetic studies in mice to the transduction of sweet, umami, and bitter tastants (Bachmanov & Beauchamp, 2007; Roper, 2007). Receptor cells that transduce sweet or umami tastants contain different pairs of the GPCRs known as T1R1, T1R2, and T1R3: sweet tastant molecules are transduced by receptor cells that contain T1R2–T1R3 receptor pairs; umami tastant molecules are transduced by receptor cells that contain T1R1–T1R3 receptor pairs. This has been confirmed by experiments with genetically modified mice (called *knockout mice*) that lack the gene for one of these three GPCRs: mice lacking the T1R2 receptor cannot taste sweet (i.e., they don't prefer sugar water to plain water, which unmodified mice strongly do); those lacking the T1R1 receptor have reduced sensitivity to umami; and those lacking the T1R3 receptor cannot taste either sweet or umami (Chandrashekar et al., 2006).

Other experiments with knockout mice have shown that bitter tastants are transduced by receptor cells containing a category of GPCRs known as the T2Rs (Chandrashekar et al., 2006), which is thought to include 25–30 different types—T2R1, T2R2, etc. (Breslin & Spector, 2008; Drayna, 2005). The diversity of T2Rs probably reflects the diversity of toxic substances that must be avoided—the mammalian taste system evolved such that they all taste bitter.

As mentioned before, presynaptic cells are connected via a synapse to a cranial nerve fiber. When salty and sour tastant ions are transported through the corresponding ion channels—which, like GPCRs, are genetically specified proteins—in the membrane of a presynaptic cell's cilia, a chain of reactions is initiated within the cell that results in the release of neurotransmitters into the synapse. These neurotransmitters are taken up by the nerve fiber, which responds by sending action potentials to the brain.

Sour tastants are acids—for example, the citric acid in lemons and the acetic acid in vinegar. Acids contain hydrogen ions, and an ion channel that transports hydrogen ions into the cell body of presynaptic cells and that is thought to be responsible for initiating the transduction of sour tastants has been identified (Chang et al., 2010; Huang et al., 2006).

Salty tastants can be divided into two categories: everyday table salt (sodium chloride, NaCl) and other salts such as potassium chloride (KCl) and magnesium chloride ($MgCl_2$). When dissolved in water or saliva, table salt releases sodium ions (Na^+), whereas other salts release ions such as K^+ and Mg^{++}. At low concentrations, table salt adds a pleasant flavoring to food; moreover, sodium is an essential nutrient, required for the normal functioning of neurons and for a variety of other physiological functions. At high concentrations, however, salty tastants are aversive. Correspondingly, there are thought to be two distinct transduction mechanisms for salty tastants: one for the transduction of sodium ions in relatively low concentrations, termed the *epithelial sodium channel* (ENaC), and another for the transduction of a wide variety of salt ions (sodium and others) in aversively high concentrations. The ENaC was identified in an experiment with knockout mice: mice lacking ENaCs are not able to taste sodium chloride in nonaversive concentrations (Chandrashekar et al., 2010).

Assuming that taste transduction works as we've described it here (and there is still debate about many aspects of this description), the following question arises: How do receptor cells communicate to the brain the presence of the sweet, umami, and bitter tastants they transduce, given that receptor cells don't have synapses with cranial nerve fibers? Studies indicate that this is accomplished, at least in part, by what is termed **cell-to-cell signaling:** receptor cells release adenosine triphosphate (ATP) into the extracellular fluid within the taste bud, these ATP molecules are taken up by presynaptic cells, and this leads to the release of serotonin by the presynaptic cells at their synapse with cranial nerve fibers (Dando & Roper, 2009). Presumably, differences in the release of ATP and the consequent release of serotonin provide information about the type of tastant transduced by the receptor cell—sweet, umami, or bitter. Thus, presynaptic cells are thought to both transduce salty and sour tastants and transmit information about

cell-to-cell signaling In taste perception, signals from receptor cells to presynaptic cells, causing the presynaptic cells to release neurotransmitters in a way that carries information about sweet, umami, and bitter tastants.

Demonstration 13.2 Functional Anatomy of the Taste System Interact with depictions of the structures and pathways involved in the perception of taste and flavor.

Carl Pfaffmann (1912–1994). [Media Resource Center, Rockefeller University]

sweet, umami, and bitter tastants, via cell-to-cell signaling from receptor cells (Tomchik et al., 2007). In addition, the ATP released by receptor cells is thought to stimulate free endings of cranial nerve fibers within the taste bud, providing another means by which taste information from receptor cells is sent to the brain (Finger et al., 2005; Yoshida & Ninomiya, 2010).

Figures 13.16 and 13.17 illustrate many of these features of taste perception via receptor cells and presynaptic cells. Figure 13.16 shows how the three different types of receptor cells are thought to send signals to presynaptic cells and to free endings of cranial nerve fibers and how presynaptic cells synapse with cranial nerve fibers. Figure 13.17 schematically illustrates how pairs of T1R1, T1R2, and TIR3 receptors transduce sweet and umami tastants, how T2R receptors transduce bitter tastants, and how ion channels in presynaptic cells transduce salty and sour tastants.

From Taste Buds to the Brain

The American physiologist and psychologist Carl Pfaffmann was among the first to measure the activity of single gustatory neurons (in the cat as well as several other species). His initial hypothesis was that any given neuron in the taste system would respond to just one of the four basic tastes—sweet, salty, bitter, and sour (in those days, umami was not widely recognized as a separate taste category). Pfaffmann was surprised to find that most nerve fibers from the tongue to the brain responded to more than just a single taste category, although any given

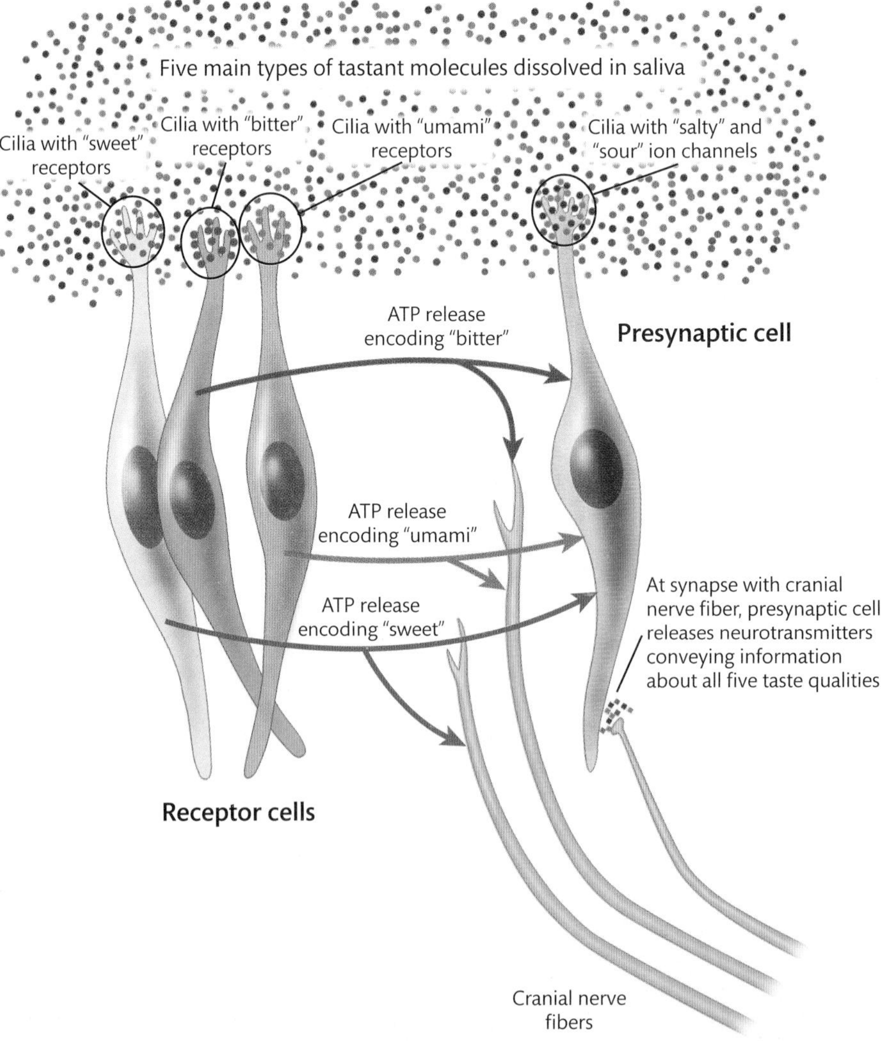

Figure 13.16 Taste Receptor Cells, Cell-to-Cell Signaling, and the Production of Action Potentials in Cranial Nerve Fibers Each of the three types of receptor cells has only a single type of taste receptor on its cilia, for transducing either sweet, bitter, or umami tastants dissolved in saliva. Each presynaptic cell has ion channels on its cilia, where the transduction of either salty or sour tastants is initiated. Presynaptic cells have a synapse with cranial nerve fibers that transmit action potentials to the brain. Receptor cells don't have synapses with cranial nerve fibers but release ATP into the extracellular fluid. Taste information encoded in this ATP release is thought to be conveyed to cranial nerve fibers by two different means: (1) the ATP can directly stimulate free endings of cranial nerve fibers within the taste bud, and (2) the ATP is taken up by presynaptic cells (a process called *cell-to-cell signaling*), which influences the release of serotonin into their synapses with cranial nerve fibers. (Adapted from Tomchik et al., 2007, Figure 7.)

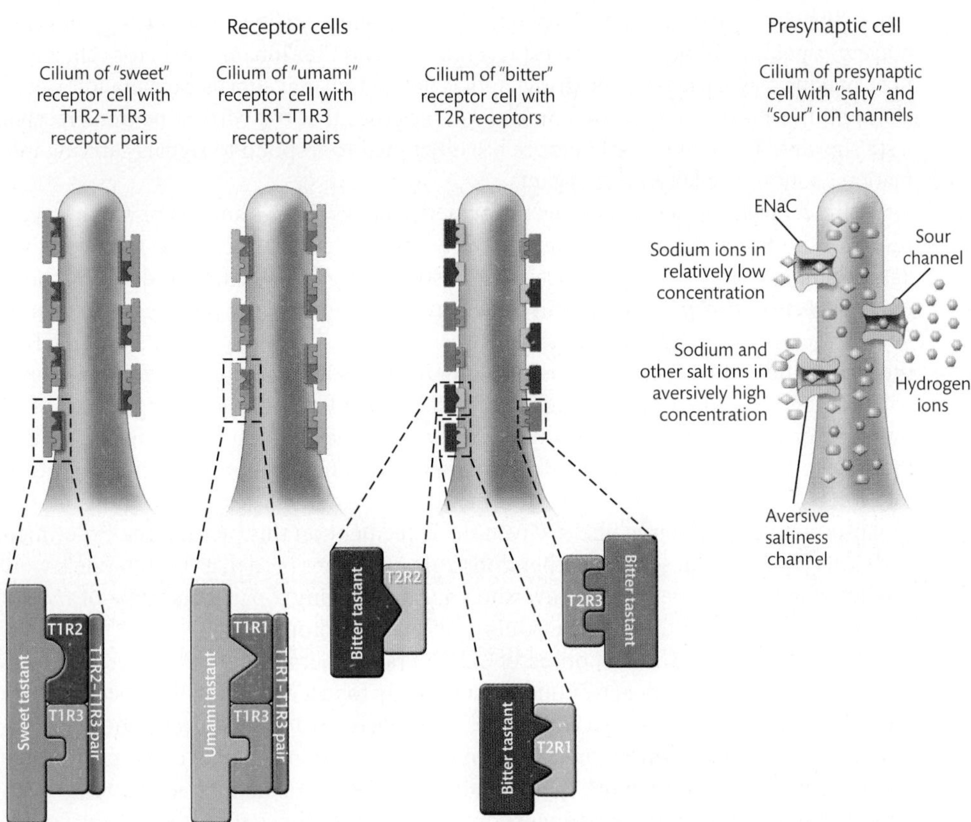

Figure 13.17 **Receptor Cells and Presynaptic Cells** This highly schematic illustration shows how TRC receptors are thought to transduce different types of tastants. On the cilia of each of the three different types of receptor cells—"sweet," "umami," and "bitter"—sweet tastants bind to the T1R2-T1R3 receptor pair, umami tastants bind to the T1R1-T1R3 receptor pair, and bitter tastants bind to various types of T2R receptors. The receptors on the cilia of presynaptic cells are ion channels—two channels for transducing salty tastants and another channel for transducing sour tastants. The epithelial sodium channel (ENaC) transduces sodium ions from ordinary table salt (NaCl), as long as the ions are in a relatively low, pleasant-tasting concentration, whereas the other "salty" channel transduces sodium and other salt ions that are in aversively high concentrations. The "sour" channel transduces hydrogen ions released by sour tastants (acids).

fiber tended to respond more strongly to one taste category than to the others. This led him to propose an alternative model of taste representation (Pfaffmann, 1955). The two models—now referred to as the *labeled-line model* and the *across-pattern fiber model*—are conceptually quite distinct, but it has proven difficult to find evidence that definitively rules out either one.

According to the **labeled-line model,** each cranial nerve fiber carries signals with information about just one of the five taste qualities, and the cortical neurons on the receiving end of these signals also respond only to information about a single type of tastant. Thus, there is a single "labeled line" from the specialized TRCs in taste buds to correspondingly specialized cranial nerve fibers to correspondingly specialized cortical neurons. In Figure 13.16, for example, the free-floating cranial nerve fiber receiving "bitter" signals could be taken as illustrating this idea, provided that this fiber responds only to "bitter" signals, not to "sweet" or "umami" signals, and provided that this "bitter" cranial nerve fiber sends its "bitter" signals to a "bitter" cortical neuron—in this case, the line label would be "bitter."

However, as suggested by the earlier discussion of taste transduction and cell-to-cell signaling, Figure 13.16 as a whole actually illustrates the **across-fiber pattern model.** According to this model, cranial nerve fibers can carry signals from multiple taste receptor

labeled-line model A model of taste perception proposing that each cranial nerve fiber carries signals with information about just one of the five taste qualities, and that the cortical neurons on the receiving end of these signals also respond only to information about a single type of tastant.

across-fiber pattern model A model of taste perception proposing that cranial nerve fibers can carry signals from multiple taste receptor types, and that the cortical neurons receiving these signals are broadly tuned to respond to signals carrying information about multiple types of tastants.

types—for example, in Figure 13.16, one of the free-floating fibers is receiving (and transmitting) signals from both the "sweet" receptor cell and the "umami" receptor cell, and the fiber making a synapse with the presynaptic cell will transmit signals carrying information about all five taste qualities. This model also proposes that the cortical neurons receiving taste signals via cranial nerve fibers are broadly tuned to respond to signals carrying information about multiple types of tastants.

Which model—if either—does the evidence favor? This is an area of much ongoing research and much debate. In weighing the evidence, let's first note that the two models agree on how tastants are transduced (as illustrated in Figures 13.16 and 13.17, though many aspects of this process are still under investigation, and the picture could change). Receptor cells are thought to transduce sweet, umami, and bitter tastants via GPCRs on their cilia; individual receptor cells typically (perhaps always) contain only one type of receptor; and transduction is thought to result in the information-carrying release of ATP by receptor cells into the extracellular fluid within the taste bud. Presynaptic cells are thought to transduce salty and sour tastants via ion channels on their cilia, and transduction is thought to result in the information-carrying release of neurotransmitters at synapses with cranial nerve fibers. Given the agreement on this picture, the experiments with knockout mice described earlier don't rule out either model, as both models would predict what these experiments have shown: mice lacking a particular type of receptor are unable to perceive tastants transduced by that receptor.

Studies in which the responses of single cranial nerve fibers were recorded have often found that single fibers respond most strongly to just one of the five taste categories (Hellekant et al., 1998)—often called *NaCl-best fibers, sucrose-best fibers,* and so forth—but other studies have found that, while some fibers respond to only one type of tastant, others respond to two or more types (Pfaffmann, 1955; Yoshida et al., 2006). The latter finding would seem to be strong evidence in favor of the across-fiber pattern model, since this model doesn't exclude the possibility that some fibers respond only to one type of tastant, whereas the labeled-line model has no place for multiple-tastant responses in single fibers. And similar evidence is provided by a study (mentioned earlier) in which the responses of individual receptor cells and presynaptic cells were measured (Tomchik et al., 2007)—results of that study support the idea of cell-to-cell signaling from receptor cells to presynaptic cells and show that the nerve fibers that synapse with presynaptic cells transmit information about multiple types of tastants. Moreover, studies with rats (Stapleton et al., 2006) and monkeys (Scott & Plata-Salamán, 1999) have indicated that neurons in the primary taste cortex (see the discussion in the next section) tend to have a fairly broad tuning profile—that is, they tend to respond to multiple types of tastants—which again supports the across-fiber pattern model.

Overall, these studies provide support for an across-fiber pattern model analogous to the well-established model of how retinal ganglion cells transmit information about color (see Chapter 5). That is, in the taste system, cranial nerve fibers are seen as carrying information about differences in taste quality based on the relative activity of a few different types of receptors (T1R1–T1R3, T1R2–TIR3, T2Rs, and three different ion channels), just as in the visual system, retinal ganglion cells carry information about color based on the relative activity of three different types of cones.

Representing Taste and Flavor in the Brain

Neural signals originating in taste receptor cells in taste buds are transmitted to the brain via three cranial nerves; the facial nerve (cranial nerve VII), which innervates the front two-thirds of the tongue and the soft palate; the glossopharyngeal nerve (cranial nerve IX), which innervates the back one-third of the tongue; and the vagus nerve (cranial nerve X), which innervates the epiglottis and the upper esophagus (Bachmanov & Beauchamp, 2007). These signals travel first to the nucleus of the solitary tract in the medulla; then, like all the other senses except olfaction, signals pass through the thalamus (specifically, through the ventral posterior medial nucleus of the thalamus) on their way to the cortex.

As shown in Figure 13.18, the first cortical areas to receive taste signals (via the thalamus) are the anterior insular cortex and the frontal operculum, which, together, constitute the **primary taste cortex.** Signals then go to the orbitofrontal cortex (where the reward value of food is thought to be represented, including both the pleasurable and the nutritional aspects of eating); the amygdala (where emotion is represented); and the hypothalamus (where hunger is represented) (Scott & Plata-Salamán, 1999). As you can see by comparing

primary taste cortex The first cortical areas to receive taste signals, consisting of the anterior insular cortex and the frontal operculum.

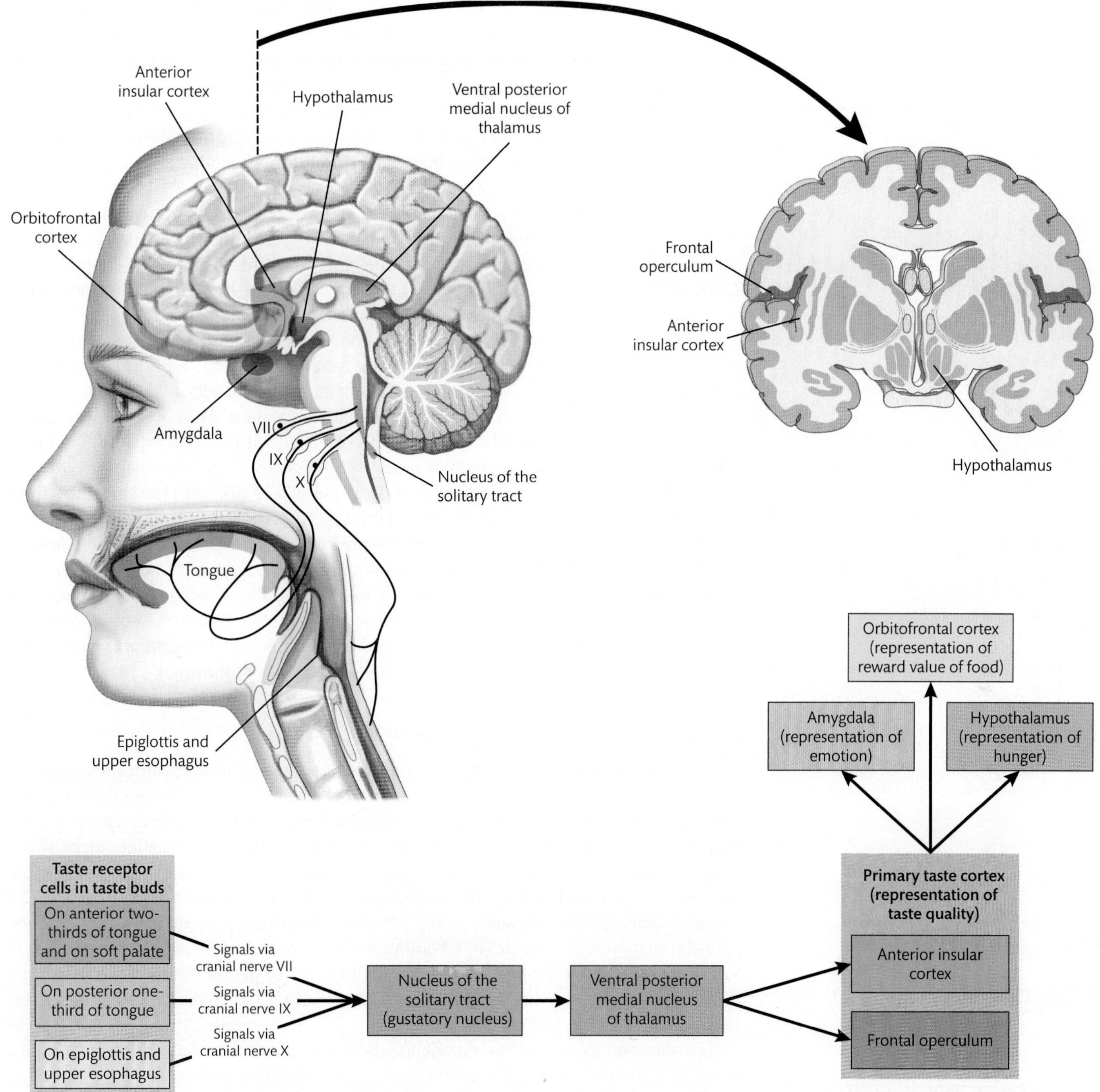

Figure 13.18 Gustatory Structures and Pathways: Mouth to Brain Signals from taste receptor cells are sent via cranial nerves VII, IX, and X to the nucleus of the solitary tract, in the brain stem. From there, signals travel to the ventral posterior medial nucleus of the thalamus and then to the primary taste cortex (the anterior insular cortex and the frontal operculum). Neurons in these areas produce representations of the qualities of tastants (sweet, bitter, umami, sour, and salty) and appear to play a role in identifying tastants. Signals are then sent to the orbitofrontal cortex, where the reward value of food is represented, as well as to the amygdala and the hypothalamus.

the diagrams in Figures 13.18 and 13.10, the orbitofrontal cortex, amygdala, and hypothalamus are also on the olfactory pathway, reflecting the tight integration and interdependence of taste and olfaction in the perception of flavor.

The orbitofrontal cortex (OFC) appears to play an especially important role in taste and flavor perception. When an animal eats, the responses of neurons in the primary taste cortex aren't affected by whether the animal is hungry or not, but neurons in the orbitofrontal cortex respond strongly—indicating high reward value—only when the animal is hungry. Thus, the OFC appears to be crucial in one of the most important functions of taste and flavor perception: to motivate organisms to eat when they're hungry, presumably based on the pleasantness of eating flavorful foods—the better something tastes, the more of it is eaten. These response patterns of neurons in the primary taste cortex versus the OFC suggest that the primary taste cortex represents taste qualities (sweet, bitter, umami, salty, and sour), which can be used to identify tastants, whereas the OFC, which receives signals not only from the primary taste cortex but also from many other sensory modalities (including olfaction, vision, and touch), represents the flavor, or reward value, of foods (Rolls, 2006).

Both the primary taste cortex and the OFC of monkeys contain multimodal neurons that respond not only to both the smell and the taste of foods (Simon et al., 2006), but also to the temperature, viscosity, fattiness, and grittiness of foods (Verhagen et al., 2004). The convergence of olfactory and taste signals in the human brain was examined in an fMRI study in which participants were asked to taste sucrose (table sugar) or smell strawberry; their neural responses were then compared with the responses of participants to tasteless or odorless control substances (de Araujo et al., 2003). Both the sweet taste and the strawberry smell activated the same region of the anterior insular cortex, a part of the primary taste cortex that also receives olfactory signals. Moreover, the strength of activation of a region in the OFC was strongly correlated with the participants' judgments about the pleasantness of the smell or taste.

In the study cited above of neural responses in monkeys' primary taste cortex to stimuli that varied in taste, temperature, viscosity, fattiness, and grittiness, about 5.5% of the neurons in the primary taste cortex responded to one or more of these factors, with a majority of them responding to two or more (e.g., one-quarter of the responsive neurons responded to both taste and temperature) (Verhagen et al., 2004). Taken together, the findings from these studies suggest that information from several sensory modalities—taste, olfaction, vision, and somatosensory perception (including both thermoreception and mechanoreception)—converges in the OFC to produce the perception of flavor.

Individual Differences in Taste Perception

Just as people lacking one of the three types of cones (a genetically determined, typically inherited condition) experience the visual world differently from people with all three cone types, so people with genetically determined differences in taste receptors experience the taste world differently. The most common of these genetic differences affects people's ability to taste certain bitter substances. The gene that codes for a specific bitter-taste receptor (T2R38) occurs in two versions, known as PAV and AVI. About 75% of people have the PAV version, which lets them detect the presence of the bitter compounds phenylthiocarbamide (PTC) and propylthiouracil (PROP) at low concentrations; such individuals are called *tasters*. The remaining 25% of people (called *nontasters*) have the AVI version and require much higher concentrations to detect these substances (see Table 13.2) (Drayna, 2005).

Furthermore, some tasters experience these and other bitter substances much more intensely than other tasters. These individuals, called *supertasters,* have about twice as many fungiform papillae on their tongues as nontasters do, and they find certain bitter foods and beverages—for example, Brussels sprouts, kale, spinach, grapefruit juice, coffee, and beer—so intensely bitter as to be practically inedible or undrinkable. An estimated 25% of people worldwide are supertasters, with women more likely than men to be supertasters, and people from Asia, Africa, and South America more likely to be supertasters than those from other regions. If you're a nontaster with supertaster friends, you're probably baffled by their extreme aversion to kale and coffee; conversely, if you're a supertaster with nontaster friends, you're probably equally baffled by their affinity for Brussels sprouts and beer. Keep in mind that nontasters and supertasters live in different sensory worlds.

Check Your Understanding

13.15 Match the basic tastes with the tastants that evoke them:

Basic Tastes	Tastants
1. Sweet	A. Acids
2. Salty	B. Monosodium glutamate and certain amino acids found in meat
3. Umami	C. Molecules such as glucose, as well as some amino acids and proteins
4. Sour	D. Many different types of molecules, often found in toxic substances
5. Bitter	E. Molecules containing a positively charged ion and a negatively charged ion that together have no net charge

13.16 True or false? The papillae within taste buds contain taste receptor cells.

13.17 Match each of the following terms with the correct letter in the table below: Aversive salty / Presynaptic cells / Sour / T1R2–T1R3 / ENaC / GPCRs / Umami / T2Rs.

Receptor cells		[E]	
[A]	Tastants	Ion channels	Tastants
[B]	Sweet	[F]	Table salt
TIR1–T1R3	[D]	Aversive saltiness channel	[G]
[C]	Bitter	Hydrogen ion channel	[H]

13.18 Fill in the blanks: Cell-to-cell signaling is a process by which __________ are thought to send signals to presynaptic cells, which then send signals to the brain via cranial nerve fibers, with information about all five __________; this is compatible with the __________ model of taste perception, but not with the __________ model.

13.19 Which region of the brain is NOT part of the primary taste cortex: the frontal operculum, orbitofrontal cortex, or anterior insular cortex?

13.20 True or false? Nontasters simply cannot detect the presence of the bitter compounds PTC and PROP, regardless of the concentration of these substances.

APPLICATIONS The eNose

Engineers have long envisioned the possibility of creating what's now generally referred to as an **eNose**—an electronic nose. The first working version of an eNose was created in 1982 (Persaud & Dodd, 1982); since that time, significant strides have been made in both the technology and the range of applications (Pearce et al., 2003). Today, eNoses are capable of

eNose An electronic nose; currently, eNoses are capable of detecting and identifying odorants, localizing their source, and even tracking odor plumes.

detecting and identifying odorants, localizing their source, and even tracking odor plumes. Scenarios for which eNoses are already in use or are under development include sampling the chemical composition of the air in environments such as deep mine shafts and the International Space Station; helping diagnose diseases such as tuberculosis, pneumonia, and certain cancers that often produce characteristic odors in concentrations too low for the human nose to detect and identify (Turner & Magan, 2004); detecting drugs or explosives; and monitoring foods for freshness and possible contamination.

How eNoses Work

An eNose consists of an array of sensors, each of which is broadly tuned—that is, each sensor responds not just to a single odorant, but to a range of substances with similar molecular structures, and any given odorant activates multiple sensors. Thus, each odorant produces a distinctive pattern of responses in the array of sensors, a code that can be used to identify the odorant. This coding scheme should sound familiar—it's a population code, like the population code used by the mammalian olfactory system (see the section "Neural Code for Odor" earlier in this chapter). However, one big difference between an eNose and the human nose is in the number of different types of sensors in an eNose (typically, no more than a few dozen) versus the number of different types of olfactory receptor neurons in the human nose (about 350).

Figure 13.19 illustrates a common technology used for eNose sensors. Pairs of electrodes are coated with polymer films, each of which conducts electricity with a different degree of resistance. When a polymer film absorbs particular odorant molecules, the volume of the film may change, which changes its electrical resistance (the change can take up to several minutes to stabilize). Each polymer-coated pair of electrodes is a sensor, and the polymer used for each sensor responds by changing its resistance in specific ways after absorbing any of a particular range of odorant molecules—this is the polymer's tuning function. The baseline resistance of each polymer is determined by exposing it to a sample of contaminant-free air (Figure 13.19, top). When the eNose is exposed to an odorant, the resistance of some of the polymers may change from baseline, increasing or decreasing to a degree that depends on both the molecular structure of the odorant and each polymer's tuning function. Any change in the resistance of a polymer indicates the presence of an odorant. Each different odorant results in a unique pattern of resistance changes (Figure 13.19, middle and bottom).

The photo at the left of Figure 13.19 shows an eNose developed by the Jet Propulsion Laboratory (JPL), with support from NASA. It contains an array of 32 sensors, a pump for drawing in air samples, a small computer, and a power source. This device spent six months on the International Space Station (ISS), where it monitored the recycled air breathed by the astronauts for various contaminants, including mercury and the gas given off during the early stages of an electrical fire. During this time, it detected Freon, formaldehyde, methanol, and ethanol at concentrations too low for humans to detect, before the concentrations reached dangerous levels.

Ultimately, the JPL eNose will be part of an environmental control system that monitors and automatically adjusts the air quality on the ISS with little or no input from the crew. NASA has established a set of spacecraft maximum allowable concentration (SMAC) values for different air contaminants that are often difficult or impossible for humans to detect at or below SMAC levels. Ammonia, for example, which is highly toxic to humans, could escape from pipes in the ISS. Exposure to ammonia concentrations of 1.5 ppm for 30 days can cause liver damage, but people can't smell ammonia at concentrations below about 30 ppm. The JPL eNose is designed to detect ammonia (and other contaminants) at such very low levels and thereby save lives. (Many other eNose applications involve detecting specific odorants—e.g., medical diagnostic applications in which an eNose can detect odorants that signal the presence of certain bacteria.)

Also useful would be an eNose that could identify the perceptual properties of novel odors, such as their relative pleasantness. In one study, an eNose was exposed to a set of 76 odors that had been rated by human smellers according to pleasantness (Haddad et

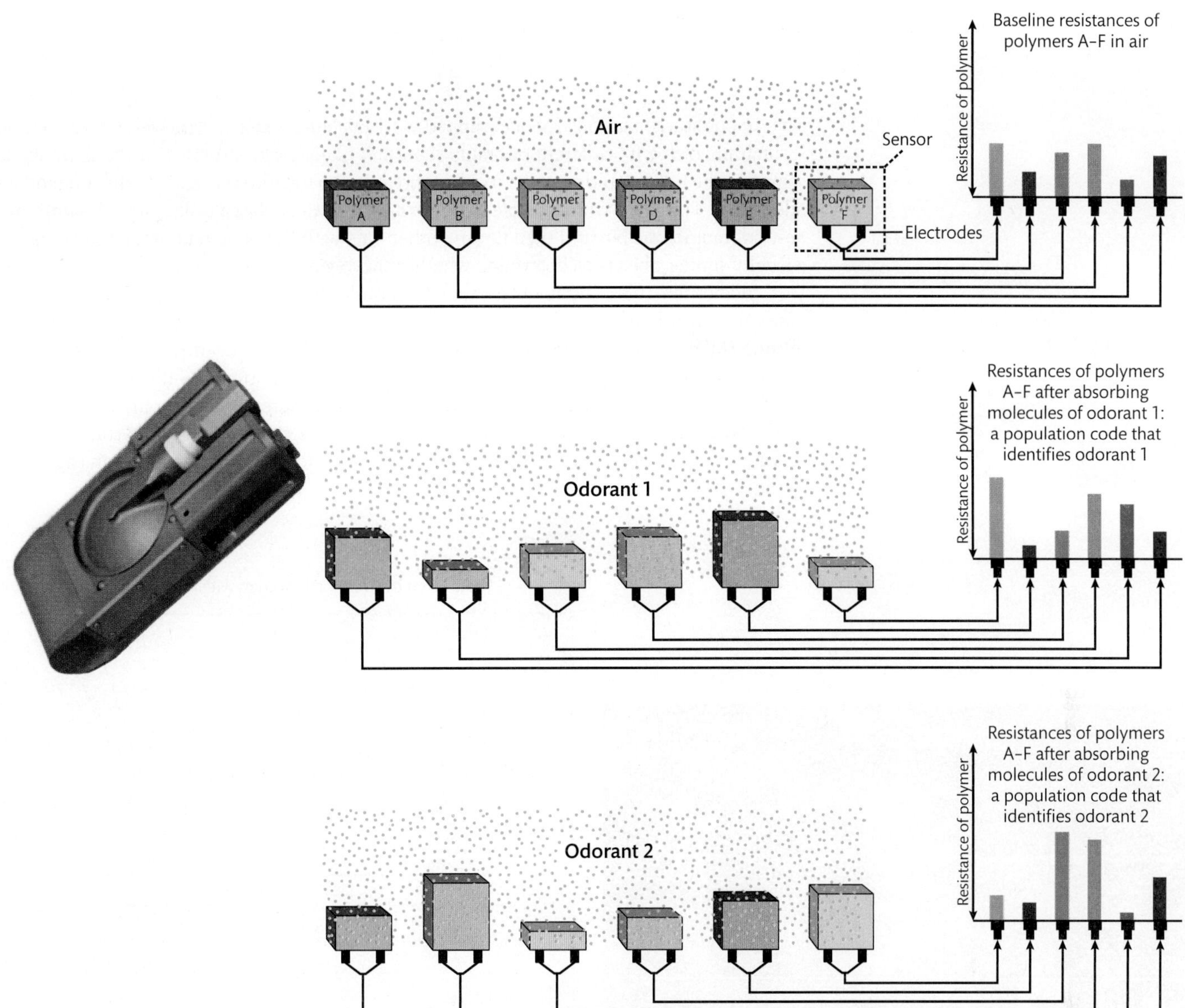

Figure 13.19 eNose Sensors The sensors in an eNose each consist of a pair of electrodes coated with a polymer film. Each sensor is coated with a different polymer. An electric current is sent through the polymer from one electrode to the other, and the electrical resistance of the polymer is measured. The polymers absorb the molecules in the air. (top) Their resistance in plain air (without any contaminants) is measured to establish the baseline resistance of each polymer. (middle and bottom) When an odorant is present, the polymer on each sensor absorbs some of the odorant molecules, which may cause a change in the volume, and hence the resistance, of the polymer, by an amount that depends on the specific odorant—that is, different odorants produce different patterns of resistance changes in the polymers, and these patterns serve as population codes identifying the odorants. The photo at left shows an eNose under development for NASA by the Jet Propulsion Laboratory, to be used to monitor air quality on the International Space Station. [NASA/JPL-Caltech]

al., 2010). The sensor responses were combined with the pleasantness ratings to develop a pattern-recognition system that the eNose could use to predict the pleasantness of novel odors, and the eNose's predictions were closely in line with the ratings of those novel odors by human smellers.

eNoses on Wheels

Prey animals often use olfaction to detect predators and determine their approximate location, so they can hide or else move in a direction away from the predator. Similarly, predators often use olfaction to detect and track prey, just as bloodhounds use olfaction to detect and track fugitives. And as discussed in the section on pheromones, male silkworm moths eager to reproduce can follow the odor plume of potential mates. Could an eNose be designed with these kinds of capabilities?

In one study, a mobile robot equipped with an eNose and a camera was put into a room containing bins with different odorants (Loutfi & Coradeschi, 2006). Using vision (via the camera), the robot could navigate to a bin and then use the eNose to sample the odorant and identify it. The robot was also able to perform other odor-related tasks, such as sampling a test odorant in one bin and then finding other bins with the same odorant, or smelling two visually similar objects to determine whether they were the same or different.

In another study, engineers designed a mobile robot with two eNoses (or "nostrils"), one on each side of its body, that could find the source of an odor by tracking the odor plume (Martinez et al., 2006). Each nostril measured the concentration of the odorant at that nostril's location as the concentration changed over time. As illustrated in Figure 13.20, various algorithms were tested for using the difference in odorant concentration at the two nostrils to control the direction taken by the robot as it tried to track the odor plume to its source. As you can see, some algorithms let the robot home in on the source rapidly, whereas others failed completely.

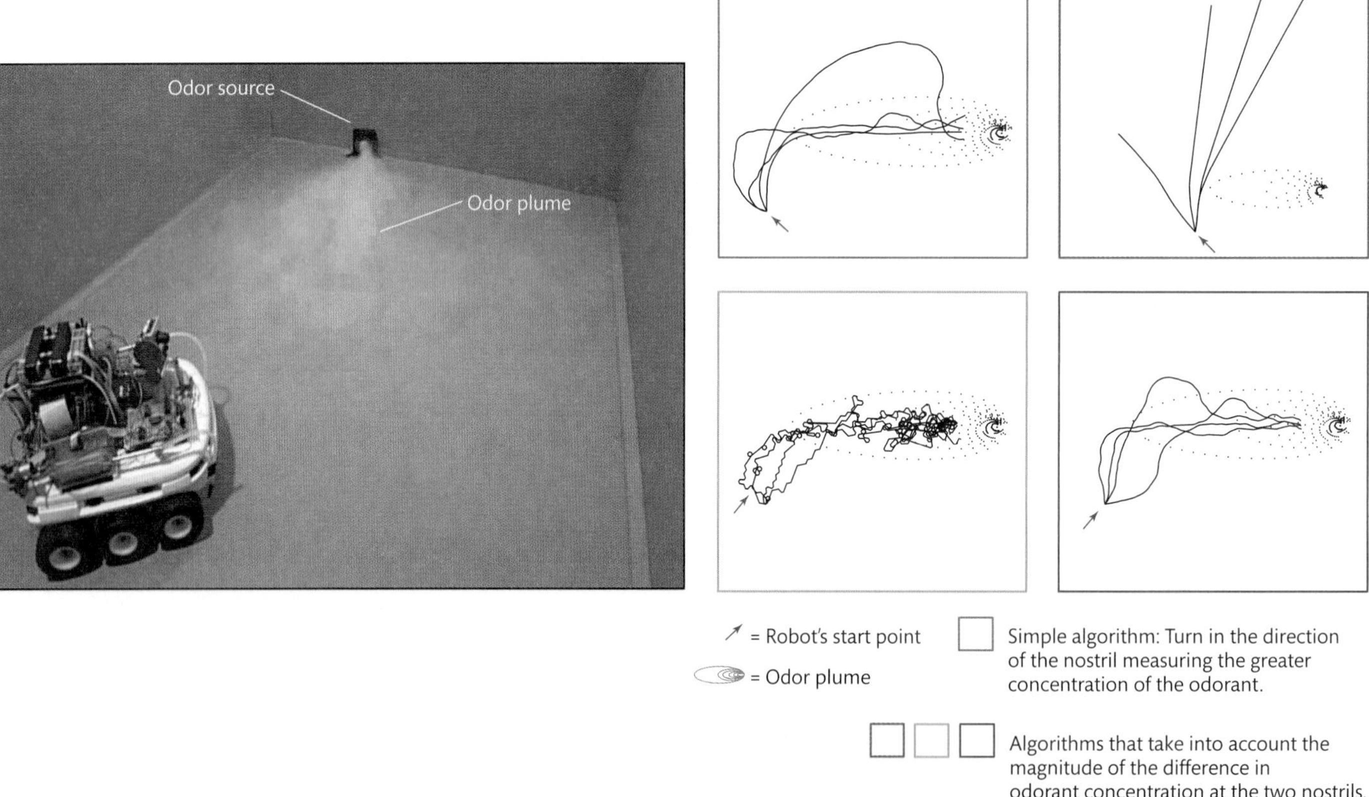
Odor source
Odor plume
Paths taken by robot on four trials with each algorithm
= Robot's start point
= Odor plume
Simple algorithm: Turn in the direction of the nostril measuring the greater concentration of the odorant.
Algorithms that take into account the magnitude of the difference in odorant concentration at the two nostrils.

Figure 13.20 Odor-Tracking eNose (left) The photo shows a mobile robot equipped with a pair of eNose "nostrils" (one on each side of its body) and placed in a room containing an odor source emitting an odor plume. The robot attempted to track the odor plume to the source. (right) Various algorithms were tested for controlling the robot's path, all based on measuring the odorant concentration at the two nostrils, as the concentration changed over time. The solid lines in each panel show the paths taken by the robot on four trials with one of four algorithms. The blue panel (upper left) shows the result of using a simple algorithm that directed the robot to turn in the direction of the nostril measuring the greater concentration. The other three panels show the paths taken using algorithms that took into account the magnitude of the difference in odorant concentration. Some algorithms were quite efficient (upper left and lower right); others weren't (upper right and lower left). (Adapted and photos from Martinez et al., 2006, Figures 4 and 9.)

Check Your Understanding

13.21 Given the number of different types of sensors in an eNose versus the number of different types of olfactory receptor neurons in the human nose, would you expect an eNose to discriminate more or fewer odors than the human olfactory system? Explain why.

SUMMARY

- Perceiving Odors We perceive odors when odorants evoke responses in our olfactory receptors. A crucial factor in detecting odorants is their concentration. The detection threshold of an odorant is the minimum concentration required for a person to detect it. The difference threshold is the minimum amount by which the concentration must change for a person to notice the difference. Odor identification ability tends to decline with age. Repeated or continuous exposure to an odorant causes adaptation to that odorant; cross-adaptation to similar odorants can also occur. Olfactory transduction occurs when odorant molecules bind to G-protein coupled receptors on the cilia of olfactory receptor neurons (ORNs) embedded in the olfactory epithelium. The ORNs' axons form the olfactory nerve, carrying signals into glomeruli within the olfactory bulb; there, the ORN axons make synapses with mitral cells and tufted cells, the axons of which form the olfactory tract, transmitting the signals to higher areas of the brain. Humans have about 350 different types of ORNs, each of which can be activated by a restricted set of odorant molecules. The neural code for odor is a population code—different odorants activate different populations of ORN types to different degrees, enabling the olfactory system to discriminate an enormous number of odorants. In the brain, signals travel along the olfactory tract to the piriform cortex (considered the primary olfactory cortex), as well as to the amygdala and the entorhinal cortex; then signals flow to the orbitofrontal cortex, the hypothalamus, and the hippocampus. The anterior piriform cortex represents features of the chemical structure of odorants; the posterior piriform cortex represents the quality of an odor as a whole. The orbitofrontal cortex and the amygdala are thought to represent the emotional dimensions of odor perception (pleasantness and unpleasantness). Odors that evoke autobiographical memories tend to relate to emotionally charged experiences from the first decade of life. Many animals emit pheromones—chemicals that evoke hormonal or behavioral responses in other individuals of the same species—which may be perceived by a vomeronasal olfactory system, distinct from the main olfactory system. The question of whether humans emit pheromones hasn't been answered conclusively.
- Perceiving Tastes and Flavors The five well-established taste categories (the basic tastes) are sweet, salty, umami, sour, and bitter. Other taste qualities that affect our overall perception of taste include hedonics (i.e., pleasantness), intensity, onset and aftertaste, and localization. These and other sensory properties—most importantly, smell—combine in the perception of flavor, the total sensory experience evoked by ingesting something. Tastants are transduced into neural signals by taste receptor cells (TRCs) within taste buds on the surfaces and inside the folds of three different types of papillae, mainly on the tongue. There are two types of TRCs—receptor cells and presynaptic cells. The cilia of receptor cells contain G-protein coupled receptors, which initiate transduction of sweet, umami, and bitter tastants; the cilia of presynaptic cells contain ion channels where transduction of salty and sour tastants is initiated. Presynaptic cells have synapses with cranial nerve fibers, which carry taste signals to the brain; receptor cells, which don't have synapses with cranial nerve fibers, are thought to send signals to the brain via cell-to-cell signaling that stimulates presynaptic cells, contributing to the production of signals with information about all five types of tastants. There are two main models of how taste signals are sent via cranial nerve fibers to the brain: the labeled-line model proposes that each cranial nerve fiber carries signals with information about just one of the five taste qualities and that the cortical neurons on the receiving end of these signals also respond only to information about a single type of tastant; the across-fiber pattern model proposes that cranial nerve fibers can carry signals from multiple taste receptor types and that the cortical neurons receiving these signals are broadly tuned to respond to signals carrying information about multiple types of tastants. Evidence favors the across-fiber pattern model, although debate remains about the exact mechanism. In the brain, signals along the cranial nerve fibers travel first to the medulla, then to the thalamus, and then to the primary taste cortex (the anterior insular cortex and the frontal operculum). Signals from the primary taste cortex go to the orbitofrontal cortex (which represents the reward value of food), the amygdala (where emotion is represented), and the hypothalamus (where hunger is represented). Some people (called *tasters*), but not others (called *nontasters*), can taste certain bitter substances at low concentrations, and some tasters (called *supertasters*) experience those bitter tastes much more intensely; the specific genetic basis for these differences has been identified.

- Applications: The eNose An eNose (electronic nose) consists of an array of sensors that change their electrical resistance when exposed to different types of odorant molecules. The pattern of resistance changes across all the sensors is a population code that can be used to detect and identify particular odorants. eNoses mounted on mobile robots can detect, locate, and discriminate odorants at different locations and can track odor plumes to their source.

KEY TERMS

across-fiber pattern model (p. 457)
anosmia (p. 433)
anterior piriform cortex (APC) (p. 443)
basic tastes (p. 451)
cell-to-cell signaling (p. 455)
circumvallate papillae (p. 453)
cribriform plate (p. 436)
cross-adaptation (p. 434)
detection threshold (p. 431)
eNose (p. 461)
flavor (p. 452)
foliate papillae (p. 453)
fungiform papillae (p. 453)
glomeruli (p. 436)
G-protein coupled receptors (GPCRs) (p. 436)
labeled-line model (p. 457)
mitral cells (p. 436)
molecule (p. 429)
odorants (p. 429)
olfactory epithelium (p. 436)
olfactory nerve (p. 436)
olfactory receptor neurons (ORNs) (p. 436)
olfactory receptors (p. 436)
olfactory tract (p. 436)
papillae (p. 453)
pheromone (p. 448)
piriform cortex (p. 442)
posterior piriform cortex (PPC) (p. 443)
presynaptic cells (p. 454)
primary taste cortex (p. 459)
receptor cells (p. 454)
tastants (p. 451)
taste buds (p. 453)
taste receptor cells (TRCs) (p. 453)
tufted cells (p. 436)
turbinates (p. 436)
umami (p. 452)
vomeronasal olfactory system (p. 448)

EXPAND YOUR UNDERSTANDING

13.1 Construct a detailed analogy between perceptual organization by the olfactory system and perceptual organization by the visual system.

13.2 A bin contains 100 scratch-and-sniff patches, each with a different familiar odor (e.g., banana, gasoline, leather, rose, etc.). If 10 people all smelled the same randomly selected patch, without any hint as to what odor it might contain, would you expect most of them to identify the odor correctly? Would you expect their odor identifications to be fairly consistent with each other, even if not correct? If they were shown a list of the 100 possible odors while making their identification decision, would you expect their identification performances to improve and/or to be more consistent? Explain your answers.

13.3 Explain why professional wine tasters are no better than the average person at detecting odors despite the training and experience that make them much better than average at discriminating, remembering, and identifying odors.

13.4 Suppose you were a participant in an fMRI experiment in which activity levels were being recorded in your anterior piriform cortex (APC) and your posterior piriform cortex (PPC). First you sniff odorants A and B, which smell different but have very similar molecular structures; then you sniff odorants C and D, which smell similar but have very different molecular structures. Which of the following statements is/are likely to be true and which is/are likely to be false?

a. Odorants A and B evoke similar levels of activity in the APC.
b. Odorants A and B evoke similar levels of activity in the PPC.
c. Odorants C and D evoke similar levels of activity in the APC.
d. Odorants C and D evoke similar levels of activity in the PPC.

13.5 A cup of cold ice cream with a scoop of chocolate and a scoop of vanilla is delicious on a hot day but not nearly as good if it's melted and has come to room temperature. Discuss the perceptual features that contribute to a difference in taste and those that contribute to a difference in flavor in the cold ice cream versus the melted ice cream.

13.6 This chapter discusses how our olfactory system uses population coding to discriminate thousands of different odors, but there's no discussion of the number of different tastes or flavors we can discriminate. Do you think you can discriminate more odors than tastes and flavors? About the same number? Fewer? Explain why you think so. Assuming that population coding is responsible for taste and flavor perception, on what variables do you think the code will be based? (Recall that the code for olfaction is based on which types of olfactory receptor neurons respond to which degrees to particular odorant molecules.)

13.7 Based on the description, in this chapter, of the ion channels that function as receptors for salty tastants, do you think you would be able to detect the saltiness of nonsodium salts in nonaversive concentrations?

13.8 On Monday, Simone ate a piece of smelly cheese with lunch. On Tuesday morning, she woke up with a head cold and couldn't smell a thing, but she again had a piece of the same smelly cheese with lunch. Which of the following areas of her brain probably showed increased activity when she ate the cheese on Monday but not on Tuesday: amygdala, piriform cortex, orbitofrontal cortex, anterior insular cortex, hypothalamus? Explain why.

13.9 Imagine an experiment in which a human participant, an eNose, and an olfaction researcher, all in separate rooms hidden from each other, are exposed to the same odorants at the same time. The eNose and the human participant then both transmit their odor perceptions by computer to the researcher, indicating how they would identify the odor, how they would rate its intensity and pleasantness, and whether the odor is one they've been exposed to before during the course of the experiment. Do you think an eNose could be constructed that would respond to the odorants in such a human way that the researcher wouldn't be able to tell which set of perceptions was coming from the eNose and which from the human? Explain your answer.

READ MORE ABOUT IT

Chaudhari, N., & Roper, S. D. (2010). The cell biology of taste. *Journal of Cell Biology, 190,* 285–296.

An up-to-date and authoritative review that summarizes current understanding about the neural basis of taste transduction.

Herz, R. (2007). *The scent of desire.* New York: Harper Perennial.

A highly accessible and engaging survey of the effects of smell on memory, emotion, and motivation.

Stevenson, R. J. (2009). *The psychology of flavour.* Oxford, England: Oxford University Press.

An in-depth treatment of how smell and taste together give rise to the experience of flavor.

Wilson, D. A., & Stevenson, R. J. (2006). *Learning to smell: Olfactory perception from neurobiology to behavior.* Baltimore: Johns Hopkins University Press.

A readable and comprehensive review of animal and human olfaction with an emphasis on the various functions of the sense of smell, including the detection and identification of nutrients, the detection of environmental hazards such as predators and fire, and social communication.

Wilson, R. I., & Mainen, Z. F. (2006). Early events in olfactory processing. *Annual Review of Neuroscience, 29,* 163–201.

A review of the neural basis of olfactory perception, from olfactory receptor neurons to the brain, in both insects and vertebrates.

Wyatt, T. D. (2003). *Pheromones and animal behavior: Communication by smell and taste.* Oxford, England: Oxford University Press.

A survey of current knowledge about animal (including human) pheromones—how they're perceived and how they affect hormonal responses and mating behavior.

GLOSSARY

A1 *see* **primary auditory cortex**

absolute threshold The minimum intensity of a physical stimulus that can just be detected by an observer.

accommodation Adjustment of the shape of the lens so light from objects at different distances focuses correctly on the retina.

accretion A dynamic depth cue—the gradual revealing ("de-occlusion") of an object as it emerges from behind another one.

achromatic light Light containing wavelengths from across the visible spectrum, with no really dominant wavelengths; perceived as more or less colorless (i.e., a shade of gray).

achromatopsia Loss of color vision caused by brain damage.

acoustic reflex A reflexive contraction of two tiny muscles in the middle ear in response to high-intensity sounds; it dampens the movements of the ossicles, which helps protect the auditory system from damage due to loud noises.

acoustic shadow An area on the other side of the head from a sound source in which the loudness of the sound is reduced because the sound waves are partially blocked by the head; it has a much greater effect on high-frequency sounds than on low-frequency sounds.

across-fiber pattern model A model of taste perception proposing that cranial nerve fibers can carry signals from multiple taste receptor types, and that the cortical neurons receiving these signals are broadly tuned to respond to signals carrying information about multiple types of tastants.

action potential An electrochemical signal that begins in the dendrites of a neuron and travels down the axon to the axon terminals.

acuity A measure of how clearly fine detail is seen.

additive color mixture A mixture of different-colored lights; called "additive" because the perceived color of the mixture is the result of adding together all the wavelengths in all the lights in the mixture.

A-delta fibers Myelinated axons of nociceptors that transmit pain signals relatively rapidly, to produce a rapid response to potentially damaging mechanical stimuli and to excessive heat.

AIP *see* **anterior intraparietal area**

amacrine cells Neurons in the inner nuclear layer of the retina.

amblyopia A condition in which both eyes develop normally but the neural signals from one eye aren't processed properly, so that fine vision doesn't develop in that eye.

Ames room A room specially designed to create an illusory perception of depth; when viewed with one eye through a peephole, all of the room's trapezoidal surfaces look rectangular.

amplitude The difference between the maximum and minimum sound pressure in a sound wave; the physical dimension of sound that is related to the perceptual dimension of loudness.

amusia A profound impairment in perceiving and remembering melodies and in distinguishing one melody from another.

anaglyph A stereogram in which the two photographs taken from adjacent camera positions are printed in contrasting colors and then superimposed; an observer who views an anaglyph with special glasses in which one lens filters out one of the colors and the other lens filters out the other color will see a single image in depth.

anosmia Loss of the ability to perceive odors.

anterior chamber The space between the cornea and the iris, filled with aqueous humor.

anterior intraparietal area (AIP) A region of the posterior parietal lobe thought to be involved in grasping movements.

anterior piriform cortex (APC) The anterior (front) portion of the piriform cortex; it produces representations of features of the chemical structure of odorant molecules.

anvil *see* **incus**

APC *see* **anterior piriform cortex**

aperture problem The impossibility of determining the actual direction of motion of a stimulus by the response of a single neuron that "sees" the stimulus only through a small "aperture" (the neuron's receptive field) and "sees" only the component of motion in the neuron's preferred direction.

aphasia An impairment in speech production or comprehension (or both) caused by damage to speech centers in the brain.

apparent motion A visual illusion in which two stimuli separated in time and location are perceived as a single stimulus moving between the two locations.

apparent motion quartet A display in which four symmetrically placed stimuli presented at alternating moments in time are perceived as two stimuli in apparent motion.

aqueous humor A clear thin fluid filling the anterior and posterior chambers of the eye.

assumption of cognitive uniformity The assumption that the functional organization of human cognition and of the brain is essentially the same in everyone.

astigmatism A condition in which the curvature of the cornea or lens is slightly irregular or asymmetrical, making it impossible for the lens to fully accommodate.

atmospheric perspective A lighting-based depth cue—the farther away an object is, the more air the light must pass through to reach us and the more that light can be scattered, with the result that distant objects appear less distinct than nearby objects.

attention The selection of some source of sensory stimulation for increased cognitive processing.

attentional cuing Providing a cue (e.g., an arrow or tone) about the location and timing of an upcoming stimulus.

audibility curve A curve showing the minimum amplitude at which sounds can be detected at each frequency.

audiogram A graphical depiction of auditory sensitivity to specific frequencies, compared to the sensitivity of a standard listener; used to characterize possible hearing loss.

audiometer An instrument that presents pure tones with known frequency and amplitude to the right or left ear; used in estimating the listener's absolute threshold for specific frequencies and to construct an audiogram.

auditory canal A narrow channel that funnels sound waves gathered by the pinna onto the tympanic membrane and that amplifies certain frequencies in those waves.

auditory core region Part of the auditory cortex, located within the transverse temporal gyrus in each hemisphere; it consists of the primary auditory cortex, the rostral core, and the rostrotemporal core.

auditory cortex Part of the cerebral cortex, tucked into the lateral sulcus on top of the temporal lobe; it consists of the auditory core region, belt, and parabelt.

auditory nerve The nerve that conveys signals from the hair cells in the organ of Corti to the brain; made up of Type I and Type II auditory nerve fibers bundled together.

auditory scene All the sound entering the ears during the current interval of time.

auditory scene analysis The process of extracting and grouping together the frequencies emitted by specific sound sources from among the complex mixture of frequencies emitted by multiple sound sources within the auditory scene.

auditory stream An assortment of frequencies occurring over time that were all emitted by the same sound source or related sound sources.

awareness Active thinking about or concentration on some source of stimulation.

axon A projection that emanates from the cell body of a neuron and that conducts neural signals to the axon terminals, for transmission to other neurons.

axon terminals Endings of an axon, where neural signals are transmitted to other neurons.

azimuth In sound localization, the location of a sound source in the side-to-side dimension in the horizontal plane—that is, the angle left or right of the median plane.

baseline firing rate A neuron's low rate of spontaneous firing at fairly random intervals in the absence of any stimulus.

basic tastes The five well-established taste categories—sweet, salty, umami, sour, and bitter.

basilar membrane A tapered membrane suspended between the walls of the cochlea; thicker, narrower, and stiffer at the base than at the apex.

Bayesian approach In object recognition, the use of mathematical probabilities to describe the process of perceptual inference.

belt Along with the parabelt, a region of cortex wrapped around and receiving signals from the auditory core region.

biased competition theory The theory that the brain resolves the competition for neural representation by selectively attending to one object and representing the features of just that object.

binding problem The problem faced by the visual system of perceiving which visual features belong to the same object.

binocular cells Neurons that respond best to the stimulation of both eyes simultaneously.

binocular disparity A depth cue based on differences in the relative positions of the retinal images of objects in the two eyes.

binocular rivalry A phenomenon in which two different images presented to the two eyes result in perceptual bistability.

bipolar cells Neurons in the inner nuclear layer of the retina.

bistratified retinal ganglion cells Retinal ganglion cells that send signals to the koniocellular layers of the lateral geniculate nucleus.

blindsight The ability to point to and sometimes discriminate visual stimuli without any conscious awareness of them.

blind spot *see* **optic disk**

border ownership The perception that an edge, or border, is "owned" by a particular region of the retinal image.

bottom-up attentional control (or *stimulus-driven attentional control*). The involuntary, unavoidable capture of attention by a salient perceptual stimulus.

bottom-up information The information contained in neural signals from receptors.

categorical perception Perception of different sensory stimuli as identical, up to a point at which further variation in the stimulus leads to a sharp change in the perception.

CDS *see* **corollary discharge signal**

cell body The part of a cell that contains the nucleus.

cell membrane A cell structure that separates what's inside the cell from what's outside the cell.

cell-to-cell signaling In taste perception, signals from receptor cells to presynaptic cells, causing the presynaptic cells to release neurotransmitters in a way that carries information about sweet, umami, and bitter tastants.

center–surround receptive field An RGC receptive field in which the center of the receptive field responds differently to stimulation than the surrounding portion of the field.

cerebral cortex The outermost layer of the cerebral hemispheres; about 2–4 mm thick and consisting mostly of gray matter (neural cell bodies).

cerebral hemisphere The two most important divisions of the brain; separated by the longitudinal fissure.

C fibers Unmyelinated axons of nociceptors that transmit pain signals relatively slowly.

change blindness Inability to quickly detect changes in complex scenes.

characteristic frequency The frequency to which each location on the basilar membrane responds most readily.

choroid The middle membrane of the eye, lining the interior of the sclera and containing most of the blood vessels that supply the inside of the eye with oxygen and nutrients.

chromatic adaptation A kind of photopigment bleaching that results from exposure to relatively intense light consisting of a narrow range of wavelengths.

ciliary muscles Tiny muscles attached to the choroid; they relax and contract to control how the choroid pulls on the zonule fibers to change the shape of the lens.

circumvallate papillae Mushroom-shaped structures (much larger than fungiform papillae) situated in a row at the back of the tongue; each circumvallate papilla contains 200–700 taste buds.

coarticulation The influence of one phoneme on the acoustic properties of another, due to the articulatory movements required to produce them in sequence.

cochlea A coiled, tapered tube within the temporal bones of the head, partitioned along its length into three chambers; contains the structures involved in auditory transduction.

cochlear duct One of the three chambers in the cochlea; separated from the tympanic canal by the basilar membrane; contains the organ of Corti; filled with endolymph.

cochlear nucleus A structure in the brain stem (one on each side of the brain); it receives signals via Type I auditory nerve fibers from the inner hair cells in the ipsilateral ear.

cognitive neuropsychology The investigation of perceptual and cognitive deficits in individuals with brain damage in order to discover how perception and cognition are carried out in the normal, undamaged brain.

cold fibers Thermoreceptors that fire at an ongoing moderate rate in response to sustained skin temperatures in the range of 17–40°C.

color circle A 2-D depiction in which hue varies around the circumference and saturation varies along any radius.

color constancy The tendency to see a surface as having the same color under illumination by lights with very different spectral power distributions.

color solid A 3-D depiction in which hue varies around the circumference, saturation varies along any radius, and brightness varies vertically.

complex cells Neurons in area V1 that respond best to a stimulus with a particular orientation; differ from simple cells in the variety and location of stimuli that generate a response.

complementary colors Pairs of colors that, when combined in equal proportion, are perceived as a shade of gray.

conductive hearing impairments Hearing impairments characterized by a loss of sound conduction to the cochlea, as a result of problems in the outer or middle ear.

cone monochromacy A condition in which a person has rods and only one type of cone.

cone of confusion A hypothetical cone-shaped surface in auditory space; when two equally distant sound sources are located on a cone of confusion, their locations are confusable because they have highly similar ILD and ITD.

cones One of the two classes of photoreceptors, named for their distinctive shape.

conjunction search Searching a display for an item that differs from all other items in the display by having a particular combination of two or more features.

consonance The quality exhibited by a combination of two or more notes from a scale that sounds pleasant, as if the notes "go together."

consonants Speech sounds produced by restricting the flow of air at one place or another along the path of the airflow from the vocal folds.

contralateral organization Opposite-side organization, in which stimulation of neurons on one side of the body or sensory organ is represented by the activity of neurons in the opposite side of the brain.

convergence A property of retinal circuits in which multiple photoreceptors send signals to one RGC.

cornea A transparent membrane at the front of the eye; light enters the eye by first passing through the cornea, which sharply refracts the light.

corollary discharge signal (CDS) A copy of an eye-movement command from the superior colliculus to the extraocular muscles, sent to the brain to inform the visual system about upcoming eye movements; used to ensure a stable visual experience even during eye movements.

corpus callosum A large bundle of axons that constitutes the major connection between the two cerebral hemispheres.

correct rejection In a signal detection experiment, a response indicating that no signal was detected on a trial when no signal was presented.

correspondence problem The problem of determining which features in the retinal image in one eye correspond to which features in the retinal image in the other eye.

corresponding points A point on the left retina and a point on the right retina that would coincide if the two retinas were superimposed—for example, the foveas of the two eyes.

cortical column A small volume of neural tissue running through the layers of the cortex perpendicular to its surface; consists of neurons that respond to similar types of stimuli and that have highly overlapping receptive fields.

cortical magnification The nonuniform representation of visual space in the cortex; the amount of cortical territory devoted to the central part of the visual field is much greater than the amount devoted to the periphery.

cortical plasticity The ability of the adult cortex to change the way it's organized.

cribriform plate The part of the skull immediately above the nasal cavity; the axons of ORNs pass through a grid of tiny holes in the plate.

cross-adaptation In olfaction, reduced sensitivity to odorants that are chemically or perceptually similar to odorants to which the person has been continuously or repeatedly exposed.

crossed disparity A type of binocular disparity produced by an object that is closer than the horopter—you would have to "cross" your eyes to look at it.

C-tactile mechanoreceptors (CT mechanoreceptors) Mechanoreceptors that are a type of free nerve endings only present on hairy skin; they respond to slow, gentle touch and send signals to the insular cortex.

CT mechanoreceptors *see* **C-tactile mechanoreceptors**

cycle In a sound wave, a repeating segment of air pressure changes.

d′ In signal detection theory, the difference between the mean of the curve showing the strength of perceptual evidence (e.g., the number of action potentials) when no signal is presented and the mean of the curve when a signal is presented; depends on the physical intensity of the signal and the participant's perceptual sensitivity, but not on the participant's decision criterion.

dark adaptation The process of adjusting retinal sensitivity (changing the operating range) as the person moves from a bright environment to a darker one; the reverse process is called *light adaptation*.

dB *see* **decibels**

DCML pathway *see* **dorsal column–medial lemniscal pathway**

decibels (dB) A physical unit used to measure sound amplitude; logarithmically related to sound pressure measured in micropascals.

decision-making bias In a signal detection experiment, a participant's tendency to be liberal or conservative in deciding whether a signal was detected, indicated by the value of the participant's decision criterion.

deletion A dynamic depth cue—the gradual hiding (occlusion) of an object as it passes behind another one.

dendrites Projections that emanate from the cell body of a neuron and that receive signals from other neurons.

depolarization Part of the sequence of events of an action potential, during which an inflow of positively charged ions causes the membrane potential to become markedly more positive.

detection threshold The degree to which the concentration of an odorant has to change for a person to notice a difference in the intensity of the odor.

deuteranopia A condition in which a person has L-cones and S-cones but lacks M-cones.

dichotic listening Listening to one message in the left ear and a different message in the right ear.

dichromacy A condition in which a person has only two types of cones, instead of the normal three; in all such cases, the person has a limited form of color vision but cannot discriminate as many colors as a person with all three cone types.

difference threshold (or *just noticeable difference [JND]*) The minimum difference between two stimuli that allows an observer to perceive that the two stimuli are different.

diopters Units used to express the power of a lens; diopters = 1/(focal length).

dissociation In cognitive neuropsychology, a pattern of brain damage and impaired function in which damage to some specific brain region is associated with impairment of some specific function but not with impairment of another function.

dissonance The quality exhibited by a combination of two or more notes from a scale that sounds unpleasant or "off."

distal stimulus A perceived object or event in the world.

distance In sound localization, how far a sound source is from the center of the head in any direction.

distributed coding Representation of objects by patterns of activity across many regions of the brain.

Doppler effect The frequency of a sound emitted by a moving sound source is higher in front of the sound source than behind it; the frequency rapidly decreases as the sound source passes the listener.

dorsal column–medial lemniscal pathway (DCML pathway) Pathway for signals involved in tactile perception and proprioception; travels up the spinal cord on the ipsilateral side, crosses to the contralateral side in the medulla, and then goes through the ventral posterior nucleus of the thalamus and on to the somatosensory cortex.

dorsal pathway A visual pathway that runs from V1 and V2 into MT and then to the parietal cortex; represents properties that relate to an object's motion or location and that can be used to guide actions.

double dissociation In cognitive neuropsychology, a pattern of brain damage and impaired function in which damage to some specific brain region is associated with impairment of some specific function A but not with impairment of another function B, along with a pattern (in a different patient) in which damage to a different region is associated with impairment of function B but not with impairment of function A.

dynamic range The range of amplitudes that can be heard and discriminated; when applied to an individual auditory nerve fiber, the range of amplitudes over which the firing rate of the fiber changes.

dynamics The manner in which loudness varies as a piece of music progresses.

eardrum *see* **tympanic membrane**

echolocation Sound localization based on emitting sounds and then processing the echoes to determine the nature and location of the object that produced the echoes.

edge completion The perception of a partially hidden edge as complete; one of the operations involved in perceptual interpolation.

edge enhancements A process by which the visual system makes edges as visible as possible, facilitating perception of where one object or surface ends in the retinal image and another begins.

EEG *see* **electroencephalography**

electroencephalography (EEG) A functional neuroimaging technique based on measurement of the electrical fields associated with brain activity.

electromagnetic radiation A physical phenomenon that is simultaneously both a wave and a stream of particles.

electromagnetic spectrum The entire range of wavelengths of electromagnetic radiation.

elevation In sound localization, the location of a sound source in the up–down dimension in the median plane—that is, the angle above or below the horizontal plane.

Emmert's law Size–distance invariance of retinal afterimages—the perceived size of an afterimage is proportional to the distance of the surface on which it's "projected."

endogenous opioids Compounds that belong to a class of substances called *opiates;* released by the body in response to painful or stressful experiences.

endorphins Endogenous opioids that have an inhibitory effect on pain-related neural signals in many areas of the central nervous system, reducing the perceived intensity of pain.

eNose An electronic nose; currently, eNoses are capable of detecting and identifying odorants, localizing their source, and even tracking odor plumes.

EPs *see* **exploratory procedures**

EPSP *see* **excitatory postsynaptic potential**

equal loudness contour A curve showing the amplitude of tones at different frequencies that sound about equally loud.

Eustachian tube A tube connecting the middle ear and the top part of the throat; normally closed but can be briefly opened (e.g., by swallowing or yawning) to equalize the air pressure in the middle ear with the air pressure outside.

excitatory neurotransmitters Neurotransmitters that have an excitatory effect on the postsynaptic neuron, increasing the probability that an action potential will be initiated.

excitatory postsynaptic potential (EPSP) The effect of an excitatory neurotransmitter, making the postsynaptic neuron's membrane potential more positive.

exploratory procedures (EPs) Hand and finger movements typically used by people to identify objects haptically.

extraocular muscles Three pairs of muscles around each eye that enable us to move our eyes very rapidly and accurately and keep the eyes always pointed in the same direction.

FAI mechanoreceptors Fast-adapting mechanoreceptors with Meissner corpuscle endings; they have relatively small receptive fields and are relatively densely arranged near the surface of the skin.

FAII mechanoreceptors Fast-adapting mechanoreceptors with Pacinian corpuscle endings; they have relatively large receptive fields and are relatively sparsely distributed relatively deeply in the skin.

false alarm In a signal detection experiment, a response indicating that a signal was detected on a trial when no signal was presented.

familiar size A size-based depth cue—knowing the retinal image size of a familiar object at a familiar distance lets us use its retinal image size to gauge its distance.

farsightedness *see* **hyperopia**

feature integration theory (FIT) The theory that the brain solves the binding problem by selectively attending to one object and ignoring any others.

feature search Searching a display for an item that differs in just one feature from all other items in the display.

Fechner's law A statement of how the perceived intensity of a stimulus changes as its physical intensity changes ($S = k \ln I/I_0$, where S is the perceived intensity, k is the Weber fraction, and $\ln I/I_0$ is the natural logarithm of the ratio of the stimulus intensity, I, to the intensity, I_0, of the same stimulus of the absolute threshold).

FFA *see* **fusiform face area**

field of view The portion of the surrounding space you can see when your eyes are in a given position in their sockets.

figure A region of an image that is perceived as being part of an object.

filter theory of attention The theory that all sensory information is registered as physical signals but that attention selects only some of those signals to be interpreted for meaning, with the rest being filtered out.

firing rate The rate at which a neuron produces action potentials, usually expressed in terms of spikes per second.

FIT *see* **feature integration theory**

flavor The total sensory experience evoked by ingesting something; it includes the perception of the basic tastes, the perception of other attributes of tastants such as pleasantness and intensity, and other sensory properties, the most important of which is smell.

floaters Shadows on the retina thrown by debris within the vitreous humor; perceived as small, semitransparent spots or threads that appear to be floating before the person's eyes and tend to move with the eyes.

fMRI *see* **functional magnetic resonance imaging**

focal length The distance from a lens at which the image of an object is in focus when the object is far away from the lens (at "optical infinity").

foliate papillae Ridgelike folds of tissue located on the sides of the tongue near the back; a few hundred taste buds are tucked into each fold.

formants Frequency bands with relatively high amplitude in the harmonic spectrum of a vowel sound.

Fourier analysis A mathematical procedure for decomposing a complex waveform into a collection of sine waves with various frequencies and amplitudes.

Fourier spectrum A depiction of the amplitudes at all frequencies that make up a complex waveform.

fovea A region in the center of the retina where the light from objects at the center of our gaze strikes the retina; contains no rods and a very high density of cones.

frequency The physical dimension of sound that is related to the perceptual dimension of pitch; expressed in hertz, the number of cycles per second of a periodic sound wave.

frontal lobe One of the four lobes of each cerebral hemisphere; separated from the temporal lobe by the lateral sulcus and from the parietal lobe by the central sulcus.

functional magnetic resonance imaging (fMRI) A functional neuroimaging technique based on measurement of the changes in blood oxygenation associated with brain activity.

functional neuroimaging An array of techniques for measuring brain activity in healthy volunteers carrying out carefully designed tasks.

functional specialization The specialization of different neural pathways and different areas of the brain for representing different kinds of information.

fundamental frequency The frequency of the lowest-frequency component of a complex waveform; determines the perceived pitch of the sound.

fungiform papillae Tiny mushroom-shaped structures located along the edges and top of the front two-thirds of the tongue; each fungiform papilla contains 3–5 taste buds on its upper surface.

fusiform face area (FFA) An area in the fusiform gyrus of the IT cortex; a functional module that responds selectively to faces.

ganglion cell layer The layer of the retina that contains retinal ganglion cells.

glaucoma A condition in which the intraocular pressure is too high for the person's eye, most commonly caused by blockage of the openings that let aqueous humor drain from the anterior chamber.

glomeruli Small, more or less spherical structures in the olfactory bulb; within the glomeruli, the axons of ORNs make synapses with the dendrites of mitral cells and tufted cells.

Golgi tendon organs Sensory organs that provide information about muscle force for proprioception.

GPCRs *see* **G-protein coupled receptors**

G-protein coupled receptors (GPCRs) A large family of proteins that function as receptors; they provide a mechanism for molecules outside a cell to influence the inner workings of the cell.

grandmother cell A neuron that responds to a particular object at a conceptual level, firing in response to the object itself, a photo of it, its printed name, and so on.

gray matter The cell bodies of neurons making up the cerebral cortex.

ground A region of an image that is perceived as part of the background.

gyrus An elongated bump on the surface of the cerebral hemisphere.

hammer *see* **malleus**

haptic perception Actively using touch to perceive and identify objects by their 3-D shape and other material properties; involves the integration of information from tactile perception, proprioception, and thermoreception.

harmonic A component frequency of a complex waveform that is an integer multiple of the fundamental frequency; the first harmonic is the fundamental frequency; the second harmonic is twice the fundamental frequency, and so on.

hearing impairment A decrease in a person's ability to detect or discriminate sounds, compared to the ability of a healthy young adult.

helicotrema An opening in the partitioning membranes at the apex of the cochlea; provides an open pathway for the perilymph to carry vibrations through the cochlea.

hertz (Hz) The number of cycles per second of a sound wave, the physical unit used to measure frequency.

heterochromatic light Light that consists of more than one wavelength.

heuristics In perceptual organization, rules of thumb based on evolved principles and on knowledge of physical regularities.

hit In a signal detection experiment, a response indicating that a signal was detected on a trial when a signal was presented.

horizontal cells Neurons in the inner nuclear layer of the retina.

horopter An imaginary surface defined by the locations in a scene from which objects would project retinal images at corresponding points.

hue The quality usually referred to as "color"—that is, blue, green, yellow, red, and so on; the perceptual characteristic most closely associated with the wavelength of light.

hue cancellation An experimental technique in which the person cancels out any perception of a particular color (e.g., yellow) in a test light by adding light of the complementary color (e.g., blue).

hyperopia (or *farsightedness*) A condition in which the optic axis is too short and accommodation cannot make the lens thick enough to focus light from a nearby object on the retina, so the light comes to a focus behind the retina, and the image on the retina is blurry; the person can see distant objects clearly but not nearby objects.

Hz *see* **hertz**

ILD *see* **interaural level difference**

illusory contours Nonexistent but perceptually real edges perceived as a result of edge completion.

image clutter A characteristic of visual scenes in which many objects are scattered in 3-D space, with partial occlusion of various parts of objects by other objects.

image enhancement A technology used in night-vision devices; dim light is amplified by converting photons into electrons, amplifying the number of electrons, and then using the electrons to produce a pattern of varying intensities on a phosphor-coated screen.

inattentional blindness Failure to perceive a fully visible but unattended visual object.

incus (or *anvil*) A small bone in the inner ear; one of the ossicles; transmits sound energy from the malleus to the stapes.

inferior colliculus A structure in the midbrain (one on each side of the brain); a stop on the ascending auditory pathway.

inferotemporal cortex (IT cortex) The cortex in the bottom part of the temporal lobe; one of the object-selective regions of the visual system.

inhibitory neurotransmitters Neurotransmitters that have an inhibitory effect on the postsynaptic neuron, decreasing the probability than an action potential will be initiated.

inhibitory postsynaptic potential (IPSP) The effect of an inhibitory neurotransmitter, making the postsynaptic neuron's membrane potential more negative.

inner hair cells Neurons in the organ of Corti; responsible for auditory transduction.

inner nuclear layer The layer of the retina that contains bipolar cells, horizontal cells, and amacrine cells.

inner synaptic layer The layer of the retina that contains the synapses among bipolar cells, amacrine cells, and RGCs.

interaural level difference (ILD) The difference in the sound level of the same sound at the two ears.

interaural time difference (ITD) The difference in arrival time of the same sound at the two ears.

International Phonetic Alphabet (IPA) An alphabet in which each symbol stands for a different speech sound; provides a distinctive way to write each phoneme in all the human languages currently in use.

interposition *see* **partial occlusion**

intraocular pressure The pressure of the fluids in the three chambers of the eye.

ion An atom that has an imbalance in the number of protons and electrons and that therefore has an electric charge.

ion channels Small pores in the cell membrane of neurons through which certain ions can flow into or out of the cell.

IPA *see* **International Phonetic Alphabet**

IPSP *see* **inhibitory postsynaptic potential**

iris The colored part of the eye—a small circular muscle with an opening in the middle (the pupil) through which light enters the eye.

Ishihara color vision test A test using configurations of multicolored disks with embedded symbols that can be seen by people with normal color vision but not by people with particular color vision deficiencies.

isomers Different possible shapes of molecules, such as the all-*trans* retinal and 11-*cis* retinal shapes of photopigment molecules.

IT cortex *see* **inferotemporal cortex**

ITD *see* **interaural time difference**

JND *see* **difference threshold**

joint receptors Sensory organs that provide information about joint angle, probably to signal when a joint has reached the limit of its normal motion.

just noticeable difference (JND) *see* **difference threshold**

key The scale that functions as the basis of a musical composition.

koniocellular layers Layers of the lateral geniculate nucleus containing neurons with very small cell bodies.

labeled-line model A model of taste perception proposing that each cranial nerve fiber carries signals with information about just one of the five taste qualities, and that the cortical neurons on the receiving end of these signals also respond only to information about a single type of tastant.

larynx (or *voice box*) The part of the vocal tract that contains the vocal folds.

LASIK Surgery to reshape the cornea in order to correct disorders of accommodation.

lateral geniculate nucleus (LGN) Part of the thalamus (one in each hemisphere); receives visual signals via the axons of RGCs.

lateral inhibition Inhibitory neural signals transmitted by horizontal cells in retinal circuits.

lateral intraparietal area (LIP) A region of the posterior parietal lobe in monkeys that is involved in the control of eye movements, including intended eye movements; an analogous region exists in the human brain.

lateral occipital cortex An area of the occipital lobe; one of the object-selective regions of the visual system.

lens A transparent structure near the front of the eye that refracts the light passing through the pupil so that the light focuses properly on the retina.

LGN *see* **lateral geniculate nucleus**

light Visible illumination; a type of electromagnetic radiation, corresponding to a small slice of wavelengths in the middle of the electromagnetic spectrum.

lightness constancy The tendency to see a surface as having the same lightness under illumination by very different amounts of light.

linear optical trajectory (LOT) A strategy for catching a fly ball by which the fielder runs in a path and at a speed such that the ball appears to travel upward in a straight line at a constant speed.

linear perspective A size-based depth cue—parallel lines appear to converge as they recede in depth.

LIP *see* **lateral intraparietal area**

LOT *see* **linear optical trajectory**

loudness The perceptual dimension of sound that is related to the physical dimension of amplitude; how intense or quiet a sound seems.

luminance contrast A difference in the intensity of illumination at adjacent retinal locations.

macular degeneration A condition characterized by damage to the photoreceptors in a region in the center of the retina; the leading cause of severe visual loss in the United States.

MAE *see* **motion aftereffect**

magnetoencephalography (MEG) A functional neuroimaging technique based on measurement of the magnetic fields associated with brain activity.

magnitude estimation A behavioral method used in psychophysical experiments to estimate perceived intensity directly; the experimenter assigns an arbitrary number (e.g., 100) to represent the intensity of a standard stimulus, and then the participant assigns numbers to other stimuli to indicate their perceived intensity relative to the standard.

magnocellular layers Layers of the lateral geniculate nucleus containing neurons with large cell bodies.

malleus (or *hammer*) A small bone in the inner ear; one of the ossicles; transmits sound energy from the tympanic membrane to the incus.

manner of articulation In the production of consonants, the nature of the restriction of airflow in the vocal tract.

McGurk effect In the perception of speech sounds, when auditory and visual stimuli conflict, the auditory system tends to compromise on a perception that shares features with both the seen and the heard stimuli; if no good compromise perception is available, either the conflict is resolved in favor of the visual stimulus or there is a conflicting perceptual experience.

mechanoreceptors Sensory receptors that transduce mechanical deformations of the skin into neural signals that are sent to the brain.

medial geniculate body (MGB) A structure in the thalamus (one on each side of the brain); the next stop on the ascending auditory pathway after the inferior colliculus.

medial intraparietal area (MIP) A region of the posterior parietal lobe involved in planning reach movements.

MEG *see* **magnetoencephalography**

Meissner corpuscles Specialized endings of FAI mechanoreceptors, where transduction takes place.

melody (or *tune*) A sequence of musical notes arranged in a particular rhythmic pattern, which listeners perceive as a single, recognizable unit.

membrane potential A difference in electrical potential across the cell membrane due to a difference in the concentrations of positive and negative ions inside and outside the cell.

Merkel cells Specialized endings of SAI mechanoreceptors, where transduction takes place.

metamers Any two stimuli that are physically different but are perceived as identical.

method of adjustment A behavioral method used in psychophysical experiments; the participant observes a stimulus and adjusts a knob that directly controls the intensity of the stimulus.

method of constant stimuli A behavioral method used in psychophysical experiments; the participant is presented with a fixed set of stimuli covering a range of intensities that are presented repeatedly in random order, and the participant must indicate whether or not each stimulus was detected.

MGB *see* **medial geniculate body**

midget retinal ganglion cells Retinal ganglion cells that send signals to the parvocellular layers of the lateral geniculate nucleus.

minimum audible angle The minimum angular separation between a reference sound source and a different sound source emitting a tone of the same frequency that yields 75% correct judgments about the relative horizontal positions of the two sources.

MIP *see* **medial intraparietal area**

miss In a signal detection experiment, a response indicating that no signal was detected on a trial when a signal was presented.

mitral cells Relay neurons within the glomeruli in the olfactory bulb; the axons of mitral cells and tufted cells form the olfactory tract.

modular coding Representation of an object by a module, a region of the brain that is specialized for representing a particular category of objects.

modularity The idea that the human mind and brain consist of a set of distinct modules, each of which carries out one or more specific functions.

molecule Two or more atoms bound together by electromagnetic forces.

monochromacy A condition in which a person has only rods or has only rods and one type of cone; in either case, the person is totally color-blind, perceiving everything in shades of gray.

monochromatic light Light that consists of only one wavelength.

monocular depth cues Cues that are based on the retinal image and that provide information about depth even with only one eye open.

motile response A response by outer hair cells that magnifies the movements of the basilar membrane, amplifying sounds and sharpening the response to particular frequencies.

motion aftereffect (MAE) A visual illusion in which a stationary element of the visual scene appears to be moving in a direction opposite to the direction of motion experienced during the immediately preceding time interval.

motion parallax A dynamic depth cue—the difference in the speed and direction with which objects appear to move in the retinal image as an observer moves within a scene.

MT An area in the middle temporal lobe consisting of neurons that respond selectively to the direction and speed of motion of stimuli.

multisensory integration A function of brain areas in which signals from different sensory systems are combined.

muscle spindles Sensory organs that provide information about muscle length, as well as information about isometric forces on muscles, for proprioception.

myopia (or *nearsightedness*) A condition in which the optic axis is too long and accommodation cannot make the lens thin enough to focus light from a distant object on the retina, so the light comes to a focus in front of the retina, and the image on the retina is blurry; the person can see nearby objects clearly but not distant objects.

natural selection The basic mechanism of biological evolution, whereby adaptive traits are more likely to be passed on to offspring through genetic inheritance and to become increasingly prevalent in a population.

NCCs *see* **neural correlates of consciousness**

near point The closest distance at which a person can bring an object into focus; presbyopia is characterized by a progressive increase in the distance from the eye to the near point as the person ages.

nearsightedness *see* **myopia**

nerve A bundle of axons that travel together from one location in the nervous system to another.

neural code A pattern of neural signals that carries information about a stimulus and can serve as a representation of that stimulus.

neural correlates of consciousness (NCCs) Correspondences between neural activity and conscious awareness.

neural signals Information-carrying electrochemical signals produced and transmitted by neurons.

neurons Cells of the nervous system that produce and transmit information-carrying signals.

neurotransmitters Chemical substances involved in the transmission of signals between neurons; neurotransmitter molecules released into a synapse by the neuron sending a signal bind to receptors on the neuron receiving the signal.

night-vision devices (NVDs) Devices to enable vision in total or near-total darkness.

nociception The perception of pain.

nociceptive pain Pain that arises from tissue damage due to physical trauma.

nociceptors Sensory receptors that transduce the physical stimuli associated with damaging mechanical, thermal, or chemical events; included among the free nerve endings in the epidermis and dermis.

noise In the study of neural activity, slight random variation in the number of action potentials produced by neurons in response to a fixed sensory stimulus.

noncorresponding points A point on the left retina and a point on the right retina that wouldn't coincide if the two retinas were superimposed—for example, the fovea of one eye and a point 4 mm to the right of the fovea in the other eye.

nuclear layers The three main layers of the retina, including the outer nuclear layer, inner nuclear layer, and ganglion cell layer.

NVDs *see* **night-vision devices**

object variety Refers to the fact that the world contains an enormous variety of objects.

occipital lobe One of the four lobes of each cerebral hemisphere; separated from the parietal lobe by the parieto-occipital sulcus.

octave A sequence of notes in which the fundamental frequency of the last note is double the fundamental frequency of the first note.

ocular dominance columns Cortical columns consisting of neurons that receive signals from the left eye only or the right eye only.

oculomotor depth cues Cues that are based on feedback from the oculomotor muscles controlling the shape of the lens and the position of the eyes.

odorants Molecules that olfactory receptors "recognize" and respond to by producing neural signals that the brain represents as perceptions of different odors.

off-center receptive fields Receptive fields of RGCs with center–surround structure in which the RGCs decrease their firing rate when the amount of light striking the center of the receptive field decreases relative to the amount of light striking the surround.

olfactory epithelium A patch of tissue in the upper reaches of each nasal cavity; the epithelium contains ORNs and is covered by a layer of olfactory mucus.

olfactory nerve The axons of ORNs, carrying neural signals from ORNs to the olfactory bulb via tiny holes in the cribriform plate.

olfactory receptor neurons (ORNs) Neurons that transduce odorant molecules into neural signals.

olfactory receptors G-protein coupled receptors in the cilia of ORNs.

olfactory tract The axons of mitral cells and tufted cells, carrying neural signals from the olfactory bulb to higher areas of the brain.

on-center receptive fields Receptive fields of RGCs with center–surround structure in which the RGCs increase their firing rate when the amount of light striking the center of the receptive field increases relative to the amount of light striking the surround.

operating range The visual system's sensitivity to the range of light intensities within the current scene; the visual system adjusts its operating range according to current conditions.

optic array The spatial pattern of light rays, varying in brightness and color, entering your eyes from different locations in a scene.

optic ataxia A deficit in the ability to guide movements visually.

optic axis An imaginary diameter line from the front to the back of the eye, passing through the center of the lens.

optic chiasm The location where the optic nerves from the two eyes split in half, with half the axons from each eye crossing over to the other hemisphere of the brain.

optic disk (or *blind spot*) Location on the retina where the axons of RGCs exit the eye; contains no photoreceptors.

optic flow A dynamic depth cue—the relative motions of objects and surfaces in the retinal image as the observer moves forward or backward through a scene.

optic nerve Nerve formed by the bundling together of the axons of RGCs; it exits the eye through the optic disk.

optic tract The continuation of the optic nerve past the optic chiasm; the right optic tract consists of axons from the RGCs in the right half of each retina, and the left optic tract consists of axons from the left half of each retina.

organ of Corti A structure in the cochlea situated on the basilar membrane; consists of three critical components—inner hair cells, outer hair cells, and the tectorial membrane.

orientation columns Cortical columns consisting of neurons with the same (or very similar) orientation tuning.

orientation tuning curve A curve on a graph that shows the average response of an orientation-tuned neuron such as a simple cell to stimuli with different orientations.

ORNs *see* **olfactory receptor neurons**

ossicles Three small bones (the malleus, incus, and stapes) in the middle ear that transmit sound energy from the tympanic membrane to the inner ear.

otolith organs Part of the vestibular system; consist of the utricle and the saccule; responsible for signaling when the head is undergoing linear acceleration or being held in a tilted position.

outer hair cells Neurons in the organ of Corti; serve to amplify and sharpen the responses of inner hair cells.

outer nuclear layer The layer of the retina consisting of photoreceptors (but not including their inner and outer segments).

outer synaptic layer The layer of the retina that contains the synapses among photoreceptors, bipolar cells, and horizontal cells.

oval window A membrane-covered opening at the base of the cochlea; vibrations of the membrane transmit sound energy from the ossicles into the cochlea.

Pacinian corpuscles Specialized endings of FAII mechanoreceptors, where transduction takes place.

pain An unpleasant sensory and emotional experience caused by potential or actual tissue damage; pain can arise from a wide range of different causes and can evoke an equally wide range of perceptual experiences.

papillae Tiny structures on surfaces in the mouth, mainly on the tongue; three different types of papillae contain taste buds.

parabelt Along with the belt, a region of cortex wrapped around and receiving signals from the auditory core region.

parahippocampal place area (PPA) An area in the parahippocampal gyrus of the IT cortex; a functional module that responds selectively to large-scale spatial layouts such as landscapes and buildings.

parasol retinal ganglion cells Retinal ganglion cells that send signals to the magnocellular layers of the lateral geniculate nucleus.

parietal lobe One of the four lobes of each cerebral hemisphere; separated from the frontal lobe by the central sulcus, from the temporal lobe by the lateral sulcus, and from the occipital lobe by the parieto-occipital sulcus.

partial occlusion (or *interposition*) A position-based depth cue—in scenes where one object partially hides (occludes) another object, the occlusion indicates that the former is closer than the latter.

parvocellular layers Layers of the lateral geniculate nucleus containing neurons with small cell bodies.

perception The later steps in the perceptual process, whereby the initial sensory signals are used to represent objects and events so they can be identified, stored in memory, and used in thought and action.

perceptual bistability A phenomenon in which an unchanging visual stimulus leads to repeated alternation between two different perceptual experiences.

perceptual grouping The process by which the visual system combines separate regions of the retinal image that "go together" based on similar properties.

perceptual inference In vision, the interpretation of a retinal image using heuristics.

perceptual interpolation The process by which the visual system fills in hidden edges and surfaces in order to represent the entirety of a partially visible object.

periodic sound waves Waves in which the cycles of compression and rarefaction repeat in a regular, or periodic, fashion.

PET *see* **positron emission tomography**

phantom limb Perception of a missing limb, as if it were still there, even though the part of the somatosensory cortex that previously received signals from the limb no longer does so.

pharynx The uppermost part of the throat.

pheromone A chemical substance emitted by individual organisms that evokes behavioral or hormonal responses in other individuals of the same species.

phonemes The smallest units of sound that, if changed, would change the meaning of a word.

phoneme transition probabilities For any particular sequence of phonemes, the chances that the sequence occurs at the start of a word, in the middle of a word, at the end of a word, or across the boundary between two words.

phonemic boundary The voice onset time at which a stop consonant transitions from being mainly perceived as voiced to being mainly perceived as voiceless.

phonemic restoration A kind of perceptual completion in which listeners seem to perceive obscured or missing speech sounds.

phosphenes Brief, tiny bright flashes in the person's field of view not caused by light but by any of a variety of other causes.

photoisomerization A change in shape by a photopigment molecule from one isomer (11-*cis* retinal) to another (all-*trans* retinal) when the molecule absorbs a photon; initiates the transduction of light to a neural signal.

photons Single particles of light; a photon is the smallest possible quantity of electromagnetic radiation.

photopigment A molecule with the ability to absorb light and initiate transduction.

photopigment bleaching A photopigment molecule's loss of ability to absorb light for a period after undergoing photoisomerization.

photopigment regeneration The process whereby photopigment molecules change back into the 11-*cis* shape after photoisomerization.

photoreceptors Retinal neurons (rods and cones) that transduce light into neural signals.

pigment epithelium A layer of cells attached to the choroid; photoreceptors are embedded in it.

piriform cortex The brain region considered to be the primary olfactory cortex, because it's the only region that both receives signals directly from the olfactory bulb and is known to be dedicated solely to olfaction.

pitch The perceptual dimension of sound that corresponds to the physical dimension of frequency; the perceived highness or lowness of a sound.

pixels Picture elements in the display screen of a color monitor; a pixel consists of three subelements, each designed to emit the light of one of three primary colors—red, green, or blue.

place code Frequency representation based on the displacement of the basilar membrane at different locations.

place of articulation In the production of consonants, the point in the vocal tract at which airflow is restricted, described in terms of the anatomical structures involved in creating the restriction.

point-light walker A display in which biological motion is made visible by attaching small lights at critical locations on an organism's body (e.g., at a person's arm, leg, and hip joints) and then shooting a video of the organism in motion in darkness.

population code A consistent difference in the patterning of the relative responses of a population of differently tuned neurons; used to compute perceptual features such as the orientation of a visual stimulus.

positron emission tomography (PET) A functional neuroimaging technique based on measurement of the changes in blood flow associated with brain activity, using a radioactive substance introduced into the blood.

posterior chamber The space between the iris and the lens, filled with aqueous humor.

posterior piriform cortex (PPC) The posterior (rear) portion of the piriform cortex; it produces representations of the quality of an odor as a whole, regardless of whether the odor is simple or complex.

postsynaptic membrane The membrane of the dendrite or cell body receiving a neural signal.

PPA *see* **parahippocampal place area**

PPC *see* **posterior piriform cortex**

preferred orientation The stimulus orientation that tends to produce the strongest response from an orientation-tuned neuron such as a simple cell.

preferred stimulus The type of stimulus that produces a neuron's maximum firing rate; for RGCs with on-center receptive fields, the preferred stimulus is a spot of light that exactly fills the center of the receptive field.

presbyopia A common condition in which the lens becomes less elastic with age, characterized by a progressive increase in the distance from the eye to the near point as the person ages; as in hyperopia, accommodation can't make the lens thick enough to focus light from nearby objects.

presynaptic cells A type of taste receptor cells in which the receptors take the form of ion channels where transduction of salty and sour tastants is initiated.

presynaptic membrane The membrane at the axon terminal of a neuron producing an action potential.

primary auditory cortex (or *A1*) Part of the auditory core region.

primary colors Any three colors that can be combined in different proportions to produce a range of other colors.

primary somatosensory cortex (or *S1*) A subregion of the somatosensory cortex; the first area to receive somatosensory signals from the ventral posterior nucleus of the thalamus; divided into four side-by-side strips known as areas 31, 3b, 1, and 2.

primary taste cortex The first cortical areas to receive taste signals, consisting of the anterior insular cortex and the frontal operculum.

primary visual cortex (or *V1*) The part of the occipital lobe where signals flow from the lateral geniculate nucleus.

principle of univariance With regard to cones, the principle that absorption of a photon of light results in the same response regardless of the wavelength of the light.

proprioception Perception of the position and movement of body parts, based on the information in neural signals from specialized sensors within those body parts.

prosopagnosia A type of visual agnosia in which the person is unable to recognize faces, with little or no loss of ability to recognize other types of objects.

protanopia A condition in which a person has M-cones and S-cones but lacks L-cones.

proximal stimulus A physical phenomenon evoked by a distal stimulus that impinges on the specialized cells of a sense.

psychometric function A curve that relates a measure of perceptual experience to the intensity of a physical stimulus.

psychophysical scaling The process of measuring how changes in stimulus intensity relate to changes in the perceived intensity.

psychophysics A field of study concerned with relating psychological experience to physical stimuli.

pupil An opening in the middle of the iris, through which light enters the eye.

pupillary reflex The automatic process by which the iris contracts and relaxes to control the size of the pupil, in response to the relative brightness of light entering the eye.

pure tone A sound wave in which air pressure changes over time according to a mathematical formula called a *sine wave,* or *sinusoid.*

random dot kinematogram A display in which a grid is filled with tiny, randomly placed black and white square dots and in which the dots in a region of the grid are then moved rigidly together as a group; the shape of the region is visible when the dots move but not when they're still.

random dot stereogram (RDS) A stereogram in which both images consist of a grid of randomly arranged black and white dots, identical except for the displacement of a position in one image relative to the other; an observer who views a random dot stereogram in a stereoscope or as an anaglyph will see a single image with the displaced portion in depth.

rapid serial visual presentation (RSVP) An experimental procedure in which participants must note whether a particular type of scene occurs in a series of photographs presented at a very high rate (3 to10 photos per second).

RDS *see* **random dot stereogram**

receiver operating characteristic (ROC) In a signal detection experiment, a curve representing the quality of a participant's performance.

receptive field The region of a sensory surface that, when stimulated, causes a change in the firing rate of a neuron that "monitors" that region of the surface; the receptive field of an RGC is the region of the retina occupied by the photoreceptors to which the RGC is connected.

receptor cells A type of taste receptor cells containing receptors that initiate transduction of sweet, umami, and bitter tastants.

refractory period Following an action potential, a brief period during which a new action potential cannot be initiated.

relative height A position-based depth cue—the relative height of the objects in the retinal image with respect to the horizon—or with respect to eye level if there is no visible horizon—provides information about the objects' relative distance from the observer.

relative size A size-based depth cue—under the assumption that two or more objects are about the same size, the relative size of their retinal images can be used to judge their relative distances.

representations Information in the mind and brain used to identify objects and events, to store them in memory, and to support thought and action.

resting potential The membrane potential when a neuron is at rest (about −70 mV).

retina The inner membrane of the eye, made up of neurons, including the photo receptors that convert the light entering the eye into neural signals.

retinal ganglion cells (RGCs) Neurons in the ganglion cell layer of the retina.

retinal image A clear image on the retina of the optic array.

retinitis pigmentosa (RP) An inherited condition in which there is gradual degeneration of the photoreceptors over many years, often leading to night blindness and "tunnel vision."

retinotopic mapping An arrangement of neurons in the visual system whereby signals from retinal ganglion cells with receptive fields that are next to each other on the retina travel to neurons that are next to each other in each visual area of the brain.

reverberation time (RT) The time for a sound to decay effectively to zero.

RGCs *see* **retinal ganglion cells**

rhythm The temporal patterning of events in a musical composition, encompassing tempo, beat, and meter.

ROC *see* **receiver operating characteristic**

rod monochromacy A condition in which a person has rods only, with no cones.

rod monochromats Individuals with a very rare genetic disorder in which the retina develops with rods but without cones; used in dark adaptation experiments to establish the curve for rods.

rods One of the two classes of photoreceptors, named for their distinctive shape.

round window A membrane-covered opening at the base of the tympanic canal in the cochlea; serves as a kind of "relief valve" for the pressure waves traveling through the perilymph.

RP *see* **retinitis pigmentosa**

RSVP *see* **rapid serial visual presentation**

RT see **reverberation time**

S1 *see* **primary somatosensory cortex**

S2 *see* **secondary somatosensory cortex**

SAI mechanoreceptors Slow-adapting mechanoreceptors with Merkel cell endings; they have relatively small receptive fields and are relatively densely arranged near the surface of the skin.

SAII mechanoreceptors Slow-adapting mechanoreceptors; they have relatively large receptive fields and are relatively sparsely distributed relatively deeply in the skin.

saccades *see* **saccadic eye movements**

saccadic eye movments (or *saccades*) Brief, rapid eye movements that change the focus of gaze from one location to another.

saccadic suppression The visual system's suppression of neural signals from the retina during saccadic eye movements.

saturation The vividness (or purity or richness) of a hue.

SC *see* **superior colliculus**

scale A particular subset of the notes in an octave.

sclera The outer membrane of the eye; a tough protective covering whose visible portion is the white of the eye and the transparent cornea at the front of the eye.

secondary somatosensory cortex (or *S2*) A subregion of the somatosensory cortex; receives signals from area S1.

selective attention Attention to some things and not to others.

semicircular canals Part of the vestibular system; three mutually perpendicular hollow curved tubes in the skull filled with endolymph; responsible for signaling head rotation.

semitones The 12 proportionally equivalent intervals between the notes in an octave.

sensation The initial steps in the perceptual process, whereby physical features of the environment are converted into electrochemical signals that are sent to the brain for processing.

senses Physiological functions for converting particular environmental features into electrochemical signals.

sensitization A mechanism that decreases the response threshold of nociceptors, so that even very low level stimulation of an injury site can cause pain.

sensorineural hearing impairments Hearing impairments caused by damage to the cochlea, the auditory nerve, or the auditory areas or pathways of the brain.

sensory receptors Specialized neurons that convert proximal stimuli into neural signals.

sensory substitution device (SSD) Any artificial aid in the process of acquiring information via one sense that is usually acquired via another sense.

shape constancy A type of perceptual constancy—the tendency to perceive an object's shape as constant despite changes in the shape of the object's retinal image due to the object's changing orientation.

shape–slant invariance The relation between perceived shape and perceived slant: the perceived shape of an object depends on its perceived slant, and vice versa.

signal detection theory A framework for measuring how people make decisions based on noisy perceptual evidence; provides a way to measure perceptual sensitivity apart from the decision-making style.

simple cell A type of neuron in area V1 that responds best to a stimulus with a particular orientation in the location of its receptive field.

single-cell recording A technique used to measure the membrane potential.

size constancy A type of perceptual constancy—the tendency to perceive an object's size as constant despite changes in the size of the object's retinal image due to the object's changing distance from the observer.

size–distance invariance The relation between perceived size and perceived distance: the perceived size of an object depends on its perceived distance, and vice versa.

size–distance relation The farther away an object is from the observer, the smaller is its retinal image.

size perspective A depth cue in scenes in which the size–distance relation is apparent.

smooth pursuit eye movements Eye movements made to track a moving object or to track a stationary object while the head is moving.

somatosensory cortex A region of the cerebral cortex in the anterior parietal lobe; receives signals carrying sensory information via the ventral posterior nucleus of the thalamus.

sound spectrogram A graph that includes the dimensions of frequency, amplitude, and time, showing how the frequencies corresponding to each vowel sound in an utterance change over time.

sound waves Waves of pressure changes in air caused by the vibrations of a source.

spatial summation A property of retinal circuits with convergence in which signals from photoreceptors in some small space on the retina summate (add up) to affect the resonse of the RGC in the circuit.

SPD *see* **spectral power distribution**

spectral power distribution (SPD) The intensity (power) of a light at each wavelength in the visible spectrum.

spectral reflectance The proportion of light that a surface reflects at each wavelength.

spectral sensitivity The degree to which a photopigment molecule absorbs light of different wavelengths.

spectral sensitivity function The probability that a cone's photopigment will absorb a photon of light of any given wavelength.

spectral shape cue A pinna-induced modification in a sound's frequency spectrum; it provides information about the elevation of the sound source.

spinothalamic pathway Pathway for signals involved in nociception and thermoreception; crosses over to the contralateral side within the spinal cord and then goes through the ventral posterior nucleus of the thalamus and on to the cortex.

SSD *see* **sensory substitution device**

staircase method A behavioral method used in psychophysical experiments; the participant is presented with a stimulus and indicates whether it was detected, and based on that response, the next stimulus is either one step up or one step down in intensity.

stapes (or *stirrup*) A small bone in the inner ear; one of the ossicles; transmits sound energy from the tympanic membrane to the incus.

static monocular depth cues Cues that provide information about depth on the basis of the position of objects in the retinal image, the size of the retinal image, and the effects of lighting in the retinal image.

stereocilia Small hairlike projections of the tops of inner and outer hair cells.

stereogram Two depictions of a scene that differ in the same way as an observer's two retinal images of that scene would differ; an observer who simultaneously views one image with one eye and the other image with the other eye (as in a stereoscope) will see a combined image in depth.

stereopsis (or *stereoscopic depth perception*) The vivid sense of depth arising from the visual system's processing of the different retinal images in the two eyes.

stereoscopic depth perception *see* **stereopsis**

Stevens power law A statement of the relationship between the physical intensity of a stimulus and its perceived intensity ($S = cI^n$, where S is the perceived intensity of the stimulus, I is its physical intensity, the exponent n is different for each perceptual dimension, and c is a constant that depends on which units are being used for S and I).

stimuli The objects and events that are perceived (distal stimuli) and the physical phenomena they produce (proximal stimuli).

stimulus-driven attentional control *see* **bottom-up attentional control**

stirrup *see* **stapes**

strabismus A disorder of the extraocular muscles in which the two eyes are not aligned with one another, resulting in a double image, which impairs binocular depth perception.

subtractive color mixture A mixture of different-colored substances; called "subtractive" because the light reflected from the mixture has certain wavelengths subtracted (absorbed) by each substance in the mixture.

sulcus An indentation between two gyri on the surface of the cerebral hemispheres.

superior colliculus (SC) A structure near the top of the brain stem (one in each hemisphere); its principal function is to help control eye movements.

superior olivary complex A structure in the brain stem (one on each side of the brain); a stop on the ascending auditory pathway, receiving signals from both cochlear nuclei.

surface completion The perception of a partially hidden surface as complete; one of the operations involved in perceptual interpolation.

synapse A tiny gap between the axon terminal of one neuron and the dendrite or cell body of another neuron.

synaptic layers In the retina, two layers separating the three nuclear layers—the outer synaptic layer and inner synaptic layer.

synaptic vesicles Within axon terminals, tiny sacs that contain neurotransmitter molecules.

tactile agnosia An inability to recognize objects by touch, which can result from damage to the parietal cortex, specifically to area S2.

tactile perception (or *touch*) Perception that results from the mechanical deformation—indentation, vibration, or stretching—of the skin.

task switching A rapid shifting of attention from one task to another and back again.

tastants Molecules that taste receptors "recognize" and respond to by producing neural signals that the brain represents as perceptions of different tastes.

taste buds Structures that contain taste receptor cells, within papillae in the mouth.

taste receptor cells (TRCs) Elongated neurons, packed within taste buds, that transduce tastants into neural signals.

tectorial membrane A membrane that lies above the hair cells in the organ of Corti.

temporal code Frequency representation based on a match between the frequencies in incoming sound waves and the firing rates of auditory nerve fibers.

temporal lobe One of the four lobes of each cerebral hemisphere; separated from the frontal lobe and the parietal lobe by the lateral sulcus.

texture gradient A size-based depth cue—if surface variations or repeated elements of a surface are fairly regular in size and spacing, the retinal image size of these equal-size features decreases as their distance increases.

thalamus The most important subcortical structure involved in perception; most neural signals pass through the thalamus on their paths from the sensory organs to the cortex.

thermal imaging A technology used in night-vision devices; infrared radiation emitted by objects and surfaces in a scene are converted into a visible electronic image.

thermoreception The ability to sense the temperature of objects and surfaces in contact with the skin.

thermoreceptors Sensory receptors for the detection of temperatures within the range of about 17–43°C; included among the free nerve endings in the epidermis and dermis.

timbre The difference in sound quality between two sounds with the same pitch and loudness; for complex periodic sounds, timbre is mainly due to differences in the relative amplitudes of the sounds' overtones; the perceptual dimension of sound that is related to the physical dimension of waveform.

tinnitus A persistent perception of sound, such as a ringing or buzzing, not caused by any actual sound.

tip links Tiny fibers connecting the tips of adjacent stereocilia on hair cells; increased tension on tip links pulls open ion channels in the membranes of the stereocilia.

tonotopic map An arrangement of neurons within auditory brain regions such that the characteristic frequencies of the neurons gradually shift from lower at one end of the region to higher at the other end.

top-down attentional control (or *voluntary attentional control*) Deliberately paying attention to something in order to get information needed to achieve goals.

top-down information An observer's knowledge, expectations, and goals, which can affect perception.

topographic agnosia A type of visual agnosia in which the person is unable to recognize spatial layouts such as buildings, streets, landscapes, and so on.

touch *see* **tactile perception**

transduction The transformation of a physical stimulus into neural signals.

transpositions Two versions of the same melody, containing the same intervals but starting at different notes.

TRCs *see* **taste receptor cells**

tritanopia A condition in which a person has L-cones and M-cones but lacks S-cones.

tufted cells Relay neurons within the glomeruli in the olfactory bulb; the axons of tufted cells and mitral cells form the olfactory tract.

turbinates Bony convolutions of tissue protruding into the nasal cavities, functioning to disperse air evenly throughout the nasal cavities.

tune *see* **melody**

tympanic canal One of the three chambers in the cochlea; separated from the cochlear duct by the basilar membrane; filled with perilymph.

tympanic membrane (or *eardrum*) A thin, elastic diaphragm at the inner end of the auditory canal that vibrates in response to the sound waves that strike it; it forms an airtight seal between the outer ear and the middle ear.

umami A basic taste evoked by tastants such as MSG and certain amino acids found in meats; it generally signals the presence of protein in food.

uncrossed disparity A type of binocular disparity produced by an object that is farther away than the horopter—you would have to "uncross" your eyes to look at it.

uniform connectedness A characteristic of regions of the retinal image that have approximately uniform properties.

unilateral visual neglect A condition in which a person has difficulty attending to stimuli on one half of the visual field (almost always the left half), as a result of damage to the contralateral posterior parietal cortex.

utility In signal detection theory, a measure of the overall satisfaction resulting from a given decision.

uvula A flap of tissue that hangs off the posterior edge of the soft palate; it can close off the nasal cavity.

V1 *see* **primary visual cortex**

V4 An area in the occipital lobe consisting of neurons that respond selectively to the color of stimuli and to the curvature of edges.

variable views The different retinal images that can be projected by the same object or category of objects.

ventral pathway A visual pathway that runs from V1 and V2 into V4 and then to the inferotemporal cortex; represents properties that relate to an object's identity, such as its color and shape.

ventral posterior nucleus (VP nucleus) A nucleus of the thalamus; part of both the DCML pathway and the spinothalamic pathway.

ventriloquism effect The tendency to localize sound on the basis of visual cues when visual and auditory cues provide conflicting information.

vergence eye movements Eye movements that occur when the gaze shifts between focusing on objects at different distances.

vestibular canal One of the three chambers in the cochlea; separated from the cochlear duct by Reissner's membrane; filled with perilymph.

vestibular system The sense organs used to produce neural signals carrying information about balance and acceleration; includes the semicircular canals and the otolith organs.

vestibulo–ocular reflex An unconscious compensating movement of the eyes during head movements in order to maintain a stable gaze.

visible spectrum The portion of the electromagnetic spectrum in the range of about 400 to about 700 nm; within this range, people with normal vision perceive differences in wavelength as differences in color.

visual agnosia An impairment in object recognition.

visual angle The angle subtended by an object in the field of view.

visual neuroprosthetic devices Devices designed to help the blind see; relay signals from a camera or photocells to implanted stimulators that activate the visual system.

visual search Searching for a specific target in a scene containing one, a few, or many objects.

vitreous chamber The main interior portion of the eye, filled with vitreous humor.

vitreous humor A clear, somewhat gel-like fluid filling the vitreous chamber of the eye.

vocal cords *see* **vocal folds**

vocal folds (or *vocal cords*) A pair of membranes within the larynx.

voice box *see* **larynx**

voice onset time (VOT) In the production of stop consonants, the interval between the initial burst of frequencies and the onset of voicing.

voicing In the production of consonants, specifies whether the vocal folds are vibrating or not (i.e., whether the consonant is voiced or voiceless).

voluntary attentional control *see* **top-down attentional control**

vomeronasal olfactory system In many species, an olfactory system that senses pheromones; it is distinct from the main olfactory system used to smell most substances.

VOT *see* **voice onset time**

vowels Speech sounds produced with a relatively unrestricted flow of air through the pharynx and oral cavity.

VP nucleus *see* **ventral posterior nucleus**

warm fibers Thermoreceptors that fire at an ongoing moderate rate in response to sustained skin temperatures in the range of 29–43°C.

wavelength The distance between two successive peaks of a wave; different types of electromagnetic radiation are defined by their differences in wavelength.

Weber fraction The constant k in Weber's law ($JND = kI$).

Weber's law A statement of the relationship between the intensity of a standard stimulus and the size of the just noticeable difference ($JND = kI$, where I is the intensity of the standard stimulus and k is a constant that depends on the perceptual dimension being measured).

white matter The myelin-covered axons of cortical neurons, making up the interior parts of the cerebral hemispheres; these axons connect neurons located in different parts of the cerebral cortex.

zero disparity A type of binocular disparity in which the retinal image of an object falls at corresponding points in the two eyes.

zonule fibers Fibers that connect the lens to the choroid; they pull on the lens to change its shape.

REFERENCES

Adams, D. L., & Horton, J. C. (2009). Ocular dominance columns: Enigmas and challenges. *The Neuroscientist, 15,* 62–77.

Adelson, E. H. (1993). Perceptual organization and the judgment of brightness. *Science, 262,* 2042–2044.

Adelson, E. H., & Movshon, J. A. (1982). Phenomenal coherence of moving visual patterns. *Nature, 300,* 523–525.

Ahveninen, J., Jääskeläinen, I. P., Raij, T., Bonmassar, G., Devore, S. Hämäläinen, M., . . . Belliveau, J. W. (2006). Task-modulated "what" and "where" pathways in human auditory cortex. *Proceedings of the National Academy of Sciences, USA, 103,* 14608–14613.

Albright, T. D. (1984). Direction and orientation selectivity of neurons in visual area MT of the macaque. *Journal of Neurophysiology, 52,* 1106–1130.

Amedi, A., Stern, W. M., Camprodon, J. A., Bermpohl, F., Merabet, L., Rotman, S., . . . Pascual-Leone, A. (2007). Shape conveyed by visual-to-auditory sensory substitution activates the lateral occipital complex. *Nature Neuroscience, 10,* 687–689.

American Medical Association. (2008). *Guides to the evaluation of permanent impairment* (6th ed.). Chicago: American Medical Association Press.

Andrews, P. R., & Campbell, F. W. (1991). Images at the blind spot. *Nature, 353,* 308.

Angelaki, D. E., & Cullen, K. E. (2008). Vestibular system: The many facets of a multimodal sense. *Annual Review of Neuroscience, 31,* 125–150.

Arnott, S. R., Binns, M. A., Grady, C. L., & Alain, C. (2004). Assessing the auditory dual-pathway model in humans. *NeuroImage, 22,* 401–408.

Atchison, D. A., & Smith, G. (2000). *Optics of the human eye.* Boston: Butterworth-Heinemann.

Attneave, F. (1971). Multistability in perception. *Scientific American, 225*(6), 63–71.

Awh, E., Armstrong, K. M., & Moore, T. (2006). Visual and oculomotor selection: Links, causes and implications for spatial attention. *Trends in Cognitive Sciences, 10,* 124–130.

Bachmanov, A. A., & Beauchamp, G. K. (2007). Taste receptor genes. *Annual Review of Nutrition, 27,* 389–414.

Bach-y-Rita, P., & Kercel, S. W. (2003). Sensory substitution and the human–machine interface. *Trends in Cognitive Sciences, 7,* 541–546.

Bahill, A. T., & Karnavas, W. J. (1993). The perceptual illusion of baseball's rising fastball and breaking curveball. *Journal of Experimental Psychology: Human Perception and Performance, 19,* 3–14.

Bahill, A. T., & LaRitz, T. (1984). Why can't batters keep their eyes on the ball? *American Scientist, 72,* 249–253.

Bantick, S. J., Wise, R. G., Ploghaus, A., Clare, S., Smith, S. M., & Tracey, I. (2002). Imaging how attention modulates pain in humans using functional MRI. *Brain, 125,* 310–319.

Barlow, H. B. (1953). Summation and inhibition in the frog's retina. *Journal of Physiology, 119,* 69–88.

Barlow, H. B. (1972). Single units and sensation: A neuron doctrine for perceptual psychology? *Perception, 1,* 371–394.

Barlow, H. B., Blakemore, C., & Pettigrew, J. D. (1967). The neural mechanism of binocular depth discrimination. *Journal of Physiology, 193,* 327–342.

Barlow, H. B., & Hill, R. M. (1963). Evidence for a physiological explanation for the waterfall phenomenon and figural aftereffects. *Nature, 200,* 1345–1347.

Barlow, H. B., Hill, R. M., & Levick, W. R. (1964). Retinal ganglion cells responding selectively to direction and speed of image motion in the rabbit. *Journal of Physiology, 173,* 377–407.

Baylor, D. A., Nunn, B. J., & Schapf, J. L. (1987). Spectral sensitivity of cones of the monkey *Macaca fascicularis. Journal of Physiology, 390,* 145–160.

Beck, J., & Gibson, J. J. (1955). The relation of apparent shape to apparent slant in the perception of objects. *Journal of Experimental Psychology, 50,* 125–133.

Becker, H. G. T., Erb, M., & Haarmeier, T. (2008). Differential dependency on motion coherence in subregions of the human MT+ complex. *European Journal of Neuroscience, 28,* 1674–1685.

Beckers, G., & Zeki, S. M. (1995). The consequences of inactivating areas V1 and V5 on visual motion perception. *Brain, 118,* 49–60.

Behrmann, M., Geng. J. J., & Shomstein, S. (2004). Parietal cortex and attention. *Current Opinion in Neurobiology, 14,* 212–217.

Bende, M., & Nordin, S. (1997). Perceptual learning in olfaction: Professional wine tasters versus controls. *Physiology & Behavior, 62,* 1065–1070.

Bendor, D., & Wang, X. (2008). Neural response properties of primary, rostral, and rostrotemporal core fields in the auditory cortex of marmoset monkeys. *Journal of Neurophysiology, 100,* 888–906.

Bhattacharya, M. R., Bautista, D. M., Wu, K., Haeberle, H., Lumpkin, E. A., & Julius, D. (2008). Radial stretch reveals distinct populations of mechanosensitive mammalian somatosensory neurons. *Proceedings of the National Academy of Sciences, USA, 105,* 20015–20020.

Bhutta, M. F. (2007). Sex and the nose: Human pheromonal responses. *Journal of the Royal Society of Medicine, 100,* 268–274.

Biederman, I. (1987). Recognition-by-components: A theory of human image understanding. *Psychological Review, 94,* 115–147.

Biederman, I., Mezzanotte, R. J., & Rabinowitz, J. C. (1982). Scene perception: Detecting and judging objects undergoing relational violations. *Cognitive Psychology, 14,* 143–177.

Bingel, U., Lorenz, J., Glauche, V., Knab, R., Gläscher, J., Weiller, C., & Büchel, C. (2004). Somatotopic organization of human somatosensory cortices for pain: A single trial fMRI study. *NeuroImage, 23,* 224–232.

Blake, D. T., Hsiao, S. S., & Johnson, K. O. (1997). Neural coding mechanisms in tactile pattern recognition: The relative contributions of slowly and rapidly adapting mechanoreceptors to perceived roughness. *Journal of Neuroscience, 17,* 7480–7489.

Blake, R., & Shiffrar, M. (2007). Perception of human motion. *Annual Review of Psychology, 58,* 47–73.

Blanche, P.-A., Bablumian, A., Voorakaranam, R., Christenson, C., Lin, W., Gu, T., . . . Peyghambarian, N. (2010). Holographic three-dimensional telepresence using large-area photorefractive polymer. *Nature, 468,* 80–83.

Blauert, J. (1997). *Spatial hearing: The psychophysics of human sound* (rev. ed.). Cambridge, MA: MIT Press.

Boring, E. G. (1940). Size constancy and Emmert's law. *American Journal of Psychology, 53,* 293–295.

Born, R. T., & Bradley, D. C. (2005). Structure and function of visual area MT. *Annual Review of Neuroscience, 28,*157–189.

Braddick, O. (1993). Segmentation versus integration in visual motion processing. *Trends in Neurosciences, 16,* 263–268.

Bradley, D. C., Troyk, P. R., Berg, J. A., Bak, M., Cogan, S., Erickson, R., . . . Xu, H. (2005). Visuotopic mapping through a multichannel stimulating implant in primate V1. *Journal of Neurophysiology, 93,* 1659–1670.

Bregman, A. S. (1990). *Auditory scene analysis*. Cambridge, MA: MIT Press.

Bregman, A. S. (1993). Auditory scene analysis: Hearing in complex environments. In S. McAdams & E. Bigand (Eds.), *Thinking in sound* (pp. 10–36). Oxford, England: Oxford University Press.

Bregman, A. S., & Rudnicky, A. (1975). Auditory segregation: Stream or streams? *Journal of Experimental Psychology: Human Perception and Performance, 1,* 263–267.

Breslin, P. A. S. (2000). Human gustation. In T. E. Finger, W. L. Silver, & D. Restrepo (Eds.), *The neurobiology of taste and smell* (2nd ed., pp. 423–462). New York: Wiley.

Breslin, P. A. S., & Spector, A. C. (2008). Mammalian taste perception. *Current Biology, 18,* R148–R155.

Brincat, S., & Connor, C. E. (2004). Underlying principles of visual shape selectivity in posterior inferotemporal cortex. *Nature Neuroscience, 7,* 880–886.

Brisben, A. J., Hsiao, S. S., & Johnson, K. O. (1999). Detection of vibration transmitted through an object grasped in the hand. *Journal of Neurophysiology, 81,* 1548–1558.

Britten, K. H. (2004). The middle temporal area: Motion processing and the link to perception. In L. M. Chalupa & J. S. Werner (Eds.), *The visual neurosciences* (Vol. 2, pp. 1203–1216). Cambridge, MA: MIT Press.

Broadbent, D. E. (1958). *Perception and communication*. London: Pergamon Press.

Broca, P. (1986). On the site of the faculty of articulated speech (E. A. Berker, A. H. Berker, & A. Smith, Trans.). *Archives of Neurology, 43,* 1065–1072. (Original work published 1865)

Brodmann, K. (2005). *Brodmann's localization in the cerebral cortex* (L. J. Garey, Trans.). Boston: Springer. (Original work published 1909)

Brown, P. K., & Wald, G. (1964). Visual pigments in single rods and cones of the human retina. *Science, 144,* 45–52.

Brownell, W. E., Bader, C. R., Bertrand, D., & de Ribaupierre, Y. (1985). Evoked mechanical responses of isolated cochlear outer hair cells. *Science, 227,* 194–196.

Buck, L. B. (2004). Olfactory receptors and odor coding in mammals. *Nutrition Reviews, 62,* S184–S188.

Buck, L. B., & Axel, R. (1991). A novel multigene family may encode odorant receptors: A molecular basis for odor recognition. *Cell, 65,* 175–187.

Bülthoff, H. H., & Edelman, S. (1992). Psychophysical support for a two-dimensional view interpolation theory of object recognition. *Proceedings of the National Academy of Sciences, USA, 89,* 60–64.

Buneo, C. A., Jarvis, M. R., Batista, A. P., & Andersen, R. A. (2002). Direct visuomotor transformations for reaching. *Nature, 416,* 632–636.

Burnham, R. W., Evans, R. M., & Newhall, S. M. (1957). Prediction of color appearance with different adaptation illuminations. *Journal of the Optical Society of America, 47,* 35-42.

Burns, M. E., & Lamb, T. D. (2004). Visual transduction by rod and cone photoreceptors. In L. M. Chalupa & J. S. Werner (Eds.), *The visual neurosciences* (Vol. 1, pp. 215–233). Cambridge, MA: MIT Press.

Burton, H. E. (Trans.) (1945). The optics of Euclid. *Journal of the Optical Society of America, 35,* 357–372. (Original work ca. 300 BCE)

Bushnell, M. C., Goldberg, M. E., & Robinson, D. L. (1981). Behavioral enhancement of visual responses in monkey cerebral cortex: I. Modulation in posterior parietal cortex related to selective visual attention. *Journal of Neurophysiology, 46,* 755–772.

Butler, R. K., & Finn, D. P. (2009). Stress-induced analgesia. *Progress in Neurobiology, 88,* 184–202.

Byrne, A., & Hilbert, D. R. (2003). Color realism and color science. *Behavioral and Brain Sciences, 26,* 3–64.

Cain, W. S. (1988). Olfaction. In R. C. Atkinson, R. J. Herrnstein, G. Lindzey, & R. Duncan Luce (Eds.), *Stevens' handbook of experimental psychology* (2nd ed., pp. 409–460). New York: Wiley.

Calkins, D. J. (2004). Linking retinal circuits to color opponency. In L. M. Chalupa & J. S. Werner (Eds.), *The visual neurosciences* (Vol. 2, pp. 989–1002). Cambridge, MA: MIT Press.

Carney, L. H. (2002). Neural basis of audition. In S. Yantis (Vol. Ed.) & H. Pashler (Series Ed.), *Stevens' handbook of experimental psychology: Vol. 1. Sensation and perception* (3rd ed., pp. 341–396). New York: Wiley.

Carr, C. E., & Konishi, M. (1990). A circuit for detection of interaural time differences in the brain stem of the barn owl. *Journal of Neuroscience, 10,* 3227–3246.

Castaneda, B., & Gray, R. (2007). Effects of focus of attention on baseball batting performance in players of differing skill levels. *Journal of Sport & Exercise Psychology, 29,* 60–77.

Cavada, C., & Goldman-Rakic, P. S. (1989). The posterior parietal cortex in rhesus monkeys: I. Parcellation of areas based on distinctive limbic and sensory corticocortical connections. *Journal of Comparative Neurology, 287,* 393–421.

Chalmers, D. J. (1995). Facing up to the problem of consciousness. *Journal of Consciousness Studies, 2,* 200–219.

Chalmers, D. J. (2004). How can we construct a science of consciousness? In M. Gazzaniga (Ed.), *The cognitive neurosciences* (3rd ed., pp. 1111–1119). Cambridge, MA: MIT Press.

Chandrashekar, J., Hoon, M. A., Ryba, N. J., & Zuker, C. S. (2006). The receptors and cells for mammalian taste. *Nature, 444,* 288–294.

Chandrashekar, J., Kuhn, C., Oka, Y., Yarmolinsky, D. A., Hummler, E., Ryba, N. J., & Zuker, C. S. (2010). The cells and peripheral representation of sodium taste in mice. *Nature, 464,* 297–301.

Chang, R. B., Waters, H., & Liman, E. R. (2010). A proton current drives action potentials in genetically identified sour taste cells. *Proceedings of the National Academy of Sciences, USA, 107,* 22320–22325.

Chaudhari, N., & Roper, S. D. (2010). The cell biology of taste. *Journal of Cell Biology, 190,* 285–296.

Chen, L. M., Friedman, R. M., & Roe, A. W. (2009). Area-specific representation of mechanical nociceptive stimuli within SI cortex of squirrel monkeys. *Pain, 141,* 258–268.

Cherry, E. C. (1953). Some experiments on the recognition of speech, with one and two ears. *Journal of the Acoustical Society of America, 25,* 975–979.

Chiu, Y.-C., & Yantis, S. (2009). A domain-independent source of cognitive control for task sets: Shifting spatial attention and switching categorization rules. *Journal of Neuroscience, 29,* 3930–3938.

Chowdhury, S. A., & DeAngelis, G. C. (2008). Fine discrimination training alters the causal contribution of macaque area MT to depth perception. *Neuron, 60,* 367–377.

Clark, G. M. (2003). *Cochlear implants: Fundamentals and applications*. New York: Springer.

Clark, G. M. (2006). The multiple-channel cochlear implant: The interface between sound and the central nervous system for hearing, speech, and language in deaf people—A personal perspective. *Philosophical Transactions of the Royal Society of London, Series B: Biological Sciences, 361,* 791–810.

Clark, G. M., Busby, P., Dowell, R. C., Tong, Y. C., Blarney, P. J., Nienhuys, T. G., . . . Franz, B. K. (1987). Preliminary results for the Cochlear Corporation multi-electrode intracochlear implants on six prelingually deaf patients. *American Journal of Otology, 8,* 234–239.

Clark, W. C., Smith, A. H., & Rabe, A. (1955). Retinal gradient of outline as a stimulus for slant. *Canadian Journal of Psychology, 9,* 247–253.

Clarke, S., Thiran, A. B., Maeder, P., Adriani, M., Vernet, O., Regli, L., . . . Thiran, J.-P. (2002). What and where in human audition: Selective deficits following focal hemispheric lesions. *Experimental Brain Research, 147,* 8–15.

Cleland, T. A., Morse, A., Yue, E. L., & Linster, C. (2002). Behavioral models of odor similarity. *Behavioral Neuroscience, 116,* 222–231.

Colby, C. L., Duhamel, J.-R., & Goldberg, M. E. (1996). Visual, presaccadic, and cognitive activation of single neurons in monkey lateral intraparietal area. *Journal of Neurophysiology, 76,* 2841–2851.

Coleman, P. D. (1968). Dual rôle of frequency spectrum in determination of auditory distance. *Journal of the Acoustical Society of America, 44,* 631–632.

Colloca, L., & Benedetti, F. (2005). Placebos and painkillers: Is mind as real as matter? *Nature Reviews Neuroscience, 6,* 545–552.

Coltheart, M. (2002). Cognitive neuropsychology. In J. Wixted (Vol. Ed.) & H. Pashler (Series Ed.), *Stevens' handbook of experimental psychology: Vol. 4. Methodology in experimental psychology* (3rd ed., pp. 139–174). New York: Wiley.

Connor, C. E., Hsiao, S. S., Phillips, J. R., & Johnson, K. O. (1990). Tactile roughness: Neural codes that account for psychophysical magnitude estimates. *Journal of Neuroscience, 10,* 3823–3836.

Connor, C. E., Pasupathy, A., Brincat, S., & Yamane, Y. (2009). Neural transformation of object information by ventral pathway visual cortex. In M. Gazzaniga (Ed.), *The cognitive neurosciences* (4th ed.). Cambridge, MA: MIT Press.

Corneil, B. D., Olivier, E., & Munoz, D. P. (2004). Visual responses on neck muscles reveal selective gating that prevents express saccades. *Neuron, 42,* 831–841.

Cornsweet, T. N. (1970). *Visual perception.* New York: Academic Press.

Costafreda, S. G., Brammer, M. J., David, A. S., & Fu, C. H. (2008). Predictors of amygdala activation during the processing of emotional stimuli: A meta-analysis of 385 PET and fMRI studies. *Brain Research Reviews, 58,* 57–70.

Cowey, A. (2010). The blindsight saga. *Experimental Brain Research, 200,* 3–24.

Cowey, A., & Vaina, L. M. (2000). Blindness to form from motion despite intact static form perception and motion detection. *Neuropsychologia, 38,* 566–578.

Cox, I. J., Ghosn, J., & Yianilos, P. N. (1996). Feature-based face recognition using mixture–distance. *Proceedings of IEEE Conference on Computer Vision and Pattern Recognition,* pp. 209–216. doi:10.1109/CVPR.1996.517076

Craig, A. D. (2003). Pain mechanisms: Labeled lines versus convergence in central processing. *Annual Review of Neurosciences, 26,* 1–30.

Craig, A. D., Chen, K., Bandy, D., & Reiman, E. M. (2000). Thermosensory activation of insular cortex. *Nature Neuroscience, 3,* 184–190.

Crick, F., & Koch, C. (1990). Towards a neurobiological theory of consciousness. *Seminars in the Neurosciences 2,* 263–275.

Culham, J. C., Cavina-Pratesi, C., & Singhal, A. (2006). The role of the parietal cortex in visuomotor control: What have we learned from neuroimaging? *Neuropsychologia, 44,* 2668–2684.

Culham, J. C., & Kanwisher, N. (2001). Neuroimaging of cognitive functions in human parietal cortex. *Current Opinion in Neurobiology, 11,* 157–163.

Cumming, B. G., & DeAngelis, G. C. (2001). The physiology of stereopsis. *Annual Review of Neuroscience, 24,* 203–238.

Cummings, D. M., Emge, D. K., Small, S. L., & Margolis, F. L. (2000). Pattern of olfactory bulb innervation returns after recovery from reversible peripheral deafferentation. *Journal of Comparative Neurology, 421,* 362–373.

Curcio, C. A., Sloan, K. R., Kalina, R. E., & Hendrickson, A. E. (1990). Human photoreceptor topography. *Journal of Comparative Neurology, 292,* 497–523.

Cutting, J. E., & Vishton, P. M. (1995). Perceiving layout and knowing distances: The integration, relative potency, and contextual use of different information about depth. In W. Epstein & S. Rogers (Eds.), *Handbook of perception and cognition: Vol 5. Perception of space and motion* (pp. 69–117). San Diego, CA: Academic Press.

Dagnelie, G. (2006). Visual prosthetics 2006: Assessment and expectations. *Expert Review of Medical Devices, 3,* 315–325.

Dagnelie, G. (2008). Psychophysical evaluation for visual prosthesis. *Annual Review of Biomedical Engineering, 10,* 339–368.

Dallos, P., Wu, X., Cheatham, M. A., Gao, J., Zheng, J., Anderson, C. T., . . . Zuo, J. (2008). Prestin-based outer hair cell motility is necessary for mammalian cochlear amplification. *Neuron, 58,* 333–339.

Dalton, P. (2002). Olfaction. In S. Yantis (Vol. Ed.) & H. Pashler (Series Ed.), *Stevens' handbook of experimental psychology: Vol. 1. Sensation and perception* (3rd ed., pp. 691–746). New York: Wiley.

Dando, R., & Roper, S. D. (2009). Cell-to-cell communication in intact taste buds through ATP signalling from pannexin 1 gap junction hemichannels. *Journal of Physiology, London, 587,* 5899–5906.

Dannemiller, J. L., Babler, T. G., & Babler, B. L. (1996). *On catching fly balls* [Peer commentary on "How baseball outfielders determine where to run to catch fly balls" by M. K. McBeath, D. M. Shaffer, & M. K. Kaiser with response]. *Science, 273,* 256–257.

Darian-Smith, I., Johnson, K. O., & Dykes, R. (1973). "Cold" fiber population innervating palmar and digital skin of the monkey: Responses to cooling pulses. *Journal of Neurophysiology, 36,* 325–346.

Darian-Smith, I., Johnson, K. O., LaMotte, C., Shigenaga, Y., Kenins, P., & Champness, P. (1979). Warm fibers innervating palmar and digital skin of the monkey: Responses to thermal stimuli. *Journal of Neurophysiology, 42,* 1297–1315.

Darwin, C. (1988). *On the origin of species.* In P. H. Barrett & R. B. Freeman (Eds.), *The works of Charles Darwin* (Vol. 15). New York: New York University Press. (Original work published 1859)

Dawson, W. J. (2011). How and why musicians are different from nonmusicians: A bibliographic review. *Medical Problems of Performing Artists, 26,* 65–78.

de Araujo, I. E., Rolls, E. T., Kringelbach, M. L., McGlone, F., & Phillips, N. (2003). Taste–olfactory convergence, and the representation of the pleasantness of flavour, in the human brain. *European Journal of Neuroscience, 18,* 2059–2068.

DeFazio, R. A., Dvoryanichikov, G., Maruyama, Y., Kim, J. W., Pereira, E., Roper, S. D., & Chaudhari, N. (2006). Separate populations of receptor cells and presynaptic cells in mouse taste buds. *Journal of Neuroscience, 26,* 3971–3980.

Dees, J. W. (1966). Accuracy of absolute visual distance and size estimation in space as a function of stereopsis and motion parallax. *Journal of Experimental Psychology, 72,* 466–476.

de Gelder, B., Tamietto, M., van Boxtel, G., Goebel, R., Sahraie, A., van den Stock, J., . . . Pegna, A. (2008). Intact navigation skills after bilateral loss of striate cortex. *Current Biology, 18,* R1128–R1129.

Desimone, R., Albright, T. D., Gross, C. G., & Bruce, C. (1984). Stimulus-selective properties of inferior temporal neurons in the macaque. *Journal of Neuroscience, 4,* 2051–2062.

Desimone, R., & Duncan, J. (1995). Neural mechanisms of selective visual attention. *Annual Review of Neuroscience, 18,* 193–222.

Desimone, R., Schein, S. J., Moran, J., & Ungerleider, L. G. (1985). Contour, color and shape analysis beyond the striate cortex. *Vision Research, 25,* 441–452.

De Valois, R. L. (2004). Neural coding of color. In L. M. Chalupa & J. S. Werner (Eds.), *The visual neurosciences* (Vol. 2, pp.1003–1016). Cambridge, MA: MIT Press.

De Valois, R. L., Smith, C. J., Kitai, S.T., & Karoly, A. J. (1958). Responses of single cells in different layers of the primate lateral geniculate nucleus to monochromatic light. *Science, 127,* 238–239.

Devos, M., Patte, F., Rouault, J., Laffort, P., & Van Gemert, L. J. (Eds.). (1990). *Standardized human olfactory thresholds*. Oxford: Oxford University Press.

DiCarlo, J. J., & Johnson, K. O. (2000). Spatial and temporal structure of receptive fields in primate somatosensory area 3b: Effects of stimulus scanning direction and orientation. *Journal of Neuroscience, 20,* 495–510.

DiCarlo, J. J., Johnson, K. O., & Hsiao, S. S. (1998). Structure of receptive fields in area 3b of primary somatosensory cortex in the alert monkey. *Journal of Neuroscience, 18,* 2626–2645.

Dickinson, S. J., Leonardis, A., Schiele, B., & Tarr, M. J. (2009). *Object categorization: Computer and human vision perspectives*. Cambridge, England: Cambridge University Press.

Dong, Y., Mihalas, S., Qiu, F., von der Heydt, R., & Niebur, E. (2008). Synchrony and the binding problem in macaque visual cortex. *Journal of Vision, 8,* 1–16. doi:10.1167/8.7.30.

Doty, R. L. (2001). Olfaction. *Annual Review of Psychology, 52,* 423–452.

Doty, R. L. (2010). *The great pheromone myth.* Baltimore: Johns Hopkins University Press.

Doty, R. L., Shaman, P., Applebaum, S. L., Giberson, R., Siksorski, L., & Rosenberg, L. (1984). Smell identification ability: Changes with age. *Science, 226,* 1441–1443.

Dougherty, R. F., Koch, V. M., Brewer, A. A., Fischer, B., Modersitzki, J., & Wandell, B. A. (2003). Visual field representations and locations of visual areas V1/2/3 in human visual cortex. *Journal of Vision, 3,* 586–598.

Downing, P. E., Jiang, Y., Shuman, M., & Kanwisher, N. (2001). A cortical area selective for visual processing of the human body. *Science, 293,* 2470–2473.

Drayna, D. (2005). Human taste genetics. *Annual Review of Genomics and Human Genetics, 6,* 217–235.

Drews, F. A., Pasupathi, M., & Strayer, D. L. (2008). Passenger and cell phone conversations during simulated driving. *Journal of Experimental Psychology: Applied, 14,* 392–400.

Dricot, L., Sorger, B., Schiltz, C., Goebel, R., & Rossion, B. (2008). The roles of "face" and "non-face" areas during individual face perception: Evidence by fMRI adaptation in a brain-damaged prosopagnosic patient. *NeuroImage, 40,* 318–332.

Driver, J., & Vuilleumier, P. (2001). Perceptual awareness and its loss in unilateral neglect and extinction. *Cognition, 79,* 39–88.

Duchaine, B. C., & Nakayama, K. (2006). Developmental prosopagnosia: a window to content-specific face processing. *Current Opinion in Neurobiology, 16,* 166–173.

Duchaine, B., Yovel, G., Butterworth, E. J., & Nakayama, K. (2006). Prosopagnosia as an impairment to face-specific mechanisms: Elimination of the alternative hypotheses in a developmental case. *Cognitive Neuropsychology, 23,* 714–747.

Duncan, G. H., & Albanese, M. C. (2003). Is there a role for the parietal lobes in the perception of pain? *Advances in Neurology, 93,* 69–86.

Duncan, J., & Humphreys, G., & Ward, R. (1997). Competitive brain activity in visual attention. *Current Opinion in Neurobiology, 7,* 255–261.

Edin, B. B. (1992). Quantitative analysis of static strain sensitivity in human mechanoreceptors from hairy skin. *Journal of Neurophysiology, 67,* 1105–1113.

Eichenbaum, H. (1998). Using olfaction to study memory. *Annals of the New York Academy of Sciences, 855,* 657–669.

Eimas, P. D., & Corbit, J. D. (1973). Selective adaptation of linguistic feature detectors. *Cognitive Psychology, 4,* 99–109.

Einstein, A. (1905). Über einen die Erzeugung und Verwandlung des Lichtes betreffenden heuristischen Gesichtspunkt [Concerning an heuristic point of view toward the emission and transformation of light]. *Annalen der Physik, 17,* 132–148. (Translated and reprinted in 1965 in "Einstein's proposal of the photon concept—A translation of the *Annalen der Physik* paper of 1905," by A. B. Arons & M. B. Peppard, *American Journal of Physics, 33,* 367–383.)

Eisthen, H. L. (1997). Evolution of vertebrate olfactory systems. *Brain, Behavior and Evolution, 50,* 222–233.

Elbert, T., Pantev, C., Wienbruch, C., Rockstroh, B., & Taub, E. (1995). Increased cortical representation of the fingers of the left hand in string players. *Science, 270,* 305–307.

Epstein, R., & Kanwisher, N. (1998). A cortical representation of the local visual environment. *Nature, 392,* 598–601.

Eskandar, E. N., & Assad, J. A. (2002). Distinct nature of directional signals among parietal cortical areas during visual guidance. *Journal of Neurophysiology, 88,* 1777–1790.

Fang, F., Boyaci, H., & Kersten, D. (2009). Border ownership selectivity in human early visual cortex and its modulation by attention. *Journal of Neuroscience, 29,* 460–465.

Farah, M. J. (2004). *Visual agnosia* (2nd ed.). Cambridge, MA: MIT Press.

Feddersen, W. E., Sandel, T. T., Teas, D. C., & Jeffress, L. A. (1957). Localization of high-frequency tones. *Journal of the Acoustical Society of America, 29,* 988–991.

Federer, F., Ichida, J. M., Jeffs, J., Schiessl, I., McLoughlin, N., & Angelucci, A. (2009). Four projection streams from primate V1 to the cytochrome oxidase stripes of V2. *Journal of Neuroscience, 29,* 15455–15471.

Felleman, D., & Van Essen, D. (1991). Distributed hierarchical processing in the primate cerebral cortex. *Cerebral Cortex, 1,* 1–47.

Fernald, R. D. (1997). The evolution of eyes. *Behavior, Brain and Evolution, 50,* 253–259.

Fernandez, E., Pelayo, F., Romero, S., Bongard, M., Marin, C., Alfaro, A., & Merabet, L. (2005). Development of a cortical visual neuroprosthesis for the blind: The relevance of neuroplasticity. *Journal of Neural Engineering, 2,* R1–12.

Ferretti, A., Del Gratta, C., Babiloni, C., Caulo, M., Arienzo, D., Tartaro, A., . . . Romani, G. L. (2004). Functional topography of the secondary somatosensory cortex for nonpainful and painful stimulation of median and tibial nerve: An fMRI study. *NeuroImage, 23,* 1217–1225.

Finger, T. E., Danilova, V., Barrows, J., Bartel, D. L., Vigers, A. J., Stone, L., . . . Kinnamon, S. C. (2005). ATP signaling is crucial for communication from taste buds to gustatory nerves. *Science, 310,* 1495–1499.

Fitzgerald, P. J., Lane, J. W., Thakur, P. H., & Hsiao, S. S. (2004). Receptive field properties of the macaque second somatosensory cortex: Evidence for multiple functional representations. *Journal of Neuroscience, 24,* 11193–11204.

Fitzgerald, P. J., Lane, J.W., Thakur, P. H., & Hsiao, S. S. (2006a). Receptive field properties of the macaque second somatosensory cortex: Representation of orientation on different finger pads. *Journal of Neuroscience, 26,* 6473–6484.

Fitzgerald, P. J., Lane, J. W., Thakur, P. H., & Hsiao, S. S. (2006b). Receptive field (RF) properties of the macaque second somatosensory cortex: RF size, shape, and somatotopic organization. *Journal of Neuroscience, 26,* 6485–6495.

Fletcher, M. L., Masurkar, A. V., Xing, J., Imamura, F., Xiong, W., Nagayama, S., . . . Chen, W. R. (2009). Optical imaging of postsynaptic odor representation in the glomerular layer of the mouse olfactory bulb. *Journal of Neurophysiology, 102,* 817–830.

Fodor, J. A. (1983). *Modularity of mind: An essay on faculty psychology*. Cambridge, MA: MIT Press.

Formisano, E., Dae-Shik Kim, D.-S., Di Salle, F., van de Moortele, P.-R., Ugurbil, K., & Goebel, R. (2003). Mirror-symmetric tonotopic maps in human primary auditory cortex. *Neuron, 40,* 859–869.

Foster, D. H. (2011). Color constancy. *Vision Research, 51,* 674–700.

Friesen, C. K., & Kingstone, A. (1998). The eyes have it! Reflexive orienting is triggered by nonpredictive gaze. *Psychonomic Bulleting & Review, 5,* 490–495.

Frye, R. E., Schwarts, B. S., & Doty, R. (1990). Dose-related effects of cigarette smoking on olfactory function. *Journal of the American Medical Association, 263,* 1233–1236.

Gabriel, K. J., Koehnke, J., & Colburn, H. S. (1992). Frequency dependence of binaural performance in listeners with impaired binaural hearing. *Journal of the Acoustical Society of America, 91,* 336–347.

Gallivan, J. P., McLean, D. A., Valyear, K. F., Pettypiece, C. E., & Culham, J. C. (2011). Decoding action intentions from preparatory brain activity in human parieto-frontal networks. *Journal of Neuroscience, 31,* 9599–9610.

Gandevia, S.C., Smith, J., Crawford, M., Proske, U., & Taylor, J. L. (2006). Motor commands contribute to human position sense. *Journal of Physiology (London), 571,* 703–710.

Gauthier, J. L., Field, G. D., Sher, A., Greschner, M., Shlens, J., Litke, A. M., & Chichilnisky, E. J. (2009). Receptive fields in primate retina are coordinated to sample visual space more uniformly. *PLoS Biology, 7,* e1000063.

Gegenfurtner, K. R., & Sharpe, L. T. (Eds.). (1999). *Color vision: From genes to perception*. Cambridge, England: Cambridge University Press.

Gelstein, S., Yeshurun, Y., Rozenkrantz, L., Shushan, S., Frumin, I., Roth, Y., & Sobel, N. (2011). Human tears contain a chemosignal. *Science, 331,* 226–230.

Getty, D. J., Pickett, R. M., D'Orsi, C. J., & Swets, J. A. (1988). Enhanced interpretation of diagnostic images. *Investigative Radiology, 23,* 240–252.

Gibson, J. J. (1950a). *The perception of the visual world*. Boston: Houghton Mifflin.

Gibson, J. J. (1950b). The perception of visual surfaces. *American Journal of Psychology, 63,* 367–384.

Gibson, J. J. (1966). *The senses considered as perceptual systems*. Boston: Houghton Mifflin.

Gibson, J. J. (1979). *The ecological approach to visual perception*. Boston: Houghton Mifflin.

Gibson, J. J., Olum, P., & Rosenblatt, F. (1955). Parallax and perspective during aircraft landings. *American Journal of Psychology, 68,* 372–385.

Gilbert, A. (2008). *What the nose knows: The science of scent in everyday life*. New York: Crown.

Gilchrist, A. L. (1977). Perceived lightness depends on perceived spatial arrangement. *Science, 195,* 185–187.

Gilchrist, A. (2006). *Seeing black and white*. Oxford: Oxford University Press.

Ginsberg, S. P. (Ed.). (1984). *Cataract and intraocular lens surgery: A compendium of modern theories and techniques*. Birmingham, AL: Aesculapius.

Goldberg, J. M., Wilson, V. J., Cullen, K. E., Angelaki, D. E., Broussard, D. M., Büttner-Ennever, J. A., . . . & Minor, L. B. (2012). *The vestibular system: A sixth sense*. New York: Oxford University Press.

Goodale, M. A. (2011). Transforming vision into action. *Vision Research, 51,* 1567-1587.

Goodale, M. A., & Milner, A. D. (2005). *Sight unseen: An exploration of conscious and unconscious vision*. Oxford, England: Oxford University Press.

Goodale, M. A., Milner, A. D., Jakobson, L. S., & Carey, D. P. (1991). A neurological dissociation between perceiving objects and grasping them. *Nature, 349,* 154–156.

Goodwin, A.W., Browning, A. S., & Wheat, H. E. (1995). Representation of curved surfaces in responses of mechanoreceptive afferent fibers innervating the monkey's fingerpad. *Journal of Neuroscience, 15,* 798–810.

Gordon, J., & Ghez, C. (1991). The muscle receptors and spinal reflexes: The stretch reflex. In E. R. Kandel, J. H. Schwartz, & T. M. Jessell (Eds.), *Principles of neural science* (3rd ed., pp. 564–580). New York: Elsevier.

Graves, A. B., Bowen, J. D., Rajaram, L., McCormick, W. C., McCurry, S. M., Schellenberg, G. D., & Larson, E. B. (1999). Impaired olfaction as a marker for cognitive decline: Interaction with apolipoprotein E epsilon-4 status. *Neurology, 53,* 1480–1487.

Gray, C. M., König, P., Engel, A. K., & Singer, W. (1989). Oscillatory responses in cat visual-cortex exhibit inter-columnar synchronization which reflects global stimulus properties. *Nature, 338,* 334–337.

Gray, R. (2002). Behavior of college baseball players in a virtual batting task. *Journal of Experimental Psychology: Human Perception and Performance, 28,* 1131–1148.

Gray, R. (2004). Attending to the execution of a complex sensorimotor skill: Expertise differences, choking, and slumps. *Journal of Experimental Psychology: Applied, 10,* 42–54.

Greenberg, S., & Ainsworth, W. A. (Eds.). *Listening to speech: An auditory perspective*. Mahwah, NJ: Erlbaum.

Grefkes, C., & Fink, G. R. (2005). The functional organization of the intraparietal sulcus in humans and monkeys. *Journal of Anatomy, 207,* 3–17.

Grill-Spector, K. (2003). The neural basis of object perception. *Current Opinion in Neurobiology, 13,* 1–8.

Gross, C. G., Rocha-Miranda, C. E., & Bender, D. B. (1972). Visual properties of neurons in inferotemporal cortex of the macaque. *Journal of Neurophysiology, 35,* 96–111.

Grossman, E. D., Battelli, L., & Pascual-Leone, A. (2005). Repetitive TMS over STSp disrupts perception of biological motion. *Vision Research, 45,* 2847–2853.

Grossman, E. D., & Blake, R. (2002). Brain areas active during visual perception of biological motion. *Neuron, 35,* 1167–1175.

Guinan, J. J. Jr, & Cooper, N. P. (2008). Medial olivocochlear efferent inhibition of basilar-membrane responses to clicks: Evidence for two modes of cochlear mechanical excitation. *Journal of the Acoustical Society of America, 124,* 1080–1092.

Guldin, W. O., & Grüsser, O. J. (1998). Is there a vestibular cortex? *Trends in Neuroscience, 21,* 254–259.

Haddad, R., Medhanie, A., Roth, Y., Harel, D., & Sobel, N. (2010). Predicting odor pleasantness with an electronic nose. *PLoS Computational Biology, 6,* e1000740. doi:10.1371/journal.pcbi.1000740

Hager, G. D., Okamura, A. M., Kazanzides, P., Whitcomb, L. L., Fichtinger, G., & Taylor, R. H. (2008). Surgical and interventional robotics: Part III. Surgical assistance systems. *IEEE Robotics and Automation Magazine, 15,* 84–93.

Halpern, B. (2002). Taste. In S. Yantis (Vol. Ed.) & H. Pashler (Series Ed.), *Stevens' handbook of experimental psychology: Vol.1. Sensation and perception* (3rd ed., pp. 653–690). New York: Wiley.

Hannaford, B., & Okamura, A. M. (2008). Haptics. In B. Siciliano & O. Khatib (Eds.), *Springer handbook of robotics* (pp. 719–739). Berlin: Springer.

Harrower, M. R. (1936). Some factors determining figure–ground articulation. *British Journal of Psychology, 26,* 407–424.

Hartline, H. K. (1938). The response of single optic nerve fibers of the vertebrate eye to illumination of the retina. *American Journal of Physiology, 121,* 400–415.

Hartline, H. K. (1940). The receptive field of optic nerve fibers. *American Journal of Physiology, 130,* 690–699.

Hartline, H. K., & Ratliff, F. (1958). Spatial summation of inhibitory influences in the eye of Limulus, and the mutual interaction of receptor units. *Journal of General Physiology, 41,* 1049–1066.

Haxby, J. V., Gobbini, M. I., Furey, M. L., Ishai, A., Schouten, J. L., & Pietrini, P. (2001). Distributed and overlapping representations of faces and objects in ventral temporal cortex. *Science, 293,* 2425–2430.

Haynes, J. D., & Rees, G. (2005). Predicting the stream of consciousness from activity in human visual cortex. *Current Biology, 15,* 1301–1307.

He, J. (2003). Corticofugal modulation of the auditory thalamus. *Experimental Brain Research, 153,* 579–590.

Hecht, S., Shlaer, S., & Pirenne, M. H. (1942). Energy, quanta, and vision. *Journal of General Physiology, 25,* 819–840.

Hegdé, J., & Felleman, D. (2007). Reappraising the functional implications of the primate visual anatomical hierarchy. *Neuroscientist, 13,* 416–421.

Hellekant, G., Ninomiya, Y., & Danilova, V. (1998). Taste in chimpanzees. III: Labeled-line coding in sweet taste. *Physiology & Behavior, 65,* 191–200.

Helmholtz, H. L. F. von (1925). *Helmholtz's treatise on physiological optics* (J. P. C. Southall, Trans.; 3rd ed.). Washington, DC: Optical Society of America. (Original work published 1866)

Henderson, D., Bielefeld, E. C., Harris, K. C., & Hu, B. H. (2006). The role of oxidative stress in noise-induced hearing loss. *Ear and Hearing, 27,* 1–19.

Henderson, J. M., & Hollingworth, A. (1999). The role of fixation position in detecting scene changes across saccades. *Psychological Science, 10,* 438–443.

Hendry, S. H. C., & Reid, R. C. (2000). The koniocellular pathway in primate vision. *Annual Review of Neuroscience, 23,* 127–153.

Hering, E. (1964). *Outlines of a theory of the light sense* (L. Hurvich & D. Jameson, Trans.). Cambridge, MA: Harvard University Press. (Original work published 1878)

Herz, R. S. (2007). *The scent of desire.* New York: Harper Perennial.

Herz, R. S., & Engen, T. (1996). Odor memory: Review and analysis. *Psychonomic Bulletin & Review, 3,* 300–313.

Herz, R. S., & Schooler, J. W. (2002). A naturalistic study of autobiographical memories evoked by olfactory and visual cues: Testing the Proustian hypothesis. *American Journal of Psychology, 115,* 21–32.

Herz, R. S., & von Clef, J. (2001). The influence of verbal labeling on the perception of odors: Evidence for olfactory illusions? *Perception, 30,* 381–391.

Heywood, C. A., & Kentridge, R. W. (2003). Achromatopsia, color vision, and cortex. *Neurologic Clinics, 21,* 483–500.

Hickok, G., & Poeppel, D. (2007). The cortical organization of speech processing. *Nature Reviews Neuroscience, 8,* 393–402.

Hodos, W., & Butler, A. B. (1997). Evolution of sensory pathways in vertebrates. *Brain, Behavior and Evolution, 50,* 189–197.

Hofbauer, R. K., Rainville, P., Duncan, G. H., & Bushnell, M. C. (2001). Cortical representation of the sensory dimension of pain. *Journal of Neurophysiology, 86,* 402–411.

Hofman, P. M., Van Riswick, J. G., & Van Opstal, A. J. (1998). Relearning sound localization with new ears. *Nature Neuroscience, 1,* 417–421.

Hollins, M., Fox, A., & Bishop, C. (2001). Imposed vibration influences perceived tactile smoothness. *Perception, 30,* 1455–1465.

Hollow, R. D., Dowell, R. C., Cowan, R. S. C., Skok, M. C., Pyman, B. C. & Clark, G. M. (1995). Continuing improvements in speech processing for adult cochlear implant patients. *Annals of Otology, Rhinology, and Laryngology, 166,* 292–294.

Holway, A. H., & Boring, E. G. (1941). Determinants of apparent visual size with distance variant. *American Journal of Psychology, 54,* 21–37.

Horton, J. C. (1984). Cytochrome oxidase patches: A new cytoarchitectonic feature of monkey visual cortex. *Philosophical Transactions of the Royal Society of London, Series B: Biological Sciences, 304,* 199–253.

Horton, J. C., & Hocking, D. R. (1998). Monocular core zones and binocular border strips in primate striate cortex revealed by the contrasting effects of enucleation, eyelid suture, and retinal laser lesions on cytochrome oxidase activity. *Journal of Neuroscience, 18,* 5433–5455.

Horton, J. C., & Hoyt, W. F. (1991). The representation of the visual field in human striate cortex. A revision of the classic Holmes map. *Archives of Ophthalmology, 109,* 816–824.

Howard, I. P. (2002). *Seeing in depth: Vol 1. Basic mechanisms.* Toronto, Canada: I. Porteus.

Howard, I. P., & Rogers, B. J. (2002). *Seeing in depth: Vol 2. Depth perception.* Toronto, Canada: I. Porteus.

Howard, J. D., Plailly, J., Grueschow, M., Haynes, J. D., & Gottfried, J. A. (2009). Odor quality coding and categorization in human posterior piriform cortex. *Nature Neuroscience, 12,* 932–938.

Hsiao, S. (1998). Similarities between touch and vision. In J. W. Morley (Ed.), *Neural aspects of tactile sensation* (pp. 131–165). New York: Elsevier.

Hsiao, S. (2008). Central mechanisms of tactile shape perception. *Current Opinion in Neurobiology, 18,* 418-424.

Hu, J., & Lewin, G. R. (2006). Mechanosensitive currents in the neurites of cultured mouse sensory neurones. *Journal of Physiology, 577,* 815–828.

Hua, L. H., Strigo, I. A., Baxter, L. C., Johnson, S. C., & Craig, A. D. (2005). Anteroposterior somatotopy of innocuous cooling activation focus in human dorsal posterior insular cortex. *American Journal of Physiology: Regulatory, Integrative, and Comparative Physiology, 289,* R319–R325.

Huang, A. L., Chen, X., Hoon, M. A., Chandrashekar, J., Guo, W., Tränkner, D., . . . Zuker, C. S. (2006). The cells and logic for mammalian sour taste detection. *Nature, 442,* 934–938.

Hubel, D. H. (1995). *Eye, brain, and vision* (2nd ed.). New York: W. H. Freeman and Company.

Hubel, D. H., & Wiesel, T. N. (1962). Receptive fields, binocular interaction and functional architecture in the cat's visual cortex. *Journal of Physiology, 160,* 106–154.

Hubel, D. H., & Wiesel, T. N. (1968). Receptive fields and functional architecture of the monkey's striate cortex. *Journal of Physiology, 195,* 215–243.

Hubel, D. H., & Wiesel, T. N. (1974). Uniformity of monkey striate cortex: A parallel relationship between field size, scatter, and magnification factor. *Journal of Comparative Neurology, 158,* 295–305.

Hübner R., & Hafter, E. R. (1995). Cuing mechanisms in auditory signal detection. *Perception & Psychophysics, 57,* 197–202.

Hudspeth, A. J. (2008). Making an effort to listen: Mechanical amplification in the ear. *Neuron, 59,* 530–545.

Huettle, S. A., Song, A. W., & McCarthy, G. W. (2009). *Functional magnetic resonance imaging* (2nd ed.). Sunderland, MA: Sinauer.

Hurvich, L., & Jameson, D. (1957). An opponent-process theory of color vision. *Psychological Review, 64,* 384–404.

Hutchison, W. D., Davis, K. D., Lozano, A. M., Tasker, R. R., & Dostrovsky, J. O. (1999). Pain-related neurons in the human cingulate cortex. *Nature Neuroscience, 2,* 403–405.

Huterer, M., & Cullen, K. E. (2002). Vestibuloocular reflex dynamics during high-frequency and high-acceleration rotations of the head on body in rhesus monkey. *Journal of Neurophysiology, 88,* 13–28.

Hyde, K. L., Lerch, J. P., Zatorre, R., Griffiths, T. D., Evans, A. C., & Peretz, I. (2007). Cortical thickness in congenital amusia: When less is better than more. *Journal of Neuroscience, 27,* 13028–13032.

Hyde, K. L., Peretz, I., & Zatorre, R. J. (2008). Evidence for the role of the right auditory cortex in fine pitch resolution. *Neuropsychologia, 46,* 632–639.

Ikeda, D. M., Birdwell, R. L., O'Shaughnessy, K. F., Sickles, E. A., & Brenner, R. J. (2004). Computer-aided detection output on 172 subtle findings on normal mammograms previously obtained in women with breast cancer detected at follow-up screening mammography. *Radiology, 230,* 811–819.

Ishihara, S. (2011). *Ishihara's tests for colour deficiency*. Tokyo: Kanehara Trading.

Ittelson, W. H. (1951). Size as cue to distance: Static localization. *American Journal of Psychology, 64,* 54–67.

Ittelson, W. H. (1952). *The Ames demonstrations in perception.* Princeton, NJ: Princeton University Press.

Jacob, S., Zelano, B., Hayreh, D. J. S., & McClintock, M. K. (2002). Assessing putative human pheromones. In C. Rouby, B. Schaal, D. Dubois, R. Gervais, & A. Holley (Eds.), *Olfaction, taste, and cognition* (pp. 178–195). Cambridge, England: Cambridge University Press.

Jameson, D., & Hurvich, L. (1959). Note on the factors influencing the relation between stereoscopic acuity and observation distance. *Journal of the Optical Society of America, 49,* 639.

Jampel, H. D. (1997). *Glaucoma: A guide for patients*. San Ramon, CA: Health Information Network.

Janal, M. N., Colt, E. W., Clark, W. C., & Glusman, M. (1984). Pain sensitivity, mood and plasma endocrine levels in man following long-distance running: Effects of naloxone. *Pain, 19,* 13–25.

Jeffress, L. A. (1948). A place theory of sound localization. *Journal of Comparative Psychology, 41,* 35–39.

Jenkins, W. M., Merzenich, M. M., Ochs, M. T., Allard, T., & Guic-Robles, E. (1990). Functional reorganization of primary somatosensory cortex in adult owl monkeys after behaviorally controlled tactile stimulation. *Journal of Neurophysiology, 63,* 82–104.

Johansson, G. (1973). Visual perception of biological motion and a model for its analysis. *Perception & Psychophysics, 14,* 195–204.

Johansson, R. S., & Flanagan, J. R. (2008). Tactile sensory control of object manipulation in humans. In E. Gardner & J. H. Kaas (Eds.), *The senses: Vol. 6. Somatosensation* (pp. 67–86). Amsterdam: Elsevier.

Johnson, B. A., & Leon, M. (2007). Chemotopic odorant coding in a mammalian olfactory system. *Journal of Comparative Neurology, 503,* 1–34.

Johnson, E. N., Hawken, M. J., & Shapley, R. (2008). The orientation selectivity of color-responsive neurons in macaque V1. *Journal of Neuroscience, 28,* 8096–8106.

Johnson, K. O. (2002). Neural basis of haptic perception. In S. Yantis (Vol. Ed.) & H. Pashler (Series Ed.), *Stevens' handbook of experimental psychology: Vol. I. Sensation and perception* (3rd ed., pp. 537–583). New York: Wiley.

Johnson, K. O., & Lamb, G. D. (1981). Neural mechanisms of spatial tactile discrimination: Neural patterns evoked by Braille-like dot patterns in the monkey. *Journal of Physiology, 310,* 117–144.

Jonides, J., & Yantis, S. (1988). Uniqueness of abrupt visual onset in capturing attention. *Perception & Psychophysics, 43,* 346–354.

Julesz, B. (1960). Binocular depth perception of computer generated patterns. *Bell System Technical Journal, 39,* 1125–1162.

Julesz, B. (1971). *Foundations of cyclopean perception.* Chicago: University of Chicago Press.

Jusczyk, P. W. (1999). How infants begin to extract words from speech. *Trends in Cognitive Sciences, 3,* 323–328.

Kaas, J. H., & Collins, C. E. (Eds.). (2004). *The primate visual system*. New York: CRC Press.

Kaas, J. H., & Hackett, T. A. (2000). Subdivisions of auditory cortex and processing streams in primates. *Proceedings of the National Academy of Sciences, USA, 97,* 11793–11799.

Kaas, J. H., & Hackett, T. A. (2008). The functional neuroanatomy of the auditory cortex. In P. Dallos & D. Oertel (Eds.), *The senses: Vol. 3. Audition* (pp. 765–780). Amsterdam: Elsevier.

Kaas, J. H., Nelson, R. J., Sur, M., Lin, C. S., & Merzenich, M. M. (1979). Multiple representations of the body within the primary somatosensory cortex of primates. *Science, 204,* 521–523.

Kadohisa, M., & Wilson, D. A. (2006a). Separate encoding of identity and similarity of complex familiar odors in piriform cortex. *Proceedings of the National Academy of Sciences, USA, 103,* 15206–15211.

Kadohisa, M., & Wilson, D. A. (2006b). Olfactory cortical adaptation facilitates detection of odors against background. *Journal of Neurophysiology, 95,* 1888–1896.

Kamitani, Y., & Tong, F. (2006). Decoding seen and attended motion directions from activity in the human visual cortex. *Current Biology, 16,* 1096–1102.

Kandler, K., Clause, A., & Noh, J. (2009). Tonotopic reorganization of developing auditory brainstem circuits. *Nature Neuroscience, 12,* 711–717.

Kanizsa, G. (1979). *Organization in vision: Essays on Gestalt perception*. New York: Praeger.

Kanwisher, N. (2001). Neural events and perceptual awareness. *Cognition, 79,* 89–113.

Kanwisher, N., McDermott, J., & Chun, M. (1997). The fusiform face area: A module in human extrastriate cortex specialized for face perception. *Journal of Neuroscience, 17,* 4302–4311.

Kapreli, E., Athanasopoulos, S., Papathanasiou, M., Van Hecke, P., Keleki, D., Peeters, R., . . . Sunaert, S. (2007). Lower limb sensorimotor network: Issues of somatotopy and overlap. *Cortex, 43,* 219–232.

Karlson, P., & Lüscher, M. (1959). "Pheromones": A new term for a class of biologically active substances. *Nature, 183,* 55–56.

Kaufman, L., & Rock, I. (1962). The moon illusion. II: The moon's apparent size is a function of the presence or absence of terrain. *Science, 136,* 953–961.

Kellman, P., & Shipley, T. (1991). A theory of visual pattern interpolation in object perception. *Cognitive Psychology, 23,* 141–221.

Kersten, D., Mamassian, P., & Knill, D. C. (1997). Moving cast shadows induce apparent motion in depth. *Perception, 29,* 171–192.

Kersten, D., Mamassian, P., & Yuille, A. (2004). Object perception as Bayesian inference. *Annual Review of Psychology, 55,* 271–304.

Khalsa, P. S., Friedman, R. M., Srinivasan, M. A., & LaMotte, R. H. (1998). Encoding of shape and orientation of objects indented into the monkey fingerpad by populations of slowly and rapidly adapting mechanoreceptors. *Journal of Neurophysiology, 79,* 3238–3251.

Kilpatrick, F. P. (1952). Elementary demonstrations of perceptual phenomena. In F. P. Kilpatrick (Ed.), *Human behavior from the transactional point of view* (pp. 1–15). Hanover, NH: Institute of Associate Research.

Kilpatrick, F. P., & Ittelson, W. H. (1953). The size–distance invariance hypothesis. *Psychological Review, 60,* 223–231.

Kim, C. Y., & Blake, R. (2005). Psychophysical strategies for rendering the normally visible "invisible." *Trends in Cognitive Sciences, 9,* 381–388.

Klatzky, R. L., & Lederman, S. J. (1999). Tactile roughness perception with a rigid link interposed between skin and surface. *Perception & Psychophysics, 61,* 591– 607.

Klatzky, R. L., Lederman, S. J., & Metzger, V. A. (1985). Identifying objects by touch: An "expert system." *Perception & Psychophysics, 37,* 299–302.

Klatzky, R. L., Loomis, J. M., Lederman, S. J., Wake, H., & Fujita, N. (1993). Haptic identification of objects and their depictions. *Perception & Psychophysics, 54,* 170–178.

Kleene, S. J. (2008). The electrochemical basis of odor transduction in vertebrate olfactory cilia. *Chemical Senses, 33,* 839–859.

Kleinstein, R. N. (1984). Vision disorders in public health. *Annual Review of Public Health, 5,* 369–384.

Knecht, S., Dräger, B., Deppe, M., Bobe, L., Lohmann, H., Flöel, A., . . . Henningsen, H. (2000). Handedness and hemispheric language dominance in healthy humans. *Brain, 123,* 2512–2518.

Knill, D. S. (2007). Robust cue integration: A Bayesian model and evidence from cue-conflict studies with stereoscopic and figure cues to slant. *Journal of Vision, 7,* 1–24.

Krubitzer, L., Huffman, K. J., Disbrow, E., & Recanzone, G. (2004). Organization of area 3a in macaque monkeys: Contributions to the cortical phenotype. *Journal of Comparative Neurology, 471,* 97–111.

Krubitzer, L. A., & Kaas, J. H. (1990). The organization and connections of somatosensory cortex in marmosets. *Journal of Neuroscience, 10,* 952–974.

Krumhansl, C. L., & Kessler, E. J. (1982). Tracing the dynamic changes in perceived tonal organization in a spatial representation of musical keys. *Psychological Review, 89,* 334–368.

Kuffler, S. W. (1953). Discharge patterns and functional organization of mammalian retina. *Journal of Neurophysiology, 16,* 37–68.

Kung, C. (2005). A possible unifying principle for mechanosensation. *Nature, 436,* 647–654.

Kveraga, K., Ghuman, A. S., & Bar, M. (2007). Top-down predictions in the cognitive brain. *Brain and Cognition, 65,* 145–168.

Kwak, K.-C., & Pedrycz, W. (2007). Face recognition using an enhanced independent component analysis approach. *IEEE Transactions on Neural Networks, 18,* 530–541.

Kwong, K. K., Belliveau, J. W., Chesler, D. A., Goldberg, I. E., Weisskoff, R. M., Poncelet, B. P., . . . Turner, R. (1992). Dynamic magnetic resonance imaging of human brain activity during primary sensory stimulation. *Proceedings of the National Academy of Sciences, USA, 89,* 5675–5679.

Lackner, J. R., & DiZio, P. A. (2000). Aspects of body self-calibration. *Trends in Cognitive Sciences, 4,* 279–288.

Ladefoged, P., & Maddieson, I. (1996). *The sounds of the world's languages.* Oxford, England: Blackwell.

Lahav, A., Saltzman, E., & Schlaug, G. (2007). Action representation of sound: Audiomotor recognition network while listening to newly acquired actions. *Journal of Neuroscience, 27,* 308–314.

Laing, D. G., Legha, P. K., Jinks, A. L., & Hutchinson, I. (2003). Relationship between molecular structure, concentration and odor qualities of oxygenated aliphatic molecules. *Chemical Senses, 28,* 57–69.

Lamme, V. A., & Roelfsema, P. R. (2000). The distinct modes of vision offered by feedforward and recurrent processing. *Trends in Neuroscience, 23,* 571–579.

Land, M. F., & Fernald, R. D. (1992). The evolution of eyes. *Annual Review of Neuroscience, 15,* 1–29.

Landis, B. N., Scheibe, M., Weber, C., Berger, R., Brämerson, A., Bende, M., . . . Hummel, T. (2010). Chemosensory interaction: Acquired olfactory impairment is associated with decreased taste function. *Journal of Neurology, 257,* 1303–1308.

Landy, M. S., Maloney, L. T., Johnston, E. B., & Young, M. (1995). Measurement and modeling of depth cue combination: In defense of weak fusion. *Vision Research, 35,* 389–412.

Langguth, B., Hajak, G., Kleinjung, T., Cacace, A., & Møller, A.R. (Eds.). (2007). *Progress in brain research: Vol. 166. Tinnitus: Pathophysiology and treatment.* Amsterdam: Elsevier.

Large, E. W., & Palmer, C. (2002). Perceiving temporal regularity in music. *Cognitive Science, 26,* 1–37.

Lederman, S. J., & Klatzky, R. L. (1987). Hand movements: A window into haptic object recognition. *Cognitive Psychology, 19,* 342–368.

Lederman, S. J., & Klatzky, R. L. (2009). Haptic perception: A tutorial. *Attention, Perception, & Psychophysics, 71,* 1439–1459.

Lee, D. N., & Aronson, E. (1974). Visual proprioceptive control of standing in human infants. *Perception & Psychophysics, 15,* 529–532.

Lee, T. W., Wachtler, T., & Sejnowski, T. J. (2002). Color opponency is an efficient representation of spectral properties in natural scenes. *Vision Research, 42,* 2095–2103.

Leonard, R. (2002). *Statistics on vision impairment: A resource manual* (5th ed., pp. 1–49). New York: Arlene R. Gordon Research Institute of Lighthouse International.

LeVay, S., Hubel, D. H., & Wiesel, T. N. (1975). The pattern of ocular dominance columns in macaque visual cortex revealed by a reduced silver stain. *Journal of Comparative Neurology, 159,* 449–575.

Levitin, D. J. (2006). *This is your brain on music.* London: Plume.

Levitin, D. J., & Rogers, S. E. (2005). Absolute pitch: Perception, coding, and controversies. *Trends in Cognitive Sciences, 9,* 26–33.

Lewis, J. E., & Maler, L. (2002). Blurring of the senses: Common cues for distance perception in diverse sensory systems. *Neuroscience, 114,* 19–22.

Lewis, L. B., Saenz, M., & Fine, I. (2010). Mechanisms of cross-modal plasticity in early-blind subjects. *Journal of Neurophysiology, 104,* 2995–3008.

Liberman, M. C. (1982). The cochlear frequency map for the cat: Labeling auditory-nerve fibers of known characteristic frequency. *Journal of the Acoustical Society of America, 72,* 1441–1449.

Liebenthal, E., Binder, J. R., Spitzer, S. M., Possing, E. T., & Medler, D. A. (2005). Neural substrates of phonemic perception. *Cerebral Cortex, 15,* 1621–1631.

Lieberman, P. (2007). The evolution of human speech: Its anatomical and neural bases. *Current Anthropology, 48,* 39–66.

Lieberman, P., & Blumstein, S. E. (1988). *Speech physiology, speech perception, and acoustic phonetics.* New York: Cambridge University Press.

Lissauer, H. (2001). A case of visual agnosia with a contribution to theory. In S. Yantis (Ed.), *Visual perception: Essential readings* (pp. 274–292). Philadelphia: Psychology Press. (Original work published 1890)

Liu, T., Hospadaruk, L., Zhu, D. C., & Gardner, J. L. (2011). Feature-specific attentional priority signals in human cortex. *Journal of Neuroscience, 31,* 4484–4495.

Livingstone, M. S., & Hubel, D. H. (1984). Anatomy and physiology of a color system in the primate visual cortex. *Journal of Neuroscience, 4,* 309–356.

Logothetis, N. K., Pauls, J., & Poggio, P. (1995). Shape representation in the inferior temporal cortex of monkeys. *Current Biology, 5,* 552–563.

Loutfi, A., & Coradeschi, S. (2006). Smell, think and act: A cognitive robot discriminating odours. *Autonomous Robot, 20,* 239–249.

Luck, S. J. (2005). *An introduction to the event-related potential technique.* Cambridge, MA: MIT Press.

Lumpkin, E. A., & Caterina, M. J. (2009). Mechanisms of sensory transduction in the skin. *Nature, 445,* 858–865.

Ma, M. (2007). Encoding olfactory signals via multiple chemosensory systems. *Critical Reviews in Biochemistry and Molecular Biology, 42,* 463–480.

Mack, A., & Rock, I. (1998). *Inattentional blindness.* Cambridge, MA: MIT Press.

Macmillan, N. A., & Creelman, C. D. (2004). *Detection theory: A user's guide* (2nd ed.). Mahwah, NJ: Erlbaum.

Mahon, B. Z., & Caramazza, A. (2009). Concepts and categories: A cognitive neuropsychological perspective. *Annual Review of Psychology, 60,* 27–51.

Malach, R., Levy, I., & Hasson, U. (2002). The topography of high-order human object areas. *Trends in Cognitive Science, 6,* 176–184.

Malach, R., Reppas, J. B., Benson, R. R., Kwong, K. K., Jiang, H., Kennedy, W. A., . . . Tootell, R. B. (1995). Object-related activity revealed by functional magnetic resonance imaging in human occipital cortex. *Proceedings of the National Academy of Sciences, USA, 92,* 8135–8139.

Malnic, B., Hirono, J., Sato, T., & Buck, L. B. (1999). Combinatorial receptor codes for odors. *Cell, 96,* 713–723.

Maloney, L. T., & Wandell, B. A. (1986). Color constancy: A method for recovering surface spectral reflectances. *Journal of the Optical Society of America A, 3,* 29–33.

Manfredi, M., Bini, G., Cruccu, G., Accornero, N., Berardelli, A., & Medolago, L. (1981). Congenital absence of pain. *Archives of Neurology, 38,* 507–511.

Maresh, A., Rodriguez Gil, D., Whitman, M. C., & Greer, C. A. (2008). Principles of glomerular organization in the human olfactory bulb—Implications for odor processing. *PLoS ONE 3*(7), e2640.

Marr, D. (1982). *Vision.* San Francisco: W. H. Freeman and Company.

Marr, D., & Nishihara, H. K. (1978). Representation and recognition of the spatial organization of three-dimensional shapes. *Proceedings of the Royal Society of London Series B: Biological Sciences, 200,* 269–294.

Marr, D., & Poggio, T. (1979). A computational theory of human stereo vision. *Proceedings of the Royal Society of London Series B: Biological Sciences, 204,* 301–328.

Martin, P. R., & Grünert, U. (2004). Ganglion cells in the mammalian retinae. In L.M. Chalupa & J. S. Werner (Eds.), *The visual neurosciences* (Vol. 1, pp. 410–421). Cambridge, MA: MIT Press.

Martinez, D., Rochel, O., & Hugues, E. (2006). A biomimetic robot for tracking specific odors in turbulent plumes. *Autonomous Robot, 20,* 185–195.

Masland, R. H. (2001). The fundamental plan of the retina. *Nature Neuroscience, 4,* 877–886.

Mather, G., & Harris, J. (1998). Theoretical models of the motion aftereffect. In G. Mather, F. Verstraten, & S. Anstis (Eds.), *The motion aftereffect: A modern perspective* (pp. 157–185). Cambridge, MA: MIT Press.

Mather, G., Verstraten, F., & Anstis, S. (Eds.). (1998). *The motion aftereffect: A modern perspective.* Cambridge, MA: MIT Press.

Matin, E. (1974). Saccadic suppression: A review and an analysis. *Psychological Bulletin, 81,* 899–917.

McAlpine, D. (2005). Creating a sense of auditory space. *Journal of Physiology, 566,* 21–28.

McBeath, M. K., Shaffer, D. M., & Kaiser, M. K. (1995). How baseball outfielders determine where to run to catch fly balls. *Science, 268,* 569–573.

McCaffrey, R. J., Duff, K., & Solomon, G. S. (2000). Olfactory dysfunction discriminates probable Alzheimer's dementia from major depression: A cross validation and extension. *Journal of Neuropsychiatry and Clinical Neuroscience, 12,* 29–33.

McClintock, M. K. (1971). Menstrual synchorony and suppression. *Nature, 229,* 244–245.

McDermott, J. H., Lehr, A. J., & Oxenham, A. J. (2010). Individual differences reveal the basis of consonance. *Current Biology, 20,* 1035–1041.

McGurk, H., & MacDonald, J. (1976). Hearing lips and seeing voices. *Nature, 264,* 746–748.

McMahon, S., & Koltzenburg, M. (2005). *Wall and Melzack's textbook of pain* (5th ed.). Edinburgh: Elsevier/Churchill Livingstone.

Mehta, M., Johnson, J., & Rocafort, J. (1999). *Architectural acoustics: Principles and design.* Upper Saddle River, NJ: Prentice-Hall.

Meijer, P. B. (1992). An experimental system for auditory image representations. *IEEE Transactions in Biomedical Engineering, 39,* 112–121.

Melrose, D. R., Reed, H. C. B., & Patterson, R. L. S. (1971). Androgen steroids associated with boar odour as an aid to the detection of oestrus in pig artifical insemination. *British Veterinary Journal, 127,* 497–501.

Mendelson, J. R., & Grasse, K. L. (2000). Auditory cortical responses to the interactive effects of interaural intensity disparities and frequency. *Cerebral Cortex, 10,* 32–39.

Mendez, M. F., & Cherrier, M. M. (2003). Agnosia for scenes in topographagnosia. *Neuropsychologia, 41,* 1387–1395.

Merzenich, M. M., Kaas, J. H., Wall, J., Nelson, R. J., Sur, M., & Felleman, D. (1983). Topographic reorganization of somatosensory cortical areas 3b and 1 in adult monkeys following restricted deafferentation. *Neuroscience, 8,* 33–56.

Metzinger, T. (Ed.). (2000). *Neural correlates of consciousness: Empirical and conceptual questions.* Cambridge, MA: MIT Press.

Middlebrooks, J. C., & Green, D. M. (1991). Sound localization by human listeners. *Annual Review of Psychology, 42,* 135–159.

Millan, M. J. (2002). Descending control of pain. *Progress in Neurobiology, 66,* 355–474.

Miller, S. L., & Maner, J. K. (2010). Scent of a woman: Men's testosterone responses to olfactory ovulation cues. *Psychological Science, 21,* 276–283.

Mills, A.W. (1958). On the minimum audible angle. *Journal of the Acoustical Society of America, 30,* 237–246.

Milner, A. D., & Goodale, M. A. (2006). *The visual brain in action* (2nd ed.). New York: Oxford University Press.

Minnaert, M. (1954). *The nature of light and color in the open air.* New York: Dover.

Miron, D., Duncan, G. H., & Bushnell, M. C. (1989). Effects of attention on the intensity and unpleasantness of thermal pain. *Pain, 39,* 345–352.

Møller, A. R. (2006). *Hearing: Anatomy, physiology, and disorders of the auditory system* (2nd ed.). Amsterdam: Elsevier.

Mombaerts, P. (2004). Genes and ligands for odorant, vomeronasal and taste receptors. *Nature Reviews Neuroscience, 5,* 263–278.

Monsell, S. (2003). Task switching. *Trends in Cognitive Science, 7,* 134–140.

Moore, B. C. J. (Ed.). (1995). *Hearing.* San Diego, CA: Academic Press.

Moore, B. C. J. (2012). *An introduction to the psychology of hearing* (6th ed.). Bingley, UK: Emerald Group.

Moore, C. I., Stern, C. E., Corkin, S., Fischl, B., Gray, A. C., Rosen, B. R., & Dale, A. M. (2000). Segregation of somatosensory activation in the human rolandic cortex using fMRI. *Journal of Neurophysiology, 84,* 558–569.

Moore, D. R., & King, A. J. (1999). Auditory perception: The near and far of sound localization. *Current Biology, 9,* R361–R363.

Moore, T., & Fallah, M. (2004). Microstimulation of the frontal eye field and its effects on covert spatial attention. *Journal of Neurophysiology, 91,* 152–162.

Moran, J., & Desimone, R. (1985). Selective attention gates visual processing in the extrastriate cortex. *Science, 229,* 782–784.

Moray, N. (1959). Attention in dichotic listening: Affective cues and the influence of instructions. *Quarterly Journal of Experimental Psychology, 11,* 56–60.

Morrot, G., Brochet, F., & Dubourdieu, D. (2001). The color of odors. *Brain and Language, 79,* 309–320.

Motter, B. C. (1994). Neural correlates of feature-selective memory and pop-out in extrastriate area V4. *Journal of Neuroscience, 14,* 2190–2199.

Mountcastle, V. B. (1957). Modality and topographic properties of single neurons of cat's somatic sensory cortex. *Journal of Neurophysiology, 20,* 408–434.

Mountcastle, V. B., Poggio G. F., & Werner, G. (1963). The relation of thalamic cell response to peripheral stimuli varied over an intensive continuum. *Journal of Neurophysiology, 26,* 807–834.

Movshon, J. A., Adelson, E. H., Gizzi, M. S., & Newsome, W. T. (1985). The analysis of moving visual patterns. In C. Chagas, R. Gattass, & C. Gross (Eds.), *Pattern recognition mechanisms* (pp. 117–151). New York: Springer.

Munoz, D. P., & Everling, S. (2004). Look away: The anti-saccade task and the voluntary control of eye movement. *Nature Reviews Neuroscience, 5,* 218–228.

Murata, A., Gallese, V., Luppino, G., Kaseda, M., & Sakata, H. (2000). Selectivity for the shape, size, and orientation of objects for grasping in neurons of monkey parietal area AIP. *Journal of Neurophysiology, 83,* 2580–2601.

Murphy, C., Cain, W. S., Gilmore, M. M., & Skinner R. B. (1991). Sensory and semantic factors in recognition memory for odors and graphic stimuli: Elderly versus young persons. *American Journal of Psychology, 104,* 161–192.

Narayan, S. S., Temchin, A. N., Recio, A., & Ruggero, M. A. (1998). Frequency tuning of basilar membrane and auditory nerve fibers in the same cochleae. *Science, 282,* 1882–1884.

Nassi, J. J., & Callaway, E. M. (2009). Parallel processing strategies of the primate visual system. *Nature Reviews Neuroscience, 10,* 360–372.

Neitz, J., & Neitz, M. (2011). The genetics of normal and defective color vision. *Vision Research, 51,* 633–651.

Newsome, W. T., Britten, K. H., & Movshon, J. A. (1989). Neuronal correlates of a perceptual decision. *Nature, 341,* 52–54.

Newsome, W. T., & Paré, E. B. (1988). A selective impairment of motion perception following lesions of the middle temporal visual area (MT). *Journal of Neuroscience, 8,* 2201–2211.

Newton, I. (1952). *Opticks: or, A treatise of the reflections, refractions, inflections, and colours of light.* New York: Dover Publications. (Original work published 1704)

Niimura, Y. (2009). Evolutionary dynamics of olfactory receptor genes in chordates: Interaction between environments and genomic contents. *Human Genomics, 4,* 107–118.

Nondahl, D. M., Cruickshanks, K. J., Wiley, T. L., Klein, R., Klein, B. E. K., & Tweed, T. S. (2002). Prevalence and 5-year incidence of tinnitus among older adults: The epidemiology of hearing loss study. *Journal of the American Academy of Audiology, 13,* 323–331.

Oakley, B., & Witt, M. (2004). Building sensory receptors on the tongue. *Journal of Neurocytology, 33,* 631–646.

O'Connor, D. H., Fukui, M. M., Pinsk, M. A., & Kastner, S. (2002). Attention modulates responses in the human lateral geniculate nucleus. *Nature Neuroscience, 5,* 1203–1209.

O'Craven, K. M., Rosen, B. R., Kwong, K. K., Treisman, A., & Savoy, R. L. (1997).Voluntary attention modulates fMRI activity in human MT–MST. *Neuron, 18,* 591–598.

Ogawa, S., Tank, D. W., Menon, R., Ellermann, J. M., Kim, S. G., Merkle, H., & Ugurbil, K. (1992). Intrinsic signal changes accompanying sensory stimulation: Functional brain mapping with magnetic resonance imaging. *Proceedings of the National Academy of Sciences, USA, 89,* 5951–5955.

Ohki, K., Chung, S., Kara, P., Hübener, M., Bonhoeffer, T., & Reid, R. C. (2006). Highly ordered arrangement of single neurons in orientation pinwheels. *Nature, 442,* 925–928.

Ohki, K., & Reid, R. C. (2007). Specificity and randomness in the visual cortex. *Current Opinion in Neurobiology, 17,* 401–407.

Okamura, A. M. (2009). Haptic feedback in robot-assisted minimally invasive surgery. *Current Opinion in Urology, 19,* 102–107.

Olausson, H., Wessberg, J., & Kakuda, N. (2000). Tactile directional sensibility: Peripheral neural mechanisms in man. *Brain Research, 866,* 178–187.

Olausson, H., Wessberg, J., Morrison, I., McGlone, F., & Vallbo, A. (2010). The neurophysiology of unmyelinated tactile afferents. *Neuroscience and Biobehavioral Reviews, 34,* 185–191.

Oliva, A. (2005). Gist of the scene. In L. Itti, G. Rees, & J. K. Tsotsos (Eds.), *Neurobiology of attention* (pp. 251–256). San Diego, CA: Elsevier.

Oliva, A., & Torralba, A. (2006). Building the gist of a scene: The role of global image features in recognition. In S. Martinez-Conde, S. Macknik, M. Martinez, J.-M. Alonso, & P. Tse (Eds.), *Progress in brain research: Vol. 155. Visual perception. Part 2: Fundamentals of awareness, multi-sensory integration and high-order perception* (pp. 23–36). Amsterdam: Elsevier.

Oliva A., & Torralba, A. (2007). The role of context in object recognition. *Trends in Cognitive Sciences, 11,* 520–527.

Ooi, T. L., Wu, B., & He, Z. J. (2001). Distance determined by the angular declination below the horizon. *Nature, 414,* 197–200.

Orban, G. A., Kennedy, H., & Bullier, J. (1986). Velocity sensitivity and direction selectivity of neurons in areas V1 and V2 of the monkey: Influence of eccentricity. *Journal of Neurophysiology, 56,* 462–480.

Ostrowsky, K., Magnin, M., Ryvlin, P., Isnard, J., Guenot, M., & Mauguière, F. (2002). Representation of pain and somatic sensation in the human insula: A study of responses to direct electrical cortical stimulation. *Cerebral Cortex, 12,* 376–385.

Oyster, C. W. (1999). *The human eye.* Sunderland, MA: Sinauer.

Packer, O., & Williams, D. R. (2003). Light, the retinal image, and photoreceptors. In S. K. Shevell (Ed.), *The science of color* (pp. 41–102). Washington, DC: Optical Society of America.

Pacione, L. R., Szego, M. J., Ikeda, S., Nishina, P. M., & McInnes, R. R. (2003). Progress toward understanding the genetic and biochemical mechanisms of inherited photoreceptor degenerations. *Annual Review of Neuroscience, 26,* 657–700.

Palmer, A. R. (1987). Physiology of the cochlear nerve and cochlear nucleus. *British Medical Bulletin, 43,* 838–855.

Palmer, S., & Rock, I. (1994). Rethinking perceptual organization: The role of uniform connectedness. *Psychonomic Bulletin & Review, 1,* 9–55.

Palmeri, T. J., & Gauthier, I. (2004). Visual object understanding. *Nature Reviews Neuroscience, 5,* 291–303.

Pantev, C., Oostenveld, R., Engelien, A., Ross, B., Roberts, L. E., & Hoke, M. (1998). Increased auditory cortical representation in musicians. *Nature, 392,* 811–814.

Paré, M., Behets, C., & Cornu, O. (2003). Paucity of presumptive Ruffini corpuscles in the index finger pad of humans. *Journal of Comparative Neurology, 456,* 260–266.

Parker, A. J. (2007). Binocular depth perception and the cerebral cortex. *Nature Reviews Neuroscience, 8,* 379–391.

Parker, A. J., & Newsome, W. T. (1998). Sense and the single neuron: Probing the physiology of perception. *Annual Review of Neuroscience, 21,* 227–277.

Parr, W. V., Heatherbell, D., & White, K. G. (2002). Demystifying wine expertise: Olfactory threshold, perceptual skill and semantic memory in expert and novice wine judges. *Chemical Senses, 27,* 747–755.

Pashler, H. (1998). *Attention*. East Sussex, England: Psychology Press.

Pasupathy, A., & Connor, C. E. (2002). Population coding of shape in V4. *Nature Neuroscience, 5*, 1332–1338.

Patel, A. D. (2008). *Music, language, and the brain*. New York: Oxford University Press.

Pearce, T. C., Schiffman, S. S., Nagle, H. T., & Gardner, J. W. (Eds.). (2003). *Handbook of machine olfaction: Electronic nose technology.* Weinheim, Germany: Wiley-VCH.

Pegna, A. J., Khateb, A., Lazeyras, F., & Seghier, M. L. (2005). Discriminating emotional faces without primary visual cortices involves the right amygdala. *Nature Neuroscience, 8*, 24–25.

Penfield, W., & Rasmussen, T. (1950). *The cerebral cortex of man. A clinical study of localization of function*. New York: Macmillan.

Pentland, A., Moghaddam, B., & Starner, T. (1994). View-based and modular eigenspaces for face recognition. *Proceedings of IEEE Conference on Computer Vision and Pettern Recognition*, pp. 84–91. doi:10.1109/CVPR.1994.323814

Peretz, I., & Zatorre, R. J. (2005). Brain organization for music processing. *Annual Review of Psychology, 56*, 89–114.

Perrett, D. I., Rolls, E. T., & Caan, W. (1982). Visual neurones responsive to faces in the monkey temporal cortex. *Experimental Brain Research, 47*, 329–342.

Persaud, K., & Dodd, G. (1982). Analysis of discrimination mechanisms in the mammalian olfactory system using a model nose. *Nature, 299*, 352–355.

Petersen, S. E., Baker, J. F., & Allman, J. M. (1985). Direction-specific adaptation in area MT of the owl monkey. *Brain Research, 346*, 146–150.

Peterson, M. A., & Gibson, B. S. (1994). Must figure–ground organization precede object recognition? An assumption in peril. *Psychological Science, 5*, 253–259.

Petit, C., Levilliers, J., & Hardelin, J.-P. (2001). Molecular genetics of hearing loss. *Annual Review of Genetics, 35*, 589–646.

Pfaffmann, C. (1955). Gustatory nerve impulses in rat, cat, and rabbit. *Journal of Neurophysiology, 19*, 429–440.

Phillips, D. P. (1987). Stimulus intensity and loudness recruitment: Neural correlates. *Journal of the Acoustical Society of America, 82*, 1–12.

Phillips, J. R., Johansson, R. S., & Johnson, K. O. (1990). Representation of Braille characters in human nerve fibres. *Experimental Brain Research, 81*, 589–592.

Phillips, J. R., Johnson, K. O., & Hsiao, S. S. (1988). Spatial pattern representation and transformation in monkey somatosensory cortex. *Proceedings of the National Academy of Sciences, USA, 85*, 1317–1321.

Plack, C. J., Oxenham, A. J., Fay, R. R., & Popper, A. N. (Eds.). *Pitch: Neural coding and perception*. New York: Springer.

Plantinga, J., & Trainor, L. J. (2005). Memory for melody: Infants use a relative pitch code. *Cognition, 98*, 1–11.

Poggio, G. F. (1995). Mechanisms of stereopsis in monkey visual cortex. *Cerebral Cortex, 5*, 193–204.

Poggio, G. F., & Fischer, B. (1977). Binocular interaction and depth sensitivity in striate and prestriate cortex of behaving rhesus monkey. *Journal of Neurophysiology, 40*, 1392–1405.

Poremba, A., & Mishkin, M. (2007). Exploring the extent and function of higher-order auditory cortex in rhesus monkeys. *Hearing Research, 229*, 14–23.

Poremba, A., Saunders, R. C., Crane, A. M., Cook, M., Sokoloff, L., & Mishkin, M. (2003). Functional mapping of the primate auditory system. *Science, 299*, 568–572.

Posner, M. I., Nissen, M. J., & Ogden, W. C. (1978). Attended and unattended processing modes: The role of set for spatial location. In H. L. Pick & I. J. Saltzman (Eds.), *Modes of perceiving and processing information* (pp. 137–157). Hillsdale, NJ: Erlbaum.

Posner, M. I., & Raichle, M. E. (1994). *Imaging of mind*. New York: Scientific American Library.

Potter, M. C. (1976). Short-term conceptual memory for pictures. *Journal of Experimental Psychology: Human Learning and Memory, 2*, 509–522.

Potter, M. C., & Levy, E. I. (1969). Recognition memory for a rapid sequence of pictures. *Journal of Experimental Psychology, 81*, 10–15.

Prado, J., Clavagnier, S., Otzenberger, H., Scheiber, C., Kennedy, H., & Perenin, M. T. (2005). Two cortical systems for reaching in central and peripheral vision. *Neuron, 48*, 849–858.

Price, D. D. (2000). Psychological and neural mechanisms of the affective dimension of pain. *Science, 288*, 1769–1772.

Proske, U., & Gandevia, S. C. (2009). The kinaesthetic senses. *Journal of Physiology, 587*, 4139–4146.

Proske, U., Wise, A. K., & Gregory, J. E. (2000). The role of muscle receptors in the detection of movements. *Progress in Neurobiology, 60*, 85–96.

Ptito, A., & Leh, S. E. (2007). Neural substrates of blindsight after hemispherectomy. *Neuroscientist, 13*, 506–518.

Quinlan, P. T. (2003). Visual feature integration theory: Past, present, and future. *Psychological Bulletin, 129*, 643–673.

Quiroga, R. Q., Reddy, L., Kreiman, G., Koch, C., & Fried, I. (2005). Invariant visual representation by single-neurons in the human brain. *Nature, 435*, 1102–1107.

Rabin, M. D., & Cain, W. S. (1984). Odor recognition: Familiarity, identifiability, and encoding consistency. *Journal of Experimental Psychology: Learning, Memory, and Cognition, 10*, 316–325.

Rainville, P., Duncan, G. H., Price, D. D., Carrier, B., & Bushnell, M. C. (1997). Pain affect encoded in human anterior cingulate but not somatosensory cortex. *Science, 277*, 968–971.

Raizada, R. D. S., & Poldrack, R. A. (2007). Selective amplification of stimulus differences during categorical processing of speech. *Neuron, 56*, 726–740.

Ramachandran, V. S. (1992). Filling in the blind spot. *Nature 356*, 115.

Ramachandran, V. S., Rogers-Ramachandran, D., & Stewart, M. (1992). Perceptual correlates of massive cortical reorganization. *Science, 258*, 1159–1160.

Ratliff, F. (1965). *Mach bands: Quantitative studies on neural networks in the retina*. San Francisco: Holden-Day.

Rauschecker, J. P. (1998). Parallel processing in the auditory cortex of primates. *Audiology and Neuro-Otology, 3*, 86–103.

Rauschecker, J. P., & Scott, S. K. (2009). Maps and streams in the auditory cortex: Nonhuman primates illuminate human speech processing. *Nature Neurosciences, 12*, 718–724.

Recanzone, G. H., & Sutter, M. L. (2008). The biological basis of audition. *Annual Review of Psychology, 59*, 119–142.

Redelmeier, D. A., & Tibshirani, R. J. (1997). Association between cellular-telephone calls and motor vehicle collisions. *New England Journal of Medicine, 336*, 453–458.

Reed, C. L., Caselli, R. J., & Farah, M. J. (1996). Tactile agnosia. Underlying impairment and implications for normal tactile object recognition. *Brain, 119*, 875–888.

Reed, C. L., Klatzky, R. L., & Halgren, E. (2005). What vs. where in touch: An fMRI study. *NeuroImage, 25*, 718–726.

Reichardt, W. (1961). Autocorrelation: A principle for the evaluation of sensory information by the central nervous system. In W. A. Rosenblith (Ed.), *Sensory communication* (pp. 303–317). New York: Wiley.

Reid, R. C., & Alonso, J.-M. (1995). Specificity of monosynaptic connections from thalamus to visual cortex. *Nature, 378*, 281–284.

Rensink, R. A., O'Regan, J. K., & Clark, J. J. (1997). To see or not to see: The need for attention to perceive changes in scenes. *Psychological Science, 8*, 368–373.

Reynolds, D. V. (1969). Surgery in the rat during electrical analgesia induced by focal brain stimulation. *Science, 164,* 444–445.

Reynolds, J. H., Chelazzi, L., & Desimone, R. (1999). Competitive mechanisms subserve attention in macaque areas V2 and V4. *Journal of Neuroscience, 19,* 1736–1753.

Riesenhuber, M., & Poggio, T. (2002). Neural mechanisms of object recognition. *Current Opinion in Neurobiology, 12,* 162–168.

Rodieck, R. W. (1998). *The first steps in seeing.* Sunderland, MA: Sinauer.

Roffler, S. K., & Butler, R. A. (1968). Localization of tonal stimuli in the vertical plane. *Journal of the Acoustical Society of America, 43,* 1260–1266.

Rogers, B. J., & Graham, M. E. (1979). Motion parallax as an independent cue for depth perception. *Perception, 8,* 125–134.

Rogers, R. D., & Monsell, S. (1995). Costs of a predictable switch between simple cognitive tasks. *Journal of Experimental Psychology: General, 124,* 207–231.

Rolls, E. T. (2006). Brain mechanisms underlying flavour and appetite. *Philosophical Transactions of the Royal Society of London, Series B: Biological Sciences, 361,* 1123–1136.

Roorda, A., & Williams, D. R. (1999). The arrangement of the three cone classes in the living human eye. *Nature, 397,* 520–522.

Roper, S. D. (2007). Signal transduction and information processing in mammalian taste buds. *Pflügers Archiv—European Journal of Physiology, 454,* 759–776.

Rose, J. E., Brugge, J. F., Anderson, D. J., & Hind, J. E. (1967). Phase-locked response to low-frequency tones in single auditory nerve fibers of the squirrel monkey. *Journal of Neurophysiology, 30,* 769–793.

Rose, J. E., Hind, J. E., Anderson, D. J., & Brugge, J. F. (1971). Some effects of stimulus intensity of response of auditory nerve fibers in squirrel monkey. *Journal of Neurophysiology, 34,* 685–699.

Rosenholtz, R., & Malik, J. (1997). Surface orientation from texture: Isotropy or homogeneity (or both)? *Vision Research, 37,* 2283–2293.

Roskies, A. L. (1999). The binding problem [Special issue]. *Neuron, 24,* 7–125.

Ross, H. E., & Plug, C. (2002). *The mystery of the moon illusion: Exploring size perception.* New York: Oxford University Press.

Royet, J.-P., Zald, D., Versace, R., Costes, N., Lavenne, F., Koenig, O., & Gervais, R. (2000). Emotional responses to pleasant and unpleasant olfactory, visual, and auditory stimuli: A positron emission tomography study. *Journal of Neuroscience, 20,* 7752–7759.

Rozin, P., & Millman, L. (1987). Family environment, not heredity, accounts for family resemblance in food preferences and attitudes. *Appetite, 8,* 125–134.

Rubin, E. (2001). Figure and ground. In S. Yantis (Ed.), *Visual perception: Essential readings* (pp. 225–230). Philadelphia: Psychology Press. (Original work published 1921)

Rubinstein, J. S., Meyer, D. E., & Evans, J. E. (2001). Executive control of cognitive processes in task switching. *Journal of Experimental Psychology: Human Perception and Performance, 27,* 763–797.

Ruggero, M. A., & Rich, N. C. (1991). Furosemide alters organ of corti mechanics: Evidence for feedback of outer hair cells upon the basilar membrane. *Journal of Neuroscience, 11,* 1057–1067.

Rushton, W. A. (1965). Visual adaptation. *Proceedings of the Royal Society of London Series B: Biological Sciences, 162,* 20–46.

Rushton, W. A. (1972). Pigments and signals in color vision. *Journal of Physiology, 220,* 1–31.

Saffran, J. R., Aslin, R. N., & Newport, E. L. (1996). Statistical learning by 8-month-old infants. *Science, 274,* 1926–1928.

Salzman, C. D., Murasugi, C. M., Britten, K. H., & Newsome, W. T. (1992). Microstimulation in visual area MT: Effects on direction discrimination performance. *Journal of Neuroscience, 12,* 2331–2355.

Samuel, A. G. (1981). The role of bottom-up confirmation in the phonemic restoration illusion. *Journal of Experimental Psychology: Human Perception and Performance, 7,* 1124–1131.

Schenkman, B. N., & Nilsson, M. E. (2010). Human echolocation: Blind and sighted persons' ability to detect sounds recorded in the presence of a reflecting object. *Perception, 39,* 483–501.

Schepers, R. J., & Ringkamp, M. (2009). Thermoreceptors and thermosensitive afferents. *Neuroscience and Biobehavioral Reviews, 33,* 205–212.

Schild, D., & Restrepo, D. (1998). Transduction mechanisms in vertebrate olfactory receptor cells. *Physiological Reviews, 78,* 429–466.

Schiller, P. H., & Logothetis, N. K. (1990). The color-opponent and broadband channels of the primate visual system. *Trends in Neurosciences, 13,* 392–398.

Schiller, P. H., & Tehovnik, E. J. (2008). Visual prosthesis. *Perception, 37,* 1529–1559.

Schlief, M. L., & Wilson, R. I. (2007). Olfactory processing and behavior downstream from highly selective receptor neurons. *Nature Neuroscience, 10,* 623–630.

Schluppeck, D., Curtis, C. E., Glimcher, P. W., & Heeger D. J. (2006). Sustained activity in topographic areas of human posterior parietal cortex during memory-guided saccades. *Journal of Neuroscience, 26,* 5098–5108.

Schneider, D. (1974). The sex-attractant receptor of moths. *Scientific American, 231,* 28–35.

Schnitzler, H.-U., & Kalko, E. K. V. (2001). Echolocation by insect-eating bats. *BioScience, 51,* 557–569.

Scholz, J., & Woolf, C. J. (2002). Can we conquer pain? *Nature Neuroscience, 5,* 1062–1067.

Schreiner, C. E., Read, H. L., & Sutter, M. L. (2000). Modular organization of frequency integration in primary auditory cortex. *Annual Review of Neuroscience, 23,* 501–529.

Scott, T. R., & Plata-Salamán, C. R. (1999). Taste in the monkey cortex. *Physiology & Behavior, 67,* 489–511.

Semaan, M. T., & Megerian, C. A. (2010). Contemporary perspectives on the pathophysiology of Meniere's disease: implications for treatment. *Current Opinion in Otolaryngology & Head and Neck Surgery, 18,* 392–398.

Shadlen, M. N., & Movshon, J. A. (1999). Synchrony unbound: A critical evaluation of the temporal binding hypothesis. *Neuron, 24,* 67–77.

Shaffer, D. M., Krauchunas, S. M., Eddy, M., & McBeath, M. K. (2004). How dogs navigate to catch frisbees. *Psychological Science, 15,* 437–441.

Shahin, A. J., Bishop, C. W., & Miller, L. M. (2009). Neural mechanisms for illusory filling-in of degraded speech. *NeuroImage, 44,* 1133–1143.

Sharpe, L. T., & Nordby, K. (1990). Total colour-blindness: An introduction. In R. F. Hess, L. T. Sharpe, & K. Nordby (Eds.), *Night vision: Basic, clinical, and applied aspects* (pp. 335–389). Cambridge, England: Cambridge University Press.

Sharpe, L. T., Stockman, A., Jägle, H., & Nathans, J. (1999). Opsin genes, cone photopigments, color vision, and color blindness. In K. R. Gegenfurtner & L. T. Sharpe (Eds.), *Color vision: from genes to perception* (pp. 3–51). Cambridge, England: Cambridge University Press.

Shepard, R. N. (1982). Geometrical approximations to the structure of musical pitch. *Psychological Review, 89,* 305–333.

Shepard, R. N. (1990). *Mind sights.* New York: W. H. Freeman and Company.

Sherrington, C. S. (1906). *The integrative action of the nervous system*. New York: C. Scribner and Sons.

Shevell, S. K., & Kingdom, F. A. A. (2008). Color in complex scenes. *Annual Review of Psychology, 59,* 143–166.

Shigemura, N., Shirasaki, S., Ohkuri, T., Sanematsu, K., Islam, A., Ogiwara, Y., . . . & Ninomiya, Y. (2009). Variation in umami perception and in candidate genes for the umami receptor in mice and humans. *American Journal of Clinical Nutrition, 90,* 764S–769S.

Shim, J., Carlton, L. G., & Kim, J. (2004). Estimation of lifted weight and produced effort through perception of point-light display. *Perception, 33,* 277–291.

Silver, M. A., Ress, D., & Heeger, D. J. (2005). Topographic maps of visual spatial attention in human parietal cortex. *Journal of Neurophysiology, 94,* 1358–1371.

Simon, S. A., de Araujo, I. E., Gutierrez, R., & Nicolelis, M. A. L. (2006). The neural mechanisms of gustation: A distributed processing code. *Nature Reviews Neuroscience, 7,* 890–901.

Simons, D. J., & Levin, D. T. (1998). Failure to detect changes to people during a real-world interaction. *Psychonomic Bulletin & Review, 5,* 644–649.

Simpson, W. A. (1993). Optic flow and depth perception. *Spatial Vision, 7,* 35–75.

Singer, T., Seymour, B., O'Doherty, J., Kaube, H., Dolan, R. J., & Frith, C. D. (2004). Empathy for pain involves the affective but not sensory components of pain. *Science, 303,* 1157–1162.

Snyder, L. H., Batista, A. P., & Andersen, R. A. (2000). Intention-related activity in the posterior parietal cortex: A review. *Vision Research, 40,* 1433–1441.

Sobel, N., Prabhakaran, V., Zhao, Z., Desmond, J. E., Glover, G. H., Sullivan, E. V., & Gabrieli, J. D. E. (2000). Time course of odorant-induced activation in the human primary olfactory cortex. *Journal of Neurophysiology, 83,* 537–551.

Solomon, S. G., & Lennie, P. (2007). The machinery of colour vision. *Nature Reviews Neuroscience, 8,* 276–286.

Sommer, M. A., & Wurtz, R. H. (2006). Influence of the thalamus on spatial visual processing in frontal cortex. *Nature, 444,* 374–377.

Stamford, J. A. (1995). Descending control of pain. *British Journal of Anaesthesiology, 75,* 217–227.

Stapleton, J. R., Lavine, M. L., Wolpert, R. L., Nicolelis, M. A. L., & Simon, S. A. S. (2006). Rapid taste responses in the gustatory cortex during licking. *Journal of Neuroscience, 26,* 4126–4138.

Stein, B. E., & Meredith, M. A. (1993). *The merging of the senses*. Cambridge, MA: MIT Press.

Stern, K., & McClintock, M. K. (1998). Regulation of ovulation by human pheromones. *Nature, 392,* 177–179.

Stettler, D. D., & Axel, R. (2009). Representations of odor in the piriform cortex. *Neuron, 63,* 854–864.

Stevens, K. A., & Brookes, A. (1988). The concave cusp as a determiner of figure–ground. *Perception, 17,* 35–42.

Stevens, S. S. (1961). To honor Fechner and repeal his law. *Science, 133,* 80–86.

Stevenson, R. J. (2001). The acquisition of odour qualities. *Quarterly Journal of Experimental Psychology A, 54,* 561–577.

Stevenson, R. J. (2009). *The psychology of flavor*. Oxford, England: Oxford University Press.

Stevenson, R. J. (2010). An initial evaluation of the functions of human olfaction. *Chemical Senses, 35,* 3–20.

Stevenson, R. J., & Boakes, R. A. (2003). A mnemonic theory of odor perception. *Psychological Review, 110,* 340–364.

Stevenson, R. J., Oaten, M. J., Case, T. I., Repacholi, B. M., & Wagland, P. (2010). Children's response to adult disgust elicitors: Development and acquisition. *Developmental Psychology, 46,* 165–177.

Stewart, L. (2008). Fractionating the musical mind: Insights from congenital amusia. *Current Opinion in Neurobiology, 18,* 127–130.

Stiles, W. S., & Burch, J. M. (1959). NPL colour-matching investigation: Final report. *Optica Acta, 6,* 1–26.

Stirling, P. (2004). How retinal circuits optimize the transfer of visual information. In L. M. Chalupa & J. S. Werner (Eds.), *The visual neurosciences* (Vol. 1, pp. 234–259). Cambridge, MA: MIT Press.

Stockman, S., MacLeod, D. I., & Johnson, N. E. (1993). Spectral sensitivities of the human cones. *Journal of the Optical Society of America (A), 10,* 2491–2521.

Stoerig, P., & Cowey, A. (1997). Blindsight in man and monkey. *Brain, 120,* 535–559.

Stone, E. M. (2007). Macular degeneration. *Annual Review of Medicine, 58,* 477–490.

Strayer, D. L., & Drews, F. A. (2007). Cell-phone-induced driver distraction. *Current Directions in Psychological Science, 16,* 128–131.

Strayer, D. L., Drews, F. A., & Crouch, D. J. (2006). A comparison of the cell phone driver and the drunk driver. *Human Factors, 48,* 381–391.

Strayer, D. L., & Johnston, W. A. (2001). Driven to distraction: Dual-task studies of simulated driving and conversing on a cellular phone. *Psychological Science, 12,* 462–466.

Suga, N., & Ma, X. (2003). Multiparametric corticofugal modulation and plasticity in the auditory system. *Nature Reviews Neuroscience, 4,* 783–794.

Supa, M., Cotzin, M., & Dallenbach, K. M. (1944). "Facial vision:" The perception of obstacles by the blind. *American Journal of Psychology, 57,* 133–183.

Suzuki, Y., & Takeshima, H. (2004). Equal-loudness-level contours for pure tones. *Journal of the Acoustical Society of America, 116,* 918–933.

Svaetichin, G., & MacNichol, E. F. (1958). Retinal mechanisms for chromatic and achromatic vision. *Annals of the New York Academy of Sciences, 74,* 385–404.

Swets, J. A. (1988). Measuring the accuracy of diagnostic systems. *Science, 240,* 1285–1293.

Swets, J. A., Dawes, R., & Monahan, J. (2000). Psychological science can improve diagnostic decisions. *Psychological Science in the Public Interest, 1,* 1–26.

Sylvester, C. M., Shulman, G. L., Jack, A. I., & Corbetta, M. (2009). Anticipatory and stimulus-evoked blood oxygenation level-dependent modulations related to spatial attention reflect a common additive signal. *Journal of Neuroscience, 29,* 10671–10682.

Takeuchi, H., Imanaka, Y., Hirono, J., & Kurahashi, T. (2003). Cross-adaptation between olfactory responses induced by two subgroups of odorant molecules. *Journal of General Physiology, 122,* 255–264.

Tanaka, K., Saito, H., Fukada, Y., & Moriya, M. (1991). Coding visual images of objects in the inferotemporal cortex of the macaque monkey. *Journal of Neurophysiology, 66,* 170–189.

Tanner, W. P. Jr., & Swets, J. A. (1954). A decision-making theory of visual detection. *Psychological Review, 61,* 401–409.

Tarr, M. J. (1995). Rotating objects to recognize them: A case study on the role of viewpoint dependency in the recognition of three-dimensional objects. *Psychonomic Bulletin & Review, 2,* 55–82.

Tarr, M. J., & Pinker, S. (1989). Mental rotation and orientation-dependence in shape recognition. *Cognitive Psychology, 21,* 233–282.

Taylor, J. B. (2009). *My stroke of insight*. London: Plume.

Tirindelli, R., Dibattista, M., Pifferi, S., & Menini, A. (2009). From pheromones to behavior. *Physiological Reviews, 89,* 921–956.

Todd, J. T. (1985). Perception of structure from motion: Is projective correspondence of moving elements a necessary condition? *Journal of Experimental Psychology: Human Perception and Performance, 11,* 689–710.

Todd, J. T., & Mingolla, E. (1983). Perception of surface curvature and direction of illumination from patterns of shading. *Journal of Experimental Psychology: Human Perception and Performance, 9,* 583–595.

Tomchik, S. M., Berg, S., Kim, J. W., Chaudhari, N., & Roper, S. D. (2007). Breadth of tuning and taste coding in mammalian taste buds. *Journal of Neuroscience, 27,* 10840–10848.

Tong, F., Nakayama, K., Vaughan, J. T., & Kanwisher, N. (1998). Binocular rivalry and visual awareness in human extrastriate cortex. *Neuron, 21,* 753–759.

Tononi, G., & Koch, C. (2008). The neural correlates of consciousness: An update. *Annals of the New York Academy of Sciences, 1124,* 239–261.

Tootell, R. B. H., Hadjikhani, N. K., Vanduffel, W., Liu, A. K., Mendola, J. D., Sereno, M. I., & Dale, A. M. (1998). Functional analysis of primary visual cortex (V1) in humans. *Proccedings of the National Academy of Sciences, USA, 95,* 811–817.

Tootell, R. B., Reppas, J. B., Kwong, K. K., Malach, R., Born, R. T., Brady, T. J., . . . Belliveau, J. W. (1995). Functional analysis of human MT and related visual cortical areas using magnetic resonance imaging. *Journal of Neuroscience, 15,* 3215–3230.

Tootell, R. B., Silverman, M.S., De Valois R. L., & Jacobs, G. H. (1983). Functional organization of the second cortical visual area in primates. *Science, 220,* 737–739.

Tracey, I. (2005). Nociceptive processing in the human brain. *Current Opinion in Neurobiology, 15,* 478–487.

Tracey, I., & Mantyh, P. W. (2007). The cerebral signature for pain perception and its modulation. *Neuron, 55,* 377–391.

Treisman, A. (1960). Contextual cues in selective listening. *Quarterly Journal of Experimental Psychology, 12,* 242–248.

Treisman, A. M. (1969). Strategies and models of selective attention. *Psychological Review, 76,* 282–299.

Treisman, A., & Gelade, G. (1980). A feature-integration theory of attention. *Cognitive Psychology, 12,* 97–136.

Trifonov, Y. A. (1968). Study of synaptic transmission between the photoreceptor and the horizontal cell using electrical stimulation of the retina. *Biofizika, 13,* 809–817.

Tsao, D. Y., Freiwald, W. A., Tootell, R. B., & Livingstone, M. S. (2006). A cortical region consisting entirely of face-selective cells. *Science, 311,* 670–674.

Tsunozaki, M., & Bautista, D. M. (2009). Mammalian somatosensory mechanotransduction. *Current Opinion in Neurobiology, 19,* 362–369.

Turner, A. F. P., & Magan, N. (2004). Electronic noses and disease diagnostics. *Nature Reviews Microbiology, 2,* 161–166.

Ulanovsky, N., & Moss, C. F. (2008). What the bat's voice tells the bat's brain. *Proceedings of the National Academy of Sciences, USA, 105,* 8491–8498.

Ungerleider, L. G., & Mishkin, M. (1982). Two cortical visual systems. In D. J. Ingle, M. A. Goodale, & R. J. W. Mansfield (Eds.), *Analysis of visual behavior* (pp. 549–586). Cambridge, MA: MIT Press.

Valeton, M. J., & van Norren, D. (1983). Light adaptation of primate cones: An analysis based on extracellular data. *Vision Research, 23,* 1539–1547.

Van Essen, D., & Zeki, S. M. (1978). The topographic organization of rhesus monkey prestriate cortex. *Journal of Physiology, 277,* 193–226.

Vaney, D. I. (1994). Territorial organization of direction-selective ganglion cells in rabbit retina. *Journal of Neuroscience, 14,* 6301–6316.

Van Eyken, E., Van Camp, G., & Van Laer, L. (2007). The complexity of age-related hearing impairment: Contributing environmental and genetic factors. *Audiology and Neuro-Otology, 12,* 345–358.

Vega-Bermudez, F., Johnson, K. O., & Hsiao, S. S. (1991). Human tactile pattern recognition: Active versus passive touch, velocity effects, and patterns of confusion. *Journal of Neurophysiology, 65,* 531–546.

Verhagen, J. V., Kadohisa, M., & Rolls, E. T. (2004). Primate insular/opercular taste cortex: Neuronal representations of the viscosity, fat texture, grittiness, temperature, and taste of foods. *Journal of Neurophysiology, 92,* 1685–1699.

Vicario, G. (1982). Some observations in the auditory field. In J. Beck (Ed.), *Organization and representation in perception* (pp. 269–283). Hillsdale, NJ: Erlbaum.

Vogten, L. L. M. (1974). Pure-tone masking: A new result from a new method. In E. Zwicker & E. Terhardt (Eds.), *Facts and models in hearing* (pp. 142–155). Berlin: Springer-Verlag.

Vollrath, M. A., Kwan, K.Y., & Corey, D. P. (2007). The micromachinery of mechanotransduction in hair cells. *Annual Review of Neuroscience, 30,* 339–365.

von Békésy, G. (1960). *Experiments in hearing.* New York: McGraw-Hill.

von der Heydt, R. (2004). Image parsing mechanisms of the visual cortex. In L. M. Chalupa & J. S. Werner (Eds.), *The visual neurosciences* (Vol. 2, pp. 1139–1150). Cambridge, MA: MIT Press.

von der Heydt, R., Peterhans, E., & Baumgartner, G. (1984). Illusory contours and cortical neuron responses. *Science, 224,* 1260–1262.

von Kriegstein, K., Patterson, R. D., & Griffiths, T. D. (2008). Task-dependent modulation of medial geniculate body is behaviorally relevant for speech recognition. *Current Biology, 18,* 1855–1859.

Wade, A., Augath, M., Logothetis, N., & Wandell, B. (2008). fMRI measurements of color in macaque and human. *Journal of Vision, 8*(10), 1–19.

Wager, T. D., Rilling, J. K., Smith, E. E., Sokolik, A., Casey, K. L., Davidson, R. J., . . . Cohen, J. D. (2004). Placebo-induced changes in fMRI in the anticipation and experience of pain. *Science, 303,* 1162–1167.

Wagner, C. R., & Howe, R. D. (2007). Force feedback benefit depends on experience in multiple degree of freedom robotic surgery task. *IEEE Transactions on Robotics, 23,* 1235–1240.

Wald, G. (1935). Carotenoids and the visual cycle. *Journal of General Physiology, 19,* 351–371.

Wald, G. (1968). Molecular basis of visual excitation. *Science, 162,* 230–239.

Wallach, H. (1948). Brightness constancy and the nature of achromatic colors. *Journal of Experimental Psychology, 38,* 310–324.

Wallach, H., & Floor, L. (1971). The use of size matching to demonstrate the effectiveness of accommodation and convergence as cues for distance. *Perception & Psychophysics, 10,* 423–428.

Wandell, B. A., & Silverstein, L. D. (2003). Digital color reproduction. In S. K. Shevell (Ed.), *The science of color* (pp. 281–314). Washington, DC: Optical Society of America.

Warren, R. M. (1970). Perceptual restoration of missing speech sounds. *Science, 167,* 392–393.

Warren, W. H., & Hannon, D. J. (1988). Direction of self-motion is perceived from optical flow. *Nature, 336,* 162–163.

Warren, W. H., Kay, B. A., Zosh, W. D., Duchon A. P., & Sahuc, S. (2001). Optic flow is used to control human walking. *Nature Neuroscience, 4,* 213–216.

Wässle, H. (2004). Parallel processing in the mammalian retina. *Nature Reviews Neuroscience, 5,* 747–757.

Watanabe, M., & Rodieck, R. W. (1989). Parasol and midget ganglion cells of the primate retina. *Journal of Comparative Neurology, 289,* 434–454.

Weinstein, S. (1968). Intensive and extensive aspects of tactile sensitivity as a function of body part, sex, and laterality. In D. R.

Kenshalo (Ed.), *The skin senses* (pp. 195–222). Springfield, IL: Charles C Thomas.

Weiskrantz, L., Warrington, E. K., Sanders, M. D., & Marshall, J. (1974).Visual capacity in the hemianopic field following a restricted occipital ablation. *Brain, 97,* 709–728.

Weiss, J., Pyrski, M., Jacobi, E., Bufe, B., Willnecker, V., Schick, B., . . . Zufall, F. (2011). Loss-of-function mutations in sodium channel Nav1.7 cause anosmia. *Nature, 472,* 186–190.

Weisz, C., Glowatzki, E., & Fuchs, P. (2009). The postsynaptic function of type II cochlear afferents. *Nature, 461,* 1126–1129.

Wernicke, K. (1995). The aphasia symptom complex: A psychological study on an anatomical basis. In P. Eling (Ed.), *Reader in the history of aphasia* (pp. 69–80). Amsterdam: John Benjamins. (Original work published 1875)

Wertheimer, M. (2001). Laws of organization in perceptual forms. In S. Yantis (Ed.), *Visual perception: Essential readings* (pp. 216–224). Philadelphia: Psychology Press. (Original work published 1923)

Wheatstone, C. (1838). Contributions to the physiology of vision—Part the first: On some remarkable and hitherto unobserved phenomena of binocular vision. *Philosophical Transactions of the Royal Society, 128,* 371–394.

Wick, W. (1998). *Walter Wick's optical tricks*. New York: Scholastic.

Wickens, C. D., & McCarley, J. S. (2008). *Applied attention theory*. New York: CRC Press.

Willander, J., & Larsson, M. (2006). Smell your way back to childhood: Autobiographical odor memory. *Psychonomic Bulletin & Review, 13,* 240–244.

Wilmer, J. B., Germine, L., Chabris, C. F., Chatterjee, G., Williams, M., Loken, E., . . . Duchaine, B. (2010). Human face recognition ability is specific and highly heritable. *Proceedings of the National Academy of Sciences, USA, 107,* 5238–5241.

Wilson, D. A., & Stevenson, R. J. (2003). The fundamental role of memory in olfactory perception. *Trends in Neurosciences, 26,* 243–247.

Wilson, D. A., & Stevenson, R. J. (2006). *Learning to smell: Olfactory perception from neurobiology to behavior*. Baltimore: Johns Hopkins University Press.

Wilson, M. (2004). Retinal synapses. In L. M. Chalupa & J. S. Werner (Eds.), *The visual neurosciences* (Vol. 1, pp. 279–303). Cambridge, MA: MIT Press.

Wilson, R. I., & Mainen, Z. F. (2006). Early events in olfactory processing. *Annual Review of Neuroscience, 29,* 163–201.

Wilson, S. M., Saygin, A. P., Sereno, M. I., & Iacoboni, M. (2004). Listening to speech activates motor areas involved in speech production. *Nature Neuroscience, 7,* 701–702.

Witney, A. G., Wing, A., Thonnard, J. L., & Smith, A. M. (2004). The cutaneous contribution to adaptive precision grip. *Trends in Neurosciences, 10,* 637–643.

Wolfe, J. M. (1994). Guided search 2.0: A revised model of visual search. *Psychonomic Bulletin & Review, 1,* 202–238.

Woodman, G. F., & Luck, S. J. (2003). Serial deployment of attention during visual search. *Journal of Experimental Psychology: Human Perception and Performance, 29,* 121–138.

Woods, D. L., Stecker, G. C., Rinne, T., Herron, T. J., Cate, A. D., Yund, E. W., . . . Kang, X. (2009). Functional maps of human auditory cortex: Effects of acoustic features and attention. *PLoS ONE, 4,* e5183.

Wyart, C., Webster, W. W., Chen, J. H., Wilson, S. R., McClary, A. Khan, R. M., & Sobel, N. (2007). Smelling a single component of male sweat alters levels of cortisol in women. *Journal of Neuroscience, 27,* 1261–1265.

Wyatt, T. D. (2003). *Pheromones and animal behavior: Communication by smell and taste*. Oxford, England: Oxford University Press.

Yantis, S., & Jonides, J. (1990). Abrupt visual onsets and selective attention: Voluntary versus automatic allocation. *Journal of Experimental Psychology: Human Perception and Performance, 16,* 121–134.

Yeshurun, Y., & Sobel, N. (2010). An odor is not worth a thousand words: From multidimensional odors to unidimensional odor objects. *Annual Review of Psychology, 61,* 219–241.

Yin, T. C., & Chan, J. C. (1990). Interaural time sensitivity in medial superior olive of cat. *Journal of Neurophysiology, 64,* 465–488.

Yoshida, R., & Ninomiya, Y. (2010). New insights into the signal transmission from taste cells to gustatory nerve fibers. *International Review of Cell and Molecular Biology, 279,* 101–134.

Yoshida, R., Shigemura, N., Sanematsu, K., Yasumatsu, K., Ishizuka, S., & Ninomiya, Y. (2006). Taste responsiveness of fungiform taste cells with action potentials. *Journal of Neurophysiology, 96,* 3088–3095.

Young, T. (1802). On the theory of light and colours. *Philosophical Transactions of the Royal Society of London, 92,* 12–48.

Yousem, D. M., Geckle, R. J., Bilker, W., McKeown, D. A., & Doty, R. L. (1996). MR evaluation of patients with congenital hyposmia or anosmia. *American Journal of Roentgenology, 166,* 439–443.

Yu, Y.-Q., Xiong, Y., Chan, Y.-S., & He, J. (2004). Corticofugal gating of auditory information in the thalamus: An in vivo intracellular recording study. *Journal of Neuroscience, 24,* 3060–3069.

Zald, D. H. (2003). The human amygdala and the emotional evaluation of sensory stimuli. *Brain Research Reviews, 41,* 88–123.

Zald, D. H., & Pardo, J. V. (1997). Emotion, olfaction, and the human amygdala: Amygdala activation during aversive olfactory stimulation. *Proceedings of the National Academy of Sciences, USA, 94,* 4119–4124.

Zatorre, R. J., Belin, P., & Penhune, V. B. (2002). Structure and function of auditory cortex: Music and speech. *Trends in Cognitive Sciences, 6,* 37–46.

Zatorre, R. J., Chen, J. L., & Penhune, V. B. (2007). When the brain plays music: Auditory–motor interactions in music perception and production. *Nature Reviews Neuroscience, 8,* 547–558.

Zatorre, R. J., Evans, A. C., Meyer, E., & Gjedde, A. (1992). Lateralization of phonetic and pitch discrimination in speech processing. *Science, 256,* 846–849.

Zeki, S. M. (1974). Functional organization of a visual area in the posterior bank of the superior temporal sulcus of the rhesus monkey. *Journal of Physiology, London, 236,* 549–573.

Zeki, S. M., Watson, J. D., Lueck, C. J., Friston, K. J., Kennard, C., & Frackowiak, R. S. (1991). A direct demonstration of functional specialization in human visual cortex. *Journal of Neuroscience, 11,* 641–649.

Zhao, W., Chellappa, R., Phillips, P. J., & Rosenfeld, A. (2003). Face recognition: A literature survey. *ACM Computing Surveys, 35,* 399–458.

Zheng, J., Shen, W., He, D. Z. Z., Long, K. B., Madison, L. D., & Dallos, P. (2000). Prestin is the motor protein of cochlear outer hair cells. *Nature, 405,* 149–155.

Zhou, H., Friedman, H. S., & von der Heydt, R. (2000). Coding of border ownership in monkey visual cortex. *Journal of Neuroscience, 20,* 6594–6611.

Zhou, W., & Chen, D. (2008). Encoding human sexual chemosensory cues in the orbitofrontal and fusiform cortices. *Journal of Neuroscience, 28,* 14416–14421.

Zihl, J., von Cramon, D., & Mai, D. (1983). Selective disturbance of movement vision after bilateral posterior brain damage. *Brain, 252,* 215–222.

NAME INDEX

Note: Page numbers followed by f indicate figures; those followed by t indicate tables.

SUBJECT INDEX

Note: Page numbers followed by f indicate figures; those followed by t indicate tables.